PROJECT MANAGEMENT
A Reference for Professionals

PROJECT MANAGEMENT
A Reference for Professionals

edited by

ROBERT L. KIMMONS

Kimmons-Asaro Group Limited, Inc.
Houston, Texas

JAMES H. LOWEREE

Management Consultant
San Francisco, California

MARCEL DEKKER, INC.   **New York and Basel**

Library of Congress Cataloging-in-Publication Data

Project management : a reference for professionals / edited by Robert
   L. Kimmons, James H. Loweree.
         p.   cm.
    Includes index.
    ISBN 0-8247-7676-3 (alk. paper)
    1. Industrial project management.   I. Kimmons, Robert L.
    II. Loweree, James H.
 (Marcel Dekker, Inc.)
 HD69.P75P727   1989
 658.4'04--dc20   89-33170
                                                                   CIP

This book is printed on acid-free paper.

MARCEL DEKKER, INC.
270 Madison Avenue, New York, New York 10016

Current printing (last digit):
10 9 8 7 6 5 4 3 2

PRINTED IN THE UNITED STATES OF AMERICA

Preface

A functionally independent business entity is formed, with little time for assessment of the compatibility of the management team, to execute a complex assignment—within a limited time frame, under budget restraints frequently set by others, to meet quality parameters specific to the client. The total satisfaction of the management of the principals is the sole determinant of success. When the project is completed the team is disbanded, and its leader—the manager—is reassigned: new team, new objectives, new client, new environment.

The objectives stated to the project manager by his company and the client may be in conflict for contractual or other reasons. No matter! When all is said and done, the manager's own management and the client's management will determine whether or not the effort was successful, often in an arbitrary manner and without regard for extenuating circumstances. A failed project will undoubtedly sharply curtail career advancement, but a successful project may not result in immediate recognition. What kind of a profession is this? Who is capable of effective performance under the conditions stated? The profession is project management, and the person capable of producing excellence in this dynamic environment is called a project manager—a unique person in a unique profession.

The professional development of the project manager proceeds in a stepwise manner, plateau to plateau, each level a result of cumulative performance. The progress of a high-potential candidate, one with all the necessary prerequisites, will move at a pace consistent with the maturation of situational management style and sensitivity toward interpersonal relationships. Projects are built by people, and the performance of people will determine the success or failure of a project.

The performance of a project manager results from the development of a range of management skills, not innate skills but skills that are acquired through hard work. Leadership is a resultant of performance. Authority is a resultant of leadership. The road to excellence—management skills, performance, leadership, authority—is a long road with many detours, but achievable for those with a commitment to excellence.

Project management is treated as an independent profession in this book. We do not view project management as a scheduling and cost control software exercise, an unfortunate tangential trend in recent years, and we do not view project management as a discipline-oriented engineering, procurement, and construction effort. Engineering, procurement, and construction are elements of a total project, each activity enhanced through the synergism of modern computer-oriented project control systems, all as part of a total management program directed by a manager through his staff.

All management efforts have defined elements of work and utilize tools to simplify the achievement of goals. We address the elements of work and the tools of project management in terms of the uniqueness of the profession of project management. The common thread, whether it be an in-house retrofit or a mega project in a distant land, is the management of the people resources and the material resources to meet a stated objective.

We are interested in what works and why it works, and through the understanding of the *why*, we have endeavored to promulgate broad guidelines adaptable to most situations that the project manager will encounter in the vast arena of project management.

The book consists of 16 units, arranged in a progressive manner. Units 1 and 2 present the concepts of project management and the role of the project manager. Unit 3 covers the preproject formative period. Unit 4 reviews contractual issues, a vital consideration in today's litigious society. Units 5-10 track the project from release through engineering, procurement, and construction—including control programs and culminating in project acceptance. Unit 11 describes the project management role in a variety of selected fields. Unit 12 analyzes certain projects in which a specific element or resource-restraint is dominant. Unit 13 addresses the international sector, characterized by the total immersion of the expatriate team in the culture of the host country. Units 14 and 15 discuss communications and management skills. We close with Unit 16, a contemplative look at the future.

Prior to the start of work on a management or technical book, or an extended series of manuscripts dedicated to a restricted field, it is normal for the authors or editors to orient their effort toward a well-defined audience. Our initial concept was to provide guidance to an audience from those at the university level to newly appointed project managers and project staff members. It was, and is, our fervent wish that every novitiate manager be taken under the protective and instructive cloak of a mentor; failing that, we hope that the wealth of experience compiled within these covers will provide a surrogate role and accelerate the careers of high-potential fledgling managers.

As our work unfolded, however, we recognized the extraordinary depth of knowledge, literally thousands of years' worth, conveyed by the slate of contributors. We see a much broader audience today, ranging from the discipline personnel and specialists contributing to projects, who benefit from a better understanding of how their roles fit into the overall program, to the senior management personnel of those organizations that provide project management services and those entities that use the services; all should have the best understanding possible of how resources are deployed to engineer and construct capital ventures.

The cast of contributors is impressive, representing a broad spectrum of industries and institutions: engineering, construction, architecture, manufacturing, public utilities, government, academia, research, investment, and the law; engineering, personnel, and management consultancies; the Construction Industry Institute, the Business Roundtable, and the Project Management Institute.

We dedicate this effort to the young people entering the profession; to experienced managers striving for quantum advancement in position; to the contributing authors who offered their wisdom; and to our wives, Florence Kimmons and Barbara Loweree, without whose continuous encouragement there would not be a book.

Robert L. Kimmons

James H. Loweree

Code of Ethics
for
the Project Management Profession

PREAMBLE: Project Managers, in the pursuit of the profession, affect the quality of life for all people in our society. Therefore, it is vital that Project Managers conduct their work in an ethical manner to earn and maintain the confidence of team members, colleagues, employees, employers, clients and the public.

ARTICLE I: Project Managers shall maintain high standards of personal and professional conduct, and:

a. Accept responsibility for their actions.
b. Undertake projects and accept responsibility only if qualified by training or experience, or after full disclosure to their employers or clients of pertinent qualifications.
c. Maintain their professional skills at the state of the art and recognize the importance of continued personal development and education.
d. Advance the integrity and prestige of the profession by practicing in a dignified manner.
e. Support this code and encourage colleagues and co-workers to act in accordance with this code.
f. Support the professional society by actively participating and encouraging colleagues and co-workers to participate.
g. Obey the laws of the country in which work is being performed.

ARTICLE II: Project Managers shall, in their work:

a. Provide the necessary project leadership to promote maximum productivity while striving to minimize costs.
b. Apply state-of-the-art project management tools and techniques to ensure quality, cost and time objectives, as set forth in the project plan, are met.
c. Treat fairly all project team members, colleagues and co-workers, regardless of race, religion, sex, age or national origin.
d. Protect project team members from physical and mental harm.
e. Provide suitable working conditions and opportunities for project team members.

Courtesy Project Management Institute, P.O. Box 43, Drexel Hill, Pennsylvania 19026.   215-622-1796.

v

    f.   Seek, accept and offer honest criticism of work, and properly credit the contribution of others.

    g.   Assist project team members, colleagues and co-workers in their professional development.

ARTICLE III: Project Managers shall, in their relations with employers and clients:

    a.   Act as faithful agents or trustees for their employers and clients in professional or business matters.

    b.   Keep information on the business affairs or technical processes of an employer or client in confidence while employed, and later, until such information is properly released.

    c.   Inform their employers, clients, professional societies or public agencies of which they are members or to which they may make any presentations, of any circumstance that could lead to a conflict of interest.

    d.   Neither give nor accept, directly or indirectly, any gift, payment of service of more than nominal value to or from those having business relationships with their employers or clients.

    e.   Be honest and realistic in reporting project quality, cost and time.

ARTICLE IV: Project Managers shall, in fulfilling their responsibilities to the community:

    a.   Protect the safety, health and welfare of the public and speak out against abuses in these areas affecting the public interest.

    b.   Seek to extend public knowledge and appreciation of the project management profession and its achievements.

Contents

Preface   *iii*
Code of Ethics for the Project Management Profession   *v*
Contributors   *xiii*

I PROJECT MANAGEMENT   1

   1 Suitable Applications of Project Management *Regula A. Brunies*   5

   2 Organizational Factors *Arnold M. Ruskin and W. Eugene Estes*   13

   3 The Evaluation of the Contractor-Owner Project Team
      William S. Dickinson   25

   4 Basic Organizational Structure and Staffing for the Execution of
      Projects *Arthur C. Burns*   29

   5 Task Force Project Execution: Pros and Cons *Joel H. Bennett
      and Keith E. Hughes*   45

   6 The Project-Driven Organization *W. Ross Cox*   49

   7 Computer-Aided Project Management *Mark J. Humphrey
      and Michael L. McCauley*   53

   8 Owner/Contractor Relationships *William K. Wakefield*   61

   9 Contingency Reserves: A Management Control Tool *Ivars Avots*   67

  10 Project Management: A History of Its Interaction with Society
      Seymour S. Greenfield and Rebecca Yamin   81

II THE PROJECT MANAGER   89

   1 Academic Approaches to Project Management *C. B. Tatum*   91

   2 The Role of the Project Manager *Ray D. Harvey*   97

   3 Authority of the Project Manager *Emery D. Carlson*   105

   4 Choosing the Most Effective Management Style *Robert L. Kimmons* 109

   5 The Superior Project Manager *James H. Loweree*   115

III EARLY STAGES OF A PROJECT   131

   1 Project Conception *Francisco G. Anzola and Francisco J. Rojas*   133

   2 Project Viability *Herbert H. Zachow*   139

   3 Early Scope Definition *Donald G. Engesser*   145

   4 Selecting the Site *Paul B. Wright*   151

   5 Regulatory Requirements and Permits *Paul V. Morgan
      and Raymond E. Krauss*   167

   6 Financing the Project *William J. Gremp and Edward J. Higgins*   179

   7 Cash Flow Forecasting: A Systematic Approach *Fernando Sotelino
      and Michael A. Gustafson*   191

   8 Selecting the Working Partners *M. William Emmons*   207

   9 Proposal Management *Clement F. Burnap*   221

IV THE CONTRACT   231

   1 Contract Considerations and Contract Types *Matthew A. McLaughlin* 235

   2 Joint Ventures *Matthew A. McLaughlin*   249

   3 Preconstruction Phase *Tom N. Frisby, Sr.*   265

   4 Guarantees, Warranties, and Liabilities *Jerome R. Kaye*   277

   5 Risk Management and Insurance *D. J. Wardle*   285

   6 Claims Management *Sol Kutner*   297

V PROJECT RELEASE   329

   1 The Project Plan *William E. Smith*   331

   2 The Proactive Execution Plan *Warren T. Olde and M. Peralta*   335

   3 A Workshop Approach to Project Execution Planning *Claudio Pincus* 349

   4 Constructability *Walter J. Boyce*   357

   5 The Project Schedule *Kenneth O. Hartley*   365

   6 The Project Budget *Edward A. Wynant*   377

IV ENGINEERING   391

   1 Design Considerations *Carl E. Petrus*   395

   2 Mechanical Engineering *John A. Adamchik*   401

   3 Process Control *Harold H. Arndt*   407

   4 Civil, Structural, and Architectural Engineering *Michael Schiller* 417

   5 Plant Layout and Piping Design *Ralph W. Smith*   425

   6 Electrical Engineering *Richard L. Ridgway*   429

   7 Computer-Aided Design and Drafting *Allen T. Koster*   433

VII MATERIALS MANAGEMENT   443

   1 Procurement *Daniel Gilan and Kevin C. Yessian*   445

   2 Expediting *P. R. Peecook and Edward C. Stokes*   455

Contents

   3 Inspection *David P. MacMillan*   461

   4 Site Materials Management *Robert L. Wootten and John Calvin Cato*   469

VIII CONSTRUCTION   477

   1 Home Office Construction Staff *F. Sweeney Tuck*   479

   2 Labor Relations *F. Sweeney Tuck*   483

   3 Methods of Execution *F. Sweeney Tuck*   489

   4 Field Organization *Edward J. McGuire*   495

   5 Field Cost Control *Edward J. McGuire and Edward A. Wynant*   501

   6 Field Scheduling *Edward J. McGuire and Edward A. Wynant*   509

   7 Field Material Control *Edward J. McGuire*   519

   8 Productivity *Edward J. McGuire*   525

   9 Quality Assurance and Quality Control *Edward J. McGuire*   531

  10 Safety and Security *Edward J. McGuire*   537

IX CONTROLLING THE WORK   541

   1 Monitoring Progress *Michael E. Horwitz*   543

   2 Managing Costs with Precision *Charles J. Peles*   551

   3 Control of Changes *W. Ross Cox*   561

   4 Quality Assurance *John D. Stevenson*   567

   5 Document Handling and Control *Sheldon R. Salkovitch*   575

   6 Financial Audits of Capital Projects *Donald E. Law*   581

X PROJECT ACCEPTANCE AND CLOSEOUT   585

   1 Project Completion *David H. Hamburger and Herbert F. Spirer*   587

   2 Performance Tests *Michael D. Winfield, Newt M. Hallman, Daniel N. Myers, and O. J. Schneider*   617

XI PROJECT MANAGEMENT IN SELECTED FIELDS   627

   1 Electrical Utility Projects *Kenneth A. Roe and K. Keith Roe*   629

   2 Managing Tennessee Valley Authority's Design and Construction *George H. Kimmons and Elizabeth E. Patrick*   647

   3 Engineering Performance Within the Municipal Electric Utility *Ronald C. Lutwen*   653

   4 Petroleum Production Projects *Frank Chuck*   659

   5 Capital Projects for the Pharmaceutical Industry *Peter Loy*   665

   6 Offshore Oil and Gas Development Projects *Peter M. J. Fagiano, Rex Alfonso, and Lawrence Allan Boston*   671

   7 Aerospace Industry *Robert J. Sanator and Vincent Tizio*   697

   8 The Support Role of Research to Project Management *John P. Henry, Jr.*   703

XII   WHEN ONE ELEMENT IS DOMINANT   709

    1   Small Projects *John L. Zarnick*   711

    2   Fast-Track Projects: A Case History *L. D. "Don" Slepow and Alan S. Mendelssohn*   719

    3   Zero-Defect Projects: The Spirit of St. Lucie *Leo Tsakiris*   727

    4   Mega Projects: Views of a Fluor Project Manager *Roy L. Klein*   737

    5   Mega Projects: Views of a Bechtel Project Manager *Robert F. Reinhard*   745

    6   The Multiproject Environment *Robert D. Robson*   759

    7   Modular Construction *Thomas A. Mullett*   771

    8   Climatic and Remote Conditions *John H. Cassidy and R. D. Sorbo*   787

XIII   INTERNATIONAL PROJECTS   817

    1   International Marketing *William L. Kelley*   821

    2   Operational Differences on International Projects *Joseph F. Stoy*   831

    3   Executing the International Project *Arthur C. Burns*   835

    4   Staffing the International Project *David G. Turner, Jr.*   875

    5   Social Aspects of Project Management in Developing Countries *Virginia Quinn*   883

XIV   COMMUNICATIONS   891

    1   Communicating for Desired Results *Lawrence L. Bissett and H. Gilbert Weil*   895

    2   Written Communications *Henry E. Francis*   903

    3   The Stand-Up Presentation *William R. Sears*   911

    4   Records Management *Thomas B. Mitchell and Elizabeth A. Basta*   923

XV   MANAGEMENT SKILLS   931

    1   Time Management *Hebab A. Quazi*   937

    2   Effective Delegation *Ronald H. Gerstenberger*   945

    3   Problem Solving and Problem Prevention *Benjamin B. Tregoe*   953

    4   Performance Management *Philip L. Helmer*   967

    5   The Art of Negotiation *Thomas A. Haskins*   971

    6   The Personnel Department and the Project *Donald A. Spiker*   979

XVI   THE YEARS AHEAD   1003

    1   New Directions *Robert L. Kimmons*   1007

    2   Development of the Profession *John R. Adams*   1015

    3   Productivity: A Key to the Future *Richard L. Tucker and Shirley S. Tucker*   1027

    4   The Business Roundtable *Carroll H. Dunn*   1037

    5   The Effects of Changing Project Requirements *Kenneth A. Fischer*   1043

6   Relational Decision Making and Communications for Project
     Managers *C. William Ibbs*   1059

7   Project Management in the Future *M. Peralta*   1077

8   The Years Ahead *James H. Loweree*   1081

Index   *1087*

Contributors

John A. Adamchik Project Manager, Barnard and Burk Engineers & Constructors, Inc., Baton Rouge, Louisiana

John R. Adams, Ph.D. Professor of Project Management, School of Business, Western Carolina University, Cullowhee, North Carolina

Rex Alfonso Senior Manager—Offshore Construction Management, Fluor Daniel Inc., Sugar Land, Texas

Francisco G. Anzola, P.E. General Manager-Procurement, Lagoven S.A., Caracas, D.F., Venezuela

Harold H. Arndt, P.E. Staff Project Engineer, MK-Ferguson Company, Cleveland, Ohio

Ivars Avots President, Trans-Global Management Systems, Inc., Arlington, Massachusetts

Elizabeth A. Basta Records Management Analyst, Cleveland Electric Illuminating Company, Cleveland, Ohio

Joel H. Bennett Senior Vice President, C F Braun, Inc., Alhambra, California

Lawrence L. Bissett President, National Institute for Chemical Studies, Charleston, West Virginia

Lawrence Allan Boston, P.E. Senior Manager—Engineering, Fluor Engineers—Houston, Houston, Texas. Currently Consultant, New Orleans, Louisiana

Walter J. Boyce President, Boyce Consultants, Houston, Texas

Regula A. Brunies Vice President, Revay and Associates Limited, Montreal, Quebec, Canada

Clement F. Burnap Consultant, San Francisco, California

Arthur C. Burns, P.E. Vice President (Retired), The Ralph M. Parsons Company, Pasadena, California. Currently living in Glendale, California

Emery D. Carlson President, Carlson Services Inc., Whittier, California

John H. Cassidy President, J. H. Cassidy & Associates, Scottsdale, Arizona

John Calvin Cato Project Executive, H. B. Zachry Company, San Antonio, Texas

Frank Chuck, P.E. Vice President and Director (Retired), Exxon Production Research Company, Houston, Texas

W. Ross Cox, Ph.D. Project Director, CRSS Constructors, Inc., Houston, Texas

William S. Dickinson Vice President, ARCO Oil and Gas Company, Dallas, Texas

Lt.Gen. Carroll H. Dunn USA (Ret.), P.E. Project Director—Construction Industry Cost Effectiveness Study, The Business Roundtable, New York, New York

M. William Emmons Principal Associate—Contract Management, Pathfinder, Inc., Cherry Hill, New Jersey

Donald G. Engesser President, PMEx, Inc., Chatham, New Jersey

W. Eugene Estes, P.E. Consulting Civil Engineer, Westlake Village, California

Peter M. J. Fagiano Operations Director, Global Engineering Ltd., Sutton, Surrey, England

Kenneth A. Fischer, P.E. Senior Project Manager, John Zink Company, Tulsa, Oklahoma

Henry E. Francis, Ph.D. Manager Corporate Services (Retired), The Ralph M. Parsons Company, Pasadena, California. Currently living in Ashland, Oregon

Tom N. Frisby, Sr. President, The Frisby Group, Tyler, Texas

Ronald H. Gerstenberger Consultant, Amherst, New Hampshire

Daniel Gilan Senior Vice President, ANR Venture Management Company, Detroit, Michigan. Currently Vice President, ANR Development Corporation, Detroit, Michigan

Seymour S. Greenfield Chairman of the Board, Parsons Brinckerhoff Inc., New York, New York

William J. Gremp Managing Director, Merrill Lynch Capital Markets, Investment Banking Division, New York, New York

Michael A. Gustafson Crocker National Bank, San Francisco, California

Newt M. Hallman, P. E. Vice President Engineering (Retired), UOP, Des Plaines, Illinois. Currently living in Mt. Prospect, Illinois

David H. Hamburger, P.E. Principal, David Hamburger Management Consultant, Inc., Spring Valley, New York

Kenneth O. Hartley Vice President, Morrison-Knudsen International Company, Inc., San Francisco, California

Ray D. Harvey, P.E. President and Chief Executive Officer, Fenco Engineers Inc., Toronto, Ontario, Canada. Currently President and Chief Operating Officer, UTDC Inc., Toronto, Ontario, Canada

Thomas A. Haskins President, The Haskins Organization, Littleton, Colorado

Philip L. Helmer, P.E. President, Helmer Pacific Inc., Kent, Washington

John P. Henry, Jr., Ph.D. Senior Vice President, SRI International, Menlo Park, California

Edward J. Higgins Vice President, Merrill Lynch Capital Markets, New York, New York

Michael E. Horwitz, P.E., CCE Assistant Manager Project Support, Simons-Eastern Consultants, Inc., Atlanta, Georgia

Keith E. Hughes, P.E. Vice President, Santa Fe Braun, Inc., Alhambra, California. Currently Consultant, Laguna Beach, California

Mark J. Humphrey President, Professional Management Services, Bakersfield, California

C. William Ibbs, Ph.D., P.E. Associate Professor of Civil Engineering, University of California—Berkeley, Berkeley, California

Jerome R. Kaye Deputy Counsel and Assistant Secretary, Lummus Crest Inc., Bloomfield, New Jersey

William L. Kelley, P.E. Senior Vice President and Manager of Operations, Morrison-Knudsen International Company, Inc., San Francisco, California

George H. Kimmons, P.E. Manager—Engineering Design and Construction (Retired), Tennessee Valley Authority, Knoxville, Tennessee

Robert L. Kimmons, P.E., PMP President and CEO, Ebasco-Humphreys & Glasgow, Inc., Houston, Texas. Currently Managing Partner, Kimmons-Asaro Group Limited, Inc., Houston, Texas

Roy L. Klein Senior Vice President (Retired), Fluor Engineers Inc., Irvine, California. Currently living in Fallbrook, California

Allen T. Koster, P.E. Engineering Manager, Harmony Construction of California Inc., Ventura, California

Raymond E. Krauss Environmental Manager—McLaughlin Mine, Homestake Mining Company, Lower Lake, California

Sol Kutner President, Sol Kutner Associates, Inc., San Carlos, California

Donald E. Law Consultant, South Bristol, Maine

James H. Loweree Management Consultant, San Francisco, California

Peter Loy Plant Engineer (Retired), Ortho Pharmaceutical Corporation, Raritan, New Jersey. Currently Consultant, Scotch Plains, New Jersey

Ronald C. Lutwen President, SFT, Inc., Toledo, Ohio

David P. MacMillan Materials Advisor, Exxon Company International, Florham Park, New Jersey

Michael L. McCauley, P.E. Lead Project Management Engineer, Pacific Gas & Electric Company, San Francisco, California

Edward J. McGuire Senior Construction Manager, Exxon Research & Engineering Company, Florham Park, New Jersey

Matthew A. McLaughlin Vice President and General Counsel, Davy McKee Corporation, Pittsburgh, Pennsylvania

Alan S. Mendelssohn, P.E., CCE Project Control Supervisor, Florida Power and Light Company, Juno Beach, Florida

Thomas B. Mitchell Treasurer (Retired), Davy McKee Constructors, Inc., Cleveland, Ohio. Currently living in Solon, Ohio

Paul V. Morgan Manager, Davy McKee Corporation, San Ramon, California

Thomas A. Mullett, P.E. Senior Project Manager (Retired), Mobil Research & Development Corp., Princeton, New Jersey. Currently Consultant, Eustis, Florida

Daniel N. Myers Manager—Heat Transfer Section, UOP, Des Plaines, Illinois

Warren T. Olde Assistant General Manager (Retired), Exxon Engineering Project Management, Support Department, Exxon Research & Engineering Company, Florham Park, New Jersey

Elizabeth E. Patrick Project Engineer, Tennessee Valley Authority, Knoxville, Tennessee. Currently Project Coordinator with Keith & Schnars, P.A., Ft. Lauderdale, Florida

P. R. Peecook Manager of Procurement Operations, Bechtel Group Inc., San Francisco, California

Charles J. Peles Project Manager, Foster Wheeler USA Corporation, Clinton, New Jersey. Currently Senior Project Manager, Pepsico, Purchase, New York

M. Peralta Associate Administrator for Management, Office of Management, National Aeronautics and Space Administration, Washington, D.C. Currently President, American National Standards Institute, New York, New York

Carl E. Petrus, P.E. Project Manager, Environmental Resources Management, Inc., Exton, Pennsylvania

Claudio Pincus Vice President, Davy McKee Corporation, Berkeley Heights, New Jersey. Currently Senior Partner, The Quantic Group, Ltd., Short Hills, New Jersey

Hebab A. Quazi, Ph.D., P.E. Vice President Operations, Kinetics Technology International Corporation, Monrovia, California. Currently President, Martech International, Inc., Covina, California

Virginia Quinn Freelance Writer, Consultant, Washington, D.C.

Robert F. Reinhard, P.E. Vice President (Retired), Bechtel Incorporated, San Francisco, California. Currently living in Santa Barbara, California

Richard L. Ridgway Program Director (Retired), Santa Fe Braun Inc., Alhambra, California

Robert D. Robson, P.E. Executive Vice President (Retired), Lummus Canada Inc., Toronto, Ontario, Canada. Currently Consultant, Calgary, Alberta, Canada

Kenneth A. Roe, P.E. Chairman and Chief Executive Officer, Burns and Roe Enterprises Inc., Oradell, New Jersey

K. Keith Roe Executive Vice President, Burns and Roe Enterprises Inc., Oradell, New Jersey

Francisco J. Rojas, P.E. Project Manager, Lagoven S.A., Caracas, D.F., Venezuela

Arnold M. Ruskin, Ph.D., P.E., PMP, CMC Partner, Claremont Consulting Group, Claremont, California

Sheldon R. Salkovitch General Manager, Annex Manufacturing Corp., Jersey City, New Jersey

Robert J. Sanator, Ph.D. President and Chief Executive Officer, Geotel Inc., Hauppauge, New York

Michael Schiller, P.E. Manager of Project Operations (Retired), C F Braun & Co., Murray Hill, New Jersey. Currently living in Pasadena, California.

O. J. Schneider Assistant Director Field Operating Service, UOP, Inc., Des Plaines, Illinois

William R. Sears Managing Director, W. R. Sears & Co., Inc., San Francisco, California

L. D. "Don" Slepow, P.E. Director of Projects, Florida Power and Light Company, Juno Beach, Florida

Ralph W. Smith, P.E. Vice President (Retired), Santa Fe Braun Inc., Alhambra, California. Currently living in San Diego, California

William E. Smith, P.E. Manager of Operations (Retired), Brown & Root Inc., Houston, Texas

R. D. Sorbo Standard Alaska Production Company, Anchorage, Alaska. Currently Manager Major Projects, IT Corporation, Martinez, California

Fernando Sotelino First Vice President, Crocker National Bank, San Francisco, California

Donald A. Spiker Manager—Personnel, Davy McKee Corporation, San Ramon, California. Currently Management Consultant, Walnut Creek, California

Herbert F. Spirer, Ph.D. Professor of Information Management, University of Connecticut, Stamford, Connecticut

John D. Stevenson, Ph.D., P.E. President, Stevenson & Associates, Cleveland, Ohio

Edward C. Stokes Senior Vice President & Manager of Procurement, Bechtel Group Inc., San Francisco, California

Joseph F. Stoy Manager of Petrochemical Projects (Retired), Petrochemical Industries Company K.S.C., Safat, Kuwait. Currently living in Charlotte, North Carolina

C. B. Tatum, Ph.D. Associate Professor of Civil Engineering, Department of Civil Engineering, Stanford University, Stanford, California

Vincent Tizio Consultant, San Francisco, California

Benjamin B. Tregoe, Ph.D. Chairman, Kepner-Tregoe Inc., Princeton, New Jersey

Leo Tsakiris, P.E. Vice President Operations, Ebasco Services Inc., Norcross, Georgia

F. Sweeney Tuck, P.E. Vice Chairman (Retired), Fluor Daniel Inc., Sugar Land, Texas. Currently living in Houston, Texas

Richard L. Tucker, Ph.D., P.E. Director, Construction Industry Institute, Austin, Texas

Shirley S. Tucker, Ph.D. President, Tucker & Tucker Consultants, Austin, Texas

David G. Turner, Jr. Manager Corporate Personnel (Retired), Brown and Root Inc., Houston, Texas. Currently President of Turner-Eatherton Incorporated, Houston, Texas

William K. Wakefield Director—Corporate Engineering and Construction, FMC Corporation, Princeton, New Jersey

D. J. Wardle Bechtel Power Corporation, San Francisco, California

H. Gilbert Weil General Project Manager, Consultant, Bridgewater, New Jersey

Michael D. Winfield Vice President Process Services, UOP, Des Plains, Illinois

Robert L. Wootten, P.E. Construction Manager, E. I. du Pont de Nemours & Co., Augusta, Georgia

Paul B. Wright Senior Staff Engineer (Retired), Davy McKee Corporation, San Ramon, California. Currently living in Sunnyvale, California

Edward A. Wynant, P.E. Senior Engineering Associate (Retired), Exxon Research & Engineering Company, Florham Park, New Jersey. Currently Consultant, Basking Ridge, New Jersey

Rebecca Yamin Archivist/Historian, Parsons Brinckerhoff Inc., New York, New York

Kevin C. Yessian Director—Contracts and Procurement, ANR Venture Management Company, Detroit, Michigan. Currently Director of Resource Management, ANR Venture Management Company, Detroit, Michigan

Herbert H. Zachow (Retired), Atlantic Richfield Company, Los Angeles, California

John L. Zarnick General Manager, Cross & Black Inc., Engineers, Union, New Jersey

PROJECT MANAGEMENT
A Reference for Professionals

I

PROJECT MANAGEMENT

Project management is an approach that an organization may use to accomplish a relatively short-term objective in an efficient manner.

Project management is extremely broad in concept. Commonly, only a very limited view of its potential application is glimpsed. Even its actual application is frequently understated.

Ideal situations for utilizing project management exist under some of the following conditions.

1. In high priority undertakings
2. When a multidisciplinary effort is required
3. In nonrepetitive situations
4. When access to some resources is limited

Normally at least two parties are involved in a project management endeavor: the owner, client, investor, or simply the "boss"; and the project staff, as personified by the project manager. The project manager may also be known as the project director, engineer, coordinator, leader; or the program, product, or system director.

The client's role in the project may be as a single voice directing the project and making all the decisions. More frequently, the client consists of diverse groups, including management, legal, marketing, sales, research, engineering, production, operations, manufacturing, maintenance, safety, human resources, and community relations, all voicing self-interests.

In specific cases, the parent organization of the project team may be the client or owner, as would be true for an "in-house" project. The relationship of the parent organization to the project team varies. Where the project team has a mandate to perform with a great deal of autonomy, it is characterized as being "strong." Excessive intervention of functional managers in the activities of their personnel who are temporarily assigned to the project team undermines the authority of the project manager.

Numerous third parties may be involved in a project. The client and the project manager must determine who will have fundamental responsibility for coordination. The owner or client should clearly identify the underlying objective for the project. This objective should be communicated clearly to all who are involved in executing the project work. This fundamental principle is frequently violated and creates misunderstandings and inefficient use of resources assigned to the project.

Project management had existed in some form for centuries before our current nomenclature and modern concepts came into use. In the past few years, the structure and formality of project management has developed rapidly. The size, complexity, and the computerization of information processing have accelerated this development. The systems themselves are sometimes mistakenly considered as being project management.

Change is an ever present probability on most projects. Ideally, the project manager will be capable of managing change so that it is least disruptive to progress. Change should be anticipated, and should not be an excuse for poor performance. Change should be carefully controlled and tradeoffs made only when they further the objectives of the project. While change may be beneficial early in the project, uncontrolled changes later on can measurably diminish the project efforts. Changes occur in the basic concept for the project, the scope of the project, project conditions, and in the staff assigned to the work. All of these may be detrimental in varying degrees, again depending upon the stage of the project at which they occur and what preparation has been made to accept unavoidable change.

A completely successful project should fulfill the stated objectives set forth with respect to purpose, cost, and completion date of the facility, function, or other outcome. In other words, the results must accomplish the intentions, the final cost must be within the approved budget, and the schedule must have been maintained.

The specific criteria for judging the success of a given project will differ only slightly between the client's evaluation and that of the project manager and/or the parent organization. Minor differences are sometimes exaggerated to the detriment of the project. Fundamentally, a project that achieves success in the eyes of the client will also be a success from the viewpoint of the project manager.

There are a host of other attributes of successful projects which should not be forgotten. Probably foremost is that the established personal interrelationships should lead to opportunities for further assignments. The feelings should be that an efficient, professional job has been done and that there is every indication that this would be the case for any future work. That all of the people who have contributed to the work will have developed positively in their chosen career path is a secondary characteristic of a successful project.

Unit One sets the stage for the subsequent contributions. Suitable applications, organizational concepts and factors, the effect of the computer on project management, the relationships between owner and contractor, contingency management, and changing project requirements as they relate to project management are covered.

BIBLIOGRAPHY

Cleland, D. I. and W. R. King (eds.). *Project Management Handbook*. New York: Van Nostrand Reinhold Company Inc., 1983.

Kerzner, H. *Project Management: A Systems Approach to Planning, Scheduling and Controlling*. New York: Van Nostrand Reinhold, 1985.

Kerridge, A. E. and C. H. Vervalin (eds.). *Engineering and Construction Project Management*. Houston, Texas: Gulf Publishing Company, 1986

Ruskin, A. M. and W. E. Estes. *What Every Engineer Should Know About Project Management*. New York: Marcel Dekker, Inc., 1982.
Stuckenbruck, L. C. (ed.). *The Implementation of Project Management: A Professional's Handbook*. Drexel Hill, PA: Project Management Institute, 1981.

1
Suitable Applications of Project Management

REGULA A. BRUNIES *Revay and Associates Limited, Montreal, Quebec, Canada*

Many of mankind's major achievements, such as the construction of the Egyptian pyramids or the Great Wall of China, can be designated as successfully completed projects; thus they were achieved by some form of project management.

However, it was not until the twentieth century that project management entered a vastly new era, with the development of specialized techniques for planning, scheduling, and controlling the interaction of very large and technically complex projects; namely, the development of Critical Path Method (CPM) and Program and Evaluation Review Technique (PERT) in the mid-1950s. These basic concepts of network development and analysis were conceived almost simultaneously by a team from Remington Rand and E. I. duPont de Nemours for the construction of a large synthetic fiber plant and by the Space Special Project Office of the U.S. Navy Bureau of Ordnance for the management of the Polaris Missile Program. These new techniques provided the managerial tools required to apply project management effectively for advanced technology projects.

Between the mid-1950s and the 1980s the project management approach has matured; nevertheless, much of its growth has come about more through necessity than through desire.

In the 1960s, companies with complex tasks and operating within a dynamic environment began to search for new management techniques and organizational structures that could be quickly adapted to a changing environment.

However other than the aerospace industry, defense, and construction, the majority of companies in the 1960s maintained an informal policy of project managing. It was not until the 1970s, in response to the increased size and complexity of their activities, that a growing number of companies resorted to a formal project management process.

What is modern project management? A combined definition from two recent project management reference sources provides the answer:

Project management is the application of the systems approach to the management of technologically complex tasks or projects whose objectives are explicitly stated in terms of time, cost, and performance parameters. (Cleland and King, 1983.)

Project management is the planning, organizing, directing, and controlling of company resources for a relatively short-term objective that has been established to complete specific goals and objectives. Furthermore, project management utilizes the systems approach to management by having functional personnel (the vertical hierarchy) assigned to a specific project (the horizontal hierarchy). (Kerzner, 1982.)

A wide variety of undertakings exists within the public and private sectors where project management concepts are applicable and have been successfully implemented. Many forms of project management have merged, but the basic concepts and techniques apply to all. The matrix structure has been the most widely accepted form, and will likely continue to be so in situations involving complex interdisciplinary efforts and a continuous stream of projects such as in the aerospace and construction industries. In other cases, the use of temporary task forces and team building has been strongly advocated for multifunctional efforts.

However, some means of justification or measure of applicability is necessary to determine if a particular endeavor is beyond the realm of the regular functional organization and the formation of a project organization is beneficial.

Although no specific formula or simple rule can identify such undertakings, several criteria can be identified, under which the project management approach will be beneficial, namely:

> In an ad hoc undertaking concerned with a single definable end product
> In an undertaking which is of greater complexity of scope than normal
> In an undertaking with stringent time, cost, and technical performance requirements
> In an undertaking which requires a significant contribution by more than two functional organizations
> In an undertaking requiring a quick response to change and value of time
> In an undertaking which is unique or infrequent to present organization
> In an undertaking with a high degree of interdependence among the tasks
> In an undertaking where a company's reputation is at stake or where rewards of success or penalties for failure are particularly high

The following sections review the major industries as well as some of the more recent situations in which project management has been successfully applied.

AEROSPACE AND DEFENSE INDUSTRIES

Since its early origins in the Atlas and Polaris Programs, project management by whatever name--program/system/project management--has become a way of life in the aerospace and defense industries. Both are typically concerned with immense undertakings involving thousands of contractors and billions of dollars. Two-thirds of the U.S. government's research budget is allocated toward aerospace and defense each year.

Project management is applied at all levels of these industries in various organizational forms. Owners, usually government, use a project organization to monitor and control their numerous projects, while contractors and subcontractors use project management techniques extensively in the performance of their contracts.

Undertakings within these industries are usually so large that they are referred to as programs rather than projects. The term *program* implies an undertaking of a greater magnitude and longer life span than a project. However, the project management approach is equally applicable to programs and projects. The terms "program management," "project management," and also "systems management," are used interchangeably and even ambiguously in related literautre.

The Department of Defense is the largest single buyer of goods and services in the American economy. Its responsibilities include the ongoing development and acquisition of weapon systems for the purpose of national defense. Some of the problems associated with the development of such complex systems include (Shilleto, 1979):

> Constantly changing environment
> Time spans of five, seven, or even more years
> Involvement of nearly every field of technology often interdependently tied together

    Changing levels of capability of current and potential adversaries
New and untried technology
Coordination of numerous private and public organizations

Project mangement techniques have long been recognized as the most effective method of managing the acquisition of weaponry. Program managers provide a single point of responsibility and decision-making throughout the program life span. The project team is usually organized in a matrix form composed of functional specialists and project personnel.

The Aeronautical Systems Division of the U.S. Air Force is responsible for the acquisition of aircraft and related equipment. Each program within the ASD works toward the goals and objectives of the division, and is composed of many projects, each dealing with a particular component of the program. An example of a program within the ASD was the development of the F-15 fighter jet, initiated to develop the best air superiority fighter aircraft in the world. Established project management concepts and techniques were successfully integrated and implemented for the first time on a major defense system under a program manager who was given full authority and responsibility for the success or failure of the program. The F-15 organization was based on a matrix structure that integrated the project tasks (airframe, engine, avionics, armament, etc.) and functional tasks (engineering, configuration management, testing production, procurement, etc.) (Guarion et al., 1979, pp. 43-45).

NASA is another extremely large and complex organization that utilizes the various forms of project management throughout its organization. NASA headquarters, situated in Washington, D.C., is responsible for the management of the entire United States space program.

Each program within NASA is a huge undertaking in itself, requiring control and coordination of many diverse resources within and outside the organization. Time and cost parameters are associated with all programs. Each program office has many divisions which coordinate the various functional tasks within their speciality. For example, the Goddard Space Flight Center is responsible for the development and management of the unmanned space flight projects.

Each project is staffed with technical and administrative specialists to assist the project manager in the management of a project. Outside firms contracted by NASA perform their tasks within a similar project organization as well.

In the past three decades, project management has matured into an accepted approach to efficiently and effectively develop new technology and systems within the defense and aerospace industries.

ENGINEERING AND CONSTRUCTION

The construction industry has been a major contributor to the national economy, accounting for at least 10% of the gross national product (GNP) in most developed countries. Various project management structures are widely used throughout this diverse industry. The degree to which project management techniques are utilized depends mainly on the nature and size of the project, but to a lesser extent also on the owner's desire to control cost, schedule, and quality of the project.

In terms of organization, the industry is a loose conglomeration of independent designers, builders, developers, financiers, skilled craftsmen, material and equipment suppliers, and managers, who are brought together temporarily for a single project. Traditionally, design and construction have been performed relatively independently of each other by separate firms specializing in each aspect of the building process. Although project teams would be established within each firm for the purpose of carrying out their respective tasks, generally no one individual was charged with the overall planning and control of the entire project. However, as the size and complexity of projects increased and a higher degree of specialization took place within not only the type of work but also within the organization of the various firms, appointment of a formal project manager became a necessity.

The concept of project management in construction is no different than that in product development or space programs. The objective of the project manager is to plan, coordinate and control the resources involved to accomplish the completion of the project.

The growth of project management in the 1970s was accompanied by a steady improvement in the organizational structures and management techniques associated with project management. Also, rapid changes in computer technology have led to more efficient and effective control systems for both cost and schedule performance.

Thus, the use of project management has become the rule rather than the exception for certain types of projects and a viable alternative for many others.

Today project management is commonplace on not only very large, complex projects, but also on many routine projects such as new office buildings or airport facilities.

While project management is used mainly in construction to satisfy the high degree of specialization involved and coordination requires, other benefits and reasons for its use exist. Generally, design professionals are not good managers, as their education, experience, and concern lies within the technical aspects of a project rather than the managerial side. Thus, the introduction of a professional manager improves the efficiency of the overall building process through better planning and coordination not only of the construction activities but also the conceptual design, proceurement, and commissioning phases. Communication and information flow between different disciplines is enhanced, thus, eliminating many future potential problems. Weekly project review meetings help in closing the gap between separate groups and/or companies and promote cooperation among all groups involved.

When a project is to be performed under the fast-track, phased construction or design-build concept, project management is almost a necessity. If construction is to substantially overlap design, an experienced project team must be actively involved in the scheduling of design and construction, letting of contracts, control of cost and especially scheduling and coordination of the multiple prime contractors. However, before implementing the fast-track approach, the benefits of an early finish must be weighed carefully against the increased cost of construction due to the unavoidable changes, revisions, late drawings, and so on. Fast-tracking is common in industrial construction where time savings are frequently financially more interesting to an owner than the additional costs resulting from frequent change orders with the resulting necessity for more sophisticated scheduling and control methods that have been developed to minimize extra costs.

Rarely does an owner possess the necessary resources or expertise to manage a large or complex project; therefore, the services of a project management firm are imperative for such projects. Some of the services that may be rendered by a project management firm include (Caspe, 1977, p. 3):

> Preliminary studies
> Conceptual design
> Value analysis
> Detailed design
> Bid document preparation
> Contractor selection and negotiation
> Overall project planning, control, and reporting
> Equipment and material purchasing
> Construction coordination and control
> Commissioning

The extent to which these services are required by an owner is determined by his desire to control cost, schedule, and quality, as well as his in-house capabilities and resources. In some instances, the owner may prefer a "turnkey" project where the project manager has full control and authority throughout the project life cycle. The completed project is then handed over to the owner for him to "turn the key" and start production. However, most owners are reluctant to give an outside firm "free rein" on their project and typically set up their own counterpart project team to monitor or even work in direct liaison with the consultant's team.

In the construction industry, project management firms are often referred to as Engineer/Procurement/Construction (EPC), or Engineer-Construction (EC) firms. They are used almost exclusively in industrial and other complex projects involving many engineering disciplines. Matrix organizations are commonly found within these firms.

There are numerous well-documented examples of EPC firms that have successfully implemented project management techniques on various types of projects, such as process plants, transit systems, offshore oil platforms, wastewater facilities, and all types of electrical generating facilities.

RESEARCH AND DEVELOPMENT

The development of new products and the improvement of existing products and processes is essential to a business operating in today's competitive and dynamic marketplace. New products are continually replacing existing ones to satisfy new as well as traditional consumer needs. The ability of an organization to maintain a strong product line and, hence, profitable growth is directly influenced by the effectiveness of its research and development activities. However, the R&D environment has gained a reputation as one of the most difficult and turbulent environments in which to manage a project. Some of the difficulties faced by R&D management include (Kerzner et al., 1984):

Planning and scheduling of research activities
Motivation of team members
Coordination with marketing and other functional departments
Dependence on others for information and resources
Meddling of executives
Setting of priorities and the assignment of resources
Performance evaluation

In addition, many R & D organizations striving to become more efficient have stressed the need for early recognition and review of (Wolff, 1980, p. 10):

Not reinventing the wheel
Market pull
Planning for efficient manufacturing
Full realization of commercial costs and selling prices
Smooth and efficient transition to commercialization

In light of the above problems and needs, many organizations have found project management to be an effective method of (1) managing the research environment during the "upstream" or early phases of the product life cycle, and (2) coordinating the various functional departments during the "downstream" or development and initial production phases.

Research departments of large corporations are typically responsible for developing new products and extensions to existing product lines and increasing profit margins on existing products. They are usually staffed with a research director, functional managers, program managers, project leaders, and a staff of scientists and engineers. Program managers have overall responsibility for a number of specific projects and usually become involved in the development stages of new products as well. Project leaders coordinate the efforts of a team of engineers and scientists toward a common goal.

Research is best conducted in a participative environment and therefore the implementation of a project management system must be approached carefully. A fine line separates management that creates maximum opportunity for individual motivation and contribution, and one that suppresses freedom and creativity. Those who undertake research have been found to be generally creative and individualistic people who tend to resist highly formalized structures (Martin, 1980, p. 15). Therefore, traditional project management principles must be modified somewhat if this creativity is not to be stifled by an inappropriate management system. A successful approach must provide balanced benefits to the management and the research staff. Success factors for implementing project management in a research lab include (Patrick, 1979, p. 243):

Development of system to suit company's specific needs
Extensive involvement of those affected
Built-in flexibility
Education of users by experienced people

Management must emphasize and communicate to the research team their need to plan and monitor progress and develop strategies if team members are to work effectively within the system. A planning process that includes feedback and updating will enhance communications and help overcome negative comments such as "You can't schedule creativity."

As a project moves from research to development and initial production, input from many different disciplines is necessary.

The various functional departments that become involved with a product during or following research are usually coordinated by a project approach known as product management. Product managers provide specialized management attention to the product, ensuring the smooth flow across functional boundaries. They direct the efforts of finance, marketing, sales, service, and production toward accomplishing the common goal of bringing the product to market.

The use of product management has increased recently, due to the increasing complexity of the marketplace and the need for better control of the development of new products. These changes, have convinced top management to accept product management as an effective extension of their responsibilities and authority for new and improved product lines. A product manager represents to top management a single point of responsibility and accountability throughout the product life-cycle. In delegating their authority, top management also desires to maintain control, considering the importance of time and the high cost of resources involved in achieving a market launch. Product management can achieve better control through proper planning and monitoring of resource allocation. Improved planning leads to increased credibility of schedules and greater commitment of those involved. Also, risk and uncertainty in the decision-making process are minimized.

The use of project management techniques in product development has also been found to contribute to a culture conducive to innovation. Innovative organizations are typically exemplified by increased communication, participative decision-making, and the presentation of new ideas (Cleland, 1984, p. 98).

Management of the research and development phases has been separated here to explain how project management is applicable to each phase. However, depending on the nature of the research and the product, the product manager may well be responsible for both phases. If disciplines such as marketing and finance are closely involved in the research, then the product manager would likely have a mandate of coordination throughout the entire life-cycle.

The pharmaceutical industry is a good example where many companies have increased R&D effectiveness by implementing project management. During the last two decades the industry has been faced with more stringent regulatory demands and increased sophistication and competitiveness of the market. As a result, more attention has been given to the use of project management to coordinate the numerous activities involved in obtaining government approvals, as well as commercial production and marketing. Project teams responsible for planning and control are actively involved in such activities as project evaluation and selection, plant expansion discussions, preparation of applications for regulatory approvals, marketing, and strategic planning.

INFORMATION SYSTEMS

During the past decade nearly all large companies have created some type of management information system (MIS) or information resource management (IRM) department within their organization. These departments exist to provide managers with more accurate, timely, and relevant information to support the decision-making process. This requires the integration of data from the various functional departments as well as outside sources, thus, the emergence of a horizontal or project management approach to this interdisciplinary effort.

MIS and IRM departments typically develop and operate complex computer systems that help them cut across vertical boundaries to assemble data. This data is then processed and made available to the entire organization. However, they are also responsible for implementing specific information or data processing systems within the various departments. The development of a computer program or information system is a project-oriented effort which requires a degree of expertise not normally found within the specific department, as well as coordination with the existing network to ensure compatibility. Planning, coordination, and control of such undertakings and also the subsequent operation of the system can be accomplished effectively by project management techniques and is commonly referred to as data processing project management.

A systems development project can be divided into four distinct phases: systems analysis, program design and development, testing, and implementation. Each phase represents varying degrees of responsibility and coordination for the project manager. User participation during the initial phase is extremely important, as most project failures result from an inadequate or incorrect systems analysis and definition of required end results. The project manager must monitor progress closely during program design, development and testing to ensure performance in accordance with budget, schedule, and technical requirements. Successful implementation requires detailed planning as well as user involvement and training to ensure a smooth transition from manual processing to automation and user acceptance of the new system.

AD HOC MANAGEMENT UNDERTAKINGS

Many types of management undertakings are suitable for project techniques. Any unique, unfamiliar undertaking that requires interdisciplinary efforts will likely be best carried out by an ad hoc committee or task force under the direction of a project leader.

Project teams have been used successfully for the development of long-range strategies in large corporations. Widespread involvement in this planning process is necessary to gain an overall view of the situation. Teams composed of representatives of various disciplines are able to transcend corporate barriers and collect information and ideas from each department. The team may also generate ideas of their own and aid in the evaluation of alternative strategies.

The project approach is often used to organize teams within marketing departments and the advertising industry. A degree of specialization is involved in each of the various efforts required to develop a major advertising campaign or specific sales promotional material. Teams are assembled with personnel from the functional departments (design, layout, operations, media, etc.) to perform the specific undertaking. At the conclusion of the project, members return to their respective departments or are assigned to other projects.

Reorganizations, cost-reduction efforts, or mergers may be accomplished successfully through project management. The ability to change quickly and efficiently is becoming increasingly important for most organizations in today's dynamic business environment. Fluctuating interest and inflation rates and deregulation have forced banks and other financial service companies to break out of their traditional organizational structures and business roles and develop new products and services. The methods used by these companies to adapt to new environments and utilize new technology will have a major influence on their future success.

There are numerous opportunities for project management techniques within educational institutions. Some university faculties have already departed from the traditional vertical "chain of command" and department structure in favor of interdisciplinary committees. These committees, composed of faculty from various backgrounds, are formed around a single teaching and research project. A representative of each committee meets with the dean as required to formulate strategic issues.

Much of the work performed in educational development is project oriented. Teams of school board members, students, teachers, and parents have successfully developed and implemented programs to improve such areas as teaching methods and equipment, reading skills, and creativity.

REFERENCES

Adams, J. R. et al. *Managing by Project Management.* Dayton: Universal Technology Corporation, 1979.

Adams, W. T. "Program Management in Corporate Facility Planning." *Industrial Development 151*(3), May/June 1982.

Archibald, R. D. *Managing High-Technology Programs & Projects.* New York: John Wiley & Sons, 1976.

Baumgartner, J. S. *Systems Management.* Washington: The Bureau of National Affairs, 1979.

Blake, S. P. *Managing for Responsive Research & Development.* San Francisco: W. H. Freeman & Co., 1978.

Bogner, Jr., L. J., and R. B. Fireworker. "Improved Software Development through Project Management." *Data Management 18*(12), December 1980.

Caspe, M. S. *An Overview of PM & PM Services.* Drexel Hill, PA: PMI, 1977 Proceedings.

Cleland, D. I. "Why Project Management." *Business Horizons 7*(4), Winter 1964.

Cleland, D. I. *Matrix Management of Long-Range Planning.* Drexel Hill, PA: PMI, 1973 Proceedings.

Cleland, D. I. *The Contributions of Project Management to Innovation.* Drexel Hill, PA: PMI, 1984 Proceedings.

Cleland, D. I. and W. R. King. *Systems Analysis & Project Management.* New York: McGraw-Hill Book Company, 1975.

Cleland, D. I., and W. R. King. *Project Management Hand Book.* New York: Van Nostrand Reinhold Company, 1983.

2

Organizational Factors

ARNOLD M. RUSKIN *Claremont Consulting Group, Claremont, California*

W. EUGENE ESTES *Consulting Civil Engineer, Westlake Village, California*

The success of a project is greatly influenced by the organizational environment surrounding it. Some organizational factors enhance a project's chance of success, while other threaten it. Wise managers will take advantage of positive factors that may exist and will try to arrange matters so that they are reinforced. They will also try to counter or compensate for any negative factors that are necessarily present.

The following sections describe organizational factors that affect project success, their advantageous and adverse impacts and some possible counteracting adverse impacts, tradeoffs that might be required of various factors, and, finally, possible courses of action for project managers who want to enhance the success of their projects.

EFFECTS OF ORGANIZATIONAL FACTORS

The six major orginizational factors—structure, staffing, client relations, attitude toward risk, communications, and expectations—that affect project success are listed in Table 1. Included in the table are the helpful and adverse effects of these factors on project managers and possible counteractions for the adverse effects.

TRADEOFFS AMONG THE IMPACTS OF ORGANIZATIONAL FACTORS

Project managers typically cannot have everything the way they would like. In order to obtain the advantages of, say, reporting to a higher-level officer in the organization (item 5), they may have to forego the advantages of reporting to an intermediate-level officer (item 6) or advantages that come with reporting to one who considers their work to be of highest priority (item 7).

The time and energy required to counteract adverse effects that accompany one factor may compete with the time and energy needed to counteract the adverse effects of another factor. Is there time, for example, to negotiate the terms for accepting an assignment (item 18), negotiate for key personnel to work on the project (item 1), and stay attuned to the status of other projects underway (item 8)? If not, then the pro-

---

This chapter was reprinted with permission, with modifications, from the *ASCE Journal of Management in Engineering*, January 1986, pp. 3-9.

ject manager should decide which factors and counteractions will have the best payoff for their limited time and energy, and apply their efforts accordingly.

Project managers need to recognize that conflicts may be inherent in their situations and that compromises and tradeoffs may be required in order to function at all.

Similarly, general managers also need to recognize potential conflicts and prepare to deal with them. They should, for example, seriously evaluate the impact of raiding an existing project in order to staff a new project. General managers must consider carefully all the helpful and adverse effects that accompany each particular situation if they are to choose wisely.

RECOMMENDATIONS

Project managers can enhance their overall chance of success by understanding how organizations affect projects and by characterizing their own organizations. They need to identify the features that will be helpful and those that will work against them. They need further to decide which consequences are so serious that they should counteract them vigorously, which deserve a limited amount of counteraction, and which can be tolerated. They can then apply their limited resources where they will do the most good and prevent the most harm.

General managers can enhance the total success of all projects by recognizing the different ways that organization affects projects and project managers. They need to give adequate attention to each new project as it starts up and to monitor interactions among projects, so that small problems are addressed before they become big problems.

Projects operate in environments that can seriously affect performance, cost, and schedule. Indeed, how the project manager works within the project environment can make the difference between success and failure.

Table 1 The Effect of Organizational Factors on Project Managers

Factors	Helpful effects	Adverse effects	Possible counteractions for adverse effects
Structure 1. Matrix organization	Allows the organization to have specialists who could not be justified on a project-by-project basis, thus making available a good selection of talent.	Requires the project manager to negotiate for needed staff.	Plan staffing needs early and allow sufficient time to negotiate staff commitments.
	Enhances apparent capabilities for marketing.	Constrains the project manager's ability to deploy project staff.	Consolidate work packages and arrange for staff in large segments of time wherever possible.
	Minimizes overall manpower fluctuations as projects come and go, thereby minimizing staff members' anxiety about job security.	Staff has at least two types of supervisors: functional managers and private managers.	Communicate with functional managers regarding staff performance. Strive for direction of one voice and reinforce each other's directives and comments when appropriate.
		Can make it difficult to obtain commitments from project team members.	Clearly define staff duties and due dates.
2. Independent project organization	Provides a single supervisor for each staff member	Heightens staff members' anxieties regarding their next assignment after project completion.	Finish on time and prearranged staff transfers to other projects. Do not take on more staff than needed.
	Automatically provides dedicated staff whose deployment is within the project manager's sole control	Requires the project manager to use the full-time services of in-house staff assigned to the project.	Arrange for close supervision. Have a project administrator help plan and schedule work.
	Allows the project manager flexibility in hiring full time specialists and in subcontracting		

Table 1 (Continued)

Factors	Helpful effects	Adverse effects	Possible counteractions for adverse effects
3. Highly structured organization	Individuals know what they are expected to do Standards are well defined and generally observed Work is produced efficiently and quickly in proper circumstances	May produce a hostile environment. Some people chafe under the structure. Adjustments for special cases are difficult to make even when authorized.	Emphasize caring for project staff. Allow individuals whatever leeway they need to function well on as many issues as possible. Break the project into segments that are readily handled by the existing structure, rules, and procedures rather than fight the situation.
4. Open or loosely structured organization	Best for innovative and creative work. Attracts high level professionals.	Very high cost for repetitive work. Some people may flounder. Standards and procedures are not well defined nor commonly followed.	Establish well-understood procedures for repetitive jobs. Provide (or be) a mentor for inexperienced staff. Establish and enforce appropriate standards and procedures for the project.
5. Project manager reports to a division chief, vice president, or higher	Provides easy access to individuals with power and authority to resolve inter-project conflicts over priorities and resources. Reduces day-to-day competition for resources.	Project successes and problems will be highly visible to the firm's highest management. The project manager is vulnerable to receiving guidance directly from the firm's highest management (second guessing).	Prepare well, present one's own case, and answer questions. Accept appropriate guidance graciously; politely rebut inappropriate guidance.
6. Project manager reports to an intermediate level manager	May provide helpful insulation from the firm's highest management.	Lengthens the chain of people who must be consulted to resolve complicated issues	Prepare strategies in advance for obtaining resolution of complicated issues.

		Increases competition for available resources.	Enlist the aid of intermediate managers in carrying out strategies; do not let important issues die on an intermediate desk. Make plans in greater than usual detail and obtain firm staffing commitments.
7. Highest priority from the boss's viewpoint (accompanies high-risk projects)	Resources more readily available.	Makes the project manager subject to more interruption or intervention by a superior who is undisciplined.	Establish a charter for one's own responsibilities and use it as a basis for managing without prior consultation. Keep the boss informed, but do not seek advise needlessly.
8. Intermediate priority from boss's viewpoint	Resources relatively easy to obtain when needed, but does not make the project subject to constant examination and modeling.	Resources may be lost to projects of higher priority.	Keep attuned to status of other projects in progress and plan around potential conflicts.
9. Lowest priority from boss's viewpoint	Considerable freedom to act provide resources are plentiful.	Difficult to get the boss's attention on short notice and for extensive discussions.	Schedule and hold routine meetings with the boss to exchange information. Take the meeting schedule into account when planning a decision that requires the boss's input or approval. Provide extra slack in the project schedule.
Staffing 10. Full-time staffing	Project manager has good control over project staff and can rearranged priorities if necessary.	Projects can cost too much when schedules are changed drastically.	Be sure that the contract or agreement allows increases in costs when schedules are changed.
11. Part-time staffing	Uses limited resources effectively.	Staff may be more interested in their other assignments.	Keep staff interest in your project high. Be straightforward with them and create an atmosphere that helps them like your project.

Table 1 (Continued)

Factors	Helpful effects	Adverse effects	Possible counteractions for adverse effects
12. Staff committed to the project until completion	Assures the project manager that work can be done to schedule.	Staff may become restless as project nears the end.	Maintain detailed schedules right to the end. Avoid adding very small parcels of work.
13. Frequent changes in staff	May resolve other organizational problems but generally at the expense of existing projects.	Gives potential for chaos, lack of continuity, and an unhappy client.	Avoid frequent staff changes if possible. If they are inevitable, then try to make them opportunities to up-grade the staff and to better match people to needs.
14. Dedicated support services	Services can be deployed without consulting outsiders. Gives better control in meeting a well planned schedule.	Resources are generally limited to the dedicated staff. The use of additional services may be difficult to arrange on short notice.	Plan ahead. Try to arrange trades with other user groups.
15. Shared support services	If the central pool does good work and is service oriented, it can provide the best flexibility.	The availability of services may be constrained by the needs of other projects. Services must be arranged in advance.	Plan ahead. Negotiate conflicts with other using groups. Again, plan ahead. Be ready to use the services when they are ready.
16. Project manager is an expert in one field of a multi-disciplinary project	Project manager can develop project plans with insight in his or her area of expertise. Client expectations may be more easily met.	Project manager may give own area of expertise either more or less attention than it deserves vis-a-vis other areas. Project manager may try to do the project rather than manage it.	Practice self-discipline to minimize the adverse effects.

Client Relations

Condition			
17. Project manager participated in selling the work	Project manager can easily assume control of the project when it starts.		Negotiate with the principal client contact the terms under which one will accept the assignment.
18. Project manager did not participate in selling the work	Project manager may be able to introduce needed improvements in the project plan.	Project manager may have problems in accepting the approaches, budget, or schedules that were sold.	
19. Project manager participated in planning the work	Project manager can be held completely responsible for executing the work (assuming proper support).		
20. Project manager did not participate in planning the work		Project manager may have difficulty in accepting the project plan and in persuading others that the plan is viable.	Participate (preferably lead) in all the planning. If joining the project later, validate the plan or revise it starting as of the new date.
21. Project manager is principal client contact	Project manager is close to client and able to understand and meet client needs.	Project manager is subject to interruptions by an anxious or undisciplined client.	Keep the client informed on a frequent and regular basis.
22. Project manager is not the principal client contact	Can give better continuity in sales where several projects come from the same client.	Project manager may receive information late, filtered, or warped. Project manager may be unable to make timely inputs to avoid misconceptions and resolve questions.	Arrange to accompany the principal client contact when meeting with the client. Establish direct communication lines to the client with the principal contact's permission.
23. Project manager deals with a high level contact in client's organization	The project will usually get good attention and fast response and payment of invoices when the work is done right.	Project manager must be capable of satisfying the high level contact.	Negotiate for the resources and authority needed to perform at a satisfactory level before accepting the assignment.

Table 1 (Continued)

Factors	Helpful effects	Adverse effects	Possible counteractions for adverse effects
24. Project manager deals with a low level contact in client's organization	Project manager may be permitted to do the project the way he or she wants.	The work done may in fact be poorly received and payment may be withheld.	Proceed very carefully with every step and insure that the client gets higher level approvals before proceeding.
Attitudes Toward Risk			
25. Potential losses strenuously avoided	Only projects deemed feasible are undertaken.	Little patience is shown for normal and abnormal difficulties, which are believed to have been eliminated.	Project manager must visualize possible difficulties well in advance and prepare management so it will act rationally when difficulties arise.
26. Risky projects knowingly pursued	Normal and even abnormal activities are expected; contingency allowances are provided.	Risks may be underestimated and contingency allowances may be inadequate.	Examine project risks and obtain appropriate contingency allowances or create them when planning project details.
27. Success-oriented proposals favored	The organization wins a larger share of its proposals than it would otherwise.	Little or no provision exists for any difficulties.	
28. Project budgets or schedules overly generous (possibly deliberately or through insufficient validation of estimates)	Provides a comfortable situation for the project manager.	Can induce undue complacency, which can lead to overruns.	Prepare realistic budgets and schedules for the project's elements and strive to work within them despite generous conditions.
29. Total project authorized at the outset	Enables cradle-to-grave planning if uncertainties are not too significant.	Serious reconsideration of later plans may be necessary if earlier work produces significant surprises.	Treat the project as if it were phased; avoid unnecessary premature commitments.

vs.

30. Project authorized in phases	Each project phase is developed after prior work is consolidated.	Project is susceptible to stop-start directives, which upset continuity and threaten resource availability.	Develop cradle-to-grave plans based upon likely, best-case, and worst-case outcome of early phases and select an approach that is least likely to incude stop-start directives.
Communications			
31. Chain of command communications	Staff members can be protected from extraneous requests and directions.	Information may be filtered between the sender and final recipient.	Publish a communications chart at the start of the project. Check information with more than one source.
32. Everyone can talk to anyone	Essential communications can take the shortest route.	Staff members are subject to extraneous requests and directions. Information channels may be filled with material not important to the recipient. Incorrect information can be widely disseminated before it is caught.	Train staff members to check with project manager before making commitments. Hold regular project meetings to exchange and compare information.
Expectations			
33. Satisfied client	Repeat business may be developed.	Selfish interests may have to be subordinated.	Remember that satisfying one's client is the principal duty of a project manager.
34. High quality end product	The reputation of the organization and of the project manager may be enhanced.	May be seen as unwanted "gold plating" by the client.	Let the client know at the earliest appropriate time what standards will be practiced.
35. High profitability required for the project	The project manager may be easily evaluated.	May produce extreme pressure on the project manager and may create a hostile working environment.	Agree upon appropriate profit goals at the beginning.

Table 1 (Continued)

Factors	Helpful effects	Adverse effects	Possible counteractions for adverse effects
36. Performance is emphasized and rewarded *or* 37. Budget is emphasized and rewarded *or* 38. Schedule is emphasized and rewarded	Project manager knows where to put effort	Project manager may be in conflict between his or her own and the client's needs.	Remember that the principal objective of a project manager is to assure client satisfaction. Arbitrary emphasis on secondary issues may affect results on the primary goal.
39. No visible connection between performance and rewards or new assignments	Project manager can put emphasis where it seems best and can apply a reward system that is commensurate with the project's needs and resources.	Project manager uncertain where to compromise when conflicts arise among performance, budget, and schedule.	Hold conferences to establish the priority system operating in the organization.
40. Regular hours worked and vacations taken when scheduled	Extra capacity (occasional overtime) exists for exceptional circumstances. Staff members retain perspective and ability to distinguish between the important and unimportant.	Project manager must plan ahead and work around vacation schedules.	Incorporate a measure of schedule and staffing contingency to provide for unanticipated events.

41.	Much overtime worked and vacations seldom taken	High ratio of direct to indirect labor.	Little unused capacity exists for exceptional circumstances. Staff members burn out and lose efficiency, perspective, and the ability to distinguish between the important and the unimportant.	Limit assignments accepted to the actual long-term capacity of an efficient staff; see that work is done efficiently. Prune unfruitful activities and redeploy efforts.
42.	Satisfied project staff	Staff have a feeling of accomplishment and contribution to the project and may want to assist the project manager again. Staff look forward to increasing roles of responsibility in the profession with commensurate rates of pay.	Staff *may* expect the project manager to assume *all* the responsibility for their well being.	Care for and protect the project staff, but do not overprotect them or be too solicitous.
43.	Satisfied project manager	Project manager will put forth the extra attention and concern needed to make the project succeed	Project manager may be disillusioned if the organization does not cooperate in conducting the project.	Establish a cooperative relationship with all the elements of the organization.

3

The Evaluation of the Contractor-Owner Project Team

WILLIAM S. DICKINSON *ARCO Oil and Gas Company, Dallas, Texas*

The various participants in the execution of a project include the owner, engineering contractors, consultants, licensors, suppliers, vendors, fabricators, construction contractors and usually a number of others. The structure used to define the inter-relationships between all or a part of these is referred to as "project organization." This chapter will consider primarily the organization within the contractor's home office.

Over time, many varieties of organizational arrangements have been used for project execution. In the future we can expect that there will be new and different arrangements as well as some modification to ones used previously.

Even if inappropriate forms of organization are used for a project, it seems that the people involved will somehow find a way to get the job done. This involves the creation of an informal organizational structure to supplant the formal organization. Where possible, it is desirable that one should attempt to make the formal and informal structures coincide to attain increased efficiency.

FORMS OF ORGANIZATION

There are two basic organizations normally considered for projects. These are the matrix and the task force. Frequently used, also, is some combination of these two.

On a task force, the project personnel are assigned to one specific project on a full-time basis. They all report directly to the project manager. The task force concept can be used on projects that are large enough to support dedicated project personnel.

In a matrix organization, the project manager and certain key second line managers/supervisors are assigned full time, but the remainder of the personnel on the team are supplied on an "as needed" basis from a central organization. They will generally be working on more than one project at a time. The matrix is efficient for a project that cannot support a full complement of project personnel. Because of conflicting priorities and lack of consistency due to the changes in staffing, this may not be the most efficient way to achieve the project goals.

In a matrixed project the team members' loyalties may be divided between the project goals and the sometimes opposing goals of their functional groups. On small projects, a matrix organization will generally be used. Where full time participation of the team members is not required, the task force would be inefficient.

Where the workload and complexity of the project are substantial, the task force approach should be used almost invariably. If a project is complex, the need for changing personnel in a matrix organization leads to obvious inefficiencies.

SELECTION OF APPROPRIATE ORGANIZATION

Generally, the project manager should analyze the project and develop an optimized project organization to reflect the advantages and disadvantages of both the task force and matrix organizations for differing requirements.

The project manager must also consider the flow of communication between the owner project team and the engineering and/or construction project teams. The two organizations should have clearly defined responsibilities and authorities to facilitate communication between the groups. Awkward organizational interfaces lead to cumbersome and inefficient operation. The contractor's proposed organization and its interfaces should be an important consideration for the owner when selecting a contractor.

The contractual arrangement also influences the best type of organization for the work. Of course, another consideration is the traditional type of organization used by an owner or contracting firms.

Until the late 1970s, a typical project scenario might proceed in a manner similar to this. The owner would select an engineering contractor, a contractor for the engineering and procurement, or an EPC contractor who would be responsible for the engineering, procurement, and field construction. The work included in the contract would be defined in a scope of work package which would contain the process flow diagrams and preliminary piping and instrument diagrams. Sometimes the work would be started at an earlier point and the contractor might be responsible for preparation of some or all of the documents for the work package. The owner would typically have very few people assigned to the contractor's office and the contractor would have considerable autonomy. The organizational structure used by the contractor was important to the internal operation, but was not highly important to the owner.

RELEVANT TRENDS IN PROJECT EXECUTION

Especially since the mid-1970s, the size and complexity of projects had grown to the point where project failure would have a severe financial impact on the owner. Owners responded by taking a much more active role in the project execution. In addition to the financial concern, there was an equally formidable problem in the definition of the scope. Projects were so large that scope development became an important and necessary part of the work performed in the contractor's office. Significantly increased owner participation was required to effectively accomplish this effort. The net result was that the owner maintained large project teams in the contractor's office and began to take a much more proactive role in managing the project.

Several important changes resulted from this new role of the owners. First, the contractors had to accept the loss of some of their accustomed autonomy and be willing to accept the closer working relationship with the owner. Second, the organizational structures of the contractor and the owner became matters of serious consequence. Good communication flow and efficiency in execution were greatly enhanced by similar team structures on both sides. Since the projects were so large, it followed that the task force approach was used most frequently. This met with the eager approval of most of the owners, as all of the contractor personnel were involved full time on the project, and no conflicting demands were placed on the key project people.

During the early stages of this new approach, the contractor's personnel were sometimes uncertain and frustrated as to their expected roles. Ultimately however a very successful mode for project execution evolved. Initially there were hesitant and groping attempts to smooth out the marriage of the large owner team and the parallel contractor team. In retrospect, we can draw some conclusions from the successful and the unsuccessful efforts.

A contractor would sometimes try to maintain complete control over the efforts and fail to participate in free and open discussion with the client. The contractor personnel maintained a very defensive posture. Frequent and unnecessary conflict and friction arose between the two parties. Because the energy of the work force was diverted from the job at hand to the conflict between the two groups, project outcomes were highly unsatisfactory.

DETERMINANTS OF PROJECT SUCCESS

Successful projects resulted only with mutual recognition of the new relationships and the importance of close cooperation in greater team effort. New ground rules for the relationships were established based on the acknowledgment that success can only come from a joint team effort where the energy devoted to the attainment of project goals is maximized and that devoted to resolve interrelational conflicts is minimized.

If a project is successful, both the owner's and contractor's project teams will enjoy an enhanced image. If the project goes sour, both will suffer. It is appalling that some project managers still believe that they must maintain an adversarial position.

The concept of team effort does not imply that there is overlapping of work efforts or that the owner/contractor are working side by side doing the same task. Team effort is truly achieved by a clear understanding of what the prescribed function of each is. This statement implies that the duties, roles, and responsibilities must be well thought out and then written down, so that they are available in the same form and content to everyone concerned. The process of thinking through responsibilities and work assignments will often avoid activities "falling between the cracks."

EFFECTS OF CHANGES TO PROJECT ENVIRONMENT

The contractor must also realize that he has indeed lost some of the free-wheeling autonomy that he might have previously enjoyed. In his new role he must accept the fact that he will often have more "help" than he really wants.

The owner must recognize that he is now more intimately involved, and because of this, he is now a recipient of more detailed information on the contractor's daily operations. He must be tolerant of those areas of work where progress is being made by "trial and error" or where there are instances of recycling or parallel paths of effort. Monday morning quarterbacking will destroy morale and lead to a deterioration of the project teams.

The team approach should not be misconstrued to preclude constructive criticism as this is healthy and necessary to the new relationship. Problems should be jointly anticipated and jointly resolved.

Although the above discussion has been based on a task force approach with heavy owner participation, the fundamental ideas are generally applicable to a matrix approach where the owner has opted for increased involvement.

One of the necessary elements for success of a project operated by matrix is timely access to the skilled people required. This is a problem that both the owner and the contractor must face to maintain the project schedule and the efficiency of the workforce. Business cycles have great impact on "matrix" projects. During periods of low activity, specialists are generally more available provided the respective staffs have not been unduly trimmed. During periods of high activity, there is severe competition for the available specialists.

IMPORTANCE OF THE PROJECT PLAN

A second important consideration in the use of the matrix organization is the ability of the project team to control the work effort according to the plan. In the matrix organization the personnel have a dual reporting relationship (project and functional); and in addition, may be working for a supervisor who has responsibility for more than one project. Conflicts exist between demands for project progress and budget control in terms of departmental resource utilization and distribution. These conflicts can jeopardize the project when it is not possible to optimize resource allocation across a slate of several projects. Tension over manning can continue to build between the project manager and functional managers if an adverse situation persists. At this time the owner's project manager frequently becomes involved, sometimes in an adversarial rather than supportive role. These same problems may exist on a "task force" project, but they are usually more specific and more easily resolved.

CONCLUSIONS

The two extremes of project team organization are the task force and the matrix. There has been a trend toward the task force due to larger, more complex projects, a desire by the owners to maintain closer control, and a tendency on the part of the owners to insist on using task forces for smaller projects. They rationalize that intermittent inefficient utilization of manpower is offset by improved productivity resulting from a more cohesive team effort.

Each case must be considered individually and evaluated to select the project organization most appropriate for the project and for the contracting parties.

4

Basic Organizational Structure
and Staffing for the Execution
of Projects

ARTHUR C. BURNS* *The Ralph M. Parsons Company, Pasadena, California*

The project team is the equivalent of a separate company organization that has been established to perform the work. The team calls upon contractor/owner resources as required to assist them in performing this work.

There are many variations of project organization. Obviously, the organization must suit the project/contractor needs. Project organizations vary from project management utilizing departmental or even subcontracted expertise to perform work to full project task force operations where the project workers are located in a common area. Factors such as owner restraints, contractor policies, and project characteristics contribute to the actual type of project organization to be established for the project. Each project organization must be able to respond to the work performance guidelines that are imposed.

The growing trend of project operation is toward the project task force, with some modifications to suit specific project and corporate needs. The major facets of project operations, engineering, procurement, construction, operations, and followup are carried out from project inception through mechanical completion, startup, and acceptance.

PROJECT ORGANIZATION

The basic organization for any project is similar to that given in Figure 1. The project team under the project manager and his coordinating staff consists of three production groups: engineering, procurement, and construction. These are complemented by project controls and corporate support. Each project team is tailored to suit the needs of the project and also the talents and experience of project personnel.

The project manager is in charge of all project activities. On small projects, he or she may also serve as a project engineer or may manage several projects concurrently. On larger projects, he or she is supported by project engineers who are assigned to oversee specific project coordination assignments. On very large or mega-projects, he or she may be called a project director and will oversee other project managers who are assigned to manage components of the project. (A typical project engineering organization for a large project is shown in Figure 2.) Personnel assignments call for careful matching of experience and ability with project requirements.

The project work program is performed by the production disciplines: engineering, procurement, and construction. They interface with each other and are supported by

*Retired

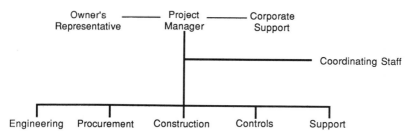

Figure 1 Basic project organization.

corporate departments such as office services, fiscal, and accounting. The project manager looks to project controls for his planning and scheduling, estimates and cost control, and material control activities.

The project organization must suit the specific time phases of the project. The initial project group provides the nucleus for expanding the organization for the prime activities. Typical project organizations are shown for conceptual, front-end engineering, production engineering, and construction work in Figures 3 through 6.

These figures show the principal work activities of the project production disciplines in summary form as the project moves through the *conceptual* and *front end engineering* work phases into the *production engineering* and *construction* activities. Throughout these phases of project work, the project manager and his team are in charge of the project operation and have total responsibility for the performance of the work. Contingent upon the contract conditions, project activities from phase to phase may overlap or the transition may be an abrupt change. Overlapping can occur when the work is performed by a single contractor. The abrupt change results from the owner's decision to complete each phase before the next phase starts.

TASK FORCE CONCEPT

A project task force is established to perform a specific project. A prime concept is to provide singular responsibility and authority for the project. The owner and contractor look solely to the project manager for directing all project activities. A key to successful task force operation calls for the team members to be located together in a central area. This is conducive to a team atmosphere, shortens lines of communications, and improves work efficiency. Key project members, located in close proximity to the project manager, have their working teams close at hand. Engineering designs and model construction are carried out in the production area of the task force. The project files are centralized, providing ready access for up-to-date information.

Each project will have its own computer terminals for use in technical, procurement, controls, and administrative work. Though a computer technician may be a member of the project team, each project discipline is held responsible for its own input and output data. Communications via the computer route are greatly enhanced. Via electronic mail programs, messages are received instantly and written conversations conducted. The ability to obtain printouts at any time simplifies the documentation aspect.

The owner's representatives are also centralized. They may be located with the contractor's project task force or in a nearby area. It is imperative that close liaison and communications be established between the owner representatives and the contractor's project task force team. The owner representatives offer guidance and approvals to ensure that they are receiving the product or service they want. The contractor's project task force is to perform the work. A good working relationship is necessary. It is important that the owner representatives deal with their counterparts in

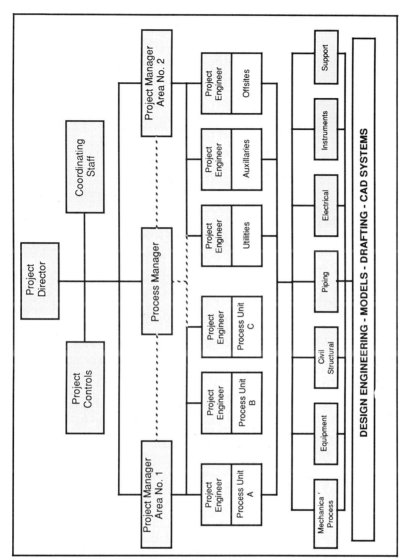

Figure 2 Typical major project organization – engineering.

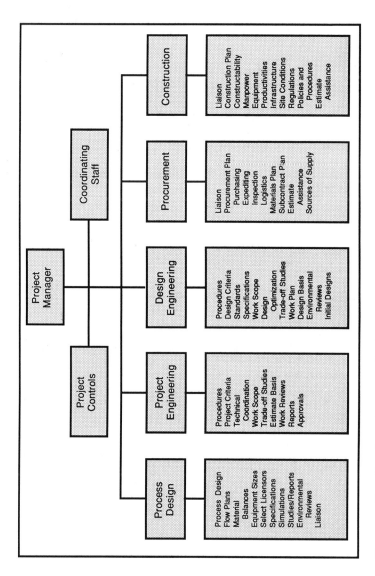

Figure 3 Functional project organization-conceptual phase.

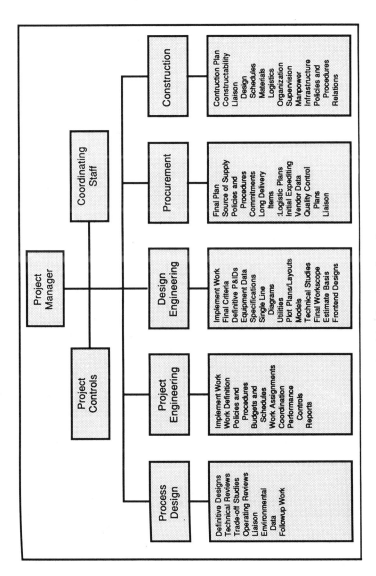

Figure 4 Functional project organization–front end work.

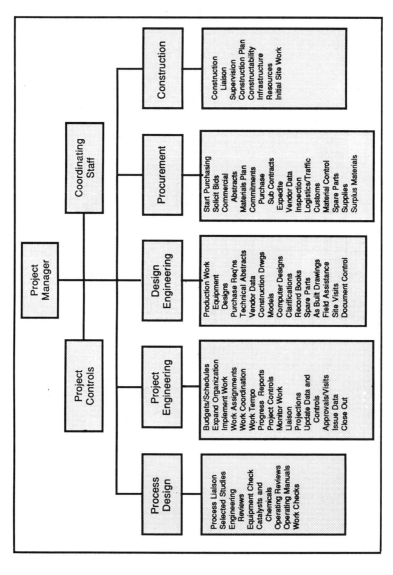

Figure 5 Functional project organization-production engineering.

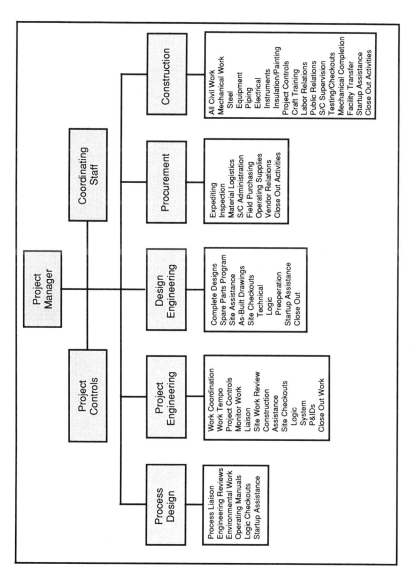

Figure 6 Functional project organization—construction.

the project task force and not with various contractor discipline workers. This breach leads to misunderstandings and upsets the work program.

As mentioned previously, under the project task force concept the project manager provides the singular representative of responsibility for the project. He represents the contractor to the owner. Internally, he represents the owner to the contractor. Operating within established guidelines, the project manager serves both owner and contractor. He must ensure that the owner receives proper and timely reports and that all available resources are used effectively so that the work is performed within limits established for time and money. The owner must be kept abreast of all project activities, especially those that may disrupt the work program. For the contractor, the project manager must establish and maintain favorable rapport with the owner, and obtain excellent performance from the project team, thereby attaining the profit goals that were established.

The success or failure of project operations is attributed to the project manager. He has both the authority and responsibility to manage the project. He selected his team; now he must establish the project tempo and establish the winning spirit. He must be a first-class motivator and get things done. The adage, "Plan your work—work your plan" begins with him. Any successful project manager has acquired that extra sense of being able to foresee trouble and avoid it. Furthermore, he must know when he is in trouble and know where to seek help in providing corrective measures. Follow-up and feedback ensure that decisions have been carried out.

Generally, when projects are performed within the contractor's offices, it is not practical or economical to attain a 100 percent task force team. Where projects are isolated such teams are formed and have proved economical. There are various work disciplines that can perform their work more effectively in their own manner and locale rather than with the task force team. Disciplines such as process designs, equipment designs, commodity purchasing, expediting, inspection, and administrative support are in this category. Their work efficiencies lie in their high degree of specialization. These disciplines do have their project representatives who are a part of the task force team and are located with the main task force team. They liaison and coordinate their discipline work programs so that the net effect is the same as if all work was performed in the task force area.

Along these lines a question may arise concerning the responsibility of work quality and performance when performed by the project task force. A simplified functional organization showing project and design engineering is presented to clarify this situation (see Fig. 7). The various technical disciplines who have assigned their personnel to the project have complete responsibility for the technical adequacy of design. This applies to adherence to codes, regulations, laws, basic criteria, and so on. The project team, via its project engineers, coordinates designs and schedules. They see that project requirements are met; as such they are called upon to approve the drawings. The project task force concept should not interfere with the various administrative functions; however, they should be able to input their recommendations and recognition of performances. The personnel assigned to the project take their direction from the project team.

It has been said that the two key people on a project are the project manager and project construction manager. Each has to manage his phase of work. The success of a project does rest with their ability to manage and delegate; however, the performances of other project members such as technical, procurement, coordination, controls, and administrative support staff all contribute toward the success of the project performance.

In summary, a project task force should be looked upon as an entity that has been established to conduct the business of carrying out a work assignment within corporate guidelines and project specifications and procedures.

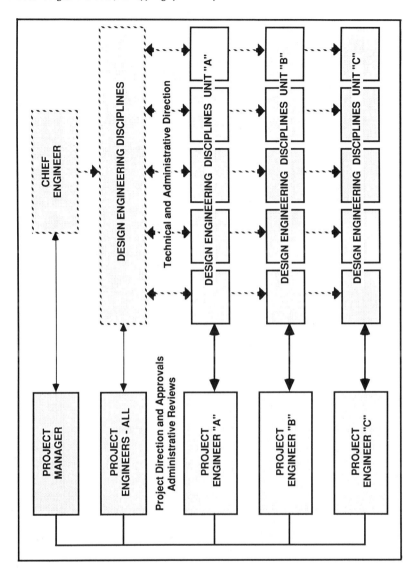

Figure 7 Project team—design engineering coordination.

KEY PROJECT PERSONNEL

The selection and assignment of project personnel must take into consideration such factors as availability, talent, experience, personality, including the ability to work as a team member and accomplish objectives. A team of all star performers does not necessarily represent a successful team. A team that allows for a complete blend of personalities will be more successful. A brief description of key project personnel follows.

Project Manager

Again it is to be noted that the project manager is the key member of the project team. He must manage the project. He delegates and coordinates the work activities, staying abreast of the work program. Through communications, oral and written, along with visits and meetings, he is fully cognizant of operations. Work status and work accomplishments are evaluated and projections made of the project's future. Any corrective measures are initiated and followed up to ensure their effectiveness.

When project responsibilities are centered at the construction site, owners may require that the project manager establish residence at the site and direct the project operations. This occurs when production engineering has been completed and full mechanical work is underway at the construction site. This move generally matches the relocation of the owner's representative from the engineering offices to the work site.

It is important not to ostracize the project manager from his project and corporate support or to impose unnecessary restraints upon him. With the continued development and usage of remote computer stations, the project manager is able to maintain his current status regarding all project matters.

Other owners consider that the construction performed at the work site is the same as, say, an engineering discipline work task. Here skilled personnel are managing and performing the work. The project manager may be a frequent visitor; however, he maintains his project location.

Both concepts have merit and have proved effective. Factors such as personalities, experience, and talents must be recognized. In any event, the project manager must be where the action is, controlling the project destiny.

Project Engineer

Project engineers are responsible for directing and coordinating the engineering activities of the project. This entails all engineering designs relating to design criteria, procurement of equipment and materials, and construction and operation of the plant. Project engineers see that the various design and mechanical engineering disciplines are provided with the project design criteria and restraints. They do not assume responsibility for the technical adequacy of engineering designs; that is the responsibility of the chief discipline engineers assigned to the project task force.

Project engineers are responsible to the project manager to ensure that the work is performed in accordance with project and company guidelines regarding economics, procedures, specifications, and standards. The definition of work scope, the establishment of interface conditions between project components, planning and scheduling, communications and engineering liaison with other departments, are key parts of his project activities.

Recognition and adherence to budgets (manpower and material costs) along with work quality are also key functions of project engineers.

It is not uncommon for project engineers to meet with vendors regarding production and subsequent delivery and cost problems. Also, they should visit the construction site and offer clarification and explanation of complex items. Design engineering specialists may accompany them on these visits.

During the latter part of construction, selected engineers will be temporarily assigned to the construction site to assist with interpretations, clarifications, and mechanical and system checkouts.

Project Procurement Manager

The project procurement manager is responsible to the project manager for all of the procurement functions of the project. He will direct and coordinate the project procurement functions of purchasing, inspection, expediting, material logistics, vendor data control, and contract administration. This work shall comply with the company guidelines modified by the specific project procedures. The project procurement manager will establish sources of supply for project materials and equipment. Project commitments may be made for bulk materials and equipment when economics so dictate.

It is important to note that the procurement manager is the official project representative to the vendors and suppliers. This is necessary because of the commercial requirements. Procurement shall be present when technical clarifications are discussed—reviewing many such clarifications may avoid unneeded changes and unwanted extra costs. Similarly, procurement shall screen vendor data review markups. Again, a technical note may entail costs that can be avoided. It is quite disconcerting to receive a cost extra because of a reduction in nozzle size from 10" to 8". While technical personnel thought, "This will save us money," the vendor states, "I have already purchased the 10" size—I must add its disposal cost to meet your revision."

Vendors and subcontractors are invited to supply separate commercial and technical bids in efforts to facilitate a contractor's review. Whereas bid leveling is a responsibility of procurement, the technical review and input is the prime consideration.

Expediting is a vital procurement tool. Invariably things do happen that cause changes and delays—many are self-inflicted. Expediting starts with the release of requirements for quotation and continues until shipment and closeout occurs. Care must be taken to ensure that the expediting expense is fruitful. The use of desk-type expediters (other than coordinators) appears marginal. The real results are achieved when vendor visits are made, shop schedules reviewed, and work schedule rearrangements made. Field expediting visits (continuous expediting where warranted) are fruitful.

Inspection (vendor quality control) is another vital activity. Approval of fabrication procedures, and periodic and continuous inspection will assure shipments that do not have to be reworked in the field. Such repairs are costly and time consuming. The quality of work is recognized as a valuable item. Many owners and contractors call for inspections to be made by certified inspectors.

Subcontract administration also is a prime discipline of procurement. The contractual terms and conditions are established and continuous administration will allow efficient and least costly activity. Procurement subcontractors are dispatched to the construction site where they perform their work under the direction of project construction management.

The use of computers in the procurement discipline is of great importance. Its use has been employed in requisitioning and buying, expediting, vendor data, and inspection monitoring.

Project Construction Manager

The project construction manager is responsible to the project manager for all of the project construction activities. (Some contractors consider this position as the prime project managerial position.) He enters the project early and, along with construction planners, participates in project events, thereby interjecting construction-oriented modes of thinking into the project. For example, based upon material delivery information, he establishes the sequence of work areas (how construction will back out of the plant). Thus all project team participants are made aware of the common work sequence and proper priorities can be established. It is disconcerting and costly to concentrate on plans and materials that require storing at the construction site awaiting their sequenced installation.

With the construction plan in hand, the selection and implementation of the construction team follows. Construction staff members are assigned, mark up meetings are held, and site preparation work is started.

The project construction manager is in charge of all site activities. He receives project direction from the project manager. He is provided construction expertise and services from the corporate manager of construction. A typical project construction organization chart is shown in Figure 8. The project construction manager, sometimes referred to as the resident construction manager, has his staff of labor relations, safety, and public relations personnel, and his production team of field engineering, production, and field administration work. Any subcontract administration is considered a part of the production group. Field quality control is the responsibility of the technical team.

The construction work is divided into work area assignments in accordance with task force activities.

Communications are ongoing. If necessary, formal or informal meetings are held daily between the construction site and the project task force team. Reports, transmittals, and communications are documented and checked to ensure that information is received. Site visits and office visits are carried out when necessary in the interest of the project work program.

Project Control Manager

The project control manager works closely with the project manager. His primary areas of activity are:

Planning and scheduling
Estimating
Cost control and trending
Progress reporting
Material control
Document control
Computer application

All project control activities utilize computer programs for developing and monitoring the work performance.

The staff under the project control manager includes a project estimator, project scheduler, project cost engineer, project material technician, project document technician, and a computer liaison representative. Depending upon the size of the project, these support personnel may serve part time assignments or be assigned full time and have additional assigned help.

The project control manager is responsible for development of procedures and programs to suit the control elements of the project. Once these are implemented, he then monitors the programs and issues reports and supplies data to the project manager. Through continuous monitoring of the project performance activities, he serves as the principal source of information relating to job status, performance, and costs. It is his responsibility to alert the project manager of any potential threats to establish schedules and budgets. The project control manager and project manager through their experience recognize the validity of data in arriving at realistic projections and project management decisions.

The material control program, whether manual or computerized, is vital. The status of equipment and materials under fabrication, as well as their scheduled shipments and deliveries, is vital to the planning of work activities. Similarly, documents such as technical data, design drawings, vendor data, and project data, require control to ensure that proper distribution of information is made and that data is issued according to schedules.

While the project control manager monitors all of the project control activities, the project manager receives composite and summary reports complete with backup information as requested. The project manager controls his project.

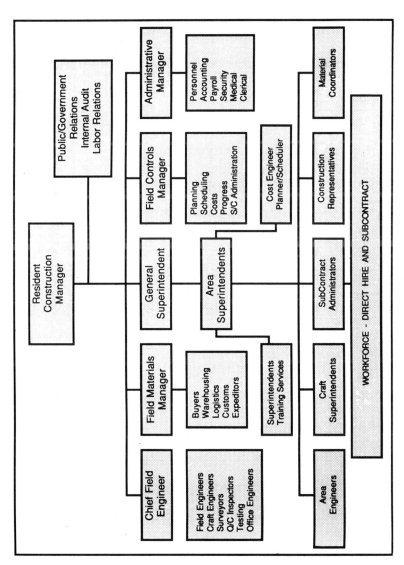

Figure 8 Typical summary, construction organization.

Project Designs Coordinator

In effect, the project designs coordinator is responsible for directing and coordinating the design engineering activities of the project. In performing these tasks, he is responsible to the project manager and also to the corporate manager of engineering to ensure that the work is performed in compliance with the project requirements and company gudielines. The definition of work scope, the establishment of interface conditions between project components, work scheduling and monitoring, data availability, design reviews, and design liaison are some of his principal project activities.

A project designs coordinator is generally employed only for larger projects. He represents the technical engineering coordinator. The technical adequacy and responsibilities always rest with the chief discipline engineers who have assigned their personnel to the project. On smaller projects, and also under certain circumstances, the coordination of design engineering is performed by project engineers who are on the staff of the project manager. These project engineers are basically charged with full coordination of all project activities under their jurisdiction.

Project Computer Coordinator

The computer department is a general corporate support department. It is necessary to provide each project with a computer coordinator. On small projects, computer coordination may be part time, while larger projects require full-time services. For project convenience, the computer coordinator may report to the project control manager. His duties are to establish and maintain computer procedures and liaison. In addition he modifies and develops various programs to best serve the project need as directed by the project manager.

Projects may have satellite computer stations that can input data and receive computer data including hardcopy printouts. For the most part the various project disciplines will input and receive their own computer data. For example, process designs and technical designs have their own technical and economic computer programs. Such computer activities are a normal part of their design operation. Similarly, scheduling, cost and estimating, and procurement handle their own programs. The computer coordinator assists and coordinates the work.

It should be noted that some projects call for the computer coordinator to input and receive and distribute all computer data. Such an operation creates a "bottleneck" and results in unnecessary expenditures of both time and money.

Project Support

The administrative manager or administrative assistant to the project manager generally coordinates the corporate support activities that are performed for the project. Such services include:

> Office services. Providing facilities, furniture and space, reproduction
>   and copies, general office services, supplies, mail, transportation
>   and travel, records, technical library, etc.
> Fiscal. Providing accounting services, contracts, insurance, internal
>   audits, taxes, financing, etc.
> Industrial relations. Providing manpower employment, personnel project
>   relocation agreements, salary administration, training, etc.
> Quality assurance. Providing guidance, direction, and approvals of specific
>   quality assurance programs and audits.

It should be noted that appreciable project support activities are not directly related to the specific advancement of the project work and, as such, are reimbursable by means of unit costs and/or overhead allowances.

Owner Organization

The owner installs his project management team in the contractor's office and also at the construction work site to guarantee prompt decision-making and to oversee the work program to ensure that the end product fulfills the established and contracted goals. Project team sizes vary with project magnitude and type of contract. Team duties may entail only periodic visits and meetings with representatives, organizing a small task force, or a large task force in excess of fifty people. The owner's team stationed in the contractor's office performs a monitoring role. They offer their services in reviews, appraisals, and expedition of work functions. The owners rely upon the contractors to execute the project work efficiently. A good harmonious relationship between the owner's and contractor's project team plays a vital role in the success of the project. The owner's team is headed by a project manager, with support talent in the fields of project coordination, planning and scheduling, cost engineering, procurement, contracts, and construction. In addition, the owner's project manager may solicit special expertise from his organization to participate in a specific project activity. Principal activities here include technical engineering, quality controls, contracts, financial audits and construction expertise.

In general, the owner's project team should reflect an organization similar to that of the contractor.

Project Work Assignments

Earlier statements outlined the basic project organization and noted that it would require modification to suit the specific needs of the project. Some of the major factors that must be evaluated when establishing a project organization are listed below.

> Type of facility, typical vs. new development
> Size of facility, small vs. multiple components
> Complexity, simple vs. intricate designs
> Location of work, local, domestic, international
> Project timetable, fast track vs. developmental
> Work scope definition, defined vs. to be developed
> Owner, requirements and experience
> Personnel, previous associations and experience, availability, talent, capabilities
> Contractual matters, definitions, restraints, interpretations

When establishing a project organization, the first priority is to identify the components of the facility. It may prove desirable to combine several components into a single project work assignment. The use of a work breakdown structure facilitates this division and combination of work. The talent of the project team, including experience and work associations are evaluated. Personnel restraints regarding magnitude of work must be fully evaluated. No one should be assigned work that is beyond his capability. Neither should there to be an assignment that does not represent a challenge. In effect, the true work assignment is tempered by many factors.

Each identifiable project component is assigned an identification number that is used throughout the project and by all of the project disciplines. These cost breakdowns tie in with the work breakdown, and in conjunction with the corporate standard code of accounts, provide a means for controlling and coordinating the project work activities. The various cost levels can be "rolled up" into a cost summary for the entire project, or specified for individual or multiple components.

Chronological work assignments are made for relatively fixed project positions. Manpower buildup, peaks, and reductions are developed for the project production groups such as engineering, procurement, and construction. The manpower loadings are based upon past experiences and specific project characteristics. They are made for each discipline involved for each group. This ensures that all facets are evaluated.

An overall manpower loading may be essentially the same; however, it lacks the assurance that each work discipline can suitably meet the project staffing requirements.

During the course of project activities, the evaluations of progress versus expenditures will serve as indicators to the project manager as to what actions are to be taken and when to implement them.

In general component assignments are made on a geographical basis. All work within defined boundaries comprise the component. This is a clearcut approach. Sometimes the work is segregated by functions and work disciplines. These cases involve an appreciable degree of increased coordination.

SUMMARY

A project task force represents an entity that has been established to accomplish a specific goal. It receives support from and its operations are monitored by the senior management of the company.

The task force principle of operation does not necessarily reflect the more economical performance; however, it generally results in the most economical project when taking into consideration the time-money-work effort and work quality.

The concept of dividing a major project into smaller components that are controllable allows each project component to operate on the task force principle. This maintains the overall objective of task force operation.

5

Task Force Project Execution: Pros and Cons

JOEL H. BENNETT   *C F Braun, Inc., Alhambra, California*

KEITH E. HUGHES*   *Santa Fe Braun Inc., Alhambra, California*

The term "task force" is used to describe a wide range of organizational structures set up to perform a specific task. In the following discussion, the nature of the task force is explained together with the differences which exist from the more permanent corporate organizations, in particular, the differences between the "task force" and the "functional" work approach where the various elements of the parent organization utilized are not under the control of a project manager.

DEFINITION

A task force can be anything from a three-man group to an organization of several hundred or several thousand people. The organization's charter is to successfully complete a specific project. The organization is assembled for that particular project and is dispersed at the completion of the project. The organization can be a very flexible one and can change over the life cycle of the project to suit the particular emphasis of the project at the time. Different task forces within a corporation can have different organizations, depending on the needs of the project being handled.

ORGANIZATION

The organization of a task force is similar to the corporate organization in the sense that the project manager as leader delegates responsibility of handling specific aspects of the project's business to various groups. The differences are (1) that the task force will not have any direct sales responsibility and (2) that the task force will rely on the corporation to handle personnel administration, legal matters, and like functions. The organization is an extremely efficient one in the sense that it is organized for one particular project, while a corporation has to worry about the future. The project's charter is well defined; and at its conclusion, it goes out of business.

A task force can be organized as an hierarchical-type organization, with each level of management fully responsible for all personnel under them; or it can be

---

Current Affiliation: Consultant, Laguna Beach, California

organized as a matrix-type organization. In general, the hierarchical type is more prevalent. However, on larger projects that involve a considerable number of separate tasks, the task force itself, can be organized as a matrix organization. An example of the latter would be a large study project where the organization may consist of many task managers who themselves need to draw upon a group of disciplines for support.

EVOLUTION

Most companies start off small, perhaps with a group of individuals, each specializing in a different aspect of an industry who together can provide the services required to perform a particular project. As the company grows, it tends to grow along departmental lines with each department providing their particular expertise for all of the projects underway at any time. In many ways this provides the best technical input for a project; the full expertise of the department and its department head is applied to every project. Uniformity throughout projects is created, and the experience gained on one project is applied to subsequent projects.

As the company grows and becomes capable of executing larger projects, the departments become more remote from the day-to-day problems of satisfying the project needs in regard to schedule and customer interface. They tend to become more concerned with maintaining their discipline organization. This creates a situation where several project managers, each responsible for one individual project, try to set priorities with the departments for the work to be done according to the project schedule. At the same time the project has to rely upon each of the departments to maintain the interfaces with other departments to ensure that continuity between disciplines is maintained.

Clients and project managers may develop a feeling of frustration and a sense of loss of control over their projects in this type of situation. Because of this, clients and project managers desire a dedicated team of people who are responsible to them, who have no conflicting demands on their time or efforts outside of the particular project they are assigned to.

APPLICABILITY

The task force approach is most applicable when the project size and duration are such that people can be dedicated to the project on a full-time basis and, ideally, when all of the people can be relocated to one common area. The close proximity of the team members to each other helps considerably with interdisciplinary coordination and also fosters an esprit de corps within the task force.

On large projects, most clients install a team of their own representatives at the contractor's office. Hence they are in favor of the task force approach since they can physically see the team at work. On cost-reimbursable projects, the client's team can readily reconcile the billings each month as they can relate them to the team members who are located in their task force area.

A project involving the part-time services of a considerable number of personnel does not readily lend itself to the task force approach and certainly not a task force relocated into a common dedicated area. Likewise, a project of short duration—less than about three months—may not warrant the physical relocation of staff to a central area. Also, by definition, the shorter duration project would probably be a smaller project where most of the advantages of a common area would not be an overriding consideration.

A "limited task force" approach is sometimes justified for those projects where a nucleus of full-time people make up a dedicated task force, but where the project requires only part-time or short-term services of others. For these projects, only the nucleus is located in a dedicated area and additional staff is called upon on an as-needed basis.

A precise decision as to the minimum size and duration of a project to be task forced is not possible. Most times the project objectives and scope will determine this. As soon as the project warrants the full-time dedication of three or four peple, you basically have a task force. For such a small group, it would be a limited task force, as this nucleus would probably require only part-time or short-term assistance from others. When the project involves the equivalent of less than 20 or 30 people at the peak, it may still be run efficiently without all personnel dedicated full-time to the project.

Most clients would not object to the work being done by a disperse group since the numbers are still small enough to keep track of. As membership approaches 50, the balance is probably tipped toward dedicating the majority to the project. When the number exceeds 50, the need for a task force invariably is almost certain.

The decision to locate the team in a central dedicated area usually depends on the duration of the project. For a project with a duration of less than three months, the cost of relocating personnel is difficult to justify. If the project duration is greater than six months, then a relocation is usually justified. Between three and six months, it depends on the project, the organization of the particular company, and the normal physical location of the people assigned to the project.

Need for tight security of information and work quarters is also a valid reason for moving the task force to a suitable common area.

PREFERENCES FOR THE TASK FORCE

The project manager will almost invariably prefer to have a full-time dedicated team that is fully under his control. Preferably it is physically located in one area so that he can, on a day-to-day basis, have his team in close proximity. Project personnel generally feel better when they are part of a dedicated team and this creates positive motivation.

Conversely, individual departmental managers are less enthusiastic about the task force approach, since their direct control over day-to-day activities of the project is diminished. They have more difficulty in controlling quality and consistency, and using personnel efficiently.

EFFECT ON QUALITY

The best quality is achieved when the greatest amount of technical expertise and experience can be focused on the project. This can be maximized in the departmental type of organization as the full resources of each department can be applied to the work. In the task force arrangement, the lead person in the task force from each department tends to be the highest level of problem-solving that is applied to the project except in a crisis situation. Obviously, this reduces the level of readily available expertise.

Systems and procedures may be set up to permit department head review of all of the major decisions made by their lead personnel on each of the task force groups. This helps to ensure that the work performed at the task force level is equivalent to that which would have been provided by the department itself. The degree of success in implementing such controls varies considerably from company to company, but is a measure used by many clients in evaluating a company's potential performance.

ADVANTAGES AND DISADVANTAGES

Reasons for using or not using a task force approach rather than a functional or departmental approach are summarized in Table 1.

OBSERVATIONS

From the 1960s into the 1980s, trends indicate an increasing acceptance of the task force versus functional approach in manpower-intensive projects. The advent of computer-aided tools with the application of high-cost equipment has caused some to reconsider that trend. The rapidly decreasing cost of hardware and availability of efficient networked systems appears to be favorable to the task force. At this time, the task force appears to be a most popular and effective organizational structure to achieve successful project execution.

Table 1 Advantages and Disadvantages of Task Force Approach to Project Management

	Task force	Departmental (or functional)
Control	Physically all people visible and easier for project management and client to "control" for complete focus on projects	Primarily department control
Efficient use of time	Standby time unavoidable if team is to be kept together throughout critical project time	Very efficient from point of view of work distribution
Changes to the work assigned	Excellent control for multiple or sequential changes	Difficult in handling changes with different people doing same work over. Could be disastrous for quick sequential changes unless monitored very carefully
Space utilization	Significant physical task forcing needs very careful scheduling to minimize space utilization	Minimum space utilization
Effect on size of organization	Requires somewhat larger organization to accomplish same level of work as functional approach. Extent of excess size depends on efficiency of manpower scheduling and discipline performance schedules	Base organizational size
Quality	Less discipline control of quality	Maximum discipline quality control
Personnel development	Provides opportunity for discipline individuals to move into leadership roles	Opportunities limited
Procurement	Tends to require "project buyers" of broader skills than commodity buying approach	Allows very efficient commodity buying approach

6

The Project-Driven Organization

W. ROSS COX *CRSS Constructors, Inc. , Houston, Texas*

The project-driven organization system breaks with the traditional approach to project execution, eliminating division of employee allegiance and reducing overhead.

Engineering and construction (E&C) companies are trimming all of the fat out of their operations and are restructuring to meet the demands of the marketplace. The project-driven organization approaches this problem from the project manager's standpoint and results in an organization that is responsive to the needs of the project and the client, while offering a minimum of internal conflict.

For a number of years, the matrix organization has been employed as the best method for executing projects within an E&C company. In many ways, it is a good system even though the objectives of the functional departments and those of project management do not always appear to be compatible.

Differences in departmental and project management objectives, as well as the dual reporting relationship, create internal conflicts for the employee which ultimately require him to divide his loyalty between department management and project management. The employee must wear two hats in an attempt to satisfy two chiefs.

While dual reporting relationships work better at some companies than at others, the problem can be eliminated and the overhead reduced at the same time. The project-driven organization employs project-oriented execution techniques specifically designed to minimize the involvement of nonproject personnel.

DESCRIPTION

In a project-driven organization, the project team operates in a task force setting and works in close association during project execution. Each member of the project team reports through appropriate project supervision to the project manager; there are no dual reporting relationships. This method enhances the allegiance of each team member to the project and to his functions on the project. All functions ordinarily attributed to department management are the responsibility of the project manager; there are no functional departments.

This approach to project execution requires greater planning together with participation and agreement of the client on three key points:

Identification of the client's objectives
The scope of services to be provided
A detailed execution plan

Planning is given much more emphasis than is traditional, and is extended to the task level. Project discipline supervisors maintain work plans that encompass the discipline's entire scope on the project and the tasks are manloaded with available or required personnel. The work plan is highly accurate regarding tasks and the personnel required to perform them for three weeks in advance and the entire plan is updated weekly. This detailed task planning permits the project to better control the scope of work.

The time devoted to preparation and maintenance of this detailed planning is well spent since the project team knows each necessary task, who is required to perform it, when it must be accomplished, and by what date specific information is needed. When the discipline supervisor is committed to achieving the plan, detail tasks will be completed on schedule and the project will be finished on time.

While manloaded task schedules are not new, they are not prepared routinely in most E&C companies. In the project-driven organization, where the project manager has full responsibility for project execution and fewer people to follow through on the completion of tasks, this method allows better coordination among disciplines of the work to be done and a higher visibility of work accomplishment.

Greater responsibility is placed on the project manager in the project-driven organization. He is responsible for training, personnel administration, salary administration, technical and nontechnical staffing, and other tasks ordinarily handled by department management. In addition, he is responsible for technical accuracy, design integrity, and the results of project execution.

TRAINING

The normal method of training personnel is to utilize an active project. Senior-level supervision is responsible for guiding subordinates through advanced methods to ensure that necessary training is performed as and when needed to support the project.

Since the project-driven organization is not constrained by functional departments, project team members who are technically able to do so often work across discipline lines. Examples of this practice are electrical/instrumentation wiring and structural/pipe support design. Personnel are encouraged to utilize their capabilities to the fullest extent.

SPECIALISTS

Specialists supply an important ingredient in the design of most process plants. On smaller jobs, their services are often required for a limited amount of time, which causes excessive overhead costs when they are not being utilized. There are two basic ways to solve the problem. One way is to contract such services, and this can be done in today's climate. As the industry rebounds, however, contracting specialists will become less viable.

Another method is to work out an agreement with specific area specialists who would like to be in business for themselves. The agreement can be for the E&C company to provide office space, furniture, local telephone, and clerical services within a defined limit in return for a priority call upon the specialist's services at a predetermined hourly rate. The experience of the parties in working together and how well the working relationship is nourished are critical to the success of such an agreement.

ADMINISTRATION

Personnel perform better when they fully understand what is expected of them. The work output of individual team members must be monitored and performance feedback given to them on a timely basis. This is workable and more objective in nature because of the detailed manloaded task schedules maintained by each project discipline supervisor. High employee motivation occurs when recognition can be seen as being commensurate with the results achieved by the employee.

The project manager establishes procedures which ensure that discipline supervisors outline expectations with each respective team member and that employee performance is reviewed on a timely basis to ascertain compliance. When performance appraisal time arrives, the ongoing process can be formalized without difficulty or surprises.

In addition to individual employee performance, the project manager establishes procedures for making group performance highly visible, such as by posting graphic indicators in the task force area. In this manner, employees can see how well their group is performing relative to expectations, as well as how well other groups are performing. Since all groups are interdependent, the competition remains friendly and motivation to achieve is greater.

MATRIX COMPARISON

The physical plant and the technology on which it is based are essentially the same whether produced under the project-driven organization concept or under the familiar matrix organization concept. What, then, are the advantages of breaking with the heretofore traditional approach to project execution in the process industry? Why should a new method be undertaken? Are there not a host of unknowns involving such a change and do these unknowns not represent a different set of problems for each company seeking to implement the new system?

As with any change, there are unknowns which surface at inconvenient times, and implementation success depends to a large extent on the backing and assistance given to the concept by top management. Possibly one of the best reasons for implementing such a concept is that it represents a way to significantly lower the cost of producing the work. Client acceptance may be a problem, however.

The market in the hydrocarbon processing industry for E&C services has been smaller than it was just a few years ago. Since the plant and technology are relatively unchanged, one viable place where savings in overall cost can be achieved is in the amount of labor required to accomplish the tasks. A major savings area is, therefore, reduction in overhead.

The functional departments which exist in the matrix organization contribute much to the overhead costs in an E&C organization. They also provide assistance to projects by ensuring that sufficient numbers of qualified personnel are on hand and available when needed, which in itself represents a sizable contribution to overhead. The project-driven organization eliminates most of this overhead since the project team is responsible for these functions and is in a better position to select the personnel needed for the specific tasks required.

Elimination of the dual reporting relationship has a significant, though intangible, benefit in that it removes conflict and allows design personnel to concentrate more on getting the job done than satisfying the real or perceived requirements of two, sometimes opposing, managers. The discipline crossover effect, particularly on smaller projects, can result in fewer personnel requirements where sufficient talent is available.

The ordeal of change is not easy and not always pleasant. But, if the E&C companies are to compete effectively, a significant reduction in the cost of producing quality work will be required. The project-driven organization represents one such method that is being pursued in the industry today.

7

Computer-Aided Project Management

MARK J. HUMPHREY   *Professional Management Services, Bakersfield, California*

MICHAEL L. McCAULEY   *Pacific Gas & Electric Company, San Francisco, California*

The basic fundamentals of project management are:

1. To plan the work
2. To work the plan
3. To monitor progress
4. To control the work (corrective action)

A computer-aided project management (CAPM) system that will facilitate the above processes can offer many benefits. The larger and more complex the project, the greater will be the accrued benefits. Some of these benefits include:

Ability to process large amounts of information
Quick adjustment to project plans during both the planning and execution
  phases
Capability of generating status reports for various levels of management
Possibility of comparing alternative "what if" scenarios

The key element in choosing and using CAPM is that the system should work for you to facilitate your work. You should not be a slave to the system! To choose the right system, you need a clear understanding not only of your requirements as project manager but also the requirements of the project itself, the project team, and senior management.

INDUSTRY NEEDS

The applications of project management are extensive and diverse. Each project is unique, and every organization has developed policies and procedures for project execution. Project management is most frequently used by one of two groups: (1) those performing the work (the contractor or consultant) or (2) those overseeing the work (the owner or operator). These two groups comprise the majority of project management users. They may have slightly different and sometimes conflicting goals and diverse reporting requirements. In spite of these differences, or possibly because of them, it is essential that both make effective use of computer-aided project management in order to achieve and maintain a high level of performance.

The Contractor / Consultant

For those persons who must perform the actual work, the first and foremost goal is to successfully bid for and be awarded a contract for the chosen project. If this first goal is met, the contractor must then manage his work as effectively as possible, so that he may maximize profit. Efficient use of computer aided project management can help him achieve both of these goals.

The contractor can use off-the-shelf software including: scheduling, resource management, spreadsheet, database, and computer-aided design (CAD). There are also special packages to help prepare bids. These application packages can be used to develop labor and equipment histograms, and to estimate cash flow. Several different construction scenarios can be studied to determine which gives the most cost-effective results. Trade-off analyses can be performed and the effectiveness of various construction sequences can be judged. All of these comparisons can be performed quickly, allowing the contractor to develop the best possible bid rapidly.

Scheduling programs calculate the amount of time a project will take, given the activities that need to be performed, the length of each activity, and the interrelationships between the activities. This type of program can be extremely valuable when investigating different construction activity sequences on large projects. A change can be made in the parameters of one activity, and the result on the overall project will be seen immediately. Numerous alternatives can be tried, and the most advantageous one used to prepare the bid.

Some scheduling programs also include resource management capabilities. The contractor can develop histograms for the critical resources, which enable him to evaluate resource requirements for varying sequences, as well as advantages of renting additional equipment, hiring additional labor, or subcontracting a portion of the work.

Electronic spreadsheets can be prepared which automatically total each line item in the estimate. The advantage here is that the contractor can easily perform "what-if" analyses where the effect of increasing the cost of concrete by $20/cubic yard or the amount of labor required by 10% can be calculated.

This type of comparison will give the contractor a feel for the sensitivity of the estimate to the various components. In turn, the contractor can weigh the risks and rewards of the project. Any contractor who knows the risks involved in a project up front and understands their possible effects is in a much better position to make a profit when the project is awarded.

A database program enables the contractor to keep historical costs and labor and equipment requirements at his fingertips. Estimates for new work can be prepared more readily with access to this historical information. Storing the data in easily retrievable form increases the organization's ability to produce a rapid and accurate estimate.

In preparing the cost estimate, it is essential to know the quantities of material required to complete the job. Digitizing equipment and CAD systems can calculate quantities more quickly and accurately than manual take-offs. In addition, like electronic spreadsheets, they tend to leave a paper trail that can easily be traced should there by any questions about how the estimate was prepared.

Once the contract has been awarded and the work has begun, computer tools can manage and track the progress of the work. The builder can determine the long range schedule effects of design changes quickly, and pass this information on to the owner so that timely decisions can be made. Expenditures can be tracked using electronic spreadsheets, and the actual costs can be compared against the plan or bid estimates. The contractor can isolate areas where the budget is being exceeded and take appropriate corrective action. Likewise, he can analyze work packages which are significantly under budget to determine if the work was overestimated, or if the work is proceeding more slowly than expected. The better understanding the contractor has of the current project status, the better are his chances of minimizing problems and completing the job with a profit.

Computer-aided management has other, not so obvious advantages as well. The benefits of keeping a working spreadsheet detailing project expenses are twofold. First, it allows the contractor to quickly and accurately summarize the applicable data and to present it to the owner in a neat and concise format. This can precipitate timely progress payments, as well as promote a good working relationship with the owner. Second, by developing the spreadsheet, the contractor paves the way for more accurate record keeping throughout the project. It encourages him to think through his expense accounting, and discourages him from stuffing receipts into a file drawer to be consolidated at a later date.

The contractor should take great pains to ensure that any information he places into his database is as accurate as possible. If he does keep accurate records, he can add them to the historical database as a basis for bidding future work.

The Owner/Operator

Understanding and using the various computer tools is highly supportive to the successful completion of the project. The owner can employ the same tools as the contractor, but with a different emphasis.

Unless the owner/operator is acting as the general contractor, he is more concerned with meeting the schedule than with the sequence of construction or the size of the construction crews. He is more concerned that the finished work complies with all codes and specifications than he is with the methods used.

Computer-based scheduling tools enable the owner to track closely the progress of the project. He can compare his estimate of progress with the contractor's status report to ensure that things are proceeding as reported by the contractor. Scheduling tools can also ensure that sufficient inspectors and material testing specialists are on site to prevent delays. Depending upon the extent of his involvement in project activities, the owner/operator should keep abreast and plan his own requirements to support the schedule.

Unknowns exist on any project. If the owner accurately and currently tracks those project matters dependent upon his action, he can more easily make timely decisions regarding project mitigation options. He may also use "what-if" scenarios to investigate these options. The owner can modify data quickly in order to look at the effects of schedule acceleration should these become of interest. If a schedule delay occurs, the owner may look at the consequences and study recovery plans.

Electronic spreadsheet and database programs can track payments to the contractor and assure that all work items have been accounted for. Even if the contractor submits receipts for all payments, mistakes are possible, and payment is sometimes requested for the same work more than once, or for work that has not been completed and accepted. If the owner maintains a detailed spreadsheet and database, he can search the available data quickly and determine exactly what work has been invoiced and paid. Research through more conventional accounting records can be time consuming and the data may be poorly indexed and spread over many pages. Thus well-ordered spreadsheets can facilitate information access.

One of the most laborious tasks for the project manager may be that of producing summary reports for senior management. If computer tools have been used to manage the project, summary reports are easy to develop. In addition, with the advent of color plotters and laser printers, production of graphs and charts for these reports and for visual presentations has become very easy. For the project manager this means less time spent on assembling information for reports as well as the ability to develop more meaningful and interesting formats for management reports.

NEEDS OF PROJECT MANAGEMENT

The following discussion will analyze the capability of CAPM to fulfill the needs of project management. These are approached from the viewpoint of (1) the project manager, (2) the project itself, (3) the project team, and (4) the senior management. All four views should be considered carefully before forming any opinion as to what kind of a system is required. If the project team has a low level of experience, a much different management style might be used. This could influence the optimum type of management system to be considered.

Project Manager's CAPM Needs

There are four broad categories of project management styles:

1. A great need to know project detail and a high level of control over the CAPM system
2. A great need to know project detail and low control over the CAPM system
3. Little need to know project detail and low control over the CAPM system
4. Little need to know project detail and high control over the CAPM system

The first project management style asks that the project plan be developed in great detail, and that the details go into the system database and be readily accessible at all times. The project manager in this case wants the project team to plan and monitor their work at a relatively low level, reviewing it at frequent intervals. The level of detail will depend on the size and complexity of the project. The CAPM system is also required to be highly responsive. The project manager will not be the individual sitting at the terminal, but he will want the system to process a large amount of data in a short turnaround time.

The second style requires that the project plan be developed in great detail, that the details go into the system database, but does not require that the details of the plan be readily accessible. The project manager asks that the project team plan and monitor the work at a relatively low level. He may not review all of this information, but examine it only selectively. He knows that detailed information is available if required. This style allows the project team more freedom in working their own plans, but still requires them to pass the detail into the system. The CAPM system in this case does not need to be highly responsive.

The third style does not require the development of a very detailed project plan for the system database or that the information be readily accessible. The project manager wants the project team to plan and monitor their own work. This style allows the project team greater freedom in working their own plans and does not require them to pass all of the details into the system. This approach is characterized as "management by exception." The CAPM system for this management style does not need to be highly responsive.

The fourth management style is uncommon. This style requires that the project plan not be developed in great detail for the CAPM system database. The project manager wants a high degree of control over the database and wants it to be readily accessible. This system will favor the project manager that has little need to manage the details through a CAPM system, but who may be required to supply numerous status reports to various levels of senior management. These reports will be summary in nature. The system in this case needs to be highly responsive but not necessarily to manipulate large amounts of detailed data.

The project manager should keep in mind that his effectiveness depends on his ability to control a project through early implementation of corrective action. The CAPM system's capability of processing "what-if" scenarios should help the project manager make informed decisions as to the best path of action to overcome any negative situations.

These are broad styles based on generalities, but they are a starting point to use in assessing the management style comfortable to the project manager and which is appropriate for a given project. The following discussions on project needs and team needs may also help in choosing the right style for the project.

Project CAPM Needs

There are three major areas of need for the project from a CAPM system. (1) constraints, (2) viewpoints, and (3) technical complexity. This first area, deals with the issues of schedule, cost, physical parameters, and visibility.

If there is a project completion deadline, and there has been no benefit of input from a planning phase, the schedule may be difficult to attain. The CAPM system will need both strong planning and monitoring capabilities.

How critical and/or sensitive are the objectives of the project to the final costs? If working to a very tight budget, a CAPM system strong in planning and monitoring cost elements is indicated. Is there a need to integrate both cost and schedule with a common work breakdown structure (WBS)? What are the physical restraints of the physical project such as access within the areas of the physical facilities, the climate, or communications? These parameters may dictate the characteristics of the optimum type of CAPM system for the project.

Viewpoint deals with what corner of the project you are managing from. The four major corners are:

1. The owner
2. The architect/engineer (A/E)
3. The general contractor
4. The subcontractor

Each of these see the project from a distinctly different viewpoint. Therefore, each has a distinctly different need in managing the project. There may be occasions when several of the corners may involve the same entity and will need to take into account the needs of both when selecting a CAPM systems.

The owner's viewpoint is that of the entire project. The owner controls the major schedule deadlines and the budget. The owner's CAPM needs would be a system that will allow the project to be treated from that overall perspective. The system will probably need to link with other systems to provide that overall look at the project. The system may need to handle more than one project so that the owner can see the effects of one project versus another.

The architect/engineer is concerned with the design and engineering phase of the project. The A/E may also be required to perform construction inspection. Two key needs for a CAPM system for the A/E are resource allocation and multiproject capability. The A/E is selling the expertise of his people; therefore, these resources are critical to getting the job done right, within budget, and on time. These resources are relatively constant and the ability for the system to allocate resources across many projects is an important function.

The general contractor's viewpoint is the overall construction effort. Key issues of concern are: compatibility with the owner's system, if this is a contractual requirement for reporting purposes; the ability to coordinate and track subcontractors, equipment, materials, and labor; and the ability to forecast the requirement for labor and consumables.

The subcontractor's viewpoint is a particular portion of the construction effort. Key issues of concern are: compatibility with the general contractor's system, if contractually required; the ability to track equipment, materials, and labor; and the ability to forecast future labor and material needs.

The third area, technical complexity, deals with the number of individual engineering and construction disciplines whose work must be integrated and coordinated.

Generally, the more disciplines involved and the attendent interaction, the more so-phisticated the CAPM system will need to be.

Project Team CAPM Needs

The project team will include those who encompass a viewpoint similar to that of the project manager as well as others who have different viewpoints. There are three major concerns when looking at the project team in terms of which CAPM system will best serve their needs.

1. Experience level of team members
2. Interfaces between team members
3. Commitment of team members

First is the experience level of the team members. A project team with a great deal of experience may not need the benefits of a detailed planning tool and tracking system. A project team with little or no experience may need to plan the work in detail and then to track the work at that level of detail.

Second is the intensity of interaction between team members, including both those who have similar viewpoints and those with differing viewpoints. Team members from different disciplines often have very different viewpoints and these must be taken into account in managing the project. Generally, a high intensity of interaction be-tween members within a single viewpoint requires minimal CAPM capabilities, but a high intensity of interaction between different viewpoints requires a more comprehen-sive system to plan and monitor these interfaces.

Finally, commitment is the cornerstone of project success. Specific intermediate milestones are agreed to by team members in order that the project proceed as planned. The greater the commitments, particularly those between differing viewpoints, the greater the system needs in planning and tracking these critical points in the project plans.

Senior Management CAPM Needs

The key element required by senior management from a CAPM system is summary infor-mation. Summary information should include key schedule deadlines, cost forecasts, and corrective action scenarios or records of corrective action taken. Senior manage-ment, generally, should not have to take the time to study the progress and forecasts on each project in detail. Another key issue is the form of presentation desired. What are the needs of senior management? Will a simple format suffice, or is something more elaborate desired?

ORIENTATION AND TRAINING

Before computer-aided project management can be used effectively, the users must have a certain amount of knowledge both in the concepts of project management and in the CAPM system itself. Without this knowledge the computer-based tools may re-quire more work than they save as well as cause confusion.

Requirements

It appears obvious that anyone using computer-based tools should have a basic know-ledge of how they work. Many users, however, do not fully understand the tools that they are using. There are a variety of reasons for this unfamiliarity including:

Inexperience with the hardware and software

Complexity of the tools makes learning difficult
Inability to understand basic project management
Lack of desire to fully understand all of the capabilities of the system
Insufficient time to investigate each of the features of the system
Belief that the system is understood when it really is not

The use of any CAPM system by those who do not understand its capabilities and limitations is disastrous. It is extremely important that everyone connected with the project team have some understanding of the tools employed on the project. At least one person on the project team must have an intimate working knowledge of the computer tools, their capabilities and weaknesses, how the information is processed, and how the reports should be interpreted. This individual should serve as a focal point to all team members for assistance in using the system. Through experience with the various machines and programs, the project manager and his staff can build a working knowledge of the system. This working knowledge can prove invaluable when problems must be solved under a time constraint. In such a situation, the project team must have access to all pertinent data and know how to isolate data relevant to the question at hand, and not be confused by superfluous information generated by the computer. Misinterpretation of data can give the team members a false sense of security or lead them to incorrect conclusions when attempting to resolve a problem, resulting in unnecessary expense and wasted time.

Along with this understanding of the tools, those involved with obtaining, reading and interpreting the output must have a basic understanding of project management concepts. To accept computer-generated reports at face value, without validating them using project management experience and common sense is a form of Russian roulette. It is easy to slip into a false sense of security that is engendered by the neatly printed reports.

A working knowledge of project management concepts has always been required to direct such an operation. Previously, calculations were done manually and those making the calculations had to understand the concepts in order to get the correct results. With the computer anyone who can push buttons can generate computer reports, but the data generated may be erroneous if the operator does not fully understand the software being used. Such erroneous data must be found and corrected before any decision is made based on that data. Scheduling programs used for resource leveling and constraining are frequently misused by those who do not understand the principles, and the interpretation of schedule information may be wrong. Just because the computer calculates an answer does not ensure that the answer is correct unless the CAPM system has been used correctly. The best safeguard against accepting misleading data is to understand the methodology behind the program.

Responsibility

The responsibility for orientation and training of the project team in the proper use of the CAPM system rests squarely with the project manager. The project manager must live with all of the decisions made on his project. This means that ultimately his performance rests on decisions made based on the CAPM information.

If the project manager cannot obtain experienced people, and does not have the time or the budget available for training, then a complex computer program is probably not the best choice.

The project manager should always take full advantage of all of the avenues of training which may be available, including the hardware supplier, the software developer, the computer operations group of his own company, and any experience available from the project team members.

Fortunately, with the proliferation of computer usage in schools and universities, the younger team members are likely to have better backgrounds and understanding. Most user manuals are well written and the programs themselves are easier to use.

Personal computers have become more powerful, and software programs feature many advanced features with easy-to-use formats.

SYSTEM DESIGN

A survey of systems currently available found that one of two methodologies appears to be employed by the systems designers.

1. Incorporate as many capabilities into the software as possible and develop the user interface as an afterthought.
2. Develop the user interface first, making the product easy to use, and then add features to increase the scope of the product's capabilities.

Both methods have benefits and limitations. Both serve the needs of different categories of users.

The first methodology is reflected in the current mainframe-based software, as well as those personal computer-based products which are scaled-down versions of mainframe products. These application packages often offer advanced capabilities, but extract the price in lack of "user friendliness." Enhanced capabilities can be of great benefit to the project manager if properly used, but a full-time computer analyst is usually required to assist with entering data, report configuration, database maintenance, and user consultation and assistance. Some features offered by these products are desirable and even necessary on very large projects where the higher overhead costs can be justified. These systems may tend to insulate the project manager from the actual data, forcing him to rely on others to tend to the data processing.

The second methodology has been employed on personal computers to date. These programs forego some of the advanced features and enhancements, making the program easier to use. These programs were developed specifically for the small machines and were not downsized from existing mainframe products. Their main advantage is their simplicity, which allows the project manager and other team members to have a "hands-on" role in data processing. Familiarity with the data can make problem mitigation easier and faster, as well as being more inclusive of all of the related factors. This type of interface also allows the project manager an opportunity to interact more closely with his team members. The portable, easy to use PC may be used to supply up-to-date information at team meetings.

When selecting a computer product to use on a specific project, the availability of hardware should be addressed. The simpler programs require only floppy disk drives and monochromatic monitor, making them ideal for use both in the office and at the jobsite. The more advanced programs may require hard disks, color monitor, plotters, and, in the case of the most sophisticated programs, a mini- or mainframe computer with the associated terminal(s). The more hardware required, the more limited will be its portability to various locations and accessibility to it by project team members.

In summary, systems design is a series of compromises. Obtaining high-powered, advanced software means sacrificing user friendliness and transportability. When more advanced software is required for a more complex project, these concerns will be secondary. When choosing a CAPM system, make certain that it fills only the actual project requirements. Technological overkill can be detrimental to the basic reasons for acquiring a computer-aided management system.

8

Owner/Contractor Relationships

WILLIAM K. WAKEFIELD   *FMC Corporation, Princeton, New Jersey*

The working relationship between an owner and a contractor is one of the most crucial determinants of project success. A positive working relationship can help overcome the problems which inevitably arise on all projects. Conversely, small problems can become insurmountable if the relationship is poor. Although some of the owner's and contractor's objectives may differ, it is critical to recognize that, insofar as possible, the major objectives are the same. This will allow a cooperative, not adversarial, relationship to develop and be maintained.

In the succeeding paragraphs the impact of several factors on the owner/contractor relationahip will be reviewed. Among these factors are:

Type of contract
Relative capabilities of owner and contractor
Personalities of key managers
Scope of work
Third-party involvement
Contractual liabilities
Senior management support

Regardless of the impact of these factors, perhaps the most important element for success is that both owner and contractor understand their respective roles. Success requires continuous communication of this understanding.

TYPE OF CONTRACT

Although there are many contract types, they can be broadly split into two categories: cost reimbursable and lump sum. The two major types include conditions which can affect the owner/contractor relationship.

Under a fixed price, the contractor has agreed to perform a given scope of work under given conditions for a fixed sum of money. The scope of the contract is perhaps the most fundamental requirement and requires full understanding by both parties. The scope should include both specifications and job procedures. The specifications must include details of the quality required as well as the facility description. If specifications are unclear, differences of opinion will strain the owner/contractor relationship. Job procedures should give the contractor as much freedom to manage the job as the owner can allow. The more requirements for owner review and approval, the more the contractor will feel that the owner is affecting his ability to complete the project and, therefore, his profitability. In short, the owner has to be very specific in *what* the contractor is to provide, but should minimize his requirements as to *how* the work is performed.

Under cost-reimbursable contracts, the owner takes most of the risks, has more control, and therefore, has more to say about *how* the work is done. Because the scope of work and the contractors responsibilities are usually less defined, the owner and contractor must effectively communicate their respective roles. The contractor has an obligation to let the owner know if he feels the scope of the project and/or his responsibilities are changing.

RELATIVE CAPABILITIES OF OWNER AND CONTRACTOR

The relative organizational and individual capabilities of the owner and contractor can affect their relationship. Many owners have a project management organization which includes specialists whose job it is to oversee the contractor's work. This overview has to be carefully managed. If initial checking shows that a contractor is fully competent in a given discipline, the degree of checking should be reduced. Continued detailed review can be a significant demotivator to the competent contractor specialist, and his productivity and efficiency may decline. Also, the owner's total engineering and project management costs will be higher than required.

Conversely, if the initial checking shows a weakness, the owner may want to increase the level of checking, have contractor personnel changed, or both. If these steps do not correct the situation, or if an owner simply wants to perform a particular discipline himself, the owner may decide to become a "doer" rather than a "checker." Mixing roles has to be done very carefully. If the discipline to be performed by the owner directly is one that involves significant interaction with other disciplines, such a move could be a mistake. For example, cost control and forecasting require input from virtually all members of a project team. An owner person who is unfamiliar with a contractor's organization, procedures, and people is at a distinct disadvantage in trying to replace a contractor person. If an owner installs one of his people into a contractor's organization, it is imperative that both parties fully understand how the responsibilities are being shifted. Obviously, shifting responsibilities based on relative capabilities is easier on a reimbursable cost project than under a fixed price contract.

If it is clear at the outset that a combination of owner and contractor personnel will achieve the best results, it is probably best to abandon the traditional roles and establish a joint owner/contractor task force. This avoids putting the owner in a combined overseer/doer role and avoids dilution of the contractor's organizational responsibility. The single task force puts the major overall management responsibility on the owner, and the contractor's principal responsibility is to provide quality people and systems as requested.

In summary, an effort should be made to use the best of both owner and contractor resources. However, it needs to be done carefully to avoid demotivation, duplication of effort, and compromise of a contractor's responsibility.

PERSONALITIES OF KEY MANAGERS

As in any undertaking, the personalities of key managers on a project have a great influence on the project success. The owner and contractor project managers are the most critical. Their personalities must be compatible and complementary. They will set the tone for their respective teams.

The manner in which individual team members interact is also important to project success. Owner specialists in an overview role have to be careful not to appear to be superior to their contractor counterparts. Contractor specialists have to recognize

that the owner will have preferences and that changes to what they have proposed
do not necessarily mean that they were wrong. Experience has shown that even strong-
willed, competent specialists can work constructively and with respect. On the other
hand, this is not always the case, and both project managers must be alert for relationship problems. If they exist, they must be corrected through coaching or changes
in personnel. If not corrected, problems eventually can involve other team members.

As part of the contractor evaluation and bidding stage, the owner must assess
the compatibility of key team members and consider making changes in personnel proposed by the contractor and even to his own team. Correcting a potential problem
before the project starts is much easier than doing so after it has begun to affect
project performance.

The ideal situation is one where both project teams are strong, knowledgeable,
have a mutual respect for each other's capabilities, and understand their respective
roles.

SCOPE OF WORK

Two elements of work scope, the degree of definition and the size, affect the owner/
contractor relationship and how a project should be organized. The less defined the
work, the more need there is for owner/contractor cooperation and communication.
For example, front-end conceptual work such as process or architectural scoping requires a close, face to face working relationship. At this stage, the contractor needs
to understand the owner's requirements, preferences, financial guidelines, and other
criteria. These are difficult to transmit completely in a written specification. If communication is poor, the contractor can be frustrated by lack of direction and/or the
owner can be disappointed if the contractor's work product is not what he wants and
requires major rework. Often the front-end work is best handled by a joint owner/
contractor team rather than by the owner working strictly in an overview mode.

The opposite end of the scope spectrum might be construction-only of a portion
of a project. For example, site grading can be clearly defined in a specification and
minimum day-to-day communications are required. The owner/contractor relationship
can be primarily a formal contractual one as opposed to the more intimate one required
for conceptual work.

The size of the project also impacts the relationship. The larger the scope, the
more the need for formal communications. This does not mean that informal communication and close, personal relationships are unimportant. They always are. However,
they cannot be relied upon to keep a large, complex project on course. They need
to work within the framework of a comprehensive project coordination procedure.

INVOLVEMENT OF A THIRD PARTY

Managing the relationship between owner and contractor becomes significantly more
difficult when a third party is involved. This third party could be an architect/engi-
neer (A/E), an overall project manager, or a construction manager. Even in a two-
party arrangement it is difficult to have both working to the same objectives, and
a third party does not improve the situation. For example, if an A/E is preparing
designs and specifications on behalf of an owner, he usually has no incentive to ensure
that designs are the most cost effective to meet owner needs. If constructibility is
not considered and the design is "gold plated," it is the owner who pays. If the design is incomplete and results in costly extras from the constructor, again, it is the
owner who pays. Often A/Es work on percentage fees, so the more the facility costs,
the more profit they make. As costs increase and schedule dates are missed, the
owner becomes frustrated with both contractor and A/E. Often, the constructor
blames the A/E for design problems, and the A/E blames the constructor for poor

performance. Regardless of the merits of the situation, the owner is in the middle, and relations with both parties deteriorate to the overall detriment of the project. There are some things which can be done to avoid this situation.

Use a design-build contract. Here, using fixed-price bidding, the owner contracts with a constructor to build to the owner's general specifications and project requirements. The constructor hires an A/E to do the required design work. The owner then deals only with the constructor and is insulated from any disputes between the constructor and A/E.

Establish cost and schedule incentives for both parties to bring their objectives more closely in line with the owner's.

Establish very detailed coordination procedures so all parties are clear on their responsibilities.

Stay intimately involved in communications between the other parties to ensure that the owner's requirements are being properly fulfilled.

In summary, involvement of a third party should be avoided if possible. However, if project requirements or available engineering and construction skills make it necessary, it must be managed very carefully.

CONTRACTUAL LIABILITES

The more liability the contractor accepts for engineering errors, poor workmanship, and consequential damages, the greater the potential for an adversarial relationship, particularly under reimbursable cost. Under reimbursable cost, contractors are often working on a limited fee. This means the owner is better able financially to accept the risks than the contractor. Even if a contractor accepts higher risks, the hidden costs to the owner may not justify the coverage. These hidden costs include:

Conservatism in design and construction
Loss of productivity due to excessive checking
Strict monitoring of the causes of errors
Loss of productivity, momentum, and focus on what is important if management spends its time arguing about liability

A good case can be made for having the owner accept essentially all liability under reimbursable cost contracts. When the owner retains a high level of control, asking contractors to take the risks without the control can be self-defeating.

The situation differs under lump sum contracts. Here the owner has given essentially all the responsibility to the contractor, and it is reasonable to expect him to accept full liability.

In any kind of contract, it is important to recognize that the relative liabilities and the management of the liabilities can have a significant impact on the owner/contractor relationship.

SENIOR MANAGEMENT SUPPORT

Although relationships at the project team level are the most critical, both owner and contractor managements can help maintain good relationships. Both organizations should have project sponsors who monitor progress and attitudes and communicate frequently. By so doing, they can often detect relationship problems before they become serious. They can resolve disputes by bringing a perspective that the teams might not have, and they can elevate disputes so that they do not interfere with day-to-day working relationships.

Senior management should also promote social and other team-building activities. Project picnics, athletic teams, and informal get togethers can be extremely effective in team building. They let people get to know each other outside the pressures of the project. Project logos, hats, jackets, safety awards, and other forms of recognition or merit can also promote team building.

Overall, senior management can have a significant impact on the project team relationship and, therefore, on the overall owner/contractor relationship.

SUMMARY

The relationship between the owner and contractor is clearly a key to project success. The factors discussed are the major ones which can affect the relationship either positively or negatively. Awareness of the factors and good communications can promote a positive relationship and identify and correct potential negative impacts. The key point is that the relationship can be managed to insure a positive experience as well as a successful project.

9

Contingency Reserves:
A Management Control Tool

IVARS AVOTS *Trans-Global Management Systems, Inc., Arlington, Massachusetts*

Contingency reserves are special provisions for uncertainties affecting the cost of a project. The term "reserve" is used here in a management context and not in an accounting context. Contingency reserve can be an effective tool in project cost control. However, it must be given proper management visibility and, like any other project cost element, its use must be monitored carefully.

In the past decade, much publicity has been given to large construction project overruns which have exceeded traditionally accepted levels of contingencies because of the nature of the uncertainties that modern projects must face. In the past, engineers were able to explain overruns by looking at finite and measurable items, such as unit quantities, wage rates, manhours, and productivity. Since the 1970s, these factors no longer cover a large portion of the overrun spectrum. Project managers must now deal with the effects of such intangible factors as organization and communications structures, environmental protection movements, increased government regulation, and a host of first-of-a-kind projects. While potentially devastating to project cost budgets, these intangible issues are largely beyond traditional engineering training and experience.

CONTINGENCIES IN PROJECT COST ESTIMATING

Uncertainties have the greatest impact on the project during the initial cost estimate. If an estimate does not adequately consider the real exposure of the project to traditional and intangible risks, significant cost overruns will be inevitable. An estimate which provides full value for all possible risks will kill the project at the start, or result in excessive costs to the owner. A carefully developed contingency estimate bridges the gap between these two extremes.

The degree of uncertainty to be dealt with depends on the phase of the project. The construction industry recognized this early on, and guidelines such as those illustrated in Figure 1 have become standard. As shown, the expected variance during the research and development phase may be as high as 40% of the total costs of the project. This variance gradually decreases as design and construction progress. Contingency reserves can be used to cover for the unknowns during this process.

In contrast to an approach that reflects the experience of a company over many projects, some contingencies are set arbitrarily by management after estimates have been prepared. Often, the principal purpose of such a contingency is to establish

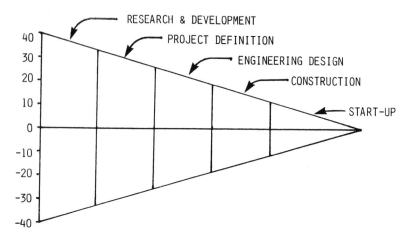

Figure 1 Effect of project phase on contingencies.

the maximum budget or the price of the project and it may be justified by little more than a "feel" for the competition or the market.

Contingencies are not equally effective management tools in all types of contracts. In cost-reimbursement contracts, the contractor profit is protected even if the work performed exceeds the planned contingency, and the contractor may have little direct incentive to introduce new management techniques for cost control. In unit price contracts, contingencies are sometimes included at the unit price level to increase profit leverage if the contractor expects quantity variations in his favor. If the actual quantities increase but the unit cost remains the same, the cushion provided through the contingency results in a sharp increase in the contractor's profit.

THE MANAGEMENT OF CONTINGENCIES

From a management viewpoint, a project should be well defined, with the contingency reserve as low as possible, permitting price setting by management based on a sound, realistic cost basis. Since the key determinant of the size of the contingency is anticipated uncertainty, every effort should be made to reduce these uncertainties. The importance of project definition and identification of specific potential risks should be emphasized.

For effective management control, contingency reserves must be related to specific risks reflected in the project estimate and must be a part of the cost control program. The following steps are typical of a sound contingency management system: (Murray and Ramsour, 1977)

1. Assess the project risk factors
2. Develop and document logical estimating assumptions
3. Assign specific responsibility for contingency reserve
4. Emphasize the early recognition of potential scope changes and cost increases
5. Control the use of reserves by limiting the size of transactions and by requiring specific approvals for transfers
6. Report any changes in the reserve at the appropriate level in the project control system
7. Analyze the rate of reserve consumption in relation to the project status

SETTING UP THE CONTINGENCY RESERVE

One approach to setting up a contingency reserve is to separate it into general and specific categories (Fig. 2). The general reserve should cover estimating variances, additions to lump-sum portions of the contract, and other like items. The specific reserve includes allowances for escalation, increases in specific line items, and uncollectable contract claims. When properly monitored, these contingencies can yield useful management information, but may fall short of an effective management system. Also, many practitioners believe that escalation allowance should be treated separately from the contingency. This is particularly true when contracts provide for changes in payment or renegotiation in accordance with a published inflation index.

In another approach, specific contingencies are assigned to each cost category: labor, materials, and subcontracts. Such differentiation permits recognition of the specific uncertainties related to each cost category, which then can be identified with separate phases of the project.

A further refinement of the contingency requires that it be related to elements of the work breakdown structure. This can be done at several levels of the structure or even at the work package level. The advantage of such a detailed breakdown is that experience can be developed as a basis for readjustment of the contingencies. This approach provides fairly good control over the contingency, but the amount of detailed recordkeeping and evaluation involved permits its use only on relatively small projects.

A key principle in applying contingency reserves is that factors not a part of the original estimate must not be involved. The reserve may not be used to cover up a negative performance variance. Each reserve expenditure must be recorded and

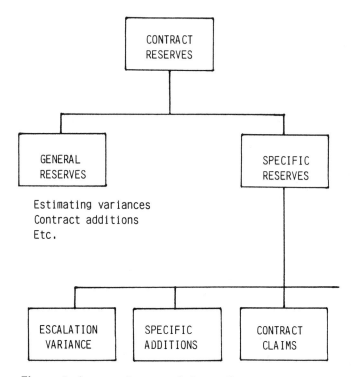

Figure 2 A general approach to contingency reserves.

reported along with cost performance at the appropriate level of detail. Actual reserve expenditures must be tracked and projected expenses estimated to assure that an adequate balance remains to cover future uncertainties.

The contingency's place during the project is illustrated in Figure 3. The contingency is included in the budget as a separate item and is transferred to the working budget only upon authorization of the responsible manager. As the work to which the contingency applies is accomplished, the planning and actual contingency allocation can be compared and the trends projected to completion. If the contingency was too generous, part of it can be transferred to another work element or released to the overall project level. After completion of the work element, any unused portion of the contingency budget can also be returned to the project level. This approach establishes control over the use of the contingency and permits more accurate estimating of the cost at completion. The current readjusted working budget at any given time during the execution of the project includes the original working budget as well as that portion of the contingency which has been allocated to this budget. Extending and implementing this approach to various elements of the project at various levels leads to periodic reports of costs incurred and progress achieved, as well as the amount of the contingencies applied and reserved for the future. This gives management additional information about the project not otherwise available and permits greater project cost control.

TECHNIQUES FOR IDENTIFYING UNCERTAINTIES

The principal problem in the development of contingency reserves is identifying and assessing the potential effects of uncertainties. Several analytical procedures can be used to set the original contingency levels, reassess them during project execution, and refine the process for future projects.

The simplest way of measuring the expected uncertainties is the statistical technique which was used in the original PERT application (Program Evaluation and Review Technique). This technique involves making three time estimates (optimistic, most

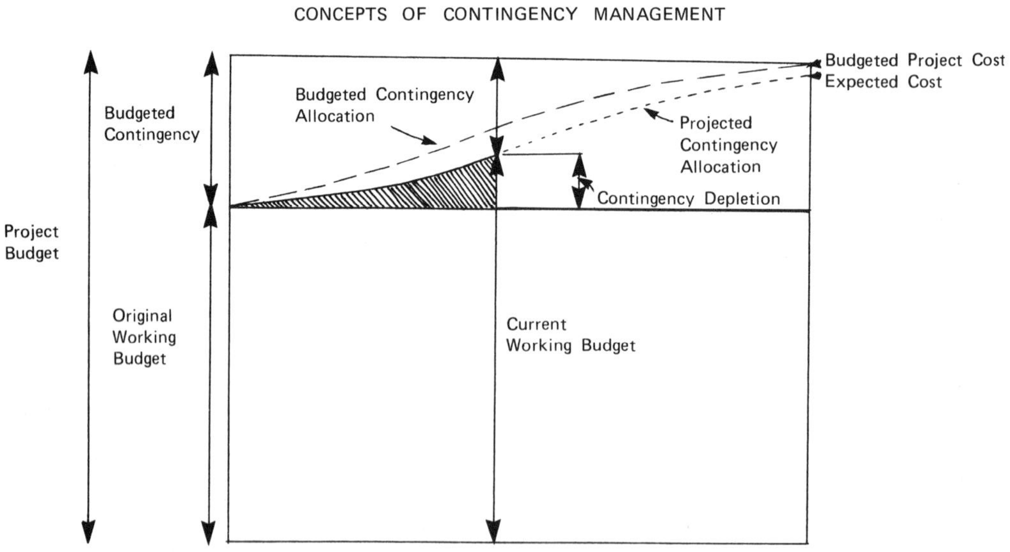

CONCEPTS OF CONTINGENCY MANAGEMENT

Figure 3 The concept of contingency management.

likely, and pessimistic) and using a simple formula [(a + 2b + c)/4] to combine them into an expected duration. While this technique made it possible to calculate the variance for each activity, as well as for the total network, the procedure was not widely accepted. The growing popularity of successive estimating, also based on three estimates, has brought renewed interest to this PERT technique.

From a theoretical standpoint, contingency reserves can be subjected to various statistical manipulations. Cost engineers talk about the central limit theorem; symmetrical and unimodal distribution curves, and the central value of the probability distribution. All are familiar terms to statisticians and mathematicians, but they mean little to most project managers. Most project managers prefer a specific completion date over a statistically calculated probability of completion. It was this probabilistic feature of PERT that was most objected to by project managers. The contingency management system must be simple and readily understandable, therefore these statistical techniques are not generally used.

Techniques that can identify and quantify the areas of project uncertainty include (1) successive estimating, (2) influence diagramming, (3) cost relevance analysis, and (4) other techniques.

Successive Estimating

In successive estimating, the estimator not only estimates the cost for each of the project elements, but also assesses the uncertainty associated with each element, either indicating a range within which the estimate may vary or by making three separate estimates as in PERT scheduling. By expressing these uncertainties as standard deviations and calculating variances, it is possible to quantify the uncertainty for the estimate as a whole.

Successive estimating takes into consideration intangible factors. The intial estimate is refined by identifying a range of uncertainty. Successive estimating does not result in a new plan but rather analyzes "snapshots" or elements, which enables the planner to devise a new plan. By focusing on those elements with the highest degree of uncertainty and cost, the planner may be able to break them down further, and find that the uncertainty is reduced or that it cannot be further reduced. When he finds that successive refinements are no longer significant, the contingency reserve must take over.

Barrie and Paulson, in their book, *Professional Construction Management,* report that reaching the point where further subdivision is not practical takes only about 20% of the effort of conventional estimating approaches and that the estimators are also much more aware of where the uncertainties in the project really lie.

Influence Diagramming

Influence diagramming is used to describe the entire project situation in terms of potential outcomes derived from action alternatives, risk factors, and given quantities. Sensitivity analysis is then used to simplify the diagram and to isolate areas where further analysis is necessary.

In the influence diagram, the relationships between the various components are shown by lines. Figure 4 illustrates a case where an architect must choose a modular system for a multiunit residential building. If we assume that this project is planned for sale, then the outcome to be considered is the net present value of the profit from the project. The type of modular system chosen will have an effect on the construction duration and cost per unit as well as on the physical dimensions of the building. Here we have assumed that the choice of a system will determine the exact dimensions of the unit. Both the calculated volume per unit and building location will influence the sales price per unit. The final value or the net present value of profit, is obtained from the cost per unit, sales price per unit, and the construction duration. According to the assumptions used in this example, these three factors are among the risks

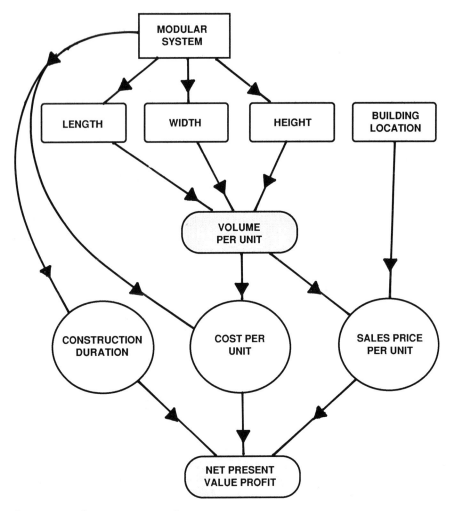

Figure 4 Influence diagram for selecting a building system.

to be considered in making this decision and will serve as the parameters used to determine the appropriate contingency reserves (Ashley and Avots, 1984).

Influence diagramming is a highly sophisticated technique, and although the principle is readily recognizable, its full use includes sensitivity analyses and fairly advanced statistical techniques, rarely appreciated by the project manager. However, such information can be processed and simplified by a technical staff and presented to the manager for use in contingency determination.

Cost Relevance Analysis

Cost relevance analysis focuses specifically on cost overruns and provides detailed checklists which can be applied to a specific project or its elements. The lists have been developed through a cause-effect analysis program which showed that all the so-called "causes" of overruns can be traced back to one of four basic factors or to a combination of the four: (1) initial underestimate; (2) scope and design changes; (3) decreases in productivity; (4) increases in basic costs. Figure 5 shows the initial

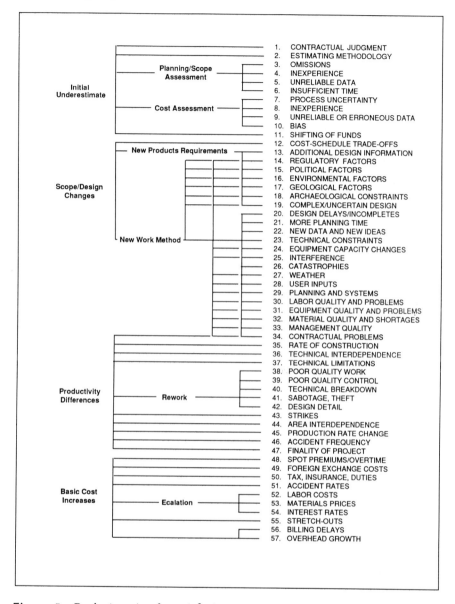

Figure 5 Project cost-relevant factors—overruns.

list of 57 cost-relevant factors. These have been expanded to cover over 100 detail factors. While the technique is primarily intended to help in tracking progress trends that lead to cost overruns, the factors may be used beneficially in determining potential uncertainties and the related contingency reserve needs (Avots, 1983).

Other Techniques

In addition to the above, useful techniques for evaluating uncertainties by recalling the problems of past projects will help management to implement corrective measures on their own projects. These techniques include: (1) the risk alarm system, (2) the construction project risk-analysis database, (3) ambiguity analysis, and (4) expert systems for analyzing project risks.

The risk alarm system was developed in Japan to identify areas on a project where management needs to direct attention in order to avoid problems. The system employs a large database to store a wide range of information on potential problems and preceding activities which can be used to mitigate the problems. This stored information can also be used to identify areas of uncertainty where contingency reserves may be called for (Niwa et al., 1979).

The construction project risk database was compiled from literature and in-depth interviews with construction managers. It lists about 700 specific problem areas. The user can input various data on problems that would be encountered during the course of the construction project. These data are then manipulated to compare the upcoming project with past projects to expose the potential risks associated with characteristics that are similar to the past problems. Contingency reserves can then be tailored on the basis of this information (Bliudzius and Ashley, 1985).

The ambiguity analysis technique is based on the following considerations (McCaskey, 1982):

1. Project is subject to different value orientations, political or emotional clashes
2. Nature of problem is itself in question
3. Contradictions and paradoxes appear
4. Symbols and metaphors are used in describing problems
5. Information (amount and reliability) is problematical
6. Goals are unclear, multiple, or conflicting
7. Multiple, conflicting interpretations of project objectives
8. Time, money, or attention are lacking
9. Roles are vague, responsibilities unclear
10. Success measures are lacking
11. Cause-effect relationships are not well understood
12. Changes to participation in decision making

The impact of the above characteristics illustrated by problems reported on the Alaska Pipeline, the Bay Area Rapid Transit project, the British development of the North Sea, and the construction of a number of process plants in the United States and summarized in Table 1, correlates very closely to the cost overruns experienced on these projects. This comparison indicated that ambiguity and potential change are important indicators to be considered in setting up the contingency reserve (Avots, 1984).

Expert systems, which mimic the behavior of experts in a particular field, are an added source in the determination of project uncertainties and related contingencies. An example is a system which analyzes project performance and identifies any variances from schedule and the causes. Employing such a program on a what-if basis can help planners identify potential risk areas in advance and make appropriate contingency allowances (Nay and Logcher, 1980).

Table 1 Ambiguity and Change Rating of Selected Projects (* Indicate Estimated Severity of Condition)

Characteristic	Trans-Alaska	BART	North Sea Oil	Process plants
Participants' frame of reference	Owners, contractors, project manager, and outside parties had different concepts of the world ***	Same as for Trans-Alaska ***	Owners had a different outlook from labor and regulators **	Owners had a different outlook from contractors **
Clarity of the nature of the problem	Started with a different product Designed as-you-go ***	Used new technology without clear vision of effects Political problems **	Inadequate design criteria, lack of codes and standards **	Questions of technological feasibility **
Adequacy of coordination	Coordination modes were changed. Previously found unsatisfactory ***	Coordination modes did not keep up with changing pressures on project **	Conflicts between organizations were not well mitigated **	Technical/construction management coordination unsatisfactory **
Amount and reliability of information	Little available ***	Political events impossible to predict ***	Information about geological conditions was incomplete *	Reliability of technical data was not known *
Contradictions or multiple goals	Environmentalist objectives vs. efficient production **	Political aspects brought mutiplicity of goals **	Lack of experience vs. ambitious schedule **	Assumed that new technology will work *

Table 1 (Continued)

Characteristic	Trans-Alaska	BART	North Sea Oil	Process plants
Understanding of cause-effect relationships	Environmentalists not concerned with cost/ schedule **	Politicians not concerned with project cost effects **	Regulators and labor not concerned with cost effects *	"Cost growth" was not well understood
Different value orientations and conflicts	Regulatory issues, labor and local interests, environmentalists ***	Involved municipalities had different value orientations **	Unions took advantage of situation *	Product marketers were pushing technology *
Adequacy of time, money, attention	Constraint of time and timing *	Money sometimes ran out **	Constraint of time and timing *	Money was usually a constraint *
Multiple or conflicting interpretations	Arguments between owners and construction manager *	Political interests caused different interpretations **	No	No
Clarity of roles and responsibilities	Roles of construction manager, owner, land management were vague **	Problems with role of municipalities *	No	No
Total score	23	21	11	11

IMPLEMENTING CONTINGENCY MANAGEMENT

A basic principle of using contingency reserves for management control is to identify them with specific uncertainties and assign responsibility to specific individuals. Such individuals must have a direct-line responsibility for the work to be performed and often are known as cost account managers.

Good practice requires that the cost account manager participate in the development of the reserve, its use, and eventual transfer to another area. When a work breakdown structure is used, as it should be on any sizeable program, contingencies can be assigned to various levels of the structure and managed by the same individuals who control the elements at those levels. Caution is urged, however, since creating too many levels of contingencies creates additional management problems.

In simple projects the project manager may be given a contingency budget to be applied over a specific period of time or for a specific purpose. When added scope is negotiated, the result is an increased budget, and the amount of the reserve used can be returned to the pool.

A certain amount of contingency, often known as the general reserve, should remain under the direct control of top management. This is particularly true if management has been instrumental in setting the contract price. In buy-in situations where it is expected that parts of the original estimate will be overrun, the general reserve should come out of general funds and not project funds. This will maintain realistic working budgets and not penalize the project for decisions made by senior management.

Figure 6 shows how contingency reserves are applied over the life of a project. The first column reflects the project estimate along with the expected scope changes and escalation allowances. Separate reserves are shown for the project manager and general management. The second column reflects the situation after the project is underway. A working budget has been developed which includes the original scope plus adjustments necessary to reflect the actual work methods to be used. These methods may differ from those assumed in the original estimate, since new information about the project becomes available after the work has begun. In this adjustment process, some of the contingencies set aside for scope changes and escalation may be actually incorporated in the working budget. The project manager still has some reserve left and the general reserve has not been touched.

The third column shows the situation still later in the project, when considerable revisions to the scope have taken place. The revised working budget now includes a revised breakdown of the various scope and contingency elements. However, some reserve for known scope changes remains under the control of the project manager. As before, the general reserve has not been used, indicating a potential increase in the profitability of the project (Murray and Ramsaur, 1977).

MANAGEMENT CONTROL THROUGH CONTINGENCY RESERVES

For management control, all reserve allocations must be recorded and reported periodically along with other project cost information. The proper uses of the contingency are:

1. To create a new budget for newly identified work within the scope of the project. This could be an item that was not expected when the original budget was set up or an item that was completed but which must be redone.
2. To increase the budget for work which has been grossly underbudgeted. It is appropriate to make such a budget correction early, and not to wait until the account is overrun.
3. To temporarily create a new budget for scope that has been added to the project, but for which the additional budget monies required have not yet been

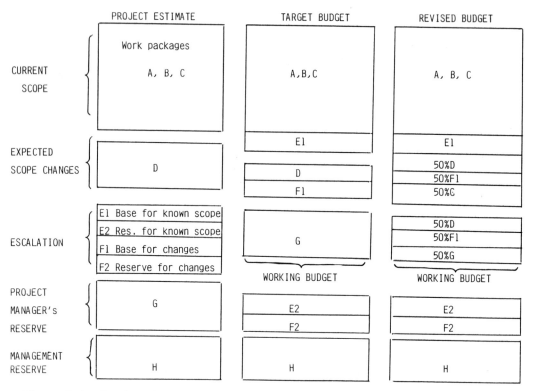

Figure 6 Application of contingencies over the life of the project.

    authorized. The contingency reserve should be replenished as soon as the budget has been adjusted.

4. To offset significant effects of unforeseen rate changes for labor, overhead, etc., during the course of a project.

    The contingency reserve should not be used to increase the budget after work has started on a work package or merely to reduce a cost overrun.

CONCLUSION

The success of the contingency management process depends on (1) identifying project uncertainties and relating them to specific contingency reserves; (2) establishing procedures for the proper use of the contingency reserves; and (3) establishing an information system showing each responsible manager what contingency reserves apply to the work under his control, how they are being depleted, how the trends appear for the remainder of the project, and when it may be possible to transfer balances to other less successful areas or to the general reserve.

REFERENCES

Ashley, D. B., and I. Avots, "Influence Diagramming for Analysis of Project Risks." *Project Management Journal*, March 1984, pp. 56-62.

Avots, I. Construction Risk Identification & Prevention Techniques. German Project Management Association, Hamburg, Germany, June 1982.

Avots, I. Cost Relevance Analysis for Overrun Control. *International Journal of Project Management, 1*(3) (August 1983), pp. 142-148.

Avots, I. Towards Control of the Intangible Project Risk Factors. Project Cost Management, International Project Management Association, Zurich, Switzerland, October 1984, pp. 68-76.

Bliudzius, P. A., and D. B. Ashley. A Construction Project Risk Identification Relational Database. Report No. UTCEPM-85-4, The University of Texas at Austin, December 1985.

Lichtenberg, S. Real World Uncertainties in Project Budgets and Schedules, 1981. Proceedings of the PMI/INTERNET Joint Symposium, Boston, MA, pp. 179-193.

McCaskey, M. B. The Executive Challenge: Managing Change and Ambiguity. Pitman, 1982.

Murray, J. W., and W. F. Ramsaur. Project Reserves a Key to Managing Cost Risks. Proceedings of the Project Management Institute Annual Seminar/Symposium, Drexel Hill, PA, October 1977, pp. 294-299.

Nay III, L. B., and R. D. Logcher. An Expert Systems Framework for Analyzing Construction Project Risks. Report from the Center for Construction Research and Education, Massachusetts Institute of Technology, February 1980.

Niwa, K., et al. Development of a risk Alarm System for Big Construction Projects. Proceedings of the Project Management Institute Annual Seminar/Symposium, Drexel Hill, PA, October 1977, pp. 221-229.

Traylor, R. C., et al. Project Management Under Uncertainty. *Project Management Journal*, March 1984, pp. 66-74.

10

Project Management:
A History of Its Interaction with Society

SEYMOUR S. GREENFIELD   *Parsons Brinckerhoff Inc., New York, New York*

REBECCA YAMIN   *Parsons Brinckerhoff Inc., New York, New York*

BEGINNING—CONTROL FOR SOCIETY'S BENEFIT

Civil engineering is as old as civilization. In fact, project management may be at the root of civilization. Some anthropologists argue that managing large-scale irrigation works gave rise to state institutions (Wittfogel, 1959). In Mesopotamia, China, and even in Mesoamerica, the political and economic power amassed for organizing irrigation systems provided the framework for organizing the earliest states. The project managers were the politicians. They may also have been the priests. Whether or not the theory holds, there is no doubt that large public works projects played a significant role in the evolution of civilization.

Public works did more than legitimize leadership in these early societies. They imposed order on an essentially chaotic world; they demonstrated control of natural forces for the benefit of humankind. Mayan temples reached for the heavens, Egyptian pyramids sought to defy the ravages of death, Roman aqueducts carried water where none flowed naturally, and roads made foreign territory into familiar ground. Public works projects demonstrated control, and civil engineers provided the expertise to seize that control. Using human ingenuity and energy and harnessing animal power and strength, corps of engineers erected a manmade infrastructure—a buffer between human society and the natural world.

The environment for civil engineering projects has changed over time. During the industrial revolution, man's ability to control natural energy sources accelerated technological development (Hendricks et al., 1975, p. 17). The infrastructure buffer zone, in urban areas at least, began to dominate the landscape and impose limits on human activity. Although engineers ceased to serve the state, they still saw themselves as custodians of the common good. With crusaderlike dedication, says Samuel Florman (1976), nineteenth-century engineers were committed to applying technological advances in ways that would benefit all people. They consistently defined their work in terms of its service to humanity. "Engineering is the act of directing the great sources of power in nature for the use and convenience of man," wrote Thomas Tredgold in 1828 (quoted by Florman,, 1976, p. 19). In the same vein, American engineer William Barclay Parsons proclaimed, "It is not the technical excellence of an engineering design which alone determines its merit but rather the completeness with which it meets the economic and social needs of its day."

Parsons' career epitomized the entrepreneurial approach to the profession at the turn of the century. He considered design of New York City's first subway his "life's

work"—a large-scale project that would give him the opportunity to apply his engineering skill and talent and would also make a substantial contribution to making New York
City a better place to live. Parsons understood the subway's implications for influencing expansion of the city northward; he fought against Tammany Hall's desire to keep
its constituency at bay within the slums of the inner city; and he aligned himself
with financial backing (i.e., August Belmont, Jr.) that could bring the project to
fruition (Katz, 1979). Parsons and his peers not only managed the engineering details
of complex public works projects; they were deeply involved in the political maneuvering
and funding for the projects. They were entrepreneurs, but they were also humanitari-
ans interested in influencing and guiding the growth of society. They were battling the
unforeseen results of the industrial revolution and were determined to bring it under
their control.

In the high tech environment of the twentieth century, however, engineers found
themselves losing control. They were less likely to be involved with the conception
of projects or in their political and financial aspects. They were hired to fulfill the
needs of the client. The ultimate responsibility of project management—to bring the
project in on time and within budget—was not to the public but to the client. The
engineer had to balance the demands of the client with the technical standards of the
profession. He also had to abide by the requirements of state and local building codes,
consider aesthetics to whatever degree allowable, worry about his own profits, and
deal with human displacement. The greatest challenge for project management in this
period was to mediate between the demands of the client and the needs of the contractor. Price became an overriding concern and time translated into dollars. The client
wanted to spend as little of both as possible, the contractor had to get the thing built,
and the project manager had to oversee the process.

SOCIAL RESPONSIBILITY IN A COMMERCIAL CLIMATE

Retaining a sense of social responsibility in a climate that valued rapid, commercially
profitable development as the ultimate good was difficult. No one guessed or even
thought about its possible cumulative consequences. This lack of attention to the
future was combined with a complacent belief that all this development was good for
the people and that the public need not be consulted about individual projects because
market forces created the need for public projects and market forces reflected the
public will.

Indeed, these presumptions often were correct. In New Jersey, for instance, a
project was conceived and completed that enhanced the environment, satisfied a public
need, and stimulated commerce with no directives other than a good working relationship between the client (the New Jersey Highway Authority) and the consulting engineers (Parsons Brinckerhoff headed the effort which involved 16 engineering firms
and 56 prime contractors). Begun in 1952 the 173-mile-long Garden State Parkway
was completed in four short years. The project entailed acquiring 5253 parcels of
land, relocating 2000 building owners, designing and building 459 bridges, constructing 121 entrance and exit ramps and 11 across-the-road toll plazas, and laying over
7,700,000 square yards of bituminous surface pavement. The resulting highway gracefully follows the natural curves of the land linking the industrialized centers of the
north with the seaside resorts of the south. Safety factors, including the across-
the-road toll gates, wooden railings to block the glare of oncoming headlights, and
exceptionally wide medians, contributed to a fatality rate far below the national average. It is a safe and a beautiful highway which serves a public need as well as the
commercial viability of the state's southern vacation communities.

Southern California's Century Freeway, however, is a very different story. Also
conceived in the 1950s, the construction of a 17.2-mile connection between Los Angeles
International Airport and the city of Norwalk, has been held up for more than 20 years.

Originally, the issue was displacement of people. An estimated 21,000 people living along the route on 6000 parcels of land were to be relcoated. The state was to take 7000 dwellings including about 3900 single family and 3000 multifamily units. The complexity and the sensitivity of the situation—the 10-lane highway was designed to pass through economically depressed areas—led to some rather innovative approaches to dealing with the problems. First, the state pioneered the idea of providing replacement housing even if it meant building it, a concept that became state law in 1968 (*Engineering News Record*, July 20, 1972). Second, a multidisciplinary team of consultants including planners (Gruen Associates) was hired to devise a plan that would blend the route into the communities. Their work (19 studies) became a model for later federal legislation and cleared the way for dealing with the housing problem, but passage of the National Environmental Policy Act in 1969 created new obstacles concerning air and noise pollution which further delayed the project.

Declared part of the interstate system in 1969, the Century Freeway, or I-105, is obviously a part of the system that did not go so smoothly. However, much of it did and engineers are justifiably proud of the network of highways they put in place across the country—a veritable scaffolding for post-World War II development. The Interstate Highway Act, the enabling legislation passed in 1952, came with regulations. Detailed designs and contract documents, for instance, were required for the first time. Satisfaction of such regulations added to the complexity of project management. Again, it was up to the project managers to make it all work. In addition to satisfying the client and keeping the contractors happy, project managers were called on to integrate procedures necessary to meet the requirements defined in the regulations. The Interstate Highway Act provided 90% of the funding for thousands of miles of highways which put a generation of engineers productively to work.

The strings attached to public funding added a dimension of complexity to project management, but the world itself had become a more complex place. Urbanization had transformed much of rural America into a suburban sprawl and cities were in a state of decline. To reverse that process was more than a construction problem. In San Francisco, what has been called a "huge social experiment-in vivo" was begun (Webber, 1979, p. 1).

Fearing the kind of deterioration already in progress in other metropolitan centers around the United States, San Francisco took a preemptive step. The city retained Parsons Brinckerhoff to make a feasibility study for a rapid transit system to serve the nine counties of the San Francisco Bay area. In the context of the late 1950s, it became clear that transportation systems were inextricably intertwined with land use and one could not be planned without the other. The task was not simply to design a subway for one of the most beautiful cities in the world; it was to choreograph a number of components that, in combination. would ensure the future of a viable downtown district, would stimulate business within the city, and create regional centers—offices and retail shop—rather than an untamed explosion of suburbs. It was intended to lure people out of their automobiles, transport the disadvantaged to new job centers, and bring remote regions within the Bay Area into the economic and cultural mainstream.

Without analyzing the actual effects of Bay Area Rapid Transit (BART) here, it is interesting to note that even the president of the Board of Directors of the BART district lamented a certain lack of fit between what was delivered and what people wanted (or knew they wanted after the fact). "A rapid transit agency must dovetail its route planning and engineering studies with that of an existing regional plan concurred on by a region's cities and satellite cities," wrote Arnold Anderson in 1969 (Anderson, 1969, p. 22). "A rapid transit agency should demand and receive a more precise definition of the social role the community expects rapid transit, through its policy makers, to play."

Although project conception and management of BART had integrated many factors not considered previously, public participation had not been part of the planning process. There was no existing science for eliciting public opinion about the project (except through passage of a funding referendum) and, as a result, public use of the system has been different than what was anticipated. BART was an experiment which produced invaluable data for future planning. It also reflected the interdependence of a multitude of factors in planning and designing and constructing a major civil engineering facility in the mid-twentieth-century United States.

BART, the Century Freeway, and Garden State Parkway, and undoubtedly many other projects incorporated procedures later mandated by legislation—replacement housing, multidisciplinary planning, aesthetic sensitivity, long-range economic goals—to name just a few. It was not just environmental legislation that transformed project management in the late 1960s. It was the complexity of completing civil engineering projects in a populous, urbanized, increasingly aware society in combination with the noticeable deterioration of the environment. The National Environmental Policy Act (NEPA) did not spring out of the blue. Legislation never does.

PROJECT MANAGEMENT AFTER PASSAGE OF NEPA

Passage of the National Environmental Policy Act (NEPA) in 1969 did make a difference. In spite of engineers' previous concern with environmental issues (see Florman, 1976, Part 1) and involvement with complex projects, there was no mandate to incorporate procedures to protect the environment into projects and, more importantly, there was no money for it. Individual engineers were as concerned as any informed citizen with environmental degradation: air and water pollution, poisonous substances in food, and unsafe automobiles. They were concerned but could not manifest these concerns on tight budgets for pennywise clients. In addition, the monitoring and measurement of environmental impacts needed a different kind of expertise. Engineers and project managers, in particular, had to learn to talk to a whole new group of professionals: political scientists, sociologists, archaeologists, ecologists, biologists, planners. They had to learn to explain engineering to nonengineers and to understand and incorporate nonengineering concerns into engineering projects.

No science of environmental analysis existed when NEPA was passed (Hendricks et al., 1975). There was no formal professional approach to environmental assessment, and just as the engineers did not understand the language or premises of the new specialists in their midst, the specialists did not understand each other. With only the vague guidelines of NEPA to go on, these specialists had to figure out how to evaluate the positive and negative impacts of proposed engineering projects on the environment and how to enlist public participation in the planning process. In the meantime, project managers had to integrate a whole new sphere of activities into an already complex process.

But projects did get done. The environmental impact statement for a rapid transit system in Atlanta, Georgia (MARTA, the Metropolitan Atlanta Rapid Transit Authority) was one of the first. Completed in 1972 this 350-page document plus appendices includes technical evaluations of such things as wetlands, first- and second-generation forests, historic and archaeological resources, as well as public input on station and route lcoation, parks, and desired economic development. Learning from BART, the planners involved local government in planning how to maximize the impact of the system in a positive way on their communities. Future land use was considered in relation to existing trends and zoning recommended, where appropriate, to create particular kinds of development. Many of the issues dealt with in the BART project were a part of the environmental review process for MARTA.

There is no question that environmental review adds to costs. An Atlanta newspaper headline read, "$50 Million in Transit Shifts," for MARTA caused fundamentally by design changes due to natural resource considerations. But it also adds intangible benefits. As Norman E. Hill points out in his article, "National Environmental Policies and the Effect on Productivity Through Regulations" (1976),

"Under the concepts developed in these laws productivity cannot be measured strictly by the use of the gross national product. Productivity must be seen as more than merely producing goods and services; rather it must be seen as the success of society in producing conditions desired by its people . . . Environmental controls have been essential to increase the productivity of society in yielding both tangible and intangible benefits which are valued by the citizens."

It is also possible for environmental review to make money by winning proponents for projects which will have tremendous economic benefits. In the case of the New York City Convention Center, completion of an EIS provided the opportunity to evaluate exactly how beneficial the proposed facility would be to the city. The study estimated a total annual economic output attributable to the facility at approximately $832 million in 1979 and total gross tax revenues for such a year at $82.3 million (*New York Exposition and Convention Center Final Environmental Impact Statement*, 1980).

The environmental review process has had both direct and indirect effects on project management. Directly, it has meant that the opinions of other than engineers must be brought to bear on decision making for engineering projects. This includes incorporating community input, which is neither automatic nor easy to elicit (see Hoover, 1975, 1981). It is up to project management to coordinate the efforts of a multidisciplinary team and facilitate the necessary communication between its many players.

Indirectly, environmental review has imposed a kind of quality control on the component parts of projects, as everyone from the designers to the economists must explain their work and justify their recommendations.

Management is charged with learning enough of the language of the many called-for disciplines to make informed choices on the hiring of consultants and intelligent evaluations of the adequacy of their work. Management must also keep totally abreast of the requirements for implementing the environmental review and permitting processes early enough so as not to interfere with or interrupt a project's progress. This has probably been the greatest stumbling block and the reason for such negative feeling toward the whole review process.

ADAPTATION TO THE REGULATORY CRISIS

Just as the environmental crisis was the result of an accumulation of errors, what some consider the regulatory crisis is the result of an accumulation of too many regulations. "As Congress passed each law," notes Norman Hill, "it examined only the incremental burden of that law. The overall burden of the many regulations emerged as an unexpected side effect . . . The concern for the adverse and unexpected effects of regulation brings home the principle of ecology that everything is related to everything else" (Hill, 1976, p. 220). But steps have been taken to remedy this situation.

The Environmental Protection Agency (EPA) has made an effort to consolidate the permitting process ("A Guide to the Consolidated Permit Regulations," 1980). In 1980, the agency made a commitment to "cut permitting costs by developing a standard permit application form for all of its permits programs, and by streamlining the procedures for processing permits." This makes it possible to collect all standard information on a single application form even when a facility requires more than one EPA permit. The consolidated permit regulations also standardized the steps involved in processing permits so that permitees do not have to learn different procedures for different permit programs, and it establishes predictable points of public involvement.

Some states, likewise, have instituted one-stop permitting with a single agency acting as a clearing house for other agencies requiring environmental review. The single agency determines what permits are necessary for a project, thereby freeing project management from the time-consuming and frustrating process of sorting out all of the requirements and hopefully avoiding delays caused by failure to complete the necessary steps.

Scoping, a process begun at the outset of a project requiring an Environmental Impact Statement (EIS), has also facilitated environmental review. As defined by the Council on Environmental Quality, scoping involves public participation in the determination of the scope of the EIS so that the document can be effectively managed. "Scoping is intended to ensure that problems are identified early and properly studied, that issues of little significance do not consume time and effort, that the draft EIS is thorough and balanced, and that delays occasioned by an inadequate draft EIS are avoided" (*Environmental Reporter*, 1983, p. 562).

Both consolidated permitting and scoping reflect agency adaptation to the needs of managing projects requiring environmental review. There has also been an adaptation within the profession to managing such projects, to working with joint ventures, and incorporating environmental concerns into the decision making process. Even more significant has been an evolution toward conceiving of projects in more holistic terms. New York City's Westway is an excellent example.

The steering committee for planning the West Side Highway included representatives of all relevant state and city planning and transportation agencies and community boards as well as a study staff of engineers, architects, planners, economists, and lawyers. They wanted more than a replacement for the old road. They wanted to create jobs, reduce degradation of the environment, and regain access to the river.

Taking these specifications into account, the resulting plans for the highway proposed to create over 36,000 man years of work—an estimated $285 million in direct wages—and significant opportunities for minority businesses. Much of the highway was designed to run underground to reduce pollution with pedestrian access to the waterfront provided above. As a transportation corridor it would serve the needs of distributing goods and would include special provisions for commuter bus service. The project reflects an educated awareness within the engineering profession to view transportation systems in a larger social context and to participate in multidisciplinary approaches to their design.

Although both agencies involved with enforcing environmental laws and project managers have evolved methods for expediting regulatory requirements and automatically incorporating them into civil engineering projects, there is room for change. Some laws and their interpretation in the courts remain inflexible to the point of absurdity, obstructing much-needed infrastructure projects. The H-3 Highway, a part of a 51-mile Interstate and Defense Highway System on the island of Oahu, Hawaii is a case in point.

H-3 has been in litigation since 1972 with all issues decided in favor of the project except Section 4(f) of the Federal Aid Highway Act. The proposed 15-mile-long highway will provide a much needed connection between several residential communities and a Marine Corps air station on the windward side of Oahu with the rapidly growing area on the leeward side of the Koolau Mountain Range to the west of downtown Honolulu, an area including the Pearl Harbor naval complex, the island's largest employer.

The particular issue affected by 4(f) is the fact that the H-3 alignment runs along the edge of Hoanaluhia Park. This park was created during the planning stages for the highway in a coordinated effort between the state's H-3 project, the county's flood control project (which was to include the park), and a local Greenbelt project (Kawaguchi, 1985, p. 6). In other words, the park did not exist before the road was designed.

By the time construction of the flood control project and associated park were authorized, final designs for H-3 were being prepared and parts of it were already under construction. The original boundaries of the park were well away from the boundary of H-3 but two expansions, the second defined by the county as a buffer zone between the park and proposed highway, brought the park up to the H-3 boundary. In November 1978 the U.S. District Court ruled that the protection of Section 4(f) applied to Hoanaluhia Park on the basis of "constructive use," specifically, noise and visual impacts. In compliance with the court's decision, the State and Federal Highway Administration investigated a no-build alternative and a realignment through a section of a nearby town, all at considerable expense. The alternatives were declared not "prudent and feasible" by the U.S. Secretary of Transportation in 1980, but the court did not give the project a go-ahead until 1982; a decision that was quickly appealed. In 1984 the Ninth Circuit Court reviewed the District Court's decision claiming 4(f) requirements were not satisfied and the project remains in limbo.

From the standpoint of project management the kinds of delays attendant to the H-3 project are disastrous. While waiting for court settlements, a project can lose key staff. Changes in technology may lead to design modifications, and economic shifts invariably wreak havoc with budgets. Mobilization and demobilization of study and design teams is both costly and demoralizing. These problems are clearly beyond the control of project management. No matter how effectively design has been staged to fit environmental regulations, delays in the courts completely upset schedules. Considering the expense and waste of time and energy, it would appear that certain aspects of the legislative process are out of control and need reexamination.

PROJECT MANAGEMENT IN THE PRESENT

There is no one environment for project management. It is a changing environment. It has never been simple and, as with any evolutionary process, it gets more complex. The passage of NEPA in the late 1960s did not transform project management; it formalized approaches to concerns that had always been part of managing large civil engineering projects. It also reasserted a basic principle of civil engineering: control over the natural world for the good of human society.

Although NEPA made mandatory the participation of specialists whose expertise was not part of engineers' training, overall project management was still left to the civil engineers. It is the civil engineers who remain the catalysts, the integrators, the ones who pull it all together (Lammie and Shah, 1979; Novick, 1982). It is up to project management to implement the environmental review process when necessary and to integrate its results into design. Environmental review is not something extra any more; it is certainly not something to be avoided. If begun early enough and performed competently, environmental review becomes just one more of the many components of a project to coordinate.

That environmental review has become an integral part of civil engineering is perhaps best illustrated by the proposal of the Research Council of the American Society of Civil Engineer's Environmental Impact Analysis Branch of an Eighth Fundamental Canon to the ASCE Code of Ethics. The canon directs ASCE members "to perform services in such a manner as to husband the world's resources and the natural and cultured environment for the benefit of present and future generations." As directors of civil engineering projects, project managers are in a position to make sure that directive is realized.

ACKNOWLEDGMENTS

The authors take full responsibility for the contents, but gratefully acknowledge productive conversations with several of their colleagues at Parsons Brinckerhoff: Alvars U. Delle, James R. Brown, Robert Schaevitz, Dean T. Anson II, Henry L. Sanger, and Stanley Kawaguchi.

REFERENCES

Andersen, A. "BART: More Than Just a Fast Ride." Reprinted from *San Francisco Business*, August 1969.

Andersen, A. "Council on Environmental Quality Guidance on Naitonal Environmental Policy Act Regulations." *Environmental Reporter 14*(13), July 29, 1983.

Andersen, A. "A Guide to the Consolidated Permit Regulations," U.S. EPA, Office of Water Envorcement (EN 335), Washington, D.C., May 1980.

Andersen, A. "Court Injunction Orders More Studies, Hearings on Los Angeles Freeway." *Engineering News Record*, July 20, 1972, p. 22.

Glorman, S. C. *The Existential Pleasures of Engineering.* New York: St. Martin's Press, 1976.

Hendricks, D. W., Evan Vlaches, L. Scott Tucker, and Joseph C. Kellogg (eds.). *Environmental Design and Public Projects.* Water Resources Publications, Fort Collins, CO, 1975.

Hill, N. "National Environmental Policies and the Effect on Productivity Through Regulation." *The Civil Engineer's Role in Productivity in the Construction Industry*, Vol. 1. New York: American Society of Civil Engineers, 1976, pp. 219-235.

Hoover, J. "Citizen Participation in Alternatives Analysis." Reprint of paper presented at a Seminar on Alternatives Analysis, San Francisco, CA, January 20, 1981.

Kawaguchi, S. K. "Hawaii's H-3 Highway: Is It Time to Say Enough for the Environment?" Delivered at American Society of Civil Engineer's Conference on Intrastructure, San Diego, June 5-7, 1985.

Katz, W. B. "The New York Rapid Transit Decision of 1900: Economy, Society and Politics." HAER IRT (original line).

Lammie, J. L. and D. P. "Raj" Shah. "Managing Joint Ventures for Large Construction Projects." Reprinted from *Issues in Engineering*. ASCE, January 1981.

Lammie, J. L. and D. P. "Raj" Shah. "Project Management-Pulling It all Together." ASCE preprint 3674, October 23-25, 1979.

Novick, D. "The Challenge of Multidisciplinary Design Teams." From Lecture on Civil Engineering Design, University of Florida, March 2, 1982.

Parsons Brinckerhoff Quade and Douglas, Inc. on behalf of New York Convention Center Development Corporation. "New York Exposition and Convention Center Final Environmental Impact Statement" (3 vols). March, 1980.

Parsons Brinckerhoff Quade & Douglas, Inc. "West Side Highway Project Environmental Impact Statement." April 25, 1974.

Webber, M. M. "The BART Experience—What Have We Learned?" Monograph No. 26, Institute of Urban and Regional Development and Institute of Transportation Studies, University of California, Berkeley, 1976.

Wengert, N. I. "Environmental Law." In *Environmental Design and Public Projects*. Hendricks et al. (eds.). Kellogg Water Resources Publications, 1975, pp. 339-397.

Wittfogel, K. "The Theory of Oriental Society." In *Readings in Anthropology*, Vol. II. Morton H. Fried (ed.). New York: Thomas Y. Crowell Company, 1959, pp. 94-113.

II
THE PROJECT MANAGER

UNIT OVERVIEW

When a company has a need to perform a complex assignment within a finite time frame and outside of the formal line organization, a project is born, and a manager is assigned to guide the project. The manager–the project manager–has the unusual task of blending a range of diverse disciplines into an effective team, with little time for preparation, leading and directing the team to meet a statement of objectives laid down by management, and when the assignment has been completed, releasing the team. What kind of person does it take to excel in this temporal and fluid environment?

The difficulty in choosing the format and content of a unit on the project manager is one of selectivity. We are discussing a range of assignments from in-house retrofits to mega projects, with a corresponding range of responsibility and authority, and, within reason, we want to address the demands of the different roles. After much discussion we chose to focus on the following topics: the views of the academic community, a general dissertation of various project roles, the issue of implied authority, styles of management, and the characteristics of the superior project manager.

There is an element of disagreement between the writings of the different authors, and this is as it should be, for project management is in transition from its founding on a technical base to the exceptionally demanding business environment of the mega project. But, it is still a profession where an individual is asked to complete a task, or series of tasks, over a relatively limited time period, and meet the accepted parameters of cost, schedule, quality, and client satisfaction.

One consideration common to all views is the need to work hard at and be attentive to interpersonal relations, for projects are built by people, and people will determine the success or failure of a project. Although there appear to be divergent views on management styles, a critical analysis will show that all authors recognize that management styles are situational: in a constant environment a basic style is recommended; different styles are suggested for different environments. Certain intangibles are covered at length: the personality of the project manager, the development of leadership, and the ever-present issue of implied authority~complex issues lacking definitive guidelines, but areas where certain identifiable practices will enhance the performance of the manager and increase the probability of project success.

Performance results from the development of management skills. Leadership is a result of performance. Authority is a result of leadership. The road to excellence in project management is up to the individual.

1

Academic Approaches to Project Management

C. B. TATUM *Stanford University, Stanford, California*

At several universities, teaching curricula and research include many topics related to project management. Generally, however, the subject of project management is treated as a management responsibility falling between general management and operations management, and it therefore does not receive specific attention in many management programs.

An appropriate mix of technical and managerial skills is essential for effective project management. This requires an adequate technical background for making major project decisions and to avoid getting "snowed" by technical specialists assigned to the project. Even in the matrix organization, with its corps of discipline specialists participating on the project team, the project manager must use his technical knowledge to make decisions to resolve conflicts between disciplines. Without a solid technical background and understanding of engineering criteria and design operations, the project manager will soon lose credibility with the engineers assigned to the project and their functional supervisors.

Managerial skills are necessary to effectively discharge their general management duties and control the large organizations under their jurisdiction. While they receive support from several functional departments, project managers must direct finance, personnel, client relations, and various administrative activities on their projects. The conflict inherent in the matrix structure frequently requires well-developed interpersonnel skills.

Different requirements and organization format place many demands on project managers. Compared with other business or manufacturing organizations, projects generally have well-defined objectives. One of these is to work the organization out of business by completing the project—an objective very different from a manufacturing organization. The changing phases of an engineering and construction project also place varied demands on project managers.

We will discuss here the academic approach to project management, specifically from the perspective of graduate programs which focus on construction engineering and management. The most numerous include coverage of project management. Several of these programs include topics which provide the basics for project involvement and progression to project management. We will discuss some of these including project organization, organization behavior, project planning, progress and performance monitoring, quality management, and materials management. As described here, and as taught at several universities, these topics do not form a complete treatment of project management. However, they do provide important techniques for the prospective project manager. We will also discuss the relationships between project management and university research, and certain conclusions regarding academic approaches to project management.

PROJECT ORGANIZATION

A tendency to associate matrix organizations with project management is apparent in academic approaches and among many practitioners. This approach fails to recognize other organizational alternatives which may better fit certain project situations. It also overlooks many dimensions of structure which are not shown on organization charts and the necessity for change as the project progresses through various stages.

Broader Views of Organization Structure

The organization chart shows the grouping and the size of major elements. Academic approaches, which take a broader view of project organization, add the location of decision making and the means of coordination as other important elements of structure (Mintzberg, 1979). This broader view is especially important because projects require that both the technical requirements of the functional discipline and the performance requirements of the owner be satisfied. This dual focus (Davis and Lawrence, 1977) increases the need to define where different types of decisions are made in the organization and how the work of the many separate disciplines will be coordinated.

Project Situation and Organization Structure

The external influences on the project (the environment) and the major operations required to meet the objectives (the technology) make up the situation (Mintzberg, 1979). Contingency theories of organization design state that situation determines structure (Scott, 1981). The elements of situation for projects are significantly different from ongoing organizations and are very dynamic. Academic approaches to project management that recognize these differences include analysis of a given situation facing a project and using expanded elements of structure to design organizations most appropriate for meeting the situation (Tatum, 1986).

Changes Over Phases of the Project

Projects pass through a series of phases: conceptual planning, preliminary engineering, detailed engineering and design, construction, testing and start-up, and completion. Each phase requires changes in project organization. Academic coverage of project organization includes anticipating the changes necessary at each phase transition and using broader views of organization to tailor the structure to the requirements of the situation.

ORGANIZATION BEHAVIOR

Project organizations make special demands of both managers and subordinates. Projects work themselves out of business; employee motivation therefore differs from that found in manufacturing and other ongoing enterprises. This means that leadership patterns of effective project managers differ. Because of the frequency of change on many projects and the intense demand for results despite this ambiguity, interpersonal skills are necessary for effective project management. Academic approaches to this subject include the study of theories of motivation and leadership and the development of skills.

Theories of Motivation and Leadership

Several theories of employee motivation and effective management are relevant to project management. Mazlow's hierarchy of needs and investigations of satisfiers and dissatisfiers by Hertzberg indicate that satisfaction derived from completing work tasks becomes important once the basic needs for food and shelter are met. Investigations of motivation and leadership in construction indicate that successful completion of work is a very important motivator. Understanding these elements of motivation and their consequences for leadership style is important for potential project managers.

Practical Leadership Skills

Theories of motivation and leadership give potential project managers a conceptual framework; practical skills are very important in applying this knowledge. Skills that can be taught through group assignments and practical exercises include: delegating and coordinating group activities, reaching a group decision, resolving a conflict, and conducting a meeting. These exercises can be included in several types of courses to reinforce the student's learning experience.

PROJECT PLANNING

Many authors and developers of computer software have strongly implied that project planning, using network-based techniques, is the critical task of project managers. Project planning and scheduling are major topics in many project management courses. This section describes academic approaches which emphasize planning techniques, and includes fundamental planning techniques, applications, and software systems.

Fundamental Planning Techniques

Understanding and taking full advantage of network-based planning requires mastery of several fundamental techniques. These include: network calculations to determine total durations and to identify critical paths, time-cost tradeoff calculations, and allocation of resources and calculation of resultant impacts on the schedule (Moder et al., 1983). Experience in manually performing these calculations gives a firm understanding and a basis for their useful application. Many academic approaches use both "i-j" (activity-on-arrow) and precedence diagramming (activity on node) representations to broaden understanding of network techniques.

Applications

Full understanding of the benefits of network-based planning systems requires involvement in their application. One academic approach requires student analysis of case studies of realistic project requirements, development of networks which capture the constraints present in these situations, calculation of durations for these activities, and use of fundamental techniques for analysis and refinement of the plan. This approach generally involves group work, which provides additional experience in group problem solving.

Computer Software

The wide range of planning software available today presents a challenge in selecting the academic approach that uses the limited time available for covering this topic to the best advantage. Even small companies are likely to use systems which offer a full

range of capabilities and operate in environments from microcomputers to main frames.
The more complex systems, which include all of the techniques for network analysis,
generally require extensive instruction to learn the basics of the system. Since this
time is not available, a more realistic approach involves using microcomputer-based
software to illustrate selected techniques and demonstrate the advantages of computerized systems for some applications.

PROGRESS AND PERFORMANCE MONITORING

Monitoring engineering and construction progress is the second key element of project
control. This includes measuring both actual progress and the resources used to
achieve this progress. Comparison of these two measures against the project plan
indicates status and pinpoints problem areas. Academic coverage of project monitoring includes scope determination and work breakdown, definition of progress and performance measures, and techniques for integrated monitoring.

Scope Determination and Work Breakdown

Several estimating techniques define the scope of a project at various points in the
project life cycle. At the conceptual stage, parameter costs, cost-capacity factors,
and several cost indices are used to estimate project costs based on scope and timing
as compared with completed projects. As the detailed engineering progresses, more
precise estimates are based on quantities of construction materials and resources necessary to install these quantities. Academic coverage of project scope determination
generally focuses on the estimating techniques used at each stage of the project (Bar-
ries and Paulson, 1984).

The work breakdown structure and the work packages it contains are used to
organize both the estimates of project scope and the measures of progress and performance. Academic coverage of work breakdown emphasizes the need for information
organized by project, geographic area, work type, resource usage, and responsibility
for performance (Halpin, 1985). This conceptual understanding of work breakdown
is essential to take advantage of the many capabilities offered by current database
systems.

Techniques for Integrated Monitoring

Following the lead of the federal government, several owners now require project monitoring using integrated time-cost techniques. Based on the earned value concept,
these systems introduce new terminology to emphasize the time dimension when evaluating project costs and the productivity dimension when evaluating progress (Moder
et al., 1984). Because these techniques are being used more often, project control
courses should indicate an illustration of their use.

QUALITY MANAGEMENT

The importance of quality assurance and quality control has increased in proportion
to the complexity and special requirements of completed facilities. As with project
planning and monitoring, quality control is a cycle which requires: (1) definition
of requirements and performance standards; (2) measurement of the results of operations; (3) comparison of these results against the standards; and (4) taking action
based on the difference. This action may involve feedback to either operations to
correct the source of a problem or to planning to revise unrealistic requirements or
standards. Academic approaches to quality management include: types and sources
of quality requirements, a technical description of quality methods, and an overview
of quality management activities.

Quality Requirements

Drawings and specifications should define all of the quality requirements. But other sources may apply: permits, codes and standards; special owner requirements; and many types of regulations. Therefore, an awareness of unexpected sources of quality requirements is important in planning quality programs.

Quality Control Methods

Quality control comprises: inspection, testing, tracking, and documenting (Parsons, 1972). Inspection includes both visual and technical examination of materials and completed construction. The types of testing used on construction projects include laboratory, destructive, nondestructive, in-place, and service. A technical understanding of these quality control methods is an important basis for planning and managing quality control programs.

Quality Management

Managing quality assurance and control activities requires specific steps to assure that all necessary requirements are defined and that actions are taken to comply with these requirements. Equally important is that quality management programs avoid setting excessive requirements. Once the requirements and the methods for ensuring compliance are defined, the quality program generally involves preparing a manual, developing necessary procedures, and planning for inspection, testing, and documentation. Academic coverage of quality management should include both the technical components of quality and the management actions necessary to plan and implement effective programs.

MATERIALS MANAGEMENT

Materials are a vital link between design and construction. Delivery of materials to the construction forces must comply with the construction schedule. Timely placement of major orders is also critical for receipt of vendor information. This information is necessary for design and for vendor detailing of materials prior to fabrication.

On many projects, the responsibility for materials supply is severely fragmented. Engineering, procurement, construction, and project management all play an important role in ordering materials and managing suppliers. This fragmentation and the construction inefficiencies caused by late delivery of material highlight the opportunity for improved performance through increased attention to materials management.

Academic approaches to materials management should emphasize the tradeoff between four types of materials costs: purchase, transportation, storage, and shortage (Barrie and Paulson, 1984). To help prospective project managers understand the complexity and fragmentation of materials supply, covering the many steps required in this process is important. This description should emphasize planning and establishing ways to monitor the status of materials.

PROJECT MANAGEMENT AND UNIVERSITY RESEARCH

Project management has garnered attention as a research topic at many universities. It is also related to many areas of management research. In addition, investigation of many management techniques has provided important assistance to project management. Examples include advanced techniques for network scheduling, simulation of construction operations, computer applications, and improved productivity.

CONCLUSIONS

A solid technical competence is essential for effectively managing technically complex projects. Project managers must have a fundamental understanding of the activities performed by each critical discipline involved in the project. Project management does not fit well into most of the academic programs currently offered in either engineering or business. But a combination of technical and managerial skills is essential.

Current examples from construction engineering and management programs illustrate a workable approach to preparation for project management. This includes introducing concepts and techniques having general applicability, illustrating applications of these techniques, and integrating these concepts in case studies based on realistic situations and problems. Project management presents an important opportunity for increased academic attention–both in teaching and research.

REFERENCES

Barrie, D. S. and B. C. Paulson, Jr. *Professional Construction Management.* New York: McGraw Hill, 1984.

Davis, S. M. and P. R. Lawrence. *Matrix.* Reading, MA: Addison-Wesley Publishing Company, 1977.

Halpin, D. W. *Financial and Cost Concepts for Construction Management.* New York: John Wiley and Sons, 1985.

Mintzberg, H. *The Structuring of Organizations.* Englewood Cliffs, NJ: Prentice Hall, 1979.

Moder, J. J., C. R. Phillips, and E. W. Davis. *Project Management With CPM, PERT, and Precedence Diagramming.* New York: Van Nostrand Reinhold Company, 1984.

Parsons, R. M. "Systems for Control of Construction Quality." *Journal of the Construction Division*, ASCE, March, 1972.

Scott, W. R. *Organizations: Rational, Natural and Open Systems.* Englewood Cliffs, N.J.: Prentice-Hall, 1981.

Tatum, C. B. "Designing Construction Organizations–An Expanded Process." *Journal of Construction Engineering and Management*, ASCE, June, 1986.

2

The Role of the Project Manager

RAY D. HARVEY* *Fenco Engineers Inc., Toronto, Ontario, Canada*

In the past, the concept and role of a project manager has been associated with engineering-related activities. Today the role is more and more associated with a broad business base—a business role.

The basic role of a project manager is often compared to that of a general manager in a small to medium sized company, and while this is true, there are some fundamental differences that make the requirements and approach to project management much more demanding. The project manager lacks the authority of the general manager and usually must depend on the functional managers in the line organization to provide him with the expertise and support that he requires to meet project objectives. He must also be prepared to build up a fully operating and productive team from a standing start and to meet scheduled key dates and budgets within this framework. Later he must also be prepared to disband what, by this time, is a successful operation, to match the downturn of the workload on the project.

Because the title project manager is used universally for a diverse array of industries covering such fields as public works, transportation, industrial, mining, petroleum, energy, defense, and manufacturing, and because projects within this spectrum can range from small to large to mega size, it is almost impossible to define the role of the project manager precisely or briefly. The scope and extent of his responsibilities are very much dependent on the recognized practice of the industry he serves, the size of the projects, and whether or not he represents the owner, the vendor, or the engineer/contractor. We will emphasize the essentials of leadership and the leadership role the manager plays in the success of the project. We will identify the main parameters that are common to good project management and then discuss how the role of the project manager will change to meet the many situations that arise in a project. The manager must build up confidence within his team to motivate them. He must exhibit strength, leadership, and direction at all times. At the same time he should understand that his success is dependent on the quality of his back-up support, the depth and quality of the systems and procedures practiced by his organization, and the experience of the functional personnel that support the total project management concept.

PROJECT DEFINITION

The term project can embrace everything from a small study or modification to an existing plant to a complete "grass roots" installation requiring extensive infrastructure

---

Current affiliation: UDTC Inc., Toronto, Ontario, Canada

and an investment of millions and sometimes billions of dollars. For the first type
of project the role of the project manager will be more technically biased than in the
second, where his skills as a manager and administrator of many complex and interrelated functions will be needed. The majority of the subjects he must deal with will
be less technical and more commercial in nature, and at times totally community related.

Irrespective of size and complexity, every project passes through similar phases
in its development. All of these phases may or may not be the responsibility of the
project manager, again it depends on the preferred work procedures and practice
of the industry in question. For instance, in projects related to public works or buildings (see Fig. 1), it is quite common for the responsibility of the project manager to
be separate from that of the architect, engineering consultant, and contractor, each
of whom may be independently appointed by others but coordinated by the project
manager. On the other end of the scale, it is quite usual for the total responsibility
for a medium to large project in the process industries to be entrusted to an engi-
neer/constructor who would have accountability and responsibility for project management, engineering, procurement, construction, and cost and schedule maintenance
for the project (see Fig. 2).

QUALITIES OF A PROJECT MANAGER

Having emphasized the disparity in the term "project" from industry to industry and
how this may be interpreted, the question then arises how best can we define the quality and qualifications required in the project manager. The role will differ depending
on whether the manager is acting for the owner, the engineer, the constructor, or
supplier. Amid these divergent influences there emerges a list of qualities a project
manager must possess:

> Recognized leader with organizational ability
> Breadth of experience in related projects
> Ability to communicate and work with others
> Ability to coordinate both simple and complex functions
> Ability to encourage maximum input from team members
> Sensitivity to human relations, including tradesmen
> Complete understanding of the resources, systems, and procedures of his company
> Ability to develop and maintain favorable relations with the client

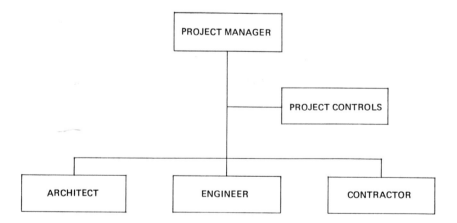

Figure 1 Typical project organization (public works).

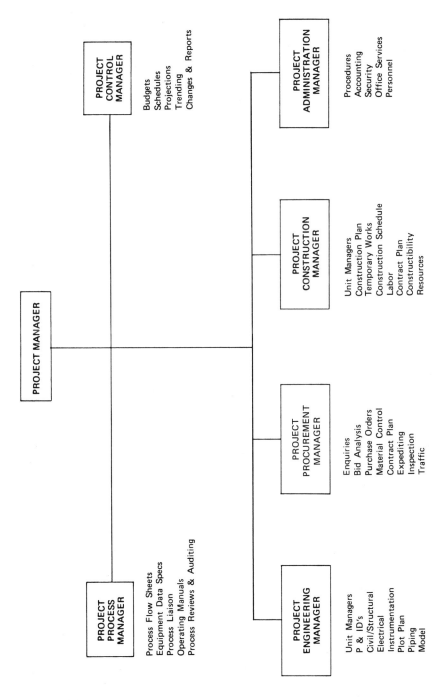

Figure 2 Typical project organization (process plant).

Let's review several of the aforementioned qualities.

The Team Leader

The project manager must be recognized as the team leader with demonstrated ability to make mature decisions based on minimum information, since projects do not always wait while managers study. He must have the confidence to delegate and have a keen understanding of the delegation process. He must maintain a broad perspective of problems and how they relate to project objectives, so that when proposed solutions to technical problems are presented he will be able to implement a sound course of action. He must have a grasp of all interactions between cost, schedule, and technical performance. Weak decisions, and worse, decisions by default, will result in team confusion and ultimately project chaos.

Client Relations

There is no consideration more important than the development and maintenance of good relations with the client. At project initiation there should be a complete understanding of the scope of work—not just the written word but what your client counterpart thinks the words mean. Produce for the client the project he has requested, within the cost and timeframes established, and within the ground rules laid down by the contract. If you can achieve this and at the same time make the client manager look good to his boss, thus furthering his career, you will have good client relations.

Contingency Planning

The cost control and scheduling departments perform a monitoring function for the manager and become his eyes and ears for the maintenance of budgets and schedules. The manager must be prepared to implement effective contingency plans promptly at the first sign of trends away from targets, and, as experience is gained, initiate corrective action in advance of trend reports.

On large projects, sophisticated computer programs are used to produce trend data. This may or may not be a blessing: reports can and do run late; reports are bulky, and if overviews are used to add clarity, further time is consumed; lastly, managers can become overdependent on documentation and lose sight of the forest for the trees.

A good approach to help in problem anticipation is for the manager to involve himself deeply in the formative phases of the project, such as preliminary estimating, risk analysis, and contingency considerations used to set the budget estimate, principal work breakdown structures, and schedule logic.

The manager must then convey to the team the need for an understanding and awareness of how and when various activities under their control fit into the total program.

Organization for the Project

This is, of course, a subject unto itself, deserving extended treatment. We will cover only one point here: the project procedures manual, a title that varies between organizations. All too often the preparation of this manual is viewed as a chore, something of little value to the project manager, but which has to be done. Nothing could be further from the truth. This manual establishes the firm scope of work—by statement and reference, the project organization—with names, duties, and responsibilities, the systems and procedures to be used, the approvals required, and the distribution of documents. It covers all phases of a project including design, procurement, construction, and start-up. It defines the use of corporate procedures, policy manuals, and computer programs.

Completion and issue of the manual provides the manager with an opportunity to walk through the project at a general staff meeting, and further, an opportunity to establish leadership as he reviews the project and the team assignments and responsibilities.

PROJECT EXECUTION

A project may be defined as an undertaking involving human and capital resources. Once a project has been authorized a commitment has been made: to complete the project on time, within budget, to the satisfaction of both the client and your management, your team, and yourself. During the course of the project resources must be commited by the manager in a judicious manner, for the benefit of all entities. This means maintaining a steady build-up of manhour and cost expenditures from project inception to a peak, which occurs during the last third of the program. If the initial build-up period is too slow or inefficient, there will be serious adverse repercussions on the last third of the project. Either additional hours must be spent to correct inaccurate work, additional manpower must be assigned to make up for lost schedule time, or the schedule must be extended, with a resultant increase in cost.

Standard project execution techniques recognize trade-offs between the expenditure of resources required for conceptual and design engineering and those required for procurement and construction. The project manager should allow a project to develop in a systematic stepwise manner, each step taking its appropriate time in the overall schedule period. On completion of each step, there is a pause and review time to ensure that the work completed to date is firm and approved before releasing resources to the next stage. This ensures that there is a single directional flow of information and that work is done in sequence, at its correct time in the project schedule, in the most efficient manner without unnecessary recycle and rework.

The main project execution steps are:

Project Initiation. This covers project definition and concepts, capital cost estimates, and project feasibility
Basic Engineering. This commences after the appropriate approvals and authorization by the owner. Key definitive parameters covering design criteria, control estimates, and schedules are established.
Production Engineering and Procurement. This phase covers the completion of design and drafting and the bulk of the equipment and commodity procurement.
Construction. This covers site development, field work, and erection.
Start-Up. This covers start-up and initial operations.

Throughout the above execution steps the project manager's major responsibilities may be defined as follows:

Project team organization and mobilization
Project initiation, direction, control
Client liaison
Contract administration
Project procedures manual
Scheduling, estimating, cost control
    Monitor, review, approve
Change orders
    Initiate, review, approve
Engineering approvals
    Flow sheets and plant layout
    Single-line electrical diagrams
    Engineering specifications
    Major equipment designs

    Procurement approvals
        Procedures, bidders list
        Major bid tabulations, purchase orders
    Construction approvals
        Planning, organization, subcontracts
    Commissioning and start-up approvals
        Organization, responsibilities, procedures
    Progress reports

THE MEGA PROJECT: THE PROJECT MANAGER AS A BUSINESS MANAGER

Today's larger projects place increased demands on the skills of the project manager. This is particularly so where the impact on the environment and the socioeconomic fabric of a small community may be totally disrupted by the influx of large numbers of construction workers. Many local community services including schools, hospitals, transportation, and recreational facilities are severely strained. Local regional and municipal budgets are unable to cope with the demand for expanded services because of short lead times and short duration of impact. Considerable demand is therefore placed on the project planning procedures and the need to look ahead jointly with the community to smooth out the effects of the project's impact on both the community and the project schedule. This has been a particularly sensitive factor with some of the large energy and resource projects built in the northern regions of the United States and Canada, where attempts have been made to minimize the impact on the environment and the local native communities. In the latter case, extensive training programs have been implemented to encourage and utilize indigenous people during the construction phase.

James Bay Hydro Electric Power Project

The giant James Bay Hydro Electric Power Project cost $14.7 billion and employed a peak labor force of 18,000 people. The logistics of the construction site camp facilities and support services, including airport, shops, schools, sports, recreation, restaurants, religious, and medical facilities, and the need for strict security because of the remoteness of the site, placed heavy demands on project management resources. This example is presented to stress how mammoth logistics place a much different emphasis on the type of person needed to fill the project management position.

Mass Transit Projects

The management approach to new mass rapid transit systems in large cities is an excellent example of the mega project. These projects are usually government funded and because of the need to plan route corridors through developed areas are clearly politically sensitive. A number of alternative routes must be planned and studied in depth and presented to local municipal councils and the public before final decisions on a right-of-way can be established. This presents the project management team with a different set of circumstances which must be addressed and which are over and above the more normal design, engineering, procurement, construction, and start-up problems experienced on other projects.

    The role of the project manager becomes highly complex in that he now is called on to show a considerable degree of diplomacy together with fine-tuned negotiation skills in dealing with several levels of government ministries. The public at large critiques his progress at every milestone and he soon realizes that he is unable to win the plaudits of all the critics all of the time. Add to this the complexity of combining public and private resources within his project organization because invariably in the bigger cities the elected officials will wish to retain management control through a small group while utilizing consulting firms and contractors to implement the work.

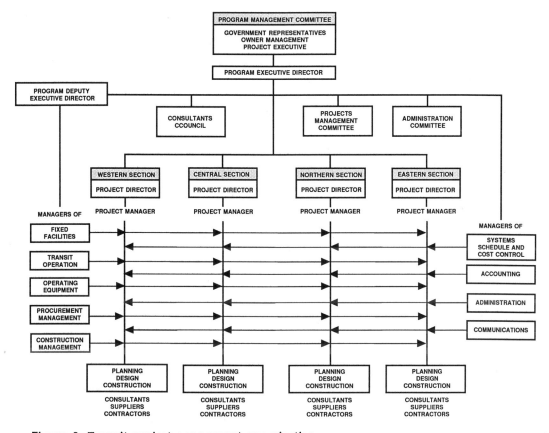

Figure 3 Transit project management organization.

Such an organizational structure is illustrated in Figure 3. The project staff group is structured in a "matrix-type" organization with the project subdivided into geographical areas, each headed up by a project director charged with the responsibility for implementing the work in his sector. Each project director will draw on the expertise and input of managers responsible for the technical quality of the work (left side of the chart) and managers responsible for administrative aspects (right side of the chart). The project directors use the resources available in the private sector for planning, design, and construction, thus ensuring maximum sharing of the pie to all local resources, including engineering, architectural, and other professional consultants, product and equipment suppliers, and support services as well as contractors for construction of the physical works.

SUMMARY

It is clear from the foregoing that no matter what project or industry we serve, versatility and flexibility are essential qualities of a project manager. Circumstances sometimes call for him to be a hardnosed leader, driving his team to meet project objectives as might be the case for a lump-sum turnkey contract; other circumstances require the skills and persuasion of a politician and diplomat to obtain necessary approvals and permits that allow a project to proceed through a tortuous and tedious pattern of public acceptance. Whatever the circumstances it is clear that the role of the project manager is vital to the success of the project and he deserves and must receive the full support of his team and his management.

3

Authority of the Project Manager

EMERY D. CARLSON   *Carlson Services Inc., Whittier, California*

Modern project management is defined by Harold Kerzner as "the planning, organizing, directing, and controlling of company resources for a relatively short term objective that has been established to complete specific goals and objectives."

In recent years, professional project management has been used in such diverse industries as aerospace and defense, manufacturing, processing plants, electrical generation, crude oil and natural gas exploration and production facilities, and for computer hardware and software development, among others.

Each of these types of projects benefits from the modern-day project management methodology and the discipline and structured approach to the many complex and highly technical activities involved. Although the form and type of project organizations vary widely, the project management approach calls for the definite assignment of responsibility and authority. It is important that the senior management of the company responsible for carrying the project through its life cycle assign the required authority to the appointed project manager. This delegated authority must then be communicated to all members of the project team and the organization. Unlike military and corporate organizations, the typical project is always a unique one-of-a-kind undertaking. The organization also changes constantly, as it moves through the conceptual, implementation, and project turnover stages.

The project manager's interaction with his key staff may be likened in some respects to that of the conductor with the members of a symphony orchestra. The orchestra leader can achieve near perfect understanding of his directions to the orchestra based upon his own skills, together with the benefits of the extremely selective process of qualifying only the best musicians as members, and the practice and rehearsals used to achieve a product of extremely high quality. The orchestra's performances are also immediately evaluated by experts in the form of music critics and concert buffs.

Project management cannot achieve this level of precise control or technical perfection. The project plan is neither developed to the same extent with respect to specific actions required by the musicians nor with the precise timing that is possible with a musical composition. The project manager must, therefore, provide a different type of management by exercising his authority and communications with his staff in such a way that the project staff receives the appropriate messages at the right time. Only in this way can the individual actions of the players be coordinated to ensure harmonious project execution.

RANGE OF AUTHORITY

Senior management must define the levels of authority to be delegated to the project manager and to the functional managers. An organization where the functional managers have the greater authority is a functional organization structure. When the project manager's authority is stronger, it is a projectized organizational structure. When the project and functional managers share authority, the organization has what is known as a matrix organization structure.

In a matrix organization, particularly, the authorities have to be carefully designated. This will greatly reduce conflict during the execution of the project.

COMMUNICATIONS SKILLS

The project manager and his key subordinates need keen communications and human relations skills to develop cohesive work groups within the framework of the project organization. Conflicts must be resolved quickly and in a fair and effective manner in order to maintain morale at a high level.

Maintaining positive working attitudes under the umbrella of the typical project organization requires clear lines of information and authority.

BALANCE OF POWER

In the matrix organization using personnel from the corporate project group together with personnel on loan from corporate functional organizations, the authority to negotiate and make decisions must be equalized for both project and functional managers within the limits of their competency. This system utilizes the problem-solving expertise of the appropriate experts under the authority of the senior supervisor involved. When agreement cannot be reached, the problem and the alternative solutions are passed up to the next higher manager for review and decision.

A balance of power between functional managers and project managers must be maintained by corporate senior management who will have determined the respective areas of authority to be delegated to the project manager and the functional managers. In addition, it is necessary that these delegated authorities and responsibilities be defined, understood, accepted, and maintained throughout the project as well as within the functional organizations. Correspondingly, the respective accountabilities must be clearly promulgated by senior management who must also stand firmly behind their performance demands.

USE OF PERCEIVED POWER

All power to be held by the project manager, especially in a weak matrix organization, is not derived from actual delegated authority. Depending upon the project manager's own managerial skills, much power can come from "perceived" authority. This is the authority that the project staff "thinks" that the project manager has. Many very successful project managers have tremendous authority which is largely "perceived." In organizations where authority is not clearly defined, there is a great disparity in the authority of the individual project managers due to differences in the perceived power.

Project managers with good track records and who are forceful leaders always operate with a great deal of perceived authority.

SUPPLEMENTAL RESOURCES AVAILABLE TO THE PROJECT MANAGER

The experienced project manager will make use of four resources in expanding his perceived authority. These are (1) his personal power, (2) his persuasive influence, (3) his style of leadership, and (4) his ability to confer status.

Personal Power

The project manager's power emanates from several sources:

1. From his special expertise derived from skills, knowledge, background, and his demonstrated ability to implement these traits successfully.
2. From his charismatic ability to obtain the cooperation of people through his personality, take charge attitude, and continual display of confidence
3. From his ability to fulfill the needs of others and to reward them appropriately
4. From his ability to withhold rewards or take away rewards where performance has not been adequate—a form of implied and coercive power.

Persuasive Influence

The project manager may derive some of his authority from his ability to use his influence or to use that of other people to gain acceptance of certain facts, ideas, and particularly, desired behavior from the project staff on a voluntary basis.

Style of Leadership

If the project manager's personal style does not conflict with his manner of operation, this can be a substantial asset to consolidating his authority. This is particularly true if his leadership style is reinforced by complementary styles on the part of his immediate subordinates. Regular and friendly dissemination of reliable and current information about the project and its personnel is important. Visible recognition of good ideas, special accomplishments, and other contributions by project team members is a good influence builder.

Status-Building Rewards

Careful distribution of certain status-building rewards can enhance the authority of the project manager. Examples might be awarding new job titles, assignment of staff automobiles, and providing special office furnishings.

SUMMARY

A project manager should soon recognize that the proper blending of power, influence, leadership style, and status rewards will greatly enhance his perceived authority. The judicious and thoughtful use of these four tools can add measurably to the authority derived from the formal organization charts, and they will contribute greatly to the beneficial use and maintenance of his authority. With practice they can be combined and tailored for each of the many situations that the project manager and his key supervisors handle every day.

REFERENCE

Kertzner, H. *Project Management for Executives*. New York: Van Nostrand Reinhold Company, 1982.

4

Choosing the Most Effective Management Style

ROBERT L. KIMMONS* *Ebasco-Humphreys & Glasgow, Inc., Houston, Texas*

The knowledgeable project manager understands that he can markedly influence the performance of the entire project staff by the style he uses to manage his immediate team. He needs to identify the appropriate style pattern for the ultimate success of the project. His style will be selected for those conditions actually present on the project at that time. The manager should feel comfortable with the style he has chosen.

LEADERSHIP VERSUS MANAGEMENT STYLE

The term "leadership style" is used deliberately rather than the more common "management style." The generally accepted differences between "management" and "leadership" are appropriate when speaking of project managers. The project manager usually has substantially less real delegated authority over the project team than the functional managers to whom they report over a long period of time. The project manager's authority is limited to that which is *perceived* or *desired* by the team members. In the matrix organization, the project manager usually does not have the authority to employ, terminate, increase salaries, give promotions, or perform most of the other hallmarks of authority that are held by the functional managers. The project manager who can excel in his role is truly a leader.

The project manager's leadership style may be looked on as "the type of working relationship that a project manager chooses to utilize with those involved with his project." We will also see the importance of selecting the right styles for use with involved parties outside of the project team.

BACKGROUND

Early characterization of management styles advanced the idea of opposing behaviors: autocratic or "task-related" and participative or "relationship-based." Autocratic behavior was best used for "high-pressure short-duration" situations, while participative behavior was thought to work better for situations of "lower pressure and longer duration." There was also a widespread belief that each manager had a fixed unbending style of management. Much of these early ideas have a degree of validity, but our knowledge of human interaction has advanced in recent years.

In project management we should never confuse the *participative* style of management with the *permissive* management which is sometimes evidenced in project work.

---

*Current affiliation: Kimmons-Asaro Group Limited, Inc., Houston, Texas

109

Permissive management is also referred to as "management by abdication." The chances of success using this type of management on a project are so remote that we can dismiss the permissive style as being an unacceptable leadership style. A successful project where the project manager has abdicated his responsibility usually means that a competent and forceful subordinate has taken over the reins.

Yeager and Raudsepp state that every manager can be seen as occupying a position on a continuum of power-related behavior that ranges from passive on one end of the scale, to assertive in the middle, and to aggressive at the opposite end. Furthermore, each of the manager's subordinates can be categorized according to the same continuum. The authors postulate the effects of the various relationships that can evolve from managers and subordinates who exhibit differing power-related behavioral positions.

CURRENT UNDERSTANDING

Hersey and Blanchard conclude that there is no "single, all-purpose" best management style, but that the leader's behavior should be adapted to the demands of each situation. This statement is extremely important to the project manager as it represents the clue to selecting a truly effective leadership style for use in a project environment. These authors identify four basic leader-behavior styles:

1. High task, low relationship
2. High task, high relationship
3. Low task, high relationship
4. Low task, low relationship

In this analysis the "task" orientation means that the manager concentrates on the elements of work. The "relationship" orientation means that the manager is more concerned with people.

The authors grade the "maturity" of the followers from low to high. This type of maturity is related to the tasks at hand and has nothing to do with the age or overall experience of the individuals. The four basic leadership behaviors may be related to the level of maturity as follows:

Immature: S1 High task, low relationship
Moderate: S2 High task, high relationship
Moderate: S3 Low task, high relationship
High: S4 Low task, low relationship

Blanchard and the Zigarmis modify this concept by introducing *development* levels in place of *maturity* levels. The development levels refer to different combinations of competence and commitment. These may be summarized as:

D1 Low competence, high commitment
D2 Some competence, low commitment
D3 High competence, variable commitment
D4 High competence, high commitment

Recognizing that people at different levels of development need to be handled differently, the authors state that the appropriate leadership styles may be matched with the corresponding development levels. Table 1 below shows these relationships in simple terms.

Table 1

Development level of followers	Suggested leader behavior
D1 Low Competence, High Commitment	Directing
D2 Some Competence, Low Commitment	Coaching
D3 High Competence, Variable Commitment	Supporting
D4 High Competence, High Commitment	Delegating

HOW TO GET STARTED

At the start of a project, the project manager probably will not be familiar with the personalities, experience, and work habits of all of his key players. In fact, it is possible that he will not have worked with many of them previously. He will need to analyze the characteristics of his co-workers very early in the project and make a conscious decision as to what leadership style will be most effective. The effective project manager will use discussions with people that he has not known well previously to start a good bidirectional communication link as well as to improve communication with previous associates assigned to his project. Asking the right questions will enable him to hone in on the style he plans to use initially with each project team member. Leadership styles may be chosen at any one of the four levels, but should move only in sequence from directing to coaching to supporting to delegating (S1 through S4). It is extremely difficult to move style in the opposite direction. Team members can accept an orderly "easing off" of control more readily than they can a "tightening."

Nothing is more disturbing to a follower than inconsistency in a manager. By carefully planning the style which he will use and how he will use it, the project manager can be much more consistent in his relationships with the team members.

Blanchard and the Zigarmis point out that style can be modified relative to situations or people. This would be true on a project where some team members might have worked with the project manager before. Their work would be much more familiar to him and he would know what to expect, whereas for those who are working with him for the first time, the project manager has a narrower knowledge base to work from. The project manager should use the style which he thinks will be most effective for each individual for the assigned role.

The project manager may also choose to deal with a person using more than one leadership style. This would be especially true if the follower plays more than one role and is required to work in areas where he has varying levels of knowledge and experience.

In a matrix structure, the project manager may not have too much choice of the people assigned to work with him. The selection is often left almost entirely to the functional manager. The project manager must manage to get the best performance out of each person working on the project. In a weak matrix, the project manager's actual authority may be extremely limited, and he may operate almost entirely on the basis of perceived authority.

PREFERRED MANAGEMENT STYLE

Each of us tends to use the management style we are most comfortable with and that appears to produce the best results. For some this is a very autocratic position; for others it may be extremely participative in nature. Between these two extremes are various degrees of style.

The project manager will already have some ideas about his own customary management style. There are published questionnaires (e.g., Stanton) to assist in identifying a preferred style. If project team members have been working with him for some time, the project manager could ask them to evaluate him using these forms. The results could be quite revealing.

The style or styles the project manager uses must always be compatible with what the project manager is. He can almost never successfully select a style that reflects a personality, set of ethical values, or a base of experience that is not him. Very few people in the world are good at being "top sergeants" in the work atmosphere and "buddies" after office hours. Most of us should not try.

SELECTING THE PROPER LEADERSHIP STYLES

The project manager needs to do four things once the project team members have been named:

1. Obtain copies of experience records and performance evaluations for the proposed project team members.
2. Hold individual discussions with each team member outlining the objectives and unique problems anticipated during project execution. Free interchange of ideas should be encouraged during this discussion.
3. Based on what is known plus what is learned during these discussions, make a preliminary determination as to the type of management style he will be using with each of the team members.
4. Outline to each team member the proposed relationship (management style) that he proposes to use. This has not been usual in the past, but will accelerate the formation of the relationship.

The philosophy of management styles is still evolving. It will be some time before it can be considered a firmly defined science. The style selection process is important to project performance and requires the project manager to analyze the anticipated conditions in his forthcoming relationship with each of the key players. The positive approach he must take should be based on consideration of all of the known factors. Communication almost certainly will improve as a result of this process.

GENERAL OBSERVATIONS

The preceding points will be more useful for a project manager after reviewing the following general observations:

1. On most projects, the project manager will be dealing usually, but not always, with mature, experienced people.
2. On smaller projects, the project manager will be responsible for doing at least a portion of the "technical" work. Those reporting to him may be less experienced. A more authoritarian style might be appropriate.
3. The larger and more complex the project, the more mature and experienced the staff reporting directly to the project manager will be. Here he should probably start with the coaching style. If, in addition, he knows the people well, he may go directly to a supporting style.
4. The project manager's style with each of his followers will indirectly affect their own style in managing their subordinates. This is a determination that must be separately investigated, analyzed, and implemented.
5. Under many circumstances, we may generalize that, where the project manager is dealing with experienced, mature subordinates, he should elect to start

with the "coaching" level of management and be fully prepared to move in a deliberate manner toward "supporting" as circumstances justify.

6. There have been some very successful project managers who have been complete autocrats. In fact, they are generally the most revered and remembered. The many unsuccessful autocrats have been long forgotten. It is extremely difficult to be a successful autocrat. Talents are required that most of us do not have. One of the ugly traps that befalls an unpopular autocrat is that of willful obedience.

We will now move into a discussion of how the project manager may actually make use of a "participative" style of management to enhance the project team's probability of success.

PROJECT INITIATION

At the beginning of the project there are certain steps that set the form and tone of the project. During this period, the project manager must direct a host of activities, and at the same time, create an environment of participation among project team members by inviting them to share in these tasks. This will gain commitment from the participants.

Definition of Scope

Regardless of how the project has been defined initially the project manager should redefine the work to be accomplished in sufficient detail and prior to committing any substantial resources to the work. His definition should identify all of the products or "deliverables" as well as all of the identifiable activities necessary to complete the assigned work.

Project Plan

The project plan will designate who is going to do the work, how it will be done, and in what sequence. The plan considers the various organizations involved in the execution and the impact of the project on the organization, as well as the effect of the functional groups on the project. Producing the plan is an iterative process, and it is necessary to recycle the developing concepts to optimize the plan.

Project Schedule

The project schedule takes the plan of execution and the activity sequences outlined therein and puts them on a time scale. Comparisons are made to determine if the plan is feasible. If not, the plan is reworked.

Project Budget

Once the work has been defined, scoped, planned, and scheduled, the project budget may be produced. It will not be the first budget, or estimate, but it is foolish to try to produce a rational budget without knowing what the work is, how it will be done, and how long it will take.

Performance Assurance Plan

Performance assurance is also done according to a preset plan, which defines the monitoring, controlling, and corrective actions to be used during project execution.

Several preliminary project activities largely determine the course of the project. Relatively firm control should be exercised to assure that all of the important elements are in place. A "directing" leadership style will probably be of benefit at this time. Advancing to "coaching" and "supporting" styles with some or all of his team can come when the time is ripe. If this has been a truly participative effort, the project manager will be left with a highly motivated and committed team.

FOCUSING LEADERSHIP STYLES OUTWARDLY

On large projects or a project that has a high public visibility, the project manager's attention and efforts may be focused primarily outward from the project. Here, the project manager must, in addition to his own staff, analyze how he will "manage" his boss, as well as public relations, the media, and other groups that may exert influence on the project. In dealing with the boss, Gabarro and Kotter point out that "you are not going to change either your basic personality structure or that of your boss." This implies that you should learn what your boss expects of you. Unfortunately, many bosses tend to use a management style which varies from complete "hands off" when things appear to be going right to a "Ghengis Khan" role at the first sign of a wobble. This is a pattern which the project manager can anticipate should his boss fall into this mold.

CONCLUSION

Understanding the importance of the right leadership style is an asset to a project manager only if he takes advantage of the knowledge available to him. He holds all of the keys in this area to improve project performance measurably. He must make his own decision as to whether the additional effort is worthwhile.

BIBLIOGRAPHY

Yeager, J. C. and E. Raudsepp. *Who's in Charge Here?* Hydrocarbon Processing. Houston, TX: Gulf Publishing Company, 1981, p. 317.

Hersey, P. and K. Blanchard. "Making It As a Manager in the Eighties—Situational Leadership. *Chemical Engineering*, June 1, 1981, p. 73.

Hersey, P. and K. Blanchard. *Management of Organization Behavior: Using Human Resources*, 3rd Ed. Englewood Cliffs, NJ: Prentice-Hall Inc., 1977.

Blanchard, K., P. Zigarmi, and D. Zigarmi. *Leadership and the One Minute Manager*. New York: Morrow & Company, 1985.

Stanton, E. S. *Reality-Centered People Management*. New York: AMACOM, 1982.

Gabarro, J. J. and J. P. Kotter. "Managing Your Boss," *Harvard Business Review*, January-February, 1980, pp. 92-100.

5

The Superior Project Manager

JAMES H. LOWEREE *Management Consultant, San Francisco, California*

Project management is a unique profession. An entire business cycle takes place over a short period of time: you form a management team, execute a project, and then disband the team. It is not surprising that unique people are required to manage projects.

If we identify a high potential candidate—a person qualified by reasons of education, skills, experience, knowledge, intelligence—all the prerequisites, the question is raised: Will he, or she, succeed in project management, and to what degree?

To predict success or failure in the abstract is treacherous, but on a census basis we can draw certain conclusions in relative safety. If we place this high potential candidate at the entry level, say Level 1, the probability of advancement to Level 2, a level of general competency, is reasonably assured when an effective management style has been developed and a sensitivity toward interpersonal relationships has been demonstrated. The move to Level 3, the superior project manager, is a quantum step and requires the understanding and implementation of practices that will be referred to here as the unique personality of the superior project manager.

The best description of the superior project manager may still be the off-stated truism: You'll know when you meet one! Whom exactly will you meet? A person with panache, charisma? Possibly, possibly not. Presence? Definitely! But when you know this person better you will find substance, an extraordinary level of competency. In time, you will realize that this competency and the skills exhibited by the superior project manager are acquired skills, not innate skills. A high-potential candidate possessing all the prerequisites can become a superior project manager.

Performance results from the development of management skills. Leadership is a resultant of performance. Authority is a result of leadership. The superior project manager is an acknowledged leader with total project authority. And it all started with hardwork: the development of management skills.

MANAGEMENT STYLES

Much has been written regarding the most effective style of management for the execution of projects. If there were only two fundamental schools of thought, they might be (1) that there is a basic style that is best suited to the environment of projects, and (2) that the environment of projects is highly variable, and each individual project requires a style tailored to the specific project environment. Although reasonable arguments can be made for either approach, a compromise is suggested here.

You, as a project manager, will normally function in a relatively constant environment determined by your company, your clients, and your subordinates, peers, and superiors. Few of us are capable of mounting a variety of styles in any endeavor,

let alone an activity as complex as project management. Develop a style that works
for you in your normal course of business, and hone it to a high degree—a basic style,
a point of reference. All successful project managers have a basic style that meets
their normal business needs. However, they go one step further: they vary their
style as project conditions vary; and, they are prepared to deviate from their basic
style dramatically to protect their project from any serious threat to the achievement
of project goals.

Four fundamental though extraordinarily different styles of management have been
used in project management, and are still practiced today. They are Active/Dominant,
Active/Persuasive, Passive/Conforming, Passive/Controlled. For our specific purposes, the terms are defined as follows.

Active:	Awareness, high visibility
Passive:	Reactive, low visibility
Dominant:	Dictatorial, competitive
Persuasive:	Influences others through force of personality or diplomacy
Conforming:	Agreeable, tactful, procedural, careful, exacting
Controlled:	Predictable, orderly, protective, patient, close-to-vest

The Active/Persuasive style is probably the best, and is the recommended basic style.
Consider, however, the benefit of a Passive/Conforming style, low key, agreeable,
as an adjunct to employ on noncritical routine daily matters. Not every issue is critical
on a project, and this low-key secondary style will go a long way toward keeping the
team loose, and will provide emphasis as you shift back into your basic style on pressing issues. The spirited half-time Knute Rockne speech is wasted when you're ahead
by five or six touchdowns, and, if abused, is less effective when you're behind in
the game.

The Active/Dominant style, the hallmark of the stereotyped project manager of a
bygone era, although still practiced in many quarters is not recommended for reasons
covered in the literature over the past 20 or 30 years. This style produced a host of
characters and unforgettable anecdotes; what is forgotten is the preponderance of
failures of young managers who attempted to emulate the revered, or feared, dictatorial
boss. It may be necessary, however, to employ this style in one highly specific situation. Simply stated, when the house is on fire it's time for a fire hose, not a democratic discussion. But, use this style with great care; after all, your staff knows
the house is on fire too, and a burst of dominant authority on your part may not only
be unnecessary but counterproductive.

There is a limited role for the Passive/Controlled style, and that is on sheltered
projects within highly structured organizations, where the project role is more one
of coordination than management.

A difficulty in implementing any management style is found in the classical observation: there may be significant differences between what you are, what you think
you are, and what you are perceived to be by others. Two solutions are offered:
(1) seriously consider a personality evaluation by a consulting firm competent in this
area; (2) listen to your supervisor during personnel reviews, and encourage a two-
way dialogue with your subordinates during their personnel reviews.

Your style, interpersonal relations, and personality may have more to do with
the performance of your project team, and the success or failure of your project, than
your knowledge and experience.

HUMAN RELATIONS

Human relations—your interactions with others—has received a high degree of attention in recent years in the general field of management, and will receive more attention
in the future, for at long last the obvious has been recognized: people will perform at

or above their potential when sufficiently motivated. In the field of project management, as in all business endeavors, people will determine the ultimate result—your
client, your peer group, your management, your staff.

The 60-year-old CEO may be a confirmed X, but it would be a mistake to think
that he is looking for an X when he surveys high-potential 40-year-old candidates
to fill a senior management position. If he were a 40-year-old executive he would undoubtedly be a Y; CEOs are thoroughly aware of current management trends.

Your Client

If you receive high grades in all phases of project management, but have difficulty
in dealing with your clients, all your valuable talents will be wasted—you will not be
a successful project manager.

Do you keep your temper in check and practice self-control? One immature display
of temper will cost dearly, with no second chance. Do you compromise in the best
interests of the project, but say "no" in a constructive and effective manner when
"no" is the answer? Do you see the project through the client's eyes? Do you understand the problems of the client project manager? Do you talk out problems, one on
one, with your counterpart, or do you follow a narrow "need to know" philosophy?
Can you lose a few battles to win the war? Do you have to be right all the time? Do
you sense that the client wants to say "no" rather than "yes" to your requests?

It is frequently true that what the client says, what the client means, and what
the client really needs are not one and the same thing. It can be a mistake for you
to take immediate action on what the client says. It can also be a mistake to unilater-
ally decide what is best for the client. Iterative dialogue founded on trust and respect will usually lead to logical joint agreements on action issues.

It is a personal and career tragedy to have a successful project, one that meets
or beats all targets, and have the client ask for another project manager on the next
job. The few things you do wrong in the area of interpersonal relationships often
have a more powerful effect on your career than all the things you do well. Conversely, a failure to meet one or more project targets seldom results in irreparable damage
to the relationship between your company and the client when the team-to-team relationship has been positive.

Complex Client Relation Problems

The most common family of problems brought to the attention of senior management
by project managers are complex client relation problems. This is unfortunate for
two basic reasons: (1) most executives are not too enthusiastic when client relation
problems are brought to them, except when they absolutely belong in the executive
suite, and then it is best to prepare a concise analysis of the available options with
a recommended course of action in advance; (2) referral of client relation problems
to senior management, even infrequently, will be accepted prima facie that you have
difficulty in the handling of clients, a view not in your long-term best interests.

With experience your ability to cope with a variety of client relation problems will
improve. This enhanced knowledge can be random or structured. An approach is
suggested that will help in the resolution of complex client relation problems and, at
the same time, will permit the orderly development of a building-block file for future
problem resolution.

> Complex client relation problems must be reduced by a separation of variables
> technique to several single-variable problems, that is, reduced to identifiable
> parts. Each single-variable problem—frequently a well-understood problem—
> should then be attacked independently and in parallel with the other single-
> variable problems in order to minimize solution time.

A complex problem is a multivariable problem, complex in structure.
A simple problem is a single-variable problem, simple in structure.
The definition of simple and complex does not relate to the difficulty of solution.
A complex problem is a mix of simple problems.

The advice often given to new project managers to sort out the facts, sort out the issues, is, in lay terms, equivalent to the preceding. When you analyze a complex problem your initial reaction may be bewilderment and confusion. Soon, however, you will see parts A, B, and C. And, you will discover that you have a solution to A, you see a possibility for B, but C isn't coming into focus. Go to work on A and B. As you proceed the solution to C may become apparent; then again it may not. If not, you have a bona fide reason to involve senior management. The ultimate result could be that the problem cannot be resolved; there are problems that persist throughout a project, but the analysis may lead to a manageable accommodation.

In each instance write a brief summary of the case for your case file, and identify a building-block problem and solution. At a later date amend the file to reflect the actual effectiveness of the implemented solution. In time you will have an excellent building-block file, permitting rapid resolution of routine problems, and conserving your time resource for critical matters.

The most difficult client relation problem is one where the personality or capability of the client project manager impacts negatively on the project. Compound this with vague communication lines within the client organization and you have a major project problem. In a real project the analysis of several apparently unrelated problems revealed the "C" case to be just this. A series of very carefully presented discussions led to a definition of team responsibilities and restructured management communication lines within the client organization to the benefit of the project. This was a fortunate result and led to a successful project, but only came about when the root cause problem was identified amid a sea of confusion.

You can accelerate your career advancement if you can develop an approach to difficult client relation problems. Follow the suggested method, or develop your own—the specifics aren't important—but do have a method.

A Client's Viewpoint

The author, as Manager of Projects for an international energy contractor, many years ago asked a major client for a briefing on the client's point of view toward contractor's project managers. Sam Re, retired General Manager, Project Management Department, Exxon Research and Engineering, offered many thoughts, all worthy of documentation here. In his capacity as GM-PMD, Sam, from the early 1960s through the early 1970s, had responsibility for over 75 projects in 15 countries with a capital expenditure of several billion dollars. During that period Sam worked with all the major energy contractors.

Of the many comments passed on to Sam Re by his project managers, six recurrent comments were identified.

> The project manager does his job, works hard, is an excellent organizer, but keeps things too close to his vest. We learn about problems too late to take corrective action—no options left. The best example is inaccurate contractor mechanical completion dates—an exercise where the contractor casts a date but withholds certain assumptions and conditions. Based on contractor input, the central engineering group passes on a fixed date or range of dates to an affiliate operating company. The operating company then proceeds to enter into supply agreements and, if overseas, selected expatriate agreements. The date is missed—at considerable expense, and to the extreme embarrassment of the central engineering group. What is the future of that project manager, and in the worst scenario that contractor, with that client?
> The project manager knows his job but brushes us off when we make suggestions.

He argues at length on changes. And we're always discussing whether this is a legitimate change or whether it is something the contractor should have done. He can't seem to understand that this is our plant.

The project manager is competent but very abrasive. Whenever we make a change his frustration is obvious, his staff reacts similarly, and everything is in complete turmoil. Eventually our only concern was getting this man off the project.

The project manager talked about broad issues, but everything, and we mean everything, was an extra.

He's extremely defensive. He, his staff, his company can do no wrong.

He did not set a good example at social functions. He drank too much, said too much.

Several of the preceding comments are specific to the contractual agreement, namely, lump sum or reimbursable. And, only one side of the story is presented–some may take umbrage. But, that is not the point. The point is that a contractor project manager should know how a client views certain issues, what is said behind closed doors, what is important to the client. The manager can elect to swim against the tide, and sometimes this is necessary, but the manager is fortunate if forewarned and prepared for a reaction.

Sam then identified four issues that wove their way through all six comments, and offered constructive suggestions.

1. A failure to establish a good relationship and a sense of trust.

   Dedicate the same degree of effort to this consideration that you dedicate to the classical cost, schedule, quality considerations. Get to know your man.

2. Try to understand the problems of your counterpart.

   In the heat of battle, beset with client delays, try to put aside your problems, display some empathy, juggle schedules and work packages, etc., rather than complain.

3. Learn to lose the occasional battle.

   You're going to lose some anyway so make some points by conceding truly unimportant issues gracefully. Don't get into memo exchanges, replete with detailed support. When you dig your heels in be sure it's when it counts.

4. A general and highly visible inability to handle interpersonal relationships with the client, his own management and staff, and various third parties.

   Don't be overly defensive. Keep your cool. Conceal your frustrations. When you slip up, say so. Recognize that the client may not always be right in his judgment, but he is always the client. And, by your actions respect the views of your management, your staff, and third parties–this will not be lost upon your client.

Your Peer Group

It is said that managers are appointed by their superiors; leaders are chosen by their subordinates. This is true in a wide range of activities, from the military to a manual workgang. The definition falls short when applied to project management, particularly in a matrix environment, where recognition of leadership by your peer group is mandatory.

A project may be viewed as a sphere of activity superimposed upon a functional organization. As a project manager, protect your sphere of activity and respect the spheres of influence of your peer group functional leaders.

If you operate in an inner sphere, you're merely rotating. Your project will be insecure; your subordinates will lose respect for you; your peers will riddle you with frequent incursions. Orbit the full project. Venture out when threatened, but only with purpose. Respect the spheres of influence of others and so yours will be respected. Your leadership will be recognized; your authority will grow. The interactions within a matrix-style organization are most complex, but the starting point is the level of mutual respect that exists between a project manager and the functional peer group.

Your Management

Ambitious project managers seem to find their way into the oak-paneled environs with regularity. Initially the reception will be favorable; the aggressive project manager has an appeal to the hard-driving executive. Be careful, however, for there's a fine line, an invisible line, the "I've had enough line," where an overly aggressive and continual exposure suddenly becomes wearisome.

Management, first, last, and always, will look at the well-being of the total organization. Whether your objective is to protect your project, or self-advancement, there are caveats to be observed. First, pressuring management to commit more personnel from the functional groups will surely alienate the functional managers. When it is imperative for you to take this step, be prepared to take the heat—it's your job. However, needless annoyance will mean the loss of your credibility with management. Second, your organization, like all organizations, has a limited pool of qualified people. An increase in your staff causes a reduction in other staffs. Management is looking at all projects, not just your project. Management likes project managers who meet all project targets with a minimum expenditure of professional services, thus creating capacity for new work.

Be cheerful in your dealings with management. Never display anger. State your business in a logical thoughtful way. Avoid smart remarks—they'll draw a laugh; they'll also leave a lasting negative impression. Finally, never forget that your qualifications for a future executive position are being evaluated every minute that you are sitting in front of a senior executive.

Your Staff

Everything that can be written about interpersonal relations applies to your staff. Your staff will determine your performance as a project manager. If your relationship with the client, your peer group, and your management is positive, it's a good bet that you will have a good relationship with your staff.

Proof of a strong bond with your staff will be self-evident when people want to be on your team; when they say it has been a rewarding experience working with you; when career development results from their association with you.

Ethics

The subject of ethics can be introduced at any point in a treatise on project management. It is discussed here because unethical behavior spawns mistrust, and trust is the cornerstone of human relations. When combined with good judgment, a synergism of trust results—a powerful force in human relations. The magic words are: I trust him/her; I trust his/her judgment. When these words are applied to you as a project manager, your effectiveness as a manager will be enhanced. In many cases, one-on-one discussions will replace letters, reports, and meetings; your views will be accepted.

THE UNIQUE PERSONALITY OF THE SUPERIOR PROJECT MANAGER

Many years ago an associate developed a form to evaluate project managers for the annual review. Ten personality factors were rated on a scale from 1 to 10; thus a score in the 90s would indicate an exceptional individual. The problem was that a manager could receive a score of one in a category—such as human relations—and theoretically still record a very high score. An improved version was developed based on an extended interview covering five principal topics: management abilities, human relations, general business knowledge, personal characteristics, and project performance, with a narrative style used for the final evaluation.

The results of the rating program supported preliminary recommendations that certain high-potential individuals should be considered for project management, and verified that the competent managers in the group had effective management styles and knew how to handle interpersonal issues. When a matrix was prepared summarizing the personality traits of the best managers a pattern emerged, and seven unique personality traits were identified. These managers could be favorably identified with most of these unique characteristics.

The seven unique personality traits are: Take Charge Attitude—a need to manage; An Achiever—results oriented; A Thinking Person—judgment and common sense; Relevancy of Perfection—perfection is a fallacy; Time Management—an irreplaceable resource; The Pieces of the Puzzle—how everything fits together; A Single-minded Purpose in Communications—conveyance of a message.

Take Charge Attitude

Our manager has an all-consuming need to manage and direct the efforts of others; an almost religious zeal to exceed goals, to be the best, to bring out the best in others. The dominant mode of this individual is tempered by a high degree of self-control and the total rejection of thoughts of self-importance; the success of the project is paramount. The result is an extraordinarily effective and unusual style of participative management, exercised by a controlled, driven, self-motivated team leader.

The destructive nature of self-importance should be clearly understood. This is an undesirable trait in anyone, but in a project manager working closely with his staff and the client, it is fatal. Self-importance magnifies highs and lows, successes and failure—from unbridled euphoria to uncommunicative depression—and it rubs off on the project team. We expect a bit more stability in our leaders.

Challenges, obstacles, problems—they bring out the best in this manager, for he is confident that he and his team can work their way through any upset, no matter how serious. Yet, there isn't a need to seek out adversity, for the goal of this manager is a smooth record-setting project. But, if a problem were to arise that, after an evaluation of all alternatives, would require an action that might threaten his career, he would have the strength to move without hesitation.

An Achiever

Our manager is proactive, not reactive. A proactive person attacks a problem vigorously when it is clearly identified. The superior proactive person operates one or two planes higher. The first level is the ability to recognize a problem in its infancy. Early problem identification permits options; late problem identification creates a severely restricted option environment. The second level requires the imagination to recognize the potential for a problem long before conception, and take steps to prevent it from happening. In many cases this managerial ability not only eliminates the problem potential, but the situation evaluation results in a course change that produces an improvement in some other phase of the project.

Achievers make decisions—studied, timely, clear, risks evaluated, assignments defined, followup defined. In project management, two conditions generally exist that are normally foreign to the line manager, and which radically change the normal approach to decision-making.

First, the project manager will make perhaps ten significant decisions per week to one for the line manager. There are two choices. He can make one or two decisions, and be right, a perfect score. Unfortunately, the other issues will be decided by default; even the weakest project manager can improve upon decisions by default. Or, he can make ten decisions, hoping that seven or eight are sound, and the few missed won't be too damaging. Top project managers certainly shoot for ten out of ten, but they learn to live with a lesser accuracy, rejecting totally decisions by default.

Second, there is usually precious little time to study the issues. Let's say a critical decision must be made based on a minimum of facts and a pressing need to move fast. One month later it is apparent to all that the wrong decision was made, but, fortunately, certain events have transpired that provide an opportunity to reconsider the earlier decision. You, the project manager, reverse your decision. Are you flexible or indecisive? Or, you decide that it is best to continue on course, everything considered. Are you stubborn or firm? Your staff, peer group, and client will decide, and for the superior project manager that decision was made a long time ago.

Achievers are results-oriented. You get results by your ability to plan and organize for execution by and through the total organizaiton. This, of course, means the skillful application of the principles of delegation. When a project manager is referred to as a delegator, this isn't a compliment. The message is that he lays off work on others, perhaps work that he should do himself. Because of this negative connotation, the valuable art of delegation didn't receive acceptance in the project management game until recent years, concurrent with the recognition of the effectiveness of the participative style of management.

Good delegation requires a well-prepared package, the assignment to qualified personnel, milestone scheduling, and a monitoring program with a light touch. Good delegators work hard. On a major project the project manager will be monitoring a myriad of delegated packages at any point in time. The superior project manager keeps many balls in the air at all times, through the use of the total organization, through a total comprehension of the synergism of delegation.

A Thinking Person

Our manager is a thinking person. When you meet someone who shows good judgment or common sense you are apt to consider these traits as innate, something you wish you had, or had more of. What you have met is a thinking person, a capability parceled out in roughly equivalent batches to everyone demonstrating even minimum project skills. The limits on our reasoning processes vary with the individual, but not the ability to initiate the process.

Judgment and common sense are not inborn. They are the endproduct of thinking through a problem. And thinking results from putting in the effort. Mentally lazy people rarely show good judgment; don't confuse this with the old hand spouting advice to the newcomer—lazy people dissertate well in familiar waters.

When the top manager goes against the grain and pulls off a coup, it didn't just happen. He thought his way through the problem for hours and hours, and what emerged was something called good judgment by his associates.

Have you ever seen a top executive glance through a report and point out a fundamental fallacy? Experience—certainly! But what kind of experience? He was not searching for a fallacy, and probably did not expect to find faulty logic or inaccurate facts. He was "thinking his way" through the report.

Think! Then trust your judgment in matters of importance. Effort promotes thinking, thinking promotes judgment.

The Relevancy of Perfection

Our manager understands there are few perfect solutions to general management problems, and even fewer perfect solutions to project management problems. He hopes to find good solutions to most problems; failing that, he will force an acceptable level of tolerance so he can get on with the main event—the project. He doesn't seek per-

fection. Perfection is a flaw in a project manager, a tradeoff that encourages strategies by default in more critical areas; we have just so much time, and as we seek
perfection the project inexorably moves ahead.

The fallacy of perfection notwithstanding, and with full recognition of personal
time pressures, the manager will still seek better ways to achieve objectives. This
apparent dichotomy is resolved by a fundamental consideration in project management.
It is imperative that the manager reserve time for himself, unscheduled time to just
sit back, relax, and mull over issues. Take a step back from the battlefield. Review those doubts you have about a strategy. Role play some nagging interpersonal
issue. Shake off the impact of the totally unsatisfactory meeting you just left.

Cost, Value, Quality Relationships

The relevancy of perfection is best illustrated by an analysis of the relationship between Cost, Value, and Quality. Although the outstanding project manager may be
unaware of the formal concept, his every action is consistent with the principles of
the relationship. The following thoughts, first expressed by J. C. Emery several
years ago, have been editorialized and extended by the author to fit the unique demands of our profession.

A qualitative graphic representation of value versus quality is in the shape of
the classical S-curve familiar to engineers. The cost versus quality relationship is
in the form of a reverse S-curve. An overlay will show that cost exceeds value for
low-quality and high-quality regimes.

In lay terms, the cost of a PVC bolt in a lawnmower exceeds its value; it wouldn't
last more than a few mowings. The cost of a titanium bolt in a lawn mower exceeds its
value; it would outlast the lawnmower. There is a regime of intermediate quality, or
optimum value, where value exceeds cost: a low-alloy steel bolt. The optimum was
best described by Oliver Wendell Holmes:

> Have you heard of the wonderful one hoss shay,
> That was built in such a logical way
> It ran a hundred years to a day?

Quality is a generic term: we could substitute information, or perfection, or some
other term representative of a measured activity.

I will offer you a system that provides maximum information at the lowest possible
cost. Do you accept? I would certainly hope so! This type of offer doesn't come
along too often. Let's review just what it is you accepted. We know that cost exceeds
value in the low and high quality (or information) regimes. There is an intermediate
regime where the curves cross and value exceeds cost—this is the optimum regime.
Several conclusions can now be drawn.

An optimum system doesn't supply all useful information, since some information
costs more than it's worth.

A system can provide maximum information at the lowest possible cost and be a
very bad system.

A blend of man and machine may produce a more cost-effective product than either
alone. Many computer applications are carried past the optimum—the optimum
point may be for man to "trim" the computer.

A well-known example of "optimum" engineering is the preparation of piping isometrics for field fabrication. To achieve an engineering accuracy above about
97% requires additional home office expenditures in excess of normal field fix-
up costs.

There are exceptions: nuclear power plants, pharmaceutical plants, or any "zero
defect" project.

Opportunities exist to exercise options when any outside activity, such as a technological advancement, changes the C/V/Q relationship: a better product

may be produced at the same cost; or, the same product may be produced at
a lower cost.

What does all this mean to the project manager? We have all been trained since child-
hood to do the best job at all times. In project management, best means optimum, not
maximum quality. Optimum produces the best project, measured against project parameters; maximum quality costs money, and doesn't produce the "best" job!

Time Management

Our manager appreciates that a project is an activity of limited duration, thus time
is a valuable resource and time management is a necessary project management technique. Some guidelines follow and many more could be added:

Budget your time. A good idea is to maintain one-week and two-week lookaheads.
    Devote an hour at home on the weekend to forward planning.
Don't fill your daily calendar, unless absolutely necessary, such as for major re-
    view meetings. Allow contemplation time each day.
Steer clear of details. Avoid an excessive interest in your area of expertise.
Develop delegating skills to the highest level you can attain. There are many
    balls in the air at all times. You can't watch them all; don't lose sight of
    those that count.
Plan your time as well as you planned the project.

If you go home at night saying, What did I do today? Where did the day go?, you
have a problem. You're in a reactive mode; the job is running you.
    A true "open-door policy" sounds participative, but it really doesn't work. A
better way to convey the thought that you are a person and not a title is to tour the
office or jobsite each day. But, don't make decisions on the tour.

The Pieces of the Puzzle

Our manager has an exceptionally keen understanding of how everything fits together
on the project—the pieces of the puzzle; his company, the client organization, third
parties.
    A key word is knowledge, if knowledge means the comprehension of the role played
by each element and how each element relates to the project: technology, business,
company, client, industry, environment, government, and so forth. Knowledge does
not mean that you have to be expert in each element. A common misapprehension is
that the project manager should have a strong technical background. Under certain
conditions, yes; small technical hands-on projects, and certainly for "zero-defect
projects." But, in general, why technical? Why not business or government? Why
anything? Given a choice, a strong business background would be advantageous in
today's market place.
    A technical background has been viewed as mandatory because (1) project manage-
ment developed from a technical base; (2) client staffs are formed from technical groups
and clients want technical people across the table. The concept of project management
as a management function is a relatively new development.
    The author has known and admired project managers with liberal arts backgrounds,
and purchasing, construction, and accounting backgrounds. However, to keep things
in perspective, a technical background is a plus in project management. In one specific
area, however, it is irrelevant, and that is the execution of a mega project in a developing country—a full-time management program, with a broad assignment of responsibility and accountability to the staff.
    If you don't truly accept the CEO concept in project management, then, in counter-
point, it follows that you expect the CEO of a major corporation to be expert in the

technology of the corporation, unless you have two definitions for a CEO. This perhaps is the crux of the shifting sands of project management as we move toward the end of this century–do we really consider the project manager to be the CEO of a complex business enterprise!

A Single-Minded Purpose in Communications

Our manager's sole purpose for all communications is the conveyance of a message, either for information or action.

The spoken word covers a range from one-on-one discussions through meetings to formal presentations. The written word ranges from brief memos through lengthy letters to formal reports. The manager neither speaks to hear himself nor writes letters "to himself." Language skills are highly developed for the purpose intended– the message; but, our manager is not obsessed with grammar, a time-robbing preoccupation.

To demonstrate the communication skills of the superior manager, we will concentrate on meeting management, the most difficult form of communication, and the one with the highest potential for gain or loss. A 4 hour staff meeting attended by 10 people equates to one management week. There had better be a clear return for this investment. The direct cost is significant, but, more importantly, the staff is unavailable to manage for a half day.

Meetings may be classified by type. The reader is urged to take advantage of the wealth of information available in the literature.

For our purposes we will arbitrarily define the types of meetings as follows:

Type 1 Information sharing: Organized exchange of data and information
Type 2 Problem solving: Options and alternatives reviewed
Type 3 Decision making: Select course of action from options and alternatives
Type 4 Planning: Future options and alternatives
Type 5 Evaluation: Review results achieved

A meeting may be of one type, or several types, with a single objective, or multiple objectives. In general it is preferable to have a single objective in a meeting, and attack compound issues in two meetings—predecision and decision—or stepwise in a series of meetings. The purpose of the meeting should be clearly stated, and well-established procedures should be followed (notice, agenda, action assignments, follow-up, and so forth).

Here is how the superior project manager might handle a major problem through a series of meetings.

An issue has developed and the client management has requested the project manager to attend a meeting, giving no inkling of the topic. At the very outset of the meeting the topic is stated, and the project manager realizes it is an exceptionally delicate issue, one that could impact his company and himself. The client management had planned a 1/2/3 meeting (information, problem solving, decision making). The project manager quickly concludes that this is an issue that clearly belongs with his top management. Accordingly, the project manager applies all his skills to convert the meeting to a 1 (information) type, holding the client at bay, listening, avoiding a decision, and reassuring the client that the issue will get his undivided attention and a prompt response. It is imperative that the manager listen closely and gather all the facts, evaluating to the best of his ability the true seriousness of the issue, the real concerns of the client, the solutions the client will accept, and the degree to which the client will pursue solutions.

The manager then sets up a meeting with his management. An advance briefing is usually in order unless there is a history of management hipshooting or over-reaction, in which case it is best to hold back until the meeting. The internal management meeting may take place in two parts: a 1/2/3 meeting with 3 covering such issues as the priorities and participation of management; followed by a 3 meeting where the company position is finalized. It is important for the manager to ascertain the true feelings of his management.

Assuming that an internal agreement has been reached to proceed with a management-to-management meeting, the final meeting will be a 3/4/5 meeting (decision-making, planning, evaluation). Whatever agreements result must meet the needs of the client and be achievable by your company, a commitment will have been made.

We have all seen serious and delicate issues handled in a variety of ways. Project Manager A, a marginal manager, may make a decision at the first meeting, or misread the situation, or minimize the issue to his management, or take some other ill-advised action. Project Manager B, an average manager, will take all the right steps but compress events, failing to think his way through the issues, and trap his management into taking actions or proposing solutions based on a shallow and subjective briefing. Project Manager C, a superior manager, will immerse himself in the problem, and with an understanding of all the nuances help his management in the development of a sound company position. The result of well-orchestrated exercises of this type is not only a good solution to the project problem but a significant enhancement of the stature of the project manager within his company.

LEADERSHIP AND AUTHORITY

We come now to the qualities most recognized in the superior project manager, and most coveted by all, leadership and authority.

Leadership—The First Resultant

Leadership is the resultant of everything we have covered: management style, human relations, unique personality. The environment of project management must first be understood in order to evaluate the leadership role of the project manager, for as Fiedler so convincingly said, all leadership is situational. Leadership isn't an abstract quality; rather it is the ultimate fit of the individual and the environment. This individual we have created isn't a straw man, for we haven't manufactured the perfect project manager; we've described a real person—the superior project manager.

From the moment a project is released, except for a brief and fleeting honeymoon period, the project manager is placed in a measurable position against many targets—targets normally set by others. The potential for conflict exists daily. The degree to which you measure up to the challenge of project life will determine your performance, with your report card filled out by your associates and your client. Leadership results from performance. Performance results from the effective application of the management skills that we have discussed.

It would be erroneous to oversimplify any of these issues, for what we have described is a participative directive manager, a most unusual blend of classical management styles. But, achievable; and when mastered, rewarding. Leadership is an exciting word, carrying a mantle of mystique. When we dissect this mystique, however, we find each of the parts represents an acquired skill, and romanticism is left for the romantics.

Authority—The Second Resultant

Leadership is the first resultant, while authority is the second, in the natural progression: Management Skills, Performance, Leadership, Authority.

Project managers have a great deal of responsibility. A frequent complaint of project managers is that their authority, particularly in a matrix environment, is incompatible with their responsibilities. As projects grow in size and complexity the responsibility of a project manager increases, but the definition of responsibility is a constant—to complete the assigned task satisfactorily against the four classical parameters: cost, schedule, quality, and client satisfaction. Authority, however, is a variable, since the accepted definitions of the authority of a project manager are somewhat loose. The authority of a project manager is an implied authority, specific to the individual, and a result of his track record.

This author has never met a top project manager who wanted his authority defined. The top project manager will resist all efforts to have his authority defined in a position description. Why? As noted, the authority of a project manager is variable, specific to the individual. This also means, to the top project manager, that his authority hasn't been limited! The real authority of the top project manager is enormous. Any reasonable definition of his authority would be too limiting. Further, top project managers will avoid polarization of issues with functional managers, since they won't gain anything; they essentially have unlimited authority provided they don't abuse it, but when a choice is forced upon senior management the decision to support the formal line organizaiton is almost inevitable.

Authority, just as leadership, is something bestowed upon you by others. Accept it, gratefully and humbly. And remember the natural progression that leads to essentially unlimited authority: Management Skills, Performance, Leadership, Authority. Use this powerful weapon sparingly and with purpose.

THE SUPERIOR PROJECT: THE FINAL RESULTANT

Before we end our critique of the superior project manager we should briefly examine what this person is supposed to do in a superior way. The final objective of the superior manager is to produce a superior project.

Three important factors should be considered in the evaluation of overall project performance.

> What is the definition of a successful project?
> What are the determinants of success?
> How can we tell if a project is going to be successful?

Definition of a Successful Project

The definition of a successful project is the time-honored big four:

> Completed on or ahead of schedule
> Completed within the budget
> Technical conformance
> Client satisfaction

Determinants of Success

Murray, Fisher, and Baker listed 206 determinants that might contribute to the success or failure of a project. They canvassed the project management field and concluded that 116 items were directly related to the success of a project. Further research demonstrated that 15 determinants strongly affected the success of a project; 34 tended to influence the outcome; 25 were associated with performance. The determinants were then classified as follows:

Positive determinants:	Significantly improve the probability of success
Negative determinants:	Significantly decrease the probability of success
Linear determinants:	Contributing determinants that either improve success or diminish failure, or impede success or encourage failure

If positive determinants are present and negative determinants are absent, success is most likely. If negative determinants are present and positive determinants are absent, failure is most likely. With a mix of positive and negative determinants~the "normal" situation—linear determinants come into play, and the opportunity for project management influence is enhanced.

The project manager's influence on a project isn't appreciated by many project managers, and is discounted by far too many senior managers. It is difficult to quantify the project management role. To prove that a manager reduced costs by 5% or improved the schedule by one month is difficult. But even the most doubting senior manager will grudgingly admit that a project manager turned a project around. It is interesting that we question a marginal improvement in the outcome of a project but acknowledge a quantum improvement!

The determinants were grouped into six categories: project manager, project team, parent organization, client organization, managerial techniques, preconditioning and other factors. The project manager, directly and indirectly, influences the first five categories, and depending on the issue may influence the sixth.

The aim of this review of determinants of success is not to explore in detail the ingredients of the successful project, but to demonstrate from an entirely different viewpoint that the project management role is the single most dominant factor affecting the outcome of most projects.

We should take one last look at the "big four" mentioned above: schedule, budget, quality, client. Historically the adjectives "meet or beat" are used with these terms to define the successful project. This is an oversimplification. When all factors are positive, success can only be measured by the degree to which the manager "beats" the targets. When all external factors are negative and dominant and clearly beyond the reasonable control of the project manager, success should be measured by the degree to which the manager "mitigates a disaster."

Will a Project be Successful?

At any point in time during the execution of a project it is imperative that the project manager, his company, his staff, and the client have a realistic and demonstrable assessment of the performance of the project against all targets.

R. L. Kimmons observed that unequal emphasis may be placed on one or two of the four principal characteristics of project success. Unfortunately, by completion time it is too late to apply remedial action if all of the objectives have not been achieved. He proposed a method to evaluate the four characteristics on a planned on-line basis.

The concept of the evaluation program, called Graduated On-Line Diagnosis, follows:

1. Examine each of the areas periodically; a Graduated approach.
2. The program should be an integral part of the project control system—not batch; an On-Line approach.
3. A comparison should be made of actual conditions against targets at selected checkpoints; a Diagnostic approach.

There are four general checkpoints suitable to most projects, as follows:

Formation: A point early in the project when the definition has been established and the target schedule and budget set.

Build-up: Basic work has been accomplished and a build-up in the rate of resource utilization is imminent.

Production: Production effort is at a peaking plateau and resource utilization is at its maximum.

Phase-out: The ratio of the production-phase rate of progress to resource utilization decreases markedly.

A matrix may then be prepared with the four diagnostic areas arranged vertically: budget (costs), schedule (planning and scheduling), quality (technical conformance), client (relationships); and the four checkpoints arranged horizontally: formation, build-up, production, phase-out.

The program is suitable for engineering, or procurement, or construction, or any discrete element, such as civil engineering, piping engineering, and so on. The four project checkpoints may be shown on the % Physical Progress/% Time Expended S-curve.

This program neither replaces nor duplicates the standard project control programs used within the company. This program is the project manager's program, prepared by him with staff assistance, with the entries limited to those specific items that, in the judgment of the manager, could impact project targets.

There are other milestone programs that will meet the needs of the project manager; some competent managers keep no more than a very informal checklist of critical milestones; others rely on their "feel." It is suggested, however that a more formal program be used on all but the simplest of projects, and that the program be developed concurrently with the development of the network logic diagram.

Many times throughout the project the manager will be asked by his management or by the client to give his personal forecast of certain targets, normally completion date and final cost. He should be able to answer such questions at any time, without preparation, but it is prudent to take time, review all pertinent control documents, and then run a status check of his milestone list. In the end the best forecast is the "gut feel" of the experienced project manager after an objective appraisal of the range of uncertainties in selected milestones. The maintenance of an on-line diagnostic program keeps all issues squarely in front of the manager in the "heat of battle."

SUMMARY

It's up to you! The road to excellence in project management is open to anyone with the basic prerequisites and the commitment to hard work.

The first step is to take a good hard look at yourself, evaluate your strengths, assess your weaknesses. The second step is to prepare a program for self-improvement. The third step is commitment, a commitment to excellence.

A high energy level (don't neglect physical fitness), and a good sense of humor (ease back on that intensity), will make the path easier. Not all people find a truly rewarding professional role in life; those who manage projects may, and this may be the uniqueness, captivation, and fascination of the profession.

A final caution. Success, like leadership, is situational; the environment will accelerate or delay your development. If the environment is favorable, the probability of success will be enhanced. If the environment is marginal, success may or may not result. If the environment is negative, or the philosophy of the company isn't compatible with the project management concept; then you must make a basic career decision.

BIBLIOGRAPHY

J. C. Emery. Cost/Benefit Analysis of Information Systems, from *System Analysis Techniques*. Couger and Knapp.

Murray, Fisher, and Baker. 1974 Annual Meeting. Project Management Institute.

R. L. Kimmons. Try Graduated On-Line Diagnosis. 1977 Annual Meeting, Project Management Institute.

Leo F. McManus, The L. F. McManus Company. Lecture on Management Styles. The Presidents Association, American Management Association: Top Management Briefing, Miami, Florida, March 1976.

III

EARLY STAGES OF A PROJECT

UNIT OVERVIEW

The process of project development can be orderly, but frequently it is not. A project may evolve smoothly, explode into action abruptly, or drag on endlessly without visible progress. A project may start out before the people who will be part of the project management for either the owner or the contractor become involved.

A new project starts out in the project development or similar type of organization of the owner firm. The early stages of a project should see progressive development of the project definition. Several different ideas may be introduced; some of these become outdated or superseded. Therefore, continuous updating of the project description is necessary. The earliest projections of cost and schedule must always be tied specifically to the project as it is contemplated at that time.

The owner first perceives a need or a competitive advantage and proposes alternative solutions to fill that need. This is project conception.

Any one, or all of these solutions, may be feasible; that is to say that technically they can be done. The first step in project development is to separate the nonfeasible alternatives from the feasible.

Next, the feasible alternatives are further investigated to determine their viability from an economic standpoint. Once a project has been deemed both feasible and viable on a preliminary basis, further definition of the project is needed. The more clearly a project can be described the less chance there will be for misunderstandings and future mistakes. The accuracy of the preliminary cost estimates depends on the extent of the definition. For some projects, site selection is a very important step. Location plays a great part in the ultimate economics of the project and should never be taken lightly. Even where there is little question about the location, taking a brief look at alternatives should not be ruled out.

Further constraints by regulatory requirements and restrictions will probably be imposed on future projects. Early evaluation of the extent of this involvement is necessary, and careful planning of permitting is essential for these projects.

The most important hurdle of all for most projects is that of obtaining the funding. Financing is a complex subject, and most project managers are not experts in this subject. A basic understanding of the financing technique for a project, if not vital, is at least extremely helpful to the manager charged with running the project. A parallel topic is that of projecting cash requirements throughout the life cycle of the project. Any instance of a shortage of funding may have grave consequences to the project execution.

Once the project has been defined and funded, it may be necessary to augment the owner's staff to accomplish the work. This may be done by contracting help from another firm. To do this a Request for Proposal (RFP) or an Invitation for Proposals is written to one or more qualified firms stipulating extent of the work and the conditions under which the work will be done. The answer to the RFP by the contractor is known as a Proposal, and contains the commercial, technical, and project execution response to the RFP.

Even though the project manager is not present during these early stages of the project, he will benefit from an understanding of what has gone on before his assignment.

BIBLIOGRAPHY

Emerson, C. *Project Financing.* The Financial Times Business Enterprises Limited, London, 1983.

Emmons, M. W. Project Management Starts Before Contract Award. Proceedings of the Project Management Institute, Drexel Hill, PA, October 1978, pp. II-L.1-II-L.10.

Johnston, D. C. (Ed.). *Managing Finances.* Symposium Proceedings, Atlanta, GA, Engineering Management Division. American Society of Civil Engineers, New York, May 1984.

Kerridge, A. E. *Make Your Own Econometric Model.* Hydrocarbon Processing, Gulf Publishing Company, Houston, November 1985, pp. 217-223.

Powell, T. E. "A Review of Recent Developments in Project Evaluation." *Chemical Engineering,* November 11, 1985, pp. 187-194.

Wynant, L. "Essential Elements of Project Financing." *Harvard Business Review,* May-June 1980, pp. 165-173.

1

Project Conception

FRANCISCO G. ANZOLA and FRANCISCO J. ROJAS *Lagoven S.A., Caracas, D.F., Venezuela*

Conception of an industrial project is the initial step in the process of defining the actual scope of a project. Project conception generally starts with a manifestation of a requirement or an opportunity that will benefit the corporate interests, and culminates when one or more preliminary options have been formulated which will, theoretically, satisfy the company's expectations as originally presented.

The process presented here, although illustrated by an industrial project, has features directly translatable to conceptual evaluation in many diverse applications. The fact that the project in question has been deferred is not uncharacteristic of the fate of many programs during the conceptual phase.

STAGES OF PROJECT CONCEPTION

Initial conceptualization of a project has various degrees of complexity, depending on the nature of the specific project and the particular analysis and approval procedures used by a company.

The company's planning strategy may require formulation of programs involving several projects. Conception of the overall program should then precede conception of the individual specific projects.

The conceptual stage involves the following activities:

1. Definition of a requirement or an opportunity that commands the interest of the company
2. Formulation of a set of preliminary alternatives capable of fulfilling the initial requirement
3. Selection of alternative(s) that might satisfy the requirements in terms and conditions attractive to the company

A brief description of each of these activities in a specific situation and in an organized environment follows.

DEFINITION OF THE REQUIREMENT OR OPPORTUNITY

The continuity of efficient operations and the opening of new business areas are the main drives for capital investments for industrial firms. Investment opportunities are

133

detected through operational analysis of current performance and by forecasts of the most likely future scenarios.

Initially, the scope of any new investment is likely to be vague. Subsequent definition involves consideration of all available relevant facts, required resources, and constraints associated with the original idea.

PRELIMINARY FORMULATION OF ALTERNATIVES

Project conception continues with development of alternatives capable of fulfilling the expressed objectives. This preliminary formulation of alternatives is important as it sets the pace of the subsequent definition and elaboration of the project scope. During this phase, the company calls upon the experience and creativity of its technicians, managers, and directors to generate an adequate group of alternatives to fulfill the expressed need.

INITIAL SELECTION OF ALTERNATIVES

After the alternatives have been identified, comparative analyses are made in order to select the most beneficial and to reject the least attractive. The selection process implies a basic feasibility analysis of each alternative and the establishment of criteria that will allow the identification of the most attractive options. At this point, further consideration of the rejected alternatives is terminated along with the need to prepare elaborate definitions for them.

The cost, schedule, profitability, and other salient advantages and disadvantages of each of the selected alternatives are assessed in terms of order of magnitude. Differences among the options are sought still without establishing precise project parameters.

CASE STUDY

The project presented was taken from a strategic program, developed by an international energy company.

The Company

The company is an integrated corporation engaged in production, refining, marketing, and transportation of crude oil and refined products. It is further integrated with four other operating companies, a foreign purchasing organization, a research and development center, and the parent organization.

The Scenario

The company has total proven oil reserves composed of 58% light crudes and 42% heavy and extra heavy crudes. For some time there has been concern over the high proportion of heavy and extra heavy oils.

In 1976 the company owned 12 refineries with an atmospheric distillation capacity of over 1.4 million barrels per day. Distribution of products from the refining plants for the year 1976 was:

Products	Percent
Gas	1.9
Gasoline and naphthas	18.6
Kerosene and gas oils	16.5

Products	Percent
Residual fuels	59.9
Asphalt	3.1
Total	100.0

As can be seen, the processing pattern was aimed at production of high-residual fuels, while the allocation to light products (gasoline, kerosene, and gas oils) appears moderate. This processing structure established operational inflexibilities since deep conversion processes were very limited.

From the mid-1970s, the international market for residual fuels became intensely competitive. The American market, of great importance to this company, experienced a pronounced decline in the consumption of residuals. Some power plants began conversion to coal firing. Demand for light products, chiefly gasolines and naphthas, is projected to increase considerably over the short and medium terms.

The Strategic Plans

In 1976, the corporation defined the following strategic guidelines in petroleum refining:

To increase the production of gasolines to a minimum of 110,000 barrels per day by 1983

To provide operational flexibility to the existing refining product profile to face market changes

To adapt existing refineries to process heavy crudes

To generate the necessary naphtha to satisfy the petrochemical demand

The Preliminary Formulation of Alternatives

The corporation formulated a set of alternative programs. Three options emerged from these.

1. Change feedstocks of existing refineries
2. Build new refineries
3. Modify existing refineries

The Initial Selection

The head office of the corporation and its affiliated companies analyzed the various alternatives to develop a refining strategy. Figure 1 is the decision flow chart associated with the initial selection of alternatives. After choosing the modification program as being the most appropriate, the 12 existing refineries were analyzed and four were selected as potential candidates for modification on the basis of the following factors: (1) location of the refinery; (2) size of the refinery; (3) degree of obsolescence

The next step was formulating the necessary modification projects and developing a master schedule for the overall program. The decision criteria used were:

1. Cost of the modifications
2. Schedule of execution
3. Degree of conversion of heavy fractions into light products
4. Profitability of the invested funds

As a result of the above process, a program of modification for four refineries was defined. This program was comprised of five main projects, scheduled to commence operation between 1979 and 1983. The case study continues with one of these projects which was known as the MPRA project.

Alternatives	Decision
Change feedstocks of existing refineries	Rejected because:
	Would require additional light and medium crudes
	Would not lead to increased flexibility
	Would not substantially change the distribution of products
Build new refineries	Rejected because:
	Existing refineries would not be adapted to process heavier feedstocks
	Would not maximize use of the company's assets
Modify refineries	Accepted because:
	Fulfills strategic guidelines
	Maximizes utilization of the company's assets

Figure 1 Decision flow chart.

THE PROJECT

Many of the expectations and a considerable portion of the resources of the modification program were concentrated in the Modification of the Refining Profile of the Amuay Refinery, or the MPRA project. This project was to be executed at the Amuay Refinery in northwestern Venezuela.

Figure 2 presents a block diagram of the main plants to be added by the MPRA project and their interrelations with the existing refinery units.

CONCLUSIONS

The methods employed are limited by the uncertainties and insufficient information available in the initial stages of a project. Because of its qualitative and comparative nature, it is not capable of providing exceedingly fine distinctions between competing projects. It does, however, provide intial guidance in eliminating some of the unattractive alternatives and the downstream work associated with their more rigorous definition and evaluation. In later phases, with diminished uncertainty and improved information both qualitative and quantitative, more elaborate models of analysis will produce better decisions on the project scope and its conditions of execution.

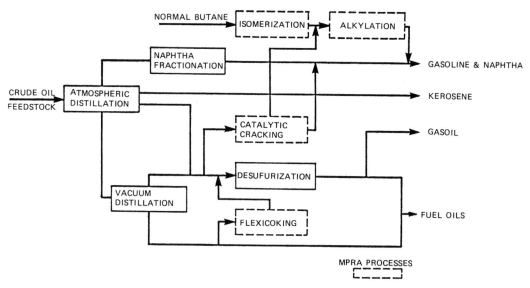

Figure 2 MPRA project block flow diagram.

BIBLIOGRAPHY

Archibald, R. A. Managing High-Technology Programs and Projects. John Wiley & Sons, Inc., New York, 1976, pp. 18-21.

Rudd, D. F., and C. C. Watson. *Strategy of Process Engineering.* John Wiley & Sons, Inc., New York, 1968, pp. 11-33.

Sounder, W. A. Project Evaluation and Selection. In *Project Management Handbook.* Edited by D. I. Cleland and W. R. King. Van Nostrand Reinhold Company, New York, 1983, pp. 185-206.

2

Project Viability

HERBERT H. ZACHOW* *Atlantic Richfield Company, Los Angeles, California*

If you want to build something, you have to find someone with a need. In almost all cases, the project manager is responsible for building a facility whose need or value is perceived by someone else.

The reason for undertaking most projects is economics. There is a belief that the new facility will add to the wealth of the entity building it. Perhaps there is a requirement for continuing operations, as in the case of a pollution abatement facility. The project may serve a public need, such as a new bridge or an airport. In each case, someone must perceive a need and a value.

DETERMINING VIABILITY

Determination of the value of a project is usually not the responsibility of the project manager or the project team. The value is determined by a group or groups within the owner organization. Among the groups usually involved are marketing (how much can be sold and at what price?), manufacturing or production (what is the probable cost of producing the product and what raw materials will be used?), finance (cost of money), and others who provide information on environmental, regulatory, safety, tax, and other issues appropriate to the specific project. The ultimate test of project viability is whether it accomplishes the stated objective (makes more money, permits an existing facility to continue operation, allows an increase in market share, etc.) or not.

The owner's management group that is in place after the facility has been put into operation will be responsible for the ultimate success of the project in fulfilling the objectives. The role of the project team in assuring project viability is to build a quality project within the constraints of time and money set forth by the owner. Since some of the objectives differ, there must be a clear understanding of the separation between those responsible for what will be built (the owner's management) and those resonsible for the building (the project team).

Understanding the techniques used by owner management to guide its actions can greatly assist the project team in responding to changes, and in many cases suggest opportunities for improvement within the project.

*Retired

In determining the long-term economics of a project, cash flow generated is the most important element. Cash flow in its simplest terms is the money left after all the costs of production, including raw materials, and selling costs have been deducted from the selling price. The amount of cash flow over the life of the facility will determine the value of the project, perhaps the ability of the entity that had the facility built to remain in business. Unfortunately, this definition is not sufficient to handle most real-life situations, since income taxes and the offsets to them are a part of almost all business undertakings.

Before income taxes, if a proprietor purchased a facility used to generate revenue and if the revenue (selling price) less all of the production costs left him or her enough money to pay the banker for the use of money and something was left over (a profit or net income) for the proprietor to spend for his or her needs or for additional facilities, the business prospered. However, governments always seem to need additional sources of revenue, and taxing the profit of prosperous proprietors was an obvious move. At this point the definition of profit becomes critical for it determines how much the proprietor must pay in income taxes. If he is to remain in business, there must be a way for the proprietor to recover the cost of the facility before determining his profit. Thus, with an income tax, the concept of depreciation or payment for a facility over its useful life or some other acceptable time period becomes very important. Net income after tax includes all of the previously described elements minus depreciation and taxes on income. True income taxes are a percentage of revenue, less production costs, etc., less depreciation. But depreciation is a noncash item, that is, it does not generate or require cash. Thus cash flow after tax is net income after tax plus depreciation. The importance of depreciation is its effect on the net income, and therefore, the amount of income taxes to be paid. This is a grossly simplified situation. Today's concepts of accelerated depreciation, investment tax credits, or other tax or credit regulations intended to encourage investment in new equipment, can and do, substantially alter the after-tax cash flow. To evaluate a project without proper awareness of the influence of taxation on the project value would lead to undertaking projects that have no chance for success, or in taking actions that work to the detriment of the project.

While cash flow may be the vital element in project worth, it does not in itself answer the question: How valuable is the project? Here one must deal in comparatives rather than absolutes. If the money to build your project were not spent on the project, it would have been spent on another project, invested to generate other income, not borrowed or whatever is currently in vogue with the financial group. In comparing investment opportunities, the project cost and the cash flow over a given time period become important. If project A and B have the same level and timing of cash flow but Project A costs twice as much as Project B, then Project B is the better investment. Unfortunately, projects and investment opportunities are not that simple, and do not appear or end at the same times. To rationalize varying project costs and cash flow patterns and levels, a concept of the time value of money is essential. If you were offered one million dollars tax free now or one million dollars tax free five years form now, almost all would take the money now for we know that we could generate added money by investing the one million dollars for five years. We know the time value of money.

Basic to almost all economic evaluation procedures is the use of discounted cash flow (the time value of money). One million dollars five years from now is today worth one million dollars less the interest that could be earned by investing the money. Thus the elements which must be known are: the time, five years in the example, and the interest rate. If the interest rate were 10% per year, $620,920 today would be equal to one million dollars five years in the future. Of somewhat less importance is the frequency of compounding the interest (annually in the example). Compounding monthly, daily, or continuously would give a somewhat lower current investment value than $620,920, but would not change the relative value of investments. However, in most

Example: Project Z

Basis:

    Project life: 10 years   Construction time: 2 years
    Interest compounding: Continuous

$$\text{Annual discount factor:}\quad \left(\frac{1}{e^{R}}\right)^{P} \cdot \left(\frac{e^{R}-1}{R}\right)$$

R = Annual interest rate/100
e = 2.718. . . . .
P = Time from point of analysis, years

Construction cost: $50,000 M
After tax cash flow–Post completion of construction

Period (years)	Cash flow ($M)
0 - 1	10,000
1 - 2	15,000
2 - 3	20,000
3 - 4	20,000
4 - 5	20,000
5 - 6	20,000
6 - 7	20,000
7 - 8	20,000
8 - 9	20,000
9 - 10	20,000

Example 1 Project Z: Net Present Value

Period (years)	Cash flow ($M) (A)	Discount factor (B)	DCF (A) (B)
	Point of analysis: Start of project		
	Annual interest rate: 15%		
0-1	-25,000	.92861	-23,215
1-2	-25,000	.79926	-19,982
2-3	10,000	.68793	6,879
3-4	15,000	.59211	8,882
4-5	20,000	.50963	10,193
5-6	20,000	.43865	8,773
6-7	20,000	.37755	7,551
7-8	20,000	.32496	6,499
8-9	20,000	.27969	5,594
9-10	20,000	.24073	4,815
10-11	20,000	.20720	4,144
11-12	20,000	.17834	3,567
			23,699

Net present value + $23,699 M

Example 2 Project Z: Rate of Return

Period (years)	Cash flow ($M) (A)	Discount factor (23% interest) (B)	DCF (A) (B)	Discount factor (24% interest) (C)	DCF (A) (C)
Point of analysis: Any convenient time (start of project in example)					
0-1	-25,000	.89333	-22,333	.88905	-22,226
1-2	-25,000	.70978	-17,745	.69935	-17,484
2-3	10,000	.56395	5,639	.55013	5,501
3-4	15,000	.44807	6,721	.43275	6,491
4-5	20,000	.35601	7,120	.34041	6,808
5-6	20,000	.28286	5,657	.26778	5,356
6-7	20,000	.22474	4,495	.21064	4,213
7-8	20,000	.17857	3,571	.16570	3,314
8-9	20,000	.14188	2,838	.13034	2,607
9-10	20,000	.11273	2,255	.10253	2,051
10-11	20,000	.08956	1.791	.08065	1,613
11-12	20,000	.07116	1,423	.06344	1,269
			1,433		-488

$$\text{Rate of return} = 23 + \frac{1433}{1433 + 488} = 23.7$$

$$\text{Rate of return} = 24\%$$

Example 3 Project Z: Payout Period

Period (years)	Cash flow ($M) (A)	Discount factor (B)	DCF (A) (B)	Cumulative DCF
Point of analysis: Start of plant operation Annual interest rate: 15%				
-2-1	-25,000	1.2535	-31,337	-31,337
-1-0	-25,000	1.0789	-26,972	-58,310
0-1	10,000	.92861	9,286	-49,024
1-2	15,000	.79926	11,989	-37,035
2-3	20,000	.68793	13,759	-23,276
3-4	20,000	.59211	11,842	-11,434
4-5	20,000	.50963	10,193	-1,241
5-6	20,000	.43865	8,773	7,532

$$\text{Payout period} = 5 + \frac{1241}{1241 - 7532} = 5.1 \text{ years}$$

situations, construction expenditures and operating income are a continuous flow of funds, therefore, continuous compounding is favored by many as the basis for analysis.

The most commonly used comparison techniques are net present value and rate of return. In net present value (NPV) the question answered is: At a point in time, what is the value of all monies spent and to be earned? To make this calculation the cost of the facility, cash flow, the discount rate (interest rate), and the time of the analysis relative to the other events must be considered (see Example 1). In a rate of return analysis the question answered is: What rate of interest must be earned on an equal investment to return the same amount as the project? (see Example 2). Each of these techniques has advantages and pitfalls. Used with care each will provide guidance to selecting the best projects. For a project team the technique used by the client in evaluating the project is the method most likely to provide the proper guidance.

Other concepts often used are payout period and investment efficiency. Both techniques usually use a discount rate acceptable to the financial arm of the client. Payout addresses the issue of how long after the project begins operation will the funds expended be recouped. Or, when does the cumulative cash flow become positive (see Example 3). Investment efficiency gives some insight into the relative worth of a series of investment choices. In its simplest terms investment efficiency is the discounted cash flow resulting from the operation of the facility divided by the discounted cash flow of the cost of constructing the facility. Using this measure, projects can be ranked by their capacity, over the entire life of the project, to return cash related to the investment required. For most cases ranking of investment opportunities is outside the realm of a project manager's activities. However, as projects evolve, there are changes to the cost and schedule. Those responsible for operating the facility and marketing the product re-examine their earnings. The investment efficiency may change, and lead to changes in the emphasis placed on the project, which undoubtedly will affect the project team's direction.

Significant elements in the economics of a project include raw material cost, operating cost, and sales realizations. Of these elements, the project team may have a material effect on the operating costs. A clear understanding of the expected operating labor, utility consumptions, expected maintenance costs, and the quality of the product made, is essential to the layout of the facility and selection of the proper equipment. While it may seem obvious that tradeoffs exist between operating labor and automation, utility consumption and equipment design, maintenance cost and equipment size and location, these critical issues are often not clearly defined early in the project. A tradeoff to the issues of labor costs, utility consumption, and maintainability is the cost of the facility being constructed. Each group, those reponsible for the design and construction, those who will operate the facility, and those responsible for the sale of the product, play important roles in assuring success of the project. Too often, once a project team has begun its work, the operators and marketers leave the scene, reappearing only when the project is near completion. Only then do they realize how valuable their ideas would have been during design and construction. In some cases, their arrival on the scene results in modifications and rework of the facilities. Delays in start-up, and increased construction costs caused by last minute changes are avoidable, and everyone must fulfill his or her role to avoid them.

Risk exists in almost all endeavors. Construction projects are no exception. Indeed many companies have sophisticated programs to assess the risk associated with a project. Most programs are directed toward ascertaining the probable cost of the project, for this is the world of the project personnel. However, greater risks to a project arise from forces external to the basic construction effort. Delays in obtaining needed permits, higher cost for funds used during construction, technological advances from within the client organization and by competitors, are a few examples of the external factors that need to be considered in determining the risks surrounding a project.

While qualitative identification of higher risk elements may be relatively easy, quantification of the overall project risk is more difficult. A frequently used technique is "Monte Carlo simulation." Using a mathematical description, which includes the range that the element may cover and the likelihood of occurrence, a random selection of outcomes for each element is combined into an overall prediction of the range of results for the project. Risk analyses using the Monte Carlo technique are usually run using a computer-based simulation model. A frequent failing of the Monte Carlo technique is that we think we know more about the project than is true. This often results in the selection of relatively narrow ranges for the elements, yielding a very limited range of risk for the project. If projects of a similar nature have been completed, their outcome may be as good, if not a better, guide to range of risk.

In assessing the risks to successful completion of a project, an exercise in conjuring up outlandish possibilities and their effect on the project is probably time well spent. This is especially true if the participants in the exercise come from varied backgrounds and hold different points of view. A synthesis of their views often results in the identification of high-risk areas that should receive more intensive examination to reduce the overall risk.

Risk analysis is most often used to determine the range of cost outcomes; however, it can also be used to determine the most likely project schedule. For projects with severe weather constraints (Arctic or North Sea construction) or other time constraints (modification during unit shutdown) a schedule risk analysis may be of more value than the cost risk analysis.

To the dismay of project managers, a business decision made by the owner will interrupt the smooth flow of a project. At the root of almost all such decisions is the cash flow of the entity building the facility. There may be a budget crunch because cash flows from other sectors of the business are not up to expectations, resulting in a need to reduce budget allocations for the project. Or there may be a market opportunity requiring that production from the project be available sooner than originally expected. For projects that experience substantial cost or schedule overruns, either forecast or incurred, a review of the ultimate cash flow may suggest that abandonment is the least costly alternative. Another frequent reason for accelerating or delaying a project is the effect of tax regulations.

CONCLUSION

An underutilized resource to improve business decisions related to projects is examination, conducted shortly after the facility has begun operation, of the causes of difficulty or reasons for success. Such an analysis is difficult. If things are not going well, it may become a search for a scapegoat rather than an examination to avoid repetition.

While often considered an unnecessary and time-consuming burden for the project team, maintaining complete and sufficiently detailed records may pay handsome dividends if they permit the client to take maximum advantage of investment tax credits or other revenue enhancement opportunities. However, one must take care not to create unnecessary and expensive record keeping.

A good working relationship with those following the fortunes of the enterprise, its data requirements, and its cash flow can let the project team maximize their contribution to the success of their project while avoiding unexpected and unpleasant surprises.

3

Early Scope Definition

DONALD G. ENGESSER   *PMEx, Inc., Chatham, New Jersey*

Early definition of project scope begins with project inception, which is most difficult to define. It concludes with the establishment of a documented design basis and consistent estimates and schedules that have been approved by management. Achieving this definition requires input from a number of groups including marketing, business, technical, operations, and management.

Most key areas of project activity must be addressed, at least superficially, during this phase. The engineering activity must be controlled to ensure that jobhours are not wasted. Activities conducted during this phase include market evaluation, analysis of raw material availability and quality, development of basic project objectives, development of design and operating philosophies, screening of alternative cases and configurations, and preparation of schedules, early cost estimates, and economic analyses. These activities must be monitored closely and integrated. The objective is to determine the overall viability of the project and to establish the economic optimum bases for design of facilities to be included.

Physical aspects must be defined including capacity, feed, product slate, plant location; however, development of the basic project execution and permanent operating organizations must also be initiated. Process design resources must be secured. Anticipated requirements for engineering specialists and other engineering support services are identified. In addition, the specific objectives of the project must be developed and documented during this phase to ensure that a consistent approach to the project by all those to be involved.

Four major components are involved in early scope definition: (1) project philosophy, (2) technical definition of the project, (3) early scheduling and cost estimates, and (4) organizational and procedural definition. The work output from these components combine to provide a consistent foundation for the more detailed work in subsequent stages of the project.

PROJECT PHILOSOPHY

A key activity that should be conducted during the conceptual stage of each project is the development of a project philosophy—a statement of the objectives of the project. This should be a written memorandum, carefully prepared and agreed to by the managers who will be involved in the development and approval of the project, the operation of the facilities, and the marketing of the products. Preparation of such a document will help ensure that subsequent decisions by the various groups are based upon a consistent rationale.

The scope of the project philosophy is broadly inclusive; it addresses facilities, proposed execution, organization, productivity, to name a few aspects. A checklist of items to be included in the project philosophy memorandum follows:

Basic project objective
Schedule objective
Cost objective
Design standards for: reliability, operability, maintainability, manning standards, energy efficiency, environmental, health and safety
Desired return on investment for incremental investment both for one-time opportunities and for discretionary investments that could be made after completion of the project.
Service factor target and maintenance plans
Parts/equipment interchangeability desires
Automation targets
Participation of local industry
Provision for future expansion
Construction/operating labor considerations

Obviously many of the above items can give rise to conflict if not applied consistently during the life of the project. For instance, pursuit of *minimum* initial cost will necessarily conflict with a minimum operational manning objective and a minimum maintenance cost objective. Such potential conflicts must be discussed and resolved *before* the project gets underway if subsequent delays and costly inconsistent decisions and decision reversals are to be avoided. The mechanism for achieving resolution of these potential problems is the project philosophy document. Once it is developed and approved by all concerned parties it can be used as the foundation for project decisions throughout all subsequent stages of the project. This key document warrants major attention during the formative stages of each project.

TECHNICAL DEFINITION OF THE PROJECT

The initial technical definition of the project can be developed either in parallel with or subsequent to the development of the project philosophy. It should not, however, precede the project philosophy. Technical definition is an interactive process that should involve technical, business, and marketing personnel. A product slate must be developed, product specifications must be established, sales volume targets set, and packaging and transportation considerations also addressed. In addition, all fundamental technical requirements that affect subsequent design alternatives must be considered. Some of the critical items that should be addressed, at least on a preliminary basis, include:

Feed/raw materials (sources, quality, availability)
Utility needs (availability and reliability)
Product distribution plans (packaging, storage, handling, and transportation)

Screening studies are undertaken to select the manufacturing process and the source of utilities and to establish economic parameters. An infinite number of approaches exist to conduct this work, from use of "in-house" engineers to total use of contractors. The specific approach chosen is a function of the owner's technical resources and the technology involved. However, one important consideration should be kept in mind with respect to use of nonowner resources. At this stage of project development it is best to use contracts/agreements that secure the required technical resources and still provide the owner with maximum freedom for future steps. The organization that can provide the best technical assistance at this stage often would not be the optimum organization for the subsequent detailed definition and construction phases. It is very important that any agreements made to secure technology or engineering assistance do not commit the owner for subsequent activities.

Care should be taken to ensure that all reasonable design alternatives are considered and evaluated. Optimization should involve direct comparisons of alternatives with capital and operating cost estimates for each of the alternatives. Often there is a tendency to "do it the way they did it last time." This approach should invariably be questioned and not be accepted unless substantiated by economic comparative data.

During the later stages of the formative design period, attention should be focused on the inherent technical risks of the selected design approach. It is important that the major technical risks be clearly identified and highlighted, so that in subsequent activities decisions are made with the full cognizance of these risks.

SCHEDULING AND COST ESTIMATES

Every estimate is dependent on three factors: the design, the costing basis, and the project execution basis. To the extent that these elements are not defined at the early stages of project development, the estimate must predict the cost impacts. As the project becomes better defined, fewer predictions are required and estimate accuracy increases. While early estimates are less accurate than later estimates, project control must be established in the formative period, and early estimates must form the basis for that control.

Initial estimates and schedules typically must be derived from rather gross parameters based upon previous experience. Prorations of previous estimates and schedules or use of curve data derived from previous designs must be used. Still, it is important to define the bases for these estimates and schedules as carefully as possible. Control of the project requires base points, and the first estimates and schedules are the first base points. Thus the first estimate should be supported by the best possible definition of the hardware involved so that as various design alternatives are pursued, the project manager will have some indication of how close the current project facilities are to the facilities assumed in the cost and schedule bases.

As engineering proceeds, alternative assumptions are developed and the cost and schedule effects of the alternatives are evaluated relative to the base case. Optional incremental investments are evaluated on an economic basis. As an example, self-generation of power rather than purchasing power might be evaluated. Ultimately, the result is the optimum project configuration selected for further development.

The project manager must think through the estimate and schedule requirements thoroughly during these early stages, and decide when it is appropriate to commit to proceeding with the project and the quality estimate and schedule that are required to make that commitment. The timing of this decision should be determined from the schedules of the design, estimating, and scheduling activities for the project. The technical development of the project must be sufficiently advanced to support development of the quality estimate and schedule required for this important decision. Often a date for the go/no go decision is set rather arbitrarily—independent of the technical development of the project. This may be a serious error unless capital costs are unimportant and speed is the only criteria to be considered during the evaluation of the project.

It is essential to project control to establish milestones at which the project will be intensively reviewed by the appropriate groups. Such check points should be formalized and made the focal point for business, operations, and design reviews by groups other than those directly responsible for the progression of the project. These milestones should be incorporated into an overall project work plan that ties together all major project elements and decisions. Preparation of this first schedule and establishment of project milestones is the first step in the preparation of a project execution plan.

Control of changes during the formative period for a project is very difficult since firm control points have not yet been established. Usually the best approach is to define the technical basis for initial estimates and schedules as clearly as possible. As development proceeds, major changes from the initial assumptions should be recognized, and their cost and schedule impacts evaluated, as they occur. In addition, intensive reviews should be scheduled periodically to evaluate costs and schedules as the project basis is firmed up. Major surprises can usually be avoided; and, if costs or schedules appear to be getting out of hand, appropriate action can be taken before the basis has been firmly established.

The project manager must always ensure that the previously defined project philosophy is being consistently applied as decisions are made. The project manager should determine the project's exposure or cancellation costs and ensure that advance funding requirements are documented and adequate funds are available prior to full appropriation of funds.

ORGANIZATIONAL AND PROCEDURAL DEFINITION OF THE PROJECT

The development of a project is an interactive process. Each time an element or activity is reviewed, it is further refined, but the fundamental direction of development is not changed. As design development proceeds, so must the organization and procedural development of the project. Estimate accuracy is a function of both technical and execution definition, so organizational and procedural decisions must also be made during the early stages if estimate and schedule accuracy are to be improved as desired.

The project manager must forecast the labor environment that the project will be facing. Will it be tight, will there be ample labor, will union or open shop construction be utilized? Will the project be handled on a subcontract basis or will direct hire of the contractors be followed?

Development of procedures for coordinating all those to be involved in the project must be initiated. These procedures must consider all aspects of the project including:

Protection of technology
Routing of correspondence
Handling of procurement
Contracting and subcontracting
Securing of spare parts
Inspection and expediting of materials and equipment
Quality assurance
Handling of changes
Accounting, invoicing, and payment
Use of scale models
Project reporting
Development of mechanical catalogs
Metric or English units
System for drawing preservation
Development of operating manuals
Environmental health
Safety
Site sanitation during construction
Site security
Insurance
Equipment protection during shipping and storage
Definition of completion

The final development of all of these procedures must necessarily extend beyond the early development stage. However, it is important that the project manager firm up requirements and definitions as early in the development of the project as possible.

A particularly important procedure for early development is change control. A formal procedure that mandates written change definition, pricing, and scheduling must be introduced into the project as soon as a design basis has been established. Without enforcement of such a procedure, project control will almost certainly be lost during early development.

Public and government concerns should be carefully considered. The overall process required for government approvals msut be understood and requirements for public hearings, and complex data submissions need to be established. For modestly sized domestic projects located in established industrialized areas, only limited government interface may be required to ensure compliance with established regulations. However, for a very large project, remotely located, many fundamental agreements must be reached, some of which can be critical to the development of the project. These agreements can range across economic, social, and political lines and can require the application of appreciable resources for extended periods of time. Typically legal, governmental relations, and technical specialists will be required to support the project manager. Realistic evaluation of these interactions and their time requirements is essential to the orderly development of such prospects.

Project team concepts must also be developed. The size of the team, the management approach to be taken, and the source of the team personnel and specialist technical support must also be established at least conceptually.

CONCLUSIONS

All of the above activities and decisions impact the project execution plan—in fact, they represent elements of the project execution plan. All these decisions must be documented. In many firms standardized procedures, applicable to all projects, have been developed. To the extent that standardized approaches are applicable, specific documentation is not needed for each project.

4

Selecting the Site

PAUL B. WRIGHT* *Davy McKee Corporation, San Ramon, California*

SITE SELECTION: AN ESSENTIAL PART OF PROJECT MANAGEMENT

Plant location is a significant factor in the development of an industrial project. The importance of the site selection process is emphasized by M. D. Bryce (1960), who reminds us that industrial plants have been built in locations where sufficient or suitable process water was lacking, where local fuel sources proved inadequate, or where the local raw materials turned out to be either insufficient, unsuitable, or unexpectedly expensive.

The hazards of site selection are greatest when a remote location has been selected because of an assumed special advantage—usually an available raw material or low-cost fuel supply. A plant situated in a remote location may be at a great disadvantage: far from service and supply sources, distant from skilled labor supplies, and far from markets. The special cost advantage of cheap raw materials or fuel can make up for such inherent disadvantages, but only if the advantages are as real as expected.

Bryce shows how the entire success of an industrial development project can be jeopardized by inadequate attention to choosing the site. Successful development of an industrial project can be enhanced by giving due attention to:

Recognition of site selection as a distinct step in the development of an industrial project

Establishment of a suitable procedure for selecting the site of an industrial plant

Giving approrpiate attention to all factors, objective and subjective, in selecting the site

Site selection is seldom mentioned as being within the scope of project management. This is probably because the evaluation and selection of a site generally takes place during the very early stages of a project and before there is a well-defined project to manage. However, even if he has not been involved in the site selection, it is important that the project manager understand the reasoning that led to the choice of a particular construction site.

Selection of the most desirable site is only one activity in the orderly development of a project. The site-selection process must fit into the schedule of all other project activities and should be a source of information to other scheduled work including environmental reports, economic evaluations, permit applications and the basic design of the plant. Although identified as an early stage activity, site selection frequently overlaps with both the conceptual and the execution phases of the project.

---

*Retired

The emphasis on site selection as part of the total development will vary considerably from project to project. For some minerals projects, where the raw material supply is a specific ore deposit and the market is reached by shipping from a nearby port,
the entire process may involve consideration of only local sites. The other extreme is
site selection for an international project where potential locations in numerous countries must be considered before attention is directed to the general areas within one
country and to locally available sites.

Regardless of the complexity of the site selection for any project, the site for a
planned industrial plant is selected somewhere between the initial economic evaluation
of the project and the engineering and construction of the plant. The simplified sequence of phases in the development of an industrial project is generally as follows:

| Project conception and |
| process development |
     | Economic evaluations |
       | Site selection |
         | Permitting |
           | Engineering and construction |

Although the development of an industrial project can be shown and discussed as a
sequence of phases, there is strong interdependence between the phases. Each phase
must rely on work accomplished as part of some other phase. Permitting makes use
of information and data developed by both site selection and by engineering. Economic
evaluations of the project depend on information from the project conception and process development phases, and to some extent, from site selection. Site selection uses
economic evaluation data as a basis for comparing alternative sites. However, each
phase of development has definite goals and objectives. The sole purpose of the site-
selection phase is to select a plant site which will optimize the economic benefits of the
project and will not present insurmountable obstacles to the completion of the industrial plant and the attainment of these benefits.

Frequently, the economic feasibility of an industrial plant project depends entirely
on selection of a suitable plant site. Plants which are high energy users are generally
highly site dependent for economic success. Raw material and labor requirements
can adversely affect economic feasibility of the project if the plant site is not carefully
selected. Therefore, the phase sequence during the development of a project shows
an overlap of site selection into the economic evaluation and the process development
phases. For a highly site-dependent project, complete evaluation of project economics
is not possible until the site criteria have been established and examination of potential plant sites is underway. The selection of a suitable site, after considering all
significant factors, can easily be the most important decision in the development of a
project.

SELECTION MISTAKES AND FATAL FLAWS

Mistakes can lead to erroneous conclusions in the site selection process. There are
three categories of mistakes:

1. Excessive time and money spent on preliminary evaluation of numerous sites
2. Unrealistic evaluation of factors
3. Failure to recognize fatal flaws in otherwise desirable sites

The first mistake can be extremely costly to the project if a high percentage of the
budget is expended on the preliminary evaluation of a large number of sites and insufficient budget remains for detailed evaluation of the choicer sites. This can be avoided
by proper planning and supervising of this phase of project development.

The second mistake can lead to selection of an inappropriate site if either inaccurate site information is evaluated or if the evaluation is unrealistic. This mistake can be avoided by the assignment of experienced and qualified personnel to the site selection phase of project development.

The third mistake can be costly and will likely delay development of the project. It is imperative that unacceptable sites (locations with fatal flaws) be eliminated from consideration early in the process. The classic example of this mistake is the Mystic Chemical Company. After spending millions of dollars on the ideal site for their new plant, it was discovered that the location was the only habitat of the red-headed muggywart, and that laws prohibit development in the area. Sites with fatal flaws are best eliminated before large sums are spent on their evaluation and development.

Some common mistakes in the site selection process are listed by A. S. Damiani (1971) in his review of evaluating site selection factors:

Miscalculating labor costs
Inaccurately estimating labor reservoir
Failing to anticipate growth
Carelessly checking the site
Failing to predict local impact of new plant
Inadequately appraising support facilities
Producing misinformation on utility costs and problems
Underestimating importance of taxes

Damiani comments further on the use of consultants with specialized knowledge and experience to supplement the site selection activities as a means of avoiding such mistakes.

An orderly process for identifying site requirements, screening potential sites, analyzing site factors, and searching for fatal flaws is presented by Lovett (1982). The process includes the following:

Establish key criteria for plant site:

    Absolute requirements
    Desirable attributes

Identify proper geographical regions:

    Raw material sources
    Product distribution patterns
    Labor requirements
    Waste-disposal requirements
    Environmental permitting requirements
    Characterization of industry served

Select candidate sites:

    Key criteria
    Land availability
    Property size
    Access
    Utilities
    Permitting situation
    Waste-disposal facilities
    Labor availability/union status

Screen candidate sites:

    History of community acceptance
    Layout of property
    Availability of rights-of-way

Availability of utilities
Existence of land preserves and endangered species
Proximity of nonattainment areas
Proximity of hazardous waste-disposal areas
Availability of labor force
Inherent time delays
Permits required and permit lead time

Compare screened sites in detail:

Capital investment costs
Operating costs
Qualitative factors

Fatal-flaw analysis of best site.

Recommend primary and optional sites.

The fatal-flaw analysis of the best site is a significant part of this seleciton process. It includes a more detailed analysis of environmental factors, community influences, and legal ramifications than is conducted on any other site. The analysis involves gathering data to be used in permitting and in establishing the impact of site development on the environment. Property title is investigated to determine any obscure restrictions on either use or access, soil borings are made to verify soil conditions, and any potential archaeological or historical sites are investigated. If no fatal flaws are identified, most of this work is usable for completing tasks necessary for plant construction. Lovett recommends that the best-site property should be optioned before completing the fatal-flaw analysis to assure its availability.

A more detailed procedure for the identification of "no-go conditions" and for using this procedure to establish the most favorable site is described by J. R. Nagy (1981) in his discussion of evaluating risks. He cites two reasons for applying this type of analysis to the site selection process. First, the increasing complexity of the factors involved in selecting the site for a new industrial site have made the process of site selection both costly and time consuming. Second, the pressures of a design and build development schedule demands the rapid identification of problems and assessment of sites. When it is necessary to make rapid progress to meet a fixed project development schedule, concentrating on risk factors which make siting prohibitive can be both cost and time effective. A classification of various types of risks and a system for the evaluation of these risks follows.

KEYS TO SUCCESS IN SELECTING THE SITE

Selection of the most advantageous site for an industrial plant generally follows these fundamental steps:

1. Establish site criteria. List separately what is required and what is desired for the plant site.
2. Establish selection factors. List separately the objective and subjective factors to be considered in selecting the site.
3. Select the general territory. Whether it be a country, state, or geographical area, such as the Central Gulf coast, narrow the search to a general area to be considered.
4. Select the specific area. Whether it be a town, county, or small geographical area, such as the Minneapolis-St. Paul metropolitan area, continue to decrease the size of the area to be considered.
5. Select the site. Evaluate locations within the specific area and select the most advantageous site.

This orderly sequence of steps is the least costly approach to an unrestricted and logical selection of the site for a new industrial plant. However, in real life it is more likely that the site selection will not follow this ideal sequence. Political considerations may take priority, the company may own property which is included as a site to be evaluated, or financing arrangements may require that only sites in one area will be considered. It is frequently necessary to make a final evaluation of several desirable sites in widely separated areas. This does not imply that these fundamental steps are not correct. The initial step in any site selection is to define the objectives of the seleciton process, identify any restraints and special requirements, and to plan the work accordingly. Begin by estbalishing a criteria for the site to be selected.

The key to successful site selection is planning and team effort. Subjective factors are of major importance, so a one-man team is undesirable for either planning or execution of the site selection. Whether the team consists of two, three, or fifty people will depend on the scope of the evaluation and the size and complexity of the project. Planning should be done by a small group including key people from the selection team plus management representation. Experienced people should establish the objectives of the selection study, prepare a schedule and budget for the study, select the personnel and organization of the study team, prepare a preliminary list of mandatory and desirable requirements for the site, and a preliminary list of factors to be considedred in the evaluation of both areas and specific site locations. Planning should include a definition of objectives for the formal reports to be completed and issued as part of the site-selection procedure and target dates for their issue. The schedule and target dates for site selection should be compatible with the project development schedule.

The site-selection process was summarized in two steps by Merims (in Landau, 1966) in his procedural guide for industrial plant development. The first step, selection of the general location for a plant, requires the economic evaluation of alternative areas. This evaluation includes comparisons of costs for transportation, labor, and utilities, in addition to the variable costs of plant construction. The second step, to select an actual plant site within the selected general area, requires a more complex evaluation to obtain the best combination of the following:

Taxes, subsidies, and regulations
Pollution restraints
Living conditions, facilities, and climate
Plot characteristics
Labor availability and type
Intangibles

W. B. Speir (1970), in his review of the site seleciton process, concludes that all but three or four of the best sites can usually be eliminated by evaluation of the major variable costs, without being too concerned about intangible and noneconomic factors.

FIELD INVESTIGATIONS OF SITES

Field investigations of both the areas and sites being considered are a necessary part of any plant-siting study. The cost of such work should be realistically estimated and included in the study budget. Travel, subsistence, and the cost of any contract services are all a part of this cost of field investigations. Local promotional agencies can frequently be used on some information-gathering activities as a means of reducing the time and cost of a field investigation. However, all information so obtained should be carefully verified.

Two documents should be prepared in advance of such field investigations: (1) A specification listing the primary requirements of the desired site including all physical requirements of the site, but omitting any requirements based on confidential or sensitive marketing plans. (2) A comprehensive checklist of local conditions as a form to be completed with numerical data, names, and hard facts. These documents provide a specific objective for the field investigation of each site and assure a uniform and complete compilation of site information. Time should be allowed for checking and verifying information before the site visit is complete. If several team members are involved in the visit their information should be cross-checked to avoid any conflicting data when the visit is complete. This will also permit arrangements to be made for any follow-up necessary to complete and to clarify site information.

Check lists of questions on local utility and transportation conditions are illustrated by D. H. Lehmer and J. H. Dennis (1977) in a general discussion of the site selection process. Their list of transportation information includes over fifty questions on all types of transport for any site being considered. Such checklists are a necessary part of the preparation for an effective field investigation.

A potential site which appears unattractive on the basis of preliminary information is not likely to become highly desirable after the field investigation is completed and information evaluated. On the other hand, highly desirable sites are frequently far less attractive after field information is evaluated. During preparation for the field investigation of multiple sites, it is often possible to eliminate one or more of the sites from serious consideration and to concentrate on sites with greater potential. This preliminary screening is important for field investigation activities and can be cost effective to the site-selection process.

SITE EVALUATION FACTORS

Site location factors are classified by P. A. Brown and D. F. Gibson (1972) as three distinct types:

1. Objective factors which can be evaluated in monetary terms
2. Subjective factors which cannot be evaluated in monetary terms
3. Critical factors which may preclude the location of a plant at a particular site regardless of other conditions

These three basic types of site-related factors in locating industrial plants can be grouped into those concerned with either production or distribution:

Production-related factors

Raw materials
Labor
Energy
Water
Wastes

Distribution-related factors

Transportation
Markets

Both production- and distribution-related factors

Climate
Taxation
Political
Governmental restrictions

Several types of checklists, or lists of factors, can be used in gathering information and evaluating potential sites for an industrial plant. Many such lists are included in the literature, ranging from six general factors to a detailed list of 1700 site information items. The appropriate list to use for any specific evaluation is somewhere between these extremes. In reality, two lists should be used. (1) A checklist of all information items to be obtained for each site being investigated. This is a working tool for the investigation team. Each item is an objective to be answered by a simple yes or no, a quantity, a name, or some other hard fact for each site being investigated. (2) A list of parameters for comparison and evaluation of the several sites being considered. This list is generally much shorter than the first list, items are more general, and many items may be subjective in nature. An example of this second list is presented by Granger (1981) and is included herewith as a Site-Rating chart (Table 1). This Site-Rating chart may be used either for preliminary screening of area, or for final comparison and site selection. Only sites providing the required conditions and passing the preliminary screening should reach this final comparison stage. At this time, more detailed information on the few remaining sites will be considered, and more sophisticated systems of comparing parameters will be used to make the final site selection.

One of the more comprehensive lists of site-selection factors is available in workbook form (Conway Publications) and includes both a checklist to aid in establishing the site criteria and a checklist of over 1700 factors for a site-selection study. Such an extensive list can be valuable in developing the list of factors to be considered in selecting the site for a specific project. This list has been developed over a number of years and is published annually as a planning tool for the site-selection phase of complex development projects. Factors are classified into the following categories:

Marketing
Work force
Transportation
Fuels, utilities, and communications
Materials and services
Federal, state and local government programs
Water and wastes
Ecological concerns
Quality of life
Climate
Specific site data
Additional factors for international projects

Financial inducements by groups representing municipal, country, or state government agencies may be offered for the location and development of industry in an area. Such inducements may be in the form of tax relief; zoning or code adjustments; revenue bonds for financing construction; or the development of utilities, roads, or rail access to the site. The value of such offers may offset minor disadvantages inherent to the area. In all cases, a thorough investigation should be conducted and hard evidence obtained on the availability and timing of such offers. These inducements should be evaluated as any other factor in the siting process and decisions made only on the results of a complete and realistic evaluation.

MATHEMATICAL METHODS OF SITE SELECTION

The term "operations research" refers generally to the application of mathematics and logical model building to the decision-making process. Various techniques are included in this field of applied technology. It is only natural that some of these techniques are being applied directly to the selection of sites for industrial plant facilities. In fact, any experienced site selector has probably made use of such methods to evaluate possible plant locations.

Table 1 Site-Rating Chart

LABOR
  Attitude
  Availability:
    Executive
    Engineering and technical
    Skilled
  Nonskilled
  Labor costs
  Labor stability
  Cost of living
  Construction labor
  Special labor laws

TAXES AND FINANCIAL INDUCEMENTS
  Business taxes required:
    Incentives
    Forgiveness–how long?
  Property taxes
  State and local taxes:
    Industrial
    Personal
  Inventory taxes
  Construction taxes
  Workmen's compensation
  Other
  Financial inducements

TOPOGRAPHIC AND SITE CONDITIONS
  Overburden
  Subsoil
  Contours
  Natural resources
  Relationship to highways
  Is railroad:
    Onsite
    Close by
  Seismic zones

UTILITIES
  Availability of gas, electricity, oil,
    and coal
  Can they meet demand?
  Cost of gas, electricity, oil, and coal
  Environmental impact on atmosphere
  Potable water available, gpm
  Fire protection water available, gpm
  Process water available
  Effluent requirements
  Sewers available
  Environmental impact of wastewater

ENVIRONMENTAL CONSIDERATIONS
  Ambient air-quality standards
  Quality of wastewater-receiving waters
  Quality of:
    Water supply
    Natural gas
    Coal
  Suitability of site for sanitary landfill
  Environmental impact of new plant on:
    Air
    Water
    Land use
  Attitude of local environmental groups
    toward new plant
  Special state or local environmental laws
    affecting plant operation

CLIMATE
  Rainfall
  Degree-days
  Wind velocity and prevailing direction
  Heating costs
  Elevation above sea level
  Ambient temperature
  Relative humidity

SERVICES
  Fire protection
  Police and security
  Maintenance of access roads
  Property maintenance
  Local support
  Waste hauling services

FREIGHT AND TRANSPORTATION
  Rail to site
  Good truck availability
  Cost of rail:
    Shipping
    Receiving
  Cost of truck shipping
  Availability of mass transit for employees

DEMOGRAPHICS
  Living conditions
  Historical background
  Schools and enrollment
  Number and type of churches
  Civil organizations
  Media representation
  Recreational facilities
  Cultural activities

One of the better introductory discussions on this topic is by H. A. Stafford (Conway Publications) in his 1979 book on the principles of industrial plant location. Stafford provides a guide on the application of operations research methods to the site selection process and includes references for more specific information on these methods. A significant technique in this type of application is the use of linear programming for the analysis of plant location factors. In complex evaluations, where problems of plant size, plant production mix, and plant location must all be considered, the use of linear programming and other related techniques may be used to determine optimum conditions. This is a developing field of computer application and current operations research literature offers state-of-the-art information on its use.

The actual application of linear programming as a basic analytical tool in the site selection process is described by F. C. Weston, Jr. (1972). His example makes use of a mathematical model where time is a principal parameter, thus permitting evaluation of variable costs over a five-year period, combined with capital costs for each alternative site. A sensitivity analysis of selected variables is an essential part of this evaluation.

Linear programming provides a basis for the formal, structured analysis of complex evaluations. It is an essential technique where multiproduct production and distribution factors are necessary considerations. It is less essential where subjective and environmental factors predominate the site selection process.

Mathematical methods can be used to evaluate subjective factors in the site selection process. The typical method is a two-step comparison process. First, each subjective factor is compared with each of the other subjective factors and the relative importance established. This comparison only determines if a factor is less important, equal in importance, or more important than each of the other factors being evaluated. These decisions are assigned numerical values and used to calculate the factor weight for each subjective factor being evaluated. Second, each site is compared with each of the other sites on the basis of a uniform description of each site. This comparison determines site suitability in the same degrees as in the first step. The site weight for each site being considered is calculated as above. These values for factor and site weights are combined in a mathematical mode to compare sites on the basis of critical, objective, and subjective factors.

A manual matrix system for the evaluation of subjective selection factors is described by J. E. Granger (1981). This procedure assigns each factor a numerical value of 1 to 4 to fix the relative weight in relation to other factors being considered. Those factors with the greatest impact on plant siting rate a 4 while those of least importance are assigned a 1.

A point value system is then used to grade each site on how it ranks for each factor and results are compared. Point values of 1 to 10 are used, with the higher values assigned to sites that rank best. These values are generally assigned on the basis of data on conditions for the general area of the site, such as state or country, rather than for the exact site location. Each point value is multiplied by the factor weight value to give a score for each site for each factor. These values are tabulated to form a matrix of factors, sites, and scores. The score totals are compared, the highest total score being the most favorable site.

As a further comparison of the more favorable sites, a sensitivity analysis is performed on the matrix. By changing the relative weights of selected factors, certain desirable features can be emphasized to more clearly identify the best site. For example, factors related to operating costs may be increased, while those representing initial capital costs are decreased. A summation of scores on this basis will show if such changes are significant to the more favorable sites. Such modifications of the matrix will show that certain sites can be dropped from consideration and that further evaluations can concentrate on a small number of the more favorable sites.

ENVIRONMENTAL ASPECTS OF SITE SELECTION

Any discussion of the site selection process is not complete without a review of the environmental aspects of the plant location decision. In recent years these environmental concerns have grown to be a major factor in selecting the site for an industrial plant. A recent presentation by H. D. Leonhardt (1984) affirms the importance of the previously mentioned fatal-flaw analysis and warns of the complexity of the many environmental rules and regulations. Part of his discussion recommends that two lists be made for each potential site being considered. The first is a list of expected emissions from the proposed plant and is essentially the same for all sites. This list of emissions should include:

1. The estimated emission rate of all air pollutants in both pounds per hour and tons per year.
2. The estimated flow of each wastewater stream with the estimated untreated concentration of pollutants in each stream.
3. The estimated discharge of hazardous and nonhazardous wastes in both weight and volume on a daily and annual basis.
4. The estimated requirements of raw and treated water on a daily and annual basis.

The second is a list of the environmental resources in the area for each site being considered. This list of resources should include:

1. Existing and planned water supply and sewage or waste-treatment systems in the area with information on how much capacity is being used and how much is actually available.
2. Any restrictions that are either pending or have been placed by the state and federal authorities on the water supply and sewage or waste-treatment systems in this area.
3. Available PSD (Prevention of Significant Deterioration - Clean Air Act) increments. Inventory of emissions from existing facilities in the area.
4. Location of any Class I areas. (Pristine areas protected under PSD.)
5. Location of any nonattainment areas. (Areas that are not in compliance with air quality standards.)
6. Capacity of nearby streams to accept wastewater flow from the site being considered.

These two lists will provide the basic information to establish relative costs of meeting the environmental requirements for each site being considered and the need for alternative solutions to minimize these costs. With this approach, either optimum or acceptable solutions can be established for each site being considered. Any environmental restraints which will effectively prevent the construction and operation of the plant at a site should be identified by the fatal-flaw analysis.

Although permitting is not a part of the site selection process, the site selector should be aware of both the requirements and of the relative cost and time to obtain the necessary permits for building a plant on each site being considered. Data-gathering activities started during site selection will continue during the permitting phase of project development. The assistance of professionals from the environmental sciences is required during all phases of project development to cope with both the complexities of environmental factors and the compliance requirements of the many regulatory agencies that may be involved. Even if no regulatory agencies are involved, such as in some foreign areas, there is a need for environmental considerations to assure public safety and acceptance during construction and operation of the planned industrial plant.

Environmental impact statements are generally a required part of the permitting process for any new industrial plant site. Environmental impact evaluations are one part of the site selection process and are preliminary to the preparation of an environmental impact statement for the selected site. The information required for these environmental studies is listed by Hales (1976) in his discussion of environmental impact assessments. His discussion can be applied to both preliminary evaluations and to final studies of the selected site.

Environmental impact statements are expensive to complete and are mandatory only for the selected site, not for all sites being considered. Environmental evaluations are necessary during all stages of the site selection process, including the fatal-flaw analysis, and provide the basis for further work on the environmental impact statement during the permitting process.

FOREIGN SITE SELECTION

Evaluation of foreign sites generally follows the same course as for domestic sites. However, when the more underdeveloped countries are included, additional significant factors may be involved in the site selection process. A systematic approach to evaluating foreign countries for an industrial plant site is presented by Davis (1979) (Table 2) and is based on his experience in global planning.

Foreign nations can be classified into three categories for site selection and facilities planning purposes:

1. Developing countries (e.g., Turkey, Indonesia, Somalia)
2. Transitional countries (e.g., Brazil, Taiwan, Chile)
3. Sophisticated countries (e.g., Australia, France, Sweden)

The factors to be considered in selecting the country for a plant site can be classified into ten elements:

1. Business environment
2. Business structure
3. Capital sources
4. Tariffs and taxes
5. Transportaiton and communication
6. Raw materials and servcies
7. Labor
8. Facilities construction or acquisition
9. Land acquisition
10. Energy

A qualitative model is developed by combining the country categories with the planning elements and showing the unique attributes to be considered for each combination in the site selection process. Such a matrix is presented by Davis with a discussion on its application. The emphasis is on the third world countries where unusual and unique factors may be significant. For example, the literacy rate of the labor market is not a typical site selection factor. However, in evaluating several developing countries, or areas within such countries, it becomes an important factor.

In evaluating developing countries, the lack of reliable economic statistics is a frequent problem. The best sources of such information may be the local branches of foreign banks, the embassies, investment banks, and private sources such as SRI International and Business International.

A procedure for success in international site elections is summarized by L. C. Hoch (1982) in the following six steps:

Table 2 Foreign Plant Site Selection Evaluation Elements

	Developing nation	Transitional nation	Sophisticated nation
Business environment	Government popular support; Agrarian: Industrial mix; Human rights and terrorism	Trade partners; Inflation; Nationalistic sensitivity	Strength of currency; Military alliances; Trade balance with U.S.
Business structure	Corporate law heritage: British, Latin, Dutch; Directors, resident vs. nonresident; Applicability OPIC insurance	Local partner requirements; Foreign expatriate limitations; Sanctity of contract with government	Corporate disclosure requirements; Advantages of joint venture; Degree of freedom: Management decisions
Capital sources	Debt: Equity requirements; International bank outlets; Existence of savings institutions	Priority sectors for foreign investment; Convertibility of currency; Development bank	Fixed asset grants and subsidies; Local capital market; Savings propensity
Tariffs and taxes	Tax holiday; Free trade zones; Preferential tariff to U.S., EEC, Japan	Export subsidies; Import restrictions; Repatriation of dividends, interest, royalties	Affiliation with customs union; Value added tax; Tax treaty with U.S.
Transportation and communication	Telex and telephone; Adequacy of domestic distribution; International airport	Satellite communication; National airline world routes; Truck and rail service	Computer service companies; Freight rates to suppliers and customers; International airlines serving hub airports

Raw materials and services	Basic industrial infrastructure	Degree of industrial integration	Comparative advantage of local procurement
	Spare parts availability	Quality of local workmanship	Natural resources
	Capacity and quality of industrial gases	Development of local suppliers	Portfolio of journeyman skills
Labor	Literacy rate	Geographic concentrations	Industrial democracy
	Ethnic tensions	Skilled labor matrix	Training subsidies
	Strike ban	Control of industrial growth	Wage and salary formula
Facilities construction or acquisition	Local construction industry	Construction quality, existing facilities	Make vs. buy analysis
	Building materials availability	Industrial parks	Environmental regulations
	Building permit processing time	Local architects and engineers	
Land acquisition	Foreign ownership allowed	Industrial parks	Appreciation return of real property
	Fee-simple or long-term lease	Rent control	Density of industrial areas
	Zoning/land use	Gov't developed alternatives to urban areas	
Energy	Availability	Sources and costs	National energy policy
	Reliability	Nuclear sites	Crude oil as percent imports per capita consumption
	Capacity expansion plans	Consumption trends	

1. Formulation of objectives
2. Establishing the requirements
3. Preliminary investigation
4. Screening
5. Field investigations
6. Final selection

This procedure follows the expected sequence of first defining the site requirements followed by area investigations and specific site evaluations. However, Hoch considers it a mistake to begin field investigations of foreign sites before conducting substantial preliminary research, using U.S. sources of information on the countries being considered. He emphasizes two important parts of international site selection procedures; the preliminary investigation and screening to narrow the scope of further investigations and evaluations. On the basis of this preliminary evaluation, some countries and areas can be eliminated and the time and cost of field investigations reduced. Final selection then follows the normal procedure of systematic cost tabulations supplemented by a full evaluation of subjective factors related to each site.

SELECTED BIBLIOGRAPHY

The literature on the selection of industrial plant sites has been reviewed and the following references chosen as practical how-to information for the project manager and the site selection team. Anyone involved in the site selection procedure should review several of these references as a background of information on this subject. This bibliography is not intended to provide information on site conditions, but to provide a better knowledge and understanding of the factors to be considered and the methods of evaluation and presentation.

This bibliography, presented in alphabetical order, emphasizes both the changing and the unchanging nature of the site selection process. Many factors and procedures, especially those related to technical and economic comparisons, remain essentially unchanged. Others, primarily the social, environmental, and political considerations, have emerged as major factors in the selection of a plant site. The site selector should be aware of these trends and realize that the site selection process will respond to them.

Several references are included primarily for their bibliographies covering some of the more specialized aspects of the site selection process. Wendell (1973) includes references on linear programming and mathematical modeling. Rowe (1980) lists references to publications relating to the field of urban studies from 1950 to 1980. Cornuejols and Thizy (1982) provide additional references on mathematical methods of site selection. Finally, Williams and Massa (1983) supply references to a wide range of site selection subjects.

BIBLIOGRAPHY AND NOTES

Brown, P. A., and Gibson, D. F. "A Quantified Model for Facility Site Selection."
    A.I.I.E. Transactions 4(1):1-10 (1972). Describes how a computer program can
    be used to evaluate both objective and subjective factors.
Bryce, M. D. *Industrial Development*, First Edition. New York: McGraw-Hill
    Book Co., 1960. Chapter 7 includes site selection as one part of analyzing the
    technical feasibility of a project. Bryce examines the problem of not giving
    adequate consideration to site selection in establishing the feasibility of a
    project.

Conway Publications, Inc., 1954 Airport Road, Atlanta, GA, 30341. Publishers of journals and books relating to development of industrial plants of all types. An important source of current site selection information. *Principles of Industrial Facility Location*, 1979, by H. A. Stafford. *Industrial Development* (issued six times a year). *Site Selection Handbook* (issued four times a year). *New Project File and Site Selection Checklist* (a project workbook). *The Good Life Index* (current social factor conditions).

Cornuejols, G., and Thizy, J. M. "Some Facets of the Simple Plant Location Polytope." *Mathematical Programming 23*(1), 50-74 (1982). A polytope is simply a group that originates from two or more sources. Several classes of facets and their integer polytopes are described. Bibliography.

Cross, F. L. (Ed.) *Industrial Plant Siting*. Technomic Publishing Co., Westport, CT, 1975. Introduction by R. Barbaro reviews the changed emphasis on many site selection factors. The chapters by Mr. Cross discuss the methods of site selection with emphasis on environmental concerns.

Cuno, C. W. "Economic Factors in Chemical Plant Location." *Industrial and Engineering Chemistry 21*(8), 738 (1929). Mr. Cuno was a frequent contributor to publications on the site selection process. See also his Chapter 26 in the Second Edition of the *Chemical Engineering Handbook*, McGraw-Hill Book Co. (1941). It is noted that space in this handbook devoted to the factors of chemical plant location decreased from nine pages in the second edition to zero pages in the recent sixth edition of 1984.

Damiani, A. S. "Selecting a Plant Site? Evaluate Facts, Figures and Facilities." *Plant Engineering 25*, 40-41 (April 1, 1971). Shows one method to tabulate cost factors for comparison of sites. Lists common and costly mistakes in site selection.

Davis, W. E. "A Primer on Locating Facilities in Foreign Countries." *Industrial Development 148*(3), 1979. A global facility planner describes a systematic approach to site selection in foreign lands. An introduction to planning the foreign project.

Granger, J. E. "Plantsite Selection." *Chemical Engineering 88*(12), 88-115 (1981). A step-by-step discussion of the procedure for locating the site for a new chemical plant. Includes references to sources of information.

Greenhut, M. L. *Plant Location in Theory and in Practice*. University of North Carolina Press, Chapel Hill, 1956. A textbook on the general theory of plant location. Reviews the work of von Thunen, Alfred Weber, and E. M. Hoover.

Hales, L. "Environmental Impact Assessments." *Plant Engineering 30*(9), 231-233 (1976). An introduction on how to prepare the environmental impact assessment.

Hoch, L. C. "Site Selection for Foreign Operations." *Industrial Development 151*(3), 7-9 (1982). Six steps to success by a site selector who has been there.

Holmes, W. G. *Plant Location*, First Edition. New York: McGraw-Hill Book Co., 1930. One of the first publications on industrial plant location to recognize a need for the engineer and the economist to combine their talents in the site selection process.

Landau, R. (ed.). *The Chemical Plant: From Process Selection to Commercial Operation*. New York: Van Nostrand Reinhold Co., 1966. A procedural guide to the steps involved in the conception, design, construction, and operation of an industrial plant. See Chapter 6 for Plant Location and Site Considerations by Robert Merims.

Lehmer, D. H., and Dennis, J. H., "Zeroing in on a New Plant Site." *Consulting Engineer 48*(4), 59-64 (1977). A discussion of operating concerns, financial inducements, trends and timing, specific problems, resources, site engineering, and scheduling problems relating to the site selection process.

Leonhardt, H. D. "Environmental Aspects of the Site Location Decision." *Industrial Development 153*(4), 23-27 (1984). Includes an introduction to the nomenclature used in discussions of environmental topics.

Lovett, K. M. "When You Select a Plant Site . . ." *Hydrocarbon Processing 61*(5), 285-293 (1982). Introduces a step in site selection called the "fatal flaw analysis." This is similar to the red flag waved by J. R. Nagy.

Nagy, J. R. "Site Selection: Using Red Flags to Management's Benefit." *Industrial Development 150*(1), 10-14 (1981). Early identification of disaster risks can reduce the number of prospective sites. Presents a generalized schedule of the site selection process.

Rowe, J. E. *Theory of Industrial Plant Location.* Monticello, IL: Vance Bibliographies, 1980. Primarily a bibliography on industrial plant site selection in the field of urban studies. Covers 1950 to 1980.

Speir, W. B. "Chosing and Planning Industrial Sites." *Chemical Engineering 77*(26), 69-75 (1970). A review of the typical site selection procedure with a seven-point outline of the preferred and required features of the site to be selected.

Warner, J. L. "Significance of Location Upon Production Costs." *Transactions of American Institute of Chemical Engineers. 32*(1), 193-220 (1936). His Exhibit A has been widely copied as a graphic display of the many factors influencing site selection.

Wendell, R. E. "Location Theory, Dominance, and Convexity." *Operations Research 21*(1), 314-320 (1973). A discussion of the nature of optimal solutions to plant location problems. Mathematical conditions are developed to guarantee optimal locations. Bibliography.

Weston, F. C. "Quantitative Analysis of Plant Location." *Industrial Engineering 4*, 22-28 (April, 1972). An introduction to the use of linear programming in the site selection process. The model described is a simplified version of an actual application.

Williams, E. A., and Massa, A. K. *Siting of Major Facilities.* New York: McGraw-Hill Book Co., 1983. Shows how the site selection process can handle an extremely comprehensive set of information in an orderly manner. Emphasis is on public works type of projects. Bibliography covers 1960 to 1982.

5

Regulatory Requirements and Permits

PAUL V. MORGAN   *Davy McKee Corporation, San Ramon, California*

RAYMOND E. KRAUSS   *Homestake Mining Company, Lower Lake, California*

IMPACT OF REGULATORY REQUIREMENTS ON PROJECT MANAGEMENT

The project manager's response to regulatory requirements can make or break the schedule, the budget, and in some cases cause the scuttling of a major project entirely.

Legislative bodies and administrative agencies have proliferated in the past two decades, engendering vast quantities of rules and regulations. Often dominated by attorneys and under the constant scrutiny of the media, the regulatory bodies have become increasingly bound by procedures. The bottom line for the project manager is twofold: (1) additional time, often exceeding a year, to accommodate public notice, review, and approval; and (2) additional staff to attend to the details and complexities of the permitting process.

The long lead times necessary to process most major permits conflict with other project milestones. Engineering decisions may be pushed ahead of the ideal timing to provide the level of detail necessary for permit applications. Regulatory agencies are usually oblivious to the seasons, so inclement weather constraints are not considered. Public controversy routinely extends permitting schedules by months and litigation can extend into years.

The manager of a major project will depend upon a team of specialists to accomplish project permitting on a timely basis. A typical team may be composed of the following:

Technical specialists who develop the project documents, environmental site and detailed project descriptions, and the rationale and justification for the design and siting decisions made.

Attorneys familiar with the permitting regulations and procedures to assure that the permitting process is correct legally and thus not subject to challenge.

A public spokesman who speaks at the project permit proceedings and who represents the project to the media.

Schedulers to assure that the timing of the permitting fits the project engineering and construction schedules.

A team leader to coordinate the activities of the team. This individual may also be the public spokesman.

Some projects also may utilize the expertise of public relations and governmental relations specialists.

The work of the project permitting team, without exception, must be founded upon a technically sound project. Project area site characteristics must be adequately known

and described. Area seismicity, foundation characteristics, hydrology, and other
site characteristics, if misrepresented, can cause lengthy delays and occasional costly
redesign. Clear, concise, complete project descriptions are essential. Much time can
be lost in preparing additional information in response to agency requests. Clear
communication channels between the permitting and project design teams are important.
Permitting requirements may dictate design decisions, making timely feedback from
the permitting team essential. The project design must be shown to be responsive
to the permitting constraints.

OVERVIEW OF NATIONAL REGULATORY AND STATUTORY REQUIREMENTS

The specific permits required for a project depend on the project location and the
jurisdictions involved. A discussion of international regulations here is impossible;
therefore, we will use a generalized discussion of the United States to illustrate some
of the principles involved. Many of these will be almost standard, however, some
will be even more stringent in other localities.

Federal law establishes certain requirements in the areas of air and water quality
which generally result in state or regional regulatory programs. The Clean Air Act
mandates a "prevention of significant deterioration" (PSD) air-quality analysis for
projects exceeding certain thresholds, requires emission controls for all projects, and
establishes air quality standards. The Environmental Protection Agency (EPA) oversees state and regional implementation. The Clean Water Act mandates a National
Pollution Discharge Elimination System (NPDES) permit that sets criteria on the
quality of water discharged. The Army Corps of Engineers administers a "404
Permit" regulating uses that impact U.S. waters. The Fish and Wildlife Services
protect endangered plants and animals.

The EPA has been provided with many new, powerful laws which pervade all aspects of most projects. Chief among these are the Safe Drinking Water Act; the Resource, Conservation and Recovery Act (RCRA); the Comprehensive Environmental
Response, Compensation and Liability Act (CERCLA); and Superfund Amendments and
Reauthorization Act (SARA). The impact of EPA and its various mandates and regulations can be measured by Part 40 of the Code of Federal Regulations (CFR) which
documents the EPA Regulations. In the first year after EPA was established, there
were fewer than 700 pages in 40 CFR which now has grown to almost 9,000 pages.
Another measure of the explosion of regulations is that the average project is controlled by over two dozen federal codes.

Federal mandates are often administered and supplemented by additional state
regulation. In addition to air and water, state regulation often covers areas such as
fish and game, cultural resources, impacts on state highways, and the like.

Often the broadest jurisdiction is reserved for local government. In many states,
local government has the authority to regulate "land use" which the courts have interpreted to include practically every aspect of a project. Local discretion usually allows
outright denial of a project without any more justification than that the use is "not
suitable."

Federal law and most state laws require some form of "environmental review." The
National Environmental Policy Act (NEPA) requires preparation of an Environmental
Assessment (EA) or an Environmental Impact Statement (EIS) prior to consideration
of permit applications. State laws are usually similar. As the first official step in
most permitting efforts, completion and approval of the appropriate environmental
document sets the stage for the subsequent project permitting. Intervention by private citizens and groups, called intervenors, frequently occurs at this juncture in the
process. At this stage, the project manager should be able to judge likely success
and the time frame for the permitting process based on the feedback from the environmental review and the resistance shown by the intervenors.

Construction permits, including local demolition, grading, building, and electrical, should be routine. Local interpretation of the various codes can greatly impact project costs. Large projects in small jurisdictions can overwhelm the local capacity to review and approve drawings.

An example of the permitting for a major project in a complex jurisdictional setting is Homestake Mining Company's "McLaughlin Gold Mine" located in northern California, a hub of current environmental activism.

THE MCLAUGHLIN GOLD MINE

Obtaining the necessary permits for development of the McLaughlin Gold Mine was very complex because of the geographic location of the project and the fast track schedule. To meet the schedule demands, a proactive approach was used by the permitting team, and a number of innovative techniques were developed to assure timely execution of this task. Coordination between the permitting team, the engineering design group, the field construction staff, and agency personnel was accomplished using a modified critical path schedule approach. This resulted in the completion of a state-of-the-art gold mining and processing facility well ahead of schedule, despite the requirement for more than 300 environmental and construction permits.

Objectives

The permitting team's objective was to keep ahead of the engineering and construction efforts in obtaining all necessary environmental and construction permits for this project, the largest gold mine and processing complex to be built in California in modern times. Although gold mining has played an important role in California's development, it is now considered mainly to be of historical and recreational interest. There have been a few recent reworkings of the motherlode gold mines. In 1976, Homestake's exploration geologists, using new technology, discovered the largest gold mine of the twentieth century in California near the juncture of Lake, Napa, and Yolo counties. This discovery was at the Manhattan Mine, a part of the historic Knoxville mining district where mercury has been extracted since the 1850s.

Description of the Site

The ore body is located at the northern tip of Napa County, home of the Napa Valley vineyards (see Fig. 1). It is some 70 air miles north of San Francisco, the center of a strong environmental movement. The ore body is transected by the boundary between Napa and Yolo Counties. Geotechnical studies examined 37 candidate sites before the tailings pond was sited in Lake County, about five miles to the northwest of the ore body. The waste rock dump, located after the same geotechnical studies, is partially on lands under the jurisdiction of the Bureau of Land Management (BLM). The project involves lands in three different air-quality districts, two state fish and game regions, and is subject to the jurisdiction of a variety of state special purpose agencies. This combination of multiple county, state, and federal authorities complicated the permitting process. None of the agencies had experience in permitting large modern gold-mining facilities. Fortunately, the BLM staff had overseen the permitting of large mines in other areas of the country.

The ore body is located in a remote area, 18 miles from the nearest state highway. Prior to the mine development, it was served by unimproved or poorly paved county roads. The nearest utility services were also about 18 miles away. Groundwater is of

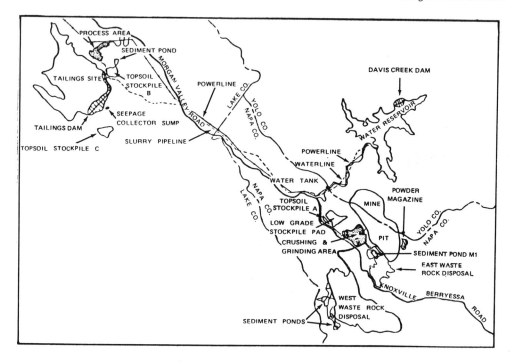

Figure 1   Northern California site of the McLaughlin Gold Mine.

poor quality and in very limited supply. The surface streams are dry for half the
year. In addition to constructing the mining complex, substantial infrastructure development was required.

Techniques Used

To accomplish the overall permitting objectives, the team adopted a proactive approach.
This called for early identification of all parties involved in the process and anticipation of all concerns and needs of these parties. Interested parties included regulatory agencies, project neighbors, environmental groups, and potential intervenors,
as well as contractors, vendors, and other direct beneficiaries of the project.

The needs of the agencies are outlined in the statutes and the administrative
rules and regulations. Individual tailoring was required for information submittals
involving special technical studies to meet specific or area concerns. Some individual
citizens were fearful of change and suspect of large corporations. Their fears were
reinforced by the abandoned mining facilities left behind from activities which predate
today's environmental legislation.

The goal of the proactive approach was to provide the materials required to fulfill
the permitting requirements and to allay the concerns and fears of agency personnel

and involved citizens. This was to be done, insofar as possible, in advance by anticipating all questions. Design studies were prepared for issues expected to be raised
such as water quality from waste rock and tailings. Being prepared for such questions creates a confident and positive project image, rather than one which is reactive
and defensive.

Regulatory staff were invited to review and provide comments on siting and design
study work programs while the scope of work was still flexible and change was possible
without serious cost impact. Similarly, regulators and potential intervenors were consulted about project siting and design during the conceptual phase when suggestions
could be incorporated into the project reasonably.

The Permitting Team

The team was composed of full- or part-time members from the Homestake Mining Company's (HMC's) McLaughlin Gold Project and the corporate headquarters in San Francisco as well as from the Environmental Services Group of Davy McKee Corporation
(DMC), the firm responsible for engineering, procurement, and construction of the
project.

A decision was made that personnel working at the mine and living in that community would make all public statements and provide testimony, if at all possible.

Part-time team members also included attorneys, engineers, and technical
specialists who brought specific expertise to the project. These specialists rendered
valuable technical support to the primary team members who would assume key roles
on the McLaughlin operating staff after project completion.

One of the team's early tasks was to conduct comprehensive environmental baseline studies. This work was coordinated by D'Appolonia Consulting Engineers. Teams
of scientists examined over 10,000 acres which could have been used for some aspect
of the mining proejct. The findings were published in a three-volume publication "Environmental Report, McLaughlin Gold Project." A fourth companion volume "Project
Description/Environmental Assessment (PD/EA)" was prepared when sufficient engineering information had become available. These four volumes served as the basic
source of information provided to each of the various agencies involved in permitting
the project, as well as to other interested individuals and organizations.

Immediately following the public announcement of the McLaughlin discovery, the
permitting team initiated a series of meetings with various agency, community, and
service groups. Most of these meetings were supported with slides showing current
and future activities at the mine. These meetings served to keep the community informed about the progress of the project and provided individuals with the opportunity
to obtain direct answers to their questions. Misinformation regarding the project was
clarified during these sessions.

Preparation of permit applications began with early consultation between the permit team members and representatives of the regulatory agencies. This allowed for
some standardization of requirements. Of particular concern were the current workloads and the turnaround times during the reviews, hearings, and appeals. Regulatory staff were invited to tour the project site. Those lacking mining experience were
offered orientation trips to similar installations in Nevada. This early consultation
was essential in maintaining tight schedules during the formal permitting process.

DMC's Environmental Services Group was assigned responsibility for preparing
the permit application documents. This group was supported by the legal and technical consultants assigned to the permitting team. All of the nondiscretionary (e.g.,
building permits, grading permits, etc.) construction permits, and permit modifications were the responsibility of the DMC group. As these permit applications were
developed, they were issued to HMC for technical and legal review prior to submission

to the appropriate agency. The discretionary permits usually required the signature of an officer of HMC, whereas most of the balance of the permits were signed by DMC as agent for HMC.

Scheduling of a comprehensive list of all required permits was accomplished with a modified critical path method (CPM). The schedule contained the necessary information required for the preparation of each permit application. This allowed permitting to become fully interrelated with the engineering design and construction phases of the project, assuring that pertinent information became available to the permitting team on a timely basis and removed the possibility of constraints on the engineering and construction schedules. The CPM network became lengthy and complex because of the large number and diversity of permits required. The schedule was monitored closely, updated monthly, and modified on a timely basis to insure that it did not become cumbersome and unworkable. Approved permits were placed in a separate format allowing the CPM network to deal only with the permit applications under preparation or review.

A number of meetings were held during the early phases of the project to communicate with individuals and agencies who had similar authority and jurisdiction. Meetings were established for the counsels, the planning departments, building inspection departments, and the public works departments of the three counties. These representatives were guided through the entire extraction process as it was being engineered and were introduced to the scheduling procedures as well as to the details of the permit applications. The chief purpose of these meetings was to acquaint the individuals with the complexity of the project and the project schedule. Feedback from these sessions allowed the permitting team to anticipate permit processing time and to schedule submittals accordingly. Prior to the submittal of permit applications, regulators were familiar with the process and the different types of materials that they would receive. Schedules for the submission of the various drawings and specifications were developed and provided to each agency.

A number of exhibits were prepared. In some cases these exhibits were excerpts from the environmental report and the PD/EA. Enlarged color drawings showed the overall site plan, mining plan, crushing and grinding area, process area, soils, geology, vegetation, areas prone to landslides and wildlife habitats. Perspective drawings were made showing both before and after views of the more important structures such as the mine, reservoir, waste rock disposal area, process facilities, and the tailings dam and reservoir.

It became apparent immediately that a large number of people living in the immediate proximity of the project site could not look at a blueprint and visualize what the completed plant would look like. Visual aids, graphic presentations, and other innovative communication techniques were used to convey this information to those persons lacking a technical background. A particularly effective exhibit was a butt mosaic using color aerial photos of the area with superimposed overlays showing the locations of the various project components. Later, a three-dimensional topographic scale model of the project area was prepared. This exhibit proved to be most effective in showing the location of the various project facilities. Inserts showed the mine, tailings, and process areas after reclamation. The model was useful in describing project facilities and their locations to public officials, agency representatives, and to those persons residing adjacent to the site. Physical models to scale of almost all of the project facilities were built for engineering, construction, training, maintenance, and future planning. Several of these models were also used at public exhibitions in combination with other graphic and photographic materials. Video tapes, showing major construction activities, were also run at these exhibits.

A monthly newsletter, *McLaughlin Gold Project Report*, was published. The four-page tabloid reported progress, highlighted various aspects of the project, featured the people involved, and made liberal use of the figures and photographs to convey accurate information. This report was distributed to public officials, agency representatives, interested citizens, employees, construction workers, and the general public.

Environmental Impact Report/Environmental Impact Statement

Early in the development of the project, HMC worked with representatives of the three counties and the BLM to develop a single Environmental Impact Report/Environmental Impact Statement (EIR/EIS) which would be acceptable to each agency. A committee, the Environmental Data Advisory Committee (EDAC) was established with membership from each of the three counties and the BLM.

Napa County was selected by EDAC to act as the lead agency for the preparation of the EIR/EIS. Lake and Yolo Counties were established as responsible agencies under the California Environmental Quality Act (CEQA). The BLM served as the lead agency under the National Environmental Protection Act (NEPA) to assure that the document also met federal requirements. These procedures were formalized in a Memorandum of Understanding, signed by HMC, the three counties, and the BLM.

EDAC initially met to review the environmental baseline data included in the environmental report and to determine its adequacy as the basis for the EIR/EIS. The PD/EA, submitted to each of the various jurisdictions, was then used by Napa County and the BLM in the preparation of the joint EIR/EIS as provided by the Memorandum of Understanding. A third-party consultant was selected by EDAC to prepare the EIR/EIS. HMC was required to fund the contract and Napa County administered the contract and supervised the work. A total of 25 public hearings, workshops, and EDAC meetings were held in various locations in the three counties to accept agency and public comments on the draft document. The draft EIR/EIS was then reissued as a proposed final document. The final issue was certified by the lead agencies on July 6, 1983, nine months after the lead agency permit applications were submitted and the process begun.

The EIR/EIS contained 195 mitigations of which 72 were volunteered in the PD/EA by HMC. These mitigation measures covered areas such as environmental monitoring, seismicity, erosion control, hydrology, surface water quality, ground water quality, aquatic wildlife, terrestrial wildlife, vegetation, climate, air quality, noise, vibration, transportation and circulation, visual resources, land use, socioeconomics, cultural resources, public health, safety, energy, and reclamation/revegetation.

The EDAC members agreed to allow the individual counties to accept and approve permit applications associated with early construction activities once the EIR/EIS was certified. These early construction activities were beyond the requirements of the major county, federal, and state permit applications, which were then being processed.

Lake, Napa, and Yolo County Permits

The Lake County Department of Public Works issued a temporary encroachment permit which provided for repair of winter damage and smoothing out curves on the Morgan Valley Road. This permit was significant because it made moving the heavy construction equipment to the site possible. On September 2, 1983, Lake and Napa Counties issued grading and encroachment permits to allow for the improvement and realignment of approximately 18 miles of county roads. Later the Yolo County Public Works and Transportation Department issued a permit to construct three miles of the Rayhouse Road.

Other early permits allowed for the construction of internal roads, picnic area, construction staging areas, aggregate crushing facilities, concrete batch plants, top soil stockpiles, sediment ponds and dams, electric transmission lines, and a park and ride facility for construction workers.

The use permits in each of the three counties included approval under the State Surface Mining and Reclamation Act (SMARA), of reclamation plans, as well as various rezonings and the cancellation of a Williamson Act agreement in one of the counties. Lake County permitting included approval of ten individual "Specific Plans of Development" covering the areas of noise mitigation, socioeconomics, traffic management, erosion and sediment control, emergency response, fire management, solid waste disposal,

spill contingency and hazardous waste plans, local hiring and training, and environmental monitoring. During construction, the permitting team processed nine minor
modifications to the Lake County use permits. In Napa County, eight modifications
to the use permit were approved while only four were required in Yolo County.

"Authorities to Construct" and "Permits to Operate" were required from each of
the three air-quality districts with authority to regulate air-quality impact of the mine
and processing facilities. The permit for the truck shop and for the crushing and
grinding facilities involved eight emission points (sources) while the mine had a number of nonpoint emission sources. There were 23 air-emission points in the process
area. In addition, 23 air-quality permits were obtained for construction facilities such
as concrete batch, asphalt batch, and aggregate crushing plants.

A total of 38 individual building permits were required among the three counties.
The two required in Yolo County were administered by Napa County as a matter of
convenience. The facilities in Napa County required 32 individual permits; but the
more complex facilities in Lake County were all covered by one permit. Three additional building permits were required by Lake County for facilities added at the end
of construction and not covered by the original plans. This demonstrates certain differences in operating philosophy between two county agencies charged with enforcing
the same uniform building code.

The Environmental Health Departments of Lake and Napa Counties issued permits
for a total of four potable water systems and five sanitary and industrial waste ponds.

Federal and State Permits

Critical path scheduling indicated that the first permit applications necessary for the
project were for water appropriations in two streams serving the project area. When
the various facilities of the mine complex were all finally located, two additional water
appropriations were filed along with a temporary water appropriation used during construction.

The BLM approved the project in two stages. The first stage authorized early
construction activities; the second stage approved the entire operation. Modifications
to the Plan of Operation allowing for construction changes resulted from a redesign
of the waste rock sediment control facilities and the addition of a continuous water-
quality-monitoring station downstream of the project activities. Four right-of-way
grants, two for roads, one for a transmission line, and one for water wells, were required. Three modifications to these grants accommodated design changes.

The Central Valley Regional Water Quality Control Board issued the National Pol-
lutant Discharge Elimination System (NPDES) and Waste Discharge permits. The latter
included approval of a solid waste disposal area. These permits were issued in two
stages: the first allowed for early construction activities, and the second for operation of the mine.

The California State Division of Safety of Dams (DSOD) held jurisdiction for three
structures at the project: the tailings dam, the Davis Creek Reservoir dam, and the
M-1 Sediment dam. An additional nine sediment dams and various check dams constructed for the project were not subject to DSOD's jurisdiction. The DSOD approvals
were granted in stages throughout construction based upon field inspection and test
data. Each construction phase was requested and authorized in writing upon completion
of the previous phase. The end result was a very site-specific approach to insure
the safety of the dams being constructed in a seismically active area. This approach
resulted in a substantial commitment of time from the field engineers and an ongoing
uncertainty regarding final cost of the structures.

Encroachment permits were given by the California Department of Transportation
(CALTRANS) for improvements to Route 53, in the vicinity of the park and ride facility. Required improvements included widening of Kugelman Road and Route 53 and
installation of a temporary traffic signal at that intersection. Approval of this permit
was supported by the California Highway Patrol and several Lake County agencies as

it tended to facilitate the traffic generated by construction workers entering and leaving the park and ride lot during the three shift changes each day.

Regulation of the tailings disposal facility by the state Department of Health Services depended upon a determination of the "hazardousness" of the waste based on an extraction test and a fish bioassay. Analysis of the pilot plant-produced tailings indicated that the McLaughlin tailings would not be hazardous. The Department agreed that a Health Services permit would not be required, subject to further testing of the tailings during operations. Subsequent tests of the tailings confirmed that McLaughlin tailings were nonhazardous. Members of the technical staff of the Department were invited to review the siting studies and site investigations and to provide input to the dam design and monitoring plans.

The 73 stream alteration permits obtained from the California Department of Fish and Game represented the greatest number of permits issued by a single agency. This was because of the large area covered by the project: 21 miles of county roads reconstructed, many miles of private access roads, transmission lines, slurry pipelines, and 12 dams. In all, there were 327 permits obtained for the McLaughlin mine as shown by Table 1.

The conceptual design study for the McLaughlin Gold Mine recommended locating the process facility in a meadow in the Morgan Valley, four and one-half miles from the ore body, with the tailings pond located one-half mile further north in a valley over one more ridge. A study was conducted which evaluated engineering design, economics, and environmental impact of alternative sites for the processing plant. The meadow, bisected by Hunting Creek, maintained a shallow water table which would have increased the cost of foundations for the process facility and required more berming to assure that accidental spills would not reach Hunting Creek. The pumping-under-pressure of the tailings slurry containing cyanide was an environmental concern. This study resulted in the selection of a new process site on top of a hill, adjacent to the tailings pond. Tailings could now be piped downhill to the tailings pond and not into area streams. The grading of this hilltop to accommodate the process facilities provided material usable in the construction of the tailings pond dam.

The serpentine soils in the area support 26 species of threatened plants that were identified during the baseline studies. These plant populations faced a high potential for destruction during the construction of the facilities. Early in the engineering design phase, meetings were arranged between the botanist who conducted plant studies and the design engineers involved in planning routes for the project facilities. Working together, these two groups established priorities, and the 26 threatened plants were ranked according to their rarity. These early meetings allowed adjustments to the location of roadways, pipelines, transmission lines and facilities to be made to avoid endangering as many threatened plants as possible. Where this was impossible the plants were preserved preferentially based upon the earlier ranking of rarity. This early cooperation helped to minimize the cost of engineering changes. The initial findings were confirmed in the field; and plant populations located close to construction were flagged or fenced to assure no inadvertent disturbances. These efforts reduced disturbance of threatened plants to the minimum.

Members of the California Native Plant Society and graduate students from the University of California at Davis were enlisted in a program to transplant or propagate many of the threatened plants in test plots in the project area. On several occasions construction equipment was made available to aid in the transplanting of these plants from the construction areas to the test plots.

When the EIR/EIS was certified on July 6, 1983 by Napa County as the lead state agency and the BLM as the lead federal agency, it contained some 195 potential mitigations. A total of 72 of these mitigations had been proposed by HMC in the PD/EA. By proposing our own mitigation measures, the requirements were ultimately more cost effective and thus more acceptable to HMC than they might otherwise have been.

During the baseline studies, a variety of historic and prehistoric archaeological sites were located by a team from the Anthropological Studies Center of Sonoma State

Table 1 Permits Obtained

Permit type	Number
County	
Air/Construct/Operate	29
USE/SMARA and Modifications	31
USE/Construction	1
Variance	2
Specific Plan of Development	2
Williamson Act Cancellation	2
Potable Water	4
Underground Hazardous Tanks	5
Helicopter Pad	1
Road Encroachment	5
Explosives	2
Building	38
Plumbing	3
Electrical	15
Mechanical	9
Grading and Dams	6
Water Wells	4
Sewage	5
Burning	9
Road Construction Approval	5
Road Acceptance	5
Environmental Impact Report	1
Subtotal	184
Federal and State	
Forestry	4
NPDES	2
Waste Discharge	2
Stream Alteration	73
Solid Waste	1
Dam Construction	3
Road Encroachment	2
Road Approval	2
Helicopter Pad	1
Pressure Vessels	11
State Architect	1
State Lands Commission	1
Burning	5
Corps of Engineers "404"	1
Water Appropriation	5
Hazardous Waste Variance	1
Plan of Operation and Modifications	3
Right of Way and Modifications	7
Explosives	2
Underground Hazardous Tanks	11
Radio	1
Environmental Impact Study	1
Road Construction Approval	3
Subtotal	143
Total	327

University. Those sites which could not be avoided during construction were immediately studied further in detail. The information contained at those sites was carefully documented; and the sites were then released for construction. Sites not subject to direct disturbance but adjacent to construction areas required protection. The location of these sites is classified information to protect them from vandalism. The security of this information had to be maintained during construction; yet it had to be made available to the engineers and constructors so that they could maintain the integrity of the sites. A drawing was prepared for superimposition upon the general facilities plan locating these archaeologically interesting sites. These areas were referred to as "Restricted Environmental Areas" or REAs." This REA designation was given to all of the archaeological, historical, and threatened plant sites, providing a tool which could be used by the engineers and contractors to avoid these areas, and yet maintain the security required by the archaeologists. REA sites that were in close proximity to the construction activities were fenced for further security. This work was coordinated by one of the archaeology team members, who was assigned to the site during the height of construction.

An important milestone for the permitting team was the agreement reached with EDAC that the jurisdictions could approve various early construction activities, including the production of aggregate from the overburden of the ore body. This provided a source of base, subbase, drain rock, and sand needed for the construction of the county roads and various project facilities. The construction of county roads, construction camps, park and ride facilities, a transmission line corridor, and site grading was allowed to proceed in advance of the issuance of the final permits. These early activities allowed more economical and feasible use of construction personnel and equipment and greatly improved adherence to the fast track schedule.

More than 1500 engineering drawings required approval by various agencies, most by the Lake County or Napa County Building Inspection Departments. Coordination with these agencies began early in the design engineering phase. Many meetings were held with building department personnel to prepare a timely schedule of their review and approval of the drawings. To improve this coordination, the chief mechanical design engineer visited the Lake and Napa County Building Inspection Departments weekly during the peak of this review process to provide timely and efficient transfer of information to the agencies to help expedite their approvals.

Although project impacts in Yolo County were limited to the construction of a fresh water reservoir and the county population is remote from the project area, a small core of dedicated project opponents developed in the Capay Valley, which is located about 10 miles east of the mine. HMC felt that it was important to actively solicit support for the project from other residents of Yolo County. To improve the dissemination of project information to interested citizens in the county, an office was opened in Woodland, the county seat. The facility was staffed by HMC employees and copies of the permitting documents and the various exhibit materials were displayed for public review. These efforts contributed to a better understanding of the project by the citizens of Yolo County and to the formation of a group of active project proponents who were visible during the permit public hearings.

As the permit hearings continued it became clear that the technical basis for the project was sound; and that opposition to the approval of the permits was limited to a very small number of people who were philosophically opposed to all mining.

The focus of the hearings was gradually reduced to the adequacy of the proposals for HMC's monitoring plan and a further review of monitoring issues specific to Yolo County. Workshops were held to provide a more detailed presentation of technical issues by individual experts and HMC personnel. The workshop format provided more time for response to questions from elected, appointed, and staff personnel and interested citizens. After various technical issues in these workshops were resolved, the normal hearing process continued.

One byproduct of multiagency jurisdiction was that different seed mixture requirements were recommended by various agencies in the individual permitting process for revegetation and reclamation. To resolve this regulatory quandary, a meeting of representatives from all of the involved agencies was arranged to reach an agreement on a single seed mixture. The result was a great simplification of the bidding, supervision, and implementation of the revegation subcontracts.

Many of the mitigations required by the various agencies and included in the EIR/EIS related to sediment and erosion control. Both temporary and permanent sediment control structures were placed during construction. Additional structures were placed along the Morgan Valley Road for 14 miles west of the project area. Ultimately about 100 temporary and permanent structures were located throughout the project area, and maintained over the entire course of construction while the revegetation and permanent construction were completed. During construction, an annual report on sediment and erosion control was prepared and issued to the various agencies. The California Department of Fish and Game stated that the streams were actually cleaner during the construction phases than they were before construction began.

The concrete batch plants used during construction were computer controlled and equipped with baghouses to control dust emissions during loading and batching. Despite these controls, particles of unwetted cement were being expelled from the concrete mixing truck drums during batching. A sheet-rubber bonnet designed to surround the batching port along with a fan and baghouse cured the problem. The solution required the cooperation of the owner, engineer, subcontractor, and the various air-quality agencies.

A series of wells were drilled to dewater the eventual mine pit. This ground water, though of poor quality, was used for compaction and dust control during construction. However, water that had accumulated behind two early sediment dams was unavailable for dust control until the project water appropriations were approved. This situation required approval of a temporary water appropriation.

A full-time traffic director was employed to work with the various trucking companies who obtained in excess of 700 wide or heavy-load permits issued by CALTRAN. The most complicated of these were the series of permits required to transport three 400,000-pound, 60-foot-long autoclaves. The autoclaves arrived from West Germany, where they had been fabricated, in the port of Oakland and were offloaded and moved by barge to the port of Sacramento. Custom-built trailers were used to haul them overland to the process site. The permits authorizing movement of these loads were obtained by the subcontractor; they were very restrictive, limiting travel to the daylight hours on Mondays through Thursdays. Delivery of the first autoclaves took much longer than expected. After meetings with CALTRANS and the California Highway Patrol, authorization was given for travel seven days a week, 24 hours a day. This helped to maintain the tight construction schedule.

CONCLUSIONS

Permitting of a major gold mine in an area known for its environmental concern, with complex jurisdictional problems, and following a fast track schedule required a proactive approach with modified CPM scheduling. This approach resulted in fast and efficient permit approvals without the delays and pitfalls often encountered when a permitting team finds itself in a defensive posture. Public opposition to the mine, though potentially large, never coalesced. This is seen as being primarily the result of the early availability of technically sound answers to the questions raised. Ultimately those few who publically opposed the project were perceived by their community as being extreme in their views.

The proactive approach is also not without pitfalls. Comprehensive studies of a multitude of issues can increase permitting costs. In some cases, studies were undertaken that were never used. There also may be a feeling that a proactive approach may sometimes result in well educated, well organized, and vocal project opponents.

On balance, the McLaughlin Mine permitting team was satisfied that the proactive approach was essential to the successful and timely completion of the project.

6

Financing the Project

WILLIAM J. GREMP *Merrill Lynch Capital Markets, Investment Banking Division, New York, New York*

EDWARD J. HIGGINS *Merrill Lynch Capital Markets, New York, New York*

INTRODUCTION

The spiraling cost of conventional long-term debt and equity has made the financing of new construction increasingly difficult. Deferring this financing runs the risk of encountering inflated costs in the future. While the rate of inflation has slowed, long-term interest rates remain relatively high and stock prices are quite volatile. It is essential that corporations maximize returns on their producing assets and minimize the amount of capital placed at risk on construction of such assets. Project financing techniques enable a corporation to achieve these objectives.

CHARACTERISTICS OF PROJECT FINANCING

Project financing allows a corporation to reduce its construction and operating risks and to lower its cost of obtaining capital by allocating the costs and benefits of owning and operating a facility among other participants, customers, suppliers, governmental entities, and outside debt and equity investors.

Project financing substitutes the acquired asset and the expected revenues derived from its use for a permanent commitment of the participant's credit. Each participant will normally commit its credit in varying ways to the success of the project, sometimes only for a limited period or on a contingent basis. Some project financing requires direct commitment on the part of a financially viable subsidiary to avoid indenture limitations on parent company.

BENEFITS

Project financing techniques offer the following benefits to the participants.

The corporation's credit standing is preserved because of a reduced capitalization impact resulting from the limited or more contingent nature of any direct credit commitment.

There is maximum leverage on the corporation's direct equity investment.

Tax benefits may be distributed optimally among the participants and investors.

Risks and rewards of developing and financing the project preserve the participant's ability to engage in future projects or to undertake projects too large or complex to handle alone.

The way is open to reassign the participants' ownership interest during the design, construction, and later, the operating phases.

Access is open to a very broad range of retail and institutional investors, commercial banks, and governmental sources of funds through the variety of available financing techniques.

OPPORTUNITIES

Project financing opportunities designed to appeal to the capital-intensive industries, as well as to newcomers faced with capital expansion requirements, are listed in Table 1.

STRUCTURING THE PROJECT FINANCING

Effective structuring is the most important part of successful project financing. The objectives of the financing, the overall cost of funds to finance the project, and the marketability of the financing components will be determined by the creativity and judgment exercised during the structuring process. Several principal considerations to be addressed in this process are summarized below.

Selecting a Financial Advisor

Potential project participants should use care in seeking experienced and professional financial counsel. Investment banking firms are a good starting source, having direct access to and knowledge of, the investment preferences of all segments of the public and private capital markets, including commercial banks.

Evaluating Feasibility

Potential participants, in close cooperation with their financial advisor, should evaluate the feasibility of the project financing from the following perspectives:

What are each participant's business reasons for participating?
What share of ownership does each participant wish to retain?
What level of risk is each participant to accept?
Are the anticipated cash flow and tax benefits of the project sufficient to justify each participant's investment?
Will the project's anticipated cash flow, tax benefits, and indirect credit support mechanisms be sufficient to attract capital from outside debt and equity investors?

Careful analysis from these perspectives will clearly define the financing objectives of the potential participants and accurately assess the credit support they are willing to provide the project.

Determining the Participants

A project's financial feasibility depends on the credit strength, expertise, and the roles of the potential participants as well as the economics of the project itself. In some cases, for example, the attractiveness of a project to outside investors will be substantially enhanced if one or more financially strong participants has a particular need for the project's output. In other cases, participants will contribute the requisite resource(s) needed to generate the output. In still other cases, participants will

Table 1 Project Financing Opportunities by Industry and Type of Project

Industry	Types of projects
Electric utility facilities	Cogeneration facilities Coal conversions of generating facilities Hydroelectric facilities
Natural resources	Cogeneration facilities Pipelines (oil, gas, and coal slurry) Fuel storage facilities Refinery facilities Port facilities Synthetic fuels Development and production equipment Sale and acquisition of exploration and production facilities Mining facilities
Raw material and manufacturing	Cogeneration facilities Steel facilities Alumina and aluminum facilities Chemical facilities Miscellaneous metal facilities Automobile, truck, and heavy machinery manufacturing facilities
Alternative energy	Windpower generating facilities Solar concentrator facilities Photovoltaic generating systems District heating and cooling facilities
Environmental	Solid waste/resource recovery Sewage and industrial waste treatment facilities Water supply and treatment facilities
Transportation	Aircraft Railroad cars and equipment Mass transportation facilities
High technology	Telecommunications equipment Satellite transmission equipment Computer equipment
Governmental	Infrastructure financing

contribute special expertise gained from development of the technology employed in the project or general experience gained from participation in similar ventures.

Assuming that creditworthy entities have expressed a strong interest in participating in the project's development, the financial advisor should thoroughly analyze each potential participant's objectives, contributions, and qualifications. To assure the feasibility of the project financing, the financial advisor's analysis must conclude that, for each participant, a joint approach will provide a more efficient and lower overall cost of financing the project and marketing its output than would result from using alternative financing mechanisms. A joint approach will often be appropriate for projects that involve the development of a captive supply of a particular resource and the securing of a guaranteed market for the project's output, the construction of a substantially larger and more efficient facility, or the implementation of a new technological process.

Once the participants have been selected, a financing plan should be developed, properly allocate the risks and rewards of the project among the participants, customers, suppliers, government entities, and outside debt and equity investors.

Developing the Financing Plan

To maximize the nonrecourse character of the transaction, the financing plan should be based on the nature of the asset being financed and the attendant cash flow from that asset. Obviously, the plan must provide sufficient credit support necessary to successfully sell the component parts of the financing. Generally, accurate assessment of the requisite credit support requires designing a financial model that enables the financial advisor to test the economic sensitivity of the proposed plan to a wide range of variables. In addition, the plan should optimally balance the advantages of full project ownership and control by the participant against the economic advantages available from selling a substantial percentage of the ownership interests and accompanying tax benefits to interested third parties and outside investors. The plan should also incorporate a provision for additional financing that may result from unexpected delays, a major scale-up in project size, or operating problems. Selected prospective lenders should be contacted to ensure the acceptability of unique features in the financing plan. Finally, even if they are not going to be asked to rate the project financing, the rating agencies should be contacted to assess the impact of the financing on each participant's existing ratings.

Setting Objectives

The financing plan should endeavor to achieve, for each participant, as many of the following objectives as possible by properly allocating the risks and rewards of the project:

1. Preservation of participant's credit standing. Project secured financings generally do not constitute direct liabilities on a participant's balance sheet. As a result, the participant may be able to avoid indenture restrictions on issuing additional debt as well as minimize dilution of its capitalization ratios. Since the transaction is structured to allocate risks among participants, interested third parties, and outside investors in a way that limits the impact on each participant's balance sheet, the future financial flexibility of the participant is preserved. For example, an agreement to complete construction of a project and then maintain it in good working order, as opposed to a full guarantee of the loans incurred to finance the project, enables the participant to employ its credit over time in a large number of projects rather than just one.

2. Maximum leverage. In a typical project financing, 65% to 75% of the project's total capital needs can be obtained through borrowings secured by the physical assets being financed and the anticipated revenues and tax benefits arising from the construction and operation of such assets, as well as by limited commitments from the participants and from interested third parties. The credit strength of the participants as well as industry precedents should be studied to determine the degree of leverage the project can support and the corresponding returns on the participants' and investors' investments.

3. Optimization of tax benefits. Generally, there are significant tax benefits, such as the investment tax credit, the energy tax credit, the research and development credit, and ACRS depreciation deductions, arising from the construction and operating of a project. A properly structured project financing can employ a variety of structures, including leasing, limited partnerships, and joint venture agreements, to allocate efficiently the tax benefits to the parties with the strongest need or desire for them. For example, the participants may achieve substantial cost savings by selling a significant ownership

interest in the project, including the associated tax benefits, to interested
third parties and outside investors.

4. Ownership flexibility. During the long lead time of the planning and development of financing a project, a participant's estimate of its need for the resource produced by the project may change. A properly constructed project
financing can enable a participant to shift its ownership interests during the
planning, construction, and even operating phases with a flexibility that
might not be possible if it had financed the facility directly.

5. Access to new sources of capital. The variety of available project financing
techniques enables participants to access the broadest possible range of retail
and institutional investors, commercial banks, and governmental funding
sources. For example, project financings have successfully accessed the
public and private taxable and tax-exempt debt and equity markets, have
utilized leveraged leasing and limited partnerships and other tax-oriented
financing vehicles, and have taken full advantage of a variety of governmental
loan guarantee and grant programs. Project financing structures also often
offer a blended credit stronger than that of most of the individual participants.
The combination of a stronger credit and the opportunity to receive significant
tax benefits generates investment interest among a wider range of retail and
institutional investors than those who would purchase a conventional offering.
The blended credit created by a project financing structure may also allow
the participants to avail themselves of a higher level of commercial bank financing, since the commercial bank can treat the project loan as a loan to
the joint venture, not to the participant, thereby avoiding legal lending limits
applicable to loans to a single participant.

Creating the Legal Entity

The participants and the financial advisor must decide whether the legal form of the
venture undertaking the project financing should be an existing or a new entity. Selecting the most appropriate form of entity requires an analysis of all relevant tax,
legal, and financing considerations. The alternative which maximizes all of the anticipated benefits will be the most appropriate form of the entity: partnership, corporation, trust, joint venture, or some combination thereof. In some circumstances, separate and distinct owning entities may be created for the construction and operating
periods. Careful consideration should also be given to whether the facility should
be owned or leased. If leasing is the preferred method, a comparison should be made
between the benefits of a leveraged lease versus a single investor base. In all cases,
the financing plan should ensure that the selected entity produces the strongest possible credit, perhaps stronger than any of the participants individually, so as to maximize the likelihood of accomplishing the financing at the lowest overall cost of capital.

Evaluating the Credit Support Mechanism

Investors must be convinced that the anticipated project revenues will be sufficient
to cover operation and maintenance costs, pay debt service, and produce a satisfactory rate of return on any equity investment. Often, however, investors, particularly
debt investors, both retail and institutional, also will look for further assurance of
payment from a participant or third party. In addition, a project financing often must
meet applicable state law tests of "adequate security" in order for certain institutional
investors, such as insurance companies, to be allowed to invest in the project.

A wide range of participant, customer, and interested third-party credit supports
may be acceptable to institutional and retail investors and should be carefully analyzed
to determine those which satisfy investor needs yet minimize credit commitment by
project participants. For example, while many project financings have difficulty meeting one major test of adequate security—an interest coverage test—they often meet

another—a contractual arrangement for the purchase of the project's output by a satisfactorily strong entity. Participants can make initial equity investments on a subordinated basis, and agree to provide additional funds should cost overruns occur during
construction or should project revenues during the operating phase prove insufficient
to meet applicable working capital or net worth maintenance tests. Participants can
also fully or partially guarantee debt service during certain phases of the project as
well as pledge additional security tax benefits which are associated with ownership
of the project. Customers may be asked to sign agreements relating to the purchase
of the project's minimum payment, tolling, or throughput and deficiency contracts.
Specialized shipping projects may include lease/character/hire agreements. Natural
resource projects may incorporate advance payments, production payments, and royalty
assignments. Interested third parties such as suppliers and contractors may provide
credit facilities or performance bonds or guarantees. Governments and government
agencies can provide government guarantees, export credits, and political risk insurance. Participants or other parties can also obtain irrevocable letters of credit from
commercial banks or policies from insurance companies to further secure their obligations.

Allocating Risks

A properly structured financing plan will allocate risks among participants, investors,
customers, and interested third parties. Of course, as investors assume more risks,
the cost of any borrowing and the required rate of return on any equity investment
increases proportionally. Similarly, the potential maximum price paid for the project's
output generally declines as customers and governmental entitites enter into long-
term contracts for purchase of the output and provide other indirect credit supports.
Some of the approaches frequently used in allocating typical risks encountered in a
project financing include:

1. Completion. Usually, investors' most fundamental concern is noncompletion
    of project construction due to unanticipated cost overruns caused by inflation,
    environmental or technical problems, government regulation, construction
    delays, material unavailability or currency fluctuations. Therefore, prior
    to the commencement of construction, it is essential that participants, inves-
    tors, and other parties agree as to how construction completion is assured.
2. Construction financing. All parties must understand by whom, and when,
    all of the necessary equity, debt, and insurance, in appropriate types and
    amounts, are to be supplied during the construction period. Participants
    are generally required to make a substantial initial equity investment and are
    often required to agree to make additional equity contributions should the
    construction cost of the project exceed its initial budget. Additional construc-
    tion cost overruns can be funded through several sources: bank stand-by
    credit arrangements, commitments from interested customers or governmental
    entities, or, as a last resort, by the investors themselves.
3. Construction contracts. To assure that project construction will be completed
    at its expected cost, investors must be given a detailed cost estimate prepared
    by an engineering firm with recognized expertise in design and construction
    of similar projects. Investors prefer that the construction contract be a fixed-
    price turnkey arrangement with a firm that has a record of finishing projects
    on time and under budget. The construction contract should also incorporate
    rigorous performance tests to ensure that the facility produces product at
    the expected levels.
4. New technology. If the proposed facility utilizes a new technological process,
    investors may be unwilling to assume any construction completion risk, in part
    because such projects often prove to be more expensive to construct than
    initially predicted.

In certain ventures it is impossible to predict the scale at which the project will prove economic. In such cases, the participants may have to provide unconditional guarantees of completion.

Operation

Since a project financing derives its principal security characteristics from the nature of the asset being financed, it is essential that project operation continue. As a result, investors often insist that the participants be required to guarantee to keep the project in operation. In many cases, a formula-based limit can be placed on the participants' operating guarantees. If, however, a relatively new technology is being employed, the participants may have to guarantee performance and agree to pay debt service when the project is not working. Satisfactory recompense sometimes can be provided to the investors through performance insurance.

Marketing of Output

Investors want to ensure that sufficient demand will exist for project output for the duration of their investment at a price that will cover operation and maintenance expenses, pay debt service, and provide a satisfactory rate of return. Prior to financing, an independent consulting firm is often asked to prepare an economic feasibility study that analyzes the participants' demand and price projections and evaluates current and potential competing sources of supply.

Long-Term Contracts

To ensure that the project output will be sold at sufficient prices, investors often prefer that 50 to 100% of the output be covered under long-term contracts with financially sound customers. If possible, the contracts should incorporate a price escalator to cover increases in operational expenses and a floor price to cover working capital needs. If the project is in an industry where guaranteed price escalators and floor prices are not the norm, or where contracts do not have to be honored if the price of the output proves noncompetititve, investors must be convinced that the participants' operations will be highly efficient. In such cases, investors may also demand a call on the revenues of the participants' existing profitable operations.

Revenue Shortfall

Even successful projects may encounter interim revenue shortfalls due to short-term declines in demand for output, or price cuts due to a temporary oversupply from other sources of the product. To guard against such declines, the anticipated annual revenues of the project should amply cover maximum annual debt service.

1. Reserve funds. In addition to the sufficiency of anticipated revenues, it is often advisable that the financing plan incorporate a debt service reserve fund which must be maintained at a specific level, such as maximum annual debt service. The financing agreements should be structured so that in years subsequent to any year in which the debt service reserve fund is tapped, revenues will be applied, after payment operation and maintenance expenses, first to pay debt service, second to refill the debt service reserve fund, and finally to make distributions to participants and to third-party equity investors.
2. Production payments. In certain nonrated private placements, a production payments approach can be used instead of a debt service reserve fund. In projects secured by production payments, the participants agree to pay debt service on the loan by pledging a certain percentage of the proceeds from the

sale of resources produced by the project (such as oil, gas, or coal). It is not considered default if those proceeds are not sufficient to cover debt service. Instead, the deficiency is added to the amount due at the end of the loan term.

Tax

Project financings may contain certain tax risks to investors, ranging from failure to secure a tax credit because the project is not in service by a specified date, to recapture of tax benefits due to the participants' abandonment of an ongoing, but uneconomic, project. In addition, tax law changes, such as increased property taxes or changes in the depreciation schedules prior to the project being placed into service, or pronouncements by the Internal Revenue Service, may also adversely impact on the feasibility of a project.

Indemnification

Investors generally start with the position that they want to be idemnified against all tax risks, including actions taken or not taken by the participants which adversely affect the tax status of the transaction, changes in the investors' financial position or tax rate which make them unable to use the tax benefits, or the invalidity of any tax ruling relating to the transaction. In most cases, participants can narrow the scope of the indemnity to cover only actions or inactions by the participants or the invalidity of a tax ruling. In all cases, however, the participants will have to provide some indemnity against their own actions or inactions which adversely affect the transaction.

Abandonment

Participants may abandon a project which proves too costly to operate and is likely to be unprofitable throughout its life cycle. Abandonment means that the participants must forfeit at least their initial equity contributions, and possibly assume a portion of the debt as part of their balance sheet obligations. If a project is only marginally economic, a negotiated settlement between the participants, interested third parties, and investors may be possible. The settlement will probably require a payment of liquidated damages to equity and debt investors. Additional payments may be required if the abandonment causes a recapture of the investor's tax benefits.

Infrastructure and Raw Material Supply

Investors will generally insist that the participants or a local governmental entity guarantee that the project's infrastructure requirements, including transportation, power, and water are provided on an ongoing basis in a cost-effective manner. Similarly, investors also usually insist that long-term arrangements be made to supply all of the requisite raw materials and resources that are not provided by the project itself.

Alternate Supply Sources

In cases where a particular resource is essential to the success of the project (for example, coal for a power plant), investors will insist that the project have guaranteed access to a substitute source of supply in the event that the primary supplier is unable to fulfill its contract. A secondary source of supply is essential if the primary supplier is a foreign company or country, if doubts exist with respect to the life of the resource, or if the project participants are unable to negotiate a supply contract which extends beyond the final maturity date of the financing.

Life of Natural Resources

In projects involving the development of natural resources, insufficient supply sources can jeopardize the project's financial viability. Investors expect extensive, verified geologic data to ensure that the proved recoverable resources are one and a half to two times the amount expected to be developed. In some cases, investors may want to further minimize the reserve risk by requiring the producer to make up shortfalls from other sources or through open market purchases. Alternatively, the producer can agree to supply a minimum amount of the resource from other sources or to make direct payments to purchasers and investors.

Regulatory and Political

The economic success of a project financing may be predicated upon continuing regulatory approvals and governmental incentives. Therefore, investors usually insist that regulatory approvals, tariffs, and other agreements crucial to the future of the project be as binding as possible, if not irrevocable. To protect against political and regulatory risks, it may be advisable to involve both the local governmental entity and local private lending institutions as much as possible in the design, financing, operation, and ultimate success of the project.

Recent experience has shown that as many environmental permits as possible should be obtained in advance of financing. If permits can be obtained only after the project commences operation, participants will have to commit to take all of the actions necessary to secure the requisite approvals. The participants will also have to assume at least some responsibility that the operation of the project will continue to conform to the representations that are made in obtaining the environmental permits. Insurance should be obtained to cover major risks, such as oil spills, discharge of hazardous waste, or contamination of air and water caused by the project's production process.

For international projects the allocation among participants, investors, and third parties of the risks of expropriation, governmental rights to join in profitable ventures, and currency inconvertibility, is negotiated on a case by case basis. If significant concerns exist with respect to the political environment of the project, some governments and governmental agencies will provide insurance to cover investors against political risks.

MARKETING A PROJECT FINANCING

Marketing Strategy

A principal responsibility of the financial advisor is to develop a comprehensive marketing strategy which implements the financing plan in an optimal manner. Careful consideration should be given to the appropriate issue types and size(s), and to timing for raising requisite outside equity and debt. For example, the benefits of financing project construction through short-term debt with a permanent debt issue upon construction completion should be compared against the advantages of employing permanent debt financing at construction commencement. In all cases, prior to the start of construction, all of the parties to the financing—participants, interested third parties, and outside investors—should have a clear understanding of how the project will be financed.

Determining Potential Investors

In developing the financing plan, the financial advisor and participants will make several decisions which either widen or narrow the range of eligible investors. The more risks that the participants wish the investors to bear, the greater the burden is on the participants and financial advisor to insure that the investors are sophisticated. Sophisticated investors (primarily insurance companies, pension funds, and banks), will, of course, recognize when they are the only viable source of funds and will act accordingly in the negotiations. Therefore, it is advisable that in negotiating with investors the participants remain flexible for as long as possible with respect to how much project risk they are willing to accept. A willingness to discuss the possibility of accepting greater risk, therefore gaining access to a wider range of investors, may enable the participants to persuade the sophisticated investors to reduce their demands.

Equity Financing

Equity funds have a variety of sources, including:

> Participant equity contributions
> Investors seeking tax benefits, cash flow, and capital appreciation
> Combined offerings of debt and equity to institutional investors
> Public equity offerings in the U.S. and Eurodollar markets
> Government aid

The financing plan will almost always provide for equity investments from the participants and perhaps from interested third parties and outside investors. The investment can be in the form of cash, equipment, expertise, or technology. Government entities may fund feasibility studies or grant resource rights. Participants can also make advances during the construction period in the form of subordinated loans. Purchasers with a strong need for the output, or suppliers needing a market for their input, may also be potential equity investors. Individual investors may contribute equity in return for cash flow, tax benefits, and capital appreciation under a leveraged lease or a limited partnership. Certain large projects requiring substantial amounts of debt may also be candidates for a private placement of an offering which combines debt and equity. For example, an insurance company may be persuaded to provide funds to the project as a lender on the basis that it will receive an additional return on its investment if the net cash flows of the project exceed a certain level. On occasion, a portion of the equity required for a project financing may be sold on a public offering basis.

Construction Period Debt Financing

Construction period debt financing can be obtained on a taxable or, where appropriate, on a tax-exempt basis, primarily from three sources:

1. Commercial paper backed by a bank credit facility
2. Permanent debt issue that includes construction period financing
3. Commercial bank loans

The choice among these alternatives depends on the size and complexity of the project as well as on the credit quality of the entity seeking the financing. In general, commercial paper backed by bank credit facility and rated at least A-2/P-2 is a less costly means of financing the construction of large projects than is a loan from a consortium of commercial banks. However, participants in projects that do not obtain a rating, that are relatively small, or highly complex, may find that a commercial bank loan is the only viable short-term financing alternative. In all cases, the short-term financing alternative employed should provide for a permanent debt takeout at the conclusion of the construction period.

The participants can eliminate the need for a guaranteed permanent debt takeout by financing the entire project through a permanent debt issue prior to the start of construction. An advantage of permanent debt financing is that interest during construction can be capitalized as a part of the issue.

Permanent Debt Financing

Long-term debt financing for the project can be provided through one or more of the following:

1. Public debt offerings in the U.S. and Eurobond markets
2. Private placements in the U.S. and European markets
3. Single or syndicated commercial bank long-term loans
4. "Club" commercial bank long-term loans
5. Government entity loans

The selection of the permanent debt financing alternatives for the project depends, in large part, on the credit quality of the project and upon how sensitive the project is to changes in interest rates. Also important are the expected operating life of the project and the corresponding maturity of the debt. The choice of a fixed or a floating rate will be determined by the sensitivity of the project's economics to upward movements in interest rates as well as by the estimation of the potential savings (in a market with a normal upward sloping yield curve) resulting from the difference between current higher overall cost of the long-term fixed rate issue and the current lower overall cost of the floating rate issue. Maturity may also be a consideration since floating rate loans often have either shorter maturities than do fixed rate issues or, alternatively, interim rate renegotiation provisions.

Fixed-rate public offerings are a good way of securing long-term funds if the debt can obtain an investment grade rating from at least one of the major rating agencies. Private placements of a rated issue can also be an attractive means of obtaining fixed rate funds, if institutional investors have substantial amounts of money to invest in a market environment where there are a relatively limited number of corporate debt offerings. Nonrated projects, on the other hand, are generally better sold on a private basis. In that case, the choice is whether to place a fixed or floating rate issue with institutional investors or agree to a long-term floating rate loan with commercial banks.

For long-term floating rate loans, the financial advisor should compare the terms and conditions available from institutional investors and from commercial banks. If a floating rate loan from a commercial bank appears to be the best alternative to finance at least a portion of the debt, then the participants and financial advisor should agree upon a strategy of how to approach the banks. The traditional approach is to initiate negotiations with one or more of the banks with whom the participants have either the strongest banking relationship or the banks who have expressed an interest in developing a significant relationship. The most appropriate commercial bank is then asked to take the lead position in negotiating the loan and in syndicating it to other banks. A less traditional approach, which has produced favorable results in certain situations, is for the participatns and financial advisor to act as the syndicator and obtain the funds on a "club loan" basis. In a club loan, negotiations with a variety of prospective commercial banks are handled on an individual basis, thereby giving the participants the flexibility they would have in negotiating a private placement with a group of institutional investors.

Project financings for U.S. corporations that have international aspects may be eligible for loans from government-sponsored institutions such as the World Bank.

Government Assistance

Governmental entities can provide financial assistance to a project both directly—through grant programs and through guaranteeing or subsidizing loans—and indirectly—through price guarantees and expanded tax benefits. For example, the U.S. government pro-

vides substantial assistance to U.S. shipbuilders by guaranteeing loans under the
Title XI program. Some cogeneration facility financings have benefited from the U.S.
Department of Housing and Urban Development's Action Grant (UDAG) program under
which a grant of funds or a below-market rate loan can be provided. Certain water
and sewer projects may be eligible for government construction grants. A few state
governments have enhanced the attractiveness of alternative energy projects, such
as solar and wind power, by providing special energy tax credits. Many states have
enacted legislation authorizing the issuance of tax-exempt revenue bonds to finance
projects such as resource recovery facilities. A variety of projects may benefit from
tax abatements provided by local municipalities.

In transactions involving foreign participants, suppliers, or interested third parties, certain governments will provide bilateral aid or export credit financing. Export
credit financing may involve direct loans, insurance, interest rate subsidies, and
assistance in hedging against dramatic rises in price and currency fluctuations.

Leasing

Lease financing may be appropriate for projects in which the participants (1) cannot
currently use all the tax benefits associated with ownership of the project, (2) can
benefit from off-balance sheet financing, or (3) wish to utilize a new source of funds—
the lease equity market. Through lease financing, participants may transfer ownership of all or a portion of the project to an equity investor or investors who will receive all or a portion of the tax benefits of ownership. The participants will then
lease the facility back from the owners, thereby retaining the right to operate the
facility and having access to its output.

Transferring tax benefits to an equity owner who can use the benefits currently,
can significantly reduce the participants' overall cost of financing the project. However, transferring ownership of the project to equity investors may result in a diminution of flexibility even in a finance lease where the participants may repurchase the
project at the end of the lease term for 10% of its original cost. Secured lenders and
equity investors characteristically require certain maintenance and transfer covenants
to protect their investments.

In certain cases, the participants can mitigate their diminution of flexibility with
respect to the project by transferring less than 50% of the ownership of the project
to outside investors. Under this approach, the cost of the financing to the participants is higher than where more control is relinquished because of the smaller amount
of outside equity investment. If debt is issued to replace the funds which would
otherwise have been available form an equity investor, the aggregate amount of debt
service will increase. Any increase in the cost of debt service will be partially offset
by the availability of additional tax benefits to the participants.

Lease financing may be employed in conjunction with both taxable and tax-exempt
debt. However, the tax benefits available to participants of other equity investors
in the case of a lease which involves tax-exempt debt generally may be reduced significantly if a municipality is either the lessee or the lessor of the project. Carefully
structured financing arrangements must be employed to assure that full tax benefits
will be available to the equity investors in a project financing where both a lease and
a municipal entity are involved.

CONCLUSION

Project managers should realize the immense impact of financing costs on their projects.
They must understand the financing conditions which affect the project and work to
minimize any adverse effects which the execution plan and changes to the plan will
have on project financing efficiency.

7

Cash Flow Forecasting:
A Systematic Approach

FERNANDO SOTELINO and MICHAEL A. GUSTAFSON   *Crocker National Bank,*
San Francisco, California

When considering the evaluation and structure of the financing of a project, it is necessary to properly identify, define, and forecast the multiple cash flows. There are cash flows relevant to (1) the project sponsor in making decisions regarding continuing with the project and how to finance it; (2) lenders in measuring the project's ability to service debt; and (3) the host government in assessing project economics from the country's standpoint. Refined cash flow forecasting techniques, which are fundamental in project financing situations, are equally applicable to any non-asset-based lending situation such as debt rescheduling or leveraged buyouts, where timely repayment of debt depends largely on future cash flows to be generated by the entity being financed.

The guidelines for cash flow forecasting and analysis presented herein attempt to be:

1. General. It can be easily applied to most, if not all project situations.
2. Complete. It allows for generation of the cash flow forecasts relevant to each of the project participants.
3. Consistent. It does not allow for contradictory interpretation of results.
4. Flexible. It allows for easy assessment of the impact of changes in key project parameters on each participant's appropriate measures of risk and return.

A case study, a modified version of a successfully financed copper mining venture in Latin American, is used to provide an example of the cash flow forecasting methodology and to illustrate the process of selection of the proper measures of risk and return. This case study involves three participants: the Latin American mining company, who is the project sponsor and who is making the major equity investment; the financial institutions who are providers of the bank debt portion of the financing; and an agency of the host government which is making the remaining equity investment and may provide subsidized subordinated debt to the project.

Following this, the concluding remarks compensate for any specificity occasioned by the case study approach, by reviewing, in a generalized form, the key methodological steps and the principal practical "tips" previously illustrated.

THE COPPER MINING PROJECT

The project consists of an expansion of an existing copper mine, undertaken by the Latin American Copper Company (LACC, or simply the "Company"). The technical and economic assumptions regarding the Company's existing operations and expansion plans may appear quite simplified; this has been done to avoid excessive forecasting detail and focus on the relevant cash flows and measures of risk and return which are the ultimate goals of the analysis. The concepts and methodology remain valid regardless of the complexity of the actual situation.

Before presenting the case study, it should be noted that the analysis and cash flow forecasts were developed using two central ideas. First, that in analyzing a project it is helpful to split the problem into two separate, though not completely independent, decisions: (1) go/no go (unlevered); (2) how-to-go (capital structure). Second, that once one cash flow, the *total equity cash flow*, has been defined carefully and specifically, it can serve as the basis for the derivation of all other cash flows. This saves time and helps avoid mistakes.

Initially, the decision regarding whether to go ahead with the project (go/no go) focuses on the inherent economic attractiveness of the venture, measuring the ability of the project to generate cash flow returns which are sufficient to compensate for resources committed and risks undertaken by potential project sponsors. The cash flow of primary interest in this analysis is the *incremental* unlevered cash flow available for distribution among the parties underwriting project risks. In most cases this is the total equity cash flow. Sensitivity analysis at this stage is used to quantity the major technical and economic risks to be shared by project participants.

The decision regarding the financing of the project (how-to-go) is then an attempt to find the capital structure, consistent with market terms and conditions and sound financial management policies, which will best: (1) match planned outflows with cash inflows; and (2) increase the returns and/or reduce the risks for one or more project participants (usually the shareholders).

Here the relevant cash flows are those which allow for assessment of the project's overall ability to service debt as well as the *incremental* levered cash flows accruing to each project participant.

PROJECT FUNDING: CASH FLOW CHOICES

LACC currently has 147 million metric tons of proven copper sulfide ore reserves. The existing mine complex consists of an open pit-mining operation and a conventional flotation plant with a processing capacity of 20,000 metric tons of ore per day. The company sells copper concentrates primarily to Japanese custom smelters. The mine has been in operation for 5 years, fine copper production last year was 108,240 metric tons, and the Company currently has assets of $175 million and a net worth of $135 million.

Due to a recent increase in proven reserves, LACC is considering doubling the treatment capacity of its flotation plant to 40,000 tons per day, including the required additional mine equipment (the "Project"). Project capital expenditures and working capital increases have been estimated at approximately $210 million. The construction period is expected to be one year, which includes a three-month start-up phase.

The Project is to be funded by a combination of equity, straight debt, supplier credits and/or commercial bank term loans, and subordinated debt. The Company's shareholders are willing to commit a maximum of $50 million to the Project. A government development agency, which is also a minority shareholder, might be willing to lend approximately $40 million to the Company in the form of subordinated notes, depending on the ability of the Project to generate foreign exchange reserves. Commercial banks cannot be expected to offer loans with maturities longer than ten years.

The Project is expected to increase the value of the firm because:

1. It will solidify the Company's position as a low-cost copper producer by taking advantage of economies of scale. Because of the expansion, cash production costs are expected to decrease 7.0¢/lb. and all-in costs 11.0¢/lb.
2. The potential earnings stream from the sulfide ore reserves will be realized sooner, even though a substantial capital investment will be required.

The go/no go decision requires modelling the cash flow effects of the following alternatives:

1. The unlevered expansion case, involving a large capital expenditure today with resulting economies of scale and earlier usage of sulfide ore reserves.
2. The unlevered no-expansion case, involving a smaller capital expenditure in the future in order to mine and process the recently discovered reserves only when flotation plant capacity becomes available.

The unlevered expansion is compared to the unlevered no-expansion in order to determine the incremental cash flow effects. If the decision is to go ahead with the Project, a third case is required:

3. The levered expansion case, which considered the effects of debt financing on the unlevered expansion.

To save time and facilitate comparison of the different cases, one general cash flow model can be built to represent all three cases. The unlevered expansion can be viewed as a special case of the levered expansion where equity capital is the only source of funds, and the unlevered no-expansion where a different mining plan is followed and certain capital expenditures and expenses are avoided or delayed. Cash flows should be defined in the most general terms, that is in accordance with the levered expansion, so that they remain valid when analyzing all cases.

Unlevered Cash Flows and the Go/No Go Decision

The cash flow model used to analyze the LACC expansion has the following general characteristics:

1. Detailed capital expenditure schedules with appropriate allowances for real and inflationary price increases and overrun contingencies. Ongoing capital expenditure requirements are separated from those expenditures tied to the expansion.
2. Copper concentrate and byproduct silver production schedules, which are based on the Company's mining and stockpile usage plans and data on ore grades, recovery factors, and product grades. Table 1 illustrates the production schedules generated for the LACC analysis.
3. Revenue flows based on a concentrate product value, which takes into account precious metals prices, smelting and refining charges and losses, transportation charges and losses, and real and inflationary price adjustments.
4. Direct costs broken out for the mining and ore treatment operations and split into fixed and variable components where applicable, and indirect costs for both current operations and expected increases due to the expansion. All costs should be broken down into the currency of occurrence, escalated at the appropriate inflation rate, and then converted to U.S. dollars. Certain incremental costs independent of both current operations and the proposed expansion (i.e., exploration expenses) were left out of the unlevered analysis and only included when considering debt financing.

Table 1 Unlevered Expansion Case: Economic and Production Assumptions

	0	1	2	3	4	5	6	7	8	9	10
Economic assumptions											
U.S. inflation (%)	4.2	4.2	4.9	5.1	5.1	5.1	5.1	5.1	5.1	5.1	5.1
Domestic inflation (%)	15.0	15.0	15.0	15.0	15.0	15.0	15.0	15.0	15.0	15.0	15.0
Copper real escalation (%)	-2.4	3.0	3.0	2.0	2.0	1.0	1.0	–	–	–	–
Silver real escalation (%)	-2.4	0.5	2.7	2.0	–	–	–	–	–	–	–
Copper price (¢/lb)	75.0	80.5	87.0	93.2	100.0	106.1	112.6	118.4	124.4	130.7	137.4
Silver price ($/troz)	9.20	9.63	10.37	11.12	11.69	12.28	12.91	13.57	14.26	14.99	15.75
Local currency devaluation (%)	9.4	9.4	8.8	8.6	8.6	8.6	8.6	8.6	8.6	8.6	8.6
Local currency /US$ FX rate	50.0	54.7	59.5	64.6	70.2	76.2	82.8	89.9	97.7	106.1	115.2
Production assumptions											
Ore mined:											
Sulfide mined OP (000 MT)	6,000	6,000	13,000	13,000	13,000	13,000	14,000	14,000	14,000	14,000	14,000
Waste ore mined (000 MT)	12,000	12,000	26,000	26,000	26,000	26,000	28,000	28,000	28,000	28,000	28,000
Ore treated:											
Sulfide mined (000 MT)	6,000	6,000	13,000	13,000	13,000	13,000	14,000	14,000	14,000	14,000	14,000
Sulfide from stockpile (000 MT)	1,000	1,000	1,000	1,000	1,000	1,000	–	–	–	–	–
Sulfide to concentrator (000 MT)	7,000	7,000	14,000	14,000	14,000	14,000	14,000	14,000	14,000	14,000	14,000

Ore grades:													
OP Sulfide grade (% Cu)	1.80	1.80	1.80	1.80	1.80	1.80	1.80	1.80	1.80	1.80	1.80	1.80	1.80
Sulfide from stock grade (% Cu)	1.50	1.50	1.50	1.50	1.50	1.50	1.50	–	–	–	–	–	–
Sulfide grade (% Cu)	1.76	1.76	1.78	1.78	1.78	1.78	1.78	1.80	1.80	1.80	1.80	1.80	1.80
Sulfide Ag content (gpt)	20.0	20.0	20.0	20.0	20.0	20.0	20.0	20.0	20.0	20.0	20.0	20.0	20.0
Recovery:													
Sulfide Cu recovery (%)	88.0	88.0	88.0	88.0	88.0	88.0	88.0	88.0	88.0	88.0	88.0	88.0	88.0
Sulfide Ag recovery (%)	80.0	80.0	80.0	80.0	80.0	80.0	80.0	80.0	80.0	80.0	80.0	80.0	80.0
Product grades:													
Concentrate grade (% Cu)	32.0	32.0	32.0	32.0	32.0	32.0	32.0	32.0	32.0	32.0	32.0	32.0	32.0
Concentrate Ag content (gpt)	331.1	331.1	327.1	327.1	327.1	327.1	327.1	323.2	323.2	323.2	323.2	323.2	323.2
Production													
Concentrate production (MT)	338,250	338,250	684,750	684,750	684,750	684,750	684,750	693,000	693,000	693,000	693,000	693,000	693,000
Silver in concentrate (kg)	112,000	112,000	224,000	224,000	224,000	224,000	224,000	224,000	224,000	224,000	224,000	224,000	224,000
Fine copper production (MT)	108,240	108,240	219,120	219,120	219,120	219,120	219,120	221,760	221,760	221,760	221,760	221,760	221,760

5. Working capital (cash, receivables, inventories, and payables) should be re-
    lated to production, sales, or cost figures using historical financial statements
    as a starting point when possible. The following working capital accounts
    were included in the LACC analysis: cash on hand, accounts receivable, raw
    materials and supplies, work in process, stockpile inventory, finished goods,
    prepaid expenses, accounts payable, and accrued expenses. The resulting
    working capital amount is referred to as required working capital, as opposed
    to working capital which includes short-term investments and short-term debt.

On the basis of the above, the total equity cash flow can be calculated for the expansion case, as illustrated in Table 2. As can be observed, under the subtitle External
Funding, drawdowns of bank debt and subordinated debt are made equal to zero,
since we are, at this point, interested in the calculation of the unlevered equity cash
flow. The interest charges and principal repayments shown in Table 2 refer to the
"old" debt, already existing in the books of LACC. The same exhibit, if generated
for the no expansion case, would also show such interest charges and principal
repayments, but would show equity investment equal to zero as no expansion would
be taking place.

The go/no go decision is to be made on the basis of the incremental unlevered
total equity cash flow, representing the difference between the expansion total equity
cash flow (last line of Table 2) and the no expansion total equity cash flow, as shown
in Table 3 for the first ten years.

Assessment of the project's inherent economic attractiveness should be conducted
through calculation of the net present values of the incremental cash flows. Many
complex methods exist for estimating discount rates, but in general the rates used
should take into account the risk-free opportunity cost of money, the general business
risk of the company, financial risk, and any perceived additional new venture risks.
In the case of the LACC expansion, the discount rate used for assessing the incremental unlevered equity cash flow was 15%, resulting from a risk-free rate of 10% and
an additional 5% for business risk. Although the operation of the project was to be
no different from current operations, a small increment of 2% was added to the discount
rate in years 1 and 2 to account for any start-up risks. The resulting net present
value (NPV) of the incremental unlevered total equity cash flow is $15 million, show-
ing that the Project should indeed add to the value of the firm.

Calculation of internal rates of return (IRRs) can also be useful, but certain pitfalls exist, for example:

1. IRRs give no indication of the amount of the investment.
2. IRRs assume that the required return for resources committed and risks under-
    taken remains constant from year to year.

Sensitivity analyses should be performed to determine the degree to which project
returns are affected by changes in key technical and economic parameters. For
example, Table 4 shows the impact of a variation in copper prices on the present
value of the incremental unlevered equity cash flow. Under the base case, if
management were to believe that the discount rate to be used in the face of the risk
to be taken was 18% or more, then the expansion should not be undertaken. Also
copper prices 5% below the base case would make the expansion alternative a marginal
project when compared to the no-expansion option (Table 4).

Levered Cash Flows and the How-to-Go Decision

Several cash flows relevant in determining the appropriate capital structure of the
project over time and the risk/return relationships among the various project participants, can be categorized as given on p. 198

Table 2 Unlevered Expansion Case: Cash Flow Analysis (000 $)

	1	2	3	4	5	6	7	8	9	10
Operating cash										
Net earnings	-18,527	33,437	34,947	31,839	40,942	51,217	53,880	56,653	59,539	63,885
Noncash charges	25,000	43,468	44,289	44,204	34,480	24,773	25,081	25,405	25,745	23,522
Change in required working capital	-3,384	38,927	195	-265	-1,245	7,129	5,661	5,948	6,250	6,568
Capital expenditures	192,520	5,465	5,744	6,037	6,345	6,668	7,009	7,366	–	–
Unfunded operating cash	-182,662	32,512	73,298	70,272	70,322	62,193	66,292	68,744	79,034	80,840
External funding										
New bank debt drawdown	–	–	–	–	–	–	–	–	–	–
Subordinated debt drawdown	–	–	–	–	–	–	–	–	–	–
Equity investment	195,000	–	–	–	–	–	–	–	–	–
Funded operating cash	12,338	32,512	73,298	70,272	70,322	62,193	66,292	68,744	79,034	80,840
Cash available to service debt										
Interest charges and fees	4,500	3,300	2,100	900	–	–	–	–	–	–
Beginning excess funds and reserves	–	–	–	–	–	–	–	–	–	–
Cash for debt service	16,838	35,812	75,398	71,172	70,322	62,193	66,292	68,744	79,034	80,840
Debt service										
Senior debt interest and fees	4,500	3,330	2,100	900	–	–	–	–	–	–
Senior debt repayments	10,000	10,000	10,000	10,000	–	–	–	–	–	–
Cash for subordinated debt service	2,338	22,512	63,298	60,272	70,322	62,193	66,292	68,744	79,034	80,840
Subordinated debt interest and fees	–	–	–	–	–	–	–	–	–	–
Subordinated debt repayment	–	–	–	–	–	–	–	–	–	–
Cash after debt service	2,338	22,512	63,298	60,272	70,322	62,193	66,292	68,744	79,034	80,840
Distribution of remaining cash										
Change in short-term debt	–	–	–	–	–	–	–	–	–	–
Ending cash reserves	–	–	–	–	–	–	–	–	–	–
Dividends	2,338	22,512	63,298	60,272	70,322	62,193	66,292	68,744	79,034	80,840
Ending excess funds	–	–	–	–	–	–	–	–	–	–
Equity cash flow										
Equity investment	195,000	–	–	–	–	–	–	–	–	–
Dividends	2,338	22,512	63,298	60,272	70,322	62,193	66,292	68,744	79,034	80,840
Total equity cash flow	-192,662	22,512	63,298	60,272	70,322	62,193	66,292	68,744	79,034	80,840

Table 3 Incremental Unlevered Equity Cash Flow (in $1,000)

Year	Expansion	No expansion	Increment
1	-192.6	1.4	-191.2
2	22.5	5.2	17.3
3	63.3	12.3	51.0
4	60.3	19.2	41.1
5	70.3	25.5	44.8
6	62.2	10.4	51.8
7	66.3	12.2	54.1
8	68.7	12.5	56.2
9	79.0	9.4	69.6
10	80.8	12.5	68.3
11	81.8	13.5	68.3
12	142.6[a]	27.8	114.8
13	—	29.5	-29.5
14	—	30.7	-30.7
15	—	31.9	-31.9
16	—	33.1	-33.1
17	—	34.4	-34.4
18	—	35.8	-35.8
19	—	60.0	-60.0
20	—	59.0	-59.0
21	—	56.2	-56.2
22	—	117.0	-117.0

[a]The expansion alternative would lead to full depletion of ore reserves by the end of year 12. The significantly larger amount of the equity cash flow in this year results from the liquidation of then existing current assets, mainly receivables and inventories.

1. Those which allow for assessment of the Project's overall ability to service debt, namely:
    a. The cash flow available to serve each type of debt
    b. The debt service cash flows
2. The incremental cash flows accruing to different project participants, such as:
    a. The total equity cash flow, which is defined just as in the unlevered analysis, but now includes the effects of debt financing
    b. Individual equity sponsor cash flows, which are easily derived from the total equity cash flow
    c. Individual lender cash flows, which include drawdowns, debt service, and any profitsharing or equity interest due the lender
    d. Government cash flows, for example the incremental change in the country's foreign exchange reserves due to either avoided or actual foreign exchange flows

The organization of Table 5, Cash Flow Analysis, is an important step and deserves some explanation. The first subtotal in the table, "Unfunded Operation Cash," represents the cash generated by normal operations before any external funding, including

Table 4 Impact of Copper Price on Go/No Go Decision

Discount rate	Copper price (in ¢/lb)	Net present value (× $1,000,000)	Decision
17% on years 1 and 2, 15% thereafter	Base case	15.3	Go
	-10%	-15.9	No go
	-5%	+2.0	Almost indifferent
	+15%	+30.6	Go
20% on years 1 and 2; 18% thereafter	Base case	-1.0	Almost indifferent
	+10%	-35.5	No go
	-5%	-14.9	No go
	+5%	+14.2	No go

any required increases in working capital or fixed assets, and the second subtotal, "Funded Operating Cash," includes external long-term funding obtained for the Project. The third subtotal, "Cash for Debt Service" is obtained by adding back interest charges, and represents the cash flow which is available to meet all debt service payments. The line item "Beginning Excess Funds and Reserves," may or may not be included in the calculation of "Cash for Debt Service." In the LACC example it represents a cash reserve required by lenders, and is therefore considered cash available to service debt; however, it should not be included in the determination of the cash generated in a given year which is available to service debt. Cash available after debt service is then distributed among short-term debt, short-term assets, and dividends. Note also that most of Table 6 breaks out the individual cash flow of each project participant and is easily derived from line items contained in Table 5.

Table 7 provides a summary of the major measures of risk and return based upon Tables 5 and 6. Discount rates were chosen to reflect the riskiness of the various cash flows; in addition, certain cash flows are actually composed of two or more underlying cash flows and their NPVs are calculated as the sum of the NPVs of the underlying cash flows.

The how-to-go decision can be thought of as:

1. Determining the amount of debt service the Project can support in each year
2. Fitting the available financing alternatives into this optimal debt service schedule, in such a way as to minimize financial cost

A good indication of a project's ability to service debt is the debt coverage ratio (DCR), which may be different for the project as a whole and for each lender, and is defined as the ratio between cash available to service debt and debt service cash flow.

A DCR of less than 1.0 means that cash flow is insufficient to service debt. The larger the DCR, the greater the amount of comfort afforded to lenders and project guarantors.

Given the risks inherent in the Project and the Company's past financial performance, it was expected that lenders would require a DCR, taking into account all senior and subordinated debt service, of 1.5 or higher. With an equity investment of $50 million and subordinated debt of $40 million, the balance to be financed with senior debt amounts to $120 million. Table 8 illustrates the calculation of the maximum new senior debt LACC could support under the base case scenario and assuming a minimum DCR of 1.5.

Table 5 Levered Expansion Case: Cash Flow Analysis (000 $)

	1	2	3	4	5	6	7	8	9	10
Operating cash										
Net earnings	-23,783	9,016	22,415	35,246	31,470	42,872	46,655	50,540	54,790	60,024
Noncash charges	25,000	44,125	44,947	44,862	35,137	25,430	25,739	26,062	26,403	24,180
Change in required working capital	-3,498	38,921	188	-219	-1,250	7,123	5,655	5,943	6,244	6,562
Capital expenditures	199,095	5,465	5,744	6,037	6,345	6,668	7,009	7,366	–	–
Unfunded operating cash	-194,380	8,755	61,430	74,290	61,512	54,511	59,730	63,294	74,949	77,642
External funding										
New bank debt drawdown	115,000	5,000	–	–	–	–	–	–	–	–
Subordinated debt drawdown	40,000	–	–	–	–	–	–	–	–	–
Equity investment	50,000	–	–	–	–	–	–	–	–	–
Funded operating cash	10,620	13,755	61,430	74,290	61,512	54,511	59,730	63,294	74,949	77,642
Cash available to service debt										
Interest charges and fees	4,500	21,563	20,500	18,700	15,400	13,000	10,600	8,200	5,300	1,500
Beginning excess funds and reserves	–	620	4,376	20,000	20,000	20,000	20,000	20,000	20,000	20,000
Cash for debt service	15,120	35,938	86,306	112,990	96,912	87,511	90,330	91,494	100,249	79,142
Debt service										
Senior debt interest and fees	4,500	17,563	16,500	14,700	11,400	9,000	6,600	4,200	1,800	–
Senior debt repayments	10,000	10,000	10,000	30,000	20,000	20,000	20,000	20,000	20,000	–
Cash for subordinated debt service	620	8,376	59,806	68,290	65,512	58,511	63,730	67,294	78,449	79,142
Subordinated debt interest and fees	–	4,000	4,000	4,000	4,000	4,000	4,000	4,000	3,500	1,500
Subordinated debt repayment	–	–	–	–	–	–	–	–	20,000	20,000
Cash after debt service	620	4,376	55,806	64,290	61,512	54,511	59,730	63,294	54,949	57,642
Distribution of remaining cash										
Change in short-term debt	–	–	–	–	–	–	–	–	–	–
Ending cash reserve	–	4,376	20,000	20,000	20,000	20,000	20,000	20,000	–	–
Dividends	–	–	35,806	44,290	41,512	34,511	39,730	43,294	54,949	57,642
Ending excess funds	620	–	–	–	–	–	–	–	–	–
Equity cash flow										
Equity investment	50,000	–	–	–	–	–	–	–	–	–
Dividends	–	–	35,806	44,290	41,512	34,511	39,730	43,294	54,949	57,642
Total equity cash flow	-50,000	–	35,806	44,290	41,512	34,511	39,730	43,294	54,949	57,642

Table 6 Levered Expansion Case: Project Participant Cash Flow Summary (000 $)

	1	2	3	4	5	6	7	8	9	10
Shareholders										
Equity investment	50,000	–	–	–	–	–	–	–	–	–
Dividends	–	–	35,806	44,290	41,512	34,511	39,730	43,294	54,949	57,642
Total equity cash flow	-50,000	–	35,806	44,290	41,512	34,511	39,730	43,294	54,949	57,642
Majority shareholders equity investment	37,500	–	–	–	–	–	–	–	–	–
Majority shareholders dividends	–	–	28,645	35,432	33,210	27,609	31,784	34,635	43,959	46,114
Majority shareholders cash flow	-37,500	–	28,645	35,432	33,210	27,609	31,784	34,635	43,959	46,114
Lenders										
New bank debt drawdown	115,000	5,000	–	–	–	–	–	–	–	–
New bank debt repayment	–	–	–	20,000	20,000	20,000	20,000	20,000	20,000	–
Interest on new bank debt	2,400	14,100	14,400	13,800	11,400	9,000	6,600	4,200	1,800	–
New bank debt fees	1,775	163	–	–	–	–	–	–	–	–
New bank debt cash flow	-110,825	9,263	14,400	33,800	31,400	29,000	26,600	24,200	21,800	–
Subordinated debt drawdown	40,000	–	–	–	–	–	–	–	–	–
Subordinated debt repayment	–	–	–	–	–	–	–	–	20,000	20,000
Interest on subordinated debt	2,000	4,000	4,000	4,000	4,000	4,000	4,000	4,000	3,500	1,500
Subordinated debt fees	400	–	–	–	–	–	–	–	–	–
Subordinated lender cash flow	-37,600	4,000	4,000	4,000	4,000	4,000	4,000	4,000	23,500	21,500
Existing bank debt cash flow	14,500	13,300	12,100	10,900	–	–	–	–	–	–
Lender cash flow	-133,925	26,563	30,500	48,700	35,400	33,000	30,600	28,200	45,300	21,500
Government development agency										
Minority shareholders cash flow	-12,500	–	7,161	8,858	8,302	6,902	7,946	8,659	10,990	11,528
Subordinated lender cash flow	-37,600	4,000	4,000	4,000	4,000	4,000	4,000	4,000	23,500	21,500
Government agency cash flow	-50,100	4,000	11,161	12,858	12,302	10,902	11,946	12,659	34,490	33,028
Foreign exchange										
Trade balance	-180,416	135,161	177,486	195,700	209,686	221,326	233,814	245,740	266,016	279,584
Services balance	-26,757	-28,207	-53,812	-60,290	-55,112	-45,711	-48,530	-49,694	-58,449	-59,142
FX effect before capital flows	-206,991	106,954	123,674	135,410	154,574	175,615	185,284	196,046	207,567	220,442
Capital flow balance	194,380	-8,755	-25,624	-30,000	-20,000	-20,000	-20,000	-20,000	-20,000	-20,000
FX effect after capital flows	-12,612	98,199	98,049	105,410	134,574	155,615	165,284	176,046	187,567	200,442

Table 7 Levered Expansion Case: Summary Measures of Risk and Return (000 $)

Year	Net earnings	Total equity cash flow	Majority shareholder cash flow	Lender cash flow	New bank debt cash flow	Government agency cash flow	FX effect after capital flows	Debt coverage (%)	Senior debt DCR (%)	Subordinated debt DCR (%)
0	-18,290	–	–	-40,000	–	–	–	46	46	–
1	-23,783	-50,000	-37,500	-133,925	-110,825	-50,100	-12,612	104	104	–
2	9,016	–	–	26,563	9,263	4,000	98,199	114	130	209
3	22,415	35,806	28,645	30,500	14,400	11,161	98,049	283	326	1,495
4	35,246	44,290	35,432	48,700	33,800	12,858	105,410	232	253	1,707
5	31,470	41,512	33,210	35,400	31,400	12,302	134,574	274	309	1,638
6	42,872	34,511	27,609	33,000	29,000	10,902	155,615	265	302	1,463
7	46,655	39,730	31,784	30,600	26,600	11,946	165,284	295	340	1,593
8	50,540	43,294	34,635	28,200	24,200	12,659	176,046	324	378	1,682
9	54,790	54,949	43,959	45,300	21,800	34,490	187,567	221	460	334
10	60,024	57,642	46,114	21,500	–	33,028	200,442	368	–	368
11	64,212	79,202	63,361	–	–	15,840	214,689	–	–	–
12	–	142,523	114,019	–	–	28,505	-52,985	–	–	–
13	–	–	–	–	–	–	–	–	–	–
14	–	–	–	–	–	–	–	–	–	–
15	–	–	–	–	–	–	–	–	–	–
16	–	–	–	–	–	–	–	–	–	–
17	–	–	–	–	–	–	–	–	–	–
18	–	–	–	–	–	–	–	–	–	–
19	–	–	–	–	–	–	–	–	–	–
20	–	–	–	–	–	–	–	–	–	–
21	–	–	–	–	–	–	–	–	–	–
22	–	–	–	–	–	–	–	–	–	–
Discount rate (%)		20.00	20.0	13.0	13.0		18.0			
New present value		92,607	76,134	-9,384	-1,473	10,242	480,540			
IRR (%)		53.1	55.6	11.9	12.6	22.9	779.6			

Table 8 Maximum New Senior Debt Service Profile (× $1,000,000)

Year	3	4	5	6	7	8	9	10
Cash available for debt service (1)	81.5	92.2	76.0	66.6	69.4	70.6	79.3	79.1
Required DCR (2)	1.5	1.5	1.5	1.5	1.5	1.5	1.5	1.5
Maximum debt service (1)/(2) = (3)	54.3	61.5	50.7	44.4	46.3	47.1	52.9	52.7
Existing debt service (4)	14.5	13.3	12.1	10.9	–	–	–	–
Maximum new debt service (3) - (4) = (5)	39.9	48.2	38.6	33.5	46.3	47.1	52.9	52.7
Subordinated debt service (6)	4.0	4.0	4.0	4.0	4.0	4.0	23.5	21.5
Maximum new senior sebt service (5) - (6) = (7)	35.8	44.2	34.6	29.5	42.3	43.1	29.6	31.2

On the basis of the maximum new senior debt service the project can support (line 7 of Table 8) and, keeping in mind a maximum term for the senior debt of 10 years, a repayment schedule was designed calling for no principal repayments in years 1 to 3 and principal repayments of 16.67% of the amount borrowed in years 4 to 9 (see Table 5). This is a rather standard type of financing and, to the extent the project can support it, one of the most easily obtainable from lenders.

A particularly useful type of sensitivity analysis of a project's ability to service debt is the "breakeven" analysis. Breakeven values and percentage change from base case which would result in the minimum cash flow generation necessary to meet debt service (DCR = 1.0) can be easily calculated. Table 9 shows breakeven copper prices for a minimum DCR of 1.0 for the final funding structure adopted by LACC. As can be observed, the breakeven price of copper goes up 10% from year 3 to year 4 indicating that an additional one year grace period should be considered, with principal repayments starting only in year 5. The cash-generating capacity of capital-intensive projects is usually lowest in the early years of operation, growing over time as operating performance targets are reached. This problem can be dealt with in several ways. (1) Debt financing can be delayed by funding the initial stages of the project completely with equity. This allows principal repayments to be pushed further out into the life of the project. In addition, estimated capital costs and funding requirements will be more accurate, and interest during construction will be lower. (2) Debt service payments can be fixed using financing techniques such as the fixed payment variable maturity (FPVM) loan (Boettcher and Sotelino, 1982). An FPVM loan allows the borrower to fix debt service payments, tie interest payments to a variable rather than a fixed rate, and adjust principal repayments to make up the difference between the two. (3) Stepped repayment schedules can be negotiated, easing the debt service burden in early years.

A FEW PRACTICAL TIPS

A discussion of the major steps of the guideline illustrated in the case study will attempt to make it generally applicable to most project situations.

Table 9 Levered Expansion Case—Breakeven Values for Copper Prices

Year	Base case copper price (¢/lb)	Total debt DCR	
		Copper	% Change from base case
3	93.2	80.4	-13.7
4	100.0	89.2	-10.3
5	106.1	90.3	-14.9
6	112.6	96.9	-13.9
7	118.4	100.5	-15.1
8	124.4	105.1	-15.5
9	130.7	112.8	-13.7
10	137.4	112.0	-18.5

Overall Methodology

The recommended approach is to separate the analysis into the following stages:

1. First, perform an unlevered analysis of the project to determine whether or not the project is likely to generate cash flow returns which will adequately reward project participants for resources committed and risks undertaken.
2. Begin the levered analysis by determining how much debt service the project's cash flow can support in each year in which financing is available.
3. Tailor the available financing alternatives to the project's inherent ability to service debt. This is done to reduce the risk of default or rescheduling and to minimize reliance on other credit supports.

Heavy debt service burdens incurred in the early years of a project can be dealt with by funding initial expenditures with equity thus delaying debt financing; and by using financing techniques which allow for gradually increasing repayment schedules. While the risk of default can be mitigated by strong construction, operation, purchase, and sales agreements, careful tailoring of debt service to the project's cash-generating capacity minimizes reliance on such contracts and reduces the risk of rescheduling.

Generating the Cash Flow

Accurate estimates of the economic returns available from a project can only be determined by considering all cash flow tradeoffs, including avoided or foregone cash flows, and the accompanying risks. Revenues, costs, and other cash flow accounts comprising the cash flow model should be broken down to allow straightforward calculation of the relevant incremental cash flows and measures of risk and return. In many cases, a number of different project concepts, plant sizes, and product mixes are viable, and each option or stage should be analyzed separately. When structuring the financing for a project, it may be more appropriate to look at the cash flows for a larger project or the company as a whole if, as in the LACC example, financing is not tied directly to the project but rather to the company or to a larger project.

The following "tips" should aid in the cash flow forecasting exercise:

1. As mentioned previously, the cash flow model must be sufficiently detailed to allow calculation of incremental cash flows; however, a common mistake is to include too much detail in the model. Accounting details which do not contribute to the final analysis should be avoided. The model should provide sensitivity analysis capability only for the variables expected to have a relevant impact on cash flows.

2. Cash flow forecasting is facilitated by keeping the analysis in nominal rather than in real terms. Escalation factors for key price and cost items should account for both inflationary and real price changes. Nominal forecasts avoid the problem that more prices and costs increase along with inflation but financing commitments, debt service, and depreciation schedules do not. People normally tend to think in terms of nominal discount rates. If certain prices or cash flows are most easily thought of or compared in real terms, they can easily be deflated from nominal to real.

3. Working capital needs should be related to current levels of production, sales, or costs whenever possible. In the LACC example, the working capital relationships used are shown in Table 10.

Since the increase in working capital is very often a significant cash requirement, assuming a fixed working capital amount can severely distort cash flows and lead to incorrect assessment of a project's profitability and ability to service debt.

Evaluation of Cash Flows

Typically, a number of different cash flows are relevant in the LACC analysis. The analysis should begin with a detailed forecast of the total equity cash flow, which can then serve as a basis for deriving most, if not all, of the other cash flows of interest.
Cash flows, either unlevered or levered, can be categoriezed as follows:

1. Equity cash flows, including the total equity cash flow and cash flows for each major shareholder or sponsor.

2. Debt cash flows, including cash flows accruing to each lender. A lender may also be a shareholder or sponsor.

3. National profitability cash flows, such as the change in foreign exchange reserves, the cash flow accruing to the host government, or some measure of the cash flow effects on the domestic economy.

Table 10 LACC Working Capital Assumption

Working capital variable	Related variable
Cash on hand	Production costs and expenses
Accounts receivable	Sales revenue
Raw materials and supplies	Concentrate production
Work in process inventory	Production costs and expenses
Finished goods inventory	Sales revenue
Prepaid expenses	Taxes
Accounts payable	Cost of goods sold
Accrued expenses	Operating expenses

Once the relevant cash flows have been determined, a number of different risk and return measures can be applied to them. The most common measures of the return provided by a cash flow are: (1) net present value (NPV) and (2) internal rate of return (IRR).

When calculating the NPV of a given cash flow, care should be taken to choose an appropriate discount rate, which may be different for different cash flows and may vary from year to year. Some cash flows may be a mixture of two or more underlying cash flows with different degrees of risk and different discount rates; the NPV should then be calculated as the sum of the NPVs of the underlying cash flows.

The caveats concerning IRR should be kept in mind. IRRs can be quite useful. For example, the IRR of a lender's cash flow can be a basis for comparison of the actual cost of alternative forms of debt, provided all hidden costs have been accounted for and assuming the same degree of credit support is being provided for all debt alternatives under consideration.

The most common measures of the ability of a project to service debt are: (1) debt coverage ratio (DCR) and, (2) interest coverage ratio (ICR).

A given DCR may or may not take into account any cash reserves or other excess funds accumulated from previous years. By not including existing cash reserves in cash available to service debt, the DCR provides an indication of the ability of the project to generate sufficient cash in the current period to meet debt service obligations. A DCR which does take into account these cash reserves, provides a measure of the amount of cash which is available to the project in relation to debt service.

All ideas and comments regarding DCRs apply to interest coverage ratios (ICRs) as well, except that an ICR measures the ability of the project to meet only interest payments, rather than interest and principal payments.

Sensitivity analysis should then provide insight into the major areas of risk for both equity and debt cash flows, and breakeven analysis is especially useful. Whereas straight sensitivity analysis requires an assessment of the likelihood of the actual event simulated, breakeven analysis may aid in understanding the magnitude of certain risks through lower or upper bounds on key parameters. Such lower and upper bounds can be particularly helpful in the design of the overall financing structure by providing the necessary guidance in the establishment of a project's borrowing capacity and associated repayment schedule as well as terms and conditions of contractual supports.

REFERENCE

Boettcher, J. H., and F. B. Sotelino, "A Look at the Variable-Maturity Loan." *Harvard Business Review*, May-June, 1982.

8
Selecting the Working Partners

M. WILLIAM EMMONS   *Pathfinder, Inc., Cherry Hill, New Jersey*

The partnership concept, once accepted by the owner and contractor, will provide the basis for a successful project. From the early planning stage, the owner must conceptualize and actively seek as a working partner that specific contractor who is best able to carry the venture (project) to a successful conclusion. The contractor's own corporate objectives must be to search out those projects which will demonstrate the abilities and thus enhance the skills, reputation, and profitability of his company.

CONTRACTING PHASE OF A PROJECT

The contracting phase of a project results in the creation of the owner-contractor partnership. It builds on the results and conclusions of the venture's development phase, accomplished by the owner, and provides the basis for the execution phase, to be accomplished by the contractor. Productive interaction between owner and contractor is the operating mode during this period . . . truly a best efforts time.

 Figure 1 outlines the basic activities to be accomplished during each project phase.

CONTRACTOR AND OWNER OBJECTIVES

The contractor and owner bring different needs to the venture; thus they establish different objectives. The contractor's objectives include (not necessarily in order of priority): winning a sufficient number of contracts to maintain a viable organization and to provide for long-term growth; being awarded contracts which will add to its library of technology and skills; and executing those contracts in such a way to provide a reasonable financial return to its owners, investors, and employees. The owner's objectives are related to finding the best contractor to complete each venture within the anticipated cost and schedule; seeing that the plant produces the quantity and quality of product expected; and ensuring that the work has been accomplished without serious accidents and that the plant operates safely, without harm to the employees or the community.

CONTRACTING PRINCIPLES

As in any undertaking, certain basic principles apply to contracting. Only the basic principles are cited here; each contractor and each owner should establish their own set of principles and communicate these to its employees, clients, and customers.

DEVELOPMENT PHASE	CONTRACTING PHASE	EXECUTION PHASE
ACTIVITIES Project Planning Market Development Process Planning Cost Estimating Basic Design	**ACTIVITIES** Contracting Plan Contractor Screening Selection of Bidders Invitation for Proposals Contractors' Proposals Bid Review Contract Award	**ACTIVITIES** Detailed Engineering Procurement Construction
. . . By Owner	. . . By Owner and Contractor	. . . By Contractor

Figure 1 Phases of a project.

Competitive Bidding

Competitive bidding strengthens industry as a whole as well as each individual company. Owners benefit through actions which optimize costs. Contractors benefit from enhanced employee creativity, higher productivity, lower costs, and improved profitability.

Single Responsibility

Awarding a single contract, covering all work required and encompassing all facilities, provides the clearest lines of communications, responsibilities, and accountabilities. Control systems can be applied with greater assurance for a successful venture.

However, in this less than perfect world, a division of work is often required to take advantage of the best available technology, skills, and capabilities in the marketplace. Figure 2 indicates both horizontal (Alternative X) and vertical (Alternative Y) divisions.

Fair and Ethical Practices

Beyond the obvious moral issues, fair and ethical practices make good business sense. It is important to establish a sense of mutual trust. The success of the partnership and the venture depends on this principle.

SEQUENCE OF CONTRACTING ACTIVITIES

As in all undertakings, contracting follows a set sequence of activities. Figure 3 sets forth the contracting sequence. The elapsed time is not indicated in Figure 3 since each contracting effort will require a different time frame depending on the type of contract, owner's reviews and approvals, project complexity, and the location as well as other factors. It is important that the contracting effort begin early in the project to allow sufficient time for decisions to be made based on appropriate information in order to avoid preempting attractive contracting strategies.

ACTIVITY	ALTERNATIVE X		ALTERNATIVE Y		ALTERNATIVE Z	
	ONSITES	OFFSITES	ONSITES	OFFSITES	ONSITES	OFFSITES
ENGINEERING	A (1)		A	B	A B	C D
PROCUREMENT						
CONSTRUCTION	B				E	

A, B, C, D AND E INDICATE SEPARATE CONTRACTORS.

Figure 2 Project execution alternatives.

THE CONTRACTING PLAN

The architect develops the plans before the cathedral can be built; and so it is with contracting. Development of the contracting plan is essential in the forging of a partnership. A plan provides participants with a sense of purpose and direction. A poorly conceived plan will result in false starts, mistakes, and frustrations.

Contracting planning consists of: (1) gathering all data and information related to the venture which will have, or has the potential to have, an impact on contracting and/or project execution; (2) analyzing such data and information, including potential effects on costs, schedule, quality, and safety; (3) structuring potential contracting strategies for the venture including qualifying and quantifying the advantages and disadvantages of each; and (4) determining the contracting strategy which will best provide the opportunity to meet the venture objectives.

The results of the contracting planning are documented for review and approval by management. The basic elements (sections) of a contracting plan are:

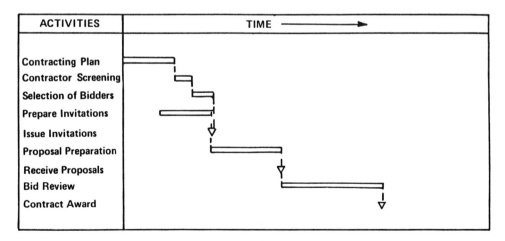

Figure 3 Sequence of contracting activities.

Purpose of plan
Project background
Contracting principles
Recommended contracting strategy
Analysis of contracting alternatives
Schedule of contracting activities
Contracting procedures
Potential contractors
Decisions and approvals needed

The contracting plan, once approved, will guide the contracting effort. It will be reviewed form time to time to verify that the strategy remains valid. Changed circumstances require a change in strategy; for example, the inability to attract sufficient
bidders for a competitive lump-sum bidding slate.

CONTRACTOR SCREENING

For most projects, there will be a number of contractors capable of performing the work.
The process of contractor screening begins with the complete list of those contractors
who appear to have the capability and experience (the "long list"), gathering up-to-
date information on their capacity, experience, capability, and interest; and selecting
a limited number (the "short list") to actually receive the Invitation for Proposals.

The Screening Telex/Letter

The screening process is in itself an application of the fairness principle. All potential
bidders receive the same information and all replies are evaluated before selecting the
final bidding slate.

The initial contact with the potential contractors is through a written document, a
screening telex or letter (telexes provide faster turnaround). The use of written documents ensures the uniformity of responses; which, in turn, simplifies screening analysis and selection of the bidders.

The screening telex/letter is a two-part document. The first part provides project
information; the second part requests information from the contractors.

The information to the prospective contractors covers:

Description of facilities
Contracting basis and timing
Key project dates
Other significant factors

The information requested from the prospective contractors includes:

Willingness to bid
Engineering personnel and workload
Tentative project execution plans
Experience
Other significant information

The replies will be tabulated and analyzed. The objective is to identify those who will
be included on the "short list." Again, a two-part analysis. First, the replies are
judged against a "musts" list: willingness to bid on the indicated basis; financial stability; no technology conflict; sufficient size of organization and skills; and ability
to work at the indicated location. There may be other items, but this list should be
kept reasonably short. The result of this review is either "yes, the potential contractor can possibly be a bidder," or "no, he does not qualify."

Second, the replies are evaluated against a list of "wants." The list contains the items which are significant to the execution of the project; each being weighted as to its evaluated impact and importance. Each contractor is rated, relative to the other contractors, for each item on the "musts" list. The weights and ratings provide the basis for the selection of the bidding slate.

Selection of Bidders

The rating-times-weighting for each item results in a component of the total. The sum of the components for each contract will identify those contractors which best meet the owner's objectives. Final selection of the contractors for the "short list" starts at this point. A broup of 6 or 8 contractors, with only small differences in their ratings, will be identified. Other subjective factors taken along with the "numbers" will determine the bidding list. The selected bidders are contacted to reconfirm their interest in bidding and the Invitation for Proposals can be issued.

INVITATION FOR PROPOSALS

The owner, who has planned the venture, established principles and guidelines for its implementation, and set economic goals, must communicate this and all other aspects of contracting and project execution to all bidders in a consistent manner. The invitation is actually a set of documents which will provide a complete basis for the preparation and submission of proposals by the bidders. The documents include:

Invitation for Proposals Letter
Information for Bidders
Proposal Form
Agreement Form
Job Specifications

Invitation for Proposals Letter

The letter is an essential part of the invitation. It is sent jointly to all bidders, thus each will know who the competitors are. If the selection of the bidding slate has been done properly, the degree of competition will increase immediately. The letter contains only the key items: a listing of the content of the invitation, the protocol and owner contact during bidding, and the bid due date and submittal conditions.

Information to Bidders

If each bidder were left to his own devices to prepare a response, the comparison by the owner would be chaotic. The Information to Bidders and the Proposal Form are developed to avoid that situation. The Information to Bidders is a memorandum which gives in detail the ground rules and procedures which each contractor must follow in preparing and submitting the proposal. In developing this document it should be remembered that the contractor's proposal will only be as responsive as the instructions which are provided. Well developed instructions will make the contractors' preparation more efficient and effective. It will also make the owner's selection of the successful contractor easier.

Proposal Form

The Proposal Form serves as the base document used by the contractor in submitting a proposal. When completed, it will include all of the required commercial terms. It is developed in parallel with the Agreement Form so that all required data and information is requested and supplied. Copies are completed, signed by an officer of the contractor, and submitted to the owner with the other proposal documents.

Agreement Form

The Agreement Form is prepared by the owner and contains the proposed terms and conditions to be used as a basis for the contractual agreement between the parties. Said terms and conditions will govern the rights, duties, obligations, responsibilities, and liabilities of the owner and the contractor during the execution of the project. The Agreement Form is both an administrative document to guide the actions of the parties during project execution, and a legal document which must be valid before the courts. It is important that after award it become a day-to-day tool of the project teams.

The owner should prepare standard documents, developed with input and approved by its legal, tax, financial, risk management, and other staff functions, to use as the base document for all contracts. This will assure more efficient contracting, consistency in the approach to contractors, and easier responses from contractors.

Job Specification

The Job Specification is a collection of documents which taken as a whole define (1) the administrative and procedural requirements related to the performance of all work to be done under the contract (a Coordination Procedure), (2) the basic standards related to the design, quality, safety, and operability of the facility components and the overall facility (general and specific Standards and Practices), and (3) a description of the facilities to be engineered and constructed (Basic Design Specifications).

The complete Job Specification will be a part of the Invitation for Proposals for lump-sum contracting. Only the Coordination Procedure and a brief description of facilities (nonconfidential) is needed for reimbursable cost contracting; the remaining portions will be issued to the successful contractor after award.

CONTRACTOR PROPOSALS

The Invitation for Proposals is issued to the selected bidders for preparation of proposals. The key to preparing a proposal which will favorably impress the owner is a thorough knowledge of the content of the Invitation for Proposal documents. Questions about unclear points should be raised with the owner. Site visits should be made to clarify the documents and for a first-hand understanding of potential problems.

The contractor's proposal must address the needs of the specific project; general boilerplate will not suffice. Alternative project execution schemes should be evaluated; and, from these, the contractor can choose those elements which will provide the owner with the lowest cost facility, consistent with the requirements of the Invitation for Proposals. The contractors' proposals will consist of these separate sections:

1. Commercial Proposal
2. Project Execution Proposal
3. Technical Proposal

Commercial Proposal

The Commercial Proposal will consist of the Proposal Form, completed and signed by an officer of the contractor, including all requested attachments. This section contains all business terms (lump-sum prices, reimbursable cost fees, overheads, and fixed rates) and the exceptions taken, the alternatives proposed, and comments to the Agreement Form and Job Specification. It is the most sensitive portion of the proposal and is submitted as the "sealed bid."

Project Execution Proposal

The content of the Project Execution Proposal is defined in detail in the Information to Bidders. It will contain:

> Corporate organization charts
> Experience, similar projects, and location
> Project execution plan
> Project organization chart
> Key personnel proposed
> Workload charts
> Preliminary schedule
> Details on techniques and procedures

Technical Proposal

The content of the Technical Proposal will vary more than any other portion of the contractor's proposal. It may contain a full description of the proposed technology plus extensive technical details on equipment and materials; and at the other extreme, a technical proposal may not be required at all. The latter case would apply to a reimbursable cost project with no contractor involvement in technology or process design.

BID REVIEW: GENERAL

Proposals are submitted by the contractors as required by the Invitation for Proposals to the person designated, and at the time and location specified. The contractor's work has been completed for the moment. They must now await the owner's response. It is often said that the contracting planning is the most important step in contracting, and it may well be. If the owner does not plan and implement the bid review effectively, the whole process can be "blown" by not selecting the best contractor, by adding project risks, and by placing the project objectives in jeopardy.

Bid review requires a sensitive balancing of facts versus judgments, objective versus subjective reasoning, work tasks versus costs, time versus price, and risks versus opportunities. Although basic principles apply to all bid reviews, procedures must be tailored to meet the needs of each bid review.

Bid Review Principles

The bid review is a complex effort. Certain basic principles or elements are:

> Bid review planning
> Dedicated bid review team
> Sequential review
> Reviews with bid reviews
> Owner-contractor interactions
> Contract signed at award

Bid Review Planning

By planning the bid review and documenting it formally (Bid Review Plan), all of the owner's participants in the bid review will have to "buy in." The plan will be the only guide and basis, providing for an effective effort. The planning should address all aspects related to both the project and the contracting. The following typical Table of Contents indicates the comprehensive nature of the Bid Review Plan.

Table of Contents

Project Background

Contracting Background
    Strategy
    Screening
    Bidders

Invitation for Proposals

Contractors' Proposals

Bid Review: General
    Location
    Objectives
    Sequence
    Award

Bid Review Team

Bid Review: Specifics
    Bid opening
    Documentation/internal communications
    Communications with bidders
    Initial review/select contenders
    Visits to contenders
    Evaluation of key personnel
    Selection of contractor for award

Contract Award
    Award recommendation
    Award/sign contract

Attachments should be included to further explain or provide working forms.

Dedicated Bid Review Team

Qualified personnel to review the various elements of the proposals must be selected, relieved of their normal duties during the bid review period, and fully informed of the project and contracting details. A typical team is shown in Figure 4.

Sequential Review

There is a standard two-step procedure for bid review. First there is a complete initial review of all proposals to determine complete content and identify the leading contenders. This requires a comparison of business terms and an evaluation of the technical and project execution proposals. Competitive business terms and acceptable technical and execution proposals determine the contenders.

Second is a thorough, in-depth review of the proposals submitted by the selected contenders. This is a time-consuming task; whereas the initial review may take up to four days, the detailed review takes up to four weeks or longer in some cases.

Reviews within the Bid Review

The Bid Review Team Organization (Fig. 4) provides the clue to the review-within-bid review concept. Three separate reviews are made: technical, project execution, and business (commercial). Each is conducted as a closed review; after each team has completed its work, the conclusions are shared and the melding of the comparisons and evaluations lead to the selection of the best contractor.

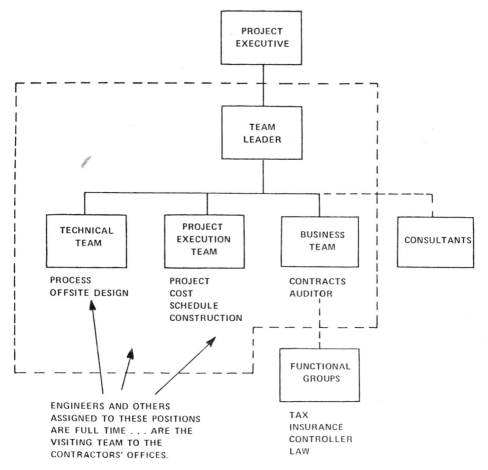

Figure 4 Bid review team organization.

Owner-Contractor Interactions

Interaction between the owner and contractor will be extensive. Formal, written documentation will be the rule; the normal mode is owner-question/contractor-answer. The owner needs to clarify and understand the proposal, and to "upgrade" each proposal to its best possible position. The contractor also wants to achieve the best position for its own proposal.

During the bid review all normal or abnormal actions should be examined in light of the fairness and ethics principle. Concern with business ethics, and any apparent or real conflicts, should be a primary guide in owner-contractor interactions.

Contract Signed at Award

All activities whether commercial, contractual, technical, or project execution must be completed by the time the contract is awarded so that the contract can be signed and execution can commence without extraneous interference from unsettled matters.

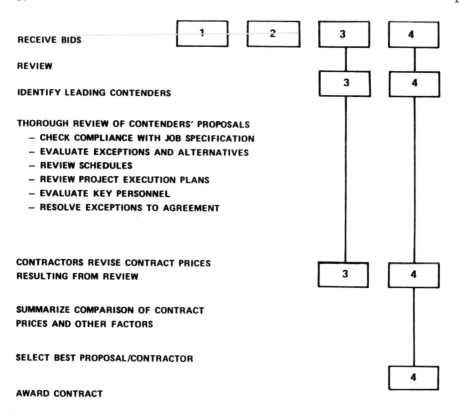

Figure 5 Lump-sum bid review.

LUMP-SUM BID REVIEW

The objective of a lump-sum bid review is to determine which contractor offers the lowest lump-sum price and conforms to all of the technical, project execution, and contractual requirements. Figure 5 charts a typical lump-sum bid review.

Since lump-sum prices are quoted, relatively little work is required in the review of business terms. The major effort is in the technical review. Specialists in process technology and design, and in machinery and other equipment, materials, safety, and control systems will review the technical proposals to ensure that the plant and facilities being proposed conform to the Job Specification.

Review of the project execution proposal assures the owner that the contractor can successfully complete the project. Any exceptions or comments on the Agreement Form are resolved during the review. After all aspects of the proposals have been evaluated and resolved, and the bid review team is satisfied with all elements, the selection of the contractor for award can be made.

REIMBURSABLE COST BID REVIEW

The objective of a reimbursable cost bid review is to determine which contractor offers the best combination of business terms and technical and project execution capability. Figure 6 charts a typical reimbursable cost bid review. The reimbursable cost bid review will consist of a detailed review of all portions of the contractor's proposal.

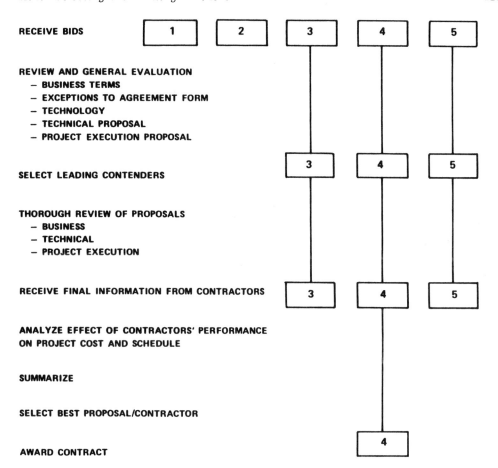

Figure 6 Reimbursable cost bid review.

Commercial Proposal

The commercial proposal includes business terms and contractual considerations. Business terms consists of salaries and wages, payroll burdens, departmental overheads, fixed rates, and fees. An estimate is made of the cost of each contractor's engineering, procurement, and construction management services using the contractor's quotations and the owner's estimate of hours to be expended. These costs are summarized to compare the costs quoted by the various contractors. Figure 7 shows a typical summary. The comparison of business terms indicates the relative competitiveness of the bidders. It is not, however, the primary selection criterion, as is normally the case for lump-sum bid review.

Project Execution Proposal

The project execution proposal will contain details in the plans, systems, techniques, and procedures which the contractor will use in executing the project. These are grouped into four categories: (1) detailed engineering; (2) procurement/purchasing; (3) project controls; and (4) field construction.

Each category is reviewed to identify strengths and discover weaknesses. Contractors are encouraged to modify procedures to eliminate weaknesses and thus bring

	CONTRACTORS			
	A	**B**	**C**	**D**
FEES	XXX	XXX	XXX	XXX
ENGINEERING & PROCUREMENT				
SALARIES AND WAGES	XXX	XXX	XXX	XXX
PAYROLL BURDEN	XXX	XXX	XXX	XXX
DEPARTMENTAL OVERHEADS	XXX	XXX	XXX	XXX
TOTAL ESTIMATED SERVICES	XXX	XXX	XXX	XXX
CONSTRUCTION MANAGEMENT				
SALARIES AND WAGES	XXX	XXX	XXX	XXX
PAYROLL BURDEN	XXX	XXX	XXX	XXX
ALLOWANCES	XXX	XXX	XXX	XXX
TOTAL ESTIMATED SERVICES	XXX	XXX	XXX	XXX
OTHER SERVICES (As Applicable)	XXX	XXX	XXX	XXX
TOTAL ESTIMATED COSTS	XXX	XXX	XXX	XXX
DIFFERENTIAL COST	BASE	+	+	+

Figure 7 Summary of business terms.

its proposal into its best position. The analysis considers the following items in each category. This list will be modified to include other items for specific project requirements.

> Detailed engineering
> > Project organization
> > Office capacity
> > Availability and quality of personnel
> > Key project personnel
> > Project team effectiveness
> > Coordination of work functions
> > Standards and procedures
> > Use of models and computers
> > Familiarity with codes
>
> Procurement/purchasing
> > Project organization
> > Procedures
> > Paper flow
> > Availability and quality of personnel
> > Knowledge of markets
> > Interaction with engineering
> > Familiarity with codes
>
> Project controls
> > Project organization
> > Procedures
> > Paper flow

>   Use of computers
>   Availability and quality of personnel
>   Reporting systems
>   Interaction with engineering and field personnel
>
> Field construction
>   Project organization
>   Quality control procedures
>   Safety awareness and procedures
>   Reporting and communications
>   Availability and quality of personnel
>   Knowledge of local labor

After the analysis, each contractor is rated in each of the categories of project execution indicating the relative strength of each contractor. These ratings, and the differences they represent, are quantified in terms of the impact on the cost of the project
and on the scheduled completion date. For example, a lower rating in procurement/
purchasing will result in higher cost of equipment, materials, and subcontracts; and
detailed engineering ratings will impact on engineering productivity and quantities of
bulk materials.

The Technical Proposal

The technical proposal normally will be a brief document, not the detailed document in
a lump-sum proposal. The review, analysis, and evaluation is similar to that performed for the project execution proposal.

Bid Review Summary

The results of the three separate reviews are combined. Then considering all items,
factual and qualitative, the selection of the contractor for the award is made.

CONTRACT AWARD

After contractor award selection, an Award Recommendation is prepared to (1) present
the recommendation to management, and (2) to document the results of the bid review
for the records. After approval by senior management, all open items are resolved
with the selected contractor. The contract documents are modified to reflect all owner-
contractor agreements, and the contract is awarded and signed.

SUMMARY

The partnership created in the contracting phase of a project, following well established techniques and procedures, has a firm foundation. The venture can be successful; the owner and the contractor can meet their respective objectives. But success
is not assured. It is now in the hands of the contractor's and the owner's project
management team . . . the next act.

9

Proposal Management

CLEMENT F. BURNAP *Consultant, San Francisco, California*

After project conception and the planning and organizing steps that follow, a proposal is requested from those who will compete for the work to be contracted out. This commonly will include the engineering, procurement, and construction (EPC) responsibilities. Most contracts are awarded on the basis of proposals submitted in response to an inquiry issued by the owner.

Each proposal of significance should be considered as an intensive project in itself. The proposal effort is headed up by a proposal manager; or, more accurately, a proposal project manager.

The knowledge of proposal management is directly relevant to the subject of project management. Many, if not all, of the attributes of a project manager must be found in a proposal project manager. Some skills, such as rapid and effective writing, are mandatory skills for the proposal project manager.

In the following paragraphs, the characteristics of a proposal project are presented, along with the need for preparation of material for future proposals and the preproposal activities essential for the success of the proposal effort. The activities involved in the actual preparation of the proposal will be presented together with an outline for a typical EPC proposal. The accommodation of owner-imposed modifications to the standard proposal format is discussed. Commercial/compensation terms are covered to give the project manager some of the available alternatives on contractual arrangements.

CHARACTERISTICS OF A PROPOSAL PROJECT

The more important characteristics of a proposal project are:

1. Proposal projects are high-priority, short-duration efforts. They must be completed to the owner's schedule requirement regardless of the workload and other demands on the contracting organization.
2. The owner's specification for preferred payment method must be adhered to, at least in the basic proposal. Alternates which offer benefits to both parties may be suggested for the owner's consideration.
3. The owner frequently will specify a particular format for the proposal and for presentation of the requested information.
4. The owner may express a clear preference as to the location where the project work will be done. The engineering company may suggest alternate arrange-

ments that give the owner a more cost-effective project without sacrificing the required contact. The base proposal, however, must be as responsive as possible.

5. The owner may have a preference, openly expressed or merely implied, for the construction labor arrangement. If this preference has not been made clear in the Request for Proposal (RFP) or in discussions with the owner, it should be determined at the earliest possible time in the proposal effort so that the proper construction program may be planned.

6. A proposal project requires forming a team of representatives from sales, project management, technical, and support functions. Many of these have responsibilities over and above the proposal project. These workloads must be considered and respected insofar as is possible.

7. Proposal projects are normally costed against corporate overhead, and therefore will be tightly budgeted and be closely monitored by senior management.

Most of these proposal project characteristics are identical to those of the projects themselves. Significant differences stem from the much shorter schedule and resource constraints which make it difficult to complete the proposal effort on schedule and within budget.

These characteristics along with other more specific factors must be considered in planning the proposal project to produce a competitive proposal which meets the requirements of both the owner and the contracting company.

PREPARATION FOR FUTURE PROPOSALS

Because of time restraints and the repetitive nature of much of the data used in proposals, it is helpful to collect as much as possible of the proposal information in advance. This is especially true for the following areas:

Proposal project managers should be identified in advance. In a company with a significant continuing proposal load, a group may be formed consisting of former project managers with verbal skills and the proper personality to allow them to function in the pressure cooker environment of proposal preparation. These individuals must have a high tolerance for working under tight schedules, stringent budgets, with borrowed personnel, and being the object of continual criticism which is not always constructive.

A proposal publication staff should be in place to be fully effective. These individuals will have skills in editing, use of word processing and reproduction equipment, as well as graphic arts capability. They should be able to work effectively with the masses of material in various stages of progress to assure that all of it comes together according to the schedule.

A technical information data base including the full range of the types of projects offered by the company, including feasibility studies, engineering projects, as well as full-scope projects for various types of facilities.

Standard scopes of services should be developed that can be readily customized for the particular project on the word processing system. Much of the particular information for various projects is quite similar and only requires bringing it into conformance with owner requirements or with those of the particular facility of location.

The company should have developed comprehensive definitions for the various levels of effort associated with producing cost estimates of varying accuracies. This is particularly important for developing proposals for feasibility studies.

Work plans should also be developed for the various basic types of projects. These can be of general information which can then be modified to conform with plans for the specific project under consideration.

A data bank is helpful to standardize commercial terms and conditions together with listings which define those costs included in overhead and those which are not. This is particularly helpful in reimbursable contracts to control changes to the standard "checklist" and the resultant changes in the reimbursable unit costs.

Qualification material should be updated frequently in several different standard formats such as:

> Project performance data, schedule and costs
> Descriptions of past projects
> Resumes of key personnel
> Writeups on support areas such as:
>> Project controls
>> Procurement procedures
>> Material management
>> Quality assurance practices

Typical writeups should be prepared in advance for various other parts of the proposal. These will be modified to suit the Request for Proposal (RFP) or Inquiry document. Among others, these writings include:

> Introduction
> Project organization
> Schedule
> Project controls
> Compensation

PREPROPOSAL EFFORT FOR SPECIFIC PROPOSALS

Preparing a proposal may start as soon as there has been a positive indication that the company will be included on the bid list and preliminary information is available on the project. Early efforts would include:

Preliminary assignments for the anticipated proposal would be made based upon the schedule for the RFP release and the due date of the proposal. These assignments would include the proposal project manager, the project manager proposed to head the project, and the proposal publication and technical support personnel. In addition, the lead estimator, lead scheduler, key technical personnel, procurement and construction representatives as indicated by the nature of the effort would be selected.

The preliminary proposal plan, schedule, and budget should be blocked out. The proposal plan would define the outline of the proposal and the preliminary assignments for the work. The schedule would indicate dates for completion of the preliminary drafts, jobhour and cost estimates, the final draft dates, the necessary dates for approval, and the publication and delivery dates.

A rigorous assessment should be made of the major technical aspects of the project to identify the company's strengths and weaknesses. Immediate and specific actions should be planned to bolster corporate capability where this is required and to develop the personnel and background information to cover these critical areas.

When the RFP is received, it is reviewed and a bid/no bid decision is made based upon any new information which has been made available as well as that developed in the preproposal work which has been done.

PROPOSAL EFFORT

Assignment of Proposal Team Members

As soon as the decision to bid has been confirmed, the assignment of proposal team members is formalized. Assigning those who participated in the preproposal work is desirable, but not always possible.

Kick-off Meeting

The project manager calls a kick-off meeting, at which time task assignments and the corresponding schedules are made. The proposed project manager should meet with the proposal project manager to coordinate the project planning prior to the kick-off meeting so the project strategy and philosophy can be communicated to the proposal team at the kick-off meeting.

At the kick-off meeting, technical, legal, and compensation considerations are reviewed, and assignments of responsibility are made including:

Proposed project manager:
    Definition of scope of work
    Stating the project objectives
    Project plan and strategy
    Description of the proposed project organization
    Development of the organization chart
    Identification of special and unusual services that are required with corresponding assignments of write-up responsibility by technical specialists.
    Project schedule showing services performed in the time sequence determined by the work plan
    Estimate of jobhours required for the project
    Cost estimates as required by RFP
Proposal project manager
    Set the proposal schedule allowing sufficient time for preparing, reviewing, and editing draft material; for reviewing and approving final proposal; and time required for printing and delivering the proposal
    Establish the proposal jobhour and cost estimates
    Prepare first draft of letter of transmittal and all sections of the proposal except the qualification (these are summarized later)
    Specify the qualification material needed for the proposal and review the available qualification material to determine what is appropriate and identify what must be developed
    Set up the master dummy book in the exact order that the final proposal is to be submitted
Proposal publication editor:
    Edit resumes
    Develop qualification section
    Initiate the legal review of the terms and conditions imposed by the RFP
    Establish requirements for graphic arts work, including covers, tabs, charts, and illustrations
    Track progress of proposal work to assure that sufficient time is available to complete printing and assembly of the proposal

Preliminary Review of Proposal Text

All material will be typed on the word processor, double spaced, with wide margins for easier editing. Each page will be identified by the appropriate section and page number together with the date of issue or revision. Typed drafts should be checked carefully against the original drafts to assure that nothing has been inadvertently omitted. Copies of the typed drafts should be sent to interested parties, including the contract draft, for information.

Editorial changes and other modifications to the typed drafts will be posted on the sheets contained in the master dummy. Retyping will normally be limited to the final corrections to the text, except where major revisions are required.

Final Review

When the text is essentially in final form and all changes have been incorporated into the typed text, it is submitted for review of operations management and for the final legal review. All major changes from this last text review should be flagged so that the signoff can be obtained quickly.

Publication and Signoff

After the review, and after any additional changes to the typed text have been made, the proposal is printed. Camera-ready material is checked against the dummy book to assure that all changes have been incorporated, and the specified number of copies are reproduced, collated, and bound.

Final approval is now given by the signoff set by senior management.

Delivery of the Proposal

After the required signoffs have been made, the proposal is delivered in accordance with the schedule and method established by the owner and/or the established plan.

TYPICAL EPC PROPOSAL CONTENTS

Following is a summary of the contents of the typical cost reimbursable proposal for engineering, procurement, and construction services.

Introduction and Summary

The RFP conditions are summarized and the general approach to the work by the contractor is indicated.

The various sections of the proposal are recapped. This is desirable to clarify the proposal content to the new readers and to introduce them to the method in which the material is to be presented.

Project Description

This material is taken largely from the Request for Proposal. It may also include information that has been obtained by site visits, during prebid conferences, and in other contacts with the owner or other knowledgeable sources. The project description may indicate the battery limits of the project, and specify the work items that are the responsibility of the owner so that it is clear that this work is not included in the contractor's scope of services.

Scope of Services

This section details the services that the contractor will provide. It includes the services that will be performed and the documents that will be produced. All services should be well defined, not openended, even in reimbursable cost proposals. Services should be listed according to the division of the project organization assigned the responsibility for that work. Table 1 shows a typical listing of services for project management as it would appear in a proposal.

Table 1 Scope of Project Management Services for a Typical Project

---

Maintain relations with owner

General administration of contract with owner and management of contract communication with owner

Plan, coordinate, and control all project activities of the contractor's project staff

Mobilize personnel at the specified locations where the work will be done

Provide direction and coordination for overall project work required in providing the services offered

Establish, monitor, and maintain project security

Provide office space and clerical support for owner's representatives

Review and issue all data furnished by owner to project staff

Participate in preparation of project criteria

Establish with the owner, the project coordination procedures including interfacing with the owner on such project activities as engineering and design, estimating, procurement, project planning, scheduling and control, construction management, approvals by the owner, and document distribution and control

Maintain project file

Maintain liaison and communication with the owner and with public officials as agreed

Develop an overall project milestone schedule

Review the contractor's standard chart of accounts for the specific type of project with the owner and arrange for any special requirements

Prepare a definite estimate of project costs

Prepare cash flow requirements

Prepare and issue quarterly project expenditure reports for the project

Prepare and issue a monthly project program and cost status report

Prepare a final report upon completion of the project

Obtain final turnover statement

Deliver all project material to the owner at the end of the job

Close out all areas of project administration

All of the documents that are to be furnished as part of the contractor's services should be listed. A brief description of what each will include will be helpful.

Work Plan and Schedule

The project work plan is developed in response to the stated objectives of the owner or as defined by the sales representative and the objectives of the contracting firm for the specific project. The work plan presents the strategy for achieving all of these objectives in performing the scope of services. All assumptions made for the preparation of the work plan should be spelled out carefully. The plan consists of sequencing the work activities and further development of how they will be executed. The work plan may be presented in graphic form showing the interrelationships between the various activities.

Project Organization

Material included in this section describes the proposed project organization, and details the responsibilities of each of the key members of the project team.

An organization chart depicting the proposed project team will be drawn. The standard project organization should be modified for each specific project to best respond to the particular owner's organization and to the interfaces required by the conditions of the RFP. It is especially important to analyze what type of organization is best suited to the job requirements—a task force is favored by many owners who feel it is easier for the contractor's project manager to maintain control over time charges and personnel assignments.

The interface with the supplier of technology should be carefully defined, and the technical review responsibilities must be clearly assigned.

The resumes of experience for each of the key members of the project team should be included in this section. They should be limited to no more than two pages unless there are specific reasons for more extensive coverage. The resumes should be indexed or should be arranged in alphabetical order for each reference. If the resumes require many pages because of the length or the number of individuals covered, it may be better to include them in the Appendix.

Estimates, Hours, Cost

All of the information presented in the preceding sections of the proposal must be taken into account in preparing the estimates for work.

It is important that the estimates be prepared based strictly upon the scope of services, the work plan, and the proposed schedule.

The various estimates from each of the sources charged with their preparation are consolidated and a final cost estimate prepared for the work. Confidential cost data is entered in those estimates by the corporate estimators or financial group.

For proposing home office services, including project management, engineering, procurement and controls, reimbursable costs are based upon a jobhour estimate. This may be backed up by a manning chart showing numbers of people by discipline and by pay grade. In addition, the salary ranges for each pay grade may be submitted.

The cost estimate will include direct salaries for all technical and nontechnical personnel, as well as indirect costs such as travel, communications, computer use, and reproduction.

In addition to the costs listed above, a preliminary estimate of the total project cost may be required at this stage to check validity of the cost estimate for the services. This estimate is usually done using the standard Code of Accounts for the contractor unless the proposal requires it to be done using the owner's Code of Accounts.

The consolidated estimate is reviewed by the responsible members of the project team, and by such representatives of functional management as have been delegated this responsibility.

Compensation

After the estimates have been reviewed, the commercial terms are finalized by adding those discretionary figures such as burdens, contingencies, overlays, and fees required by the format of the bid. This information is presented in the Compensation section of the proposal.

The basic terms and conditions for reimbursable-type proposals will specify compensation through payment or compensation for costs incurred in performance of the services performed and through the proposed treatment of the fee.

Services

Compensation is usually based upon the following elements of reimbursable cost:

Salaries and wages together with a stated percentage to be added to cover payroll
   burdens

Commercial terms for compensation for jobshop or contract personnel who are not
   regular employees of the contractor

A stipulated percentage to be applied to direct costs to cover corporate overhead
   for such items as nonreimbursable selling, administrative and management costs
   of the contractor' organization

Out-of-pocket costs for outside services

Costs incurred in issuing purchase orders not otherwise reimbursed

Payment of travelling and living expenses for personnel on assignment out of the
   contractor's office

Fee

The RFP defines the fee structure desired by the owner. This may call for the fee to
be quoted to cover only the profit to the contractor or it may include all or many of
the contractor's indirect costs. The preparation of the "checklist" of reimbursable
costs is extremely important. Any proposed checklist must be reviewed and checked
very carefully because of its potential effect upon the profitability of the work.

Payment

The payment schedule terms must be carefully studied to determine the effect on the
contractor's cash flow. It is preferable to set up a system of advance or anticipated
payments to assure that the contractor is not financing the work without providing
for the cost of borrowed money in his proposal. This, of course, becomes very important where major equipment and bulk materials are being purchased for the contractor's
account. A change order formula should be included in the proposal.

Qualifications

The Qualification section of the proposal contains all relevant material arranged in the
proper manner to strengthen confidence as to the contractor's capability in the mind
of the owner's management. Much of this material will be taken from that previously
collected in the files of the contractor. It must always be reviewed to make sure that
the information presented is accurate, pertinent, and forceful. The proposal manager
should not stint on the editing of this section of the proposal.

MODIFICATIONS TO THE STANDARD PROPOSAL

Many owners have a very specific format which requires that the contractor depart
from a standard proposal format. It is best to follow the specified format as it will
help to simplify the proposal evaluation process in the owner's offices.

CONCLUSION

Successful and effective management of proposals requires assignment of qualified personnel to the proposal effort; advance preparation of the support organization and proposal information and data prior to the receipt of the RFP; clear delineation of the
results and timing expected from the proposal effort; close coordination between proposal management, project management, functional management, and senior management of the firm; and strict adherence to a realistic publication schedule.

Above all, a winning proposal requires the ability to identify those things the owner really needs, to respond in a sensitive manner to his concerns, and to convince him that your firm is uniquely qualified to provide the best and most economic job.

IV
THE CONTRACT

OVERVIEW

In today's litigious society, contractual agreements reached prior to the initiation of a project, and the actions and reactions to those agreements throughout the course of the work, may very well determine the success or failure of the venture.

The inclusion of a discussion on contracts in a general treatise on the management of projects is offered with some trepidation. The complexity of modern projects and the general tenor of the current environment clearly demand competent legal counsel. Experienced project managers don't play lawyer; nor do they operate in a vacuum, using experts as decision makers. They have a basic understanding of all phases of their project, and evaluate the recommendations of experts for implementation within the context of project-specific conditions.

In many organizations the project manager may not have decision-making authority regarding contractual issues, or the manager may be assigned after contract award, but when the opportunity to participate is available, the manager should take the initiative. Once a project is released, it's your contract, your project.

The concepts used to arrive at the content of this unit on the legal aspects of project management are twofold: first, fundamental business considerations, or project management prerequisites; second, extended discussions of issues common to the management of projects in the engineering and construction industries. Extended discussions include: the advantages and disadvantages of lump-sum and reimbursable contracts as perceived by the owner and the contractor; joint venture contracts; and, the management of risks and claims—peripheral areas in the past, vital areas today.

CONTRACT CONSIDERATIONS AND CONTRACT TYPES

A contract is an agreement to do or not to do something. The services to be supplied by one party, and the costs and fees to be paid by the other party, and all of the conditions affecting this exchange (the principal considerations) are agreed upon during the negotiation process. The well-written contract serves as a legal and operational memorandum of understanding of the agreements reached between two parties.

Basic contractual issues are covered: why have a contract; the limits; why it should be in writing; and a basic check list applicable to the engineering and construction industry. Two principal contracts, cost plus and lump sum, receive extended treatment.

JOINT VENTURES

A joint venture approach should be considered when the combined strengths of two or more entities result in a joint organization with unique credentials in a targeted business area. A joint venture is a relationship where each party needs the other to achieve a common mutually beneficial objective. Without this synergistic consideration, there is seldom justification for the formation of a shared business venture.

Several basic considerations are covered: a joint venture is defined; the choice—joint venture or corporation; the factors favoring the joint venture; and typical terms to be evaluated for inclusion in a joint venture agreement.

PRECONSTRUCTION PHASE

A considerable number of construction awards are based upon documents prepared by an architect/engineer for an owner, as differentiated from turnkey work. The cost and duration of the construction program is thus largely determined by the quality of the preconstruction process initiated by the owner and architect/engineer. All too often the documents, prepared to meet the objectives of the owner, aren't critically reviewed for "constructability." When detailed specifications are prepared by the owner's representative, that is, architect/engineer, the financial and contractual risks of the contractor are far more limited than realized by the owner.

The contractual positions of the owner and contractor are reviewed in detail; a comprehensive summary of 116 projects analyzed by the National Electrical Contractors Association (NECA) is presented to show the principal reasons for poor project cost/schedule performance, and, by inspection, how the preconstruction phase impacts performance; finally, a lengthy checklist is included to guide the owner in the preparation of construction bid packages.

GUARANTEES, WARRANTIES, LIABILITIES

There are four distinct categories of "express" guarantees in the design/construction industry: design/mechanical; field workmanship; equipment (vendors); performance (process). These guarantees are express in that they are set forth in the agreement as opposed to "implied"—created by the law regardless of the contractual terms.

The express guarantees are discussed in detail; the concept of implied guarantees is reviewed; the elements of guarantees—coverage, time frame, liabilities—are described; and certain other liabilities, such as tort, are covered.

RISK MANAGEMENT AND INSURANCE

Two kinds of risk are found in the business community: one dynamic, one static. Dynamic risks, generic to market, management, and political sources, can result in either profit or loss. Static risks, those that typically arise from loss or damage to property, or personal injury, and usually transferable to insurance underwriters for a price, only result in losses.

A diverse category of available coverages is discussed, including property insurance, casualty insurance, workers compensation, and surety bonds. The pros and cons of "wrap-up" insurance, a program applicable to very large projects, are presented.

CLAIMS MANAGEMENT

The management of claims is an integral part of the entire project management program. Claims management is incorrectly considered to be the handling of claims after problems arise. When this thinking is corrected, most disputes can be settled as they occur. A good claims management system should be in place prior to contract award, and readily implemented as disputes develop.

A claims management program divides a project into four management phases: contract formation, contract performance and administration, claims/dispute resolution, and preparation for litigation support.

All parties should bear in mind that effective management of changes and conflicts as they arise is far more economical than waiting until money has been wasted, the schedule devastated, and both sides have moved toward legal action. If, however, the claim leads to litigation, the prospect of building cooperative relationships between the parties is dim, leaving one simple objective: to win. The least time-consuming and most economical way to achieve this is with a well-prepared claim.

REFERENCES

Contracts

Construction Briefings, Federal Publications.
Werbin, I. V. *Legal Guide for Contractors, Architects, and Engineers.* Central Book Company, 1961.
Restatement of the Law Second. American Law Institute, 1981.

Risk Management

Rosenbloom, J. S. *A Case Study in Risk Management.* Englewood Cliffs, N.Y.: Prentice-Hall.
Angell, F. J., and Pfaffle, A. E. *Insurance and Risk Management.* Insurance Advocate.
Advanced Study Group No. 208. *Report on Construction and Erection Insurance.* London: The Insurance Institute of London.
Mehr, R. I., and Hedges, R. A. *Risk Management in The Business Enterprise.* Homewood, Ill.: Richard D. Irwin.
The Forum—Tort and Insurance Practices Section. American Bar Association.

Claims

Levin, P. *Claims and Changes: Handbook for Construction Contract Management.* W. P. L. Associates, 1978.
Rubin, R. A. *Construction Claims: Analysis, Presentation, Defense.* New York: Van Nostrand Reinhold, 1983.
Richter, I., and Mitchell, R. S. *Handbook of Construction Law and Claims.* Reston, Va.: Reston Publishing, 1982.

1

Contract Considerations and Contract Types

MATTHEW A. McLAUGHLIN *Davy McKee Corporation, Pittsburgh, Pennsylvania*

A contract is an agreement or promise to do or not to do something. We will discuss here contracts and contract types principally from a functional viewpoint and specifically from the viewpoint of the project manager.

It is sometimes said that contracts exist only for "legal" reasons. The implication is that they serve no functional purpose or even that they do more harm than good, and in any event are an expensive nuisance "to be put behind us as quickly as possible." Unfortunately, these views are valid if the contract isn't negotiated, written, and implemented knowledgeably and skillfully.

Properly used, a contract can aid in the achievement of project goals. The project manager should view it like any other project tool, such as drawings, tools, labor, equipment. The manager should understand the principles of the contracting process and the content of the specific contract to be used for the project, so that it may be used as an efficient and effective tool in the execution of the project.

The contract negotiation process will define the basis for the principal considerations: the services to be rendered by one party, and the costs and fees to be paid by the other party. Apart from arriving at a court-enforceable document, the contract negotiating process can identify potentially contentious issues and develop sound business understandings. A well-written contract can serve practically as well as legally as a memorandum of the agreements reached between two parties, defining the rights and obligations of the parties in most common and many complex situations.

If you conclude that a substantial part of the following material deals with matters you or others normally delegate to lawyers or contract administrators, you will not be wrong. However, legal and contract administration considerations are not ends unto themselves. They bear on and are a part of project execution. Accordingly, your knowledge of what your experts are doing and have done should be sufficient to assure that the contract element is an integrated and effective element of the total project.

You will also be correct if you conclude that it is unlikely that all of the following suggestions can be implemented on any project, and that in certain instances they should not be. Our purpose is to provide a basis for the establishment of objectives and the identification of tradeoffs, so that you can contribute to the process of contract negotiation effectively.

BASIC CONSIDERATIONS

Why Have A Contract

In abstract theory a contract is not essential to the performance of a project. Most of life's activities are carried on without contracts. However, contracts are useful where performance involves substantial, complex, or extended commitments, and particularly where they are interdependent. The contract is used to define these commitments and the liabilities inherent in nonperformance on the part of either party. It provides a record of the commitments and the agreements—a basic project reference document. It provides a foundation for court decisions if one party refuses to perform.

Understand What You Want To Do, The Limits, and How the Contract Can and Does Affect These Factors

A workable contract should define what it is you want to do, what others are to agree to do, and any limits on the obligations on either party. These principles are basic to all good contracts.

The completed and signed contract should be studied in detail to fully understand how it will impact the objectives of the project and your style of management. In skilled hands, the consequences of deficient words and agreements can be minimized; in clumsy hands, valuable rights, though agreed upon and reflected in the contract, are lost.

If you are not directly involved in the contract negotiations, try to understand what is happening and what has happened in the contracting process. Long after senior management, sales, tax specialists, counsel, and other intermediaries have departed the immediate scene, you will have to live with the die they have cast. It is possible that the agreement may be inadequate and the wording ambiguous regarding the intent of the agreement. Ask questions, seek clarification; you are responsible for implementing the contract.

Get It In Writing and Get It Signed—But Don't Give Up If You Haven't

There are practical reasons why you should always have a written contract.

1. Although in certain cases an oral contract can be enforced, there are rules that require that certain contracts be in writing. These rules can be quite complicated. The moral is to avoid the problem by getting the contract in writing.
2. A written contract will minimize disputes and confusion about what was agreed —a problem which can and will arise on projects of extended duration and complexity. You want to minimize arguments about who agreed to provide exactly what, when, how, and the terms of payment.

If it is necessary that a specific contract be in writing in order for it to be enforceable, it is also normally required that it be signed by the party against whom it is to be enforced. By signing the contract, the parties are manifesting in a practical way that the specific document is their "legal handshake." However, if faced with a situation where only an oral agreement was made and the other party won't perform, don't abandon hope too quickly. There are circumstances—highly specific—under which such an agreement can sometimes be considered binding and enforceable.

As a a last resort, if you cannot enforce the contract or obtain enforcement, you may be able to recover for the goods and services you have supplied based on their reasonable value to the other party, but if you haven't yet provided the services or goods, you may not be able to recover your costs, or you may recover only a portion of your costs, since the value measured is normally the value to the recipient.

Frequently there are practical reasons why a contract cannot be signed before the work commences. Every day that you work without a written contract leaves you exposed to the risks discussed.

Include All Important Terms and Contingencies

Unless certain essential items have been agreed, the contract, oral or written, cannot be enforced because no one, including the courts, will be able to determine the essential terms. There are many cases involving contracts where a term as essential as price has not been agreed upon. A contract must, at the least, include a description of what is to be done and the price to be paid for the goods or services.

A contract must include not only the legally required minimum provisions, but to the extent feasible, provisions covering all elements important to your performance, including those which deal with contingencies either likely to occur or, although relatively remote, could result in an unacceptable level of liability exposure or financial loss.

To be sure that all essential elements have been adequately covered, you should have a checklist; reviewed and adjusted to fit the needs of the project. A basic checklist should include at least the following items for a contract for engineering or construction services.

> Description of the Work. What is to be designed or built? What is the scope of participation for each party to the contract? Are all interfaces well defined?
>
> Commercial Terms. What is the price? If the contract is cost plus or guaranteed maximum, what is included/excluded? Are there incentive terms, with crystal clear parameters?
>
> Payment Terms. What are the conditions: milestones, approvals of owner, approvals of a third party, such as a governmental agency? Where is payment to be made, when, in what currency, and who is to bear the risk of exchange controls and fluctuations?
>
> Schedule. When is performance to be completed? Are there interim milestones? What are the consequences of late performance? Unless limited, a party is liable for the consequences of failure to perform on time. In the absence of a specific provision, performance will be required within a time frame considered to be reasonable under the circumstances, a distressingly imprecise standard. Delays resulting from failure to deliver necessary approvals or plans on time are usually compensable. Clauses that prohibit damage claims for delay are generally enforceable, though not necessarily equitable.
>
> Changes. In general, unless the contract includes a provision for changes, a party to a contract cannot alter the agreed performance without the consent of the other party. A change provision should describe the conditions under which a change can be made and the consequences. Is prior written approval required? Can or must the work proceed if there is a disagreement about whether or not a directive constitutes a change? A provision requiring prior written approval of a change as a condition for payment is usually enforceable. Change management is a severe test of the intent and working relationship of the parties to a contract.
>
> Force Majeure. It isn't always clear which party is to be responsible for the schedule delays and financial losses associated with certain events classified as Force Majeure or events "beyond your control." Not every event "beyond your control" frees you from liability, for example, bad weather common to the area, casualty destruction, such as by fire, of work in process, insofar as the need to replace it is concerned. A contract should be explicit with respect to this type of liability, no matter how unlikely.
>
> Insurance. Insurance is not required to be provided unless specified. If there is no insurance, however, the party with the liability may be without funds

to satisfy its obligations, thus, a provision requiring a wide range of insurance coverages is almost standard in modern contracts. Unnecessary multiple insurance coverages with redundant costs, more common than one might think, should be identified and corrected.

Subcontracting. Subcontracting is permitted unless specifically prohibited by the contract. It is normal to see a contractual provision giving the client the right of approval of subcontractors. Clients frequently require a list of potential subcontractors for approval as part of a proposal, or provide their own list of approved subcontractors. Overly restrictive subcontracting clauses can involve considerable costs for the prime contractor, and may not be in the best interests of either party to the contract.

Guarantees and Liabilities. Unless specifically limited you can be liable for all of the foreseeable economic consequences of your failure to perform, including consequential damages, such as loss of profit or production. Descriptive words can be construed as guarantees, unless the contract provides otherwise. Liability is not limited to the period or the remedy in the guaranty clause unless expressly limited. In some states you may be liable on a "negligence" theory even where your liability is otherwise expressly limited, unless negligence is expressly limited.

Taxes. Are sales, use, gross receipts, and in foreign countries, income taxes included in the price or are they reimbursable? An unexpected foreign income tax can totally consume the profit on a project, and then some.

Termination. Unless the contract so states neither party can terminate except for substantial default of the other without being liable for all costs and profits.

Default. Is there a right to notice and to default?

The preceding are only some of the major elements to be considered and then only certain aspects of those elements—a starter list. Have a basic checklist suitable to your business with modification to suit the specifics of the project in question. A good list should precede the drafting of a contract and will assist greatly in the orderly development of a good contract.

The Contract Should Be Clear, Concise, and Complete

Even an inexperienced project manager knows that unclear, overly elaborate, and/or incomplete drawings and specifications invite delays and/or extra costs. The same is true for a contract.

Good contract language is good English or whatever language is used for the contract. Certain words such as "assignment," have a reasonably well understood legal meaning and should be used where appropriate, however, most legal concepts can be expressed in relatively simple language and sentence structure. To the extent that the language is simple, there is less risk that the idea will be obscured, misstated, or misunderstood, or even not agreed. If you don't understand what you read, ask; there is always the possibility that it doesn't make sense. Another way of testing language is to restate the language or apply it to a hypothetical situation and see if the others involved agree; if not, you may have no agreement in fact.

Good contracts are concise. They should cover the necessary points in a straightforward manner. Each issue should be addressed in a contiguous set of provisions. Although there is no single "right" order, provisions should flow logically from one issue to the next. The same issue should not be dealt with differently in different provisions. Language and structure should be consistent. Cross references and definitions should be used where they will help. You would not begin a contract with a clause on "assignment," then move to "changes," then "subcontracting," followed by "payment." You would not deal with changes in two or three different separate provisions in different ways; however, cross references can be appropriate, such as a reference in the "price" provision noting that the lump sum is subject to adjustment for changes. You would, however, define what is to be supplied as "the Work" or "the Supply" to avoid repeating pages of description, but you should thereafter be consistent in your use of the defined term.

The contract should be complete in the sense that there should be a single document or set of clearly integrated documents readily and clearly identified as "the contract." Although contracts can be made up of separate documents not signed by both parties—a letter proposal accepted by a responding letter for example—it is at best risky to have a series of documents, items, proposals, etc., which serve as the basis for work but which have not been clearly identified as the final contract documents. You will probably find that such documents are neither clear nor concise, and are in conflict on one or more significant points. Worse yet, there may be a dispute about which documents form the contract; for example, a document you thought was superseded may later be claimed, even in good faith, to be part of the contract, imposing obligations such as warranties which you thought you didn't have. You may find that you have no specific contract at all! Documents incorporated by reference must be completely identified; don't refer to "specifications" if you mean "Specifications Dated March 11, 1986, Rev. 2." Where a contract is made up of several documents which conflict on important terms don't rely on a clause stating that one document has precedence; straighten out the conflict.

The preceding does not mean that a contract must necessarily be short or simple. A complex situation usually calls for complex treatment. A detailed contract may be necessary when the division of work and the attendant responsibilities are unique. But, this does not mean that clarity has to be sacrified.

Use Standard Contract Forms; Don't Let Them Use You

There is nothing wrong with the use of well-prepared standard contract forms. In fact, it would be foolish not to use standard forms where suitable. Forms are essential for many aspects of the project, such as multiple purchase orders and subcontracts, where the same "legal" terms are generally applicable.

Each form should, however, be reviewed to be sure it is suitable for the purpose to which it is being put and that necessary changes have been made; clauses deleted, modified, added. For example, should there be special warranty or limitation provisions? And, while it may be satisfactory if there is no problem, the use of a purchase order form with, say, two paragraphs on delivery and nothing covering field activities to obtain field construction services leaves you with an inadequate tool should a performance problem arise.

Don't Be Too Perfect

Notwithstanding what has been said, the objective is to arrive at a workable contract position.

> As a practical matter, particularly after negotiation, you can usually hope at best to arrive at a contract form which lacks much in terms of good English but which is clear enough for the purpose.
> You may decide that it is impractical to obtain the clarity you would wish on certain issues or even that the attempt to do so will only produce an immediate confrontation, so you may elect to run the risk with something less than perfection. This is not inconsistent with the "principle of clarity" stressed throughout this discussion; rather, we introduce here a conscious tradeoff to serve a practical consideration.
> After analysis you may conclude that certain factors, such as good engineering, a quality estimate, and a history of excellent relations with the client, justify accepting less than contract perfection in terms of completeness or liabilities.

Do not, however, willingly accept or use a contract which does not address your understanding of the work or is vague on points which may very well arise. It is one thing to run the risk on a liability provision based on an assessment that the problem will never arise or that less than perfect language is the best you can obtain; it is quite another if the language is fuzzy on matters such as price and payment terms, or issues known or suspected to be potentially contentious.

The specialist—the lawyer or the contracts administrator—ferrets out what he needs to know. Help him. But, help yourself as well; what do you need to know? Don't misstate necessary information on facts and contingencies. Otherwise, you may wind up with an excellent contract which simply doesn't deal with the important aspects of your project.

Get Competent Advice Where You Need It

You may know enough about basic contracts to feel you don't need specialist help. You may find, however, that advice or review or participation by a lawyer is desirable. Engineers are not adverse to second opinions or reviews on complex engineering problems, and lawyers frequently seek opinions of other lawyers on legal strategies. Lawyers with excellent reputations in contract law are not at all reluctant to seek the opinions of their peers. There is a real need today to involve specialists in the development of the contract, including those with expertise in the fields of taxes, patents, and insurance, among others. The lawyer or contract administrator can work with these specialists for you, and probably more efficiently.

Ideally, the manager and the legal staff should form a cohesive team, with each party understanding enough of the other's needs and skills to produce a good legal/functional document. Though some will disagree, it is essential for the specialists (legal, taxes, etc.) to recognize that their role is one of contributors to a project where the corporate accountability has been delegated to a project manager, and their role is analogous to the roles of key project staff, such as engineering and construction management.

Understand What the Contract Means

The point to keep in mind in considering these suggestions is that they should be applied with knowledgeable judgment. In this connection never fall into the error of denying that the problem or risk is there. Too many projects have fallen victim to an analysis such as the following: I want the project; I don't want the risk; therefore, there is no risk; therefore, I don't have to be on guard to provide for and minimize it. Rationalization of risk is a great deterrent to project success. This rationalization may not even be a conscious act; in fact, for goals-oriented people it is an insidious negative, effortlessly suppressed by the enthusiasm of positive action.

TYPES OF CONTRACTS

General

Engineering and construction contracts usually fall into certain contract categories based on the form of payment.

1. Cost plus. Most costs are reimbursable.
2. Lump sum. A fixed price has been established for the defined work.
3. Guaranteed maximum. Most costs will be reimbursed up to a fixed limit.

There are numerous variants of these basic contracts consisting of hybrids where part of the work is lump sum (engineering and procurement) and part is cost plus (the field program). Frequently we see a lump sum for certain defined elements, but

other areas are recognized as insufficiently defined, and an alternative contractual
treatment is used. One form is a guaranteed maximum in which both parties share to
some extent in the overrun or underrun.

Although these forms are identified in accordance with the pricing method used
they are commonly understood to have certain other characteristics. The specific
terms of the contract will control, not the generic name.

Our discussion will be from a legal/functional viewpoint, with certain legal issues
addressed to show practical consequences rather than purely legal opinions.

Cost-Plus Contracts

A cost-plus contract is one, definitionally, where the contractor is reimbursed for
substantially all of its costs. A conventional cost-plus contract represents a tradeoff
where one or more of the following principal factors are present.

> The project is not sufficiently defined for a realistic lump sum.
> Schedule requires the work progress on several fronts at the same time rather
> than in normal sequence.
> The owner or prime contractor wishes to exert a relatively high degree of control
> over vendor/subcontractor selection and management of the work.
> The cost of the project and other such factors make it unlikely that a contractor
> will be able and/or willing to accept lump sum or guaranteed maximum risk.
> The owner or prime contractor believes that it has a better grasp of or control
> over certain risk factors, such as quantities, than the contractor.

Some commonly occurring factors or misconceptions are as follows:

> If a contract is called "cost plus," all costs are reimbursable. On the contrary,
> only those costs are reimbursable which are defined as being reimbursable.
> Normally, even in a broadly reimbursable contract, indirect costs, and fre-
> quently, fringes are reimbursed by a formula based on a percentage of reim-
> bursable salaries. What is included in the two categories should be defined,
> including adjustments for escalation, as an example.
> The contractor has no liabilities. On the contrary, unless the contract specifically
> limits liabilities the contractor can be fully liable for any legally defined de-
> fects or discrepancies found to be its legal responsibility. This isn't neces-
> sarily a fair or practical basis for imposing liability. Contractors believe that
> it is better to arrive at an allocation-of-risk provision under which the con-
> tractor's liability is limited in proportion to the scope of its participation, its
> control, access to contingencies, and other factors.
> A cost plus contract does involve other risks. If the contract is cancelled, is
> there a charge to cover costs for other work foregone or reduction in person-
> nel such as severance pay?
> All of the usual provisions such as for changes and termination need to be included.
> There is no automatic right to terminate or make changes under a cost-plus
> contract.
> From the contractor's viewpoint equitable adjustments should be made in the con-
> ventional lump-sum provisions covering liens, indemnities, and patents. Even
> in a lump-sum contract certain limitations are appropriate, but the contractor
> will argue that the same risk with regard to these factors under a cost-plus
> contract is not proper. Liens frequently result because the contractor has
> resisted claims or taken risks on subcontractor selection in the interest of
> the owner. Money neither accrues to the cost-plus contractor from these
> items nor is there a contingency to cover it; thus the contractor will argue
> that its liability should be limited to a failure to pay vendors amounts paid to
> it by the owner, but this will not be the case if the usual lien provision is used.

The contractor will argue that the same principle should apply to patent indemnity unless the scope of work of the contractor includes patent searches or contractor proprietary information and its fee is commensurate. In the case of indemnity for property damage and personal injury—except possibly personal injury due to contractor's negligance—the contractor will argue that the liability should be limited to amounts unrecoverable from specified insurance. It must be stressed, however, that these provisions will only operate if appropriately drafted and that greater liability can be imposed on the contractor by express provision or by general law.

The contract should be administered with the same care as a lump-sum contract, particularly with regard to costs, changes, and schedule. Owner and contractor should be aiming for the best technical and economic result feasible; sloppy handling of the factors mentioned can result in disappointment and additional costs for both, and even major litigation if there is a substantial surprise.

Assumption of a function does not necessarily mean assumption of risk or responsibility. Even when it does, the party with the risk may not recognize it. On cost-plus work the owner may think that by breaking the work down into parts such as engineering, purchasing, and separate contracts for elements of construction which it contracts out directly, it has saved the cost and manning charged by a general contractor. However, if those functions of coordination and management are not handled by someone there can be substantial unnecessary costs including liability for a failure to coordinate. A corresponding error on the part of a contractor is to think the owner has recognized or assumed the risk involved.

A disproportionate share of those project disputes which become "legal matters" have their genesis in projects in which the work was subdivided into separate parts by an owner with neither the staff nor the knowledge to appreciate the risks of what it was doing or to control them. This condition is often aggravated by one or more contractors taking an overly narrow view of the need to assure integration of their work as a matter of execution and result.

A cost-plus contract is not the solution for a poorly defined or managed project. Cost-plus contracts need skilled owner-contractor coordination and management and should not be used in an effort to paperover project problems, but only where there is confidence that sufficient knowledge exists about what is wanted and what it should cost so that risks can be assessed and controlled.

Even where you are not in the contract chain on a project, you can be directly liable to other contractors, or the owner in the case of subcontractors. Although many states still limit liability for economic losses—excluding physical injury or property damage, as compared to a direct contract—others don't. Your best protections are specific contract provisions which the other party should be obligated to pass on to its subcontractors and suppliers, provisions defining and limiting your role and liability for functions you have undertaken or may be deemed to have undertaken.

Lump-Sum Contracts

A lump-sum or fixed price contract is one, definitionally, where the price is fixed for a defined scope of work. Lump-sum contracts are most useful when the factors are substantially the reverse of those for a cost plus contract. A lump sum is apt to be most useful when, within reasonable limits, the project is defined, work will progress in an orderly sequence, the contractor is to have a relatively high degree of control, and the contractor has the resources to bear and capability to assess the risks. Some commonly occurring factors or misconceptions are as follows:

If a contract is lump sum, all risk lies with the contractor. On the contrary, if the owner does not fulfill its express or implied responsibilities it can be liable for as much or more than it would if the work had been cost plus. For example, in the absence of an express agreement to the contrary, the owner usually has an implied warranty for the adequacy of any plans or information supplied, and a general disclaimer won't necessarily limit this liability. The owner will be responsible for interference caused by its own delays; interference can include late approval, changes, hindered access, or interference by other contractors. The contractor can default and/or go broke, and the owner may not be able to foresee this; this risk can be reduced through bonds and retentions as well as contractual provisions, but may be expensive.

The contractor may find that he or she does not have the expected degree of control over the work when despite the owner's obligations, the owner has failed to perform or because certain of the owner's obligations have been reversed by express contractual provisions.

In a lump-sum arrangement the contractor may be in deep trouble before the owner realizes it, since the owner doesn't have the day-to-day detail available under a cost plus job. Therefore, the owner will usually seek contract provisions specifying the supply of reasonable information to enable it to assess progress in relation to costs; this can include not only information on schedules and progress, but also information on orders to major vendors and subcontractors. The owner may also want to reserve the right to demand and in some cases will require a partial lien waiver and releases from major suppliers or subcontractors and certification that certain goods have been delivered and have been paid for.

If the scope of work is not clearly defined in detail, the cost of the work may exceed that under a cost plus contract because of claims for extras. In such cases there may be not only the direct cost for the extra work itself but also for overhead and the cost for processing claims, including legal fees.

Guaranteed Maximum Contracts

A guaranteed maximum contract is one, definitionally, where the cost of the work is reimbursed up to a specified level. In the case of a true guaranteed maximum, the contract is in reality a lump-sum contract. Guaranteed maximum contracts are most useful when one or more of the following factors are present.

1. There is doubt about the amount of contingency required.
2. From the owner's viewpoint a guaranteed maximum contract can have the advantages of a cost plus contract and a lump-sum contract if the contractor is willing to accept the maximum but permit cost plus administration by the owner. Obviously well-advised contractors will not want to permit this in either language or practice; rather they will insist that the contract and its administration be approached substantively from a lump-sum viewpoint.
3. A modified form of guaranteed maximum which can be more or less like either a lump-sum contract or a cost plus contract depending on the allocation of the financial risk between owner and contractor, is one in which the contractor and owner share in the underrun or overrun.

Contractors usually do not like guaranteed maximum contracts. They involve the risks of lump-sum contracts but usually not the potential for profit since owners will usually demand all or a substantial part of the savings. This does not mean that a guaranteed maximum contract always produces a net benefit for the owner as compared to other forms; for example, the contractor will have less incentive to save and will want a very adequate contingency.

Paradoxically, the owner's own personnel, particularly if more concerned with operations than capital costs, may press to have contingent funds spent for extras.

Some commonly occurring factors or misconceptions are as follows:

The contractor will expect all costs up to the maximum to be reimbursed including costs for make-good. This will not necessarily happen unless the contract so provides. On the other hand, the owner may resist payment for make-good even though he, rather than the contractor, has the benefit of the contingency. This is particularly true in the case of postcompletion guaranty work.

Because costs are reimbursable, the contract can be administered as a cost plus contract forgetting that there is a maximum. On the contrary, the risk is that one or both parties may be lulled into doing this to the great loss of both, since no one will be acting as a responsible party for the consequences. In fact, changes should be promptly identified and documented to protect both owner and contractor.

Contingent funds are a windfall to be spent on extras without accounting. On the contrary, there can be a tendency to assume that a contingency is sufficiently great to excuse failures to control costs or identify changes, especially during the early phases of the work. Since the contingency is visible, there may also be owner pressure to release contingencies too early or for items which should be considered changes. In many cases it is not until near job completion that major needs for the contingency arise or are identified.

The contractor does not need the same control over the work as on a lump-sum job. On the contrary, a contractor should neither by contract or practice cede control to the owner without a corresponding adjustment in accountability and cost. From the owner's viewpoint, actions contrary to this advice can be as costly to the owner as to the contractor.

In the case of arrangements for sharing underruns, owners may wish to limit the share in the underrun to avoid an incentive to overestimate.

A target arrangement, rather than a strict guaranteed maximum, pursuant to which underruns and overruns are shared in certain percentages can be a useful form of incentive for both owner and contractor. Under such an arrangement the contractor is not responsible for all costs incurred over the guaranteed maximum, but also does not have all savings under the guaranteed maximum. A target arrangement can thus create incentives while still facilitating cooperation, especially in a case where the risks of a true guaranteed maximum would be too great.

Unit Price Contracts

A unit price contract is based on a fixed price for a defined unit of supply, such as a fixed price per cubic yard of concrete poured including labor. Unit price contracts can then be further refined into a species of guaranteed maximum target or incentive contracts with the maximum or target being tied to an estimated or guaranteed total quantity.

A point frequently overlooked on unit price contracts by both clients and contractors is that the units used may be based on important factors not stated in the contract. A price per cubic yard of concrete may be based on a minimum quantity to be purchased, thus justifying the installation of a batch plant. If the actual quantities are significantly less, the batch plant may not be economical. Or, the opposite can happen, where quantities significantly exceed the estimate, and a batch plant might have paid out. A price per cubic yard of fill might be based on a certain quantity available from a convenient source; an increase in the quantity could result in excessive costs if other sources have to be used. The buyer should specify what changes are permitted without adjustment in the unit price, and the seller should specify those factors which will require a change in the unit price. Failure to make a provision for a quanity adjustment in unit price work is a prime condition for an ultimate resolution in the court room.

Allowances to Cover a Lack of Definition for an Element of Work

In the scope of work for a construction project there may be certain elements that are not sufficiently defined to be included in a lump-sum or guaranteed maximum contract. One solution, if the item can be identified reasonably well in fact and words, is to provide that its cost will be reimbursed, or that an allowance will be included to cover an estimated target quantity, to be adjusted for the actual quantity or cost under an agreed-to formula.

The Project Management Contract

We reserve until last a brief discussion of one of the most difficult contracts of all: the increasingly popular project management contract. A functional description of project management is difficult at best. To define contractually a project management assignment will test the skills of the legal staff, not to mention the senior marketing and sales personnel, and the project manager, and, for that matter, the executive suite. The project management contract must be developed with the utmost care, with a keen understanding of scope and liabilities; a classical "what if" exercise.

Interestingly enough, the spurt of international mega projects in the Third World during the 1970s was not the prime arena for abusive litigation and excessive claims. The enormous scope and vast complexity of these projects more often than not was characterized by a close relationship between the client and the project management contractor, with the contractor truly functioning as the management arm of the client. The extension of the concept to small and intermediate projects, and particularly domestic projects, produced a rapid escalation in litigation and claims. Unsophisticated clients and contractors, and perhaps sophisticated principals who elected to "play dumb," were the root cause of uncertainty about the viability of this approach.

The project management contract, when used in good faith, is a most useful addition to the contracting industry. Be prepared, however, for new and unusual claims, since the ultimate scope can far exceed the understanding or the intent of either of the parties to the contract. Litigation can be complex, since sorting out the facts and the intent is no easy matter for an arbitrator or a court.

LUMP-SUM VERSUS REIMBURSABLE CONTRACTS: SOME VIEWS FROM INDUSTRY

The two principal turnkey contracts entered into by an owner and a prime contractor in the process plant industries are the lump-sum contract and the reimbursable contract. There are advantages and disadvantages to each type, as viewed from the perspective of each party. Here we will discuss certain of these viewpoints as conveyed by senior executives to the writer over a period of years. These views may be considered by the reader to be arguable, but please note that only the expressions that have come through time and time again are included. The material is aimed primarily at the young project manager as an orientation assist.

The comments relate primarily to the domestic petroleum and chemical sector, a sector where we have seen significant developments in contractual format, due to the influence of the large energy companies. Certain comments may have universal application; others will have only limited application to international projects, projects in undeveloped countries, and government projects.

The owner and contractor considerations that follow are presented as they are usually perceived by the principals, with selected editorial comments and clarifications as deemed appropriate.

Lump-Sum Considerations: Perceptions

Owner
    Advantages
        Lower price
        Budget control
        Reduced owner staff
        Better contractor personnel

    Disadvantages
        Reduced involvement
        First cost versus quality
        Start-up surprises
        Inquiry program/package
            Extends schedule/expensive

Contractor
    Advantages
        Higher profit potential
        Minimum owner participation

    Disadvantages
        Higher loss potential
        Cost of bidding
        Probability of award
        Resource allocation
            Proposals versus projects

Principal Advantages and Disadvantages: Overview

The principal advantage to owners is budget control; the secure feeling that the appropriation for expenditure (AFE) is protected, although it has been amply demonstrated that substantial additional costs can be incurred by an owner on lump-sum contracts. The principal advantage to contractors is the opportunity to make a good profit.

The principal disadvantage to owners is the reduced involvement in "their" project. The principal disadvantage to contractors is, surprisingly, the cost of bidding, an expensive exercise, and a highly interactive consideration: a heavy commitment reduces the potential for loss, and increases the probability of award, at the expense of a reallocation of resources from profitable work.

Reimbursable Considerations: Perceptions

Owner
    Advantages
        Involved
        Competitive contractor markups
        Few surprises
        Fast track potential

    Disadvantages
        Potential overrun
        High staff costs
        Weaker contractor personnel
        Contractor home office costs
            Opportunity for "loading"

Contractor
    Advantages
        Normally will not lose money
        Reasonable bidding costs

    Disadvantages
        Profit levels modest
        Heavy owner participation

Principal Advantages and Disadvantages: Overview

The principal advantage to owners is their total involvement in all phases of the project. The principal advantage to contractors is financial predictability.

The principal disadvantage to owners is the potential for a budget overrun. The principal disadvantage to contractors is limited profit, although for large reimbursable projects the base-load nature of these projects gives the contractor marketing flexibility.

General Comments on Schedule

The relationship between the method of contracting and the project schedule is complex, variable, and strongly influenced by many factors. To form definite opinions about the relationship in the absence of project-specific knowledge is a gross over-simplification. Certain generalities are more often true than not but can be totally erroneous in a given situation. It is often said that control of schedule is difficult when an element of field work is let on a lump-sum basis to a subcontractor. Margin-ally true. To extend this to a prime contractor with turnkey responsibility on a major project is illogical since far too many factors interact to even remotely consider the validity of any generalities. Nevertheless, a few directional comments will be offered here, but consider the caveats, unstated, to be there.

A contractor must at all times consider the impact of schedule on fixed and variable costs and the allocation of resources. On the one hand, it may be advantageous to stretch a schedule, using minimum staff. On the other hand, it may be advantageous to advance the schedule to reduce overhead charges. A turnkey contractor, left to his own devices, will prefer to delay a field start in order to maximize engineering and procurement completion, with the expectation of improving field productivity. This concept is not always saleable to the client, and the debate continues, and will continue, regarding the optimum overall project strategy.

The client role on a large reimbursable project is frequently a compromise between marketing pressures (push the job), and engineering pressures (study the options). One of the two roles will be "policy," but in most instances will be conditioned to the pressures of the other role.

If, in the preaward phase, a project has been developed "in-house" over a long time frame, data will be available to prepare a complete bid package. This often leads to a firm basis for "tight" lump-sum bidding, so called "nuts and bolts" bidding. If, on the other hand, there is a "beat the market place," or "product obsolescence" consideration, the reimbursable "fast track" or "bootstrap" approach may be best.

A 50-Year Contractual Profile

Prior to World War II, the contracting industry was characterized by a functional approach. In the late 1940s, contractors, and particularly the major energy contrac-tors, reorganized to service projects in a matrix style, undoubtedly influenced by certain war time projects, such as the Manhattan Project. Although most projects were lump sum, the issue of lump sum versus reimbursable was not significant, and legal staffs were minimal. It was normal to see contracts processed by a contracts administrator, and a legal staff consisting of one lawyer and one contracts administra-tor was common.

Throughout the 1950s, serious concerns developed, initially on the part of owners, about the cost of lump-sum bidding, since it was apparent that the costs recycled to the owners in the form of increased overhead. A breakthrough occurred in the early 1960s, when several major energy companies decided to employ a reimbursable contract strategy for their larger projects, reasoning that it is our money and our project, thus we will provide the overall venture management, with a contractual format com-patible with the new strategy. During the 1960s and 1970s, we saw an explosive growth of the "involved" and "educated" client; initially visible on "mega" projects, but gradually evolving as a standard approach on most projects.

This change in project strategy resulted in a comparable growth in the size of the legal staffs of contractors, and an ever-increasing contractual complexity, with the new buzz word "litigious" applied to the engineering and construction industry as well as contemporary society. The concepts of the "involved" client and contractual terms as a major element of negotiation in turnkey construction work are basic to the modern contracting business and a project manager who yearns for the good old days when they "just let me do my job" is in the wrong business.

The energy business has been depressed for most of the 1980s, with the result that it has been "contracts to the forefront"—a buyers market. Not too many years ago, contractors could say that a job was never lost on contractual terms. Today many a job is won on contractual terms, including concessions on extensive assumptions of liability. During normal cyclical downturns in new plant construction it is common to see an upsurge in the award of lump-sum contracts. Paradoxically, the most recent downturn has evidenced a shifting of views on lump-sum versus reimbursable contracts by owners and contractors. Although the lump-sum contract is very much in evidence, many owners prefer reimbursable contracts, since the contracting industry has been operating anywhere from a significant underrecovery of overhead to marginal profits, and there are bargains available in reimbursable work at low overlays. The contractors, on the other hand, see benefits in lump-sum work, particularly the negotiated lump sum. In any case, however, the contractual considerations of the 1980s are key elements in the determination of the profit or loss position in the contracting industry.

2
Joint Ventures

MATTHEW A. McLAUGHLIN *Davy McKee Corporation, Pittsburgh, Pennsylvania*

A joint venture approach to the marketing, organization, and execution of a project should be considered when the combined strengths of two or more entities result in a joint organization with unique credentials in a targeted business area. A joint venture is based on a complementary relationship: one party may lack one or more major elements needed for market penetration, such as technology, design-construct capabilities, geographic location, or financial strength; the other party should be able to compensate for these areas of weakness, thus forming a strong team capable of mounting a viable marketing program.

A highly specific but highly powerful joint venture approach has been developed over the past 25 years in the execution of complex projects in underdeveloped nations, where sophisticated expatriate contractors venture with local firms for legal reasons, or to circumvent an extended cultivation program.

A joint venture is a relationship where each party needs the other to achieve a common mutually beneficial objective. Without this fundamental consideration there is seldom justification for entering into such a shared business venture.

To provide a meaningful discussion of a very broad subject, we will focus on the joint venture as it is used by firms engaged in the design and construction of projects. It should be understood, however, that the vehicle has universal application to the production of goods and the provision of services in any industry.

Adherence to certain principles will assist the manager in setting up and running a successful joint venture.

1. Know enough about the joint venture approach to be sure it is the proper organizational approach to meet your objectives.
2. Participate in all formative phases: contractual, tax, accounting, and financial, to be sure the specific joint venture has been structured to meet the needs of the specific project.
3. Play "what if" to the point of exhaustion. Joint ventures can be deceptively simple until a problem arises; then the problem can be much more serious than would have been the case in a conventional project organization.

WHAT IS A JOINT VENTURE? IS IT THE RIGHT FORM?

To decide whether a joint venture is a suitable form of organization for a particular project and to proceed accordingly requires some basic knowledge about the joint venture form.

249

Definition

A simple definition of a joint venture is an association of two or more parties for the achievement of a business objective, with some degree of joint control by the participants, in which each party makes some contribution and will in some manner share in the profits.

This definition can vary, because, within certain very important limitations, the parties can structure the joint venture according to their needs. This flexibility can be very helpful; it can also result in confusion, misunderstanding, and financial loss if a joint venture is used where it is inappropriate or if clear agreements are not reached in a timely fashion and followed on all critical points.

A joint venture is flexible because it is primarily the product of a contract or agreement between the participating parties. The parties have broad authority to establish matters such as the scope of the joint venture, the identity and authority of those who will manage it, what each party will contribute, the time frame for each participant's input, and how profits and losses will be shared.

Joint ventures can be made between corporations, partnerships, individuals, and even other joint ventures, or any combination of these entities.

Joint venture contributions can include almost anything: cash, technical expertise, services, tools, equipment, office space, and the commercial advantage or "inside track" with a prospective buyer. The contributions can vary in any manner the parties choose: by percentages; by specific limits such as a dollar limit on the contribution of a party; by stated conditions, such as a threshold or ceiling for sharing of losses by one of the parties.

The parties can also fix their own arrangements for profit sharing. Although it is normally considered that no joint venture exists unless there is a requirement that payment to a participant depends on the profitability of the entire joint venture—otherwise the participant's role is no different than a supplier or investor—there can be infinite variations in how profits are shared. Profit sharing can be based on percentages, or allocation of profits primarily to one or the other partner up to certain limits; further, profits need not be shared in any fixed proportion, or in proportion to the value of contributions.

The basis for sharing of losses need not be the same as for the sharing of profits. It isn't necessary between the participants in a joint venture that a given participant share in losses at all.

Apart from the need to be sufficiently clear about all major elements of a joint venture, there are several other aspects to joint ventures which can affect their attractiveness in specific cases and which should be understood before a joint venture is elected.

Analogy to Partnerships

For most legal purposes a joint venture is like a partnership. Thus under many legal systems each participant is considered to be present for legal and tax purposes wherever sufficient joint venture activity takes place even though all such activity is carried out by one of the other participants. Until the contrary is established, it should be assumed that each participant must be in compliance with the laws and regulations every place the joint venture is carrying on activities incident to the venture's business, if such compliance would have been required if the participant had itself performed the activity. It the joint venture is performing a project in another state, each joint venturer may have to be licensed to do business and to have all required licenses, such as contracting licenses, even if individually it has no employees in that state. In addition, the joint venture itself may have to be separately licensed. For example, the California courts at one time ruled that unless a joint venture had a contractor's license it could not enforce payment of its contract against the owner even though the participants in the joint venture were licensed.

Tax Consequences

Generally there is no separate legal existence for tax purposes between the joint venture participants and their joint venture as there is in the case of a corporation and its shareholders. Thus for tax purposes, the revenues, profits, and losses of the joint venture flow through to each participant in accordance with their agreed share in the venture. This lack of separate identity between the joint venture and its participants makes each participant generally liable for taxes to the extent of his or her participation in profits and losses of the joint venture in any jurisdiction where the joint venture is carrying on activities, even if the participant has no direct role in those activities. The participant will incur these tax effects as they are incurred by the joint venture, that is, taxation will not depend on any formal distribution of profits or assets or actions by the joint venture, as differentiated from a stockholder in a corporation, taxed only when a dividend is declared and paid.

The tax consequences may be advantageous where the participants and the venture operate in one state or country, since participants will usually want to consolidate their share of venture profit or loss with those from their other operations in computing their taxes, otherwise there could be a tax liability on overall operations in excess of what it would have been had the share of joint venture loss been taken into account.

Even where the joint venture is pursuing a foreign project, these tax consequences are usually advantageous or at least neutral for engineering or construction projects, assuming careful tax planning. This is not necessarily true, however, if joint venture operations are carried out in more than one country, or participants from more than one country are involved. Under many legal systems actions by a participant carrying out joint venture functions are joint venture actions, especially if the profit incident to those actions is to be shared. For example, a non-U.S. participant may be unwilling to file a U.S. tax return but may be forced to do so because part of the joint venture activities, such as engineering, is being carried on in the United States by another U.S. company participant, and part of the non-U.S. participant's share of the profits is deemed, for tax purposes, to flow from its fellow participant's U.S. engineering activities; worse yet, the non-U.S. firm may find that its own country's tax system gives no relief from double taxation in such a case.

These tax consequences do not always exist, but until the contrary is established, it should be assumed that each participant and the joint venture must comply with all tax requirements where the joint venture or its participants engage in activities on the venture's behalf.

A final comment is that for U.S. tax purposes, the formal designation of the relationship is not conclusive; if sharing of profit and loss and other characteristics of a joint venture are found, the association will be taxed as a joint venture even if the parties call it something else, such as a prime contractor-subcontractor relationship.

Contractual Liability

Joint venture participants are generally liable directly and without limit to any third parties for contractual liabilities and negligence of the joint venture. Statements previously made about the flexibility in allocating profits and losses among participants in a joint venture apply only to the relations among the joint venturers themselves; they do not apply to the rights of third parties unless a third party expressly agrees to this. It is not practicable to obtain agreements from each party with which the venture deals limiting the liability of the participant's to the assets of the joint venture, and such limitations are of no use with regard to negligence claims. It should be noted that if the joint venture follows a practice of contractually limiting its liabilities to joint venture assets, and if certain other critical factors are present such as continuing existence, centralized management, and free transferability of interests, the joint venture may be treated as a corporation for U.S. federal income tax purposes.

Dealings with Third Parties

Each joint venture has broad authority to bind the joint venture and the other participants in dealings with third parties. In theory there are some limits on what rights a
third party may claim against a joint venture and the other participants based on the
commitments made by one of the participants if, in purporting to bind the joint venture,
the participant is clearly acting beyond the scope of the joint venture or the authority
delegated to it. For practical purposes, however, the courts will generally favor the
third party and resolve any doubts against the joint venture and the other participants.

Obligations of Participants to the Venture

Each joint venturer owes the other joint venturers a duty of trust and fairness. Each
party has an obligation to act in the interests of the joint venture, to keep the other
participants advised, to deal fairly with the venture in all transactions, and not to
take individual advantage if it would disadvantage the joint venture or deprive the
joint venture or other participants of opportunities incident to the conduct of the joint
venture. These duties are greater when a participant has a management or leadership
role in the joint venture.

In practical terms, if in doubt and in the absence of specific agreement saying otherwise, the law will resolve doubts against the party which seems to have taken unfair
advantage; it is not enough to simply adhere to the letter of the contract or even the
minimal standards applicable to other commercial transactions, and it makes no difference that relations between the parties are poor. If a joint venture is formed to pursue
a project and there is an opportunity for new work from the same customer, in the absence of agreement to the contrary, a participant may be found to have a duty to give
the joint venture and the other participants notice of this and a fair chance to pursue
the new work even in the absence of any specific agreement requiring such notice or
joint participation in new work, or even an indication that the customer would entertain a bid for the new work by the joint venture or the other participants.

Since a joint venture can be found to exist at an early stage through a course of
dealing even where the parties may not have so designated the relationship, this factor
alone makes it essential to have clear understandings about the nature and duties of
the participants during the formative period.

It is possible to offset some of these consequences by specific agreements. However, even where such agreements are possible, remember that people have precon-
ceptions about the rights and obligations which flow from the form of a particular transaction. Thus, irrespective of contractual language, designated subcontractors will
tend to behave like subcontractors taking direction from the party designated as prime,
expecting a subordinate role in the management of the project and no participation in
its profit; whereas, designated joint venturers will tend to expect to behave like partners with rights of active participation and joint control. While special agreements
can to some degree alter these expectations and the actions consequent from them, such
agreements to the extent they "run against the grain" will be difficult to implement.
If significant problems can be visualized for normal business activities, it is highly
likely that a joint venture is not the right form for the particular purpose.

JOINT VENTURE VERSUS CORPORATION

Having established certain factors which should be present if a joint venture form is
to be elected, it is appropriate to consider the major alternative to a joint venture
where two or more parties wish to associate on a joint basis in pursuit of a business
objective: this is the corporation.

Discussion

Unlike a joint venture which is formed and largely governed by the agreement of the parties as interpreted and amplified by court decisions over the years, a corporation must be formed pursuant to statutory law of a particular state or country. This law will contain some fairly detailed requirements about what must be done both at formation and thereafter, although the law in the United States often permits more flexibility than that of certain other countries.

Properly formed and run, a corporation has a legal and financial existence separate from its stockholders and management. Generally it is a separate taxpayer. If the corporation is run properly from a tax viewpoint, its stockholders are only liable for taxes on dividends declared by the coproration and profit from transactions with the corporation. And, if the corporation is properly formed and managed, its stockholders will be liable only for the consequences of the corporation's dealings and actions to the extent of the corporation's assets, including the investment of the stockholders in the corporation.

Although there are many technical and other differences including the fact that a corporation must be formed, registered, and operated in accordance with specific laws, the foregoing considerations are the major functional differences between the unincorporated joint venture and the corporation.

If a corporation limits the liability of its stockholders, why then not use a corporation in all cases? The reasons are several.

Time and Effort

It takes extra time and effort to set up a corporation, particularly where special licenses or registration are required. In some countries the establishment of a corporation may require special approvals; in certain cases limitations may be placed on the percentage of interest which foreign stockholders may own and the management power they may exercise compared to stockholders who are nationals of the country.

Procedures

The corporate form has its own rigidities. There must be stockholders and stockholder meetings, boards and board meetings, and officers. More importantly, corporate law generally foresees the corporation operating under its own management elected by a majority of the board and the board by a majority of the stockholders, with profit participation either being related to arms-length dealings between the corporation and the shareholder, or in strict proportion to shareholdings. These consequences can often be avoided or offset by special charter and by-law provisions, by stockholder agreements, and by agreements between the corporation and its shareholders; however, if there is no advantage to the corporate form, there is no reason to elect it and incur the effort to minimize or eliminate the consequences which otherwise flow naturally from it.

Limited Liability Not an Issue

The characteristics of incorporation may not be important or even practically available. If those dealing with the corporation require the guaranty of the participant stockholders and there is adequate insurance to cover exposure of the participants to all risks, limited liability will be of no determinative advantage.

Duties to Others

The majority shareholder and the management have a duty to the minority shareholders, and indirectly, to the corporation's creditors not to conduct any of the corporation's affairs contrary to the common interest of the corporation. A corporation does minimize some of the problems incident to the joint venture form of organization.

Independence of Action

Limitation of liability and separate identify for tax purposes usually require that the corporation have substance in terms of personnel, assets, and some independence of management, as well as that transactions between the corporation and its stockholders be on an arms-length basis, that is, both the tax authorities and the courts may not recognize the corporation for tax or liability purposes if its transactions are structured solely to balance the accounts of the corporation to meet the agreed financial needs of the stockholder owners. To the extent the criteria of independent existence are lacking, the desired tax and liability limitation characteristics may be diminished or lost, and to provide these criteria may involve financial and operational costs which are unacceptably high or practically unachievable.

Tax Consequences

A flow through of tax consequences to the participants is often desirable, especially for associations formed for carrying out engineering and construction projects. It may be so important as to exclude from consideration the corporate form even where it would be feasible for purposes of limiting liability. While a detailed discussion of tax consequences is outside the present scope, it should be noted that under the federal income tax law, unless a stockholder owns at least 80% of the stock of a corporation, it is usually not possible to combine the stockholder's interest in profit from the corporation's operations against a loss on other operations of the participant unless a dividend is declared—even then there is a tax on a dividend, albeit a reduced one; further, the stockholder's share of the corporation's losses may not be combined against profit from other operations of the participant unless the corporation is liquidated, and then only as a capital loss available for use against other capital gains.

It should be evident then that in some cases a joint venture will be more useful than a corporation; and some cases where it cannot be justified at all. Generally, in the case of an association formed to carry out an engineering and construction project, the preference will be for a contractual joint venture.

Complex Organizations

One or more corporations may be formed or used to advance the purposes of a joint venture. In such a case the corporation does not displace or supersede the joint venture; it merely becomes a tool for carrying out its objectives. In the case of a foreign project, it may be easier or safer or of tax advantage for the joint venture to operate through a corporation in the country where the project is located; in such a case the participants will decide how the corporation will be structured and will establish its charter, bylaws, board, and contracts to be consistent with joint venture objectives and rules. This does not mean that the problems mentioned with regard to corporations are eliminated; they exist, usually in more complex ways. However, the needs of the specific case may well justify this complexity as the best and easiest method of carrying out the joint venture. As stressed elsewhere, knowledge and care are the watchwords in establishing a joint venture corporation and its interrelationship with the participants to avoid mistrust, overreaching, and legal problems.

OTHER JOINT VENTURE CONSIDERATIONS

We have discussed the joint venture form of organization and compared it to a corporation, the major alternative if a joint association is desired to achieve a business objective. Parties may also work together under other contractual relationships, including prime contractor–subcontractor, licensor-licensee, and direct contract between the party for whom you are working and the other party whose services are needed. If there is a choice about the form of the relationship, it should be considered that a joint venture is more likely to be useful when one or more of the following factors are present.

1. The would-be participant requires some additional element(s) beyond what is available in its own organization to enable it to seek and perform the project, and the other joint venture participant is able to supply what is missing. The element could be technology, construction capability, financial or bonding capacity, or even the ability to meet the requirement for local participation in the case of certain foreign projects.

2. Certain risk-profit considerations may direct complementary participants toward a joint venture. Participant A may have a need to spread the risk on a very large fixed-price project; Participant B may agree to accept the shared risk provided there is an opportunity for commensurate shared profits.

3. The other participant should be solvent and able to perform its obligations and bear its share of any losses. It will do no good if one of the objectives is special supply or risk sharing if the other participant proves not to have the resources and money to respond when the need arises.

4. The other participant should be capable of assuming joint responsibility. This consideration leads immediately to a complex and frequently highly subjective evaluation of the best role for your company: joint venture, prime contractor, subcontractor. If your company has the option to act as the prime contractor, with the other party as a subcontractor, even though as prime you have the ultimate responsibility for the performance of a subcontractor, you will generally find it easier to shed an incompetent or insolvent subcontractor than it is to shed a co-venturer. Alternatively, as a subcontractor, your company will be responsible only for the work it does. These issues, as they related to the profit-risk potential, are often the organization determinants.

5. The other party should be trustworthy and sufficiently sophisticated to carry out its role as a partner. It is difficult enough to deal with anyone in any form of transaction when these elements are deficient; it is much more difficult in a joint venture relationship. Needless to say, deficiency in these factors compounds some of the other problems discussed, such as management and limitation of risk. One point to be emphasized is that sophistication means the skill or ability to understand and carry out the assigned role; it does not mean that the participant be capable of running the joint venture independently. A participant selected to meet a local content requirement, with say a 20% interest in the joint venture, ideally should recognize that this indicates a limited role, and it would not be expected to understand the complexities of a grassroots project.

6. If a party's participation is relatively small, for example, in terms of contribution and share of profit and loss, the complexity of a joint venture relationship is probably not worthwhile to either party.

7. Where the problems described, or other factors, reveal inherent weaknesses in a joint venture approach, the manager should ask whether there are other potential participants or other forms of relationship: prime contractor-subcontractor, where your company wants sole management control; licensor-licensee, where technology is the primary requirement; direct contract between the owner and the supplier, where it isn't necessary to route supplies through the principal contractor.

In the end, this isn't a perfect world, and a joint venture may be necessary under less than ideal conditions. If care is exercised in formation and operation, and if the limitations of the selected co-venturers are understood and accepted, problems can be minimized and favorable results achieved.

THE TERMS OF THE JOINT VENTURE AGREEMENT

Timing

The justification for a joint venture approach, the selection of other participants, and the commencement of work on a joint basis can occur over a relatively short time frame. It is important both legally and practically to agree on all of the principal details concerning the joint venture as promptly as possible and to document them in an appropriate joint venture contract. The reasons for this are:

1. A joint approach to the pursuit and execution of work requires clear understandings about the division of labor, the duties, and the rights and responsibilities of each participant prior to venture start-up. Prompt attention to these elements will assist in selecting the team and implementing operation and other necessary contributions from the different organizaitons.

2. Prompt action on these critical matters will also minimize commercial misunderstandings and potential legal problems. Don't leave details to be worked out at a later date, since what might be a detail within an established organization can be a significant commercial, staffing, or legal issue in a joint venture. If prompt agreement isn't reached, and substantive issues arise, it could be left to a court to impose its own terms on the parties on the basis of general law; terms which the parties might not have agreed to at all. For example, suppose award of the project is delayed, are the parties still bound to work together if it is reactivated eighteen months later? Are the bid costs shared and if so how? Who is finally responsible for fixing bid terms, or is the responsibility divided, and if so what disclosures or agreements must be made to the other participants? Who is authorized to deal with the owner during negotiations and are the other participants to be present?

3. From a legal standpoint it is usually a sound practice to have a written document covering basic issues prior to the initiation of activities when two or more entities agree to pursue a common business objective. A few examples may be of interest.

> While the law requires a contract in order for a joint venture to exist, the contract need not be written and can be implied from the acts and communications of the parties.
>
> When a project is being pursued in association with others, such as a potential major subcontractor, it is important to define the relationship if only to negate the existence of a joint venture.
>
> Even if a prime contractor-subcontractor relationship clearly exists, an agreement is useful to avert misunderstandings and claims about the extent to which the parties should be entitled to rely on each other and be bound to each other. Can the prime, having used the expensively prepared bid of the subcontractor as part of a successful bid, then obtain competitive bids from others? Or, may the subcontractor refuse to sign a bid after the prime's bid has been accepted and the prime has bound itself to the owner in reliance on that bid?

4. Finally, given all the other matters to be dealt with in pursuing a project and executing it, if the pursuit is successful there is every reason to eliminate the uncertainties between or among joint venture participants as quickly and as completely as feasible in order to minimize interference or delay in project pursuit and execution.

It is obvious that the joint venture details should be worked out early in the bid process stage. In most cases it will be possible to define terms relevant to all the critical areas. Even where this is not possible, agreement should be reached on as many points as possible, and explicit recognition of those areas where agreement is yet to come. Even if it is not possible to define the basis for achieving such future agreement, something should be said about the plan for ultimate resolution of open points.

Content

Once the joint venture form has been selected, the participants identified, and the time to define and document the joint venture has arrived, the parties must address the major issues and reach agreements to be embodied in appropriate contract documents. The following guidelines are offered.

Scope

The objective of the joint venture should be identified with reasonable clarity and completeness. If it is a construction project, the owner, the location, and the general nature of the project should be stated. There is a tradeoff here between specificity, desirable to keep the applicability of the joint venture from being too broad and covering work elements not intended to be included, and the inadvertent exclusion of objectives that may appear to be too detailed but which are, in fact, discrete and identifiable work packages.

This is the heading under which doubtful areas should be delinated. If the object of the joint venture is a construction project, it would be advisable to spell out that, while it extends to normal changes under the contract with the owner, it does not extend to other work at the same site with the same owner, assuming this is your intent.

Negotiation and Start-Up Phase

The joint venture will be actively incurring costs before it is at all certain that the actual project will move forward or that the joint venture will obtain it. Thus there should be agreement on these points.

1. The identity of the lead role in the initial phase, including negotiations. Committees are unwieldy instruments for dealing with details. There should be agreement on the authority given the lead participant. The lead should keep the other participants reasonably advised on commercial and legal considerations. It is unusual for the lead to have power to finally commit or sign contracts on behalf of the joint venture without specific approval.

2. Whether or not all participants should be present at all meetings, and if not, what advance notice and consultation is required. It is standard practice for all major participants to receive advance notice of meetings with the prospective buyer and to have an opportunity to participate. To minimize claims, it is advantageous for the other participant to make sure notices are issued even if not required. On larger projects, authority to negotiate with prospective suppliers may be delegated to one participant subject to guidelines, usually the final approval of selection of major suppliers and price.

3. Identification of the resources that each participant is to supply during this phase and the conditions of supply. Pursuit of a large project may require hundreds of thousands of dollars and months of effort. In most cases it is probably best to leave the decision on a participant's commitment to individual reasoned judgment since it is unfair to expect a blank check; if the parties cannot agree at this fluid stage about what each should supply, the venture has a bleak future. Nevertheless, it may be desirable to specify certain principal items that a participant is to supply in connection with a bid, with an estimate of the time and cost for each activity.

4. Who is to bear the costs incurred during this negotiation or start-up phase? Often each party bears its own costs. In specific cases, where one party's share of the costs is disproportionate, the other party may agree to bear part of the costs up to certain limits. Another possibility is to provide for recovery of start-up and bid costs partially or completely after the joint venture goes into operation with such recovery being payable before profit distribution. Needless to say, the categories of such costs and the support required for them should be defined with the same care as other costs to be recovered if the joint venture goes forward.

5. When does the joint venture terminate if it does not become operational? This may not be a problem if the purpose of the venture is to pursue a project and the work is awarded to another. However, potential projects may hang in abeyance with no clear date of final resolution, or the successful bidder may approach one of the joint venture participants with an offer for it alone to perform part of the work. To cover this, it is usual to spell out several likely occurrences which will terminate the work. One is award of the work to a competitor. Another is failure to award the work or to execute a contract by a specified date, usually fixed to provide ample margin for normal delays.

Allocation of Functions

In ordinary situations each participant could simply pitch in. But, this is seldom satisfactory. In more elaborate ventures, there may be substantial differences in what each venturer is to supply; one may provide the basic and detailed engineering, and another construction capability. These functions should be described in sufficient detail to identify them adequately from both the viewpoint of the joint venture and each participant. This is particularly important if the participant's supply is to be on a fixed price and/or individual responsibility basis.

This is also the heading under which to address the question of what special rights of control, if any, a participant wishes to exercise over work in its area of special responsibility. As in other elements, there are tradeoffs, even where one party has a superior bargaining position and can impose its own terms. If a participant is to be charged with special responsibility for a function, such as design, it may be legally and practicably advisable to consider affording it more unilateral authority in that area, even though this may work against the other participant's desire to exercise joint control of all elements critical to the venture. And, consider the discussion on liability, management, and transactions between the joint venture and the participants.

Status and Name

If it is a joint venture say so: ambiguity on the status of the relationship is undesirable. Agree on the name under which the joint venture will trade. If for some reason the names and separate identities of the venturers are not to be disclosed, special registration may be required under the laws of the states where the venture will operate.

Management

A rudimentary management framework should be agreed. If there is no specific agreement, each participant has authority to act for the joint venture and to bind the other parties.

It is usual to establish a management committee made up of one representative from each sponsor. This committee should be given authority to set policy and exercise broad control over day to day management. Legally a committee can manage the day to day operations of the joint venture. However, this is unworkable in practice.

Policy can be defined as anything the parties wish. Subject to the caveat that you should not make the joint venture inoperable by reserving too much detailed control to the committee, it is preferable, if you are a minority participant with a junior role in operations, to have a comprehensive list of items requiring committee approval. At a minimum these should include major changes in joint venture scope, transactions between the joint venture and a participant, approval of major contracts, changes in top management of the joint venture, and any action contrary to or amending the venture agreement. For less important, but still significant elements, it may be sufficient to require that certain issues and the steps suggested to be taken be proposed to the participants or the committee in advance, even if a majority participant or sponsor will have the final decision-making authority; sunlight can be a powerful deterrent to overreaching or rash action.

The committee should vote by participant percentage interest. It is usual to require approval by one representative of each participant on all critical issues, the criteria of criticality being subject to definition. A participant certainly does not want two other participants to be able to vote for a reduction in its profit share and an increase in its liabilities.

In some cases, one participant is named as project sponsor with rather broad authority to run the project. This isn't necessarily bad for the other participants if the sponsor is capable and trustworthy and keeps the others informed.

It is standard practice to name a project manager who will run the joint venture's day to day operations subject to the terms of the joint venture agreement and joint venture policy established by the committee. One method of selection is to let the major participant or sponsor nominate the project manager with approval by the committee. Another approach is to provide that the project manager serves only as long as he or she remains acceptable to all participants; although there is some theoretical danger that the manager will become indecisive trying to please all interests. This danger is less likely to arise in a project situation where good political relations with major joint venture participants are a critical element for the manager's success.

Further details on management should be dealt with in standard project procedures.

Interest in Profit and Loss

The arrangements for sharing of profit and loss are endless and are preeminently a matter for commercial judgment and bargaining. A simple across the board provision for sharing of all profit, funding requirements, and loss can be administratively simple and discourage subsequent nonproductive maneuvering and disputes. This approach may not be suitable for a participant whose share of the profit and control is relatively small, or where the participant is dependent on the performance of another participant, or can not realistically share the risk. Saddling a minority participant with an exposure it cannot afford or control produces a difficult partner, and a weakened joint venture. In some cases, special allocation of profit and losses to specific activities or geographic areas may reduce the risk of multistate taxation. Participants should be obligated to pay their share of any losses promptly. In this connection consider the discussion of working capital, currency of account, and liabilities.

Bank Accounts

Where joint venture funds are to be kept and who is to disburse them should be addressed. Usually this is a routine matter. However, it can be important if a participant is financially shaky or the location of the depository is subject to exchange risk. The extent to which account signatories are or should be bonded should be discussed with qualified advisors.

Working Capital

It is likely that at some point the joint venture will need working capital, if for no other reason than that distributions to the participants will have depleted the cash accounts.

The agreement should specify the proportions and circumstances in which working capital is to be contributed. Normally the obligation to fund is shared. It is usual, but not necessary, that it be in the same ratio as shares of profit and loss.

If one party funds in excess of its share by agreement or by necessity, the extent to which interest should be paid and at what rate should be considered and defined. In the absence of specific agreement the funding may be viewed as a contribution covered by the participant's profit participation.

If multiple currencies are involved, the question of who bears this risk and how it is computed can be very important. If both disproportionate funding with deferred payment and multiple currencies are involved, the complexities and exposures can become mind boggling and can require very detailed provisions.

Current funding of working capital needs in agreed ratios is usually simplest with the matters of currency adjustment and interest being dealt with as contingencies in the event of a default through a failure to fund currently. The basis should be favorable to the party forced to bear a disproportionate share of the funding obligation to discourage such defaults.

Provision should be made for interim distributions of profits and excess cash subject to projected working capital needs.

Transactions Between the Joint Venture and a Participant: Reimbursements

It is believed that the best way to view transactions between the joint venture and a participant is in the same way as a transaction between the venture and a third party, with two exceptions: there should always be adequate advance disclosure and approval of any such proposed transaction; and, the bases of the transaction should be clearly agreed.

If the participant's costs are to be reimbursed, the nature of the work to be done and the bases of reimbursement including fringes and overhead should be spelled out. The extent of manning should be adequately defined and controlled. If the joint venture is for performance of a prime contract on a reimbursable basis, it is usual to provide that the costs the owner will reimburse are correspondingly reimbursable to the participant.

Where the share of profit and loss are in reasonable proportion and the participants knowledgeable, reimbursement should work reasonably well where it is normal for the participant to work on that basis. If not, as in the case of manufactured equipment, lump sum may be more appropriate, but the major elements of the basis of supply, including price and payment terms should be defined with the same precision as in any lump-sum purchase and any changes should be documented to reduce disagreement. For the same reason the question of payment to be made in the event of owner termination should also be addressed.

The joint venture and its participants may incur costs capable of advance definition but which are nevertheless appropriately shared, assuming such costs are not specifically agreed to be within one participant's realm of responsibility and are not the result of defective performance on its part which the others have not agreed to share. For example, if there is an uninsured casualty, or an owner claim, the joint venture and the participants may incur costs for which the joint venture should pay and to which the participants should contribute in proportion to their share of working capital and, if a loss is finally made, their share of losses. It is difficult to define what costs should be covered except to say that such costs will be reimbursed if directly related to and arising out of the work under the joint venture. Normally such consequential losses as loss of other work, excess capacity, and the like should be excluded. Reimbursability may be further defined and limited by provision on the liability for specific work.

Normal practice should be to reimburse costs monthly and to pay lump sums on a schedule adjusted for actual progress. If there is to be any delay in payment this should be dealt with as a form of funding under the heading working capital; a delayed payment is no more than a loan by the creditor participant to the joint venture benefiting the other participants in proportion to their shares.

Provision should be made that all costs recoverable from the joint venture are to be adequately documented, and if reimbursable should be subject to audit.

Books of Account

Accounting records should be kept for the joint venture in as much detail as would be expected in any business. If there is any question, particularly in a venture involving foreign interests, the basis of accounting should be stated. For U.S. companies, it usually will be U.S. generally accepted accounting principals. If records must also be kept on some other basis to meet foreign requirements, this should be noted as well as who pays if it is unduly expensive. There should be specific agreement that each party can, at its own expense, audit and copy the joint venture books. The books should be retained for a specified period sufficient to meet legal requirements.

Currency of Account

The currency of account should be specified if foreign participants are involved so that receipts, disbursements, and liabilities are in a common currency.

It may be necessary to spell out the bases on which the joint venture will deal with a foreign participant. Will the foreign participant bill its currency for work it does or costs it incurs? If payment is deferred, will the deferred payment be calculated in the foreign currency? In certain countries a payment denominated in the foreign currency deferred for a year at U.S. interest rates will only be worth a fraction of its value at the outset. One solution for current accounts is to have the foreign participant bill in its currency on the terms agreed by the participants to be conventional for that currency; the joint venture then pays as it would in the case of any third-party supplier, with the cost including any exchange loss booked in the specified currency of account of the joint venture. Of course as far as venture profits and losses are concerned, the foreign participant's share should be calculated and paid in the agreed currency of account for the joint venture.

Participant Support to the Joint Venture

As in the case of support at start-up, there should be agreement on participant support to the joint venture. Frequently this is covered by a general statement that the participant will, with proper regard to its other operations, make available such part of its organization and facilities as may be necessary in connection with the prompt and efficient performance of the joint venture. Such a generalization is fine where the joint venture is working on a cost-reimbursable contract. It may be both too broad and not sufficiently precise if specific supply is required of a participant or the costs and reimbursability are not sufficiently defined; in such a case the basis of supply should be further defined. Note also with regard to this heading, and that relating to transactions between the joint venture and the participant, that in the absence of agreement for specific payment for its work before joint venture profits are computed, the participant's recovery may be limited to its specified share of joint venture profit and nothing more.

Interests in Joint Venture Property

Normally the agreement provides for assets to be disposed of and the proceeds taken into the joint venture account for purposes of computing profit and loss. If disposition is other than on the open market on an arms-length basis, or is to a participant, the bases for this should be approved by all participants.

Insurance

This issue may not even be mentioned in the joint venture contract. However, the participants will want to assure that the joint venture and their interest in it is properly insured.

Blanket corporate policies do not necessarily extend to the joint venture and if they do they do not necessarily cover the other participant's liability to third parties. If the other participant is not adequately insured and an insurable loss occurs, the joint venture relationship and contract could leave the insured participant exposed but uninsured for the uninsured portion of this loss.

Whether and the extent to which a participant's corporate policy should be extended to the joint venture or the other participants should be carefully considered with insurance and legal personnel.

Default

There should be agreement on what would happen in the event of default. The general legal rule is, that in the event of default, the other participants may either terminate the joint venture as to the defaulting participant and proceed to completion without it or continue to consider the participant as part of the joint venture and sue it for what was promised. A further rule is that if the defaulting participant has contributed some asset which continues to be used by the remaining nondefaulting participants, it will be considered that the second option has been elected. Finally, it is usually necessary to give notice to the defaulting joint venturer. To some extent these consequences can be altered by specific agreement.

It is advisable to include provisions to the effect that, in the event of default, notice will be given to the defaulting party after which it will have a specified number of days to make payment if the default relates to the payment of money or to commence and diligently proceed with cure if it is some other default. If payment or cure does not proceed within the specified limits, the interest of the defaulting party in the venture may be terminated but the joint venture may continue to use any contributions previously made and may recover any damages suffered as a result of the default.

Normally, if a joint venture participant is to supply anything other than money, consideration should be given to defining the extent to which it will be liable to the other participants if that supply proves to be defective or deficient in some respect, including adherence to delivery schedule. Although each participant is going to be fully liable to third parties for the joint venture's breach of any contract or act of negligence which damages the third party, whether or not the particular participant was responsible for the defect, the innocent participant may be able to recover on any of several bases from the participant whose failure to perform caused the damage to be incurred. There seems to be no reason why these exposures may not be limited by specific contractual provisions to the extent that they are subject to such limitation in other circumstances, a perhaps doubtful point given developments in law in the United States. The extent to which such limitation should be proposed or accepted will depend on the extent to which a participant will benefit or lose from limited liability or broader liability.

Many joint venture agreements contain broad provisions to the effect that the bankruptcy dissolution or similar action relating to the insolvency of a participant will terminate its interest as in the case of default. Such provisions were generally considered valid under the old bankruptcy law. The extent to which they may be valid under current law is debatable and in any event is beyond the scope of this discussion. If there is any significant concern about the solvency of a participant, avoid it as a coventurer; if this cannot be done, this point should be investigated in more detail with competent counsel. Incorporation of such a bankruptcy termination provision is advisable as a matter of routine.

Temination

It is usual to include a provision to the effect that the joint venture will terminate upon completion of all anticipated work and obligations of the participants to each other and to third parties. Though this is generally no more than a statement of the applicable law, it will also serve to further confirm the limited scope of the joint venture.

Assignment; Successors

For the same reasons that it may be advisable to include restrictions upon a contractor's right to subcontract the work to assure that the performance will be that which was contracted for, similar provisions should be considered for the joint venture agreement.

Generally, under U.S. law, a party cannot be prohibited from assigning or pledging its rights to payment and such assignments can result in significant complexity if the assignee claims rights to proceeds, especially if broad rights of setoff or counterclaim are sought to be preserved against the participant. Special provisions can be drafted to minimize problems arising from such assignment of proceeds.

Entire Agreement

Although it is often considered a boiler plate provision, a clause should be included to the effect that the agreement constitutes the entire agreement between the parties, superseding any previous agreements and understandings and that any amendment in order to be effective must be in writing, referenced to the contract, and signed on behalf of both parties. The reason for such a provision is that there will often be a number of communications between the parties which, depending on how they are read, may be interpreted to impose a variety of obligations not all consistent with one another. While the courts will not necessarily give total effect to such a contract provision, which is called an integration clause, it does have some legal and practical significance.

In closing, it should be emphasized that while it is not anticipated that management would involve itself in all the details of the negotiation and drafting of the contract covering the joint venture, it should do so on all substantive points. The contract writing process in itself serves several useful functions beyond the purely legal. First, it is a checklist of items which ought to be addressed by the joint venture participants. Second, it acts as a catalyst for achieving agreement on those points. Third, in the commercial sense of the term as well as the legal it serves to create a memorandum of the agreement which the parties have reached. Fourth, the basic agreement need not consist of more than twenty pages, although special lump-sum supply provisions could greatly add to this.

One final thought. If a joint venture participant is going to have only a financial interest in the results of the joint venture, with management being undertaken by others, the question arises as to whether or not the participation is not some form of security. Even if registration under the federal or state securities laws is not required, it should be recognized that the law is rather more solicitous of an investor than of someone engaging in normal commercial transactions. If an investment relationship is found, there may also be found to be a correspondingly greater duty on the part of the other participants to make full disclosures to the investor of all aspects and risks associated with the venture, even where the investor is rather sophisticated. Generally this aspect will not be a major problem in the normal commercial joint venture. It may have some significance where the primary requirement of the other participant is funding.

3

Preconstruction Phase

TOM N. FRISBY, SR. *The Frisby Group, Tyler, Texas*

Before the shovel enters the ground, the cost and duration of the construction program will have been largely determined by the quality of the preconstruction process, a process initiated by two entities: the owner and the architect/engineer, neither of whom will always have a total understanding of construction or the needs of a construction contractor.

The first entity, the owner, wants a building in which to manufacture, educate, sell his wares, or whatever. But the owner is not a constructor, and the erection of a building is not his goal; he wants space, space to ply his trade, to perform an economic function. The owner may be highly knowledgeable as to his trade, or even the kind of building he wants, but he is not normally immersed in the day to day business of construction; yet through his decisions, and nondecisions, he will greatly affect the construction cost and schedule.

The second entity, the architect/engineer, prepares the plans and specifications for the facility required to meet the objectives of the owner. The "constructability" of the documents prepared by the architect/engineer will have a major influence on the cost of the construction program.

The term contractor, as used here, refers to a construction contractor, building a facility under contract to the owner, using documents developed and provided by the architect/engineer.

DEFINITION PHASE

Our studies reveal that a well-planned preconstruction phase is absolutely critical to a cost- and schedule-effective construction project, no matter how small or large.

For our purposes, we shall term the "design" or "preconstruction" phase as the *definition phase*. It is imperative that the best definition be provided to the contractor as a basis for bid preparation.

Definition Phase: Owner

Facility requirements	*Management requirements*
Function	Team members
Space	Contracting technique
Quality	Commitment to preconstruction phase
Budget	Time and resources
Schedule	Accountability of parties

Facility requirements
   Return on investment
   Operation and maintenance
   Expandability and flexibility

Management requirements
   Decision making
   Funding

Definition Phase: Architect/Engineer

Facility requirements
   Space
   Systems
   Subsystems
   Quality
   Budget
   Value analysis
      Tradeoff decisions
   Schedule
   Design interfaces
   Soils analysis
   Design analysis
   Constructability

Management requirements
   Feasibility
   Adequacy of contract documents
   Logistics
   Risks
   Contingencies
   Roles and relationships
   Contracting techniques
   Degree of accountability

The preceding listings represent the actual division of definition responsibility between owner and architect/engineer as applied to certain commercial building projects. The divisions between facilities-oriented and management-oriented functions are arbitrary, and are intended to emphasize that a management involvement is critical, the nature of which depends on the management approach of the specific principals. As we move from relatively simple and contained projects to highly complex programs, the listing would naturally expand, and at the level of a mega project would encompass a detailed independent report, with several supporting volumes.

THE OWNER

Of all the participants, the owner has the greatest impact on cost. An owner's decisions on the size, scope, and schedule for the project will have the most substantial bearing on the ultimate cost. Yet, many owners, at the outset of a project, do not fully analyze the project in light of their needs, with the project definition thus becoming one of progressive disclosure.

Whether building a factory, a school, or an office building, it is imperative that the owner commit to the evaluation of space and quality requirements at the outset. The owner should know what is needed and what resources will cover the cost. The owner who contracts with an architect without having done a critical self-analysis of the requirements, and the capacity to fund those requirements, will in all likelihood reap the consequences of such inadequate preplanning. As a result the project often grows in size, with a design phase characterized by indecision, scurrying about, frustration, and too little time to do too much. The consequence is inadequate construction documents laden with time bombs certain to explode and adversely affect the construction of the project, with multitudinous changes and resultant contractual claims.

The point is that the quality of the design and construction phases is directly related to the owner's commitment to define the program requirements clearly; to fund the design phase adequately; and to provide the time necessary to perform the design properly. The constructability quality of the design phase will determine just how effectively money and time can be managed in the field program, yet as a percentage of total program cost the design effort is normally only 5 to 15%.

The owner must also consider the degree of accountability to be assigned to the parties. A major malaise in the construction industry is what can be called "design

by disclaimer," the legal technique by which owners may attempt to transfer the risk
of design errors and/or omissions to the contractor. It is an underlying principle that
accountability is the very lifeblood of productivity. The owner must establish requirements such that each party in the construction process will accept full accountability
and responsibility for his phase of the work without, a priori, attempting to avoid it
by exculpatory, disclaimer, and/or hold harmless clauses, or other contractual devices.

It is imperative that the owner develop a full understanding of his implied contractual duties, and how to avoid the pitfalls that can result in financial distress. An owner
who is aware of the numerous duties which generally are not explicitly written into the
construction contract and the breach of which can add substantially to the cost of the
project, will insist on both a well-disciplined and effective design phase as well as a
"tight ship" in the construction phase.

As the design phase gets underway, the owner and architect/engineer should understand these duties clearly, and establish a plan to discharge them in such a manner
as to avoid subsequent damages due to their nonfulfillment. To begin with, in most
construction contracts the financial risks undertaken by the contractor are more limited
than one might realize. In cases where detailed specifications are prepared by the
owner's representative (i.e., architect/engineer), there is a relatively narrow fence
around the contractor's potential financial liabilities.

As Figure 1 indicates, the owner is not always cognizant of the potential economic
risks he is taking. The contractor's liabilities are set forth inside the "fence" in
Figure 1, whereas it is the owner's "deep pocket" which must bear the financial consequences of those risks outside the contractor's fence. As a general guideline, if
it isn't inside the fence, consider that it's outside. Without getting into an extensive
and perhaps debatable legal discussion, through the concept of "quantum meruit"–what
it's worth–a protective umbrella may be placed over the contractor's fence, further
protecting his limited liabilities.

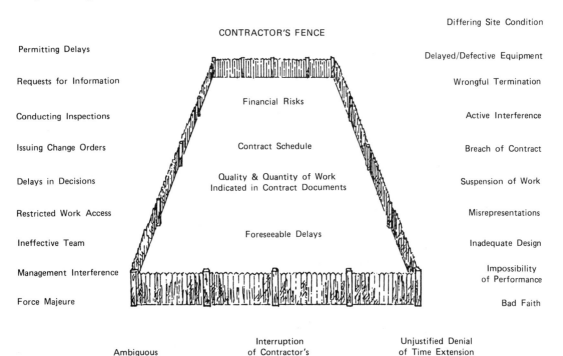

Figure 1 Potential economic risks of owner.

THE ARCHITECT/ENGINEER

The owner's program requirements are basically a statement of his problem: a structure to perform a given function within specified parameters of time and money. It is the responsibility of the architect/engineer to solve the problem and represent the solution in the form of construction specifications and drawings of sufficient clarity and completeness to enable construction contractors to bid and construct the project productively with only minor difficulties in interpreting those documents. The preconstruction phase is not just a design phase. It is the time to present realistic proposals to meet the owner's requirements and develop an efficient management program which will avoid the extra costs that can arise from violation of the duties set forth.

Design versus Construction

The architect will sometimes perform functions, or select materials or methodologies which, in an engineering vacuum, are adequate, but from a construction productivity perspective, may be catastrophic. Consider the following:

Soils

The engineer will commission a soils report. Often, because of budgetary constraints in the design phase, a limited number of test holes will be drilled to determine soil characteristics and on which to base structural calculations. The limited number of holes may be adequate for structural calculations, but woefully inadequate for informing the construction contractor of the subsurface conditions which may be encountered. If conditions differ from what is reasonably anticipated from the soils report, the owner may be required to pick up the extra costs, including delay damages, caused by the changed conditions.

To illustrate, an engineer on a large military housing project ordered a soils report. Twenty-five test holes were drilled at random around the site. Few were in the actual construction area. The contract documents specified a drilled pier configuration, whereby a pier is drilled by augur, a cage is inserted, and concrete is poured into the hole. A standard prebid site investigation was set forth in the bid documents and the prospective bidders were warned that site information, such as soils reports, were not to be relied upon. Having only 30 days to bid the job, which was in excess of $20,000,000, the contractor relied instead on the log of the test borings which disclosed no boulders and what he considered to be a static water condition, as opposed to water under pressure which could cause caving of the sandy-type soils at the base of the holes.

When the drilled pier operation began, the contractor encountered boulders, water under pressure, caving soils, and other conditions inconsistent with the economic use of drilled piers. The owner denied the contractor's claim for substantially increased costs associated with drilling the piers and for delay damages on the basis of the "exculpatory" clause requiring the contractor to do a prebid site investigation and which disclaimed any responsibility for the accuracy of the soils report. It was determined that the contractor should prevail, however, because generally an owner must stand behind the data it sets forth in the bid documents even though the disclaimer of reliability of the data was written in the proposal.

The owner ended up paying for a hugh claim which was totally avoidable. By drilling enough test holes to provide sufficient information for potential construction problems, as well as for design solutions, the engineer would have determined for himself that the subsurface conditions were incompatible with drilled piers and prevented a serious impact to the job in terms of both time and money.

Tolerances

Construction of a building, or any project, is not a controlled process such as a manufacturing process. Imperfect materials, such as wood framing or concrete forms, are used by journeymen who may not be craftsmen of the "old school" in field conditions. Is it any wonder that even good contractors do not always achieve the tolerances that architects specify?

The minimum tolerance requirements that the owner can live with should be specified. If the specified tolerances are unreasonably "tighter" than what the industry is accustomed to, the result is often unnecessary costs, and the specified tolerances still may not be achieved. Again, the area of tolerances is one in which design cannot be isolated—it must be integrated sensibly with the real world of construction. Examples are legion: requiring a factory smooth finish on concrete panels poured in the field; tolerances on floor slabs of 1/4" in 6' that are not necessary; requiring code welds for noncode applications, architectural finishes on the inside walls of clarifiers in sewage treatment plants . . . and the list goes on.

Construction Methodologies

Maximum flexibility. Reasonable latitude should be given to the contractor relative to methodology. Care should be taken to avoid designs which dictate uneconomical methodologies.

Design interfaces. Frequently, each functional design is adequate, but the interface between functions may not receive adequate attention. For example, tolerance build-up between systems is a common problem. Or the electrical hook-up of mechanical equipment is left unclear. These examples can cause unnecessary disputes, slow down a project, and increase its cost. Interface design review as an integral part of the design phase is strongly recommended.

Schedule. The construction schedule dictated by the contract documents is a critical factor in productivity. We know, on the one hand, that a relatively tight construction schedule will generally produce a higher level of productivity and lower net cost than an unnecessarily long schedule. On the contrary, a too tight schedule that forces the contractor to stack crews and use overtime can equally adversely affect productivity. Time is money; the same is true of the sequence and production flow of the construction operations. Employing a construction consultant during the design phase to recommend a reasonable construction schedule may be desirable.

Fast tracking. Phased construction can enhance productivity. However, every part of a small project, and at least the ground work and civil parts of a larger job, should be complete upon release for construction, for if numerous design changes and revisions are subsequently issued, the contractor's productivity will be lowered.

Doing It Right

Exculpatory clauses and other contractual arrangements for transferring or shielding design risk are poor substitutes for good project management. Seldom do they prevent production problems on the project. The architect/engineer has a myriad of legal duties as set forth in Figure 2. The best way to avoid the consequences of these liabilities is to "do it right," avoiding pitfalls by using his technical capability rather than legal trappings. The preconstruction phase should and can be a "productivity planning" phase. The owner should insist upon it. The architect/engineer should commit to it.

CASE STUDIES

The National Electrical Contractors Association (NECA), in its publication, *Guide to Electrical Contractors Claims Management*, Volume II, provides the following enlightening study.

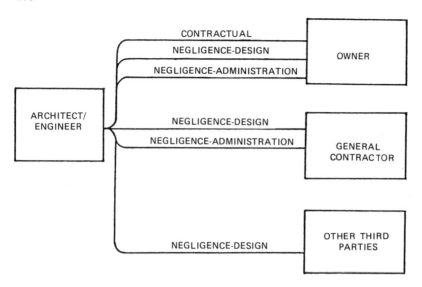

Figure 2 Potential liabilities of the architect/engineer.

Scope of Survey

The report is based on 116 project cost reports furnished by members of NECA. The original estimated prime electrical cost of these projects, excluding overhead and profit, ranged from $1700 to $5,900,000. The data furnished for each project included:

1. Original estimated prime cost
2. Final prime cost
3. Cost overrun
4. Schedule overrun
5. Reasons for cost/schedule overruns
6. Project description by classification

Figure 3 is a summary of the 116 projects included in the study grouped by project classification.

Relationship of Project Size, Schedule Overruns, Cost Overruns

Table 1 indicates that the magnitude of both schedule and cost overruns tends to increase as the project size increases. The ranges of overruns actually experienced are also shown in Table 1. Ranges normally are more significant than averages for purposes of evaluating the probable reasonableness of cost overruns claimed for individual projects in comparison with the experiences of others.

Figure 4 illustrates graphically the correlation between project size, magnitude of time overrun, and extent of cost overrun. This indicates, for example, that, of projects in the $200,000 cost range which experience schedule distortions, a schedule overrun averaging about 44% would be typical and would result in a cost overrun averaging 20%. The cost impact of a smaller project would be proportionately higher in ratio to the magnitude of schedule overrun. Projects of $2 million or higher might be expected to experience greater percentages of both time and cost overruns than smaller projects, but the ratio of cost overrun percentage to schedule overrun percentage would be slightly lower on the average than for smaller projects.

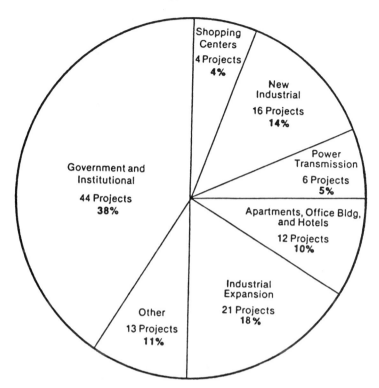

Figure 3 Number and types of projects included in study:
 89 projects (77%) had substantial cost overruns.
 27 projects (23%) had less than substantial cost overruns.
  0 projects (0%) had no cost overruns.

116 projects (100%) total

Also reported:
 79 projects (68%) had substantial schedule overruns.
  5 projects (4%) had less than substantial schedule overruns.
  7 projects (6%) had accelerated completions.
 11 projects (10%) had no schedule deviations.
 14 projects (12%) did not report any schedule information.

116 projects (100%) total

Reasons for Cost Overruns

The project reports used in this study included the reasons for the cost overruns. There were 18 different reasons cited, with 50 project reports listing one reason, 58 project reports listing two or more reasons, and 8 project reports which did not include any reasons. Table 2 is a summary of the reasons reported.

It is evident that too many projects end up in trouble, resulting in cost and schedule overruns. Many, perhaps most, are preventable by the owner complying with the checklist shown in Table 3 during the preconstruction phase.

Table 1 Summary of Data Submitted on Schedule and Cost Overruns

Estimated prime electrical cost	Magnitude of reported schedule overruns		Magnitude of cost overruns	
	Average (%)	Range (%)	Average (%)	Range (%)
Under $100,000	43	10-200	18	5-83
$100,000-300,000	48	12-87	19	2-99
$300,000-600,000	49	17-150	22	3-62
$600,000-1,000,000	49	10-105	25	13-49
Over $1,000,000	56	10-250	26	5-56

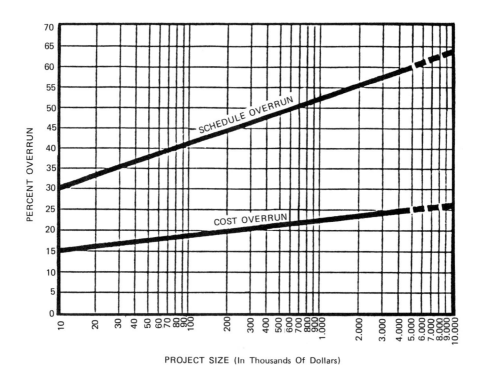

Figure 4 Typical relationship of project size, schedule overrun, and cost overrun.

Table 2 Summary of Cost Overruns

Line	Reason	No. of projects	%
1	Schedule overrun	84	78
2	General contractor scheduling and coordination	22	20
3	Change orders	22	20
4	Other trades behind schedule	16	15
5	Delays in delivery of materials	11	10
6	Design problems	10	9
7	Weather	10	9
8	Extra manning	9	8
9	Strikes	8	7
10	Schedule acceleration	7	6
11	Materials	6	6
12	Administrative	5	5

Table 3 Owner Checklist

Item	Specific questions
I. Master plan	a. What is the specific land use to be.
	b. What is present marketability (demand, absorption rates, best usage, etc.)
	c. What is long-term marketability. What flexibility do you desire.
	d. What are the functions required.
	e. What is the approximate square footage required.
	f. What are the items or functions the building must have.
	g. What are the optional items or functions you would like to consider.
	h. What is the level of quality your studies indicate is required.
	i. What governmental restraints exist: environmental impact study zoning ordinances
	j. What is the economic feasibility return on investment cash flow Use at least three models (best case, worst case, probable case)
	k. At what cost level is the project: marginal not feasible

Table 3 (continued)

Item	Specific questions

l.   What is your effective timing for completing the project.
     What financial effect would a schedule overrun
     of 10%, 30%, 50% have on the market and eco-
     nomic feasibility of the project.
     What financial effect would a cost overrun of
     5%, 10%, 15% have.

m.   How much cash can you honestly afford to front-
end for the planning and design phase.
     What resources do you have to cover unantici-
     pated cost overruns.

n.   What operation and maintenance factors are you
using in your analysis. Are they realistic. What
effect would increasing or decreasing this factor by
10-15% have on cash flow.

II. Team members

a.   What is the experience record of the architect/engi-
neer on this type project.

b.   What is the present capability of the architect/engi-
neer.

c.   What have other users said about the architect/engi-
neer's performance. What have contractors had to
say.
     quality
     design or overdesign
     errors or omissions
     schedule performance
     cost performance
     accountability
     operation and maintenance
     timeliness of decisions

d.   What special requirements are there which may demand special expertise.

e.   Do team members have adequate insurance coverage.

f.   How does architect/engineer intend to:
     Work with manufacturers' representatives.
     Integrate "constructability" in design.

f.   If fast-track or construction management is to be
employed, what is the architect/engineer's experience with these arrangements.

h.   If construction management concept is to be used,
what is the track record of the construction manager.
Check with others who have used CM. Check with
craft contractors who have worked on his project.
What responsibility is the CM willing to assume for
scheduling and coordination.

i.   Have you been completely realistic and honest with
team members regarding program requirements and
financial considerations.

j.   Are you willing to accept your own responsibility
for decision making, funding, etc.

Table 3 (continued)

	k.	Do you have an adequate staff for discharging your obligations during the preconstruction phase.
III. Working relationship in design phase	a.	Is there a schedule for design development and construction phases.
	b.	Is there an established system for decision making and design reviews.
	c.	Does adequate time exist for the design phase. Is "speed" overemphasized at the expense of quality and a productive construction phase.
	d.	Are soils investigations given proper consideration. Do you as owner have a full understanding of the significance of soils investigations on design and construction.
	e.	Are program requirement goals consistently evaluated during the design phase.
	f.	Are you assuring that design will be basically complete and not require change prior to construction. Are you willing to accept full consequences of the changes which do occur after construction begins.

4

Guarantees, Warranties, and Liabilities

JEROME R. KAYE *Lummus Crest Inc., Bloomfield, New Jersey*

The principal objective of a project contract is positive—the achievement of stated project goals. Unfortunately, there is also a negative side, namely the liability on the part of the contractor for failing to achieve the objective completely, or at least in all of the essential aspects contemplated by the parties. That part of the contract which deals with the most obvious manifestation of this negative side is found under the heading of "Guarantees" or "Warranties" or sometimes, for good measure, both. What's the difference?

In the early days of the common law, there was a difference. Purists and professors of law may still insist there is a difference. A guarantee is given by one party that the performance of another party will meet a certain standard. A warranty is given by one party that his performance will meet the specified standard. That's a bit of an oversimplification, but for our purposes it really does not make much of a difference. The fact is that the contractor is promising that his performance will meet the standards spelled out in the contract and the owner is concerned that those standards adequately define that what is being "bought" will meet his expectations. Whether the contract calls this "Guarantees" or "Warranties" or vice versa is probably nothing more than tradition.

TYPES OF GUARANTEES

In the typical full-scope project agreement, there are generally four distinct categories of "express" guarantees. These guarantees are express in that they are fully set forth in the agreement of the parties, as opposed to "implied," that is, created by the law regardless of the words of the parties in the contract. Whether implied guarantees, or implied warranties, as they are usually called, arise in our type of projects is a question we will touch on later.

Express Guarantees

The four types of express guarantees are:

1. Design/mechanical
2. Field workmanship

   3. Equipment (vendors)
   4. Performance (process)

Design/Mechanical

This type of guarantee is usually referred to as a design guarantee or a mechanical
guarantee. However, it is really broader, depending on the nature of the work to be
done by the contractor. It is actually intended to establish that the contractor will
perform his home office work against a standard of care which is appropriate in the
industry. It may apply not only to the engineering performed by the contractor, but
also to the purchasing services he may be furnishing, including inspection and expediting. It may apply not only to the design and drafting, but also to the requisition
and specification writing. In short, it is a guarantee that the contractor will do the
office work in accordance with recognized and accepted standards.

Field Workmanship

The name clearly indicates the nature of this guarantee. It is the standard against
which the construction portion of a project is measured.

Equipment (Vendors)

It is not unusual for the contractor merely to obtain and pass on from manufacturers
and vendors guarantees with respect to the quality and soundness of the equipment
being delivered. This must be distinguished from the guarantee expected from the
contractor that the proper and adequate equipment has been specified. It assumes
that the contractor has performed correctly, but the manufacturer or vendor has not.

Performance (Process)

This is the category of guarantees in which the contractor assures the owner that specific performance characteristics will be achieved by the facility which is being designed and/or constructed. When the process to be practiced in the facility is one
which is designed and licensed by the contractor, this kind of guarantee presents a
relatively straightforward situation. Difficulties arise when the process is licensed
by a party other than the contractor. In that situation, the owner will often want the
process guarantees flowing from the licensor through the contractor to the owner. In
this way, the owner tries to avoid having two parties, as least one of whom must of
necessity be responsible, pointing fingers at each other and leaving the owner holding the bag. Of course, the other side of the coin is that such an approach can put
that bag squarely in the hands of the contractor, who has been forced to accept the
full contractual responsibility in his arrangements with the owner, but who has a recalcitrant process licensor who will not accept liability and claims that the contractor
has improperly carried out his part of the design or construction effort. Indeed there
may be certain performance guarantees (e.g., utilities consumption) where the detailed engineering contractor may actually be the one essentially responsible for the
success or failure of the guarantee.

Implied Warranties

In addition to express guarantees, those which the parties have specifically bargained
for and included in their contract, there may be implied warranties. These are guarantees which have been created by law simply because of the relationship that exists between the parties.

   The most well-known implied warranties are those created by the Uniform Commercial Code, which has been adopted in all states except Louisiana in substantially
the same form. The Code provides for implied warranties of merchantability and fitness for the purpose. Merchantability means generally that the goods which have been

sold are suitable for the ordinary purposes for which such goods are usually sold. Fitness for the purpose means that goods which have been sold are suitable for the particular purpose for which they have been sold. As you can see, there is considerable overlap in the two concepts. However, there is a substantial question as to whether those warranties apply to projects of the kind we are considering. The Uniform Commercial Code by its terms applies to the sale of goods. It seems quite clear that a contract for engineering and design services alone or in conjunction with construction services is not one for the sale of goods. If you add procurement services, particularly where the contractor is purchasing equipment and materials for the project in his own name, one could argue that that portion of the contract is one for the sale of goods and therefore the Code applies. However, we are not aware of any case which has actually held that way and there have been those that have specifically refused to apply the Code to construction contracts. Nevertheless, in perhaps an excess of lawyerly caution, it is typical of contractors' attorneys to include in the project contract a specific disclaimer of any implied warranties.

While the Uniform Commercial Code warranties probably do not apply to construction projects, there is a type of statutory warranty that clearly does apply. For the most part, it is found in locations outside the United States, particularly in those countries whose system of law is based on the European Continental Civil Code, rather than the Anglo-Saxon common law. This is a statute which imposes on the architect or designer of a structure, liability in the event that the structure collapses before a specified period of time elapses. While a usual guarantee period extends for one year to, in some cases, two years, the guarantee period for these so-called "fall-to-ruin" statutes is generally at least ten years. This type of statutory guarantee is not usually found in the United States. One exception, as you might expect when you consider that its system of law is based on the French Napoleonic Code, is the state of Louisiana.

ELEMENTS OF GUARANTEES

Coverage (Scope)

The coverage or scope of the so-called design or mechanical guarantee may be framed in terms of a guarantee against defective design. It may also be framed in a positive fashion, that is a guarantee that the work or service will be performed in a professional manner or in accordance with accepted professional standards. There are those who feel that such a guarantee is imprecise and that it leaves open to varying interpretations the standard against which the work is measured. This is true to a certain extent regardless of how this guarantee is worded. Unlike performance guarantees, where the project's performance is judged against precise, objective calculations, the mechanical or design guarantee is frequently not susceptible to precise measurement. One is called upon to judge whether the performance is one which a competent individual, skilled in his profession, could be expected to achieve.

The guarantees obtained from manufacturers and vendors are fairly standard. They provide that the equipment and materials being furnished will be free from defects in materials, workmanship, and design and will conform to the specifications in the order. On occasion, they may include that the goods will be new and of good quality. Of course, since the sale of the equipment and materials from the manufacturer or vendor either to the contractor who purchases in his own name or to the owner where purchases are made either directly by the owner or in the owner's name are clearly sales of goods covered by the Uniform Commercial Code, the equipment and materials will be covered by the implied warranties of merchantability and fitness for purpose. However, it should be noted that the Code expressly allows for a disclaimer of those warranties so long as it is done in a clear and conspicuous manner. Today most knowledgeable and sophisticated vendors will make that disclaimer. Finally, some owners will also insist on a warranty of title. This is not the type of warranty regarding the quality of the goods, but rather is directed toward the ownership of the goods free and clear of any liens or other interest of third parties.

The scope of the usual field workmanship guarantee needs little explanation. It is directed toward the achievement of construction free of defects in workmanship and in accordance with the applicable plans and specifications.

The scope of performance guarantees depends, of course, on the nature of the project. In the typical process industry contract, one would normally expect to find guarantees of capacity, product quality, yield, or product recovery, and consumption of utilities.

Time Frame

Typically, design guarantees extend for 12 to 18 months. Sometimes it is both, viz, the guarantee runs from 12 months after completion of all construction of the facility, but not more than 18 months after mechanical completion. By mechanical completion, of course, it is generally meant that the facility is capable of being started up although final insulation, painting, etc. may not yet have been completed. When the contractor is not responsible for construction of the facility, there is justification for capping the design guarantee period at a specified time after completion of engineering or, since it is not always easy to determine just when engineering is fully completed, a specified time after the date of the contract may be stated. Of course, in the latter instance it would be appropriate to extend that cap for delays attributable to the contractor.

As a rule, the guarantee period for equipment is based on the date the equipment is first placed into operation, extending for one year from that date, although occasionally owners may wish as much as a two-year guarantee. However, since the vendor normally has no control over how long his equipment may remain after delivery before it is put into operation, it is typical for a cap to be put on the guarantee period based on the shipment or delivery date. That cap is most frequently 18 months.

The field workmanship guarantee almost invariably is 12 months after completion of construction.

Occasionally, owners have sought performance guarantees applicable throughout a given period of time, such as the first year's operation. However, this is not the norm. Performance guarantees, particularly in the process industry, are usually based on a test run carried out over a period of time which is sufficient to be representative of the facility's long-run operations. That period generally ranges from 24 to 72 hours, although runs of as much as 144 or 168 hours are occasionally required. Another time frame that may be imposed on the performance guarantee is one which requires the test run to be completed, or at least commenced, within a specific period of time after mechanical completion, when the facility would normally be turned over to the owner for his start-up. What that time period should be depends on the given circumstances of the particular facility, but several months would not be an inappropriate time. That time would also be subject to extension for delays attributable to the contractor. As in the case of the design guarantee, if the contractor is not responsible for construction of the facility, a time cap based on completion of the engineering or the date of execution of the contract would be appropriate.

Liabilities

Under fixed-price contracts, the extent of the contractor's liability for a breach of any of the guarantees (design, field workmanship, performance) is quite straightforward. The contractor is responsible for the cost of corrections to the plant or its work, whether they consist of redoing engineering or procurement services, paying for replacement of additional equipment or materials, or replacing or installing field work. That liability is generally subject to a maximum monetary limit, which usually reflects all or a significant portion (not less than half) of the contractor's anticipated profit. Excluded from the contractor's liability as a general rule are consequential damages, such as loss of profits, downtime, and interest charges during construction.

In the case of performance guarantees, there may be an alternative form of liability, often at the contractor's option, but sometimes at the owner's or as agreed by the parties. This is to provide for the payment of liquidated damages in the event of certain failures, the most usual of which is for failure to meet utilities consumptions or product yields. Occasionally, there may be liquidated damage formulas provided also in connection with the plant capacity guarantee, at least where the capacity does not fall below some specified percentage, such as 95%. This type of liability may also be found in cost-reimbursable contracts.

The greatest controversy over the extent of the contractor's liability for breach of guarantees arises in the case of cost-reimbursable contracts. Contractors generally take the position that their liability in such cases should be limited to reperforming their services, specifically re-engineering and redoing procurement and construction supervisory services. There are a number of strong arguments for that position, among them that there is no place in a cost-reimbursable contract for the contractor to establish a contingency to protect against potential guarantee claims, that the nature of a cost-reimbursable contract is such that the contractor is acting essentially like the owner's agent, and that the imposition of liability forces the contractor into a potential conflict of interest between his obligation to perform the work in a cost-effective manner and the desire to avoid liability by overdesigning the facility. An additional, and quite significant argument is that, since in the first instance the costs of equipment, materials, and installation are for the account of the owner, there is no incentive to the contractor to save on the costs if the result might be that the contractor himself may bear the costs arising out of what might later be determined to be a breach of a guarantee.

Nevertheless, there may be circumstances which do not permit this limited type of liability. In that case, there are still some principles which should be applied to recognize the essential difference between a fixed price and a cost-reimbursable contract and produce a more equitable result. The most significant one is that the contractor's liability in a cost-reimbursable contract should be limited to the incremental costs of the breach of guarantee. That is, only those costs which the owner incurs as a direct result of the breach should be for the contractor's account. As an example, if the contractor neglected to provide a required piece of equipment which would have cost $20,000 had it been purchased in the normal procurement effort but which cost $25,000 at the time its omission was discovered, the contractor's liability would only be $5,000. Similarly, if the omitted equipment would have cost $10,000 to install at its normal time in the construction schedule, but in fact cost $17,000 because of a subsequent labor rate increase as well as the need to redo some previously installed work, the contractor would assume the difference of $7,000.

Other variations on liability under a cost-reimbursable contract might be for a sharing of costs between owner and contractor, either on the basis of sharing each dollar of costs or on the basis of alternating slices of cost between the parties. Another variation, which actually is found at times in fixed-price contracts, is to avoid frequent controversies over relatively small matters by providing for a dollar deductible with the owner bearing the costs up to the deductible amount, and the contractor assuming the liability above that amount, or a dollar threshold, with the contractor bearing all the costs for a breach provided that the costs of correction exceed the threshold amount—if they do not, the costs are borne by the owner.

OTHER LIABILITIES

In addition to the typical guarantee and/or warranty considerations described so far, there are certain other liabilities which may normally flow from the quality of a contractor's work or lack of it, not including such specialized types of liabilities as patent or copyright infringement.

Tort (Negligence)

The liabilities described up to this point share one common element. They are all breaches of contract. Another type of legal liability is a tort; a personal wrong. This covers such things as the ordinary automobile accident, an accident on commercial premises, slander or libel, assault and battery, and so on. The common elements in this liability are negligence or intentional harm. Increasingly today, there is another category of tort based on what is known as strict liability. As yet, "strict liability" has not been a significant factor in our type of projects.

There are cases in some jurisdictions which have held that a contractor is liable for negligent performance of his contract or a portion of it. This is completely separate and distinct from liability for failing to comply with a particular clause or clauses in the contract, including the guarantees. The real significance of this kind of liability is that it is normally not subject to any limits of liability which are spelled out in the contract unless the contract specifically applies the limits to tort liability.

Compliance with Laws and Regulations

A requirement that a contractor comply with all applicable laws and regulations is effectively a specialized type of guarantee. This is especially true of requirements of laws as they apply to the project itself, as opposed to requirements which apply to the contractor's performance of the work. A clearer distinction can perhaps be seen in considering the application of OSHA (the Occupational Safety and Health Act) to the contractor's employees' workplace and the workplace of the owner's employees, the project itself. The nature of this requirement as a type of guarantee is emphasized when one considers the distinction made earlier between fixed-price contracts and cost-reimbursable contracts. In the former, the failure to include particular facilities, such as safety rails or platforms, should be the financial responsibility of the contractor, since he has agreed to furnish for his fixed price a project meeting legal requirements. In the case of the cost-reimbursable contract, it seems obvious that the owner should bear the cost of required safety facilities just like any other portions of the project. In either type of contract, however, the expense of fines and penalties imposed for noncompliance by the contractor should be borne by the contractor.

One difficulty encountered in this area is the proliferating nature of laws and regulations. They are not static. The body of law applicable to our projects is constantly growing. It seems only fair then that the contractor's compliance obligation relate to the law as it exists at the time he performs his work, or at least that the financial consequences from noncompliance with laws or regulations enacted after the relevant work is performed are not borne by the contractor. This flows from the very nature of the contract in a cost-reimbursable project. In the case of a fixed-price contract there should be provision for adjusting the price as a consequence of changes in laws and regulations.

If this text had been prepared 10 to 15 years ago, it would perhaps have called for special consideration in the area of environmental laws and regulations. Because of the evolutionary nature of that field of regulation, it was difficult to predict with certainty what measures would be required by environmental authorities. Hence, it was not unusual for contracts to provide that the owner would be responsible for establishing the requirements for compliance with environmental laws and regulations and the contractor's obligation would be restricted to meeting the requirements established by the owner. As the education process, both from the standpoint of the authorities and of the owners and contractors, has evolved, there is less and less justification for this special treatment.

Personal Injury and Property Damage

While not really a guarantee or warranty issue, there is one large liability issue that ought to be mentioned. That's the issue of liability for personal injury or property damage. Unfortunately, from the contractor's standpoint, owners sometimes like to get the contractor, in effect, to give them an insurance policy against personal injury and property damage. They do this by a clause that seeks to get the contractor to indemnify and hold harmless the owner for any and every thing that happens in the performance of the contract. While contractors may be willing to accept that kind of liability if it results from the contractor's negligent or willful acts, namely, those for which the law would hold the contractor liable even without a contract clause, the "blank check" clause seems excessive for a business in which risk is an ever-present factor. The result frequently is that some kind of limit, often relating to the contractor's insurance, is contained in the clause, particularly as it relates to the owner's property and the project in quesiton.

5

Risk Management and Insurance

D. J. WARDLE   *Bechtel Power Corporation, San Francisco, California*

Few business enterprises are free of risk: most are faced with two kinds of risk, one dynamic, one static.

Dynamic risks are those that arise from unexpected changes in the value of the capital investment generic to market, management, or political sources, namely risks that can result in profit as well as loss.

Static risks are those that arise from loss of or damage to physical assets, loss by fraud or criminal violence, loss because of damage to the property of others, and loss of income owing to the death or disability of key employees, namely risks that can lead to losses only.

The management of such risks is a vital part of the overall concept of sound project management and serves to protect the assets of the entrepreneur against catastrophic loss. The assumption of risk by the entrepreneur should at all times bear a reasonable relationship to the amount of money invested and the profit expected to be derived from the enterprise over a fixed period of time.

To manage these risks successfully the entrepreneur should properly assess the risks based upon:

1. All of the risks as they really are, in terms of type, dollar amount, and time exposure
2. Complete, reliable, and accurate information
3. The knowledge that inevitably some predictions may go awry, and be willing to recognize the need for contingency plans

Having analyzed the risks, the entrepreneur then should apply the golden rules of risk management:

1. Don't risk more than you can afford to lose
2. Don't risk a lot for a little
3. Consider the odds

We will discuss the foregoing principles as they relate to the design and construction of major commercial developments and facilities. Except as otherwise noted, the project manager shall be deemed to be the senior representative of the prime contractor responsible for the design, procurement, and construction of the project.

RISK ANALYSIS

The prudent owner, who perceives, plans, organizes, and decides to proceed with a
project, must, in so doing, analyze the risks associated with the enterprise in order
to reach the final decision to proceed to construction. The owner's risk analysis will
form the basis of the proposed design, procurement, and construction of the project
in a timely manner. The prime contractor, through its project manager, must then
analyze the risks inherent in the owner's proposed construction contract, including
risks that are insurable and those that are not. While the prime contractor can transfer certain risks to the insurance industry "for a price," he must decide if he can
afford to assume the uninsurable risks associated with the proposed contract–including
perhaps, certain liability to and indemnification of owner, and liability to third parties.
The prime contractor must take into account any contractual releases of liability and
any insurances that may be provided for the benefit of the prime contractor by the
owner and/or third parties; for example, in many instances of "Mega Projects" in recent years, owners have elected to furnish Project Wrap-up Insurance Programs for
the benefit of all parties involved in the construction phase of such projects.

THE TRANSFER OF RISK TO INSURANCE UNDERWRITERS

The transfer of risks to insurance underwriters can be accomplished by placing and
maintaining throughout the term of the project a variety of property and casualty insurance policies.

Property Insurance

In the majority of business enterprises, the principle "asset" is in the form of property
that is owned by the business. Any loss or damage to the property is a direct loss
to the financial worth of the enterprise. In addition, to perform certain limited operations, the same enterprise may rent, lease, or "borrow" property from third parties
on the understanding that it assumes the full risk of loss or damage to such property
in its care, custody, and control. As a result, any loss or damage to same will represent a similar reduction in the financial worth of the enterprise.

An example of the foregoing stems from the construction industry wherein the prime
contractor and its subcontractors typically are held to be liable under contract for all
risks of loss or damage to the work under construction by them until such time as the
work is completed and finally accepted by the owner. A discussion follows on the more
common forms of property insurance that are carried by a prime contractor during the
construction phase of a project.

Builder's Risk

Otherwise known as "Contractors Installation Risk" or "Course of Construction Insurance," this type of property insurance is designed to insure the new work under construction against the risk of physical loss or damage. The extent of the coverage and
limits to be furnished must be determined after taking into account the size, nature,
location, and schedule of the project under construction.

Whereas only the perils of loss by fire need to be insured in certain circumstances,
it is normal to provide at least Fire and Extended Coverage, or the broadest protection
of all, namely, "All-Risks."

The following is a summary description of the insured perils under Builders Risk
Insurance.

Fire. A Standard Fire Policy represents a basic contract of property insurance
and serves to protect the insured against direct physical loss and/or damage to the
specified property by "hostile" or "unfriendly" fire and/or lightning. The policy spe-

cifically excludes loss by fire or other perils caused directly or indirectly by (a) enemy attack by armed forces, (b) invasion, (c) insurrection, (d) rebellion, (e) revolution, (f) civil war, and (g) usurped power. Loss by reason of explosion or riot also is excluded, unless fire ensues but then covers the fire damage only.

Fire and Extended Coverage. This form of insurance, commonly referred to as Fire & E.C., consists of a Standard Fire Policy plus one or more forms or endorsements that adapt the basic contract to the protection needs of a specific policyholder. The normal Extended Coverage Endorsement will add the perils of windstorm, hail, explosion, riot, riot attending a strike, civil commotion, aircraft, vehicles, and smoke.

All Risk. Unlike a Standard Fire Policy, the All-Risks Policy is far from standard. Such insurance is usually tailored to suit the particular needs of the insured and can provide the broadest form of property insurance available at the time. As a result, in concept, it represents insurance against all risks of physical loss or damage to the insured property, except as otherwise excluded.

The property insured is the new work under construction, including all materials, equipment, supplies, and labor destined to form part of the permanent facility. The term of the insurance normally applies while the property is in storage at or on the project site awaiting installation, during construction, installation, or erection, and until such time as the work is completed and accepted by the owner's representative. In projects involving the installation of mechanical and/or electrical equipment or systems, it is important to understand when "owner's acceptance" of the work takes place under the terms of the contract, that is (1) upon "mechanical completion," including "precommissioning tests" where applicable, or (2) following commissioning and start-up, or (3) following a prescribed period of commercial operation. In the case of (3), the contracting party ultimately may assume the risk of physical loss or damage to the work until such time as the certain performance tests have been completed and have been met over a prescribed period of time to prove the satisfactory output of the facility or work. Whereas (1) is a normal construction-type situation, and as a result, does not impose any significant additional risk upon the Builders Risk Insurers, (2) and (3) introduce significant additional exposures and cost of insurance by reason of the need to "power operate" the mechanical and/or electrical equipment and systems that form the heart of a process or production facility. This may only be possible when "feedstocks" or "raw materials of production" have been introduced into the "process flow lines" or "production lines" of the plant. Such circumstances require careful analysis by the insured and by the insurer to understand the exact nature and extent of the new risks involved, namely (a) the raw feedstock/production materials of the owner have been added to the risk, (b) "operating" risks have been added to the more static risks of construction, and (c) physical loss or damage to the property may arise out of the act of owner's operating personnel, in addition to the acts of the construction personel—all of this is vital underwriting information which must be fully understood and noted by the underwriters prior to exposure under the Builders Risk Policy.

Whereas the basic Builders Risk Policy insures the property at the project site, frequently coverage is expanded to "while the insured property is en route" to the project site via inland transportation and "while property is held in interim or temporary storage" away form the project site but excluding while at the vendor's plant and excluding any property otherwise insured under a warehouse-to-warehouse Ocean Marine Cargo Insurance Policy. The need for this additional coverage will greatly depend on the final terms of procurement for permanent materials, equipment, and supplies. If such property is purchased FOB/project site, the risk of physical loss or damage remains with the vendor until the property is so delivered. In the event neither the vendor's cargo insurer nor its transportation company's insurer or the vendor is able pay for 100% of the loss or damage that occurs, then the Builders Risk Insurer will be called upon to settle the claim and pursue its rights of subrogation against the defaulting parties.

Since the sole reason for Builders Risk Insurance is to protect the party or parties insured thereunder against physical loss or damage to property "under construction"

in which it or they have an insurable interest, it is essential that the policy contains
a clear statement to confirm the insurer's agreement to waive any and all rights of subrogation it may have or acquires against the party or parties insured thereunder. The
following example will serve to illustrate the benefit of such a waiver of subrogation:

    a. Parties A and B are subcontractors to the prime contractor and each are named
       insureds on the project Builder's Risk Policy.
    b. Party B causes physical loss or damage to the project property in which Party
       A has an insurable interest.
    c. Party B has no insurable interest in the particular section of the project
       damaged by it under (b) above.
    d. The insurer pays the claim filed by Part A.
    e. Without a recommended waiver of subrogation, the insurer would be entitled
       to subrogate against Party B (even though Party B is a named insured on the
       same policy) to recover the payment made by it to Party A.
    f. The recommended waiver of subrogation, if included in the policy, would serve
       to protect Party B from any such subrogation action by the insurer.

Also such insurance should confirm that it is primary insurance for the prime
contractor and owner.

Ocean Marine Cargo

This is a special marine property insurance designed to insure against physical loss
or damage to any goods which are subject to ocean or air shipment, insuring under
all-risks conditions, including, if possible, war and strikes and covering on a warehouse-
to-warehouse basis; in other words, each shipment is insured for the entire distance,
including any regular inland transportation prior to and/or following the ocean leg
of the journey. Such insurance should contain an insurer's waiver of rights of subrogation in favor of the prime contractor and owner and is often provided through an "Open
Cover" form, subject to a maximum limit of any one shipment. Extra large and/or
valuable single shipments are usually the subject of a separate endorsement to the
policy issued prior to the date of shipment stating the type of goods, the value, and
time, dase, and method of shipment.

Such insurance should be deemed primary insurance for the prime contractor and
owner but excess to any insurance carried by the ocean/air shipping company.

Contractor's Equipment

Routinely carried by contractors and subcontractors in the building industry, this
form of insurance is an essential element in the protection of the assets of those organizations that operate and/or use, in the course of their day to day operations, a significant quantity of equipment which is owned by them and has a high aggregate replacement cost value.

This form of insurance is usually expanded to insure similar items of equipment
that may be leased, rented, hired, or borrowed from third parties for which the operating contractors or subcontractors are responsible, that is, that they assume under
contract the risk of loss or damage. Motor vehicles licensed to operate on the public
highway are frequently covered under this form for direct physical damage rather
than under a separate automobile policy which covers both physical damage to and
liability arising from the operation of such motor vehicles. Project owners often require contractors and subcontractors to carry such insurance to mitigate the risk of
serious delays in the construction schedule caused by contractor and/or subcontractor bankruptcy arising from major equipment losses. Such insurance should be en-
dorsed to provide an insurers waiver of subrogation in favor of the owner and its
representatives.

Casualty Insurance

The operations of most business enterprises must be carried out in an environment that involves the persons and property of nonrelated parties, namely "third parties." As a result, in today's highly litigious society, and particularly in the United States, the entrepreneur must keep fully informed at all times of the ever-changing environment that surrounds, is alongside, or is likely to be damaged in any way by his particular operations. Because it is extremely difficult to predict accurately the frequency and extent of claims that will be filed against the business enterprise, the entrepreneur will be well advised to transfer the principal risks to underwriters of casualty insurance. There are various forms of casualty or liability insurance that will serve to protect the interests of the prime contractor who is designing and/or building new facilities. A summary description of such insurance follows.

Comprehensive General Liability Insurance

A typical insuring agreement states that:

> The Insurer agrees to defend in the name of the Insured any civil action brought against the Insured, and to pay on behalf of the Insured all sums which the Insured shall become obligated to pay by reason of liability imposed by law or assumed by the Insured under any written contract as is defined herein for bodily injury and/or property damage and/or personal injury sustained by any person or organization or of those parties indemnified by the Insured under contract.

Based upon the foregoing, it is clear that, subject to the terms and conditions of each specific policy, Comprehensive General Liability Insurance will serve to protect the prime contractor if bodily injury/personal injury and/or property damage has been sustained or is alleged to have been sustained by a third party as a result of the prime contractor's operations. However, it is important to remember that notwithstanding, for example, the specific extensions under the policy such as "loss of use," bodily injury/personal injury, and/or property damage must first occur, or be so alleged, for the insurer to defend and/or pay any claim/suit for damages. In many instances, this form of insurance is expanded to include Owned and Nonowned Automobile Liability Coverage.

The limits of such insurance must be determined only after due consideration of the nature and location of the operations involved, the period of exposure, the liabilities assumed by the prime contractor under its contracts with the owner and others (including any indemnification and hold-harmless agreements therein contained), and an overall analysis of the risk. Policy limits on a "per occurrence" basis may be further restricted under the policy by aggregate limits, namely Annual Aggregates or Policy Term Aggregates—the exhaustion of such aggregate limits could cause the prime contractor to become uninsured or expose other excess liability insurance carried by the prime contractor to the same risk. At the time of this writing, the insurance industry is giving serious consideration to a proposal to change the policy base from "per occurrence" to "claims made."

Many projects cover the design and construction of new works/facilities within or immediately adjacent to existing facilities/plants/operations. Such existing facilities/plants/operations may be owned by (1) "pure third parties" or, in some cases (2) by the same organization that is deemed to be the "owner" of the new works/facilities. In both cases, the prime contractor is automatically exposed to two very major risks, namely

(a) Causing physical loss of or damage to the existing facilities/plants/operations.
(b) Causing consequential damage to the existing plant operations such as loss of use, interruption of production, loss of sales, default in contracts for the supply to others of plant output in the form of goods, energy, products, etc.,

Claim amounts in this area can reach monumental proportions and are ever increasing. In assessing this particular risk, the entrepreneur must pay particular attention to the risk of causing physical damage or interruption to underground utilities that either serve the existing plant/facilities/operations or transport products from the existing plant/facilities/operations. While the physical damage loss sustained may be minor, the claim for consequential damages may be of serious proportions.

To the maximum extent possible, the prime contractor should seriously consider transferring these types of risks to the insurance industry. While the owner of the existing plant/facilities/operations normally would be expected to carry and maintain Direct Property Insurance and Business Interruption Insurance at all times, the prime contractor should make every effort to have his Comprehensive General Liability Insurance cover liability for causing damage to the existing plant/facilities/operations (referred to as (a) above) of owners (1) and (2) (referred to above). Also, the same insurance should be expanded, to the maximum extent possible, to cover liability for resulting consequential losses (referred to as (b) above).

Airport Construction Liability Insurance

This form of insurance is more or less a variation of the Comprehensive General Liability Insurance referred to previously. It is designed specifically to take into account the special risks associated with the performance of construction work within the so-called "airside operations" of an existing operating airport, for example, immediately adjacent to or on the runways, taxiways, parking areas, maintenance areas, hangars, etc., that are in use by operating aircraft. Whereas, the "owner" of the runways, etc. is likely to be a department of federal, state, provincial, or municipal government, the aircraft owners generally are a highly complex group of pure "third parties." The working environment is special by reason of the high risk of causing physical loss or damage to aircraft and causing bodily injury and/or death to the crew and passengers therein. Any single occurrence is likely to result in very major claims upon the entrepreneur causing the loss by reason of the high price of aircraft, the high density of crew and passengers contained within the relatively fragile hull of any airplane, and the relatively long response time needed by pilots of moving aircraft (on the ground or in takeoff or landing modes) to avoid obstacles in the line of motion. Imagine if you will, the consequences of the unexpected presence of a construction contractor's pick-up truck within the direct line of a Boeing 747 commercial jet-liner that is about to touch down or takeoff.

Thus, the limits of this form of insurance related to construction operations at a commercial airport must take into account the nature and specific location of the work and the possibility of such major disasters occurring. For instance, to require limits of up to $300 million dollars per occurrence would not be unreasonable at certain major U.S. airports. The same risks must be examined in the case of construction operations at foreign airports, although a lower level of claims filed and awards handed down by the courts in a particular host country may determine that limits of U.S. $100 million dollars per occurrence or less would be reasonable in the circumstances.

Few prime contractors operate their own aircraft as part of their direct construction operations. In the event aircraft are to be employed, for example, in the transportation of personnel and/or materials and/or equipment, the prime contractor normally charters such aircraft on a fully operated, fueled, and maintained basis from third-party aircraft charter companies. Under the terms of a typical aircraft charter agreement, the charterer should be required to furnish hull, liability, and cargo insurance to meet the requirements established by the prime contractor. Such insurance should include the project owner and the prime contractor each as additional insureds and the policy should contain an insurer's waiver of subrogation right in their favor.

Watercraft-Hull and Protection and Indemnity Insurance

This is marine insurance, and as one would expect, is special in both its coverage and application. It is designed to take into account the unusual risks associated with the ownership, charter, and/or operation of watercraft over and above a minimum size, length, weight, or capacity. Such insurance normally is carried by either the owners or operators of such marine equipment and deserves special consideration by those involved in the project management of marine-type developments and facilities, such as offshore oil/gas platforms/pipelines, piers and jetties, marine terminals, lock and dam construction, within or alongside existing inland waterways.

Aircraft-Hull and Liability Insurance

As the description implies, this is aviation insurance designed specifically to protect the owners of aircraft against (a) the risks of physical loss or damage to aircraft while on the ground (stationary or while in motion), during takeoff, or in landing and while in flight, and (b) liabilities incurred to third persons including injury or death to passengers, arising out of the ownership, maintenance, and/or operation of such aircraft.

The coverages provided are tied closely to the regulations of federal governments and provide for clear distinctions between fixed-wing and helicopter aircraft, commercial and private aircraft, passenger and cargo aircraft, or a combination thereof.

The underwriters need to be made fully aware of the geographical zone of operations, such as the country or countries involved, the scheduled routes to be followed, the frequency of operations, the airports to be used, and the nature and extent of the cargo. If the use of aircraft is planned as part of certain construction operations, such as the hoisting, carrying, and placing of permanent equipment and vessels in refinery construction, such insurance must be designed to take into account all such intentions based upon the submission of comprehensive underwriting information to the insurers or prospective insurers.

The limits, deductibles, period of coverage, and other terms and conditions attached to the policy should take into account all of the foregoing.

Professional Liability Insurance

Such insurance is required only if the prime contractor is responsible for performing architectural/engineering design, project management, medical and/or other professional services in connection with a particular project. A typical insuring agreement reads as follows:

> The Company will pay on behalf of the Insured all sums, in excess of the Insured's deductible, which the Insured shall become obligated to pay as damages if such legal liability arises out of the performance of professional services for others and if such legal liability is caused by an error, omission, or negligent act of the Insured or any person or organization for whom the Insured is legally liable; provided always that such professional services are performed for, or in connection with, the Project specified in the Declarations.

The prime contractor's legal liability stems from its failure to perform its professional services in accordance with, or to meet, an expressed standard of performance—usually set forth in its prime contract with its client, or otherwise laid down or generally accepted in the industry or profession. Wherever possible, such a standard should be stated clearly in the contract between the parties, to reduce the possibility of a misunderstanding as to the standard that will be used to determine if legal liability exists.

In the event that legal liability is alleged to exist, the insurer must defend any suit or action and pay damages awarded, if legal liability is judged to exist. Such damages may include those caused by, or on account of, resulting bodily injuries or resulting property damage or resulting consequential damages, such as business interruption/loss of use. Also, such damages may well include the cost of reconstructing, modifying, adding to or removing structures/facilities that are improperly designed and are then constructed in accordance with the faulty design and which do not function satisfactorily, or physically deteriorate or collapse.

This type of insurance normally is written on a "claims-made" basis and the prime contractor, therefore, must insure not only during the performance of its professional services, but for a reasonable minimum of time thereafter, unless the owner is willing to specifically release and indemnify the prime contractor by contract with respect to any legal liability arising out of the professional services after an agreed-upon date. Also, Professional Liability Policies are normally subject to an aggregate limit, that is, either annual, policy, or project aggregate.

In certain circumstances, it may be possible to reduce the risk transferred to the Professional Liability Insurer by obtaining the agreement of the Comprehensive General Liability Insurer to cover liability of the insured for injuries to persons or damage to property arising out of professional services, such as design, inspection, and project management services, in the same manner and to the same extent as liability for injuries and property damage arising out of the insured's nonprofessional operations. At this time the market for Professional Liability Insurance is very limited in terms of capacity and number of underwriting companies.

Workers' Compensation and Employer's Liability

Workers' Compensation legislation was first introduced to provide for payment of limited benefits, determined according to law, for injury or illness emanating from worker's employment, without regard to the fault of the employer. Thus, while the legislation promised the prompt payment of agreed-upon limited benefits to the disabled worker, the legislation also intended such compensation to represent the single exclusive remedy available to the worker in such circumstances.

As one noted authority on the subject stated, "Since inception in the USA, a striking feature of the Workers Compensation Laws of the different states is their dissimilarity—they differ not only in detail but in every major feature." In recent years these laws have been subject to significant changes. More recently, increased litigation in different U.S. courts has placed very unusual, if not alarming, interpretations upon the Workers' Compensation Statutes, which has resulted in serious erosion of the original "exclusive remedy" concept, by allowing legal experts to circumvent Workers' Compensation Laws and file claims based upon common law. Significant court awards based upon common law have been obtained in this way. As this trend continues, we anticipate a further decline in the effectiveness of the Workers' Compensation Laws.

In the meantime, the prime contractor must continue to comply with the requirements of the Workers Compensation Laws in the United States and elsewhere and to pay the increasing premiums associated with insurance to cover the risk of work-related injury and/or illness to prime contractor's workers. The need for improved and increased safety programs, rules, and practices has never been greater in the construction industry. We will make no attempt to discuss, even in general terms, the Workers Compensation Laws of the various jurisdictions where the prime contractor may perform services. However, the following notes as to how Workers' Compensation Insurance is organized in the United States and Canada may be helpful to the reader.

United States

In six states (Nevada, North Dakota, Ohio, Washington, West Virginia, and Wyoming), Workers' Compensation Insurance must be obtained through exclusively operated monopolistic W.C. funds. Private insurers are not permitted to write W.C. Insurance in these six states.

In 13 states (Arizona, California, Colorado, Idaho, Maryland, Michigan, Minnesota, Montana, New York, Oklahoma, Oregon, Pennsylvania, and Utah), established W.C.

funds are now operated by the state to provide an additional market for W.C. insurance; i.e., they are in competition with the regular private insurers and operate as domestic monoline insurers.

In all other states, Workers Compensation Insurance is available from regular private insurers.

Canada

In Canada, Workers' Compensation Insurance (or Coverage, as it is referred to) is furnished through and by each of the individual Provincial Workers' Compensation Boards or Commissions. Because the coverage so provided does not include Employers Liability Insurance, it should be added by endorsement to the Comprehensive General Liability Policy. Like the first six states referred to above, the provinces operate the workers' compensation funds on a monopolistic, exclusive, noncompetitive basis.

Elsewhere

The prime contractor must comply with any current Workers' Compensation Laws in force in the country where the work is to be carried out. In addition, special arrangements need to be made with respect to Workers' Compensation Insurance covering prime contractors' U.S. expatriate and foreign contract personnel.

Other Miscellaneous Forms of Insurance

From time to time the prime contractor may find it necessary, if not desirable, to place one or more of the following more exotic forms of insurance:

1. Performance Guarantee or Efficacy Insurance
2. Dicennial Guarantee/Liability Insurance
3. Force Majeure Insurance
4. Delay in Completion Insurance
5. Liquidated Damages Insurance

As we go to press, the foregoing forms of insurance are not "readily available" from the insurance markets of the world.

"Wrap-up" Insurance Programs

The concept of a "wrap-up," in effect, literally bundles the owner, contractor, subcontractors, and other parties involved in the project, including on occasion, the architects and engineers, into one Workers' Compensation, Public Liability, and Builders' Risk Insurance agreement that is provided, paid for, maintained, and controlled by the owner. While the size, nature, location, schedule, etc., of a project may be such that an owner-controlled "Wrap-Up" Insurance Program is the only sensible arrangement, the debate on the "pros and cons" of such programs continues. Here are a few of the points under debate that clearly reflect the complexity of the concept.

In Favor

1. The program provides the same coverage for all insured parties.
2. The owner hopes to obtain broad insurance coverage at low rates.
3. When the insurance is in effect, the owner knows the exact extent and quality of the coverage provided. Hopefully the policies will provide adequate limits to protect contractors and subcontractors against liability claims filed against them by the owner and third parties.
4. Under the Worker's Compensation Coverage, the owner is able to arrange for:
   a. A cash flow premium payment plan.

    b. A dividend or retro plan to reduce premiums paid as a result of favorable claims experience.

    c. A project-wide claims/safety organization created and maintained on behalf of all contractors and subcontractors at the project site.

Against

1. Contractors and subcontractors are denied the opportunity to use their normal insurance programs.
2. Because of anticipated deficiencies in the "Wrap-Up" program, contractors and subcontractors may have to provide their own insurance as back-up protection.
3. It may be necessary for contractors and subcontractors to provide Completed Operations Liability Coverage and excess limits to cover losses shared with the other parties insured under the "Wrap-Up" program.
4. Under Workers' Compensation Coverage contractors and subcontractors do not receive any dividends they might otherwise earn if their own insurance policies were at risk.

It is important to recognize that in certain states of the United States, the use of "wrap-up" insurance programs is prohibited by law.

CONSTRUCTION METHODS AND SAFETY PRACTICES

The prime contractor is able to control, in large measure, the static risks associated with its operations and those of its subcontractors in the design and construction of a project. This is accomplished mainly by (1) the employment of sound, well proven methods of construction, (b) the adherence to strict safety rules and practices, and (c) a strong professional team of managers expert in their respective fields.

    The best loss/accident record that the prime contractor can enjoy is a no-loss/accident record. If achieved the following benefits will be realized:

1. No construction manhours will be lost and there will be no interruption of the planned schedule for the project.
2. No costs will be incurred by the contractor that are not otherwise recoverable from the client.
3. No time or compensation will be lost by valuable employees.
4. No losses will be reported to the contractor's insurers and, as a result, there will be no cause for immediate or future increases in the cost of project-specific insurance (this is particularly important as far as Workers' Compensation Insurance costs are concerned). Also, a perfect or near-perfect loss/accident record of a contractor is of immense importance if ongoing corporate insurance protection is to be continued and/or maintained at a reasonable cost—this has special significance in view of the present chaos in the insurance industry.
5. The contractor's no-loss/accident record will serve to enhance its reputation as a safety conscious employer who will continue to attract high-quality construction personnel to a safe place to work.

SURETY BONDS

Any discussion of risk management and insurance would be woefully incomplete without a brief reference to the traditional forms of Surety Bonds associated with the design and building of major commercial developments and facilities.

    From the late 19th century, Surety Bonds have been written in the United States by private corporations and, today, they are an essential part of everyday business transactions to assure that promisors will carry through their respective promises to promisees. In today's economic and highly litigious society, any entrepreneur who plans to build and provide funds for a construction project, to design and oversee such a project, to provide legal advice for it, or to analyze the risks attached to such a project should consider requiring, at least, the following types of Surety Bonds:

Bid Bonds guarantee that a bidder will, in fact, upon award, enter into the contract at the bid price and at that time furnish the specified performance and payment bonds. The issuance of a bid bond in itself serves to give the owner the additional security of knowing the contractor has satisfied a very comprehensive prequalification review by the surety of the contractor's finances, previous experience, and capacity to perform the contract.

Performance Bonds protect the owner from financial loss caused by the failure of the contractor to build the project in accordance with the terms and conditions of its contract. For the money lender, the bond provides assurance that if the contractor is paid, the project that secures the loan will be completed in accordance with the terms and within the time frame of the contract.

Payment Bonds guarantee that all of the laborers, subcontractors, and suppliers who furnish labor, services, equipment, and/or materials to the contractor for the performance of the contract will be paid even if the contractor defaults. Also, the payment bond relieves the owner from the risk of financial loss arising from liens filed by unpaid laborers, suppliers, and subcontractors. In addition, such a bond helps smooth the transition from construction to permanent financing by eliminating liens.

Furthermore, the above described bonds

1. Reduce the possibility of a contractor diverting funds from the project
2. Provide protection against one of the major perils of building (i.e., contractor failure)
3. Provide the catalyst that enables the open, competitive bidding system to function smoothly in the United States.

6

Claims Management

SOL KUTNER *Sol Kutner Associates, Inc., San Carlos, California*

The principles of contract and claims management are the same for all parties involved in construction: owner, project manager, general contractor, subcontractor, architect, and engineer. Contract and claims management are integral parts of the entire project management program and should be considered an integral part of the administrative process of any construction project.

Though problems inevitably develop during actual construction due to priority conflicts between owner and contractor, both parties are in business, and the essence of business is to make a profit. The owner wants the best product at the least cost and the contractor wants to complete the project with the highest possible profit. That is the way it should be. The key question for everyone is: how do I maximize profitability of the project? Good contract and claims administration are the answers.

PROBLEMS ARE MANAGEABLE

Project managers who carefully consider conflicting priorities on a daily basis throughout the entire project will find that discord is predictable and controllable. Keen observation shows clear evidence of developing problems, and early attention mitigates their impact and increases management control. One goal should be paramount: to design, build, and complete the project in the agreed time for the agreed price according to the applicable contract documents and all necessary changes thereto. It can be done!

PROFESSIONAL MISCONCEPTIONS

Many problems which lead to contractual disputes and claims are rooted in a misconception of the claims process. Claims management is incorrectly and unprofitably considered as the handling of claims after problems arise. When this concept is corrected, most disputes can be settled as they occur. Even more important is the ongoing ability to avoid lost revenue, flared tempers, wasted resources, and long legal battles.

Claims management is to project management what regular physical exercise and checkups are to good health. It is preventive in nature. What's more, efficient management of work changes and claims provides the highest possible return by avoiding expensive confrontation when possible, and substantiation of disputed positions when unavoidable.

DEVISING A SYSTEM

Establishing a system to control and document disputes as they develop is the basis for good claims management. This should be done prior to the contract award. Moreover, during contract review and intermittently during the life of the project, it is nearly always cost effective to bring in an objective expert/consultant on contracts and claims to identify potential problems and recommend corrective measures. It is also highly advisable for both owner and contractor to seek professional advice (claims and/or legal) at the first sign of any seemingly significant action along the way. A few dollars spent early can save significant sums of money when problems first surface and are still manageable.

MAJOR MANAGEMENT PHASES

A good contract/claims management program starts by dividing the job into four phases as follows:

Phase I Contract Formation. Preparation of a fair contract clearly indicating both parties' rights and obligations and a means of resolving problems will help assure smooth, productive, contract management and work performance. A timely, thorough review should not reveal blatantly unfair clauses, but if it does, they should be refuted.

Phase II Contract Performance and Administration. When the contract has been awarded, thorough documentation and detailed schedule/cost reporting programs are of utmost importance. This facilitates presentation and payment of valid claims in a timely manner, saves costly conflict, and enhances all-around profitability. It should be homework gladly done because it is invaluable when the need inevitably arises.

Phase III Claims/Dispute Resolution. This relates to owner-contractor problems that are inevitable; often arising over changes to the work. Management of these changes and subsequent claims can profoundly impact on both cost and profitability of a project. Proper planning and preparation in prior phases can avoid many expensive difficulties.

Phase IV Preparation for Litigation Support. Occasionally, even parties showing continuing good faith cannot resolve a dispute. Though it is essential to avoid litigation at almost any cost, the only reasonable action is impeccable preparation should a formal disputes resolution process become inevitable.

In summary, all participants should be mindful throughout the project that effectively managing changes and conflicts as they occur is far more profitable than waiting until the money has been spent, the schedule has been devastated, and both sides are moving toward legal action. Though the perfect contract document has never been written, a negotiated settlement is always preferable to a lawsuit.

PHASE I: CONTRACT FORMATION

Good Faith and Clarity: Good Partners

Good faith is presumed by both parties to an agreement. However, if either party exhibits suspicion, distrust, or malfeasance both parties suffer.

If good faith is present, in fact, and the contract is clearly worded and definitive, chances are good for the orderly handling and acceptance of responsibilities when changes arise and disagreement escalates into a claim. In a good faith environment the contractor promises, in effect, that the work will be done as directed and the owner pledges, similarly, that payment will be rendered for the work done. Under these conditions, spurious claims are not made, and valid claims are not ignored.

While clarity is essential, no contract can state everything in complete detail. That would demand a document encyclopedic in both scope and volume. Therefore, various and far more practical formal and informal administrative procedures are required to implement the contract and keep the work progressing. We shall discuss these suggestions in detail.

Cost-Plus Contracts

Cost-plus contracts are typically used on large, fast-track projects. In this instance, "fast track" means that construction starts prior to completion of all drawings. A firm price cannot be established since the precise scope of work is uncertain and, therefore, incompletely defined, though all costs are covered by contract agreement. However, the work must commence.

Under these contracts, production and work forces may be increased as necessary to meet time restrictions and imposed work conditions. In fact, work may be accelerated or delayed by the owner without significant impact on the contractor, who will be reimbursed accordingly for additional expenses.

Occasionally, claims occur on cost-plus work when substandard performance or noncompliance with the terms and conditions of the contract occur. Generally speaking, however, this type of contract assures the contractor of the lowest risk. Alternatively, it will most likely not produce the lowest cost to the owner.

Lump-Sum Contracts

Most competitively bid construction contracts are lump sum, so most problems arise and most claims are made under this type of contract. In theory, there is a predetermined price for a specific and well-defined scope of work and a fixed schedule of performance under defined terms and conditions.

Concept

To understand lump-sum contracting and the significance of costs and time, it is important to understand the concept of the lump-sum contract "baseline" (Fig. 1). The contract-defined scope, schedule, and conditions (both contract and working) constitute the baseline. A claim is a request by the contractor for money or time, due to a change in any of the three basic elements of the contractual baseline. Each change increases the job cost and decreases profit for the contractor, unless an appropriate adjustment is made to the contract.

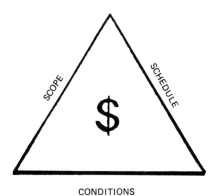

Figure 1 Lump-sum baseline.

Attitude

Lump-sum contracting requires a particular mind-set and method of operation. The attitude is aggressive, as well as cost and profit oriented. Time is of the essence and risk is ever present.

Price and Cost

The lump-sum fixed price provides the lowest possible financial risk for the owner. Alternatively, it provides the highest risk for the contractor, for any variance affects his cost and may result in a claim. When work is changed the contractor is supposed to negotiate the price and perform the work. The contractor may then seek additional compensation. This is where most disputes develop.

Changes

All changes should be considered in terms of deviation from the baseline. The question is, "what element has changed?" Is the change somewhere along the scope, schedule, or contract/working condition lines? The schedule is the most easily affected element of the contract baseline, since any delay, acceleration, disruption, or distortion of performance constitutes a change that may entitle a contractor, and obligate an owner, to additional compensation. "Time is money" is not just proverbial, but factual. Failure by either party to recognize this relationship will be costly.

Managing Changes

The major elements of scope, schedule, and conditions of a lump-sum contract must be used as the baseline against which to measure the validity of a potential change or claim. Invariably, failure to do so leads to disputes.

Baseline Perception

The contractor is usually inclined to view the baseline narrowly and the owner to view it broadly, each thinking that pattern is to his advantage. Sometimes this is true, but inflexibility leads to unresolved claims that lead to disputes, which require an unbiased third party (arbitration, litigation) to determine deviation from the baseline and make a judgment. That judgment can be very expensive to one or both of the parties. An unwritten rule of thumb is the fewer third parties involved in settling a dispute, the greater the chances the original parties will reach a reasonable settlement.

Seven Contract Sections

Generally, there are seven sections of a construction contract, but regardless of the specific number of sections, each of the following items should be included and clearly detailed.

1. Agreement (usually one or more pages dealing specifically with issues and signed by both parties)
2. General terms and conditions (common to most contracts; i.e., "boilerplate")
3. Special terms and conditions unique to this contract (including a description of the responsibilities of the owner, architect/engineer, and contractor)
4. Pricing
5. Technical specifications
6. Drawings
7. Other relevant documentation such as geotechnical reports or other special studies that vary from contract to contract

Preaward Phase

The preaward phase of the project is critical. It provides the foundation for all rights and obligations from which the contractual baseline is derived. In a negotiated contract, it is the last opportunity for the owner and contractor to modify their agreement prior to signing the contract against which all future actions are measured.

A contractor's right to obtain additional funds must be proven against the baseline. If that baseline is verifiable as an accurate representation of the agreed-upon scope, schedule, and conditions of the project, differences between the contractor and owner will be minimal and many potential disputes avoided.

Rights and Obligations

All rights and obligations must be set forth in the contract document for the protection of all parties involved. When the owner or contractor wishes to do something that is unclear in the contract, disagreement may ensue. Presumed good faith between the parties implies that each will endeavor to respect the rights of and meet the obligations to the other. Neither party will delay nor handicap the performance of the work and will cooperate according to terms agreed upon in the contract. Ultimately, this is to the parties' mutual best interests.

The owner and contractor can create a project which invites a minimum of potential disputes. Or, they can create one with many built-in problems by agreeing to contract clauses which give one party excessive rights and the other inadequate remedies. This often happens when contractors are too anxious to get on with the job and neglect doing their homework. Perhaps the most important issue involving the rights and obligations of both the owner and contractor involves changes to the contract.

Exchange of Promises

The contract document is an exchange of promises for future performance, whereby each party to the contract has specific rights and obligations. The owner has the right to require additional work from the contractor by issuing a change notice, and this right is accompanied by an obligation to pay for the work (Fig. 2). The contractor is obliged to perform work changed by the owner, and has the right to be paid.

The two most important events that will most frequently take you to court are:

1. Breach of contract by the owner in failing to pay the contractor for progress, approved changes, or any other payment legitimately due.
2. The contractor's stopping work in any manner, or ultimately, walking off the job and abandoning the contract.

It is said that the conduct of the owner or contractor can carry the case. That means there is a time for the owner not to pay the contractor and a time for the contractor to walk off the job, but those are only in cases where there is definite and provable bad faith and abuse of one party by another. Both are very serious actions and are foolishly undertaken without advice form an attorney and a claims expert.

Review of Key Clauses

As previously suggested, there are several key clauses calling for special attention in the review of any construction contract. Some are intended to mitigate risk and all require careful examination and analysis.

1. Schedule
2. Extension of time
3. Progress payments

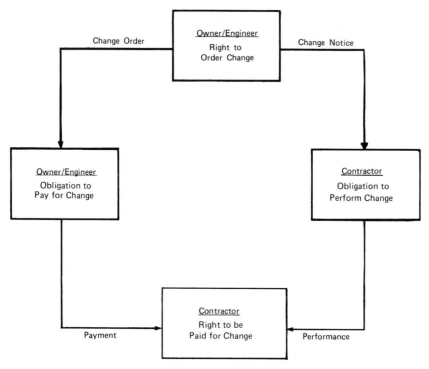

Figure 2 Rights and obligations of the parties.

4. Escalation
5. Changes and extra work
6. Variation in quantities
7. Changed conditions (including differing site conditions)
8. Exculpatory (holding harmless) language
9. Dispute resolution
10. Limits of liability
11. Liquidated damages
12. Allocation of responsibility and risk

These may be called the "what if" clauses. What if a problem occurs? What if the owner wants a change? The manner in which contracts accommodate these potential problems and the good faith efforts of both parties will largely determine the severity of any difficulties that occur.

Clause Constraints and "What Ifs"

Constraints of cost, schedule, conditions, and knowledge preclude writing a perfect contract or the flawless execution of work under ideal conditions. That is why the contract should be examined carefully prior to execution. Questions to ask include:

1. What if the contractor must have an approved schedule or cost breakdown (initial and revised) prior to owner's obligation to pay for work performed and the two parties cannot agree on the schedule?
2. What if the contractor is obligated to perform all disputed work at his own cost without interim payments until the dispute is resolved?
3. What if the engineer's decision is final?

4. What if the contractor is responsible for consequential damages?
5. What if there is no dispute resolution clause?

Evaluation and Interpretation

Pre-execution evaluation of a proposed contract should include detailed study of the entire document, but particularly the wording on the twelve problem clause areas in construction contracts listed above. If they all address the issues in a fair manner, then project life will be easier, and futile last-ditch efforts to resolve differences can be avoided.

PHASE II: CONTRACT ADMINISTRATION AND PERFORMANCE

Formally Speaking

Contract administration is the art and science of managing a project, using the contract document as the source for valid actions, rights, and obligations. It involves recording relevant events and data on a regular basis, being alert to problems as they emerge, and making an effort to avoid or correct them before they cause major time or cost overruns.

The practical result of an effective contract administration program for each project is higher productivity and increased profit. Because money, time, and protracted dispute resolution procedures are significantly reduced, the financial "bottom line" is significantly improved. The principles of contracting and contract administration are similar for all parties in the contractual hierarchy.

Post Contract

Once the prime contract has been awarded, a series of subcontract awards and purchase orders follow (Fig. 3). Each step down the award ladder involves a different contract, but all the common principles and pitfalls still apply. The owner awards the contract to the general contractor, who in turn issues purchase orders for goods and hires subcontractors for field labor services. The subcontractors also issue purchase orders and hire their own subcontractors. Each level has an accountable manager and each level from the top of the diagram ladder is responsible for everything that happens,

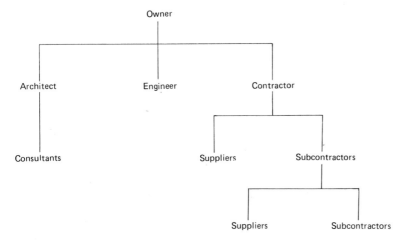

Figure 3 Owner/architect/contractor relationships.

contractually, on the lower rungs. Because the awarding party generally writes the contract, it reflects the preparer's natural preferences and also includes protective clauses that pass on the risks ("pass-through clauses") to the next level.

Contractors and Subcontractors

A contractor has two sources of craftsmen: direct hire and subcontract. These resources are equally important in accomplishing the primary objective of completing the work and should be treated accordingly. However, often this is not the case. Contractors are inclined to manage direct hire work, while treating subcontractors as second-class citizens. This is particularly unwise since the contractor is responsible and liable for all aspects of performance under his contract. If a subcontractor has a problem, the owner should and will look to the contractor for its resolution. Therefore, it behooves the contractor to continuously oversee his subcontractors' performance, problems, and well being. If only one subcontractor fails to perform proficiently it may cause a contractor to incur costs that not only negate his own profit, but may ultimately produce a loss on an otherwise profitable project.

Contractor Balancing Act

Contractors have a dual problem: balancing their interests between owners and subcontractors. Standing contractually between the owner and the subcontractor creates potential claim situations for the contractor with either of these two parties. However, it is avoidable. The contractor can, and should, stipulate in each of his subcontracts that the subcontractor is obligated to the contractor via "pass-through" clauses in the subcontract for all the prime contract clauses and requirements of the owner in the same manner that the contractor is obligated to the owner. In fact, many owners stipulate in the prime contract that all subcontracts shall incorporate specific clauses such as regulatory requirements (OSHA, etc.) payments, liens, and various other performance obligations. Very often, all the terms/conditions of the prime contract are incorporated by reference in each subcontract. While this does not create a contractual relationship between the subcontractor and the owner, it does inform the subcontractor of precisely what rights and remedies the prime contractor has in his agreement with the owner.

Diligence with Subcontractors

If the contractor is not diligent both in the subcontract preparation and administration, he may be liable to the owner for that subcontractor's failure to perform and will encounter difficulty in recovering any costs from that subcontractor. Perhaps the best example of this situation is when the contractor specifically obligates the subcontractor to meet scheduled milestones, but neglects to make him liable for liquidated damages (as a pass through to the owner) for late performance.

Another, sometimes devastating, example is when the contractor agrees to payment clauses in the subcontract allowing the subcontractor to demand payment from the contractor prior to his receipt of payment from the owner.

Basic Subcontractual Relationship

In many respects, the contractor and subcontractor perform as a team, but theirs is a contractual relationship with both parties responsible for good administrative practices. One important practice is the contractor's obligation to pass through to his subcontractor payments he receives from the owner on the subcontractor's behalf. This includes progress, retention, and change order payments. The contractor violates fiduciary responsibility, and risks exposure to serious legal consequences for diversion of funds, if he fails to pay a subcontractor monies received on his account.

Similarly, a subcontractor should be sure of payment clauses in the subcontract to provide pass-through payments to him from the owner through the contractor.

Liability Upon Termination

A special situation exists when the owner terminates the contractor. The contractor must make final payments and terminate all subcontractors, though the contractor is generally exempt for payments not yet received from the owner. However, there are exceptions where liability exists. One example is when the subcontractor has performed properly, while the contractor has not, and the owner terminates the contractor for cause; namely that the contractor fails to perform. In such case, even though the contractor has not been paid by the owner, the contractor is still obligated to pay the subcontractor.

Subcontractors and Vendors

By definition, a contractor purchases material, equipment, and supplies from a vendor through a purchase order. It is as important for the contractor to plan, schedule, and monitor the performance of vendors and administer purchase orders as it is to manage direct work. This complicates claims analysis and entitlement when concurrent delays exist.

In a Word

Subcontractors are key participants in the successful performance of the contractor. As such, the contractor must manage subcontractors in a professional and businesslike manner, and both parties must work at maintaining good relations and full awareness of mutual responsibilities and contributions. It only works as a team effort.

Scheduling

Scheduling is important to success in the construction industry. Few endeavors are more difficult than planning and scheduling a major engineering/construction project. Each element of the work is planned as a function of time. Contractors must adjust all resources to meet the constraints of scheduled start, end, and milestone dates. Success requires close adherence to a carefully prepared, realistic schedule. It is not surprising that a common axiom in project management is,"plan your work and work your plan!"

Scheduling Purpose

There are many methods of scheduling work on a construction project. Their common purpose is to facilitate predetermined, sequential, production management. When the sequence of work is disrupted, time and money are inevitably lost and, depending on the circumstances, may not be recovered.

CPM Most Effective

The CPM (critical path method) schedule is currently the most effective method of establishing effects of delays on project operations. It is accepted as the most common analytical basis for evaluating effects of time-related problems such as changes to the work, delays, changes to sequential work activities, and acceleration of activities on the entire project. While it is possible to use the conventional bar chart schedule for some of these evaluations, this is much less effective in portraying the impact on related or dependent activities. The CPM clearly shows interrelationships between work activities and subsequent effects from impacts to antecedent activities, making it a valuable management and claims analysis tool.

Schedule Preparation

Most construction contracts require preparation of a schedule for approval by the party awarding the contract. Unfortunately, contractors, subcontractors, and suppliers frequently produce token schedules that are approved by the owner/engineer/construction manager. While appearing to be adequate, they are incomplete in scope and detail, and may contain defects in logic that will surely lead to trouble.

The CPM schedule should be developed realistically in both graphic and tabular printout format, enabling project personnel to visualize the flow and interrelationship of work activities. It is also desirable to "cost load" the CPM network, that is, to distribute the total contract price into all the CPM activities consistent with the contractor's estimate. Therefore, the sum of all the cost-loaded activities will equal the total contract price.

Review, Revision, Approval

Most contracts require the contractor to submit his CPM schedule to the owner for review and approval. It is important that the contractor makes this a formal presentation, since it will constitute the official schedule baseline for the project. In addition, the contractor's progress as measured against the owner-approved cost-loaded CPM schedule may also be used for progress payment calculations. In this context, the contractor should revise his CPM schedule as frequently as necessary (or as required by the contract/owner) and obtain the owner's approval of each revision before proceeding with its use.

Schedule Float Time

A common problem relates to "who owns the float?" Practically speaking, float is the time available between the completion of an activity and the necessary start date of the following activity. It is important that the contractor position himself for entitlement to this float by establishing a need for the flexibility it provides. The contract can determine float use, but when it is silent on a multicontractor project, available float is generally used by the party who first establishes a need for it. Therefore, for claim purposes and to expedite subsequent construction activities, it is important that the contractor position himself in his early management planning to claim this float before another party beats him to it. There is, however, a current legal trend that, absent a specific contractual stipulation, schedule float will be available to the contractor as a management planning tool.

Schedule Compliance

Schedule compliance has different significance for various parties to the project.
For the owner and construction manager, it means an obligation to:

1. Provide owner-furnished equipment and material on time
2. Coordinate concurrent contracts
3. Provide access and facilities on time
4. Expedite changes to the work and contract
5. Review and analyze constructor schedule submittals in a timely manner

For the architect and engineer, it means an obligation to:

1. Produce complete drawings and documents on time
2. Provide timely review and response for vendor/contractor submittals and requests for information
3. Provide timely review of change orders

For the contractor, it means an obligation to:

1. Man the job as scheduled
2. Manage resources effectively (including subcontractors)
3. Maintain planned production

All parties are responsible for meeting their obligations on schedule and not interfering with the rights of other parties. The smallest schedule slippage is frequently an indicator of potential problems.

Continuing Responsibilities

Owners, architects, and engineers are inclined to overlook their own continuing obligations to others once the price has been fixed and the contract signed. They often try to burden the contractor with full responsibility for timely completion at the expected price. This causes ongoing difficulties and resentment. In fact, all parties to the contract have an expressed or implied duty to assure that the progress of other parties is not disrupted and must make every reasonable effort to help maintain the project schedule.

Monitoring

Careful monitoring of performance facilitates early detection of problems and makes timely adjustments possible. It calls for constant comparison of actual conditions with the baseline established by the contract. Most importantly, it helps everyone manage deviations that constitute changes to the baseline, minimizing potential claims and disputes.

Manpower and Equipment

Manpower and equipment schedules assure resource "leveling" of both labor and equipment and reflect projected needs over the course of the project. Consistent monitoring and necessary adjustments make it possible to forecast accurately variances from the original resource requirements.

Control

Monitoring the schedule and cash flow usually presents an accurate picture of the job's progress, but monitoring in itself does not provide project control. Control is made possible by monitoring progress against schedule and making adjustments as necessary.

The S Curve

The "S curve" is a powerful summary tool for management control. The precise shape and slope of the S curve will vary, depending on the specific elements which comprise its component data. It plots actual progress in either percentages or dollars as a function of time. It integrates all estimates; labor, equipment, material, and overhead, into one classic curve. Contract changes or actual performance alter the shape of the curve, suggesting potential difficulty for the contractor to meet scheduled milestones and end dates. It is a strong signal of project problems that need quick attention. While there are many more sophisticated curves for analyzing various aspects of the work, the S curve remains the fundamental management summary tool.

Schedule, Time, and Money

A clear, comprehensive schedule facilitates early analysis of delay or acceleration impact, and will minimize claims, by allowing appropriate time extensions as variances occur. Many owners learned the hard way that the cost of a change-order time extension is substantially less than that of a postconstruction claim settlement. By the same token, meticulous monitoring and a clear schedule document are excellent defenses against spurious delay claims.

Documentation

Documentation may be defined as the contemporaneous planning, formatting, recording, organizing, and storing of all relevant information on a project. It may take the form of:

Correspondence
Diaries
Exception reports
Computer printouts
Photographs
Handwritten memos to the file
Drawing records
Payroll records
Cost records
Manpower and equipment records
Telephone records
Daily job log
Meeting minutes
Changes to the work
Change orders
Payment application files
RFI log (Request for Information)
ITC log (Instructions to Contractor)
NPC log (Notice of Potential Claim)
NPD log (Notice of Potential Delay)

There is no getting around the fact that documentation is paperwork, and in the construction business, paper is worth its weight in dollars. In fact, it is absolutely vital to good business practice and, ultimately, to profit or loss.

Document Categories

Organizationally, documentation has various categories. For instance, a daily progress report is the bread and butter of documentation and should contain references to areas and quantities of work activities; likewise, manpower and equipment reports, and labor hour and payroll records. In addition, daily weather reports, and status of work on hold due to "held" drawings must be included.

In the Beginning

As the job begins the contractor should walk the jobsite with an official owner's representative, discussing and noting site conditions. These findings should be recorded in an original site inspection report that may later be support for a claim.

Minutes and More

Minutes of all meetings must be recorded and kept. Prebid, preaward, preconstruction, and progress status reviews represent formal interactions where problems are raised with concurrent opportunities to avoid or resolve them. They must not be discarded. Dated photographs with written descriptions are excellent sources of problem verification, as are file memos, cost records, and any documents showing job status and payments.

Change Orders

Since a change order involves offer and acceptance, it is a form of contract unto itself. Every change order amends the existing contract, changes the original baseline, and, in a manner, creates a new contract that necessitates bilateral agreement. The burden lies separately with the contractor and owner to satisfy themselves, before signing, that each truly accepts all changes and conditions. Therefore, it is crucial to keep a change-order file and log documenting the dates of the problem discovery; of the request for change order; the date that plan revisions or shop drawings were submitted with a pricing request; the change order quote date; the change order request settlement; analyses of cost and schedule effects; and any delay caused by the problem or change order.

Still More Documentation

Additional pertinent project documents include drawings, all drawing revisions, requests for information, and requests for clarification, as well as notices of potential delay and potential claims relating to proposed change orders. Similarly, correspondence and records of telephone conversations should be kept, though it is sometimes difficult to determine how much of a conversation should be documented. This is a sensitivity that must be cultivated.

Multiple-part speed memos are easy, effective records, that send a message, allow for return comments by the recipient, and provide both correspondents with a complete record of the issue obviating the necessity of going through slower formal office channels. Of course, like all other forms of correspondence, they should cover the five w's (who, what, where, when, and why) and should be sequentially numbered.

Though all of the above can be accomplished by the use of simple, standard forms, many contractors just muddle through without bothering. This can be a devastating practice when evidence for a claim is required.

Accuracy

All reports must be complete, accurate, and objective. This is especially true of the following subjects:

1. Identified problems
2. Pertinent statements and actions, including instructions by the owner, engineer, architect, and construction manager, as well as contractor instructions to subcontractors and suppliers
3. Changed or unforeseen conditions
4. Changes in the work

An Elastic Work Force

There is an abstract but real concept of an elastic work force, or flexible relationship between work activities, meaning that no element of work is rigid enough to require a fixed amount of time. Work duration can be altered by overtime, added equipment, more or less manpower, and any number of positive or negative elements. Though the concept is valid, in practical application problems are often generated by the owner's false perception of infinite elasticity of work performance, together with the contractor's failure to evaluate the practical limit of elasticity or its impact on the contractor's cost of performance.

Small Favors

Small favors performed by a contractor at the request of an owner seem innocent enough, one by one, within the concept of recognized elasticity, and are generally accommodated without quibbling. Problems occur because often they are asked for and performed without proper monitoring and documentation. Many small favors can affect a project like the proverbial "death by a thousand cuts." One or two don't hurt much; lots will have a severe impact on the project baseline and, therefore, on profits.

Document Summary

Durint the course of a project, paperwork will seem superfluous, bothersome, and not worth doing or keeping. Contractors and owners are inclined to think of documentation as a nuisance overhead cost instead of an essential administrative cost. Who actually performs the documentation is unimportant; how it is charged is relatively unimportant. What is important is that it be done properly. During analysis of a claim, seemingly minor items affecting the work are often of unexpected importance. Therefore, it is difficult to exceed reasonable detail in any appropriate documentation and this should be thought of as insurance, rather than a bother.

Early Warning Signs

Early warning signs that a problem exists and requires close monitoring should trigger corrective actions before performance, costs, and/or schedule are affected. Examples include:

Owner/architect/engineering-directed changes

1. Additional work from changes, revisions, amplifications, or clarifications to drawings or specifications.
2. Additional work not indicated in drawings or specifications.
3. Directed acceleration to shorten schedule.
4. Directed compression to accommodate more work in same time frame (constructive acceleration).

Owner/architect/engineer failure to perform (potential breach)

1. Unanticipated work from defective or deficient drawings or specifications.
2. Work interruption, disruption, or stoppage.
3. Late owner-furnished equipment, material, or anything furnished in condition unsuitable for use. Untimely review of required shop drawings.
4. Failure of owner's other contractors to perform.
5. Refusal to grant legitimate extensions of time.
6. Failure to disclose information.
7. Unwarranted rejection of work.
8. Defective agency performance by a construction manager, including delays due to owner/architect/engineer procrastination.
9. Excessive changes to the work.
10. Arbitrary or capricious behavior regarding contractor responses to nonconformance and punch list rework.

Contractor's rights: external factors

1. Force majeure (acts of God, weather, war, civil disturbances, etc.).
2. First-, second-, or third-tier strikes.
3. Differing site conditions.
4. Added costs to comply with new or revised laws, regulations, or procedures.

Contractor's rights: interference with planned work operations

1. Work, work methods, or sequence different from that specified or expected.
2. Area or site congestion.
3. Area or site unavailability.
4. Multiple occupancy of area or site.
5. New or revised schedule requirement.
6. Increased requirements for inspection, standards, quality control, or tests.
7. Shifting of schedule "windows."
8. Productivity losses due to overtime or extra shifts.
9. Late owner progress payments.
10. Owner's financing institution interference.

More About Clauses

When early warning signs of problems appear, always refer to the contract to determine whether a related clause either directs something specific or prohibits it. Difficulties arise when a clause is silent on an issue. A cardinal rule is that *a contract must be interpreted in its entirety.* If there are parts of a contract that obliquely relate to the subject, they are relevant. Therefore, if disagreement occurs during the performance phase of a project regarding an issue on which the appropriate clause is silent, the following guidelines should be used in evaluating the issue:

1. Find other parts in the contract that relate to the subject not mentioned in the clause at issue
2. Determine the practice followed and precedence established on the project
3. Research normal industry practices under similar circumstances
4. Determine, wherever possible, what is reasonable in view of the circumstances

PHASE III. CLAIM/DISPUTE RESOLUTION

Changes

Change management is probably the most significant administrative problem in construction. It is the area that leads to most claims, disputes, and eventually to arbitration or litigation. Effective use and maintenance of a critical path method schedule, detailed cost records, and complementary, contemporaneous documentation facilitates early analysis of change impacts and avoids excessive expense by resolving claims or disputes before legal action is necessary. Unfortunately, there is an inclination by many contractor/engineers in field management to become mired in a comfort zone of resolving technical problems. They overlook the fact that, under it all, construction is similar to all other businesses in its primary objective: to make a profit. That objective is achieved, as in any other business, by good management practices. However, since the construction business is unique in its tendency toward small profit margin vis-à-vis high-risk exposure on virtually every project, exceptionally efficient management practices must be the rule to achieve profitability.

Validation

To validate a change or claim, you must compare it with the contract baseline of scope, schedule, and conditions (Fig. 1). Again, the question is, "what has been changed?" Something different must have happened and it must qualify for consideration. Was it the scope of work? Was it the schedule? Was it the contract conditions? Was it the working conditions?

In General

A change can go the preferred route of agreement between the parties and result in a potential change order (PCO), or lacking that agreement, it becomes a claim. If the ordered change is directed and performed, then there is another opportunity for settlement as the contractor submits documentation to the owner of the effect of performing the work substantiating a claim for additional time and/or money. Should this procedure also fail to produce an agreement, the claim becomes a dispute. If the contractor proves his case and wins, he will be paid by an award of the court or by the change order he sought in the first place. If the owner is right, the contractor will not be paid and will incur legal costs as well as other losses.

Mechanisms

A well-written contract provides appropriate clauses as mechanisms for handling construction changes and unforeseen and undetailed events such as: changed conditions;

design changes; defective specifications; excessive quantity variations; delays; disruptions; and acceleration.

Change Rights and Obligations

Once more, all parties to the contract have specified rights and obligations (Fig. 4). The owner has the right to request changes and the contractor is obligated to perform them, even though he may not agree about need or timing. However, that is not a one-way street. In addition, most contracts also require the surety to be notified of all changes to the contract. While it is implicit in any contract that the owner has the ability to pay for the work including changes, it behooves a prudent contractor to obtain written assurances of adequate available funding. The contract protects the contractor by obligating the owner to compensate the contractor for changed work, providing the contractor performs the changed work in accordance with the contract terms and conditions. Similarly, the contractor's performance of services and payment bond protect the owner and provide assurance that the contractor will complete the work and pay his bills, or else the surety will do so.

Change Management

Poorly managed changes cause a negative progression. A good contractor change management program will significantly minimize claims, conflicts, and disputes. To work efficiently, it must be an integral part of project management. Therefore, responsibility for the program is not limited to the person assigned to process the contract changes or related complications. It works best when each person, knowledgeable of targeted events, is alert to changes which alter the originally defined baseline. However, under any circumstances it is essential to pursue the equitable resolution of changes to the work as quickly as possible, within the context of the contract, and in a manner which preserves the good relations between the owner and contractor.

Points of View

As noted previously, each change must be evaluated to determine its impact on the contract baseline and whether it affects the overall performance and outcome of the project.

From the contractor's point of view, a change management program should be implemented at the beginning of the project to avoid performing additional services without suitable compensation. Similarly, the owner should have an on-site representative to monitor changes and assure full representation and protection. The changed work should not be excessively costly. The owner should be aware that most changes to the work will cost more than if they were included in the baseline scope of work and priced in the initial bid.

Haste Makes Waste

Too often, owner and contractor rush into the performance of changed work. The owner wants it done without delay and, since neither party wants to interfere with job momentum, the contractor frequently proceeds without proper and formal agreement with the owner, thus sowing the seeds of a future dispute. Of course, the owner has less incentive to settle a disputed change after the work has been done. The prevailing party in a dispute is usually the one with superior documentation and on-site, authoritative representation.

Know Your Contract

To effectively administer performance and manage changes, it is essential to know your contract intimately. This is no perfunctory matter.

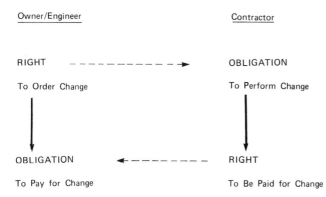

Owner/Engineer   Contractor

RIGHT — — — — — — — — — →   OBLIGATION

To Order Change   To Perform Change

OBLIGATION ← — — — — — — —   RIGHT

To Pay for Change   To Be Paid for Change

Figure 4 Rights and obligations of the parties.

From the independent contractor's perspective, this document sets out rights re-garding interference by others with the contractor's planned and agreed-upon work and financial operations. It is mandatory for all parties to be aware of their respective rights and obligations and to work out a smooth method of handling problems before they occur.

Change Progression and Deterioration

To understand fully how claims and disputes develop and are settled, the order of progression must be examined. When changes to work are not properly managed, a definite sequence occurs, as follows:

> *Changes* to the work create
> > *delays* that cause
> > > *disruption* of ongoing activities that
> > > > *impact* activities,
> > > > > *compress* activities,
> > > > > > *accelerate* activities, and cause
> > > > > > > *overruns* leading to
> > > > > > > > *claims* and *disputes.*

Changed Circumstances

Frequently, the owner orders changes to an activity of work just as it is about to take place. When this happens, performance conditions will deviate from the original base-line conditions. If the change is significant, or there are excessive changes, and the owner and contractor do not agree on a timely change order, then the aforementioned sequence usually develops.

Delays

Since the contractor is rarely permitted under a lump-sum contract to perform changed work without a change order or other formal documentation, if he follows the rules, the progress of that portion of the project is halted until the owner completes the paperwork.

Owners and contractors tend to plan and schedule project work with an optimistic (no delay) outlook, ignoring the fact that interruptions and delays are almost inevitable and will affect costs. Delays vary in duration and effect, and, depending on management performance, are either avoidable or unavoidable. The consequences of delays, however, are usually negative and frequently serious. They may be categorized as shown in Table 1.

Table 1 Consequences of Delays in Project Schedules

Category	Excusable[a]	Compensable[a]	Example
1	Yes	Yes	Suspension of work, changes to work, extra work, late delivery of owner-furnished material and equipment, late access to work site, unreasonable and noncontractual delay in receiving/approving shop drawings
2	Yes	No	Weather, strikes, force majeure, acts of God, government actions
3	No	No	Contractor-caused delays or events under his control

[a]Always refer to specific contract clauses for entitlement.

Excusable Delays

Excusable delays are beyond the contractor's control, entitle him to extension of time under the contract, excuse him from liquidated damages, and relieve him from performance obligations related to such delays. They are compensable if due to the owner's failure to meet obligations, and noncompensable if beyond control of both contractor and owner.

When compensable (for even a few hours), the contractor is entitled to reasonable costs incurred. When excusable, but noncompensable, both parties absorb their own costs. When nonexcusable and noncompensable, the contractor is entitled to neither an extension of time nor additional compensation, but is liable for liquidated damages and, possibly, for breach of contract for nonperformance.

Example of Cause and Effect

The owner's delayed review of contractor drawings and other submittals is a common cause for claims and often goes undocumented by the contractor, though his work depends on timely owner approval, and such delay may immediately impact contractors schedule and costs. Such neglect by the owner or his architect/engineer must be documented by the contractor to prove cause and effect, if any. Similarly, the contractor's failure to submit his drawings or material samples or equipment selection or substitutions in a timely manner may impact the owners ability to respond in a timely manner, thus the owner would be excused from performance.

Concurrent Delays

When concurrent or overlapping activities cause more than one delay, the contractor has an opportunity to make an analysis as part of the claim. If one delay is allowable and compensable and another is not, the contractor should carefully position himself to benefit from the compensable (owner-caused) delay by claiming it before claiming a noncompensable (weather, etc.) delay. Similarly, the owner should review and confirm that these same concurrent delays have been properly analyzed to assure that the contractor does not get improper extension of time with concomitant compensation.

Disruption

As the project continues without progress on the delayed activity, disruption affects the craftsmen, assigned equipment, and supplies on hand. Time is lost reassigning resources to productive work. Other activities dependent on the completion are stalled, eventually causing progressive disruption of the entire project.

Impact

Many owners, engineers, architects, and contractors fail to consider the full impact of changes. Although a contract change order may compensate the contractor for direct costs on a negotiated lump-sum or time-and-materials basis, it seldom reflects the progressive impact on original work that was delayed, disrupted, or somehow affected by the change. There is a definite negative sequence that begins with any change to the work and seems to be little understood. In fact, for simple protection, though it is rarely done, a contractor should immediately submit a Notice of Potential Claim (NPC) for time and/or money whenever the owner changes the scope of activities without concurrently issuing a change order. A contractor should also always reserve his rights on any change order from which impact costs may flow. If no reservation is made, the contractor's rights are forfeited.

As the amount of possible work in the affected activity diminishes, the contractor's craftsmen become disoriented. A what-do-we-do-next condition exists, and the contractor must scramble to keep his work force busy. At best, only one section of the job is affected, but quite often there are repercussions and "ripple" effects on other portions of the work, or even on the entire project.

Compression

When the disagreement is finally settled, or if the contractor is ordered to proceed before settlement, a work compression may develop. More work must be completed for that particular activity in the remaining time than is set forth in the original schedule. More craftsmen are added, more confusion ensues, and efficiency plummets.

Acceleration

An acceleration of the project follows as the contractor adds manpower and equipment, attempting to speed up and complete the project as close to schedule as possible. Acceleration occurs when:

1. The original scope of work must be performed in less than the originally scheduled time
2. Increased scope of work (changes or extra work) must be performed in originally scheduled time
3. The original scope of work must be performed in the originally scheduled time, but actual working conditions are not as represented

Reasons

Acceleration may be owner directed for reasons related or unrelated to contractor performance. There may be constructive acceleration when, due to owner insistence, the contractor is directed to meet a schedule milestone, and circumstances entitle him to a time extension which the owner refuses to grant. Assuming the contractor has proper documentation, the court/arbitrator may find that, since the contractor had no control over the situation, even if the contract prohibits payment, he should be paid.

Finally, contractor-directed voluntary acceleration occurs for reasons unrelated to owner demands or owner delay circumstances and is not compensable.

Instruction

The contractor should, whenever possible, obtain written instruction from the owner directing acceleration. However, when the owner fails or refuses to issue such direction, the contractor must establish entitlement to compensation for constructive acceleration by written request for extension of time. If the owner still rejects the request and directs the contractor to adhere to his original schedule, there will be an indisputable record of the events.

Overruns

Cost and time overruns invariably develop as a result of acceleration. There is a ripple effect on all related work, reducing efficiency and further impacting and aggravating the remaining activities. The biggest problem on overruns for the contractor is calculating costs for loss of productivity.

Dispute

If attempts to negotiate a settlement continue without success, the disagreement becomes a dispute. By definition, the dispute phase occurs when a third party resolves the disagreement by applying independent judgment. This is done through arbitration or litigation, and frequently represents a breakdown in the system of good faith negotiations between the parties. A growing trend is toward the use of nonbinding mediation, that is, the use of an independent third party agreed to by both parties.

Claim Posture

A claim is usually associated with a disagreement that, if not controlled, will escalate into a dispute that strains communications and generates an unnecessary adversarial posture between parties to the contract. Experienced managers who know their contract and who communicate their position clearly, early on, and in a cooperative, good faith manner are the winners. They are able to solve problems to everyone's advantage by maintaining a positive, professional relationship that is basic to a cooperative effort leading to timely completion of a project. When the change progression leads to a claim, however, that relationship is often tense, and further strain should be prevented wherever possible to avoid the next step toward litigation.

Claim Preparation

One of the contractor's responsibilities is to prepare his claim clearly and comprehensively. It should be thoroughly documented, and the pricing approach must be credible. The scope of the claim package will vary with magnitude and complexity of the situation, and frequently an expert claims consultant and legal representative should be brought in for advice. In any event, the contractor preparing and assembling the claim should consider a format including the following sections:

1. Letter of transmittal
2. Title page
3. Table of contents
4. Introduction
5. Executive summary (for large, complex claims)
6. Chronological narrative of claim development
7. Major issue discussions
8. Schedule/delay analysis
9. Pricing analysis
10. Contract analysis
11. Special reports or analyses
12. Supporting documentation
13. Summary

Simple or Complex

For minor claims, a letter format with appropriate details and attached documentation is sufficient. A multivolume approach is required for complex claims of significant value. In either case, the claim must be clearly written and organized to relieve the reviewer and analyst of unnecessary labor in understanding it. The goal is to inform and convince, not to confuse and annoy.

Important Details

Charts and graphs are helpful in making a point, while computer printouts, unless carefully prepared, are difficult to read, dull, and ineffective. Use numerous paragraph headings, and divide long chapters into major sections. Likewise, use reasonably wide margins with at least 1-1/2 line spacing. Place volumes in three-ring or spiral binders for ease of reference.

The text should be written in straightforward, nontechnical language, so that an average "layperson" can understand the issues, follow the development of events, and logically conclude the point of the claim on the basis of the material presented. A professional writer can usually organize and present the text with clarity and objectivity that is difficult for involved engineers.

Contract Claim Procedure

The following list is the sequential procedure of a properly handled claim. We will discuss some items to a greater extent than others, depending on their gravity.

Identification is the recognition that some modification has been made that departs from the baseline.

Notification is simply the contractor alerting the owner as soon as possible that there is a potential claim situation (Notice of Potential Claim form). This is essential. Late notice or failure to notify the owner of a problem or potential problem can create serious problems in negotiation of a claim and handicaps a contractor's ability to obtain additional compensation or extension of time. Well-written construction contracts stipulate that the contractor must give the owner notice of an event within a limited time. This notice properly informs the owner of problems and affords him an opportunity to mitigate damages. Such notice requirements are often strictly applied by courts and various Boards of Contract Appeals.

Examples of situations requiring written notice that are frequently ignored by the contractor and which often result in claims are: (a) differing site conditions; (b) changed working conditions; (c) delays to the work; and (d) impacts to the performance of the work.

Documentation is the recording of the identification and whatever happens after that. It is the factual statement of circumstances: the "what, where, and when."

Analysis of events is the "why" of what happened. It has to justify entitlement in its analysis of the factual events. The contractor must prove there is a causal connection between the event precipitating the loss and the resulting costs.

Contract analysis is an interpretation of the contract relative to the event, including analysis for entitlement specific to the claim issues where the contract is silent.

Cost analysis begins with documentation, and is the quantification of the claim. Essentially that consists of direct costs of labor (and fringes), equipment (rental and operating) costs, and material, plus indirect costs, which are consumables (small tools, field overhead costs, and other costs that it takes to support the craftsmen). It may also include various impact costs, inefficiency (or loss of productivity) costs, and home office overhead costs.

Schedule analysis interprets delays to the performance of certain activities, as well as effects on the project as a whole. This requires comparisons of the initial approved CPM schedule with subsequently revised, approved CPM schedules.

Assembly of the claim contains appropriate narratives, analyses, graphs, charts, and so forth.

Presentation of the claim document is made by the contractor to the owner, preferably in person, briefly guiding the owner through the claim. The contractor has prepared and assembled the claim. Now the owner does his homework by analyzing the claim. Each has now established his position.

Negotiation begins, and if good faith is present, most of the time a dispute will be avoided and a change order will be issued. An expert consultant can often help with this negotiation in convincing one side or the other that either the claim issues are inadequate to succeed with litigation, or there is another method whereby a negotiated settlement can be achieved.

Pricing the Claim

The contractor must ensure that any claim presented to the owner contains a thorough description of all costs incurred as of an identified cutoff date, as well as those he thinks will develop from the problem. The owner is entitled to a reasonable level of detail for his understanding and analysis. Similarly, any backcharge or counterclaim which the owner presents against the contractor should be as complete and thoroughly prepared as the claim the owner expects from the contractor. The standards are the same.

A claim may be priced by several methods or a combination, as follows: (1) estimate of anticipated costs (forward pricing); (2) existing contract unit prices; or (3) actual costs.

Forward and unit pricing are most appropriate prior to performance of the work, while actual cost pricing can only be used during or after the performance. Since estimates and costs are subject to analysis, interpretation, and judgment, the final (agreed-to) price usually comes from negotiation.

Most owners prefer forward-pricing lump-sum estimates or unit prices because they get advanced information on increased costs of work claimed by the contractor, together with a chance to consider alternatives or modify a proposed change. Whatever the pricing approach, there is *no good reason for a contractor to lose money on change order work*.

Lump-Sum Estimates

A lump-sum estimate for a proposed change order should incorporate every reasonable anticipated cost and a contingency allowance to accommodate unforeseen worst-case conditions. If the owner and contractor disagree on a lump-sum price and the owner orders performance of the changed work on a cost-plus basis, the owner's cost should not differ significantly from any of the pricing approaches. There are various options available to an owner to limit his exposure such as incorporating a "not to exceed" cost clause, providing an incentive shared savings/overrun cost clause, or utilizing an unattractive fee on cost-plus work to encourage reasonable lump-sum pricing.

Lump-Sum Pricing Elements

Most claims are based on a discrete (single) change or issue that is simple to analyze. In such case, preparation of a lump-sum forward-pricing claim should include the following elements:

1. Identification of the changed work (drawings, specifications, owner's direction)
2. Estimated quantities of work by category
3. Estimated rates of productivity for each work category

4. Estimation of required craftsmen manhours for various work categories
5. Composite crew costs, if necessary
6. Estimated quantities of material
7. Estimated quantities of equipment (plus fuel and maintenance costs)
8. Estimated nonmanual supervisory and support personnel
9. Small tools and consumables
10. Manual crafts hourly rates
11. Labor burden: social security and unemployment taxes, union benefits, insurance, etc.
12. Material costs
13. Sales tax
14. Equipment rental costs
15. Nonmanual supervisory and support personnel salaries
16. Burden and fringe benefit costs for salaried personnel: social security and unemployment taxes, insurance, vacation, sick leave, etc.
17. Field overhead costs: office facilities, cars and trucks, heat, electricity, toilets, telephone, office equipment, computers, cleaning services, etc.
18. Home office direct project-related support services
19. Home office general and administrative costs
20. Profit

These cost items apply to subcontractors pricing as well as the contractors. In addition, the general contractor is allowed a nominal markup on the subcontractors price to compensate for his additional overhead costs and a reasonable profit.

Simplify

To avoid extensive and detailed estimates and calculations, it is common practice to combine various cost elements and reduce their analytical and summary level. For example, a single percentage calculation is acceptable to combine:

1. Indirect costs as a function of and related to hourly wage rates for craftsmen
2. Cost of salaried people, small tools, and consumables as a percentage of craftsmen hours
3. Indirect overhead field costs as a percentage of direct field costs of labor, material, and equipment

The owner can simplify the entire matter by requiring the contractor to provide overhead percentage and profit factors to be used for all change cost calculations. These may be:

1. Stipulated by the owner in the contract
2. Stipulated by the contractor in its bid submitted with the owner's RFP (Request for Proposal)
3. Negotiated by the owner and contractor at any time

Analysis

In forward-priced changes or claims, a thoroughly documented and recorded analysis of forecasted claim costs and costs actually incurred during performance will significantly enhance amicable agreement between contractor and owner, should they fail to reach earlier agreement.

Just the Facts

Resolution of most claims involves legal and technical issues, but usually hinges on the facts, making contemporaneous documentation essential. Elegant legal interpreta-

tions are seldom successful in settling a dispute out of court. Disputed technical de-
terminations are also rarely a factor in claim analysis. Facts—pure, simple, documented
—are usually the basis for resolution of a claim on a negotiated basis.

Existing Contract Unit Prices

Contracts frequently include unit prices for various items of work and stipulate their
consideration for change order work. It is important to understand that a unit price
is a mini lump sum that includes all elements of a lump sum in terms of the baseline
scope, schedule, and condition.

Though some flexibility is provided because the exact number of units need not be
known before work is performed, too many contractors overlook or forget that their
obligation to perform changed or extra work on a unit price basis is predicated on the
assumption that conditions for performing the work are the same as those under which
the unit prices were originally estimated. When conditions are significantly different,
the agreed-upon unit prices are inappropriate and should not be used. In this situation the agreed-upon contract unit prices should be renegotiated to reflect the changed
conditions; likewise, an extension of time, if appropriate. It makes no sense for a contractor to accept insufficient payment for changes and absorb unnecessary losses, but
that is often what happens due to lack of sophistication or careless administration of
both lump-sum as well as unit price changed or extra work.

Actual Costs

On a total cost-plus contract, the contractor should recover all costs for performing
change order work because they are reimbursable within the guidelines of the contract.
However, it is quite possible for a contractor to lose money on cost-plus change order
work on a lump-sum contract. This happens when the contractor inaccurately captures
and records costs, leaving uncompensated stray costs charged to baseline work. It
also happens when he cannot or does not evaluate such impact costs as additional nonmanual supervision, indirect effects on concurrent and subsequent work, or simply
increased administrative costs for changed work.

The contractor must have a comprehensive system of cost reporting that accurately
reflects amount and distribution and allows thorough accounting and reconstruction
of the work done and costs incurred. He must be able to prove that he not only ordered material and received it, but also must establish that he used it on the specific
work performed. Incurred costs must be recorded in a manner consistent with the
schedule records and documented events. It is very difficult to prove a claim if the
claimed costs and related events are incompatible. Again, the key is establishing the
causal relationship between these aspects of the claim. The clear burden for establishing this rests with the contractor.

Total Cost Claims

Contractors generally submit total cost claims because:

1. Multiple impacts from numerous changes ripple and intertwine through concurrent and subsequent work activities so subtly that it defies identification
2. They have not done their homework; that is, they have had cost overruns,
   have not kept their costs segregated, and are unable to identify costs related
   to a series of changed work

A Difficult Method

Total cost claims are difficult to negotiate, and the ensuing disputes are difficult to
prosecute in terms of establishing the owner's liability versus the contractor's entitle-

ment. However, the contractor must be able to establish that at least the following four conditions existed:

1. The nature of the work was so affected by problems not his fault that the multiple cost impacts are impossible to segregate and accurately identify
2. The contractor's bid was reasonable and properly prepared
3. The contractor did not cause added costs due to his mismanagement or inefficiency
4. The actual documented costs were reasonable under the circumstances

Impact Claims

Unlike straightforward "discrete" claims for increased costs due to a single, clearly identifiable event or change, impact claims are always of a secondary nature, the product of a previous event, and consequently difficult to analyze. Their difficulty grows with their size.

There are three basic approaches in determining impact costs on a construction claim, as follows:

1. *Total Cost Approach* Validate the bid as a reasonable cost, increasing it as necessary to correct specific shortcomings. If the previously noted qualifying conditions have been met, then the impact is total actual cost less the adjusted bid price.

It is particularly convincing if there is a portion of the work that was not affected, and cost records show that the contractor performed this work at his estimated price. Alternatively, if the contractor has recorded costs for performing the same or similar work on other unimpacted jobs, or if the nearest competitive bidder's prices were close, this would also help to establish his bid price as reasonable. This approach is frequently described as the "measured mile" method.

2. *Impact Factors Calculation Approach (Postconstruction)* Validate the contractor's bid as described in Item 1; then, use impact factors developed and published by organizations such as MCA, NECA, and the Business Roundtable. These studies substantiate the deleterious effect of extended overtime, poor owner management, poor drawings, weather, acceleration, stacking of trades, and other impact factors on productivity. Highly subjective in application, these factors are easily disputed, but extensive research in decreased productivity has helped prove the validity of their harm and can aid in the recovery of compensable cost to the contractor.

3. *Discrete Impact Cost Approach (Concurrent Analysis)* Establish validity of the contractor's estimate, and use this as the baseline for work activities. Provide a comprehensive daily survey of all construction activities, noting work performed, craft hours, and other specific costs, together with problems encountered and the observed source of impacts. An established baseline estimate and continuous, detailed, documented observations allow the contractor to make an analysis which, though still somewhat subjective, will significantly reduce conjecture as to how he reached a total value of impact and its distribution to various causes. Similarly, the owner should also use the awarded contract value as the baseline for analysis, particularly if the contract requires a cost-loaded CPM schedule which includes equipment and man-loading data.

Cause and Effect

Even in cases of established entitlement to additional compensation, a contractor must prove that increased cost was incurred. He must substantiate the specific relationship between cause and effect of a given event; namely changed work or performance under conditions different from the baseline, resulting in allowable, increased costs. Most increased costs are recoverable with proper calculation and documentation, and need not turn into disputes. A more detailed and definitive cause/effect analysis should provide a more appropriate settlement. This applies to both contractor and owner, that is a counterclaim should have the same level of detail and documentation as a claim.

Interest Costs

Unless the contractor can clearly establish that the additional costs are identifiable, actual, related to the claim issue, and necessarily incurred, interest costs are usually not recoverable. Generally, financing costs are included in the baseline and considered part of doing business. The contractor must borrow the money for specific reasons related to the claim events, and generally will not be compensated for the "use" or "time/value" of his money.

Asserting a Claim

The basis of any claim presentation or defense is "what might have been." The underlying wisdom in that message is to recognize and track early signs of problems that deviate from the baseline.

The Theme

Every claim must have a theme, theory, or major concept. The focus must not be only on separate issues, but on the whole situation because any major problem affects other areas of the project. A single-issue or limited approach overlooks the compounding effect of problems and reduces maximum recovery. Similarly, the owner's analysis should consider the deleterious aspects of problems caused by and the responsibility of the contractor.

How It Works

Every claim for money and/or time must have a valid cause, which also has a measurable, verifiable, and documented effect, qualifiable under the acceptance criteria of the contract. The costs of such effect also must qualify.

Providing appropriate notice which complies with contract requirements is done so both parties are fully aware of events and potential consequences. A complete factual analysis must be compiled containing extensive documentation consistent for both cost and schedule, using the initial, approved schedule as the valid baseline, and focusing on the other party's errors, or failure to perform, or failure to meet obligations.

The total obligation is on the party presenting the claim to adequately assemble, present, document, and explain it. Major claim elements are schedule, costs, and contract eligibility. All must meet acceptable levels to qualify for consideration. All available resources (legal counsel, expert advisor) should be used to analyze and prepare a claim.

Impact claims are particularly difficult because they require describing what should have happened, but didn't! Because of multiple factors and their "domino" effect, it may be difficult to identify the schedule impact and extent of delays. Therefore, the quality of the analysis and presentation is very important. Of course, the theme must effectively hang together, but a successful claim depends as much as anything on management commitment and a single-minded determination to win.

Defending a Claim

On the defense side, first seek to identify the basic theme of the offense—whether or not the contractor has been astute enough to develop a claim theme—and neutralize it. When the credibility of the theme is challenged, or the logic of entitlement placed in doubt, the contractor's expectation is lowered.

As with the assertion of a claim, the defense requires a complete factual analysis, incorporating evaluation of all known relevant data. Without at least a threshold level of contemporaneous documentation on hand available to either party, it is usually fruitless to proceed with negotiations unless there are compelling reasons.

Procedures

Examine the baseline schedule for discrepancies in logic and timing. The other party will point out your weaknesses, so be prepared. If documentation appears adequate, probe for the loose thread. Look for a complementary cost/schedule level of detail and attack the weak areas. You will find them because most contractors prepare their own claims and do so inadequately relative to the facts, the theories, the contract, and the rights and obligations of both parties. This is distinctly to the owner's advantage.

Examine the claimed initiating cause or contract clause. If inappropriate, it is cause for immediate rejection. Rights must be stated or implied in the contract and based on either contract or case law. Examine the claimed effect, as well. Is there a sound cause/effect relationship? Can it be rejected on the basis of contractor actions? Analyze documentation (cost/schedule records) with professional help, if necessary.

Determine whether the contractor has complied with relevant notice requirements.

The analysis of and written response to a claim must be prepared with the same care as used in claim preparation. The facts must be assembled, documented, and presented objectively, always focusing on the contractor's legal, contractual, and performance weak points.

Asserting/Defending in General

Many procedures are similar, some identical, in asserting or defending a claim. For instance, one detail-oriented person should be responsible for preparing or analyzing a claim. The entire contract should be reviewed with legal counsel and a claims expert, discussing interpretation of contract clauses; particularly, when prescribed contractual obligations have not been met and options for action are limited. Problems frequently encountered in this area relate to notice, schedule revision, extension of time requests, and reporting requirements.

Both claim and defense should be presented in the most effective format possible. They should be simple enough for anyone to read, be organized in sections or volumes, and should include all relevant documents, graphs, charts, photos, and cost/schedule comparison data. There is equal responsibility for thorough, good faith claim analysis and presentation by the contractor and response by the owner. Objective, professional conduct by both parties should enable amicable negotiations to conclude with a settlement both parties are willing to accept.

PHASE IV: PREPARATION FOR LITIGATION SUPPORT

The time to smile, shake hands, think about rapport, and maintain a friendly relationship has passed. Litigation is like war, and in a war there will be a loser, so it's time to pull out all the stops and concentrate on winning.

Typical construction litigation involves multiple claims, issues, and theories, usually resulting in factually complex cases. The key to successful prosecution or defense of such litigation is the same key often overlooked in contract administration and claim management, only advanced a few steps. It is the thorough investigation, organization, and analysis of facts and documentation. A thorough, well-prepared claim and analysis will significantly diminish the time, effort, and expense of this phase.

Since the claim has escalated into a forced third-party resolution, this assumes that attorneys have been hired and will be responsible for the overall litigation effort. As litigation "managers," they will prepare the program with the client's support.

The Team

By virtue of licensing, an attorney is an agent of the court, and under ordinary circumstances must be hired to represent a party who is establishing (filing) suit and needs court access. An attorney assigned to the legal dispute will function as team leader with the client's project personnel, percipient witnesses, and experts called upon to support their case. Attorneys know the law and claims consultants know claims theories, and with their guidance the contractor's or owner's personnel should be able to identify the factual causes of the dispute through reference to proper documentation and familiarity with project events. This group of knowledgeable field resources should comprise a winning team employing singular, cooperative, focused determination. This applies equally to the owner's team as well as the contractor's team. The party to a dispute which fields the better team will often win the battle, frequently with an inherently inferior case.

Privilege

A legal shelter known as "client/attorney privilege" protects the team from unwanted intrusion in, or access to, any communication or work product prepared at the request of, or under the direction of, legal counsel for or with his client in anticipation of litigation. The opposing side can subpoena certain documents, but cannot easily obtain others because of this privileged relationship. Therefore, since it would be foolish to volunteer information unnecessarily to the other side, it is important that any such written information be noted and segregated between "discoverable" and "protected" documents.

Litigation Management Plan

Designing a well-developed and well-managed plan will minimize litigation costs. As team leader, legal counsel should prepare a litigation plan, outlining what is expected of and what will be done for the client. However, in the final analysis, it is up to the client to maintain control and see to it that what should be done on his or her behalf is done. Litigation should be treated as a construction project. The attorney is now in the lead position, but the client, contractor, or owner should still take a management interest and management point of view. In the case of litigation, that view should be one of strict observance, meticulous communication and documentation, and "prepared helpfulness," with a touch of wariness. That means that the client should never allow the litigation to "run away" simply because he is too preoccupied with other activities to fulfill his continuing management role. Major litigation often consumes several years and several million dollars, during which time opportunities for settlement may be overlooked due to management inattention. Winning is the responsibility of the entire team.

Litigation in Practice

As practiced in the United States, litigation is an adversarial exercise about which most professionals, other than attorneys and claim consultants, are neither knowledgeable nor comfortable. Therefore, it behooves each party to the litigation to assign a senior company officer to be responsible for managing the entire effort with all the skills and resources available to him. It is only in this manner that the overall company objectives and business judgment can be brought to bear on the key issues and the whole litigation effort kept in focus. It is not uncommon for total litigation costs to equal or exceed the final award value.

The Plan

The litigation plan should include major activities (what is to be done), assignment of resources (who is to do what), as well as major milestones, schedule, budget, and document control. If the contractor uses a claim consultant, then the claim should serve as a positive factor in support of the litigation, and the attorneys should work cooperatively with the consultant in getting the best all-around advice for their client.

If the claim is poorly prepared, the attorney will probably direct that it be done again to meet a certain threshold quality for litigation. A properly prepared claim significantly shortens preparation for litigation (therefore, litigation costs), and a good attorney can use it as the basic building block for the legal argument.

Monitoring

Implementing a monitoring program is just as important for litigation as it was all through the project and claim administration. In some cases, attorneys dislike being "watched over" by the client; however, it is the client's case, he is paying the fee, and the conclusion will affect him most directly. Litigation can be very expensive, as previously stated so the client must assign a senior management representative to scrupulously perform this monitoring function and make periodic reports. When at risk, don't be "frozen out" or allow issues to drift out of control.

Work Facilities

A "war room" should be established with controlled access to those people directly assigned to or otherwise involved in the case. In this room there should be work tables, photocopying facilities, and lockable, fireproof containers for storage of vital documents.

The Legal Theory

Just as there must be a unifying strand or theme running through a claim, there must be a binding legal theory that neatly ties together all the major relevant events and facts of the case for litigation: one relates to the contract tenets; the other relates to the law. They certainly should support each other.

Litigation involves the education and persuasion of a third party, which mandates that theory and arguments be convincing, reasonable, and sustainable.

A good theorem is to be sure you don't fall over your own feet into the enemy camp; there is no longer room for negotiation. Casual dialogue with the opponent should be held to a minimum, and consultation with counsel should be frequent and ongoing. The rules have changed, and the situation is now an adversarial one in which there will be a winner and a loser. While the opportunity for settlement should always be kept as the preferred option, both the contractor and owner must be wary of "Trojan Horses" and control any urges to engage in an unrestrained conversation with the adversary.

In the end, a well-developed theory, effectively presented, followed, and supported by documented facts, will be the best offense (or defense) and will maximize chances to prevail in the dispute.

Plan and Manage

Planning and managing a litigation support effort is similar in many respects to planning and managing a construction project. Although some of the rules are different because of the adversarial nature of the legal system, essentially it is a repeat case of "plan the work, work the plan."

The contractor/owner (in addition to paying all the legal bills) functions in two positions relative to litigation counsel: in a support position, providing resources, facilities, and information necessary to litigate the case; in a management position, consulting and making decisions.

Arbitration of a major dispute is time consuming, expensive, procedurally oriented, and disruptive to normal contractor/owner operations. Litigation is more so. Both essentially represent a failure in the good faith relationship between the parties.

SUMMARY

Contract and claims management should be integral and natural to an entire management program. The common goal of all parties—owner, contractor, subcontractors, and workers—should be to design, build, and facilitate the project in the agreed time for the agreed price. While not always easy, this is definitely achievable and profitable when good contract and claims management techniques are properly applied.

Problems leading to claims and disputes are wisely looked on as preventive, if detected early, and not something to be dealt with, or healed, when they have become serious. An expert consultant hired at the first sign of trouble can provide cost-effective and rewarding advice.

In the risk-present and time-sensitive business of construction, almost any delay, acceleration, or distortion of work progress and performance impacts the contract baseline of scope, schedule, or conditions. This translates into a loss of money. The first preventive step to avoid possible loss of profit is careful attention in the preaward phase when the foundation for rights and obligations is being laid. This is when complete pre-execution understanding of the contract and contract clauses is vital in terms of explicit directions, prohibitions, and silences. This is where promises count: when they are understood in full, and in writing.

Good contract administration and performance equate to project harmony, bringing all the parts together effectively and on time. This means managing subcontractor resources as members of the team; it means careful scheduling of each element of work as a realistic function of time; it means conscientious monitoring of early warning signs of problems and of inevitable changes to the work; and, it means painstaking documentation of all pertinent project events and resultant communication. In other words, alert, all-around attention to detail and recognizing the opportunities will assure reasonable profitability for the contractor while simultaneously assuring the owner of reasonable project cost.

Again, change administration is the most significant management problem in construction and the one that most often leads to claims, disputes, and eventually to arbitration and litigation; each more serious, more complex, and more expensive than the former. Good change management is a combined team responsibility. Everyone must be alert to any change that will impact the contract baseline, and do something appropriate about it. The alternative is poor change management, unavoidably giving rise to a negative sequence, as changes to the work create delays that cause disruption of activities, which in turn impact, then compress, then accelerate activities, causing price overruns and resulting in claims and disputes!

Claims preparation involves a strong theme fusing cause and effect. It must be meticulously documented, and have a credible pricing approach and a comprehensive format, including various pertinent analyses, narratives, and schedule delays. Whether the claim is complex, as an impact claim always is, or relatively simple, the text must be clear, nontechnical, and easy to follow.

The properly handled claim procedure begins with identification of the problem and ends with negotiating in good faith between the parties to avoid litigation and provide a mutually acceptable settlement. Unless the procedure gets out of hand, there is no good reason for a contractor to either lose money or make a windfall on change order work, and successful resolution is virtually dependent on complete analysis and documentation of the facts. Of course, this holds true in the defense, as well as the assertion of a claim.

If the claim leads to potential litigation, the time for building cooperative relationships between the parties has vanished, the system of good faith has failed, and there is but one simple objective: to win. This can be achieved in the least time-consuming and least expensive way with a well-prepared claim and analysis of the facts.

Always keep in mind that claims will be resolved eventually by one means or another, but they can be very expensive and their successful resolution is often a matter of financial survival for the contractor. Similarly, for the owner, excessive cost over-runs frequently turn an otherwise profitable project into a financial fiasco. In summation, there are generally three opportunities to settle a claim between two parties: when it first arises, during the closeout phase of the project, and "on the courthouse steps." As Thomas Jefferson once said, "Some are born good, some make good, and some are caught with the goods." If a claim cannot be settled prior to arbitration or litigation, it should be looked on as an opportunity for gain. An opportunity to "make good." Remember, one will win and one will lose.

V

PROJECT RELEASE

UNIT OVERVIEW

The award or release of the project signals that the initial planning activities may be started. In the case of lump-sum projects, these efforts start with the preparation of the bid.

The tone of the project is set by the initial activities which are programmed by the project manager. The project enviornment harbors very difficult interpersonal and organizational relationships. Directing a project requires a very professional level of planning. A written plan communicates the project manager's strategy for achieving the project objectives.

Existing documents such as the client's inquiry; the proposal, as modified and amended during the negotiation period; the contract and the preliminary work plans done during the proposal preparation form the basis for the project manager's planning endeavors.

Before execution planning starts, the project manager must provide a complete scope definition of the work to be included. For a lump-sum contract, this would have been done before bidding the work.

The planning process must be simple and practical. Planning is hard work and no one is going to do it unless it shows a good payout. A written plan is required, which focuses attention on specific items and will emphasize importance of early planning.

The plan defines the strategy by which the stated project objectives will be achieved. The experienced project manager will have an in-depth constructability analysis made of alternative or improved ways of accomplishing project tasks. This review will concern itself with layout optimization, and sequencing and simplification of operations.

Successful communication of a good execution plan to the project team, the client, and to the project manager's parent organization is important to project success.

The execution plan is the basis for all of the schedules, detailed cost estimates, the control budget, and quality and performance assurance programs for the project, leading to the development of the work breakdown structure (WBS) which integrates the work, schedule, and costs into a trackable and controllable program. Performance baselines are established during project planning.

Two other early stage documents issued by the project manager are (1) the coordination procedure and (2) an early work schedule (EWS). Coordination procedures, or job instructions, are merely the administrative procedures to be used on the project. The early work schedule tracks activities which cannot wait for release of more formal schedules. It contains a running list of the activities which must be started during the early weeks, the name of the responsible individual, and the completion date for each activity.

Much emphasis is placed on early planning. However, planning does not stop with the initial plan. It is a continuous process which is finetuned whenever necessary. When events occur that adversely affect or are disruptive to the plan targets, corrective action must be taken to restore the integrity of the schedule or budget.

REFERENCES

Bennis, W. J., and Nanus, B. *Leaders: The Strategies of Taking Charge.* New York: Harper & Row Publishers, Inc., 1985.

Cleland, D. I., and King, W. R. *Project Management Handbook.* New York: Van Nostrand Reinhold Company, 1983.

Datz, M. Develop Project Scope Early. *Hydrocarbon Processing.* 161-177 (September 1981).

DeBono, E. *DeBono's Thinking Course.* New York: Facts on File, 1986.

Dinsmore, P. C. Planning Project Management: Sizing Up The Barriers. 1984 Proceedings of the Project Management Institute, 16th Annual Seminar/Symposium, Philadelphia, October 1984, pp. 195-200.

Fangel, M., Rendbaek, O., and Koop, E. Master Project Planning in Tough Practice. 1981 Proceedings of the Project Management Institute, 13th Annual Seminal/Symposium, Boston, pp. 247-256.

Kimmons, R. L. Use a Matrix for Project Plans. *Hydrocarbon Processing.* 177-180 (February 1978).

McConkey, D. D. *How to Manage by Results,* Fourth Edition. New York: Amacon Book Division, American Management Associations, 1983.

Pincus, C. Plan Better with Team Building. *Hydrocarbon Processing.* 357-370 (November 1979).

Sloat, F. W., Gannon, A., and Simard, R. L. The WBS—More Than Just a Cost/Schedule Integrator. 1982 Proceedings of the Project Management Institute, 14th Annual Seminar/Symposium, Toronto, Ontario, Canada, pp. IV-K.1/IV-K.5.

1

The Project Plan

WILLIAM E. SMITH* *Brown & Root Inc., Houston, Texas*

Once project viability has been established and a decision to proceed has been made, a detailed, written "Plan of Execution" for the project should be drawn up. A plan is a structured sequence of events leading to a desired set of objectives. It must show who is to do what, when, and how, and include all major decisions required. The plan becomes a vehicle for communication with all project participants and is a prerequisite for detailed scheduling of the work and for the preparation of a definitive cost estimate.

Planning is not the same as scheduling. The plan must precede the schedule. The schedule then develops the calendar for the execution of the plan. The lack of a properly prepared project plan is a leading cause of poor project execution. It is important that the project plan of execution be developed early in the project, prior to starting any of the major activities.

The plan is not a static document, however, and should be revised during the life of the project whenever appropriate due to changing conditions. This does not mean that the plan can be changed anytime there is a forecasted schedule or cost overrun. The plan is changed precisely to avoid negative variations from the cost and schedule targets by doing things differently than called for by the initial plan.

INFORMATION REQUIRED FOR PLANNING

Before a proper plan of execution can be prepared, certain information, listed below, must be available.

1. The type of project, its capacity, and location(s)
2. The scope of work to be performed
3. A preliminary cost estimate
4. The site visitation report
5. A preliminary schedule of major milestone objectives
6. Pertinent contract requirements
7. Special design and/or construction requirements
8. Climate restrictions
9. Environmental studies, feasibility reports, etc.
10. Proposal documents

---

*Retired

PLAN PARTICIPANTS

The project manager should take the lead in preparing the project plan of execution. However, it is important that participation by the engineering, procurement, construction, and other pertinent groups be enlisted in the planning process. Through such participation, the plan gains acceptance by those who must implement it. This is vital to successful execution of the plan. Once the plan has been drafted it should be presented to management for review and comment. This will usually result in some modification which will make it more viable and assure allocation of the necessary resources for proper execution. Once the plan is in final draft form, the client should be formally presented with the plan. After the client approves, the final project plan of execution is published and distributed to all project participants.

COMPONENTS OF THE PLAN

The components of the project plan of execution will vary widely from project to project depending upon type and location. A single process unit located on the U.S. Gulf Coast might require only a simple plan consisting of two or three pages, whereas a large petrochemical or mining complex located at several sites in an underdeveloped nation with insufficient infrastructure might require a sizable volume. The format of the plan should be in accordance with the work breakdown structure of the participating organizations.

The following items should be included in any project plan:

1. Division of responsibilities between the owner, contractor, and any third parties involved in the project
2. The engineering plan
3. The procurement plan
4. Logistics planning (material control)
5. The quality control plan
6. The construction plan
7. The financial plan
8. The commissioning and startup plan

Most organizations engaged in engineering and construction have standards and procedures covering routine aspects of the work. The project plan of execution should stress those aspects which are unique to the specific project rather than the routine activities.

DETAILS OF PLANNING

The planning process should start with the final milestone—mechanical completion or startup test run depending upon the scope of work—and proceed from there. This assures focus upon the ultimate objective of timely completion. A checklist for planning follows:

Construction planning
1. Facility turnover sequence
2. Temporary facilities, offices, warehousing, etc.
3. Tool and equipment requirements
4. Labor availability and productivity
5. Camp requirements
6. Work week and productivity impact
7. Climatic affects on field work

8. Field engineering assistance required
9. Extent of subcontracting
10. Field organization and staffing

Procurement planning
1. Procurement sources (equipment-materials)
2. Home office vs. field procurement
3. Long lead time items
4. Expediting
5. Logistical planning

Engineering planning
1. Source(s) of technology
2. Codes, specifications, and standards to be utilized
3. Utilization of consultants
4. Early work
5. Requisitioning priorities
6. Drawing priorities
7. Vendor data requirements
8. Utilization of scale models
9. Manpower requirements
10. Approval requirements
11. Organization and staffing
12. Utilization of prefabricated modules

Quality control planning
1. Audit of design and equipment for conformance to specifications
2. Checking of calculations and drawings
3. Shop inspection of equipment and fabricated items
4. Certification of materials
5. Certification of welding procedures
6. Receiving and inspection of equipment and materials
7. Jobsite storage and environmental protection of equipment and materials
8. Construction inspection

Logistics planning. Some projects require extensive planning, considering shipping limitations, port facilities limitations, customs, inland transport, etc., as well as consideration of weather restraints.

Financial planning
1. Cash flow requirements
2. Progress payments and billing frequency
3. Impact of financial sources

Commissioning plan
1. Preoperational checkout and turnover
2. Commissioning operations
3. Initial operations
4. Performance testing

Job closeout
1. "As built" drawings
2. Client-required manuals and records
3. Record retention
4. Final job report
5. Release of retention

2

The Proactive Execution Plan

WARREN T. OLDE*   *Exxon Research & Engineering Company, Florham Park, New Jersey*

M. PERALTA   *National Aeronautics and Space Administration, Washington, D.C.*

Ask almost any experienced project manager about doing execution planning, and the reply will be: "Sure—it's paramount to the success of a project." Certainly, some type of execution planning has been done since the advent of project management. But, over the years, execution planning has evolved through various forms and has meant different things to different people. So, some discussion of what is execution planning is appropriate.

For decades, some form of execution planning has been practiced in building new projects or, for that matter, modernizing existing facilities. Earlier, this planning generally took the form of lists of activities presented as some type of schedule (bar chart or equivalent). This became the project execution monitoring tool. As time passed, the techniques became more sophisticated. In the early 1960s, with the development of computerized scheduling methodology (CPM, PERT), industries' planning efforts often became synonymous with the development of schedule logic, basic for input into computerized programs.

To other managers in the project business, usually the clients, this was not enough; and the search for better ways to plan, communicate, and execute continued. This latter effort was geared to augment the computerized scheduling methodology, not supplant it. These augmentations often took the form of written documentations outlining the fundamentals upon which later schedule logic work was based. These documents were sometimes called "project execution plans," with content and impact being wide variables depending upon the industry, a company within a given industry, and a management within a given company.

Over time projects grew in size and complexity, and so did execution plans. The advent of contracting of mega-sized projects in the 1970s spurred some clients to expend great effort in developing plans that set the desired execution parameters from project inception through plant commissioning, virtually a soup-to-nuts approach. These documents tended to be one-time plans covering every conceivable aspect of the project. Most of the data accumulated proved to be informational or historical, having little relevance to the actual work execution. Thus these voluminous documentations were of limited utility during the intense work phases of the project.

---

*Retired

A NEW PLANNING INITIATIVE

As the 1990s approach, industry still sees a wide variety of project execution plans, and with it a continually forward-looking attitude on project execution planning. Several new initiatives on this important aspect of project work are evolving. This chapter will address one such initiative: a viable, utilitarian technique, presented in a simple, clear, crisp way, which has become a highly efficient communicating medium throughout all execution stages of a project.

In essence, this execution planning initiative is a living working document that provides key input on how a project is to be built. It focuses on strengthening the management of risks that are inherent throughout a project's work phases and augments the documents that define what is to be built.

A broad definition of this new project execution planning initiative would be: "A proactive identification, analysis and documentation of key project parameters and of expected beneficial or adversarial key events/activities, at any point in time during the project execution period, that may impact on the decision making process and, thus, the well-being of the project."

This initiative is not intended to cover detailed day-to-day project planning efforts or project procedures. Rather, it is a broad foundation for development of these plans and procedures in conjunction with other more routine data that are available for the project (specifications, standards, contract documents). In this regard, it is not unlike the execution planning efforts of clients in the 1970s, but this particular initiative differs mainly in its proactive project risk management posture and its presentation method, which foster continuous updating to reflect increasing needs for specificity as the project moves forward.

WHY AN EXECUTION PLAN

At this point, one could expect to be asked "why is such an execution plan necessary?" While the answer is likely obvious to highly experienced project people, the uninitiated may well benefit by some advice on this point. In the past, client and contractor upper and middle managements have had varying degrees of success in effectively setting and/or communicating project execution parameters. True, efforts were made as described above, but subsequent follow-up and incurrence of too many preventable adverse incidents indicated that project people and/or systems had ignored, forgotten, or otherwise not sufficiently considered those parameters. This often led to project crises and reactive corrective measures, usually too late, and the well-being of the project was, at best, scarred.

Normally, the degree of influence and significance of decision making are greatest in the early phases of a project, and these aspects diminish as the project progresses. Also, history indicates that when projects have gotten into trouble, a significant factor has been the lack of adequate early and continuous execution planning. It soon became apparent that more definitive, formal, and direct proactive execution planning measures were necessary. The objective was to eliminate or, at least, largely reduce those past shortcomings in project planning that caused later extensive reactive corrective measures which consume so much of management's time, create excessive use of project resources, and result in unnecessarily high project costs.

These forces dictated the need for (1) proactive identification of potential project impediments along with subsequent action plans to eliminate or reduce adverse impacts; (2) proactive plans to take advantage of the positive factors available to the project; and (3) a hardhitting and simple communicating mode throughout all levels of management and project staffs, including both client's and contractor's.

Potential credits accruing to a project by implementing this type of execution planning could amount to millions of dollars annually depending upon the size and number of projects being executed by any given company. In any case, high-quality execution planning is essential for projects requiring clearly expressed concepts and efficient execution.

A VIABLE TECHNIQUE

This planning initiative normally has four primary parts and one secondary part, although the technique is flexible enough to accommodate any particular client's or contractor's special project needs. The four primary parts involve the identification and documentation of (1) the client's basic project objectives and how to address the relative values of these objectives, (2) the roles and responsibilities of the major parties involved in a project, (3) the contracting strategy/plan, and (4) major potential execution impediments and positive aiding factors. The secondary part covers general information that assists the understanding of the plan or project at any point during the execution phase.

Basic Project Objectives

The primary part that addresses the client's basic project objectives is essential for achieving clear execution concepts, and it has a major impact on later execution. It is, perhpas, the most difficult part to prepare, because clients sometimes are reluctant to admit that the often-used simplistic objectives of attaining a "safe facility of high quality, at low cost and by a fixed completion date" are, in reality, unrealistic. In fact, at any point in project execution these seemingly simplistic objectives are not normally compatible. They often impede and confuse the decision-making process when the client's or contractor's project execution people attempt optimization to meet all of these apparently equally important objectives. This adverse situation is also often compounded by clients having a few (or many) other obscure objectives that appear on the decision-making scene at various points in an execution program. These obscure objectives (use of local resources, conservation of energy, financing requirements) are sometimes imposed on a project quite informally and without enough thought as to their impact on the ability to meet any formally expressed objectives for a project.

In view of the above, prudence dictates that the client's basic project objectives should be addressed directly, including establishing the relative values of each objective and guidance on how the relative values should be used in making tradeoff decisions at various points in the execution program. Objectives and their relative values can change as the project progresses. So, the documentation on this primary part needs to be done at the inception of a project, and needs to be reviewed and updated, as appropriate, through the various execution phases. This assures the client that the project objectives are clear, and good dissemination to the client's and contractor's project managements and staffs will gain solid understanding of the objectives, thus enhancing chances of their being met.

Figure 1 is an example of how to approach documenting a client's initial basic project objectives using six basic, prioritized objectives covering safety, quality, costs, schedule, and use of local resources. The figure also addresses some specific considerations in applying the prioritization of the objectives.

Often, clients have more than six objectives, some of which can be obscure as previously mentioned. For best results, all objectives should be identified, prioritized, and the intent of evaluating one objective versus another or all others should be stated as clearly as possible. If this primary part of project execution planning is done well, the client will be rewarded by having project staffs highly informed and able to make sound judgments that are consistent with the established objectives.

As a final point, as briefly cited earlier, objectives can change at any stage of the project. When this occurs, the client should ascertain what if any impact this will have on the project, and then issue appropriate revisions to this part of the execution

<u>SAMPLE</u>

CLIENT'S BASIC PROJECT OBJECTIVES

<u>XYZ REFINERY PROJECT</u>

BASIC OBJECTIVES AND RELATIVE VALUES

The Client's objectives for this project, in order of priority, are as
follows:

1. Maximize construction, operations and maintenance safety.
2. Attain a quality, reliable facility with a high service factor.
3. Complete project on schedule.
4. Maintain capital investment within budgeted amount.
5. Minimize operating costs.
6. Enhance business opportunities for local vendors and subcontractors.

Prioritizing the Client's objectives is intended to assist the decision-making
process in those situations in which objectives conflict and compromises are
necessary. For significant conflicts in objectives, agreement must be reached
with the Client's Facilities Manager regarding the optimum solution before
implementation. If achieving reasonable trade-offs on prioritized objectives
is deemed impractical in any specific circumstance and does not constitute
good risk management or solid business practices, the particular circumstance
must be reviewed with the Client's Facilities Manager to address the possibility of changing priority of the Client's objectives.

APPLICATION OF RELATIVE VALUES

The following expands on the intent and guidance on the application of relative values in connection with attaining the stated basic objectives:

1. Maximize Construction Operations and Maintenance Safety

    a. Operations and maintenance safety requirements will be incorporated
        into the fundamental design basis from which detailed engineering and
        procurement will proceed.

    b. Personnel and plant safety have the highest priority in making choices
        between design, cost or schedule alternatives. Thus, no deviations
        from the basic safety requirements are allowable without the expressed
        written approval of the Client's Facilities Manager.

    c. Design of facilities will comply with acceptable environmental health
        standards, including:

        (1) Existing and reasonably anticipated legal requirements are to be
             met.

        (2) Unacceptable risks involving potential danger or nuisance to
             refinery employees, contractor personnel, visitors and neighbor-
             ing communities shall be eliminated from the work.

Figure 1

(3) Special attention shall be given to strictly limiting worker exposure to harmful materials, heat and noise consistent with government health/safety criteria.

d. Construction safety shall not be compromised in any way and Contractor(s) shall develop job site safety programs consistent with the Client's safety standards and shall use best efforts to achieve a zero target of fatalities or permanent disabilities and a 25 percent or less OSHA/BLS (comparable industry) severity and case rate record.

2. Attain a Quality, Reliable Facility With a High Service Factor

a. Facilities minimum acceptable quality requirements will be incorporated into the fundamental design basis and augmented by other contract documents (e.g., Client's standards).

b. The fundamental design basis and the detailed engineering for the project shall be compatible with meeting a two-year run length.

c. Each utility system shall be designed so that a single failure will not result in a total loss of that utility, in the loss of a critical item of equipment (e.g., gas compression, feed pumps), nor in an entire processing facility shutdown.

d. Any unique (e.g., "first of a kind") equipment items or designs, regardless of cost, shall be approved by the Client's Facilities Manager prior to inclusion in the project.

e. Any recommended deviations from the fundamental design basis to improve safety posture or gain cost/schedule advantages shall be submitted to the Client's Project Manager for consideration and disposition.

3. Complete Project on Schedule

a. Significant financial credits can accrue to the Client for early commissioning of the facilities. Completion incentives (after tax) vary from approximately 50k$ per day (contractor overheads) on/before December 1, 19xx up to approximately 300k$ per day on/after March 1, 19yy.

b. Schedule performance must be compatible with the planned refinery turnaround scheduled for a 6 months period starting June 1, 19xx.

c. Schedule performance must also be compatible with the Client's planned turnover sequence/schedule for process and utility systems and units.

d. Opportunities to improve schedule performance, even at some higher capital investment, shall receive strong consideration. All execution staff people (Client's and Contractor's) should make views known, in this regard, for the Client's Project Manager's review and disposition.

Figure 1 (cont.)

4. Maintain Capital Investment Within Budgeted Amount

   a. Opportunities to reduce capital investment shall be pursued vigorously during the engineering, procurement, and construction phases of the project, insofar as the above higher priority objectives are not compromised.

   b Contractors shall be encouraged to perform investment optimization studies which appear to have reasonable potential for cost savings. Such cases shall be reviewed with the Client's Project Manager before proceeding with the detailed studies.

   c. The economic criteria for discretionary incremental investment decisions, at any point in time, shall be as advised by the Client's Project Manager.

5. Minimize Operating Costs

   a. Facilities shall be designed for economically justified energy conservation.

   b. Operability and maintainability (including manning requirements) will be given high priority in the evaluation of facilities alternatives.

   c. The facilities design shall be reviewed at designated execution milestones to assure that facilities can be maintained at low cost and with minimum maintenance manpower.

   d. Discretionary investment items, regardless of return, which indicate a reduction in operating and/or maintenance manning, shall be reviewed with the Client's Facilities Manager for potential inclusion in the project.

   e. Where economically feasible, multiple equipment items (e.g., machinery, instruments, electrical) shall have interchangeable parts so as to minimize spares inventory and facilitate maintenance and operator training and reduce warehousing costs.

6. Enhance Business Opportunities for Local Vendors and Subcontractors

   a. Potential local vendors who can offer materials/services for the project will be placed on the vendors list.

   b. Selected local vendors and subcontractors who meet project requirements shall have a full and fair opportunity to bid and be awarded work based on the lowest evaluated total cost.

   c. If requested to do so, Contractor shall give any local supplier/subcontractor a full, fair and courteous hearing on matters that are justified in connection with its business.

   d. New local supply sources offering comparable materials, better service and/or lower evaluated costs shall be favorably considered along with other vendors.

   e. No cost premium is to be paid for selection of local vendors/subcontractors over other qualified sources who provide comparable materials/services. On this project, there is no minimum requirement regarding how much business must be awarded to local vendors/subcontractors.

* * * * * *

Figure 1 (cont.)

plan. After dissemination to those parties involved in the project work, the client may expect further feedback relative to expected impacts of the changed objectives, probably some of which were not ascertained earlier. This situation generally introduces some major execution impediments, the handling of which will be discussed later in this chapter.

Roles and Responsibilities

The second primary part covers roles and responsibilities of the various major organizations involved in the execution of a project. For the most part, this effort should be primarily directed toward the client's internal organization, although the client's interfaces with other organizations which are expected to work on the project should also be addressed. The extent of the latter is a function of the terms and conditions of any contract between the client and the other organization. Typically, the contract between the client and a prime engineering, procurements, and construction (EPC) contractor carefully defines the roles/responsibilities of each party to the contract. Thus, execution plan coverage would likely be limited to only special aspects that need further clarification for optimum understanding. However, when nonprime EPC contractors or consultants provide services on a project, it is advisable to clearly define their roles and responsibilities vis-à-vis the client, the prime EPC contractor(s), and other organizations (other contractors, consultants) who are also involved in the project. Each of these facets are discussed further below.

Within a client's organization, the need for defining each organizational subpart (department, division, group) and key individual's (project manager, facilities manager) role in a project, and responsibilities commensurate with that role, is paramount. In this regard, interfacing activities are particularly important, especially when some potential overlapping of responsibilities is perceived. Once the client's internal roles and responsibilities are established, most of them remain fixed throughout the life of the project. Some, however, will change as the project progresses, and when this occurs, the execution plan should be updated accordingly.

This aspect of execution planning covers a wide range of topics, and the degree of coverage in the plan is a function of the way a client normally operates. Certainly, all possibilities cannot be addressed here, but a few examples of client's topics in establishing internal roles and responsibilities follow:

1. Project development stage. Setting the design philosophy, product quality criteria, conducting engineering and topographical surveys, delineating local code requirements, conducting soils investigations, preparing cost estimates, processing appropriations, establishing pollution control criteria, obtaining government permits and licenses, acquiring free construction site access, preparing fundamental design basis documents, setting contracting strategy, performing contracting activities (select bid slate, solicit and evaluate bids, award contract), establishing client's project team needs, setting reporting/communications criteria, setting approval authority levels, and developing the initial execution plan.

2. Project execution stage. Involvement in quality control activities, selection of equipment and material supply sources, initiation and approval of changes, accounting and auditing, cost and schedule forecasting, traffic and customs clearance, jobsite security and safety, labor relations, public relations, spare parts selection/purchasing/warehousing, facilities checkout and acceptance, execution plan updating, start-up training and manual preparation.

The topical examples cited above represent a broad cross-section of considerations. Clients who are sophisticated in project planning and execution generally have ready-made check lists to aid in the process of pinpointing roles and responsibilities for a particular project. Less sophisticated clients may have to generate the topics to be addressed without benefit of having experience data or they may resort to obtaining aid from experienced consultants. In any case, a well-disciplined approach in this area will eliminate unnecessary duplication and gaps in a client's project-oriented activities.

Roles and responsibilities of third parties (contractors other than the prime EPC contractor, consultants, client's affiliated organizations) should also be defined and documented in the execution plan. Coverage can occur in several ways, typically:

> Referencing a contract between the client and a third party (e.g., a consultant hired to provide specific services). This approach normally avoids unnecessary duplication of data and chance of promulgating conflicting information. However, care must be taken to sanitize portions of such contracts (commercial terms) before copies are given to the prime EPC contractor or other third parties for informational purposes.
> Fully define the roles/responsibilities of the third parties for the particular project in the execution plan. This may be preferable when, for example, a consultant may be under a long-term, broad-based contract with the client and services provided to the particular project are limited in scope.
> As appropriate, clearly delineate, in the execution plan, interface activities roles/responsibilities between each third party and other third parties and the prime EPC contractor.
> Any combination of the above which suits the situation at hand.

The type of third-party coverage is exemplified as follows: A soils consulting firm has been hired by the client to survey the planned construction site, take test data, evaluate the data, and prepare a soils report for the use by the prime EPC contractor in its civil design work. In this case, it is reasonable for the EPC contractor to fully understand the scope of the consulting firm's work plus have direct access to the firm's engineering, who prepared the soils report, during the subsequent civil design effort and, possibly, later during construction. Thus, the interface roles/responsibilities vis-à-vis these two parties and the client should be delineated in the execution plan, and providing the EPC contractor with a sanitized copy of the client's contract with the soils consulting firm, principally the work scope definition portion, is appropriate.

This example is also representative when execution plan coverage is warranted for the prime EPC contractor to augment the roles/responsibilities defined in the contract between the client and the EPC contractor.

Contracting Strategy/Plan

In the early development of an execution plan, the contracting strategy becomes the third primary part. This is a challenging exercise that has to consider all aspects of the project to be contracted (project type, location, contracting environment, client policies/practices) and then evaluate the viable contracting alternatives (e.g., cost-reimbursable, lump-sum, splitting of EPC contracts). Selecting the optimum contracting mode and then developing a detailed plan to carry out the contracting effort (e.g., screening for interest, bid slate selection, solicitation and evaluation of bids, contract award) is a highly significant step in the project execution program.

Major Execution Impediments and Aiding Factors

The fourth primary part, which addresses potential major impediment and aiding factors, is the heart of a good execution plan and the risk-management efforts on a project. Here is where everyone involved in a project should contribute to the before-the-fact efforts to identify those major problems which may have an adverse impact on meeting the client's defined objectives. Proactively identifying those factors which should aid efforts to meet the defined objectives is also beneficial. These identification activities should be ongoing during the life of a project, whether as organized, pre-planned sessions or as random events by individuals or groups. The first key to success in this effort is to generate a project-related activism wherein fertile minds expose issues that need to be addressed and innovativeness prevails in developing actions to eliminate/mitigate problems or take advantage of aiding factors. The second key to success is to have the managements involved support and ensure that plans of action developed for each documented issue will be sustained.

The method of documentation is utilitarian and follows a simple format:

1. Identify the problem (or aiding factor) along with a brief explanation as to why it is a problem (or aid) and potential impact on the client's prioritized objectives.
2. Establish a goal to be reached that will alleviate the problem (or make best use of the aiding factor) along with a target date for achieving the goal.
3. List action plans, in major milestone form, that should lead to achieving the goal—include interim dates for expected completion of milestone actions along with who has the responsibility to carry out the specific actions.
4. Identify the management individual within the organization, normally the client or prime EPC contractor, who has the overall action responsibility, so that individual can appropriately follow-up.

Documentation should be crisp, clear, and normally limited to a single typewritten page (see Figs. 2 and 3 for typical examples). Experience indicates that this is a highly effective mode of communicating. Also, if more than one page is necessary, it is likely that there is more than one problem (or aid) to be documented.

For best utility, documentations should be kept current, via appropriate revisions, on a prearranged schedule or at random, as the situation dictates. In any event, periodic follow-up reviews by the manager responsible is certainly necessary to ensure continuing attention to each major issue that has been raised, including revising the previous action plans if necessary to attain the established goal. Once the goal has been met, the specific documentation may be retired to an inactive file.

The decision as to what type of major problems (or aids) should be addressed in this fashion varies from job to job and situation to situation. A good rule of thumb is that if the issue in question is likely to have a significant impact on the client's objectives or their priorities, document it for special treatment in the execution plan. Otherwise, good judgement is the basis for such decisions. Erring on the conservative side is reasonable, especially during the earlier phases of a project when the degree of influence and significance of decision making is highest. Also, if later reviews indicate that, for example, a previously identified potential project impediment never developed or did not develop to the extent expected, the action plans can be shelved or modified accordingly. If an aiding factor fails to materialize as expected, look for further potential impediments.

General Informational Data

The secondary part of an execution plan is a compilation of background and informational historical data. These data are important to the understanding of the project and the execution plan developed for the project. But, it is also important that the data not clutter the primary parts of the execution plan, and bury these prime aspects that need constant attention during the active stages of project execution. Relegating the data to an addendum role in a second volume accomplishes this goal. In this way, the data are readily available "on-the-shelf" when needed, but remain in a secondary posture.

SAMPLE

EXECUTION IMPEDIMENT/AIDING FACTOR

XYZ REFINERY PROJECT

☐ IMPEDIMENT   ☒ AIDING FACTOR

Sequence No.:   AD-1

Responsibility: D. Smith, Contractor Engineering Manager

IDENTIFICATION:

A new XYZ unit is being added adjacent to an existing five year old XYZ unit. This new unit essentially duplicates, including layout and configuration, the previous unit. This offers many opportunities to use technical data (e.g., mechanical, instrument, electrical) generated for the older unit, thus possibly significantly reducing engineering, procurement and construction planning manhours plus improving schedule performance.

GOAL:

Establish and implement techniques/procedures to make maximum use of available technical data to enhance duplication efforts and realize potential related cost savings.

ACTIONS	BY	WHEN
• Establish availability of old data, collect, and give to EPC contractor	J. Jones (Client PE)	2/15/8x

• Digest data and establish extent of usage for:
  - Civil/Structural Designs
  - Vessels/Exchangers
  - Piping/Stress Analyses/MTO
  - Machinery
  - Instruments
  - Electrical
  - Insulation
	H. Hall (Contractor, Design Coordinator)	4/1/8x

• Establish precise usage techniques/procedures for each discipline and implement program.	H. Hall	5/1/8x

* * * * * *

Figure 2

SAMPLE

EXECUTION IMPEDIMENT/AIDING FACTOR

ABC CHEMICAL PROJECT

[X] IMPEDIMENT   [ ] AIDING FACTOR

Sequence No.: I-6

Responsibility: J. Doe, Client Facilities Manager

IDENTIFICATION:

Obtaining government permits for construction to proceed is normally onerous
and, thus, needs a well-planned program involving the client and contractor.
State, county and city administrations have extensive permit requirements for
safety and environmental control. Laws are in effect that require various
levels of approval for portions of the project prior to start of construction.

GOAL:

Obtain all required government permits in a timely fashion so as not to impede
construction progress.

ACTIONS	BY	WHEN
• Establish which permits are required.	A. Law (Client Law Dept)	7/1/8x
• Develop detailed plan for obtaining permits, including information needed (e.g., forms, calculations, drawings, specification data), activities schedule, points of contact and responsibilities of persons involved.	B. New (Contractor PM)	9/1/8x
• Submit final permit applications to appropriate authorities.	D. Day (Client Construction Coordinator)	3/1/8y
• Monitor progress through approval channels and obtain final permits.	D. Day	7/1/8y

* * * * * *

Figure 3

Many client and contractor project management people rely on the background/informational data to indoctrinate others on the various aspects of a project. The data are often used to prepare presentations and reconciliations. So, the data are of value, but not on a day-to-day need basis, and being on-the-shelf ready for use is an acceptable practice.

The types of data that should be considered for this execution planning treatment are variable. Mostly, it is best to include data which set the parameters for the execution plan at any point in time. This may include such data as descriptions of facilities, preliminary project schedules, studies of various options considered in setting the planning bases, early survey data (local resource availability, local environmental conditions), issues that were proposed for inclusion in the primary parts of the execution plan but were abandoned (and why?), etc. Generally, the choice of what to include is left to those with the responsibility for preparing each original execution plan and later updates.

EXECUTION PLAN TIMING

Knowing when execution plans should be developed, relative to a time-line of project progression stages, is a significant part of the overall project planning effort. Starting with the concept of "having the execution plan fit the needs of the project at any point in time," client's managers with the execution planning responsibility need to establish the timing and content of the initial execution plan effort and of subsequent updates.

Typically, at project inception and when an initial project budget estimate is to be prepared, the client's execution planning should begin. At this stage, it is reasonable to establish first-pass basic project objectives and early roles and responsibilities (refer to Project Development Stage roles and responsibilities examples cited earlier in this chapter). Also, it is appropriate to address the potential contracting strategy for the project and other issues (potential major execution impediments and aiding factors) that can have a significant bearing on the initial budget estimate. In essence, the four primary parts of the execution plan are covered, but only to the degree necessary to satisfy the concept of "fit the needs . . . at any point in time." The primary goal is to provide good data for cost and schedule estimates necessary for budget preparation while considering the size and complexity of the project. At this point, the secondary part, General Informational Data, can also be assembled for subsequent use.

Later, as the project moves toward a more definitive budget estimate(s) stage, the entire execution plan should be reworked by the client, this time to confirm that previous decisions, assumptions, etc., relative to objectives, roles and responsibilities, and execution issues are still valid. If not, these aspects should be updated to reflect current thinking. Also, this is the time for the client to address additional roles and responsibilities (refer to Project Execution Stage examples cited earlier) plus additional potential impediments and aiding factors that are indicated. At this point, the client's contracting mode should be established and become a part of the client's execution plan. Also, the historical part of the plan should be updated as needed.

After contract award, the client's execution plan should be shared with the prime contractor(s) selected for the engineering, procurement, and construction of the project, excluding, of course, the client's contracting strategy/plan and other sensitive parts that are not necessary for the contractors to know for doing the work. Subsequent major updates of the overall plan during the EPC contractor's work execution phase are generally necessary only when there is a change in the client's objectives, priorities of objectives, roles and responsibilities, or when a significant number of major new impediments or aiding factors are predicted or encountered either by the client or the contractor(s). With these exceptions, the client's project management team and the contractor's staff are expected to work together to routinely monitor the impediment/aiding issues section, update the write-ups as appropriate, and generate new issue write-ups for incorporation into the execution plan as the project detailed work moves ahead.

EXECUTION PLAN UTILIZATION

In general, the use of execution plans is variable since individuals and organizations react differently to the concept. However, it is highly important that the plan must not simply evolve; rather it should be planned and implemented in an orderly and disciplined fashion to give the utmost assurance of achieving the client's objectives. The people and organizations with a high degree of discipline relative to implementing this new execution planning initiative will find it to be a highly valuable mechanism for project management people at all levels. Typically, it becomes an excellent communicating medium by highlighting the client's objectives and priorities, thereby significantly aiding in the decision-making process in the management of project risk factors for both the client's and contractor's project management people. Also, clear delegation of responsibilities can only enhance the interactions between the parties involved in executing the many project work activities.

The capturing of major potential execution impediments and positive aiding factors in a simple, clear documentation is highly useful. First, the process of generating these types of issues is healthy because addressing them early, before options may disappear, presents the opportunity to proactively "do something constructive" about each situation. Second, the fact that managements endorse and monitor the action plans provides high incentives for the managements' staffs to follow through more effectively. Third, staffs often feel a kinship toward the issues because they normally play a continuing role in the generation and updating process—and they know that managements (client's and contractor's) are highly informed on staff activities relative to these issues—this facilitates positive, often innovative, staff actions to gain recognition. Fourth, the routine review and updating of issue write-ups, and continuing proactive generation of new write-ups, results in highly enhanced control of key project activities—those that have the greatest potential for impacting on the client's project objectives.

It is important to reiterate that the execution plan does not replace day-to-day project planning efforts or project procedures. The execution plan does, however, often lead to modifications of the day-to-day work planning and changes to detailed project procedures. These are natural outgrowths of any good project execution plan.

PLANNING DISCIPLINE HAS A HIGH RETURN

Effective execution planning and implementation discipline can have a high payout for both the client and the contractor(s). Some broadened credits, lower project costs and resource usage were discussed briefly earlier. There are however, numerous significant other credits, many of which not only affect the project in hand but also can have a lasting impact on the client and contractor(s). Some of these credits are:

1. Quality anticipatory execution planning will improve work proficiency and, thus, contractor's engineering, procurement, and construction productivity. For example, it can enhance the timely addressing of critical design issues and the purchase and delivery of critical equipment and material. These, in turn, will reduce design recycling, accelerate receipt of necessary design data from suppliers, and culminate in faster and better deliveries of drawings, equipment, and material to the construciton site. Obviously, construction proficiency is highly dependent upon these timely deliveries, and if this cascading effect can be controlled even just a little better than in the past, better field worker productivity will result in benefit for all.

2. Working habits can be enhanced by forcing key supervisors (e.g., design, construction) and subordinates to "think ahead" rather than mostly being re-active. In fact, it is reasonable to use this execution planning initiative within the functional groups in the client's and contractor's organizations. These functional group planning exercises can be considered subsets of the overall project execution plan and should be managed within each functional group. Only those group issues which have the potential for impacting on the client's objectives should be elevated to the overall project execution documentation level.
3. Client and contractor(s) relations should be improved via closer communications and better understanding of mutual goals and problems. The potential synergistic effect can only aid in meeting the client's objectives, and all parties will benefit accordingly.
4. Worker satisfaction from having planned and executed well, and receiving acknowledgment, accordingly, can have a lasting effect, and will doubtless favorably impact the next assignment, as success breeds success.

THE BOTTOM LINE

The bottom line is that better project execution planning will aid in project risk-management efforts and have a significant positive impact on project cost, schedule, quality, and safety performance, thus enhancing chances for attaining a high success ratio in project work. The execution planning initiative covered in this chapter is a strong step in that direction.

3

A Workshop Approach to
Project Execution Planning

CLAUDIO PINCUS*   *Davy McKee Corporation, Berkeley Heights, New Jersey*

Activities at the beginning of a project are, by nature, hectic. Initial efforts often are perceived as ill-defined. Key members assigned to the project seldom have adequate time to fully participate in the planning effort. An intensive planning workshop will alleviate some of these pressures while helping to create a cohesive team that will significantly increase the probability of project success.

Most project managers recognize the importance of issuing a complete project plan of execution. Project plans of execution determine the organization, strategies, schedules, and their interrelationships.

The key team members, under the leadership of the project manager, are responsible for developing these plans to assure project success. The plans of execution must conform to the contractual requirements, as well as to the objectives of the client and the parent organizaiton. A planning workshop concentrates these efforts at an early stage of the project and insures more timely, comprehensive, and conclusive results. The participants become parties to the plans. Because of a better understanding, they are able to assert improved leadership in carrying out the plans.

The workshop can transform a group of individuals of different backgrounds, experiences, and personalities, into a homogeneous working team. Motivation will be increased by direct involvement and a more complete perception of those factors that will influence the project results.

The quality of the team relationship improves when members understand the roles, responsibilities, difficulties, and the restrictions of each other. The workshop allows the project manager to make adjustments to the teams' project job description. Standards of performance may also be settled at this time.

THE PLANNING FUNCTION

The three main contributors to a project are the client, the parent organization (the project team's management organization), and the project team. Written plans will balance the objectives of these parties. Incomplete plans may evolve at a time of crisis, and may not reflect an overall strategy which all parties should agree to at the beginning of the project.

Project plan development most often occurs in one of the following ways:

> *By decree.* The project manager directs the work of the project team and informs them only of short-range plans. The project manager has sole responsibility

---

Current affiliation: The Quantic Group, Ltd., Short Hills, New Jersey

for the interpretation of objectives and for any planning adjustments or corrections.

Crisis plans. Plans are neither precisely defined nor published. They are oriented
    toward "averting the crisis."

Committee plans. Many team members develop partial plans during periodic pro-
    gress review meetings. The resultant plans are again, generally short-range
    and inconclusive.

Increasing demands and more sophisticated techniques render these methods insufficient.

An effective plan of execution must incorporate many aspects besides schedules.
Critical paths, bar charts, or other time-oriented reports have been confused with plans
of execution. These scheduling documents reflect highly sophisticated techniques worked
out by "isolated" control groups and are directed toward time and logistic considerations.

PLAN OF EXECUTION

A plan of execution details the how? who? when? and where?. It is an answer to the
What? and is in accordance with the why? The *what has to be done* represents the
scope of work as well as the project specifications. The *why* defines the project objectives to the client and the parent organization's satisfaction.

Answers to the above questions must be compatible. They cannot be prepared
independently of each other. To positively affect the project, those responsible for
the execution must jointly develop a balanced strategy.

When developing the plan of execution, the following guidelines should be considered:

What are the specific objectives to be met?
What is the work breakdown?
Who must do what, where, and when?
What are the obstacles in performing the work?
What are the major decisions which must be made? (When, and by whom?)
What is the sequence of work?
What is the difference between the execution of this job and normal procedures?
How must the involved groups interrelate?
How will the accomplishments in achieving specific targets and goals be measured?

An intensive workshop is used to develop the plan of execution and accelerate the
formation of a cohesive project team. This is done by creating an environment conducive to meeting these two main objectives.

1. To formulate the plans, strategies, organizational structure, and relationships
    for successful execution according to requirements and with the participation
    of the involved parties.
2. To obtain a cohesive project team in which members understand their specific
    responsibilities, authority, and standards of performance as interpreted by
    the project manager and in accordance with the requirements of the parent
    organization.

THE INTENSIVE WORKSHOP APPROACH

The workshop brings together the key members of the project team during the early
stages of the project, preferably for a brief but undistrubed concentrated period of
time. Substantial preparation is required by all participants prior to the workshop.

Conditions Necessary for a Workshop

In implementing an intensive workshop approach to planning a project, the following conditions are essential:

> There must be full commitment to the concept on the part of the project manager as well as the parent organization.
>
> Each participant should receive a full explanation as to the purpose, expectations, and guidelines of the workshop.
>
> The workshop must be held in the early stages of the project, but only when sufficient information is available.
>
> Advanced preparation of a detailed workshop agenda in order to maximize necessary participants' interaction is essential.
>
> Extensive preparation must be completed by participants prior to the meeting.
>
> The project manager must lead preparation of individual plans by outlining his basic project strategy as it affects those plans.
>
> The workshop must be oriented toward discussion periods rather than long technical dissertations.
>
> The physical environment established for the workshop must provide for uninterrupted sessions in a conducive atmosphere.

The workshop approach should not be considered without the full endorsement and participation of the project manager. The project manager must control the planning and decision-making process.

Workshop Design

The workshop agenda requires careful preparation to achieve the objectives. Some subjects will be informational in nature, while others require well-organized discussion periods with maximum member involvement. Sessions may be designed in different formats, each one requiring a different type of preparation, leadership, and direction. To fulfill the objectives, it is suggested that the agenda be organized in three major phases. Each of these three phases is discussed in more detail in the following paragraphs.

Interaction of the Parent Organization and the Project Team

The agenda for the first series of workshop sessions must include these subjects. The parent organization's representative must take an active role in presenting the views to the participants.

> Parent organization's view of the project
>> What did the parent organization sell?
>> Contract description
>> Parent objectives
>
> Client's view of the project as seen by the parent
>> Project objectives
>> Client project team
>> Importance of schedule/costs/technology

Those involved in the development of the execution plan must incorporate the commitments made before contract award, the essence of the contracts, the parent organization's objectives, and the goal of the client.

The first series of sessions must deal with the transition of "ownership" of the project from the parent to the project manager (team), who will actually execute the project.

Before assigning most team members to the work, the parent organization will have to finalize client negotiations. To reach that stage, preliminary project plans were developed, commitments were made, the project manager and other individuals were selected, costs were established, and contractual documents were signed. All of these aspects should be viewed as to their impact on the stated objectives of the parent organization. The results of the efforts during the negotiations influence the ultimate success of the project.

The objectives of the parent organization can vary with the elements included in the contract, the financial status, the economic outlook, the in-house availability of resources, and the type of technology. Individuals involved in the planning must know those management objectives that affect the project execution. Misunderstanding of management goals could result in misdirection, perception or lack of management support, and finally, frustration of personnel.

The contract stipulates the legal obligations of all parties. A good comprehension of the contract delineates the legal obligations of all parties and affords an understanding of how to best influence the project results.

The parent organization's perception of the client's objectives is important since it influences the preliminary project strategy during the negotiation phase. The client must indicate the proper balance between schedule, cost, and technology for each specific project.

Interaction of the Project Team Members

A possible agenda for this series includes the following topics:

A. Overall project plan
B. Project manager's view of the team members' roles
    Project team organization
    Definition by the project manager of the responsibility, authority, and standards of performance.
C. Project team members view themselves and others
    Communications
    Relationship with parent (matrix)
    Relationship with client project team
    Project meetings
    Reports
D. Specific work plans
    Technical considerations for each discipline
    Sequence of work
    Interaction with and dependency upon other groups
E. Performance assurances
    Time, cost, and quality controls
    Client relationships

The core of the intensive workshop consists of a series of well-planned sessions in which team members develop actual working plans.

The level of participation will depend on the perceived importance of the planning process, the quality of the work plans, and the leadership shown by key individuals.

An orderly and productive effort depends upon the full commitment of the project manager. The project manager asserts the type of leadership exercised throughout the project. Since the emphasis during this phase serves to clarify the interface with other team members, participants must maximize the preparation. Each person should realize that every team member must understand each other's work plan, restrictions, interfaces, and degrees of responsibility.

These series of sessions can be divided into five groups:

1. Overall project plan
2. Project manager's view of the team members' roles
3. Project team members' view of roles of others
4. Specific plans for each group
5. Performance assurance

Overall Project Plan. The project manager must define for the team the parameters which constitute project success or failure. As such, the project manager must outline the overall project plan. This description will explain the general view and also set the guidelines for the remaining development. If necessary, at this time, the project manager may clarify the scope of work.

Project Manager's View of the Team Members' Roles. The project manager explains the project organizaiton using the organizaiton chart to show the functional interrelationships. The organization should be explained within the context of the project objectives. Organization charts are only graphical representations of reporting relationships. These sessions are an opportunity for the project manager to add to his knowledge of the personality of each of the team members.

Often, project managers working in matrix-type organizations lack the opportunity to fully explain the position description for all members. If this effort is routinely accomplished as a departmental function, the project manager must tailor it to fulfill specific needs. Each team member should receive a written description which delineates relevant duties, responsibilities, and authorities in the areas of planning, organization, leadership and direction, control and working relationships. Descriptions should include decision levels for each activity. To facilitate team work, other members should develop awareness of other pertinent position descriptions. Everyone should receive a standard of performance for each position description category. A good understanding of the basis of evaluation by the job leader may improve employee motivation. A project assignment in a matrix assignment may create a feeling of isolation with regard to individual career growth. Clear and timely preparation of both documents will avoid many future misunderstandings and may result in the foundation for team building.

Project Team Members' View of Roles of Others. For an orderly execution, team members should agree as to how to deal with third parties. Specifics are worked out by them under guidelines provided by the project manager.

Areas covered will include internal lines of communication, relationship with the parent organization, client, and vendors, project meetings, reporting procedures, documentation, as well as other pertinent subjects.

An informal group environment is the suggested vehicle for these constructive discussions. Each participant becomes involved in the development of the agreement.

The integration process between all major groups, with different areas of responsibilities, accelerates by exploring such questions as the "How will they communicate?" "How much work can overlap?" and "What is the basis of the decision-making process?"

A well-structured session which encourages a frank exchange of ideas will set the stage. Though the matter might not result in resolution at this time, future relationships will benefit substantially from these discussions.

The relationship with the parent organization must be considered. The project can be executed within a matrix organization using either a departmental or task force approach. Team members must conclude how to obtain the maximum benefit when dealing with departmental management. Disagreements involving availability, quality, and timing of resources may result. During this part of the workshop, the project manager outlines the procedures for communications, individual responsibilities, and finally, the process for any necessary escalation of conflict. Helpful devices may include round table discussions and/or cases to illustrate the subject.

Specific Plans for Each Group. Most of the workshop will be devoted to the specific work plans. These will cover technical and commercial considerations of such groups as basic design, engineering, procurement, manufacturing, and construction.

Each major discipline must develop and present a specific plan of execution in conformance with the project requirements and objectives. Refer to the guidelines for plan development given at the beginning of this chapter for preparation of this plan. Major emphasis should address the following aspects:

Major considerations to be faced
Obstacles in performing the work
Sequence of work, schedule
Decisions to be made—When and by whom?
Interaction with other groups
Plans for achieving specific targets and goals

Individuals from diverse technical backgrounds and responsibilities will be instrumental in the execution of each specific plan. The presentation format must aim toward promoting an understanding between these individuals.

The presenter should specifically identify the obstacles that the group will face, how they plan to overcome the obstacles, and how others will interface with them.

A conference set-up is desirable, and suitable graphic aids for this session should be employed. At the end of each presentation, a discussion period allows time for clarification.

Performance Assurance. The work plans, as presented by the major disciplines, require support by the control procedures for effective performance assurance and corrective action. Each one of the control groups must then also develop plans to assist the others. Specific methods must be designed to fulfill the requirements.

Commonly, the control group engineers may perceive a lack of understanding and support from upper and intermediate project management. The workshop presents a good opportunity for schedule and cost engineers to "sell" their techniques and assure themselves of direct involvement during the project by participating in the development of specific work plans. While developing plans, the key question is: "What can we do to assist those responsible for budgets and schedules?" Sophisticated techniques are oriented to developing better control systems, but must not be imposed on result-oriented individuals.

During the final discussions the specified work plans and assurance performance have to be modified and issued to all parties. Only after considering and incorporating the input from all parties can the benefits of a workshop be reaped.

Interaction of the Client and the Project Team

Scope (clarifications?)
Organizations
Objectives
Relative importance of cost/schedule/technology (within the contract requirements)
What is project success?

The workshop may culminate at a meeting with the client's representative. The project members have completed a series of sessions to determine all aspects of the plan and can present them to the other party. Also, the client's team has been involved in the conception of the general plan before contract award. An exchange of ideas will then test the compatibility and the proposition feasibility.

A preconceived image of each other could result form prior job executions, recommendations, or performance during contract negotiations. This first major session, devoted solely to discussions of the execution approach may facilitate future communications, reporting, and the problem-solving process.

Whenever a meeting is possible, within the context of contract agreement, both the project and client teams can enhance the possibilities for project success. The workshop will have served as the vehicle for this desired result.

Benefits and Implementation

The environment created in a workshop atmosphere will result in the following benefits:

> The project team's early concentraiton toward planning
> Organized input into the plan by each of the involved parties
> More comprehensive and conclusive results since the workshop leads to a written plan
> A more timely plan due to early concentrated effort
> An opportunity for the project manager to form an early impression of members of the project team
> A chance for all participants to know the other team members and their distinct project roles
> Higher probability for individual commitment to the plan because of the opportunity for interaction and discussion
> Early participation in planning and plan interpretation which tends to minimize later conflict among project team members

The workshop presents a unique environment which encourages all individuals to present their views. To maximize participation, each member must perceive the potential benefits of a successful workshop as it affects their work. Motivating factors that will encourage participation and preparation include:

> Direct identification with the work as "my project" and "my team"
> New and strengthened relationships between key members
> Direct recognition from management
> Understanding everyone's plans will facilitate each individual's future work per author
> Possibility of career growth

Many benefits will result from preparation and participation in the workshop; however, it remains essential to issue written work plans shortly thereafter. These comprehensive documents should facilitate dissemination of the agreed plan results throughout the remaining organization.

Workshop efforts are incomplete until the establishment of follow-up procedures. As conditions change, execution plans may require modification. Team cohesiveness may be diminished. The project manager must assess the need for corrective action.

SUMMARY

Comprehensive plans of execution must be developed at the beginning of the project. These plans, which include schedules, strategies, and organization, respond to the project requirements in accordance with parent and client objectives.

A workshop is a conducive environment for the completion of this task. Members become instrumental in the development of the plan when a well-designed compact series of sessions covers the required aspects. Participants' motivation may be improved by identification with "my project" and "my team."

Again, the level of participation by the project team depends upon the perceived importance of the workshop, the quality of the work plans, and the leadership demonstrated by key individuals.

4
Constructability

WALTER J. BOYCE   *Boyce Consultants, Houston, Texas*

My idea of constructability includes all of those things that make a particular project easier, faster, safer, and less expensive to build.

Although their main purpose is to minimize costs and close loopholes, contract provisions and project financing constraints can create obstacles to good performance. Formal agreements have become a necessity; but, almost invariably, they tend to create an adversarial relationship between the owner and the contractor which makes project execution more difficult.

Major equipment costs account for about a quarter of the total installed cost of a typical project. The remaining 75% is the target of most of the constructability cost reductions.

There are basic ideas that will make engineering design, procurement, and construction easier, less costly, faster, and safer. Some of these concepts are discussed here.

ENGINEERING

Layout

The arrangement of the equipment required for a project is a key element of the concept of constructability. Layout may be best viewed from the standpoint of accessibility—access for people and construction equipment to the equipment, piping, electrical, and instrumentation systems being installed. The access considerations must include construction, operation/production, safety, and maintenance. The layout must be finalized very early in the project. It is rarely given the attention it deserves. Too often, layout tends to repeat past mistakes and provides no opportunity for a fresh approach incorporating what was learned on past projects. Probably no single item can influence costs more than the layout. Input from all of the best minds—engineering, construction, operations, or maintenance—should be considered.

The best way to achieve a good layout is to use a block layout model. No drawings are made for this model. The model comes first, and the drawings come later. A layout model furnishes a good, three-dimensional look and is easy to use for testing ideas for alternative plant arrangements. The layout model speaks all languages.

Running piperacks, cable trays, roads, and drainage ditches before placing the equipment helps to provide a clean layout. There will always be some adjustments necessary. When the equipment is spotted first, there will be be more jogs and irregularities in the interconnecting systems. Layout of equipment and process elevation requirements will determine the structural needs. Good constructability design means that nothing is higher than it needs to be, so that support is at the lowest possible point, and so that only what must be enclosed is enclosed. Once a structure becomes necessary, this same structure is used for other items. Good constructability means that you don't custom design a building if a pre-engineered building will do. You don't build a new structure for access to equipment if that piece of equipment can be located next to an existing structure. And you don't locate a piece of equipment without knowing how you are going to get to it with pipe, electrical, and other services. Remember that straight pipe is cheap when compared with the in-place cost of structures, valves, and fittings.

Equipment Design

Equipment design is important to the constructability concept. You should use standard equipment items wherever possible. Here equipment is viewed only from a constructability approach—considerations such as support, access, and fabrication. Constructability calls for equipment with skirt supports, nozzles properly located for access, standard length exchangers with standard supports, and standard vessels. Nozzles sometimes require an exact position on a vessel, but most have at least some location flexibility. Nozzles are not randomly located nor are they located by some vague rule of thumb. Access to equipment is determined by layout, and all nozzles and other items requiring access are brought to that location. Structural work is simplified and costs are reduced. Heat exchangers with standard tube lengths and supports are ideal but are rarely possible. Two or three standards are usually obtainable with a few special or oddball items. Again, the reason for standardization is accessibility. Similar heat exchangers can be lined up with a common top elevation. A cable tray/walkway is set on top for access to valves, relief valves, and instrumentation.

Setting equipment in place requires planning the lift. Lifting lugs are considered the best solution, but their disadvantages are often ignored. The primary disadvantage is cost, but lifting lugs present objections even after erection. The lug may penetrate insulation, intensifying weatherproofing and corrosion problems. The lug can be cut off after erection, but this adds to the cost. Most equipment nozzles are strong enough for lifting the piece into place. A special lifting blind flange may be required, and may be used for lifting several vessels. With advance planning, such interchangeability is another reason for standardizing the size of manholes.

Manholes are necessary in most vessels and can be made to serve double duty. Large pressure vessels can be designed with two manholes, one top and one bottom. All other connections, including provision for inlet, outlet, relief, level, and temperature hookups, can be made through the manhole flange. This simple procedure means that the vessel design and fabrication can proceed earlier, and that nozzles may be added and nozzle sizes may be changed without changing the code vessel. Conventionally placed nozzles cannot be located to the best advantage until the layout is finalized and the access location is known.

Foundations

Foundation design using the constructability concepts can result in substantial savings. Mat-type foundations use more concrete, but much less labor. When the layout for the equipment has been done with mat foundations in mind, the volume of concrete can be minimized. Some of the readily apparent advantages of mat foundations are:

"Finished floor" productivity as work is "out of the mud"
Increased safety during construction
Improved schedule
Fewer design and construction jobhours required
More flexibility in minor equipment location

No differential settlement calculations required
Lower cost

Equipment does not have to have a plinth; grout will keep base plates out of water. Only the major anchor bolts are set. Cinch anchors are used in place of the minor bolts. Supports for horizontal vessels and heat exchangers can be steel if fireproofing is not required. When fireproofing is required, the supports are doweled into the mat and poured later.

Piperacks

Because of the large quantities involved, piperack work can be the source of substantial savings. Concrete rack supports, poured in a horizontal position, and set into empty holes before pouring the foundation can save both time and money. Work can start earlier than with comparable steel supports as no prefabrication is required. This method also reduces conflict with painting and fireproofing during the heavy piping, electrical, and instrument field work.

The decisions of what and what not to fireproof are eliminated. Detailed knowledge of the precast piperack is very important because of the opportunities to make provision for future additions. With a major piperack a part of the design, other structures may be eliminated.

Another cost saver is to use a low-level piperack wherever possible. These racks are good for use in tank farms, runs between units, and other pipe runs that do not require location of equipment or vehicular traffic underneath. The advantages of these racks are many, among them:

Added safety during construction and maintenance
Lower costs of piping erection, piping insulation, painting, electrical installation, instrument installation
No material or labor costs for scaffolding
Costs of flushing and testing are reduced

Where a road crossing is required over a low-level piperack, it is done by ramping up over the rack with removable precast slabs over the rack itself.

Unit prices from a firm quotation on an actual project showed labor jobhours for installation of low-level (no scaffolding) piperacks to be 50% of elevated racks.

Structures

Structures are to be used only when required. Required structures should be standardized. Column sizes should be the same for constructability; one size is preferred. The speed of duplicating design, fabrication, and erection efforts offsets the small savings achieved with a very tight design. Never make structures higher than necessary.

Preengineered steel and concrete buildings are cost effective. Steel has an advantage in shipping because of both weight and reduced damage. Concrete has an advantage in both maintenance and general availability. When concrete metal forms are used at the construction site for making the pieces required, the schedule may be improved.

Architects may not like to work with preengineered building blocks. They like to start from scratch and develop unique and innovative buildings. When an architect will employ conceptual thinking, the standard components of a preengineered system can be made attractive and utilitarian.

Piping

The most complex systems in a process plant are usually piping systems. Here, again, the constructability concepts offer great savings in time and money. Some points to note are:

Changes in direciton are more costly than a few extra feet of straight pipe.

A change in direction should also be used for expansion.

Plan pipeways to minimize individual pipe supports.

Minimize the number of different piping specifications groups. Each specification group adds to the items to be bid, purchased, shipped, received, sorted, stored, issued, connected, inspected, and tested. In addition, it forever complicates plant record keeping, maintenance, repairs, and plant modifications.

Pipe should be mechanically cleaned, prime-coated, and marked before shipping. Marking should be from end to end to help inspection in the field.

Control valve stations should be a spool item completely assembled, including flush provision, when shipped. The flush provision should be full-line size. The control valve installation should use block valves and bypass valves the same size as the control valves.

Line reduction and change in direction often uses a 90-degree ell and a reducer. The purchase price and welding costs are less when reducing ells are used.

Expansion loops are hard to plan; but if all loops are outside of the piperack and held at the same elevation, four 90-degree ells are used versus six 90-degree ells. The 6-ell design also traps the line.

Electrical

Constructability can be improved by considering the following approaches. Each project has different conditions. In general, a substation should be as central as safety permits. Distribution of intermediate voltage to area substations should be by underground cable in ducts. There are two reasons for this: direct burial cable costs more than the cables used in ducts; and often the cable size cannot be determined until late in the design and therefore delivery is late. The site would be disrupted after other underground work is finished.

Area substations and area control rooms should be located together in a two-storied building, with a false floor above the control room and under the motor control center. This arrangement facilitates power, control, and instrument work. From the control and MCC building, cable trays should be strong enough to span piperack supports and to carry a couple of men. When handrails are added, these can also be used as walkways.

Instrumentation

The instrument discipline appears to be less subject to constructability considerations than piping and electrical. In the design offices, the split of discipline responsibility may differ for design of instrumentation and the interconnecting pipe and wire. Some procedures can be used to reduce costs.

Small connections from large pipes to instruments should be shown on the piping and instrumentation diagram and on the working model, if one is used. They do not have to be shown on the isos or spool drawings. These connections, along with the vents and drains, require many hours of engineering and fabrication. There is a good chance of mislocation, misorientation, or damage to these appendages during shipment or erection of the spools.

A procedure that has been found to be very satisfactory is to have the field instrument engineer locate and mark the lcoation of these instrumentation connections in the field after the spools have been erected. The field cost of welding these connections may be somewhat more than shop welding, but the connections will always be correct and accessible. Savings in this instance are in the simplification of the engineering, fabrication, and reduced field correction required.

When flexibility in the piping or instrumentation standards can be permitted, there is nothing wrong with drilling and tapping many of these instrument connections when the pipe walls are thick enough.

PROCUREMENT

The constructability concept is very applicable to the procurement activities on a project. Close liaison between the equipment engineers and the equipment buyers is necessary.

Simplified Specifications

All required equipment should be described by the engineers in a general way with as few limitations as possible. The buyers then find what is available as standard design or "off-the-shelf" items. This does not mean lower quality. A Cadillac is "off-the-shelf"—a Cadillac with a Ford transmission and a Chrysler carburator is not. Most quotations should be obtained with a duty spec of about one page. When the quote has been received, engineering should analyze it against the actual requirements. Change only what must be changed, and buy it with negotiated spare parts prices for future delivery.

Buy/Build Decisions

When deciding whether to buy or to build in the field, costs must be compared on an all-inclusive basis. These costs must include design, procurement, expediting, inspection, crating, shipping, receiving, uncrating, warehousing, issue to construction, and erection. The cost to ship a caged ladder may exceed the cost of the ladder.

> Thin-wall stainless-steel tanks, hoppers, and even handrails may be less expensive than carbon steel when the total costs of sandblasting and painting both sides and repair of painting is considered. The extremely high costs of site labor in remote locations, as in the Arctic or in the Middle East, will sometimes swing customary approaches to alternative ones. Constructability recognizes each project as different and takes these factors into account.
>
> Assembly line-type field fabrication of ladders, stairs, cable trays, walkways, push button stands, and handrails can also be cost effective when well planned. This type of field work can be used as fill-in activities, welding tests, or training.

Vendor Drawings

Vendor or supplier drawings may be divided into two categories: critical, or those that are necessary to allow design to proceed; and noncritical, or those that are for record purposes only or which may not even be required at all. Noncritical vendor drawings include such standard catalog items as pumps, fans, and valves (including relief and control valves). These include the type of item that would have as a certified drawing an 8-1/2 × 11 inch page from the same catalog that the order was placed from. Custom-designed items such as columns, tanks, vessels, and heat exchangers are also noncritical for design to proceed. For these items, when the vendor's dimensional drawing is not in accord with the buyer's drawing, the vendor's drawing is wrong.

Constructability favors the reduction of design jobhours. Certified drawings should not be requested unless they are truly necessary. By reducing the number of items calling for certified drawings, those that really need them receive more attention. The lack of a certified drawings is very often used as an excuse for lack of progress or for not starting a design. When it is known that the vendor will not be supplying a certified catalog page, this excuse cannot be used.

CONSTRUCTION

Constructability concepts are most rewarding in the construction phase of a project. Construction input has been considered during the planning and early design stages, and there should be no surprises.

> The warehouse should be built first and used during the construction period for protection of equipment and supplies. Field fabrication of items may be done inside the warehouse, taking advantage of these activities on rainy days. Construction offices may also be located inside the warehouse. A preengineered warehouse is the lowest cost weather protection in most areas. In some cases, the temporary construction storage and shop areas have cost more than the permanent facilities on an area basis. There is an additional cost to remove them at the end of the job.
>
> Low-level piperacks will add considerably to the ease of construction. Actual contract unit prices for pipe installation, insulation, painting, and testing have been found to be approximately half the price when compared to conventional racks which required scaffolding. Storm ditches under the piperacks will give access to the bottoms of the pipe and will also save plot area.
>
> Mat-type foundations, horizontally precast concrete piperacks, open trench and swail storm drainage, a simplified straight line oily water sewer system, and ducts for underground ables should facilitate completion of the underground work.
>
> The underground oily water sewer system requires a somewhat different approach when using mat-type foundations. There is no reason not to run these drains through the neutral axis of the mats. The cleanout will be on one side of the mat and will drain to the other side. Vertical connections for equipment drains, etc. can be simplified with equipment layout, a straight line of pumps, etc.
>
> Work that can be done at ground level eliminates expensive scaffolding. All columns should be completely dressed out before erection. Design for one-side access makes this easier. Constructability calls for this philosophy on all vertical vessels that would otherwise require scaffolding.
>
> The value of a block model during the conceptual and planning stages cannot be overstated as a communication tool.
>
> Likewise, the design model is important to the design and construction phases of the project. The completed design model in the field is a big advantage to constructability. Accessibility to the model for visibility is encouraged, but the model must be protected from damage. Such events as a hard hat falling onto a model with complex piping are unnecessary disasters.
>
> Commodity materials should never be purchased on the short side. The tremendous cost of the total investment with no production cannot justify an approach which leads to a "for want of a nail" situation. When a substantial purchase order is being negotiated, it should include a very reasonable restocking fee. The owner then should have the option of buying leftovers for operating stock.

SUMMARY

Applying the constructability concept to the individual project will save money and time. The criteria for each project should be carefully scrutinized on an individual basis using the project objectives to determine the most important items. The following 10 rules of constructability should be applied:

> Constructability Philosophy Summary (the "kiss" approach)
>
> 1. Keep it simple and straight

2. Keep it same size
3. Keep it shop standard
4. Keep it square and squatty
5. Keep it specification simple
6. Keep it standard size
7. Keep it support simple
8. Keep it standards simple
9. Keep it schedule sacred
10. Keep it standard for site

5

The Project Schedule

KENNETH O. HARTLEY   *Morrison-Knudsen International Company, Inc.,
San Francisco, California*

Much has been written about the development and growth of modern scheduling techniques from their origins in CPM (critical path method) and PERT (project evaluation and review technique) in the late 1950s. These techniques, which are appropriate for computerization, were derived in part from bar graphs and the even earlier Gantt charts of the 1910s. Since that time most project management practitioners have become familiar with the standard techniques and many of the variations thereof, including ADM (arrow diagramming method), LOB (line of balance), and GERT (graphical evaluation and review technique), depending upon their specific requirements. In doing so we have also become conversant with such terms as early and late start, early and late finish, float (free, total, and negative), networks, subnets, fragnets, and the like.

The specifics of these scheduling techniques and definitions of terms have already been described very well elsewhere. Additionally, many organizations, including owners, engineers, contractors, and government agencies, have also developed their own project scheduling standards and procedures. Consequently, it is assumed that the reader is already familiar with the basic project scheduling techniques. The following paragraphs concentrate instead on those items which have been found to enhance development and use of the project schedule on major engineering/construction projects. The examples presented are representative of those encountered on large contracted projects and with which the reader is undoubtedly already familiar. However, similar conditions although of varying magnitude and criticality exist on virtually every project within the broad spectrum of industries which apply current management techniques.

Application of the methods described will obviously not guarantee a successful project, but should ensure production of a more meaningful project schedule and an overall beneficial project scheduling effort. Use of the term "project schedule" herein implies all basic scheduling documents including network diagrams, bar charts, histograms, progress curves, and computerized reports and listings.

SCHEDULE PURPOSES AND OBJECTIVES

Before embarking on development of the project schedule it is advisable to examine its basic premises and to have them clearly understood by all project participants. At a minimum, the following purposes and objectives should be established:

The project schedule is more than merely a scheduling document; it is a management tool, which is used as a basis for decision making. As such, the schedule is used by the project management team to: plan, schedule, monitor, control, report, forecast.

The project schedule is used by all project participants and should influence and will be influenced by activities of owners, engineers, contractors, vendors, utility companies, operators, and government entities alike, but in varying degrees.

The project schedule is a dynamic document which reflects both the project baseline (execution plan) and subsequent events which influence the original plan as the project proceeds.

The project schedule incorporates all direct project activities, at varying levels of detail, and interrelates those activities and necessary resources to predetermined milestones.

The project schedule establishes the relative priorities for all activities and focuses attention on those activities critical to achieving the earliest project completion date.

In order to achieve maximum benefits, project participants must be directly involved in the schedule preparation and fully committed to achieving the objectives set forth in the approved project schedule. If the project schedule is to be viewed as a means of wallpapering the various project offices its value is meaningless.

Acknowledgment of these scheduling premises is critical to ensuring a common goal for all project participants and will help to avoid misunderstandings during execution of the work. A statement regarding the intent and significance of the project schedule should be included in the basic project strategy or execution plan documents.

SCHEDULING SYSTEM SELECTION

Many different corporate-standard scheduling systems exist today which incorporate both computerized and manual methods. Most combine some in-house proprietary programs with those provided by several well-known project control software firms. Selection of the appropriate system to be used on a given project depends on several important variables.

These should be examined as early in the project as possible, preferably while the project is in the conceptual stage or in the bidding stage of a contracted project. On the latter type project, the owner will undoubtedly want to know how the scheduling issues will be handled before selecting a contractor. At this time the reasonable expectations from the project schedule should be established. The extent of the scheduling effort should be fully evaluated through a cost/benefit analysis. This analysis should examine the cost of developing and maintaining the project schedule versus the tangible and intangible benefits, including the positive corporate prestige to be obtained in meeting or bettering the schedule objectives.

One of the important elements is to examine the project itself. If the project is straightforward and short-lived without a large number of participants and interdependencies, a simple bar chart with periodic updating is usually sufficient. When the interrelationships between project participants and activities are critical to the project or when the time constraints assume critical significance, a network-based scheduling system should be examined. The use of computerized systems either on mainframes, minis or micros, will be dictated by the amount of detail to be processed and the anticipated frequency of updating.

Another important facet to analyze is the computer hardware and software already available in-house. Usually if the principal project participants have used the system successfully in previous applications, the probability of their acceptance and use again will be heightened. A review of the past experience of the users, both at management and supervisory levels, will also indicate the users' relative degree of sophistication and their potential for accepting another system should it be deemed more appropriate for the project. For a megaproject, which may have stand-alone computer capabilities, the use of any systems previously acquired for existing in-house use may not be readily transferrable to the project due to licensing agreements with proprietary software vendors and the availability of resources to support the system.

If it is determined that a sophisticated scheduling system is required from an outside source, there are several important factors to consider:

Total cost of system, either purchased or leased, and the reimbursability of same
Compatibility with in-house data processing hardware and expertise
Vendor support availability (particularly in the international environment)
Communications systems requirements and availability
Systems training required and provided
Compatibility of the system with the systems used by other project participants
Familiarity of scheduling personnel with the system
Validation of new system results, using sample of own or similar project data
Capability of system to produce desired and/or contracturally required results

Another option is to develop a unique scheduling system which is a combination of an existing in-house system and available outside project control packages. This option may combine the best features of several computerized and manual scheduling methods and include the knowledge and background of the responsible scheduling engineer.

SCHEDULING SYSTEM DEVELOPMENT

Regardless of the basis for the selected scheduling system it must be structured to the specific project to facilitate its use and to maximize resultant benefits.

The scheduling system should be well defined for reference by all project participants as early as possible after project initiation. The project procedures manual should include at least one section on the scheduling system to be used. Without being unduly cumbersome, this reference should be sufficiently detailed to inform the users of how the schedule will be developed, used, maintained, and updated. It should include responsibility flow diagrams which indicate the interrelationships for development of the supporting data for the scheduling effort, distribution of the schedules and accompanying reports, and identification of the project participants. Usually sample schedule formats are also included, as is a description of the schedule update cycle.

Of particular significance is the integration of the scheduling system with the work breakdown structure (WBS), cost control estimate, materials management system, and project progress report. It is important that these relationships be properly described and the adopted alphanumeric coding structure be consistent not only within the overall project cost and scheduling control system but also throughout all phases of the project.

The scheduling system should be installed on the project immediately, using whatever portions of the overall scheduling system are available. Schedule consciousness must be adopted early in the project due to the long-term effects of not meeting the initial project targets. In the beginning the system may be rather rudimentary and consist only of the master contract schedule, the list of milestones, and some short-interval working schedules, all of which are discussed in the following section. By starting the process early it will be easier to integrate the more detailed schedules as they are completed.

SCHEDULE PREPARATION

Project schedules, by their very nature, are evolutionary documents and their application is often dictated by the amount of detail which they contain. As the project progresses, more information will be available and the schedule will be appropriately refined to reflect the available data.

As stated earlier, there are many variations on the basic scheduling techniques within the overall guidelines provided in many instances by an organization's standard practices. However, within each of those frameworks there is often much latitude for the individual scheduling engineer to apply his/her own innovations in order to make the schedule work better for the specific project. In general, use of these particular techniques should be encouraged, provided that certain general practices are not violated.

The project schedule is an important tool for use by all project participants. Hence, it must be an easily understood, practical, pertinent, and current document. Care must be taken to avoid developing a project schedule which is so unwieldy, cumbersome and complex that it can only be used by the scheduling engineer. In order to maximize use of the document on the project, these precepts should be of foremost concern to the scheduling engineer.

General Considerations

There are several basic parameters which govern the preparation of all project schedules. Recognizing that all project schedules have at least the following common ingredients, it is well to understand the principal concerns associated with each.

1. The project participants' involvement is critical in preparing any schedule. Lack of this involvement has probably caused more schedules to be discarded than any other reason. Schedules should not be developed in a vacuum without benefit of the knowledge of those individuals who know the most about their respective project areas. Their assistance is essential in all phases of the project scheduling effort. In many respects the scheduling engineer functions as a coordinator who assembles and integrates the thoughts and plans of all the project participants.

2. Activities should be identified to describe the project in sufficient detail to satisfy the schedule objectives. Care should be taken to ensure that the activities are neither too broad nor too detailed for the intended purpose of the schedule. A conceptual schedule for a specific project at initiation may well have only a few very general activities, while subsequent issues may have several thousand activities. Essentially the best scheduling approach is to start with a broadly defined schedule and work toward a more detailed one. Activities selected for inclusion in the schedule should be describable in terms of times required for execution, definable completions, and responsibility assignments (controllable elements). Those activities occurring in the immediate future (three to six months) should be defined in more detail than those which follow. Later these subsequent activities can be more accurately described.

3. Durations should be assigned to each activity based on documented previous experience of the organization and other project participants, and either historical performance or quoted data from outside vendors and contractors. As a general rule, the assigned durations should have a 50% probability of achievement in order to establish a realistic overall schedule. If durations are assigned on a different basis, this basis should be clearly understood by all project participants so that proper considerations can be applied in their uses of the schedule. This is particularly necessary for the production personnel who must commence planning for operating the completed facility long before the project is finished. To facilitate early project scheduling, standard durations are often established for similar activities and these are later adjusted as project experience dictates. Development of these standard durations may be facilitated by referencing the project estimate (if it is available at this early stage in the project) and final historical data from other completed projects.

4. Interrelationships of the identified project activities should be analyzed to reflect the restraints between and among them. Proper identification of these logic ties can frequently eliminate bottlenecks in the subsequent execution of the project. Care should be exercised to include only those which are meaningful. Day-to-day working relationships which affect specific activities are usually best omitted from the schedule. Those which convey major decisions or actions between activities and significantly affect the subsequent activities must be included.

5. Responsibility centers should be identified for the execution of each activity. These centers may be either individuals or organizational entities. It is desirable that these responsibility centers be indicated on the scheduling documents as a means of focusing attention on project planning and performance.

6. Resource assignments should be made to either individual activities or groups of similar activities. The types of resources typically allocated include general manpower staffing, specific skills, equipment, space, infrastructure (when in a remote location), and materials. Resource requirements can usually be obtained from participants on previous projects, completed project data, individual experience and, when available, a detailed cost control estimate.

7. Formats of the project schedule may vary within a given project depending on the planned use of the documents, type of work being scheduled, and preferences of the individual project participants. Regardless of the schedule presentation format used, the concerns identified above must be considered in its development.

Project Master Schedule

At the beginning of a project, there is often very little definitive information available from which to develop a schedule. However, by careful examination of the project authorization documents and discussions with the originators of these documents, enough data can usually be found to prepare a generalized overall project schedule. As a result, the first project schedule may well consist of only a few activities and the identification of major target milestones. This document is commonly referred to as the project master schedule or master contract schedule. It may be part of the documentation for the owner's authorization to commit funds and is frequently found in an owner's bidding documents or a contractor's proposal documents, and as such, often provides the basis for contracting of services. Typical activities included in this schedule are broad functional categories of project work (engineering, procurement, construction, and commissioning). Depending on the project specifics, each of these categories may be further divided into project areas, respective engineering disciplines, procurement of long lead time delivery items and bulk materials, applicable construction disciplines, and commissioning of individual project systems.

Also included in the initial schedule is identification of "key milestones" either on which the schedule depends or which are established by the schedule itself. Examples of the former type milestones include date of project approval, contract award, funding and site availability, external utilities provision, and sales commitments for the final product. The other characteristic milestones include those usually associated with the start and completion of general activities (engineering completion, placement of major equipment purchase orders, jobsite mobilization, and mechanical completion). Dates for these milestones are often extracted form the schedule for use in senior management progress reporting.

The format for the project master schedule is typically a bar chart due to the usual lack of activity detail and discrete restraints identifiable at the time of preparation. If critical interrelationships can be identified at this stage of the project a time-phased logic diagram may be used to signify their importance to the overall project.

Project Detailed Schedules

Having either established or been provided with an overall project master schedule, the schedule should be divided into finite components for more detailed analysis. Typically this is accomplished by segregating the project into its traditional functional categories: engineering, procurement, construction, and commissioning, with appropriate divisions for areas and subareas. Another approach is to divide the project into areas or subareas first which then can be executed as semi-independent miniprojects within the overall project. This latter approach will probably also require converting these miniprojects into their functional categories. For most large contracted projects the former approach is preferred because of the traditional organizational mode of project execution where the engineering and procurement are often accomplished in one location and the construction in another. Either approach, however, requires that all functional activities be integrated to provide a complete perspective of the individual project areas and subareas.

A few special comments are appropriate for each of the functional schedules:

Engineering

In preparing the engineering schedule the most valuable source documents are the drawing and specification lists which identify each document by area, number, and title. These lists are usually divided first into engineering discipline (architectural, structural, electrical) and then into project areas. While this helps responsible engineering discipline supervisors plan and manage their activities, it is an illogical split for the project schedule. All engineering documents pertaining to each project area must be integrated with each other, the procurement activities, and construction or production needs. Only in this manner can execution of an entire project area be properly planned and controlled.

Rather than attempt preparation of an engineering schedule on a drawing-by-drawing basis, it is usually easier and more effective to schedule the drawings in packages divided according to discipline as they would normally be issued for bidding, fabrication, or construction. In this way the engineering discipline supervisor has the flexibility of completing the individual drawings in each package in whatever sequence he/she chooses, provided the scheduled completion date for the package is maintained.

Equally important in preparing the engineering schedule are the interfaces for three elements of the procurement cycle: (1) preparation of bills of materials and purchase requisitions, (2) technical review of vendor proposals, and (3) review of the vendor submittals, both preliminary and certified, and their incorporation into the engineering packages. The engineering schedule cannot be finalized until these restraints are properly identified.

Another activity to be included in the engineering schedule is the provision for owner comments and approvals by the owner or reviewing agency. Omission of this activity in the schedule usually leads to a very optimistic engineering schedule.

After completion of the schedule, the scheduled start and completion dates are entered on the appropriate source lists to facilitate use by the responsible engineering personnel.

Procurement

Availability of an equipment list and/or a set of flow sheets is vital in preparing a comprehensive procurement schedule. Use of standardized subnetworks showing engineering and procurement activities for the itemized listing of equipment can greatly simplify the scheduling effort here. Typical activities to be included in the procurement schedule are: development of bidders lists; preparation and issue of bid packages; vendor bidding period; technical and commercial bid tabulations, evaluations, and recommendations; award order; submission and review of vendor documents; fabrication; and delivery

International bidding requirements and foreign construction locations can substantially increase the durations for procurement activities, as well as add more activities to the procurement cycle, such as staging, ocean packaging and freight, import licensing, customs clearance, and inland transport.

A specialized element of the procurement schedule is that of individual vendor schedules. For complex and critical equipment items, as well as for strategic materials such as structural steel, it is recommended that requirements for provision of detailed fabrication, production, and delivery schedules be included in the purchase order along with provisions for access of project scheduling personnel to the vendor scheduling process.

Another element of the procurement schedule deals with the contracting and subcontracting process for various project services, principally in the areas of engineering/consulting and construction. It is important to stress in the bidding process that schedules are required for the contracted services and will be incorporated not only in the overall project schedule but also in the contractural documents. Thus, it is also desirable to ensure that the scheduling systems used by all project participants are compatible and that all scheduling information is provided in a consistent manner.

Construction

Many feel that the construction schedule is the easiest to prepare of the four functional categories on a large contracted engineering/construction project. Examples of this phase of the project schedule in other industries may include the manufacturing and assembly of production units or the compilation and integration of many documents into a complete publication. Regardless of the type of project, this is primarily due to the ease of visualizing actual materials being assembled and/or equipment being installed. Yet it is this arena where the various elements identified in the engineering and procurement schedules must be integrated. As a general rule, all structures and major equipment, along with supporting piping and electrical utilities, should be shown on the construction schedule. Care must be taken that the background of the responsible scheduling engineer does not lead to a distorted number of construction activities in the area of his or her expertise. A reasonable balance should be stressed in order to maximize schedule benefits. Areas of consideration include the scheduling of special construction equipment which must be shared by the entire project and the availability of infrastructure to accommodate the manpower required to execute the work. Another area of concern in scheduling the construction aspect of the project is the availability of skilled craftspeople in a given jobsite location and their productivity level.

Early in the project it is usually sufficient to include a single checkout and test activity for each major system in the construction portion of the schedule. Other activities occurring near the checkout and test timeframe include correction of punchlist items and cleanup of the various project facilities. Durations for these activities are frequently estimated based on previous experience. Both of these activities relate directly to the project mechanical completion milestone. Therefore, as the project proceeds toward this target, these activities need to be better defined and appropriately scheduled. Lastly, refurbishing and renovation activities, if appropriate, as well as demobilization should be included in the construction schedule.

Commissioning

Project commissioning activities are usually accomplished by a specialized group involving engineering, construction, and operations personnel. Since the concluding event in this arena is the turnover of a fully operational project, completion and commissioning of the various systems must be sequenced so that an effective transition from construction to operations can be achieved in an orderly and timely manner. Thus, development of this functional schedule is critical to the operations, maintenance, and production plans of the owner. It is at this juncture where the project schedule and the owner's plans are merged. Only with a well-planned series of interfaces can the completed facility undergo the required checkout and turnover activities which are necessary to attain the subsequent production goals.

It is important not only to establish responsibilities for developing this schedule as early as possible in the project but also to initiate efforts on the commissioning activities themselves. Special activities to be identified in the commissioning schedule include completion of startup, operations, and maintenance manuals; delivery of special commissioning tools and chemicals; provision of required utilities; acquisition of services of skilled vendor representatives; development of turnover procedures; and completion of operator training.

Functional Schedule Integration

Although it may appear that each of the functional schedules can be done independently of the others, the converse is actually true. While project participants may only be using a specific functional schedule, the timing of the activities in that schedule depends on completion of the preceding activities. The more closely the activity approaches the critical path of the project the greater its influence will be on the timing of all preceding and succeeding activities.

Therefore, it is necessary to integrate the project schedule's functional components. When combined they must represent a valid perspective of the work to be accomplished and properly indicate the timing for completion of the project activities. As part of the integration process, a careful check should be made of all interrelationships between the activities. A thorough examination of the critical path is also an absolute necessity. This must be accomplished to ensure that the logic relationships not only are legitimate but also connect the appropriate activities.

Review and Approval

As stated earlier, a project schedule is only as good as the project participants' commitments to making it work. Their involvement in its preparation with respect to their areas of expertise is vital. A recycle of the preliminary product is also important. Information supplied regarding a single activity may assume an entirely different perspective when viewed in relationship to other activities. The performance of an activity in parallel with others versus its sequential execution may completely change the entire schedule. Thus, it is advisable to convene a meeting of the responsibility centers and the project director for the purpose of reviewing the overall schedule before its publication. The project schedule should be issued as a representative joint venture production of the combined responsibility centers, each of whom has indicated commitment to it by affixing his or her signature on the basic document.

PROJECT SCHEDULE UTILIZATION

Maximum benefits can only be attained from the project schedule through its continual use by the project participants. The scheduling engineer has the responsibility for ensuring that the document is provided to the proper project personnel in a timely manner and that it is updated periodically to reflect progress and changing project conditions.

Use of the project schedule differs with the varying supervisory levels of the organizaiton. Consequently, the project schedule should be developed so that only the applicable segments need to be provided to the individual supervisors and managers.

For first-line supervision it is possible that the level of detail will not be satisfactory for the day-to-day or hour-to-hour scheduling required to perform the work. Here the supervisors will rely on the project schedule to set target completions and will prepare more detailed short interval schedules for their own purposes. For example, a schedule for the concrete construction superintendent may be detialed to show building foundation, equipment pads, and slab on grade. In turn, he or she will further divide the schedule into individual building column footings and grade beams, individual equipment foundations, and segments of the floor slab. In this manner proper planning and

control of manpower, equipment, and materials can be exercised. Experience
has shown that the project schedule portrayed in bar chart format is most
beneficial here.

At the functional manager level, the project schedule must reflect the applicable
discipline schedules and the manner in which they relate to each other: the
relationships of the underground utilities, concrete construction, structural
steel, building enclosure, equipment installation, electrical and piping services,
and the architectural finishes. Generally the level of detail in the project schedule
is sufficient for use by the functional manager without further detailing. Time-
phased logic diagrams and summary level bar chart presentations are valuable
at this level.

At the project director level, project information should be condensed to provide
data relative to milestones and summary level bar charts by functional categories or project areas.

At the executive level schedule information should be consolidated even further
to provide an overview of planned, forecast, and actual project major milestones.

Monitoring and updating the project schedule should be done on a systematic and timely
basis. The easiest way to accomplish these tasks is through use of the basic schedule
documents. Supervisors should be responsible for performing these tasks within their
respective area and should be assisted in doing so by the scheduling engineer. This
joint effort should produce consistency among the various supervisors and managers
and help to ensure accuracy of the provided data. Items to be considered in this update include: remaining durations for those activities already started, completed activities, identification of any other activities to be added to the schedule, and any
changes in the planned method for executing the work which would result in logic
modifications. The scheduling engineer is then responsible for consolidating the
current data into the project schedule. The monitoring and updating cycle should
coincide with the project requirements for reporting of cost, schedule and progress
data.

Management reporting via the project schedule can be accomplished by using a milestone listing showing the planned, forecast, and actual dates for accomplishment of
certain activities. Another graphic approach is through use of target reporting where
summary level bar charts showing the original schedule are maintained, with the periodically revised schedules shown beneath the original schedule bars. In this manner
improvement or slippages in the schedule can be readily seen and attention focused
on those which need expediting.

Progress review meetings using the project schedule as the primary agenda are
very useful. These meetings are usually coordinated by the scheduling engineer and
are attended by key supervisory personnel and the project director. They are held
immediately after issuance of the schedule update and progress report. In these sessions those activities which are behind schedule are reviewed in some detail with the
responsible supervisor identifying the problems causing the delays and actions being
taken to mitigate these delays. Assistance required from other supervisors and the
project director should also be indicated. The sessions also serve as "brain storming"
opportunities for exploring means of accelerating overall completion of the work.

SCHEDULE FORECASTS

A project is continually changing and the schedule should be "statused" to reflect these
changes on a current basis. As originally prepared, the project schedule is a baseline
describing what activities are required to meet the project objectives. That baseline
is maintained with schedule performance planned in accordance with it and progress
measured against it in terms of scheduled accomplishments. All project efforts should
concentrate on making the schedule happen as delineated in the baseline.

However, changes often occur which make attainment of the baseline schedule
either impossible or economically unfeasible. When this happens it is necessary to make
a schedule forecast, that is, a prediction or projection of the schedule based on the
project performance to date and the current outlook. In this situation, honesty is the
best policy: seldom do things improve markedly. When indications are that changes
are having a significant (greater than 10%) effect on the schedule, it is advisable to expend the effort to review the project schedule completely and make a formal schedule
forecast. This regrouping often has a positive impact on performance of the entire
project team due to the schedule's new realism and the team's sense of goal attainability.

A project schedule forecast should not be undertaken lightly. It should be done
only after all methods for accelerating the work to meet the baseline schedule have been
explored and the concomitant cost/benefit analysis of taking corrective action has been
made. This cost/benefit analysis must include considerations of the actual project costs
and benefits as well as those overall objectives of the owner, that is, market position
and conditions and return on investment. The schedule forecast is developed in a
manner similar to the detailed schedule preparation described earlier. The forecast
should focus on those areas on or near the project critical path and those which are
significantly behind schedule.

SCHEDULE POSTSCRIPT

Although no two projects are identical, there are often many similarities in the types
of projects performed. Therefore, the project schedule may play an important role
on subsequent projects and should be regarded as one of the project assets. To
maximize its use on future projects, the following steps are necessary:

A section of the project final report should be devoted to the project schedule,
    identifying the achievements versus the baseline schedule, the reasons for
    any significant deviations, and key schedule issues encountered together with
    how they were overcome.
Copies of the principal project schedule documents should be retained, including
    network diagrams; target versus actual bar charts of manpower, resources
    and quantities; histograms comparing actual use with those scheduled; and
    various progress curves based on the schedule data.
Also important is a brief document describing the scheduling techniques used,
    their effectiveness, and recommendations for future improvements.

SUMMARY

The project schedule is an important planning and control tool for the project management practitioner. Equally important is the staff which prepares this document and
assists the project team in using it to complete the project in a timely manner. Regardless of the apparent quality of the documents produced, the efforts expended may be
of limited value if the project schedule is not used by the project participants. Experienced and adaptable scheduling personnel are necessary to ensure that positive
results are obtained.

There are many variations in the project schedule format and techniques. As project management practitioners become more familiar with them and personally experience the benefits which can be obtained from their application, they will become their
greatest proponents. Further, as more scheduling systems become available for microcomputers and mainframe computers are not longer required, the project manager with
desktop scheduling capabilities will become the established norm. Utilization of the
methods described herein will assist him/her in obtaining the maximum benefits from
the scheduling effort.

BIBLIOGRAPHY

Bent, James A. *Applied Cost and Schedule Control.* New York: Marcel Dekker, 1982.

Guthrie, Kenneth M. et al. *Managing Capital Expenditures for Construction Projects.* Craftsman Book Company of America, 1977.

O'Brien, James J. (ed.). *Scheduling Handbook.* New York: McGraw-Hill, Inc., 1969.

Stuckenbruck, Linn C. (ed.). *The Implementation of Project Management. The Professionals Handbook.* Reading, MA: Addison Wesley Publishing Company, 1981.

6

The Project Budget

EDWARD A. WYNANT* *Exxon Research & Engineering Company, Florham Park, New Jersey*

The project budget is the basis for fiscal control throughout the life of the project. Estimates and budgets differ. An estimate precedes and is the basis for the development of the budget. The budget may be higher or lower than the estimate and represents a set of conditioned numbers, submitted to and approved by management, which are used to monitor and control the costs of project activities.

Developing and budgeting projects entails a multifaceted and coordinated effort involving various skills, functions, and responsibilities. In large industrial corporations this means devoting considerable resources to increase the chances that the venture will be considered. Areas of expertise required run the gamut of business and engineering skills and tools including market surveys and analyses, financial analyses, cost estimating and scheduling, planning and budgeting cycles, and investment advisory committee reviews. Most corporations have established procedures for budgeting and project appropriations. These may be very similar in nature.

We will deal primarily with the aspects of the budgeting process especially as it applies to the owner, and, where appropriate, contractor involvement in this process.

CAPITAL EXPENDITURE PROGRAMS

Most successful corporations plan for their capital expenditure programs a number of years into the future. Initially, a project may appear within the overall program with only the total preliminary estimated cost with proposed start/completion dates. These major programs require a sophisticated approach to the budgetary process. For routine minor projects, involving moderate capital expenditures, operating groups are usually responsible for developing their own budget programs. For major capital projects the procedures are complex and usually require expertise from the owner's project management and technical organizations; and, where required, contractor assistance. Programs involving capital expenditures and expansions covering planned projects are sometimes referred to as "Cap Ex." "Cap Ex" programs are essential to corporate health and growth. The reliability of the project cost estimates is critical to the success of these programs.

Current affiliation: Consultant, Basking Ridge, New Jersey

An axiom among owners says that "only when a contractor has a lump-sum price does he feel that 'hard money' is at stake." However, to an owner all committed projects are "hard money." Every expenditure required for project activities from early feasibility studies through startup of the facility comes out of the company coffers and can be recovered only if the venture proves profitable. Accurate budgeting is important to ensure the validity of decisions regarding venture viability and to minimize losses from abandoned ventures.

Many owners do not maintain the skills in-house to facilitate independent development of project budgets. Frequently owners develop preliminary budgets and proceed through early project approval phases utilizing semidetailed estimating techniques. Contractor assistance is then obtained to develop detailed cost estimates to be incorporated in venture analyses and used for finalizing the appropriation of funds.

THE CONCEPT OF PROJECT PHASES

Owners can minimize the amount of capital at risk by staging approvals of project funding. The term "advanced funds approval" is used to imply the same concept. Approval stages should be tied to project phases to reflect the additional information available about the project as it proceeds through development. At each approval stage, the owner has a quantification of the funds at risk should he decide to terminate the project. Implementation of projects involves several distinct phases. For purposes of describing the budgeting/project approval stages, these phases are broken down as follows:

Project Conception

Project evaluation through the feasibility and screening studies.

Project Inception/Project Development

Owners begin definitive planning and proceed into basic engineering work which may be supported by a contractor.

Contracting

Most owners do not maintain in-house capability to perform full detailed mechanical design, procurement, and construction. All of the activities required to engage a contractor to perform these services such as capability surveys, contractor screening, bid solicitation, bid preparation, and evaluation of the bids are a part of this phase. To some extent these activities can overlap with the preceding phase.

Project Execution

This phase may be divided into two subphases: mechanical design and procurement, and construction. Many major contractors maintain an integrated expertise and capability to handle the work of both subphases. Others specialize in one or the other. Construction of the Alaskan pipeline, the largest construction project ever undertaken by private enterprise, illustrates use of both types of contractors. The mechanical design and procurement for the pipeline was performed utilizing the services of one major engineering contractor, while the construction was performed by five separate joint ventures composed of independent contractors. The mechanical design, procurement, and construction of the pump stations and southern terminal facilities were done by one major prime contractor.

Figure 1 illustrates the four project phases, and lists the types of activities that take place during each.

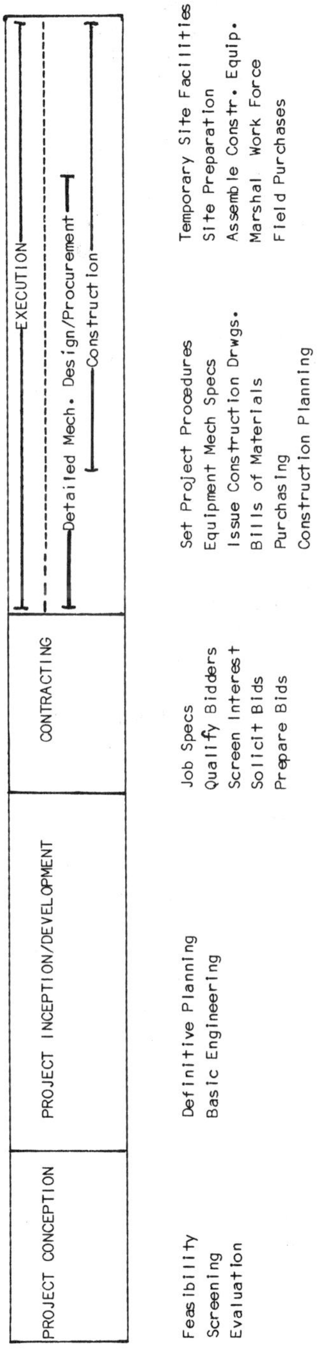

Figure 1 Project phases.

PHASED PROJECT APPROVALS

Project phases provide convenient and logical milestones for establishing project approval stages. Project phases are sometimes broken down differently by combining phases or subdividing them in some other manner. Most important is that the division into project phases must provide discreet, stand-alone check points at which additional information may be reviewed and project desirability evaluated before proceeding further.

Owners and their front-end contractors working during project conception should establish cost engineering practices to clearly define the degree of project development required to prepare cost estimates of a satisfactory level of accuracy at the various approval stages. These cost engineering practices are applied in conjunction with broader owner policies governing the project budgeting process. Based on sufficient estimating experience, statistical accuracies can be established for estimates at each phase of development to assist in defining the amount of risk at each approval stage. Experience shows that the reliability of cost estimates depends more on the degree and accuracy of project definition than the actual estimating information. The estimating methodology should include all elements of project costs. It is not so important that some elements are estimated in great detail as it is to be sure that others which may be poorly defined are not overlooked.

Estimate contingency should not be relied upon to cover standard elements of cost.

PROJECT CONCEPTION APPROVAL

The owner must approve early project studies and estimates without a real knowledge of the order of magnitude of the ultimate project cost. This is a recognized cost of doing business. Costs during the conceptual phase of the project can extend over a lengthy period of time, especially if repeated studies are called for. The owner should determine a rough project cost at the earliest possible moment and make a "go/no go" decision based on an early estimate and a corresponding preliminary viability calculation. This first approval stage will cover only funds for early studies.

PROJECT INCEPTION/DEVELOPMENT

The next stage of approval usually entails authorization for continuing expenditures to develop the project conceptually. This stage of approval authorizes work on definitive planning and basic engineering. At the beginning of this phase, the owner selects a case for development based on the earlier screening studies. A milestone is reached when a design basis has been completely defined. The owner's representative will agree or will modify and make specific changes to this basis. Cost estimates are made reflecting this revised and firmer basis and upon the additional project information developed to date.

CONTRACTING PHASE

If work is authorized to continue, the owner can now proceed to prepare a job specification for contract bidding and do any additional basic engineering work required to facilitate the mechanical design work.

PROJECT EXECUTION PHASE

The greatest amount of money is put at risk at this stage of approval. Up to the point of committing the entire project and proceeding with an integrated detailed mechanical design and procurement effort, the project can be terminated at a relatively nominal cost. After execution has seriously begun, cancellation has a significant monetary implication. A project that has been allowed to reach the execution phase and then is shut down by spiraling forecasts, may be characterized as a "once in a career" project. This underlines the importance of a reliable and accurate budgeting process to the responsible project manager.

Depending on the location of the interface between the owner and the contractor, an additional approval step may be introduced into the project. At the completion of the basic engineering work a more detailed and accurate cost estimate may be prepared prior to appropriating funds for the entire project. This step requires assuming a risk of losing a portion of the engineering work necessary for the additional details.

PROJECT ANNUAL BUDGETS

The fiscal or budgetary practices of some owners call for breaking project costs into estimated annual expenditures in order to make appropriation of funds on a fiscal year basis. Such procedures only complicate accounting and reconciliation requirements and do little to improve project cost control. The additional resources required can detract from real project control. A schedule change of project activities can completely throw off the timing of expenditures but not, in fact, alter the total project cost forecast. From a project position, the budgeting of funds should be on an activity basis and not made to conform artificially to a calendar basis.

TYPES OF ESTIMATES AND METHODOLOGY

It is not the intent here to provide the techniques necessary for project cost estimating and scheduling. Those involved in project management should be aware of the necessary skills and should understand the underlying philosophy.

The degree of complete and positive knowledge or "firmness" at any stage of project definition is the most important element in estimating accuracy. Estimating methodology should reflect the amount and type of information available at the various approval stages. An estimate developed in conjunction with early feasibility studies, if it is prepared and presented in great detail, can delude project sponsors into attributing far greater accuracy than can possibly be justified.

PITFALLS OF EARLY ESTIMATES

The $7.8 billion Trans-Alaskan Pipeline System (TAPS) project represents a remarkable achievement in terms of cost management skills required to bring a complex project to a successful completion. Built during years of rampant inflation from 1974 to 1977 and requiring some 150 million construction jobhours, the successful completion of this work is worthy of note.

However, the feasibility estimate prepared in 1968 projected the cost for the TAPS project to be $900 million. The detailed estimate conveyed a grossly misleading impression of the accuracy of the number. The $900 million dollar estimate was undoubtedly an accurate picture of costs on the basis provided, which largely reflected pipeline design and construction in much friendlier environments. While it was recognized that much of the construction would be over permafrost, very little was known about design requirements in the hostile Arctic region and it was not possible at that time to accurately assess the impact of these conditions on facilities to support life and work. *Alaska Pipeline Stipulations*, the federal government's book on design and construction conformance requirements, would not be issued for several years. The feasibility estimate would have been much more reliable if these ground rules had been available. The work put into the cost details of the known scope was largely invalidated because of the great number of major unknown factors which would be encountered later.

The TAPS project is only one instance which demonstrates problems with early cost estimates. The Business Roundtable (BRT) Construction Industry Cost Effectiveness Project Report A-6 "Modern Management Systems" dated November 1982 found that early estimates have a wide range of variability: "most often they are notoriously low." Owners' budgets are often set during early stages of the project definition and without a rigorous analysis of the accuracies of individual costs. The BRT study group said that the figures developed early in a project are often only very crude estimates. The owners have very unrealistic expectations for the accuracy of these early figures.

A Rand Corporation analysis of estimates of more than forty oil and chemical process plant pioneer plants built from the late 1960s to the early 1980s showed that, on average, costs more than doubled in going from R&D phase estimates to final costs. Even after the project definition phase, the final cost increase was one and two-thirds above the estimate. Rand found a scarcity of systems for tracking project cost history. It is not surprising that they found that cost estimates today are no more accurate than they were in the 1960s. Rand identified two very significant managerial obstacles to accurate estimates:

1. Project advocates force justification of why the early numbers should not be less.
2. Most companies are not willing to invest the resources necessary to develop better estimating practices.

The Business Roundtable Report A-6 (1982) concludes that "In almost all cases, the ineffectiveness of project management is directly traceable to the lack of modern management systems that help management to establish and achieve realistic goals for schedule, cost and quality."

Estimating methodology should consider the amount of valid information available at various approval stages; and different estimating approaches should apply at different project phases. The accuracy of past estimates at various phases of projects should be recorded, so that the project sponsor can gauge the degree of risk involved in funding at each phase of the project. The major commitment of project costs, the point at which continuing means incurring significant unrecoverable costs if the project is cancelled, occurs upon release of the project execution. The estimate at this point should be the most definitive that can be prepared, and even so will be somewhat conceptual in nature as many of the detailed execution plans are still being formulated and only predictions of project performance can be used.

A COLLABORATIVE EFFORT

There are far more poor estimates than there are poor efforts by estimators. The preparation of estimates used for setting budgets should include contributions by the entire technical organization. The project manager should see that the estimating effort is properly orchestrated so that all of the individuals involved in developing the project should agree with and, in a sense, "own" the estimate and have a high level of commitment to it. The amount ultimately budgeted should be a fair representation of their combined efforts.

ESTIMATE CLASSIFICATION SYSTEMS

To develop accurate statistics as mentioned above, basic definitions of the various types of estimates and their requirements should be established so that information collected from the various projects will be comparable. Keeping this same system will permit a valid comparison of the performance predicted and realized on subsequent projects. Continuity is also important for the wide acceptance, understanding, and use of the system throughout the company. Everyone involved in project approval and implementation must be able to assess the degree of risk associated with decisions based upon estimates made at various stages during the project.

It stands to reason that the more diversified the operations of a company, the more difficulty there will be in establishing the basic estimate class definitions and requirements. A company whose capital projects are all similar (all chemical manufacturing plants) will be able to use "pat" terms to define the estimating requirements for these traditional projects. These terms are more likely to be universally understood. In those companies where the nature of the capital projects is diverse, the terms and requirements need more exact and explicit definition. The system needs to be broader and applicable to a wider spectrum of usage. These objectives should be kept in mind when specifying an estimate classification system:

> The system should be capable of covering all types of estimates that are contemplated.
> The system should be rigid enough that there can be an understanding and dependence on the degree of reliability of each class.
> Various departments/sections should be responsible for specific input to the estimates.
> The system should be reviewed periodically to avoid proliferation of estimate classes and unnecessary, obsolete, or redundant statistical information.

When developing an estimate classification system, the following subjects need to be considered:

> Effects of new technology
> Different estimating methods for different stages of project development
> Effects of project size on relative costs
> Uncertainties involved with pioneer projects
> Accuracy versus cost of developing information tradeoffs at various stages of project development
> Unusual project conditions:
>> joint venture ownership
>> complex project financing
>> unconventional project organization
>> permitting/regulatory difficulties
>> new business/geographic areas
>> unique project development approaches
>> "hostile" environment
>> extended project durations
>> uncertain economic environment
>> revamp, retrofit, or expansion projects
>> stringent resource restraints

Figure 2 shows the relationship between estimate classes and project phases. Estimate classes are from "unclassified" to "E" through "A" in increasing order of accuracy. Project activities are shown as they relate to the estimate classifications.

Figure 3 is a suggested matrix defining a sample estimate classification system. It is more detailed than many such systems. This additional detail is provided to enhance understanding of the subject and increase the range of application. For example, an estimate may not be classified as a Class "B" estimate unless all of the requirements stipulated for a Class "B" estimate have been fulfilled.

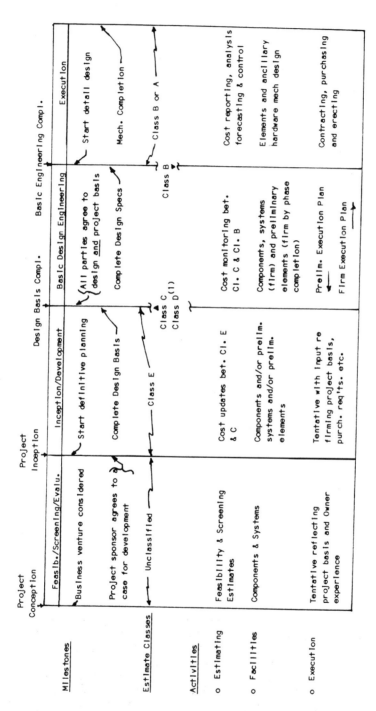

Figure 2 Relationship between estimate classes and project phases.

(1) Estimates are classified as D when they are prepared at the design basis point but do not meet all the criteria for a Class C designation. E.g. Revamp projects, projects with significant new technology or projects lacking information on other estimate criteria such as lack of firm information on regulatory requirements.

```
                                                           ●  Firm
                                                           o  Preliminary
                                                           x  Implicit
```

```
                        PROJECT ESTIMATES
                   SAMPLE ESTIMATE CLASSIFICATION
```

Information Required	Un-Classif'd	E	D	C	B	A
1. Project Milestones						
a. Business venture considered	●	●	●	●	●	●
b. Project sponsor selects case for develop.	o	●	●	●	●	●
c. Definitive planning started	x	●	●	●	●	●
d. Complete design basis	x	x	●	●	●	●
e. All parties agree to design & project basis	x	x	o	●	●	●
f. Design specs completed	x	x	x	o	●	●
g. Start detailed design	x	x	x	x	o	●
2. Facilities Definition						
a. Site location and size						
- General location	o	●	●	●	●	●
- Size Parameter (e.g. bbls of thruput, tons of solids feed, etc.)	o	●	●	●	●	●
- Yield chart and product slate	o	o	●	●	●	●
b. Onsite and offsite unit configuration						
- Onsite and offsite areas defined	o	o	●	●	●	●
- Major facilities layout defined by unit blocks	x	x	●	●	●	●
- Individual equipment layout	x	x	o	o	●	●
- Grade elevations established for major areas	x	x	●	●	●	●
- Critical layout considerations	x	x	●	●	●	●
c. Site selection						
- Identification of alternate sites	x	o	●	●	●	●
- Land for final site purchased or optioned	x	o	●	●	●	●
d. Engineering Survey						
- Meteorological conditions	x	x	●	●	●	●
- Seismic data	x	x	●	●	●	●
- Hydrographic data	x	x	●	●	●	●
- Topographical data	x	x	●	●	●	●
- Local codes	x	x	●	●	●	●
- Available infrastructures	x	o	●	●	●	●
- Utilities availability/reliability	x	o	●	●	●	●
e. Lab work - demonstration runs						
- Lab testing of resource characteristics	x	x	●	●	●	●
- Lab or pilot testing for process or equipment selection	x	x	●	●	●	●
- Lab or pilot testing to provide design parameters	x	x	●	●	●	●

Figure 3

PROJECT ESTIMATES
SAMPLE ESTIMATE CLASSIFICATION (Cont'd)

Information Required	Un-Classif'd	E	D	C	B	A
f. Soils and Hydrographic data						
- Soils investigation	x	o	o	o	●	●
- Heavy loads identified	x	x	o	o	●	●
- Costly pile foundations identified	x	x	o	o	●	●
- Foundation design parameters	x	x	●	●	●	●
- Foundation design	x	x	o	o	●	●
- Unusual mobilization features	x	x	●	●	o	●
- Approx. elevations for major blocks	x	x	●	●	●	●
- Approx. elevations for major equipment	x	x	o	o	●	●
- Source of borrow material identified	x	x	●	●	●	●
- Survey and topo maps available	x	o	●	●	●	●
- Unique soils and civil features ident.	x	x	●	●	●	●
- Ground water conditions ident.	x	x	●	●	●	●
- Bathymetric data available	x	o	●	●	●	●
g. Owner project practices						
- Establish engineering standards	x	x	o	o	●	●
h. General offsites						
- Buildings, shops, labs definition	x	x	o	o	●	●
- Mobile Equip.	x	x	o	o	●	●
- Maintenance facilities defined	x	x	o	o	●	●
- Warehouse facilities defined	x	x	o	o	●	●
- Accomodations definition	x	x	o	o	●	●
- Port, rail, airport facil. defined	x	x	o	o	●	●
- Communications system def.	x	x	o	o	●	●
- Access roads/railroad def.	x	x	o	o	●	●
i. General						
- Optimization studies						
+ Process selection	x	x	●	●	●	●
+ Feedstock system	x	x	●	●	●	●
+ Product movement system	x	x	●	●	●	●
+ Utility supply method	x	x	●	●	●	●
+ Major driver selection	x	x	●	●	●	●
+ Purchased vs. generated power	x	o	●	●	●	●
- Additional studies required						
+ Areas leading to go/no-go decision	x	o	●	●	●	●
+ Unique features	x	o	●	●	●	●
+ Areas critical to operability	x	o	●	●	●	●
+ Areas critical as to technical risk	x	x	●	●	●	●
+ Areas typical of previous experience	x	x	o	o	●	●
+ Areas typical but large increase in size	x	x	o	o	●	●
j. Reviews						
- Reviews to agree on project basis	o	o	●	●	●	●
- Reviews of facilities description at various phases	o	o	●	●	●	●
- Reviews for safety	x	o	●	●	●	●
- Reviews to agree on changes which alter direction or intent	o	o	●	●	●	●
- Reviews to agree on modifications to job philosophy	o	o	●	●	●	●

Figure 3 (cont.)

PROJECT ESTIMATES
SAMPLE ESTIMATE CLASSIFICATION (Cont'd)

Information Required	Un-Classif'd	E	D	C	B	A
3. Execution Definition						
a. Schedule						
- Project milestones defined	o	o	•	•	•	•
- Project Execution strategy defined	o	o	o	•	•	•
- Source of resources and req'ts. defined	x	o	o	•	•	•
b. Contracting strategy						
- Owners objectives & procedures defined	o	o	o	•	•	•
- Contract survey	x	o	•	•	•	•
- Develop/review strategy with owner	x	o	•	•	•	•
c. Project Execution Planning						
- Define project background	o	o	•	•	•	•
- Define project environment	o	o	•	•	•	•
- Finalize contracting plan	x	x	o	•	•	•
- Define materials procurement procedures	x	x	o	o	•	•
- Define field construction execution basis	x	x	o	o	•	•
- Define management milestones	x	o	o	o	•	•
- Define project organization	x	x	o	o	•	•
- Define project control system	x	x	o	o	•	•
- Develop coordination procedures	x	x	o	o	•	•
d. Contract award	x	x	x	x	o	•
4. Regulatory Requirements						
a. Laws, regulations and other statutory requirements						
- Concession terms agreed	x	o	•	•	•	•
- Requirements for using local materials, firms and personnel	x	o	•	•	•	•
- Work permits	x	o	•	•	•	•
- Visa requirements	x	o	•	•	•	•
- Certification	x	o	•	•	•	•
- Permitting requirements	x	o	•	•	•	•
- Government agency approval req'ts.	x	o	•	•	•	•
- Sociopolitical requirements	x	o	•	•	•	•
b. Environmental						
- Environmental field survey	x	x	o	•	•	•
- Environmental design criteria	x	x	o	•	•	•
- Contacts and agreements with authorities	x	x	o	•	•	•
- Toxics control review	x	x	o	•	•	•
- Environmental impact statement	x	o	o	•	•	•
5. Estimating						
a. General economic level of location	x	•	•	•	•	•
b. Cost survey	x	o	•	•	•	•
c. Project Feedback/histories						
- For industrialized locations						
+ From country	x	•	•	•	•	•
+ From general area	x	o	o	o	•	•
+ From project location	x	x	o	o	o	o
- For LDC's/hostile locations						
+ From country	o	•	•	•	•	•
+ From general area	x	•	•	•	•	•
+ From project location	x	o	•	•	•	•

Figure 3 (cont.)

CONTINGENCY

Various definitions of "contingency" have become institutionalized in various companies and sectors of the construction industry. The perspectives of owners and contractors differ with their different requirements and responsibilities. Even within one organization, there are varying interpretations of the word. Within a single organization, contingency must be defined so that all of the individuals involved with assessing and assigning contingency have a mutual understanding of the term as it applies there.

A theory which the author supports is that contingency should correct for estimate basis. Not estimating basis (although this is one element of contingency), but *estimate* basis, i.e., the "organizational product." This means tying it into the historical performance experience of the organization. (For another good argument for keeping accuracy statistics, see foregoing section on Estimate Classification Systems.) Each element of project cost growth (analyzed after the fact) should be addressed in developing the amount of contingency to include for each class estimate, that is, estimating errors/omissions; normal project changes to facilities definition; average degree of precision in defining field conditions, e.g., soil conditions; minor changes in execution basis, e.g., switching from direct hiring to subcontracting portions of the work, and so forth. Of course, this means the amount of contingency included will vary with the class of estimate.

Following this concept in defining contingency leads to a logical conclusion about what it should cover. It does not make sense to make contingency all-inclusive because the budgeting process would be adversely impacted. For instance, cost growth due to project *basis* changes should not be included in contingency analysis. That is, if an owner embarks on a venture to construct a football stadium at a sports complex and then changes it to a race track, the budgeting process should start all over rather than the same appropriation being continued with the hope that contingency will cover the change in basis. The same is true for *scope* change. "Scope" in this sense is meant to infer size or capacity. For example, if the football stadium venture had envisioned a facility with a seating capacity of 35,000 and later on this is changed to 70,000, the budget scope has been altered and contingency should not be designed to cover it. Differentiating between "basis" and "scope" change may be a matter of symantics. However, the point is that in either case trying to provide for this type of change in the project contingency would burden the project budgets unduly and probably kill many viable projects.

Additional perspectives on project contingencies have been expressed by Clark and Lorenzoni (1985).

Contingency, although assessed on a line item basis, is best expressed as a single figure in the budget. As the project progresses, approved transfers may be made from the single figure to the line item to facilitate project control.

CHANGE OF SCOPE

It is particularly important that a definite scope be established early on any project proceeding on a reimbursable basis. On this type of project there is great difficulty in fixing scope, and there may be confusion in what is included in the estimate and what isn't. All estimates must be accompanied by a list of assumptions which were made for that particular estimate. The probable validity of these assumptions must be evaluated during the assignment of contingency.

Change control throughout the job is of the utmost importance in keeping a handle on project expenditures. Tight control over introduction of unnecessary changes and modifications will reduce problems in adhering to the project budget. Approved changes must be incorporated into the budget in a timely manner.

RECAPPING THE BUDGET PROCESS

The budgeting process is not an "event" but rather a series of continuing activities. These activities are tied into project phases, culminating in approval stages. Each approval stage is a decision point. Cost engineering practices should be established to clearly define the degree of project development required to prepare acceptable cost estimates at each of the approval stages.

The degree of firmness in the project definition and development is the most important element in improving the accuracy of cost estimates and, consequently, improving budgeting. The budgeting process should be well-disciplined and controlled by formalized policies. When a contractor is called upon to assist in the preparation of studies and budgets, the owner should establish the parameters by which the contractor works. The owner should be intimately involved, as he will ultimately assume the financial obligation. The owner has an interest in conserving capital, and the budgeting process should minimize funds at risk without inhibiting cost optimization. Approval stages should be set to provide termination of the project without incurring unnecessary capital loss.

The bottom line is that every effort should be made to facilitate a "go" project. The budgeting process should encourage bringing projects to a successful fruition and not act as an impediment to capital investments. Capital expansion programs are essential to the growth and well-being of industry.

REFERENCES

Clark, F. D., and Lorenzoni, A. B., *Applied Cost Engineering*, 2nd ed. New York: Marcel Dekker, 1985.

Modern Management Systems. Construction Industry Cost Effectiveness Project Report No. A-6, 1982. New York: The Business Roundtable. P. 1.

VI
ENGINEERING

UNIT OVERVIEW

The engineering portion of a project is seen by many of the participants as being the key phase. Others view engineering as only a preliminary step necessary for reaching the important part of the work—the field construction. Neither viewpoint is wholly valid, but both have elements of truth.

Another way of looking at engineering is that it is really just a continuation of the detailed planning process. Engineering drawings and specifications are viewed as being no more than extensions of the overall project plan, whose purpose is to detail what is planned for installation at the jobsite in order to fulfill the project objectives.

Chapters in this unit are directed toward making the project manager's job easier. Knowing certain aspects of the engineering work which have caused problems on past jobs, the project manager can anticipate potential troublespots. No effort is made to enter into or explain the technical considerations of the engineering disciplines.

DISCIPLINE INTERFACES

A perennial problem on projects is communication across interfaces between engineering disciplines. In some organizations there appears to be an almost insurmountable wall between the people in different disciplines. Unfortunately, this is rarely seen by higher level functional managers; or, even more unfortunately, it may be actually encouraged by middle managers in a frantic effort to protect "turf." Project organizations have adjusted to a need to improve communication by assigning interdisciplinary coordination to a project engineering manager or a project design supervisor whose authority extends across all engineering disciplines for the given project. On smaller projects, this function must be filled by the project manager, who should be aware of the pitfalls implicit in neglecting this role. The project manager needs to demonstrate leadership by building up an esprit de corps encompassing all of the engineering personnel so that they all see the success of the project and their part in it as being paramount.

SAFETY

One of the few negatives in a project management career is the tremendous responsibility that the project manager personally assumes, by virtue of his role, for the many human lives that are affected by the project.

The project manager's concern for safety falls into one of two broad areas: (1) the proper design of the plant to assure that safe operation and maintenance are possible, and (2) the program and procedures adopted to ensure that the field construction operations are conducted in a safe manner.

Obviously, the project manager cannot check all of the design work personally to assure that it is completely safe, nor can he be present at all times during the field construction. Within the project, he must delegate the responsibility for a safe design and for a safe jobsite. He must personally make absolutely sure that the proper safety design reviews have been identified, scheduled, held, and the findings and recommendations implemented. He must be sure that a specific construction safety program is in place in the field, that it is being monitored, and that it is effective in eliminating accidents.

IMPORTANT OBJECTIVES FOR THE PROJECT MANAGER

1. Make sure that the amount of engineering done is the absolute minimum to conform to contractual requirements and to permit the downstream work (procurement and construction) to be efficiently completed.

2. The project manager must have complete confidence in the engineering discipline leaders assigned to the project. He must then set the tone for expected performance, putting in place an effective system of two-way communication with these leaders. Meaningful communication between disciplines must be encouraged.

3. Make sure that produciton work does not start in any engineering discipline until the information and data available can support that effort. Staff accordingly, initially tending to be stingy on numbers of people assigned to downstream work.

4. After the production design work has started, do not approve unnecessary changes. Allow only those changes that are required to make the plant work, that are required for safety, or those that will save substantial amounts of money or schedule time.

5. The early stages of engineering are most productive in saving money. Be sure that the plant layout is finetuned to construction, operational, and maintenance efficiency.

6. Be ruthless in editing specifications to eliminate all vestiges of unnecessary requirements which only add to the cost of the work.

7. Provide checking in proportion to the criticality of the activity. Do not duplicate checking, especially of noncritical items. Determine where there has been a history of problems, and anticipate these by reinforcing the checking.

8. Use standard materials and equipment items wherever possible. For piping and electrical bulk materials, reduce number of different types to a minimum. Use special items only where a standard will not work.

BIBLIOGRAPHY

Blake, R. R., and Mouton, J. S. Improve the Work Flow Between Departments (part one). *Hydrocarbon Processing* 135-153 (October 1983).

Bradford, M. Supply Side Process Engineering, *Hydrocarbon Processing* 111-120 (January 1985).

Bush, W. D. When You're a Project Engineer. *Hydrocarbon Processing* 263-275 (November 1980).

Jenett, E. Guidelines for Successful Project Management, *Chemical Engineering* 70-82 (July 9, 1973).

Kern, R. How to Manage Plant Design to Obtain Minimum Cost (twelve in a series). *Chemical Engineering* (May 1977 to August 1978).

Kletz, T. A. Make Plants Inherently Safe. *Hydrocarbon Processing*, 172-180 (September 1985).

Kletz, T. A. Eliminating Potential Process Hazards. *Chemical Engineering* 48-68 (April 1, 1985).

Swartz, M., and Koslov, J. Piping and Instrumentation Diagrams. *Chemical Engineering* 85-89 (July 9, 1984.

Tomfohrde, J. H. Design for Process Safety. *Hydrocarbon Processing* 71-74 (December 1985).

Wells, G. L. Safety Reviews and Plant Design. *Hydrocarbon Processing* 241-261 (January 1981).

1

Design Considerations

CARL E. PETRUS   *Environmental Resources Management, Inc., Exton, Pennsylvania*

The project manager must be deeply involved early in the project in establishing the guidelines for the detailed design of the project. Although delegation of detail to his key specialists is an absolute must for the survival of the project manager on most projects; he must, nevertheless, pay close attention to the key plant design decisions at the start of the project. The project manager's skill and hard work in covering all major design considerations at the start of his project is the thread that will hold his team together throughout the project in producing a cohesive, optimized design. We will deal with how the project manager should approach some of these considerations.

DELEGATION

Most project managers are promoted into their jobs after years of hard work and demonstrated proficiency in one of the specialized engineering disciplines required for a project. More often than not, they were extremely good at their previous job. Once assigned as a project manager, an individual must resist the temptation to remain deeply involved in his previous field. Too often, new project managers allocate a disproportionate amount of their available time to their specialty, because they are comfortable in dealing with it and with the personnel doing the work. While he cannot ignore the work output from his own field, the project manager should spend proportionately less time there, since he should be able to review this portion of the work with a minimum investment of time. It is the unfamiliar fields where he should concentrate his efforts. In this way, he will expand his knowledge into new areas and will also be able to anticipate and solve upcoming problems on his project.

COMMUNICATION

An important function of the project manager at all times during the course of a project, but particularly during the design phases of a project, is to foster communication among the project staff. A regular weekly staff meeting is an excellent forum for the key project staff members to describe their current work progress and to highlight urgent information needs or decisions that must be made to keep their work on track. The project manager should also be reasonably accessible to key staff members, striking a sensible balance between the extremes of an open door policy in which his time is dominated by numerous visitors, and a closed door policy in which no one can reach him. The project manager should also provide a presence in the design work areas. He should show his interest and concern for work progress by holding random discussions with various designers and engineers on their current work. He should attend all meet-ings with the owner or equipment suppliers when key decisions or commitments are likely to be made. He should also see that relevant notes are quickly written and issued for all important meetings. Another important aspect of communications, and a key to a successful design effort, is the early preparation of a detailed scope of work by the project manager. After his initial meetings with the owner, the project manager must make a written record of all pertinent information about the project and description of the work to be performed. All reference materials: plotplans, site surveys, soils surveys, flow diagrams, process descriptions, photographs, should be included. As the project manager contemplates the various aspects of the project, many new ques-tions will arise for which he must obtain answers. Similarly, his staff of discipline engineers will find further questions and information needs as they review the work scope in light of their areas of the design work.

   Writing the work scope is often the creation of a living document, requiring numer-ous revisions and updates throughout the course of the design phase as new informa-tion and scope changes appear. The work scope should include a general description of the process and utility areas, with good descriptions of the limits of the work, such as interfaces with existing facilities or with other design engineering companies. After the various discipline engineers have reviewed the project manager's work scope, raised new questions, and obtained the required answers, it is a good idea to have each disci-pline engineer write their own work scope for their portion of the work. These spe-cialized work scope writings should also include specific directions and instructions on how the work will be done in that particular discipline. Thus, civil engineering in-structions will include a definitive description of the civil work to be done and will spec-ify all building codes to be followed, design criteria such as wind and seismic loads, specific soil data for foundation design, and other similar design information. Similarly, instructions for all other engineering disciplines, as well as purchasing, accounting, inspection, traffic, and so on should be developed to serve as a guide for the people doing the work in each discipline. Close review of these discipline work scopes will assure the project manager that all requirements of the job will be met, that no dupli-cation or overlap of effort will occur between disciplines, and that no unrequired work is planned.

COMPANY STANDARDS

On a typical plant project, there may be as many as three different sets of engineering standards that will be applied to the design of a plant. If a process licensor is involved, he or she will have process, equipment, metallurgical, and layout requirements specific to the process which must be adhered to in order to protect the licensor's guarantees. The owner normally has written standards that have been developed over many years of plant operation, and which they, too, want incorporated into the design of the plant. Finally, engineering contractors also have standards which their engineers, designers, inspectors, and construction forces are used to working with. Obviously, there will often be conflicting requirements among the standards of the three parties involved. If three different company standards covering pressure vessels, for instance, were to be referenced on a purchase order for a distillation column, the inherent conflicting requirements would cause significant confusion from the inquiry stage through final inspection and shipping of the column. While this procedure will serve to get the in-quiry out early in the project schedule, it usually results in an increased manhour ex-penditure and, often, a delay in delivery time and increased final cost of the equipment.

   When faced with multiple company standards, the project manager must decide at the outset how best to incorporate such standards into a single document with no con-flicting requirements. The following options are generally available to him:

1. A complete rewrite of the standards into project specifications which incorporate the requirements of all companies and which resolve all conflicting requirements. This option is generally the most expensive in terms of engineering costs.
2. Select one of the multiple company standards, and write an addendum to that standard, incorporating any additional requirement of the other applicable standards. Unless the owner insists on using his documents as the base standards, using the contractors standards will generally minimize project costs of design, inspection, and construction management, because the personnel involved in these functions will be most familiar with their own company standards.

It is important to remember that either of the above options requires a review by all parties of the documents produced, whether those documents are new project specifications or addenda to existing specifications. Another consideration to keep in mind is that a review by the owner and licensor of project specifications or addendum to specifications prepared by the engineering contractor does not relieve the engineering contractor of his responsibility to follow the specifications and requirements of the owner and licensor. The project manager should therefore see that all exceptions to, or violations, of owner or licensor standards are fully discussed with all interested parties and that all such decisions are documented in writing.

DESIGN REVIEWS

The project manager must determine the minimum number of design and specification reviews by outside sources (owner and licensor) to satisfy the requirements of the contract. The more often a drawing is reviewed, the more comments and design changes will be made, resulting in possible cost and schedule impact. Engineering documents can be issued for approval, review, information, inquiry, purchase, design, construction, as well as for other reasons. As these documents are transmitted to outside parties, the letter of transmittal should clearly state what action, if any, is required of the addressee. If a drawing is being issued for design after owner comments have been obtained and incorporated into the new issue of the drawing, it is not in the best interests of the project to receive a second set of comments on the drawing after detailed design has begun. A short note on the transmittal letter stating that the owner's comments have been incorporated into this issue of the drawing and that no further action is necessary should prevent a second round of owner's comments. In short, wherever possible, have the owner and licensor perform a single review on only those engineering documents that they should review to satisfy the contract. Unfortunately, no one set of rules can cover all the possible combinations of owner/licensor/contractor responsibilities. At the start of each project, the project manager should establish the review requirements for each type of engineering document. He should watch for any abuse of approval requirements during the course of the project.

For reimbursible-type projects involving a process licensor, an engineering contractor, and an owner, some generalizations can be made. Table 1 shows how a project of this type normally handles review and approval requirements. The process licensor issues a process design package at the start of the contractor's work and reviews a sufficient amount of the contractor's work to insure that his requirements will be met. The licensor will normally approve all process flow diagrams, piping and instrumentation flow diagrams (P&IDs) covering the process, all process equipment specifications, the plotplan, and the preliminary model or piping planning drawings. He is normally not issued detailed piping, structural, foundation, architectural, and electrical drawings since the engineering contractor has design responsibilities for these areas.

The owner and the process licensor generally review and approve the same items. In addition, on a reimbursible contract project, the owner retains control of spending

Table 1 Typical Review and Approval of Engineering Documents
for a Reimbursable Project

Document	Licensor	Owner
Process flow diagram	R, A	R, A
Process equipment specifications	R, C	R, A
Process P&IDs	R, A	R, A
Utility P&IDs	I	R, A
Utility equipment specifications	I	R, A
Plot plans	R, C	R, A
Piping planning or model	R, C	R, A
Detail piping design	NI	I
Structural design	NI	I
Foundation design	NI	I
Architectural design	NI	R, A
Electrical power and control	NI	I
Instrumentation	NI	I

R	review
A	approve
I	information
NI	not generally issued
C	comment

and quality of purchased equipment by reviewing and approving all process equipment, instrumentation, and utility equipment specifications. He also approves utility system P&IDS, which the licensor does not. Once the owner approves the plot plan and preliminary model or piping planning drawings, the general arrangement of the plant is fixed, including steel structures, piperacks, and buildings. Detailed drawings of piping, structures, foundations, and electrical control and wiring are provided to the owner for information only. One exception will usually be architectural details of buildings, which the owner has a right to approve to control the outward appearance of his plant. Of course, the owner has the option of commenting on any document, even if it is issued for information only.

OTHER REVIEWS

The project manager should also determine if agencies other than the licensor and owner will review any engineering documents. These agencies could include the owner's insurance carrier, or permitting agencies such as EPA or local zoning agencies. An insurance carrier review of process flowsheets, P&IDs, and plotplans may be required. If the owner is a large company, it may be self-insured, and would not require these reviews. In any event, the need for these reviews should be determined early in the project so they can be scheduled along with the owner and licensor reviews. A change that can easily be handled at small engineering cost early in the project will invariably cost a great deal more if made after detailed design is underway.

FINAL ENGINEERED PRODUCT

The degree to which a plant must be designed and the types of drawings and engineering documents needed will be determined, to a large extent, by the construction and purchasing plans for the project. The project manager must be sure that the right extent of design is planned. He cannot allow each engineering discipline to proceed with their "standard" design package unless it fits the project's requirements for procurement and construction. Soon after the start of a project, the project manager must determine precisely how the plant will come together. Who will purchase and furnish various types of bulk materials (pipe fittings, valves, structural steel)? Which construction trades will be direct-hired in the field, and which will be provided through subcontractors? What schedule forces and restraints will affect these decisions? For instance, on the subject of piping fabrication and erection alone, the following questions must be answered in order to plan for the right level of piping design required on the project.

    1. Will piping erection be by direct hire of pipefitters in the field? If so, the engineering contractor's home office has responsibility for providing all piping materials to the field, either in the form of random pipelengths, fittings, and valves, or as finished pipespools fabricated in a shop away from the plant site. Piping design manhours must be included to prepare piping material takeoffs to purchase materials for the field-fabricated piping, but may not be necessary for the shop-fabricated pipespool materials if the shop fabricator has been given responsibility for providing his own materials. However, if delivery of these materials is foreseen as a schedule problem, the engineering contractor may buy all, or a portion of these materials in advance, requiring a full material takeoff by the piping designers. In addition to extra manhours for material takeoffs, a higher degree of design is usually provided when piping erection is direct-hired, including preparation of field-fabricated pipespool drawings with individual material lists, and pipespool erection sequences for all pipespools.

    2. Will piping erection be subcontracted? If so, the supply of piping materials can be assigned to the subcontractor, requiring no piping materials purchasing effort and material takeoffs by the engineering contractor's office. Often however, deliveries of piping materials force the engineering contractor to make a preliminary purchase of these materials long before the design work is complete and before a piping fabricator or erector is selected. In addition, if piping fabrication and erection are subcontracted, it is often possible to reduce the amount of piping design done in the engineering contractor's office. Piping orthographic drawings, without isometric drawings, material lists, and erection sequences, are usually sufficient to define the work required of a subcontractor.

    3. Will small piping, 3/4-inch and less, be completely designed in the office, or will this piping be field routed? How detailed will vessel trim and instrument installation drawings be? Will materials be summarized or just indicated on the drawings? Questions such as these drastically affect the manhours required for piping design, and subsequently, project costs. Similar questions for structural steel, reinforcing bar, and electrical wire and gear, will affect other areas of design.

The plan for procurement and construction on a project, often called the material and subcontract coordination plan, is generally prepared early in the project by the project manager. It is reviewed in detail with the engineering, design, procurement, and construction specialists and revised as necessary during the project as conditions change. Each engineering and design discipline leader should prepare a written work scope and a corresponding manhour budget for his work sphere, carefully delineating the planned degree of design. The project manager should give these plans careful review to be sure the design requirements for his particular project will be met, and that no unnecessary extra work is planned.

In general, if any construction trade is direct hired in the field, as opposed to subcontracting the work, a higher level of design and material summarizing is usually necessary in the office. This is because it is the responsibility of the office to provide all required materials to the field in a timely manner, a task which can be transferred to the subcontractor when the field work is subcontracted.

Another aspect to getting a custom-tailored final engineering product at optimum engineering costs is for the project manager to specifically state whose services are, and whose services are not, required on his project. For instance, if the licensor furnishes a complete, firm process design, with all process equipment data sheets fully prepared, there should be no need for the contractor's process engineers to devote any time to the job. Similarly, if the licensor provides approved P&IDs for the plant, the role of the contractor's system engineers will be greatly reduced. In short, the project manager must program the contractor's engineering organization to plan for just the right amount of input from each discipline during the course of his project.

2
Mechanical Engineering

JOHN A. ADAMCHIK   *Barnard and Burk Engineers & Constructors, Inc.*, *Baton Rouge, Louisiana*

Regardless of the project approach—task force, matrix, or other—the performance of the mechanical equipment specialists dramatically affects the tone of the project. The project approach will certainly affect the type of mechanical engineer or specialist you will need for best performance.

Each project is different, and each has its own unique problems. The general responsibilities of the mechanical engineering team are discussed and suggested guidelines are given where appropriate. The project manager should be knowledgeable of a number of key areas including qualified staff, project documents, documents produced, documents reviewed, interfaces, and schedule.

STAFF

The experience and background of the mechanical engineers needed depends on the project approach used. For a true task force organization, it is desirable to have people with a general background who can handle all of the equipment associated with the project. If the project is sufficiently large, the generalist will probably serve as the discipline leader; and appropriate specialists will support him. In a matrix or modified task force the project manager will need equipment specialists over the duration of specifying, ordering, and inspection of the mechanical equipment.

PROJECT DOCUMENTS REQUIRED/PRODUCED

Table 1 lists the documents needed for the mechanical equipment engineer to complete his work properly and identifies the source of the documents. This table also lists the documents that will be produced by the mechanical discipline.

DOCUMENT REVIEW

The mechanical engineer is responsible for reviewing the P&IDs, vendor drawings, and the model or the orthographic drawings. He reviews the P&IDs to identify all instrumentation and equipment supplied by the vendor and to be sure all instruments and equipment being supplied are shown. Vendors' drawings and data are reviewed for compliance with specifications and to assure that information needed by the other disciplines is shown on the drawings or the data sheets. Review of the model and/or

Table 1 Document Information Requirements

Information needed	Furnished by
Mechanical specifications:	
Owner's general specifications	Project
Project general specifications	Project
Specific project requirements	Project
Industry standards	Mechanical
Engineering requisitions;	
Project equipment list	Project
P&IDs	Project
Mechanical specifications	Mechanical
Standard drawings (vessels)	Mechanical
Utilities and site data	Project
Process data sheets	Process
Thermal ratings (S&T exchangers)	Process
Skirt heights (vessels)	Process/piping
Cathodic protection	Electrical
Electrical requirements	Electrical
Electrical area classifications	Electrical
Instrument requirements	Instruments
Fabrication requirements:	
Nozzle orientation	piping
Platform requirements	Piping
Ladder requirements	Piping
Platform clip location	Civil
Pipe support clip location	Piping
Technical bid evaluation:	
Engineering requisition	Mechanical
Purchasing plan	Purchasing
Vendor quotes	Purchasing
Bid closeout	Project
Commercial bid tabulation	Purchasing/project
Fabrication requirements to vendor:	
Nozzle orientation	Piping
Platform requirements	Piping
Ladder requirements	Piping
Platform clip location	Civil
Ladder clip location	Civil
Instrument level sketches	Instruments
(size/rating/location transmitted by nozzle orientation sketch)	
Grounding clip requirements	Electrical
Erection requirements:	
Construction requirements	Construction
Platform design schedule	Civil
Ladder design schedule	Civil

orthographic drawings should ascertain that the equipment is properly piped and that all interconnecting piping and connections are shown.

DISCIPLINE INTERFACES AND SCHEDULE

It may seem unusual that these two go hand in hand, but in the case of the mechanical engineer the information interchange with other disciplines must be done on schedule to avoid unnecessary delays at the start of the job. At project inception, there is no detailed schedule, and the mechanical engineering effort must recognize the requirements of the other disciplines. It is essential that the mechanical engineer furnish the other disciplines with good preliminary data so that their work can start. To do this effectively, the mechanical engineer should have a realistic early work schedule and communicate the work plans and the equipment status by means of suitable, timely reports.

ENGINEERING REQUISITIONS

An engineering requisition (ER) document is used to transmit all of the necessary process and mechanical equipment information to the other disciplines, the client, and to the vendors. This requisition is composed of the specifications, data sheets, and design notes.

The ER is issued and updated periodically as required. The initial issue is generally for inquiry; the second issue normally occurs after a purchase order number is assigned and the successful vendor selected. Circumstances may require revision of the ER between the initial issue and issue of the purchase order.

SPECIFICATIONS

Normally the specifications will consist of the client specifications, the engineering contractor specifications, and industry standards and codes. The type and restrictiveness of the client and contractor specifications vary with individual clients and contractors. Industry standards vary with the segment of industry served. Some codes, such as the ASME codes are normally recognized and used by all industries.

DATA SHEETS

The mechanical engineer receives the process data sheets containing process data developed by others. It is his responsibility to add the mechanical requirements of the project. The completed data sheet should identify the specific requirements for the service necessary for the subsequent design and for the vendors to bid the supply of each piece of equipment.

DESIGN NOTES

Design notes cover information specific to the equipment service not covered on the data sheets. These notes include the specific requirements set by plant personnel.

The As-Purchased Requisition

The "as-purchased" ER is a revision that incorporates the vendor data on the equipment item as initially purchased. This ER is important, since what is written here is incorporated into the actual purchase order and represents the understanding as to what has actually been bought.

ER Revisions

Although the piece of equipment is defined by the initial purchase order; realistically, there will be changes as the work progresses. The ER is revised to handle and control these changes, as well as to keep the definition of the equipment current. As a rule of thumb, the mechanical jobhours required for developing and processing ERs represent about 20% of the total mechanical jobhours.

TECHNICAL BID EVALUATION

The technical bid evaluation, commonly called the "bid tab," is the formal review by the mechanical engineer of the vendor bids from which he will make a decision as to which vendor best meets the project specifications for the particular piece of equipment. In addition, the recommended vendor must be the most economical for the service and meet delivery requirements.

The procedures for the formal technical bid evaluation are:

1. A preliminary review of the quotations as they are released
2. A pricing and technical tabluation
3. Designation of the apparent low bidder
4. Conditioning of the vendors offerings to put them in agreement with all terms/conditions (generally confined to the lowest bid or the two lowest bids)

Preliminary Review

All quotations are reviewed for a statement of compliance with the inquiry documents, or a list of exceptions taken. The clarity of the offering, the completeness of technical data, the pricing, the delivery, and the drawing issue dates are all reviewed. If any of this information is missing, followup is required.

Tabulation

A pricing tabulation is made of all quotations received to determine the apparent low bidders. The higher bidders and those which do not conform are eliminated from further consideration. The special purchasing conditions are reviewed by procurement specialists to determine any commercial reasons which might disqualify a bidder. Depending upon the project procedures, approximately three bids are selected for a complete technical evaluation.

Conditioning

The quotes are conditioned initially from a pricing standpoint. The apparent low bidder is then conditioned technically. Conditioning questions are made either by telephone or in writing to the vendor; however, all responses should be made in writing addressed to the same individual to whom the initial bids were addressed.

Formal Recommendation

A written formal recommendation or designation of the low bidder should be prepared by the engineer. Pertinent points of the recommendation are:

1. A statement that the equipment is in complete conformance with the project specifications. If there are exceptions, these must be listed. If variances are required by the client, this fact should be highlighted.
2. Technical details should be described as they were evaluated.
3. Extra appurtenances and supplies that need to be purchased should be listed.
4. Outstanding items requiring clarification and which require written confirmation prior to issuing the purchase order.

VENDOR DATA

Vendor data is critical to the successful execution of the project. The vendor data must be received in a timely manner and in compliance with the project specifications. The information needed by the design disciplines is vital to the orderly design process.

Once the vendor data has been received, it should be routed for proper review, review comments noted, and the documents returned to the vendors as expeditiously as possible. Ten working days should be adequate for the turnaround. Rapid approvals are necessary to avoid any slippage in delivery of critical equipment.

SHOP VISITS

Shop visits are generally associated with shop inspection and shop expediting. On large dollar value orders, shop visits are recommended at the beginning of the order. This visit will serve to further clarify intent and fabrication procedures and to assure that vendor and engineering contractor are in accord. Any discrepancies brought to light on this visit should be resolved immediately. A successful meeting at the beginning of an order will eliminate most of the problems that will arise during detailed engineering.

The engineer may make a further visit to expedite drawing approval. To conserve schedule time, it is sometimes a good idea to conduct "on-board" drawing approvals. This is a valuable technique based on real need, but it should not be overdone.

The engineer will also make shop visits to conduct or witness tests of the completed equipment items. The equipment specialist should be used for shop performance and mechanical testing. It is much easier and less costly to fix or repair equipment in the shop than it will be in the field, and is much less disruptive to the schedule. The project manager should not be tempted to "skimp" on trips by mechanical specialists to participate in final inspection and to witness tests of key equipment items. A few dollars saved here will not offset the costs stemming from later field problems.

SITE

In some cases, it will be beneficial for the equipment specialist to go to the jobsite to check the installation of critical equipment and participate in the field testing and commissioning.

The project manager should realize that these shop and site visits can contribute substantially to the smooth and rapid startup as well as to the experience and capability of mechanical engineers on subsequent jobs.

SUMMARY

The project manager should be aware of the status of each piece of equipment from the definition stage through inquiry, bid tabulation, ordering, fabrication, shipping, and installation. Each piece of critical equipment must be followed each step of the way. The project manager depends on the mechanical specialists for this information. In turn, the project manager must be sure that the mechanical specialists are kept a-breast of developments which might affect the mechanical efforts. Utilize the experience and knowledge of mechanical specialists in making decisions. Encourage field trips and site visits by mechanical engineers where these will pay a dividend to the project. General rules of thumb that may be applied to home office mechanical hours are as follows:

> When the requisition is issued, you should be at about 20% of the jobhours for the item.
> When the formal bid evaluation is issued, you should be at 45% of the jobhours.
> When the vendor drawings are returned approved, you should be at 95% of the jobhours for the item.
> The remaining 5% is for resolution of questions from the field.

3

Process Control

HAROLD H. ARNDT *MK-Ferguson Company, Cleveland, Ohio*

The finished facility must be capable of operation in conformance with the process concept. Proper design of the process controls assures this operability.

The process concept calls for specific time sequences, flow rates, mix times and rates, pressure buildups or letdowns, stops and starts, opening and closing of valves, all according to a set pattern. With today's robotic equipment, with sophisticated temperature, pressure and flow sensors, and computer controls, changes can be detected and controlled in milliseconds. Other equipment where slower response times are indicated is available.

Process and control engineers have a vast storehouse of equipment from which to choose. In the following paragraphs, types of equipment are listed together with the types of companies that make the equipment, design the control schemes, and assemble the equipment into operating process control systems. The high priority concerns of the project manager are pointed out. Because of the rapid growth and current importance of computerized process control, this is covered in some detail.

TYPES OF PROCESS CONTROLS

Pneumatic

Pneumatic hydraulic controls are the oldest and, in many cases, the least expensive. Some pneumatic and hydraulic controls date back more than 2,000 years. Many of the older process plants worldwide use pneumatic controls or a combination of pneumatic and electric controls. New plant design, where the process is suited to these control characteristics, continues to specify pneumatic controls. Conversely, many older plants previously equipped with pneumatic controls, are being retrofitted with electronic or some combination of computerized control.

Electronic

Electronic controls came into widespread use because of their versatility, sensitivity, and rapid response time. As electronic controls became cost competitive with pneumatic instrumentation; and, as maintenance costs reached a standoff, these systems were designed into the majority of new process plants.

Programmable Logic Controller (PLC)

Programmable logic controllers (PLCs) were introduced to control a specific area of a process system and are generally associated with speed control, on-off sequences,

and other similar controls. PLCs are easily changed, as the logic chips can be changed
or reprogrammed quite readily. PLCs lend themselves to batch-type processing with
many on-off, start-stop, open-close and time-related operations. As the system price
of the PLCs became competitive with electronic instrumentation and on-line programming
became available, they became a natural choice for processes suited to its characteristics.

Computer

The computer, initially, was used only in very large process units where a high operating efficiency could be achieved to offset the large investment cost.

The great flexibility and large memory capacity of the new mini- and microcomputers
and their comparatively low cost, allowed more and more new plants to use computer-
controlled processing. In most new plants, the process and control engineers tend to
use some form of PLCs and/or computer control in some combination. The computer's
advantages allow it to be used to control very complex processes with a fraction of the
crew size. These plants can consistently produce a higher quality product with less
waste. In some cases, a smaller plant or unit can be operated unattended using a computer.

Combination System

Combined process control systems are more common today. Old plants convert only
a portion of the plant at a time; and, in many systems, it is not cost effective to
change. In both new plants and old, certain types of processes are more suited to
one type of control system. Rather than specifying an inefficient or cost-ineffective
system, process and control engineers design a combination system for the plant.

DIFFERENCES IN CONTROL AND DATA GATHERING

Process Control

Process control is the control of the process recipes (formulae) to produce a product
from one or more feedstocks. The control of the process breaks down into controlling
temperatures, pressure, flows, distances, speeds, and levels in terms of rates and
times in addition to some other less common elements.

The ability to combine all of the control functions of a given process with an adequate and efficient control system at an economical cost is the principle objective of
the process control design engineers.

Data Gathering

Data gathering is the collection of information by means of instrumentation for purposes
other than process control. Data gathering, although important, is not process control.
In fact, processes can be controlled without data gathering. However, most plants
have data gathering capability mixed in with the control design. There are several
reasons for this. First, the process design engineer will often need data to confirm
pilot plant or research work that preceded the scale-up for the full-scale process unit.
Second, data gathering may be added to process units to obtain information for further
enhancements to the process or expansions to the process unit. Third, data gathering
may be required in conjunction with the quality control function. Fourth, data gathering may be used as a part of a maintenance program for determining equipment servicing intervals, repairs or replacement.

For processes in the research and development state, data gathering in pilot plants
and semiworks plants may be the primary requirement. Here, process and control engineers must work closely with the instrument engineers. The control system selected
may be dictated by the necessity for integration with the data gathering requirements.

Process control is often only secondary to data gathering in the overall instrumentation of these special applications.

TYPES OF FIRMS INVOLVED WITH PROCESS CONTROL

Instrument Manufacturers

There are a number of instrument manufacturers that have remained just that. They have not, to any great extent, tried to enter into the design and manufacture of process control systems. They specialize in making one or more of the various types of instruments. These include instruments for controlling temperature, pressure, flow, level, speed, time, distance, as well as for analytical applications. When looking for a specific instrument it is best to go to an instrument manufacturer for data and information for your specific needs rather than a controls system manufacturer.

Pneumatic or Electronic Control Systems Manufacturers

The pneumatic or electronic control systems manufacturers in the process control industry are typically giants in the industry. They have also tended to specialize in specific industries; it is easy to consult with a few firms for your specific needs.

PLC Manufacturers

Only a few programmable logic controller manufacturers have emerged. However, in conjunction with other computer products, some of the newer computer process control companies have introduced PLCs into their line of products. PLCs have only a limited marketplace fit. It is difficult for a new company to get a share of a market that is already dominated by a few well-known suppliers.

If you require information about potential applications of PLCs in process control, you should talk to the PLC manufacturers. You probably will not have to talk to more than three or four companies to get answers to your questions.

Computer Manufacturers

The computer process control industry has grown and developed rapidly in the recent past as the capability and cost of mini- and microcomputers have improved dramatically.

The large process control companies have added computerized process control equipment to their product lines. The smaller companies have added computerized process systems using both proprietary hardware and software. New companies have emerged with their own hardware and software.

This has added a new dimension to the process control manufacturing business. It has allowed small new companies to compete with large, high-volume and highly successful firms. The software capabilities of a small firm merged with the proper hardware can produce very competitive systems that are tailormade to a specific process. The flexibility and short schedule possible with this approach have frequently been very profitable.

Manufacturer of a Combination of Items

Some companies offer products and services that include two or more of the above types of equipment and services. Many owners should take advantage of the services of a company that can supply complete control systems, or break down the systems into major subsystems. It is possible to buy each major subsystem from a large integrated company. Doing so brings a large number of specialists to work on your specific problem or problems. A few of these firms presently control the major share of the market.

The remaining manufacturers that offer a combination of equipment and services are specialty companies that cater to specific segments of the process control industry.

The large integrated companies have large R&D groups and large sales support groups offering complete presentations on what they can do for you currently, as well as what you may expect or plan for in the future. When developing an overall process control philosophy for your company or for a new facility, you should use this resource to the fullest.

Consultants

There are numerous consultants in the process control field. Some of these are oriented toward hardware and control applications, and some toward the process end of the business. With increased computer usage, some consultants do nothing more than programming to a given client's specifications. These specialized consultants may have little or no knowledge of either process or process control.

Use of consultants should be very carefully thought out. If the level of work so justifies, it is advisable to train your own staff. Consultants are then used only to solve very special problems.

Selection of consultants should be given the same attention you would use in selection of control equipment. You should carefully evaluate the projected costs involved relative to the references and track record of the consultants considered. There should be a clear understanding as to the scope of the services included.

Engineering/Architectural Firms

When an owner is building a new plant, modifying an old plant, or just changing the control system, an engineer/architect is often employed. There are then at least three parties involved: the owner of the plant, the engineer/architect, and the vendor supplying the equipment.

Engineer/architectural firms range from small specialty firms to large integrated "do it all" firms. The choice depends largely on the scope of work and what specialties are required from the engineer/architect. If the process control system is only a part of a large new process plant, then the process control capabilities of the engineer/architect will not be of primary concern. However, if the plant modification is to change the control system or if you have already selected the control system based on other criteria, you may narrow your selection of the engineer/architect to a very few who have this specialized control experience.

Care should always be exercised in evaluating the process control capability of an engineer/architect. Changes and advances are occurring faster in this area of process plant technology than any other.

Construction Firms

Construction firms are also to be chosen with equal care. Installation of pneumatic or electric controls is a completely different "ball game" from the installation of computerized control systems where the environment of the control system can be extremely important.

On many large project installations, the calibration and checkout of instruments on the process control systems are subcontracted to specialty firms. This is generally a very intelligent approach to proper process control system installation, calibration, and checkout. If computerized controls are involved, it is wise to contract the installation and checkout of the computer portion to the vendor supplying this equipment on a turnkey basis.

You should not try to save small amounts of money in installation, calibration, and checkout of highly sophisticated equipment costing millions of dollars. You should budget for the maximum efficiency; and try to minimize repair, rework, and lengthy schedule extensions required for recycling field work.

PRIORITIES

In selecting, designing, procuring, installing, and starting-up a process control system careful planning should be used to avoid the many pitfalls which have plagued projects in the past. The project manager should keep in mind certain high priority considerations which are discussed in the following paragraphs.

Selecting the Proper Control Approach

You should select the control system at an early stage of the project in conjunction with the process design. This may be during the pilot plant work, or even before. Les Kane, Equipment Editor of *Hydrocarbon Processing* magazine, editorialized in the June 1984 issue "Any advanced control project requires proper planning and getting the basic controls right first" (Kane, 1984).

If the process plant owner is building a new plant to be controlled by a highly sophisticated control system and the plant is to be built by an engineering/construction contractor the plant owner may choose the control system to be purchased prior to award of the E/C contract or before the start of the design and the start of the equipment purchasing cycle.

The control approach should be thought out early and the decision as to what approach should be used must be made early. Otherwise, both schedule and project costs will be adversely affected. Most certainly additional charges for changes will be introduced and process inefficiencies or compromises will result.

COORDINATING THE DESIGN EFFORTS

Close coordination of the design efforts is essential for maintaining schedule and staying within the project budget. Those areas requiring careful monitoring of the interfaces are process, mechanical equipment, layout, electrical including grounding, piping, environmental, safety, computer and computer communications, construction, checkout, and start-up.

The project manager must see that the responsibilities for work assignments are carefully spelled out. We have seen in some organizations some confusion among the process, instrumentation, and the electrical disciplines with regard to responsibilities. The project plan will spell this out clearly. Planning must be done for each project and should not depend on past history or custom to let people know what is expected. The timely receipt of accurate, complete vendor data is important to the design effort. If PLCs or computer systems are to be used, the programming of these systems will require special coordination.

1. The equipment driven by the PLC or computer must be coordinated with the program writer.
2. The software checkout. This may require the owner to send a team to the vendor's plant.

Coordination of the design effort can be very simple for an ordinary pneumatic or electronic control system or very complex for a large computerized control system. When planning the work, be sure to take into account coordination efforts.

DOCUMENTATION

Documentation of the process control system is the body of communication to all of the other disciplines, to the field installation groups, and to the owner for operating and maintenance training. Documentation must be complete, comprehensible, timely, and correct to assure completion of the project on schedule and within budget. Never fall into the trap of allowing one person to hold all of the process control philosophy and design direction in his mind without proper documentation. This may have disastrous consequences for the project and for the plant.

As the control system becomes more complicated, the problems of documentation multiply. Software documentation can become very difficult and should be thoroughly thought out at the start of a given project. Items to include in the plan are:

1. Who is responsible for the software packages?
2. Who handles the licensing agreements for the software packages?
3. What revisions of the software packages are to be used with the system purchased?
4. Who is reponsible for maintaining a baseline software system?
5. Are the various software packages compatible with each other?
6. Who tests and filters all of the software problems/questions?
7. Who determines if a certain problem stems from hardware, software, or documentation deficiencies?

These are just some of the items that must be considered in making a normal computerized control plan. For a larger and more sophisticated system, there are more such considerations. The actual implementation of the process control plan for a complex plant will require many highly talented, experienced people and a large sum of money. A detailed plan to sensibly budget sufficient funds must be developed. Attempts to cover unbudgeted items after the initial appropriations and to maintain schedule can only lead to grief.

PROCUREMENT COORDINATION

Procurement activities for a pneumatic or simple electric system do not represent difficulty for the project. However, as the systems and projects increase in size, complexity, and sophistication, the coordination of the procurement activities can become important and should be a high priority item in the project plan.

Considerations in procurement planning include:

1. What equipment, systems, or software is the owner providing?
2. Who is responsible for expediting the equipment and the documentation for owner-procured materials?
3. Who has control of changes for owner-procured materials?
4. Are the specifications of owner-procured materials compatible with those for E/C or A/E-procured materials?

The E/C contractor is frequently responsible for coordinating the systems where the owner has set the criteria for the system and:

1. The input and output devices are purchased from one vendor
2. The instruments from another vendor
3. The computer from still another
4. The software from yet another

The coordination of this effort must be very carefully planned and thought out; and the plan communicated to the project staff, the owner, and each vendor.

START-UP ACTIVITIES

Starting up a new plant calls for certain lead-time process control activities. If the project is an expansion of an existing control system or a duplication of an existing control system, the lead time for start-up activities is greatly reduced and will probably pose no problem.

For a new process control system the problems of training, maintenance, and testing become large in terms of time and cost. Again, this is compounded if the new system is sophisticated and computerized.

The owner's operators and maintenance forces may require on-the-job training experience, preferably prior to or during the system start-up and initial field checkout. Software training, operator application training, new equipment maintenance training, and lead times for these items should be considered in preparing the plan and schedule. You may want to consider using consultant assistance during the checkout/start-up and first time use of the equipment after the operating and technical support people have returned from the various courses and training periods.

COMPUTERIZED CONTROL

Because of the rapid development of the use of computerized process controls, this topic is being covered separately. The use of computerized controls will continue to increase because of the ability to perform a multitude of control functions with a small inexpensive package together with continual hardware and software advancements.

Complex Systems

The most sophisticated type of process control architecture is one that allows a plant to operate unattended while feeding recipes into the system together with product specifications and processing times. The plant manager lays out the desired inventories, the product selling prices, and the algorithms for plant operating costs, raw material costs, schedules, accounting data, and the integration of the plant data into the corporate management and accounting systems. The process control system then requests the proper inventory of products, produces a schedule showing raw material requirements, lead time, and inventory requirement and finished product quantities inventory. This system also provides a complete accounting plant balance sheet, profit and loss statement, and income sheet. The system also produces a management report with alternatives for different product mixes depending upon sales and price projections for the product mixes fed into the system. Many plants operate in this manner today. These plants will have operator assistance in starting and stopping operations, spot checking product quality, performing maintenance, reviewing records, and performing some scheduling functions. Plant employees also support delivery and shipping activities, assure that equipment breakdowns are corrected quickly and efficiently, and handle plant turnarounds.

Because of the savings of the automated plant, a large investment is possible for the computerized control system. Once the decision is made to follow this control philosophy, efforts should be directed toward assuring allotment of and safeguarding sufficient funding for the system. The totally computerized plant depends on a well designed, well thought out and well coordinated effort by hundreds of highly qualified technical and managerial people.

Less Complex Systems

Medium-sized control systems are less complex. But even these systems incorporate many parts of the large systems and require all of the interfaces, documentation, training, integration, and checkout of the more complex systems.

Simple Systems

A small system will consist of a PLC stand-alone microcomputer that is installed to control a single process function such as a fractionation tower, a mixing system, or a weaving machine. These small systems can be purchased preprogrammed. The operator needs only to enter the recipes, set points, alarm data, start, stop, and timing data and other specific information in order to operate this type of system.

Documentation and Training Requirements

Complexity of the documentation and training requirements of sophisticated systems depends on three factors: (1) the system architecture chosen, (2) the number of hardware vendors you choose to use, (3) the number and kind of software packages that are selected for use. As the complexity increases, training provided for the plant personnel, as well as personnel from the vendor companies, engineering contractors, and consultants increases accordingly. Documentation is required for each problem encountered, including those involving software, hardware, interface, design, and installation. All of this is in addition to the documentation required for specifications, drawings, change orders, day-to-day correspondence, memos, and meeting notes. New software packages and systems for basic process control are coming onto the market every week. To choose the package or system that best fits the need is extremely difficult. Some good guidelines to follow are:

1. Don't try to force a package to fit your needs just because someone in your organization is familiar with the software
2. Categorize the software packages available by the types of processes (batch, continuous, compatible with other plant systems) they fit
3. Prepare a long list of potential choices
4. Check the actual operating experience of these packages with users and programmers
5. Prepare a short list for competitive bidding
6. Do an in-depth bid evaluation including a visit to all potential vendors' plants and operating plants where the software packages are being used

The use of consultants in selecting and designing the computerized control system is a must unless you, your engineer, and all equipment vendors have an extensive computer background. You should try to use consultants sparingly and for specific problems. They should be subject to the same careful selection process as the hardware and software. Consultants can be very helpful and if the right choice is made, can lead to substantial cost savings. Again a word of caution about the necessity to adequately budget this function.

At this point, most A/Es do not have strong in-house computerized control system capabilities. It would be expected that this activity will either be added to their staff during the course of your project or will be subcontracted to another firm. Neither of these situations is ideal, but represent what you are likely to encounter. This condition needs to be reflected in your project plans. To work through the problem means planning, budgeting, judicious use of consultant expertise, and extra coordination.

SUMMARY

Perhaps the most important aspects of process control systems can be summarized as follows:

1. Support is available from literature, from consultants, and from process control companies and full advantage should be taken of these resources.

2. Process control is a difficult, multifaceted integration of process design, instrumentation, and operating personnel. All of these disciplines must participate and cooperate in the process control of the facility.
3. The process control field is rapidly changing, and these changes impact the system architecture for new plants. They pose a challenge for plant and corporate management.
4. The plant owner should decide on a control process early in the project. If an integrated computerized system is used, the vendor should be selected prior to starting detailed process and engineering design.
5. An early decision on five points should have high priority in the project manager's planning:

   a. Type of system architecture
   b. Control philosophy
   c. Expansion provisions
   d. Upgrading contemplated
   e. Preferred vendors

6. Special consideration should be given to the integration with plant layout, equipment, civil, piping, electrical, and grounding design and safety and environmental factors.
7. These items should be considered as having "red flags" and special planning should be developed:

   a. Thorough and complete documentation
   b. Careful planning and control of design activities
   c. Complete definition prior to application programming
   d. Schedule ample time for coordination of many software programs and revisions
   e. Necessity for thorough hardware and software testing
   f. Importance of total company commitment to control program

REFERENCE

Kane, L. Editorial, *Hydrocarbon Processing* (June 1984).

4

Civil, Structural, and Architectural Engineering

MICHAEL SCHILLER*   *C F Braun & Co., Murray Hill, New Jersey*

The project manager should be aware of some of the pitfalls that may be encountered in the civil, structural, and architectural disciplines on the project. Many of these are discussed in the following paragraphs. The focus is on procedures and practices and not on the technical aspects of engineering. The points raised, while not pretending to be an all-inclusive listing, do cover many of the more common problems.

SCOPE

Beginning a project with a poorly defined scope of work guarantees wasted jobhours and schedule delays. When engineers and architects are launched, en masse, on a project whose scope of work is ambiguous or hazy, the results can be calamitous. Aside from inevitable budget overruns caused by rework, there is the concomitant drop in morale and loss of confidence in the project leadership. So take the time to define the scope carefully before building up the staff.

Frequently restricting information on a "need-to-know" basis can be too constraining. Staff performance is better when they feel a sense of participation and a reception to their ideas. Staff must understand the contract, the schedule, the problem areas surrounding long delivery items, location of information delays and other factors critical to progress of the project. Staff will only accept ownership of the project and responsibility for solving its problems if they understand the full picture. Treat them like the professionals that they are and the staff will respond positively.

The project manager must take the time at the beginning of the assignments to be sure that the staff fully comprehend the scope of work. All of this data should be written and issued as an official document to the client for his agreement. The benefits derived will be well worth the time spent doing this. Some missing piece of information that may not seem vital now could develop into a major irritation later.

The same philosophy of providing a detailed and complete introduction of the work to the staff must extend with equal vigor to the lead engineers and their teams. Do not consider this as a waste of time. The increased work quality and productivity will be a direct measure of how fully the teams view themselves as contributing participants in a well-knit team.

The extent of engineering and the required detail will vary greatly if the work is being performed on an engineer, procure, and construct basis, or design only. Usually the advantages of providing more detail and making material takeoffs in the office

---
*Retired

outweigh the costs if the procurement and construction are being done by in-house forces. This strategy and action plan must be established at the project kickoff, and all involved must be told so that the engineering and drawings reflect the plan.

It is important also to define as early as possible, the precise limits and physical boundaries of each subcontract. This will reduce the amount of possible late rework and number of errors. Establish or confirm the interfaces between the engineering disciplines. Verify or establish boundaries between the different contracts.

Misunderstandings among engineers and contractors is not unknown. Some of the more common problem areas are the definition of interface between below and above grade piping, steam piping headers and laterals to unit heaters, fire water lines and sprinkler piping, plumbing within a building connecting to outside sewer lines, structural steel connections between adjacent structures, leveling plates and grout between a structural column and foundation. The list is endless.

Take the time to review and confirm these interfaces early in the engineering. Make sure the intent is clear, even if the method of showing it may not look very professional. The message must be completely unambiguous.

SCHEDULE

A logical and efficient schedule can only be conceived and completed if the scope of work is defined in detail, and the strategy of how to accomplish it, including a plan of all subcontracts, is fully established. There will be few instances when you will have all of the information you need at the beginning of the project. In those rare times, the work can be planned logically and sequentially and performed most efficiently. Normally one is faced with an assemblage of incomplete data, much of which will change as the job progresses. Nevertheless, a master schedule must be developed before proceeding. This single, vital document, will show all the major milestone dates and the project end date. It should also show the time span over which engineering specifications and drawings will be completed, the dates for procurement and delivery of equipment and bulk materials, the field start date, and the time span for each phase of construction.

After you have reviewed the preliminary master schedule, allow your staff leaders sufficient time to study it and ask that they bring their comments to a formal schedule review meeting. No doubt there will be valid objections and reasons why the schedule is too tight. The work may not proceed efficiently because information is lacking. The milestones and time span must be placed in a logical sequence, and the time spans shown must be achievable. You must be prepared to answer substantively all staff leader questions even if not entirely to their liking.

However, two things will happen at this time. The proposed schedule not only becomes the formal project master schedule, but through persuasion the staff leaders must accept ownership of this document as *their* schedule. It cannot be something that is thrust upon them, but must be something that they accept and will be willing to use as their own concept and work plan. Take the time necessary to accomplish these goals. The benefits to you later will be returned severalfold.

It is essential at this time that each project leader fully comprehends the scope of work that is described in this master schedule. Assemble your staff and describe the overall project to them again. Each staff leader should be asked to describe his work plan to the others, including the kinds of documents he plans to produce. You might find that some of the work has fallen into a no-man's land due to one leader expecting a certain flow of information which an upstream leader hadn't planned to produce. Subcontracted work might present a special set of circumstances and information requirements to the staff leaders.

The master schedule and the scope of work are the triggers for a detailed work plan, displayed in a work schedule, with appropriate time spans and manhour budgets. All of these must be in accord with the master schedule and the contracted budgets.

Conflicts and problem areas must be discussed and resolved at this time, before large numbers of people are assigned to the work. Staff leaders must be permitted to review each other's schedules to be sure that each leader's work is organized to flow sequentially.

Aside from monitoring the work, conduct regular scheduled review meetings to assess progress and problem areas. When you do pinpoint a restriction to the planned flow of work be sure to develop an action plan and designate the person responsible for the corrective action. Be sure to follow this up at the next meeting. The first item on your agenda should be the responses to the action plan.

The lead scheduler must have free and direct access and be able to speak freely to the project manager. The scheduler's confidential assessments of progress and potential problems, including his recommendations for resolving them, are an invaluable input to the project manager.

At times you will be asked if a schedule is feasible or where you think a schedule is impossibly short, or you will be faced with buying and erecting certain items long before final information is available. Do not be quick to say a schedule cannot be completed on time. There may be ways, especially if the client is willing to spend a little money to buy time. An example of such tradeoffs is paying a premium to place the foundations and to erect structural steel before winter sets in so that three months in the overall schedule are saved. Be inventive in devising possible solutions.

Here are examples of some ideas that have been used successfully in the past. A manufacturing facility was planned to be housed in a new single-story building. A preliminary layout of all the equipment was made, but no vendor drawings were available to allow checking of the work. The schedule demanded that the foundations be placed. Increasing the thickness of the floor slabs allowed freedom of placement of most of the apparatus except for some large ball mills. Only the ball mill area remained untouched until the foundations were designed. Raising the roof an additional two feet clear of the floor, and designing the roof beams to carry an additional point load allowed conveyors to be located freely later in the most desirable position dictated by engineering, and eliminated construction delay. Equipment drainage was connected with small pipe above the floor, eliminating a possible delay for equipment location. Pipe was arranged so as not to form a tripping hazard. The lines were then led to a number of small sump pumps set into the floor, which pumped the drainage to a central tank above grade.

For a large steel process structure, preliminary design layouts showed the location of large and small reactors, pumps, blowers, heat exchangers, drums, and other pieces of apparatus. Because of long delivery and fabrication times for structural steel, it was imperative that the steel drawings be released for fabrication before vendor drawings were available. In some instances, apparatus had been specified but had not been purchased. The solution was to replace the steel flooring on all floors with a concrete slab. The concrete was designed for a live load sufficient to carry all but the heaviest pieces. For the heavy reactors, the steel beams and girders were placed just outside the perimeter of the reactor, allowing it to be finally supported on the concrete. This scheme allowed the steel to be released immediately, and since all future floor penetrations would go through the floor slabs, there was ample time to detail them later.

ENGINEERING

This volume is not intended to be a civil or structural engineering text. It is assumed that the quality of the engineering and design is not under discussion. However, to ensure that the client understands the basis on which engineering will proceed, all engineering disciplines must define the criteria they will use in their design. The more detailed this document, the less likelihood of surprises and change later. It should include loadings, both structural and meteorological, dimensions such as aisle and roadway widths, surfacing and architectural materials selections, and so on. This specification should be reviewed in detail with the customer, and have his written approval.

The more complicated the site and soil characteristics for foundations, the greater the benefits in investing in a comprehensive soil report. This report should focus on the specific problems of the project and offer practical solutions. This is impossible unless the soils consultant is given a detailed description of the planned project, the types of structures and their loadings, and as many qualifiers as possible. The engineer and the soils consultant must understand each other's problems to produce the most economical and practical design.

For instance, there is no point in insisting on preloading a site so that spread footings are feasible rather than piling if the schedule cannot accommodate a year's delay. On the other hand, if it can, it is certainly a viable and low-cost solution. If the groundwater table is high, this should be known early. It can wreak havoc with the costs of large underground piping systems.

If possible, do not get trapped into specifying something that is impractical, but may be nice to have. Compaction requirements called for should be achievable without a great deal of imported, expensive fill material or complicated machinery. The bedding for underground piping should be the minimum that is acceptable. Settlements for foundations should be reviewed thoroughly. Be practical in your demands from the soils consultant, and look for the same practical reality from engineering. It is easy to get boxed in and end up with an expensive solution that leaves no one pleased with the outcome. Do not demand more than you need before you really know what you can live with. It is too easy to ask for an ultrasafe solution, and then walk away from the problem assuming it is now someone else's responsibility. The final measure of success lies with you.

Errors in location and elevation can be reduced by keeping all the figures positive. Establish a vertical datum at elevation 100 feet, so that all elevations, including those below grade, remain a positive number. Similarly, when selecting a baseline, locate it in such a position that your entire facility remains in one quadrant, preferably northeasterly.

The use of field-welded connections for heavy steel structures has waxed and waned over the years. Should you encounter this issue, it is usually worth the effort to investigate its use with a steel erector. Conversely, be sure that the mechanical and electrical engineers have some idea of the sizes of the vertical and horizontal gussets that they may encounter at the intersections of structural members. Too often pipe lines have had to be redirected due to the obstruction of a gusset plate.

With an early understanding of the scope of work, and the boundaries of various subcontracts to be let, design and drafting can be laid out to match these limits and interfaces. Assignments must be given in detail, with the budgeted hours expected for the work. Communications must be free, and decisions made must be put in writing and distributed to all involved. The project manager must participate in the recognition and solution of technical problems, but should not remove technical responsibility or ownership from the engineer.

Know your client, his concerns, his problems, and his point of view. If they have any existing facilities ask if you can visit them. In developing a new project you should know if it is a shortlived venture requiring a low first cost and little concern over maintenance costs, or a longlived venture with the reverse requirements. Does the customer plan to own their own maintenance cranes, rent them, or will they require built-in monorails with permanent trolleys attached? The same philosophy holds through the design and selection of materials, from architectural criteria to drainage systems.

BUILDING AUTHORITY

Many of your project assignments may not fit the building code, nor was the code written to cover all types of work. However, if the project is somewhat run-of-the-mill, and after reading the building code you feel you have a good, economical, and safe fit, with no problem areas, then proceed with the design.

Many projects, especially those which have process or chemical engineering bases, may not be easily or economically interpreted within some building codes. The primary intent of most codes is to provide a safe environment, especially worker safety from environmental mishaps, fire, and the like. The building code's purpose is not the same as that of insurance companies, where the carrier's concern includes loss of production as well as structural damage.

Most codes are general, and not specific to particular industries. As floor areas and heights increase, so do requirements for access, egress, fire resistance, and ventilation needs. These code requirements appear mandatory, and there may often be no correlation between their demands and the size of the permanent working population to be housed. The codes seem to assume a certain population per square foot of floor area, and base their safety practice on that assumption.

If assigned to a project that will occupy a comparatively large area with a minimum number of permanent occupants, plan a visit at the earliest possible date, with a senior building official of the agency issuing the necessary permits. Describe the process completely to the official, using plot and floor plans, show what you believe to be a safe working arrangement and explain why. Sketches should show all the pieces of equipment, access and egress routes. Describe type of construction, heights of floors, exterior and interior wall materials, fire protection systems, structural fireproofing, if any, location of hydrants, distance between buildings, and other relevant information.

Answer all questions truthfully and completely, and demonstrate to the best of your ability why your recommendations offer a safe design. Defend your position with facts and good industry practice. This may take more than one meeting. However, it should end with a clear understanding as to what the governing authority requires, documented in a complete set of meeting notes.

A word of caution—do your homework. Before visiting the building authority, have a full understanding of the local code requirements and all of the various options open to you. There is no substitute for being prepared for these meetings, which should be initiated in a friendly, cooperative atmosphere.

In some areas of the country, a number of different governmental agencies must be satisfied before construction can commence. Other than the building official, they could include the fire marshal, state environmental agencies covering liquid wastes and air, and flood control agencies if any earth moving is necessary.

Avoid embarrassment. Be sure that either you or one of your senior staff is an engineer licensed to practice in the particular state. Building officials have been known to threaten terminating any further discussions with engineers not registered in their state.

If you have a turnkey project, that is, complete responsibility for engineering, purchasing, and construction, it may be possible to get a partial construction permit to do the foundations only, even though the rest of the drawings are still not complete. Usually, all risks then reside with the engineer in case of any error or change required by the permit-granting agency.

CODE CONSIDERATIONS

There will be times when state codes and prudent engineering judgment may be in conflict—specifically in areas of high seismic risk. A state code may not show any requirement for earthquake-resistant design, yet the seismic probability charts indicate the area to be a zone 2 or even zone 3.

If the project entails primarily grade-mounted equipment, or lightly loaded vessels housed in a single-story building, then considerations of how to proceed may not need to extend any further. However, if the work involves heavily loaded floors in a tall structure, then the problem may be more complicated. You may be in compliance with the state requirements even if you ignore the problems of earthquake design. However, this conflict should be explained to the client in complete detail. While there may be a substantial difference in insurance premiums associated with the various courses of action, there will be a substantial increase in the cost of engineering and materials if the structure and foundations are designed to resist seismic forces. The final decision must rest with the client, but the decision must be made with knowledge of all the facts at hand.

One additional consideration should be investigated. It is always a good idea to check local practice. There are probably good and valid reasons for what is accepted locally. Vary from it with caution.

RETROFITS

Where work involves retrofitting, enhancing, or rebuilding an existing facility, the potential for errors is great. Existing drawings should be studied but not trusted, whether it be an elevation, location, dimension, or datum.

If your problem is localized in a small area, save time by referencing an existing point of location. But if your new facility traverses various units, the opportunities for error increase geometrically. There have been instances where existing surveying monuments were in disagreement with each other and, hence, buildings were not accurately located. Elevations of floors were off, and so on. New designs must accommodate these inaccuracies, with final fitups being done in the field. Use angle seats and slotted holes to make up final connections. If you are doing engineering only, place the responsibility for field measurement and fit on the constructor. Your other choice is to make a complete new survey.

When gathering information for your design, client security requirements can be served by clearing your requirements with the plant manager. Explain what you will be doing, such as the need for taking Polaroid-type photographs. There are advantages in using a Polaroid-type camera. All photos must be logged and cleared with the client's office and returned at the end of the project. Similar measures should be taken with all existing drawings.

Make sure all your information is accurate before launching a construction effort. Problems such as confirming location of existing underground piping or electrical conduits in congested areas warrant spending money to dig trenches early in the project. Certainty of information in these early stages will reduce expensive rework and delays later. Use licensed surveyors when gathering or confirming early information. Haphazard taping from element to element will inevitably lead to trouble. If the situation is truly complex and messy, consider setting up your own monuments and coordinate grid system and elevations. Do not assume alignments are accurate. A structural steel column may not be plumb nor be the precise dimension called for in the steel handbook. When designing a new element abutting an existing structural steel column, leave some working room between the old and the new to allow for mill tolerances, misalignment, and ease of construction.

PROCUREMENT

The lead engineers must be involved and participate in procurement at the conceptual stage. You must obtain the client's concurrence as to what is to be subcontracted, and what is to be purchased by the owner or engineer. More frequently than not, you may need to go out for bids with incomplete drawings, and yet obtain protection on the pricing.

The engineers must contribute their thoughts on what unit prices will be required. One of the more complex subjects is structural steel, especially if bids are based on preliminary drawings. Naturally, if the drawings are complete and checked, you can go for a lump-sum bid and your problems are minimal. However, a very fast schedule may force you to get bids on very much less than complete drawings.

In a competitive market, the fabricator will try to come up with a good price based on what he sees on your drawings. Since the definition is inadequate, you must be sure that the fabricator gets a clear and complete picture of how the final drawings will look, and you must document this information as part of his bid prices. Fabricators have been known to demand extras or to seek significant changes to their unit pricing for any of the following reasons: less repetition of steel that requires more detailing; greater complexity of work; different mix of steel, such as many more lighter weight beams were added than heavier ones; more or less steel than they saw on the original sketches; a slip in schedule which affected their shop. Some of their claims may certainly be justifiable, but to reduce future headaches on both sides, do the best you can to describe all of these areas in your request for quotation.

On subcontracts, be sure that all the limits are defined and contractor responsibility is assigned for the connection at the interface. Review the benefits of combining contracts, such as excavation and backfill for foundations, underground piping and underground electrical. Be sure that you are covered in the contract for delays of one subcontractor by another, or by late delivery of apparatus purchased by the engineer.

Subcontractors must be required to follow all the drawings or get written permission if they wish to deviate. Sometimes the first one on site sees no reason to follow a complicated route, not understanding the problems of those who will be following shortly behind him and whose space he will be occupying, making a complex problem even messier. Be sure that your contruction planner is involved and coordinates the sequence of erection of the different contractors.

CONSTRUCTION

If your office has a construction department, or if you have a construction planner on your staff, get him assigned to your staff early in the development of your project. Make sure the planner reviews the plot plan and provides his input on such matters as ease of access of cranes, erection sequence of the project, method of delivery of materials, and the like.

He should also provide a description of the facilities available for the constructor, including a working arrangement for storage of materials; warehousing security; utility requirements for construction, including temporary power and telephone; and location of the construction fence and gate.

He should also review the planned materials of construction and advise of any problem areas that he can foresee. He must be available to the lead engineers to discuss options, ease of construction, materials selection and methods as they may affect price, constructability, and union rules. He should be available to all subcontractor bidders to be sure they understand on-site work rules.

CLOSEOUT

It is common to find as engineering nears completion and the number of staff has dwindled, that the engineering calculations have not been assembled. Be sure to alert staff leaders to keep up-to-date records and calculations and to dispose of all unnecessary or revised sheets. The leaders should keep the calculations current with pages numbered and titled. Many states demand that copies of these calculations, stamped with a professional engineer's seal, be submitted with your request for a building permit.

5

Plant Layout and Piping Design

RALPH W. SMITH* *Santa Fe Braun Inc., Alhambra, California*

Job hours included in plant layout and piping design account for approximately 40% of home office engineering time and some 30% of construction field labor of most industrial process plants. As such the performance of this discipline weighs heavily in the successful execution of such a project.

PLANT LAYOUT

The piping engineering discipline is the focal point of plant layout and plot plan development. The objective is to devise the most economical plant layout while providing an operable plant that can be readily maintained. A consideration, sometimes forgotten, is the constructability of the plant; and that the design must take into account the field schedule and the delivery of equipment to the site. Thus, design may not necessarily be that leading to the least expensive first cost of the plant, but the total costs including the operating and maintenance costs as affected by the layout.

Working with process, mechanical, and civil/structural engineers, the plant layout engineers develop the initial planning studies. Layout starts based upon the P&IDs, the site topography, access and other information, specifications, preliminary process and mechanical data for major equipment items and additional requirements from the owner. When a preliminary consensus has been reached, a planning model may be constructed and used as a communication tool for better visualization of plant layout.

The project manager should be aware of ten key concepts as the conceptual layout is developed. For all plants, safety considerations are primary and take priority over any other of these concepts.

1. For facilities located inside a building, the architects will play an important part in the plant layout. In a design office more accustomed to designing outdoor plants with the piping designers taking the lead in plant layout, this may cause a problem.
2. The layout should be made on a rectangular grid. Preferably all coordinates for the layout should be in the same quadrant to reduce confusion. All elevations should be based on a theoretical plant base selected so that all figures are positive.
3. Location of large towers and furnaces should be done first. Location should follow the logic of the process flow.
4. Preliminary piperack location should be developed taking into account the pipes entering/leaving the plot.

---
*Retired

5. Equipment serving the same system should be logically grouped together. For instance, the pumps and exchangers should be located near the tower that they mutually service.
6. Lengths of large diameter alloy pipe should be minimized consistent with other considerations.
7. Alignment of the plant should consider the prevailing wind direction.
8. Layout of instruments should consider the operational practices of the owner/operator.
9. Location of all equipment items must be considered in the layout to assure adequate access for maintenance equipment/labor crews.
10. Construction sequencing and erection procedures should be taken into account. The preliminary model should be reviewed with construction planners or, preferably, with the nominated construction manager.

Until the plant layout has been established, very little productive work can be done by the design disciplines. Development and approval of the layout and, consequently, the plot plan should be a high priority item for the project manager. Meanwhile, disciplines other than design depend upon the firm plot plan issue to develop detailed procurement and construction schedules and the preliminary material takeoffs.

Piping's role is especially crucial during the early phase of project development. Certain key activities of this discipline should be monitored closely by project management in the interest of overall project performance. These seven piping discipline activities, when executed in a timely and effective manner, will go far in assuring a successfully completed project.

1. Design approach
2. Staffing
3. Piping materials
4. Equipment orientation
5. Supplier drawings
6. Pipespool design
7. Pipespool fabrication

DESIGN APPROACH

There are two design approaches used today for translating the piping systems contained in the process and piping and instrument flow diagrams to the fabricated piping erected in the industrial process plant. These are (1) orthographic plans and elevation drawings and (2) an engineering model.

Either of these may be the basis for the piping isometrics and pipespool drawings used for fabrication and erection of the piping in the plant. Frequently today, a combination of the two systems is used. Models are used for complex processing units, and orthographics for less complex facilities including interconnecting pipeways and piping for the tank farm areas.

Where the plant design is relatively simple, or where the work involves revamping or retrofitting, the best approach is not always apparent. Project management together with the piping discipline should select the design approach, considering the economics of design and schedule most appropriate for the specific project requirements.

A third approach used by a few of the larger engineering firms consists of modeling the plant entirely within the computer data bank. All input is made to the computer to permit drawing isometric views of the plant; plans, sections, and elevations at any point in the plant; and isometric drawings of all piping. Some of this software has been developed by the engineering firms, and a few systems are available commercially.

Another approach, sometimes useful in maintenance operations, plant upgrading, revamp and retrofit work, involves the use of special photographs which can be used as a background for indicating the desired modifications which may be shown to exact scale. The project manager should evaluate this approach carefully, as the cameras and techniques necessarily employed can be expensive and time-consuming.

STAFFING

False starts for piping engineering can be extremely costly in terms of rework and lower performance. This is the result of prematurely starting the piping work on a broad front when it can be based only on incomplete and assumed upstream design data. Project management should exercise control over the design staffing buildup to ensure that work proceeds on reasonably firm and accurate data.

The initial piping design staff should be made up ideally of a small nucleus of experienced layout and planning designers. They should establish all of the layout parameters in terms of equipment spacing, arrangement, and elevations together with pipeway widths and heights. These parameters should be consistent with the operating, maintenance, and safety guidelines and requirements for the project. Piping routing included with the layout should be limited to the large diameter piping and the critical process and utility lines. Detail should be kept to a minimum so that changes caused by the firmed up design basis can be readily incorporated with little disruption and expenditure of jobhours.

PIPING MATERIALS

Seemingly endless quantities of different individual piping items are available. These include various configurations, materials, and wall thicknesses of pipe and fittings. Piping designers should give proper emphasis to reducing the number of different items on a project, particularly with regard to carbon steel materials. Wherever possible, the design should adhere to the standard items readily available from the suppliers. Cost tradeoffs should be made to use additional wall thickness over the design minimums to reduce the total number of piping items.

The project manager and the piping designers need to realize that where large numbers of different piping items are used, corresponding increases in cost of design, procurement, handling, storing, construction, and surplus disposal are inevitable. It rarely pays to buy small quantities of special materials where a more standard item of slightly better characteristics can be substituted.

SUPPLIER DRAWINGS

Realizing that supplier drawings are a key to completion of many of the piping isometrics, the project manager should focus on two problems. The first is rapid placing of the purchase orders for equipment. Many equipment suppliers are reluctant to order materials, start detailed shop drawings, or start specific plans for the shop fabrication without a written purchase order in hand. Sometimes even written letters of intent or telex orders do not really carry the import of the actual purchase orders. Next, the processing and approval of the vendor drawings needs to be carefully expedited. Most equipment delivery dates are based on times measured from receipt of approved drawings. The recycling of vendor drawings between engineering contractor and supplier can result in serious delays in shipment. The receipt of final supplier drawings is needed to complete the engineer's design drawings.

Many delays can be avoided if the known needs are indicated to the equipment vendor at the time of the inquiry. If the purchase order for air coolers includes ladders and platforms, a sketch should be included with the inquiry showing the preferred platform and ladder arrangement. The preferred location of the lube oil reservoir should be given with the inquiry for large compressors. The shell and tube heat exchanger inquiry should contain preferred foot spacing and nozzle orientation. Other usual problems involve late receipt of supplier data for inline instruments and rotating equipment, which can hold up the release of significant numbers of pipespools for fabrication. The piping work should also take into account the field schedule, assuring that the delivery of the pipespools from the shops is in accord with the field erection schedule.

PIPESPOOL DESIGN

Almost invariably, the design, fabrication, and delivery of the prefabricated pipespools falls on the critical path in a process plant project. The project manager and the piping discipline leader must concentrate on expediting the completion of that information necessary for the production of the isometrics including the plot plan, process and instrumentation flow diagrams, piping specifications, special criteria from the operations, maintenance, and safety departments, the engineered equipment data, and the nozzle orientation information.

The piping design itself must be continuously reviewed to assure that the configuration of the piping is as simple as possible consistent with the job requirements. Every flange, every fitting, and every weld represents additional cost to the job. Each must really be needed for the plant to operate safely and satisfactorily to justify the extra cost.

PIPESPOOL FABRICATION

Pipespools may be fabricated at the job site or in a commercial pipe shop. Many jobs look to a combination of two sources.

Most spools are made in a vendor's shop for reasons of economy. The shop, by virtue of a higher mechanization and a relatively permanent cadre of craftspeople and supervision, can operate more efficiently than a temporary field facility. The required quality of work may be more easily achieved in the shop environment.

Before inquiries are issued to vendors for pipespool fabrication, a reasonably accurate estimate of pipespool quantities differentiated by material and size is required as a part of the bid documents. Fabricators need these for pricing the work, allocation of shop space, and for estimating equipment and personnel requirements for the work. Project management needs to verify the reliability of the estimates in consideration of the appreciable amount of downstream planning which is based on these estimates.

The project manager should realize that some scheduling conflicts are inherent in most fabrication orders. The vendor will be inclined to give priority to the largest pipespools and the spool sizes with the greatest volume to maximize his upfront cash flow. The field piping erection program requires a mix of pipespool sizes by geographic area to optimize piping erection productivity.

Recognizing the potential for conflict, project management must assure that the production schedule is agreed to, and that the purchase order contains the proper language to exercise reasonable control over the sequence of work in the shop. Continuous onsite expediting may be necessary to coordinate manufacturing, shipping, and coordination with the job site where the schedule is especially tight.

SUMMARY

Special attention by project management to these few key piping engineering activities can improve performance dramatically. It is not a time-consuming task for project management; but the timing of project management involvement and attention is crucial.

6

Electrical Engineering

RICHARD L. RIDGWAY* *Santa Fe Braun Inc., Alhambra, California*

One of the project manager's biggest problems is the individual engineer's overwhelming desire to do a good job. A better job than the project warrants or that the contract calls for. The problem is greatest when dealing with electrical engineering and design personnel.

It has been my experience that people untrained in electrical engineering believe that there is something mysterious about electricity; and, as a result, they go to great lengths to avoid learning any electrical engineering theory. Even bankers and lawyers working in an engineering environment pick up a smattering of mechanical, civil, or even chemical engineering, but throw up their hands and close their minds when someone starts talking electricity.

The net result is that electrical engineers and designers have seldom had to find economic justification for their work. They simply maintain that these are the levels required by existing codes or by that wonderful phrase "good engineering practice." Most often any differences are settled with this retort. Unfortunately, this attitude is not confined to an engineering contractor's organization. It is equally true in the client's engineering department.

Normally, the client's project manager's interest in controlling project cost and schedule is equal to the contractor's project manager. As a result, the contractor's project manager can usually rely on the client's help in controlling the natural tendency of his people to demand more sophisticated and costly designs than can be justified by the particular application. But this is not so for electrical work, where the client shows the same unwillingness to understand or challenge the mysteries of the electrical world.

THE IMPORTANCE OF SOME ELECTRICAL KNOWLEDGE

The best advice that I can offer my fellow project managers is to throw away your inhibitions and learn a little about electrical engineeirng. It is not all that hard. You need not become proficient in transmission line design or electronic circuitry, but you should have sufficient knowledge to be as critical of what comes out of the electrical discipline as you are of what comes out of mechanical, piping, chemical, or civil.

Fortunately for those with little expertise in electrical matters, the economics of the electrical work do not warrant much of the project manager's time or energy. In most industrial or process plant projects, direct electrical material and labor runs from five to ten percent of the total estimated cost of the project. One can best put this statistic into perspective by realizing that most projects carry a contingency which is of the same order of magnitude. A discussion of the things that affect the magnitude

---
*Retired

429

of the cost of the electrical work would probably be most helpful to the nonelectrically oriented project manager.

MAJOR CONTRIBUTORS TO ELECTRICAL COSTS

When a new unit or process line is being added to an existing facility, it must be determined whether or not the existing plant has enough main substation capacity to supply the addition. Often the existing facility's power supply is insufficient to support the proposed expansion. Under these conditions, the cost of the new work must include the cost of expanding the main substantion. It is usually desirable to increase the capacity of the main substation beyond the immediate needs of the proposed expansion, which increases the cost of the immediate electrical work, but may save money for the owner in the long run.

In the case of a new grass roots project, a high-voltage main substation will almost invariably be included. However, the cost of the peripheral facilities associated with grass roots facilities tends to again reduce the electrical cost percentage.

Another important feature affecting the electrical cost of the project is the philosophy of the owner in providing redundancy. Dual feeders versus single feeders, single-ended substations versus double-ended, the quantity of motor-driven spare equipment such as spare pumps and compressors, are all examples of redundancy that affect electrical costs as a percent of total cost. Three 50-percent pumps as compared with one service pump plus a 100-percent spare, for example, could save the overall project cost, but increase the cost of the electrical work because of the additional starter and feeder.

The cost of high-voltage substations as well as the increased costs for redundancy are both highly weighted toward increased material cost with small labor cost increases. Further, transformers, substation equipment, and switchgear are relatively long delivery equipment items and must be ordered early in the project. Since this equipment is almost always bought on a fixed-price base and involves a small amount of field labor, the cost impact of the electrical work is pretty well fixed early in the project. Once approved, cost control of this part of the electrical work should not cause concern to the project manager.

SCHEDULE CONSIDERATIONS

As pointed out above, the major electrical equipment requires a long lead time and can be the determining factor in the overall project schedule. The project manager must be sure that all such equipment has been identified and that ample time has been allowed for preparation of the corresponding specifications, requisitions, purchase orders, and delivery when approving the overall project schedule.

OTHER COST CONSIDERATIONS

Four other items that can seriously affect the electrical costs are (1) the amount of automation desired, (2) how much data collection is specified, (3) is cathodic protection required, and (4) the extent of electrical heat tracing needed. Automation could include a computer as well as several programmable controllers. The real effect of these four items is to materially increase the amount of control wiring and the number of electrical connections to be provided in the field. These items are labor intensive; and, as such, have only a minor effect on the cost of electrical material, but a very major effect on the amount of electrical field labor necessary for the installation.

The definitive extent of these four items is often not clearly defined in the project design basis. Due to time and competitive pressures, it is easy for the electrical engineers, designers, and estimators to underestimate the extent of this part of the work. Although jointly, this group is responsible for early definition and pricing of the work for the budget, they have little control over subsequent growth of the work due to differences in interpretation of philosophy and specifications. The amount of automation is usually controlled by the process, chemical, and instrumentation engineers. The amount of data collection can be ultimately dictated by operating or marketing people, who may not have been directly involved at the definition stage of the project.

The extent of the electrical heat tracing is controlled by the process, mechanical, and piping engineers. Piping will usually lay out the plant to minimize alloy piping at the expense of longer carbon steel runs, while giving little or no thought to the amount of heat tracing required. The magnitude of cathodic protection is a function of existing soil conditions, and may not be quantifiable until long after the assumptions for the project budget and schedule are set.

QUANTITY/SCHEDULE RELATIONSHIPS

The electrical engineers have little actual control over these aspects of the project work; and, unfortunately, neither does the project manager. The best that can be hoped for is that they are given very careful consideration before budgets are set and schedules are fixed. In the overall picture, the effect of a poor evaluation of the scope of the electrical work is much more pronounced on the schedule and the costs of schedule overruns than on the cost of the electrical direct material and labor.

In the opinion of many people, the project manager's two primary responsibilities are to complete the project on time within the budgeted cost. The cost of the electrical work is sufficiently small so that the incremental differences should not warrant a great deal of the project manager's time. A 20 percent overrun in the electrical direct material and labor would usually mean only approximately one percent of the overall job cost. The effect on project schedule and costs of the attendant schedule delay costs are another matter.

IMPORTANCE OF ENGINEERING DISCIPLINE COORDINATION

The home office electrical work is almost always the last to be completed, and electrical contractors are always among the last to complete work in the field. Information developed within the electrical group has a minor effect on the work of the other engineering disciplines, but the work done by the chemical, mechanical, piping, and instrumentation disciplines always impacts on the electrical design substantially. For example, a reliable load summary must be available to the electrical engineer before substation and switchgear equipment can be specified. As already discussed, these items must be ordered early because of long delivery lead times.

Process engineers are usually responsible for deciding how much process equipment is to be motor driven. The mechanical engineers, working with the process engineers, must size the motor drivers. They are responsible for developing a reliable motor list early in the project so that electrical engineers may produce the electrical single line drawings and other electrical data. The civil engineers must furnish information on cranes and hoists, the architects develop building loads, the piping engineer specifies motor-driven valve requirements and heat tracing, and the instrument engineers must specify the extent of the electrical instrumentation as well as the extent of the emergency power system.

The project manager's main concern during engineering is that the other disciplines furnish all of the information to electrical on time and in the proper sequence for electrical to perform their work on schedule. To do this, the project manager must acquire a good idea of exactly what the electrical discipline does and exactly how they do it.

COORDINATION OF CONSTRUCTION TRADES

A similar situation exists with the construction phase of the work. The other trades have to be fairly well along with their work before the electricians can start. Obviously power equipment must have been set before the electrical craftspeople can hook it up. The same holds true with communication equipment, instrumentation, and control equipment such as computers, and data collection and monitoring equipment. Cable pulling is a multiple person operation; but, due to space limitations, hookup of most of the electrical equipment and terminal blocks is a one-man operation and can proceed only as fast as one man can work. Neither the project manager or the construction manager have the luxury of improving the work schedule by saturating the area with electrical craftspeople.

An overrun in electrical labor costs may not be too serious; but, because of the indirect costs associated with schedule delay and the fact that it is difficult to accelerate the field electrical work for reasons already explained, an underestimation of overrun of the electrical craft labor can be disastrous for the project. The electrical work is concentrated late in the project. Schedule delays cannot practically be recouped by increasing the number of craftspeople, so the end date for the overall project slips with corresponding indirect costs of production loss, etc. The project manager should see that other trade work is performed in the proper sequence to allow the electricians to start their work on time and to proceed in an orderly fashion.

SUMMARY OF PROJECT MANAGEMENT CONCERNS WITH THE ELECTRICAL DESIGN, BUDGET, AND SCHEDULE

We see, then, that the project manager's concern with electrical is probably more with schedule than with the direct cost of electrical materials and labor. Rather than depend on others to properly schedule the electrical work, the project manager should learn exactly what the electrical discipline does, what information they need to do their work, and the proper sequencing and timing of their activities. At the very least, an understanding of the possible effects of underestimating electrical labor on the schedule, and that ground lost because of this is very difficult to regain, is essential. The project manager must work very closely with the electrical discipline group to promote open communication to keep him up to date on potential problems. By understanding the content of the electrical scope, budget, and schedule and the relationships between these three, the project manager has a fighting chance of knowing how serious these problems are and the magnitude of their possible effect on the project.

7

Computer-Aided Design and Drafting

ALLEN T. KOSTER   *Harmony Construction of California Inc., Ventura, California*

Engineering designs and drawings are the graphic means of transmitting technical information and instructions from the engineering designer to all others who are engaged in the project construction process. The two primary purposes of these designs are (1) to identify the materials required for the project and (2) to show where and how the materials are to be used.

For a very simple task, it may be sufficient to produce a rough sketch of the proposed installation using materials that are on hand or readily obtainable.

For larger projects, it is necessary to produce more formalized drawings and material lists in order to control errors and to enable the project to be completed with a minimum of confusion and within a definite period of time.

New techniques, tools, and engineering aids to assist designers and drafters in meeting the requirements of economical design and acceptable project schedules are being developed continually. The mechanical drafting machine combined the functions of the T-square and triangles. Drafting templates, lettering sets, electric pencil sharpeners, and electric erasers are all examples of aids adopted to improve the productivity of designers and drafters.

The computer is one of the latest devices to find a place in assisting project execution. A standard tool for many years in engineering calculations, the computer has been programmed to produce engineering designs and drawings. It is ideal for handling a variety of complex assignments composed of many necessary, noncreative and repetitive tasks involved in engineering designs.

EARLY USES OF COMPUTERS BY ENGINEERING AND CONSTRUCTION COMPANIES

Computers were called "number crunchers" when engineering companies first began to take advantage of the speed at which the machines could handle complex mathematical calculations. The first day-to-day usage was in the accounting field to store data and manipulate the many arithmetic functions of corporate and project accounting. Process engineers soon started using computers for process design calculations. Heat and material balances, heat transfer calculations, plate-to-plate fractionation tower calculations, and line size computations were some of the early process engineering uses of the computer.

Some early mechanical engineering uses involved pipe stress problems. Prior to the advent of the computer, piping stress analysis was done either by graphic solution or by solving several simultaneous equations. A great deal of experience was necessary to reduce the pipe stress problem to a manageable size. A simple three-plane piping configuration normally took 40 hours to solve manually; the computer routinely solves the same problem in seconds.

PROBLEMS WITH EARLY COMPUTER USAGE

Many problems associated with computer usage inhibited acceptance of the computer for use in design applications. Here was a new and expensive technology entering the production scene with a unique terminology, new operating methods, and a new mystique of control and programming. To cope with these unique features, skilled technicians were hired. It was inevitable that communication barriers and conflicts would arise between the new computer experts and the future users who had an interest in adopting this new tool but who were unfamiliar with the new technology. Data entry at that time required that individual bits of information be keypunched and stored on input cards. This method produced errors and inaccuracies that the new technical user had to search out and correct prior to making the calculation run on the computer. The keypunch system of data entry was slow and cumbersome. To make matters even worse, engineering programs were assigned lower priority than the financial and accounting programs, and so were frequently delayed in the computer que. The new technical user had a sense of frustration and lack of control when his program ran into problems because of his input errors. An adage born during this era has endured to become standard computer terminology: "Garbage in–garbage out."

Increased use of the computer was inhibited by a lack of trust in the results. Fear of new and unfamiliar technology was accentuated by program designs lacking data validation and internal checking routines. Communication gaps developed between technical users and computer programmers because users were unable to fully describe all of the required design steps in sufficient detail for the program to be written. The computer programmer was interested in designing a program that would run most efficiently on the computer; and such a program was often not the most efficient for the user. A signal reason for the ineffective use of the newly developed programs was the lack of adequate program documentation and the failure to properly train the new users. Companies, after approving the capital funds to acquire the hardware, often did not foresee the additional money required for software development or education of the engineers. The lack of communications inhibited the technical use of the computer until a better understanding was reached between the computer programmers and the technical users.

Another problem complicating the acceptance of the computer was that program documentation was difficult to keep current because of (1) problems with priorities, (2) the pressure for rapid development of engineering programs and the continuous debugging and enhancement of these programs, (3) the shortage of competent programmers, and (4) the high turnover during this period of both programmers and engineering personnel.

EXPANDED USE OF THE COMPUTER FOR DESIGN APPLICATIONS

Despite these difficulties, it was evident that the computer had enormous potential for technical applications. As engineering workloads increased and projects became more complex, there was a need for more accurate and faster processing of project information.

Piping material takeoffs, bills of material for procurement, and control of the material through the delivery and erection were specific areas where improvement of current methods was urgently called for. Long delivery material had to be ordered far in advance of firm design information and early material takeoffs resulted either in omissions of critical materials or in expensive surpluses because manual accounting was inadequate to meet the needs of these larger, complex projects.

Piping isometrics were first introduced to the project activities to assist with material control and with piping erection. The handdrawn piping isometric detailed a portion of a process line and listed all of the material required for fabrication and erection of the line. The earliest computer material summary systems tabulated and summarized all pipe line material with a resulting improvement in material accounting.

The electrical designers had many applications for the computer such as the studies required for loads, for short circuits, and system voltage drops. Pressure vessel and heat transfer designs were applications that were added to the computer's growing list of technical applications. The technical users were drawn to the computer as a design aid wherever there was an opportunity to improve productivity and eliminate tedious calculations. Additionally, college graduates now entering the field, demonstrated proficiency in computer use and began to bridge the communication gap between the users and the programmers.

BREAKTHROUGH IN COMPUTER USAGE AS A DESIGN AID

As the engineering design industry began to master the computer intricacies, excellent proprietary programs became available for either outright purchase or on a timesharing basis. The best of these new programs were well designed and were accompanied by excellent documentation. Support for the user was available when difficulties were encountered with program use.

Timesharing introduced another feature that ultimately led to accelerated computer usage. The access to the host computer was accomplished through a cathode ray terminal (CRT), which eliminated the cumbersome cardpunch system of data entry. Input data could be checked and errors corrected prior to running the programs, eliminating many costly reruns.

The timesharing CRT, usually located at or near the designer's work station, had the effect of placing enormous computing power at a designer's fingertips. The advantage of the CRT was immediately evident and had a beneficial influence on later design applications. The actual hands-on use of the computer did much to dispel some of the concerns and reservations once common among the users.

ADVANCED COMPUTER TECHNIQUES AND AIDS

Operational pressure for improvement to the handdrawn piping isometrics and material lists continued. Computerized isometrics were made possible by the development of the two-axis, numerically controlled, flat-bed drafting plotters. Computer programs were developed that could list the line materials sequentially when specific instructions were input concerning the material specifications, material description, and the distance and direction defined between piping control points. The computer was programmed to produce a plot tape that controlled the action of an automated drafting machine in such a manner as to produce a finished isometric drawing together with the material list for that isometric. With the piping material captured in the computer memory, the material summaries, material requisitions, and purchase orders could be readily produced. Many other activities associated with piping material control could also be achieved, such as the tabulation of insulation and painting requirements, field inventory control and piping erection control. The piping isometric became an even more valuable tool as the controlling document for the design and erection of process plant piping. Piping isometrics became one of the first computer-aided drawings to be used effectively in the construction industry.

Some organizations produced piping isometric and material control programs for their exclusive in-house use. Others made their programs available to the industry on a purchase or a lease-royalty basis. One of the earliest in-house programs used in the engineering/construction industry was the PIC program developed by the Lummus Com-

pany. Another system that received widespread acceptance was the Compaid by Davy
Computing Limited, which was available for outright purchase. In addition, Compaid
was made available at a number of timeshare locations such as McDonnell Douglas Computing Services in St. Louis, Missouri and Multiple Access Limited in Montreal, Quebec.

The achievements reported for the computer-aided isometric piping and material
control systems were directionally consistent throughout the industry. All users reported a reduction in the jobhours required to produce isometrics. Because of differences in bookkeeping practices, quantitative figures are not meaningful.

One user of the Compaid system found that there were three measurable improvements:

1. A consistant reduction in jobhours per isometric on large jobs, showed an im-
    provement of some 45% using Compaid over manual isometrics/material control
    from orthographic drawings. A corresponding reduction of 36% was made using
    Compaid rather than manual isometrics/material control from an engineering
    model.
2. The total cost of producing a computerized isometric drawing with a material
    list was evaluated to be approximately 20% less than producing the same infor-
    mation with manual isometrics from an engineering model. This, of course,
    depends on the billing rates selected for the computer and use of the program.
3. By far the biggest cost effect evidenced using the computerized isometric sys-
    tem was in the reduction of engineering errors. Historically, field rework due
    to engineering errors fell in the 4-8% range (piping rework hours as a percent
    of total direct piping field hours). After the incorporation of the Compaid
    system, piping rework fell to a range of from 1.5-3.8%.

Computer-aided design for the civil engineering discipline received a large assist with
the development of the finite-analysis programs, which made possible static and dynamic
analyses of very large and complex structural systems while, at the same time, varying
design and operating conditions. The data was easy to input and verify and the results
were quickly received. The program capacity was extremely large and, for the first
time, allowed analysis of complete complex structural systems which produced superior
and very economical civil/structural engineering designs. Time would never have permitted the analysis of these complex structural systems manually. Innovative designers
developed computer programs that produced solutions for complex problems such as
foundation designs for rotating machinery on soil and on piles. As a result of the widespread acceptance, many of these programs have become industry standards.

Some of the complexities involved in electrical engineering were also assisted by
new computer programs. One of these was the Instrument Wiring System (IWS) developed by Bonner and Moore, which was capable of producing a point to point wiring
schedule for installation of field wiring. This computer program also has a graphic
capability which permits visual analysis of the instrument electronic loops. The IWS
has a side benefit of improving the communication between the design groups because
of the details available in the output reports.

Word processing has had an impact on the performance of projects and has been
used effectively to produce material specifications, material requisitions, and project
standards that could be kept current by periodic revisions with a minimum of additional
effort. There has been a continuous improvement in the word processing systems from
the early days of the Magcard and the IBM MTST.

The overall project management effort has been significantly aided by the computer
programs that were developed for timekeeping, engineering, scheduling, estimating,
and cost control. The project benefited from computer-generated reports because of
the easy availability and the variety of information available.

The development of computer-generated piping design and plant layout drawings
has been attempted by several organizations. A few of these systems have been used
in production with varying degrees of success. The computer-generated orthographic

piping drawings have the capability of interface checking against design parameters and producing input to a piping isometric program. The computer-generated piping drawings have not yet been as successful a communication tool as the engineering design model.

Computer-aided design's primary objective is to improve the quality of design, increase design productivity, and improve overall project communications. Although the piping design model is not a computer system, many design organizations have incorporated the plastic model as their standard with a high degree of success. In this system of design, the piping designers and model builders work in close coordination and construct the model from study sketches. The design model replaces the need for piping plan and elevation drawings and becomes the focal point of the project detail design resulting in a well-coordinated engineering design. The model lends itself very well to interfacing with computer input for piping isometrics.

PROBLEMS ENCOUNTERED WHEN ADOPTING NEW DESIGN TECHNIQUES

When new design techniques are introduced or production systems are modified, the production personnel tend to view them with suspicion as being a threat to their jobs. It is obvious that improved productivity eventually results in fewer personnel required for execution of the project. For the individual, this negative consideration is more than offset by the increased value of the work that he is producing. When computer aids are used, he is usually quick to realize that tedious, repetitive activities are significantly reduced.

Project teams tend to resist the introduction of new techniques or system changes on their projects. There is sufficient experience in the past to warrant their resistance. When computers were first used on project work, many problems resulted due to insufficient preparation and training of the personnel involved. This resistance can be overcome by proper planning, close coordination, and education of the personnel involved.

Corporate management has resisted the increased use of the computer because of the high investment costs in hardware and development and maintenance of the software. During the early days money was invested in software programs without achieving the desired results. These failures were expensive and the expended funds had to be written off. There was resistance from some shortsighted senior management personnel who saw no wisdom in reducing project job hours which were, after all, the basis for income on the prevalent cost-reimbursable jobs.

Management resistance may be reduced by thorough planning, training, and a successful track record of incorporating new computer programs. The need to maintain a company's competitive position has always been a strong incentive to adopt productivity improvements such as afforded by computerized engineering and design methods.

Resistance from traditional clients of engineering/construction firms has been essentially nil. These clients may have been the driving force behind the operational upgrading which stems from computerization. Client representatives readily accept those computer aids which have been proven, and have adopted a positive and supportive position for reaching out to new programs which promise operational improvement.

Training has always been an integral part of an engineering contractor's annual budget. The computer has changed the emphasis considerably from "how to do" to "how to use various computer programs to do better." In the past, weeks of training were necessary to develop a drafter's lettering. This emphasis has been changed to teaching keyboard usage. The basic training has not been materially changed, but the emphasis has been redirected significantly.

Departmental systems and procedures have been impacted due to the computer's requirement for accurate input. The human mind has a great capacity to accept questionable data without being diverted from its objective. The computer has little tolerance for such data. As a result, procedural modifications have had to be instituted and the execution of certain work either had to be expedited or postponed until acceptable data became available. The net effect on project performance has been acceptable, since the productivity improvements produced by the computer design have more than offset any possible schedule delays. The use of a computer causes attention to be focused on an engineering department's procedural weaknesses. This fact requires detailed analysis of all procedures and production systems to protect the integrity of the systems prior to introduction of a new computer program. The net result has been better and more efficient handling of work through a design production office with an improvement in internal and external communication.

JUSTIFICATION FOR COMPUTER DESIGN AIDS

The cost of developing computer programs, testing, and documentation is very expensive. The purchase of proprietary computer programs for a mainframe computer is less costly, but still can be very expensive. To justify the installation of a proposed computer system, it is necessary to analyze the application thoroughly and prepare a cost justification, payout calculations, and a return on investment analysis. The cost justifications are generally based on improved productivity of the work task and a shorter project schedule. A careful analysis must be made and methods developed for verifying the results once the new computer system or design aid has been installed. Many computer design installations have been made based on a faulty justification; and, as a result, additional applications have been delayed. Millions of dollars have been poured into some computer-aided engineering programs with a complete loss of time and expense. Early attempts at computerized piping isometrics using programs so poorly written and associated drafting equipment so cumbersome to use, that the cost of the isometric was several times that of a handdrawn iso. Sometimes poorly designed programs were pressed into service on projects in production resulting in added costs and project delays.

Computer-aided design justifications have generally been evaluated on the basis of a limited area of usage, such as specific work tasks in an engineering department only. It has been established that when computer-aided designs are incorporated in the design effort, there is a cascading benefit throughout the entire project. Many of these benefits are difficult to forecast and perhaps even more difficult to measure. The fact remains that more accurate information in greater detail is available earlier, and that more accurate and economical designs are possible with the computer.

DEDICATED COMPUTER SYSTEM FOR DESIGN AND DRAFTING

The previous discussions have centered on experiences using a large mainframe computer as a design aid. The aircraft industry developed design systems called computer-aided design and computer-aided manufacturing (CAD/CAM) programs that operated on mainframe computers. These computer programs are large and complex and have the capability of producing digital tapes which control a manufacturing operation. The CAD/CAM system was not readily justifiable for everyday design/drafting use because of the high operating cost. The dedicated minicomputer system was the logical choice for an engineering design aid. Many companies, such as Autotrol, Calcomp, Calma, Computervision, Computrol, and Intergraph entered into the field of producing systems designed for engineering drafting production. The most successful applications were made by manufacturers who developed software which was tailored to fill the needs of a particular industry, such as architecture, electronics, automotive design, or process plant design. The software capabilities had a decided influence on the selection of a system supplier.

The usual configuration of a computer-aided design (CAD) system includes a mini-computer, disk drives, unit controller, multiple interactive input stations, digitizer input stations, electrostatic and ink plotters, and various software packages. At the start, the equipment is usually located in a central area. The arrangement usually is chosen to facilitate the close initial supervision, the startup, training and development of standard operating procedures and design symbology.

The task required by the designer is brought to the CAD center in the form of a very rough sketch. The sketch is discussed with the CAD operator so that the designer's needs are clearly understood and there is agreement on the output requirements. The operator then manipulates the appropriate input devices and produces the designer's sketch within the computer's memory as well as visually on the CRT screen. When the operator completes the drawing to the required detail, the completed drawing is generally made on an electrostatic plotter, the output of which is adequate for a check print. This check print is then marked with changes and corrections by the designer and returned to the CAD operator. The changes are made to the data file. A final drawing is prepared on the ink plotter using high-quality plastic film. The final drawing is returned to the designer, backchecked, and then issued and handled in the production cycle in the same manner as any other drawing. The CAD system itself has a very detailed document control procedure program that permits accurate control of all drawings produced by the system and which is capable of producing reports for performance assurance and accounting purposes.

JUSTIFICATION FOR COMPUTER-AIDED DRAFTING

The physical work entailed in producing an engineering drawing is easy to measure. It is a simple matter to compare the productivity of a CAD-produced drawing with a drawing produced by conventional methods. In the payout calculations used to justify a CAD installation, the productivity improvements for the various categories of drawings that are planned to be produced are the basis for the justification of the installations. The design capabilities of the CAD system are not generally taken into account because of the difficulty in evaluating design tasks. These are best left until after the installation and until experience and experimentation can direct the future development of the new system. The drafting productivity improvements that can be expected with a CAD system range between 3 to 1 to as high as 10 to 1 depending upon the type of drawing that is being produced and the degree of experience of the operator. The average overall productivity improvement for drafting tasks seems to be in the order of 5 to 1.

A typical justification of a new CAD system would incorporate the anticipated staffing requirements over a five-year period which are used to calculate the payroll costs. The billing costs must take into account low efficiencies anticipated initially during the training period, and a lower utilization of the system for billable work during the early months. A new system will probably be started on a single-shift operation, but should ideally be increased to three shifts within a fairly short period. The machine rate per hour should be fixed. In doing this there must be a very careful balance between recovery of the investment costs, and a realistic charge to the project. In all cases, the total cost using the computer must offer a definite saving over the manual mode. The assumed productivity will be adopted for the justification, and the total annual revenues for each of the first five years can be calculated.

The operating expenses are estimated including all payroll costs, maintenance of the system, cost of supplies and consumables. An important factor during the first year will be the startup costs which should include training costs. Using the revenues generated and the operating costs, the profit/loss before taxes and depreciation may be calculated. The remainder of the calculation may be done in accordance with the applicable taxation and depreciation rules.

During the startup period, emphasis should be given to maintaining a high degree of morale within the CAD group. There will be many instances where easier ways to do things will be found and these must be adopted readily. It has been found helpful to have outside expertise available to help solve specific input problems initially. This help is much more readily available today than only a few short years ago.

Whenever a new system is introduced some analysis must be made of the risk involved to ongoing projects. A backup position must be identified before going into the program so that there can be no question of the projects being completed as planned. In some cases this may be using dual systems (computer and manual, or new computer system and old computer system) for a period on that project or projects on which the new equipment is started up.

EXPECTED PROBLEMS AND SOLUTIONS

New CAD systems have been installed in a central location because of the many associated benefits explained earlier. The selection and training of personnel must be done carefully. The individuals selected should have a broad knowledge of all disciplines included in the organization. They should be innovative, motivated, and capable of contributing to the future development of the new engineering tool.

The major problem encountered in the CAD systems based on a minicomputer central processing unit is the response time experienced by the operator as a result of multiple entries of input occurring simultaneously. The initial solution to improving response time hs been directed at improving the operator's techniques and the application of system discipline. There will always be a need to improve the response time until the capability of the CAD system can be made to interact with the user at an acceptable pace. Normally response time gets progressively longer as the system is used more and approaches its maximum capacity. Finally, the response time is improved by increasing computer capability.

FUTURE DEVELOPMENTS

After the CAD system has been in place and accepted as a normal part of the company design procedure, there must be a continuing analysis to determine methods of improving the design service and to identify new applications within the organization. There is a necessity to stay current with the rapidly developing CAD field.

Trends in the computer industry and pressures within the engineering/construction companies indicate that the future lies in a group of software data base modules tying all of the organizational structure together in one comprehensive program. Each module will be capable of functioning independently, while also being capable of being integrated into an interactive master project system.

The microcomputer will be used effectively as a preprocessor for every level of project activity. The drafting board will disappear and will be replaced by a computer-input terminal which will have access to several levels of computer capabilities available to the organization. Design information, project progress, and costs together with other necessary project information will be at the fingertips of the project manager permitting projects to be executed more efficiently to tighter schedules and budgets.

SUMMARY

The computer has had a distinct impact on the execution of engineering/construction projects in the past decade. The impact can be measured in productivity improvements in every engineering discipline and all other areas of project execution. The quality of the designs produced are significantly better than they were in the preceding decade and there has been a correspondingly significant reduction of engineering errors as a result of computer applications. There is every expectation that these improvements will continue as the full potential of the developing computer technology is realized.

VII

MATERIALS MANAGEMENT

UNIT OVERVIEW

The development of materials management has lagged behind other areas of project execution. One probable reason is that, in most firms, responsibility for the various procurement activities has been split between engineering, purchasing, and constructtion. Modern materials management has tended to assign full responsibility and accountability to a materials manager within the project organization.

A characteristic of most successful projects is a smooth and efficient flow of material to the jobsite. Efforts expended to maintain this flow are well invested. Elimination of double handling is an important consideration, but it has to be weighed against not having the material when it is required. The cost of paying for equipment and bulk materials in advance of when they are required should be balanced against possible disruptions in the field schedule if they are not at the site. Generally, it is preferable to have everything at the site early rather than have to wait for even a few items. It is to this end that the procurement planning and control is focused.

This unit stresses the need for detailed planning for specifying, requisitioning, purchasing, expediting, inspection, shipping materials, and equipment. Once the plan has been developed, it must be communicated to all of those involved, and then the work must be monitored and controlled against the schedule targets established by the overall project plan. Because of the number of people involved in procurement activities of one sort or another, coordination of efforts is essential.

The first chapter in this unit covers the prepurchasing, purchasing, and post-order activities. The second chapter deals with the types of expediting commonly used to assure delivery of the materials to the point of use.

Chapter 3 discusses how inspection procedures insure that equipment and material orders comply with the purchase order requirements and specifications. The last chapter in this unit talks about the site material management.

Project managers should be aware of the immense variety of tradeoffs available to them to meet project objectives.

For projects with very short schedules sole source negotiation for equipment and commodities might resolve time constraints by eliminating the time required for competitive bidding. There have been many instances where long lead time equipment from other plants or surplus commodity materials have been purchased to eliminate fabrication/manufacturing time. For projects where money is tight, used equipment may be considered. In tightly funded projects, expanding sources of supply can sometimes result in savings, as might be the case with international procurement.

The vendor print approval cycle should be monitored carefully. This source of time slippage often contributes to inordinate delays in completing manufacturing or fabrication. For critical path items, field trips by engineering personnel may be scheduled to the vendor's engineering office, the plant, or the shop to expedite decisions.

The project manager must assure that everyone involved on the project understands the priorities given to each of the purchase orders. Critical path material must be given the attention necessary to remove all barriers to its on-time delivery to the jobsite.

BIBLIOGRAPHY

Battle, R. K. and B. F. Robertson. The Management of Change: Bechtel's Evolutionary Approach to Project Material Management. Proceedings of the Project Management Institute, Drexel Hill, PA, October 1985.

Clark, R. L. Improve Equipment-Source Inspections. *Hydrocarbon Processing*, April 1982, pp. 213-242.

Graham, S. A. and L. F. Ray. Managing Bulk Material Delivery. An Hierarchical Approach. Proceedings of the Project Management Institute, Drexel Hill, PA, September 1986, pp. 213-221.

Guaspari, J. I Know It When I See It. AMACOM, American Management Association, New York, 1985.

Kerridge, A. E. How To Evaluate Bids for Major Equipment. *Hydrocarbon Processing*, May 1984, pp. 141-154.

Kinsley, Jr., G. R. Hedging Currency Risk When Buying Foreign Equipment. *Chemical Engineering*, April *20*, 171-174 (1981).

Shillitoe, W. How to Handle Procurement in Developing Countries. *Hydrocarbon Processing*, December 1982, pp. 62-67.

Stukhart, G. and L. C. Bell. Construction Materials Management Systems. Proceedings of the Project Management Institute, Drexel Hill, PA, October 1985.

1

Procurement

DANIEL GILAN* and KEVIN C. YESSIAN   *ANR Venture Management Company*
Detroit, Michigan

An important factor contributing to the successful execution of a project is the implementation of proper procurement activities. Procurement functions are highly sensitive and visible activities as exemplified by the extreme inflationary period of the 1970s. The complexity of product evaluations combined with worldwide procurement require a high level of talent within the procurement organization.

PLANNING THE PURCHASING EFFORT

One of the very first and critical elements to any EPC (engineer, procure, construct) schedule is the proper examination of the major components of purchasing and the time relationships to securing the best possible price without sacrificing quality. This planning effort should be broken down into manageable segments: equipment, commodities, and subcontracts. Each major area will consist of multiple level steps within each segment allowing the appropriate personnel to track the segments for which they have responsibility.

Equipment Planning

Depending on the type of project control estimate prepared prior to the detail design, it may be necessary to extract additional information to assist with the equipment procurement planning effort.

Typically the preliminary data sheets developed during the estimate stage will allow preplanning of the equipment purchasing effort.

Lead times for equipment deliveries are crucial to setting schedules and priorities for the detail design and construction activities. The lead times for compressors, pumps, and large vessels should be obtained early, based on current availability. Items which can be purchased from international sources should be identified and evaluated as to transit time and the overall erection time after receipt. The method and type of manufacture will need to be coordinated with the design engineering and construction efforts to determine the preferred method of assembly—partial or full, modularized, or skid-mounted.

If field assembly problems are anticipated, consideration of the transfer of the assembly to the fabricator/manufacturer may be warranted. Freight limitations on the final size, weights, and configuration must be reviewed, evaluated, and coordinated with the overall project approach.

Current affiliation: ANR Development Corporation, Detroit, Michigan

Commodity Planning

The largest single effort in many project purchasing efforts is the piping. Planning of the piping program is a joint effort between engineering and procurement. If the control estimate includes quantities with line sizes, types of material, and preliminary plot plans, purchasing will have an opportunity to focus on minimizing delivery problems. The piping plan should examine possible alternatives, including the extent of field fabrication and whether material supply should be part of the shop fabrication purchase order. The purchasing plan should evaluate the pros and cons of such alternatives, considering the project circumstances. The commodity plan should also address the overall isometric/orthographic schedule.

The capabilities of the various vendors must be carefully assessed, considering the following schedule restraints:

Receipt of the engineering isometric/orthographic drawings
Preparation of the shop drawings
Takeoffs for the bills of material
Material identification
Duration of shop fabrication
Preparation and methods of surface-coating application
Inspection
Loading
Time required for transport to site

The issue of drawings should coincide with the field need dates to ensure that the proper sequence has been achieved. Fabrication priorities should be dictated by the engineering and construction schedules. Projects with a large number of fabricated spools will generally benefit from a computerized material control program. Some fabricators have this capability and this should not be overlooked during the qualification survey.

Separate planning and custom reports are usually necessary for reinforcing steel, structural steel, in-line instruments, valves, and heat tracing. The various manufacturers should be informed of the reporting requirements prior to award of any purchase orders.

Single point of purchase versus duplicate sources of supply should be evaluated even though the upfront economics do not warrant splitting the requirements. Two sources of supply may prove to be highly beneficial if the engineering effort is delayed or if the overall schedule needs to be accelerated. The subsequent effects on the single source vendor may impact their ability to perform.

PURCHASING ORGANIZATION REQUIREMENTS

Once the macro review of the purchasing plans has been completed, the organizational requirements may be addressed.

The organization should be developed to support the requirements of the overall program. For each project centralized versus decentralized purchasing should be evaluated. A detailed manpower loading schedule should be made to ensure that sufficient personnel are available for the work over the entire schedule. Major disciplines to be considered include:

Procurement management
Buyers (by specialty)
Expeditors
Inspectors
Traffic Specialists

Warehouse personnel
Procurement clerical personnel

BIDDERS LISTS

An approved bidders list (ABL) should be made and approved for each category of
equipment, material, or subcontract required for the project. The ABL provides a
direction for the buyer or subcontracts administrator in soliciting competitive bids.
This list also provides a close tie to design engineering. The ABL should be developed
taking into account the current performance history of each firm including both technical and financial strengths. The ABL should be structured by categories, for example:

Major equipment item
Ancillary equipment
Commodities and consumables
Instrumentation

The bidders list should be approved by the client and by both the engineering and
construction contracting firm(s). Some firms do not prequalify vendor/subcontractors
prior to soliciting. However, this may necessitate a substantial amount of additional
job hours to be spent in downstream procurement activities. A key element to developing an approved bidders list is a careful evaluation of each potential supplier. Prequalification of a firm can be accomplished by various means. One method is by using
a prequalification questionnarie to be completed by the potential suppliers. Information
solicited and used for evaluation would include:

Management capability
Technical capability
Fabrication/manufacturing capability
Labor/management relations history
Labor contracts expiration
Past performance
Financial position
Industry expertise

Typically, the ABL is developed well in advance of the completion of detailed design.
The bid list is reviewed before the individual request for quotation is released, to
allow for fine tuning and incorporation of the current performance data.
    Worldwide procurement will complicate ABL preparation, but good bidder evaluation
is all the more necessary to avoid downstream material management problems.
    Many projects will have restricted purchasing as a contractual or legal requirement.
The "Buy American" restriction on projects calls for a specific review to ensure compliance with these stipulations. Other countries may have equally or more restrictive
constraints on importing of project components.
    When the ABL is prepared, there are two facets of the procurement effort which
should be pursued: (1) standardization and (2) package combination/blanket orders.

Standardization

Long-term operability and maintainability are usually high on the owner's list of objectives. Savings from standardization result from several areas:

1. Purchasing job hours can be greatly reduced
2. Lower costs of expediting and inspecting

3. Simplification of receiving and warehousing
4. Reduction of paperwork through the procurement effort

The prime candidates for a standardization program might include:

Equipment:
  motors
  transformers
  switchgear
  panelboards
  motor control centers
  batteries
  invertors
  motor starters

Instruments:
  analyzers
  annunciators
  control panels
  control systems

Mechanical—rotating equipment:
  crushers (roll, impact)
  feeders (belt, plot, screw,
      vibrating)
  fans and blowers
  pumps (centrifugal, vertical,
      vacuum, hydrocarbon chemi-
      cal, water, firewater, sump,
      lube oil, boiler feedwater,
      chemical injection, positive
      displacement)
  reducing gears
  V-belt drives
  agitators
  lube oil coolers
  mechanical seal flush coolers
  hydraulic systems

Mechanical—fabricated:
  conveyors (belt, screw)
  dust collectors (baghouse,
      centrifugal)
  scrubbers
  scales
  filters
  ejectors, eductors, and vacuum
      jets
  vent silencers
  elevators
  cranes, monorails, and hoists
  HVAC equipment
  fire hydrants
  static mixers
  davits
  insulation rings

Commodities:
  electrical
      grounding materials
      communication devices
      lighting fixtures (indoor, outdoor)
      cable (segregated- and nonsegre-
          gated-phase bus)
      pushbuttons
      pilot lights
      relays (control, protective)
      metering devices
      wiring terminals
      terminal blocks
      receptacles
      electric tracing systems
      cable trays

  instrument
      pressure relief devices (safety
          valves, rupture discs)
      steam turbine governors
      vibration detection devices
      control valves
      solenoid valves
      valve actuators and operators
      instrument air pressure regulators
      conservation vents and vacuum
          relief valves
      flame arrestors
      UPS devices
      instrument wiring
      thermocouple assemblies
      electronic transmitters
      local indicators
      valve I/P transducers
      limit switches
      fire protection devices
      orifice plates
      analog panel instruments
      displacement-type level instru-
          ments

  mechanical—auxilliaries for conveyors
      belting
      bushings
      idlers
      pulleys
      bearings
      gears
      wipers
      holdbacks

mechanical-auxilliaries except
    conveyors
mechanical seals
packing
couplings (disc, gear, dia-
    phragm)
bearings

piping
    valves (gate, globe, ball,
      butterfly, plug, needle,
      check, diaphragm, knife)
    valve packing
    valve bonnets
    hangers, supports, anchors
    steam tracing manifolds
    gaskets
    steam traps and strainers
    in-line strainers and filters
    expansion joints
    back flow preventors
    tube fittings
    hose connections
    coating and wrapping materials
    cathodic protection materials
    piping (steel, spiral welded,
      plastic, glass-lined, cast
      iron, concrete)

structural
    anchor bolts
    conveyor support structures
    pipe support structures
    pipe sleeperways
    pile caps
    building siding
other
    bolting materials (bolts, washers,
      nuts)
    fire fighting equipment (hose,
      sprinkler heads, portable
      extinguishers)
    plumbing insulation
    thermal insulation
    accoustical insulation
    refractory
    acid brick
    paint systems
    lube oil and greases
    welding rods
    building hardware
    vessel and tower packing
    portable safety devices
    fencing materials

Once the standardization program has been established, additional benefits can be realized in the form of blanket purchase orders and package combinations.

Blanket Purchase Order Agreements

Blanket purchase orders can be developed from those items listed in the standardization program. Additionally, major project agreements can cover fabricated structural steel and fabricated pipe spools. These agreements can be structured to provide specific or nonspecific items. Once the source of supply has been established, these items can be further spelled out within the detailed package specification and/or incorporated within the individual subcontract packages.

The development of blanket orders requires a close interface with the engineering and estimating groups to ensure that optimum benefits materialize. Some things that should be kept in mind are:

1. Added purchasing power by increasing volume in combining requirements typically offers additional savings as opposed to individual purchases.
2. Prices are protected for a period of time which satisfies the benefits of cost containment. A de-escalation clause might be introduced depending on market conditions. The appropriate indices can be traced via the Standard Industrial Classification (SIC) of an item or the Bureau of Labor Statistics (BLS).
3. Specific items are released from the blanket agreement in accordance with takeoff quantities in the approved design. This provides for the highest level of control to minimize surplus at job completion. This method provides for bulk receipt at the construction site.
4. The necessity of negotiating individual prices is eliminated, and the control is centralized in purchasing and accounting.

PROCUREMENT CONTROL

Each project needs a set of tracking systems to ensure that the procurement cycle
target dates are being met. Here we will focus on these cycles through the placement
of the purchase order or the signing of the subcontract. There are two separate cycles
to consider: that of the engineered equipment and commodities, and that of the subcontracted work. The individual steps will vary depending upon the contractual conditions, but typical examples of the two cycles follow:

Equipment/Commodity Procurement Cycle Planning Schedule

1. Receipt of the engineering requisitions including technical specifications by
    purchasing
2. First review of inquiry package
3. Check to ensure conformance of standardization program
4. Check to ensure conformance of the consolidation program
5. Confirmation of approval of the engineering specifications by project, manage-
    ment, and the client
6. Determine special terms and conditions
7. List spare parts (if required)
8. Final review of requisition/contract/inquiry package
9. Issue inquiry package with recommended bidders list to client for approval
10. Receipt of client approval for inquiry package and bidders list
11. Issue inquiry
12. Clarification meeting
13. Bids due
14. Bid clarification meeting(s)
15. Bid evaluation complete
16. Issue award recommendation to client for approval
17. Receipt of client approval
18. Preaward meeting
19. Purchase order award

Subcontracting Procurement Cycle Planning Schedule

1. Receipt of engineering specifications from engineering
2. First review of scope of work/contract or inquiry package
3. Confirmation that engineering specifications have been approved by all tech-
    nical disciplines, the project manager, and the client
4. Review by construction of scope of work/contract/inquiry package
5. Final review of scope of work/contract/inquiry package
6. Issue scope of work/contract/inquiry package with recommended bidders list
    to client for approval
7. Receipt of client approval for scope of work/contract/inquiry package and
    bidders list
8. Issue inquiry
9. Clarification meeting and site visit
10. Bids due
11. Bid clarification meeting
12. Bid evaluation completed
13. Issue award recommendation to client for approval
14. Receipt of client approval
15. Preaward meeting
16. Subcontract award

In both of the above cycles, each step requires a certain amount of time to implement prior to proceeding to the next step. This task cannot be undertaken solely by purchasing personnel, but requires a close interface with the project control functions and with the project manager. Forecast or anticipated dates are inserted to provide a structured planning tool. Appropriate contingency time should be considered to allow for unexpected problems including the forced extension of a bid due date. The overall cycle should be meshed with the project schedule. Depending on the complexity of the project, computer-assisted programs can be used to provide current status and consistent formats. Variances can be pinpointed and corrected before they adversely affect the project schedule.

THE MATERIAL COORDINATION PLAN

The material coordination plan (MCP) specifically orchestrates which party, engineer, client, or subcontractor, is responsible for each of the procurement activities. It provides an additional tool for project coordination and control. The MCP designates responsibility for each type of material required for the project and should cover equipment, commodities, and subcontracts. The MCP becomes more important as the complexity of the project increases. In the environment of today's projects, it is not uncommon to see many contractors working together under a joint venture agreement or in a partnership arrangement. As the dispersion of responsibilities grows, the need for a master list documenting the project procurement plan becomes increasingly necessary.

PURCHASING CONTROL FORMS

Prior to requesting formal bids, the format and proposed usage of all of the purchasing documents or forms should have been resolved. Where two or more design firms are working together on the same project, standardization of the purchasing documents should be considered. A checklist of some of the forms which will be needed follows:

   Request for quotation: Instruction to bidders
   Purchase order terms and conditions
   Subcontract terms and conditions
   Purchase order and purchase order acceptance form
   Subcontract form
   Subcontract support
   Packaging, marking, invoicing and shipping instructions
   Special terms and conditions
   Bid tabulation forms

The forms listed above highlight the major instruments used in securing goods and services. Procedures must be written to support the objectives and methodology of using each form. Careful conformance to these procedures will reduce future conflicts from an administrative, as well as from a legal, standpoint.

THE BIDDING PROCESS

Request for Quotations

It is essential that the project have a tracking system for the Request for Quotation cycle covering the time from when the bids are solicited to the time they have been received.

Bid Evaluation

Once the bids have been received, distribution should be made to the appropriate personnel by means of a predetermined distribution sheet. Depending upon the policy of the particular company, the involved parties will receive either priced or unpriced copies of the bidder's quotations according to their need. Some companies restrict knowledge of the bid price to one or two commercial people while giving only unpriced copies of the bids to the technical specialists. Other companies believe that a true technical evaluation cannot be made without knowledge of the comparative prices. If there is any possibility of the prices becoming known prematurely, access must be restricted. Policy sometimes dictates that the bids be opened in a public meeting. The proper ethical aspects of the procurement professionals should be observed completely.

The assigned purchaser will commence review of the bids, and development of a preliminary bid tabulation sheet. Questions about the technical and commercial aspects of the bids should be handled solely by the purchaser during the evaluation period. Many of the bids can be evaluated and the process concluded without further recourse to the bidders.

Companies have different practices regarding bid evaluation. Some demand that all bids be fully evaluated, technically and commercially. Frequently, however, the bids are screened for price and only those two or three apparent low bidders receive the full evaluation. Proper evaluation of a complicated bid, for example for a compressor train or a process control system, is time consuming and costly. There appears to be merit in reducing the evaluation effort where the end results will be the same and fairness to all bidders assured.

Preaward Meetings

In the case of more complicated orders after the technical review has been completed and the purchaser has made a preliminary bid tabulation, individual, preaward meetings should be held with two or three of the bidders. The agenda for these meetings must be customized depending on the purchase order content; however, there are certain typical topics that should be covered including questions about the following areas of the bid:

    Technical
    Purchasing
    Inspection
    Expediting
    Engineering/Purchasing/Vendor contacts

The meetings should be attended by representatives of purchasing, project engineering, the engineering disciplines involved, the vendor, and the client. Minutes of these preaward meetings should be written, and written confirmation of any clarifications and/or changes agreed to by the vendor should be immediately forthcoming.

Purchase Order

The purchase order should be written and delivered to the successful vendor as soon as practicable after all approvals have been given. If there are many changes to the initial bid, or if additional work has to be done to bring the purchase order into compliance with the decisions reached in the preaward meeting, it is usually better to issue the initial purchase order based on the original bid with the stipulation that it will be supplemented in accordance with decisions agreed to in the meeting. Usually little productive work is done on an order until the actual purchase order is received, regardless of telexes or letters of intent.

TRAFFIC

Coordinating material deliveries and ensuring that goods will move from the point of fabrication/manufacture/distribution to the jobsite requires some very detailed planning. Traffic here means developing the appropriate methods that should be employed to minimize transportation problems while optimizing the cost of transport. Traffic involvement begins at the early planning stages and continues through bid tabulation and concludes only with the actual delivery of the material to the jobsite.

Bid Evalutation

Freight should be itemized as a separate cost in the bid tabulation and also the purchase order. The freight program should be analyzed carefully to select the most appropriate form of transportation: rail, air, barge, overseas carriers, contract haulers, commercial carriers, and the like.

As a result of deregulation in the U. S. trucking industry, the overall potential savings are well worth the efforts involved in these evaluations. Freight cost on a project can represent as much as 5 to 10 percent of total material costs.

Traffic considerations will be an integral part of several of the bid evaluations. In some cases the freight cost will be the determining factor in vendor selection. Individual bids should be requested on the basis that the weight, freight costs, routing, and transport plan be presented together with the other commercial terms. The traffic group will then make a determination as to whether the freight cost should be included in the purchase order.

The traffic review should include an evaluation of the vendor's technical ability to handle the transport of the goods as well as the cost effectiveness of his proposal.

Transport Constraints

The traffic group will need to identify any constraints imposed upon deliveries by the various transportation means available for shipment to the site. With this information, a preferential routing guide can be customized for the site.

Early in the traffic program development all codes and regulations associated with movement of material from likely points of shipment to the jobsite should be reviewed including:

Permitting requirements
Tariff authority
Load restrictions
Rail restrictions
Air service restrictions
Small package carrier limitations
Tax laws
Frost laws

The Traffic Program

The traffic program should take an umbrella approach in reviewing all shipments to the project site including:

Overseas shipments (heavy lifts, light lifts, oversized shipments)
Full truck loads
Less than full truck loads
Freight forwarded requirements
Custom clearance procedures/requirements
Import duties

Bonding/power of attorney requirements
Consolidation of shipments (overseas shipment, less than truck load shipments)
Freight damage handling
Insurance requirements

Some particularly large or heavy pieces of equipment will require extensive field study to determine even one acceptable means of moving the material to the jobsite. In some cases, special transport equipment may need to be leased or fabricated especially for the task.

Additional savings can be obtained by reviewing all items to be imported and arriving by overseas shipments. A conference rate or project freight rate can be secured once points of manufacture/fabrication have been determined. A competitive freight quotation can be developed listing all items to be imported, with weight, size, shipping schedule, and other pertinent data. Delivery slippages must be avoided by building adequate protection into the contract.

Once an ocean carrier has been selected, a similar approach can be used for barge shipments. The onloading and offloading requirements from the points of exportation to destination are reviewed.

The heavy lift program should be designed to cover all such shipments from the various points of origin, and all intermediate points of handling through to the offloading at the jobsite.

Additional freight contracts for major bulk commodities such as structural steel, pipe spools, and the like can be secured with carriers to enhance freight savings as well as to facilitate coordination of the shipments.

Coordination of Site Deliveries

Coordination of shipments to the site during peak construction is often overlooked in planning the project. If receiving dock space is limited, eliminating less than full truck load shipments can cut down on the numbers of carriers converging on the site. A consolidated freight agreement can be used to combine all less than truckload shipments. Full truck loads are then programmed to arrive at the site by an exclusive carrier competitively selected. This program may be especially beneficial for remote project sites.

If the site is already congested, as in an existing plant, an area away from the site should be considered for a marshalling yard. Although some double handling will be necessary, the added control over site traffic will compensate.

CONCLUSION

The project manager should recognize that the proper planning and execution of purchasing activities are important determinants to project success.

2

Expediting

P. R. PEECOOK and EDWARD C. STOKES   *Bechtel Group Inc., San Francisco, California*

The objective of expediting is to provide an adequate flow of equipment and material to a jobsite at the required time and in the proper sequence. An inherent part of this objective is the task of ensuring that suppliers meet the schedule promised when accepting the purchase order or contract.

Placing the orders and then trusting the suppliers to fulfill their commitments may or may not accomplish this objective. Additional effort is usually required to get orders delivered when they are needed at the jobsite. Some businesses place a higher priority on prompt delivery than others; as a result, expediting systems vary in sophistication ranging from a month-at-a-glance calendar to those that make use of extremely complex computerized tracking systems. Procurement groups who order maintenance and operating supplies are less likely to be concerned with delays than are engineering/construction organizations where an entire construction project could be brought to a halt by late delivery of essential components and materials.

There are, therefore, relative degrees of emphasis placed on the expediting of orders within certain groups. It is also probably true that the majority of orders require little or no expediting at all. However, for those managers who are working on projects where an hour's delay can mean thousands of dollars in additional expense and working with materials and equipment where close tracking and follow-up is mandatory if satisfaction is to be achieved, professional expediting can require substantial resources.

ORGANIZATION

Within the larger procurement organizations, there are usually many departments: Purchasing, Contracting/Subcontracting, Expediting, Inspection, Traffic, and Material Control. These functional groups are closely related and form a full materials management capability that begins with the identification of equipment, materials, suppliers, and subcontractors and extends through to issue to field forces for installation.

The Expediting Department, generally under the direction of procurement management, can be subdivided into sections and subsections. Major engineering and construction firms typically divide their staff into two categories: (1) project expediters, who concentrate on specific projects, and (2) shop or area expediters, who visit the suppliers' plants.

Recognizing that, for a project, the project team is the basic building block, the expediters, contract specialists, buyers, inspectors, and traffic personnel would be integrated within the task force. This is more true for very large projects requiring several full-time personnel; but it should always respond to the needs of the project. Operating under a matrix organizational concept, the procurement team typically is managed by the project procurement manager who reports to the project manager. Administrative responsibility and functional guidance remain under the procurement management of the functional organization.

EXPEDITING METHODOLOGY

While the actual expediting of suppliers does not normally start until an order has been placed, expediting may participate in the procurement cycle at a much earlier point by furnishing information on existing labor situations, workload conditions, manufacturing lead times, and performance history of the various suppliers and subcontracting firms.

To assist in developing a bid list of acceptable suppliers, expediting may perform capability surveys and obtain information on their past and current performance. On critical orders, expediting should participate in bid clarification and preproduction meetings with suppliers to address potential problem areas, obtain commitments on schedule, designate key supplier contacts, discuss the supplier's sources of material, and determine that the supplier has the knowhow and a viable plan to meet the project requirements.

Expediting also monitors the issue of material requests for quotations and return of supplier quotations in order to support the overall procurement effort.

By monitoring the supplier's engineering, procurement, and manufacturing functions and relating these to the project's engineering and construction schedule requirements, expediters identify potential problem areas and initiate action to resolve them before they become sufficiently serious to impact the project schedule. This is called "preventive expediting."

There are two distinct types of expediting: project and area. Although both functions have a common goal, there are significant differences in their mode of operation.

PROJECT EXPEDITING

Project expediters may be located in the project office or at the jobsite. It is they who generally initiate the expediting effort. They should work very closely with engineering and construction to facilitate coordination and communication. To assure a smooth flow of work, project expediters must maintain personal contact with all members of the project team involved with each particular order including: planners and schedulers, suppliers, buyers, area expediters, subcontractor buyers, field buyers, supplier quality inspectors, design engineers, the project manager, and construction.

To maintain this contact the project expediter must function as a central figure in this group, coordinating with or generating action through all of those listed, to ensure that the scheduled events take place in accordance with project needs.

Post Award Activities

Order Entry

The expediter's responsibilities are to identify and generate action to resolve any exceptions or constraints that prevent the order or contract from entering the supplier's cycle; and, as applicable, obtain shop order number, names, and telephone numbers of the appropriate supplier contacts, the schedule for submittal of engineering information, and the preliminary shop or site scheduling information.

Engineering

The expediter will monitor and expedite the processing and final issue of engineering drawings, data, and documents to assure that suppliers receive initial design data, follow supplier drawing and data submittal to assure that it conforms to the committed dates and the project schedule, and perform inhouse followup expediting to assure the prompt coordination, review, approval, and return of documents to the supplier.

Material Acquisition

The prime supplier has the responsibility to take all necessary measures to obtain raw material and components on time to meet his delivery commitments; however, expediting should follow and expedite subsuppliers for critical orders as appropriate or necessary. Expediting should focus on the prime supplier to verify that the purchase and delivery dates of material will support the supplier's fabrication/manufacturing/construction schedule.

As applicable, expediting should coordinate with the project quality control inspectors for programmed or spot inspections at the subsuppliers' plants.

Fabrication/Manufacturing

The production and assembly phases of fabrication/manufacturing require intensive expediting, because rework or upgrading of components may be involved. Progress may be delayed due to prior work lagging in the supplier's schedule. At this stage, suppliers may also subcontract some functions. If milestone events on the supplier's schedule do not occur on time, prompt action to recover the lost time must be initiated.

Testing and Customer Acceptance

Expediting coordinates with the inspection function to exchange information and identify potential quality problems that may signal a slippage in the supplier's schedule. Particular attention should be given to the supplier's testing schedule to ascertain test stand availability, arrange for the presence of any engineering or owner witnesses stipulated by the project procedures, or any other quality constraints that can be foreseen.

Packing and Shipping

Expediting works closely with traffic to coordinate the scheduling and followup of shipments from the supplier's plant to the jobsite. Traffic should be provided with the necessary data to enable them to arrange for special transportation and permits and to effectively trace all shipments.

Schedules

The supplier's manufacturing schedule is required for all major purchase orders. It is used to determine if the delivery lead times and milestone dates are sufficiently realistic to support the committed shipping dates. Expediting should also compare the supplier's periodic progress reports with the original schedule to verify that sufficient progress is being made to meet the required end dates.

AREA EXPEDITING

Area expediters are located geographically in major industrial areas. In a broad sense they act as the eyes and ears of the project expediters. They visit suppliers to maintain direct personal liaison with the key plant personnel, visually observe the work in progress, and initiate on-the-spot action to resolve schedule problems. The area expediters' local knowledge and experience with the suppliers are vital assets in assuring that manufacturing schedules will be maintained. Moreover, they are considerably less expensive to employ than would be the case of sending in "outsiders" who are unfamiliar with the area and the supplier concerned.

Using a team approach on the purchase orders they cover, the project expediter handles the "inside" project problems and the area expediter the "outside" project problems. Primary responsibility for determining the scope and frequency of the area expediting visits and for keeping the project informed rests with the project expediter.

Area expediting activities begin when an assignment is received, with an initial visit to the supplier. During this visit the purchase order should be reviewed with the supplier; future contacts established for information on the engineering, procurement, production, and shipment of material; and the initial area expediting report prepared and discussed with the supplier, covering the significant aspects of the purchase order.

Normally, when the purchase order is being covered by area expediting, supplier visits are scheduled every two weeks. This may vary, and on critical or very large orders or where serious problems exist, it may be necessary to assign a full-time resident expediter. Conversely, visits for orders with very long lead times and lengthy periods between milestones should be adjusted to the production activity.

Area expediting assignments should be made on an as-needed basis. Key factors to be considered in determining the assignments are:

Magnitude and complexity of the order
Overall project schedule
Order criticality
Experience with supplier
Experience with material being supplied
Expediting job hour budget on project

Magnitude and complexity is a factor especially on large orders for steam generators, compressors, turbines, ash-handling systems, or skid-mounted packages.

The overall project schedule dictates time pressures and identifies those delays in material deliveries that will adversely impact project completion. Critical path orders must be on time to allow other related work to proceed on schedule. Such orders are frequently covered by area expediters.

Suppliers who have had problems meeting past commitments should be considered for area expediting coverage while those suppliers with good records will receive less attention. Orders for valves, structural steel, pumps, control panels, and large compressors are routinely included in area coverage.

Budgeted jobhours may be a constraint on assigning area expediters. However, the successful project manager will not allow a tight jobhour budget to be translated into the false economy which introduces much more serious problems later in the job.

Resident expediters are very expensive, both in the jobhours charged and attendant support costs, and are used only in cases of extreme urgency. They usually signal a supplier with serious problems.

Expediters used the term "kicking iron" to mean that the area expediter was present in the shop, witnessed the work in progress, and confirmed the status personally. "Kicking iron" will quickly reveal any variance between the supplier's actual progress and what is being reported by written or oral progress reports.

The area expediter is responsible for identifying the individual within the supplier's plant capable of resolving problems. On most occasions, a brief conference between the area expediter and the supplier's representative will suffice. However, if the problem continues, it should be escalated until it reaches the person whose real authority can resolve the matter.

Area expediting is an excellent source of information on shop capacity, equipment availability, and labor activities such as contract expirations, vacation periods, inventory shutdown, and threatened strikes. Such information is very useful when considering placing future orders or when monitoring progress of current contracts.

Area expediters use a number of standard strategies, including early morning phone calls and surprise visits to suppliers' plants. They also bargain and negotiate, which can involve some compromise on delivery schedules, assistance in expediting the supplier's subvendors, or authorizing overtime to expedite delivery of subvendor materials. Threatening to withhold progress payments and future orders are also options.

EXPEDITING REPORTS

Area Expediting Reports

These reports are prepared for the project expediter and submitted within 24 hours of the visit. Many companies now routinely use electronic communication with the project and jobsite offices to rush these reports which give the detailed status of the order, outline any problem areas, and recommend solutions.

Status of Major Equipment and Material Reports

These reports reflect the current status of all active orders and give current traffic and logistical information pertinent to delivery. The report is issued to project and client representatives, to engineering and construction, and is used in project planning, particularly jobsite scheduling.

Critical Item Reports

This report is prepared by the project expediter and outlines on-going problems and the corrective action underway to resolve them. The status of orders which are behind schedule and which contain material critical to jobsite construction, is highlighted and the latest expediting forecasts as to predicted shipping and delivery dates are contained in these reports.

Computerized Expediting Status Reports

State-of-the-art computerized material status and integrated tracking systems are used for the rapid transmittal of information and forecasts to the user (jobsite). Using satellite telecommunications networks which link the project team at the design office, the jobsite, and international procurement offices, up-to-the-minute status and delivery information can be accessed immediately by any user via CRT or hardcopy printouts. The more sophisticated systems allow for multiple sorting capability to produce exception reports, segregating critical data and specific items from the overall volume.

NEW EXPEDITING CONCEPTS

There are other expediting concepts being used by industry today that merit consideration. The "dual function expediter" combines purchasing and expediting functions into a single position. With intensive training and on-the-job coaching it has proven to be efficient and cost-effective during the appropriate phases of the project. The concept offers an additional option for consideration in the business development, planning, and budgeting aspects of potential new work. It is particularly useful in lump-sum projects and operating plant services.

The "project-dedicated expcditing specialist" is a "roving" expediter who works at supplier plants (supplementing area expediting), jobsites, or project locations. This concept allows for comprehensive detailed expediting of key or problem orders and affords direct project continuity. It is particularly effective in system turnover and nuclear plant fuel load modes.

Start-up expediters work directly under operating plant services on long-term temporary assignments at the jobsite. This concept offers valuable experience and exposure while effectively and efficiently employing knowledgeable personnel to support this critical project phase.

Seconded expediters are those who work with the client organizations providing technology transfer as well as assistance in developing systems and procedures in support of the client's in-house programs. The concept offers valuable experience and strengthens project/client relations.

SUMMARY

Today, a new professional and important management function is emerging at many companies. The expediter is a professional troubleshooter, concerned specifically with keeping production on schedule and assuring that materials and equipment arrive at the point of use on time.

Experience has shown that expediting success depends to a large extent on three essential elements:

1. Providing the supplier with a clear definition of requirements
2. Holding the supplier to commitments by timely followup of key milestones
3. Convincing suppliers through a businesslike and resolute approach that correcting and avoiding problems to meet commitments is a matter of mutual interest.

3

Inspection

DAVID P. MacMILLAN   *Exxon Company International, Florham Park, New Jersey*

Proper inspection is the key in enabling a project to meet its quality assurance objectives and to provide for subsequent successful startup and operation. Quality assurance must be a multifunctional effort of the owner, the contractors, and vendors each striving to assure that the project fully meets the planned end use.

Quality assurance establishes the proper end-use requirements and sets up multiple layers of selective sampling to accomplish them. This process is focused on preventing errors or catching mistakes as early as possible. This "multiple-layer" approach is applied throughout the life of the project, starting with the design and continuing through detailed engineering, vendor engineering, manufacturing, fabrication, erection, and ultimately, facility startup as shown by Figure 1.

In the following paragraphs, the role of inspection in the quality assurance process will be addressed commencing with the need for an early inspection strategy and then stressing the execution of that strategy during inspections performed at vendors' shops and at the construction site.

INSPECTION STRATEGY/QUALITY ASSURANCE EXECUTION PLAN

The inspection strategy is formulated at a very early stage of the project and well before the actual placement of materials and equipment purchase orders. This strategy is designed to translate the owner's philosophy into the quality goals for the project. Strategic use of resources is planned in proportion to the criticality of the individual components or systems, making sure that the quality and reliability specified are realized. The inspection strategy for a portion of the facility could very well be "zero defects" if the criticality is such that it requires a level of assurance of that magnitude.

The quality assurance execution plan should be developed from the outlined strategy and should be geared to satisfactorily achieve each of the project's quality goals. The formulation of the execution plan requires input from both the owner and the contractor as expressed by their project management and inspection personnel. The plan defines the degree and the type of inspection coverage which will be employed and is based on equipment lists, procurement strategy (worldwide versus home country) as well as the philosophy of vendor selection. The plan should establish and document all communication procedures between engineering, the inspectors, and vendors so that all parties are aware of the requirements for satisfying the project's quality goals. Critical process/service conditions, exotic material usage, the expected level of vendor quality control all will be specifically addressed by provisions in the inspection plan to furnish operational guidelines so that all owner and project requirements can be met.

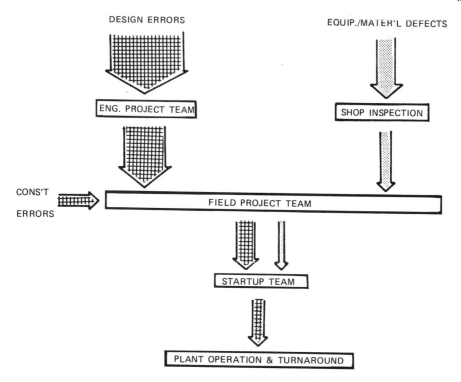

Figure 1 Sifting out errors: multiple-layer sampling.

Individual projects have their own identity and the execution plan must be tailored
to fit the project.

SHOP INSPECTION

Shop inspection is sometimes referred to as source inspection. It covers all inspection
activities conducted at the vendor's fabrication facility.

Shop inspections consist of conducting sequential examinations and/or tests of material or equipment for compliance with all of the provisions of the purchase order. Shop
inspection verifies that the quality of workmanship is appropriate to satisfy the specified service. These examinations and tests generally include:

    Monitoring the effectiveness of a vendor's own quality control techniques
    Evaluating a vendor's quality standards, which may lead to establishing stricter
        acceptance norms if the existing ones are inadequate
    Destructive and nondestructive testing
    One or more forms of mechanical or electrical testing
    Mechanical running and performance tests
    Review of documented data covering tests not witnessed
    Surface examinations
    Dimensional tests

Remember that quality can never be inspected into a product—it must be built in. Quality must be achieved during the manufacturing or fabrication, not during inspection.

It is the vendor's ultimate responsibility to achieve the required quality of the product. However, the inspector should always work with the vendor proactively to identify any conditions which could create the need for costly rework or cause time-consuming delays during manufacture.

WHY PERFORM SHOP INSPECTION

Depending upon the degree of shop inspection required, these costs can average between 0.5 and 1% of the total project investment. There may be budgetary pressures to reduce or eliminate inspection in the shop. Inspection costs could be trimmed by inspecting and repairing defects at the site. Arbitrary cutting of shop inspection costs will lead to increased total project costs.

Good source inspection prevents many errors or catches them at an early stage before costly repairs are necessary.
Defects reaching the field are an order of magnitude more costly than shop repairs.
Major defects for items reaching the field late cause significant disruption to the construction schedule and even delay project completion.

In summary, an investment made in an effective shop inspeciton effort results in lower total project costs.

INSPECTION PLANS

Consistent with the quality assurance execution plan, an inspection plan is made to allocate and prioritize inspection resources according to the criticality of each order. Inspection classifies each order as "critical," "major," or "minor," based on the technical features, size, and criticality of the order. Critical orders would usually include large towers, reactors, boilers, large process compressors, and drivers. Major orders would include drums, towers, heat exchangers, air fin exchangers, and field-erected tankage. Minor orders could include pipe, small electric motors, valves, and tubes. These classifications would change markedly depending upon the demands of the specific project.

The inspection plan for each critical or major order would typically call for a complete inspection on a progressive basis. This type of an inspection would involve:

Monitoring the effectiveness of the vendor's quality control techniques
Evaluating the vendor's quality standards
Witnessing destructive and nondestructive tests
Witnessing mechanical or electrical tests
Witnessing mechanical running and performance tests
Reviewing documented data
Examining surfaces
Checking dimensions

Further, a preinspection meeting will be arranged for all critical and some major orders. Appropriate management, engineering, purchasing, and inspection personnel will attend these meetings.

For minor orders, the inspection plans might call for only a partial inspection, and some of the interim examinations covered by a complete examination would be eliminated. An example of partial inspection would be for bulk pipe at a warehouse done by randomly checking diameter, wall thicknesses, and length. Partial inspection can also cover complete inspection of only a portion or partial shipment of the order. If the inspection results are satisfactory, inspection of the balance of the order may be waived. On the other hand, if defects are found in the initial check, the sample size would be increased.

The inspection plan for other minor orders may call for only a final inspection conducted on the finished product through visual and dimensional checks, together with a review of test data and mill certificates. The use of a final inspection only is specified when experience indicates that it is reasonable to look at the finished product to determine if the necessary quality requirements have been met. It may take several days to complete such a final inspection, depending on the complexity of the item. The inspection procedures used are similar to those used when a complete inspection is made except that the interim examinations and perhaps some testing are not required. If this type of final inspection for a particular commodity results in rejection of the products, complete sequential inspections of future work may be required or the vendor may be disqualified.

There may be other small value noncritical orders where the cost of shop inspection may not be justified. In these cases the plan may call for inspection to be waived at source of supply or for inspections to be done upon receipt at the jobsite.

In summary, the inspection plan assigns and prioritizes the inspection resources according to the criticality and technical complexity of each order. It further defines in detail the type and mode of all inspection tests and examinations which the inspector will follow to assure that the vendor has provided a product of the specified quality.

PREPARING FOR SHOP INSPECTION

Qualified Inspectors

After the inspection plan has been written, qualified inspection personnel must be assigned to implement the inspection activities.

A good qualification process will involve structured interviews that establish an individual inspector's proficiency to inspect one or more specific materials or types of equipment. Inspection of some critical items may be so specialized that only persons with a great deal of experience should be considered for this work.

The shop inspectors may be provided by the owner or supplied by a contractor or qualified inspection agency. In addition to the shop inspectors, major projects will have a lead inspector or quality assurance manager who would direct the shop inspection efforts.

Operations Procedures

In addition to their inspection expertise, the inspectors must understand and be capable of following the inspection operating procedures for the project. These procedures define the roles of the owner, contractor, and inspection personnel and all of the interfaces present to adequately perform the inspection function. The procedures must reflect an understanding of the inspection responsibilities and coordination, define specifically who takes what kind of action and when, and describe the appropriate communication channels. For complex pieces of equipment or those items requiring very sophisticated fabrication techniques, specialized engineering personnel may be called in to witness a portion of the tests. All major inspection activities such as issuing assignments, scheduling inspection visits, and issuing rejection reports are also defined in the procedures. Other important activities that should be addressed in the written procedures are:

    Early engineering interface and review of specifications for inspection requirements
    Supplier evaluation, experience, and completeness of inspection requirements
    Designation of type of inspection and specific instructions to the inspectors
    Distribution of complete purchase order packages
    Disposition of rejected materials or equipment
    Inspection reports

The procedures should be reviewed carefully and concurrence and approval reached prior to starting the inspection activities.

Inspection Input to Specifications and Vendor Capabilities

The quality requirements must be clearly stated in the purchase specifications, especially those involving inspection and witnessed tests. A review of these requirements should be a standard part of the inspection function. The lead inspector should determine that all of the inspections and tests stipulated are feasible and unambiguous.

The inspection function provides valuable input as to the qualifications of potential suppliers and can assess the degree of appropriate capability, experience, and expertise to adequately supply acceptable quality products according to the promised schedule. For critical materials or equipment, inspection will call for the vendor to submit a quality assurance plan to demonstrate how he intends to meet the quality requirements of the order. This plan would outline the vendor's quality control organization, detail the qualifications of the personnel to be involved, and describe the quality control procedures to be followed.

For some material or equipment it may be necessary to include vendors on the bid slate where there is little or no direct knowledge of their capability. In such cases, a shop survey should be conducted to ascertain the vendor's capability. This survey would evaluate the manufacturer's fabrication facility and investigate adequacy of shop space and equipment, successful experience and capability with similar orders, appropriate quality control procedures, and organization and quality of work in progress. The vendor who successfully satisfies these requirements would be deemed an acceptable supplier from a capability standpoint.

PREINSPECTION MEETINGS

For critical orders, the inspection plan should always include a preinspection meeting to focus on preventative inspection to anticipate and mitigate any potential problems which may result in costly repairs and delivery delays. The objectives of the meeting are to: (1) clarify the inspection requirements, (2) avoid rejections, and (3) identify any misunderstandings or conflict between the order and the vendor's plans. Typically discussions cover the materials specified, manufacturing and fabrication methods, examination and testing requirements, vendor quality control activities, and witness and hold points.

The meeting should be held at the vendor's shop where the work will be done. This is to assure the availability of the vendor's key production people with minimum disruption to the shop production schedule. Typical attendees at the meeting will be the inspector; the vendor's key people from engineering, production, quality control, and customer service; the purchaser's welding engineer and, if delivery is critical, the purchaser's expeditor. The meeting should be held before shop work has started; but, preferably, after the vendor has issued his initial set of shop drawings. The inspector will clearly document the results of the meeting. He will include all agreements and clarifications and will make necessary modifications to his inspection plan. All attendees should receive a copy of this report, as well as any other party who will be affected.

THE ACTUAL INSPECTION

The inspector is expected to create a positive relationship with the vendor. He should demonstrate a dedication to the end result and infuse a spirit of cooperation to see that the work is completed in full compliance with the specifications.

Upon receipt of the inspection assignment, the inspector should thoroughly review the purchase order and specification requirements and develop an individual order inspection plan containing all of those steps considered necessary to meet the order requirements and comply with the overall inspection plan. As inspections are conducted, the inspector will issue a notice detailing the inspection performance, the results, and what is to be the next inspection.

Purchase orders that include requirements for advising the purchaser or for conducting witnessed inspection tests stipulate that the vendor notify the appropriate personnel of the date and the time of the inspection. This should be done in writing in so far as is possible.

If the inspection results are satisfactory, the inspector releases the vendor to proceed with the next fabrication step or to ship the material in the case of final inspection. If materials are found not to meet the applicable specifications, a rejection notice is issued detailing the specific reason for the rejection. The vendor is required to correct the deviation or offer an alternative solution for engineering approval.

Upon completion of the inspection, a final release for shipment is issued by the inspector. A final report including any pertinent performance or compliance data should be issued with details as to the inspections conducted and the results. Clear, precise, and rapid communication of the inspection results is important for the following reasons. First, the release or rejection notice immediately advises the vendor of the inspection outcome. Second, the notice alerts the project, in the case of rejections, that some form of engineering corrective action may be necessary. Third, the final inspection report informs those receiving the equipment exactly what has been inspected and the results of those tests.

FIELD INSPECTION

As was the case with shop inspection, field inspection also is a key factor in a project's quality assurance plan. Field quality control must be exercised by all project participants to assure the quality requirement described by the project specifications, industry and national standards, and local codes are constructed into the project. Further, the quality of workmanship must be acceptable and consistent with good construction practices.

It is the responsibility of the construction team to assure that quality deficiencies and errors do not remain in the completed facilities. Safety and operating considerations dictate the resolution of all variances before the owner accepts custody and starts commissioning the facility. The construction team must guard against poor quality installations; their efforts are the last line of defense against poor quality and inferior workmanship.

The field quality control philosophy should be based on the concept of preventative inspection. Preventative inspection should be practiced in order to avoid defects or to identify them early before expensive and time-consuming rework is necessary. This is accomplished by carefully preparing quality control procedures for installation, material control, and qualifications of craftspeople. Further, implementation of these procedures closely monitors construction quality through adequate and effective spot checks, verification, and witness points to ascertain that acceptable quality is being achieved.

FIELD MATERIAL QUALITY CONTROL

Material quality control at the construction site ensures that the correct materials have been received, that they are properly stored and preserved, and that the correct material and equipment are installed. Receiving inspection is performed to determine the acceptability of incoming material. First, the material is visually examined for damage or missing components. Second, if applicable, the certified mill test reports and any functional test documents covering the material are reviewed. Third, materials may undergo a quality control inspection to assure that they meet the specified requirements.

In some circumstances the field inspector may uncover material and equipment defects that were not discovered during shop inspection. In these cases, the field inspector should advise his shop inspector counterpart to take remedial action to prevent defects in future shipments and avoid repeat performances. Field inspection must also inspect incoming bulk materials purchased locally such as anchor bolts, reinforcing steel, structural steel, and materials furnished by subcontractors.

The field receiving effort should also check that bulk materials are correctly identified and marked to avoid misapplication. Some projects, in addition to color code marking for piping components, require alloy piping materials to be 100% checked with a portable elemental analyzer capable of sorting one alloy from another.

Project personnel are responsible for appropriately storing and preserving the material. Material must be preserved in an acceptable condition from receipt until turnover for start-up operations. Special attention should be given to electrical circuitry, instruments, and machinery to protect materials against dirt, moisture, weather effects, and accidental damage.

INSTALLATION QUALITY CONTROL

Installation quality control ensures the correct materials are properly installed. Prior to the start of every work activity, quality control procedures should be approved and agreed to between the owner and contractor. These procedures should include detailed job checklists, specific to the project, with the necessary forms to document the installation and test data. These checklists will define all required tests and which tests the owner needs to witness.

Also, the construction team should be staffed with qualified field inspectors. The field inspection staff will support the project field engineers. Typically the field inspection staff will have appropriate expertise in welding; nondestructive testing; and instrument, electrical, and rotating equipment installation. The inspectors should be alert to the project requirements and provide sufficient ongoing quality inspection to achieve early detection of deficiencies to permit sufficient time to take corrective action.

Inspection relies heavily on the detailed job checklists which serve as a basic tool and a central component in a field inspection effort. Checklists are prepared for practically every major work activity such as site preparation, concrete work, pile driving, steel erection, piping erection, equipment setting, machinery installation, insulation and painting. These checklists serve as the basis of an inspection plan. As work is inspected, each item is signed off from the checklist, and the completed checklist serves as the formal inspection report.

In most refinery and chemical projects, the largest work activity is piping fabrication and erection; and these items should receive a corresponding amount of quality control attention. Before any welding is done, inspection assures welding procedures have been approved and verifies that welders have been qualified by examining test welds made to a given weld procedure. Inspection keeps records of each welder's work and matches this work to the type of welds for which he has been qualified. Welders must mark all of their welds with a unique stamp and inspection follows the quality of each welder by this unique marking through radiographic tests. If quality problems arise with a welder, he must either be requalified or dismissed. Inspection monitors such specific welding procedures as preheat, the use of the proper welding rod, and other pertinent requirements.

Hydrotesting

After a piping system has been erected, it is prepared for the hydrotesting by removing all equipment that could be damaged by the test and installing test blinds. Prior to the hydrotest, an intensive check must be conducted to assure that the installation conforms to the drawings and all installed components have been made from the specified materials. The hydrotest is conducted with all welds exposed and unpainted. Trenches for underground lines are not backfilled prior to acceptance of the piping system. During the hydrotest, all welds are physically checked for leaks. The system must hold test pressure throughout the test. Following acceptance of the test, blinds are removed, components are reinstalled, and required painting or installation is completed.

Water in sufficient quantity for hydrotesting may be a serious problem at some sites. Plans should be made well in advance where this is the case. Disposal of this water may also create a problem.

SYSTEM TURNOVER

The last step in the quality control cycle is the turnover to the owner of a completed system, including all work activities (equipment, piping, civil, electrical, insulation, and paint). In this step, a turnover package is prepared which includes all of the inspection checklists with appropriate drawings, test documentation, and nondestructive testing results. The startup personnel then conduct an independent visual check to assure the system conforms to the drawings and job specification. After successful completion of this check, the system is turned over for commissioning and startup.

SUMMARY

Shop inspection and field inspection are the two key ingredients in a quality assurance program for a successful project. Inspection plans should be aimed at preventing defects. However, if defects do occur, the inspection plan should make sure that they are caught early to avoid costly rework and disruptive schedule delays.

Lastly, a successful quality assurance program relies on the cooperative, proactive, and coordinated actions of many parties to assure that potentially damaging defects are caught before the project is put into operation.

4

Site Materials Management

ROBERT L. WOOTTEN   *E. I. du Pont de Nemours & Co., Augusta, Georgia*

JOHN CALVIN CATO   *H. B. Zachry Company, San Antonio, Texas*

BASIS FOR SYSTEMS DEVELOPMENT

Materials management is the management process for planning and controlling all necessary efforts to make certain that the right quality and quantity of materials and equipment are appropriately specified in a timely manner, are obtained at a reasonable cost,
and are available at the point of use. The materials management effort for a particular
project may be split between the owner, engineer, and the contractor. Herein lies
the basic problem of maintaining the essential continuity of the materials management
functions from material definition to erection. This problem has plagued the construction industry for years and has contributed heavily to lower productivity and high
levels of surplus material.

BACKGROUND OF CURRENT ACTIVITIES

The construction industry has recognized the value of materials management through
research conducted by the Business Roundtable's Construction Industry Cost Effectiveness (CICE) Study and the Construction Industry Institute (CII) research programs. Industry leaders have focused their attention beyond the traditional engineering design effort and normal construction activities to include materials management
as an integral third element of project management. Control of materials and equipment,
usually 50 to 60% of a project's cost, is recognized today as essential to project success.

In order to be more cost effective, the problems caused by the fragmentation of
the materials management responsibilities have to be overcome. Some of these problems
will be corrected through reorganization of the corporate structure to place responsibility for all materials management functions into one group or department. The other
significant contribution to a more unified approach is the continued enhancement of
totally integrated computerized tracking systems: databases that can interconnect the
corporate functional and project structures and interface with other materials management systems as required.

WHAT IS BEING DONE TODAY

The Business Roundtable's CICE study established that materials management has a
major impact on project costs and schedules. This impact can be favorable and cost
effective. When not properly implemented it can also have the opposite effect, con-

tributing to low productivity and higher project costs. These findings led the Construction Industry Institute to define the principal characteristics of materials management. The CII has a mission to provide information and concepts that prove the value of total materials management in improving overall project performance.

Improvement Already Realized

Most of the improvements that have been realized to date have been on the front end of the material procurement cycle. That is, from the material definition stage through purchasing and expediting. Most owners and engineering firms have actively utilized computers in these areas for several years.

Payoff for the Next Steps

The transition from this phase to the site activities has lagged primarily due to the fragmentation caused by the three-party system: owner, engineer, contractor. Fully integrated systems or systems that can interface with another system will solve this problem. Progress is being made in this area; and, as a result, it is now recognized that site materials management can provide significant cost savings through improved labor productivity and reduced material costs. The Business Roundtable and the Construction Industry Institute research places potential labor savings alone in the range of 6%.

Site materials management has received less attention from owner and contractor management. This function, often called "field material control," has been a craft function, and its success has been largely dependent upon the skills and experience of the individual craft supervisors and the working craftspeople. Within the last decade an increasing number of progressive contractors have recognized that project management intervention in the planning and implementation of the material control effort is essential to the successful execution of their projects. They further believe that highly qualified, professionally trained personnel are required to manage this important function.

Site/Off-Site System Interdependence

Site materials management has been seen to have well-defined and restricted limits of responsibility which started only with the receipt of materials at the jobsite and ceased as soon as the materials were released to the crafts. Site materials management in this context included receiving, on-site inspection, storage, warehousing, materials protection, distribution to the crafts, and response to shortages. It has not always been recognized that site materials management is impacted by all of the other related procurement activities: material takeoffs, material specifications, procurement, expediting, and inspection. Equally important, site material management impacts on the other elements by defining site needs in terms of quantities, quality, and timing. Schedule requirements, especially those necessitated by changes in design or scope, have the most impact on the overall materials management system. As a result, site materials management cannot be a standalone function.

Industry Emphasis on Materials Management

The Business Roundtable and the Construction Industry Institute have served as catalysts in setting materials management as a priority item to improve construction industry cost effectiveness. As a consequence, industry has begun to respond. The advantages of knowing with certainty that all of the proper materials will be available within project schedules and budgets is recognized by both contractors and owners. As a result, enhancement of their existing materials management systems is underway and entirely new systems are being developed to meet the needs of tomorrow's projects.

Site Materials Management

Construction site materials management basically comprises the functions of receiving, storage and protection, and issue to the field. These activities should be managed jointly. In turn, they must be fully integrated with the other materials management functions: material takeoffs, purchasing, quality management, expediting, and shipping, to provide an overall coordinated approach without regard to location or departmental responsibility. Then the actual construction plan has to be integrated into the system to insure that the material flow is consistent with drawing releases and available craft labor. When these functions are not properly managed, individually and collectively, shortages and surpluses occur. More importantly, costly labor delays result when the required quantity of materials of the proper quality is not on hand when needed. In order to achieve a smooth, timely, efficient flow of materials, all parts of the system must function well. This means that early emphasis must be put on good planning and excellent communications within the respective organizations of the owner, engineer, and constructor as well as between the three firms themselves.

Once the scope of materials management responsibilities has been defined and lines of communication established, the contractor can organize the site materials management effort to best meet the needs of the project.

Anyone involved in materials management, be they the owner's, engineer's, or contractor's representatives, should understand the basic elements of a successful materials management system. It has often been necessary only to understand those items for which one had a direct accountability or which impacted one directly. The lack of a management-directed, integrated effort has contributed heavily to the decline in labor productivity in the construction industry.

FUNCTIONS OF THE MATERIALS MANAGEMENT SYSTEM

A well-defined list of characteristics has been identified by research into the materials management activities of the more progressive contractors and owners. These characteristics can be categorized according to the following list of functions.

> Planning and communications
> Materials requirements and engineering interface
> Vendor inquiry and evaluation
> Purchasing
> Quality assurance and control
> Expediting and shipping
> Warehousing, receiving, and distribution
> Field material control
> Computer systems

CHARACTERISTICS OF MATERIALS MANAGEMENT

While site materials management is normally only responsible for the warehousing, receiving, distribution, and the field material control functions, a working knowledge of the other functions is essential to the success of the overall project effort. The following listing of the nine materials management functions gives their key characteristics in effective firms

1. Planning and communications

   Senior management involvement to ensure organizational involvement
   Project procedures prepared

Formal training and education programs conducted for users and materials
   management personnel
Materials plan prepared for each project
Master codes and specifications used
Material control systems exist
Postproject reviews used
Owner's and contractor's senior management are promptly informed of materials
   progress and problems
Internal meetings held to improve communications
Owner and contractor aware of restrictions on materials management effort
Materials management functions are integrated between owner, design engineer,
   and contractor

2. Material requirements and engineering interface

   Material requirements identified early
   Master specifications automatically merged with project requirements
   Bills of materials prepared and computerized
   Bulk materials linked to equipment requirements
   Timely, electronic transmission of data

3. Vendor inquiry and evaluation

   Formal procedures used for screening vendors
   Coordinated procedure for evaluating vendor proposals
   Vendor performance monitored
   Commitments and schedule requirements computerized
   Use of quality evaluations on vendors

4. Purchasing

   Purchasing data fully integrated into materials management system
   Purchase order data automatically transferred from requisitions
   Purchase orders adapt easily to changes
   Status of purchase orders reported
   Prevention of duplication of purchases
   Purchases of critical items tracked

5. Quality assurance and quality control

   Quality requirements in specifications
   Project specifications include physical inspection
   Vendors responsible for quality control
   Quality plan and quality assurance manual exist
   Nonconforming materials rejected prior to shipment
   Positive material identification established in materials management system

6. Expediting and shipping

   Priorities of expediting are pre-established
   Frequency of expediting and reporting in timely manner established
   Expediting information exchanged with managers
   Vendor's schedule matched to project schedule
   Traffic plans include alternative modes
   Defined plan of action to respond to expediting effort

7. Warehousing, receiving, and distribution

   Field materials operations actively supervised and physically secured in order
      to maintain accurate inventory

Warehouse storage laydown area plan established
Materials individually protected to meet the quality assurance requirements
Receiving data entered into system when it happens
Shortage and damages reported
Warehouse central inventory data maintained, including locations

8. Field material control

   Material control integrated with other project control systems
   Priorities of material allocation are adjusted to work priority established by
       each craft discipline
   Material control system provides history and status
   Shortages and surpluses are forecast
   Shortages are acted upon promptly
   Receiving, distribution, and issue data entered
   Crafts plan material requirements well in advance
   Warehouse requests checked promptly to see if valid
   Periodic inventories conducted and inventory data adjusted with provisions
       for audit trail

9. Computer system

   Computer systems provide flexibility to tailor system for each project's require-
       ments
   Computer system provides current, timely information
   Information updated and examined at line item level
   Data terminals conveniently located in the field and home offices
   Integrity of system maintained for accuracy and auditability

FUNCTIONS SPECIFIC TO SITE MATERIALS MANAGEMENT

While cost-effective materials management systems address all of the functions of materials management in a planned and organized way, three of the functions have a more
direct and definite impact on site productivity: (1) planning and communications, (2)
field material control, and (3) computer systems.

Planning and Communications

Any state-of-the-art materials management system must be based primarily on excellent
skills and procedures for planning and communication. A serious deterrent to the development of construction materials management has been lack of an organized planning
effort. Progressive contractors and owners today acknowledge that this is an urgent
need.

Once the need for planning and communications has been established, a definition
of the planning effort is necessary. Several key areas must be addressed by the owner,
engineer, and contractor. The nature and volume of materials and equipment for the
project must be determined. All of the parties need to clearly identify, discuss, and
agree upon the way that the activities on the materials management cycle are to inter-
mesh. Once this has been accomplished the three parties can establish definite requirements for the system. Items to be resolved include the data required, the report format,
and the report frequency. Lines of communication and required interfaces are then
established accordingly.

The pivotal interface in the project execution process is that between the design
engineer and the contractor's site materials management organization. Effective two-
way communication between the two organizations is absolutely essential to the success
of any materials management effort. Another crucial interface is between the contractor

and the owner's project control group which provides input for cost, schedule, and
quality assurance tracking.

Field Material Control

Receiving, holding, and dispensing the materials to the field, all part of the field material control process, are important to the site materials management system. More importantly, material control provides valuable information for craft work planning. Field
supervisors can actually perform withdrawal-of-material simulations. Their work can
then be scheduled based on known availability of materials, thereby avoiding false starts
and possibly costly rework. Shortages and surpluses are quickly and easily forecast.
Shortages can then be acted upon promptly and supervision can schedule around them
if necessary. Thus, a major interface exists between the field material control function
and field activities. How well this interface is managed by the materials management
and project organizations will have a major influence on site productivity.

The Computer System

A third crucial function for all projects of sufficient size and complexity is the computer
system. While it is entirely conceivable that a small owner and/or contractor can operate a successful materials management program without using a computer, the increasingly lower cost and flexibility of computers, and the greater variety of hardware auxiliaries and software will soon make the use of computers more attractive on smaller
jobs. Larger owners and contractors have found the use of computer systems to be a
cost-effective project management tool.

A wide range of computer systems is currently in use for construction materials
management. In a very general sense, computer systems can be classified as belonging to one of two categories:

1. Database systems that track the status of engineered equipment and critical
   items
2. Comprehensive integrated systems that address all materials management functions for both engineered equipment and bulk materials

Of the two categories, the comprehensive integrated system has higher development
costs, but also produces more tangible cost-saving benefits.

To be effective, any computer system should exhibit the following characteristics:

The system must be capable of adapting to the unique conditions of the project
   at hand, including the project type and size, and the owner's preference with
   respect to schedule, quality, and cost. Commercially marketed systems often
   do not meet this requirement.

The system must be capable of providing current information. This usually means
   that "on line" systems are preferred to "batch" systems.

The system must be capable of tracking materials to the desired level of detail without "overcontrolling" items that would be better monitored with a "min-max"
   system.

Computer hardware configurations that are currently being used for materials
management include large home office mainframe computers, on-site minicomputers,
and, in some cases, microcomputers. Home office mainframes provide tremendous storage and computing power, but require communications methods that may be costly and
cumbersome to use. An on-site minicomputer works well when the owner or contractor
has a continuing use of the computer after the project has been completed. The use
of single-user microcomputers (PCs) for materials management is somewhat controversial.
Microcomputers have not been generally well suited to materials management because

they have been essentially single-user computers. The purpose of an effective materials management system is to facilitate communications between several system users. Microcomputers have been used effectively as personal productivity enhancing tools, and there is potential for developing systems on micros and transferring the system to a larger computer or for using microcomputer networks.

Finally, it should be noted that commercially available software packages that adequately meet the materials management needs of the construction industry are somewhat limited. This may be attributed to the fact that they need to be more general than specific. As a result, most of the state-of-the-art systems have been developed "in-house."

VIEW OF THE FUTURE

While there may be some discussion of the specifics, the future of construction materials management is fairly clear. The value of a planned materials management effort and its contribution to overall project success will become more widely understood and accepted by both owners and contractors. Planning and execution of materials management will become second nature just as scheduling, cost control, and quality assurance are today. Senior management will become more supportive of the materials management effort. As a result, it will receive its proper stature as a full partner in modern management techniques. Integrated management systems will become commonplace with material management data flowing smoothly into the rest of the project control systems.

Materials will be managed based on input from project schedules and the quality assurance program. Technical skills required for materials management personnel will be identified and used to acquire and/or train personnel. Users will be trained to understand and effectively use the resources provided by the system.

Other traditional barriers will fall. Turf protection will become less and less of an issue as all parties better understand the need for an integrated proactive effort. Craft acceptance and the use of site materials management as a service has already been demonstrated by contractors having state-of-the-art systems.

The biggest hurdle currently is the inability of individual owners and contractors to improve their current materials management programs without difficulty or to develop entirely new systems. In some cases, the problem is a lack of understanding of the potential of materials management to improve project performance. This will become less of a concern as the efforts of the Business Roundtable and the Construction Industry Institute proceed and the level of awareness continues to grow.

A more significant problem is one of individual companies not knowing how to effect the changes that will actually produce for them a state-of-the-art materials management system that best meets their needs. The work of the Construction Industry Institute will provide definition of the functions which a company's system should address. Perhaps, even more important, will be the results of research on the costs and benefits of materials management. It is believed by many that greater recognition and understanding of the benefits will drive management of individual companies to initiate the effort necessary to achieve state-of-the-art materials management systems.

Ultimately, the benefits of effective materials management will accrue to the projects. Labor productivity will improve because of the ability to plan and schedule work on the basis of known material availability. Material shortages during the life of the project and material surplus at the end of the project will be minimized. Both the owner's and the contractor's cash flow considerations will be better managed through the use of more accurate and timely information on materials. Finally, integration of proactive materials management systems with scheduling, estimating, cost control, and quality assurance systems will provide owners and contractors the ability to improve the planning and execution of projects and to achieve maximum cost effectiveness.

BIBLIOGRAPHY

CICE Report A-6. Modern Management Systems. New York: The Business Roundtable, 1982, pp. 24-29.

Attributes of Materials Management Systems. Austin, TX: Construction Industry Institute, 1985.

VIII

CONSTRUCTION

UNIT OVERVIEW

Construction—the last bastion of defense! If a project is proceeding well prior to the initiation of the field program, a good construction effort will secure the project. A poor effort will undo all past achievements; only the sour taste of the final result will linger, perhaps indefinitely with that client. If, on the other hand, the project is in trouble when the dirt-moving starts, a good construction effort can bail it out, and, conversely, a poor effort will put the nail in the coffin. This is construction in a nutshell—a pressure-packed fishbowl business.

We start this unit with an analysis of the role of the home office construction staff, vital to both the pure construction company and the full-service turnkey organization. The duties are many—procedural, technical, personnel—and, depending on the company organization, can include the following: assignment of field staff; monitoring field projects; participation in estimates, schedules, proposals; construction equipment supply; QA/QC procedures; rigging calculations; safety and security procedures; personnel practices; and labor relations, to name a few. An interesting history of the development of labor relations laws and regulations in the United States is included. The home office staff should work with the project team from the start and maintain a review position thereafter to assure the "constructability" of the designed plant.

A general discussion of the methods of execution of construction projects ranges from domestic direct hire and subcontracted strategies to Continental European practices, offshore construction, the programs utilized in lesser-developed countries, and the mobilization of low cost labor on a worldwide basis.

Detailed discussions follow on field organization, cost control, scheduling, and material control. An in-depth analysis of strategies to optimize field productivity includes comments on "measured productivity" programs and certain traps to avoid if the results are to be valid. Lastly, quality assurance and quality control concepts and procedures for safety and security are covered.

1

Home Office Construction Staff

F. SWEENEY TUCK*   *Fluor Daniel Inc., Sugar Land, Texas*

The duties and responsibilities of the Manager of Construction and the home office staff are diversified. The size of the organization is dependent upon business volume, but the responsibilities are the same, regardless of size, and each member of the staff should have extensive field experience.

The manager of construction normally reports to senior management, but, under the project management concept his or her primary responsibility is to serve and satisfy all of the project managers with active construction projects. The manager of construction must understand that construction is just one part of the project, albeit very important, and must act as a team player for the overall benefit of the project and the company.

ASSIGNMENT OF FIELD STAFF

The development of an organization and the assignment of the right people to the right jobs are the most important responsibilities of the manager of construction. The quality of field jobs will only be as good as the personnel he or she assigns.

A nucleus of capable construction managers, craft superintendents, inspectors, schedulers, materials people, and so forth, should be available for assignment to field jobs as required. The manager of construction is expected to maintain the nucleus with as little overhead cost as possible since they must be moved from job to job with minimum standby time.

The manager of construction must train these field supervisors, guide them, lead them, inspire them—and keep them happy. The ability to attract and keep capable field supervisors is a true measure of this manager's value to the company.

MONITORING FIELD JOBS

The project managers expect the manager of construction to provide them with a quality project. And senior management expects all construction jobs to be executed well. These objectives can be achieved only if the manager of construction has a suitcase and likes airline food and motels. And, a cooperative and supportive family.

Only so much about the performance of a construction job can be learned from written reports. The manager of construction must make periodic visits to each jobsite to ascertain that the team is functioning properly. He or she must "walk the job" with key supervisory staff to be satisfied that quality, cost, and schedule requirements are being met. All staff members should be visited to assure that their attitude and

---

*Retired

479

morale are high. A checklist of things to look at, such as warehousing, fabrication yards, equipment maintenance, construction methods, and the like should be used to be sure nothing is overlooked.

If the volume of company business is large, various assistants may be available to help in this monitoring. Regardless of the number of locations or the jobs, the manager of construction or a totally qualified assistant must monitor performance. And the project manager should demand that this be done.

ASSIST HOME OFFICE ESTIMATING

The preparation of field labor and indirect cost estimates should be prepared by professional estimators, usually working for a department other than Construction. But the home office construction group must assist the Estimating Department in the preparation of field estimates. Generally, the manager of construction should approve the field cost estimate before a bid is submitted.

The key members of the Home Office Construction Department (HOCD) should have extensive expertise in measurement of field productivity for all crafts. They should know the factors that affect field labor productivity. They should be able to advise the Estimating Department of expected performance ratios for every craft at the proposed site.

These key members should be able to outline to the Estimating Department the expected requirements for construction indirects. This includes supervisory staff, nonmanual staff, construction equipment, tools, construction buildings, construction utilities, supplies, and so forth.

ASSIST HOME OFFICE SCHEDULING

It is generally preferred to have master schedules and construction worksheets prepared by a group in a department other than construction. Key members of the HOCD should advise the Scheduling Department on such items as construction sequence, task durations, and proper manpower loading. HOCD should approve and commit to the construction schedule, with the concurrence of the project manager.

HOCD should monitor all scheduling reports from the field, and should audit schedule performance and procedures at the site. If a job is falling behind schedule, recovery programs should be develped at the site with project management and field staff.

ASSIST ON PROPOSALS AND SALES PRESENTATIONS

HOCD is expected to write the execution plan for field work for proposals. They must prepare organization charts and assign candidates for all key field supervisory positions. They must discuss construction execution plans and construction expertise in an effective manner in sales presentations.

OPERATE CONSTRUCTION EQUIPMENT COMPANY

Many major construction firms have found it advisable to own and operate a construction equipment company to assure that well-maintained and safe construction equipment is on hand when required by the construction team.

It has been found that this strategy can provide a good source of income, although profit on owned equipment isn't the prime reason for ownership. Generally, a construction contractor can provide equipment to a major project more economically than it can be rented from third parties, due to captive use and resultant high utilizaiton factors.

The contractor should have a centrally located yard where equipment can be maintained and repaired, and stored when idle. Rail loading facilities should be available.

One way of obtaining high equipment utilization is to own about 80% of your equipment requirements and go outside for short-term needs. Construction tools and minor equipment, such as welding machines, compressors, and pumps, can be very efficiently owned. Ownership of vehicles is borderline.

Management of the construction equipment company requires good financial management, mechanical expertise, and construction knowhow. The head of the equipment rental company should report directly to the manager of construction.

QA/QC SURVEILLANCE AND STANDARDS

Construction must be performed to a satisfactory level of quality or the contractor cannot remain in business. Cost overruns and schedule failures have often been forgiven because a plant was of excellent quality, started up quickly, and performed well. HOCD must set the QA/QC policies, the QA/QC procedures, and the field QA/QC organization. These policies, procedures, and organization must be clearly defined and strongly enforced.

RIGGING CALCULATIONS AND STANDARDS

Here the penalties for failure are injuries and deaths, property damage, financial loss, and schedule failures. This responsibility cannot be left to the "seat of the pants" rigger.

All rigging calculations, excluding standard lifts, should be approved by the rigging specialists of HOCD. A standard lift is a lift within the allowance capacities of a single crane, properly positioned, stationary.

These specialists must be capable structural engineers but with field rigging experience; practical hands-on knowhow.

CONSTRUCTION PROCEDURES

Construction procedures tend to be technical and complicated; such things as welding procedures, including qualifying, preheat, postheat, and stress relieving. But this isn't all. A short list would include rigging, fabrication, vessel erection, tube rolling, hydrotesting, and cable pulling.

Again, we cannot leave procedures to the "seat of the pants" craftsman. Yes, we need the skill of the craftsmen: their technical skills are most impressive. But for many detailed tasks, there are procedures that are best, and proven effective. HOCD should determine these procedures, write them, update them, and monitor their use.

CLIENT CONTACTS

Clients are vitally interested in the effectiveness of contractor construction organizations. Construction cost can be 20 to 40% of the total project cost. Clients are smart construction people, and becoming more so. They know the difference between poor performance and good performance, on a daily basis, or over any time frame.

Clients respect and admire construction people who produce excellent results. They want "repeats" of good jobs. They want that "good team" back on the next project.

The manager of construction and his key people should get to know the client personnel connected with each project at all levels. The construction management team can "sell" their company.

LABOR RELATIONS AND SAFETY

Management of labor relations is often the direct responsibility of the manager of construction, who may delegate some of these functions to the Head of Labor Relations. But the manager should maintain contacts with labor leaders at all levels.

Last but not least, HOCD should set all safety policies, procedures, and monitor all field safety programs.

2

Labor Relations

F. SWEENEY TUCK*   *Fluor Daniel Inc., Sugar Land, Texas*

INTRODUCTION

The project manager should have a general knowledge of the complex system of rules, regulations, and decisions governing the conduct of construction labor activities. An understanding of the process of collective bargaining and the complexity of labor agreements will give the project manager a better perspective of the impact that labor problems can have on a project. A well-prepared prejob conference and an accurate job assignment list are two excellent ways to help prevent labor problems in the field. Let's review the broad nature of federal labor laws and the relationships of the construction worker, the contractor, and the union.

HISTORY OF LABOR LAWS AND REGULATIONS

Although the Norris-LaGuardia Act was passed in 1932, it was not until 1935 that the U.S. Congress enacted the first of three major acts which are the foundation of our national labor policy: the Wagner Act. This act protects the rights of workers relating to wages and working conditions. Commonly referred to as the National Labor Relations Act (NLRA), it established the principle that employees should have the right to organize into labor unions and bargain collectively in matters concerning wages and working conditions. The act outlined the rules by which employers must conduct their relationships with employees:

> It is an unfair labor practice for an employer to discriminate against an employee for labor activities, i.e., his right to organize, bargain collectively, or engage in other lawful activities for mutual aid or protection.
> Employers are required to bargain in good faith with the duly authorized representatives of an elected union.

The Wagner Act also created the National Labor Relations Board (NLRB) and charged it with the responsibility to administer and enforce the National Labor Relations Act.

During the next dozen years, the strength and membership of the unions increased enormously. Unfortunately for the labor movement, however, a succession of criminal abuses by some labor leaders, work stoppages, strikes, and restrictive work practices occurred over a period of time, and public opinion mounted against the unions. In 1947 Congress passed the Taft-Hartley Act, also known as the Labor Management Relations Act. It amended the Wagner Act in almost all aspects, retaining the principles

---

*Retired

of exclusive representation and unfair labor practices of employers. For the first time Congress imposed controls and restrictions on organized labor union activities. It added a list of unfair labor practices by the unions.

> Unions cannot interfere with an employee's right to participate, or not participate, in union activities.
> If a union has been designated as the bargaining agent by a majority of the employees through a proper election the union must bargain in good faith with the employer.
> It is an unfair labor pratice for a union to encourage or cause an employee to stop work to enforce a secondary boycott or for purposes of jurisdictional disputes.
> Unions are prohibited from charging excessive dues as a condition of becoming a member.
> It is an unfair labor practice for the union to force an employer to pay for services not performed.

Although the Taft-Hartley Act did not solve all the problems plaguing the construction industry it did establish the Federal Mediation and Conciliation Service, gave the President power to intervene when national health or safety was involved, and limited political contributions of both labor and business.

The third labor act, the Landrum-Griffin Act, passed by Congress in 1959 can be separated into two parts. First, it established a code of conduct for unions, union officials, employers, and "middle men" serving as labor relation consultants. Second, it amended the Taft-Hartley Act and added a number of new provisions.

Also known as the Labor-Management Reporting and Disclosure Act, Landrum-Griffin sought to guarantee inalienable rights to union members, to protect the public from unscrupulous union leaders, and to insure democratic elections in unions.

Under the provisions of the act, labor organizations, employers, employees, and labor consultants are required to report to the Secretary of Labor on matters that affect the organizing and bargaining rights of employees. Labor unions are required to file annual financial reports and inform union members of their policies and procedures.

The act sets minimum standards for conducting union elections, establishing union trusteeships, and makes it mandatory for every labor organizaiton to have a constitution and a set of bylaws.

The amendments to the Taft-Hartley Act were a compromise of labor and management, but in the end it was felt to have favored the employers. The restrictions on strikes, boycotts, and picketing outweighed the voting rights sought for permanently replaced economic strikers and the prehire and seven-day union shop contracts won by the unions.

Other federal laws affecting employees' rights have been enacted by Congress prior to 1935 and after 1958:

> 1926 Amended 1934, 1951, and 1966. The Railway Labor Act. Established procedures for settlement of disputes between railroads and unions through the National Mediation Board. Gave the President the power to establish an Emergency Board to investigate if a strike is threatened. The union cannot strike during the 30-day investigation or for 30 days following the Emergency Board's report to the President.
> 1931 Davis-Bacon Act. Sets minimum wages and fringe benefits for construction employees working on federal government-financed projects. The Secretary of Labor is charged with the responsibility of determining the prevailing wages in an area for the type of construction work to be performed. Contractors and subcontractors are required to pay the minimum wages and benefits published for the area.
> 1934 The Copeland Anti-Kickbacks Act. In addition to outlawing "kickbacks" from employees to employers the act also makes it illegal for an employer to withhold compensation to which an employee is entitled.

1932 Norris-LaGuardia Anti-Injunction Act. Limits the power of the federal courts to issue injunctions against labor union activities.

1938 The Byrnes Anti-Strikebreaking Act. Forbids the transportation of out-of-state persons to interfere in labor matters.

1939 Fair Labor Standards Act. Also known as the Wage and Hour Law. Set minimum wages, maximum hours, and overtime pay. It also established child labor standards.

1946 The Hobbs Anti-Racketeering Act. To obstruct, or impede interstate commerce by robbery and extortion is a felony under the Hobbs Act.

1958 Welfare Fund Disclosure Act. Requires administrators of welfare and pension funds to file detailed reports and gives the Secretary of Labor the authority to investigate and the power to enforce the provisions of the act.

1964 Civil Rights Act. Title VII Equal Employment Opportunity. It is unlawful to discriminate in the employment or union membership of an individual because of race, color, religion, sex, or national origin.

1967 Age Discrimination in Employment. Employers and labor unions are prohibited from discriminating against persons between 40 and 65 years old.

The test of interstate commerce must be applied to determine who is covered by the provisions of the Naitonal Labor Relations Act. The interrelationship of the employee, employer, and labor union may exist as defined by the provision of the act, yet none may file a complaint with the National Labor Relations Baord. The standard used to determine eligibility is based on the annual dollar volume of business of the employer or the volume of goods that the employer buys or ships to other states. Interpretation by the courts has been so broad that practically all construction work of any magnitude falls within the jurisdiction of the Board.

COLLECTIVE BARGAINING: LABOR AGREEMENTS/PROJECT AGREEMENTS

There is little doubt that unions make a substantial contribution to the construction industry. They tend to establish a stable work force within an area and through negotiated labor agreements establish area economic conditions. In order to bid a project effectively the contractor must have knowledge of the work force available and the precise area wage rates by craft.

Through collective bargaining labor and management enter into contracts which form the basis of their working relationship. Wages, hours of work, and other terms and conditions are mutually agreed upon through this process.

Some contractors elect to negotiate directly with the unions while other will assign their bargaining rights to an association of contractors and bargain collectively. A well established pattern of bargaining has emerged in the construciton industry. Most local contractors will join a general contractors' association, usually the Association of General Contractors, which will bargain with the basic trades in the area. The unions will not normally join together to bargain as one group. They form geographic councils, referred to as the Building and Construction Trades Council, to coordinate their common goals.

The local trade union is chartered by the international union but maintains a great degree of independence. The local usually has the authority to negotiate labor agreements and call strikes without approval of the international.

When an association bargains with the union the first step in the process is the appointment of a bargaining committee. Representatives of member companies, legal counsel, and the association staff make up the management committee. Officers of the local union, representatives of the international union, if requested by the local, and representatives of the district council usually make up the labor committee. The bargaining process then begins.

The National Labor Relations Act specifically outlines mandatory subjects of bargaining, voluntary subjects, and illegal subjects. It isn't necessary that agreement be reached on any proposal or that either side make concessions—only that both sides bargain in good faith.

Once an agreement is reached and ratified by the union members, a written contract or "Labor Agreement" is signed which is binding on both parties, and covers all the work in the jurisdiction of the union on all construction projects.

Contractors and unions have recently incorporated project agreements in negotiating special conditions in areas where open-shop competition exists. Originally project agreements were used to standardize conditions on a specific project. Through a project agreement the union will make concessions on that specific project to relax work rules, lower wages, and modify other terms of its local agreements to help the union contractor win the bid.

Construction labor agreements usually are for a one-year term, but can be multiyear. Multiyear agreements have a stabilizing effect in an area and usually have provision for periodic wage increases during the life of the contract.

Prior to the expiration of an agreement either party desiring to change any of the terms must give at least 60 days written notice to the other party of their intent to open negotiations for a new agreement or terminate the existing agreement. Once notice has been given to negotiate a new agreement both parties are required to negotiate and bargain in good faith. Failure to do so is an unfair labor practice.

When negotiations break down the major weapons available to the union and the contractor are the threats of a strike or lockout, respectively. Union members may refuse to work and walk off the job. This is of little effect if the contractor is allowed to hire replacements. To prevent this the union customarily establishes a picket line at the employer's place of business. In the case of a lockout the contractor locks the gate and refuses to allow the employees to work without a contract. The National Labor Relations Board has established guidelines to determine when a strike or lockout is an unfair labor practice.

Contractors who work in several geographical areas of the country find it advantageous to sign national labor agreements with the international unions. National labor agreements offer employment of a given union's members to contractors who work throughout the United States and, in some cases, Canada. These agreement standardize working conditions and are a convenient way for the national contractor to coordinate his labor relations policy. Wages and fringe benefits under national agreements are usually the same as the local agreements.

The National Labor Relations Act, Section 8(F), established a unique procedure for the construction industry, the use of prehire agreements. Prehire agreements allow contractors, who may not have any employees on the payroll, to negotiate a union shop agreement to establish terms and conditions of employment prior to bidding a project. The union shop agreement does not assure the union of representation and can be challenged at any time. The contract may require the employees to join the union within 7 days after employment, but until the union can demonstrate that it represents a majority of the employees the employer is free to change or modify the terms and conditions of a prehire agreement.

A common practice in the construction industry is the use of hiring halls. A labor agreement may require the contractor to give notice to the union of job opportunities available for referral. The union must refer applicants on a nondiscriminatory basis regardless of whether or not they are members of the union. The selection of foremen, as well as any other employee, is at the sole discretion of the contractor. It is not unusual for the contractor to give preference to union referrals for foremen and general foremen but the levels of supervision above the general foremen are hired directly by the contractor.

Taft-Hartley outlawed the use of closed-shop agreements where an applicant must be a member of a union prior to employment. It does allow contractors and unions to enter into union shop agreements which require an employee to join the union within a specified period of time after employment, but not less than 30 days—the one exception being the building and construction industry. In addition, Section 14(B) allowed individual states the right to forbid union membership as a condition of employment. To-date, 20 states have enacted laws outlawing union membership. These "right-to-Work" states are: Alabama, Arizona, Arkansas, Florida, Georgia, Iowa, Kansas, Louisiana, Mississippi, Nebraska, Nevada, North Carolina, North Dakota, South Carolina, South Dakota, Tennessee, Texas, Utah, Virginia, and Wyoming.

PREJOB CONFERENCE/MECHANICS OF ASSIGNMENTS

National contractors are required to hold a prejob conference prior to the start of field construction work on each project. It is their responsibility to advise the international unions, local unions, and officials of the International Building and Trades Council of the meeting. As a matter of courtesy all the local unions are usually invited, even though only the major ones may have work on the project.

Contractors present the policies and procedures of the company, scope of work, jobsite work rules, safety rules, and jurisdictional work assignments. The prejob conference is an opportunity for contractors to discuss and agree with the unions on any peculiarities of a project prior to the start of work. It is much easier for contractors to manage a project and get on with the work if they have advance union acceptance of their procedures.

On a union construction project there may be as many as thirteen craft unions involved in the field work. This sometimes leads to disputes between the unions over who will perform a certain task. Section 8(B)(4)(D) of the Taft-Hartley Act protects the employer from getting caught in the middle of such disputes and makes it an unfair labor practice for a union to strike to force an employer to assign work to one union or the other. The National Labor Relations Board has the power to settle jurisdictional disputes but has allowed the construction industry to develop its own methods of resolution. The most recent national plan, which has now been abandoned, was developed by the National Contractors Association, the Association of General Contractors, and the Building and Construction Trades. It is the plan for settlement of jurisdictional disputes in the construction industry. The plan establishes the method by which contractors make job assignments.

Assignments are made to signatory unions based on "Agreements of Record" published in the "Green Book" by the AFL-CIO Building and Construction Trades Department. This book contains a partial list of jurisdictional agreements and decisions. The Jurisdictional Handbook, prepared by the National Contractors Association, is a more extensive list of agreements and understandings reached between the major crafts which do not appear in the Green Book. The Green Book is complemented by a small Blue Booklet and a small Red Booklet. They are both very important and vital to field management.

The Blue Booklet contains the "Procedural Rules and Regulations of the Impartial Jurisdictional Disputes Board and Appeals Board Procedures." It contains specific instructions as to making an assignment, the investigations to be made, and procedures to follow in submitting a dispute to the Impartial Board and the Appeals Board.

The Red Booklet contains the "Enforcement Procedures" authorized by the Building and Construction Trades Department for the impartial umpire to use to prevent work stoppages on a project. The procedure provides for fines against the union and legal proceedings by the employer.

At the prejob conference the contractor presents a list, as complete as possible, of the work and which union is assigned to perform each part of the work. The unions are required to review the assignments and resolve any disputes among themselves. Once agreement is reached on any disputes the assignments are considered to be final and binding on all parties. Should a dispute arise after construction begins and the two disputing unions cannot resolve the problem, the contractor is bound to make an assignment to one of the unions. This assignment cannot be changed without a directive by the Impartial Jurisdictional Disputes Board. The decisions of the Impartial Jurisdictional Disputes Board can be appealed to the Joint Administrative Committee. There are many other voluntary plans in the construction industry which deal with the settlement of jurisdictional disputes.

LOCAL UNIONS, BUSINESS AGENTS, AND JOB STEWARDS

Labor unions are structured to operate within geographical areas such as a city, county, district, state, or region. The union is referred to as the "local" union, and is chartered by the international union and is subject to its constitution and bylaws. The jurisdictional area assigned to locals of different unions often vary extensively. For instance, one carpenter local may cover two states while the same area may have two electrical locals responsible for the electrical work.

Every local is required to have a constitution and bylaws to govern its operation. The authority of the local union lies with the membership. They elect the officers and business agent, ratify all labor agreements, vote on strikes, and control other matters of union policy.

The officers usually serve without pay except for actual time spent on union business. The Business Manager conducts the day-to-day affairs of the union and is paid a full-time salary. Every project is appointed a job steward to police the jobsite and report to the business manager any violation of the union rules by the contractor. As a rule, labor agreements require the job steward to be a working steward. He must work at all times except when conducting union business and only with prior approval of his supervisor. The job steward is usually the first man hired in his craft and the last one terminated. He is a key element in the execution of a successful field labor relation policy on a project.

The business manager is the spokesperson for the union, and has primary responsibility to protect the work of the union within the local jurisdiction. The business manager has practically unlimited authority to act on behalf of the union with contractors: dispatching manpower to jobs, handling grievances, preparing for contract negotiations, coordinating strikes, and acting as the general go-between for the employees to the contractors. The business manager is responsible for the financial status of the local and must file detailed reports with the international union and government agencies.

The local union has a great deal of autonomy, but the international union maintains the right to control any irresponsible behavior of the local.

OPEN SHOP

The recent trend in the construction industry has been from union to open shop construction. Today approximately half of the total construction volume is performed with nonunion labor.

Open shop does not mean antiunion, rather that a contractor hires its employees and conducts its business without regard to union or nonunion status. The primary difference between a union contractor and an open shop contractor is its labor relations policy. The open shop contractor is responsible for recruiting, hiring, training, disciplining, promoting, and discharging its employees, unlike the union contractor, who depends on the local union for its skilled labor force.

The open shop contractor is not faced with jurisdictional strikes over work assignments or work stoppages due to economic issues. The open shop contractor defends the right to spend as much time managing, assigning, and working with employees as deemed appropriate. The contractor believes in the principle that employees are paid according to ability and performance. The hourly wage is less in open shop work but the contractor usually provides the means, through overtime work, for employees to equal or exceed the annual salary of the union worker.

3

Methods of Execution

F. SWEENEY TUCK* *Fluor Daniel Inc., Sugar Land, Texas*

The construction execution plan is one of the first and most important items that must be settled. We will discuss the principal approaches or options available. The project manager should take the lead in the selection of the construction execution plan.

The decision as to the construction execution plan may be limited by certain factors. One of these factors might be site location; domestic U.S., Europe, less developed countries (LDCs), offshore. Another factor might be the labor situation: closed shop, open shop, third country nations. Other factors include client preference and schedule requirements. All of these factors will be discussed here.

DOMESTIC CONSTRUCTION

Direct Hire

In the twenty to thirty years following the Second World War, most of the heavy industrial construction in the United States was performed on a direct-hire, union, reimbursable basis. The 30 or more members of the National Contractors Association (NCA) executed most of their larger projects on this basis.

The NCA members had national agreements with most of the building trades. These agreements enabled them to move into almost any area of the United States and be supplied with a well-trained, experienced workforce. Wages, benefits, and work rules were well established and fairly uniform. The NCA members developed field supervisory staffs that were experienced and capable.

One of the big advantages of the direct-hire, union, reimbursable basis was that large projects could be organized and started long before the plans and drawings were completed. To meet fast-track schedules, it was impossible to obtain lump-sum competitive bids.

Another advantage was that there was a single organization directing the work rather than a large number of independent subcontractors. As a result, except for civil-type projects, there weren't many large-size mechanical subcontractors available in the United States. The NCA contractors had the supervisory expertise and the access to available craftspeople to perform the difficult projects requiring close coordination.

The advantages mentioned above, however, were gradually outweighed by the adverse cost impact. Both unions and contractors contributed to the high costs that began to affect many projects. Lack of dedication by both parties caused higher costs as compared with competitively bid projects by more aggressive contractors and more dedi-

---

*Retired

cated craftspeople. The clients found themselves required to insist upon lump-sum competitive bidding in order to obtain more realistic construction costs.

Multiple Subcontracts

An execution plan designed to obtain lower construction costs by means of competitive bidding received increasing attention. Although this approach frequently results in an extended construction schedule, it has generally been found that lower construction costs can be obtained.

Before embarking on this course, it is best to canvass the area to verify that qualified and interested local subcontractors are available. It is important that they have access to their usual workforce, and that they are comfortable in the area.

A determination of the number of subcontracts that the project is to be divided into is quite important. For the most part, specialty contractors should be used. Not much is to be gained by packaging different types of work together unless it is a normal subcontracting procedure. An obvious example would be that earthwrok and electrical would not be put in the same subcontract. On the other hand, it would be perfectly normal for a building contract to include many typical building crafts or trades; concrete, steel, plastering, brickwork, painting, etc.

As mentioned above, use of multiple subcontracts on a competitive bid basis will result in an extended construction schedule. There are at least two major items that cause this. One is that you must allow extra time for preparation of subcontract inquiries, preparation of lump-sum bids, analysis and award, as well as separate mobilization periods. Another is that subcontractors on a lump-sum project tend to understaff more than contractors on a reimbursable direct-hire project.

The multiple subcontract approach has some added costs due to: (1) extra quality control actions required; (2) overall job schedule extension; (3) duplication of construction facilities; and (4) greater coordination costs expended by the client or the project management contractor. But, even with these and other added costs, the overall construction cost will usually be lower on a multiple lump-sum contract basis than on a reimbursable direct-hire project. The client has to make the decision as to whether he wants the project on the lowest cost basis or the earliest completion basis.

Under certain conditions for large domestic projects a blend of direct-hire, lump-sum subcontracts, and reimbursable subcontracts should be investigated. The managing contractor (MC) on a large project will normally have, or should have, a full-range integrated team, with depth at all positions: a management team. The MC may elect to do certain work direct hire (critical work), work of the type where the MC has know-how or a strong supervisory pool, or merely to get the "feel" of the job. Specialized highly controllable work that can be clearly scoped for bidding purposes would be subcontracted on a lump-sum basis, i.e., earthwork. Consideration should then be given to a reimbursable strategy for principal subcontracts; candidates would include structural, piping, electrical, and instrumentation, all highly interactive areas.

The advantages are threefold: (1) the deterioration of schedules inherent in the lump-sum approach is mitigated; (2) the MC retains control of the subcontracted work; (3) the potential for major subcontractor contractual claims is virtually eliminated. In today's litigious society you may think that funding needs are stabilized when lump-sum subcontracts are let; they aren't. Large projects with multiple lump-sum subcontracts are characterized by large and multiple claims. Claims are not resolved easily, since the basis usually centers on the allegation that the MC didn't permit work initiation and/or work continuity compatible with the execution plan submitted with the proposal, or clearly intended; overheads are up, productivity is down, profits have vanished, etc. In many cases this is true, and even where the claims are spurious it is not uncommon to see negotiated settlements or court awards. The drain on productive management is considerable. Needless to say, the managing contractor must provide a qualified subcontract administration staff to implement a program of this type effectively.

CONTINENTAL EUROPEAN CONSTRUCTION APPROACH

The following comments are general in nature but apply to most continental European countries. They do not apply to Great Britain. All in all, the approach in continental Europe results in a construciton performance superior to that achieved in reimbursable direct-hire projects in the United States.

In most of Europe, construction unions are fairly loosely organized and weak. As a rule there are few hiring halls except for unskilled laborers. As a result, the major contractors maintain their own employees on a year-round basis, often several years. The employee looks to the contractor for gainful employment, rather than to the union. This results in greater productivity.

The contractors are divided on a craft or discipline basis: electrical, piping, structural steel, rigging, furnaces, machinery, brickwork, concrete, and so on. They have excellent procedures for bidding on a unit-price basis with excellent quantity breakdowns. These can be calculated into lump-sum prices that can be adjusted for final quantity changes. In this manner, bids can be prepared prior to completion of final drawings.

Each contractor provides its own construction facilities including bunkhouses, equipment, storage sheds, tools, and canteen. They also set their own work hours. They seem quite independent and uncoordinated, but the final result is good. There is a sufficient supply of efficient contractors, and lump-sum or unit price bidding is an established way of life for them.

CONSTRUCTION EXECUTION IN LDCs

Here we are really talking about two types of lesser developed countries. The first is a country where there is a limited supply of construction labor. Examples include most of the Middle Eastern countries (Saudi Arabia, Kuwait, United Arab Emirates). The second is a country with a very large population but a limited number of skilled craftsmen, especially in the mechanical crafts. Examples include Indonesia, Mexico, China, and India.

In the first category, Saudia Arabia has a very small population leaving it no choice but to import hard-working, low-paid craftspeople. Korea has proven to be an ideal exporter of diligent, skilled, low-cost contractors. Large Korean companies such as Hyundai, Daelim, Daewoo, Samsung, and many others have made a tremendous impact around the world. However, other countries such as Indonesia, Phillipines, Pakistan, India, and Turkey have also provided excellent craftspeople at competitive rates.

In the second category, Indonesia, etc., with tremendous populations, lack sufficient skilled craftspeople, especially in the mechanical trades. Because of very high unemployment in these countries, it is against national policy to import workers. As a result, the U.S. contractors on projects in these countries have no choice but to train local workers. Excellent craft-training techniques have been developed and it has been found quite practicable to construct large mechanical process plants in countries in this classification, with the result that several of these countries now export labor.

CONSTRUCTION EXECUTION OFFSHORE

The expansion and development of offshore oil and gas production has required the introduction of new execution plans. Water depths have increased from 50 feet to over 1300 feet in the past 35 years. Twenty-five percent of the world's oil production is now done from offshore facilities. Construction of these facilities has required innovative thinking and new execution plans.

One aspect of offshore construction is the requirement for very large and expensive items of equipment. Derrick barges have increased from 100-ton capacity thirty years ago to over 10,000-ton capacity today. Lifts weighing more than 2000 tons are quite common. Offshore labor costs can be four to five times the cost of onshore fabrication yard labor. The large derrick barges are extremely valuable in reducing offshore "hook-up" labor manhours. One of the most important items in an offshore execution plan is the determination of sizes and weights of modules and decks.

Other major equipment items required for offshore construction are quarters barges, pipe lay barges, and, of course, crew boats, tug boats, and helicopters. Equipment costs represent a major percentage of offshore construction costs, perhaps three times the percentage of equipment costs required for onshore construction projects.

There are a limited number of firms with complete offshore construction equipment and expertise. American firms include Brown & Root, McDermott, Sante Fe, and Raymond. French firms are ETPM and Bouygues. Italian firms are Saipan and Micoperi. The Dutch firm Heerema is highly regarded and has good equipment, as does the Korean company Hyundai. There are also several other firms with limited equipment capability.

Despite high labor and equipment costs, much offshore work is let on a fixed-price competitive basis. Contractors usually have protection clauses covering bad weather, but otherwise are conditioned to giving firm prices. Korean firms have been very competitive and have obtained much of the offshore work in Saudi Arabia and India.

The project execution plan must address all of the following facets: fabrication facilities, towing, derrick barges, hook-up, nationalism, and labor rates. There is a "best" way to do every offshore job, and the right decisions must be made at the start.

LOW-COST LABOR

In the mid-1970s the Koreans burst upon the international construction scene. They have made quite an impact. They have been followed by the Indonesians, the Filipinos, the Pakistanis, the Indians, and the Turks. The Peoples Republic of China is now exporting construction labor and many are predicting that they will be the leading exporter of construction labor in the coming years.

The Koreans began in heavy process plant construction when American companies were required to hire and train Korean workers for facilities built in Korea. The Korean workers were then taken by American contractors to the Middle East. At first they were contracted for work on an all-in hourly rate basis that included travel and living costs.

They came on a single-status basis; accepted quite bare living conditions; worked extremely long hours; were diligent and skilled; behaved themselves; and were accepted by the host countries. Most of their wages either went back to their families or to the government. Their overseas time worked also counted in lieu of military service.

Major Korean firms then proceeded to contract for much of the work themselves. They provided their own supervision, equipment, and tools, but their contracts were usually for construction labor only, excluding engineering and the supply of plant equipment.

In recent years major Korean firms have accepted contracts covering equipment, materials, yard fabrication, and field labor. The major firms are Hyundai and Daewoo for offshore work. For onshore work, in addition to Hyundai and Daewoo, the firms of Daelim, Samsung, and KHIC are strong.

The Koreans have developed their own engineering skills, principally in the area of detail design. But in the near future we can expect them to enter into most of the engineering fields on a turnkey basis.

DETERMINE EXECUTION PLAN AT OUTSET

We have covered normal execution plans for various areas around the world. There is a best execution plan for each area and for each project. The execution plan must be determined very early in the project. The engineering approach, the purchase of engineered equipment, the procurement of the commodity materials, the preparation of subcontracts, and the scheduling and cost control efforts, all must be tailored to the execution plan.

4

Field Organization

EDWARD J. McGUIRE *Exxon Research & Engineering Company, Florham Park,
New Jersey*

The success of the field erection phase of a project will be determined by how well the
goals established for the project are met. In setting goals, corporate desires for safety,
quality, cost, and schedule need to be considered. Two important factors that will
determine how successful a construction project will be are the adequacy of the site
management organization and the relationship between the contractor and the owner.

On most large projects, new organizations for both contractor and owner will be
established. The forming of these organizations will be the most important task that
the respective managements will face. Some of the characteristics of these organizations are:

Many people working together for the first time
New procedures, at least new for the people using them
Short time available to mobilize and demobilize

TYPE OF CONTRACT

Organization structure should be developed based on the type of prime contract and
the execution strategies. In staffing these organizations, the capabilities of contractor
and owner personnel must be considered. For large projects, it may be necessary to
supplement permanent staff with professional project management personnel hired for
the project if capabilities or experience among permanent staff are lacking.

The two most commonly used types of prime contracts are lump sum and reimbursable. There are numerous variations within these two categories of contracts. The
type of prime contract will have a large effect on the size and structure of the owner's
organization. The execution strategy chosen by the contractor will have the largest
effect on his organization.

OWNER'S ORGANIZATION

Characteristics of the two types of prime contracts and the effects these have on the
owner's field organization are as follows:

Lump sum

   1. Primary characteristic is that the financial risk rests with the contractor.
   2. Owner's field team must be capable of
       a. controlling extras
       b. performing desired level of quality assurance
       c. encouraging contractor to meet safety goals
       d. interpreting contract terms

Reimbursable cost

   1. Primary characteristic is that financial risk remains with the owner but control
       of expenditures and performance is through the contractor's organization.
   2. In these contracts, positive and open relationships must exist between contrac-
       tor and client organizations. Contract boundaries and responsibilities must
       be respected.
   3. The owner's project team must be
       a. experienced
       b. able to motivate contractor through encouragement and cooperative efforts
       c. capable of appraising the contractor's cost, quality, schedule, and safety
           performance in a positive way

CONTRACTOR'S ORGANIZATION

Contractor organizations will be affected to some extent by the type of prime contract,
but not to the same degree as the owner's. The structure of the contractor's organization will be determined to a much greater extent by the execution strategy with regard to field labor. Figures 1 and 2 show two typical organizaitons for a major petrochemical project. In Figure 1 field labor will be hired directly by the prime contractor.
In Figure 2 field labor will be hired by subcontractors.

DIRECT HIRE

Figure 1 depicts a direct-hire field execution scenario. In this case craftspeople work
for foremen and superintendents. In Figure 1 the superintendents control an area—
onsites or offsites. On some projects it may be more logical to organize the superintendents along craft lines and then assign area coordinators to control workers in
each area.
      The role of the office manager in this type of organization includes the major areas
of personnel, timekeeping, and payroll. However, even in this type of execution, on
large projects there will be numerous subcontracts and a subcontract supervisor will
be required.

SUBCONTRACT

Figure 2 depicts an execution scenario where field labor is hired by subcontractors.
The role of the subcontracts administrator is a senior position. The office manager's
role is reduced because the payroll and other employee activities are reduced.
      The organization in Figure 2 shows activity supervisors. As with direct hire jobs,
this is one way of organizing. Other ways include an area basis or a subcontract basis.

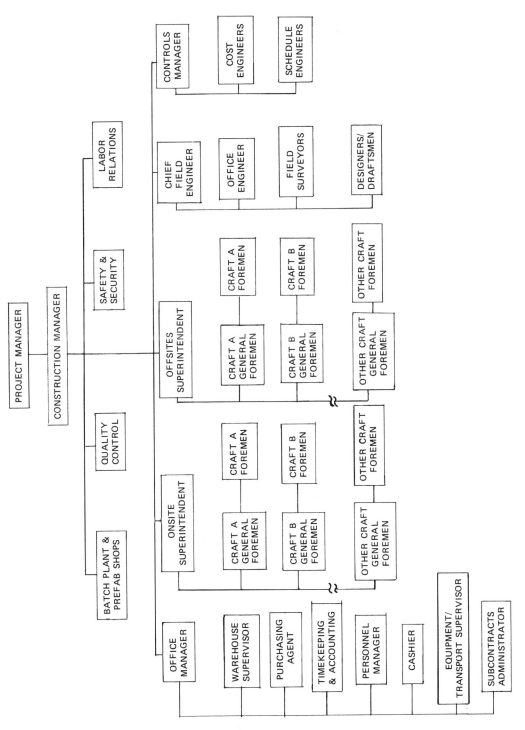

Figure 1 Typical contractor's field organization (direct hire program).

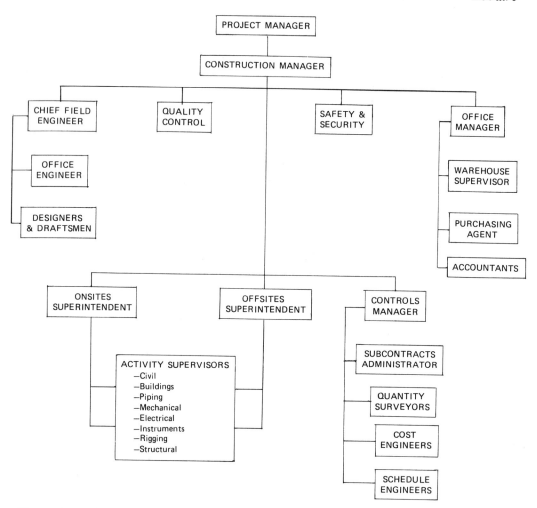

Figure 2 Typical contractor's field organization (subcontract program).

QUALITY CONTROL

Both Figures 1 and 2 show quality control reporting to the construction manager. This is shown to emphasize that the senior person at the site has responsibility for quality, as well as safety, cost, and schedule. However, it may be desirable to have some independent quality assurance function. This can be accomplished by establishing a QA manager who assists the quality control manager but reports directly to the project manager or elsewhere within the contractor's organizaiton.

ORGANIZATION SIZE

A client organization's involvement can vary from no representation at the site to a very substantial presence. The most effective client organization is one which is the minimum size necessary to match the owner's philosophical way of handling risks and motivating/evaluating the contractor.

The size of the contractor's organization will also depend on execution strategy. For direct-hire strategies, this may vary from 4 to 5 staff members (superintendent, accountant, scheduler, two general foremen) on small projects (less than 150K field manhours) to several hundred personnel on projects with over 10 million manhours.

INTERESTS

For effective relations to exist, each organization should understand and respect the other organization's interests. Contractual arrangements should respect these interests as much as possible. Examples of these interests are:

Owner
> Earliest completion
> Costs within budget
> Smooth startup and long run length with low maintenance
> Safe construction

Contractor
> Maximizing profit
> Pleasing owner by meeting goals established if return business is possible
> Maintaining good image in the industry
> Safe construction

SUMMARY

The experience and quality of personnel in a contractor's field organization, along with diligent implementation of field procedures, will determine the degree of success of the construction phase of a project. Developing effective teams and positive relationships between contractor and client is an important task of the respective managers. Contractual boundaries along with areas of risks and interests must be respected. However, unhealthy/destructive relationships often develop. These should be guarded against as they deflect management's ability to pursue safety, quality, cost, and schedule goals.

5

Field Cost Control

EDWARD J. McGUIRE and EDWARD A. WYNANT* *Exxon Research & Engineering Co.,
Florham Park, New Jersey*

Field costs are often divided into two categories defined as follows:

> *Direct costs* which include materials, labor, and subcontract expenditures associated with the actual installation of permanent physical components of the plant.
> *Indirect costs* which are all other field expenditures. Sometimes referred to as "hidden costs," these expenditures support the direct activities (examples would be supervision, warehousing, equipment rental, catering, etc.).

Both direct and indirect expenditures can result from labor costs (wages paid for labor hired directly by the prime contractor), material purchases, or subcontracts. The technique used to control these costs is basically to (1) establish a good budget, (2) know where expenditures are being made, (3) forecast final expenditures, (4) identify problem areas by comparing expenditures with budgets, and (5) apprise managers and supervisors of this information early so that actions can be taken to achieve economies.

Cost engineering is the technology used to collect and analyze cost data. We will suggest ways of using cost engineering reports and forecasts to control and reduce field expenditures, and introduce control techniques that can be used to track and control field costs.

COST/WORK BREAKDOWN STRUCTURE

As mentioned, field expenditures can be divided into two primary categories. These categories are then generally subdivided to create a cost breakdown structure (CBS) as follows:

> *Indirect Costs*
>   Supervision and other staff functions
>   Temporary facilities (offices, warehousing)
>   Construction equipment and tools
>   Other support services
>   Supplies
>   Consumables (weld rod)

Current Affiliation: Consultant, Basking Ridge, New Jersey

Direct Costs
   Labor costs
   Material purchases
   Subcontracts

Direct costs are then subdivided into various accounting codes to reflect the actual work (foundations, structural steel). This breakdown is often referred to as a work breakdown structure (WBS). It is the division of the job into a WBS that is used to calculate progress.

Indirect costs for services can include both purchased services or wages paid to labor hired directly to perform services. These services will include items such as warehousing, janitorial services, material handling, guards, and canteens. Whether services are purchased through a subcontract or are performed by labor hired directly, expenditures should be tracked using tracking curves.

FIELD LABOR COSTS

The costs per hour for labor hired directly by the contractor include wage rates and burden rates (social security rates, insurance, other taxes). Wage rates are controlled by union agreements or, in the case of merit shop, by competition. Burden rates are governed by taxes, corporate employee policies, insurance, and so on.

The actual costs paid are equal to the hours worked times the wage plus burden rates. The major component of this equation that is controllable in the field is the actual hours worked. For direct costs, field labor hours are minimized by maximizing the effectiveness of the hours worked or "the productivity" of the worker. For indirect costs, field labor hours can be minimized by increasing effectiveness and by working only on necessary activities. Hours spent on indirect activities should be tracked and compared to budgets established for the activity and then reviewed with the responsible manager.

CONTROL OF INDIRECT COSTS

Whether the result of expenditures for labor, for materials, or to subcontractors, indirect costs can be substantial on a project. These commonly represent 40% or more of the total field expenditures on major projects. They also represent the expenditures over which field management can have the greatest control.

How much money and effort is put into indirect costs can have a marked effect on the productivity of labor working on direct cost activities. For example, not spending an appropriate amount on small tools can make labor ineffective if there is a waiting period for tools or delays are caused because tools wear out too soon. It is up to field management to properly balance these expenditures to achieve the lowest overall cost.

Managers/supervisors who will be responsible for each indirect cost center must be assigned to these cost centers early. Joint reviews must then take place on a scheduled basis for each account or cost center. At each of these reviews cost engineers, the responsible manager, and site management should review expenditures and forecasts. Budgets should be available to establish guidelines but actual expenditures need to be justified on a needs basis. Site management must take an active roll in these reviews.

Costs can be made visible by tracking curves (see Figure 1) or by appropriate lists (see Table 1). Lists are needed for high cost single items such as supervisory staff and major equipment. Tracking curves should be used for all indirect accounts, including those for which lists are available.

As is apparent in Figure 1, when tracking costs it is necessary to make sure that forecast curves and actual cost curves are on the same basis. If one is on the basis

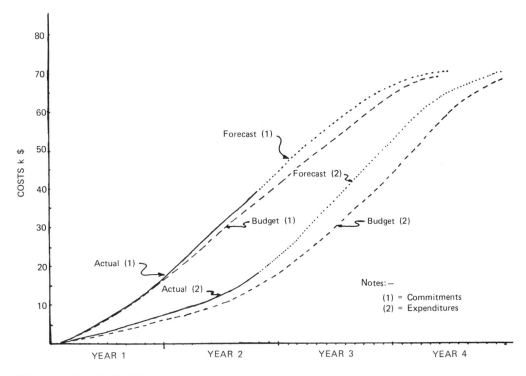

Figure 1 Typical indirect account tracking curve.

of commitments and the other on the basis of expenditures, there will be large apparent "savings" or "overruns" which are in fact not real.

DIRECT COSTS: LABOR

Field labor costs are controlled by controlling the hours of work. In the direct cost accounts, the way a facility is designed will have a very great effect on the amount of labor required to erect it. In addition to labor savings which can be achieved by properly selecting designs during the engineering phase, the opportunity for savings once in the field is still significant. It is not unreasonable to target for a 20% productivity improvement over previously established norms for the type of work in question. More importantly, however, the possibility of poorer-than-budget productivity is even much greater. Experience has shown that labor expenditures can exceed budgets by up to 100% when projects are lacking in effective field planning and overall project coordination.

In striving to attain the highest level of productivity and/or avert field labor overruns it is important that labor budgets are available from the project control estimate. The breakdown of these budgets should conform to the manner in which the project is being executed and should be reflected in the WBS. The entire field supervisory staff from the construction manager on down to the first level of foreman must be aware of the budgeted labor hours as they apply to their scope of responsibility.

As in the case of field schedule control, the product of the cost engineering department cannot be viewed as independently generated merely to fulfill cost reporting requirements. The field line management has a vested interest in insuring the relevance

Table 1 Typical Indirect Account Tracking Lists

List #1 Purchased Construction Equipment Schedule

Item	Equipment No.	Description	Cost ($) Budget	Actual	Resale value ($) Budget	Actual	Total cost ($) Budget	Actual	Over (+)/under (-) budget ($)	Status
1	P1	Pickup truck	15,000	13,000	2,000	(1,000)	13,000	(12,000)	(-1,000)	Purchased
2	S1	Sedan	13,000	14,000	2,000	2,000	11,000	12,000	+1,000	Sold
3	S2	Sedan	13,000	14,000	2,000	(2,000)	11,000	(12,000)	(+1,000)	Purchased
4	C1	18 T crane	180,000	150,000	80,000	(60,000)	100,000	(90,000)	(-10,000)	Purchased
5	C2	15 T crane	150,000	(150,000)	70,000	(70,000)	80,000	(80,000)	(0)	Still required

Etc.

( ) = Forecast

List #2 Rented Construction Equipment Schedule

Item	Equip. No.	Description	Date req'd Budget	Actual	Date released Budget	Actual	Rental rate (K$) Budget	Actual	Months req'd Budget	Actual	Cost (K$) Budget	Actual	(K$) Over (+) under (-)
1	C4	60 T crane	8/1/74	9/1/74	12/1/76	(12/1/76)	3.2	4.2	28	(27)	89.6	(113.4)	(+23.8)
2	C5	60 T crane	1/1/75	12/1/74	12/1/76	(12/1/76)	3.2	4.0	23	(24)	73.6	(96)	(+22.4)

Etc.

( ) = Forecast

of the field workhour budgets. This management should make sure that the control estimate is continuously recast to reflect any changes made to the execution strategy.

As actual engineering designs are completed, required quantities of materials to be installed will be different from the original estimates. For this reason, the budgets for each account must be updated to reflect these quantity adjustments. This quantity adjusted budget (QAB) for field labor should be updated periodically to incorporate design changes or other changes not attributed to field performance.

Measuring actual performance against the aforementioned budgets requires accurate collection of performance data. Care must be taken to ensure that this is feasible when setting up the WBS. Line management should guide cost engineering in setting up the WBS so that it is relevant to the project execution. It will require dedicated personnel to collect labor expenditures and progress data, as well as foreman training in this regard. Too ambitious a control procedure or a less than conscientious effort on the part of the foremen in filling out time cards can render the system meaningless. Conversely, a reliable control system will benefit the project in many ways. Performance trends reveal where corrective action may be required. By knowing how actual performance stacks up to the budget, cost forecasts can be prepared. And, labor requirements can be fine-tuned based on knowing the actual labor expenditures required to accomplish the planned work.

A project cost forecast for direct labor accounts is developed by extrapolating the actual performance to date to the end of the project. This should be modified to reflect any planned changes in field construction methods or procedures. This gives line management the opportunity to have the cost control engineer evaluate the impact of execution alternatives on the cost forecast. In this manner project costs can be optimized. Once a change in the construction plan is agreed to, cost engineering can incorporate its impact in the forecast. As an example, say a cost engineering analysis indicates that concrete/civil work will significantly overrun the direct labor budget. The construction manager determines that the production rate can be increased by using equipment with greater capacity and with essentially no increase in crew size. Thus in this case it becomes a tradeoff of labor savings vis a vis added equipment costs and a decision can be made to utilize the most attractive alternative.

There are many reasons for pursuing various execution schemes. The experienced construction manager generally knows several good construction approaches. However, a wise construction manager will include cost as a consideration in deciding which approach to take and will see that execution alternatives are evaluated.

PRODUCTIVITY

Labor productivity, or effectiveness, should be tracked for each of the direct labor accounts. There are many ways to express labor productivity, but for simplicity we will define it as follows:

$$\text{Labor productivity} = \frac{\text{Physical \% complete}}{\text{Percent of budget labor hrs expended}}$$

The percent of hours expended should be calculated by dividing the actual hours used on an account in the WBS by the quantity adjusted budget for that account. An example follows:

Assume review of an erection account:

Hours originally estimated	30,000 hrs
Original quantity	300
Quantity as designed	330
QAB = 30,000 hrs × 330/300	33,000 hrs

Quantity installed	200
Hours expended	18,000 hrs
Physical percent complete	
= 200/330 × 100	60.6%
Percent hours expended	
= 18,000/33,000 × 100	54.5%
Productivity = 60.6/54.5 =	1.11

Productivity measured in this way will vary over the life of a project. The actual values determined will depend on the method used to calculate percent complete (this is primarily dependent on when credit is taken for quantities installed) and on factors affecting the actual efficiency of labor in the field. A typical plot is shown in Figure 2. Historical plots are useful for the type of work being measured and the system being used to determine percent complete.

By monitoring productivity and comparing the values obtained to those expected, deviations can be observed and the necessity of taking corrective action determined.

SUBCONTRACT COST CONTROL

Subcontracts can be issued to cover both direct and indirect work activities. For direct activities executed through the use of subcontracts, the major way to control costs is through clear contracts with a well-defined scope of work, control of changes, avoiding claims, and assisting the subcontractor wherever possible in the execution of his assigned work. For indirect activities executed by a subcontractor the main concern is to work only on those activities that are necessary and to follow good contracting procedures.

Most of the principles outlined in the foregoing sections for control of labor costs when labor is hired directly by the prime contractor are applicable to controlling sub-

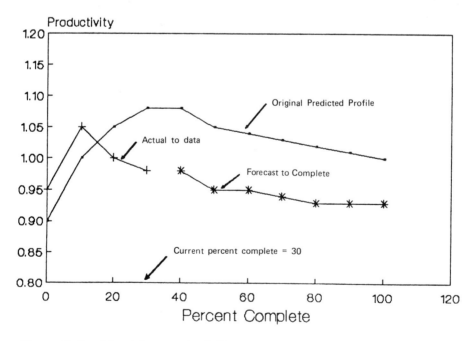

Figure 2 Tracking labor productivity.

contract erection costs. However, it must be recognized that a different set of conditions exist. In the case of unit price or fixed price subcontracts, the subcontractor is primarily responsible for controlling labor hour expenditures since, in theory, the subcontractor has assumed that risk. Therefore for the construction manager, field subcontract cost control takes on a different emphasis.

The construction manager should review with cost engineering the subcontracting strategy. The control estimate will not always anticipate every subcontract order. In the interest of improving execution efficiency the construction manager may have rearranged some of the original plans for executing the work; direct hire vis a vis subcontract. It will be necessary to recast the control estimate to reflect any change in execution strategy.

The next order of business is for the construction manager and the responsible supervisors to review the comparisons of the bid package for each of the subcontracts with the control estimate. This is because subcontract bids are usually a literal and strict interpretation of the bidding documents, whereas the control estimate is designed to anticipate a realistic, all-inclusive final cost. The construction manager will need to impart some insight to the normally less experienced cost engineer in "conditioning" the bids, making sure all bids being reviewed reflect the same scope of work. Even then it is necessary to add a "subcontract growth allowance" to the priced subcontract to make the subcontract value on the "bid tab" (what is approved by management before the subcontract is awarded) realistic.

In many ways administration of subcontract work requires more discipline on the part of the construction manager than does direct-hire work. Cost impact for productivity losses due to some fault of the prime contractor (late material deliveries) becomes readily visible in the form of subcontractor claims. Also, to the construction manager it may appear that if subcontracts are tightly written, only extras need be policed since quantities will have been determined in the design.

However, things don't always work out that way. The aim is to make subcontracts as straightforward as possible with easy to apply unit prices (all-in $/cy of concrete for various types of foundations). Because of the complexity of tying down the number of variables to bid a straightforward unit price, subcontracts often contain a complicated pricing schedule. In analyzing performance, comparison should be made to the anticipated costs turned up from the subcontractor's bid at the time of the bid analysis. The bid analysis was based on a certain method of execution and a subcontractor performing differently than this basis may effect higher total costs even applying the same unit prices. For example, a civil subcontract covering excavation and concrete foundation work includes a unit price for dirt haulage. In estimating the subcontract value it may have been assumed that the haulage price would be paid only once per cubic yard excavated. However, due to the sequence of work the subcontractor is obligated to move the dirt from place to place several times. This will, of course, result in higher costs for dirt haulage because of the possibly less than optimum work plan.

The construction manager should concentrate on helping the subcontractor to be as efficient as possible. In general this will result in optimizing project costs and both parties will benefit.

CONTRACT CHANGES

Changes to the contracts must be strictly controlled and documented. This applies to the prime contract and to subcontracts. Changes are disruptive to the ongoing construction program and if not documented properly can result in a basis for claim later. By documenting changes and requiring various levels of approval, the need for the change to actually be implemented can be ascertained.

Figure 3 shows a typical change form that can be used to obtain the proper level of review and approval of a change. Not only can changes be very disruptive to field

TO: CONTRACTOR CONSTRUCTION MANAGER   CHANGE NO.＿＿＿ REV.＿＿

                                              DATE ＿＿＿＿＿＿＿＿＿＿＿

ACTION REQUESTED

        ( ) ESTIMATE COST/SCHEDULE EFFECTS ONLY

        ( ) ESTIMATE COST/SCHEDULE EFFECTS AND
            PROCEED WITH CHANGE

        ( ) CHANGE IS AUTHORIZED, PLEASE PROCEED
            AGREED EFFECT ON COST ＿＿＿＿＿＿＿＿＿
            AGREED EFFECT ON SCHEDULE ＿＿＿＿＿

        ( ) CHANGE REQUEST IS CANCELLED, DO NOT
            PROCEED

DESCRIPTION OF CHANGE:

DRAWINGS AND SPECIFICATIONS AFFECTED:

REASON FOR CHANGE:
        (Note...it might be desirable to develop a series of categories for
            changes so that reconciliation can be easily made later
            to determine the reasons for changes. These categories can
            also help when evaluating the need for a change).

APPROVALS

        OWNER'S REPRESENTATIVE ＿＿＿＿＿＿＿＿＿＿＿＿＿

        DESIGN ENGINEER ＿＿＿＿＿＿＿＿＿＿＿＿＿＿＿＿＿

ACCEPTANCE

        CONSTRUCTION MANAGER ＿＿＿＿＿＿＿＿＿＿＿＿＿

Figure 3 Change form.

operations, but they can also be a concern from a quality standpoint. Therefore, any
change should have the proper engineering design review and documents modified as
required.

REWORK

Rework in the field can result in a significant expenditure of funds. This rework can
result from three areas: engineering errors, construction errors, and owner requests.
    The latter category (owner requests) should result in a change to the prime con-
tract. However, it is necessary sometimes to authorize a minor change as "rework"
in order to progress the work expeditiously. Of course it is necessary to get adequate
engineering reviews of any rework that change designs and possibly later issue a
change to capture the costs of all the miscellaneous owner requests.
    In order to adequately control these expenditures, rework tracking curves should
be developed and reviewed periodically with the groups involved.

6

Field Scheduling

EDWARD J. McGUIRE and EDWARD A. WYNANT* *Exxon Research & Engineering Co.,
Florham Park, New Jersey*

INTRODUCTION

Schedule control is essential to the success of any construction project. Major projects
are a complex effort to mobilize and coordinate large numbers of personnel, materials,
and equipment. Continual monitoring of the plan for potential bottlenecks, correctness
of original assumptions, and actual progress are necessary in order to identify problems
early and to forecast completion dates with increasing accuracy. Good schedule control is to develop a plan, implement the plan, monitor execution of the plan, and make
changes to the plan when necessary in order to meet schedule target dates.

Schedule control is also needed in order to keep the owner advised for his planning
needs: (1) start-up manpower (including the hiring and training of plant operating
personnel); (2) scheduling feedstocks; (3) scheduling of product shipments. The
owner generally has large costs at stake and, therefore, a great interest in accurate
schedule reporting.

We will cover here the general background of accepted techniques for scheduling
and schedule control. Scheduling during construction relies on a "master schedule"
to establish the overall logic for the field activities and then the use of long- and short-
range analyses to form the basis of field control.

MASTER SCHEDULE

The master schedule is generally a logic network-type schedule that reflects project
execution plans, the construction strategy, equipment delivery estimates, and engineering plans. The construction part of the master schedule should include only an amount
of detail sufficient to guide other project phases and predict the completion date of
the project. It should reflect the owner's requirements for start-up or occupancy.

Whether a logic network-type schedule or a bar chart form, the logic in the construction section of the master schedule must include:

1. An anticipated backlog of materials, an orderly construction manpower build-
   up and rundown, seasonal weather conditions, and local vacation and holiday
   customs
2. Starting dates of each construction phase which should be realistic, making
   allowances for engineering, material procurement, and mobilization

---

*Current affiliation: Consultant, Basking Ridge, New Jersey

3. Anticipated labor shortages which may result from other large projects in the area
4. Back-up data such as:
   a. Projected progress curves
   b. Manpower curves, including a summary of skilled craft requirements where shortages are expected
5. Identification of the need for early completion of certain portions of the project to suit the owner's needs

The project execution strategy is developed by the project manager, the construction manager and by "line" management as well as including input from project specialists such as experienced planners. This strategy is translated into an execution plan which, in turn, provides the basis along with other project documents (drawings, specifications) for the master schedule. Thus, the master schedule is not developed in a vacuum by technical specialists, but is, rather, a reflection of the thinking of those ultimately responsible for the success of the project.

Using the project master schedule as a starting point, more detailed schedules can be developed as needed in the field to control the job. These more detailed schedules will:

1. Provide easy-to-read information to the various field groups to indicate how their work must progress in order to be consistent with the overall plan
2. Provide a basis for preparing up-to-date schedules to be used during initiation of subcontract activities since large cost claims can result if a subcontractor arrives too early or too late
3. Allow coordination of the schedules of others and tie-ins to facilities and utilities which other contractors and/or the owner may be handling
4. Allow identification of problem areas regarding schedule and, where possible, correct them early enough to prevent schedule slippages or cost overruns (productivity may be low, supervision inadequate, etc.)
5. Allow preparation of accurate completion forecasts so that operational planning can proceed

FIELD SCHEDULING ACTIVITIES

Field schedules developed from the master schedule fall into two categories: long range and short range. Long-range scheduling generally relies on such techniques as specialized logic diagrams, equipment and drawing delivery projections, manpower planning (resource planning), and physical progress measurement. Short-range scheduling generally relies on detailed logic networks for parts of the project, "look ahead" schedules, "punch lists," and field observations of actual work versus planned activities. These schedules must be consistent with the overall progress and logic anticipated in the master schedule.

Using both long- and short-range scheduling techniques, problems can be identified early and completion dates accurately forecasted. Construction sequences and priorities can be revised to reflect other changes, delays, etc., that may occur. Short-range schedules are particularly important when there are many interfaces involved as during start-up or if there is revamp-type work to be performed on existing facilites.

Field-scheduling activities must reflect a continuous exchange between field "line" management and the field scheduler. Many successful construction managers take a direct hand in scheduling field activities and it is up to the field scheduler to quantify these actions. In any event, team spirit in field-scheduling activities is the aim and a bureaucratic approach to field scheduling wherein a scheduling "department" produces a document which tends to be an "end in itself" should not be acceptable. If field-scheduling activities are to contribute to the effectiveness of the field construction effort they must also be a reflection of the agreed execution strategy.

FIELD SCHEDULING TOOLS (TECHNIQUES)

The following is a discussion of the types of schedule control tools available and some guidelines as to where each should be used. Each of these tools must be developed for the individual project, using the master schedule as a basis. There are numerous computer software programs now available to assist in this effort. However, our purpose is to present only a fundamental understanding of these tools.

Logic Networks

Several types of logic networks are in use on projects. Basically, whether the type of network used is "critical path method" or something else, these tools generally show the relationships of the various tasks in a project. This will include:

Tasks that have to be completed before others can start
Identification of "critical activities" . . . any delay to these activities will delay
the project

For details of how to set up and use the various types of network scheduling tools available, the reader is referred to other books on the subject.

Critical activities and deliveries in the master schedule must be monitored continuously. This includes such items as delivery of critical equipment, initiation of work in critical areas, and progress of work on critical field fabricated items. Detailed logic networks, or "fragnets," must be developed to show the logic for certain activities. These are magnifications of the master schedule and include a lot more detail (for example, one step in the master schedule may be "erect boiler," whereas the detailed breakout logic network would show possibly 30 or more tasks, in their proper sequence, that are necessary to erect the boiler). This detail was not needed when the master schedule was developed but becomes necessary to control the field activities.

Examples of the need for breakout logic networks would include:

Control of the erection of any major equipment item that consists of many tasks
(installation of HVAC systems, field fabricated tanks and process vessels,
major heavy lifts, etc.)
Coordination of the efforts of several individual crafts
Other activities where there are numerous interfaces involved

Sampling

To monitor the schedule logic effectively and continuously, and to identify problem areas early, techniques such as "sampling" or taking a "snapshot" of the work should be used. Basically, these techniques mean to monitor daily performance (snapshot), or performance for a week or so on a specific task (sampling). Examples would be number of piles driven per day in a pier, number of trays installed per week when traying a process tower, and number of tests per week during a testing program. The emphasis here is to define manpower limitations or productivity problems early enough so that corrective actions can be taken while there is still time. Judgment must be applied to these snapshots or samples so that proper conclusions are reached.

Look-Ahead Scheduling

Frequent updates of schedules are required to direct project activities on a daily basis. These schedules are particularly required when project activities are impacting directly on the activities of others (as during the completion phase of a project or where "turn-arounds" are part of the project). These updates have four basic forms: (1) simple logic network diagrams, (2) bar charts, (3) look-ahead-type lists, and (4) punch lists (lists of outstanding work).

During the life of a project, "look-ahead" schedules should be prepared at set periods of time (usually every 2 weeks) and show work that should be done during an upcoming period (1 to 2 months) consistent with the "master schedule." These types of summary schedules are useful for:

Balancing manpower and/or equipment utilization
Identifying to field management upcoming activities that must be prepared for
Coordination of activities with other groups

Often a major petrochemical construction project will include turnaround or revamp work in an operating unit. A very intense scheduling program is required to successfully complete this type of work because: (1) the unit will probably be out of service during the revamp activity and any delay in getting it back "on stream" will be very costly to the owner, and (2) there will be a lot of work by others going on simultaneously, presenting complex coordination and interface problems. During the revamp work itself, daily meetings, daily reports, daily worklists, and daily "look-ahead" schedules are required to keep all informed and to progress the work as smoothly and quickly as possible.

Schedule Statusing

Schedule statusing is an integral part of the foregoing techniques. It is particularly crucial to the use of short-term scheduling or look-ahead schedules. All schedules, no matter how sophisticated, are useless if not implemented in some manner. This is not to say that they must be rigidly adhered to. A certain amount of flexibility in project execution is essential to permit construction management to take advantage of opportunities to optimize the construction effort. However, "statusing" against the plan/schedule is important to the assessment of actual performance and in forecasting the schedule outcome.

Purists in the application of critical path method (CPM), program evaluation and review technique (PERT), and other similar techniques endorse total reliance on schedules employing these techniques and the statusing thereof. The authors, however, favor the more practical approach described above. In this manner, schedule implementation is achieved through a continuous monitoring of the construction progress against the master schedule and updated "look-ahead" schedules. In that there is usually some flexibility in schedule decisions, the field construction management has to be well informed in order to make the correct decisions.

Milestone Reviews/Assessments

On nearly every project, large or small, there comes a time when it is necessary to perform a major schedule update, to take stock of what has been accomplished and where the project is headed. It is usually desirable to formalize these updates in milestone reviews or assessments. The larger the project, the more structured or formalized the update. As an example, the construction of the Alaska Oil Pipeline, a project involving over 175,000,000 manhours of effort, included several such milestone reviews.

However, it is not only on the large super projects that milestone reviews can be beneficial. Even a small project involving a few thousand manhours of effort and directed in the field by a staff of two or three line managers can benefit by milestone reviews. The timing and/or need for these reviews should be determined based on specific project circumstances and characteristics. For large projects two or three reviews scheduled to coincide with the 25, 50, and 75% progress points or some key project milestones are suggested. For small projects one major update at about the 50% construction progress point may be appropriate.

Charting

Charting and other wall displays depicting project status have proven to be particularly effective in schedule control during field construction. They generate interest in schedule performance among key decision makers who see regular project reports as well as throughout the entire project organization. Making charts accessible to viewing by craftsmen can promote healthy competition and pride in accomplishment.

Imaginative charting is most effective but care should be taken to make it meaningful. Overall progress, production rates on a week to week or monthly plot, amount of different kinds of work completed, manpower, are good candidates for charting.

Charting is useful to line management because it usually displays a powerful message in a succinct way. A quick glance or brief critique of the charts covers a lot of ground. Keeping things simple promotes the greatest efficiency on a construction site and charting can be made consistent with that philosophy. There is much to be said for the simplicity of a wall chart displaying accomplishments on a single but significant item. Complicated reports, although essential to the overall construction effort, can easily overburden key line individuals with unnecessary paper.

PROGRESS MEASUREMENT

The master schedule and the basic logic for this schedule must be continually monitored. Logic monitoring is achieved by watching material deliveries, subcontractor performance, engineering progress, construction equipment availability, and other activities/ events using the short- and long-range scheduling techniques discussed above. An overall view of the schedule can be effectively achieved by measuring progress. Two methods of progress measurement should be used: (1) physical percent complete and (2) resource utilization.

Physical Percent Complete

The most basic technique for overall monitoring of a schedule is to calculate physical percent complete and compare this to a forecasted progress curve based on the master schedule. Calculation of physical percent complete is probably the most widely used tool for schedule monitoring. In order to use this technique, an accurate method for forecasting and then calculating physical progress must be established. A forecasted progress curve should be developed and then the actual progress curve plotted for comparison. One method for doing this is described below. This method should only be used to calculate progress based on "direct work accounts" and not based on expenditures in indirect accounts.

Forecasting Progress

Bar graph schedules for direct activities and the control manhour estimates for these activities should be established using a work breakdown structure (WBS). The WBS must reflect the agreed accounting code system that will be used to collect field time charges. The bar graphs developed are based on the master schedule and these should also be consistent with the WBS breakdown. The data can then be combined as follows:

1. Spread the total manhours for each direct activity code in the estimate over the time shown on the corresponding bar graph of the construction schedule. This distribution is not made uniformly. It should take into account the need for a gradual buildup of manpower, engineering drawings, and a backlog of materials (Table 1).

Table 1 Simplified Construction Master Schedule

Account code	Activity	MH (1000s) esimate	wf	J	F	M	A	M	J	J	A	S	O	N	D
1.00	Foundations	30	.15	(4)	(6)	(8)	(8)	(4)							
2.00	Equipment	10	.05				(4)	(4)	(2)						
3.00	Electrical	30	.15					(2)	(6)	(6)	(6)	(4)			
4.00	Pipe	70	.35			(4)	(6)	(8)	(8)	(10)	(10)	(10)	(8)	(6)	(4)
5.00	Instruments	30	.15							(4)	(4)	(6)	(8)	(6)	(2)
6.00	Insulation and paint	30	.15							(4)	(4)	(6)	(6)	(6)	(4)

Notes: 1. The above is a very simple master schedule and is presented to illustrate calculation procedures only.
2. The number in brackets ( ) is the hours scheduled to be used that month.
3. Account code is a simplified work breakdown structure.

2. Using the control estimate of hours for each direct account, a weight factor (wf) for each account can be calculated as follows:

$$wf = \frac{\text{Total estimated hours for account}}{\text{Total estimated hours for total project}}$$

3. After a distribution is made for each code and bar graph, the forecasted man-hours for each month for that code divided by the total forecasted manhours for that code for the job represents the forecasted progress for that code for that month (Table 2).
4. The cumulative percent complete for each code for each month of the project should then be calculated.
5. The total forecasted cumulative percent complete for each month is then equal to the sum of each individual account percent complete multiplied by the wf for that account (Table 2).

The above method for calculating a forecasted percent complete curve assumes that the productivity for an account does not vary with time. Because the measuring procedures for calculating the physical percent complete are not 100 percent accurate, the apparent productivity will vary with time. If historical data is available it may be desirable to adjust the predicted percent complete for each account based on an expected productivity at that stage of the project. However, this is not usually done because of the difficulty in accurately predicting the shape of the productivity profile.

Measuring Percent Complete

A method for calculating actual physical progress (percent complete) must be established for each account code. Once this is done, overall physical percent complete can be calculated as follows (Table 3) and plotted against the forecast (Fig. 1):

1. List each account and its corresponding weight factor (wf) as found above.
2. Examine and observe progress every month on each account code. Using the procedures established, tabulate actual physical progress. Physical progress is defined as the percentage calculated by dividing the physical portion of the work completed by the total physical quantity scheduled to be built.
For example, 50 square feet of concrete paving has been placed out of a total for the project of 200 square feet. Then 25% of that account has been completed. To allow for the fact that some physical quantities are easier to install than others (as a foot of 2-inch pipe compared to a foot of 30-inch pipe), account codes can be further subdivided to allow for weighting of the various activities within that account code.
3. After tabulating the physical progress for each account code, these are then combined with the corresponding wf and added up to a total percent representing the physical state of completion of the job.

Earned Workhour Concept

A variation to the physical progress measurement technique described above is the earned workhour concept. The system utilizes workhour estimates and component weighting the same as the technique described in the foregoing. As work is completed, workhours are "earned" according to pre-established budgets for the work irrespective of the actual number of workhours expended to perform the work. Progress is calculated as a percent of earned workhours accumulated to the total budgeted hours. The system facilitates combining different types of work (cubic yards of concrete or tons of structural steel) in that all the units are the same (workhours). It also facilitates productivity calculations by simply comparing earned workhours to actual expended hours.

TABLE 2 Simplified Scheduled Progress Calculation (month of June)

Account code	Activity	(A) MH (1000s) estimate	(B) wf	(C) Sched mo. hr	(D) Sch. mo. % compl.	(E) Wtd. mo. % compl.	(F) Cum. hours	(G) Sch. cum. % compl.	(H) Wtd. cum. % compl.
1.00	Foundations	30	.15	0	0	0	30	100	15
2.00	Equipment	10	.05	2	20	1.0	10	100	5
3.00	Electrical	30	.15	6	20	3.0	8	26.7	4
4.00	Pipe	70	.35	8	11.4	4.0	22	31.4	11
5.00	Instruments	30	.15	0	0	0	0	0	0
6.00	Insulation and paint	30	.15	0	0	0	0	0	0
					Total	8.0			35

Notes: 1. (D) = 100 × (C)/(A)
       2. (E) = (D) × (B)
       3. (G) = 100 × (F)/(A)
       4. (H) = (G) × (B)

Table 3 Actual Progress Calculation (month of June)

Account code	Activity	MH (1000s) estimate	wf	% Actual progress	% Wtd progress
1.00	Foundations	30	.15	95	14.3
2.00	Equipment	10	.05	82	4.1
3.00	Electrical	30	.15	25	3.8
4.00	Pipe	70	.35	27	9.5
5.00	Instruments	30	.15	0	0
6.00	Insulation and paint	30	.15	0	0
				Total	31.7

Resource Utilization

The physical percent complete method is a necessary tool for monitoring the project's construction schedule. However, because the accuracy of this method can vary depending on the accuracy of the procedures used, other indicators and trends must be watched, and other proven scheduling tools used at the appropriate times. Another tracking system is called resource utilization.

Worker requirements should be monitored relative to the forecasted manpower. This should be done for the project as a whole, for individual areas, and for critical crafts where shortages are possible. This technique is referred to as "resource utilization" tracking.

Using the monthly workhour totals developed for the forecasted progress curve, the required monthly number of workers can be determined. First divide the monthly workhour totals by the hours worked each month. Next add personnel for indirect labor and then adjust this total for absentees (varies from 6% to 30% depending on the location), holidays, and other lost hours (such as weather) to get total people required "on-the-rolls." Adjusted monthly personnel figures are then plotted to form the projected labor requirement curves.

In addition to evaluating the practicability of achieving labor peaks predicted by the projected personnel curves, hiring rates should also be reviewed. In establishing hiring rates, normal attrition (voluntary and involuntary terminations) must be considered (can be 15% per month or higher in certain locations for certain crafts). For example, to raise the personnel on a project from 200 to 300 in a month would require that 138 (100 plus .15 × 250) people be hired if the attrition rate is 15%.

Craft requirement curves should be developed for the overall project and for critical crafts (pipe fitters, welders). When establishing craft requirements, allowances should be made for craft people required in indirect accounts. As a further note, most direct accounts (pipe, electrical) are worked on by various crafts (laborers, fitters, welders), and therefore correct "mixes" of the various crafts for each account must be estimated in order to establish the numbers of craft people required.

People actually working at the site should then be plotted against the curves developed above. If the number of people working tracks above or below the projected curve, the contributing factors should be analyzed. This will allow management to accurately predict costs, predict schedule completions, or take appropriate actions.

The benefit of the resource utilization technique over the method of strictly looking at the physical percent complete is that it is not as greatly affected by procedures

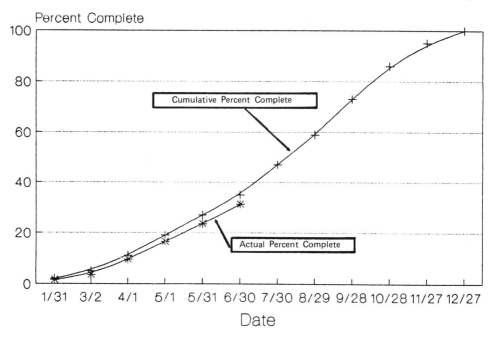

Figure 1 Tracking cumulative and actual percents complete.

for calculating physical percent complete. On the other hand, looking only at personnel employed or workhour expenditures does not allow the engineer to identify things such as estimating errors or productivity problems.

REPORTING

Monthly reports should include summaries of the schedule analysis work done. This generally includes:

> Physical progress charts and curves
> Charts showing actual personnel working on the site versus estimated requirements (overall and for "critical" crafts)
> Written reports on critical activities and critical deliveries
> Summary of forecasted and target completion dates

Progress reports should be concise and present sufficient data to indicate why the conclusions regarding schedule were reached and to provide a general understanding of how the project is progressing.

7

Field Material Control

EDWARD J. McGUIRE   *Exxon Research & Engineering Co., Florham Park, New Jersey*

Control of materials in the field is an integral part of the overall material management and control system that should be initiated during the engineering phase of the project. The process of managing materials is not complete once materials have been received at the site, but continues until the facilities are constructed and turned over for operation. If the process is not continued throughout the construction period, costly problems can occur.

In a recent publication, the Construction Industry Institute defined the total materials management function as

> Materials Management can best be defined as the planning and controlling of all necessary efforts to insure that the correct quality and quantity of materials and equipment are appropriately specified in a timely manner, are obtained at a reasonable cost, and are available when needed. The materials management process combines and integrates the individual functions of project planning, material takeoff, vendor inquiry and evaluation, expediting and transportation, field material control, and warehousing.

Good material management programs can have a significant impact on many parts of the field construction effort. Examples are as follows:

> Recent studies have shown that craft productivity can be affected by up to 6% or more
> Adequate final quality of the completed facility depends on getting the right material installed in the right location
> Surplus material is costly
> Field warehousing space and storage yards are expensive and must be minimized

FIELD MATERIAL CONTROL SYSTEM BASICS

As with any control system, basic steps apply to the control of materials in the field: (a) develop a plan, (b) execute the plan, (c) monitor and analyze performance, and (d) correct deficiencies noted.

When developing the field material control plan, it is important to understand the responsibilities of the field organization with regard to the overall material management system for the project. These responsibilities will include:

Purchasing of certain materials
Receiving material and then properly protecting materials while in storage
Providing information to site management regarding material receipts in a way that
    permits adequate planning/kickoff of other activities
Controlling inventories and providing materials to craft people in a timely manner
Identifying shortage so that additional material can be purchased as required
Disposing of surplus materials

FIELD PURCHASING

Engineered materials (equipment, fabricated steel, fabricated pipe) are normally purchased in the home office. On many large industrial projects critical or "engineered"
bulk materials (piping materials, electrical cables) are also purchased in the home office.
However, there is usually a substantial amount of materials that are purchased in the
field. It is important that a clear understanding be reached on what will be purchased
where and that this understanding be reflected in the field material control plan.

Field purchasing can include permanent materials (concrete), consumable materials
(welding rods), temporary materials (field office supplies), subcontracts and service
agreements. A field purchasing procedure needs to be prepared that addresses the
following items:

Preparation of requisitions
Selection of bidders
Issuing of requests for quotations
Preparation, review, and approval of bid tabulations
Issuance of purchase orders
Expediting and inspection of field orders

Authority approval schedules should be prepared and included in the field purchasing procedure. These schedules show who can approve what level of expenditure.
The schedules must reflect corporate policies and be consistent with site management
philosophies on the delegation of authority.

Details within the field purchasing procedures should address the following points:

Selection of bidders. Prospective bidders should be evaluated to determine that
    they can perform adequately before being asked to bid. This evaluation should
    include a review of past performance, quality control procedures, capacity
    to meet required production rates, financial stability, etc. Unqualified firms
    must not be invited to provide bids.
Bid tabulation, review, and approval. Bids should be received and evaluated in a
    consistent manner. Recommendations for award and approval of selected ven-
    dors should be clear. For cost-control purposes, bid tabulations should clearly
    compare recommended purchase value against the established budget, and large
    discrepancies investigated.
Expediting. Field expediting should be conducted in a way that insures timely
    delivery of materials. Clear information must be provided by expediting re-
    ports to field management on the latest anticipated delivery dates so that other
    activities can be planned or corrective action initiated.
Quality control. Who will do inspections, how these inspectors must be notified,
    how rejections will be handled, and so on need to be stated.
Close-out of purchase orders and subcontracts. Procedures need to state how to
    close out orders and subcontracts once all materials and services have been
    received. These procedures are necessary to insure that outstanding claims,
    backcharges, or other items are identified.

FIELD WAREHOUSING

Plans for the receipt, storage, and issuance of materials can be complicated, and if not properly prepared early can result in productivity problems later. The size and layout of the site warehouse and storage yards, and the receiving, inventory control, and issuing procedures are important parts of the plans.

Site warehouses can be very substantial in size (40,000 to 60,000 square foot warehouses are not uncommon on very large process plant sites). The actual size of the warehouse at the construction site will depend on:

Existing facilities that can be used for storage.

The types of materials to be stored. Some materials must be stored indoors for weather protection (instruments, insulation materials). Other materials must be stored indoors because they are small or valuable.

If tool storage is to be included in the warehouse, space must be provided.

The possibility of having to segregate some material when received while awaiting inspections or other functions before acceptance into inventory.

The types of bins or racks and the equipment to safely access these.

Access for receiving and issuing of materials.

One method of reducing the size of the field warehouse and the cost of carrying a large inventory—a cost that can be considerable over the time span of a large project—is to rely on vendors to maintain a large inventory of materials at their locations and then supply the field on an "as-needed" basis. The site warehouse can then maintain a low inventory. Obviously there are numerous precautions to be taken when relying too heavily on vendor stocking or disastrous problems with field productivity and schedule can result. Some precautions that can be taken when considering relying on vendor inventory are:

Investigate the reliability history of the vendor

Periodically review the vendor's inventory

Constantly monitor the performance of the vendors

MATERIAL PRESERVATION

Warehousing procedures must address the preservation of materials while in storage and until equipment is placed in operation. Extremely costly repairs and delays can occur if this is not done. Some of the critical equipment requiring protection are:

Rotating machinery (pumps, compressors, engines, bearings, spare shafts)

Electrical and electronic equipment (motors, instruments, switch gear)

Machined surfaces (flanges, valves)

Records will have to be kept for some equipment. These are necessary for site quality control and quality assurance monitoring and to establish a record to insure that guarantees remain valid.

TEMPORARY ACCESS AND STORAGE AREAS

Many materials to be received and stored at a construction site will not require indoor storage—large process vessels, structural steel, most fabricated pipe, etc. However, large lay down or open storage areas will be required to store this equipment. When developing plans for these areas, consideration should be given to the following:

Size of areas: for large process type plants, total temporary areas, including
     offices, warehouses and open storage areas, can be three times the actual pro-
     cess areas
Logical layout of the areas to permit easy identification and retrieval of material
Size of access roads for handling equipment
Security and protection of the public
Lighting
Material preservation needs for material stored inside or outside

On some sites it will be necessary to receive very large pieces of equipment. Plans
need to be developed early for receiving facilities (docks, railroads), storage areas,
if required, and access to the installation location.

RECEIVING, INVENTORY CONTROL, ISSUING

Large volumes of expensive materials will be controlled in the field. Procedures which
cover the receipt, storage, and issuance of these materials will be necessary in order
to assure proper stewardship of this function.
Receiving procedures need to cover the following:

1. Adequate identification by purchase order, vendor, description, quantity,
    and date of receipt
2. Required receiving inspections consistent with the quality control plan
3. Overage, shortage, and damage (O S & D) reports which must be properly filled
    out
4. Daily receiving logs should be distributed to management on a "need to know"
    basis

Inventory procedures should clearly identify where material is stored and the quantity of each item that is on hand. For some bulk materials a "min/max" system may
need to be established so that, as material is used and the inventory reaches a certain
level, new purchases are made. The inventory procedure must be integrated with the
issuing procedure so that a record is kept of where material is used. The issuing procedure should cover:

Approval authority to requisition from warehouse inventory
Clear description of usage
A check of usage against engineered material takeoffs

Material substitutions can cause serious problems and should not be permitted without the proper engineering evaluation and approval. If a material substitution is approved, there may need to be a reordering of the material, cancellation of other orders,
and/or documentation on "as-built" drawings/documents.

CONSUMABLE SUPPLIES AND TOOLS

Consumables are usually defined as materials that are "used up" or consumed during
the construction project. These can be materials that do not form a part of the final
plant (fuels, grease, gases) or materials that form a part of the final plant (welding
rods). The Quality Control Plan for the project must address those consumables that
could have an effect on the quality of the final constructed facility. Some of these
materials (weld rods) will require close monitoring and control from a preservation and
use standpoint. They also may require a degree of inspection to insure that the correct quality material is received.

Tight procedures on the use of consumables will be required to prevent losses. This is particularly true in the case of fuel. Good records are needed on what vehicles and equipment are refueled and at what intervals. In some locations, if construction equipment and vehicles are confined to the construction site, it may be possible to purchase fuel without paying highway and other usage taxes. This should be investigated, but will require additional controls in order to insure that laws are not violated.

Procedures for the control of tools on the site need to cover the following:

1. Location of tool rooms.
2. Contents of tool kits issued to each craft person.
3. Assignment of tools not included in kits–small power tools generally. This procedure should cover to whom the tool is issued and for how long.
4. Safety inspection frequencies for tools, such as small power tools.
5. Safety precautions and how to qualify personnel to operate certain tools.

Tool room supervisors should be asked to provide periodic reports on tools requested by the field personnel but not available in the tool room. The supervisor should also collect other information that would help evaluate the efficiency of the tool room operation and adequacy of the existing procedures–average length of wait at the tool room for a craft person, damage to tools returned, etc.

It will also be necessary to periodically conduct site inventories of small tools and equipment in order to determine losses. This can be more easily done if the tool control procedures permit assignment of tools to a particular person or crew for a specified time limit.

DISPOSAL OF SURPLUS

There will always be a surplus of materials throughout the life of a construction project. This surplus will consist of everything from packing crates to expensive pieces of construction equipment. Procedures need to be established that cover:

How to declare an item surplus.
How to solicit and receive bids for the sale of the surplus. Some purchase orders may contain clauses which require the original vendor to take the surplus at some agreed-to price.
Who must approve the proposed disposition of an item.
How to handle monies received and how to account for these monies.

Substantial amounts of money can be involved in the disposal of surplus, and thus surplus materials represent an asset to the owner or contractor. Precautions must be established to protect these assets. Procedures used to dispose of the assets must be tight and auditable.

8

Productivity

EDWARD J. McGUIRE *Exxon Research & Engineering Co., Florham Park, New Jersey*

Productivity is usually defined as the quantity of work accomplished in the field for
a specified amount of labor effort–cubic yards of concrete in place per manhour, for
example. Some owners and contractors compute a "measured productivity" by comparing "actual productivity" with "budgeted productivity." A measured productivity of
1.0 would mean that the results of the field effort are equal to the results anticipated
in the budget.

Several flaws are inherent in the implementation of productivity measurement programs. Two common failings will be discussed here: budget quality and rework considerations.

Measured productivity programs require realistic budgets, otherwise the programs
are meaningless. All too often field performance reports–both good and bad–are clearly counter to the jobsite observations of senior project and construction staff personnel.
The problem frequently lies in the quality of the budget. Budgets should serve as
the basis for performance evaluation. The project plan must reflect constructability
and the budget must be compatible with the agreed-to construction execution plan.

Measured productivity programs collapse when budgeted work-unit targets are not
adjusted for rework caused by design changes. A pipeline 20 feet in length that took
40 hours to construct will have been installed for 0.50 feet per manhour. If another 20
feet of pipe has to be added as a result of a design change and requires an additional
40 hours to install, an "apparent productivity" of 0.25 is recorded if the budget is not
adjusted for the design change. The budget might have been 0.40, the actual is 0.50,
the record will show 0.25–and there goes the program! Credence has to be given to
the classical lament of the construction team: we are evaluating the budget.

The way in which a facility is designed, procured, and contracted for can have a
substantial effect on the productivity of field labor. And there is no more important
activity than the preparation of the overall project plan–the strategy and philosophy
of the team.

A case in point is the execution of grassroots mega refinery projects. Grassroots
refinery projects more often than not have a series of critical paths, usually centered
on the process unit complex, with the pipefitter craft controlling. Productivity in this
craft can be greatly enhanced by building a "fly wheel" into the basic project plan.
Tank farm piping, offsite sleeperway piping, ancillary units, and other "noncritical"
units should be scheduled over an extended period, starting relatively early in the
program, and following an "on-off" concept. A pure focus on critical path method
(CPM) criticality without an understanding of resource allocation (the "blinders syn-

drome") often is detrimental to overall jobsite productivity. The results of flywheel planning are manifold:

Long, flat manning plateaus, rather than sharp peaking
Development of "on-site" manpower pools
Training of craftsmen in the methods of the owner and the contractor
Job continuity, leading to rank-and-file support—teamwork

Many factors affect the productivity of field labor, some controllable by management and labor in the field, some not. We will discuss techniques which have been found over the course of time to contribute to good field performance.

EXECUTION STRATEGIES TO ADDRESS PRODUCTIVITY

Strategies need to be developed early in a project so that appropriate actions can be taken later to optimize productivity. In developing actions, tradeoffs will have to be evaluated and judgments made, for example, additional expenditures during the engineering phase to save field manhours. The project execution strategy must explore at least the following areas, in addition to the review and confirmation of and agreement on realistic budgets, and the initiation and completion of sound basic planning.

Organization
Compatibility with the contract
Constructability
Work continuity
Industrial relations

Organization

This subject becomes more important as a project's size increases. However, philosophies that govern required strategies should be similar. These philosophies are:

Cooperative attitudes between owners, engineers, and constructors should be encouraged. Team-building and other techniques should be used.
Contractual boundaries must be respected.
Organization structures must be as simple and clear as possible.
Capabilities of personnel must be closely reviewed.
Management should establish goals and guiding principles for the project and communicate these widely.
Authority and accountability should be delegated to as low a level in the organization as possible.

In developing the strategies to follow on any specific project, the importance of some of the above philosophies will vary. However, on large projects where new organizations are being formed and new relationships being established, these philosophies become much more important. Management is responsible to establish appropriate audit controls to make sure personnel are performing in the desired way.

Compatibility with the Contract

How a project is contracted will have a significant effect on the field labor productivity. This must be considered when developing contracting strategies. Some points to remember are:

    How a facility is engineered and how materials are procured will have an effect
       on how easy it is to build.

    The interests of the various parties—owners, engineers and constructors—basically
       have to do with making money for their organizations. Contracting strategies
       should respect these interests and try to align these interests with an interest
       in optmizing the field productivity.

An example of a case where the interests of the engineer/procurement contractor
may not be "aligned" with increasing field productivity would be to award that contractor a lump-sum contract to supply designs and materials to the field. His interests
then are in keeping his engineering effort to a minimum and purchasing the materials
in the least costly fashion without regard to ease of field assembly.

Constructability

Constructability can be defined as the consideration of construction needs during planning, engineering, and procurement. How well this is done will depend on the ability
of the organization to obtain and use construction knowledge and experience during
the early phases of the project. Personnel with construction experience should be assigned to project teams early and these personnel should: (1) have strong interpersonal skills, (2) have broad experience in construction and engineering, and (3) have
the ability to identify major issues which offer most payout.

    The constructability of a facility is enhanced when:

    Design and procurement policies make the facility easier to build. For example:
        Schedules are sensitive to construction needs
        Appropriate offsite or onsite preassembly techniques are used
        Design details are standardized and configured to permit easy construction
    Access for construction equipment is adequate and sufficient laydown areas are
       provided.
    Weather conditions, soil conditions, etc., are considered and designs are developed
       to facilitate construction.
    Design details permit the use of advances in construction technology—automatic
       welding, foamed-in-place insulation, etc.
    Designs reflect safe construction.

Work Continuity

Execution strategies must address the question of work continuity. Simply put, this
means "don't start until there is sufficient engineering and materials at the site to support continued field activities being performed in a logical sequence." Some examples
of this would be:

    Don't start foundation work if, in order to keep personnel busy, they have to be
       moved many times on a site
    Don't erect pipe spools if some are missing from a system
    Don't bring additional workers onto the site if there isn't a sufficient backlog of
       work and an assurance of future work releases to keep them busy

Industrial Relations

Industrial relation requirements vary depending on where the project is to be constructed (city, state, country). Some projects will be constructed in an "open shop" (nonunion) environment and others will have union involvement. Regardless of where a
plant is constructed, productivity will be affected by how industrial relations are ap-

proached and what policies are established. The interests and morale of construction workers must be considered or industrial unrest will develop.

Construction workers are a cross-section of the community in which they live. As with most people, they are becoming better educated and better informed. This enhanced sophistication, along with the fact that they live in a free enterprise system, creates certain occupational inducements—a pleasant place to work, good pay, knowledge of how their efforts affect the project, etc. Strategies and policies should be established which address these interests, for example:

> How can management minimize "them vs. us" attitudes?
> A project identity that is important and credible should be established.
> What training is required for supervisors . . . are supervisors adequately recognized?
> Do work hours optimize performance and meet worker desires—shift patterns, overtime, etc.?
> Are relations with unions supportive of improved field performance?
> Are field discipline procedures clear and do they reflect a firm and fair attitude?
> What programs are required to communicate with employees and show that they are valued—induction training, "open days", newspapers, tool box meetings, etc.?
> Are field support facilities adequate—toilets, eating areas, water, etc.?

Obviously, how the above items are addressed on a specific project will vary depending on the size of that project and how the project is contracted. However, if one is to get the most and best productivity from the project team personnel, all of the above should be considered.

PRODUCTIVITY MEASUREMENT

It is extremely important that cost control/reporting systems be developed to measure both physical quantities installed and field labor effort expended. When measurement systems are in place and budgets are known, targets which are achievable should be established and communicated to supervisory personnel. Actual productivity by type of work should be analyzed versus established targets and communicated to supervisors in a way that is supportive of their efforts. This communication must recognize that some supervisors will have productivities lower than others simply because of the nature of their work. Productivity is highly dependent on engineering, procurement, and management systems and may not reflect how hard people are working. The real value of a supervisor is to improve the productivity to the best of his ability by improving management systems, communications, and the motivation of his employees.

FIELD PROGRAMS TO IMPROVE PRODUCTIVITY

Field programs should be developed which are geared to improving systems, work methods, morale, and abilities of personnel. What programs are used will depend on the specific project. Some suggested programs are as follows:

Management Commitment

Management commitment is achieved when:

> Contractual interests are aligned.
> Middle management feels that they have a role in establishing policies; management committees, organizational development programs, etc., can help.
> Goals and philosophies are identified and supported by management.

Unless owner and contractor management are committed to a strong productivity performance, it won't happen.

Communication Programs

Communication programs are necessary to satisfy employee desires to know what is going on and to feel a part of the project. These programs will have a marked effect on morale and include:

Tool box talks
Induction programs
Newsletters
Management/worker presentations

Problem Identification/Solving

It is important that the capabilities of all employees to identify and solve productivity bottlenecks be tapped. When doing this, it is important that the stature of supervision and middle management be respected. Thus, it may be more important to establish programs which reach those groups before extending programs to all workers on a site. The size and timespan of a project will determine how many personnel can get involved in this activity.

Problem identification/solving techniques can include:

Committees
Individual effort
Foreman circles
Quality circles

Work Methods Improvement

How a job is approached and the flow of work will impact on productivity. Work methods improvement means looking at this aspect and using knowledge of procedures and methods to make improvements. There are several consultants available who specialize in this activity. Some examples of work methods improvement would be:

Use of portable platforms instead of scaffolding
Automatic welding
Site preassembly
Assembly line concepts

Surveys

On-site surveys of supervisors and employees can be valuable in identifying and eliminating bottlenecks. Some types of surveys which have proved useful are: (1) foreman delay surveys and (2) tool room surveys.

Training

Training should be evaluated as a means of increasing capabilities of craftsmen and improving morale. Training will include subjects that vary from supervisory techniques for supervisors, safety training for supervisors and craftspeople, to welder training and other skill-enhancement programs.

SUMMARY

The apparent field productivity in terms of quantities installed for a given amount of labor effort is dependent on (1) how well the facility is engineered and procured, (2) how motivated the field labor and supervisors are, (3) how efficient field procedures and systems are, and (4) how supportive management is of the field effort. We have discussed some strategies that should be developed early in a project if productivity is to be optimized, and some field programs which can be used to improve field performance.

9

Quality Assurance and Quality Control

EDWARD J. McGUIRE   *Exxon Research & Engineering Co., Florham Park, New Jersey*

Quality control and quality assurance are terms that are quite often used synonymously to describe the programs which control the quality of work and assure management and others that the constructed facilities meet specifications. We will generally refer to quality control as the project systems that insure quality is built-in (craft training, inspection procedures, inspector training, record keeping, analysis) and the "feedback" mechanisms which cause corrections to be made when deficiencies are found. Quality assurance will refer to independent functions that monitor the quality control programs to assure organizations that desired results are obtained. These assurance monitoring functions may be performed by personnel working for the prime contractor, the owner, or government agencies; often these personnel are independent of the site organization.

Procedures and certification requirements are becoming more complex depending on the type of facility being constructed, the location of the project, and the owner involved. This is particularly true for nuclear plants in any location and for process plants built under some governmental jurisdictions. Failure to follow correct procedures and to collect adequate certifications can and often does result in costly and time-consuming investigations and rework. Achieving good quality on a project will depend on the plans developed early in the life of the project, on the capabilities of the personnel involved—craft people, supervisors, inspectors—and on the commitment to quality exhibited by management.

It is not the purpose here to describe in detail the requirements of any code, specification, or governmental agency. We will cover the general concept of quality control as it applies to the construction phase of any project. Detailed requirements for a specific project will have to be developed by those responsible for the execution of that project.

QUALITY ASSURANCE/QUALITY CONTROL PLAN

A quality control (QA/QC) plan should be prepared early during project execution. This plan must cover QA/QC activities during engineering, procurement, fabrication, and construction. We will primarily address the principles that should be covered in the construction part of the plan. These principles should recognize and build on the parts of the plan which cover other phases of the project.

531

The QA/QC plan should describe all of the programs that will be used to control the quality of the facility to be built. The plan should not repeat requirements contained in specifications, codes, or standards, but should state how execution will be controlled so that these requirements are met. The following are essential considerations when developing the plan:

1. Statutory and owner/contractor needs for record keeping
2. Types of contracts to be used for both the prime contract and subcontracts
3. Field organization
   - Role of inspectors
   - Testing, certification and training of inspectors and craft people
   - Reporting relationships for inspectors
   - Independent quality assurance functions required
4. Material identification and certification
   - Field purchased bulk material (back fill, concrete, anchor bolts, rein-forcing steel
   - Certification of alloys and special steels
   - Segregation of materials in storage
5. Erection QA/QC procedures
6. Maintenance of records
7. Any other requirements that require special consideration

The involvement of government agencies or other groups must be recognized and plans made to allow their inspections in a timely fashion. For process plant construction this involvement can include:

1. Government certification of certain pressure containing systems, for example, steam generating systems
2. Inspection by local authorities of utility systems, occupied buildings, etc.
3. Certification by insurance companies of fire protection systems
4. Operator inspections of certain equipment before it is closed and sealed, for example, process vessels

The more hazardous the plant, in general, the greater the number of government and other agencies that will be involved. The QA/QC plan should describe the systems that will insure that the various requirements of these agencies are understood and met.

CONTRACTS

The types of contracts and subcontracts to be used at the construction site can have a significant impact on quality. This must be recognized and considered in the development of the QA/QC plan.

For fixed price (lump sum) or unit price contracts, the primary interest of the contractor (profit) may be in conflict with quality. The role of the owner's project management team in this case will be heavily orientated toward a quality control/assurance function.

With reimbursable contracts, interests of various parties may not always be as clear. In developing the QA/QC plan the interests of each party must be thought out and plans developed accordingly. Some interests may be:

Owner desires to keep costs down
Contractor providing quality above that specified even at greater cost

The project management team must recognize all interests created by contractual arrangements and describe systems and procedures to balance these interests in the QA/QC plan.

SPECIFICATIONS AND CODES

During detailed engineering, the governing codes and standards must be reviewed and specifications for the work established. The QA/QC plan should not repeat the requirements of the specifications but should refer to them and describe the systems used to insure that the requirements are met. If the requirements are repeated in the QA/QC plan, then each time a specification is revised the plan will have to be revised—a needless and time-consuming exercise, and one that leads to errors.

Preparation of the construction QA/QC plan is the responsibility of the construction project management team. The specifications for the work are the responsibility of the engineering function. When conflicts are uncovered during construction between codes, standards, specifications, and possibly the QA/QC plan, it is the responsibility of project management to see that a proper engineering resolution of the conflict is obtained.

INSPECTIONS

Inspections are conducted by inspectors, engineers, or others as the work progresses. The role of inspection personnel is basically to help the construction team make sure that the specified requirements are met. Inspectors must have some organizational independence from the craft people. This independence is more important for some activities than others, and will also depend on the contracts used for the erection work. Inspectors should not be placed in a conflict of interest position where they are under pressure to accept workmanship that does not meet specifications.

Whatever the organizational relationships, there should be healthy working relations between the inspectors and the crafts. Often the inspection personnel perform tests and keep records that the craft people are not trained to perform. Many of the tests are necessary for the work to proceed in an acceptable fashion, and thus the results of the tests are required by the craft people.

Qualifications of persons doing inspections at the site should be carefully checked. These personnel should clearly understand the specification requirements, the project goals, and the QA/QC plan. It is critical that they be trained to perform the tests they will run and qualified to conduct these tests. Additional training should be arranged as required; often local schools or companies can provide this training.

MATERIAL QUALITY CONTROL

Systems are required to control the receipt and handling of materials at the site so that the right materials are installed in the right locations. A receiving inspection may be necessary to check the certification of material before being placed in storage. This inspection should consider:

1. The degree of shop inspection already conducted and the reliability of that inspection
2. An inspection for damage or contamination during transit
3. Proper markings/identification

At some locations an elemental analyzer instrument is used to check the alloy make-up of steels as the steel is received at the site. This type of inspection is only a check of the material certifications and is not a substitute for them. The intent should always be to get the manufacturer/supplier to provide material as specified.

Locally purchased material will also require certification testing to make sure specifications have been met. Quite often there are local testing laboratories which can provide independent inspections of materials such as concrete, soils, reinforcing steel, etc.

Many bulk materials will be received at the construction site which must be properly stored and protected. It is extremely important that materials be identified and segregated while in storage. Materials such as alloy steels and impact tested steels can easily loose their identity if mixed. Certain steels and other materials will have to be protected from weather and other contamination.

The QA/QC plan and warehousing plans should detail:

How materials will be marked and stored
Preservation requirements
Transfer of markings as materials are cut and portions are used
Checking of material certificates

The material quality control plans must also cover material substitution procedures. Material substitutions should not be permitted, even if perceived to be an upgrade of the material, without an engineering evaluation. This evaluation should include the proper record keeping and preparation of as-built information so that future problems are avoided (for example "upgrading" of alloy steels can cause welding procedure problems, now or in the future, or other operational problems if not evaluated correctly).

ERECTION QUALITY CONTROL

The basic responsibility for quality during the actual erection of equipment belongs with the craft people and their supervisors. The most important ingredients in a quality job are:

Clear instructions
Use of proper materials and equipment
Skill and knowledge of the erection crews
Dedication of the erection crews to doing a good job

Inspections are conducted to assist the craft people in doing their work and to give site management an independent evaluation of the quality of the workmanship; thus inspections provide both a quality control and a quality assurance function. For the quality control systems to work, inspections must be performed early with timely feedback on problems found. In this way deficiencies can be corrected or avoided and rework costs kept to a minimum. Clear and well organized records must be kept to prove the quality of the work performed.

The QA/QC plan should contain quality control procedures for each erection activity. These procedures address the inspections to be made, the records to be kept, and the testing to be performed. Examples of activities that must be covered in the QC plan are:

Surveying
Earthwork
Foundations (piling, concrete, etc.)
Steel erection
Electrical
Pipe erection, welding, testing, etc.
Material control/certification
Machinery

The above are only examples of categories of activities that need to be considered when developing QA/QC procedures. The type of facility to be constructed and the various organizations involved will determine what procedures are actually required. Procedure and record keeping requirements of the QA/QC plan must:

1. Not add requirements that are not contained in the applicable specifications, standards, or codes for the facility to be built.
2. Be kept simple and straightforward—for this purpose simple checklists are very helpful.

QUALITY ASSURANCE

Quality assurance is an independent activity that monitors the quality control programs. The QC and QA activities quite often overlap and in many organizations the terms are synonymous. The quality assurance function is used to "assure" the following that the QC programs are working correctly:

Contractor or owner management
Government agencies
Others

The degree of quality assurance will depend on the facility being constructed and the location. This effort can be minimal or it can be a very major part of the execution of the project which, if not planned for properly, can result in significant delays or rework costs.

SUMMARY

Quality control, like any other control function, is dependent on:

1. Knowing what has to be done (specifications, codes, drawings, etc.)
2. Developing plans to meet these requirements
3. Monitoring and analyzing the results of activities at the site and materials received
4. Correcting plans, actions, procedures, etc., so that the desired quality is achieved

A QA/QC plan must be developed early which reflects the type of plant to be built, the location where construction will take place, and the requirements of the owner and other interested parties. A key portion of this plan will be the part that covers work executed at the construction site.

A project with a minimum of quality problems will result if management is committed to achieving a quality job by planning early, supporting inspectors and other quality control/quality assurance personnel, encouraging craft people to work in a quality manner, and always respecting specifications and other job requirements. Problems will result if management gives out mixed signals such as accepting poor workmanship, failing to support inspectors, and overlooking specification requirements in order to achieve a faster or less expensive result, or just not caring about quality. Like any other activity, management will achieve what they want if they show an interest in the activity.

10

Safety and Security

EDWARD J. McGUIRE   *Exxon Research & Engineering Co., Florham Park, New Jersey*

On major projects safety and security (Loss Control Management) can have significant effects on project costs and schedule. Security is concerned with prevention of loss from theft and protection of property from vandalism—or in some areas terrorist activities. Safety is concerned with the protection of personnel from physical hazards and environmental hazards that may exist on the site.

The construction industry has had one of the worst safety records of any industry over recent years. In the United States, for example, construction industry accident rates are 54% higher than the average for all industries. Despite this poor record of the industry in general, some owners and contractors through the institution of safety improvement programs have been able to reduce injury rates to 10% or less of the construction injury averages.

SAFETY IS GOOD BUSINESS

Not only do owners and contractors have an obligation—both morally and legally—to protect employees and others who work on their property, but good safety programs generally pay for themselves. When analyzed it becomes apparent that costs related to injuries can be high. Insurance costs, which are included in field labor burden rates, can range from a low of about 4% of labor costs to 15% or more. Insurance rates are based on a contractor's experience and thus contractors with good "experience modifiers" will achieve a competitive edge.

Job site accidents cause disruption and delays. The actual cost of even slight injuries can be as high as four times the visible costs. Visible costs would include wages paid while an injured person is off the job at a medical facility. Invisible costs would include loss of productivity of other members of the crew when one member is missing. Serious injuries can affect morale and productivity on the entire site, and, in very serious cases close the job.

With modern communication facilities (newspapers, television, etc.), safety is also a public relations issue. Good safety programs and statistics can have a positive impact on an owner's long-term acceptance in a community. Conversely, poor safety performance with serious accidents can have long-lasting negative effects which can enmesh management (site and corporate) in legal actions for years.

MANAGING SAFETY

Not only can safety be managed, but safety statistics can be an early indication of how well site management is performing. Safety statistics are relatively easy to collect. A safe site is one that is also productive and probably achieving other goals on cost, schedule, and quality. Techniques used to measure safety are similar to those used to manage other areas. A sample of U.S. Contractors with site-safety programs shows:

"Recordable" injury incidence rates less than 40% of the national average rate for construction ("Recordable" injuries are defined in ANSI Z16.4 as injuries which require more than first aid attention. New OSHA regulations may be more demanding as to what injuries must be recorded.)
"Lost workday" injury incidence rates below 5% of the national average rate for construction

In order to achieve good safety, senior management of the owner and the contractor organizations must be committed to, and continually emphasize, the importance of safety. Commitment and emphasis set the basis for site management and must be demonstrated by:

Discussing safety at all meetings
Setting goals and guidelines and then communicating these to all site personnel
Providing safety expertise as a resource to site management
Evaluating the safety performance of prospective contractors and not allowing contractors (or subcontractors) with poor records to bid for work

Once the above emphasis by corporate management is achieved, site management can take action to manage safety knowing that support exists. As with quality, cost, and schedule, the best way to manage is to provide individual supervisors and employees with resources/knowledge and then hold them accountable for results. Site-safety personnel should be a resource to other managers. Safety personnel should be committed to improving site performance but accountability for performance should remain with line management and supervisors.

Programs that have proven to be successful in helping assure a good safety performance include:

Site induction courses with heavy emphasis on safety
Site audits (site inspections) are highly successful when visible, and when senior site management participates. Success can be helped also if a dialogue with workers (encouraging good performance and counseling poor performance) is a part of the audit.
Use of permit-to-work systems (excavation permits, electrical lockout procedures, etc.)
Programs to maintain safety awareness (publicity, incentives, continuous training, accident investigations, weekly toolbox meetings, etc.)

A must in all site programs is that the line organization (from project manager to foreman) be held accountable for the safety of their subordinates.

INJURY OR ILLNESS

Safety programs must consider not only physical hazards on the site but also industrial illnesses that can result from environmental or chemical hazards. Industrial hygiene to prevent industrial illnesses from fumes, noise, dust, and asbestos is becoming a greater concern as medical knowledge is extended. Many states have laws which require employers to explain to employees any hazards to which they will be exposed. However, from a purely business point of view, a little prevention early can prevent serious time-consuming wrangles in the future when industrial illnesses might develop.

The National Safety Council, OSHA, and other organizations publish safety statistics which can be used as a guide to where efforts on a site should be placed to achieve the most benefit. These organizations, especially OSHA, provide guidelines and standards which are not only helpful but in many cases must be complied with by law.

The greatest sources of fatal accidents on construction sites are falls, vehicle accidents, electrocutions, and the caving-in of excavations. By concentrating on these sources of fatalities, serious accidents should be reduced. By reviewing statistics from a particular site, and other similar construction sites, other sources of injuries should be identified.

Certain equipment should be mandatory for all personnel or visitors on a site. These should be identified for the specific site and rules developed. These rules must be rigorously enforced. Requirements that should be considered are:

> Personal protective equipment (hard hats, glasses or other types of eye protection, shoes, safety belts)
> Warning devices on vehicles and mobile equipment (backup alarms, load indicators)
> Procedures to regularly inspect and certify power tools
> Permit-to-work systems

If construction is taking place in an operating industrial plant, hazards from fire, explosion, and fumes must be known. Evacuation procedures must be developed and communicated. Practices should be held. Caution must be exercised if holding unannounced practices as these can result in injuries from panic or overreaction.

FIRE

Fire is an ever-present threat which must be considered. Evacuation procedures for temporary offices should be developed and practiced. Flammable materials should be stored in suitable locations. Areas such as warehouses should be periodically inspected for compliance with safe practices. Critical documents should be protected from damage in fireproof cabinets.

PERMIT-TO-WORK SYSTEMS

Some type of permit-to-work system will probably be required for certain activities on any site. These systems basically require that all necessary inspections and decommissioning activities have taken place before work starts. These procedures should also address the possible need for locks being placed to prevent recommissioning while work proceeds. Some examples of permit-to-work procedures are:

> Electrical lockout procedures
> Hot or cold work permits in hazardous environments
> Excavation permits where buried hazards may exist
> Permission to enter a confined space

When construction activities take place in operating plants, permit-to-work systems are a must. These systems must be developed for each location jointly by the contractor and owner. The procedures which must be followed before work proceeds must guarantee that power lines, pipelines, or other facilities that can possibly be affected by construction activities are either decommissioned or protected from damage.

Permit-to-work systems are also necessary on "greenfield" or "grassroot" sites to protect workers from electrocution, buried hazards, or other hazards.

SECURITY

On all sites good security programs are necessary to:

Prevent loss from theft
Prevent injury or loss on site from vandalism (or terrorism)
Protect the public from hazards that exist on the site

How security is organized will depend on owner and contractor agreements. However, such items as fencing, lighting, gate layout, gate pass procedures, and visitor access must be addressed early. Wherever possible, private vehicles on the site should be kept to an absolute minimum. A large number of private vehicles present an uncontrollable security risk. They also can create extremely hazardous safety conditions.

SUMMARY

Safety and security programs must be developed early as a joint effort by owners and contractors. Safety is important because:

Good safety programs will have a positive effect on site moral, productivity, and public relations.
Constractors and owners are required by law to care for employees and others working on their property.
Good safety programs are good business.

Safety programs will only be effective if actively supported by senior site and corporate management.

IX
CONTROLLING THE WORK

UNIT OVERVIEW

An important characteristic of project management is the systematic approach taken to control the work. Although the most emphasized controls deal with schedule and budget, these are only two of several project elements that may be subject to control.

The control philosophy for a specific project keys from the objectives established for that project. Therefore, these objectives must be honest and clearly stated. For a project with limited funding, the control emphasis would be properly placed upon costs. For a truly "zero defect" project, the control would be narrowly directed toward quality assurance. For these special projects, a single element would receive the preponderance of the control effort. This does not mean that other elements would be ignored; only that they are placed in the right perspective. Most projects are not tied to a single objective, and the controls are necessarily broader.

The control plans are a part of the project strategy which is designed to assist the project manager in achieving the project objectives. They are developed from the definition of project scope alongside the execution plans and complement these.

The elements that are frequently targeted for control on a project are time; costs, including material management; quality of the various work products; changes introduced as the work progresses; receipt, distribution, and approval of project documents; and finally, audit of the project—financial, operational, and conformance to the contract provisions. Reasons to control other project elements may be due to specific project requirements or to compensate for previous difficulties encountered on like projects. Plans for these control programs are generated as required.

A control plan does not have to be lengthy or complex. It should state the purpose, establish what specific elements are to be controlled, set baselines or standards to control against, and provide for continuous or periodic monitoring of the work output against the baseline or standard. The plan should assign responsibilities for monitoring, and formulating and implementing corrective action. Reporting on the status of the project is particularly important. The project manager should always be aware of any significant variances that may affect reaching the project objectives.

Based upon the control plan, a budget is set for these efforts. This is sometimes forgotten in the eagerness to get on with the work or in the desire to reduce the estimated costs. The project manager should verify that the control plans have the required budget allocations.

More and more clients are insisting on the integration of work scope, costs, and schedule. These three elements are closely related and a change in any of the three will probably affect the other two. A work breakdown structure of the project with all work output defined in terms of work packages each with its own budget and schedule will simplify later evaluation of the effect of change.

Obviously, the more notice that is available about problems, the less drastic and disruptive will be the remedy. For this reason, the project manager needs effective methods of charting progress, costs, and other control measurements so that the performance trends may be easily observed. A negative trend should be investigated immediately. An evaluation should be made of the reason, the possible effects on the job, and what action plan is required to reverse the trend. Possible ripple effects of the performance variance on downstream work have to be looked at carefully.

The project manager must not be lulled into false security by an artificially inflated earned value early in the project. It is possible to take credit for work done "out of sequence" and be, where only percentages are reported, "ahead of schedule" and have a great deal of false security. In addition to the percent complete, the project manager needs to watch that all milestones are also achieved on schedule.

When, during the course of a project, one element is in serious trouble, the trending for this element is negative, and meeting the project objectives is jeopardized, the project manager must not delay in moving to rectify the problem. One alternative is to bring in a small separate task force specifically to resolve the crisis. The regular project personnel will be able to continue working in all other areas normally. This solution should only be used in appropriate situations. The special task force has to be explained carefully to the project team and the two groups must work closely together. The special task force reports directly to the project manager and should have sufficient autonomy to investigate, evaluate, and implement corrective measures effectively. As soon as the problem has been resolved, the regular project personnel should reassume control of the problem area; and the special task force should be disbanded. The project manager should resist the temptation to prolong the assignment with other problems. This would have a deleterious effect on morale and performance of the regular team.

Having the necessary control plans, the need to establish baselines and standards to control against, the regular monitoring of work against these baselines, the evaluation of planned versus actual results, the early identification of problem areas, and the firm and positive action to resolve performance variances promptly are all key steps that the project manager should employ in controlling the project to a successful conclusion.

BIBLIOGRAPHY

Bent, J. A., *Applied Cost and Schedule Control*. New York: Marcel Dekker, Inc., 1982.

Cost Engineers' Notebook. Morgantown, WV: American Association of Cost Engineers. Continuously updated.

Guthrie, K. M. and Associates, *Managing Capital Expenditures for Construction Projects*. Solana Beach, CA: Craftsman Book Company, 1977.

Kerridge, A. E., Integrate project controls with C/SCSC, *Hydrocarbon Processing*, November 1984, pp. 193-208.

Kerridge, A. E., Predict project results with trending methods, *Hydrocarbon Processing*, July 1983, pp. 125-152.

Patrascu, A., *Construction Cost Engineering*. Solana Beach, CA: Craftsman Book Company, 1978.

Wideman, R. *Max, Cost Control of Capital Projects and the Project Cost Management System Requirements*. Vancouver: AEW Services, 1983.

1

Monitoring Progress

MICHAEL E. HORWITZ   *Simons-Eastern Consultants, Inc., Atlanta, Georgia*

WHAT IS PROGRESS: A DEFINITION

Every project control system has criteria that define "progress." Progress is determined and identified to inform management that the project is or is not on the plan,
schedule, or budget. Progress implies a movement ahead, or at least in the right
direction. Progress can be shown in several ways: full completion of an activity or
gorup of activities, partial completion of an activity where a percentage of the full
accomplishment is identified, and lack of completion where the completion had been
planned/scheduled.

DETERMINATION OF PROGRESS

Progress can be expressed qualitatively in terms of milestones completed or not completed. The methods of showing progress on milestones is as varied as the methods
of showing the time relationships on schedules. Schedules show when specific activities
will be started and completed. *Qualitative* progress, then, identifies how the project
is doing with regard to the "when" criteria. Mathematically, progress is similar to
the integral of a function for an activity which starts and ends with the "limit" that
defines only the points in time during which the integration takes place.

Progress can also be expressed *quantitatively* in terms of specific units of work
performed according to a plan. The determination is not only whether the work has
started or finished but also, how the project is coming along with the mass of the work
or mathematically, the "area under the curve" during the integration of the function
activity(s).

Quantitative progress may be unitless and expressed as a percent of the total to
be accomplished, while the full accomplishment of *a milestone* is specific and complete.

For example, Pile Cap B-12 is poured. Partial completion of *an activity* can be
represented quantitatively in terms of yards of concrete poured, bricks laid, or square
feet formed. Table 1 is an example comparision showing quantitative progress, planned
and actual. This type of progress identification is useful to project personnel to show
improved productivity or that more resources are clearly needed. But the same activity expressed in percent (Table 2) is perhaps more meaningful to upper management.
The percentage method is certainly the only way to represent overall project progress.

Yards, square feet, and bricks all can be combined in the "area under the curve"
of total project dollars. Thereby, the dollars provide a bottom line that project management can use to compare dollars "planned" to be spent and dollars "actually" used.

Table 1 Comparison of Planned and Actual Progress

Activity: concrete poured	Progress	
Date	Planned yards	Actual yards
July 7	172	151
July 14	315	298
July 21	520	485
July 28	756	620

Table 2 Percentage of Planned and Actual Progress

Activity: concrete poured	Cumulative progress	
July 7	23%	20%
July 14	42%	39%
July 21	69%	64%
July 28	100%	82%

Identification of Progress

Progress can be identified in terms of four criteria: milestones reached, money spent, resources used (and their productivity), and value achieved (earned).

The primary achievement of progress on paper, the control system, should be expressed and identified in terms of real and visible things that happened in the physical system that we are trying to control. Easiest to plan and monitor in a project are milestones since the accomplishment of a start or a finish of an activity is usually very clear due to the way we select activities.

The expenditure of money is, hopefully, another sure sign of project progress as long as the project participants are honest. If money is not committed on schedule and then not actually expended on schedule, people are not going to make things happen on schedule. A project control system that has no reference to money (or at least to resources) is bound to be ineffective since the prime mover (money) and the secondary mover (other resources) must be correlated to the things to be accomplished, the activities.

A project manpower plan, related closely to the scheduled activities, is a project control necessity. If a project manager presumes to have enough people and believes that the real work will be accomplished on schedule without a carefully developed manpower plan, his presumption will quickly lead the project to failure. The secret to project success is a balance between the plan to accomplish activities and the resources to accomplish them. This balance is established on the fulcrum of productivity. If the project manager knows from past projects the manhours per unit of work and knows the rate of work that can be maintained (only so many roofers can work on a roof even if it is about to rain), he has a good chance of developing a workable project plan. The milestone activity schedule, the number of workers to accomplish the activities, and the workers' productivity are all part of the complex control system. If the project control system has meaningful display mechanisms (reports) that specifically identify how people and their productivity are affecting the outcome with respect to cost and time, the responsible manager can correct the condition causing insufficient progress and/or productivity through the manipulation of the resources at his disposal.

Identifying the value of work achieved or the earned value criteria is the most recent addition to the management "bag of tricks." It is very useful and effective since it gets into the issue of total project productivity. The earned value criteria is particularly effective because it is able to combine *all* the diverse project activities and resources into one common denominator: % progress with respect to time. It, therefore, allows management to be presented with a "bottom line" statement that will say the project is 20 percent complete. This actual percent complete can be compared to a planned percent completed.

Further criteria can be added to the project control system to achieve the Department of Defense/Department of Energy Performance Management System or "C/Specification." These project control criteria allow the establishment of indices such as budgeted cost of work scheduled (BCWS), budgeted cost of work performed (BCWP), and actual cost of work performed (ACWP). From these, specific "bottom line" statements are developed: schedule variance (SV), cost variance (CV), cost performance index (CPI), and schedule performance index (SPI).

Simple earned value criteria can be implemented easily following reasonable effort with or without a computer to compile the data, the "C-spec" can only be implemented effectively after considerable effort associated with specialized and expensive software systems.

Displaying Progress

Displaying progress has developed significantly since the first bar chart: PERT (progress evaluation and review technique) and CPM (critical path method) were standard methods until recently. Schedule graphics packages now allow the scheduler or project manager to select, sort, and sequence the total schedule until only the area of concern need be displayed for critical review. The computer has made the development and updating of performance and cumulative data much easier. Sophisticated display systems such as "QUADPLOT IV" can be developed for management who can relate to the extra visibility this technique provides.

Basis for Quantitative Analysis

In order to make the progress analysis system tell the manager what he/she needs to know, the activities on the schedule and the budgeted work packages should be reconciled. Every activity in the schedule should be matched one for one, or at least matched, to a work package or cost account item. If the project will be cost controlled with work packages, the schedule should reflect the timing of the work packages as they are released.

If the project is not controlled with work packages, the budget should be broken down and assigned to the scheduled activities. Some creative cost manipulation may be needed since money for certain activities may not be identifiable in the budget.

After the activities in the schedule have been assigned a relative value in terms of the common denominator, dollars, a method of assessing progress on each item must be determined. Sometimes progress is assessed with a nonspecific "wet thumb in the wind" or "take a quick look" approach that may be *perfectly adequate if and only if*: The activity is of short duration and represents less than 5% of the total project budget. Short duration means that the activity is only monitored twice: during the first report period, when the activity started, and during the second report period, when the activity ended. In this case, 50% at the first and 100% at the second assessment is a perfectly adequate Standard for Progress. Activities that are monitored for more than two report periods do require a more definitive schedule of progress, % complete, with respect to work completed.

Standards for Progress

The construction industry has used quantitative analysis for years because of the large capital cost of the projects and the need to monitor progress. A method of bringing a large undertaking to a bottom line has been required by many project managers. Therefore, we have standards for most construction activities based on the total cost of the completed work (Table 3).

The standards for progress on engineering activities seems to be more controversial. Sources recommended for developing a system of standards are listed in the references (Klim and Grady; Koval; Zink).

A generally accepted standard for drawing progress may be structured as shown in Table 4. Drawings are not generally identified individually on the project schedule but are monitored from a list of drawings using standards like those above.

The procurement activity on a major project accounts for significant engineering office manpower for specifying, bid packaging, evaluation, purchasing, and expediting.

Major equipment items may be monitored as specific activities on the project schedule and other equipment items may be monitored in groups or as individual line items on equipment list. A standard for procurement progress may be structured as shown in Table 5.

Earned Value

The construction industry applies the concept of earned value in the application for payment system used by the contractor to request a "draw" for the work that he has accomplished during the month. The earned value system provides a fixed payment for a defined amount of work regardless of the cost (Table 6).

When the contractor completed the foundations, his cost was $17,600 and because of his contract arrangement he is able to "draw" $18,000 showing a $400 profit at that point. However, after the framing is complete and he has paid $43,600 to do 35.8% of

Table 3 Standard for Construction Progress Pump Foundations

Work	%	% Cumulative
Excavate	5%	5%
Form	40	45
Rebar	25	70
Place concrete	25	95
Strip	5	100

Table 4 Standard for Drawing Progress

Work	%	% Cumulative
Design basis	5%	5%
Concept approval	15	20
Start DWG	10	30
Issue for project review	30	60
Issue for client approval	15	75
Issue for bids	5	80
Issue for construction	10	90
Complete	10	100

Table 5 Standard for Procurement Process

Work	% Cumulative
Complete engineering	10%
Issue specification	40
Client approval of specification	50
Issue for prices	60
Bid tabulation	75
Issue purchase order	85
Delivery to site	100

Table 6 Application for Payment System

Work	Dollars earned value	% of Contract earned	Actual dollar cost
Earthwork	$ 3,000	2.5%	$ 2,500
Foundation	15,000	12.5	15,100
Framing	25,000	20.8	26,000
Insulation	5,000	4.2	5,000
Roof	5,000	4.2	6,000
Electrical	25,000	20.8	24,000
Mechanical	22,000	18.3	25,000
Finishes	20,000	16.7	20,000
	$120,000	100%	$123,600

the total job, he has by contract only "earned" $43,000 and is now $600 in the hole. The "earned" amount of $43,000 is also known as the budgeted cost of work performed (BCWP) which is compared to the actual cost amount of $43,600 and is known as the actual cost of work performed (ACWP).

The contractor goes from bad to worse during the rest of the project and completes the work having spent $4,600 more than he has earned by contract. On this project the value of the work earned is $120,000 even though his costs were $123,600. During the course of this contractor's project, as he saw the divergence between payoff and cost grow, he attempted to control the cost and actually was able to keep the final cost from being $130,000. The system of being paid only for what he "earned" made him keenly aware of the need to control his costs.

This concept, without the personal touch, is what earned value intends to accomplish on all types of projects: construction, engineering, or manufacturing. The systems are similar and the work breakdown is the key to control. The work must be organized on paper and in the execution so that there is a defined contract or budget amount of work with a value or cost in dollars or resources.

On an engineering project, the earned value cannot be determined by inspection as easily as on a construction project. The drawings for a project do, however, have significant similarities from project to project that permit the manager to estimate the value of each part of the work.

There is no clear midpoint indication as there is in construction that the foundations are finished and it is time to start framing; therefore, someone is entitled to the "$15,000 for foundation work." These midpoints must be created by the work breakdown, and a budget for the work, or value of the work between midpoints must be assigned. With this environment established, progress measured on the basis of a

Table 7 Progress Assessment of Earned Value

Work package	Budget for work	Progress measured by standard	Earned value of the work	Cost of the work
DWGE1	100	20%	20	
DWGE2	100	20%	20	
DWGE3	100	30%	30	
DWGE4	100	40%	40	
DWGE5	100	20%	20	
Total	500	26%	130	140

standard for progress can be applied to the budget to determine an earned value which can be compared to the cost (Table 7).

In this example, the progress assessments and earned value analysis tell us that the total earned amount in this work package is 130 based on the progress of each item expressed in percent multiplied by the budget for each item. The cost of the work package was accumulated and is 140 at the point that the progress assessment was made.

In this manner the project manager is able to evaluate how he has done on all work packages in the project. Where the cost of the work exceeds the earned value of the work, the project manager knows he needs to apply corrective action in this area.

Forecasting Project Outcome from Progress to Date

The information gained through earned value analysis allows the project manager to forecast the cost outcome of the project. The progress to date, the budget, and the cost to date can be applied to formulas to determine a forecast of final cost.

There are two forecast formulas that can be averaged to provide the most likely number for cost at the end of the project. These formulas are shown below:

$$\text{Formula no. 1} = \frac{\text{Dollars (or other resource) used to date}}{\text{Percent progress to date}}$$

Formula no. 2 = [(100% − % progress) × budget] + dollars used

Formula 1 forecasts the cost at the completion of the project on the assumption that productivity for the remainder of the project will be as it has to date. Until progress is greater than 20%, this forecast formula may cause excessively optimistic or pesimistic predictions. Formula 2 forecasts the cost at the end of the project on the assumption that the budget is correct and that the remaining work will be performed with the proportional amount of the budget required to perform the remaining work. The average of the two forecast formulas results in a most likely number for the project cost. Any difference between the Formula 1 and Formula 2 forecasts indicates the uncertainty of the forecasts. The ratio of the forecasts:

$$\frac{\text{Larger forecast}}{\text{Smaller forecast}}$$

if equal to one or no greater than 1.1 indicates a high degree of certainty that the average forecast will be the final cost. Forecast formulas are not able to anticipate changes in project scope or changes in productivity.

BIBLIOGRAPHY

Cook, R. A., "Cost/Schedule Integration - PANACEA or POISON?" *AACE Transactions*, 1982, pp. E11-E16.

Horwitz, M. E., "Project Scheduling and Forecasting—A New Approach." *PMI Proceedings*, 1979, pp. 113-118.

Huot, J. C., "Productivity Defined." *AACE Transactions*, 1981, pp. 141-147.

Kimmons, R. L., "Track Projects with Quadplot IV." *Hydrocarbon Processing*, September 1979, pp. 301-310.

Klim, J., and Grady, M. B., "Productivity Evaluation of a Drafting Function in a D-E Firm." *AACE Transactions*, 1981, pp. I31-I34.

Koval, J. G., "System for Establishing Drawing Status." *AACE Transactions*, 1981, pp. H51-H56.

Makler, F., and Mazina, M., "Implementing Earned Value Reporting." *AACE Transactions*, 1980, pp. A81-A84.

Zink, D. A., "Monitoring the Adequacy of the Amount and Productivity of Egnineering and Construction Manpower." *AACE Transactions*, 1980, pp. CB1-CB8.

2

Managing Costs with Precision

CHARLES J. PELES* *Foster Wheeler USA Corporation, Clinton, New Jersey*

The project manager depends upon timely information to make those key decisions that result in effective management of project costs. The free flow of this information can be assured by establishing a cost management system that takes into account the cycle of:

    Adequately detailed and approved baselines
    Monitoring, evaluating, and analyzing current performance trends
    Identifying problem areas
    Recommending corrective action, then follow-up measures
    Forecasting future performance

The project manager will find that certain guidelines will assist in specifying how such a system can be implemented. The techniques identified below are typical of those used on a process plant design/construct project and are presented from the viewpoint of a contracting firm. The concepts are valid for a large number of other types of projects in that many of the components are similar.

A cost-conscious atmosphere is required to effectively manage costs. A commitment to cost consciousness should be evident at the start and continue throughout the project. This attitude must start with the project manager and those immediately surrounding him or her. The first part of this chapter will deal with the development of a cost management plan (CMP) during the proposal stage. The next part focuses on the critical front-end activities that must take place immediately after contract award. Administrative reporting responsibilities of the personnel assigned to the cost-management function on the project are discussed in the third part. Here, these individuals are referred to as the project cost group (PCG). Subsequent material covers specific techniques used in managing the home office, material, subcontract, and construction costs effectively.

It is necessary to recognize that a great deal of the project cost management necessarily takes place during the conceptual development. Fundamental decisions made regarding the nature and configuration of the facilities determine their minimum cost. So it is with any project. This chapter is primarily focused toward the management of expenditures so as to contain them within a reasonable margin of that minimum cost.

DEVELOPMENT OF THE COST-MANAGEMENT PLAN

At the time a proposal is made, a CMP is developed consistent with the philosophy and strategy contained in the execution plan. The CMP consists of the following components:

Current affiliation: Pepsico, Purchase, New York

551

Cost Responsibilities

The responsibilities of the project cost group (PCG) are defined here. All cost aspects of the project are covered, including home office costs, costs of equipment, bulk materials, direct labor, subcontracts, and construction indirects. For control purposes, a precise definition of the levels at which the costs will be reported and controlled is always required.

System Selection

After evaluating the project in terms of size, complexity, client requirements, and any other pertinent factors, the PCG works with the project manager to select a system or system modules that will satisfy job requirements. The selected system(s) should be consistent with the project reporting needs and the level of detail must permit adequate monitoring.

Cost Organization

To perform the work outlined in the CMP, an estimate of the number of jobhours is developed. From this estimate the staffing of the cost function during the different phases of the job is defined. Reporting relationships of these personnel are clearly set forth in the project organization chart and lines of communication are clearly specified both in terms of project and departmental reporting.

Data Flow

For the PCG to achieve its objectives, effective lines of communication must be established to and from the other groups working on the project. This part of the CMP defines the responsibilities of all of the parties in terms of the data flow required for proper utilization of the control system.

CRITICAL FRONT-END COST ACTIVITIES

Cost Procedures

On each project, the development of the CMP should begin with the contractor's standard cost reporting and management procedures. These should be tailored to fit the specific requirements of the project. The procedures should be issued to the project staff as well as to the client. The target date for issue should be within four weeks of contract award in order to provide a clear definition of those immediate steps required for an effective control system. Early issue also stresses the importance of costs and sets its priority attention status throughout the job.

Project Code of Accounts

The project code of accounts should be that normally used by the organization performing the work. It should be adjusted to reflect unique or specific requirements of the project. It should fully cover all of the work stipulated by the contract and permit accounting of costs by the organizational breakdown and by the work breakdown structures or work packages. It has to be consistent with the pre-established reporting levels as defined by the CMP. The project code of accounts must satisfy the client's needs. It is important that there be an understanding of what these real needs are. Sometimes, the contractor is saddled unnecessarily with the client's operating code of accounts, which is not designed for a design/construct project, when the only use made of the numbers is to assign costs to the proper investment account. It is much more efficient to determine what numbers the client needs, and to resolve how these can be most easily provided using the contractor's normal code. Often this may be accomplished by an automated data link conversion either on a monthly or a job completion basis.

Control Budget

A budget must be established as a control baseline as early as possible. The budgets are derived from estimates prepared using all of the design and cost information available at the time. Although budgets will be refined as the estimates are upgraded from conceptual to factored to definitive, all parties must be cognizant of the current budgets for their activities and for the execution of their work within the approved budget.

Trend Program

The trend program is a control tool developed to assist in the effective management of project costs and schedule. The essential elements of this program are:

Preparation of an original control baseline defining project scope, schedule, and cost
Identification of deviations from the control baseline on a continuous basis
Prompt evaluation and analysis of the deviations
Initiation of corrective action as required

Although project team members all have a responsibility for providing input to this control system, the PCG is the focal point for implementing and administering the program. The PCG reviews the trends figures, identifies adverse trends, evaluates the impact of these trends, and makes recommendations for corrective action to project management. Project management is responsible for actually directing and implementing any changes. In many cases, company practices make it imperative that adverse trends also be reported independently through the functional management chain.

ADMINISTRATIVE REPORTING RESPONSIBILITIES

The PCG is responsible for issuing timely cost reports designed to provide project management with an overall and comprehensive picture of the cost status of the job. These reports contain estimated, budgeted, committed, expended, and forecast information for costs and jobhours. Accompanying the report is a written analysis that identifies trends, recommends corrective action, and provides feedback on the effect of actions previously taken.

Change Order Control

A change procedure makes provision for furnishing the client with prompt estimates of the cost and schedule effects of work outside the contracted scope. Ideally, no work will be started on an identified change until the client has given approval. The project manager is responsible for seeing that change order pricing is developed as rapidly as practical to minimize its effect on job progress and the morale of the project staff.

Budget Control

Once the initial budget has been set, the PCG follows the execution plan in updating data. The plan will have necessarily stipulated the number of estimates to be made during the project and these estimates will be converted into approved control budgets. Approved changes must also be incorporated into the budget. When there are various participants in a project, the budget transfer procedure will be established to maintain budget integrity and to ensure meaningful and proper accounting/reporting of project costs.

Commitment/Cash Flow Analysis

The contractor must prepare and maintain commitment/cash flow profiles for the entire scope of the work. The client, in turn, uses this information to manage the money required to fund the project. The overall information is presented in chart form together with detailed information on home office, equipment, bulk material, subcontract and construction commitments and expenditures.

These curves are updated as additional information becomes available. As schedules are prepared, the planned commitment data are generated which keys into order dates shown by the schedule. Similarly, as purchase orders are placed, expenditure profiles are made based on the agreed terms of payment.

The PCG interfaces with accounting to maintain actual cost data. Given the long range nature of their work and the impact of the projections, the responsibility for maintenance of overall expenditure and commitment profiles should remain with the cost group.

Risk/Contingency Analysis

In order to identify and quantify cost exposures and possible schedule delays, risk/contingency analyses are performed. Risks are identified and contingencies are assigned to cover them. The objective is to improve the quality of forecasts and minimize exposure to the unexpected.

The PCG is responsible for coordinating the contingency analyses. This calls for jointly identifying specific risks with the project team members, and then summarizing and analyzing the results using techniques such as the Monte Carlo simulation method. Specific guidelines are established for management of contingency accounts. It is recommended that the risk/contingency analyses be reassessed at intervals to reflect current project developments.

HOME OFFICE COSTS

Progress/Performance Analyses

To measure progress for home office activities, one of the earned value systems is used based on taking credit for physical work completed. Specific guidelines are established using historical data for all engineering, drafting, and procurement activities. Within every discipline, each activity is further broken down into stages of completion with a weighting established for each of these milestones. Plans and schedules are developed using these earned value guidelines. This results in a true comparison of actual to planned progress when the actual percent complete is determined. Where discrepancies arise, the PCG can rapidly identify problem areas and develop corrective action plans.

Manpower projections are developed. Based on these plans and schedules, the required resources are determined. By the process of leveling, staffing required for each discipline is optimized within the constraints afforded. Actual staff utilization is compared regularly with the earned value progress data to generate the performance evaluation.

Forecasting Jobhours

Correlating the progress/performance data with the manpower analyses from each discipline forecasts of the remaining home office jobhours are made. When variances are identified, the PCG works with the appropriate disciplines to determine the proper corrective action. Manpower projections are revised based on the latest forecast.

Monitoring Wage Rates

Wage rate data are accumulated and monitored by the PCG for use in forecasting salary costs. Based on the planned expenditures of jobhours for each disciplines, a budget curve is established depicting wage rate fluctuations over project life. The curve may be influenced by such factors as varying departmental charges for supervision and administration, the experience level mix within each discipline at various stages of the project, and escalation of salaries.

Other Home Office Costs

This category includes such costs as reproduction, communication, computer, and travel and living expenses. The PCG collects and monitors these costs in tabular and graphic format. It is preferable that the project discipline leaders be responsible for not only jobhour expenditures, but for these other costs attributable to their personnel also. In order for this to be meaningful, budgets must be established for these costs and spending should be time-phased over the project life. The PCG generates the reports documenting the actual performance versus that planned. Deviations are investigated and corrective action taken.

MATERIAL COST CONTROL

Input to Bid Tabulations

A critical aspect of the material management program is the participation of the PCG in the review of the bid comparisons for purchase orders and subcontracts. Typically, the PCG should be responsible for providing the following input during the bid tabulation process:

> The current budget for the item
> Explanation of any variance from the current budget and/or forecast
> Comment on corrective action to prevent cost or schedule overruns
> Evaluate cost/schedule tradeoff alternatives as required

This provides an added measure of control by insuring that appropriate cost information is available to project management prior to making purchase order or contract awards.

Equipment

Control of equipment costs begins with the evaluation of design alternatives. Cost personnel work with equipment estimating specialists to determine alternatives on an all-inclusive cost basis. The PCG is involved in the bid tabulation of all equipment prior to the award of the purchase order, and may be called on to participate in pre-award meetings with vendors.

After the purchase order is placed, worksheets are maintained to itemize budgeted, committed, actual, and forecasts costs for each equipment item. The complete buildup of the forecast contains certain identified allowance amounts for engineering development changes, escalation, freight, taxes as well as other items for international projects.

Bulk Materials

Control of bulk material cost uses a program featuring a continuous review of forecast quantities. Very early in the project budget quantities for each type of commodity are established based on the control budget plus authorized changes. As design information becomes available, design quantities are compared to the budgeted quantities. Significant variations are reported and, where feasible, the designs are reviewed for possible optimization to decrease the variance. Emphasis is placed on developing corrective action to reduce quantity shortages or surpluses.

Sampling techniques are applied to such items as concrete, steel, piping, and bulk electrical and instrument materials to improve control and forecasting results. The PCG works with design engineers to implement this program which extends through the final takeoff. For reporting purposes, forecasts are continually updated to reflect actual design quantities and vendor prices. For construction planning pruposes, it is usually necessary to project quantity requirements at a detailed level, but generally costs can be forecast on a summary basis.

Evaluating Vendor Extras

Changes to the purchase orders result form revised specifications, drawings, and requisitions during the course of the project. These, in turn, cause changes in the purchase order prices. As changes occur, the PCG reviews the affected documents and prepares an estimate of the cost of the change.

When the vendor submits the charge for the extra work, the PCG assists with the negotiation. The result of having all of the relevant information developed beforehand means prompt resolution with a minimum schedule and cost impact to the job.

Administering Unit Price Orders

Due to the special characteristics of unit price orders for shop-fabricated pipe and structural steel, special procedures must be developed to control these commodities from the inquiry stage through resolution of any field backcharges.

Specifically, as part of the inquiry, the PCG identifies anticipated quantities by type to facilitate the bidding. Sample isometrics or steel drawings are issued with the inquiry and vendors are required to price these drawings with their own unit bids. These calculations are used initially as a basis in the bid evaluations; and later are used to resolve differences in applying the unit prices to completed work. The PCG works with procurement specialists to establish a basis for evaluating the bids and determining the low bidder. The price books of the fabricators are reviewed together with the pricing of the sample drawings prior to award to insure a clear understanding of the pricing structures. This results in fewer problems when the invoices for pipe spools and fabricated structural steel are audited.

SUBCONTRACT COST MANAGEMENT

Preaward Forecasts

In addition to the established control budget values for the subcontract packages, the PCG develops preaward forecasts based on the latest actual design quantities. As a general rule, the values in the estimate for material unit prices, jobhour/unit and wage rates are used in developing the preaward forecast unless there is a valid reason for adjusting these items. Any change in jobhour requirements falling out from the preaward forecast must be evaluated for the corresponding effect on the job schedule.

The Subcontract Selection Process

To facilitate the identification of the low bidder, it is necessary to place all of the bidders on an equivalent basis. The elements involved in this process depend upon the commercial terms called for in the bid; and they are different for lump-sum, reimbursable, and time and material contracts.

A bottom-line project final cost is established for each bidder as a part of the determination of the low bidder. Factors to be considered in each case are the following:

Lump Sum Subcontracts
Estimated values are used for:
  Supplements to the inquiry issued prior to award
  Omissions or exclusions that any bidder elected to make
  Potential growth to the subcontract after award due to changes and additions

Unit Price Subcontracts
  The definitive unit price structure submitted by each bidder is reviewed for
    accuracy and consistency
  Quantities determined by the PCG are used to price out the bid for each bidder
    using the unit prices submitted

Time and Material Subcontracts
  The PCG makes a simulation to ascertain the total anticipated costs for each
    contractor based on their quoted labor and equipment rates and material
    mark-ups.
  The preaward forecast jobhours and quantities can be used as the basis for
    the simulation.

In cases where there are anticipated differences in the general contractor's costs and/ or the client's costs because of demonstrable historical costs of administration and/or inspection of work with the various bidders, it is acceptable to credit/charge the bottom lines established in the evaluation. This can lead to misunderstandings and hard feelings unless it is properly done. Any differences should be established by personnel well acquainted with past performance and the specific amounts credited/charged should be properly and specifically documented prior to opening any of the bids.

Projecting Subcontract Costs

The projected final costs are established for each bidder regardless of how the work is to be executed. The conditioned bid of the selected contractor is used for the initial subcontract forecast. The PCG is responsible for tracking and trending all variable items included in the forecast. The forecast is continually updated with the variances and an analysis reported to the project manager for corrective action.

Subcontract Extras

When a lump-sum subcontractor is required to perform additional work because of specification, drawing, or requisition changes, the PCG independently assesses the effect of the change concurrently with the pricing of the extra by the subcontractor. When the subcontractor's request for the extra is received, the PCG assists in negotiating and resolving the cost for the extra work. When the parties are far apart, it may be necessary to look at other alternatives such as doing the extra work on a time and material basis; but it is generally better to do the extra work on the same contractual basis as the main body of work.

Unit Price and Cost Plus Subcontracts

The PCG assists in administering subcontracts of this type by:

  Specify reporting requirements in the subcontract inquiry packages
  Review subcontract package bids at preaware meetings
  Make independent checks on data submitted by subcontractor
  Track actual quantities and jobhour expenditures
  Audit subcontractors' invoices

CONSTRUCTION COST MANAGEMENT

Construction Cost Reports

Cost personnel at the jobsite issue cost reports covering costs, jobhours, quantities, and installed units on a budgeted, actual, and forecast basis. Transmission of cost data to the home office is expedited by a computer hook-up. The information contained in these field reports is analyzed and potential problems are identified. This information is given to the project manager and to the client. The cost data is used by the PCG to assess status of project cost forecasts.

Progress and Performance Data

Earned value systems are also used to determine progress in the field by taking credit for physical work completed. Historical data provide a basis for standard productivity profiles that are used as the baseline for subsequent comparison to actual values. Performance data are derived by correlating actual progress achieved with actual jobhours spent. Progress should be measured for each activity for each craft. Performance data may be reported on a summary basis by craft. This technique is utilized for subcontract labor as well as for direct labor.

Construction Jobhour Forecast

Both direct and subcontract jobhours to perform the work must be accurately forecast. The cost group uses progress and performance data to help in projecting future progress, performance, and manpower requirements. It is important to keep a tab on even lump-sum subcontractor performance so that invoices may be properly audited and so that potential problems with poor performance can be discovered at an early stage.

Construction Indirects

Initial control budgets are established for indirect construction costs by the PCG. Construction indirects include supervision, indirect labor, construction tools, temporary facilities, consumable supplies, security, and for international projects such items as travel, housing, and restaurant facilities. Prior to the field start date, the PCG works with the construction planners to time-phase the budgets based on the construction execution strategy. A package of reports, charts, and graphs are then prepared which allows the construction manager to compare actual with planned expenditures in his reports to the project manager. Forecasts are made for each category and reported on a monthly basis.

  Control is exercised by examination of all significant variances and by establishing why they are occurring. Corrective action is implemented as needed. Support is provided to evaluate the cost differences of construction alternatives where these are considered as a means to improve cost of schedule performance.

**Resolution of Field Extras, Backcharges, Claims,
and Disposal of Surplus**

The PCG contributes to the resolution of these items in the following ways:

Field extras provide prompt estimates of the cost and schedule impact of the new work. This permits the project manager to determine if the change should be initiated in a timely fashion. Check estimates are also developed for lump-sum contract extras for use in evaluation of the contractor's pricing. Alternate schemes are also priced out where this is necessary for evaluation purposes.

Backcharges. When a fabrication error occurs, remedial work in the field is sometimes inevitable. The PCG will gather the necessary supporting cost documentation for backcharging the vendor. This must be done in accordance with the terms of the purchase order. The PCG assists with the negotiations to resolve backcharges. To maximize legitimate recovery of costs associated with poor fabrication or failure to meet specifications, it is essential that the vendor be advised of any potential backcharge and be given an opportunity to make the corrections.

Claims. When a problem arises in the field that could lead to a claim from the subcontractor for additional money. The PCG will assist in resolving the problem by:

Preparing the documentation necessary to evaluate the claim or to dispute it. This may well involve the use of the detailed progress/performance analysis discussed earlier.

Assisting in evaluation of the subcontractor's claims and in negotiations to resolve payment of the claim.

Surplus disposal. At the completion of a project it may be necessary to dispose of surplus materials. The PCG establishes the value of such material and evaluates the bids received from potential buyers. For surplus material disposed of in the field or for items with buyback provisions, the PCG establishes the procedures to be used in handling the associated costs to insure that recoveries are properly reflected in the forecasts. Client agreement may be required for the procedures to be used in disposing of surplus material depending upon the terms of the contract.

CONCLUSION

One of the key parameters used to measure project success is whether or not the cost objectives were met. The primary responsibility for this rests squarely with the project manager, who is supported by the project cost group and the cost management procedures developed for the project.

The chances for project success are materially enhanced by use of the systems described here which tie all cost elements together for reporting, analyzing, and correcting. The systems are directed toward prompt identification of potential problem areas and immediate initiation of corrective action.

The continuous interface between the cost group and the rest of the project team is a valuable aspect of these systems. Following the principles outlined will insure that the project manager will have sufficient warning and the information necessary to keep the project within budget.

3

Control of Changes

W. ROSS COX   *CRSS Constructors, Inc., Houston, Texas*

Changes occur to varying degrees on all projects. Some projects by their very nature experience innumerable changes while other experience relatively few. By "control of changes," one might perceive that changes on a project are negative in nature and therefore unproductive to the project. This is not necessarily so. For some projects, changes can produce very positive responses leading to significantly greater project success. It must be determined what types of changes are acceptable and how they will be implemented into the project work in order for the project to benefit.

Control must be directed to those changes that tend to occur on all projects which are undesirable or detrimental to a project. While the number of such changes is variable, changes must be dealt with during the life of every project. The project work would ideally be performed once, in the proper order, to the required accuracy, on schedule and within budget. It is a complex job just to keep track of where a large project stands with relation to all these parameters.

INEVITABILITY OF CHANGE

A very small, well-defined project involving a small project team whose members have worked together before, is unlikely to experience many changes since most of the factors which contribute to change are absent. It is more likely that this project will experience great success, perhaps greater than achieved by the same team on the last project as long as some other variable has not emerged, such as a new technology. These people will be used to working with each other, will anticipate each other's needs, and will strive to keep the project on an even keel because of their personal relationships. Most projects do not contain these conditions.

Project managers list excessive and uncontrolled changes as one of the primary reasons for failure to achieve project objectives. The scope of work is often difficult to fully establish. Errors are discovered and must be corrected. Client requirements are modified because of a newly revised sales plan that affects the products to be produced by the completed project. Someone on the project team sees a better way of accomplishing a previously completed task. The reasons are endless.

Projects which are on the forefront of technology, those in the research and development stage and open-ended studies, are likely to experience many changes because such projects cannot be well defined at the start and a new discovery often points the project in a previously unthought direction. Budding technology is likely to contain the seed of many changes while more mature technology should produce fewer.

Even with very mature technology there is experience of ample changes occurring. This is perhaps more easily recognized on projects having lump-sum commercial terms.

These projects are usually better defined and the contractor's financial risk is greater than on projects which contain reimbursable commercial terms. The seasoning of the technology is only one of many contributing factors.

While the contractor tends to monitor changes more closely on lump-sum projects, changes on the less defined reimbursable projects are sometimes a source of conflict. Projects that lack a definitive scope of work which is mutually understood by both client and contractor are potential time bombs. It is almost inevitable that the client and contractor will be less restrained in their approaches to the execution of the work and that inclusion of a number of apparently beneficial changes will take place.

Some of these changes are likely to become urgent in nature. Documentation concerning their addition to the scope of work, the effects on the project cost and schedule, and the errors which may occur because of recycling the work to incorporate the change may be overlooked. The cooperation of the contractor in adding such changes to the project is understandable as it adds to his business success. Such cooperation can delude the client into believing there is no added cost to be paid. The result is a project out of control with a serious addition to the project budget. The effect must be explained and sold to the client's management.

Indeed, clients have been known to instruct contractors to incorporate any change the client representative requests without estimating its effect on the project and later complaining about the excessive project cost. Such conflicts are not rare, and stem from misunderstandings between client and contractor about the work which must be done to properly incorporate a change into an ongoing project as well as the disruptive effects changes have on the project work in progress or already completed.

ORIGIN OF CHANGES

Most contractors have operating systems which, when properly used, help to keep the project team organized and the project work coordinated. These systems contain procedures and practices which the contractor organization has found to work best for it over the years. As a result, changes which might otherwise occur, are eliminated. Even with good systems, changes may occur causing severe adverse conditions on a project.

At the beginning, many decisions must be made about the project and the way the work will be executed. Every project is unique in many ways, and assumptions are often made which later prove incorrect to some degree. When the error is discovered, a change results. The complexity of the project may be cause for omissions or oversights made by either client or contractor which must be added during project execution. These types of changes can be of a serious nature, increasing project cost, extending project schedule, and disrupting project work.

During project execution, new information may result from innovation or from the desire of project team members to continually make improvements. Often, project team members believe continually improving project designs constitutes a positive contribution to the project. This may be true at times, but changes made to established designs generally create severe problems.

Delay in completing a design causes schedule difficulties for those groups which must further develop the design. Revising the design, regardless of the reason, creates a recycling of work already completed. This too can cause schedule difficulties. More importantly, recycled work is actually a more serious problem, because errors often go undetected, only to surface later at an inopportune time.

Work recycling generally results in increased costs, schedule delays, and a deterioration in client-contractor relationships. If the engineering and construction are being handled by different firms, or if the construction work is being handled by a number of subcontractors, finger pointing may occur, resulting in wasted effort. The possibility of a sour project under such circumstances is high.

ADMINISTRATION OF CHANGES

The project systems employed by the contractor will likely contain procedures for han-dling changes. These procedures are intended to provide a comprehensive method of determining the effects on the project. They should also be capable of making all affected team members aware of the change so that project disruption and resulting errors due to recycle of work are held to a minimum.

There are basically three types of changes which occur: changes to a defined scope of work, contractual in nature and generally occurring on lump-sum projects; additions to the scope of work based on innovation or omissions, generally occurring on reimburs-able projects; and contractor internal changes.

Where there is a defined scope of work for the project, it is easier to determine when a change exists. Lump-sum projects generally have a defined scope, but the depth of definition varies widely among contractors. Some contractors go to great lengths to define the project, even engineering and pricing many of the details, in order to pro-tect themselves financially while maintaining competitive bids.

A defined scope of work on a lump-sum project is generally part of the contract between client and contractor. Planning and scheduling the project in accordance with this scope definition will provide a basis for the work of the project team. It will also make the project team more aware when an out-of-scope condition surfaces. A change occurring under these circumstances can be evaluated on its own merits.

On reimbursable projects, the scope of work will usually be less defined than on lump-sum projects. The major technical reasons for a project having reimbursable com-mercial terms are complexity and lack of definition of the work to be accomplished. As a result, it is more difficult to know when a change occurs. In fact, many of these projects are developmental in nature, particularly in their early stages, and do not lend themselves well to lump-sum commercial terms.

It is more difficult to determine when a change occurs on a reimbursable project since the detailed scope of work is not fully known in the beginning. On these types of projects, a definitive estimate is often made once the project has been developed through basic engineering. At this stage, the definition of the project is known and the minimum cost of the project will have been set by this definition. From this point on, changes can be determined and evaluated similarly to those on a lump-sum project. Unless market conditions dictate otherwise, reimbursable projects are sometimes changed to lump sum once a definitive estimate or scope of work definition has been established.

Contractor internal changes may occur due to errors or omissions on lump-sum projects or on the defined portion of reimbursable projects. On lump-sum projects, the contractor absorbs the cost of these changes, but on reimbursable projects the client pays for them. These changes are largely hidden since they do not represent changes to the scope of work. They may result from error corrections, innovation, improvements, or personal preferences, but they have a cost which must be paid and they often affect the project schedule, sometimes in subtle ways that are not detected immediately.

Changes can be identified by either the client or the contractor. To indicate that identifying changes is "everyone's" responsibility will guarantee that the task will not be important to many project team members. Plato told us that "when everybody owns everything, nobody will take care of anything," and the maxim is just as true today in project management. Specific team members must be made responsible for identifying changes on a project, whether produced by themselves or by others.

Once a change is identified, it must be completely defined, the effects on the project must be determined, and the results must be reviewed and approved by suitable authority prior to any implementation taking palce. This is not always easy to accom-plish. The earlier the change is incorporated, the fewer changes should have to be made at a later time. This may be true, but many changes are incorporated early and documented late in the interest of expediency. The result of these undocumented changes comes back to haunt the project later.

There are times when changes must be incorporated and times when they can be delayed. For either the client or the contractor to be bulldozed into incorporating changes without formally agreeing on the nature and cost will create problems. Changes can and should be handled with minimum financial risk to either party when it is agreed the change is necessary.

Changes are difficult and cumbersome to incorporate with the complex systems used by contractors. It is not the system that causes this difficulty, but the fact that most changes occur out of normal project work sequence. The lack of detail available concerning the tasks to be achieved on a project is one reason for this difficulty. The complex systems are helpful in discouraging changes that are not essential to the project.

EFFECTS OF CHANGES

Cost and schedule are usually affected in some way when changes are incorporated on a project. Yet, often the schedule is not changed. The overriding reason seems to be rooted in optimism. While the completion date may not be affected by the magnitude of the change, any change will have an effect on personnel, resources, or the schedule for execution of individual tasks. Such effects must be taken into consideration and planned into the project scope to be sure the project benefits from the change.

As mentioned above, the quality of the project work can easily be affected by incorporation of changes. Work recycling is difficult, and often new errors are introduced which show up at a later date. Progress on projects is in the forward direction and it is difficult to keep looking back to pick up all the effects a change causes to work in progress or already finished.

A particularly adverse effect occurs when a number of successive changes are introduced; project team member morale drops. People do not like to keep doubling back to pick up changes any more than clients like paying for them. The only way to prevent this problem seems to be to develop a flawless plan. This is not necessarily true. A flawless plan is not necessary; however complete planning and thinking through the tasks prior to the time they must be performed is vital.

Finally, the effect on the client-contractor relationship can suffer greatly if changes occur in rapid succession. The client representative will be forced to sell his management on budget increases or otherwise explain why he is unable to manage the contractor toward producing the quality project that was expected all along. The result can be anything from mild irritation to replacement of the contractor.

MONITORING THE EFFECTS OF CHANGES

One of the most difficult problems facing the project manager is keeping track of what happened when a change was incorporated. In many cases, this step is ignored or otherwise not monitored sufficiently to ensure that the change was fully incorporated and its presumed effects were accurately predicted. Once a change is approved and the work begins, the change cycle cannot be considered complete until the change and all it affects are fully, and correctly, implemented.

Some changes are obviously large enough and serious enough that they are tracked separately from the rest of the project work to determine the cost or to ensure that the change is fully implemented. Most smaller changes do not warrant this special treatment due to the cost associated with the extra tracking and reporting required. This situation must be considered when the change is approved and the appropriate method determined.

PROJECT MANAGEMENT CONSIDERATIONS

A thorough, documented and agreed-to scope of work requires both client and contractor to think through the project and anticipate possible problem areas. When the scope is translated into detailed task schedules by each discipline, it requires an in-depth analysis to accomplish. Each team member should know what work is to be done by him or her, when it is scheduled to be completed, what information is required to support the work and who else is involved. Building this type of awareness among the individual members of the project team will limit the changes and their severity since each team member will be focusing on future as well as present circumstances.

When changes do occur, someone must be responsible for following up to see that the change is fully implemented. Performance statistics must be brought up to date when a change is incorporated into the project unless the change is to be tracked separately. Budgets, schedules, and completion figures must reflect the change and must be redistributed to the project team; otherwise, a change of any type incorporated into the project, including an internal change, will result in distorted performance reporting.

Project progress reports do not reflect the effects on the project of recycling the work or the time spent evaluating changes which are not approved for incorporation. Wherever possible, these items should be included in the change procedure so that the estimating portion of the nonapproved change will be compensated for and budgets and progress will be properly reflected for reporting purposes.

Most contracts require client approval prior to incorporation of a change. Often, due to time constraints or the belief that it would be foolish to have to redo any more work than necessary, the change is incorporated first and the documentation is prepared later. This should never be allowed to occur, even when client and contractor relations are considered excellent. If a change is considered urgent, an agreement should be made whereby the contractor can recover his costs. Otherwise, development or incorporation of the change should not proceed. This is strong language and it is difficult to follow. But, contractors should expect to receive and clients should expect to pay the cost of legitimate, approved changes on the project which are not included in the existing scope of work.

Client and contractor should strive to anticipate change and to adopt a flexible attitude toward positive and necessary changes. A statement of intent made at the beginning of the project concerning what is required on the project in terms of documentation, quality, reviews, and approval cycles, would be of significant benefit in determining the acceptance of changes. Such an intent would ideally be a part of the contract, but should at least be agreed to by both parties.

A serious concern on many projects is subjective judgment about what constitutes good engineering practice or quality. Many contractors appear to believe that nothing is too good for their clients. Unfortunately, many clients cannot afford to pay the price that such an attitude commands. The project may become less viable or even uneconomical under such circumstances. The project specifications, developed within the constraints of the project intent, must guide the work and the project team members must recognize different quality levels in order to satisfactorily perform project work.

Ideally, client and contractor project managers would discuss the control of changes prior to any changes being anticipated and would agree on how the subject is to be handled when a change is identified. It is to the client's advantage to consider all changes seriously. If the contractor cannot or will not develop changes which are desired but unapproved, the end result of the client's project may be seriously flawed.

Contractors must ensure that clients receive all they have contracted for without a stream of frivolous changes being introduced. But, it should not be necessary for them to provide more work than called for in the contract, even though some appear to think this improves relations. Anyone can give valuable services away. A professional contractor must make a profit in order to survive and continue to provide services to clients.

There is always a better way of doing anything. But the project must be completed in order to justify its very existence in spite of all the possible added benefits. Perhaps the best method of controlling changes would be an early agreement between client and contractor, supported by the project team, which goes something like this:

If it will work,
If it is safe, and
If it can be maintained
Leave it alone.

4

Quality Assurance

JOHN D. STEVENSON   *Stevenson & Associates, Cleveland, Ohio*

Quality assurance is one of the most misunderstood terms in project management. This is because quality is often defined differently by the two main parties in any project, the owner, and the contractor. The term "owner" also includes the owner's agent or designee who acts on the owner's behalf.

To the owner the term "quality assurance" is typically defined as follows:

> Quality assurance comprises all those planned and systematic actions necessary to provide adequate confidence that a structure, system, or component will perform satisfactorily in service.

To the contractor, the term "quality assurance" is typically defined as follows:

> Quality assurance comprises all those planned and systematic actions necessary to provide adequate confidence that all items designed and constructed are in accordance with applicable standards and as specified by contract.

Quality assurance includes two major elements. The first is termed "quality control examination," which comprises the examination of the physical characteristics of the structure, system, material, component, part or appurtenance and comparison to the acceptance standards associated with those examinations. This element is more commonly termed quality control. In many instances, quality control has generally been broadened beyond examination or inspection to include material selection and control, manufacturing, fabrication, and installation procedures and tolerances.

The second element of quality assurance is termed "quality control administration," which is defined as the management and documentation which assure that the specified quality control examinations are carried out, and in many instances, this portion of quality control has been corrupted and has simply been called by its parent's name, quality assurance. Commonly, quality assurance has come to mean the administrative procedures and quality control the actual examinations, procedures, limits, and tolerances, which assure satisfaction of applicable standards and contract requirements.

The owner's definition of quality assurance, which may sound better because of its broader scope, is much more difficult to implement because of the necessity for the owner to know and communicate to the contractor *all* the requirements of the project in order for it to be implemented.

The owner wants a reliable, safe, and economical facility. If this desired end is not achieved, the owner tends to view this as the result of either poor project management or a breakdown in quality assurance on the part of the contractor. In general, the contractor is only responsible for what has been specified by contract between the owner and contractor and as specified by applicable codes and standards. Overall, satisfactory performance cannot be assured by the contractor independent of these specifications.

In general, the contractor's definition is preferred by the project organization since it defines the vehicles by which all project requirements are to be determined and identified.

ORGANIZATION

The project management should be responsible for the establishment and execution of the quality assurance program. Project management may delegate to subcontractors, agents, or consultants, the work of establishing and executing the quality assurance program, or any part thereof, but should retain responsibility therefore.

The authority and responsibility of persons and organizations performing activities affecting quality should be clearly established and documented. These activities include both the performing activities of attaining quality objectives and the quality assurance functions.

The quality assurance functions within the quality assurance program are: assuring that an appropriate quality assurance program is established and effectively implemented and verifying (checking, auditing, or inspecting) that such activities have been correctly performed. Persons and organizations performing quality assurance functions should have sufficient authority and organizational freedom to:

1. Identify quality problems
2. Initiate, recommend, or provide solutions
3. Verify implementations of solutions
4. Limit or control further processing, delivery, or installation of nonconforming item or unsatisfactory condition until proper dispositioning has occurred

The required authority and organizational freedom should be provided by having quality assurance personnel report to a management level within the project. Because of the many variables involved—number of personnel, type of activity being performed, and location or locations where activities are performed—the organizational structure for executing the quality assurance program may take various forms given this requisite authority and organization freedom. Irrespective of the organizational structure, any individual assigned responsibility for assuring effective execution of any portion of the quality assurance program at any location where activities are being performed should have direct access to such levels of project management as may be necessary to perform this function.

Quality assurance should be a direct responsibility of project management. In recent years, conventional wisdom has been to make quality assurance independent of project management. In theory, this permits the quality assurance organization to more effectively perform its tasks independent of the pressures of schedule and cost. In practice, it leads to a "them" and "us" mentality where project personnel actually doing the work are no longer responsible for quality. Quality, in addition to quality assurance, then becomes the responsibility of the quality assurance organization. This defeats the old dictum "quality must be built in." It is extremely difficult if not impossible and hardly cost effective to inspect quality into the work.

QUALITY ASSURANCE PROGRAM AND MANUAL

The project should have a quality assurance program for the control of the quality of specific items being designed, constructed, or procured. The program should define the organizational structure within which the quality assurance program is to be implemented and should clearly delineate the responsibilities, levels of authorities, and lines of communication for the various individuals, groups, and subcontractors involved. The quality assurance program should be documented by written policies, procedures, and instructions. The quality of all items and services, whether constructed, manufactured, or obtained from an outside supplier, should be controlled at all points necessary to assure conformance with the requirements of a quality assurance manual, which serves as a basis for demonstration of quality assurance compliance. The manual should be accepted by the owner.

The program should provide for the accomplishment of activities affecting quality under suitably controlled conditions. Controlled conditions include the use of appropriate equipment, suitable environmental conditions for accomplishing the activity, and assurance that prerequisites for the activity have been satisfied. The program should take into account the need for special controls, processes, test equipment, tools, and skills to attain the required quality and need for verification of quality by inspection and test. The program should provide for ready detection of nonconforming material and items and for timely and positive corrective actions. Management shall regularly review the status and adequacy of the program.

Indoctrination and training should be provided to personnel performing activities affecting quality as necessary to assure that suitable proficiency is achieved and maintained. It should be project responsibility to assure that all personnel performing quality functions, including personnel of subcontracted services, are qualified.

BASIC ELEMENTS OF QUALITY ASSURANCE

Design Control

Measures should be established to assure that the applicable requirements of government and industry standards and the design specifications or criteria provided by the owner for items are correctly translated into specifications, drawings, procedures, and instructions. The measures should include provisions to assure that appropriate quality standards are specified and included in these design documents. Measures should also be established for the selection and review for suitability of application of materials and design details.

These specifications should be checked for adequacy and accuracy. Design reports and the overall design should be reviewed for design adequacy and compliance with the design specifications and criteria. Design reviews and checking should be performed by or for the responsible design organization. It is recommended that design documents should be certified by a registered professional engineer.

Reports of in-process and final design reviews should be checked by management of the responsible design organizations. Design changes, including field changes, should be accepted by the organization that performed the original design unless the owner specifically designates another responsible organization. Procedures should be established among participating design organizations for the review, approval, release, distribution, and revision of documents involving design interfaces.

Measures should be established to assure that applicable regulatory requirements (codes and standards), design bases, and other requirements which are necessary to assure adequate quality are suitably included or referenced in the documents for procurement of material, equipment, and services, whether purchased by the owner or by contractor or subcontractors. To the extent necessary, procurement documents shall require the contractor or subcontractors to provide a quality assurance program consistent with the pertinent provisions of the project program.

Document Control

Measures should be established to control the issuance of all documents including changes thereto, which prescribe all activities affecting quality. These measures should assure

that documents, including changes, are reviewed for adequacy and approved for release by authorized personnel and are distributed to and used at the location where
the prescribed activity is performed. Changes to documents should be reviewed and
approved by the same organizations that performed the original review and approval
unless the owner designates another responsible organization.

Control of Purchased Material, Equipment, and Services

Measures should be established to assure that purchased material, equipment, and services, whether purchased directly by the owner or through the contractor and subcontractors, conform to the procurement documents. These measures should include provisions, as appropriate, for source evaluation and selection, objective evidence of quality furnished by the contractor or subcontractor source, and examination of products
upon delivery. Documentary evidence that material and equipment conform to the procurement requirements shall be available at the site prior to installation or use of such
material and equipment. This documentary evidence should be retained at the site and
should be sufficient to identify the specific requirements, such as codes, standards, or
specifications, met by the purchased material and equipment. The effectiveness of
the control of quality by the contractor and subcontractors shall be assessed by the
owner and the project organization at intervals consistent with the importance, complexity, and quantity of the product or services.

Identification and Control of Material, Parts, and Components

Measures should be established for the identification and control of materials, parts,
and components, including partially fabricated assemblies. These measures shall assure
that identification of the item is maintained by heat number, part number, serial num-
ber, system number, component number, part or device number, and line number, or
other appropriate means, either on the item or on records traceable to the item, as
required throughout fabrication, erection, installation, and use of the item. These
identification and control measures shall be designed to prevent the use of incorrect
or defective material, devices, parts, and components.

Initial Inspection

A program for inspection of activities affecting quality shall be established and executed
by or for the organization performing the activity to verify conformance with the documented instructions, specifications procedures, and drawings for accomplishing the
activity. Such inspection shall be performed by individuals other than those who performed the activity being inspected. Examinations, measurements, or tests of material
or products processed shall be performed for each work operation where necessary to
assure quality. If inspection of processed material or products is impossible or dis-
advantageous, indirect control by monitoring process methods, equipment, and personnel should be provided. Both inspection and process monitoring should be provided
when control is inadequate without both. If mandatory inspection hold points, which
require witnessing or inspecting by the owner, and beyond which work shall not proceed without the consent of the owner are required, the specific hold points shall be
indicated in appropriate documents.

Test Control

A test program shall be established to assure that all testing required to demonstrate
that structures, systems, and components will perform as specified in service is identified and performed in accordance with written test procedures which incorporate the
requirements and acceptance limits contained in applicable design documents. The test
program shall include, as appropriate, proof tests prior to installation, preoperational

tests, and operational tests during normal, steady-state, and anticipated transient operation, of structures, systems, and components. Test procedures should include provisions for assuring that all prerequisites for the given test have been met, that adequate test instrumentation is available and used, and that the test is performed under suitable environmental conditions. Test results should be documented and evaluated to assure that test requirements have been satisfied.

Control of Measuring and Test Equipment

Measures should be established to assure that tools, gauges, instruments, and other measuring and testing devices used in activities affecting quality are properly controlled, calibrated, and adjusted as required to maintain accuracy within necessary limits.

Handling, Storage, and Shipping

Measures should be established to control the handling, storage, shipping, cleaning, and preservation of material and equipment in accordance with inspection instructions to prevent damage or deterioration. When necessary for particular products, special protective environments, such as inert gas atmosphere, moisture content levels, and temperature levels, should be specified and provided.

Operating Status, Inspection, Test, and Acceptance

Measures should be established to indicate, by the use of markings such as stamps, tags, labels, routing cards, or other suitable means, the status of inspections, and tests performed upon individual items of the facility. These measures should provide for the identification of items which have satisfactorily passed required inspections and tests, where necessary, to preclude inadvertent bypassing of such inspections and test. Measures should also be established for indicating the operating status of structures, systems, and components of the facility, such as by tagging valves and switches, to prevent inadvertent operation. It should be documented as to exactly what is meant by owner "acceptance" of a structure, system, or component.

Nonconforming Materials, Parts, or Components

Measures should be established to control materials, parts, or components which do not conform to requirements to prevent their inadvertent use or installation. These measures should include, as appropriate, procedures for identification, documentation, segregation, disposition, and notification to affected organizations. Nonconforming items should be reviewed and accepted, rejected, repaired, or reworked in accordance with documented procedures.

Corrective Action

Measures should be established to assure that conditions adverse to quality, such as failures, malfunctions, deficiencies, deviations, defective material and equipment, and nonconformances are promptly identified and corrected. In the case of significant conditions adverse to quality, the measures shall assure that the cause of the condition is determined and corrective action taken to preclude repetition. The identification of the significant condition adverse to quality, the cause of the condition, and the corrective action taken should be documented and reported to appropriate levels of project management.

Quality Assurance Records

Sufficient records should be maintained to furnish evidence of activities affecting quality. The records should include at least the following: operating logs and the results of reviews, inspections, tests, audits, monitoring of work performance, and materials analyses. The records should also include closely related data such as qualifications of personnel, procedures, and equipment. Inspections and test records should, as a minimum, identify the inspector or data recorder, the type of observation, the results, the acceptability, and the action taken in connection with any deficiencies noted. Records should be identifiable and retrievable. Consistent with applicable regulatory requirements, the owner should establish requirements concerning record retention, such as duration, location, and assigned responsibility.

Audits

A comprehensive system of planned and periodic audits concerning both technical as well as administrative project requirements should be carried out to verify compliance with all aspects of the quality assurance program and to determine the effectiveness of the program. The audits should be performed in accordance with the written procedures or check lists by appropriately trained personnel not having direct responsibilities in the areas being audited. Audit results should be documented and reviewed by management having responsibility in the area audited. Follow-up action, including reaudit of deficient areas, should be taken where indicated. The audit function is the one area of quality assurance where it is recommended that the audit activity at least in part be performed and administered by personnel other than those assigned to the project being audited.

CURRENT LEVELS OF APPLICATION OF QUALITY ASSURANCE REQUIREMENTS

As a practical matter within owner and contractor organizations, there has always been some level of quality assurance practiced. Generally, three levels of quality assurance can be identified.

Level 3 is typically identified as a baseline and is employed on conventional industrial projects while Level 1 is usually employed on critical facility or high hazard projects such as nuclear power plants and liquified natural gas storage facilities.

Elements of a Level 1 typical critical facility quality assurance program are:
1. Provides for the development of a detailed quality assurance manual which regulates all aspects of the quality assurance program
2. Provides for the formation of a project independent* quality assurance organization to monitor project quality assurance
3. Provides for formal audit (administrative and possibly technical) of all aspects of project quality assurance
4. Provides for routine sign off by the quality assurance organization of controlled project documents
5. Mandates a formal procedure for resolutions of nonconformances identified between "as designed" and "as built" construction

Level 2, which is a compromise between Levels 1 and 3, tends to be employed on large organizationally complex conventional projects and also tends to find application in publicly funded or government projects.

Elements of a Level 2 typical government or major project quality assurance program are:

---

* A common element of existing Level 1 quality assurance programs which is not recommended.

1. Provides for the development of a quality assurance manual which regulates the quality assurance program usually by reference to applicable regulatory, contractor project and owner policy, procedures, and contract requirements
2. Provides for the formation of a project independent* quality assurance or audit organization to monitor project quality assurance
3. May provide for administrative or technical audits of selected aspects of project quality assurance
4. Requires documented resolution of nonconformances identified in the field

Level 3 quality assurance is so ingrained into typical project standard operating procedures that often it is not recognized as quality assurance. For example, the routine checking of drawings is a typical example of Level 3 quality assurance which might be identified as prudent engineering management rather than quality assurance.

Elements of a Level 3 typical conventional, heavy industry quality assurance program are:
1. Requires quality assurance program is by reference to applicable regulatory, contractor, project, and owner policy and operating procedures and contract requirements
2. Mandates a quality assurance program be the responsibility of and administered by project management in accordance with applicable regulatory, contractor, project, and owner specified policy and operating procedures and contract requirements
3. Usually includes no routine or scheduled audit function
4. Provides for resolution of nonconformance identified in the field as provided by contract. Generally, this procedure is performed by field engineers who are competent to evaluate intent of design and who are allowed to use judgement in evaluating significance of nonconformances

Project services provided to quality assurance Level 3 are considered to be provided at a baseline cost. The Level 2 quality assurance typically adds 5-10% to the baseline project cost, and Level 1 typically adds 20-30% to baseline project costs.

In many ways, Level 1 quality assurance can be described as "management-by-numbers." It is tacit recognition that the normal project management organization cannot be depended upon to produce the required level of quality when operating through the normal project chain of command and is not recommended unless it can be fully justified on an overall cost-benefit basis. Even then, the desired fix should be to change project management and not augment or make project independent the quality assurance function if desired quality levels are not being maintained.

SUMMARY AND CONCLUSIONS

Quality assurance should be a prime responsibility and function of project management. In order for quality assurance to be rationally applied, quality must be designed and constructed into the project. Quality cannot effectively be inspected in by a quality assurance organization.

Effective project management should not separate the responsibility from the accountability for quality assurance. There is a quality assurance audit function which should be performed independent of the project in much the same way that fiscal audits are typically performed independent of the line organization being audited but other quality assurance functions should be performed by the project.

_____

*Only a project independent audit organization is recommended.

The ultimate goal of any quality assurance program should be a reliable and safe facility consistent with applicable regulatory and contract requirements and not some Utopian dream where "quality assurance" is somehow going to eliminate all **errors** and problems associated with project management and performance.

5

Document Handling and Control

SHELDON R. SALKOVITCH   *Annex Manufacturing Corp., Jersey City, New Jersey*

IMPORTANCE OF DOCUMENT CONTROL

Your assignment: one of the members of a team sent as company representatives to a consulting engineering firm.

Your task: to effectively control the flow of documents sent by the contractor through your group to obtain timely approvals.

Your dilemma: you can hardly see over the pile of paper on your desk. The boss wants to know if a requisition has been approved and you are not sure that it has even been received.

It is imperative that you establish a system at the onset of the job to receive, distribute, return, and thus effectively monitor and control the continuous stream of documentation being circulated. You must also be in a position to prepare monthly status reports covering progress on document preparation and issue.

Since it would be redundant to describe control schemes for each important document, one example has been selected–the specification–and will be described in detail. The principles for any document-logging system are identical; the details will vary with the type of project and the contract requirements.

The procedures described here are not rigid; rather, they are intended to illustrate the principles. They should be reviewed and adjusted to suit the particular situation, large job or small, in-house or contracted. Further, these techniques are not theorized models. They have been utilized on jobs ranging from $20,000 to over $100,000,000 and are "job-proven successes." The objectives of an effective system of document control are twofold: (1) to assure that all of the contractual and procedural requirements are regularly adhered to in an organized manner, and (2) that the status of all of the documents is readily available at any time.

DOCUMENT FLOW SHEET

The first step in effective document control is optimization of document handling. This is done by developing a document flow sheet that shows the paths of distribution for the specification (or other document) and all associated recording and control functions involved in (1) document receipt, date stamping, and logging; (2) distribution of the copies for review; (3) expediting review comments; (4) coordinating comments; (5) finalizing comments; (6) customer approvals as required; (7) issue of approved docu-

---

ment; and (8) location of the project file copies. These paths are traced to adequately cover the control measures and documentation procedures.

Obviously each project will have very different requirements. It is essential that there be no carryover of customer-specific requirements from one project to the next. Use of out-of-date or unnecessary protocol in document processing can cause job delays and waste manpower.

On the document flow sheet, the requirements for document status should be clearly shown and the responsibility for this function definitely assigned. On a large project or one with considerable schedule pressure, this may call for a project document coordinator. On a small project, discipline leaders may be assigned the responsibility. There should be a project standard for document handling and reporting.

The flow sheet is analyzed and critiqued to determine more direct paths or more effective procedures to achieve the same results. Once the optimization has been completed, the flow sheet is made available to everyone involved in the review and approval cycle so that there is unquestionable understanding of the process.

RECORDING FUNCTIONS

In all of the following discussions, references are made to manual tracking of documents. At the present time the vast majority of document control is still done manually. Computerized recordkeeping is being used more and more; and, as the technology of information systems develops, it will tend to replace the present systems. The principles of control are precisely the same, and the computer should be viewed as a method of recording, sorting, and reporting which may be more efficient than doing these manually.

Log Books

All incoming mail is date-stamped and then forwarded in accordance with the project procedures and the document flow diagram for logging. The log book for specifications (and all other types of documents) should contain preprinted sheets. The record for each specification will be contained on a separate sheet. The entries are arranged in a logical manner depending on the specification numbering system used for easy reference.

The log book serves two purposes: (1) it records and documents the day-to-day transactions between customer and contractor, and (2) it serves as a record of the specifications which have been issued so that there will be no duplications in issuing new numbers.

Each sheet of the log book will contain the following information:

    Project number
    Project name
    Specification number
    Specification title
    Customer approval date

The above information may be presented at the top of each log sheet.

It is necessary to identify the revision number of the specification, the purpose of the revision, the dates received and returned, and the transmittal letter number.

There may be several revisions to each specification for which provision will have to be made. The status of the last revision is kept current on the log sheet with a minimum of manual entries because of the specially conceived marking techniques that are described in the following paragraphs. This information can be very repetitive and the techniques described make it easy to identify current status, yet be able to retrieve a complete history of the specification for record purposes.

Format of Log Entries

The body of the log sheet is divided horizontally into the number of revisions contemplated for the specifications. Whenever a specification is changed and reprinted/reissued for whatever reason, a new revision number is assigned. Five appears to be a reasonable and manageable number of revisions.

Logging Blocks

For each of the revision lines two large squares are printed. Where letter-size logsheets are used these will be approximately 1-1/2 inches square. The first of these squares is to reflect the handling of the original issue of the specification, and the second the handling of the reissue or republication with the comments.

Each of the two large squares is divided with a diagnoal line from the upper right corner to the lower left. Above the diagonal are five smaller squares each with a letter to identify one of the types of specification issues. The contracting engineer issues specifications for various purposes. Typical examples are:

Approval (A): Submitted for approval of flowrates, temperatures, and performance requirements. The approval issue also sets the general format of the specification and the scope of the specification or the material to be covered by the specification.

Inquiry (I): This issue releases the specification to be used to obtain proposals for furnishing the services, items of equipment, or materials covered.

Design (D): This issue releases the downstream detailed design work of the civil, mechanical, piping, electrical, instrumentation, and other design disciplines. At this point the detailed drawings may commence.

Purchase (P): This issue is a part of the purchase order or subcontract and reflects exactly the understanding at that time of what is being bought.

Construction (C): This issue of the specification is the one in which everything has been incorporated prior to starting erection/field construction.

Upon receipt of a specification, the small square indicating the type of issue is colored in with a yellow marking pen. At the same time the date of receipt of the specification is entered above the diagonal line.

The lower part of each large square is used for information about the returned specification. The date the specification is returned is noted below the diagonal line. Depending upon whether or not the client is in agreement with the current condition of the specification, it may be returned (WC) "with comment," (WOC) "without comment," or (A) "approved." Again, small squares are provided below the diagonal of the large square with the designations "WC," "WOC," and "A." The proper small square is again yellowed in. There is also a place in the lower half of the large square to note the number of the specification transmittal (STN).

For each specification revision on the logging sheet, two of the large squares are provided. This allows tracking of specifications which need to be revised to reflect customer comments before issue. The same marking procedures are used for the reissue or "republication" of the revision as for the original submission. As soon as customer approval has been given, the specification, or revised specification, is issued. The system of using the two logging blocks for each revision works whether the specification is returned with comment or without. The system is neat, orderly, and pictorial—providing a complete history of each specification at a quick glance.

MONITORING FUNCTIONS

The role of the specification logbook is to record the total job documentation for all of the specifications. To monitor, control, manage, and prepare status reports, logbooks are not the most practical format.

Another management tool is required- one that ensures timely review and approval of all major engineering documents by providing a visual map of current needs. This tool should also provide a medium whereby a monthly tally of items submitted can be made quickly and accurately. The answer to these requirements is the monthly analysis ledger sheet (MALS).

Monthly Analysis Ledger Sheet (MALS)

This document is meant to give a complete up-to-date status of each of the various types of major documents that are being controlled. A copy of the MALS is posted in a convenient location so that it is visible to the entire project team.

The MALS for specifications has a line for each specification. Upon receipt of a specification and, in conjunction with the logging process, the appropriate entries are listed on the MALS. The specification number including the revision number and the specification title are listed.

Visual Map

The current status of the specification is indicated in the visual map which provides a separate block for each of the five types of specification issues discussed above. In addition, an additional square is provided for the "first issue." This square is completely darkened if the submittal represents the original issue of the document. Another block may be used where it is important to keep track of whether the document requires an approval signature apart from transmittal approval. The actual size of the issue blocks should be about $1/2 \times 1/2$ inch.

Receipt of a particular issue is shown by drawing a diagonal line from the upper right hand corner to the lower left-hand corner in the appropriate block. The upper portion of the block is darkened. Since only that half of the block is filled in, it symbolizes that only half of the transaction is complete. When the specification has been approved and returned, the lower half of the square is darkened. If the specification is returned "with comment," instead of darkening the lower half of the square, the initials "WC" are posted there.

The right portion of the MALS provides space for noting the date on which the specification is received, the date on which it is returned, and the date of a review meeting, if required. The resubmittal data and approval date are also noted. Space is allocated for posting the transmittal number of the original and resubmitted specifications. Any special requirements created by the specific project coordination procedures may also be used in a similar fashion on the MALS.

UTILITY OF SYSTEM

The MALS fulfills a multitude of purposes on the project. It is a "picture at a glance" for the entire month's progress. Your eye can run down the "visual map" looking only for incompletely filled blocks. One can quickly find the issues returned with comment or which have not yet been returned. One need not read any information on the MALS to note which specifications have not yet received action. By noting the receipt date and allowing for the scheduled turnaround, the engineer can assess the urgency of reply. Project control is facilitated from the MALS, since the entries not completed will figuratively "stare one in the face."

For the project manager wishing to determine the day-to-day progress of the job, the MALS offers a method whereby this information is always attainable at a glance.

Progress Reporting

In addition to being an excellent monitoring and control tool, the MALS provides a quick and accurate means of reporting monthly progress. All of the information needed for these reports is routinely assembled on a daily basis. The MALS has been used very effectively for monitoring jobs with a total installed cost of over $100 million. It can be easily implemented for smaller projects. It results in a fast, effective, and accurate means for logging, monitoring, controlling, and reporting project documentation. This results in tangible cost savings.

6

Financial Audits of Capital Projects

DONALD E. LAW *Consultant, South Bristol, Maine*

WHY CONDUCT THE FINANCIAL AUDIT?

Financial audits of most business enterprises in the United States are conducted on a regular, recurring basis. This practice will continue because of the extensive problems these audits have eliminated (inaccurate, misleading financial status statements), and their continuing value (maintenance of financial control and as a catalyst for improved financial management). The financial audit is supportive to financial management responsibilities.

Financial audits are an institution which needs to be extended more regularly to large capital projects including, particularly, major construction programs. The reasons for this are similar to those which prompted legal adoption of financial audits 50 years ago, namely, risk and reporting which is often misleading and inaccurate. Why don't financial audits typically include large capital projects? Primarily because auditors tend to focus mostly on the regular, day to day business of a company. Also, in many projects, technical (engineering) interests play a dominant role during project planning and implementation. This can lead to a condition where sound financial management practices are not fully adopted, and subsequent financial risk may jeopardize project results. An audit can assess this condition and suggest appropriate change.

WHAT FINANCIAL PRACTICES ARE IMPORTANT?

Typical points of financial management interest for construction projects relate to issues such as:

> Accurate cost estimates (budgets)
> Timing of costs (cash flow)
> Justification of costs (financial analysis)
> Timeliness and accuracy of cost reporting
> Use of appropriate financial controls
> Identification of incorrect project charges
> Project status reported on a timely, meaningful basis
> Exercising appropriate authorizations before any expenditures are incurred

All of these points should be of prime interest to organizations both funding a project and those responsible for its implementation. The full development of these interests, however, requires the special skills of strong financial management supported by an effective audit program.

WHO SHOULD PERFORM THE AUDIT?

Three important variables in choosing a financial auditor are technical skills, independence, and positioning. These needs can be compromised by superficial attention. The audit can be conducted either internally (by the company's audit depeartment) or externally (by some other organization specializing in such audits). Neither group has inherent advantages; selection should be based on as precise a job of specifications as possible.

Technical skills should include qualifications in:

Financial management
Financial auditing
Operational (management) auditing
Construction management
Cost estimating
Program scheduling

Many companies do not possess internal audit capabilities covering this range of technical skills. Instead they depend on their external, certified public accountants to both identify audit requirements for construction programs, and conduct the audits. Unfortunately neither have these firms developed appropriate skills for the work, nor have they achieved an enviable audit record in this area.

Independence during an audit requires freedom from being biased by anyone having an interest in the audit's results. External auditors are often thought of as being more independent because they have no direct management ties. They are, however, dependent upon management for their tenure, and this opens the door to potential conflict. The easiest way to resolve this issue is for the auditors to be solicited by and report only to the chief executive or operating officer.

Positioning for delivery of audit results will control whether the auditing recommendations will be enacted or discarded. Even an excellent audit product may not achieve the intended effect if presented at the wrong level of management. Boards of directors who are sufficiently organized to monitor the implementation of commitments should control the action taken on audit recommendations.

WHAT SHOULD BE AUDITED?

The typical project audit should be conducted in three sequential stages:

1. Near the end of planning for design or construction
2. During the design or construction period
3. Following the completion of design or construction

Each stage will require a different mix of audit personnel, substantially different amounts of effort, will focus on different objectives, and result in different audit products.

THE STAGE I AUDIT

The Stage I audit focuses on whether appropriate approaches, systems, and procedures have been developed for the maintenance of acceptable levels of financial management during Stage II. A checklist for this audit would cover a review of proposed management approaches to:

The project budget system

Cash-flow projections
Financial controls
Authorization requirements
Accounting systems
Estimating methodology
Level of scheduling detail and cost-loading technique
Change control
Status reporting

Each element of the audit should be completed as far in advance of the actual design or construction period as possible. During each element, the auditor would first determine whether a well-documented approach had been developed. If so, he would next review the approach to evaluate its suitability for the project. Experienced auditors would compare the proposed approaches to those which, in their opinion, were appropriate to the project. Detailed guidelines should be developed by the auditor for this purpose. Lastly, the auditor would summarize his findings in a written report for management. This report would focus on changes necessary to bring proposed approaches up to the level appropriate for the project. This stage would end with management adopting a plan for implementing corrective action.

THE STAGE II AUDIT

The Stage II audit would consist of a series of reviews to determine whether the approaches developed and approved in State I were being complied with. The frequency of such "compliance audits" would vary depending on the result of each prior audit, fewer audits being required as work audited becomes more routine and consistent.

Tests of compliance would include sufficient sampling of actual cost data (payroll, material) to assess:

Accuracy
Use of correct account/activity codes
Timeliness

The Stage II audit would also include the review of monthly project status reports. The purpose of auditing these reports would be to verify both status and variance explanations. Particular emphasis should be placed on the availability of full documentation for any variances which may ultimately contribute to unfavorable project cost, schedule, or quality of performance.

Independent documentation should be developed if necessary to satisfy audit requirements. Any potential, in the auditors opinion, of subsequent litigation should receive legal review at this time.

Stage II audit results should consist of three separate report periods:

1. Periodic reports on the outcome of compliance testing; specific recommendations by the auditor where improvements are required
2. Periodic assessments of status reporting accuracy with comments and recommendations considered appropriate by the auditor
3. Special reports documenting significant variances and circumstances from which they resulted

THE STAGE III AUDIT

The primary purpose of Stage III is to provide an independent assessment of performance for the completed project.

The Stage III audit report would be prepared primarily for the project sponsor. Material generated during Stage I and II audits would be used to both assess and explain overall project results. In particular, any major variances from plan and their causes would be fully documented for use by management in interpreting project results and planning future projects.

WHO CAN BENEFIT FROM THE PROJECT AUDIT?

Most projects are undertaken with an air of optimism that belies the possibility of subsequent unfavorable performance. Using our experience, we lay our plans carefully to achieve well-defined results. As hard as we may try, however, events often not under our direct control will contribute on occasion to unwanted and unacceptable results. We find ourselves blindsided, suddenly faced with the need to explain the totally unexpected.

While no audit can provide a guarantee, the project audit as outlined here offers substantial insurance against the unexpected loss of project control—for any reason. Like most forms of insurance, the potential value of the payout is huge compared to cost. All projects should, therefore, be audited. The more sensitive the project becomes (resulting from public ocmmitments, political interests, news media coverage, regulatory commission involvement), the greater the audit's potential value in preventing loss of control.

Stage II of the audit can restore control when it appears to have been lost. Most frequently, questions regarding project performance cannot be easily answered because of poor recordkeeping and incomplete status reporting. Resulting debates of opinion can be time consuming and expensive, with or without litigation. The purpose of the Stage III audit report is to provide an analysis of project performances from an independent perspective. When this is based on the documentation developed during Stage II, it is superior to any other record available.

The full project audit may be omitted from project planning due to concern for audit costs or a lack of awareness of its contribution to rigorous project management and project performance. Awareness is a matter of education and opinion. Concern over audit cost should never prevent gaining this experience. These costs are trivial in comparison to overall project costs. They are also trivial in comparison to the audit's potential for controlling unfavorable variances (cost or schedule) and avoiding postcompletion litigation.

X

PROJECT ACCEPTANCE
AND CLOSEOUT

UNIT OVERVIEW

Regardless of the type of project undertaken, there are certain principles that should
be followed as the work is concluded:

Each component, system, or element should be verified or tested to assure that
it has been completed in accordance with the original intent, or as formally
modified during the course of project execution.

The composite work output must also be confirmed as being finished and that it
fulfills the agreed-to expectations.

This proving or testing should be done according to a formal plan. This will
smooth the transition between the development and implementation phases of
the project and its delivery to the client to begin to serve its useful purpose.
For a manufacturing facility this may be called a "commissioning plan"; or,
in other cases a "turnover plan" or some other terminology may be used.
Safety is often an important consideration during this transition period.

This testing phase must be carefully scheduled to minimize conflict with completion
of other project activities, yet still expedite the date at which the result of
the project work effort will become economically productive for the client.

The responsibility for the care and custody of plant, facility, or other result of
the project undertaking has to be carefully tracked as it passes from the project group doing the work to the owner's recipient organization. Frequently
this turnover is a legal milestone, documented in detail, and in strict accordance with a contractual procedure.

All commercial transactions conducted during the execution of the project must
be finalized. Final invoices should be paid and any claims resolved.

All data and information that can be used on subsequent projects should be put
into order so that it may be easily retrieved.

Project documentation must be completed. Extraneous and duplicate files should
be disposed of. Material to be kept should be properly filed.

Project acceptance and closeout may be the area of weakest performance on a successful project. An experienced project manager will not leave this phase of the project
to chance, but will develop a comprehensive plan for winding down the work.

1

Project Completion

DAVID H. HAMBURGER   *David Hamburger Management Consultant, Inc., Spring Valley, New York*

HERBERT F. SPIRER   *University of Connecticut, Stamford, Connecticut*

The euphoria that marks a project's beginning and the enthusiasm of work execution are usually gone when the project nears completion. Interest and excitement dwindle as project challenges become chores. The plan that brought the project to near completion is obsolete and far less managerial guidance and control are felt. Project team members have been assigned to new projects and are looking ahead to a fresh start, or see no new work in view and succumb to a natural tendency to stretch out the remaining effort. In either case, effective closeout—necessary for total project success—is not achieved. Timely and effective project completion can mean the difference between:

> Financial success or failure
> A satisfied client and the potential for future work, or a disgruntled client and the risk of possible litigation
> A firm that benefits from its projects' technological and administrative achievements, rather than one that finds that it must "reinvent the wheel" as it undertakes each new endeavor

To achieve timely and effective project completion the project manager should treat the necessary effort as a miniproject which requires a level of planning and control consistent with the needs of any other major project. The project manager must identify the issues of closure (both intellectual and emotional) and plan for their resolution. The intellectual issues (addressing unsatisfied specifications and missing deliverables; cancellation of identified tasks determined to be unnecessary; paperwork clean up; change negotiation with the client, vendors, and subcontractors; technical and financial data collection and organization for corporate dissemination; and disposition of resource), must be delineated, assigned for execution, and completed. The emotional issues (loss of interest in the remaining tasks; project team deterioration; loss of motivation; staff disposition) must also be addressed. The project manager must be able to deal with these behavioral problems in executing the work required to effect a successful project completion.

The following paragraphs cover the closeout of projects which are executed in behalf of a client in accordance with a formal contract. However, projects which are executed within an organization can be treated similarly, as most of the closeout principles and issues are relevant to the internal endeavor. The internal project sponsor becomes the client; and the project authorization, scope of work, and budget are, in essence, the contract. The need for timely and effective closeout, client or project sponsor satisfaction, and the dissemination of project information to the parent organization are essentially the same for both a contracted and an internally sponsored project.

THE NEED FOR EFFECTIVE PROJECT COMPLETION

Kickoff and execution are perceived as the glamourous and exciting aspects of the project life cycle; while the detailed effort required to complete the defined tasks, clean up the contractual loose ends, collect and disseminate project-related technical and performance information, dispose of materiel and facilities, and reassign the project staff seem to generate little interest and enthusiasm. In many cases an actual resistance to this effort exists. Timely and effective project completion (contract closeout) is important for many reasons, including:

Final payment or retention is usually withheld by a client until the project objectives have been met and the contractual terms and conditions satisfied. A delay in receipt of these funds will result in additional financial expenses which can turn a potentially successful project into a financial failure.

Stretching out project completion and/or deferring an orderly staff reduction invariably adds to the total cost of project execution, as project costs will continuously accrue during such inefficient periods of performance. Again, a potentially successful project can be turned into a financial failure.

Failure to provide a client with timely and appropriate information, drawings, manuals, training, and field assistance, required to support an otherwise acceptable system or hardware component furnished under a contract, can result in client dissatisfaction, loss of goodwill, loss of future business, increased system misuse, abuse and failure which will increase the number of warranty claims and the potential for litigation, and a general deterioration of reputation within the industry. A perfectly good product will not function properly if the user does not like it, understand it, or is not satisfied with the support furnished by the supplier.

Failure to provide a client with required information could delay or prevent compliance with the government regulations which control his operation. A client's resulting burden of lost revenues, fines, and the effort required to rectify a noncompliance situation will ultimately be reflected in his relationship with the organization he deems responsible. This can affect receipt of final payment, the final amount the client feels obligated to pay, product satisfaction, future business, and the supplier's reputation within the industry.

Untimely or delayed staff reassignment can seriously affect project financial performance, limit availability of technical skills for other projects within the organization, and negatively influence the morale of those personnel whose future within the company has not been clearly defined and are retained on a relatively inactive project.

The technology developed on a project represents the project's contribution to the future growth of the organization. To be of value, such information must be transferred from the project into the appropriate technical and other functional areas of the firm. Therefore, an orderly transfer of data is required before the project team is disbanded and the developed technology gets lost or disappears with the reassigned or discharged project team members.

Delayed termination of purchase orders and subcontracts can seriously affect vendor and subcontractor relationships. Failure to settle open purchase orders and subcontracts in a timely manner can result in added project costs resulting from a loss of the information needed for settlement negotiations, the unavailability of the right technical personnel needed to support negotiations, a general weakness in position which occurs with the passing of time, and the cost of the additional time required to reach a settlement.

In addition to the technology developed on the project, much can be learned about one's estimating skills from the final financial performance report. Further, the organization's estimating database, used to estimate the cost of future endeavors, can be expanded by the incorporation of the project's actual cost results. Therefore, the project manager must prepare a final cost report which compares actual costs with the original estimate and provides information regarding the causes of any significant variance immediately following project completion. This report must then be distributed to the appropriate functional groups for their use.

The disposition of materials, supplies, government-furnished equipment (if applicable), etc., must be accomplished in a timely fashion to minimize the cost to the project. Loss and natural shrinkage, which can be expected if unused items of value are left unattended for an extended period of time, can only be prevented by timely action.

A warranty start date must be established and confirmed by the client to limit the term of the firm's financial obligation. The sooner the warranty is set in effect, the sooner the cost for adjustments to the system or hardware will stop being charged to the project; and the sooner the warranty is set in place, the sooner this financial obligation will expire.

Since management of the warranty effort is usually a customer support or marketing responsibility, effective inauguration of this function is necessary to avoid poor warranty performance. The individual or group responsible for this effort must be cognizant of the status of the system or hardware furnished under the contract; the open issues with the client; and his concerns about the product's uses, capabilities, and limitations. The warranty manager must be furnished with all drawing, documents, and correspondence relevant to his effort following project completion.

PROJECT COMPLETION

Project completion (completing the contract) can either follow successful completion of the natural sequence of project activities directed toward meeting the specified objectives, or a sudden decision to cease the project effort in mid course. In either case, once completion has been established, the contract must be closed out, the technical and financial data collected, analyzed, and distributed to the relevant elements of the functional organization, and the project team effectively disassembled.

Natural Completion (Completing the Contract Work)

Natural completion occurs when the project has run its full term and the basic objectives defined in the contract have been satisfied and the furnished system or hardware has been deemed acceptable by the client. At this point, the major deliverables have been supplied and installed, the system or hardware has been made functional, and the specified performance tests have been executed. The client has beneficial use of the items supplied under the contract. However, all aspects of the contract's requirements may not have been satisfied as secondary deliverables may remain unfurnished, disputed items may require settlement and the necessary paperwork must be executed before the client formally acknowledges that the contract is completed and makes the required final payment.

Frequently, natural completion cannot be accomplished because the specified performance has not been attained. In such cases the dispute between client and supplier can only lead to delayed acceptance, additional cost accrual, and a further deterioration of the client/supplier relationship. Identifying and then closing the gap that exists between actual and expected performance (variance) becomes a necessary and critical step in the contract closure process. To move the project toward its natural completion, the deficiencies which cause the discrepancy must either be remedied or their existence technically justified or accepted through a negotiation with the client.

Unnatural Completion (Stop Work Notification)

Unnatural completion is the result of a conscious decision to stop all future effort on the project, irrespective of the status of the work and the achievement of the desired contractual objectives. Unnatural completion can be the result of a change in the client's needs, lack of funds, reassessment of the project's true performance benefits, revaluation of project cost, ineffective supplier execution, identification of a better solution to the client's problem, loss of client confidence in the supplier's offering or his ability to execute, or a breakdown in the supplier/client working relationship. Frequently, an apparently successful project may be suddenly terminated for one of the aforementioned reasons which may not be the responsibility of the supplier.

The difference between closing out a contract which has been completed naturally or unnaturally is largely a matter of degree rather than substance. The closeout efforts are essentially the same, but the environment in which the closeout is accomplished is significantly different. The suddenness of a stop work notice adds to the complexity of an unnatural completion. The project team may become demoralized by the bad news, little or no advance preparation has been made for an orderly closeout, management loses interest in the project and priorities are usually lowered, the client is less concerned with an equitable settlement negotiation and may be more difficult to deal with, the client may even be resistive to settlement efforts if contract cancellation is attributed to a supplier performance failure, and many more loose ends remain to be resolved. On the other hand, closure of the technical effort does not require completion of the open tasks, but does include preparation of the completed portion of the work for storage and/or transmittal to the client. In addition, the need to establish post project warranty and client support relationships no longer exists. If the project has the potential for restart, then the closeout process must prepare for future resurrection of the project organization and recovery of the completed, or partially completed, work.

COMPLETING A PROJECT IS A PROJECT

Once it becomes clear that the project has reached its natural or unnatural completion, the task of closing out the contract should be treated as a distinct project. This effort itself can be described by the classical project definition: "a one time unique goal with specific resource constraints" (Lock, 1979). With this in mind, the familiar project management principles can be applied to the process of contract closure and the conventional tools and techniques can be employed. In fact, treatment of the closure process as a new endeavor will provide the environment needed for efficient execution. The specific needs of each unique closure process will determine the nature of its plans, schedules, organizational structure, and manpower requirements.

The project manager responsible for contract closeout must recognize that the plans and controls used to bring the original project to its present state of completion are probably obsolete and should be discarded. The contract closure miniproject must be given a fresh perspective, as this process has its unique requirements and organizational constraints. A contract closeout plan is required. The planning process begins with the definition of a specific set of closure objectives which will then be used to develop a closure work breakdown structure (CWBS) which is discussed later. The CWBS becomes the major planning and control tool, serving as a "punch list" which must be fully executed before contract closure (project completion) is achieved. The CWBS should be initially formatted in terms of contractual and organizational issues and then further broken down to the task/work package level, describing functional responsibilities. The primary concern at this stage of the project is to define exactly *what* has to be done and *who* is going to do it. Task budgeting, cost control, risk assessment, and schedule are now lesser considerations which should not significantly influence the development of the CWBS. A responsibility matrix (Hamburger, 1984), reflecting the tasks/work packages defined on the CWBS and the individuals or functional groups who will be responsible for their execution, should be prepared and published as a part of the closeout plan.

The nature of a punch list suggests a greater level of independence between tasks. This, coupled with the need to close out the contract as quickly as possible, makes the use of a critical path type schedule less desirable. Rapid completion of each task will achieve the desired results before the closeout miniproject can bog down due to a loss of interest and enthusiasm by the client, management, and the project participants. Should a degree of interdependence exist between the closeout tasks, identification of the critical path will be desirable to determine the factors that constrain closeout completion. Slack time identification will be useful in making the most efficient use of the limited team assigned to the effort. Since contract closeout is characterized by a "level of effort" expenditure rate, early completion of all tasks must be emphasized to support rapid staff reductions and miniproject completion at the earliest possible time.

The cost of contract closeout comes primarily from labor expenses which are directly related to the staff size required to execute the necessary tasks and the time it takes to complete the total effort. Settlement costs related to performance shortfalls, purchase order and subcontract backcharges, contract penalties, or the cost of additional work to bring the system or product in line with the specification may be significant and many "trade-off"-type decisions between alternative approaches will be required. The negotiating ability of the project team members and the quality of the available supporting data will serve to minimize these costs.

The unique characteristics of contract closeout which alter the planning approach also have an influence on the type of person who can effectively execute the plan. Not all project managers who excel at "kicking off" and executing a project are good at cleaning up loose ends. The drive of a project manager to keep things moving often results in a tendency to overlook certain details. Selection of the right person requires an assessment of the specific traits required for the job. Of even greater importance is the selection of a supporting team, as these people must be motivated toward putting themselves out of work as quickly and as efficiently as possible. This philosophy will be foreign to most technical and administrative people found executing projects, making the important task of contract closeout team formation extremely difficult.

CONTRACT COMPLETION ISSUES

Most of the problems associated with completing a contract represent the two basic aspects of human behavior: intellectual (cognitive) elements and emotional (affective) elements. Subdivision into these fundamental categories provides the project manager with a convenient structure for identifying, and then resolving, project completion problems. The intellectual issues are primarily issues of *detail*, while the emotional issues represent issues of *spirit* or attitude. Both are of major importance if the project manager is to complete the project and effectively close out the contract. The unresolved details (intellectual issues), both external and internal to the organization, must be identified and evaluated to determine their disposition. Most details must be completed, but some may no longer be relevant and can be disregarded. Other details can be resolved through a negotiated settlement with the client, vendor, or subcontractor. The emotional issues are equally important; as the project manager must deal with the attitude and sensitivities of the client, management, vendors, subcontractors, and the project team members, in effectively implementing the contract closure process. Failure to recognize and address the emotional issues greatly inhibits the manner in which the intellectual issues are resolved.

Table 1 provides a general view of the problems associated with contract completion, presented in an indentured work breakdown structure format (Spirer, 1983). Recognition of the two basic issue classes and the specific types of problems that can be encountered in completing a contract will serve the project manager in planning and controlling an actual project closeout.

Intellectual (Cognitive) Issues

The intellectual issues relate to the specific details which must be completed in the project closeout process. Identification and expedient execution of these issues are necessary for efficient contract closeout. These issues fall into two basic categories: internal and external.

Internal issues include project details which remain to be resolved by the project team within the organization. The internal issues may be further classified as contractual and organizational. Contractual issues are related to the contract closeout process, and the organizational issues deal with the organization's needs imposed on the termination process.

External issues include unresolved details which are influenced by external entities such as the client, vendors, subcontractors, government regulatory agencies, and so forth. The external issues may be further classified as client, vendor/subcontractor, and field. Client external issues require resolution in direct dealings with the client, and vendor/subcontractor external issues are resolved with the organizations from which the project equipment, services, and support are procured. Field external issues usually relate to activities at a job site or other remote operational location. In general, external intellectual issues are resolved in direct dealings with organizations which are independent of your organization, but are related to the project through some legal document (contract, purchase order, subcontract). Completion of these items is therefore restricted by the legal constraints of the controlling documentation. The process is one of understanding the technical and commercial requirements, identifying the open issues, and fulfilling them, if possible. If not possible, negotiating an alteration to the defining documentation or negotiating a financial settlement. To execute this aspect of the closeout work effectively, one must be completely familiar with the controlling documents and the extent and quality of the work completed to that point. Additional requirements are: knowledge of the needs and abilities of the party with whom you are dealing, a willingness to compromise in settling the open issues, and negotiating skills.

Emotional (Affective) Issues

If contract closeout was simply a systematical process of resolving the intellectual issues until no open issues remained, the project manager would find contract closeout much easier to achieve. Unfortunately, the emotional problems that arise as a project nears completion complicate this effort. Emotional letdown and loss of interest are common at the end of a project, equally affecting the performance of both the project's team members and the client's representative. The project manager must be able to recognize the symptoms and effect a cure. His/her influence and control over the project team members makes this possible internally, but little can be done with a client representative who does not wish to cooperate.

The emotional issues that affect the project team and the client can be further classified as either motivational or procedural. The motivational problems affecting project team performance can be addressed using conventional behavioral practices, since the project manager has a degree of authority and influence over the project team. The same methods used to motivate the staff during the "kick off" and execution phases of

Table 1 Contract Completion Issues Work Breakdown Structure

Contract Completion Issues
    Intellectual
        Internal
            Contractual
                Identify remaining deliverables
                Perform a financial audit
                Identify certification needs
                Identify outstanding vendor/subcontractor commitments
                Screen incomplete tasks for need
                Close open work orders/work packages
                Control project charges
                Communicate closures
                Inaugurate warranty program
            Organizational
                Identify/dispose of physical facilities
                Identify project personnel
                Dispose of unused project material
                System hardware performance critique/engineering update
                Consolidate/distribute project's technical data
                Consolidate/distribute project's financial data
        External
            Client
                Confirm remaining deliverables with client
                Meet the specification or negotiate a settlement
                Negotiate open contract changes/backcharges with client
                Obtain required certifications
            Vendors and Subcontractors
                Confirm outstanding vendor commitments
                Negotiate vendor changes/backcharges
                Confirm outstanding subcontractor commitments
                Negotiate subcontractor changes/backcharges
            Site
                Prepare as-built drawings
                Demobilize physical facilities
    Emotional
        Project Team
            Motivational
                Loss of interest in remaining tasks
                Fear of no future work
                Dissatisfaction with next assignment
                Loss of project-derived motivation
                Loss of team identity
                Diversion of effort
            Procedural
                Selection of personnel to be reassigned
                Reassignment methodology
        Client
            Motivational
                Change in attitude
                Loss of interest in the project
            Procedural
                Changes in personnel assigned to project
                Unavailability of key personnel

---

the project should be used during closeout. Team spirit must be maintained, and the importance of an efficient closeout and the significance of the individual's contribution must be stressed. In dealing with the client—where the project manager's authority and influence is essentially nonexistent—one must appeal to the client's desire for contract compliance, an unencumbered contract closeout, and trouble-free postcontract operation. Since the client's desires in this regard and the executing organization's drive for the completion of work and the reassignment of the staff will frequently be in conflict, a willingness to compromise is necessary. Meeting the client halfway in effecting a closeout can overcome many of the motivational roadblocks; this will be discussed later.

Project team procedural problems are details which must be addressed and could, therefore, be considered intellectual issues. However, the manner in which these issues are handled can greatly influence the emotional stability of the project team and the success of their execution. Therefore, the problems of staff reassignment are considered to be emotional issues. Procedural issues on the client side are also considered to be emotional, as they do not represent details requiring resolution, but rather challenges for which the project manager must find creative solutions. Changes in the client's staff can significantly affect the methods used to affect a contract closeout.

USING A CLOSURE WORK BREAKDOWN STRUCTURE
TO DEFINE THE REMAINING WORK

A detailed assessment of the intellectual issues associated with the contract closeout process is fundamental to the planning effort required to define the scope of this project phase. Given an awareness of these issues, the project manager can prepare a closure work breakdown structure which will define the remaining tasks, serve as the basis for assigning responsibility, support the generation of a schedule (if needed), and ultimately become the project manager's "punch list" for controlling closeout execution. In most contract closeout situations, a comprehensive CWBS can be used as the project manager's sole tool for control of the process, since each task identified on the CWBS has its scope of work and responsible organization identified. Table 2 presents the previously discussed intellectual issues and those tasks identified as emotional issues, because of their psychological implications, in an indentured list format CWBS. The intent is to classify the effort into conveniently manageable groups. Specifically, all project closeout tasks can be defined as being either contractual or organizational. Contractual tasks deal exclusively with the contract in question and organizational tasks deal with the project's relationship with, and its lasting effects on, the organization in which it is being executed.

Contractual Tasks

Contractual tasks may be further classified as internal, client, vendor and subcontractor, and field, as each group of contract-related tasks has its unique characteristics which require specific execution skills.

Internal tasks represent contractual responsibilities which can be exclusively accomplished by the project team without external participation. Each contractual task must be identified, addressed, and resolved as a part of the contract closeout process. Agreement between client and supplier regarding contract completion will not be reached unless this is achieved.

Identify Remaining Deliverables

A comprehensive review of the contract is necessary to determine which of the specified deliverables have not been furnished the client. Deliverables can take many forms including hardware, software, documentation, training, operational support, fixtures,

Table 2 Contract Closure Work Breakdown Structure

Contract Closure
    Contractual
        Internal
            Identify remaining deliverables
            Perform a financial audit
            Identify certification needs
            Identify outstanding vendor/subcontractor commitments
            Screen incomplete tasks for need
            Close open work orders/work packages
            Control project charges
            Communicate closures
            Implement the warranty program and other follow-on activities
        Client
            Confirm remaining deliverables with client
            Meet the specification or negotiate a settlement
            Negotiate/settle open contract changes and backcharges
            Obtain/submit required certifications
            Invoice for final payment
        Vendors and Subcontractors
            Confirm outstanding vendor commitments
            Negotiate open vendor/subcontractor changes orders and backcharges
        Field
            Obtain client's punch list
            Make necessary corrections
            Prepare as-built drawings
            Prepare a final field report
            Demobilize physical facilities
    Organizational
        Technical
            Critique system or hardware performance
            Critique system or hardware technical effort
            Consolidate/distribute project's technical data
        Administrative
            Identify/dispose of physical facilities
            Identify/evaluate project personnel
            Select personnel for reassignment
            Reassignment methodology
            Dispose of unused project material
            Consolidate/distribute project's financial data

---

shipping containers, calculations, reports, demolition and/or restoration of existing facilities, permits, certifications, spare parts, and so forth. Knowledge of the remaining obligations (undelivered deliverables) is necessary for the preparation of a detailed contract close out plan. Furnishing these items as a part of a structured program will be less costly than responding to a last minute demand from the client or an auditor for their delivery. Every outstanding obligation should be evaluated to determine the additional time and cost required for completion, and its value to the client should be assessed. Given this information, the project manager can prepare for a client negotiation in which the options of financial settlement, deletion from the scope of supply, "tradeoff," or reduced content can be considered.

Perform a Financial Audit

As the project nears completion, a financial audit becomes necessary to identify the items which must be rectified during closeout. This audit should cover both client obligations (income) and the project executor's obligations (expenses). A client-related audit of the financial records includes: determining if the full value of the completed scope of work has been invoiced, matching payments received with submitted invoices, conforming change order cost proposals with a change order log, ensuring the existence of change order paperwork consistent with the negotiated changes, and verifying the amount of retention withheld by the client. An expense record audit includes: verification of payments to vendors and subcontractors, consistency between purchase order values and the amount invoiced by the suppliers, expense charges to the correct account, checking for duplicate or missing charges, identifying potential vendor backcharges, enumerating unresolved vendor change requests, and confirming appropriate retention withholding. The results of this financial audit will support closure of the client and vendor contractual issues and will ensure accurate financial data for the preparation of the final project financial reports.

Identify Certification Needs

Certifications represent a critical class of contract deliverables which are frequently deemed to be as important as the primary contract requirements. Therefore, their ultimate supply can rarely be avoided. Extreme care must be taken to identify each certification requirement and then ensure that the correct documentation is supplied, properly executed, in the specified quantity. The requirement for certification can be found in many areas of the contract including the general specification, terms and conditions, component specifications, test specifications, performance specifications, and the government and corporate regulations and standards, frequently referred to as "boiler plate." In a properly managed project, identification and accumulation of the specified certifications will not be left to the closeout phase, and this issue, therefore, should be one of identifying the few unfulfilled requirements and ensuring ultimate availability.

Identify Outstanding Vendor/Subcontractor Commitments

Every open purchase order and subcontract should be reviewed to identify all outstanding vendor/subcontractor obligations. The closeout of each order should be handled with the care and effort given the closeout of the prime contract. The project manager should classify each obligation as either mandatory, desirable, or no longer necessary in preparation for a negotiated settlement with the vendor or subcontractor. Mandatory items must be completed, desirable items can be resolved through negotiation (either completed, settled financially, or deleted from the scope in trade for other work), and the unnecessary items can be dropped from the scope of supply or used for trade in reaching a compromise. The classification decision may not always be left to the project manager's discretion. The client has the last word regarding his/her expectations which reflect the client's interpretation of the prime contract.

Completed purchase orders and subcontracts also require consideration, as their obligations may have been erroneously filled, leaving the project manager with the responsibility for correcting the discrepancy. Obviously, the project manager's clout with the vendor or subcontractor is diminished once the order is closed and the project will likely incur the cost of any corrective action required under this condition. Therefore, extreme caution is advised to avoid premature purchase order or subcontract closeout. Where possible, include retention in the purchase orders or subcontracts and link acceptance of the item or service, furnished therein, to acceptance of the prime contract's scope of supply.

Figures 1 and 2 contain general checklists for the close out of open purchase orders and subcontracts. Specific checklists should be prepared by Purchasing and

Description	Action by	Due date	Actual date

Material/Service

    Material/service as specified (latest P.O. revision)
    Proper quantity received
    Material not damaged in transit
    Packaging per specification
    Identification markings per specification
    Specified checkout/startup service provided

Paperwork (Content/Quantity)

    Invoices
    Packing lists
    Shipping papers
    Approval drawings
    Shop drawings
    Certified drawings
    Test reports
    Material certifications
    Performance certifications
    Operating instructions/manuals
    Maintenance instructions/manuals
    Catalog "cuts"
    Inspection reports
    P.O. acknowledgements on file
    Computations/engineering reports
    Progress reports
    Schedules
    Tax certificates

Payments

    Invoiced amount matches P.O. amount
    Backcharges to the vendor—identified
    Backcharges to the vendor—negotiated
    Vendor cost increases—identified
    Vendor cost increases—negotiated
    Discounts—identified
    Discounts—taken
    Payment terms satisfied
    Retention—held
    Retention—period identified

Figure 1 Purchase order closeout checklist.

Description	Action by	Due date	Actual date

Material/Service

    Material/service as specified (latest P.O. revision)
    Codes and standards satisfied
    Proper quantity received
    Packaging per specification
    Identification markings per specification
    Specified checkout/startup service provided

Paperwork (Content/Quantity)

    Invoices
    Packing lists
    Shipping papers
    Approval drawings
    Shop drawings
    Certified drawings
    Test reports
    Inspection reports
    Daily reports
    Progress reports
    Material certifications
    Performance certifications
    Time and material records
    Operating instructions/manuals
    Maintenance instructions/manuals
    Insurance certificates
    P.O. acknowledgments on file
    Punch lists
    Schedules
    Tax certificates
    "As built" drawings
    Union labels
    Underwriters approval
    Certificate of occupancy
    Release of liens
    Progress payment applications
    Change requests

Payments

    Invoiced amount matches P.O. amount
    Backcharges to the subcontractor—identified
    Backcharges to the subcontractor—negotiated
    Subcontractor cost increases—identified
    Subcontractor cost increases—negotiated
    Discounts—identified
    Discounts—taken
    Payment terms satisfied
    Retention—held
    Retention—period identified

Figure 2 Subcontract closeout checklist.

Subcontracts, relevant to the content of the primary contract; addressing the three basic areas of each order: material/service supply, documentation, and payments. Each open purchase order or subcontract should be evaluated to identify its incomplete aspects. The material/service supply requirements should be checked to determine if the specified performance and quality have been satisfied, the proper quantity has been furnished and all physical goods were received without damage. Packaging and marking requirements, if specified, should also be verified. Documentation should be checked to determine if the required paperwork, in the correct quantity, has been supplied. The payment requirements should be checked to ensure that the payments due the vendor or subcontractor are consistent with the order papers, change orders and backcharges have been reported and their costs substantiated, retention withheld and the quoted discounts considered. In dealing with a consultant subcontract, the emphasis shifts from hardware or system supply to the provision of a service, and the "subcontract closeout checklist" must be adjusted accordingly.

Screen Incomplete Tasks for Need

Once the remaining deliverables, certification needs, and outstanding commitments have been identified and evaluated, screen the incomplete tasks for need. Knowledge of your open contractual obligations should be used to determine if the tasks still in work are truly necessary. Tasks or work packages, defined at the project's onset, may no longer be relevant because of contract changes or alterations to the project execution methodology; or an originally defined effort may not have been necessary for contract completion, but remains on the list of things to be done. In other cases, tasks or work packages which are essentially completed are kept open because the individual executing the effort has some "loose ends" to clean-up. The tendency to avoid task completion adds to project cost and clouds the true picture of the project's schedule status. If the remaining effort is not necessary for contract closeout, or is not relevant to the technical and financial data-gathering process, then the task or work package should be closed out with no further expenditure of funds. Identification and closeout of the tasks or work packages which drag on after their primary objectives have been satisfied should not be left to the contract closeout phase, but should be addressed during project execution to avoid excessive costs and the misuse of limited resources. Contract closeout screening should be limited to the few tasks which remain active at the end of the project. The result of the screening process will be two lists of the open tasks and work packages—those requiring no additional effort which can be closed, and those which must be completed to meet contractual requirements. A finite punch list must be defined for each incomplete effort to be used to monitor and expedite its completion.

Close Open Work Orders/Work Packages

Once the screening process has been completed the open work orders/work packages can be systematically closed. The aim is to first reduce, and then totally eliminate the work orders which represent places for people to charge their time—a reality of project life which unjustly increases the cost of execution. First address those work orders/work packages which the screening finds obsolete. Their authorization must be formally terminated to prevent further charges. Allow the active functions to proceed to completion, but do not permit them to drag on longer than necessary. Use the punch list to monitor each active work order/work package. Stress timely execution of the open issues, and once the requirements are satisfied, formally terminate the activity. Purchase orders and subcontracts should be treated in the same way. Systematically settle each open order with the vendor or subcontractor based on your classification of their unfulfilled commitments.

Control Project Charges

As a project approaches completion, charges to its cost accounts escalate as its open charge numbers become fair game to the entire organization. Familiarity with a par-

ticular charge number makes it accessible when completing a weekly time sheet, while
others view a project nearing completion as a convenient place to "bury" some undesirable expense. Extreme care is required to avoid such inadvertent or deliberate mischarges. The cost collection system must be designed to respond to a work order termination notice so that charges made after the charge number has been formally closed
will not be accepted. The project manager, in terminating a work order, must ensure
that its charge number is closed concurrently. During the contract closeout phase,
the periodic cost reports must be reviewed more carefully to prevent undesirable or
erroneous mischarges or system abuses.

Communicate Closures

The requirements of the various closure tasks defined on the CWBS must be fully understood by the individuals responsible for their execution. The project manager's role
is to ensure communication of this information and confirm understanding.

As the closure tasks are completed and the project staff is reduced, contact between
team members also diminishes. Therefore, a conscious effort is required to ensure
flow of the necessary instructions and timely work order/work package closeout and
work cessation. In addition, suitable feedback is required regarding compliance with
the defined requirements to ensure that the closure tasks are being executed effectively.

Implement the Warranty Program and Other Follow-On Activities

Since the contractually specified warranty program and other follow-on activities are
generally executed after the contract has been closed, these efforts are usually transferred from the project team to an ongoing functional group within the organization.
Retention of a project team for the execution of this work has proven to be a costly
and inefficient use of project personnel. This staff misuse can lead to the unavailability
of key skills for other projects, a loss of morale, development of bad working habits,
poor execution, and an unhappy client. The groups receiving the new assignments
must be provided the tools needed to perform these functions properly. Therefore,
the transition into the warranty program, or any other follow-on activity, requires a
comprehensive plan and an extensive level of control. The transfer of these future
tasks to other groups may require the transfer of technical information, material,
equipment, tools, training aids, manuals, drawings, test results, files, vendor data,
and possibly, project personnel. Of major importance is the transfer of responsibility
for the post contract effort. This entails a documented internal transfer of the work,
communication of this fact to the project staff, orientation of the individual assuming
responsibility for the work, and formal client notification of the change in his point of
contact for this effort. Orientation entails familiarization with the contract scope,
the scope of the specific follow-on activity, client communication channels and procedures, existing project problems, the present status of client relations and his expectations at contract completion, and the project manager's plan for completing the remaining contract work (i.e., scope, method of attainment, and schedule).

Client awareness of an internal responsibility transfer is crucial to both contract
closure and future relations between organizations (postcontract and new endeavors).
At this critical contract stage, the client must not be confused or disturbed by a
perceived change or disruption in the project's working procedures. He should not
be permitted to manipulate his multiple points of contact by taking advantage of the
differences in their specific objectives and operating styles, or their possible internal
political differences during closeout. The project manager must remain the client's
primary point of contact and a unified front must be maintained until the contract has
been formally closed. In initiating a warranty program the client must concur with
the validity of the start of warranty, the established start date and the effectivity
period. The warranty terms are normally defined in the contract's terms and conditions,
making any additional warranty scope definition a moot point. In addition to formal

notification of the start of warranty, an introduction of the party responsible for warranty implementation to the client may be desired. Other client contact, unless a specific warranty issue arises, should not be necessary. Other types of follow-on activities (i.e., periodic inspections, follow-up training, operational assistance, performance evaluation, and maintenance service) will require a degree of client contact as his input will be needed for the planning and scheduling of these efforts.

Client-Related Issues

The client-related contractual issues are problems which must be resolved through direct dealings with the client. This requires a thorough understanding of the tasks and their true value to the project, an intimacy with the contract's technical and commercial elements, a working relationship with the client's representative built on trust and respect, an ability to negotiate the resolution of these issues, and the authority to make the commitments necessary for their resolution. Client-related tasks are discussed in the following paragraphs.

Confirm Remaining Deliverables with the Client

Once you have identified the remaining deliverables, it is necessary to confirm that the client has a similar perception of the "open" work. Items that are no longer required to meet the intent of the contract should be dropped by joint agreement to reduce the remaining effort and shorten the closure period of performance. The obvious intent of this negotiation is to achieve agreement with the client regarding the level of performance that he or she is willing to accept as satisfactory. This minimizes the remaining contract work without detracting from the quality of the supply or degrading the working relationship and long-term reputation with the client.

Meet the Specification or Negotiate a Settlement

Once the remaining deliverables have been identified and agreed to by the client, consideration should be given to your ability to meet their specifications. If the system or hardware falls short of the contract requirements, a decision must be made regarding the approach to be used to resolve the open issues. An effort should be made to modify the deliverables to achieve the specified results, but if this effort proves too costly or time consuming, a settlement may be necessary. A settlement can be reached through client acceptance as a concession, trade-off for some desired requirement not specified in the contract, or a direct cash settlement. Contracts frequently contain a "Liquidated Damages" clause which assigns a penalty for a failure to satisfy a particular specified requirement (i.e., delivery date, performance levels). At some point in the closure process it may become apparent that the requirement cannot be satisfied and the penalty must be paid. A decision to stop further efforts to attain the specified level of performance and either seek a compromise or pay a penalty requires an evaluation of the alternatives. The cost of meeting the specification must be compared with the cost and other implications of a compromise solution. In preparing for such negotiations, remember that a client who feels that the basic needs have been satisfied by your efforts, will be likely to accept a shortfall condition which does not materially affect performance of the delivered items with little or no penalty. This cooperative nature is a function of the client's basic satisfaction with your performance to date, higher confidence in your organization and its assurances of your support after contract closure, the relationship developed with the project manager and staff during contract execution, and a feeling that any negotiated settlement will not be a one-sided situation.

Negotiated/Settle Open Contract Changes and Backcharges

During the course of the project, contract changes may have been authorized by the client for which a final price had not been established, or certain work may have been performed by the client in your behalf. Before the final payment is made and the contract closed, these items must be resolved. Appropriate and adequate supporting document will be needed to settle these issues. Ideally, no change in scope should be implemented until a change in the contract (price and schedule) has been authorized by the client. However, if directed by the client in writing, certain work may be undertaken if the client explicitly agrees to pay for the actual expenses incurred or is willing to negotiate the cost at a later date. In these cases the written authorization and detailed records of your actual expenses are critical to a trouble-free settlement negotiation. Acknowledgment that the work was actually performed, in the form of time sheets signed by the client's witnessing representative, will be even more effective. In the case where the client has directed you to perform certain tasks which you as the supplier deem to be a contract change, but are considered to be part of the basic scope of work by the client, supporting paperwork becomes even more important. If such disputes exist upon direction to perform the work, the client must be notified of your disagreement and an effort should be made to secure a resolution before the work commences. If the client is not willing to compromise at that time and directs immediate execution (possibly through his legal rights defined in the contract's terms and conditions) he should be advised in writing of your disagreement and the fact that you are "reserving your rights" for future negotiations.

With this paperwork properly done, you are obliged to execute the disputed work. Witnessed records of the actual effort expended are mandatory. The client's representative will be reluctant to sign for this effort, as his or her signature could be taken as an authorization; but a qualified signature, stating that the work was "witnessed but not accepted as a change in contract scope," should be relatively easy to obtain. Resolution of this type of open issue will require a compromise settlement, unless clearcut proof of either position can be made. It is unlikely that the original opinions will change, and you must, therefore, be willing to negotiate. Litigation, although highly undesirable to both parties remains an ultimate solution. Backcharges (payment claims by the client for work performed in your behalf) represent similar situations except that the roles are reversed, and his or her right to undertake such work will probably be defined in the contract documents. Supporting documentation will also be important in this case, when attempting to negotiate a contract settlement. When advised that the client plans to undertake work in your behalf, acknowledge either agreement or disagreement and demand the maintenance of records which your field representative will sign. Negotiating a price before the work is performed will simplify the contract closure process.

Obtain/Submit Required Certifications

Certifications represent a class of documents, required under the contract, which attest to the validity of the achieved performance or scope of supply. Even though system or hardware performance satisfies the client's expectations, the contract cannot be closed unless the appropriate certifications have been furnished. The certification needs identified under the internal tasks must be fulfilled. This documentation, properly executed and prepared in the required quantity, must be collected from the appropriate source and submitted to the client for the record.

Invoice for Final Payment

Submitting the final invoice for payment represents the culmination of the closeout process, which most people assume is the final step, occurring only after every other issue has been resolved. However, expediting the cash inflow and thereby reducing the financial expenses associated with the outstanding receivables should be the project manager's primary objective at closeout. Therefore, the thrust during close out should be directed toward reducing the outstanding amount due by:

Pressing for reduction of the retention (the amount withheld from the periodic invoices to protect the client from performance shortcomings) as the outstanding obligations are fulfilled, without waiting for the completion of all work.

Preparing and submitting contract change and backcharge claims as quickly as possible.

Providing a detailed justification and all available backup material with each claim.

Developing the backup data when the work is being done and not after the fact.

In evaluating the validity of a client's claim and the cost of making the corrections required to meet his expectations, it may be cheaper to accede to an unjustified demand if the cash inflow can be expedited by making such a concession. A protracted dispute over the scope of supply can seriously delay receipt of the final payment, as this represents the client's primary leverage at the end of a project.

Making necessary concessions in negotiating backcharges and contract changes.

Expediting the completion of the contract scope of supply to enable prompt final invoicing.

Controlling invoice paperwork processing. Don't assume the corporate "system" automatically processes the correct documentation.

Vendor/Subcontractor Issues

Vendor/subcontractor tasks are issues which must be resolved through direct dealings with these supporting external organizations. In each case, the supporting effort (equipment supply, hardware fabrication, software development, technical or administrative services, construction, and so forth) is governed by a purchase order or subcontract. Execution of this legal document places the project manager in the role of client and the party furnishing the specified material or service in the role of supplier. This apparent role reversal is not difficult to accept, as the implementation and closure processes in these areas are usually managed by the project team's procurement specialists (purchasing agents, buyers, subcontract administrators), whose primary skills and training are in these administrative areas. In this capacity they are the supplier's "client" and primary contact. However, technical support may be needed from other members of the project team when the supplier has not fulfilled his contractual technical performance obligations. The procurement specialist must have a thorough understanding of the controlling documents (purchase orders; subcontracts; technical, performance and test specifications; general terms and conditions, project specifications, and the applicable codes and standards); a position regarding your supplier's completed and remaining work; a working relationship with each vendor or subcontractor; and the ability, willingness, and authority to negotiate the resolution of any open issue requiring settlement. Vendor/subcontractor tasks include:

Confirm Outstanding Vendor/Subcontractor Commitments

The "punch list" of incomplete issues developed internally for each open purchase order or subcontract must be confirmed with the applicable supplier and an agreement reached regarding which items will be completed, modified, or dropped. A change order must be issued to conform the original document to the revised scope of supply and, if necessary, to adjust the price and delivery. Upon confirming the remaining work, a schedule commitment for its execution must be obtained from the supplier. The schedule is used to monitor performance and to hold each supplier to his word. The sooner the vendor or subcontractor fulfills his open commitments, the sooner final payment can be negotiated and paid.

Negotiate Open Vendor/Subcontractor Change Orders and Backcharges

Purchase order/subcontract closeout not only requires completion of the specified work and submission of the required documentation, but also entails negotiation and payment of a final price. The payment secitons of the checklists found in Figures 3 and 4 should be used as a guide to the execution of this task. To close out a purchase order or subcontract the invoiced amount must match the value authorized in the controlling document. Quantities, unit prices, labor rates, discounts, and fees should be checked for compliance. Arithmetic—both your and your supplier's—should be checked. Make certain that items of supply have not been invoiced more than once and don't treat an invoice for retention payment as an additional obligation, if the retention has been included in a prior invoice, but not paid. As the client in this negotiation scenario, demand adequate justification and backup for the supplier's claims. Predetermined labor and material rates for changes and backcharges, delineated in the purchase order or subcontract, will simplify this process. Expect the supplier to be as thorough in his claims, as you are in making such claims to *your* client. Make this chapter required reading for the supplier. Where justified, negotiate a price reduction for work deleted from the scope or for work which you or another supplier may undertake in your supplier's place. To complete the closure process: verify completion of all work in accordance with the controlling documents, identify and take the appropriate credits and discounts, reconfirm supplier warranty and other post order responsibilities, establish applicable retentions (cost and duration), and make final payment.

Field Tasks

Field tasks are issues which must be resolved at any project location removed from the project office. The primary difficulty in addressing these problems stems from the remoteness of the activity from the organization's base of operations and the increased influence that the client may exhibit in his own "backyard." Less effective communications and a difficult-to-manage chain of command become the major obstacles to efficient field closure. Specific field closeout tasks include:

Obtain Client's Punch List

After the specified system or hardware has been delivered, installed and made functional, all deliverables must be jointly inspected with the client to determine his perception of their respective operational shortfalls. A formal "punch list" (a list of discrepancies which the client expects to be rectified before acceptance) should be requested to establish a limit of the remaining work required by the client to comply with the terms of the contract. You must help the client realize that the contract cannot go on forever and that your cooperation and support under its terms must be restricted to a reasonable level, as acknowledged in a well-defined "punch list." The "punch list," as any other request for work, must be assessed to determine its contractual validity. If the requested work is justified it should be performed, but if she claim is for work beyond the scope of the contract, the request should be treated as a potential contract change. Remember, the intent of the "punch list" is to define the limited amount of remaining work which will satisfy your client and will thereby delineate your open contractual obligations. Acceptance of added work, either as "punch list" items or as contract changes will serve to extend the closeout date. Such efforts should be avoided if possible. The benefits gained from executing additional work must be fully understood and should far outweigh the implications of a protracted project closeout.

Make Necessary Corrections

The client's "punch list" should be analyzed for contractual validity and ease of execution, and the requirements negotiated. The obvious issues should be settled quickly, devoting negotiating time to the "gray" areas. As many unnecessary items as possible should be eliminated. Trading off easy-to-achieve noncontractual items for the more difficult requirements which your client may be willing to forego should be considered. The goal of this negotiation is to limit the extent of the remaining effort, while ensuring client satisfaction with the work. An unreasonable attitude on either side can lead to a serious disruption of the closeout process. Many items on the "punch list" may not be justified, but if they can be done easily, the long-term relationship with the client will be enhanced. If an item on the list is believed to be beyond the contract's scope, negotiate its removal. If the client insists on execution, the project manager should justify his or her position and submit a formal change request. The suitability of either a fixed price or a "time and material" change order should be considered. The work in dispute should not be performed until an agreement has been reached. If directed by the client, the work should be executed and the project manager should "reserve his or her rights" for settlement at a final contract closeout negotiation. The client's views may be altered by the project manager's cooperative effort or the discovery of additional support for the claim. At the least, the claim may be used for trade in settling other issues.

All "punch list" issues should be settled quickly, since an extended execution period can be exploited by an unreasonable client for the identification of additional items of work. Vendors and subcontractors must be advised of their open responsibilities (the project manager's "punch list" which may contain additional requirements beyond those specified by your client) and their concurrence and a schedule commitment for the work must be obtained. An established retention in their order or contract will assure greater cooperation (at least to the extent of the remaining financial obligation). A vendor or subcontractor who procrastinates in either admitting responsibility, or in performing the work can seriously jeopardize the planned contract closeout. Such nonsupport, which is not an uncommon occurrence because of the suppliers limited obligations, may require execution of the work by the buyer's staff or by an alternate supplier. In such cases the delinquent vendor or subcontractor must be given formal notice of his failure to perform and the buyer's intention to execute his work. If an acceptable response is not received within a predefined time period, the work is done and its cost is deducted from the retention. If the retention does not cover the cost or retention has not been established, and the supplier is unwilling to make the necessary restitution, then legal action and/or dropping the supplier from your qualified bidder's list must be considered. Once an agreement has been reached and the responsibility for each item identified, the work should be executed expeditiously.

Prepare As-Built Drawings

If required by contract or mandated by an internal policy, "as-built" drawings must be prepared to reflect the actual configuration of the project's deliverables. The original drawings are modified at the home office, but the detailed information generally comes from the field. Collection of this data is either accomplished by a project field representative or by a vendor or subcontractor, if specified in the agreement.

Field changes to the original design to make the system "work" or to make the components fit together at installation should be recorded on a set of master drawings as they occur. This will ensure availability of a record of all change conditions required for "as-built" drawing preparation and will preclude the problems inherent in researching the changes at the end of the project when the modification may no longer be visible or accessible; the responsible party may have left the site; and memories, in fact or for convenience, grow dim.

Prepare a Final Field Report

A final field report should be prepared describing all operational, implementation, and construction problems. This report can be used to define and implement a follow-on upgrade project and to prevent a recurrence of these problems on similar projects in the future. This report should also reflect the field staff's implementation experiences and should be used by engineering and design to simplify future field efforts.

Demobilize Physical Facilities

Once the client has accepted the contract deliverables and all contractual field activities have been completed the site facility should be demobilized. All tools, test equipment, office furniture, trailers, and so on should be returned to the home office or rental agency or transferred to another site. Files, drawings, reports, photographs, test and operating data, and any other information on file at the job site should be reviewed for need. Redundant information should be discarded and the material deemed valuable should be returned to the home office files. Contract-specified spare parts should be formally turned over to the client and a receipt obtained to confirm delivery. Other material of value should be assessed and either returned to the home office, sold for scrap, or given to the client for his use. Most leftover material will have to be discarded. It may be necessary (either by contract or by a desire to retain a favorable impression with the client) to return the field site to its original state (regrading the property; demolishing temporary roads, parking areas, and work laydown areas; and possible landscaping). Therefore, don't leave the site until the client has expressed satisfaction with your restoration effort in writing.

Organizational Tasks

The organizational tasks may be further classified as technical and administrative, based on the area affected by their execution. Although these tasks have no direct bearing on the contract and the closeout process, they are extremely important to the organization, as they respond to both immediate and long-term needs. Systematic disassembly of the project organization, its facilities, and equipment represents an immediate requirement; and the collection and assimilation of project information into the organization database represent a long-term requirement. The significance of these functions makes the organizational tasks as important as the contractual tasks—they must be given equal attention. Delaying these activities in deference to the contractual tasks will diminish, or totally abrogate, their potential benefits. The longer one waits to perform these tasks the more difficult efficient execution becomes.

Technical tasks represent the functions of collecting data related to the technology developed during project execution and transferring this data from the project to the appropriate functional groups within the organization. If effectively done, the project provides more than a profit margin, as it contributes to the technology base upon which the organization has been built. Technical tasks include:

Critique System or Hardware Performance

"We've been doing it that way for years and it still doesn't work," is a tongue-in-cheek expression describing the perpetuation of a bad design long after its flaws have been recognized. Regrettably, there is more truth than humor to this saying as many organizations fail to learn from their past mistakes and continue to repeat them. To paraphrase Santayana: Those who fail to remember a project's history are destined to repeat it. Our efforts are of little value if we don't learn from our mistakes, as we will most certainly repeat them. Conversely, a financially unsuccessful project can prove to be successful, if the lessons learned in failure can benefit the organization in the long run. Prior to project closeout, or as soon as practical thereafter, the performance of the system or hardware developed under the contract should be evaluated under its operating conditions to identify its true capabilities and its fundamental weaknesses. A structured, short-term, performance test will not be adequate, as too many test conditions will influence the results. Performance tests are run in a controlled environment and are programmed to ensure successful passage. On the other hand, the operators are not really familiar with their jobs and have not "pushed" the system or hardware to its limits. In addition, "shake down" may not be completed, as the pressure for system validation, and subsequent project completion, may cause the performance test to be run prematurely. The collected performance information should be objectively evaluated by the technical groups to determine how the system or hardware *should have* been initially designed. This feedback information can serve as the base-

line for future projects and can be used as the basis for an upgrade of the product
under scrutiny.

Critique System or Hardware Technical Effort

A critique of the system or hardware technical package (drawings, manuals, computations, software, instructions, training programs) should be made for the reasons described above. The results of the critique should be transmitted to the organization's
functional groups to improve future performance and to provide a basis for improving
the evaluated product.

Consolidate/Distribute Project's Technical Data

Consolidation and distribution of the project's technical data will contribute to the organization's technical data base and should prove useful on other projects. In addition,
this information can be used to support follow-on activities such as service, warranty,
operational retraining, periodic inspections, spare parts provisioning, future upgrade
projects, and the supply of like or similar additional units. In most organizations,
retention of relevant project files for a fixed period (10, 15, or 25 years) is mandatory
in the event they are needed to support a litigation defense. The increased number
of product liability cases in recent years will attest to the need for consolidation and
retention of relevant project files for potential future use.

Administrative Tasks

Administrative tasks represent project disassembly and the collection and assimilation
of administrative data for future organizational use. If properly executed, these activities will provide benefits similar to those gained in the technical area. Administrative
tasks include:

Indentify/Dispose of Physical Facilities

The physical facilities accumulated during the project's course must be identified and
disposed of to minimize project charges. Physical facilities such as buildings, trucks,
machinery, construction equipment, office equipment, tooling, trailers, computers,
furniture, test facilities and equipment, automobiles, when no longer needed, should
either be transferred to other projects, returned to the corporate inventory, or sold
to recover their salvage value. If performed efficiently, this process will curtail internal project charges at the earliest possible time. It will convert idle, usable material into a cash inflow, improving project financial performance. If no savings can be
achieved, at least the material can be put to better use in other areas which have a
specific need.

Indentify/Evaluate Project Personnel

As part of the contract completion process the project manager must identify and evaluate each member of the project staff in preparation for his ultimate disposition. In a
large, multilocation project, awareness of all personnel and their particular talents and
capabilities by the project manager may not be practical. Yet efficient contract closeout not only requires the release of staff as early as possible, but is also expected
to ensure appropriate reassignment within the organization with minimum loss to the
outside. If not properly managed, a project can be plagued by a large number of resig-
nations, even if other job opportunities exist within the organization. The loss of key
personnel will not only disrupt the project completion process, but will also result in
the organization's loss of a significant portion of the technology developed during the
project.

Select Personnel for Reassignment

Since the contract closure process continuously reduces the remaining tasks until all
requirements have been fulfilled, commensurate staff reduction becomes a necessary
aspect of the process. A well-planned reassignment program is necessary, as the
natural conflict between the desire to put your people to work on new endeavors and
the need to maintain a suitable staff for the completion of the open work must be considered. The natural tendency for the project manager is to keep the good people as
long as possible to ensure effective execution of the remaining tasks, but both the needs
of the organization and the individual must be considered. New projects must be staffed
with the best talent available for the long-term benefit of the organization, and the
emotional and professional growth needs of the individual must also be considered. Exceptional project performance should not be rewarded by holding the individual back
when a growth opportunity arises. Balance your project's needs with the needs of
the organization and its employees. When making necessary transfers of key personnel
obtain a commitment from their new manager for the part-time use of the transferred
individual if specific problems arise.

Reassignment Methodology

Establish a formal procedure for staff reassignment. A formal project closure plan will
define your expectations for the completion of the remaining work. From this plan,
resource requirements can be defined in terms of skills, quantity, and timing. Given
this information and a statement of the parent organization's needs on other projects;
a detailed staff reduction plan can be developed, identifying the approximate date at
which each individual will become available and, if possible, indicating the expected
next assignment. Publication of a staff reduction plan will assist the parent organization in its reassignment program, allowing adequate time for selecting the best person
available for each open position. One might question the advisability of informing the
staff of their expected completion date, as their level of effort may be negatively influenced by the knowledge of this information. However, evidence of a formal plan
and an honest attempt to identify the inevitable should be useful in motivating the staff
for execution of the remaining work. Being kept in the dark when the end is obviously
near creates fears and anxieties which can destroy an individual's desire for productivity. Awareness of an expected cutoff date and adequate lead time for the loyal individual to seek a new assignment or new employment will be appreciated; and a project
manager's honesty and openness will be rewarded with productive support.

Dispose of Unused Project Material

During the course of the project large quantities of raw materials, components, rejected
parts, partially completed assemblies, test assemblies, samples, catalogs, manuals,
vendor data, files, and drawings are accumulated. These items must be disposed of
before the project can be considered complete. The project manager frequently dumps
the unused material or "walks away" from it, leaving it to be dumped by those who
have a need for the occupied space. Although time consuming, careful scrutiny followed
by rapid disposition will prove beneficial. Parts and raw material can be salvaged for
other applications or for use as spare parts, useful data can be cataloged and stored
for the record or for other applications, valuable scrap can be sold for cash and to
free storage space, and the remaining useless items can be discarded.

Consolidate/Distribute Project's Financial Data

Consolidations, evaluation, and distribution of project financial performance results
will provide feedback to management on the reasons why the project failed to perfectly
track its financial plan (budget and spending plan). This type of information will support a better assessment of the project manager's performance and, if properly used,
can improve management's skills in evaluating estimates, budgets, and spending plans

for future projects. In addition, the estimating department can use the actual data to expand its estimating database and evaluate its estimating performance on the completed project.

DEALING WITH THE EMOTIONAL ISSUES

The process through which one addresses and resolves the previously discussed intellectual issues is easily grasped and understood by most project managers, as the concepts are generally akin to their professional background and educational experiences. Dealing with emotional issues, however, requires an understanding of human behavior and the psyche; areas of study to which most technical project managers have never been formally exposed. At best, the project manager's "people skills" are self-taught or developed "on the job", yet the need for these skills grows as the project draws to a close. To deal with the emotional issues effectively, one must first recognize the issues and their causes, and then address the manner in which each person on the project is affected by them. This entails knowing the personality and psychological makeup of each project team member and each relevant member of your client's project staff; and dealing with each unique personality separately to achieve the desired motivational results. This obviously requires a major portion of the project manager's time and energy at the end of the project, when the emotional issues intensify and are more difficult to resolve.

The Issues

The emotional contract completion issues, issues shown in Table 1, are further defined as relating to the project team and the client. As previously stated, the issues affecting team spirit can be controlled to a degree by the project manager, but an uncooperative client can prove to be an insurmountable handicap if allowed to resist settlement and contract completion.

The emotional issues affecting the project team (both individuals reporting directly to the project manager and those individuals in the functional areas of a matrix organization) can be further described as being motivational and procedural. Motivational issues relate directly to the people involved in the project and the factors which either drive them or inhibit their personal dedication to the work for which they have an assigned responsibility. Specific motivational issues will be discussed in the following sections.

Loss of Interest in Remaining Tasks

The excitement of working on new concepts and applying novel approaches which characterize the kickoff and implementation phases of a project are often lost at the closeout phase, as the work becomes more tedious and less imaginative. Creative aspects of the job are replaced by clerical or administrative functions. Documentation must be completed; computations cleaned up and assembled into a usable format; data sorted and the relevant information cataloged and filed; and the loose ends which were deferred in order to address more pressing issues at the time, must now be completed. The fun has gone out of the work and the professionals needed to complete the effort no longer have an interest in the drudgery. Their time is spent either avoiding the needed effort or seeking other, more challenging assignments. Their lack of interest results in poor performance when they do get around to completing their work. Other team members may be talented in perceiving and addressing "the big picture," with little ability in dealing with the details. When confronted with the closeout effort, which is primarily concerned with details, they may be incapable of an acceptable level of performance.

Fear of No Future Work

When the end of a project is in sight, the obvious question asked by each staff member is: "Where do I go from here?" If the answer to this question is not clear and no future assignment is on the horizon then foot-dragging or slowdown becomes a reality. Fear for their future influences their actions; as their interest is diluted, either by their efforts to find other employment, or their planned or subconscious desire to extend their present assignment. Drawings become hard to complete, data and files are conveniently misplaced, tools are lost, parts for the last unit of a multiple quantity contract have been either "bastardized" or pirated for earlier unit application and are no longer suitable for their intended use, final vendor deliveries are not expedited, and even sabotage has been known to occur. In general, there is no desire to finish the project, as project completion may mean unemployment for the individual.

Dissatisfaction with the Next Assignment

As a corollary to a fear of no future work, others may be concerned with the scope and quality of their identified next assignment. The next assignment may be viewed as a demotion, the group to which an individual is to be assigned may have a bad reputation, his prior or expected relationship with the new supervisor may be unsatisfactory, or the work may appear to be unchallenging and unrewarding. Dissatisfaction with management's future plans or a fear of change can have the same results discussed above. The impact on the project may be the same, but the approach needed to understand and motivate such individuals will differ greatly from the techniques needed to deal with a fear of no future work.

Loss of Project-Derived Motivation

The concept of a project mission which is shared among project team members, has been identified as one of the practical advantages of a project structure (Middleton, 1967); and the effective project manager uses this common set of goals to build his team and develop staff loyalty during the early phases of the project. Unfortunately, as project completion nears and the mission is either achieved or recognized as unattainable, this common bond diminishes. The project team and its objectives become less important and the individual's concerns become personal. Further deterioration results from loss of interest in the project, as stated above, and from the staff reductions which occur during closeout. The project manager can also lose interest at the end of a project, as his major achievements have been recognized and management's interest in the project begins to wane. The resulting lack of management attention can certainly demotivate the project manager normally driven by a need for achievement and the reward of management recognition.

Diversion of Effort

Once the primary project objectives have been achieved and management's interest in the project diminishes, the project and functional organizations consider the project's importance reduced. This perceived loss of priority influences their attitude toward the remaining project tasks and other work becomes more important. The apparent low priority becomes the functional groups' excuse for working on the more exciting aspects of newer projects in deference to the mundane tasks of the project in close out.

The procedural issues deal with closeout processes which can influence project team motivation. As a specific closure process, each procedural issue becomes a task on a closure work breakdown structure that has specific objectives which can be satisfied by a finite expendture of effort. They have, therefore, been discussed in the section dealing with a project's CWBS. However, the project manager must not forget that proper handling of the procedural issues is necessary for a healthy approach to project team motivation and efficient contract closure.

The emotional issues relating to the client are also further classified as motivational or procedural issues. Client personnel, like the internal project staff, undergo changes in attitude as the project approaches completion. The client has either gotten the results he was looking for and is now interested in other things, or he feels that the contractual relationship has deteriorated to a point where little more can be gained. In addition, the emotional factors affecting your project staff, equally affect the client's staff. Supporting groups lose interest, are concerned about their personal futures, and feel the loss of prestige when their management lessens its interest in the endeavor. Although the project manager has no direct influence over the client and his staff, an awareness of the effect of the emotional issues on these people can be useful in his closeout relationships. Understanding their concerns and the reasons behind their lost motivation can be useful in settling the open issues, either through negotiation or by making concessions. The client motivational issues include:

Change in Attitude

In reaching the closeout phase of a project, the client's representative has gone through a difficult period, operating under pressure from both his management and his supplier(s). "Burnout" is not uncommon at this point, as the client's representative has worked hard in attaining the desired results. It is likely that the system or hardware is working at or near specification, but the client's management may be looking for the solution to specific problems that have not been resolved or they may be seeking increased performance. At the same time he can expect minimal support from the supplier, as he seeks closeout of his project. Now that the supplier has little to give, the client may resort to a tougher attitude, refusing to make concessions without major compromises by the supplier. Other clients may take an unreasonable approach, asking for more than they are entitled to by contract (either intentionally or through a biased interpretation of the agreement), before accepting the system or hardware. They try to keep the supplier committed to the project to extend his support. Others may remember the difficult relationships which occurred during the course of the proejct and may deem closeout as a "get even phase."

Loss of Interest in the Project

Once the system or hardware is in place and working, the client can lose interest in the project. His attention may turn to an improvement effort which the supplier may not be expected or required to support; other elements of his project may require greater attention now that your effort is near completion; he may be assigned to a new venture or may be planning his return to a line function within the organization; or he may be preoccupied with his personal future, which his management may have failed to address. In any case, the close working relationship that existed during the project will weaken during the closeout process. There is little benefit to the client in aiding your quest for a rapid, trouble-free closeout. In addition, your client's staff will undergo a loss of interest similar to the loss of interest experienced by your staff. They too, will be harder to deal with because of a general lack of interest, an unwillingness to finish, and a fear of an uncertain future.

Procedural actions by your client can also influence your closure effort. Staff reassignments and the thrust of other efforts can affect the level and timeliness of the client's cooperation in reaching a satisfactory conclusion to the project. With its major needs satisfied, the client's management has less interest in a contract closeout and may direct its project staff toward other areas requiring their attention. Typical client procedural issues include:

Changes in Personnel Assigned to the Project

As the project draws to a close, the client will withdraw his development team and install an operating staff. Design specialists will be needed elsewhere to initiate new ventures, while the people who will be expected to operate the system or hardware for the long-term must become comfortable with it. The cadre of new people are anxious to become familiar with the project, but have little interest in its controlling contract. The operating personnel often impose personal requirements on the supplier; requesting things they would like to have which may not have been specified in the contract. Their lack of familiarity with the contract and its terms makes closure negotiations far more complex.

Unavailability of Key Personnel

The transfer at the end of the project of key client personnel responsible for project inception and execution, is generally viewed by the client as having little effect on their effort, as specific people can be recalled as needed. However, such recall will only be effected when it suits the client's needs and not the needs of the supplier. The diversity of assignments and locations will limit their availability unless their management's needs are served; and your requests may go unheeded for an extended period, before the required individuals can be reached. Their removal from the project will also hamper the closure process as memories will falter and access to the files will become more difficult once new assignments have been undertaken.

Their Resolution

The emotional issues confronting the project manager during contract closure are similar for his internal staff and for his client, as the project seems to follow similar patterns in both organizations. In each case the work become less creative and more detail oriented, the next assignment becomes a major concern for the individual, and new assignments remove key personnel from the project or detract from their commitment to it. In addition, the two organizations grow apart as their need for each other diminishes. Although similarities in attitude and cause exist, the project manager must address the emotional issues in each area differently. The issues affecting his internal organization can be resolved using his authority, influence and power. Factors which have been enhanced during project execution, if a degree of project success has been achieved. Yet these factors will not influence and/or control the client's organization.

   In dealing with the project staff at closeout, the project manager must recognize that the team which was built to initiate and execute the project has been dispersed and the esprit de corps that held the team together no longer exists. To effectively complete a project it will be necessary to restructure the team and rekindle the spark that motivated them. This task will be more difficult than the original team-building effort because of the extensive emotional issues affecting staff behavior and his possible lack of personal motivation. In addition, the project manager will find it difficult to invest much time and energy in this endeavor, as he may perceive closeout as a short-term effort; and team-building for the short term, a waste of his time. In reality, it is the extent of the emotional issues that creates the demand for his attention to the team at closeout; and if not completely addressed, these issues will significantly hamper the closure process. The project manager must therefore, reinforce his belief in the project and the importance of an effective closeout; and then redouble his team building efforts to ensure effective performance by the parties invovled.

   The project manager's positive attitude, sense of urgency, and enthusiasm were contributing factors to the original success; and he must continue to exhibit pride in the project mission and in individual performance; using these traits to sell his plan to management and the functional groups (Hamburger, 1984). He must recognize that failure to effectively close out a contract can reverse the benefits gained during execution. Management must also reinforce these beliefs to bolster the project manager at this critical period in the course of the project. In terminating an unsuccessful project, or one that was completed unnaturally, the project manager must be convinced that the organization can still benefit from an efficient closure. Once a positive attitude has been established, the project manager will be able to reassemble a team and "sell" them on the need for an efficient contract closeout.

Addressing project closeout as a distinct miniproject will require changes in the organization. Personnel who can and will support the effort must be retained while the others, who are no longer required, should be reassigned. Proper restructuring will not only assemble the best available personnel for the job, but will also help the project manager mitigate many of the emotional problems that can effect those who are left to finish the work. To restructure an organization that will best suit the needs of the contract closure process, the project manager should:

Retain the personnel best suited to the closeout process; people who understand the project's scope and contract terms, and who can deal with the detailed aspects of contract closure.

Develop and propose a staff reassignment plan; making each reassignment decision a conscious, deliberate choice. Consider the factors affecting each decision carefully; balancing the needs of the project, the parent organization, and the individual. Support of the parent organization and individual rewards are important, but these factors must not be allowed to debilitate the project team to the point of ineffectiveness. A published plan, based on a thorough analysis of needs, will foster a positive attitude within the project organization.

Openly implement the reassignment plan, providing adequate warning of an impending change. Keep the staff informed of your planned actions to avoid the rumors and scuttlebutt that can demoralize a team. Knowing that the project manager is in control of the reassignment process will be reassuring to the staff.

Play an active role in the reassignment process. Don't wait for the parent organization to take action. Implement your plan before external forces can disrupt your closeout miniproject.

Keep the project team informed about the status of other activities within the parent organization. An honest assessment of where the organization is going and the effect of the existing backlog on each ind vidual is important. If the future is bright, a positive attitude toward completing the project will result. If little or no work appears forthcoming, and the staff is aware of this fact, motivation will be more difficult, but the destructive effect of the "rumor mill" will be reduced.

To counteract the negative effect of the emotional issues on the project organization, the project manager must apply his authority, influence, and power to the maximum extent possible. He should take advantage of the fact that he has enhanced his actual authority from the momentum of his accomplishments on the project (Brooks, 1975), maintaining and using the status he has achieved. As the team leader, he must treat the staff with respect and openly support their efforts. He must continue to assume responsibility for their technical judgments without displacing their function. Maintenance of his leadership role will pull the project team together, in spite of the negative forces which tend to debilitate an organization when the end of its effort approaches. Staff motivation must not be treated lightly, as it will require his continuous attention throughout the closeout phase of the project. To recreate the project spirit and properly motivate the contract close out staff, the project manager should:

Define the contract closeout phase as a distinct miniproject with its own unique identity. Delineate the miniproject's objectives in a form that can be understood, accepted, and supported by the close out staff.

Prepare a detailed closure plan, based on performance input from the project staff, and obtain their commitment to it. Make sure that each member of the closeout team knows his or her specific role in the process and the tasks for which he or she will be held accountable.

Provide a team identity to stress the importance of the closeout effort. A new project name for the final phase, newsletters, periodic progress reports to the staff, promotional campaigns, and a reward system should all be considered as motivational tools. A common denominator is needed to unite the widespread project activities. A modest investment in some or all of these endeavors will be rewarded by the savings that can result from an efficient contract closeout.

Schedule frequent team coordination sessions. Unlike the execution phase of a project; closeout requires extensive group participation, frequent policy communication, and continuous project closeout status reporting. Informal staff get togethers; in place of lengthy meetings, controlled by comprehensive agenda; create the casual setting needed for staff interaction and the sharing of relevant experiences. Communication will improve and new ideas will have an open forum in which they may be discussed. Meetings will be necessary during closeout, but the constraints of a formal agenda will not foster the freedom of expression needed to enhance team spirit.

Use the staff to prepare for a client or supplier negotiation. Alternative tactics must be identified and evaluated, potential client offers must be anticipated, and the possible negotiation scenarios played out before a "devil's advocate" to develop a "feel" for the possible outcome. Participation in such brainstorming sessions will create a feeling of belonging for the attendees and their diverse input will improve the project manager's negotiation position.

Employ MBWA (management by walking around) techniques; get out and meet the people. Visit the closeout staff at their work place, either in the office or in the field. These visits should be used by the project manager to narrow the geographical gaps that may exist between elements of his closeout team. Show an interest in their efforts and provide the "warm fuzzys" and "pats on the back" needed to reward their efforts during this unrewarding phase of the project. Use these informal visits to reinforce the team's project team identity.

In preparing performance evaluations, establish the importance of the closeout goals and report on the individual's performance accordingly. Commendations for a job well done, or a memo to a functional manager or the person's next supervisor should stress the significance of the individual's contribution to the contract closeout process.

The aforementioned motivational tools lose their value in dealing with the client's staff, as the project manager has little or no authority, influence, or power in that organization. Yet client support is as important as the support of his project team in attaining an efficient contract closeout. To influence a client's actions, the project manager must first identify the client's needs and desires, and then address them to gain client support in reaching a satisfactory contract conclusion. Obviously, many client wishes will be inconsistent with the project manager's closeout goals, making total capitulation unrealistic. For example, the client will seek to minimize his total investment in the project, while the project manager will attempt to recover all justifiable costs incurred in the execution of the work. However, several common project and personal desires exist which can be accommodated in an effort to motivate an otherwise noncooperative client. Addressing these issues first will break down many barriers, creating a proper environment for negotiating the issues which represent conflicting goals. Specific supportable client goals include:

Trouble-free operation of the system or hardware furnished under the terms of the contract

Minimum administrative problems associated with closing out the contract

Receipt of the specified supporting documentation (drawings, manuals, bulletins, training aids)

Availability of spare parts and service over the useful life of the system or hardware furnished under the contract

Effective implementation of any post contract program including: warranty, periodic
   inspections, operational support, operator retraining, and system upgrading
Management recognition for a "job well done," in achieving the contractual objectives, and in effecting an orderly, uneventful contract closeout
A new assignment, following successful project completion (hopefully a promotion)
   unencumbered by a recurrence of time-consuming project problems

The project manager msut realize that his goals for a successful contract closeout
will not be attained unless the client and his staff are willing to cooperate. By addressing the client's goals, stated above, progress can be made. Once the client has been
convinced that a common set of objectives exists and a degree of satisfaction has been
achieved, he will be willing to negotiate a compromise on the remaining issues. Client
motivation through support of these common goals should naturally lead to an effective
contract closeout.

A PROJECT MANAGER FOR THE JOB

The project manager who organizes and executes a project may come to the completion
phase and find that his interest has diminished for the very same emotional reasons
that affect the project team's performance. In addition, he may lack the unique attributes required for an effective project closeout. When closing a project the project
manager must believe in the need for efficient execution and must be well versed in
the requirements of the project closure process. He must take the same pride in this
phase of the project as he did in planning the initial effort and in bringing the project
to the point of near completion. Management must recognize the project manager's human frailties, providing the motivation needed to "keep him going" until the project is
completed. Project manager replacement for project closure is a distinct possibility,
as reassignment to a new endeavor may be deemed necessary by management or the
particular individual may lack the specific skills required for managing the closeout
process. Such decisions must be made with the recognition that the newly assigned
individual will lack a significant amount of project awareness, and the working relationship established with the client in executing the project will be partially or totally lost
to the replacement project manager.

CONCLUSION

The attraction of project work stems from the challenge and excitement of creating a
unique product or system to serve a client's specific needs, and achieving the desired
results within predefined time and cost parameters—as specified in a contract—makes
project work even more appealing. Unfortunately, attainment of the primary desired
results, or recognition that the results are not totally achievable, will lead to a loss of
interest in the project before an effective contract closeout can be attained. The results-oriented approach to planning and implementing a project, which provides the
initiative and motivation needed to execute the work efficiently, is not always employed
when the detailed contract closeout tasks must be completed. Efficient contract closeout is essential for ultimate project success and the future growth of the project
executing organization. The significance of an efficient contract close must be
stressed, and the project manager and his project team suitably motivated for its
attainment. The personnel retained on the project team must be detail oriented, as
contract closure is essentially a miniproject consisting of a number of specific detailed
tasks. The closeout miniproject must be planned and executed with the vigor and
intensity that marked the project's "kickoff" and implementation phases. During
closeout, negotiation and compromise characterize the relationship between the project

manager and his client; and motivation represents his primary role in dealing with the project staff. Timely project closeout can mean the difference between a project's financial success or failure; a satisfied client and the potential for additional work, or an unhappy client who may be considering litigation; and a firm that benefits from a project's technological and administrative achievements, rather than one that cannot keep up with its competition.

REFERENCES

Lock, D. *Project Management.* Epping, England: Gower Press, 1979.

Hamburger, D. H. *Project Management—A Practical Approach.* Soundview Publishing, 1984.

Spirer, H. E. In *Project Management Handbook*, Cleland and King, eds., Chapter 13. New York: Van Nostrand Reinhold, 1983. Adapted from Figure 13-1.

Middleton, C. J. *How To Set Up A Project Organization.* Cambridge, MA: Harvard Business Review Reprint Series No. 67208.

Brooks, F. P., Jr. *The Mythical Man Month.* Reading, MA: Addison-Wesley Publishing, 1975.

2

Performance Tests

MICHAEL D. WINFIELD, NEWT M. HALLMAN,* DANIEL N. MYERS, and
O. J. SCHNEIDER   *UOP, Des Plaines, Illinois*

GENERAL PHILOSOPHY

The primary objective of performance testing is to obtain accurate data that will allow specific detailed comparisons of the actual plant performance, realized against the various original design criteria, and to summarize these data in compiling an overall plant test record. The project management will assemble large quantities of data, for the record, during performance testing. Essentially all of these data will more than likely match the anticipated values from the original engineering, design, and construction work.

It is also a project management function to identify and classify any apparent errors or discrepancies. These should then be determined as being attributable to the design (both process and detailed), supply, construction, installation, and/or operational phases of a project.

Secondary objectives also exist. Performance testing represents the best opportunity for establishing the actual plant and equipment performance, which can then be used as a reference base case for later evaluation purposes. Similarly, it represents an opportunity to establish the practical limitations that exist within the plant. For example, the testing should address the question of what level of production represents the practical maximum limit, and at what level of sacrifice in quality.

This is also the time when management can choose to focus efforts upon adjusting the unit performance, as much as possible, to the realities of the marketplace. This can, and often does, involve sacrificing or ignoring some of the original design criteria.

The most important testing to be completed is that which will ultimately prove or disprove the validity of the licensor's or designer's technology. Since this can be done only by evaluating the many individual component results, each data point recorded is important. The licensor or designer may point to individual component deficiencies as the justification for failure of the plant to demonstrate represented levels of performance. Only through careful documentation during the course of the entire project can the ultimate testing of the plant be held as valid.

Proper timing of performance testing is important. Testing is normally the basis for transfer of responsibility. Ideally, operational capability should be demonstrated before transfer of responsibility of the individual components, and ultimately of the entire plant. Yet although some delay in testing can be useful, the project manager has a vested interest in initiating comprehensive testing early, so that individual component deficiencies do not hold up the entire plant completion.

---

*
Retired.

As objectives are identified and put in priority, an overall testing philosophy must be developed specifically for each project. Major testing requirements may include product quality tests, equipment tests, and catalyst stability tests.

Legal agreements may provide both the basis for testing and for determining how errors may be assigned to the organization responsible for correction. If the project team does not conduct testing, which is consistent with the plant design criteria, and consistent with the legal requirements, unfavorable settlements may result, or worse, may go uncorrected.

In some cases the legal responsibility for correction might rest with an organization that was not, in fact, responsible for the work leading to the error. This could arise when a contractor holds product quality guarantees for a plant using a proprietary catalyst that is supplied by a third party. In such situations, it can be very important that precise data be recorded in order to clearly establish the deficiency.

Specifically, such legal requirements are usually detailed in a document called the guarantee agreement. In scope, a guarantee agreement establishes the relationship between the designer and the owner with regard to performance guarantees. A good agreement should be sufficiently specific to protect the rights of both parties. However, excessive detail can severely limit the applicability of a given agreement. As a simple example, specifying an excessive number of parameters in a feedstock definition (particularly for individual units) can later prove extremely restricting in executing a performance test. Also, since there is normally a sizable time lag between formulation of the agreement and actual testing, allowances are sometimes included to consider modification of the agreement. If design feedstock becomes unavailable, provisions can be included to evaluate and reformulate the guarantees, based upon available feedstock.

A typical guarantee agreement protects the rights of both parties by including terms to establish provisions for:

1. Inspection to certify conformity to design
2. Supervision of commissioning, initial operation, and testing
3. Definition of suitable feedstock
4 Allowable operation time and conditions prior to testing
5. Testing to demonstrate operating conformance to represented capacity, yields, product quality, and catalyst durability, as applicable
6. Rectification of design errors, if any
7. Liquidated damages for failure to attain guarantees
8. Limitation of liability
9. Termination of the agreement

In this chapter, we do not provide an exhaustive discussion of the broad area of performance testing and the legal implications, but rather focus on the primary components of determining overall plant operating performance. Information on specific guidelines for equipment testing or unit performance testing can be obtained from a literature search for the applicable area of interest. The current availability of microcomputers and modems in the field office makes this an easy task. The search can be conducted using services such as APILIT, Engineering Information Inc., or Food Science and Technology Abstracts. Other hardcopy sources would include the API, ASTM, and ASME.

The project manager and staff must address many areas of testing, which can include product quality, hydraulic capacities, utility consumption, equipment performance, and catalyst performance. Although we are primarily concerned with the overall performance, comments are included to address specific areas of concern to the project manager.

BASE PERFORMANCE LEVELS

The project management team should be interested in more than just those items specifically guaranteed. A comprehensive summary of detailed observations of equipment performance while all pieces of equipment are still new and presumably performing at their optimum levels, will later prove to be an invaluable reference. Sufficient data should be gathered to evaluate individual equipment performance by comparison against vendor representations. For example, calibrated single-gauge pressure and temperature surveys should be conducted around all significant pieces of equipment, such as reactors, heat exchangers, fractionators, fired heaters, and rotating equipment. The flow, position, and pressure drop across important control valves should be measured and recorded. The utility consumption of individual pieces of equipment and major sections of the process unit and offsites should also be noted.

Since baseline testing will record such items as equipment pressure drops, temperature profiles, and vibration levels, these measurements can be checked periodically to determine if obstructions, fouling, or excessive wear are occurring. Operations and maintenance personnel can use this information when problems develop at a later date, or to determine when a piece of equipment needs cleaning. Reference to this base data by plant operations management after a long period of plant operation can enable efficient detection of performance problems such as exchanger fouling, control valve plugging, and deterioration of rotating equipment output.

UNIT HYDRAULIC LIMITS

The project management team should also use this opportunity to secure other useful information such as the maximum capacity of the unit. A capacity test is usually performed by gradually increasing the capacity of the units until a bottleneck appears, such as off-specification products, or a safety or mechanical limitation. Bottlenecks can occur in fired heaters (overfiring), distillation columns (poor fractionation), reactors (high pressure drop or poor product quality), rotating equipment, and control valves. A record of this information is most valuable when the time comes to consider expansion of the capacity of the plant.

It is usually best to conduct the capacity test before the departure of commissioning advisors so that their observations and recommendations can be obtained. For example, a plant may be able to process 120% of the design feed rate, but only at the cost of higher reactor temperatures and lower hydrogen-to-hydrocarbon ratios. The licensor can advise as to the effect on catalyst life, and the vendor representative can confirm that continued operation of the compressor or other equipment at these conditions will not have an adverse impact on the ultimate life of the equipment.

DEMONSTRATION VERSUS FORMAL TEST RUN

Often, the project manager is faced with a situation where testing cannot be conducted under the terms of the contract or guarantee agreement. One of the most common reasons for this is the lack of the design (guaranteed) feedstock. For example, the sulfur content of the feed to a distillate hydrotreater may be only 70% of the design value. Since this feed is easier to process, the unit will not be fully tested. The opposite situation can also arise. If the feed to a hydrotreater contains significantly more sulfur than design, the licensor may refuse to conduct a test run with this feedstock. As another example, the guarantee may require a 7-day test period. If the market cannot absorb the products that will be generated during 7 days at 100% charge rate, the licensor may be asked to accept a shorter test period.

If a full-scale official test run is not possible, a demonstration run can often accomplish the same objective. A demonstration run is not legally binding to either party and, thus, the conditions become more flexible. For example, licensors will usually have no objection to operating hydrotreaters with a high feed sulfur content if the refiner is willing to accept a product sulfur level that may exceed the guarantee value. If the product meets marketing specifications, both parties may be satisfied. If a demonstration run meets all of the product guarantees, it may be later redesignated a test run for record purposes. If the demonstration run does not meet all of the guarantees, it can either be repeated under different conditions, or it can be accepted with the nondesign feed or process conditions.

SINGLE UNIT VERSUS MULTIUNIT COMPLEXES

The project management team faces various alternative when multiunit complexes must be tested. The choice will depend on the sequence of unit start-ups, utility or secondary complex guarantees, the number of licensors involved, the intermediate storage capabilities, and the availability of manpower.

When considering units intended to operate together, the advantages are that simultaneous testing more closely approaches design operating conditions for the units as a whole, minimizes the period of testing, requires only minimal intermediate storage, allows close examination of how well the units integrate at design conditions, and avoids the necessity of making assumptions on complex balances such as hydrogen, fuel gas, fuel oil, and steam. The drawbacks are that it may stretch the available manpower (particularly laboratory and plant operating personnel), may require cooperation and agreement among several licensors, vendors, and subcontractors, and may be sensitive to unit interruptions.

Breaking up a complex performance test into individual unit tests has the advantages of lower peak manpower requirements, more limited scope of work to be repeated if the test is unsuccessful or is interrupted, and more flexibility with respect to unit battery limit conditions required by different licensors. The major disadvantages are that the overall period for testing is prolonged, more intermediate storage is generally required, unit integration with the complex cannot be fully evaluated, and complex material and energy balances require calculation and assumptions that can result in inaccuracies.

No single approach will work in all cases. Often some compromise such as testing of various product trains separately may be the preferred choice. It is the responsibility of the project management team to evaluate its requirements and limitations before deciding on the appropriate test method.

EQUIPMENT TESTING

The project management should assign experienced equipment specialists to review specifications in sufficient detail to assure that correct equipment was supplied. For heaters and heat exchangers, the vendor typically uses his own thermal design rating and quotes his equipment on that basis. The vendor then provides guarantees of both the thermal and mechanical performance on this basis. For rotating equipment, industry standards such as API standards are referenced to assure that conservative design guidelines are followed. The project team should review the testing requirements, which are detailed in the equipment specifications.

Typically, vendors expressly warrant equipment for the first 12 months of operation, or for 15 to 18 months from the date of shipment. Often the project schedule is such that equipment is no longer under warranty when the plant actually starts up. This situation emphasizes the need for the project team to take steps early in the project to assure that high-quality equipment reaches the field, and that the associated warranties are maintained to the greatest extent possible.

Aside from express warranties, the equipment supplied also carries implied warranties. Among other things, the equipment supplied must fit the contract description, be of average quality, be suitable for its ordinary uses, and operate within the variations permitted by the purchase agreement. Sufficient attention should be given to establishing testing that certifies that the equipment meets its express, as well as implied, warranties.

Shop Testing

Rotating equipment lends itself well to shop testing. Defects can be discovered and corrected in the shop much more easily than under field conditions. By shop testing rotating equipment the project team can be best assured that most pump and compressor problems can be found and corrected prior to delivery to the site.

Typical testing for a centrifugal compressor would include: rotor balancing, four-hour mechanical test run, and a full performance test with the specified molecular weight gas. For critical pumps, a typical testing requirement would include a performance test and NPSH suppression test.

Field Testing

In the plant design phase, critical pieces of equipment are selected for possible field testing. The main examples include heaters and exchangers. In addition to checking the installation and equipment, the field testing of equipment allows identification of inadequate equipment and may indicate the necessity of further testing, or perhaps even replacement.

Fired Heaters

During the product test run, the heater performance is evaluated by obtaining the following data around the heater: process composition and flows, sufficient temperatures and pressures to allow calculation of the heater duty, waste heat recovery flows, and sufficient temperatures and pressures to allow calculation of the waste heat recovered.. On the combustion side of the heater the following data are required: ambient air temperature, air preheat temperature, air flow, heater bridgewall temperature, flue gas temperatures into and out of the waste heat recovery system, stack temperature, fuel gas flow rate and composition, flue gas analysis draft profile, and other data to permit calculation of the heater and overall system efficiencies. In most systems, the vendor's guaranteed efficiency values (one to two percentage points below calculated) are easily reached, particularly if heater specialists have generated the thermal design.

The heater data taken should be used to make comparisons of actual heater operation against vendor representations. Observed efficiencies should meet or exceed vendor guarantees at rated capacity. Usually the heater will be running somewhat below rated capacity during the performance test. However, occasionally heaters are running at rated capacity or above during the performance test. This can arise because of underperformance of upstream heat exchange equipment.

Exchangers

Normally only heavy duty, key exchangers are fully evaluated during the test run. Properly designed exchangers will normally perform satisfactorily during the test run. One case of a badly underdesigned exchanger required more than two years to resolve. A third identical exchanger was required, since the two original units did not perform the desired duty. Complex negotiations were required to determine the cost split between the designer (contractor), fabricator, and end user.

During the performance test, a single calibrated gauge and portable potentiometer should be used to collect the following data: hot side and cold side flows, compositions

622

and temperatures, both in and out. With these data, the overall heat transfer coeffi-
cient and duties should be calculated and compared against vendor data sheets. Clean
exchangers often perform better than vendor representations. This clean performance
data will serve as a baseline from which fouling trends may be observed. The measured
pressure drop should be compared against the vendor predicted values. If the observed pressure drop is significantly greater than expected and causes flow restrictions, a design error or physical obstruction may be the cause. There have been situations where an exchanger bundle was installed backwards by a contractor, so that an
impingement baffle blocked the outlet nozzle. If no physical cause can be found to
explain the problem, the vendor should be contacted.

Pay particular attention to large items, such as combined feed/reactor effluent exchangers, which may recover as much as 80% of the exchange heat load of a process
unit. A small degree of underperformance can cause a large load to be placed on associated fired heaters.

For air coolers, measure the velocities and temperatures to obtain air side flow
and temperature profiles. Air coolers are normally designed for hot ambient air conditions, which may or may not coincide with the ambient temperature during the performance test. Poor performance may result from such mundane items as loose belts on
electrically driven fans. Check heat transfer coefficients and pressure drops against
vendor data sheets. Note gross deficiencies for further investigation and resolution.

Rotating Equipment

For both compressors and pumps, the test run is utilized to establish baseline performance and compare the test conditions versus the shop test results. Pump and compressor performance field testing should include single, calibrated pressure gauge surveys
to measure the pressure differential developed by the piece of equipment. Record flows,
temperatures, and compositions of fluids. Map performance of the equipment on pump
and compressor curves provided by the vendor. The curves used may be obtained
from the vendor catalog or from performance tests run in the shop.

Compare driver power requirements to the vendor-represented values. Check large
condensing steam turbines to ensure that steam consumption is not excessive. Measurements to check steam turbines include steam flow, temperature and pressure at the
turbine inlet. Calculate horsepower work load from the load or output end of the train.

Comprehensive field testing of a compressor can be done, but requires elaborate
measuring devices and the attendance of vendor personnel to conduct the test. If any
problems develop in the field, they may be difficult to correct. Shop testing is recommended over field testing because of better-controlled conditions and improved ability
to remedy any problems that develop.

In summary, field testing serves to establish baseline performance for the various
pieces of equipment. Gross inadequacies can be discovered during the test run screening, but when experienced process and equipment specialists have been involved in
specification and purchase of the equipment, instances of underperformance will be
very rare. Shop test everything possible, such as pumps, compressors, and fans.
For items which cannot be shop-tested, particular attention should be given to the design, specification, and purchase of the equipment. This will minimize problems in
the field and make field testing for equipment performance guarantees more of a baseline test than a measure of underperformance of poorly designed equipment.

PROCESS UNIT TESTING

The key to successful process unit performance testing is good organization by the
project manager and his team. Experience has shown that careful planning can save
time and money by avoiding repeated testing, as well as by avoiding placing individual
pieces of equipment into modes of operation that are outside the design conditions.

The complexity of a process plant makes it more difficult to test than an individual piece of equipment, but the basic testing principles remain the same. A successful test requires thorough preparation, careful execution, and proper documentation. This effort is most likely outside the capability of one individual. Accordingly, the project manager must properly assign specific responsibilities to individuals who will be able to assist with the various aspects of the performance testing.

Preparation

Careful planning and coordination is required for a successful test run. Specific duties should be assigned to the appropriate trade specialists to ensure their participation and involvement. All professional and nonprofessional staff must work smoothly together if the test is to succeed. Once the project manager has advised those involved of their individual responsibilities, he must continue to follow through to ensure that all is accomplished according to the plans. The following guidelines are suggested:

Define Operating Variables

Conduct a careful study of all plant and equipment operating variables. Design values and equipment limitations should be noted. These values, together with the actual operating conditions, should be used to develop a set of operating parameters that will be followed during the test. Since there will be a number of individuals present during testing, each representing different interests, the basis, including what and by whom, for adjusting or altering conditions during the course of the test, must be clearly established prior to testing.

Select and Analyze Feedstocks

Selection of a performance test feedstock can sometimes be quite difficult. The desired feedstock is the design feedstock, since expected equipment and process performance are already known. In the case of a licensed process, a contractual performance test may be specified that allows no options. However, if the test basis allows, and an alternative feedstock is selected, a careful feed analysis should be made, and new performance values calculated for the process and equipment using the licensor or vendor correlations.

Summarize Anticipated Test Results

Convey the goals, objectives, and duration of the performance test to all parties. This is extremely important when multiple companies or organizations are involved, since a misunderstood test basis can often lead to disputed test results. This possibility can be avoided by preparing a document listing all test objectives and procedures, and distributing it well in advance of the test so that all parties have time to properly review and agree on the test basis.

Organize Data Reporting

Develop a common procedure to collect and evaluate the data. The same procedure should be used by all organizations to avoid potential disputes caused by differing data or calculation methods. Procedures needed are detailed below.

Data collection: Establish a common system for data collection, ensuring that data are collected in consistent units of measurement. Agreement is needed on log-sheet format and frequency of plant and equipment operator readings, as well as those readings to be taken directly by members of the project management test team. Log sheets should be constructed for the process plant, feed, intermediate and product tankage, as well as all equipment to be tested. Equipment and system tests often include heaters, exchangers, pumps, compressors, columns, and hydraulic and energy surveys. The associated piping and instrument drawings should be checked for adequate temperature, pressure and flow measurement points. Agreement must also be reached by interested parties as to the data-averaging period, and which are the "official" flow or other readings. For example, it must be decided whether to use analog chart recording averages or point measurements, or similarly, totalizers or tank gauging to record flow rate data.

Sample analysis: Establish a laboratory schedule that permits daily operational analysis and evaluation. The analytical workload during a test will be much heavier than during normal operation. Thus, the cooperation of the laboratory staff is essential. The laboratory should have the opportunity of reviewing in advance the analyses required. This will ensure that schedules and staff coverage can be adjusted to avoid any adverse surprises. In addition to practicing analytical techniques involved with new or unusual analyses, it may be necessary to secure additional equipment, supplies, and reagents. It may be necessary to engage the services of an outside laboratory to ensure that all necessary data can be obtained. The laboratory schedule should include stream description, analytical method number, and sample frequency. Provisions also should be made to keep "retain" samples, which can be either duplicate or daily composites, until there has been a consensus on the test results.

Data evaluation: Standardize calculation methods. Each method should be well documented and list all formula and data sources (e.g., flow meter, temperature, pressure indicator numbers). The project manager must ensure that these are developed well in advance of the test so as to avoid any potential last minute debugging.

A typical calculation that must be standardized is the process unit's weight balance. An accurate weight balance is essential to demonstrate that feed and product flows are internally consistent with a typical order of accuracy of plus or minus 2%. There must be agreement on the calculation procedures. Otherwise, a disputed test result may occur because of disagreement on production or feed rates. This situation could easily develop if flows are calculated by different methods such as tank gauges versus orifice meters. It is also particularly important in the case where a plant test is being conducted that includes several individual process units. For example, an overall hydrogen balance can be quite complex if there are several process units that are either producers or consumers of hydrogen.

An integral part of data evaluation is data organization. Develop data, operations, and analytical summary forms to help sort the hundreds or thousands of data values generated daily.

Specify Outsider Organizational Structure

Performance testing commonly involves outside personnel, which will include vendor and/or engineering company representatives. These representatives are often responsible for specifying test conditions and adjustments. A system should be set up to accommodate them within the project organization. Preparation also should include securing more than the normal amount of maintenance personnel, as well as access to an adequate supply of spare parts and consumables. The goal is to minimize any mechanical problems that could jeopardize the testing.

Check Operability

Check to ensure that all instrumentation is operational and properly calibrated. Special attention should be given to items that have a direct influence on the performance test goals and objectives. Flow meter calibration is such an item, and it is important to confirm that all transmitters and orifice factors have been checked. On-line analyzers are another area of particular concern, and all should be serviced and operating correctly before proceeding with the test.

Adjust and check all pieces of equipment at anticipated test conditions. Analyze all streams and confirm that product yields, purities, and rates are within performance limits.

Execution

Continuous steady-state operation is required for a performance test. A test conducted during transient conditions should be avoided, since the results can be misleading or even erroneous. The period of time necessary to reach steady state is commonly referred to as the lineout. This period varies for different process units. A simple process may require only a single shift, while a complicated process may require a week before all streams have reached a steady-state value. Most performance test programs incorporate a minimum three-day lineout before starting the test.

The lineout is a critical part of the test procedure. It is the last chance to get everything right before putting the unit on test. The project manager must ensure that all aspects of the unit from operations to calculations have been checked and adjusted. Specific individuals should be responsible for the following: monitoring all instrumentation to ensure it remains operational and properly calibrated, adjusting and checking all pieces of equipment at test conditions, and analyzing all streams as necessary.

The performance test is ready to start at the end of the lineout period and should proceed smoothly if the preparation and lineout phases have been successful. Data collection and laboratory analyses should occur as scheduled allowing daily evaluation and adjustment. However, problems can occur. Utilities and equipment can fail, upstream or downstream units can have trouble; there are hundreds of possibilities. Since all upsets have an impact on the test, it is important to keep detailed and accurate records of any deviation. These deviations, and the daily observations, should be written into a performance test log. To the greatest extent possible, agreement should be immediately reached to establish the basis under which the testing may continue once it has been interrupted.

Documentation

The performance test report is the end result of the performance testing program. The importance of compiling a thorough report cannot be overstated. It is often the sole means of communication between the various organizations and companies involved in a testing procedure. Technically, it is a permanent record of everything that transpired during the test, and it presents the conclusions, observations, and data developed during the test. Legally, it is an important document, since it contains the records that may be required, should a legal dispute develop.

The performance test report should be a well prepared document, because of its importance. Information omitted will become information lost as soon as the primary parties leave the scene. The following guidelines should help in developing a well-organized, well-documented report.

Daily Results Summary

Reports should include:

1. Name, address, and location of company where testing is conducted
2. Complete legal name of process tested
3. Introduction, stating purpose of test
4. Body, containing the actual versus the anticipated test results. Discuss all events that have had an effect on test results
5. Conclusion, reviewing the results of the test in context with the original test basis including a recommendation or decision to accept or reject the goals and objectives of the test
6. Attachments to the report, including daily data, operations, and analytical summaries, and all data from equipment and system surveys
7. Deviation summary, listing all departures from testing procedure (unit upsets, equipment problems)

8. Testing log, containing record of daily events
9. Record of names and titles of personnel involved in the testing organization

Evaluation of Results

In most cases the project manager plays a critical role in evaluating the results from the test or demonstration run. If all of the guarantees were met, and there were no mechanical problems, then the decision to accept the unit is an easy one. However, if one of the guarantee values was not achieved, or if mechanical problems were encountered, the decision becomes more difficult. Judgment is needed to balance the shortcoming against the economics of putting it right. If the problem affects the capacity of the unit or the salability of the products, the economic impact is serious and obviously must be corrected. If the problem is mainly aesthetic in nature, its correction may not be economically justifiable.

If one of the guarantees was exceeded by a wide margin, a credit for the over-performance could become an issue. However, it would be more likely to arise as an issue relating to the contractor rather than the licensor. This is because the licensor's concerns are related more to underperformance during a performance test, and any credit for overperformance has usually been provided for. Examples would include royalties in his licensing provisions when the plant is to be operated continuously at a higher than represented capacity. The contractor often requests that provisions be included for overperformance credits. This may result especially from a case where the contractor faces equipment performance liabilities or utility guarantees. In this case, overperformance in one piece of equipment, or excess credit in one form of utility, might be used to offset a shortfall elsewhere. For example, the test may show significantly higher than expected high-pressure steam generation, but at the cost of higher fuel or electric power consumption.

There have been cases where all of the product quantity/quality guarantees were met, but mechanical problems prevented the acceptance of the unit by the client. In one instance, the recycle gas scrubber of a distillate hydrotreater experienced severe carryover of amine with the scrubbed gas. During the test run the unit was able to meet all product guarantees without the scrubber in operation. Even though the performance of the scrubber was not a guarantee point and did not affect the quality of the products, the project group refused to accept the unit until the carryover problem was resolved. The licensor complied with a minor revamp, even though there was not a clear cut contractual obligation to do so. The incentive was maintenance of his engineering reputation and good will to the customer.

The completed plant test record documents all aspects of plant performance capabilities. It assures licensor, designer, contractor, and owner of the quality installed. It serves as an evaluation basis, often for the entire operating life of the plant. The performance test, assuming it results in plant acceptance, is usually the last major task of the project management team. With this successful conclusion, it is certainly an appropriate time to pause and celebrate the fruitful culmination of the many years of project activity.

XI

PROJECT MANAGEMENT
IN SELECTED FIELDS

UNIT OVERVIEW

At one time, project managers were selected almost exclusively on the basis of their knowledge, experience, and technical expertise in the discipline most predominant in the specific project at hand.

Subsequently, a knowledge of project management technology assumed greater importance in this selection process. The ability to plan, schedule, budget, and control costs was a distinct advantage to the aspiring project manager.

More recently, project managers are being looked upon primarily as managers. Their managerial abilities are being given precedence over their detailed technical knowledge in either a related discipline or in the technology of project work. This is not to say that the latter talents are not important; only that the ability to manage is seen as being of greater importance.

The scope of project management techniques has expanded over the past 30 years to include many new additional industries and applications. Managing a project for a specific industry requires an understanding of any unique demands by the majority of the projects in that industry. We may conclude not only that each project has unique requirements; but also that the objectives and business conduct in each industry will impose certain blanket demands on the projects executed for that industry.

This unit considers some of the various industries which commonly employ project management as their method of introducing new facilities and operations. Among these are aerospace, electric utilities, federal and municipal entities, petroleum production, offshore or overwater facilities, and the use of research support in managing projects. Differences in emphasis and conduct of these projects are considered, each in its own general environment.

Despite the many significant differences illustrated, we cannot help but realize that the basic tenets of project management remain the same. They are repeated over and over in postulating how projects of all types may be assured success, regardless of the parent industry.

1

Electrical Utility Projects

KENNETH A. ROE and K. KEITH ROE   *Burns and Roe Enterprises Inc., Oradell, New Jersey*

Effective management of large power plant projects involves three key factors: goals, techniques, and measures.

First, clear and specific goals may be difficult to achieve; they must be attainable. With communicable goals, project personnel know what is expected of them and may measure their accomplishments against management's expectations.

Successful achievement of project goals demands effective management techniques. These techniques include establishing suitable schedules, budgets, forecasts, and reporting procedures as well as proper operating procedures. The project team must be organized around manageable units of work, and an efficient communications network must be created.

Finally, reliable and reasonably accurate means of performance measurement must be devised. Goals must be translated into action plans such as schedules, budgets, and quality standards. Actual performance is then compared against planned performance on each action plan. Timely monitoring of such measures allows prompt corrective action to be taken.

Whether a power plant is nuclear or fossil fueled will not change the basic management principles involved, but it will affect the character and degree to which management techniques are adapted to control the work. Figures 1 and 2 display typical organizational relationships and principal responsibilities of the major participants required for a fossil and nuclear project. The most noteworthy differences are:

1. On a nuclear project, more design responsibilities are placed on the architect/engineer
2. A nuclear project requires a greater number of interfaces between the project participants, equipment suppliers, and constructors
3. The A/E may provide construction management or construction services for a fossil plant

To better understand the management considerations that apply to electric utility projects, we briefly describe some of the important differences between a fossil-fueled and nuclear power plant. Table 1 compares some representative attributes for recent large nuclear and fossil plants 800 MW and larger. It can be seen that building volumes and certain bulk quantities can be as much as a factor of two higher for a nuclear plant than for a fossil-fueled plant. The relationship of the manhours required to design and construct these plants, however, are not linearly proportional to the quantities. This is because nuclear power plant work must comply with many more stringent safety requirements (e.g., design and construction to withstand loss of coolant accidents)

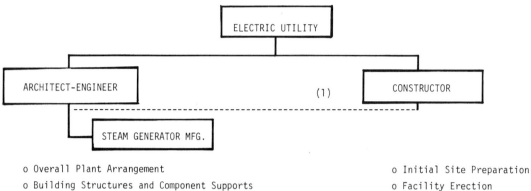

o Overall Plant Arrangement
o Building Structures and Component Supports
o Mechanical and Electrical Support Systems
o Steam Generator System
o Auxiliary Steam System
o Turbine Plant Systems
o Condenser Cooling Water System
o Particulate Removal System
o Flue Gas Desulfurization System
o Fuel Handling System

o Initial Site Preparation
o Facility Erection
o System Installation
o Final Site Preparation

(1) A-E may also provide:
  - Construction Management
  - Construction Services

Figure 1 Organizational flow chart for fossil-fueled power plant.

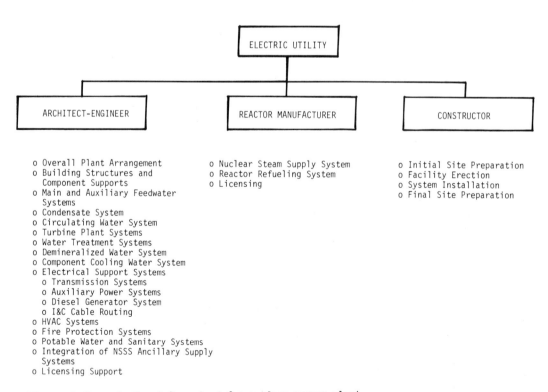

o Overall Plant Arrangement
o Building Structures and
  Component Supports
o Main and Auxiliary Feedwater
  Systems
o Condensate System
o Circulating Water System
o Turbine Plant Systems
o Water Treatment Systems
o Demineralized Water System
o Component Cooling Water System
o Electrical Support Systems
  o Transmission Systems
  o Auxiliary Power Systems
  o Diesel Generator System
  o I&C Cable Routing
o HVAC Systems
o Fire Protection Systems
o Potable Water and Sanitary Systems
o Integration of NSSS Ancillary Supply
  Systems
o Licensing Support

o Nuclear Steam Supply System
o Reactor Refueling System
o Licensing

o Initial Site Preparation
o Facility Erection
o System Installation
o Final Site Preparation

Figure 2 Organizational flow chart for nuclear power plant.

Table 1 Order of Magnitude Comparative Estimate for Large Power Projects

Description	Nuclear	Coal fired
Manhours:		
Design services	9-12 million	0.7-1.1 million
Site manual labor	27-32 million	8-11 million
Site nonmanual labor	10-14 million	1-1.2 million
Bulk quantities:		
Concrete (cubic yards)	210-250 thousand	120-140 thousand
Rebar (tons)	22-28 thousand	10-13 thousand
Structural steel (tons)	19-23 thousand	9-3 thousand
Piping (linear feet)	300-380 thousand	100-250 thousand
Cable (linear feet)	6-7 million	2-4 million
Cable trays (linear feet)	90-110 thousand	30-50 thousand
Conduit (linear feet)	475-550 thousand	100-250 thousand
Terminations (each)	180-250 thousand	100-120 thousand
Pipe whip restraints (each)	175-225	0
Building volumes (cubic feet):	17-20 million[a]	11-13 million

[a]Of this, 9-11 million cubic feet must meet the more stringent seismic criteria imposed by Appendix A, "Seismic and Geological Siting Criteria for Nuclear Power Plants," of the Code of Federal Regulations, Title 10 - "Energy," Part 100 - "Reactor Site Criteria" and Nuclear Regulatory Guide 1.29, "Seismic Design Classification."

and requires a much higher degree of sophistication in analytical methods, construction techniques, and a much greater amount of paper work associated with quality control and assurance.

The stringent requirements and increased quantities found in a nuclear plant create a unique set of criteria for the Nuclear Steam Supply System (NSSS) material and equipment suppliers that are not found in the design and construction of a fossil plant. The nuclear components are far more complex in design and have traditionally been custom built for a specific plant, which creates the need for an intensive interface between the NSSS designer and equipment vendor. Extensive testing, seismic qualification, and certification of material pedigree and component performance must be conducted by the vendor to ensure that the plant safety requirements can be achieved. Finally, NSSS components are costly and require close monitoring by project management of the vendor's cost and schedule performance.

In contrast to nuclear plants, component design for a fossil plant more closely follows a standard or proven design which results in vendor engineering data being available in the earlier stages of the overall plant design. Accordingly, the components generally are standard off-the-shelf items or components that can be constructed in a shorter period of time since they are less complex and do not require the extensive testing and certification that is required for nuclear components.

Finally, the greater complexity and stringent requirements of a nuclear project, place greater demands on the various engineering disciplines and related management and support than is true of a fossil-fueled project. Although the role and scope of the disciplines are much the same for the conventional buildings and systems of a fossil and nuclear plant, this similarity ends with the nuclear plants' steam supply system. The nuclear island and building structures' seismic and structural criteria; radiation shielding, monitoring and waste disposal; redundant and diverse instrumentation and controls and electrical power supplies; primary and secondary mechanical components and piping and related seismic and stress analysis; and nuclear design are some of the principal safety design requirements to be met to ensure the licensing of a nuclear plant. These additional design requirements can approximately double the civil/structural manhours required, increase the mechanical/nuclear manhours 6-7-fold, and the electrical manhours 3-4-fold.

Thus, in nuclear power plant project work, one must ensure that the management systems have the capacity to deal effectively with an expanded data base of planned activities. It follows that the greater the number of discrete activities, the greater the number of interfaces or interdependencies between the designers, equipment suppliers, and constructors. Unless carefully planned and monitored, an unexpected delay in any one of thousands of such interfaces can have a profound ripple effect on the overall project schedule and cost. Since power plant costs and capital financing account for approximately one-half of the total plant cost, the prevention of unexpected delays in schedule must be a major objective of project management to preclude placing an undue increased financial burden on the plant owner. It is not uncommon today for such delays to result in a plant's construction being indefinitely deferred or even cancelled due to the cost impact of the delay.

All power plants must comply with local and federal safety and environmental regulations, however, the requirements for nuclear plants go well beyond those imposed on fossil-fueled plants. Particularly, the necessity for auditable traceability of all design requirements on a nuclear project results in extensive quality assurance controls and the costs associated therewith.

The utility industry now, more than ever, must take a dedicated approach to achieving high plant availability and reliability due to the spiraling cost of power generation, whether it be through fossil or nuclear power generation. Fuel costs stop when a power plant is not operating, but capital, administrative, and maintenance costs must be paid whether a plant is producing electricity or not. Moreover, if a generating station is shut down for maintenance or repair, its usual output of electricity must be replaced by using a less economical standby station or by buying expensive replacement power from a neighboring utility. For these reasons, the reliability of a plant is crucial in determining the economics of a power plant. Additionally, public acceptance of a nuclear plant may be jeopardized due to the nature and media exposure given an unscheduled outage.

To achieve the objectives of high plant availability and reliability, the project manager, in concert with the client, should ensure that the design of a power plant use proven technology and a simple, practical design that allows for ease of inspection and maintenance of the plant components.

Power plant owners often have specific preferences with regard to types of equipment, operating and control philosophies, and maintenance provisions. Because each of these items can have a significant effect on the detailed design, close and continuous cooperation and coordination with the client is required of the project manager.

MANAGEMENT OF DESIGN ACTIVITIES

Engineering Schedule Control

All large projects require an overall integrated schedule. The schedule must integrate the engineering, procurement, construction, test, start-up, and turnover planning. Procurement must obtain vendor information to support design, while design must be completed and equipment delivered to support construction. In turn, construction must be completed in sufficient time to support test and startup.

For power plant projects, three levels of schedules are usually required with each level showing increased detail (Figure 3). Once the project is awarded, a Project Milestone Schedule is prepared. This Level I schedule illustrates, on a time-scaled logic diagram, the time requirements for license or permit acquisition, and major engineering, design, procurement, and construction activities. It is separated into the major

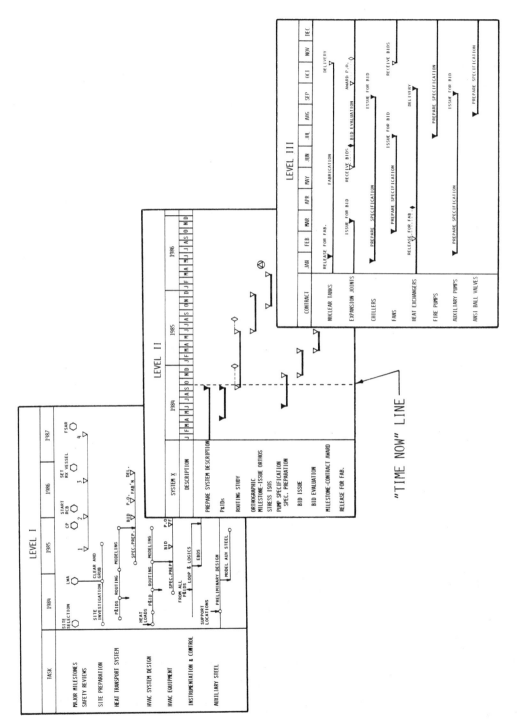

Figure 3 Project milestone schedule prepared for Levels I-III.

physical areas, and the relationships between the major events are shown. The Project Milestone Schedule is reviewed with the client and then used as a basis for preparing the more detailed schedules.

A time-scaled logic network that schedules every "deliverable" activity on the project in summary form is then prepared. Examples of activities on such a network (often called a Level II schedule) are: major studies, process and instrument diagrams, general arrangements, system descriptions, contracts, equipment specifications and deliveries, drawing groups, and major construction activities (erection of high-pressure piping). The critical path of the project is identified on this schedule. The Level II schedule is often computerized, and must provide sufficient detail to assess significant changes, but not so detailed as to demand excessive revisions. The Level II schedule is updated (usually monthly) by the use of a "time now" line and is used as a guide for preparation of still more detailed schedules: the Level III schedules.

Three distinct Level III schedules are normally prepared: a contract schedule, a drawing schedule, and a work schedule. All three schedules may be bar charts and should be updated at least monthly. The contract schedule contains a line item for each construction and prepurchased equipment contract. For each line item, specific checkpoints (such as issue for bids, award contract, release for fabrication) are used to monitor the progress. The drawing schedule lists all the drawings required for the project by number and title along with the drawing completion dates, based on the Level II schedule. Scheduled progress (in percentage completion) can then be indicated on the initial issue of the schedule and later compared with actual progress. The detailed schedule provided by each construction contractor is the third form of Level III schedule. This schedule defines the sequencing of work to be performed by the specific contractor.

The various project schedules are designed to be used together as an integral part of an overall project information system that includes engineering budget control.

Engineering Budget Control

Engineering budget control is usually based on a work breakdown structure (WBS) which organizes the project work according to: systems or facilities, activities, and functional groups or disciplines. A typical WBS first divides the project into major process or service systems and facilities. Each system or facility is then further subdivided into activities which must be accomplished to complete the systems. For each activity, the functional groups or disciplines needed to accomplish the work are identified. Figures 4 and 5 illustrate a typical nuclear and fossil project work breakdown structure.

Based upon the WBS and the manhour estimates for the project, budget is distributed to the functional groups in accordance with their requirements. Although project management requires firm leadership by a single individual, this leadership is made effective by assigning responsibility to the point of action—the point or level at which the individual or group performs the work or takes corrective action when required. Breaking down the budget by functional group assigns such responsibility. Each functional group budget is broken down into systems and then further subdivided into activities within each system.

Once a schedule has been developed, it must be resource allocated to ensure that the project cash flow requirements and available manpower are compatible with the overall schedule. In considering craft and equipment limitations, one should not schedule more work in a period than can be reasonably accomplished with the available manpower and/or equipment.

For the WBS to be effective, actual manhours expended must be entered into it on a regular basis and compared to the work accomplished to ensure that the actual progress is keeping pace with the expenditures and to preclude budget overruns. Input of actual manhours expended is usually accomplished by having all workers complete time cards on a weekly basis. Typical data entered on the card include: project,

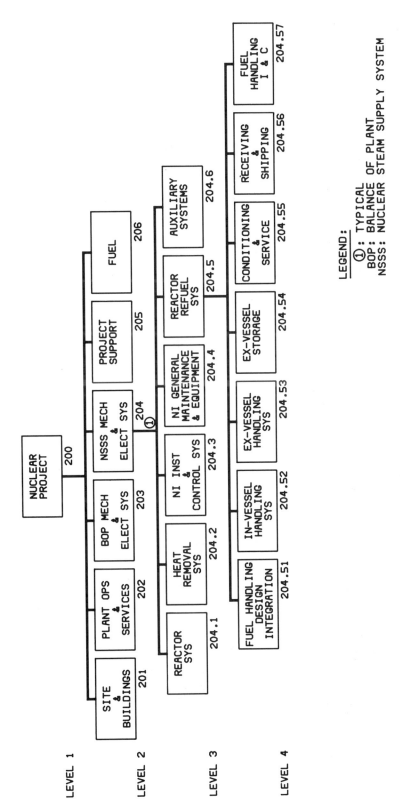

Figure 4 Work breakdown structure for nuclear power plant project.

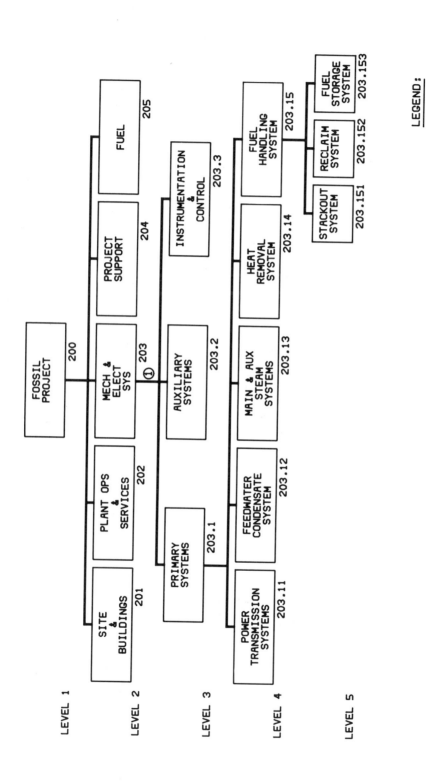

LEGEND:
① : TYPICAL

Figure 5 Work breakdown structure for fossil-fuel power plant project.

system, activity, functional group, and hours. A computerized system is required
to handle the quantity of data relating to budget control for even small fossil-fueled
power projects.

The engineering budget control system can be integrated directly with the schedule
control system if both are computerized. If not, they can at least be correlated by
using the activities from the WBS to develop the Level II schedule. From the resulting
overall project control system, a wide variety of reports can be obtained and used to
effectively manage the work. Two types of cost/schedule reports are commonly produced which correlate the manhours expended to the physical work (design/engineering)
actually completed. The first type provides all the data associated with a particular
system and the second type provides the data organized by the functional group. These
reports typically contain data relative to budgets, actual manhours or cost to date,
cost variances, schedules, schedule variances, and projections. Once this base of
cost and schedule data has been developed, it can be sorted by various parameters to
provide additional reports that are valuable in planning and monitoring work progress.

Ensuring Technical Quality

An important step toward high-level technical quality on any project is to assign competent professionals to the project who have the knowledge, experience, and time necessary to carry out the required work. This is extremely important for nuclear power
plants because of the complex and changing nature of nuclear regulations. These regulations have concentrated primarily on safety and licensing issues. Although the numerous environmental requirements and limitations that exist are applicable to nuclear plants,
they have a far greater impact upon fossil-fueled plants. This impact will undoubtedly
increase as concerns about emissions and acid rain grow.

The achievement of quality objectives ultimately becomes the responsibility of all
personnel associated with the project. The work must be carried out in strict accordance with a planned and disciplined approach to prevent conditions adverse to quality,
while assuring the prompt detection and correction of deviations.

Design Development

After the conceptual design is defined, the design continues to be developed through
the preliminary, detail, and final design phases. During this process, industry and
company standards are reviewed for applicability; engineering studies are performed
to assure that the maturing design meets established criteria, is based on proven practices, and is adequate for intended services; parts and material are selected; and acceptance criteria established.

Design Reviews

As the design develops, action is implemented at various points in the design cycle
to asure the technical quality of the design product. When the cumulative effect on
downstream costs due to incomplete, incorrect, or inadequate design is considered,
the importance of a proper design review cannot be overemphasized. In practice, design reviews can be categorized as intradisciplinary, interdisciplinary, and independent.

An intradiscipline review may consist of review by a competent peer of the responsible design engineer, and/or a review by the responsible technical staff or management.

Interdiscipline reviews are accomplished by specialty groups such as reliability,
quality assurance, constructibility, and test engineering; as well as by interfacing
disciplines/organizations that will be affected by the design or from whom design input
will be required. Intra- and interdiscipline design reviews are typically considered
part of the evolving working design.

Independent design reviews may be performed by outside consultants, off-project
personnel, or on-project personnel who have no direct responsibility for the portion of

design being reviewed. These reviews are typically performed when deemed necessary by the responsible engineering organization to evaluate a complex new design, or in the case of a nuclear plant, to satisfy the requirements of 10 CFR 50* on safety-related systems.

All design reviews should be documented, with the most complete documentation provided for any independent design review performed on safety-related items for nuclear power plant work. Independent design review documentation should include any checklists used, the names of the reviewers, issues or problems raised as a result of the review, how, by whom, and when the issues were resolved. Records of design reviews and other engineering documentation should be retained for the period specified by the contract or company policy, whichever is longer.

Fossil projects often replicate proven plant designs and, accordingly, design reviews performed on the original or "standard" plant are often applicable when supplemented by ad hoc reviews. Nuclear power plants may soon incorporate the concept of replication into the design process. Such an approach is expected to reduce the overall cost and schedule duration for these plants, in contrast to a situation wherein each plant is custom designed.

Design Control

Control of the design typically starts with the establishment of the design criteria. Later, parameters and other important requirements are recorded in an engineering log or notebook along with the basis for technical decisions such as calculations and studies. This logbook serves as an historical reference, providing the rationale for selecting specific designs. It also provides reference to the documents (specifications, drawings, etc.) used to arrive at technical decisions. All technical documents that have gone through the design review process must be approved by responsible personnel. Any changes to the technical documents should be reviewed/approved by the same organizations that performed the original review and approval.

An important tool, gaining in use for the control of design, is a plant scale model. Models have proven to be very effective in assuring design integrity and constructibility, returning their initial investment many times over in avoiding the need for rework. The development of an engineering model is an evolutionary process that begins with a basic model that is used to establish the civil/structural parameters: floors, walls, structural framing, and ceilings. The next stage is the design model, which reflects the actual design and construction of such system layouts as piping and cable trays. As the systems are installed in sequence in accordance with a predetermined priority, interferences are identified and resolved during the early stages of design rather than during construction, when changes would have much more impact on plant cost and startup schedule. Optimization of routing configruations for piping, cable trays, ductwork, and conduit is accomplished using the model as a three-dimensional visual design tool. The various design teams for each discipline use the model as the primary vehicle to ensure that the design meets operability, maintainability, and constructibility design criteria.

Ultimately, the model should be located at the construction site to facilitate final construction sequencing, component installation, and resolution of unforeseen design anomalies or interferences. The model may also be used for training plant operators as well as for planning future shutdown maintenance.

Although plastic models have been used almost exclusively in the past, computer-aided design (CAD) has enabled three-dimensional images to be produced directly as a product of design. The CAD systems are also able to automatically produce bills of

---

*Code of Federal Regulations, Title 10-"Energy, Part 50-"Domestic Licensing of Production and Utilization Facilities." Defines the criteria that must be met to license a nuclear plant.

materials and keep track of quantities and costs which will enable management to more closely control these costs. It is anticipated that the CAD models will eventually be able to perform all the functions described above for conventional modeling.

Ensuring Constructibility

To minimize construction problems, it is important for construction personnel to participate with the engineering and design team in the initial planning of the project. Matters to be addressed include contracting strategy, the planning of initial facilities, site layouts, and the development of the Project Milestone and Level II schedules. Along with test and operations professionals, construction specialists should also consult with the engineering and design team to be sure that appropriate construction, operations, and maintenance factors are incorporated into the plant design. Administrative portions of specifications should also be reviewed by construction personnel to ensure that contractors provide, at the proper time, the data that is required during construction. Specification and schedule interfaces must be carefully examined to ensure that the work will proceed in an orderly, efficient, and continuous manner. In addition, the availability of sufficient labor for the time and location of the project must be studied and accommodated in project planning.

MANAGEMENT OF CONSTRUCTION ACTIVITIES

Construction of any project requires the receipt of both material and equipment to be closely controlled to minimize on-site storage while ensuring that material is available when needed. There are basically two approaches to the management of construction activities: the force account approach and the construction management approach.

In the force account approach, the resident manager/project superintendent (often the architect/engineer) is also the constructor, responsible for the power plant from design through erection and testing. The constructor is responsible for scheduling and supplying all labor and materials necessary to achieve the contract schedule.

In contrast, the construction management approach is one in which the construction manager (often the architect/engineer) contracts furnish/erection or erection only of the construction packages on the project and oversees the performance of the contractors. The contractors (and their subcontractors) in turn are responsible for supplying the necessary labor and materials.

Construction Management Approach

For the construction management approach, basic scheduling information from the Level II schedule must be given to the subcontractors so that each may submit the required Level III schedules to the construction manager for review. In addition, the specifications must require the contractor to submit a critical path network (Level III), manpower-loaded bargraph schedule, and forecasted cash flow curve. For each subtask, the contractor should be required to submit: quantities, cost of materials, cost of labor, and total cost. The contractor should also be required to submit regular progress information (usually monthly). Such information typically includes:

Updated Level III schedule
Update of manpower-loaded bar graph schedule indicating status of each subtask
Subtask quantity fabricated and/or installed to date
Monetary amount earned to date on costs for subtask material and labor
Monetary amount earned to date on the total cost

Although there is no formula for selecting the better approach, there are a number of factors to consider. For example, the regulatory climate at the time the plant is scheduled for construction should be considered. Delays caused by regulatory agencies or extended permit acquisition could result in delay claims from subcontractors, thereby making the selection of the construction management approach inauspicious. Conversely, should the design information be in a form that is substantially complete prior to start of construction, the development of proposal packages and securing of competitive fixed price bids may make the construction management approach more appealing. In addition, particularly on multiunit sites, considerable cost savings can be realized by adopting a common-facilities approach; standardizing design between units for form reuse thereby saving time ($), and taking advantage of the learning curve from the first unit.

Ensuring Construction Quality

The construction manager assumes the responsibility for inspection/quality control using a quality surveillance program he or she has established for the site. The contractors have the prime responsibility for their quality of equipment/material and workmanship since the quality surveillance program is part of the contract document.

Meeting quality requirements is the responsibility of individual contractor's supervisors; however, the responsibility for inspection of quality may be assigned to a separate inspection discipline within the construction management organization. The field construction engineers check the construction process or the product at critical points identified in advance, use approved gauges or other measurement devices for inspection, accept or reject the product, and keep records of inspection results.

Construction of certain specialty systems requires that this inspection be carried out by the vendor/erector in accordance with the requirements of specified federal or state codes and regulations.

Construction Schedule Control

Each Level III critical path method (CPM) schedule submitted in the required format, is compared to the Level II schedule for consistency and resolution of interface activities. Not all contractors have the capability of scheduling properly (format), and the construction manager may have to adapt a submitted format to the CPM method with the contractor's concurrence. When approved by the construction manager, it is used as a baseline against which the contractor's actual performance is measured. The contractor's schedules should also be updated regularly (usually monthly) so that actual performance can be measured against scheduled performance.

When maintaining a fast-track schedule, the construction management approach permits letting contracts for those portions of work which are completed early so that construction can proceed as design on the remaining work continues. For example, equipment that requires a long lead time can be let for manufacture while the systems that include the equipment are still in design.

The construction manager conducts regular meetings (usually weekly) with contractors to assess performance, reviews work in process as well as work planned (three-week look-ahead schedule), discusses problems, and updates short-term goals so that extreme variances and problems can be avoided. It also makes contractors aware of what others are doing and minimizes access and coordination problems.

Construction Budget Control

In the construction management approach, each contract specifies that payments to the contractor are based on a construction management system (CMS). The work breakdown structure of a typical CMS monitors performance at four levels: total construction, based on quantities and/or dollars, construction package, tasks, and subtask. The data at each level is summed and presented at the next higher level using the earned value technique enabling management to have high visibility over performance to plan. Problem areas and adverse trends should be identified quickly and traced to their source. Discussions with construction contractors should deal in specifics, because CMS identifies the specific problem and work level where the problem exists. The ability of CMS to identify problems quickly permits corrective action to be applied in a timely fashion.

Cost information for each contract should be summed to provide a cost performance report for the total construction effort.

Force Account Approach

The basic difference with the force account approach versus the construction management approach previously mentioned is that the resident manager/project superintendent has direct control over craft labor, material, equipment, quality, and so on, and is responsible directly to the client. His role is much the same as a contractor under the construction management approach. However, the same types of systems outlined in the CM approach can be used to monitor progress, cost, and procurement/delivery since he also has the responsibility for specialty subcontractors engaged to perform certain phases of the project.

SPECIAL CONSIDERATIONS FOR FOSSIL-FUELED PLANTS

Rural Electrification Administration (REA) Funded Projects

For fossil-fueled power projects funded by the REA, no construction can begin until the REA administrator determines that the requirements of the National Environmental Policy Act (NEPA) have been met. This is generally based on a detailed Environmental Impact Statement.

REA Form 211 "Contract for Engineering Services" defines the engineer's scope of work and covers studies, detailed design, and resident engineering services.

Bidding procedures are governed by REA Bulletin 40-6. REA policy is to obtain at least three competitive bids for all significant purchases. REA Forms 198 and 200 specify, respectively, the terms and conditions for furnish only, and furnish and erect specifications. Major contracts, including specifications, drawings, and amendments, are subject to REA review and comment.

International Work

Many nations purchase their fossil fuels on international markets and are not committed to any particular supplier or even any specific region for long-term supplies. Therefore, accommodations for a wide range of fuel grades are often required in power plant design.

Other factors one should consider when involved with international fossil-fueled power plant projects are:

Local laws and regulations including local content laws and laws limiting foreign construction personnel
Unique design standards: 50 versus 60 Hz power systems
Units of measure: metric versus English
Language to be used for specifications and other documents
Tariffs, duties, and taxes
Infrastructure available to support equipment deliveries and construction
Availability of miscellaneous construction materials and craft labor
Foreign exchange risk
Political risk
Licenses and permits

Operations and maintenance training
Transportation of materials
Spare parts and service

SPECIAL CONSIDERATIONS FOR NUCLEAR POWER PLANTS

Nuclear Plant Licensing

The area of nuclear licensing within the Public Utilities Commission consists of three elements: technical, administrative, and process.

The technical aspects of the licensing process focus on assuring that the design is safe and that it is defensible. Assurance of safety requires in-depth understanding of individual systems along with an appreciation for systems interactions. Capability and imagination to envision system responses to a spectrum of initiating conditions are required. The easiest way to ensure that a design is defensible is by the proper application of regulatory criteria and guidance. This process requires an in-depth knowledge of the body of regulatory documents and their intent. An awareness of the current regulatory atmosphere is essential. Anticipation of impending new requirements and incorporation into design at an early stage can reduce efforts and costs over the duration of the project. A comparison with similar plant designs for which the licensing process has been completed also provides a barometer of design defensibility. A prerequisite for this approach is a familiarity with a wide range of plant designs.

The administrative scope of effort involved in the licensing function involves handling the flow of commitments associated with obtaining necessary permits, both on the federal and local level. The bulk of the effort in this area is centered on interface with the Nuclear Regulatory Commission (NRC), initially in the submittal of a safety analysis report and environmental report, and subsequently in the response to formal NRC questions and direct interfaces. Any misrepresentation to the NRC, whether intentional or not, incurs a liability to the utility and/or contractors.

While the first two elements are necessary for successful management of nuclear licensing, they are not sufficient. Licensing managers cannot afford to be swept away in the flow of technical and administrative problems. They must manage the licensing process so as to achieve the utility's objective of obtaining the necessary licenses on schedule at an acceptable cost.

One must manage the licensing process to facilitate NRC review by establishing a problem-solving atmosphere. It is important to reach a mutual understanding that the NRC staff is not being arbitrary and that the applicant is not disregarding safety. A schedule must also be established with the NRC that is realistic, and senior NRC and utility management's commitment to this schedule should be obtained. Finally, the needs of the individual NRC reviewers must be satisfied by timely and effective communication, with early identification and resolution of problems. It is at this level that the alert licensing manager can be most effective in managing the process. The NRC review will have to endorse and perhaps even testify to the safety of the plant design. Accordingly, if the design meets the same criteria as a previous similar design, the reviewer will have added confidence in the defense of the design.

It is worth noting that the process of licensing a nuclear facility has become increasingly complex over the past several years. A proliferation of regulations in the wake of the accident at Three Mile Island and the resulting increase in the number of people required to review an application, coupled with the expanded database associated with a maturing industry, have contributed to an extremely cumbersome licensing format.

The Nuclear Regulatory Commission and the Department of Energy have each submitted to Congress a proposed Licensing Reform Bill, aimed at streamlining the licensing process. These proposals have as a basis, the premise that the industry has advanced to the point where it should be possible to describe and evaluate (1) standardized plant designs on a generic basis, (2) essentially complete designs prior to plant construction, and (3) propose plant sites without plant design details.

Nuclear Plant Safety

The fundamental safety of nuclear plants is due to two key features: redundancy and conservatism.

Redundancy means providing independent duplicate parts and systems to prevent failure of an entire system if a single part or system should fail. Nuclear plants have numerous built-in lines of defense against serious accidents. There are control systems for normal operation, and then there are backup control systems. Beyond these are systems for shutting down the plant safely in case of a serious component or operator failure. Finally, there are systems to contain the effects of any accident that might happen within the plant structure.

Conservatism refers to the wide margins of safety that are engineered and built into a plant. Nuclear engineers always consider the worst probable things that could happen: earthquakes, fires, floods, tornadoes, and then build each plant to withstand these events.

Incorporating redundancy and conservatism into the already complex design and construction of a nuclear plant places additional demands on project management not found in fossil plants, which results in increased costs and schedules of longer duration.

Nuclear Plant Quality Assurance Quality Philosophy

Top management's involvement in the quality assurance program must be highly visible and sustained. It must result in a "trickle down" philosophy whereby quality is the responsibility of everyone on the project.

Engineers and Procedures

Due to the complex and often evolving nature of nuclear power plant design, there is a need for detailed procedures. These procedures standardize the methods and practices to be used in carrying out the design. These procedural constraints may be perceived by some engineers as an attempt to inhibit their thinking along creative and independent lines. This perception, if allowed to persist, can result in a loss of commitment to, and responsibility for the design on the part of the engineer. Management can counter this attitude by adopting a positive quality philosophy, through the direct involvement of the engineers in the preparation of governing procedures.

CONTRACTING WITH THE FEDERAL GOVERNMENT

When contracting with the federal government, many special contractual considerations will be encountered that are not customary in the commercial contracting arena. Some of these considerations are:

Federal Procurement Regulations

These regulations identify the principles and procedures governing what costs are allowable and allocable under a government contract; the accounting standards a contractor's accounting system must comply with; and the elaborate procedures to be followed in the event of a contract termination.

Budgeting Constraints

When contracting with the government, contractors must be conscious of the governmental funding process. The budget for a project may involve approvals by committees, subcommittees, and both houses of Congress along with approval by the President.

The budgetary approval process may require months to complete and may not be finalized until well into the next fiscal year, therefore making it very important that the contract funding is not exceeded.

Equipment Acquisition

The government has regulations controlling the entire procurement process from advertisement of bids through completion of the contract. Numerous acts and policies such as the Buy American Act, Equal Opportunity, and Minority Business, must be considered in the selection process.

Management Control Systems

On all major acquisition contracts, the government typically invokes a cost/schedule control system which the contractor's cost accumulation system must meet. The government requires that each contractor's system be validated against the system criteria established. Contractors must be aware that refining their accounting systems to meet these criteria can be costly.

Property Management

Often the government will provide special tooling, test equipment, certain facilities, or other items of equipment for use in contract performance, or permit the contractor to procure such items and charge the contract directly. There are many regulations for controlling government property while it is in the possession of contractors. Contractors must establish meticulous procedures to account for the receipt, storage, issuance, maintenance, protection, and final disposition of such government property.

INTERNATIONAL WORK

When entering into an agreement to provide nuclear or nuclear-related design and/or construction services in the international market, one must consider several factors. Federal laws regulate the conduct of U.S. firms involved in the exchange of information related to foreign atomic energy programs or engaging either directly or indirectly in the production of special nuclear material. Prior to entering into any international contractual arrangement, a contractor must secure federal approvals and define any special reporting requirements.

Special attention should be given to the procedural process of acquiring permits and licenses in the country where the project is to be constructed. In addition, local and national laws and regulations must be reviewed and evaluated to assure that the final design will be in compliance and technically acceptable.

There are several ways in which technology can be transferred to other countries:

Work could be accomplished in the foreign country through a staff of experienced people guiding and training representatives of the foreign nation while they are working on the project.

A selected work force from the foreign nation could work in the United States, gain experience, and subsequently take the technology back to their native country and serve as instructors there.

Sources of manufacturing for plant equipment could be developed in the procuring nation. This would enable the establishment of an economic and technical base for the nation to continue growth.

Regardless of the method chosen, there will be obstacles: language barriers, translation of construction and procurement documentation, adopting to the use of metric equivalents on all deliverable documentation, and instilling a disciplined approach to work through pre-established procedures and practices.

CONCLUSION

The important considerations for managing large power plant projects described in this chapter are intended to increase the reader's understanding of their proper application and utilization in a fossil or nuclear project. Specifically, effective management can be achieved through the use of goals, management techniques, and performance measurement. A project manager must have a broad knowledge of the management techniques and controls that should be applied.

The high capital cost to construct power plants and the corresponding need to maintain schedule, the utility industries dedication to high availability and reliability, and the ever-changing regulatory and licensing requirements present a challenge never before encountered by project managers. It is imperative that the unique features of each project environment (be it government, Rural Electrification Administration, international, or privately owned domestic utility) be translated into specific goals and objectives, and that the project organization be adaptable in size and configuration to meet these needs.

2

Managing Tennessee Valley
Authority's Design and Construction

GEORGE H. KIMMONS* and ELIZABETH E. PATRICK[†] *Tennessee Valley Authority,
Knoxville, Tennessee*

Since its creation in 1933, the accomplishment of the broad objectives of the Tennessee
Valley Authority (TVA) has required a massive and continuous construction effort.

In the 1930s and 1940s, dams were built on the Tennessee River and along many
of its tributaries in an effort to harness the region's abundant water resources and
provide flood control, navigation, and hydroelectric power generation. Transmission
lines, switchyards, and substations were built to provide electricity to the region's
farms and homes, where kerosene lamps had been the only source of light.

In the 1950s and 1960s, as the region's growth outstripped the capacity of the
rivers to supply all the needed electricity, large coal-fired generating plants were
built—each new one larger and more efficient than the previous one.

In the late 1960s and 1970s, TVA turned to the atom, ushering in a new era in construction: designing and building large nuclear power plants to supply the anticipated
future power needs of the region.

Unlike most other federal agencies and private power companies, TVA from its beginning has relied on its own forces rather than outside contractors for the majority
of its engineering design and construction work. This has allowed TVA greater control
and flexibility in adjusting to changing engineering standards and economic conditions,
and has provided the ability to transfer critical skills from one project to another in
an orderly and efficient manner.

This success story didn't just happen, however. It was a program that was planned, executed, monitored, and controlled in a deliberate and organized process.

HISTORY OF THE TVA STRUCTURE

During the Great Depression, in 1933, President Franklin D. Roosevelt signed into law
legislation creating the Tennessee Valley Authority, "a corporation clothed with the
power of government but possessed of the flexibility and initiative of a private enterprise." The concept of unified resource development became the basis of TVA's pro-

*Retired
[†]*Present affiliation:* Keith & Schnars P.A., Fort Lauderdale, Florida

gram. By considering all available resources as part of every project, TVA helped to
achieve the simultaneous development of navigation, flood control, power generation,
reforestation, agricultural and industrial development, and recreation.

The TVA is governed by a three-member Board of Directors appointed by the President and confirmed by the Senate. Members serve for designated 9-year terms, unlike
the heads of many other government agencies, who serve at the discretion of the President.

The original Board of Directors, appointed by President Roosevelt, included Chairman Arthur E. Morgan, responsible for engineering and construction; Director David
E. Lilienthal, responsible for the power system; and Director Harcourt A. Morgan, who
headed the fertilizer and agriculture program.

Less than three months after the TVA Act was signed, construction began on Norris
Dam, the agency's first multipurpose dam, named for Senator Norris, who was instrumental in advocating TVA's creation. While reviewing the proposed construction of
the dam, the TVA Board also examined how construction of TVA projects should be
accomplished. It decided to hire and train its own employees to construct the dam and
other projects in the planning states. The basis of this decision included the following
considerations:

> The Nation was in the midst of a depression. The Board was aware of the urgency
> of starting work as quickly as possible to reduce unemployment.
>
> If projects were contracted out, six months would be lost in preparing bid specifi-
> cations before design and construction could begin.
>
> The Bureau of Reclamation, the project's designer, strongly recommended in-house
> construction.
>
> An extensive, continuous dam construction program was planned and use of an
> in-house staff would give invaluable transferable expertise in dam design and
> construction.
>
> Because of the high unemployment rate, TVA had its pick of top engineers and
> construction managers.
>
> The uncertainties of unforeseeable foundation conditions and the hazards of severe
> flooding during construction made the flexibility allowed by in-house design
> and construction forces attractive.

An inherent element in these factors and a concern which had a major influence
in the decision to use an in-house work force, was TVA's congressional mandate to
develop the total resources of the Tennessee Valley, including the development of a
productive and skilled work force. A comprehensive training program for construction
workers was implemented that would have been unfeasible were the project built under
contract.

The course TVA was to follow through its 50 years of design and construction was
established at an early date. The agency has maintained a core of engineering and
construction personnel, using contractors to meet specialized needs and peak requirements.

PROJECT MANAGEMENT PROCESS USED DURING
HYDROELECTRIC AND COAL-BURNING PERIOD

The TVA's construction history can be divided roughly into two periods: the hydroelectric and coal-burning period, and the nuclear period. Project management processes
during each period were different and were tailored to meet the complexity of the projects under construction at the time.

Two basic characteristics of the project management process during the hydroelectric and coal-burning period were the use of the Gantt chart as the main management tool and the management of the project by a single project manager. Construc-

tion of the dams, coal-burning plants, and other civil projects was not as complex as the nuclear projects.

TVA's design division was organized along traditional disciplinary lines, with specific project design responsibility superimposed. The simple single-line schedule by feature, normally called the Gantt chart or bar chart, served adequately in the management of these projects. Once TVA organized the full construction program for one of these projects, the design, construction, and management teams were established. These teams circulated from project to project, designs were repeated, and the bar charts from completed projects became the groundwork for similar projects elsewhere. As projects were completed, and final costs were recorded, the estimates, too, became sound foundations for estimating and scheduling future projects.

The construction project manager was in complete control of the project. All project-related resource development activities were coordinated closely with the site project manager. Changes were controlled by the project manager, unless the design required change. His team had usually worked together on other projects and, together with established procedures, reliable designs, and stable estimates, projects could be managed from bar charts and daily reports of progress. As the project manager and his team transferred to other projects, new employees were introduced to and trained in the established construction methods. The result was a skilled work force that achieved recordbreaking results.

PROJECT MANAGEMENT PROCESS USED
DURING THE NUCLEAR PERIOD

In the mid-1960s, TVA entered the nuclear era. It was soon apparent that the size, complexity, and construction duration of nuclear plant construction jobs required management techniques of a different nature than those employed for dams and fossil projects. A project/discipline matrix organization was established to distribute TVA's design and construction expertise to all phases of these projects as well as to the smaller maintenance projects on the fossil plants.

The bar chart was no longer adequate for planning and controlling more than 31,000 design and construction activities on a single project, and TVA began using the critical path method (CPM). Extensive use of computer systems afforded TVA the ability to plan, schedule, estimate, and track more than a half million tasks. Computer-aided estimating and computer-aided design techniques have been added to the tools available in the management of its projects. Also, the concept of an on-site project manager with primary responsibility for the job has changed. TVA now employs a project manager overseeing both design and construction. Sustained design support and control play a more prominent role through the full design/construction cycle for nuclear construction compared with hydroelectric and fossil-generating plant construction. The project manager has responsibility for the total project schedule and budget, and approves all changes or inputs which would affect the timely completion or cost of the project.

TVA is accountable to its ratepayers and Congress for costs related to the self-financed power program which represents 95% of its expenditures. Congress and the executive Office of Management and Budget retain oversight review for the total TVA operation and appropriate funds for nonpower programs representing the remaining 5% of TVA expenditures. The amount and types of data required to meet the requirements of these constituents involve the generation of extensive facts and analysis of not only ongoing operations but also proposed future projects.

TVA Operating Plan

A key tool for measuring progress and productivity is the operating plan. The annual Operating Plan is a comprehensive work and financial plan for the next fiscal year.

It outlines goals, activities, costs, schedules, and employment levels from an organizational accountability perspective, as well as from a project perspective. The operating plan aids planning by requiring heads of offices and divisions to make future plans, estimate costs, and predict results. Providing a means for coordinating activities into a balanced overall program, it contributes also to coordination by making it necessary for offices and divisions to exchange information on project and program content, thus disclosing imbalances or inconsistencies in activities early enough to be corrected. The operating plan: (1) aids in controlling programs by comparing planned results with actual results, (2) requires an explanation of variances so that corrective action may be taken if necessary, (3) provides a mechanism for generating forecast changes for the current fiscal year's program, and (4) provides a means for preliminary development of the next operating plan. It is approved by the Board of Directors at the beginning of each fiscal year and is reviewed on a monthly basis through program summary reports.

Operating Plan Development

Budgets are built from the bottom up; that is, work activities are established at the lowest manageable level, called responsibility centers. A responsibility center is an organizational entity charged with performing assigned activities or functions either directly, or by control of subordinates. Responsibility center budgets are approved and summarized to form workplans. Workplans are summaries of scopes, schedules, costs, and cash flows for activities to be performed by the division. The project manager reviews the workplans for applicability to ensure the work is not overstated and that the estimates are reasonable. Once the workplans are reviewed and approved, they are summarized at the division level and, together with other division submittals, a base estimate of the project scope is derived. A range of estimates is produced by adding probabilistically derived contingencies to the base estimate to accommodate project uncertainties and scope changes due to design evoluation, new technology, and environmental concerns.

UNIQUE PROJECT MANAGEMENT CHARACTERISTICS OF TVA

Since 1938, TVA has operated with a general manager who is responsible for the overall coordination of all TVA program activities. The three-member Board of Directors no longer has specialized areas of management responsibility, but rather serves as the corporate policy-making body. Under this arrangement, program managers, as the client, and the project managers are responsible to the general manager and Board of Directors. Both the program managers and project managers are subject to the same general corporate policies and procedures, thus eliminating many of the organizational relationship problems normally encountered among different project participants. Since all TVA organizations eventually report to the general manager, all litigation costs normally expected between design and construction contractors are eliminated.

Considerable historical experience and records are available as well to draw from for more thorough planning. TVA managers have a large pool of diverse design expertise which can be relied upon for advice on new technology and methods. The TVA Act, by dictating the development of the total resources of the region, has created a cadre of individuals: economists, biologists, agronomists, archaeologists, geologists, and many others from which to draw expertise.

TVA has its own procurement process. It is not the exact GSA process, but it still must meet certain government standards. It is primarily based on the lowest bidder conforming to the specifications. There is an office within TVA devoted to all litigation issues involving TVA. Although governed by regulations stated in the procurement process, suits are filed daily.

Another unique characteristic of TVA as an electric energy supplier is TVA's rate-setting process. TVA sets its own rates for power whereas almost all other utilities' rates are regulated by state utility commissions. As dictated by the TVA Act, "Power shall be sold at rates as low as are feasible," and the results are power rates that are some of the lowest in the nation.

A key to TVA's success is in its cooperative relationship with the Tennessee Valley Trades and Labor Council, an organization of craft unions. Working conditions are uniform on all TVA projects; there have been few work stoppages that would impact the construction schedules. TVA and the Council have developed a large pool of skilled manpower, although there have been cases when TVA was unable to hire as many construction workers of a particular craft as it needed, and the schedules were then impacted. This problem is of minor consequence in periods of declining construction expenditures.

BENEFITS OF AN IN-HOUSE PROJECT MANAGEMENT ORGANIZATION

Some of the many reasons why TVA has maintained such a large in-house work force of designers, builders, and project managers are discussed in the following.

Consistency

The centralization of engineering design work in one organization results in consistency in design approaches as well as in drawing format and style. This consistency promotes standardized construction practices, which reduce TVA's ultimate costs. Because TVA must use the facilities it designs to carry out its responsibilities, TVA's design effort is influenced more by long-term considerations of operation and maintenance than by comparable design work by a private contractor.

The continuing availability of the original design organization during plant operation also results in long-term operating efficiencies to TVA. This is particularly important for nuclear plants where safety modifications are frequently required and for hydro plants, where knowledge of a plant's design, construction, inspection, maintenance, and operation is needed for ensuring the dam's continued safe operation.

Scheduling and Coordination

Schedules of the projects' activities tie design and construction activities together, affording a true picture of project development durations. These schedules furnish management with accurate tools for producing cash flows and determining employment levels.

The lead time required from the point where a need is identified to start of construction is considerably lengthened if a decision is made to contract the work. Scope definition, cost estimates, and conceptual engineering are done in-house. After this, either in-house design or the preparation of specifications for use in contracting must begin. From this point, the schedules for various alternatives to design and construct begin to diverge.

Changes

Once construction starts, if there are no significant changes in the project, progress depends on management, productivity, and delivery of materials and equipment whether the work is done by contract or in-house. There should be no major differences in schedule requirements for these two approaches.

When changes are required because of new regulations, differing site conditions, errors, or the need to change the scope of the project, such changes may take more time to implement under the contract approach. For example, when a required change is to be performed by a subcontractor, TVA must work through the primary contractor to obtain the desired result, a time-consuming and expensive process. Therefore, in projects where a number of significant changes are to be expected or where extremely tight schedules are required, good business practice favors in-house performance as a means of avoiding the possibility of such delays.

Fast-Tracking

Under TVA's in-house system, construction proceeding concurrently with the design effort is more expeditious than if the work were being performed by private contractors. Again, TVA is able to change priorities quickly and be more responsive to a changing environment. As a result, all project schedules allow enough flexibility to keep the total TVA program in balance.

Continuity

Experienced construction personnel, key managers, engineering, and supervisors familiar with TVA's methods are transferred from one project to another. The rotation of personnel also exposes the crafts to the continuity needed to support a stable program. Heavy or specialized equipment is shifted from job to job to fit staggered construction or maintenance schedules or to meet emergency needs. This rotation of equipment affords TVA maximum use of all equipment. This flexibility enables TVA to respond quickly to its changing design, construction, and emergency maintenance needs.

A CHANGING FUTURE

Today, TVA's future is much different than it was several years ago when TVA drastically cut its nuclear construction program. The future for TVA will involve research and development work, additions and improvements to existing facilities, and technology transfer. TVA will continue to share its knowledge and experience with local, state, federal, and international governments and agencies.

CONCLUSION

The TVA experience extends beyond the construction of projects and past the harnessing of a river to the development of a region for the benefit of the people. Through a well-managed program of unified resource development, the Tennessee Valley Authority continues to develop, keeping in balance all the resources available.

3

Engineering Performance Within the Municipal Electric Utility

RONALD C. LUTWEN *SFT, Inc., Toledo, Ohio*

Municipal projects require greater personal involvement and commitment from an engineering firm than most other types of projects. The personnel from the municipality responsible for formulating and directing a project are quite often political appointees with little or no technical background. Even those with considerable technical backgrounds are still normally subject to their area politics. Usually, the engineer has to be aware of the particular political setup of the municipality, take part in the political process, and be ready for changes in leadership within the city.

Many municipalities have little or no engineering staff; therefore, they rely on their engineering firms to a very great extent. These municipals will use the same firm year after year. Some municipals can accomplish this by purchasing professional services without being required to take competitive bids. Other municipals, who must take competitive bids, find it more difficult to keep the same engineering firm.

As a client, the municipal requires a great deal of dedication and time from its chosen engineering firm. The firm's principals are expected to have a very active role on all of these projects.

THE MUNICIPAL AS A CLIENT

Politics

All projects involving municipals require some knowledge of politics. The people who manage the city are, in general, elected to their jobs, and their tenure is subject to the wishes of the voters. The engineering firm must be aware of the political climate of the city and respond accordingly. Because of the nature of politics, these city managers continually demand that the projects in which they are involved be successful and must not provoke criticism. The engineering firm should maintain close personal contacts with these managers to be able to keep abreast of the situation at all times.

Types of Organization

There are various protocols used by cities to handle their municipal projects. Some cities have an elected mayor. Sometimes this position is a figurehead only; conversely, it may be a position of great authority. Normally the engineering firm does not deal directly with the mayor.

653

Some cities appoint a city manager, who generally has great responsibility within the city. The city manager is usually appointed by the city council and is not subject to quite the degree of political pressure as is an elected official. A city manager is generally selected based on his or her management credentials and is, therefore, usually accessible and provides a very good working relationship on municipal projects.

The city council may be responsible for final decisions on municipal projects. This can make project approvals and acceptances difficult to obtain, since these people are all very politically oriented and generally not technically adept.

Other cities appoint special bodies, such as boards or commissions to oversee various operations in the city. The board members/commissioners are usually appointed by the mayor and council; and, although politics may be involved, they generally are good managers. Many times they are also technically sound. The procedure of the board/commissioners is generally to retain a general manager who reports to them. This person is a technical manager. The engineering firm will have most of its dealings with the general manager; but may also meet frequently with the board/commission.

Services from an Engineering Firm

When a project is identified, the municipal may require the engineering firm to provide services varying from the conceptual design, to bonding assistance, and continuing on through the actual detailed engineering design. Additionally, the city will usually require construction management services from the engineering firm. Budgetary constraints of the city usually result in limiting the amount of time that city staff can devote to the project. The engineering firm will be relied upon to provide as broad a scope as possible.

The firm working for a municipality has another duty which is not usually considered as a normal function. That is to submit reports to the political bodies of the city. The principals of a firm are called upon for this, as the mayor (or city manager) and council need a savvy veteran who can gain their confidence. The engineeirng firm's representatives must be able to achieve this without delving too deeply into detailed technical areas. The audience will not have time for much detail; and, as laypersons, would probably not be able to understand much of what is presented.

An engineering firm dealing in municipal projects also needs to do a great deal of socializing with municipal representatives. In their role as "right arm" to the city "guardians," it is most important to get to know the people well and to pay frequent social visits. This allows the engineering firm to foster a stronger feeling of trust as well as to keep track of the political winds in the community.

The engineering firm should anticipate and be prepared to defend itself against verbal assaults that will be launched whenever a project encounters difficulty. Even if the firm is blameless, the tendency is for it to be singled out. The city relies on the firm for protection from problems. In addition, the elected and appointed officials of the city will quickly assign blame to others to protect their public image. The engineering firm will find the finger pointed at them.

Types of Projects

There are three types of projects that may be assigned to an engineering firm working for a municipal electric utility.

The first is the day to day service project. Usually the engineering firm will handle these by means of a continuing services agreement. Many of these types of projects will involve the future planning for the municipality's systems.

The second is the relatively small project which might typically involve replacement of a minor piece of equipment within the system. Since the city is normally required to accept competitive bids on even minor items, the engineering firm will be required to do preliminary design, write a specification, solicit bids, evaluate the bids, make a recommendation, and then carry out the project through start-up.

The third type of project is the largest, and might involve the engineering and building of a new power plant. The steps for work of this scope are very similar to those taken for the smaller projects; but requiring more time and more effort.

Design/construct or turnkey bids cannot be offered by the city's engineering firm since it is considered to be acting as their agent and must function purely as an engineering consultant.

The engineering firm generally will not utilize just one general construction contractor for a major project. Rather, the concept followed would be to divide the project into basic equipment, systems, and components and have each item of work bid separately.

A typical municipal electric power plant project will have perhaps twenty or more separate contracts. The contracts may be categorized into four classifications:

1. Equipment—f.o.b. site
2. Equipment—technical direction of installation
3. Equipment—systems furnished and installed
4. Field construction—by disciplines

A typical major project might have individual contracts dealing with the following services:

1. Steam generator, including the boiler and boiler accessories, burner management system, and pollution control equipment, installed
2. Turbine-generator and accessories including gearing, excitation system, lube oil system, hydraulic oil system, cooling system, controls and instrumentation, all delivered to the jobsite
3. Condenser and accessories, condensate and circulating water pumps, delivered to the jobsite
4. Turbine erection. Offloading the turbine, generator, condenser, and all accessories at the site and erection of these items
5. Cooling tower and accessories delivered to the site and erected
6. Substructure, including supplying and installing all concrete and imbedded metals for support of the structure and equipment
7. Structural steel, including supplying materials and installing all structural members, stairways, guard rails, roof and floor decking, and large tanks
8. Supplying the deaerator and accessories delivered to the jobsite
9. Feedwater heaters including accessories delivered to the jobsite
10. Boiler feedwater pumps including water pumps and accessories delivered to the jobsite
11. Water treatment system, wastewater treatment systems, and accessories, delivered to the jobsite
12. Instrumentation and control systems, including primary elements and accessories delivered to the jobsite
13. Stack delivered and erected
14. Coal handling, furnishing and installation of additions to the existing coal handling system as required to support the new equipment
15. Piping and miscellaneous mechanical work: furnishing, fabrication, and installation of all pipe, valves, fittings, insulation and lagging, hangers, miscellaneous tanks, receipt and installation of items 9, 10, 11 and portions of 12, 23, fire protection, chemical feed, water sampling, and HVAC
16. Transformers delivered to the jobsite
17. Switchgear and protective relaying delivered to the jobsite
18. Motor control centers delivered to the jobsite

19. Uninterruptable power supply (UPS), battery system, charger and inverter delivered to the jobsite
20. Station wiring and lighting including furnishing materials for and installation of all cable tray, conduit, auxiliary panels and transformers and wire together with installation of items 15, 16, 17, 18, and portions of 12
21. Enclosures, including materials and installation of siding, louvres, doors, and windows
22. Architectural finish, including materials and installation of upper floor concrete, roofing, roof ventilators, interior partitions (control room, restrooms, locker and shower rooms, and electrical rooms) plumbing, miscellaenous equipment foundations, interior storm drainage, and other miscellaneous items
23. Ash handling system including furnishing equipment and materials for additions to the ash handling system as required to support the new equipment
24. Painting including material supply, equipment, and labor for final painting of all items as required by the specifications.
25. Site finishing including materials equipment and labor for final grading, gravel, roads, pavement, and landscaping

SELECTION OF THE ENGINEERING FIRM

There are three recognized types of bidding procedures/contractual arrangements used by municipalities in contracting work with an engineering firm:

Continuing Professional Services

When a city selects an engineering firm to represent it on a continuing basis, the two parties enter into a continuous professional services agreement, which provides for day to day services as required. This type of agreement traditionally is renewed each year.

Negotiated Bid

If an engineering firm is retained on a continuing basis, the city may elect to contract additional services for a small or even a large project, without competitive bidding. The engineers would be required to submit a bid with an estimated price, a firm price, or a not-to-exceed price. The city checks this price against the industry norm and if satisfied that it is reasonable, enters into an additional agreement. Some municipalities cannot accept this procedure because they are required to request competitive bids.

Competitive Bids

There are three types of commercial arrangements for which competitive bids are normally solicited.

1. Reimbursable. The engineer will estimate the total charges and then invoice on an hourly basis.
2. Not-to-exceed. This is the same as reimbursable except that there is a cap on the total charges for the work.
3. Fixed price. The engineering firm bills on an agreed basis such as a payment schedule or based upon completion of milestones. This is not a preferred method of bidding for large projects, but it is frequently used on small projects.

PERFORMING THE WORK

Project Team Organization

One of the first things an engineering firm will do is to appoint the project manager to be in charge of the project. The same project manager may handle all projects being performed for the same client. The project manager will be responsible for the project and, in addition, may be responsible for dealing with the related political situations. At other times, one of the firm's principals will be involved with the city; not only to monitor the project manager's work, but also to handle the political requirements of the project.

The project team will be staffed based upon the anticipated work required. The principle difference with a municipal project is the additional amount of field time required. Since the engineering firm is required to breakdown the project into many components, and since the city does not normally have a great number of their own personnel to devote to the project, the project team will have considerable field involvement during construction and startup. The site construction manager should be responsible to the project manager.

Reporting Requirements

During the early stages of a project, especially during the conceptual design, the engineering firm should report frequently to its contact with the city.

Some boards or commissions hold weekly or biweekly meetings and the firm should present a report of progress or problems at such meetings. These meetings often are held in the evening, and the firm will be required to be represented and to devote these particular nights to the city.

When a project is in the engineering design stage, the firm should report on a monthly basis. If the report is very technical, an executive summary is needed. This report should cover progress, problems, schedule, and budget.

Special Project Requirements

The most significant requirement of a municipal project is to stay within the budget. This is true on most other projects, but it differs in degree for municipal projects. If the project exceeds the budget, the city will have difficulty in obtaining additional funding. A city normally finances this type of project with a revenue bond issue at the beginning of the project. To exceed the amount of the approved bond issue requires additional financing, creating great political problems.

Having the project come in much below budget is also a problem. Municipalities cannot, under arbitrage laws, bond for more than the project is worth. To avoid this problem, the engineering firm must develop very accurate estimates. Exact prices must be fixed on major pieces of equipment by bidding even before the project has been approved.

The engineering firm should plan on securing a minimum of 50% of the project price through firm bids. The other 50% will have to be carefully estimated. When the project has been approved and the bonds have been sold, the city should be in a position to immediately let contracts for 50% of the work.

The engineering firm's services may include processing all invoices rendered against the project and act in many ways as a purchasing agent for the city.

SIGNIFICANT ASPECTS OF A TYPICAL PROJECT

A project involved the design of necessary and required changes to a municipal electric steam power plant to add a 32 MW steam turbine generator. Adequate steaming capability to serve the new project was in place at the existing plant.

Members of the firm attended the biweekly commission meetings, and submitted a detailed bid which outlined all of the services proposed. Following a period of negotiation, the commission stipulated that a not-to-exceed price would be set. The agreement was signed on that basis and the preliminary engineering commenced.

A project team was established within the firm. The project manager and the principal most familiar with that city attended each commission meeting.

The first part of the project required sufficient preliminary engineering to develop an accurate estimate with which to go to the municipal bond market. This entailed preparation of detailed specifications for all of the major components including the steam turbine-generator and surface condenser, together with the detailed estimate for the rest of the project.

During this phase, much time was spent with the bond advisor, attending council meetings, and in going to special meetings of citizens' groups who had diverse interests in the project.

The culmination of this phase came when the electric revenue bonds were sold and the project was released. The project manager continued to report progress at every commission meeting until the bonds were sold and the detailed design underway. The reporting was then done on a monthly basis.

During construction, the project team, consisting of a lead engineer and designer from each discipline, spent a great deal of time at the site. As construction activity increased, the construction manager, who had previously been on-site only part time, was assigned full time to the site.

As construction neared completion, checkout of the electrical and mechanical systems began. The project team provided on-site technical support to assure proper system installation. An operator training program was initiated prior to actual testing and start-up of the equipment.

During preliminary operation of the equipment, the project manager coordinated the necessary engineering disciplines to provide the necessary support to conform to the start-up schedule and to interface with the city's operating personnel. Following commercial operation and acceptance, the project team completed all of the drawings and other documentation to give the city a permanent, complete record of the project.

CONCLUSION

In summary, the most significant requirement of a municipal electric project is that the engineering firm devote its resources to providing whatever services the city has contracted for and all of those additional services which are implied for the successful completion of the work. This calls for a much greater personal involvement compared with many industrial projects.

4

Petroleum Production Projects

FRANK CHUCK* *Exxon Production Research Company, Houston, Texas*

Certain information should be considered by the project manager assigned to the development and execution of crude oil and natural gas projects. Much of this has been the result of experience gained by project personnel over a long period of time. It is the collective answer by many of these project managers to the question, "what do I know now that I wish I had discovered sooner?"

CAPITAL PROJECTS FOR CRUDE OIL AND NATURAL GAS PRODUCTION

Petroleum production projects include those involving exploration activities prior to drilling, exploration drilling, development drilling, production and treating facilities, enhanced oil recovery, pipelines, and the development of equipment and procedures for accomplishing work related to these activities. They do not properly include crude oil refinery projects, petrochemical projects, or any projects related to the downstream use of crude oil, natural gas, or gas liquids.

All projects include a commonality of certain project management features such as organization, planning, funding, and execution; however, there are also variations and uniqueness of project management considerations which are peculiar to the type of project being undertaken. The following paragraphs will discuss some of the special considerations which apply to petroleum projects. No attempt will be made to detail particular project organizations, contracting and control methodology, or the mechanics of planning systems.

Preproject Activities

A number of preliminary activities must occur before a petroleum production project reaches the stage of drilling producing wells and installing production facilities. These activities can greatly influence the success of the project. Some basic considerations associated with these activities are the lease acquisition efforts and costs; exploration evaluation of the lease area with sound risk calculations; timing estimates for evaluation; obtention of permits or approvals; exploration drilling plus design and installation of facilities; and determination of whether the operation will be a wholly owned company operation, involve a joint operation with other companies, or with partial government ownership.

---

*Retired.

It is essential that all questions regarding these prior activities be asked and answered, or at least it must be recognized that an answer is unavailable, and that an area of doubt exists. These considerations all contribute to the project definition. It is universally recognized that insufficient project definition is a significant contributor to major project schedule and cost overruns.

Changes Over Life of Project

Those responsible for major petroleum production projects must maintain an awareness for events that can change project definition. This is especially true for those large-scale projects in frontier areas where a time lapse of 10 years or more can occur between the discovery of oil and gas and the first delivery of product to markets.

Characteristics of Petroleum Production Projects

Lack of Definite Data

A fundamental characteristic of petroleum production projects is the lack of sufficient data at the early stages. Prior to exploration drilling, there will be a lack of hard data on the reservoir fluids to be encountered during drilling. The driller might unexpectedly encounter deadly hydrogen sulfide or abnormally high pressure gas. Even after exploration drilling has been completed, the planners and designers will most likely have only an imprecise reservoir description upon which to base the design. For frontier area projects, there may be a lack of hard knowledge regarding environmental conditions such as ice forces, wave heights, or wind velocities. For petroleum exploitation in underdeveloped countries, there may very likely be a lack of laws regulating many of the activities related to exploration and production—with the certainty that such laws will be promulgated as the government perceives the need for them.

Need to Reduce Uncertainty

The project manager must make every effort to reduce the level and the impact of uncertainties upon the project. The more data acquired early on, and the better this data is, the greater the possibility of success for the project. Where answers are not available, programs must be established to obtain the answers. For example, a research program to obtain as much information on arctic ice as possible; its thickness, strength, movement, duration, physical properties, and other information required to confidently design drilling and production equipment for use in such environments. Likewise, for nonarctic offshore prospects, the designers require information on water depths, currents, maximum wave height, and winds. Even supposedly known and available information, such as design philosophy and operating procedures, should be clearly established, recorded, and approved early in the life of the project. This will avoid the embarrassment of constructing a facility which fails to meet the operator's requirements; and, more frequently, will avoid the expense of having to subsequently modify the facility to make it serviceable. Any assumptions made should be carefully documented; and it should be made clear that they are only assumptions. There will be key factors that will influence the success of a project that cannot be established with certainty (the value of the production over the life of the facility), so that every effort must be made to tie down all of those factors which can be determined in advance.

CONSIDERATION OF TECHNOLOGY

The planning and execution of petroleum production projects also involve technology considerations; both technology development requirements and technology application.

Technology Development

In the area of technology development, during the past decade we have seen many large-scale petroleum projects utilizing new technologies for the first time. In offshore facilities, for example, we have seen guyed towers, tension leg platforms, multiple-component gravity platforms, and submerged production systems. New technology has also been developed for deep sour gas drilling, for arctic gravel islands to serve as drilling and production platforms, for installation of facilities in permafrost areas, and for treating and handling oil and gas production. Other new technology is still under development: caisson drilling and production vessels, enhanced oil recovery methods, and automated drilling systems.

Project managers need to consider whether new technology must be developed to make their proposed project feasible, whether new technology is required to develop special drilling and production equipment and procedures, whether new technology is required for environmental reasons or to meet government requirements, and whether technology development can improve fabrication and construction operations. Consideration must also be given to what effect new technology breakthroughs might have on the economic success of a project.

Technology Application

There are also considerations to be made with respect to technology applications. The most obvious, of course, is to be sure that all of the applicable technical codes are met in the design of the project. Keep in mind that in addition to such technical codes as API, ASME, and ASTM, there may be special government codes or rules—especially for projects that exceed a decade from inception to conclusion. We need only to look at the disastrous results of changing government regulations on nuclear power plant projects during the recent past.

There are many considerations to be made regarding the utilization of newly emerging (and yet unproven) technology. Among these, is whether the new technology will really prove to be cost effective. New technology which results in lower material costs may result in higher labor costs. Contractors must be willing to develop the capability to apply the new technology in the fabrication and installation of equipment. Proprietary technology used in joint venture projects must be protected. Considerations must be made, and resolutions arrived at, before selecting fixed designs and making cost estimates.

FINANCIAL CONSIDERATIONS

The planning and execution of petroleum production projects also involve financial considerations. Most such projects involve heavy front-end charges and long project execution life, with insufficient early data. A deficient database affects the quality of cost estimates and job schedules, both of which materially affect the profitibility of the venture.

Other considerations which can affect the financial results of the project are governmental influences on the project—requirements for local procurement of materials and equipment; use of local contractors; government-supplied services such as utilities, docks, and roads; unanticipated taxation and other government policies or laws limiting the use of expatriate employees, application of pay scales, import duties, and repatriation of funds.

CONSIDERATION OF EXTERNAL INFLUENCES

There is also the need to anticipate the effect of external influences or unknown and unusual marketplace forces on the project financial results. Examples include OPEC actions affecting crude and product prices, discoveries affecting the supply of crude oil and natural gas, and political disturbances.

PROJECT DESIGN TRADEOFFS

Project design tradeoffs affect project economics. These include reservoir depletion mechanics and effect on facilities design; need for secondary or tertiary oil recovery systems; location of processing facilities—on or off shore; and prefabrication versus on-site fabrication.

ENVIRONMENTAL AND SAFETY

Project managers need to consider all of the environmental and safety aspects which may affect the success of their project. It may be necessary to execute a program to acquire environmental data to prove that construction or operation of the project will not adversely affect the envrionment. Obviously, there is a need to know the existing government environmental standards and laws. Beyond these, there is the need to consider safety of operations in sensitive areas such as the arctic, of operations with hazardous products such as hydrogen sulfide; and the need for contingency plans such as safe escape routes and relief well capability. A final word of caution would empahsize the necessity to be alert to external effects. Accidents of other operators in the same type of endeavor may result in additional requirements upon your project with a detrimental financial impact.

PROJECT COORDINATION

Project coordination in petroleum production may have some unique facets. There are other facets which are applicable to other projects, but are so vital to a petroleum production project that they merit mention even at the risk of duplication. The definition of the project is prime. The overall project scope and the functional requirements of all major components must be established at the beginning. The project definition must be in writing and must be understood and agreed to by all concerned: the project management team, the owners, the contractors, the operators, and any other entity to be affected by, or involved in, the project. The documentation of the project definition, and the agreement thereto of all concerned, will greatly reduce problems and surprises in executing the project.

Project Objectives

Objectives for the project must be clearly identified; they should be supported by a set of studies conducted to define the market and the drilling program. The project manager must understand all of this background information and its implications on the project itself.

Project Execution Planning

The project manager will also develop a project execution plan and communicate this plan to all of the entities affected by the project. Definite milestones should be established in the project execution plan, and major project reviews should be held as each of the milestones is reached. As the project progresses, it will probably be necessary to update and modify the execution plan and the milestones. Again, all such modifications should be done with the concurrence of all of the affected entities. Effective communication is the key to a smoothly run project.

Adequate technical manpower must be made available during the early phases of the project.

Communication

Constant communication between the project team, the operating organization, the owner/management and their reservoir, drilling and facilities engineering staffs, and the contractors is essential to a successful project. The interface coordination between all of the design and construction contractors and the owner's operating forces must be given high priority. For joint venture projects, the role of the nonoperators must be initially defined and respected throughout the execution. Special agreements may be necessary to protect proprietary technology utilized in joint operations.

CONCLUSIONS

An overview has been given of the more important considerations to be given by project managers to a petroleum production project. Additional material on systems for project planning, offshore structures and pipelines, and related topics is included in the bibliography.

BIBLIOGRAPHY

Anderson, P. W. P. "Design Safety Audits on Major Construction Projects." *Protection,* December 1977.

Chung, J. S. "Offshore and Arctic Frontiers." *Mechanical Engjneering,* May 1985, pp. 55-63.

Chung. J. S. "Offshore Pipelines." *Mechanical Engineering,* May 1985, pp. 64-69.

Cloyd, M. P. "Offshore Industry's Need for Project Management." *Offshore Services,* September 1977.

Vicklund, C. A. and W. S. Craft. "Management of Offshore Projects-An Industry Challenge." *Petroleum Technol.,* April 1981, pp. 585-592.

5

Capital Projects for the Pharmaceutical Industry

PETER LOY*   *Ortho Pharmaceutical Corporation, Raritan, New Jersey*

IMPORTANT CONSIDERATIONS FOR THE PROJECT MANAGER

Recent occurrences with regard to the discovery of toxic substances having been introduced into pharmaceutical products point out the very real need for strict control over the manufacturing operation for all such products. Although tragedies of this kind are difficult if not impossible to avert, it is extremely important to take all possible safeguards to prevent such tragedies.

The Food and Drug Administration (FDA) issued regulations initially known as Good Manufacturing Practices (GMP). This document and its regulations have been further amplified and developed. Today this body of regulations is known as the Current Good Manufacturing Practices (CGMP) document.

These regulations were promulgated to guide pharmaceutical manufacturers in adopting methods to prevent production of products which might be dangerous to the user.

Minute traces of pennicillin were once found to be present in a nonpenicillin product. Pennicillin can cause anaphylactic reactions in a very small segment of the population, in some cases, severe enough to cause death. Consequently, the FDA set limits on the amounts of penicillin allowed in nonpenicillin products. The allowable amounts were so low that it become almost impossible to manufacture both penicillin and nonpenicillin products in the same facility. Now the FDA requires that separate facilities be provided for the manufacture of penicillin products.

Capital projects for the pharmaceutical industry have very fundamental differences that influence the way the projects are managed.

Technological advances and social change have spurred the use of medicine and drugs. Population and average lifespans are increasing. Medical aid has become more available to the world's population. For these reasons and others, experience has shown that the pharmaceutical industry usually stands up well against economic recessions.

Pharmaceutical products are relatively high in value, rigidly specified, and produced at modest volumes. Production control is important. The raw materials used may be toxic or be controlled substances. Contamination is a constant concern.

Extremely high costs of research and product development are normal in the pharmaceutical industry. Once a product breakthrough is made, a lengthy period of testing is required by the regulatory bodies. During periods of high interest rates, the cost of money borrowed for research and development over the time involved represents a substantial portion of the total investment in the cost of a product. Patent

Current affiliation: Consultant, Scotch Plains, New Jersey

protection is possible for only a limited period. These factors reinforce the need for expeditious production once the necessary approvals for public use have been given.

The large pharmaceutical companies are very internationally oriented by nature. Companies headquartered in the United States have operations in many parts of the world. Some plants located in the United States are owned by European or Japanese companies. Often companies will take advantage of tax relief in special situations and make use of reliable and cheaper labor available to them. These widespread operations may introduce problems relating to differences in language, government regulations, or cultural backgrounds. In past years two particularly favored locations have been Ireland and Puerto Rico.

Pharmaceutical plants must produce safe products of an absolutely assured quality. Introducing an unsafe product into the market or producing a medicine or drug that fails to conform to quality specifications are tremendous ethical and financial concerns to this industry. Because of the importance to the well being of society, governmental regulations are widespread and comprehensive.

In the United States, many of these regulations are developed and managed by the Food and Drug Administration (FDA), a part of the Department of Health, Education and Welfare. To obtain federal approval to market a pharmaceutical product in the United States may take from a minimum of 2 years upward to in excess of 10 years from the initial application. An average time of 7 years is commonly used for planning purposes. The patent protection for a product is valid for 17 years form the date of issuance. This means that from the time a product is approved for sale to the public until it may be duplicated by the competition may be 10 years or less. Two of the problems being addressed by the pharmaceutical industry are (1) attempting to accelerate regulatory approval which implies finding better and faster ways to test the drugs, and (2) attempting to extend patent protection for this type of product.

Current Good Manufacturing Practice for Finished Pharmaceuticals, Current Good Manufacturing Practice for Large Volume Parenteral Drug Products for Human Use, and Current Good Laboratory Practice are the basis of some of the regulations applicable to many pharmaceutical projects. Bulk pharmaceutical products are not specifically covered by CGMP except by reference in statements in the CGMP for finished pharmaceuticals.

PRODUCT TYPES CATEGORIZED BY PROCESSING SYSTEM

Products of pharmaceutical plants may be categorized by the process involved. The three accepted classifications are:

1. Bulk manufacture
2. Recovery from natural substances
3. Dosage plants

Bulk manufacturing plants most frequently are larger and have more processing involvement than the other two. There are fewer plants of this type than of dosage plants, but more than those recovering product from natural substances. The two principal processes used in bulk manufacture are biochemistry and organic synthesis. Bulk manufacturing plants may also be classified according to the system used, either batch or continuous processing. Because of the relatively low volumes involved and the past difficulties in adequate process control, the batch process has been favored. The batch process has also been used most frequently in plants which use the same process train for more than one product. With the advent of computerized process control, there has been a trend to go into continuous processing for some products.

The fermentation process is based upon enzymatic reactions in which enzymes that have been produced by living organisms are used as catalysts in chemical reactions to make useful products. Most of us are familiar with some of the natural enzymatic processes such as starch conversion to sugars, the conversion of mile to solids, and the digestion of proteins. There are many nonpharmaceutical products produced by fermentation including vinegar, ethanol, citric acid, wine, beer, and other spirits. Examples of pharmaceutical products produced by fermentation include such antibiotics as penicillin, streptomycin, erithromycin, and cephalosporin.

Genetic engineering continues to produce many more types of bacteria and yeast. New and useful products will, in turn, be engineered based on the technological advances made possible by these.

Plants involving recovery of product from natural substances are generally smaller and less sophisticated in their technology. They are also fewer in number.

Dosage plants are those which package drugs and medicines in the proper form for customer usage. There are many more of these plants worldwide than the other two types. Frequently, packaging plants are located in Third World countries. These are generally encouraged by local import restrictions.

Products of dosage plants may be categorized into two areas: (1) nonsterile products which are oral or topical substances introduced into the digestive or respiratory systems or applied to the skin and (2) sterile products which are injected into the blood stream or subcutaneously, or used as special inhalants.

CONSIDERATIONS IN DESIGN OF PHARMACEUTICAL FACILITIES

Unless otherwise specified, the prime objective of a pharmaceutical facility is assumed to be that of producing a product of the specified quality with complete reliability. Schedule is important, but is secondary to quality. Cost also is important, but usually takes third place. The project manager should always question the relative importance of these three determinants of project success prior to starting the work. The owner has a responsibility to see that all of the personnel associated with the project have a clear understanding of project objectives.

The physical design of a pharmaceutical facility is intimately tied to sterilization and the operating procedures selected by the owner.

The project manager should have an understanding of the following important elements and activities of pharmaceutical plant design and operation. They will affect the successful completion of the project both individually and collectively.

1. Fermentation plants
   a. Batching
   b. Media preparation
   c. Innoculum preparation
   d. Fermenters and piping

2. Extraction and purification
   a. Solvent extraction
   b. Ion resin recovery
   c. Crystallization
   d. Centrifugation or filtration
   e. Membrane separation
   f. Drying
   g. Clean-in-place systems

3. Organic synthesis (sterile/nonsterile)
   a. Reactor equipment design
   b. Process equipment selection/design
   c. Clean piping system design

4. Dosage form manufacture
   a. Equipment selection

    b. Sanitary standards
    c. Purified water
    d. Clean steam
    e. Application of FDA's CGMP's
    f. Validation procedures in design

5. Subdividing and finishing (drug delivery systems)
    a. Liquid and powder filling (sterile/nonsterile)
    b. Tablets and capsules (two piece and soft)
    c. Ointments and creams (ophthalmic and topical)
    d. Microencapsulation
    e. Transdermal application
    f. Prodrugs (prodrugs are chemically modified forms of the drug which after absorption into the body convert to the active compound. This is commonly achieved through the agency of an enzyme)
    g. Osmosis
    h. Container preparation and sterilization
    i. Handling of labels, cartons, and inserts

6. Warehousing and material handling
    a. Storage of raw materials (quarantine and approved)
    b. Finished goods storage
    c. Highbay and conventional storage warehousing
    d. Handling toxic and hazardous materials in powder form
    e. Handling toxic liquids
    f. Distribution firms

7. Laboratory facilities
    a. Quality control
    b. Spore laboratories
    c. Research and development laboratories
    d. Animal rooms

8. Heating, ventilating, and air conditioning
    a. Clean room design
    b. Mass air flow systems
    c. Dust pickup and collection
    d. Control of cross contamination
    e. Control of toxic vapors

9. Auxiliaries
    a. Process control/instrumentation
    b. Utilities
    c. Solvent disposal
    d. Locker/shower rooms
    e. Cafeteria
    f. First-aid stations
    g. Offices
    h. Access roads, parking
    i. Facilities for visitors
    j. General storage

CONSIDERATIONS IN MANAGEMENT OF PHARMACEUTICAL PROJECTS

The responsibilities falling to a pharmaceutical facilities project manager are heavy. Probably no other area of project management can detrimentally affect the lives of so many innocent people. These plants must truly fall into the category of "zero-defect" projects.

There is no substitute for experience, and the project manager should assure that the project team has good pharmaceutical experience. For any areas where there may be an experience gap, the project manager should look to a pharmaceutical consultant for assistance or to review proposed plans.

Remembering the specialized nature of the pharmaceutical facility, the project manager should assure an overkill with his communication to the owner's representatives, architects, engineers, and consultants in promoting coordination of the interaction that will be necessary for a successful project.

If the project manager particpates in the site selection of the facility, he must be very sensitive to the possibility of strong community reaction to any fume exhausts, odors, liquid discharge, or noise as well as any perceived danger to the public from toxic emission or the presence of flammable or explosive materials. During the design and construction phases of the project these concerns have to be kept in mind. Problems must be anticipated, and a well-thought-out and coordinated public relations program implemented.

The project manager should see that there is absolute conformance to the owner's requirements for product quality and project security. Any suggestions for deviations involving potential improvements should be fully discussed and no changes made before approvals have been given. A great deal of procedural flexibility is needed in dealing with pharmaceutical firms. There is a wide diversity of preferred working relationships between the owners and architectural, engineering, and construction firms. Although this flexibility is required, there must be rigid adherence to the corporate and regulatory practices governing the project.

The project manager should realize the trend may be toward continuous processing for some processes because of the higher throughputs possible, toward computerized control, and toward introduction of robotics into the processes. The sensitivity of the high product quality requirements and the higher risk of a disastrous human error together with the greater difficulty of avoiding cross-contamination in the process in implementing these new techniques must be a concern to the project team.

6

Offshore Oil and Gas Development Projects

PETER M. J. FACIANO   *Global Engineering Ltd., Sutton, Surrey, England*

REX ALFONSO   *Fluor Daniel Inc., Sugar Land, Texas*

LAWRENCE ALLAN BOSTON*   *Fluor Engineers–Houston, Houston, Texas*

The design and construction of offshore oil and gas exploration and production (E&P) development project facilities has evolved rapidly from the shallow waters of 50 feet in the late 1940s to depths in excess of 1000 feet by 1980. The past, current, and future direction and form that these development projects will take is being dictated by three key criteria: (1) cost, (2) hydrocarbon demand, and (3) technology. Hydrocarbon price is a related criterion dictated primarily by supply and demand.

Throughout the 1970s, demand and free market pricing were the driving forces for offshore oil and gas development, subject to the general constraints of cost and technology. Environmental safeguards, the requirement to keep our seas and beaches clean and unpolluted, has always been of primary importance in offshore operations. These needs became even more important as regulatory agencies tied leasing restrictions and penalties to pollution control and actual histories of accidents. Technological capabilities blossomed in this environment at a somewhat faster rate than did the application of advanced project management techniques. Megaprojects proliferated, requiring ever improving and more sophisticated project management methods to organize and direct the resources required to execute these monumental endeavors. One measure of the success of the use of these management methods is emergence of on-time and underbudget projects in the North Sea and elsewhere by the early 1980s, a clear improvement over the cost and schedule overruns of the early to mid-1970s.

Just as improved execution of offshore megaprojects was being assured and the technology developed for further step-outs into deeper water for hydrocarbon extraction, worldwide demand for hydrocarbons softened because of conservation, worldwide recession, and operator oversupply. By the mid-1980s, these factors had caused the operators to invoke cost economies which have led to the cancellation of many major offshore oil and gas exploration and production development projects. Future project management approaches must reflect a new emphasis, with smaller, more effective project management teams using improved methods and material. In-depth planning strategies must also reflect this change to more effective project management. Likewise, carefully managed planning, bidding, and contract execution work is mandatory for contractors and consultants to survive in this altered business climate. It is only a

---

*Current affiliation: Consultant, New Orleans, Louisiana

matter of time before demand or technology will once more assume precedence over cost. This will again impact the increased need for project management in offshore oil and gas development, but it will not change the fundamental axiom: good project management techniques and controls, properly applied by knowledgeable personnel, can deliver the desired work products—on time, within budget, and in a safe and professional manner.

THE OFFSHORE PROJECT

In discussing project management activities as applied to offshore oil and gas design/ construction projects, it is important to provide a basis for common understanding in three areas:

1. The typical sequence of offshore oilfield exploration and production (E&P) operations
2. The nature of offshore structures and the way the projects are generally executed
3. The unique risk nature of the oil business, especially as regards offshore E&P activities

This mutual understanding will allow us to place the design and construction operations required for offshore development projects in the proper perspective when applying them to project management.

PATTERN OR SEQUENCE OF PROJECT DEVELOPMENT

The offshore search for hydrocarbons typically follows a pattern determined by economics, environment, and government regulation. The operator is an owner oil company, general partner, or operating entity for project development and operations who acts on behalf of the owners' interests. Each step strives to maximize the information obtained at the same time minimizing the costs. A key principle followed is successive refinement of that data necessary for decision making.

1. Prior to leasing

    a. Perform general area studies to determine the probable existence of hydrocarbons, and their potential nature and extent
    b. Evaluate the general financial viability of hydrocarbon production in the area recognizing the environment, the costs to find and produce, and the probable markets

2. Lease acquisition

    a. Weigh the probability of successfully finding significant amounts of hydrocarbons against the costs likely to be encountered in developing the prospect and the operator's particular needs
    b. Assess bid amounts (for royalties, production sharing, etc.) to determine what competitors are likely to bid

3. Postlease, predrilling evaluations

    a. Perform detailed seismic and geological evaluations, including calibrations against known data from oil/gas wells in adjacent properties
    b. Convert data into probable hydrocarbon reservoir predictions and select the best locations for the initial and subsequent wells to be drilled on the lease

    c. Identify suitable drilling and support specialty contractors

4. Initial exploratory well

    a. Determine the likely geology, the probable producing horizons, and the data to be gathered from various drilling, testing, and completion techniques

    b. Gather as much geological and flow data as possible by core samples fluid tests, and logging

    c. Revise earlier geological and reservoir predictions based on data gathered

    d. Evaluate whether to continue exploration operations or abandon

5. Continuing operations (go, no go)

    a. More in-depth reservoir studies, coupled with the drilling of one or more additional exploratory wells

    b. Steadily improve the operator's technical and financial data base to support decisions whether to continue to expend monies for further exploration activities

    c. Continue or abandon as justified

6. Field development planning

    a. Establish probable field configurations, production methods, preliminary facilities estimates, based on geological and reservoir data from exploration operations, and a realization of site conditions and drilling, environmental protection requirements, permitting, production, and construction considerations

    b. As warranted, bring together or hire a project development team to conceive the field development planning

    c. Successively refine development plans as additional data becomes available

    d. Select actual development facilities based on cost, market, and site conditions-interim, sequenced or full development, as appropriate

7. Development implementation

    a. Design, construct and install production facilities-fixed platforms, underwater pipelines, hydrocarbon handling (production) facilities, subsea systems, or others

    b. Drill and complete production wells (as opposed to exploration wells)

8. Field life cycle

    a. Initiate production, typically under natural reservoir conditions

    b. Perform remedial operations, as downhole and production equipment problems arise

    c. Enhance natural reservoir pressure drive (if financially warranted) to improve hydrocarbon production amounts and rates

    d. Phase-down and abandonment of facilities as production fails to meet minimum financial requirements

These are the operations, decisions, and iterations required for the exploration and development of offshore oil and gas fields and the major necessary financial commitments. Installed costs for offshore oilfields range up to hundreds of millions of dollars including all relevant costs. Such complex operations involve the application of proper management and financial controls throughout the life of the project. Project management techniques applied to the design, construction, and installation of production facilities are an extremely important control device.

THE NATURE OF THE OFFSHORE PROJECT

The components associated with most offshore platforms for drilling/producing oil/natural gas include:

> The *jacket* which is the supporting structure for the offshore platform. The jacket is set on the bottom and anchored with *piles*.
>
> The *topside* is the platform proper. It furnishes the immediate support for the modules.
>
> *Modules* are self-contained assemblies that have a unit or system functionality. Modules may be combined with other modules to expand the unit or the service. The size and weight of the individual modules is limited by the lifting equipment available for the work. Modules are described according to their function. Common modules include *drilling* modules, *process* modules, *power* modules and *living quarters* modules.
>
> The *riser* is the casing which extends from below the seabed up through the water to the platform. Drilling is done through the riser. The riser is sometimes referred to as the *suface casing*.
>
> Oil or gas is produced through the well and flows through a *pipeline* or *gathering line* to a collection platform, a production barge or vessel, or directly to shore.

The expertise for conceptual design, detailed engineering, fabrication, installation, hookup and commissioning represents a very diverse range of technical skills. It is not surprising that there are only a limited number of large international engineering/constructors who have the in-house capability of competing in every cell of the offshore applications matrix.

Structural engineering firms will tend to specialize in the conceptual and detailed design of the structural components of the platform. They will prepare designs, drawings and specifications for the jackets and the pilings while at the same time establishing the parameters for the topside. The fabrication and installation of these elements is frequently done by marine construction contractors who have very large and special equipment and experienced personnel for this type of work. The design of the topside also requires very special expertise in conservation of space and in the weight control for the topside structure and the conceptual work for each of the modules. There are several international engineering contractors who are competent for this work. Some of them specialize only in specific areas of the work. Here, again, the fabrication of the topside structure may well be done by another contractor. The structure may be set on the jacket by still a third contractor.

Module design may be done by the topside engineer, or one or more of the modules may be done by other design firms. This work may be coordinated by the operator's project personnel, or the project engineering coordination may be done by a firm charged with the overall project management responsibility.

RISKS IN OFFSHORE OPERATIONS

At the beginning of this chapter, understanding of the unique risk nature of the offshore oil business was given as a prerequisite. Very few major fields of commercial endeavor involve the level of risk and probable lack of reward accompanying oilfield E&P activities. The likelihood of finding significant amounts of hydrocarbons range from well under 1% in true wildcat operations to almost 10% in the best of infill development programs. Further complicating development is the high level of capital investment involved, the length of time to potential payoff even when exploratory work is successful, and the considerable uncertainty rendered by future oil and gas prices and governmental actions.

The above generalities apply wherever oilfield E&P operations are conducted. Conducting such work offshore anywhere in the world introduces additional complications. The in-ocean or offshore environment (ranging from mild Indonesian waters to extremely hostile arctic climate) alone adds major risks and increased potential for costs as well as loss. Distance to market, logistics, and exploration/production support requirements also combine to introduce major cost and risk implications.

The high risk offshore oilfield E&P business, when coupled with offshore operations, combines to produce a unique business climate having certain key characteristics:

1. Typically high hydrocarbon finding costs (including very significant leasing costs.
2. Long lead times prior to significant production. These typically range from three to fifteen years depending on the location, difficulty in obtaining permits, leases, development lead time and the oil/gas market itself.
3. Major capital expenditures for production support means-facilities, operations, environmental safeguards and the like.
4. The need for careful and detailed preplanning because of the extremely high penalties for errors and omissions.
5. The requirement for clear and careful recognition of ocean-related impacts.
6. The need for environmental safeguards, pollution awareness and the high cost of pollution into ocean, Arctic or beach environments.
7. The maximum utilization of all facilities.
8. Proper respect for the hazardous materials being handled.
9. The need for redundant equipment to sustain production due to the inability to obtain full maintenance service immediately.
10. An insistence upon utilizing only the most proven technology.
11. Often, a technical breakthrough is required before profitable operations can occur.
12. Major uncertainties in long-term field production predictions due to geological, reservoir, and other factors.

All of these combine to place extreme pressures on the operator's project management to bring hydrocarbon production online as rapidly and efficiently as possible.

Review of the above should confirm to the reader the very high risk nature of offshore oilfield E&P operations. Proper management dictates minimizing these risks to the fullest extent possible. One proven risk reduction tool is the utilization of project management techniques.

Project management of the total development of a successful offshore oil or gas field is actually a series of properly managed elements.

Exploration
Evaluation
Field development planning
Field and production facilities design and construction
Production operations

Coverage of the entirety of this topic is well beyond the scope of this chapter. The following pages will discuss the production story from the standpoint of project management methods applied to planning, design and construction of offshore hydrocarbon production facilities.

PROJECT MANAGEMENT: THE PROJECT EXECUTION PLAN

Project management for an offshore production facilities project is a service that provides a common direction to all project functions.

An essential part of this service is the establishment of a project management plan with effective controls to ensure that the project is properly executed within the financial and the time constraints imposed. This is called the project execution plan. The plan recognizes the three essential elements of any properly managed project—cost, time and quality. The correctness with which these requirements are addressed and the commitment to execute will determine the ultimate success of the project.

The development of the project execution plan is directed by the project manager, who works in conjunction with the representatives of the operator. The operator may provide the project manager and his staff. Alternatively he may hire an experienced project team, providing supervisory overview and authorization control.

The Project Execution Plan outlines the desired project objectives and describes the general approach to managing the project. The plan is, in turn, supported by the schedule, cost control, procurement, and administrative procedures. They provide the detail necessary to ensure that the project is completed in a timely and economical manner.

Major offshore E&P projects typically pass through three distinct phases. The role of the plan in each of these phases is defined below:

PHASE 1: Project Identification

In the project identification phase, emphasis is placed on the overall identification of the project and on its proper justification. Preliminary development plans, cost and timing estimates, and financing sources are defined in sufficient detail to allow basic project viability decisions to be made. The project execution plan, in this phase, is necessarily general in nature. It dwells on overall approaches to the project and on the project's critical elements.

PHASE 2: Project Definition

The project definition phase addresses conceptual designs, plans, and cost estimates. Viable development alternatives are evaluated and summarized. During this phase engineering companies often are engaged to assist in developing conceptual layouts, preliminary engineering and order of magnitude estimates and schedules. In the project definition phase, the project execution plan is considerably refined and supporting documents (schedules, comparison matrices, cost tables, among others) are prepared in sufficient detail to allow the subsequent detailed engineering design of all major project components. The project management approach to be used is clearly defined, including the interfaces with project representatives, engineers, contractors, and the operator's production offices.

PHASE 3: Project Execution

In the project execution phase, the project management team directs the project through detailed engineering, fabrication, installation, hook-up, commissioning and startup activities in accordance with the objectives and plans developed in the definition phase.

The project execution plan provides a coherent basis for the activities of all project personnel. Throughout the life of the project, the objectives remain constant: maximum project profitability at minimum risk, while ensuring that the project is conducted in a safe and professional manner achieving the time, budget and quality targets set.

PREPROJECT PLANNING AND ESTIMATING

Offshore oilfield E&P projects are unique in that the environmental risks during construction have a much greater impact on project viability than they do on similarly sized onshore projects. Further, these impacts occur at the time of maximum financial exposure to the project. In addition, the costs of doing remedial work offshore are often from ten to twenty times what they would be for similar onshore activities. The extra cost stems from the requirement for floating or offshore support services, as well as the uncertainty of dealing with unpredictable weather.

An excellent example of this impact is the "weather window" criterion. In the mid-1970s, the constraints of lifting capacity and motion characteristics of floating installation equipment placed major limits on the useful working season in the North Sea and other similar harsh environments. All construction contracts were geared to ensure that the platform components and major drilling/production facilities atop these platforms were loaded out, transported, and installed during the favorable April to September construction season. Lifts were in the 500 to 2000 ton range due to equipment and lifting vessel seakeeping constraints. Schedules had to be rigorously adhered to in order to meet weather window and contractual obligations (if fabrication and installation contracts are not linked). The narrow weather window and contractual terms for installation often resulted in incomplete topside facilities. After setting these then required literally thousands of premium priced jobhours for offshore completion for work which should have been done using facilities in onshore fabrication yards.

The weather window has been opened somewhat by the emergence of much larger offshore lift vessels, some with capacities ranging upward of 10,000 tons. These units employ hull shape configurations that considerably reduce their motion responses to wind and waves, and they can significantly expand the weather window. Even with these vessels, there remains a significant penalty for some offshore construction activities during the worst of the winter months. Proper project planning for engineering and onshore fabrication together with completion of the work in the fabrication yard prior to installation can minimize this penalty by insuring that all critical offshore lift activities occur during the extended favorable weather window and that offshore hook-up work is kept to a planned, absolute minimum.

PREPROJECT PLANNING

The Project Identification and Definition Phases are critical steps in a properly managed project. The extent and formalization of the planning and the studies made during these phases will vary with the prospect or field being developed and the risks involved. In any event, by the time the necessary conceptual and feasibility studies are completed for a viable prospect, the preferred field development concepts and the included components should be defined in sufficient detail to allow for development of:

1. In-depth cost and schedule estimates for all major project components
2. Financial studies made to serve as a basis for decisions to justify proceeding with the project. During the project definition phase, the following activities common to most offshore projects should be developed to support the justification to proceed:

   a. The technical basis for the engineering, design and construction of all major project components (e.g., environmental, oil/gas production and throughput platform and pipeline materials location, etc.)
   b. Review of engineering and design aspects for compatibility with available construction support equipment and capabilities and order of magnitude life requirements
   c. Formalization of the Project/Execution Plan, to include a schedule, budget and other measures for project control

The project definition will be reviewed by the operator's senior management and the operator's partners. Multiple recycles to an approved state is not uncommon and should be anticipated.

Once the operator and the partners for the planned facility are sufficiently satisfied with the technical and economic viability of the project, some variation of the project definition is submitted to the appropriate governmental authorities for their review and approval. In the United Kingdom's section of the North Sea, experience dictates that operators submit their information via a document, "Annex B" to the Petroleum Engineering Division of the Department of Energy. An outline of Annex B indicating the level of detail usually required is shown in Appendix 1. Similar, but usually less comprehensive data for United States' waters, must be submitted to the Minerals Management Service (MMS), of the Department of the Interior. The extent of the development plan data to be given to the MMS is very dependent on the lease location. The MMS justification requirements can be extensive for leases in deep waters, the Arctic, and for frontier and environmentally sensitive areas.

A "front-end engineering" step is often initiated on larger and more complex project after the operator and partners have approved the development concepts in the definition phase. Typically this work proceeds while the governmental and regulatory reviews are underway.

Front-end engineering involves:

General layout and overall design of major facilities
Establishment of detailed design and construction execution plans
Determination of any limitations on lifting weights, size restrictions, and soil capacity
Incorporation of key items from governmental and regulatory review as they are imposed

A primary purpose of front-end or preliminary engineering is to produce the documentation to allow detailed engineering to proceed expeditiously once the necessary owner and government approvals are received. Products typically produced during preliminary engineering include:

Process and utilities systems definition
Environmental safeguards and requirements
Control and safety systems
Major equipment items
Platform configuration and topsides layout studies
Construction methods and delineation of hookup requirements
Preliminary versions of construction and procurement documents

SELECTION OF ENGINEERS AND CONTRACTORS

In the project definition phase, the operator generally selects an engineering support contractor or engineer. In choosing an engineer, the operator seeks a unique combination of relevant experience, and general technical and project knowledge applicable to the particular project. The ability to rapidly discern logical development alternatives and establish realistic cost and timing data is paramount. A small number of well-qualified engineering specialists is required for this phase.

These capabilities contrast with those needed in an engineering contractor during the project execution phase. In this phase, the ability to convert the conceptual data into detailed designs, drawings, specifications, and procurement documents is required. Such in-depth work typically requires a large staff of specialists trained in a diversity of disciplines. Project definition jobhours can range from 50 to 10,000 hours, while comparable project detailed execution jobhours are 1,500 to 1,000,000. On large projects, an engineering contractor may perform the project definition and front-end engineering as well as the project execution detailed engineering for continuity and schedule purposes.

To properly access certain areas of technology, it may be necessary to bring consulting specialists onto the project task force. Over the years, such specialists have supplied technical, project, and construction related support to many offshore projects, and are economically justified in lieu of hiring specialized personnel on a direct hire basis.

ENVIRONMENTAL SAFEGUARDS AND REGULATIONS

The operator and his engineer must be fully cognizant of all applicable local, state and national environmental regulations and safeguards. The consequence of a relatively small blowout or spill of any type is costly to clean up, but can be potentially hundreds of times more costly if permitting authorities deny or hinder the permitting process. Additional studies and impact statements can be requested which may indefinitely delay the full development of a lease for which the operator may already have expended hundreds of millions of dollars in exploration activities.

Compounding the problem is the fact that there is not a single, comprehensive environmental standard to work to. The operator and the supporting engineering contractors and consultants generally work on a zero-pollutant basis: the exploratory, development and production facilities are planned and engineered to keep all polluting hydrocarbons contained and controlled at all times. Contingency plans are readied, equipment is purchased and personnel are trained to respond to accidents, upsets and even surface sheen due to diesel oil on the water. Each of these resources is maintained on a standby basis ready to be called out as needed.

There are no standards that cover all projects. The time, location and jurisdiction will determine these for each project. Project management must place environmental safeguards at the very top of its priorities in terms of researching the current governing local, state, and national requirements. Effective plans must be developed to assess and prepare for situations which can give rise to potential environmental damage. The engineering and construction on the project must provide for safe, pollution-free facilities. Contingency actions to contain and clean up any pollution in an effective and environmentally safe manner must be formulated. These costs must be included in the estimates prepared for the project from the earliest date.

Environmental planning and preparation is not inexpensive. Operators and their engineers recognize that it is much less expensive to do adequate planning, than to take a change by having anything less in the way of planning, equipment, facilities and personnel when a serious polluting situation arises.

In the United States, offshore environmental regulations are under the jurisdiction of the Department of the Interior. Permitting is by the Mineral Management Services of the Department. Each state has supplementary guidelines and regulations. Local governments such as potentially affected counties and even municipalities can also become involved in the permitting and development process.

Alaska, the Arctic, and the offshore areas of California and Florida are extremely sensitive to environmental pollutants, as are closed bodies such as Mobile Bay in Alabama. These areas are sensitive primarily because of previous shipping accidents, but also because of a very few blowouts. There have also been a few surface leaks, some of which have been of natural origin.

North Sea environmental guidelines by the United Kingdom, Norway, Denmark, and The Netherlands are extremely sensitive primarily because of heavy pollution from crude oil shipments in the recent past.

In each of the above areas, the environmental safeguards are planned, evaluated and provided by the operator and his project staff to protect populated areas, sensitive marine life, commercial and recreational interests. Damage to the enviornment may take years or even decades before the area can return to its former state.

Many other areas of the world have some form of environmental requirements; some are very demanding and sophisticated. The operator and his project staff must identify and comply with the particular requirements which apply to the project. The project development programs must meet or exceed these requirements.

A sound principle for any project calls for an environmental survey of the area to obtain background data on the following:

Identification of sensitive marine plant and animal life

Identification of commercial and recreational users of the marine resources

A survey and establishment of a baseline or current level of the condition of the offshore and near shore environment and existing pollutants in or on the water, beaches or bottom due to shipping, sewer outfalls and any industrial dumping. Adjacent areas upstream, downstream, in and about any intended offshore oil development site should be included in the survey.

PROJECT EXECUTION

Project Management Concepts

A variety of project management concepts have been employed for offshore development projects with mixed success. The best concept will depend upon the size and complexity of the project and upon the ability and related experience of the operator's staff. Project management concepts often used can be categorized into the following types:

1. Project Management Contracts. Used where an operator has limited in-house resources or experience and chooses not to develop and maintain such skills on a continuing basis. Project management is essentially vested in an independent project team which has an overall reporting relationship to and is supervised by a small operator staff. This technique is typically used by independents, smaller operators, and regional offices of major operators with large projects.

2. Project Support Services Contracts. Used to supply personnel to supplement the operator's own project staff. Utilization results in project management team mixture of operator and contractor/consultant personnel. This technique is often used when an operator embarks on a very large, one-of-a-kind project.

3. Operator Management Team with Supporting Specialists. Employed when the operator desires to maintain in-depth control over all or most portions of the project. Supporting contractor/consultant personnel, both technical and project oriented, are used to perform the majority of tasks and to report their results to decision-making representatives of the operator.

4. Contractor Management (often called "turnkey" management). Used when the operator simply defines what final products he desires (e.g., installed structures) and the operator does not wish to define methodologies for achieving the end products. This technique can be used in situations where the final products can be reasonably well defined in advance via performance criteria and specification.

Many subsets and variations of the above categories have been employed in offshore oil field development applications. Over the years, certain principles to the successful utilization of these management concepts, irrespective of the general categories of management, have emerged and are summarized as follows:

Successful projects must provide a clear understanding and definition of the roles of the operator, the engineering contractor/consultant and the fabrication and installation contractor

Project team members must be carefully selected for proper skills and experience

A positive team spirit by the operator and the contractors must be developed, along
with a willingness to subordinate individual differences to meet common project
objectives

The operator must develop a realistic expectation as to probable costs and times
for the project

Violations of one or more of the above principles nearly always result in project cost
and schedule overruns.

PROJECT MANAGEMENT TEAM FUNCTIONS

The project execution plan can be essentially subdivided into four parts: the plan
as it deals with detailed engineering; that which covers procurement/material control;
the construction plan and the project control plan.

Detailed Engineering Work

The project management team must ensure that all engineering disciplines clearly understand their roles as regards the desired work products as well as all budget and time
constraints. Usually, a project manager is assigned to overview the engineering work
on a large project, ensuring that proper interdisciplinary liaisons are in place. He
functions as a single reporting point on the project management team. On a small to
medium sized project, a project engineer will perform this function.

Most engineering units function under some form of matrix organization. This
dual reporting structure is inherently a source of conflict because of the competing
demands placed on the project engineer and the discipline supervisors in keeping a
project on time, within budget and technically correct. A matrix organization often
requires that the project engineer exhibit the tact and persuasive skills of a diplomat,
the patience of Job and the wisdom of Solomon.

Because of the environmental, time, budgetary and other such constraints, it
is imperative the project engineer keep the critical path design work on schedule.
In many offshore E&P design/construct projects, the specifications of long leadtime
items such as compressors, large switchgear, control panels and the like will dominate
the entire project schedule. The proper selection of these items as early as possible
is mandatory so that expediting personnel can function effectively in assuring their
timely delivery. These items can greatly affect the design of related control and
safety systems, electrical, piping and the design of the supporting structure itself.
Early selection of material can also affect the schedule positively, allowing the early
purchase of material. The earlier that material requirements can be finalized and
requisitioned, the earlier orders can be placed. For each month that material procurement is postponed, an additional month will have to be added to the completion date.

Procurement/Material Control Work

The role of the procurement group on the project management team is to ensure that
the project materials have been properly defined, obtained, and supplied to the construction entities. The quality and quantity of the materials are both important.
Procurement and material control activities include the commercial aspects of:

Purchase requisition preparation
Issuance of inquiries for tender
Receipt and evaluation of bids
Recommendations for purchase based on quality, delivery, and price considerations
Placement of purchase orders

Project engineering will see that the material takeoffs, specifications, and material or equipment requisitions are properly prepared. They will specify when and where the material must be delivered.

After placement of purchase orders, the project procurement personnel expedite deliveries, inspect materials and equipment, provide logistical support to construction sites, ensure proper site receiving and warehousing procedures are in place, and monitor that proper site and field materials utilization occurs. While the foregoing stresses the proper handling of larger, critical path items, the same principles and requirements apply equally to the thousands of "bill of material" items such as standard pipe fittings, pipe, electrical and instrumentation bulk material and fittings. The potentially critical nature of these lesser value items cannot be overstressed. For example, the industry has experienced several cases in which aircraft were chartered just to fly necessary valves and fittings to offshore construction sites thousands of miles away. The cost (and time lost) due to a wrongly specified and missing item may be hundreds of times the base cost of the item itself. The driving force for these extraordinary methods is money. It costs far less to spend thousands expediting missing items than to shut down a startup operation which can be bringing in millions as soon as it goes onstream. Obviously, it is far less expensive to not have to spend money to expedite lost and missing material. Well run projects recognize the value of good planning, and try to minimize these occurrences.

Procurement can greatly assist the project in meeting schedules when long lead time materials are purchased prior to and during the fabrication/installation bid cycle. This is a three to four month effort in itself. Where the fabrication contractor has fabrication-only responsibilities, significant schedule savings are possible.

Construction Work

Offshore oilfied E&P construction projects are considered unique in that:

> Construction activities often occur at several sites simultaneously. For example, on a large project with several platforms and pipelines it is ineviable that fabrication yards, pipeline and platform installation and hookup and commissioning work will be conducted nearly simultaneously to meet project deadlines and in widely separated yards. This increases personnel requirements to effectively monitor and inspect contracted work.

> A variety of governing codes for material, equipment and construction can be found (especially for electrical items) which reflect the differing origins of construction materials and the geographic dispersion of the construction sites.

> Construction work occurs in a sequenced set of steps: onshore prefabrication into large subassemblies; transportation of these subassemblies to the installation site; erection and interconnection of the prebuilt subassemblies at the offshore site; hookup and commissioning and separate startup of the several assembled units (for drilling, production, quarters, and storage).

The construction component of the project management team is responsible for the overall construction planning, work package breakdown and for interfaces with the construction contractors who are doing the actual fabrication and installation. Further, the construction component interacts with engineering and procurement to review constructability, logistics, and scheduling problems. They initiate expediting activities when "approved for construction" drawings are late, and initiate "working around" solutions when delivery of materials is delayed. Construction resolves problems related to work in the field promptly to minimize costly expediting of material and construction delays.

One of the most important construction duties is inspecting and accepting the completed subassemblies, as well as the offshore facilities. Construction is responsible for assuring that the completed facilities function in accordance with the project requirements.

Project Controls Work

A very significant part of the project management team are the project controls specialists. This group is responsible for preparing cost estimates, schedules, and reports from data provided by others on the team. Subcontract administration and quality assurance/quality control activities may be included as a part of this function.

Figure 1 illustrates the major interfaces between the project control function and the operations design, procurement and construction facets of the project management team.

PROJECT MANAGEMENT TEAM ORGANIZATION

The organization of the project management team on an offshore project must reflect the size, complexity, as well as any special requirements such as those imposed by governmental agenices.

Figure 2 indicates a typical team organization chart applicable to a medium to large offshore oilfield E&P design/construct project. Projects ranging from 35,000 to 500,000 jobhours have been handled using organizations similar to this one. The project con-

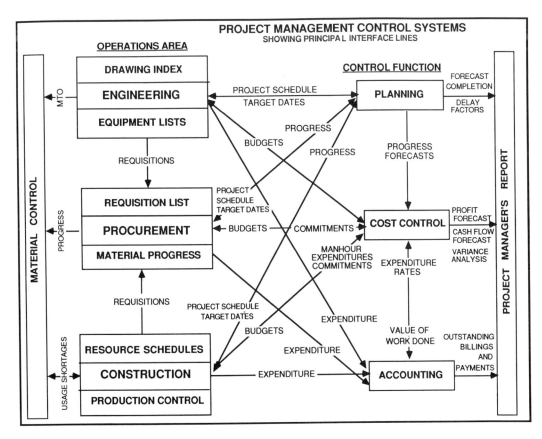

Figure 1 Principal interface lines in project management control system.

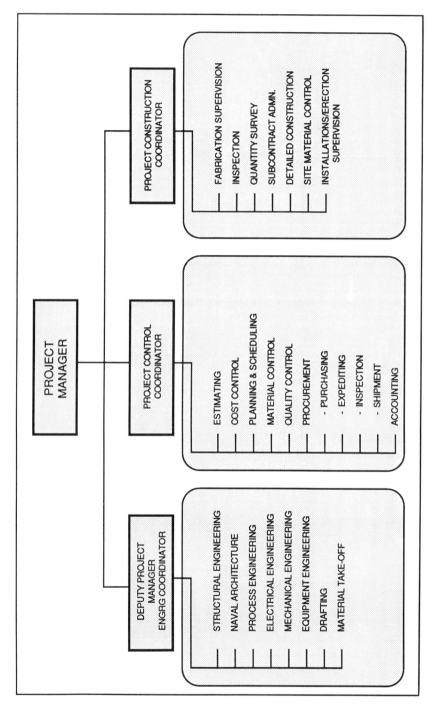

Figure 2 Typical team organization chart of medium to large offshore oil field project.

trols function is sometimes subdivided into external procurement/materials control and internal project control functions.

Very large and complex projects (typically 250,000 jobhours and more) dictate further organization refinement. Figures 3, 4 and 5 outline an example of a North Sea project where the organization used reflects three distinct project phases:

Conceptual/detailed design
Construction (onshore preassembly and field installation)
Startup and commissioning of the platform and pipelines

The downstream drilling and production operations are also addressed. While there are three different versions of the project management team as the project progresses; there is definite continuity as the three key managers, engineering, procurement and services, remain with the project on each of the three phases. The size of their staff and relative importance to the overall project varies. The project manager and these and other key staff members provide the necessary continuity to ensure proper project execution.

Small offshore projects (1500 to 15,000 jobhours) may have quite simplified project management organization structures. In some cases the project engineer doubles as the project manager and draws upon support from internal and external materials, construction, and services experts as required.

The real keys to proper project management team organization are:

The use of a flexible organization structure tailored to meet the project damands
Changing the team size and structure as the program progresses; while carefully maintaining the continuity of key personnel

Commercial Basis of Contracts Between Operators and Design/Construct Contractors/Consultants

The type of contract selected will reflect the dominant commercial environment in which the oil operation is functioning. In situations where it is imperative to have the facility functioning as quickly as possible and where the cost is secondary, cost reimbursable contracts are the norm. In situations where there is little past experience and the extent of the work required cannot be defined in detail, cost reimbursable contracts are again used.

Situations encountered in early offshore oilfield development of the middle and northern sectors of the North Sea matched both of these scenarios. Not surprisingly, major cost and timing overruns were quite common in both design and construction activities. As oil operators and contractor/consultants became more knowledgeable about the resulting work products and the proper infrastructure to support design and construction activities was put into place, the transition to contractual forms employing definite commercial constraints were logically introduced. For current North Sea design/construction work, some form of totally fixed price, fixed price with incentives, or reimbursable cost with fixed overheads contracts are in use.

Contractual relationships between operators and contractors/consultants changed rapidly as costs assumed a much greater significance because of the marginal nature of many offshore projects. Beginning in the early 1980s world oil prices started to erode. An ever-increasing price of crude oil can no longer be counted on to cover the cost and time overruns that were acceptable during the seventies and very early 1980s. Many formerly lucrative offshore oilfield investments are only marginally viable with oil prices in the $15 to $20/barrel range. Many more are no longer viable at oil prices at the $10 to $15/barrel figure.

This cost-conscious environment has placed a premium on proper project planning, estimating, contractual, and execution strategies. Very detailed plans are required to prevent later cost and timing overruns. A sample of the type of master project

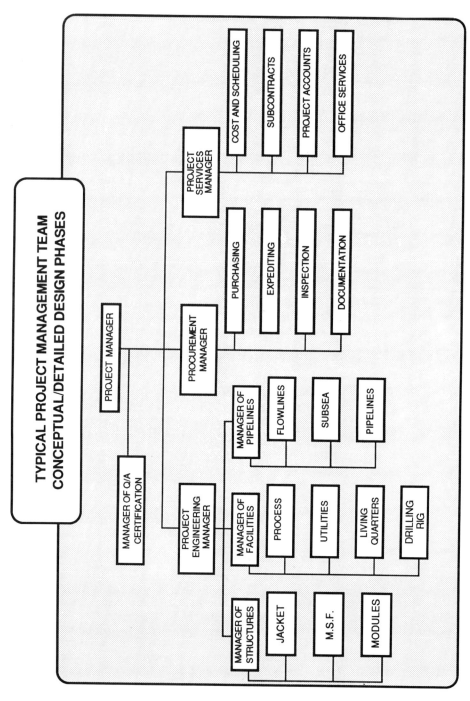

Figure 3 Conceptual detailed design organizational flow chart.

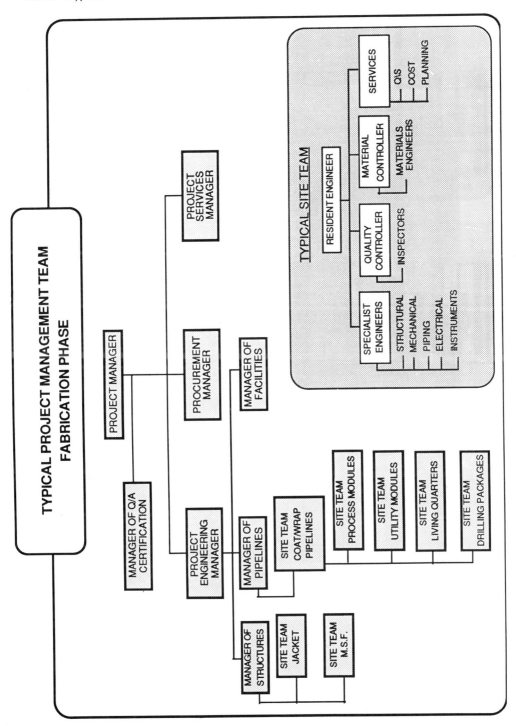

Figure 4 On-shore preassembly and field installation flow chart.

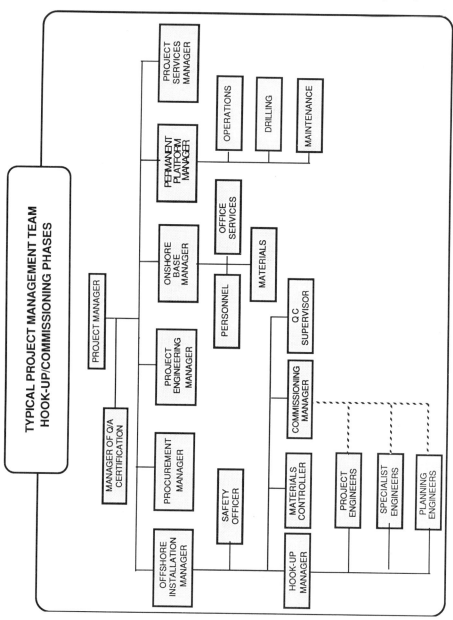

Figure 5 Startup and commissioning of the platform and pipelines.

schedule describing the major project deliverables is shown in Appendix 2. The derivative schedules for each of the major areas are much more detailed. Experience has shown the definite benefits in better executed projects of this increased complexity in project planning and management. As of the late-1980s, it is not uncommon for North Sea projects to be completed on schedule and within budget. While increased operator and contractor experience and infrastructure improvements can be credited with some of this gain, the benefits of thorough, detailed project planning and execution must also receive due credit.

From the operator's point of view, fixed price contracts are very attractive. He can budget and control his expenditures closely; a major advantage in today's very cost conscious world. Further, turnkey fixed price contracts based on defined performance criteria may reduce some of the operator's project monitoring requirements. These advantages have to be carefully weighed against the requirement for early development of in-depth design and construction contract documents. Premises and general guidance are not sufficient. While this approach may shorten construction time, long delivery items must be purchased by the operator and furnished to the construction contractor.

Ideally, all necessary preliminary engineering work would be essentially complete prior to entering into fixed price contracts for detailed design/procure/construct or procure/construct contracts. The time taken to do this preparatory work can have a major time impact on project completion.

Turnkey contracts with or without the detailed engineering portion have proven valuable in many offshore applications around the world. They are especially useful if:

> The project scope can be well defined and is unlikely to change. This is particularly true if the work scope is similar to previously executed projects
>
> The operator does not possess the internal staff (or does not wish to employ a project management team) to provide project management expertise required to subcontract the design and construction
>
> The contractor is willing to give definite performance guarantees for on-time completion along with process and mechanical system performance guarantees

Contractual relationships having a fixed price basis linked to incentives are becoming more attractive in offshore work; aside from the cost considerations, the "driving forces" toward this type of contract include:

> Recognition that engineers/contractors/consultants should be financially rewarded for properly achieving project goals, and for innovations which result in increased productivity and improved work products. Similarly, these contractors should be penalized for substandard performance.
>
> By sharing the rewards (penalties) for improved (substandard) performance between the owner and contractor/consultant both will be properly motivated in the direction of improved performance.

CONCLUSION

The foregoing summarizes the primary elements which must be considered in the execution of a successful offshore oil/gas development project.

Offshore development projects need a constant influx of new project management tools tailored to the peculiar requirements of these projects. The tools will be incorporated into the projects by dedicated operators, project managers and engineers who can effectively get the job done on time, below cost and to the specified quality requirements.

ANNEX B DOCUMENT

FIELD DEVELOPMENT AND PRODUCTION PROGRAM

EXECUTIVE SUMMARY

PROGRAM ESSENTIALS

1.1   **DEVELOPMENT AREA**

1.2   **NUMBER AND POSITION OF INSTALLATIONS**
From which the Field is to be Developed, and Use of Each Installation,

1.3   **NUMBER OF WELLS**
Provided for on Each Installation in Each Category

- **Production** (number of subsea satellite wells to be given separately)
- **Gas Injection**
- **Water Injection**
- **Other**

1.4   **DESIGN CAPACITY OF MAJOR EQUIPMENT ON EACH INSTALLATION**

- **Oil/Gas/Water Separation Facilities**
- **Water Injection Facilities**
- **Gas Compressions Facilities**
- **Gas Reinjection Facilities**
- **Gas Flaring Facilities**
- **Natural Gas Liquids Recovery Facilities**
- **Power Generation Facilities**

1.5   **FACILITIES PROVIDED**
For Use in an Oil/Gas Transportation System and the Design Capacity of the Facilities,

1.6   **OTHER MAJOR ITEMS**
Relevant to the Extraction of Petroleum.

2.0   **ANY OTHER RELEVANT WORKS**

3.0   **QUANTITIES OF PETROLEUM TO BE PRODUCED**
Maximum and Minimum Quantities of Petroleum To Be Produced During Each Calendar Year

3.1   **GAS**
Expressed as a volume in cubic meters Measured At or Calculated as if Measured at a temperature of 15 degrees Centigrade and a Pressure of 1.01325 Bar.

Appendix 1 Outline for "annex B" documentation (p. 678) required for North Sea operations in the U.K. section.

3.2 GAS LIQUIDS
Expressed as Weights in Metric Tons (and Standard Cubic Feet)

3.3 OIL
Expressed as Weights in Metric Tons (aand Barrels)

4.0 **BACKGROUND INFORMATION**

4.1 **HISTORY AND STATUS**

- **Discovery and Appraisal**
- **Licensees and Operators Involved**
- **Feasible Development Options Considered**

4.2 **RESERVOIR DATA**

- **Geology and Geophysics**

  - Seismic Data
  - Stratigraphy
  - Structural Configuration
  - Geological Model of the Field
  - Figures and Diagrams

- **Formation Parameters**

  - Petrophysical Interpretation
  - Production Logging
  - Fluid Contacts

- **Reservoir Fluid Parameters**

  - PVT Analysis
  - Reservoir Fluid Analysis

- **Reserves**

  - Hydrocarbons In Place
  - Hydrocarbon Recovery

- **Reservoir Engineering**

  - Reservoir Development and Monitoring of Performance
  - Development Drilling
  - Well Performance and Testing
  - Assisted Recovery
  - Artificial Life
  - Enhanced Recovery

Appendix 1 (Cont.)

- **Field Life and Production Profiles**

    - Field Life
    - Production Profiles
    - Injection Profiles
    - Maximum Profile
    - Gas Production Profiles

4.3   FIELD INSTALLATIONS, PIPELINES AND TERMINALS

- Field Installations

    - Structures
    - Drilling Facilities
    - Production and Injection Wells
    - Production Facilities

            General Arrangement
            Processing Plant
            Metering
            Utilities and Accommodation
            Injection Plant
            Pollution Control
            Emergency Planning

- Hydrocarbon Transportation

    - Offshore Loading
    - Pipeline Systems
    - Risers and J Tubes

- Gas Utilization

- Shore Terminals

    - Location
    - General Description of Terminal
    - Site Layout
    - Pipeline Terminal
    - Process Facilities
    - Utility Systems
    - Storage
    - Terminal Marine Loading
    - Terminal Road and Rail Loading
    - Effluent Treatment

Appendix 1   (Cont.)

- **Project Management**

  - Planning
  - Organization
  - Procurement
  - Quality Assurance
  - General
  - Studies
  - Consultation
- **Abandonment**

4.4   RESOURCE COSTS

- **General Requirements**

  - Expenditures
  - Contingency
  - Shared Facilities

- **Exploration, Appraisal and Development Costs**

  - Seismic
  - Appraisal
  - Feasibility Studies
  - Production Studies
  - Plant and Facilities
  - Field Pipelines
  - Trunk Pipelines
  - Terminals
  - Development Drilling
  - Ships and Mobile Floating Equipment
  - Capitalized Pre-Operating Costs
  - Other Expenditures

- **Operating Expenditures**

  - Wages and Salaries
  - Insurance
  - Production
  - Platform and Pipeline Maintenance
  - Well Maintenance
  - Logistics
  - Safety
  - Hire Cost of Floating Production Facilities
  - Tankers
  - Other Major Items

- **Pipeline Operating Expenditures**

  - Wages and Salaries
  - Insurance
  - Operation
  - Maintenance
  - Other Major Items

Appendix 1   (Cont.)

- **Terminal Operations Expenditure**

  - Wages and Salaries
  - Insurance
  - Operation
  - Maintenance
  - Other Major Items

- **Other Expenditures**
- **Abandonment Costs**

- **Pollution Liability Provision**

4.5   **MANPOWER RESOURCES**

- **Development**

- **Operations**

Appendix 1   (Cont.)

Appendix 2 Master Project Schedule–Main Platform.

695

7
Aerospace Industry

ROBERT J. SANATOR   *Geotel Inc., Hauppauge, New York*

VINCENT TIZIO   *Consultant, San Francisco, California*

INTRODUCTION

The aerospace industry encompasses activities ranging from basic research through product development and production to deployment and support for a wide variety of products. All of these products share the unique characteristic of flight, whether in or out of the Earth's atmosphere. Customers for aerospace industry products may be governments, notably the U.S. Department of Defense (DoD) and the National Aeronautics and Space Administration (NASA); or they may be commercial users, such as international airline carriers. Although this discussion concentrates on the government/military marketplace, much of the project management activity is similar for commercial projects, particularly at the high ends of the cost or system complexity spectra.

Management of aerospace projects conducted for the Department of Defense is highly structured and closely supervised by the customer from inception to completion. These unique characteristics arise because of the usually critical schedule requirements for defense materiel and the need for accessibility to information concerning projects paid for with public funds. Evidently, the industry is more than willing to accept these management requirements in return for the unique benefits associated with government contracting.

Aerospace companies identify potential government contract opportunities by utilizing their in-house marketing and technical specialists, as well as industry consultants to forecast the government's future needs. These needs are based on published guidance material and intimate knowledge of the defense purposes to be met with available and advanced technology. Because of the long gestation period for government contracts, a consistent approach used for identification of market targets and allocation of resources is the company's long-range or strategic plan. Depending on a company's status and business philosophy these plans, normally updated annually, cover periods of from 5 to 15 and sometimes up to 20 years.

The strategic plan introspectively analyzes the company's situation, its strengths and weaknesses, and any potential dangers to its corporate well being. With certain assumptions about the applicable marketplace, it establishes a set of target business opportunities to pursue and forecasts capturing a certain number. Critical self-assessment with regard to the target business opportunities will address questions such as:

> Does the customer view the company historically as a viable contractor? Has the company done business with this customer in the past? If so, was performance acceptable? If there were deficiencies, have they been adequately corrected?

Will the company's total resources be adequate at the proposal time? Will there be in place suitable staffing and validated functional plans and procedures?

Will the required facilities—manufacturing, test, simulation, and design—be available?

Will the commitment to research and development and the preproposal activity be made? Is the company financially able to carry out the program?

Through this self-assessment, a strategic direction for the company is selected and those resources deemed necessary to achieve successful capture of future business are defined.

PROJECT LIFE CYCLE

In the life cycle of a government aerospace project, five distinct phases are encountered. Each of these phases present different and special demands on management and the relationships with the customer: Preproposal, proposal preparation, full-scale development, production, and deployment.

Preproposal Phase

The initial, or preproposal, phase focuses on establishing the customer's needs prior to the issuance of a formal Request For Proposal (RFP). Recent years have witnessed the use of a Request For Information (RFI) during this phase. The RFI serves the useful dual purposes of providing the customer with data from the various industry competitors on what generally is available or possible for solving his problem as well as assisting the government in establishing effective requirements. Industry participants benefit from the exposure of their wares and approaches to the customer. With suitable interchange he stands to improve his position to offer winning proposals. This phase stretches over many months and can last for many years.

During this phase, the project team is relatively small, staffed with technical, marketing, and planning specialists led by a creative senior executive. The project manager ideally has the ability to develop credible plans for the project, revising them as required, and communicating them effectively to his potential customers, superiors, and team members. Close contact with the customer is essential during this phase to determine if requirements are changing.

Proposal Preparation Phase

The second phase is an intense period of activity during which competing contractors prepare their proposals. These proposals contain their solutions, at a price, in accordance with a schedule which is usually predetermined in the RFP. The objective is to win an award and nothing is spared to achieve that end. The preproposal team is fleshed out with the required depth in all of the special skills needed to prepare a professional proposal. An important step in the process is the selection and naming of a proposal manager whose function is to plan, organize, and generally supervise the proposal preparation for the project manager.

Full-Scale Development Phase

Upon award of the contract, the third phase, Full-Scale Development (FSD), commences. In many cases, a new project manager, one who has demonstrated the skills needed to conduct this demanding phase, is named. Among the characteristics sought are a suitable blend of technical and administrative skills to initiate the plan and to effectively build up the resources to meet the program schedule. The project manager must be capable of delivering excellent and timely solutions to the inevitable technical problems that arise, while carefully controlling costs within budgets. He must also take special care to ensure that all groups on the project are communicating. Engineering must coordinate with all of the other functional groups, particularly manufacturing and product support to guarantee, in addition to product technical superiority, producibility within the budgeted cost and schedules and supportability in the field. This phase can last for several years for most weapons systems, with engineering resources peaking at about the end of the first one to one and a half years.

Production Phase

It is customary for the production phase to begin while FSD activity is ongoing. This concurrent approach accepts and manages the risk associated with starting initial production before the development and qualification of the system have been fully completed. This approach can save many precious months, and even years, in fielding the product. The transition to production is often accompanied by a still further change in management and staffing as the nature of the problems encountered shifts from those typical of development (technical) to production (manufacturing, procurement, and contractual). As the buildup to peak production rate progresses, large increases in the resources dedicated to manufacturing occur and a concomitant reduction of engineering is apparent.

Deployment Phase

In the final phase, deployment, fielding of the product is completed. The project winds down in size and intensity, focusing on support to the customer in the form of spares, training, maintenance equipment, and documentation. During this phase, which continues over many years, the contractor's staff is minimal. It is usually led by a project manager skilled in working with the system's user. He should be capable of influencing effectively a product improvement program that will either extend the life of the product or enable it, through engineering change proposals, to expand its mission capability.

PRODUCT DESIGN AND PERFORMANCE

During the proposal phase, a product performance specification is developed that satisfies the RFP requirements. This "spec" is offered in the proposal submittal and in the ensuing contract becomes binding; in other words, the contractor must deliver test and evaluation articles that prove compliance with the "spec." Any shortfalls must be corrected by the contractor before production articles are accepted by the customer. The project manager is responsible for ensuring that the design specification is achievable by his organization and that it balances the customer's needs with cost-effective solutions to design/production problems. In recent years, weapons systems costs have risen sharply, creating concern about the government's ability to provide adequate and affordable defense of the nation. At the same time, concern has been rising regarding the readiness of our military forces. Concepts that have become popular, as a result, are known as "design to unit cost" and "design to life-cycle cost." In the former, the system performance specifications are individually traded off against product cost to ensure that no marginal performance requirements, beyond those absolutely required for system effectiveness, are permitted to survive and drive the cost up. Design to unit cost was successfully applied in the 1970s to the USAF's A-10 program.

Design to life-cycle cost is a concept that defines an affordable cost for the entire project, from FSD through production to deployment, including all of the operational and support costs for the system in the field up to its retirement. In reality, this concept has been applied as an umbrella, under which the cost of maintaining an operationally ready fleet of aircraft is minimized. Accordingly, contracts are written specifying the various measures of reliability and maintainability that the system must deliver: a mean time before failure and maintenance of manhours per flying hour. Readiness is enhanced as a result of meeting these requirements and the payoff is in raising the Full Mission Capable (FMC) rate of the fleet. An FMC rate of 100% means that for a wing of fighter aircraft, every aircraft in that wing is ready to perform its missions with all mission-required subsystems and equipment in a go status. Contractual commitment to parameters such as these is binding and failure to comply is no less serious than for any other performance parameter. Measuring compliance is addressed by an agreed-to life cycle cost model that is developed and presented for customer approval early in the project cycle. In the A-10 program of the USAF, this model was used to evaluate test results obtained during the FSD phase. As a result, the contractors were awarded a $3 million bonus for bettering the life-cycle cost commitments.

PRIME CONTRACTOR'S ROLE

The prime contractor's project manager can commit the company to a course of action. As the single point of contact with the customer, he represents the customer within the company. In major programs, the customer is also represented on-site by government employees, e.g., an Air Force Plant Representative Office (AFPRO), whose function is to provide surveillance and approve the contractor's product for acceptance.

The prime contractor traditionally accepts full responsibility for all activities carried out by the industrial team he has organized in accordance with his contract with the government. There is an increasing trend to government contracting to have the prime accept Total System Performance Responsibility (TSPR). This means that the customer holds the prime responsible to correct any deficiencies and discrepancies from the specification performance regardless of the origin of cause. This approach was first tried in a major way on the USAF's C-5A program (with less than satisfactory results, for reasons not entirely related to the concept and objectives of TSPR). In major aircraft programs, important subsystems are often developed and purchased by the government and provided to the prime contractor for installation/integration into the weapons system (engines, armament, and certain avionics). For these Government Furnished Equipments (GFE), associate contractor agreements are drawn up that define interfaces as well as joint and individual responsibility between the weapons system prime contractor and those parties who themselves are responsible to a government agency for a particular subsystem. In this way, a manageable approach is available to implement TSPR under a single contractor.

As the aerospace industry matured, the cost-plus contracting environment prevalent in its formative years has steadily decreased. Today, fixed-price contracting is becoming the preferred method except in the highest risk projects. The most common approach for moderate to low risk projects is to contract for the full-scale development effort by means of a fixed-price incentive-with-ceiling contract. This instrument recognizes risk by first setting a target price for the baseline effort contemplated and then an associated ceiling price somewhat higher, usually 125% of the target price. Incentive is provided for the contractor to stay close to or below the target price by designing a sliding scale of profit that diminishes to zero at the ceiling. All costs related to the baseline effort above the ceiling are the contractor's responsibility. On the premise that risk reduces further as production proceeds, production contracts are firm fixed-price agreements.

THE GOVERNMENT'S ROLE

The Department of Defense is unique as a customer to industry in exercising its capability to maintain surveillance of its contractors. It has available expert data of all of the disciplines relevant to the aerospace business from engineering, manufacturing, quality assurance, contracts, finance, to logistics support. Additionally, it has a large group of professionals with industrywide exposure to contractors working in a wide spectrum of plants on diverse projects. These resources are formidable in their ability to evaluate the true status of a project in a short time by means of on-site inspections.

Prior to contract award, the DoD conducts on-site surveys of the contractor's plant, equipment systems, and organization to assess his readiness to undertake the project. A key to readiness is the existence of a suitable management information system that can be validated in accord with the DoD's Cost/Schedule Control System Criteria. a system of monthly program statusing that has been in effect for nearly 20 years on major military programs. Deficiencies noted during the preaward survey must be addressed and management commitments obtained before contracts are awarded.

On contract award, it is usual for major aerospace programs to have development managed by the Air Force Systems Command (AFSC), through a Systems Program Office (SPO). The SPO is responsible for all aspects of the program and establishes direct lines of communication between itself and the prime contractor for the duration of the project. The AFPRO, an independent detachment for the Contracts Management Division of AFSC, works with the SPO to provide on-site surveillance of contractor activity across the board on a day to day basis as well as serving in the vital role of monitoring contractor quality assurance. In this regard the AFPRO is the agent, with delegated authority from the SPO, to accept delivered end items from the contractor and authorize payment. A key tool used by the AFPRO is the Contractor Management System Evaluation Program, a system of condition questions to assess the existence and adequacy of the contractor's procedures as well as his compliance with them across all of the functional areas operative in his plants. Shortfalls detected by the AFPRO are raised for management attention and corrective action. The AFPRO/SPO team on a major aerospace project will number in the hundreds of people serving full time.

As part of its contractual requirements, the SPO receives from the contractor a number of other reports and documents that it deems necessary for the success of the project. These are defined in a Contract Data Requirements List (CDRL) that emcompasses engineering drawings, subsystem qualification reports, test plans and reports, vendor specifications, logistic support plans, etc., that are to be delivered at agreed-to intervals. However, the key reporting instrument is the monthly Cost Performance Report (CPR), based on the contractor's validated management information system, which reports the progress for the month and cumulative to-date progress on the project. Comparisons are made between the project planned cost and schedule and the reported actuals. Variances are analyzed to determine cause impact and establish recovery plans. Timely delivery of accurate CPRs is essential to avoid difficulty with the customer, as for example, suspension of progress payments.

CONCLUDING REMARKS

One of the unique aspects of the aerospace industry's government/military marketplace is the inversion of the customer/supplier relationship. There is basically a single customer, DoD, and a number of suppliers. Further, the customer is sophisticated, experienced, and staffed well enough to specify his needs, evaluate offerings, select contractors, negotiate contracts and—in short—get what he wants. Experience shows it is advisable for industry project managers to maintain good relationships with the many DoD representatives who are "the customer." The basis for a sound relationship is evident willingness to live up to the spirit and letter of the contract. Responsiveness to the customer's needs are imperative. If his needs extend beyond the contract, prompt action should be taken to amend the contract to satisfy his needs. This should be done in an atmosphere of cooperation; development of an adversarial relationship will hinder progress in settling differences.

In the FSD phase, it is critical that a credible project schedule and concomitant resource plan be established and adhered to. Even small variances must be investigated and corrected before matters get irrevocably out of control. Design reviews should be conducted early and regularly by specialists who have little involvement with the project. Included in the reviews should be members of the SPO or their designates. Early discovery of technical deficiencies or misinterpretations of customer needs is invaluable.

A successful project relies on open and clear communication among all functional groups and with the customer. Candid airing of all significant issues with solid, credible corrective action plans, with competent people designated by name to fulfill them, is a proven way to establish confidence that there is an effective management in charge of the project.

8

The Support Role of Research
to Project Management

JOHN P. HENRY, JR. *SRI International, Menlo Park, California*

RELATIONSHIP OF RESEARCH TO PROJECT MANAGEMENT

Research programs should be designed either to:

> Support all aspects of a project from conception through operation including development. At the extreme, this activity might be called "technical service."
> In its purest form, provide intellectual input to the project concept, with no immediate expectation of a "payoff."

In most cases, research associated with a particular project should be designed to ensure that the project remains viable over time. By its very nature, therefore, the research activity is dynamic.

The dynamics of research programs that support a major project are reflected in the following steps:

> Definition or redefinition of the research topic
> Initiation of a proposal activity that should describe:
>> What is to be done
>> Who should do the work
>> What is the cost/benefit of the research
> Project initiation on agreement about the scope of the work to be carried out
> Reporting of the research progress
> Completion or termination of the work

Research and technical support of any major project are likely to consist of a number of tasks carried out simultaneously. In other words, a number of research or development activities at various stages of development will be simultaneously initiated and completed—hopefully under the management of a project research director.

Ideally, research programs will be anticipated and, following an orderly planning process, put in place so that the research design can be carried out more expeditiously. In reality, however, as a project gets under way, a series of unexpected events will occur that necessitate the inauguration of research or technical services. Often those services must be provided quickly—with no time for the orderly design that most researchers seek. Therefore, the research team that supports any major project must be made up of scientists and engineers who, in addition to having professional interests in research and technical services, must also be able to change their work course if necessary as project management needs evolve. They must thus approach the support of any major project with a "service" rather than with an "academic" concept in mind.

It is useful to examine these issues in more detail.

RESEARCH PROJECT DEFINITION

Perhaps the most difficult aspect of designing a research or R&D program is to make certain that it fits into the overall strategic objective of the project. Research in its purest form often proceeds best if it is unhindered by immediate or short-term goals or cost objectives. Research in support of any major project is more likely to drift toward the "technical services" role than to the "pure" research role.

It is important at the outset to identify the personnel and facilities needed to meet the research objectives. Therefore, the strengths of the research team must be objectively assessed as they approach the difficult questions that need to be answered to support any major project. Such an analysis will often clearly indicate areas of weakness within the research team or in the support facilities—issues that must be resolutely faced early in the design of the research program.

Among the major problems that occur in any research program is the proper definition of various "milestones" in the research process. It is critical that a research team realize that it must not only meet intermediate goals, but that those goals may change during the course of a project.

It is realistic to assume that the definition of a research program will change—often dramatically—over its course. Whether the major project for which the research is defined is part of a series of projects supporting corporate development or whether the research supports a single-purpose, stand-alone project, the acquisition and maintenance of the research team and facilities are of critical importance. A major corporate development project often has longer time perspectives for research programs than those designed to support a major stand-alone venture. Research management in support of the project must be flexible, therefore, and carefully chosen to meet the overall project objectives.

MANAGING A RESEARCH PROGRAM

Research management begins at the earliest stages of project and program design and development. Once the technical support needs for a major project are identified, it is the responsibility of the research director, in support of the project manager to:

> Complete preproposal activities/define project scope
> Develop the proposal
> Initiate the research program
> Monitor the program
> Terminate the program when necessary

Preproposal Activities/Project Definition

Even before submitting a proposal to the project team, it is important that the research director carry out detailed negotiations with the project manager to demonstrate a full understanding of the research or technical support needed to meet the overall project objectives. They should arrive at a mutually acceptable project definition. More often than not, the research program will consist of a series of interrelated tasks that can open the range of research from "theoretical" through "applied" to "technical services." The research director must understand the types of research personnel that will be needed to meet the overall project objectives, and tailor an acquisition/reward system to attract appropriate professionals. This step is critical, and must be undertaken before writing the formal proposal.

Probably the most critical element in establishing a research program as a major support role to project management is the conception and construction of the research proposal. The proposal defines program scope for both the project manager and the research director and serves as the basis for funding negotiation throughout the program.

Developing the Proposal

Once the program or series of programs has been defined, the research director, assisted by the support team members, initiates the writing of a formal proposal. This document provides the basis for fund negotiation with the project manager, and therefore the more comprehensive this document is, the less likelihood there will be of problems as the project proceeds toward completion.

Once the research program or group of programs have been defined, the proposal—as a statement of this definition—outlines the schedule of deliverables to the project director. In addition to the careful definition of the deliverables expected, the proposal must clearly state the anticipated manpower needs over the life of the program and the cost of personnel along with the necessary capital and operating costs required to support the research. The more clearly these items are defined in the proposal, the more likely the chances are for success in the support of the project.

The research proposal must also include an indication of the supplemental staff needed to accomplish R&D objectives. Rarely can a research program be fully staffed with all of the experts that might be needed to explore the avenues that might open up unexpectedly during the course of the research. The research director should anticipate the need for additional outside technical consultants to carry out the work program. In many cases, this work element is established on a cost-as-incurred basis.

The proposal should outline definite milestones as well as the target dates for deliverables. These must concur with the need dates of the project manager. The R&D team must understand the importance of meeting all of these dates to ensure the project's success.

Milestones are a measure of the effectivity of the research process. Periodic milestone reports and meetings will allow the value of the research to the project to be evaluated on a continuous basis. It is likely that the direction of the research program may have to change as its results are compared with the actual needs of the project. The original proposal will probably be revised several times; and this should be considered an opportunity for a healthy exchange of information.

If the research is achieving the results anticipated, it is likely to lead to changes in overall project direction which were unanticipated earlier in the project. Such an outcome is one of the chief values of the research effort.

Research Program Initiation

Once negotiations for the scope and the funding for the required research have been completed, the research objectives can be clearly defined with regard to the level of support required for the major project. As research is initiated, the research director and the overall project manager will agree upon a schedule of discussions to keep the joint goals of the research team and the project manager "in sync." The research director becomes responsible for initiating the proposed research activity as soon as the proposal has been accepted. He should be prepared for unexpected, additional research support requirements that may arise as the project manager encounters unforeseen technical difficulties.

The research director and key staff members proceed to lay out a formal work plan. The following items should be completely covered by the plan in as much detail as possible:

The work to be carried out "in house," as well as a statement of the outside labor support needed to achieve overall program objectives

A clear statement of the capital acquisition timing and startup of the various phases of the research effort

The need for any outside support such as licenses or other cost elements associated with acquiring the knowledge base needed to meet program objectives

The research director needs to outline to the staff both the short-term and long-term needs of and expectations for the research effort. The research director must obtain commitment from the staff, not only with regard to reaching the stated objectives of the research effort, but also the awareness that the research results must support the needs of the project. Too often, research programs go astray when the research team views its work as an "end" in and of itself, rather than as a critical element in project development.

The project plan can be presented in a suitable format which may be a PERT chart, a sophisticated computerized project management program or some other means of establishing the details of the program work schedule.

Initiation of the research program is an exciting time for the entire research team. The tone and spirit of this activity must be set at the outset by the research director if the overall program goals are to be met in the time required.

Monitoring the Progress

Objective and analytical progress monitoring is critical for any research program. At preset "milestones," the research director and the project manager should meet to discuss the program to ensure that both understand the synergy of their objectives. Research programs often "go wrong" because of inappropriate progress dialogue between the project manager and research director whose goals have become divergent.

Objectivity must be kept in mind as the research director and the project manager meet at the appropriate "milestones" of the research program. Differences of opinion will frequently arise given the exploratory nature of research. However, unless an adversarial deadlock occurs at one of the milestones, the project manager and the research director are expected to continue to direct the research effort to meet project needs. On occasion, an outside arbiter may be brought in to mediate serious disputes.

The research results that are described at the various "milestones" are likely to suggest that either the research effort or the overall project be modified. Because it is usually easier to redirect the research effort than change the overall objectives of a major project, the research should be looked upon as a dynamic process. The research work plan will probably have to be modified as a result of the interim progress meetings. This is a normal process for research designed to support major projects.

At the other end of the project spectrum, it is likely that the project manager will receive suggestions for changes in project direction from his corporate management as unforeseen events unfold and changes in corporate strategy are recognized and implemented. At this point, the dialogue between the project manager and the research director might result in establishing a need for substantial changes in the R&D support.

Monitoring R&D progress is crucial. The more frequently the two parties conduct this type of dialogue, the more likely it is that the results of the research effort will be useful for both parties. Whether engaged in pure research or in technical service, the research director should be willing to deal with the details of the R&D program. He must also try to anticipate the changes needed in this program to support the overall project objectives.

Program Termination

When a research program ceases to provide "value added" to a project, it must be terminated. The research director must be prepared to terminate entire programs or subcontracts if it becomes obvious that their outcome will not be useful to the overall project or if the expected value of the research would have only a marginal impact on the project. Thus, it cannot be emphasized too strongly that the research director must maintain "objectivity" throughout the course of his work. Research and support for any project are just that–investigation and support.

The realities of terminating the program must be recognized as soon as possible and steps taken to ensure that the process is orderly. The decision to terminate any R&D program is usually determined by one of these conditions:

1. Successful presentation of results and acknowledged completion of the work. In this case, it is important to outline maintenance steps needed to ensure that the program results remain useful and up to date.
2. The program ends in a research impasse because the project scheme of analysis simply does not work. Such a conclusion allows the research director to re-deploy the project's financial assets to other channels which may produce more useful results for the overall project.
3. The topic becomes so complicated that a research program spinoff might be preferred. In this case, the results of the R&D effort might well open up research avenues or opportunities that might benefit the project itself and also have potentially important economic benefits for the parent organization as a whole.

R&D work usually entails risk to various degrees. The research director should set up a reward system to encourage taking risks if the expected successful outcome would be of significant value to the overall project.

Termination of research programs and the liquidation of assets associated with them should be discussed at the various milestone meetings between the research director and the project manager. Successful termination of the research program is the goal of all parties. Given the nature of research, termination of activities that no longer provide project benefits for the costs they incur should be determined as early as possible to allow the manpower and capital resources to be deployed as efficiently as possible for continuing R&D work.

XII

WHEN ONE ELEMENT IS DOMINANT

If we were to canvass a broad field of experienced project managers in an attempt to define the makeup of a "statistically" normal project, we would have great difficulty in arriving at an acceptable definition, but we surely would develop a good list of the factors to be considered. If we then took those factors and evaluated ranges where each could operate without submerging the influence of others, we should be able to define a broad band of "normal" or balanced projects at least qualitatively.

We could then demonstrate that a high content of a principal factor could alter the relative importance of other factors, and at some level could be totally dominant. The other factors would be either essentially benign, or their impact so altered that only routine monitoring would be required to neutralize their importance—a supportive role. The total dominance of one element on a project is rare; the Manhattan Project during World War II comes to mind; all that counted was "how soon."

There have been many projects, however, where one element, for practical purposes, controlled the program. A well-known and common example is the "fast-track" project, where time is of the essence. There are two standard approaches to the fast-track project: (1) deliver a complete package to the contractor at the expense of a time-consuming front-end effort on the part of the owner; (2) "bootstrap" the operation with a selected and qualified contractor on a reimbursable basis. A decision by management to implement the first approach, or a qualified and limited release with the second approach, means the schedule wasn't totally dominant, and not a pure fast-track project. In the real world, however, from the standpoint of project execution by a combined owner-contractor project team, a fast-track project is one in which the directive is to complete the project on an accelerated schedule, with reasonable cognizance of other factors.

To demonstrate how one factor can become dominant, we have to tabulate the principal factors and select those that occur more frequently and with more impact than others. Accordingly, four factors have been selected based on experience and judgment to illustrate this restricted phase of project management: schedule, size, quality, resource limited.

SCHEDULE

The accelerated-schedule project is one of the most common and least understood exercises the project manager will encounter. Upon project release all clients want their
projects completed "fastest," but not at the expense of budget or quality. This isn't
a fast-track project. The fast-track project, normally under a reimbursable contract,
will compromise budget (not wastefully) and quality (not safety) to meet a critical
marketing target date.

The quality compromise requires clarification. Concessions must be accepted as
the program advances. Plant layout may not be ideal. Preferred equipment may be
unacceptable due to extended deliveries. Piping and conduit routing may not be optimal. Access for maintenance may prove to be awkward (not by plan). But, if one
month is saved to beat competition to the marketplace for a new drug or insecticide
the client will say the project was successful.

SIZE

The full range of project size is presented: the considerations for the planning and
execution of small projects; two discussions of "mega" projects by senior managers of
two of the largest EPC contractors in the world, with significant areas of fundamental
agreement on the issues, and interesting views on unconventional but successful tactics.

A concept to consider for the mega project is the "3 PM Concept". These projects
are long; people get stale; different psyches fit different time phases. Project Manager
A, strong on planning and creativity, initiates the program. Project Manager B, strong
on production, pushes the work. Project Manager C, strong on detail, wraps up the
project. Blue sky, mover and shaker, nit-picker!

QUALITY

Quality considerations are best illustrated by an analysis of the nuclear power plant
industry. These projects, referred to as zero-defect projects, also put the project
under the scrutiny of regulatory bodies, the press, and the public. An extended
chronology of a nuclear project covers the project management role in detail.

RESOURCE-LIMITED

We move into a wide field when we consider resource-restrained projects, since all
projects have limitations on resources, but we wish to emphasize dominance. Three
chapters deal with this condition: the execution of projects in a multiproject environment; a project on the North Slope of Alaska (remote location, severe climate); and,
a solution to certain resource limitations (modular construction).

1

Small Projects

JOHN L. ZARNICK   *Cross & Black   Inc. Engineers, Union, New Jersey*

The large process plant and heavy industry construction projects that dominated the 1960s and 1970s were followed by a trend to much smaller projects in the late 1970s and throughout the 1980s. Clients, dissatisfied with the inability of the major engineering and construction contractors to adjust to the changing times, were left with several options, none of which were entirely satisfactory: first, form an in-house group, with attendant overhead and limited project experience; second, award work to smaller contractors accustomed to the techniques of small project execution, but without the depth to solve complex problems; third, attempt in various ways to monitor and control the ratio of total cost to work output in the shops of the major contractors. Within the inner circles of major contracting organizations, top executives displayed their frustration and anger at the lack of progress with new "lean and mean" campaigns.

In retrospect, we have to evaluate the efforts of most contractors during this period as inadequate; lip service rather than commitment was the norm, perhaps due to a basic inability to truly comprehend the organization needed to be competitive in the small projects market, or, more likely, the mistaken belief that the halcyon days of the late 1960s and early to mid-1970s would return. That a basic lack of capital funding existed, and that the limited funds available for capital expansion would be released in a highly selective and controlled manner, were recognized too late as the new plant construction drought persisted.

The most common approach used in the engineering and construction (E&C) industry was to "beat down the hours," a practice not encouraged by clients who wanted the expenditure of productive hours, but not what they considered to be "overhead" hours. A casualty, all too often, was a cutback in "good overhead"—the expertise of supervisors, and a continuation of "bad overhead"—or, charging the job. The preceding is an oversimplification. The real culprit was "business as normal"; the time-tested procedures and policies used on normal projects for proposals, estimates, engineering, procurement, construction, and, unfortunately, project management, were applied to small projects with unacceptable results. Nobody was thinking "small" following the splurge of mega projects! And standards, fattened by years of large cost-plus work, were inviolate, as were project staff concepts, formulated in the era of the "project directorate."

An approach that gained favor within some major E&C companies was the formation of a separate profit center for the execution of small projects: a concept sound in theory, but susceptible to empire-building and reproducing the original sin on a grander scale; a concept, however, that met with limited success when two primary conditions existed—a deep management commitment, and a good backlog of projects, particularly the latter.

Several conditions have to exist for a major contractor to pursue and execute small projects successfully over an extended time frame: management commitment, streamlined project organizations, appropriate procedures and policies—from proposals and estimates through execution, flexible hands-on personnel as opposed to systems-oriented personnel, sales and marketing people who are "believers," and strong client feedback channels to top management.

DEFINITION

A small project has certain characteristics, some a question of degree, some not. If we review the literature seeking definitions of certain elements of our profession, we are stuck with the great difficulty authors have had with a definitive statement of things they understand well, such as project management, project, mega project, authority, and so forth. A classic and profound definition of a top project manager, a mega project manager, is "When you meet one, you'll know it." So it is with the small project: "When one comes along, you'll know it."

The first definition of a mega project emphasized size. Time proved this definition to be inadequate, for size without complexity wasn't enough. A basic definition of a small project is that it's small. But, this definition doesn't go far enough. The missing ingredient is simplicity. And small has to be relative to the normal level of work within a given organization, with normal defined as the utilization of standard company practices, policies, procedures, and personnel for the execution of projects.

All of us, however, have a need for one-dimensional definitions, categorizations, putting things in slots. Certain small project definitions, all of which fall short, are in common usage.

A small project has a capital expenditure range from as little as several thousand dollars to $10,000,000-$15,000,000

A small project has a professional service expenditure range from as little as several hundred hours to 40,000-50,000 hours

The preceding definitions are more often true than not, but within an organization are erroneous if the specific project clearly requires the application of standard company practices, policies, procedures, and personnel. In such a case, the project is not small, but of intermediate or normal size.

Small projects require simplified procedures and special treatment, multiple duty performance of versatile general purpose engineers, streamlined project organizations, parttime assignments, minimum use of systems, on-off help from specialists, and design and procedural shortcuts with maintenance of acceptable levels of quality.

The types of projects that may qualify as small projects, other things being equal, include pilot plants, small production facilities, modifications to existing facilities, and feasibility studies, the most common of all.

A useful management tool for small projects is a small project manual. The initial issue should be produced by a representative team directed by a senior executive. The manual should be updated as each small project, or group of small projects, is completed, to reflect methods and philosophies that have been found to work. The format can be "cook book," but must clearly cover what practices work well and what practices absolutely must be avoided. The introduction to the manual should state the philosophy of the company with respect to the execution of small projects. The body of the manual should be specific with respect to mandatory practices; best if limited to what is truly mandatory, plus a wide range of suggested practices, to encourage the versatility and flexibility so necessary for effective management of such projects.

SCOPE OF WORK

A clear definition of the scope of work is critical to all projects. Many projects have gotten into trouble early because work proceeded without an agreed-to understanding of precisely what was required, who was responsible for each element of the work, and how the work was to be executed. For small projects, these considerations are paramount since the tolerance level for a false start is nonexistent. Further, most experienced project managers will recall the time they turned out a beautiful report, to learn that it wasn't what the client wanted.

Before acceptance and release of work (a joint study and development team on an open-ended rate basis might be an exception), the what, who, and how should be spelled out in detail. On a very small job, this step is often considered unnecessary. If ever there was a need for definition it's on the very small job!

The What

A standard checklist with room for specific additions is a useful guide. On a century account basis the guide should include at least the following—subheadings can be extensive.

Regulatory	Computer systems
Process engineering	Estimating
Basic design	Scheduling
Civil engineering	Cost control
Electrical engineering	
Instrument engineering	Procurement
Piping engineering	Buying
	Expediting
Apparatus engineering	Inspection
HVAC engineering	Traffic
Machine design	
Material handling	Home office construction services
Mechanical equipment	Field construction
Protective coatings	
	Economics

The Who

Although the contractor normally does the majority of the work on a small project, there are usually several outside contributors. It takes only one outside contributor to complicate a small project. The most common situation is where the external contributor is the client, with the responsibility to provide certain key data upon project release, and possibly at fixed dates throughout the project.

The responsibility to perform certain work or to provide certain data should be stated in an assignment document. Possible contributors include: Contractor, Owner-Upon Award, Owner-After Award, Others-Upon Award, Others-After Award, Not Required. The category "Not Required" should be clearly stated in the assignment document; an almost universal occurrence on a small project is the performance of work that just wasn't required.

The How

The last step to a complete definitive scope of work is an extended narrative of how the work will be done, the timing, the documentation, and everything else to be provided to the client.

With the scope of work, milestone and completion schedules, report format, and contractual terms agreed to by contractor and client, a small project stands a high chance of being successful

ORGANIZATION

If the contractor only occasionally does small project work, the organization to plan
and execute the work will, in all likelihood, follow traditional organizational concepts
for that contractor, with perhaps a minimum attempt to accommodate the concepts of
small project management. If, however, there is a commitment on the part of a major
contractor to enter the field, or a smaller contractor wishes to establish a pre-eminent
position in the field, then certain well-established concepts should be implemented.

An executive should be appointed with full responsibility and accountability for
the marketing and execution of small projects. Depending upon the level of activity
this assignment will be part or full time. The sales personnel and project team members can either be part of a formal small projects group or function within the normal
company matrix. The determining factor is workload, but regardless of the organization the concepts that follow are generally applicable. For clarity in presentation we
will assume a reasonable workload, but below the level required to justify the establishment of a separate group; the mix of large and small projects within a matrix is the
most common and most troublesome condition.

The one person who should be full-time is the proposal coordinator. Depending on
the views of the company, this person could be the responsible executive, but assume
for the moment that he isn't. It is important that every proposal be coordinated by
the same individual: the outline, organization, schedule, and preparation of the proposal; the review of the completed proposal. At this point, the executive thoroughly
reviews the proposal and adds two elements: the organization chart and the nominees
for the key positions.

Several factors should be considered in setting up the organization chart and ap-
pointing the candidates. Foremost among these are the availability and suitability of
the candidates for the project being proposed, client preferences if any, prior relationships between available candidates and the client, and the project organization within
the company: matrix, task, full time assignments, part time assignments.

The usual approach to structuring the organization for a small project is to execute
the work with a streamlined project team. The choice of task force versus matrix may
be dictated by the client, or in the absence of a client preference, by the contractor.
It is important to remember, however, that a basic condition for a task force is continuity of work, and a basic characteristic of many small projects is part-time work. However, another basic condition of small projects is a highly efficient communications network, and this is a clear plus for the task force. The best organizational approach
for a specific project must address many issues. To set hard and fast rules is to counter the flexibility inherently needed for successful small project execution.

Several additional considerations have to be evaluated to arrive at a workable organization. These include:

> The person who heads up the small project team isn't necessarily a project manager.
> He could be a project or lead engineer, squad leader from a discipline, pro-
> curement manager, or construction manager.
> Support services normally supplied to larger projects can be handled by selected
> members of the team with help sought from the parent department only if neces-
> sary.
> Work normally performed by a discipline may be performed by a team member and
> the discipline specialist used only as necessary for special input or checking.
> The team should be on the lean side, with most members picking up multiple duty
> assignments and responsibilities. Part-time assignments, if practical, should
> be given strong consideration.
> When production work is accomplished using the matrix organization, working super-
> visors should be considered to avoid discipline assignments and resultant
> charges.

If the project, even though small, crosses many company interfaces, it is best to assign a project manager, even on a part-time basis.

If the project involves full EPC services, even if small, a project manager should be assigned full time up to the point where followup is clearly a part-time need.

Members of a small project team should be selected for their adaptability, flexibility, resourcefulness, and team-oriented attitudes. They should be capable of coping with work problems and situations outside of their normal areas of expertise. They must be willing to perform multiple duties. They must be innovative in areas of work methods, short cutting, streamlining of operations, elimination of nonessential work, and cost and schedule improvements. A small project team must have flexibility and compatibility. There is no room for rigidity or agitation.

PROJECT CONTROLS

A general position on project controls and procedures should be understood: the emphasis has to move from a reliance on systems to hands-on person-to-person verbal communications, with one exception. As we move from a "small" small project to a "large" small project we should introduce selected systems carefully.

Estimating

The single greatest mistake in estimating small projects is the use of standard tools more suited to conventional projects; the key is to estimate the project that you are going to implement. Avoid the use of historical data and administrative overlays. Avoid the inclusion of "normal" contingencies. Small projects are high-efficiency once-through programs; if this isn't the case, then the company's approach to small projects needs to be overhauled.

Scheduling

The simple bar chart approach to planning and scheduling of projects is best for most small projects, and should be evaluated for suitability for a specific project before an alternative program is selected. A useful adjunct for the project manager is a minimum-activity logic diagram with milestone highlights.

There are some notable exceptions to the proposed standard approach, generally limited to highly defined and interactive complex short-term projects. Examples include: a refinery turnaround, a changeover from conventional to computerized instrumentation systems; in short, any system where the complexity is such that it isn't reasonable to expect the players to be able to "see" the project at all times. Projects of this type benefit from a CPM or PERT approach, but with bar chart printouts.

Cost Control

There are two reasons for developing and implementing cost control programs and methodology within a contractor's organization: (1) internal considerations (allocation of resources, production of profit), and (2) external considerations (achievement of client project objectives, maintenance and growth of client relations). Often, cost control programs seem to have the mass production of paper as an objective, the project within a project syndrome. Large projects survive this approach; small projects don't.

Effective cost-control procedures for the four principal classifications of projects based on size (mega, large, intermediate, small) are drastically different. There are two approaches to the determination of the cost-control needs for a small project: review the standard company practices and select what fits, or, develop the programs you believe you need. Both approaches work, but the first has the advantage of familiarity.

A caveat that must never be forgotten: Most cost control procedures fail because the scope of work was not clearly defined or it was not understood by the team members. Meet with your team for one morning before embarking upon the project, and talk-through the scope of work. Throughout the project, maintain a timely project note system confirming all scope changes received from the client. Don't be trapped by a common misconception that small projects don't require a project note system; all projects require a project note system.

The earned value concept, a quantum leap in controls management during the 1960s and 1970s, is ill-suited to most small projects, as is its precursor, the internal project note, adjusting work quantities between disciplines. One general controls approach, contributory to performance evaluation on larger projects, should be considered for small projects, and that is the "audit system." Each week select one or two elements of work (a drawing, a specification) and have the designer explain the work to the project team. The audit system serves several purposes, including a continual awareness of scope; are we over- or underdesigning, is progress as advertised, and so forth.

Communications

Start with a basic principle: don't write letters to your staff. Meet and discuss issues. Maintain a simple indexed instruction program as a project reference document; entries should be brief, hand-printed. Visit with staff members frequently, but don't make a nuisance of yourself; once a day for a few minutes is suggested. The classical needs list works well on all projects, and is particularly well suited to the small project.

Management briefings, whether they be for the client or your own management, detract from small project performance. They take a disproportionate amount of time and require documentation not necessary to management of the project. On a normal project most of the documentation used for presentations is of a fallout nature; this should not be so for the small project. But, the client or your management may insist upon formal presentations. Try to wean them away from this approach and toward brief one-on-one discussions.

ENGINEERING SHORTCUTS

All standard company procedures and policies should be reviewed before incorporation in either a basic company approach to small projects or the execution of a given small project. Shortcuts, with maintenance of acceptable quality, should always be sought. Team members should question and challenge standard practices, when appropriate.

The ideal small project is a once-through project with a minimum of change. Be certain everything required for an efficient kickoff is on hand before starting work. Then, with the project underway, think "shortcuts" all the time. There are two principal sources of shortcuts: a company small projects practices manual, if available; a "thinking" project team.

The approach suggested is applicable to the engineering, procurement, and construction of a turnkey project. Some thoughts on engineering follow. Note that as many, if not more, opportunities exist for unique performance in the procurement, construction, and project controls areas.

Engineering considerations should include as a minimum:

Use of a standard layout drawing for overlay discipline engineering where feasible
Use of orthographic drawings, with supplementary isometrics only where required for clarity
Combining drawings where possible
Use of standard detail drawings
Use of tabulations to codify such things as standard foundations

Familiarity with area construction practices; supply only the necessary engineering to complete an issued-for-construction package

Use of 8-1/2 by 11 sketches liberally in lieu of formal drawings

Mark-up of existing drawings for revamp projects, or supplemental sketches

Use of vendor drawings to the maximum

Taking advantage of and using preliminary drawings prepared by the process/technical center or client

Condensing massive general specifications to project specifications; it is not uncommon to extract one or two applicable pages from a 50-page general specification

Questioning the need for a material takeoff: is it necessary; can others do it

Evaluating what engineering tasks can reasonably be done by a field engineer

Some of the preceding suggestions may not be applicable to a specific project, or may be unacceptable to the client. Many other good ideas will surface upon review by the team. Ideally, the principal strategies should be stated in the proposal, for commercial and client relations purposes. But other ideas will surface as the project proceeds. It is best to get client agreement promptly. It is a losing proposition to deliver a package to a client that falls short of the detail that the client had every right to expect.

SUMMARY

We have reviewed the unique characteristics of the small project and the people who staff these projects.

Some comments are offered to management for their serious consideration:

Successful small projects start with a commitment by senior management.

If the approach to the marketing and execution of small projects goes beyond once-off or a minimum level, a practices manual is a necessity.

Consider the merits of a skills inventory study to learn the depth of multitalented people in the organization.

The adaptability of the current project management corps should be reviewed. If a project manager can't "see" the project, he's not a small projects manager. He may be excellent for large projects, but keep him clear of small, fast-moving, projects.

2

Fast-Track Projects: A Case History

L. D. "DON" SLEPOW and ALAN S. MENDELSSOHN   *Florida Power and Light Company, Juno Beach, Florida*

The use of project management techniques on major construction projects is not new. In recent years, however, we have seen a trend toward more automated tools to help the project manager in doing his job. But what about the application of project management techniques to a large crash project? Do the principles still apply? Can project management work?

A case history of Florida Power & Light Company's Sanford Coal-Oil Mixture (COM) Demonstration Project provides an answer. This involved the design and construction of an on-site COM preparation plant, appropriate modifications to the power plant to accommodate this experimental fuel, and a 1-year demonstration to test the effectiveness of the fuel in a 400 mega-watt oil-fired boiler. Designing the facility around available equipment, using an abbreviated procurement cycle, and fast-track construction with engineering and procurement allowed the making and burning of coal-oil mixture to take place approximately seven months after the project began. Analysis of results and the preparation of a three-volume final report documenting the test data were also under project management direction.

To gain an appreciation of the magnitude of this accomplishment, it is first necessary to describe the importance of the project, the physical modifications made, and the results obtained; then discuss the application of project management and how it was used to make the demonstration successful.

PROJECT DESCRIPTION

Before discussing this project in detail, let's first describe how we do business on our other projects. We have been practicing project management at FPL since 1973. The Project Management Department has authority and responsibility over all activities associated with assigned major projects from the time of assignment until the project is complete. To accomplish this, project management relies on project teams comprised of departmental representatives who receive project direction from the project general manager (PGM) and receive technical and administrative direction from their home department. This is what matrix management is all about. The Project Management Department is directly responsible, through its project controls staff, for planning and scheduling, budget and cost control, estimating, and project reporting. The department is also responsible for directing and coordinating all project-related functions including engineering, procurement, licensing, quality control, construction, contract administration, preoperational testing, accounting, and inventory resources.

In April 1980, Florida Power & Light Company conducted a one-year test of a new fuel as part of its efforts to decrease its dependence on oil. This fuel, coal-oil mixture (COM), is as its name implies, a mixture of these two conventional fuels that are combined as a substitute for oil.

To achieve this, the Company formed a project organization to build and modify the required facilities and conduct the demonstration. The project's success is now history. Our success was due to the application of project management principles in an environment that precluded the use of sophisticated tools.

The work began in September 1979 when senior FPL management met with high-level officials from the Department of Energy (DOE) and committed to test burn a coal-oil mixture in a 400 MW unit starting early in 1980. The motivation for doing this was based upon the increasing cost of oil, a reduction in the quality and availability of the fuel, and the likelihood of some sort of imposed mandatory restrictions by federal and/or state authorities. Within our system there were nine 400 MW units and four 800 MW units, all designed to burn oil. In fact, FPL burned more fuel oil than any other utility in the United States. Our desire to reduce our consumption was manifested in this commitment to DOE.

It was felt that a full conversion decision to coal-oil mixture was premature, since no large commercial scale test on an oil-designed boiler had previously been done. Many technical questions remained concerning this new fuel that could only be answered by a comprehensive test program. One of the Sanford units was chosen to do the test.

Our design philosophy was to utilize as much of the existing fuel supply system as possible and make only changes or modifications to the unit that were absolutely necessary for operational or safety reasons. In other words, spend as few capital dollars as possible to accomplish the goal. Since the amount of COM required was five times the capacity of the largest preparation plant existing at that time, the decision was made to construct a facility on site to make the desired amount, 10,000 barrels of COM per day, having a coal concentration of 50% by weight.

SCHEDULE

Engineering was started on October 12, 1979. Bechtel Power Corporation was chosen as the engineer/constructor/operator of the COM preparation facility. Construction began November 29th with clearing of the COM preparation plant site. FPL management's original goal was to burn COM in February 1980. As delivery dates for equipment were determined, it became evident that this date could not be met. At the end of the year, the schedule was revised to reflect an April burn date, which was the earliest possible considering the long lead times and availability of certain equipment. Sanford Unit 4 was shutdown for four weeks in March 1980 in order to make appropriate modifications to the unit. The first COM was mixed on April 18th and this 10% by weight concentration was burned on April 20, 1980, less than five months after construction began. The overall engineering and construction schedule is illustrated in Figure 1.

PROCESS

The coal was brought in by rail cars using a newly constructed railroad siding. It was then unloaded using portable equipment and moved to either the coal pile or placed directly onto a conveyor for feeding into the facility.

The coal that entered the preparation facility was stored in one of four coal silos. As needed, it flowed to the pulverizers where it was ground to a consistency of 80% through a 200 mesh screen.

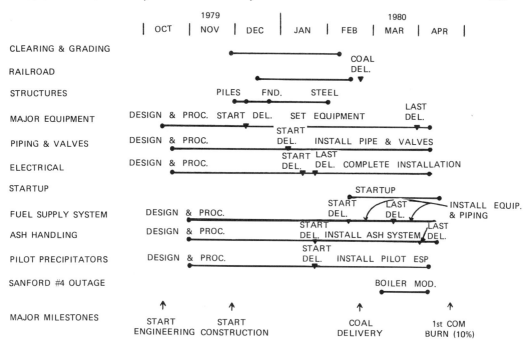

Figure 1 COM demonstration engineering and construction schedule.

The coal was then transported by air from the pulverizers to the top of the facility and through cyclone separators which separated out the majority of the pulverized coal from the air. The pulverized coal went into the storage bin located directly below. The air and the remaining fine coal particles went into baghouse filters located at the top of the facility. The coal-free air was then exhausted from the baghouse filters. The pulverized coal that was collected on the filters was knocked off and stored in hoppers at the bottom of the baghouse. It was then piped to the pulverized coal storage bin. The pulverized coal storage bin was a large cylindrical stainless-steel-lined cone designed for smooth flow of the powdered coal.

The 15,000 gallon mix tank, located at ground level, received the pulverized coal from the storage bin, as well as oil from a storage tank within the power plant and mixed it together to form the coal-oil mixture. In addition to the coal and the oil, an additive and a small amount of water were also introduced to insure stability of the mixture. Coal has a tendency to settle when mixed with oil. The additive helped to prevent this.

To produce a 50% by weight barrel of COM requires approximately 200 pounds of pulverized coal and 0.6 of a barrel of oil.

The COM was pumped from the preparation facility, at a maximum rate of 300 gpm, to a 55,000 barrel tank that had been modified for COM storage. We insulated the tank and installed four paddle mixers that slowly rotated to keep the COM in motion, which helped maintain the suspension of the coal particles in the mixture.

The COM was routed from the tank to the suction of the new burner pumps located near the tank area. These pumps took the COM and dumped it through COM fuel lines that tied into the existing fuel oil supply line in the area of the daytank. The daytank, which was used to measure the amount of oil normally burned, was bypassed when burning COM.

At the onset of the project, it was determined that the existing high-pressure, mechanical atomizing burners would not be suitable for an abrasive fuel like COM. A low-pressure, steam atomizing burner was developed by the burner manufacturer for this demonstration. During the early operations on COM, it became evident that excessive wear was occurring on the front nozzle of the burner tip. Through the efforts and imagination of the several team members, a solution to the problem was found to essentially eliminate the wear and improve combustion.

When not burning COM, the unit could revert back to oil.

To handle the ash generated while burning COM, several systems were installed for the demonstration. These included a bottom ash system, consisting of dumpster-type bins connected to the bottom of the boiler, and a fly ash system that used a modified ready-mix cement truck for transporting the ash to an on-site storage area.

Some insights into boiler behavior and performance were obtained through analysis of the data collected. We found that the superheater temperatures were slightly higher on COM than on oil. Boiler efficiency appeared to remain nearly the same on COM as on oil. The increase in excess air for COM firing slightly reduced efficiency. Burner modifications reducing air pressure drops and providing better combustion could possibly raise COM efficiency even closer to that of oil.

Early in the test it was determined that wall deslaggers had to be installed in the side and rear waterwalls of the boiler to keep the unit free from excessive ash buildup.

QUANTITIES

The Sanford COM demonstration required the installation of: 4 pulverizers, 10 pumps, 6 agitators, 230 tons of steel, 721 valves, 28,000 feet of pipe, 69,000 feet of cable, and 1,400 feet of railroad siding.

During the demonstration we achieved the following quantities:

COM produced	-	1,716,400 equiv. barrels
	-	325,800 tons
Coal burned	-	131,260 tons
Power generated	-	1,152,000 MWH
Maximum concentration	-	50%
Long-term concentration	-	42%

COST

The cost for doing a demonstration of coal-oil mixture was not small. The COM preparation plant and modifications to Sanford Unit 4 required $12.8 million in capital expenditures. An additional $5.2 million was needed to operate both facilities during the test. This total of $18.0 million, which did not include the costs for coal, oil, or additives, was partially offset by savings in fuel cost of $8.2 million from the substitution of COM for oil. Thus, the cost to the customer was $10.2 million, or about $4.50 per customer. The Florida Public Service Commission allowed FPL to recover this cost through the fuel adjustment clause during the one-year test period.

The original estimate for the project was $8.8 million, including $5.6 million for capital and $3.2 million for operating expenditures. This estimate was very conceptual in nature and was developed prior to the start of any significant engineering. As with many research and development projects, the scope of work is not often defined until some preliminary engineering work is done. This project was no exception. The scale-up from the only previous industry experience—an 80 MW coal designed unit—required a lot of imagination, innovation, some very original estimating, and resulted in the scope becoming better defined within a relatively short time frame. Once it was set, however, it did not change significantly. Most of the cost increases, in both the capital and operating areas, were a result of this solidification of the initial scope of the improvements to be made and the length and complexity of the test to be conducted. As construction was nearing completion, it was necessary to maintain a two-shift operation with extensive overtime in order to maintain schedule. This also contributed to the cost increase.

PROJECT MANAGEMENT

Why was FPL successful in what it did? The answer is the application of some basic success principles utilizing the project management framework to implement these principles. FPL management set a clear identifiable goal with a definite time frame. The project team did more than their best; they did whatever it took to get the job done using a very positive approach and positive attitude. We could not afford to take the time to discuss all the reasons why we could not do something. Every decision was based on schedule and economics.

We used a small "close knit" team, dedicated to getting the job done. We cut red tape, changed traditional ways of getting the work out, and made quick, timely decisions. Using very top management support, we bypassed strong-minded, traditionally oriented department heads, performed quick reviews of engineering by FPL, and reviewed drawings at the same time they were sent to the field for construction. Excellent communications between team members from FPL, the engineer/constructor, and the boiler manufacturer (Foster-Wheeler) were key factors.

The secret to our success lies in 17 elements that are like "motherhood and apple pie" statements. They are as follows:

1. We had top management commitment to the success of the project and the work of the project team. In fact, management was pushing very hard for progress rather than the usual case of you pushing management for support.

2. We were able to cut through company "red tape" by bending procedures to their fullest, as necessary. Approvals that normally take days or weeks were obtained in hours, often by walking through the appropriate cycle. People often delegated their authority to allow those in the project mainstream the freedom to do their job without unnecessary holdups.

3. There was excellent coordination between team members allowing information to flow in a timely manner. Personalities and personal preferences were put aside for the sake of the common goal.

4. We kept the project team small and manageable. Only those team members who were absolutely needed played an active role. Other team members contributed, as appropriate.

5. Excellent communications existed between all team members in all organizations allowing a free flow of information.

6. We let the engineer/constructor do his job. We hired him because of his expertise and his ability to do what we wanted in the short time frame. Instead of using the normal review and comment process that most projects in FPL go through, we bent the procedures and used an abbreviated version. We relied very heavily on the engineer/constructor's expertise.

7. Timely decisions were a must considering the short schedule. Telephone discussions and approvals were the rule rather than the exception in order to allow engineering and procurement to proceed in an expeditious manner.

8. The project had more or less an open checkbook, within reason. While cost was a factor, the overall potential benefits to the Company and the customer dictated that the project proceed at as fast a pace as possible. In other words, meeting the schedule became more important than holding the budget.

9. We made very few changes to the scope as agreed upon. This minimized schedule and cost impacts. In accomplishing this, we often had to give up our design preferences for some other option that met all the requirements in order not to impact the schedule. Of course, having an engineer who was familiar

with our design standards and philosophies made this approval more palatable. The minimization of scope changes should be a must for all projects.

10. We used schedules, budgets, and trends to guide the project. As previously indicated, the schedules were used for control; the others merely tracked and reported progress.

11. We had "get it done" type project managers on FPL and engineering/constructor teams. Their emphasis was not necessarily to reach compromise and satisfy all parties. It was often required to be "hard nosed" in order to keep the project on track.

12. Everyone possessed a "can do" attitude. By carefully selecting who would have the influential roles in project activities, the "foot draggers" were left out. In addition, instead of telling why something could not be done, the energies were directed toward doing it, often with surprising results. Team members in all organizations were encouraged to use their imagination and their initiative in problem solving.

13. The engineer/constructor put engineering and procurement in the field to work hand-in-hand with construction, thus resolving field problems quickly. In fact, the engineers who started the design in the home office were transferred to the field and stayed there through the startup phase. In a "small" project this is usually not the case. A $13 million capital power-plant project in FPL is considered small in our system.

14. The engineer/constructor and the boiler manufacturer had incentives to do a good job because of the possibility of future work with COM. This was a real plus for FPL in having a built-in incentive for these outside parties.

15. FPL had strong incentives because of the economics of future fuel supplies for our fossil units. While the price of oil has fluctuated, our long-term projections indicate a rise in prices and confirm our need to convert to some form of coal. The COM project has provided us with a knowledge base and an in-house level of expertise to apply to other developing technologies that could help us meet these long-term needs.

16. We used matrix management to establish strong communications and strong team control. Circumstances kept department heads out of the action—"information only." This allowed the team to proceed with its common objective. While individual department-head desires were considered, they did not control.

17. We picked a contractor who had the "total" capability of providing engineering, procurement, construction, startup, and operating services. This eliminated all bidding and contracting phases by FPL used in a typical package job where multiple specialty contractors are used. Thus, front-end time was reduced to a matter of a few weeks. By having one contractor operating under a cost-plus contract, it was easy to adapt the work output to the project needs without affecting the schedule progress. This was extremely important in doing the job quickly.

SUMMARY

Are sophisticated control systems required for project management implementation? Only when the volume of information and the duration of the project warrant it. On this project, they did not. Such basic tools as bar charts, critical action item reports, procurement status reports, etc., were used in an all manual operation and updated frequently to meet project needs. In contrast to this, FPL now uses computerized cost and schedule processors that tie automatically to accounting systems, quantity tracking systems, and to each other. Our emphasis was to provide to the project manager and his team all the information needed to control a project and do so in the format and in a time frame that supports that effort.

Can project management work on a crash project? The answer is a definite yes. This project was a one-of-a-kind project and does not represent the normal mode of operation at FPL. It was performed under ideal circumstances. The results were real. It happened because management made it happen.

3

Zero-Defect Projects: The Spirit of St. Lucie

LEO TSAKIRIS *Ebasco Services Inc., Norcross, Georgia*

On April 6, 1983, the St. Lucie Unit No. 2 Nuclear Plant started its core-load operation. By August 8, 1983, the unit was put into commercial operation. Those events in themselves should not have been particularly significant; however, when viewed from the perspective of what was happening in the nuclear power plant industry, they were indeed significant and represented an outstanding achievement. As a basis of comparison, the entire project from the construction permit in June 1977 to commercial operation in August 1983, was accomplished in a little over 6 years; 3-1/2 years better than current industry averages. In addition, where other units of a similar size have cost upward of $5 billion, this unit was built for a relatively modest $1.42 billion.

We will discuss the management of this project from the perspective of the engineer/constructor, Ebasco Services Inc., retained by Florida Power and Light Company to perform the engineering, design, and construction of this unit, as was the case for St. Lucie Unit No. 1. In all major project efforts, each of the parties: client/owner, engineer/constructor, vendors, and so on, have a particular role to perform to achieve project objectives; however, in my view, nowhere is the everyday performance more crucial and under more constant scrutiny than that of the engineer/constructor. It is here where the "rubber meets the road." The success or failure of its efforts is quickly reflected in the rate of progress of the project. The hard realities of everyday performance and of making schedules within budget restraints quickly relegate philosophical managerial theory to the halls of academia. This project is an example of a dedication to basic management practices and a determination to never lose sight of the project objectives.

BACKGROUND

The St. Lucie Unit No. 2 Nuclear Power Plant is an 890 MW unit utilizing a Combustion Engineering nuclear steam supply system and a Westinghouse turbine generator. It is located approximately 45 miles north of West Palm Beach, Florida, on a beautiful barrier island known as Hutchinson Island. This unit was intended to be a duplicate of the first St. Lucie unit, but the Nuclear Regulatory Commission insured that by the time construction was started, very little of the "duplicate" design was useful. Seismic criteria, tornado missile criteria, fire protection requirements, electrical cable-separation requirements, and more than 1000 other regulatory changes, in addition to those changes mandated as a result of the incident at Three Mile Island meant that we had to proceed practically from "scratch," taking special care that we did not assume duplication from the first unit without checking to see that it met current requirements. Another factor to be addressed was a pessimistic attitude that prevailed over the nuclear industry during this period, and a general trend to accept the most negative news concerning schedules, costs, or quality as commonplace in the industry. This attitude was one of the biggest obstacles to be overcome when dealing with vendors and subcontractors; all finding it easier to accept negative news when dealing with nuclear industry problems than to find ways to overcome the problems. We found a skepticism toward progress "as reported" and a general feeling that the "other shoe will drop," revealing the "true status."

Against this background, the management story of this major nuclear plant project can now be related.

THE EARLY DAYS

As the newly appointed project manager for St. Lucie Unit No. 2 in 1973, I received from our then Vice President of Projects, J. A. Scarola, a clear mandate concerning this project and my role in it. After informing me of the importance of the project for our company, he stated that as project manager I had the clear authority to form the project team and establish project policies. This mandate from executive management, establishing my authority in these areas, could not have been clearer. If we were to number the management lessons learned, this could be regarded as No. 1; a clear mandate and clear delineation of authority from above to conduct the business at hand.

Our staff selection included a number of "veterans" of St. Lucie Unit No. 1, with the introduction of certain key personnel changes to provide the additional engineering, construction, and management expertise necessary for this major undertaking. A degree of "personnel burnout" in the first unit team was apparent and fresh thinking was necessary.

Another important point that was established was what I'll call the "philosophy" of the project. Our company is an engineer/constructor, but it was evident that the "engineer" thinking dominated the planning and scheduling and priorities of projects, especially in the home office. Steps were taken early to establish that the object of this project was to support the construction effort, and that we all had to see that a project was constructed. The result was a complete commitment to the project objective: to build a nuclear power plant on schedule, within the established budget, without sacrificing quality or safety.

PROJECT PLANNING

The considerable time and effort spent on the initial planning and scheduling contributed significantly to the overall success of the project.

Between October 1976 and March 1977, a team of Ebasco construction supervisors developed the project master schedule. Setting the stage for all future planning, a 65-month schedule for the project—start of concrete to start of fuel load—was established and major milestones identified and fixed. The schedule consisted of an integrated engineering and construction plan and included summary start-up logic.

"Early Start" Dates

The schedule philosophy adopted by the project was to schedule and monitor all activities and material delivery dates to the "early start" date requirements. This approach provided a valuable safety factor which proved useful in minimizing the impact on the construction schedule caused by factors outside the control of the project.

Special priority was placed on engineering, design, and delivery of piping and hangers, scheduled for delivery a full 18 months prior to the "early start" dates. Hanger installation preceded pipe erection and minimized the need for temporary pipe support devices to a large degree, resulting in an orderly pipe installation program.

Although the future of St. Lucie 2 was uncertain when the Limited Work Authorization was withdrawn in October 1976, a bold decision was made to proceed without delay in accordance with previously established engineering, design, and procurement schedules. Consequently, when the construction permit was granted in June 1977, approximately 75% of the original scope of engineering and design was completed, and 40% of the engineered materials were delivered. This decision typified the total management commitment and support this project received from its inception.

Design Review

Another factor which contributed to the success of the construction effort at St. Lucie 2 was the detailed design review of St. Lucie 1 by construction personnel. The object of this review was to recommend areas in which design enhancements could be made to improve construction productivity and costs. Approximately 250 items were addressed and incorporated into the design. In addition, a design problem review (DPR) program was initiated. This program was a comprehensive review by engineering of all St. Lucie 1 changes: backfit changes, operations enhancements, regulatory requirements, and so on to ensure their consideration and disposition for St. Lucie 2. Over 1000 items were considered with approximately 350 incorporated into the St. Lucie 2 design.

Construction Planning and Implementation

Optimization of the construction effort was the result largely of the early planning and innovative thinking that went into the formulation of the overall construction plan and schedule for this project.

INNOVATIVE DESIGN AND CONSTRUCTION CONCEPTS

Reactor Auxiliary Building "Stair-Stepping" Concept

One innovative idea contained in the initial plan and schedule was the "stair-stepping" concept for the construction of the Reactor Auxiliary Building. In this plan, the building was constructed with emphasis placed on early completion of the west end of the building. The philosophy was that early completion of this end of the structure would provide an early start to the roof installation of the more critical areas of equipment in the Reactor Auxiliary Building: the control room and the reactor auxiliary control boards, the cable vault area, and NSSS auxiliary equipment.

The building during construction took on a "stair-step" appearance. As each elevation was completed, all major equipment and appurtenances were moved into that level prior to the roof installation. A considerable amount of Q deck construction was also used in an effort to minimize forming and shoring requirements. The net result was that critical areas were completed earlier, and key crafts started their work sooner.

Reactor Containment Building

Foundation design considerations were finalized as part of the original plan for simultaneous construction of both St. Lucie 1 and 2. Subsurface exploration borings indicated poorly consolidated sand with thin layers of clay to a depth of 65 feet below existing grade. To meet seismic criteria, a plant island was constructed by excavating the unsuitable material, backfilling with well-graded sand, and then compacting to required specifications. This plant island resulted in a compacted Class I fill measuring 780 feet by 920 feet by 78-1/2 feet deep. For economic reasons, the plant island was sized as small as possible by spacing the plant structures at minimum separations. When FP&L decided to delay construction, these plans were technically feasible, but subsequently required unique design and construction efforts for the second unit.

A circular sheetpile cofferdam for the Reactor Containment Building, which Ebasco believes was the first nuclear safety Class 1 cofferdam ever to be engineered and constructed, was necessary to protect the safe shutdown ability of St. Lucie 1 under all foreseeable circumstances, including earthquakes. The cofferdam was braced with internal compression beams and sized to allow excavation, concreting of the base mat and walls up to grade elevation, and subsequent backfill operations. The 180-foot-diameter circular cofferdam was constructed by driving 500 tons of sheetpiling in 72-foot lengths through compacted sand with electrical vibratory hammers. The 900 tons of horizontal bracing (walers) consisted of wide flange beams 36 inches deep, weighing 230 pounds to the foot, installed every 5 feet on vertical centers. To allow dewatering of the cofferdam, 18 deep wells were installed along the periphery. Driving of the sheeting started in June 1976, and the mudmat (working surface) was placed in late September of that year.

Another innovative construction accomplishment at St. Lucie 2 was the "slipforming" of the concrete containment shield wall for the Reactor Containment Building, in lieu of the traditional "step-form" method. This concrete cylinder has a 3-foot thick reinforced wall, approximately 190-1/2 feet high with an inside radius of 74 feet. It is supported by a ring wall, 9 feet thick and 4 feet high, which, in turn, rests on the base mat. The shield wall contains more than 1000 tons of reinforcing steel with another 23 tons of embedded materials such as electrical conduits, grounding cables, and anchor bolts. Wall placement through slipforming of 10,000 cubic yards of concrete averaged 11-1/2 feet per day, and the operation took place without interruption in only 16-1/2 days. Manpower for slipforming averaged 398 craft workers, and the crafts worked three shifts a day, 7 days a week until completion. Ebasco engineering and construction supervisory personnel also provided around-the-clock support and technical assistance. Immediately after completion of slipforming, construction on the steel containment vessel started inside the shield building.

Nuclear Steam Supply System (NSSS) Installation

An important benchmark in the Nuclear Regulatory Commission's (NRC) assessment of nuclear plant construction is the installation of the nuclear steam supply system's major equipment: reactor vessel, steam generators, and pressurizer. The project was able to meet this milestone on a progressive schedule by adopting two innovative ideas.

First, early planning and the decision to erect the containment steel vessel utilizing the "tops-off" approach. Basically, this method provides postweld heat treatment of the vessel erection before erecting the dome. Because of thinner plates, the dome did not require heat treatment and could be erected at a later time. As a result, interior concrete work started months earlier than otherwise possible and ensured that support structures were ready for NSSS installation.

Second, the interior concrete was not brought up to the operating level before setting the nuclear vessel. Instead, Ebasco engineering and construction personnel, in conjunction with the heavy rigging subcontractor and the polar crane manufacturer, simplified the "posting" arrangement for using the polar crane in setting the vessels. Using a two-shore instead of six-shore polar crane girder support system saved considerable schedule time and enabled construction forces to meet the target date of June-July 1980.

Ocean Discharge Pipe

Construction of the discharge headwall and installation of a 3345-foot-long ocean discharge pipe were completed as scheduled in October 1981. The discharge headwall is located just south of Unit 1's headwall at the dune line to the Atlantic Ocean. The structure funnels circulating discharge water into a discharge defuser pipe measuring 16 feet in diameter.

This pipe connects at the discharge headwall under the bench dune line. Running beneath the ocean floor, it stretches 3345 feet into the Atlantic Ocean. To disperse the discharge water evenly and at a constant rate of flow, the last 1368 feet of pipe contain 58 risers, 48-inch diameter, which project through the ocean floor at 24-foot intervals.

PROGRAM IMPLEMENTATION

After the initial plans and schedules were developed and techniques established for their implementation, the next phase involved carrying out these plans. We established a close liaison with our vendors, construction staff, and the client to insure rapid and effective feedback of potentially troublesome areas.

Vendor Monitoring

Vendor monitoring was under the direction of the assistant project manager. Advantages of this arrangement, especially in the critical areas of material procurement and expediting, were that vendor technical, commercial, and subvendor problems received immediate management visibility. This enabled project resources to be brought to bear to resolve problems and maintain critical material delivery dates. It also enabled close liaison with the construction site on delivery dates to allow materials and jobsite priorities to be addressed in a timely manner. We found, on some occasions, that the vendors' apparent inability to meet schedule was due to a lack of additional information they required from us. This would not have become apparent as quickly if not for these constant monitoring and feedback mechanisms.

Likewise, in construction, lead construction engineers were required to meet with the lead discipline engineers on a regular basis, to objectively review jobsite problems, and resolve them in an expeditious manner. It was important that these problems not be allowed to fester, and that neither engineering nor construction personnel take defensive attitudes. Constant management attention and a reinforcement of "team work" attitudes helped in this process.

Jobsite Craft/Management Interface

Another crucial area in the implementation of this project was the jobsite management of the construction effort. A number of steps were taken to insure a successful construction environment.

Quarterly labor-management meetings were held to open lines of communication in a nonadversarial atmosphere. This provided an appropriate forum for resolving grievances and jurisdictional disputes.

Training of electrician and welder crafts up to the foreman level was initiated, upgrading craft skills and the planning, motivation, and productivity techniques of supervisors. An attitude survey was performed with approximately 15% of the craft manpower and, as a result, a number of items were uncovered which were adversely affecting productivity, attendance, and attitudes. These items were promptly corrected, changed, or otherwise addressed, with a noticeable improvement in morale and productivity. Communications were enhanced on the jobsite through the publication of a site newsletter to report on specific as well as general information concerning the project.

The items mentioned above, with firm but fair application of labor agreement provisions and project work rules, essentially eliminated work stoppages.

The safety program in effect at the jobsite won two safety awards for the project for working over one million manhours without a lost time accident. Inadequate or non-existent safety programs lead to significant direct and indirect project costs: insurance rate increases, accident claims, loss of productivity, disrupted schedules, and wages paid to injured workers.

As a result of the construction techniques and expertise employed at the jobsite, outstanding performance as measured against industry standards was achieved.

START-UP

Start-Up Planning and Implementation

A major contributing factor to the completion of St. Lucie 2 on or near schedule was the ability to turn over components and systems to FP&L's operating department in an oderly manner. The success of this phase of the project was due to the early planning, scheduling, and implementation of a start-up program, and, probably more importantly, to the overall philosophy concerning acceptance and testing of equipment and systems, which had as its primary objective the earliest possible acceptance of equipment, components, and partial systems to enable early testing and problem identification of system components.

An overall start-up program plan and schedule was developed which required the early on-site presence of operating department personnel—35 months prior to the scheduled "start of fuel load" date. This was not just a token workforce, but rather a sizable commitment of manpower—approximately 64 people. Their early work consisted of a number of tasks, including

> Defining start-up system boundaries
> Preparing preoperation test procedures
> Establishing construction turnover sequences
> Establishing preoperation test requirements
> Determining start-up (construction and operations) manpower levels
> Establish target milestone dates

Construction/Start-Up Schedule Integration

The detailed start-up schedule and logic were then integrated with the construction schedule to develop one combined schedule that the jobsite followed, supported by home office engineering and design.

Implementation

With target milestones for start-up established, the "SCAT" program (Startup/Construction Accelerated Turnover Program) was initiated to expedite the turnover of systems from construction to operations. Essentially, this program identified portions of total systems PTSs (partial turnovers) which are then completed and turned over to operations, for early testing and problem identification of system components. Approximately 488 "packages" were identified and scheduled for turnover in priority sequence to support established start-up milestones. In addition to the PTSs, conditional turnovers were also established; operations accepted systems on a conditional basis, with an agreed-upon list of exemptions sufficiently complete to permit initiation of testing and checkout. Early acceptance of components and partial systems created time to identify and resolve equipment and start-up test performance problems with minimal impact to the overall scheduled core-load objective.

In the course of the start-up phase of the project, the construction organization objectives gradually shifted from a bulk quantity installation and area control concept to total support of start-up turnover requirements and discipline-oriented work.

CHANGE-ORDER MANAGEMENT

Changes in Scope

Concurrently, it was recognized by project management from both companies that continual increases in the scope of the project would make any milestone dates established very elusive targets.

Change Review Board

A change review board was established, comprised of engineering, construction, operations, and project management personnel from both companies, with the objective of reviewing changes arising from licensing commitments, system enhancements, and operations improvements. The purpose of the review was to determine whether it was best to implement the item prior to core load or defer to a backfit status (post-core load) to avoid impacting on construction, turnover, and start-up schedules.

In general, the criterion employed by the group was that if the item was needed to operate the system, or if it was a licensing commitment promised for completion prior to core load, it would be approved for implementation prior to the core-load date. Items not meeting this criterion were designated for backfit. This procedure insured a defined scope and helped assure realistic schedule dates.

FSAR PREPARATION AND REVIEW BY THE NRC

The project schedule was significantly threatened in 1980 during the Nuclear Regulatory Commission's caseload forecast panel review of the site and project schedule. The NRC estimate of project completion generally follows a statistical schedule model, which was developed prior to Three Mile Island and includes three curves showing the lower, medium, and upper quartile for completion. Using this model and other data obtained during their on-site visits in February and September 1980, the NRC projected a fuel load date of December 1983, 13 months later than that established by the project. Since the NRC schedule for review of the Final Safety Analysis Report (FSAR) was based on this later date, it was necessary to convince them that the project could meet our schedule. Through concerted upper management efforts, the NRC accepted the project schedule and completed the FSAR review in a record time of nine months.

To insure that the licensing effort was supportive of project objectives, an overall plan was developed for this phase of the project. The plan called for the preparation of the Design Defense/FSAR Interface Document. A well-known problem in meeting nuclear power plant schedules is the "ratcheting" that occurs during the licensing review cycle and results in unforeseen additions to the project scope and an increase in schedule. To minimize this problem on St. Lucie 2, a three-party review (Ebasco, FP&L, and Combustion Engineering) of the St. Lucie Unit 2 design against the NRC Standard Review Plans was conducted to document the degree of compliance and identify possible areas of contention. The Design Defense Documents also served to organize and develop the Final Safety Analysis Report (FSAR) for the plant.

In conjunction with this effort, a detailed three-party (Ebasco, FP&L and Combustion Engineering) integrated schedule, indicating preparation and review of primary and secondary responsibilities of all sections of the FSAR, was prepared. Ebasco was responsible for the control and production of the document.

The Environmental Report-Operating License was a two-party (Ebasco and FP&L) effort, unique in that the ER-OL presented only an update of the initial Environmental Report and did not duplicate information previously submitted.

A 25-month time span from start of DD/FSAR/ER (Design Defense/Final Safety Analysis Report/Environmental Report) to tendering of these documents was achieved.

The NRC finally docketed the FSAR and ER in February 1981, leaving very little time for the FSAR review cycle by the NRC.

Again, the combined efforts of Ebasco, FP&L, and Combustion Engineering established a unique organization for conducting what had to be an accelerated review process. The review process itself was established as an informal process whereby meetings were conducted with the different NRC branches to answer all questions, which were later formally documented. This process allowed the review to proceed expeditiously.

Seventeen integrated licensing teams were organized in 1980 with representatives from the three major participants, Ebasco, Florida Power & Light Company, and Combustion Engineering, to provide total support for the many tasks required in the licensing effort. These tasks included accelerated licensing review methods, normal licensing processes, Environmental Report-Operating License, TMI, and others. The team manager was selected from the organization with primary responsibility for the task. All team managers reported to an engineering management team consisting of the Ebasco project engineer, FP&L engineering project manager, and the Combustion Engineering project manager.

Through these efforts, the NRC team approach and formal review approach, licensing was removed from the critical path of the project by reducing the time span from the "Docketing of FSAR" to the ACRS letter recommending issuance of an operating license in 9 months versus 19 to 21 months in the pre-TMI days.

THE UNPLANNED HURRICANE DAVID

When the project was 26 percent complete, a severe storm seriously jeopardized our continued ability to meet project objectives and be ready for the start of fuel load in November 1982. The high winds of Hurricane David struck on September 3, 1979, toppling a 150-ton construction derrick being used to supply materials to both the Reactor Containment Building and the Reactor Auxiliary Building. The storm completely destroyed the derrick, composed of a 180-foot tower with a 256-foot mast resting on top of the tower, and a 200-foot boom. More importantly, the falling derrick severely damaged the Reactor Auxiliary Building under construction. Initially, lost schedule time to repair the damage and replace equipment was estimated at 13 weeks.

Immediately, Ebasco engineering and construction supervisors formulated recovery plans. A task force of construction and site engineering personnel pinpointed all damage on design drawings. Ebasco engineers assessed this damage, developed repair procedures, and determined the extent of necessary nondestructive testing of adjoining areas. Concurrently, Ebasco reviewed equipment damage with vendor representatives and expedited orders for replacement equipment. Construction plans called for additional overtime by crafts and construction supervisors to make up the extra hours required for repairs. As the recovery operation proceeded, site activity unaffected by the derrick collapse maintained its previous schedule.

The net result: by November 1980, the teamwork factor—so important in St. Lucie 2's progress to date—was able to make up the 13-week loss on the critical path schedule.

SUMMARY

The specific and general management actions employed throughout the various phases of the St. Lucie Unit No. 2 Nuclear Power Plant project have been discussed.

The theme throughout the project and most responsible for the success of the project was a "winning attitude." Innovation and creativity were encouraged from the early stages of the planning and scheduling efforts; a qualified and dedicated team of motivated professionals was assembled to implement the project activities; and, there was considerable project management attention and follow-up to insure that intermediate milestones were achieved and problems resolved on a timely basis.

The proper attitudes of teamwork were encouraged and supported, while those personnel incapable or unwilling to work in that environment were replaced in the course of the project.

We learned to rely on our own project resources and abilities and resisted pressure to bring in "outside expertise" as a solution to these challenges. This helped immeasurably in keeping the project at a manageable level and avoiding involvement by parties who did not have a vested interest in the eventual outcome of the project.

The bottom line was multifaceted. For those involved, it was a source of professional pride to have been part of a successful project, plus the more tangible benefits of career enhancement. The client received a nuclear power plant that has realized a fuel savings of $20 million/month and adds 890 MW of capacity to their system. The availability performance record of the unit since commercial operation attests to the quality built into the plant and represents additional savings to the utility and rate payers. For the corporation, it represents a major achievement which reflects the talent and capabilities of its personnel and enhances its reputation in the industry.

Last, but not least, it represents a bright spot in an otherwise negative nuclear industry. Perhaps the management lessons learned and the project's accomplishments will generate some positive feelings regarding the future of nuclear power in the electric generation industry and remain the "Spirit of St. Lucie."

4

Mega Projects: Views of a Fluor Project Manager

ROY L. KLEIN* *Fluor Engineers Inc., Irvine, California*

INTRODUCTION

The development of the mega project in the 1960s and 1970s represented a quantum leap in complexity from the sheltered projects of earlier years. The demands placed upon the project management role gave birth to and accelerated a new concept of the project manager: the total business executive.

On normal projects, the project manager has direct contact with all elements of engineering, procurement, and construction. Communications are simple and direct. Decisions can be made quickly and results observed.

Mega projects, coined from projects in the billion dollar class, elevate the project manager into broader fields of management, where he or she functions as the president of an independent corporation: a comparable organization, with a directorate; a large direct and indirect manpower base; a high level of income and expenditure, with rapid asset movement; and, in most cases, all of the problems of a multinational business.

Competent project managers, accustomed to projects that they can "see," have failed in the mega environment: staff management and delegation of significant responsibilities; management of a multicompany project organization; utilization of systems as opposed to "hands-on" control; socioeconomic considerations in foreign countries; complex consortium financing; extensive infrastructure; and, the sheer magnitude of each decision.

The mega project, however, shares a basic concept with the normal, or "standard," project, a basic and simple concept that must never be submerged by project complexities: the objectives of a mega project or of any project, are a quality facility, delivered on time, within budget.

What constitutes a mega project? How do we define it? Size, certainly. But, that is not enough! A grass-roots domestic refinery, at a certain throughput, will cost, say, $250,000,000. Increase the throughput and the project's value increases to one billion dollars. Do we have a mega project? Not from the viewpoint of the duties of the project manager, the theme of this discussion. The billion dollar refinery will clearly require a highly competent project manager, but the scope of the management role does not differ significantly from that of the smaller refinery project; equipment is larger and more costly, but there is no discernible change in the required management style or direction. Size is a prerequisite. Complexity is the difference.

CHARACTERISTICS

The majority of the mega projects built to date share certain common characteristics.

Capital-Intensive Projects

Funds to build a mega project usually exceed the financial reserves of the owner. Bank financing is one source of capital. The most common source of funding is through export credits and concessionary country to country loans or grants. The project manager must understand how to utilize the source of funding in order to plan and commit the expenditures for goods and services.

> Export Credits. Industrialized nations provide loans to support the export of their goods and services. Most of these nations belong to the Organization for Economic Cooperation and Development (OECD), which provides overall guidelines for export credits.
> Most countries providing export credits will require guarantees by a sovereign government or by a recognized first-class bank. Precedent has been set for banks to provide guarantees with limited recourse back to sponsors of major projects. Nevertheless, each exporting country's export credit agency is unique in the way it examines a project's credit and the mechanism used to provide loans.
> Commercial Banks. Since export credit agencies may not provide all necessary loan funds, it is useful to organize a group of commercial banks to provide such funding and to take a level of guarantee risk. These banks generally lend at floating interest rates for shorter periods of time.
> Under various export credit approaches, commercial banks actively participate in, and profit from, the export credit loan. Thus, they are more eager to provide commercial loans at better terms.
> Mixed Credits. Many countries combine low or no-cost developmental aid support with export credits to provide projects with financial incentives. Some countries provide interest-free grants which must be spent for their goods and services, while others provide low interest rate, long-term loans, which in theory, may be spent on goods and services from any country of origin.

Three factors must be kept in balance to assure the optimum utilization of project funding:

> Completion Schedule and Technical Quality. Many countries offer economic inducements to support exports of their goods and services. Savings from such inducements can be false economies if projects are not completed on schedule or if quality is inferior. Use of multinational development institution funding can also negatively impact on schedule as well as project cost.
> Price. Projects locked into specific country procurement by favorable financing have often experienced higher than expected costs from vendors who have no fear of competition from outside of their country.
> Financing. Project procurement based on quoted price alone may ignore the positive economies of longer term fixed-rate financing, which can significantly lower a project's time-discounted costs.

Infrastructure

Mega projects are located in remote areas. Projects like shale oil and coal gasification are normally located at the source of raw materials due to the economies of handling the materials. Such projects require provisions for the housing of employees, the building of roads, rail, and utility facilities and so on, to support the project. Hence, the owner's investment goes beyond the process facilities requirements. Infrastructure is usually provided by the owner outside the scope of the engineer-contractor. In the case of the SASOL plants in South Africa, a housing facility was developed, that today is a thriving city with a population exceeding 35,000.

People Resources

The number of people involved on a mega project is large. For the SASOL project, engineering and procurement people exceeded 2500 and for construction, in excess of 24,000. Two U.S. and four European engineering firms participated in the project. Fluor, as the Managing Contractor, developed the overall plan, specifications, procedures, and coordinated the work. The master plan organized the scope of work in such a manner that it operated as a single unit. Fluor procured the bulk materials for all six firms to optimize procurement and for control of excess material. Fluor organized and controlled the logistics to the jobsite for materials and equipment originating in the United States, Europe, and Japan. Fluor, in order to use indigenous construction labor, provided the key supervision within a single organization to manpower level the workforce and to suit the flow of engineering and materials to the jobsite.

Size

The economics for capital-intensive projects tend to improve as projects get larger. The number of people required to operate the plant doesn't increase proportionately to size; the same operators are required whether the vessel is 3 feet in diameter or 12 feet in diameter. To increase throughput, it is desirable to make the equipment as large as possible within the restrictions of proven technology and constructability. Transportation is also a limitation for equipment which can't be field erected. At some point, however, equipment can't be further increased in size, for several reasons, and process units are then designed as multiple trains, with certain significant advantages.

Project Visibility

Mega projects have a high visibility in the region or country involved. They affect the socioeconomic levels of a community. This requires establishment of a public relations program, not found in most conventional projects. Project management is called upon to provide a certain posture when the owner is particularly concerned about image and obligations. Policies are developed in this respect for conducting affairs with the media, local officials, government, and vendors.

Time to Build

The time span from when the owner begins in-house plans until the plant is completed can range from 5 to 7 years, or longer. The time to design and build is on the order of 5 years. Environmental requirements can add a year, or more. Because mega projects are capital intensive, there are milestones for decision making, feasibility studies, financial planning, and marketing considerations.

For projects to be successful, continuity of people is required. Therefore, key personnel are often assigned for the entire period, beginning in the home office and then transferring to the jobsite.

ORGANIZATION

Project Organization

The task force approach is the most effective way to organize a project to achieve performance objectives, meet schedules, and stay within budgets. This approach is used on all projects at Fluor. In the early 1960s, Fluor began analyzing hundreds of projects. The common threads running through most of the successful projects were team experience and dedication to the project. Also important was the implementation of a plan of execution and the proper use of systems and procedures.

The project task force for a large project is effectively a fully organized company. The task force builds up to maximum peak as the work becomes available. Then, on a preplanned and controlled program it winds itself down. Full-time project personnel are brought to one location. In the one location, team building is fostered for the common objective. Short lines of communication promote efficient operations. Part-time team members are not assigned to the one location, but they are responsible to the task force for their work.

There is great advantage to the owner and the project by having total responsibility under one organization and a single individual, the project manager.

Figure 1 is a basic organization chart for a mega project. The key to the vital planning and control functions of the task force is the project directorate.

Directorate

The contractor's directorate on a typical mega project is comprised of the following positions: project director, project controls director, engineering director, contracts director, materials management director, and construction director.

The directors have the responsibility for all aspects of the engineering, procurement, and construction activities. Each director has expertise in a specific area of responsibility and is a member of a team formed during the preaward stage. They develop the project execution plan: a road map of how the work will be done. They have both responsibility and authority to carry out their duties. The general functional responsibilities are:

> *Project Controls Director.* Responsible for the cost and scheduling function for engineering, procurement, and construction. Cost estimates are prepared, which form the control base for tracking costs. Early estimates are prepared on the scope definition based on factored estimates for like facilities. As the scope is further refined, machinery and equipment factored estimates are prepared. As the work proceeds, a detailed estimate is made. The entire task force must be sensitive to cost and schedule. Trend reports are generated when a change occurs from the plan, providing the vehicle for corrective action.
>
> *Engineering Director.* Responsible for the production of engineering drawings and material requirements. Area engineering managers are responsible for segments of the plant. Cost and scheduling engineers are assigned for the day-to-day work, despite the fact that they also feed back to the project controls director.
>
> Fluor has developed a phased engineering approach for the execution of a project, encompassing a sequence of discipline functions which are organized to:

1. Achieve greater efficiency in staffing the project task force
2. Minimize the premature start of work
3. Reduce recycling of information
4. Support efficient construction staffing

Each phase and its major milestones are listed in Table 1. Guidelines for each discipline identify work which should be begun and completed during the various phases. In turn, each phase is identified by the percent of total project time needed for completion.

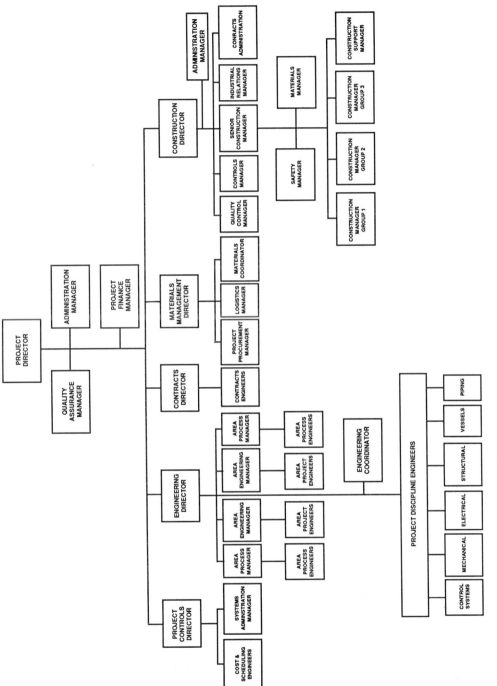

Figure 1 Key members of typical task force organization.

Table 1 Phased Engineering Approach to Project Execution

The major engineering and construction activities completed during the six engineering phases are as follows:

Conceptual engineering phase

    Process flow diagram—issue AFC[a]
    Overall plot plan—issue AFC
    Preliminary mechanical design

Preliminary engineering phase

    Mechanical flow diagram
      (P&IDs)—issue AFC
    Unit plot plan—issue AFC
    All RFQs[b] issued

Engineering design phase

    Model review
    Electrical diagram
    All equipment POs[c] issued

Early production engineering phase

    Start of construction
    Underground piping
    Underground electrical

Production engineering phase

    Piping isometrics
    Above ground piping
    Control systems details

Field support engineering

    Electrical connections
    Final fabrication and erections
    Plant check out and startup

[a]AFC: approved for construction.
[b]RFQ: request for quotes.
[c]PO: purchase orders.

Contracts Director. Responsible for the work awarded to other contractors. The quality of the documents covering contractual terms and conditions and scope definition for each contract plays a major role in the success of the job. Contracts awarded prematurely without a clear scope of work definition will have adverse effects.

    The initial planning of the directorate includes the contracting plan which defines the work, the commercial basis, and specifies when a contract is to be bid and awarded.

Materials Management Director. Responsible for ordering the equipment and materials required. Worldwide procurement introduces the element of dealing with vendors in distant places. Materials management becomes a vital function to plan and follow through from the design stage to its arrival on the jobsite. Shortages of materials or late delivery can have a significant cost and schedule impact. A tracking system that quickly translates an inspection/expediting report to all interested parties becomes a necessity in both the office and field on a mega project.

Construction Director. Responsible for all jobsite activities. How does the construction manager plan to do his work in the field? The construction plan must be his plan. Engineering and procurement must support his plan after the total plan for engineering, procurement, and construction has been adopted.

    On mega projects, physical areas for construction management must be established. Engineering, and cost/schedule control then divide the work into the same identifiable areas. These become the cost/schedule control centers in the office and the field.

    When fieldwork is approximately 10% complete, home office progress is approximately 70% complete. This is about the time key members from the task force transfer to the field for the construction support effort.

In addition to the contractor's directors, the client is an active member of the total project directorate. To ensure efficiency, the client assigns his own team to interface with the contractor's directorate staff.

Home Office Communication Lines

The project manager must arrive at a sound working relationship with corporate management. Project managers must determine when they should seek management's advice and report on the project's progress.

Further down the chain of command, section and department managers must see to it that proper technical direction is being provided to assigned personnel. This includes participation in some phases of conceptual design, planning, approving project procedures, visits to the task force, and attendance at appropriate meetings.

While these planning and control functions are in motion, the project manager and directorate must keep task force performance, project cost and schedule, client relations, and business interests in balance.

Flexibility

Despite the obvious need to adhere to the game plan, a certain flexibility must be permitted.

Each contract must be performed with slight variations because conditions for each project vary. Among those variables affecting projects are size, location of jobsite, timing of manpower availability at the jobsite, use of national resources on overseas projects, state-of-the-art technology, and project financing.

To illustrate the scope of one of these variables, manpower, Fluor established a training center for welders at the jobsite in South Africa. The hundreds of pressure vessels and heat exchangers and the miles of piping systems of SASOL Two and Three created a heavy demand for welders. Approximately 7000 welders over a period of 3 years and a like number of pipefitters were trained by Fluor, although only 1000 were required at the peak.

Qualities of the Manager

There is no better way to sum up an explanation of project management than to describe those qualities required of a project manager. The following are the key skills of those who oversee mega projects.

Anticipation. Project managers must look ahead and indulge in contingency planning. They must extend the consequences of decisions several steps further and analyze their effects on the project.

Auditing. A major responsibility of the project manager is examining and verifying the progress and quality of the project through each controlled phase.

Differentiation. The wisdom of Solomon would be helpful. The project manager must differentiate between the significant and insignificant.

Posses detailed knowledge of the project. While it is impossible to know everything there is to know about the project, the project manager should be familiar with enough details to be able to make logical decisions when priorities must be established and when conflicting conditions arise. He or she must have the ability to convey to the client that he or she has sufficient knowledge of the details of the job to ensure the client that the best interests of the project are being handled.

Delegating authority. No one person can be expected to handle everything. The ability to delegate responsibility to competent personnel is a key skill, but just as important is the maintenance of a close working relationship, of seeking counsel, and good feedback.

Flexibility. Effective leaders realize that circumstances are seldom fixed, that change is normal, and that innovation is necessary.

Sensitivity to co-workers. The project manager must realize that human personalities are the most complex variables.

Be people oriented. Project management is the art of effective leadership. The project manager must be a good motivator. Set realistic goals and objectives.

Communication. The project execution plan has little chance of working unless the project manager establishes effective channels of communication with the task force, other departments, and the client.

5

Mega Projects:
Views of a Bechtel Project Manager

ROBERT F. REINHARD* *Bechtel Incorporated, San Francisco, California*

Prior to discussing mega projects, it would be well to define the criteria to be met before a project merits the tag "mega." Size, of course, is one measure. But how to measure size? Cost alone is a poor yardstick. Factors such as location, economic nationalism, requirements imposed to get financing in place, political constraints, and the like may complicate efforts to successfully complete a project. However, these factors seldom come into play unless the job is large enough to have a high profile. The best measure of size currently available is the amount of work it takes to do the job, expressed in field manual manhours and technical engineering manhours. Generally speaking, any project which requires 2,000,000 engineering manhours and 15,000,000 field manhours will have a high profile, and consequently enough complicating factors and a long enough schedule to deserve the rank of mega project.

UNIQUE ASPECTS OF MAJOR PROJECTS

In the initial planning phase the first complicating factors related to size will begin to show. If the job is on a normal schedule, it may not be possible to do all the engineering in one shop because of the lack of manpower. In addition, on jobs outside of the United States, national and regional interests must be served, and the issue of transfer of technology to host country engineers and managers will arise. Pressure will be exerted on the client and, in turn, the contractor, to develop plans to satisfy these demands. This is usually the start of the "Project Manager's Stress Quotient," which will rise until the job is clearly over the hump and which he must endure and live with, or be replaced.

The obvious and immediate consideration is the creation of multiple interfaces between engineering firms who have never worked together, who probably use different specificiations, codes and standards, different measuring systems (English and metric, for example), different symbology, and different control systems.

When planning for construction, similar factors to those which influenced engineering will arise. Regardless of whether the job goes union or open shop, or is in an area where those terms are meaningless, there will be pressures, even immovable requirements to use local and regional contractors of unknown capability. Construction planning must include realistic assessments of manual labor requirements, field supervisory personnel and administrative staff needs, and a firm, well thought-out quality assurance/quality control program. Further, the manager must recognize the increased

---

*Retired

difficulties of formulating and implementing efficient modularization/prefabrication programs, infrastructure development, bulk material control, construction equipment usage, and all of the myriad of activities that must be carried out correctly if construction is to be an efficient operation.

Procurement of equipment and materials is another area where special interests come into play; the directed purchases to meet financing criteria, those actions required by national and regional ambitions, and naturally the client's executive whose cousin holds a high position in the government. The impact of these and similar restrictions on normal procurement operations, as carried out on smaller, less visible projects, tends to be greater than expected. To deal with the problems, a detailed, written procurement plan must be developed early in the project. The plan must integrate the purchasing, expediting, inspection, and logistics functions and allow dissemination of timely and accurate information across the project. You have to know where it's coming from, what shape it's in, and when it's going to get there if your construction planning is to be viable.

Organization Concepts

Organizing a team that can cope with these problems, plus all the other unforeseen problems which will arise during the course of the project, is crucial. The total scope of a mega project is too extensive for most of us to visualize; it must be broken down into manageable parts under the guidance of a project directorate—an advanced form of the decentralized operations and centralized control concept. Caution must be exercised so that the degree of responsibility does not exceed the span of control capability of the manager assigned to that area. The project manager will be involved to a large extent in making presentations to various political entities, to other important and interested groups, to the client, to his own management, and in soothing the ruffled feathers of other engineers and contractors working on the job, or wanting to work on the job.

The organization must be flexible. The initial organization will not be the final organization. Many of your early plans will not hold up: problem areas demanding special attention will arise; some managers will not perform as expected and may need to have their span of control shortened or may have to be replaced; some will wilt under the pressure and stress of 60-80-hour work weeks; and some will prove capable of assuming additional responsibilities, clawing their way up the ladder.

If the project is closely integrated processwise, it may be good to set up the project management group at the center of gravity for the work when construction commences. This location may or may not be at the jobsite, depending on how the project develops. The group should include the project manager, his deputy or deputies, and the managers of costs and budgets, finance and administration, procurement, subcontracts, planning and scheduling, construction, and engineering.

With multiple engineering companies funneling their output to the project, engineering interface management will immediately become a problem. This problem can be best handled by a separate group of engineers from the project management group with assigned representatives in the different offices to review and approve work and coordinate the engineering for the total project. Congruity of all engineering interfaces, with work being done by different firms in locations perhaps thousands of miles apart, is only attained by unceasing vigilance and lots of hard work.

Construction interfacing is best handled in the field by the field management group. Although it seems a simple task compared with the problem of engineering interfacing, misunderstandings can and do occur, which, if unchecked, will lead to major tensions with the individuals involved, and a deterioration of performance.

Communication: The Key

A major project will not be a success without an open, two-way communications channel between client and contractor. Teamwork, within your project team and the client's team, produces the best job. An adversarial relationship is counterproductive. This does not mean that the contractor must agree with the client at all times. But an atmosphere should exist in which differences of opinion can be rationally discussed. Sometimes however, this is not possible. In such a situation two courses of action are open: first, agree to accept the client's direction, but insist that it be in writing; second, buck it upstairs for your management to deal with. However, they won't appreciate this, so the situation had better be pretty serious, and you'd better be right.

The above touches on another facet of the communications problem; that of keeping your management advised, of getting them interested and involved in your project. This is important, because somewhere along the way management's help will be needed; be it with internal staffing problems, conflicts with other engineers and contractors, or political problems.

Also advisable, though a more difficult task, is to have a communications channel to the client's top management. One way to do this is to hold periodic formal meetings with a senior management group from the client and from the contractor, plus the client's and contractor's project managers. The agenda for these meetings should be developed by the contractor's project manager and agreed to by the client's project manager. This provides a good forum for exploring major problem areas and the actions being taken to solve them. Of course, never raise a problem in such a group without having a plan of action to resolve it.

When dealing with multiple contractors, some of whom may be widely separated geographically from the project management group, and may not even be familiar with the type of plant they are working with, it becomes very difficult to get all of the relevant information to them so that the design parameters as well as project objectives and control requirements are understood. In fact, from a distance it may be difficult for the managing contractor to figure out what it is that the other contractor doesn't understand. A coping strategy in this situation is for the managing contractor to place the required personnel in the other contractor's office to follow the work on a day-to-day basis, and have members of the managing contractor project staff make periodic visits to the offices of all third parties.

To reiterate: on major projects, it is essential that both vertical and horizontal lines of communication be established and used. Failure to do so will result in a poor job. Who can do a good job if they don't fully understand what the job is; what is expected of them?

Planning and Scheduling

Everyone pays lip service to planning. Yet many jobs are run without a formal plan or perhaps no plan at all. Some project managers on small or even medium-sized jobs use the fire-fighting technique: wait until the blaze erupts and then rush to put it out. This will not work for a major project.

A major project cannot be successfully completed without a vast amount of early planning. A written "plan of execution" should be produced as early as possible, detailing how the job will be done. It should provide a road map for the project from start to completion, including organization charts for the total job, manpower curves for engineering and construction, commitment curves for procurement and subcontracts, plans for modularization and/or prefabrication, construction equipment needs, cost control programs, schedules, labor relations plans, including recruiting plans if needed, plans for construction camps, temporary construction utilities, roads, gravel and sand, concrete, consumable supplies, jobsite warehousing; in fact, everything that will add to an understanding of the way you plan to execute the project.

When the plan of execution is completed and issued it will probably already be out of date in some areas, and ready for revision. It must be a living document, a document which will change continually throughout the lifetime of the project. The plan at any given time should contain the best possible program for executing the work.

A proven workable scheduling strategy is to produce a master milestone schedule using an arrow diagram format of no more than 300 events. This is the project manager's schedule; only he or she can change any of the milestones. When the master milestone schedule has been reviewed and approved, develop a more detailed engineering-procurement-construction schedule covering the life of the project. Review the EPC schedule monthly. When work commences at the jobsite, prepare 90- or 180-day schedules, with the first 30 days scheduled in great detail. The 90-or 180-day interval is suggested to fit a weather cycle, or a cost forecast cycle, or a key parameter cycle. At some point when the EPC schedule is firm, the 90/180-day schedule will become the working schedule for the project. As construction speeds up, the field begins production of very detailed crewed-out weekly work plans, reviewed weekly for performance against targets and serving as a basis for corrective action. Figure 1 shows the level of management responsible for the schedule hierarchy.

On average size projects the logistics and transportation functions are largely routine. Major projects pose more serious problems. Since equipment and materials will probably be procured from many parts of the world and shipped great distances by land or sea at great expense, marshalling yards to allow consolidation of loads may be required. You must have a general ideal of where everything is at any given time; including all major suborders. Thus expediting information must constantly be fed into the logistics and transportation plans to keep these plans current and to assess the risk of items missing a shipment. Plans must be made covering instances where a missed shipping date might mean the better part of a year's loss of schedule due to weather restrictions. Incessant monitoring of shipping dates and truck, rail, and ship movements is necessary to stay on top of the situation. You can't make plans to cope with a problem if you don't know the problem exists.

All major projects require extensive field labor. Many of the jobs in the Middle East, the North Slope of Alaska, and in the North Sea are now modularized, but labor is required to build the modules and to hook them up. The plan of execution should include a forecast of labor requirements by manhours, by craft, and should define the field nonmanual staff: the field supervisory, engineering, and administrative requirements. The labor plan must set out how these needs will be filled. This requires analysis of the sources of labor supply, availability, and the need for special training to augment the supply or to satisfy host country requirements. The plan must define the training programs and the facilities required to carry out the training, including the necessary equipment and instructors. Again, failure to produce a well thought-out plan and to keep it current will result in delays to the project. For a major project, labor will have to be ordered at least a month ahead of the need date, and in many cases three or four months or longer in advance.

Estimating and Cost Control

All contractors have their own estimating standards and cost control systems that they know, and are used to working with. In a major project involving multiple contractors it is wise to allow each contractor to continue to use his own system, making only those changes that are required to feed information to the project manager's organization in the format required by the project manager. The project management group then must produce the estimate and budgets for the total project. This is where problems arise. Each contractor will produce, for its piece of the work, an estimate based on parameters such as the work week, average hourly wage, camp costs, and so on, furnished by the project management group. However, these estimates will not include the factors which relate to added complexities inherent in a major project: the special needs for indirect labor, field nonmanual staff, and all the extra costs associated with a major project as compared to an average size job. A small job can't serve as a model for a major project. Looking only in the rearview mirror is sure to bring trouble. Look ahead and think through the project; the one you are going to build. Push engineering to develop scope documents as fast as possible. Identify cost trends frequently

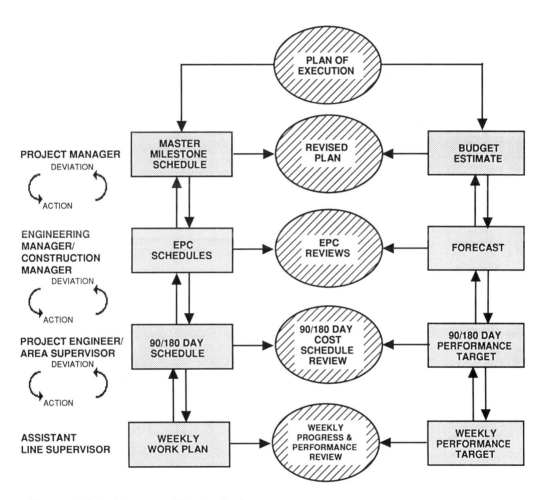

Figure 1 Schedule control by level of management.

on a periodic basis. Update the estimate by planned periodic cost forecasts throughout
the life of the job. Initiate risk analyses as part of the estimating and forecasting cycle
to evaluate contingency levels. Make sure everyone understands that contingency is
the project manager's domain and cannot be touched without his approval; it's likely
that some people will try to take more than their share. Remember, too, that systems
don't control costs; people do.

Risk Management

A control system isn't complete without some form of risk management. Simply put,
risk management is the ability to be proactive, not reactive, to situations which arise
during the project. Remember, a continual practice of putting out fires after they're
started won't produce a successful major project.

A good risk-management policy is to set up a separate body in your project management group charged with responsibility for managing risks. Have them analyze the
whole job, identify and quantify the areas of risk, and prioritize them. Then they
must develop contingency plans, sometimes called "what if" plans, to deal with any
risk areas as undesirable trends surface. Contingency planning is difficult; only the
most experienced and highly skilled people can do it well. Ceaseless review and analysis of risks is the price that must be paid if you are to have confidence in your ability
to deal with the problems that will arise. Fortunately, things don't always go wrong.
This technique will also reveal situations where things are going better than planned
and you can take advantage of this.

Bulk Material Control

Bulk material control, or the lack thereof, is the rock upon which many jobs have foundered. Again, every contractor has a system and the systems work in direct proportion
to the amount of effort expended to make them work. Granted, the expanding use of
computer-aided design will improve the overall quality of material takeoffs immensely.
Still, on a major project with multiple contractors involved, the requisitioning, receiving, warehousing, and control of bulk material remains a formidable task. If modulari-
zation/prefabrication is in the job plan it becomes more complicated. One approach
to this problem is to include a bulk material coordinator as part of the project management group; a person who is responsible for control of all bulks, including pipe spool
fabrication. This has the advantage of centralizing responsibility instead of scattering
it among many contractors, and allows more efficient control of the bulks. A great
deal of time and money can be spent on bulk material control, using computerized systems that produce printouts 18 inches thick that nobody can or will use. The best
system is the simplest possible one that will give the required degree of control and
that is cost effective. Spending a million dollars on controlling two million dollars worth
of bulks is not cost effective.

Standardization

Many arguments can be generated about the degree of standardization that should be
attempted for major projects. Operating considerations should play a major role in deciding this quesiton. How much spare part interchangeability is desired? How is the
plant warehousing going to be done? Will operators be shuffled back and forth between plant areas? How tightly are the plants integrated?

Generally speaking, the least amount of standardization which will allow the plants
to be operated and maintained efficiently is the correct amount. This would mean standardizing plant and equipment numbering systems, the symbology on process flow and
piping and instrument diagrams, and the basic material and equipment specifications.
Beyond that, the requirements of the project should be considered on an item by item
basis.

If one or several plants in the project are not integrated with the rest of the facility processwise, it would be possible to run that plant as a completely separate project, with its own engineer and constructor, with its own specifications; managing only the interfaces with the rest of the project. This would avoid some of the higher costs associated with mega projects.

SUMMARY

The foregoing comments portray management of a mega project as a formidable task, and so it is. At this time, the state of the art of managing mega projects is in its infancy; there really haven't been that many executed, so there are no pat formulas that can be used. Each mega project must be analyzed, planned, and organized to meet its own peculiar needs. The tool that is the most useful in doing this, and if you're going to manage a mega project you'd better have it, is just plain common sense. Let's now review a real-life mega project—the Syncrude Canada Mildred Lake Project.

A CASE HISTORY—HOW A MEGA PROJECT WAS MANAGED

Syncrude Canada Ltd's Mildred Lake project was awarded in March 1972. The facility was to be designed to extract bitumen from ore mined from the Athabasca Oil Sands deposits and to upgrade the bitumen into a light, sweet, synthetic crude oil (Fig. 2). The job was to proceed in two phases. The Phase I assignment was to carry out studies on:

Mining configuration and related operating costs
Mine development
Utility plant configuration

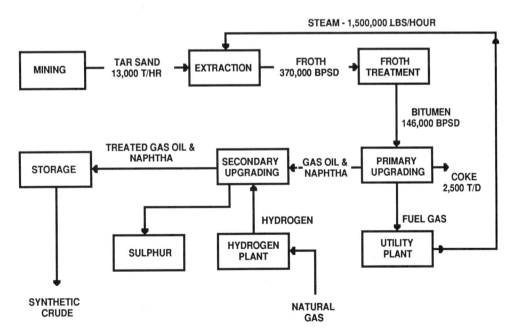

Figure 2 Simplified block process flow diagram, Mildred Lake project.

Process selection
A project plan of execution
Order of magnitude estimate

The purpose of Phase I was to provide sufficient data to Syncrude for a "go-no go" decision by August 1973.

The facility was to be located 26 miles north of Fort McMurray, Alberta, Canada. In early 1972 this was a community of 5000 people, on the banks of the Athabasca River. The nearest industrial and transportation center was Edmonton, Alberta, approximately 300 road miles south of the project site.

Syncrude turned out to be a true mega project with multiple owners, including several major oil companies, the federal government of Canada, and two provincial governments. Execution of the work involved the expenditure of 4.4 million engineering technical manhours by 15 engineering firms and the managing contractor, whose work was done in three offices: San Francisco, Houston, and Edmonton. Construction required over 34 million manual manhours of which about 25% was subcontracted and the rest done by the managing contractor's direct hire force.

Initially the execution of Phase I was managed by three men, each with more than 25 years experience with the managing contractor as well as previous experience on Canadian projects. The organization and responsibilities were as noted in Figure 3.

One of the most important documents on the job was produced during Phase I: the Project Plan of Execution, which included the following:

Master milestone schedule
Systems and controls to be used
Manual staffing, by craft
Nonmanual staffing
Construction equipment list
Labor relations and recruiting strategy
Manual training plans
Engineering plan, including work to be subcontracted to third parties
Major construction subcontracts
List of qualified subcontractors
Prefabrication plan

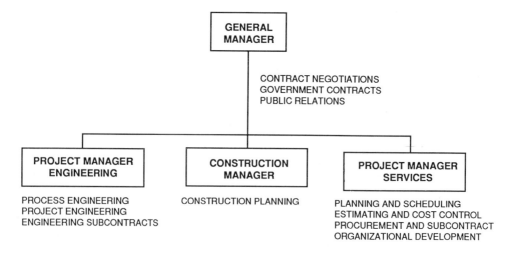

Figure 3 Organization of responsibilities for Phase I, Mildred Lake project.

      Temporary construction facilities, including buildings, recreation facilities, and
          construction utilities
      QA/QC plan
      Safety and security plan
      Procurement plan
      Project management group in Edmonton

     This document provided a road map for carrying out the work in an integrated effort. Everyone, client and contractor alike, knew where we were going and how we planned to get there. As the job developed, the plan of execution was revised to reflect changing circumstances and more complete definition of the work. As the prefabrication and modularization scheme developed, a detailed addenda to the plan of execution was written to cover that work. The effort put into the Syncrude plan of execution could have been doubled, to the benefit of the project. Yet, there were those within both the client and managing contractor's organization who believed we wasted money planning. "It won't work that way anyhow" they said. "Just get that engineering done and get the material there and build it." Fortunately, those people were in the minority. Detailed planning pays off. Remember, on jobs like these there are no little mistakes.

     It was evident from the very beginning that one of the most important keys to a successful project was going to be establishment of a workable communications network which would keep all of the players involved apprised of the plans, goals, objectives, and accomplishments of the project: client and contractor personnel, client and contractor management, third parties involved in the work, the media, and other bodies with the need to know. To bring senior management of the client and contractor fully into the picture and to provide interaction, a senior management advisory group was formed. Quarterly meetings run by the contractor's project manager were held. A formal agenda was issued and minutes were taken and published. Major project issues and policies were the main items on the agenda.

     It was agreed that all releases of data and information to any government or political body and to the media would be made by the client. The contractor would assist the client to whatever extent necessary in the development of such data and information.

     Because of the heterogeneous nature of the developing project organizations, and particularly the client's, which had seconded personnel from a number of companies, plus a large number of new hires, the contractor's project manager brought his organizational development (OD) people into the act. Periodic meetings were held between the project teams to help the teams crystallize their thinking on targets and objectives, identify potential areas of conflict, work problems, assign action items, and assist in developing a team approach to the job. Both the client and the contractor's project managers wholeheartedly supported this approach as giving the best chance for a successful project, rather than allowing an adversary relationship to develop between the two teams. This does not mean there were no arguments; plenty of heated discussions developed, but they were always settled on a rational basis.

     The scope of the effort was expanded to include problem-solving sessions with the contractor's project staff. Two people were assigned to the project management group in Edmonton and when construction picked up momentum another was assigned to the field staff. Their work continued through the job peak and into the demobilization period, which brought its own share of headaches.

     Early in September 1973, the decision was taken to implement Phase II. Anticipating this, the organization was changed to better cope with the expanded scope of work, as shown in Figure 4. The general manager moved to Edmonton to tighten liaison with the client, and stepped out of line management. The Project Manager-Services took over as project manager and an assistant project manager took direct charge of the cost and planning functions.

     Early in 1975, with the pace of work accelerating rapidly, the project manager's span of control was exceeded by the organization currently in place. The organization

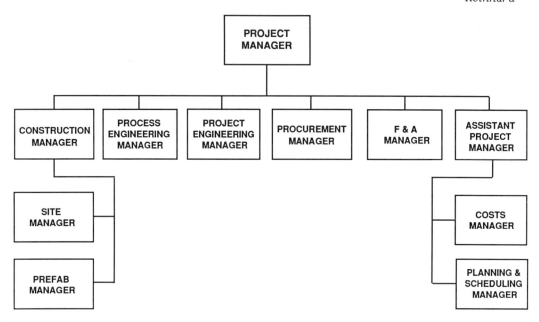

Figure 4   Alteration of organization for Phase II, Mildred Lake project.

shown on Figure 5 was put into place and managed the job through the peak period
in 1976-1977.

Estimating and cost control work started immediately after job award. Initially,
all of the estimates the client had prepared over the dozen or so years the job had been
under consideration were collected and put into a consistent format. This compilation
was used as a base from which to trend cost variations as the process selection and
mining schemes were studied, but it in no way reflected what either the client or contractor thought the final cost would be. As soon as the process plant and mining studies allowed, an order of magnitude estimate was started. This estimate was 100% factored using the contractor's historical data which was largely derived from a somewhat
similar, smaller plant the contractor had built some years before. It did not foresee
the soaring escalation caused by the oil price crisis, the costs associated with meeting
recently imposed environmental constraints, the total difference in jobsites, as well
as many other differences between the historical data and the plant that was to be built.
It was not a good estimate.

However, at the time no one recognized this. The estimate became the new cost
trend base. As process selection and the mining scheme firmed up and engineering
slowly began to produce scope documents, periodic cost and schedule trend meetings
were held between the client and contractor. As engineering progressed, the constantly rising cost trends pointed out very clearly the inadequacies of the order of magnitude estimate. We simply did not have enough data to produce an accurate factored
estimate.

It was evident that another estimate msut be prepared as soon as possible; an estimate based on as much firm data and forward thinking as possible. An engineering
cutoff date was set and preparation of scope documents for estimating was pushed to
the maximum. In November 1974 this budget estimate was completed, and after in-
depth review by the contractor's management, was submitted to the client. After intensive review by the client and others the unwelcome flood of publicity receded, the
bullet was bitten, and work went on. Periodic cost forecasts on a 4-month cycle continued throughout the project, as did cost trending. However, the budget estimate,

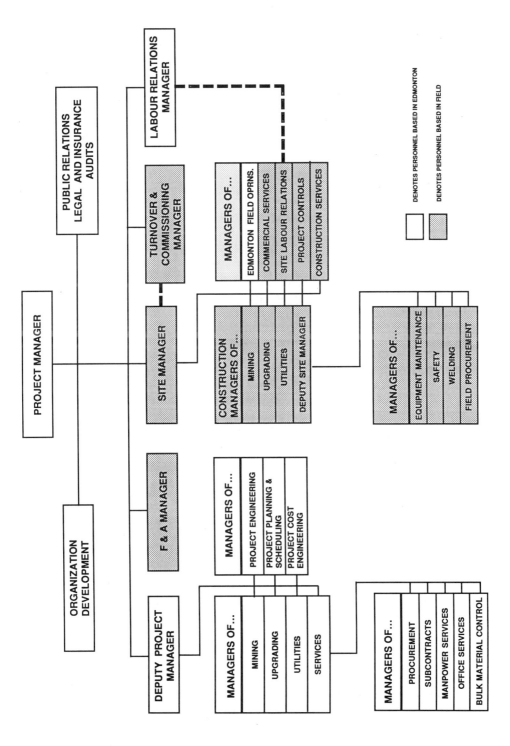

Figure 5 Final expansion of control organization, Mildred Lake project.

which was finished when engineering was 5% complete, held for the life of the job. The only increases were for changes in the scope of the work as approved by the client.

Since costs and schedule go hand in hand, development of the schedule hierarchy paralleled the cost effort. The initial master milestone schedule became hopelessly optimistic when the cost trends and later the budget estimate preparation began to reveal depth of resources and the amounts of equipment and materials required. Revision of the master milestone schedule and development of a detailed engineering-procurement-construction (EPC) schedule proceeded along with the estimate.

The EPC schedule became the project manager's principal tool in fulfilling his pledge that the completion dates would be met. In March 1975, EPC reviews were instituted. These reviews were held at the jobsite and were attended by the appropriate engineering, procurement, cost, schedule, construction, and management personnel. After an overall review by the project manager, individual groups reviewed each plant's objectives for the coming month in detail, including commitments to production goals, delivery of equipment and materials, and action items to correct actual or indicated deficiencies. These reviews were held early each month. The April 1975 review and all subsequent reviews started by looking at achievements versus plans for the month just past. Each individual was required to explain any missed objective; and excuses were not accepted. People found it very difficult to stand before their peers, who were busting their tails to meet their objectives, and say that there was no good reason why they had failed.

As engineering progressed, the center of gravity of the project gradually moved toward the field and the development of 180-day schedules was initiated. The 180-day interval was chosen because of the seasonal variation in Alberta—winter is about 180 days long and the work must be planned accordingly. The first month of the 180-day schedule was minutely detailed, and the next level of scheduling, the weekly work plan, derived from this. As time went on, the 180-day schedule supplanted the EPC schedule as the monthly review document.

The whole hierarchy of schedules was part of the effort to distribute responsibility and accountability through all levels of supervision, from the project manager down through the engineering squad leaders and the general foremen and foremen in the field. Arduous hardly described the degree of difficulty in implementing this; the excuses and reasons why it couldn't be done successfully came from both the field and the engineering offices, but perseverance finally won out. With everybody in agreement, it became possible to schedule and forecast with a great degree of confidence, which proved to be justified.

The EPC and 180-day schedules served as the basis of our risk-management effort. Close analysis of these schedules revealed potential problem areas, which were prioritized on the basis of degree of risk and potential effect on the project. These then became the subject of "problem-action" reports which were plans to deal with the risk. A good example of such a risk involved very heavy pressure vessels being fabricated in Brescia, Italy, and Victoria, British Columbia, as well as the ships for sea transport, the special railway cars for transport across Canada, and the necessity to move the vessels from Edmonton to the jobsite only when the roadbed was solidly frozen. A miss here would mean at least a 10-month delay. The actual execution went like clockwork, thanks to the good planning. This was but one of a number of such instances.

Very early in the project it was recognized that labor manhour costs at the jobsite were going to be significantly higher than those in the Edmonton area; that a number of craftspersons simply would not go to the jobsite; that there was the opportunity to set up a facility in Edmonton where work could be done under controlled conditions ensuring greater productivity. A marshalling/prefabrication/modularization facility was set up in Edmonton, where craft shacks, concrete electrical duct banks, utilidors, catch basins, manholes, pump foundations, instrument boxes, pipeway and equipment modules, electrical houses, and the like were fabricated. Equipment was insulated, structural steel fireproofed, pipe spools fabricated and assembled with all the nuts, bolts, gaskets, valves, etc., boxed or bagged and specifically identified before ship-

ment to the jobsite. Not only did this operation save money, it provided schedule protection by doing this work largely indoors where weather was not a factor and by having the items ready for the jobsite forces to install. This contributed significantly
to our success in 1977 during one 6-month period when we really broke the back of
the job by installing over 200,000 feet of pipe and 1,000,000 feet of wire and cable each
month. The project was completed in July 1978, several months ahead of the schedule
made in November 1974.

In summary, the success of the Syncrude Project was due primarily to three things:
in-depth planning; the effort made to keep communications flowing to and from all levels
of the project; and teamwork.

6

The Multiproject Environment

ROBERT D. ROBSON* *Lummus Canada Inc., Toronto, Ontario, Canada*

Since project management is, in essence, an exercise in complex communications, management in a multiproject environment differs from single-project management only in that it involves a significantly higher degree of such complexity. This is apparent when the various types of multiproject environments are defined. Generally they fall into three categories, in increasing order of difficulty.

1. A number of concurrent contracts of varying size, for different owner-clients, executed in one office of an EPC contractor.
2. A number of plant elements in a complex grass-roots facility; each engineered, procured, and constructed by separate contractors for one owner-client.
3. A number of concurrently built but separate facilities in a common geographical area, by a number of EPC contractors working under various contract conditions for different owner-clients.

All of these cases exhibit to varying degrees the salient feature of a multiproject environment: competition for limited resources. In engineering and design these resources include qualified technical people, management skills, and, in recent times, computer capacity. In procurement the resources include qualified purchasing agents, inspectors, expediters, traffic managers, etc., and material manufacturing and distribution, shop fabrication capacity, and traffic facilities. In construction the resources include craft labor, field supervisory personnel, field management and control personnel, local material suppliers, distributors, and fabrication and construction equipment.

In all cases, the project manager's prime role is to ensure that he and his counterparts cooperate and coordinate activities to ensure that each receives an appropriate and fair share of the limited resources. Obviously this requires cooperation and compromise in setting goals and determining requirements. The ability to do this is very much affected by the terms of the contracts between the various owner-clients and contractors, and by the leadership ability of the project manager, who must be able to rationalize the goals and objectives of the project with the overall goals and objectives of all participants in the circumstances that exist. A fair analogy is that of the battalion commander in a large-scale military operation as opposed to one directing an isolated limited engagement. The celebrated conflicts between Allied army commanders in France during World War II are an excellent illustration of the problems of a multiproject situation.

Current affiliation: Consultant, Calgary, Alberta, Canada

CASE 1: MULTIPROJECTS IN ONE EPC CONTRACTORS OFFICE

For the individual project manager this is the less onerous of the three types of multi-project environments, for three reasons. First, all the concurrent projects are being executed with common working and control systems, and with a large core of personnel familiar with those systems. Second, in the management of the EPC contractor their exists a focal point for the resolution of the problems of competing resources. Third, the individual project manager is a co-worker and personal friend of the managers of the other projects competing for the limited resources; which significantly aids the communication process.

Nevertheless, problems do exist, often resulting from the business aspects of the various contracts being executed. For example, the project manager fortunate enough to have the largest project "in-house," for an established client with a good future business potential, and with a reasonable project profit markup, will certainly have the least difficulty in obtaining resources for his project from the contractor's administrative management. The project manager who does not enjoy this happy situation must ensure that his requirements are adequately considered and fairly met. In such cases, almost all project managers will strongly campaign for "task force" execution as opposed to "matrix" execution.

Task force operation does increase the amount of control authority of the project manager, but it has its hazards. It is most improbable that one project will get the company's best lead civil engineers, best lead electrical engineers, best lead instrument engineers, etc. Further, a certain degree of restriction of communication has been placed between departmental managers and their discipline representatives assigned to the task force. One function of departmental managers is to oversee the technical competence exercised on all projects, and the performance of individuals from the departments assigned to the task forces. Solutions to the potential problem do exist as technical audits (quality assurance) and reviews carried out at regular and frequent intervals by persons outside of the project task force group. Ideally the audit functions should be carried out by the same individuals for all projects in this multiproject circumstance as a check of the fairness of distribution of the qualified technical resources available from the EPC contractor.

To obtain the commitment of the management of the EPC contractor to his particular project, many owners require the designation of a "project sponsor," a member of the senior echelon of the contractor's organization who will ensure that the project gets the appropriate share of the companies resources, both in quantity and quality. In concept this has its virtues; in practice it is of varying effectiveness. If all projects have "sponsors" the effect is merely to elevate the level of interdepartmental cooperation to the executive level and hence further from the problem. It also reduces the relative stature of the project manager, who in dealing with department heads, is communicating with personnel at roughly the same level in the company hierarchy and in dealing with "sponsors" is communicating with a group at a superior level. He is at a bargaining disadvantage.

The ideal solution is regular communications at the project level: between competing project managers. This requires thorough and honest assessment of project personnel requirements, updated weekly and monthly by each project manager, and leadership, either by one predominant project manager or by the contractor's "manager of projects." As always, the base for coordinated cooperative action is accurate and timely assessment of needs to permit action, rather than reaction.

Given the environment of competition for resources in a multiproject office what can the individual project manager do within his or her own group to ensure efficiency, quality, and the meeting of project goals? The obvious answer is the development of a "team" atmosphere among those assigned to the project; particularly the project engineers and lead discipline personnel. Herein lies the test of true project management capability; to take the manpower resources that are available and mold them into an effective operating team to meet the project objectives.

Prior to the 1970s, the resource of concern to the project manager in this multiproject environment was people. Now there is competition among projects for another resource: computer capacity. In some respects, this is a more difficult challenge. Computers and programs are costly, and to make them operational is a time-consuming process, compared with hiring additional personnel. Capital outlays for added capacity are significant and often complicated by company policies geared to outdated conditions and circumstances.

It is incumbent on the project manager to thoroughly evaluate the extent of computer utilization on a project during the early planning stages. With the maturing of computer-assisted engineering and design (CAD) this is as important as manpower resource planning. Which of the developed and proven systems of the company will be used? Should the project serve as a "guinea pig" for developed but heretofore unproven systems? To what extent will computerized control and management systems be used? To what extent will complex "main frame" procedures be used as opposed to "ad hoc" microcomputer systems? How much programming support will be required to modify standard programs to specific project requirements?

The project manager's responsibility is, as always, foresight, planning, and communications with the service organizations. If computer systems are to be employed on a project, the project manager must also ensure control to prevent excessive and unnecessary usage of computer time to a much greater extent than the control normally required to avoid wasteful usage of manpower resources. The computer facilitates the processing of data and the production of reports to an alarming extent and many project managers have foundered in a sea of useless information, sorted and resorted. Ultimately, too much information becomes no information. The resource is being wasted.

On projects, and particularly in a multiproject environment with, as always, a shared and limited resource, project managers must rigorously define their true needs—not wants—at project inception. Each manager must review and agree to computer usage requirements for each discipline group on the project. It is essential to institute "control through prior approval" to prevent the growth of computer usage beyond the agreed needs. Finally, each manager must be prepared to coordinate individual requirements with other project managers, accept methods for stretching the availability of the resource, and minimize the use of programs and program modifications specially tailored to his or her project, as opposed to use of "company standard programs."

CASE 2: A GRASS-ROOTS COMPLEX FOR THE OWNER-CLIENT

The multiproject environment in which a project manager must operate in this case is best illustrated by example. A common one is that of an ethylene-based petrochemical complex with downstream product facilities (oxide, glycol, polyethylene, vinyl chloride, styrene), on a grass-roots site requiring full utilities, services, and general facilities and, in a newly developed area, the infrastructure or "community" required to support the operating organization. All of these facilities would be built at one time for one owner (frequently "state-owned") but by a number of EPC contractors. Such a circumstance is most frequently met in so-called "developing nations" eager to upgrade their own natural resources and build an indigenous manufacturing industry.

Whereas in case 1, the limited shared resource is mainly technical personnel in a defined controlled environment, case 2 introduces a host of resource-limiting problems. It introduces these problems in an environment that has no established control mechanism and requires that one be developed for the particular project. The first question to be resolved is that of who must accept responsibility for setting up the control environment.

Case 2 is simpler than case 3 in one major respect, that is in the "person" of the single owner-client there exists a potential focal point for coordination and control. Unfortunately, the owner-client usually has neither the people nor the experience and systems to effectively fill this role. There are a number of alternatives to this situation:

1. The owner-client can recruit and build the control and coordination organization. This alternative has two serious drawbacks: the need to develop workable control and coordination systems in a very short timespan, and the redundancy effect (what do you do with this organization when the project is finished?).

2. The owner-client can assign to one EPC contractor the overall project management and control function. It is usually preferable that the chosen contractor for this alternative be the one responsible for EPC of the utilities, services, and general facilities. These not only tie the plant together and interface with all other units but are the first systems required to be completed, commissioned, and operated, and the first systems requiring on-site construction operations.

3. The owner-client can charge each EPC contractor with the responsibility of coordinating with the others and require that the group set up a project coordination committee for overall project control. For obvious reasons this is less likely to be successful.

4. The owner-client can set up a "project directorate" organization, letting a "project services" type contract to one company who, along with the owner will staff the directorate from his manpower pool. The contractor would also provide the project management and control systems.

    This approach permits direct owner participation in overall project management and largely overcomes the "redundancy" problem on project completion. The chosen service contractor may or may not also have EPC responsibilities for some of the facilities. Ideally he should have certain EPC responsibilities to ensure that his decisions and actions are realistic and workable on the site and can be modified quickly as events during the project may require.

    In recent years the project directorate approach has had considerable popularity among owners, but those who have experienced it in action have developed reservations. The flaw is that the one bonding agent for effective team development—allegiance to permanent ongoing company or enterprise—is missing. Personnel seconded to the directorate come from diverse organizations for a limited assignment and are loath to shed the habits, systems, and philosophies of their host companies.

Regardless of the method chosen for overall management and control there is one underlying requirement for multiproject success: consistency of contracts between the owner and all participants. Such contracts of course depend on the scope of work assigned to each participating contractor. This decision should reflect a thorough analysis of the potential problems of the multiproject environment.

Of the various areas of potential resource limitations, that of engineering and design resources is likely to be the least significant. It is unlikely that these functions will be carried out in one geographical area by all participants. For each segment of the facility the problems of case 1 will apply, but except in the case of general overall demand on engineering, the problems in each contractors design office will have little effect on those situations in the offices of others.

In the area of procurement, the multiproject environment imposes the need for coordination and control, and the extent of the need varies with the type of material being purchased and delivered to the site. Material generally falls into four categories:

1. Engineered items of major equipment
2. General commodity materials, such as piping components, electrical cable and equipment, insulation, etc.
3. Prefabricated assemblies, such as trimmed vessels, pipe spools, modular assembiles, etc.
4. Field consumables and make-up material

If procurement sourcing is restricted to one economic area or country, control must be exercised to prevent competition for limited suppliers, hence shop overloading, cost escalation, and potential delivery problems. This applies to all four of the above categories but is most crucial for specific equipment items and for prefabricated assemblies. It is complicated by the obvious desire on the part of the owner to have reasonable standardization of equipment to minimize future maintenance problems and spare parts requirements. In such a multiproject environment the immediate reaction may be to centralize all buying either under the project directorate or through the project services contractor. Unfortunately this introduces a potential project delay in the analysis of bids and the placement of orders and, most seriously, in the handling of vendor drawings.

Probably the most satisfactory arrangement is for a centralized procurement group to do the following:

1. Set the bidders' lists and coordinate placement of orders for itemized major equipment by each participating contractor. The individual contractors handle the expediting of vendor prints and possibly inspection during equipment fabrication. The centralized procurement agency handles delivery, expediting, and traffic.
2. Select prefabrication shops and let the contracts for pipe spooling, module prefabrication, etc. and handle inspection, expediting, and traffic.
3. Receive bills of material from all participating contractors for "commodity" materials, place orders, and direct delivery to point of use, whether it be to a prefabrication shop or the plant site.
4. Delegate field purchases to the erection contractor, or constructors, but subject to centralized coordination and audit.

The above items are strongly influenced by the type of contracts existing between the various multiproject participants. Obviously the split of procurement responsibility suggested above indicates either total cost-plus contracts between the owner and project contractors, or at most, lump-sum contracts for engineering and major equipment pruchases. The alternative of letting total lump-sum EPC contracts to each of a number of multiproject participants precludes the owner's or project directorate's participation in procurement and construction control; making execution of a multiproject operation more difficult to coordinate and control. This aspect, the influence on the type of contract on multiproject coordination, is even more important in the field construction phase of the project.

It is in construction that the need for multiproject coordination is most pronounced. Such coordination must include:

Identification of craft labor requirements over the schedule, the analysis of locally available labor resources, and the determination of potential craft labor resources from outside the local area

Determination of the degree of local manpower training and upgrading that can be effective, and the coordination of such programs

Setting common project labor conditions, including hours of work, work breaks, jurisdictional assignments (if the site is unionized), etc.

Provision of housing, and other social facilities for imported labor where such is not adequate at the locale of the project.

Analysis of major construction equipment availability in the area and the arrangement for supply, delivery, maintenance, and control of all such equipment, local or imported, for most efficient use

Setting common site safety and security policies

Control of all types of traffic, for both workers and material deliveries to the site

Coordination of purchasing of local materials used on the various projects

These examples suggest the advantages of having one contractor do all site construction management for a multiproject of this type. Having centralized control of
the letting of all site "subcontracts" is an extra advantage.

The difficulties of having a number of contractors executing site work on independent contracts are apparent from the preceding list of coordination areas, but are even
more pronounced if the contractors are operating under separate lump-sum EPC contracts.

In this circumstance, the following arrangements should be considered for maximum
coordination and control, and minimum problems:

The owner lets a project services contract with a major EPC contractor who:

1. Provides personnel, systems, and procedures to the project directorate
2. Coordinates equipment procurement between various participating contractors
3. Executes all procurement activities for commodities and prefabricated assemblies, including tendering, purchasing, inspection, expediting, and traffic
4. Controls traffic-delivery to site, of all material
5. Is fully responsible for construction of all facilities by either direct hire or
   subcontracts or both
6. Coordinates overall project control and reporting from all participants

In addition to the above, the owner lets separate unit or facility contracts to contractors to carry out all engineering and design functions plus procurement of major itemized
equipment, except expediting and traffic, under the overall control of the project directorate. Such contracts can be lump sum or cost plus for the defined scope of work
and services, provided the conditions under which the contractor is required to work
are well considered and spelled out in the inquiry documents.

The above arrangement simplifies the coordination responsibilities throughout the
project and facilitates the planning and coordinating of construction completion and
plant commissioning activities. As suggested earlier, there is an advantage in having
the coordinating contractor also do the engineering and procurement of utilities, services, and off-site facilities for the project.

If project considerations result in a decision to let a number of lumpsum EPC contracts for sections of the plant to separate contractors, it is most desirable that these
contractors bid to a coordinated, thoroughly defined, definition of scope. This is especially important in the case of full-service, turnkey contracts. Usually, the owner's
effort to define what is to be built far exceeds the effort to define how the work is to
be executed, particularly in the areas most affected by the multiproject environment,
namely procurement and construction. Yet these are the areas of greatest potential
for claims for extras. Many of these claims are based on intercontractor coordination
problems causing scheduling difficulties for each contractor. The inquiries, which
are the basis for bidding, must spell out in detail the program, the requirements for
intercontractor coordination, the hazards and liabilities which must be accepted by
the contractor in determining his price, and the conditions or circumstances that will,
or will not, be accepted as grounds for contract extra claims. As much or more thought
must be given to this aspect of the inquiry document as is given to the technical scope
definition.

An aspect of an intercontractor situation that is often overlooked is that of assignment terms and conditions for site management and supervisory personnel. Wide variations in per diem living allowances, transportation, and completion bonuses, lead to
morale problems among supervisors and managers, that can only be detrimental to field
execution. Owners should require bidders to spell out their assignment policies in
detail so that any significant departures from a reasonable norm can be discussed with
the bidders prior to award. An alternative is for the owner to spell out the acceptable
assignment conditions as a basis for reimbursement, but this presents a number of problems. First, the owner frequently has insufficient experience on which to base a workable assignment policy. Second, such an "imposed" policy is difficult to enforce, re-

gardless of the type of contract, but particularly on lump-sum contracts. Third, small variations in policy from contractor to contractor are not a problem, but large variations can be, hence, a rigid universal assignment policy should be avoided.

A word of caution is in order regarding special incentives for job completion in a multiproject environment. Penalty/bonus clauses as incentives for contractors to meet scheduled completion dates can be destructive to the intercontractor cooperation that is essential in a multicontractor environment. Such incentives assume that the contractor has almost total control over his performance, yet in such an environment in the field this is not the case. In general, therefore, such incentives are not recommended.

An increasingly important aspect of project execution is public relations. A multiproject environment generally is consistent with a large project, and significant expenditures have a great impact on the community in which the plant, or plants, are to be built. It should be made clear that this is an owner responsibility. Who has the authority and responsibility to talk to the media? If, for example, the decision is made to let an overall field management contract to one contractor he may be required to deal directly with the media in the event of labor difficulties or work stoppages, while the owner's own personnel handle all other aspects of publicity. If field management responsibility is divided among a number of contractors, it is probably best that the owner handle all contacts with the media, including labor problems. What must be avoided is multisource contacting with the media which leads to serious problems of contradictory statements and indicates a lack of centralized control.

CASE 3: CONCURRENT PROJECTS FOR DIFFERENT OWNERS BY DIFFERENT CONTRACTORS IN ONE GEOGRAPHICAL AREA

This is the most difficult of the various types of multiproject execution. There exists no obvious single coordination responsibility or authority, yet all the problems of case 2 apply without a focal point for arbitrary resolution. As a basis for discussion, the following is an example of such an environment.

A company decides to build a petrochemical base stock facility producing acetylene, ethylene, propylene, butadiene, benzene, and other products. These justify the building, by other companies in the area, of downstream facilities to produce ethylene derivatives, plastics, propylene-based chemicals, polybutadiene, styrene, and so on. Each of these downstream plants are independently defined and contracted by the separate companies, following policies and practices normal to the various owner companies, but varying significantly one from another. Yet all draw on the same pool of resources available in the project area: labor supervision, construction equipment, materials, supplies, etc.

This bare description of an example of case 3 indicates the potential problems facing project management. Each of the owner companies will have its own philosophies, practices, and policies for the execution of projects and the probability that these policies will be compatible in a common multiproject environment is low. Yet the success of all of the concurrent projects is dependent on setting up compatible execution circumstances and close coordination of supply and allocation of local resources.

As in case 2, this multiproject environment is unlikely to have an impact on engineering and design capacity. The marketplace, special contractor knowhow, and individual contractor capacity will make it improbable that any one EPC contractor will be awarded contracts for a number of these separate but concurrent projects. Thus, excess demand for engineering and design capacity is more likely to result from total industry demand than from demands of these projects alone. The multiproject conditions of case 1 normally can be expected to apply.

In procurement and construction, the problems discussed in case 2 will apply in case 3, but without an obvious coordination activity in existence. For overall success, such an authority must be set up. In developed industrial areas, coordinating vehicles may exist in the form of operation/owner councils, and local construction associations. In undeveloped areas, such organizations must be formed. Who takes the lead role?

Obviously in this multiproject environment, those with the most at stake are the owners. They provide the cash, and are most affected by project schedules and reap the most benefit from early operation of new facilities to provide positive cash flow. Therefore, the owner's project management personnel should take the lead in forming a projects' coordination group. The first group "on-site" and the one on whom all others depend for the operation of these facilities is probably the group building the base stock facility. Therefore it is advantageous for this owner's project manager to take the lead in forming an owner's council.

Procurement

In procurement functions, the owners' council should consider information sharing and coordination in the following areas:

1. The placement of orders for fabricated assemblies or equipment. A specific example is that of shop fabrication of pipe spools. Overloading of shops within a reasonable shipping distance is possible, to the detriment of all projects in the area both in schedule and in costs.
2. The placement of subcontracts with local firms. The same situation as for shop-fabricated piping exists with local subcontractors.
3. The purchasing of miscellaneous construction materials, make-up commodity materials, hardware, and supplies from area suppliers.
4. The reasonable standardization of commodity materials to justify supplier maintenance of spare parts in stock for future operating requirements. This is particularly important in less-developed industrial locations.
5. The demands on local construction equipment availability: cranes, welding machines, mobile facilities.
6. The material handling and traffic capacity of local transportation facilities for delivery of material to the various sites.

It is unlikely that coordination is needed or desirable for major equipment items, pumps and compressors, for example; these are likely to be purchased from areas remote from the construction sites and are specific to each facility's needs. On the other hand, some standardization between facilities is advantageous in setting up a local supply of spare parts and services for future plant maintenance. This approach applies to such items as pump seal components, electrical commodities, instrumentation, and gaskets. Obviously the desirability of standardization between owners is reduced if the multiprojects are being built in developed industralized areas where the various vendors will have service and parts warehousing facilities within reasonable travel time of the area.

One aspect of standardization cuts across both engineering and procurement functions: standardization of fire-fighting and other safety facilities. It is usual in a multi-owner complex that a cooperative approach will be taken to fire-fighting and other disaster circumstances. To facilitate such cooperation during plant operation it is desirable that all owners have a common approach to the design and procurement of safety facilities to ensure that assistance from one plant to another will not be hampered by lack of familiarity on the part of the firefighters and lack of compatibility of equipment.

Thus, very early in the projects' schedules (during the planning phase) the project manager for the "first-off" project should take the lead in organizing an owners' (preferably) or a contractors' procurement coordination council. Such a council should either establish an office, or assign the responsibility to one of the contractors to:

1. Receive preliminary quantity estimates of all material

2. Receive each contractors material procurement coordination plan
3. Analyze the area supply capability against the projected demand across the total schedule
4. Advise contractors as to sources of supply when standardization across the various plants is deemed necessary
5. Assist local suppliers to increase their capacity to meet the projected demands both during construction and during subsequent plant operation and maintenance
6. Ensure equitable distribution of resources between the various projects
7. Prevent local economy overheating through uncontrolled competitive bidding for goods and services

The above recommendations, by their implied impact on the contractors' plans of execution, suggest that the various contracts between owners and EPC contractors should be of the cost-reimbursable type. To have some or all of such contractors "turnkey lump sum" is to inhibit or prevent the type of coordination needed to benefit all owners. Under these circumstances, contractors are not truly in control of their project execution circumstances; a condition essential to lump-sum contracting. Penalty/bonus clauses also are unlikely to be applicable as applying to either cost control or the meeting of completion schedules or both. Any contractual terms that encourage an individual contractor to act independently rather than cooperatively is contradictory to the coordination recommended for this multiproject case.

Construction

In principle, all the factors discussed for procurement coordination apply to the construction phase of the various projects in case 3. The only difference is in degree; whereas procurement cooperation and coordination is desirable for optimum use of resources, it is absolutely essential for effective control of construction resources. The situation again indicates the need for a coordinating council, but in this case, it is likely that a council composed of contractors' representatives will be more effective than an owners' council.

There are a number of reasons for this. First, most owners are unfamiliar with construction operations, whereas they are familiar with procurement operations. Second, owners generally have limited experience in dealing with construction labor and its unions. These differ markedly from plant operation unions in their tenure (temporary versus permanent) and allegience (to the union rather than the employer). Third, in a large multiproject environment construction skills' training and upgrading is sure to be necessary, and it is the contractors who have developed the necessary training systems and procedures. Fourth, the contractors' management know the impact of differing work conditions, union jurisdiction, and so on, and are best able to coordinate these conditions with each other as direct managers of the work forces.

Such a council should be organized very early in project planning; probably by the contractor's project manager of the "first-off" project. Ideally the contractor's site construction manager will be assigned at this stage and will be preparing a construction execution plan and if so, he should be designated to take the initiative in the organization of a construction council. Such a council should have a representation from every prime contractor retained by the owners. In developed areas where a local construction association exists this also should be represented, as should the president of local Building Trades Council for unionized projects.

Owners' representation should be limited and ex officio. Such representatives should communicate the owners' policies and wishes and report actions and decisions to the owners' council. Recognizing that the best solutions to problems in this type of environment are "consensus" solutions arrived at by parties directly managing the resources, it is not recommended that an owner's representative act in an approval or "veto" position. If it is felt that decisions are being made which are not in the best

interests of the owners, the council representative should report this back to the owners, who in turn, will make their positions known to their specific prime contractors
by way of normal project coordination procedures.

The owner/project manager/construction manager communication links should not
be bypassed by way of a coordinating council.

Each participating contractor should supply the coordinating council the following
information:

1. The overall project construction schedule showing major milestones
2. Craft labor demand curves for both direct hire work and subcontracted work,
    by craft and across the total field schedule
3. Craft training and/or upgrading plans, systems, and procedures
4. Proposed job work rules and jurisdictional policies
5. Subcontracting plan: work to be contracted, types of contracts, estimated num-
    ber of contracts, estimated manhours for each subcontract, subcontract overall
    schedule, and subcontractor manpower requirements by craft distributed across
    the schedule
6. Expected monthly purchases of services and materials from local suppliers by
    commodity and volume
7. Expected demand for construction equipment from local sources

The coordinating council should develop, in cooperation with any existing local Building Trades Council and with governmental agencies, the labor supply picture. For
large project complexes it is unlikely that the local labor supply will be adequate; even
with training programs and skills upgrading, and in all but a few countries, it is likely
that labor will have to be imported. It would be chaotic to leave arrangements for immigration to each project contractor to work out with the host government. The same
applies for basic training programs. These usually receive government financial assistance and use services and facilities of local institutions, such as trade schools.

The fundamental difference between this case and the "single-owner" multiproject
of case 2, is that the council is a coordinating group for common problems but has no
direct impact on the execution of each project by the EPC contractor. How the safety
program, for example, is organized and run on one project is of no concern to the contractor on another project, except as each may learn from the others to improve procedures. Standardization of methods is recommended in case 2 but unnecessary in case 3.

In cases where a number of projects are executed concurrently in one locality,
a large influx of craft labor, frequently numbering in the thousands, will require a
coordinated solution to housing. Camp facilities will probably be required.

Experience has shown that one common camp facility is preferred. This is best
provided and managed by an agency separate from any of the various contractors executing the projects. This is an excellent vehicle for increasing the participation of
local people in the projects. A "common" camp provides service to all contractors for
housing of single status persons with appropriate billing to each on a manday cost basis.
It also simplifies transportation by including busing service from the common living
facility to each project site as part of the package.

The discussion of cooperation and coordination between contractors emphasizes
the initiation of programs and actions, but it must be emphasized that such actions
will bear fruit only through continuity of cooperation throughout the life of the projects.
A problem frequently encountered is "job-jumping," as one project nears completion
ahead of others. The rundown of craft levels requires the same coordination between
contractors as the build-up. Also requiring control is the common pressure to meet
an individual project's completion date and the temptation to break agreements of hours
of work, overtime, double shifting, and so on. In this situation it is essential that
the owners enforce the common policy on each of their projects to the final completion
of the last one.

One situation which, if it occurs, must be handled on a coordinated basis by all contractors is labor unrest. If a coordinating council has been formed and has done its preparatory work properly, including working in full cooperation with local labor unions, labor unrest will be minimal. There will, nevertheless, be problems on individual sites, usually interunion jurisdictional problems. The general approach to the resolution of such problems should be consistent from project to project. If a major disagreement occurs it is essential that the contractors stand together on a defensible position. On the other hand, though it should not need stating, the worst mistake is for the contractor as a group to support one of their members in an indefensible position. Sad to say this has occurred at the general expense of the projects and the owners.

In many multiprojects, there have been moves to institute project or area agreements (which differ from state, provincial, national, or international agreements) with the various construction labor unions. Frequently, these are fostered by governments as a means of isolating the particular requirements of the situation from other activities in the area, state, or country. Contractors working in other area of the state, especially smaller local firms in other types of construction, view such project agreements with suspicion since they often provide conditions and concessions to the unions to ensure labor peace, which either add an ongoing burden to the local contractor after the "big-jobs" are finished, or "syphon-off" the best craftspersons to the big jobs. It is essential that all parties involved, owners, contractors and government agencies, obtain the input of local groups in the drafting of project or area agreements and avoid clauses and conditions which will negatively affect the future of the "locals" long after the "big internationals" have left the scene.

An increasingly popular alternative in North America is "open-shop" construction. Significant labor cost savings have been demonstrated by this approach, particularly in the Gulf Coast area of the United States. But, in areas where the multiproject environment is often likely to ccur, remote and/or nonindustrialized areas, there are advantages to the "union-shop" situation. In labor supply coordination, setting of common work conditions for all projects, craft training and skills upgrading, fair allocation of labor resources among the various contractors, settlement of labor problems on a total area basis, and coordination of all aspects of the circumstance which affect labor, an organization exists to work with contractors and owners which represents the man on the job. Whether these advantages compensate for possible cost savings claimed for "open-shop" construction is something for project managers of both owners and contractors to decide in concert.

The project manager and construction manager working in this environment must be prepared for one unfortunate byproduct: comparison of project performance with others, in the areas of productivity, safety statistics, labor upsets, rework percentages, to name only a few. It is unlikely that such comparisons are either valid or fair. Comparisons, for example, of pipefitter productivity on a piping-intensive facility with a downstream facility emphasizing equipment installation with minimal piping are of little value. Their value is even less when it is considered that the measurement of productivity is inexact and that each contractor has his own methods and measuring yardsticks. Nevertheless, experience in similar cases indicates that such comparisons will be made by the owners, craftsmen, and others in the community who have no way of judging their validity. Each project manager can do his best to execute the work and avoid participating in the situation by comparing his own performance with that of the other contractors in the area. The coordinating council can also help by good public relations; making use of all local media channels to educate the total community of the progress and accomplishments of all projects and emphasizing the interrelationships and common aspects of the multiproject as opposed to individual projects.

One of the most difficult factors for multicontractor coordination is that of field management and supervisory resources. Ideally the coordinating council of contractors should:

1. Receive from each contractor projected requirements of such personnel, the numbers to be provided from his permanent staff, the numbers and types of personnel he expects to hire locally for the project, and the numbers of "project hires" he expects to import into the area.
2. Coordinate minimum job qualifications by function to prevent hiring "one level above the level of competence," hence diluting general overall competence.
3. If possible, set common salary and benefits guidelines, particularly in the matter of per diem living allowances, jobsite transportation, project completion bonuses, "R&R" provisions, etc.
4. Set up a skills-upgrading program for local hires, to leave behind a greater legacy than merely completed plant facilities, and coordinate the allocation of such personnel to the various project sites.
5. Set common, or at least compatible, end-of-job layoff policies and ensure that they are made known to all new personnel at time of hire. This includes allowances for relocation expenditures for "imported" personnel and their families.
6. Coordinate housing facilities for supervisory personnel and families.
7. Inhibit "piracy" of individuals between competing contractors, and job jumping.

Total uniformity of personnel policies among all participating contractors is unlikely, and is not essential. Reasonable variances are accepted. Wide variances cause unrest among the very people most responsible for project success: the line supervisory and management group, with obvious negative effects on performance. In such an environment there are no secrets, and special deals by one contractor cannot be kept private.

Obviously, these recommendations assume that all contractors are working under "cost-reimbursable"-type contracts with the owners. Lump-sum contracts will make such coordination and cooperation impossible, since it will be the contractors' position that his policies and expenditures are his business alone and he is at liberty to do what he thinks best to manage and execute the project for maximum profit.

CONCLUSION

For all types of multiproject circumstances the key features of project management are the "three Cs": communication, coordination, cooperation, to the optimum benefit of all participating owners and contractors. Success requires a central authority or organization through which the three Cs can be realized. In the case of concurrent projects by a number of contractors for one owner, it is proper for that owner to fill that role. In the case of multiple projects for multiple owners, coordinating councils should be established for procurement, preferably by the owners, and for construction, preferably by the participating contractors. While controlling his own project, the project manager for each must work with the philosophy that what is best for all concurrent projects will, in the final analysis, be best for his.

7

Modular Construction

THOMAS A. MULLETT* *Mobil Research & Development Corp., Princeton, New Jersey*

The components comprising a project may be assembled at the jobsite, or they may be put together somewhere else and transported to the jobsite. If the latter is the case, the preassembled portion is called a module. It might also be referred to as a packaged plant. The entire plant may be modularized, or only a portion depending upon the requirements.

A project involving modularization differs markedly from a conventional project. It might be characterized as two concurrent projects or one subsidiary project created within the main project. These two projects have all of the same types of activities; however, some of those within the subsidiary portion will have special demands and will probably have to be implemented on an earlier time frame than those on the main project.

Recognition of the unique characteristics and earlier timing of this "other project" is the key to developing an effective implementation plan for a modularized project.

Whether or not modularization is the correct approach depends entirely upon the nature of the project and the conditions that exist at the jobsite. Some projects are not feasible without modularization; others may be feasible, but are certainly not viable without the use of modularization. In most cases, modularization is not the proper approach and should not be considered.

Modularization affects the implementation plan of a project to a major extent. If a project is to be executed using modularization techniques, there must be an early recognition of the differences involved and how these will change the conventional approach to running a project. As with most conventional projects, the execution of the modularized portion of a project requires a multidisciplined effort. These efforts will involve management attention to the following:

Organization
Controls (cost and schedule)
Engineering
Procurement
Fabrication
Transportation
Construction

Current affiliation: Consultant, Eustis, Florida

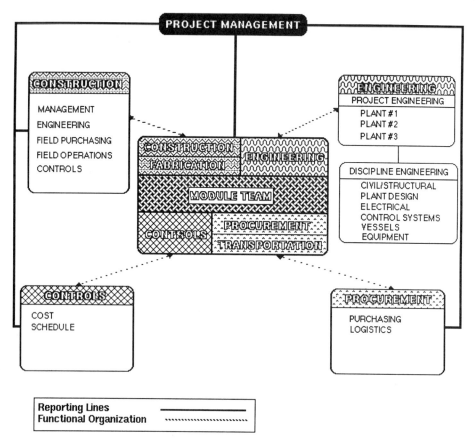

Figure 1 Module team organization.

ORGANIZATION

To effectively manage the module-related activities within the main project, the use of an identified multidisciplined module team within the project task force is recommended. A suggested organizational arrangement is illustrated in Figure 1.

In this organization, specific individuals representing engineering, procurement, transportation, construction, and the controls functions are dedicated to work as a task force within the main project organization. The module team, through its leader, is responsible to the project manager for:

Formulating the overall strategy for the engineering, procurement, fabrication, and transportation of the modularized plant components, and presenting for the approval of the project manager

Coordination of the resultant objectives and the detailed plan with the engineering, procurement, transportation, and construction activities for the main project

Supervision of operations of the module fabricator

Coordination and/or supervision of the module transport/rigging contractor

The functional group origin of the individual team members helps ensure that the special requirements of modularization are given timely and proper attention in the functional groups. Immediate availability of structural design, heavy haul, and rigging expertise on a high-priority as-needed basis to the module team is indispensable to the success of the effort. Prior experience on modular work is particularly desirable for those key members of the module team. The built-in inertia of traditional project organizational systems, procedures, and priorities must be avoided; potentially expensive surprises and delays on a modularized project can result. The new requirements cannot be accommodated with a "make do" or "business as usual" mentality.

PLANNING AND JOB CONTROL

Formulation of the strategy for implementing the module portion of the project is the first order of business for the module team. Next, is gaining the project management acceptance of the strategy. As a minimum, the strategy should provide a statement of objectives, and a detailed plan for achieving those objectives.

In developing the module strategy, the team will understand the particular reasons for the decision to modularize the project. It is important that there be real commitment to the decision among those responsible for the work. These reasons are then converted to specific team objectives. An example of such a strategy statement for modularizing a project is shown in Table 1.

The strategy, once accepted, should be expanded into a more detailed list of activities. Such a list provides a ready checklist for defining responsibilities for each of the module team members and serves as the basis for developing the project's master module schedule. A typical activities list is shown in Table 2.

In the next stages of the project, module team efforts will be concentrated in the home office on engineering and procurement. The project manager must realize that

Table 1 Modularization Strategy Statement

Objectives

1. Complete and deliver modules and subassemblies on schedule to support achievement of the project mechanical completion date
2. Shift 30% of conventional on-site construction jobhours off-site via module design/fabrication concepts
3. Optimize local content

Action Plan

1. Develop the design of the project maximizing modular features; identify all modules, subassemblies and nonmodularized equipment items
2. Prepare and establish early overall schedule of module activities
3. Monitor module design efforts via concurrent craft jobhour estimate control to ensure the shift of required jobhours offsite
4. Implement worldwide competitive procurement, with preference given to local sources where competitive in price, quality, and delivery. Award all modules and related equipment items offshore
5. By means of unit price inquiry, expedite an early selection and award to the minimum number of module fabricators (preferably one)
6. Assign responsibility for procurement of bulk materials to module fabricator with any exceptions explicitly identified
7. Obtain custom duty exemptions for offshore modules and equipment
8. Conduct logistics/transportation surveys; develop overall module transportation plan; verify local port size/tonnage/volume capability
9. Define and disseminate project QA/QC requirements to potential prefabricated component suppliers

---

Table 2 Modularization Activities List

Organization
  Develop and publish module implementation strategy
  Identify and assign responsibilities to module team members

Controls
  Compile a list of modularization activities
  Prepare and establish modularization implementation schedule
  Prepare conventional construction craft jobhour estimate
  Prepare module craft jobhour estimates on progressive design monitoring basis

Engineering
  Prepare process flow diagrams[a]
  Compile equipment lists[a]
  Conduct site/soil surveys[a]
  Prepare plot plans incorporating module concepts[a]
  Establish module foundation design concepts
  Prepare module criteria specifications
  Identify and conceptualize modules and nonmodularized equipment items
  Prepare MTOs by module
  Develop and utilize scale model to facilitate design of modules
  Define module Q/A and Q/C requirements
  Prepare module inquiry packages

Procurement/fabrication
  Establish module contracting strategy
  Qualify module assembly yards
  Secure module customs license and duty exemption

Transportation
  Conduct module logistics studies
  Qualify ocean transport charterers
  Survey existing road transportation routes and other means of access to construction site from module fabrication yard through port of entry.[a]

Construction
  Conduct site labor availability survey[a]
  Establish compatible construction sequence priorities with equipment and module deliveries
  Develop construction erection, heavy lift handling, and equipment transport requirements
  Qualify on-site contractors vis-à-vis modularization requirements

---

[a]Main project activities which are prerequisite to modularization activities.

the engineering effort for a modular project is more extensive than for a similar conventional project. Engineering budgets and schedules should be evaluated and reviewed accordingly. After sufficient progress in engineering has been achieved, bid requests will be prepared and the module fabrication/transportation contractor(s) selected. Activity now shifts to the fabrication yard, where emphasis must be placed on meeting the schedule for completion of the modules and delivery to the jobsite.

A module program entails a characteristic logical sequence of events. From the list of activities and the module program logic, a module milestone schedule is established. In developing this schedule there are significant timing issues that must be considered. The milestone schedule will serve as an important planning guide for developing more detailed schedules for each of the disciplines. At this stage of project development, a firm plan in any significantly greater detail must await further development of those activities.

In general, a successful modularized project requires even more careful planning, more disciplined execution, and earlier than usual scheduling of a number of activities than a conventional project. This must be recognized because of the critical nature of planning and scheduling considerations in a modularized project.

A typical example of a module program logic is shown in Figure 2 and of a module milestone schedule in Figure 3.

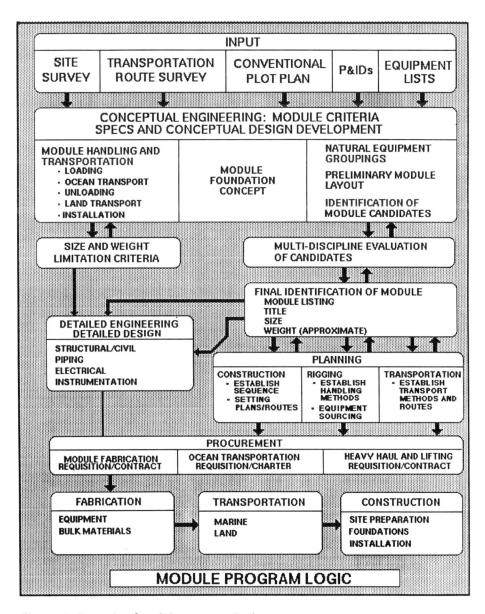

Figure 2 Example of module program logic.

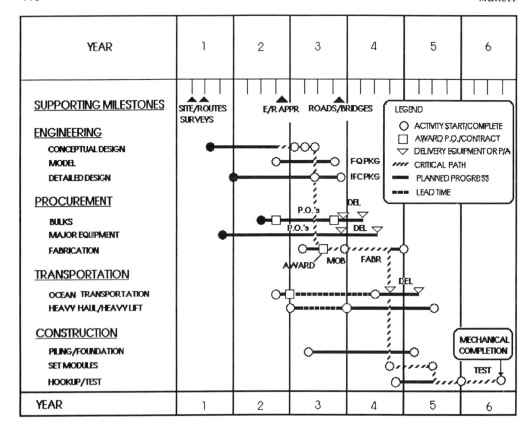

Figure 3 Example of module milestone schedule.

ENGINEERING

The engineering of a modular project requires a different approach, not only in terms
of layout and design but also in the organization of the work and the methods and controls used. Those aspects which differ significantly from a conventional project are
discussed below.

Module Terminology

A few terms and definitions in common use include the following:

   Module. A large-scale plant section fabricated and assembled in a yard, remote
       from the main construction site, with multidisciplined, skilled craft labor. The
       term *module* is used to identify preassembled units normally larger than those
       capable of shipment by road or rail.
   Subassembly. A unitized group of materials and equipment shop fabricated and
       assembled into smaller scale hardware elements at or apart from the main con-
       struction site. They are normally shipped by rail or road.
   Vendor Package or Vendor Assembly. Items of engineered equipment customarily
       manufactured and/or assembled in a vendor's shop and sold as a packaged unit.
       It usually performs a self-contained plant function.

> Field Assembly. Nonmodularized materials and pieces of equipment which are put
> together and erected at the plant site. The resultant unit has a high propor-
> tion of field labor. A common term is "stick built."

In applying these definitions, there may be some difficulty in making a decisive classification of certain items. Arbitrary classifications must be assigned. Perseverance
in having such definitions adopted for the project will pay off in improved communications, clear assignment of responsibilities, and more effective execution.

The Engineering Schedule

It is to be expected that the module engineering activities will be on the critical path
for the entire project. The successful project requires more careful planning, more
disciplined execution, and an earlier sequencing of a number of engineering activities.
Prompt identification of all module-related engineering activities and early detailed scheduling of these should get high priority. A suggested checklist of those activities impacting module engineering work is shown in Table 3.

To support the overall project schedule, it becomes evident that the electrical and
instrumentation design, frequently delayed on a conventional project, must be conceptualized and defined much earlier. Engineering decisions will have to be made on the
basis of experience and good judgment with less time to evaluate alternatives and to
optimize solutions. An individual engineering schedule for each module or group of
similar modules is of value.

Engineering Documentation System

Since a modularized plant will be designed, procured, fabricated, transported, and
erected in packaged units, all project functions must communicate and act on the basis
of the identity, description, scope, and material content of the modules. This means
that documentation must be structured accordingly, and formatted and packaged to

Table 3 Module Activities: Engineering Work Plan Checklist

---

1. Site soils survey
2. Module transportation route survey
3. PFD/P&ID development
4. Equipment listing
5. Conventional plot plan development

6. Contracting plan
7. Engineering documentation system design
8. Design criteria development
9. Fabrication criteria development
10. Rigging, handling, and structural design criteria development

11. Layout, conceptual design, and identification
12. Sea fastening and voyage protection criteria development
13. Scale modeling
14. Weight/dimensional control program
15. Quality control criteria preparation

16. Fabrication bid package preparation
17. Fabrication yard surveillance (Q/A and Q/C)
18. Mechanical completion schedule
19. Load out/sea fastening

---

facilitate all project operations. The customary classification of documentation for discipline-only is inadequate. The ability to assemble all of the necessary information on the basis of each individual module is essential and must be recognized and implemented early.

Because of the nature of the schedule, the close tolerances involved, and the complex nature of the intergroup communications on a modular project, it is extremely important that a comprehensive change-order system be established and maintained throughout the project. Changes can be minimized with the help of good planning, but they are inevitable. Project management must exercise the proper level of control on any changes introduced into the design to reduce their impact on cost and schedule.

Module Design Criteria

There are many design specifications unique to modules which engineering must ultimately fix in detail. Table 4 contains a partial listing of these. When a project involves several modules, standardization of dimensions, materials, and installed equipment should be pursued to the fullest extent practicable. Specific classes of modules can be developed to allow repetitive use of transportation and lifting equipment which, in turn, can lead to cost savings.

Three design criteria are basic and must be established as early as possible:

> Size and weight limits
> Marine and land transport means
> Site installation concept

Table 4 Module Design Specifications

Fabrication requirements
Transport, rigging, and shipping concepts
Structural design criteria
    Seismic stress
    Shipping stress

Size
Weight

Layout
Center of gravity and stability
Base frame concept
Base frame foundation and support level
System tie-ins and interfaces

Dimensional control
Modeling standards
In situ corrosion protection
Discipline details
    Structural
    Piping
    Electrical
    Instrumentation
    Insulation and fire protection
    Painting
Hydrostatic testing

Mechanical completion
Shipping protection and sea fastening

These three criteria are interdependent and are developed together. Prerequisites are comprehensive site/soils surveys and a thorough transportation route survey. The transportation survey should cover the marine and/or land routes from prospective module yards to the main construction site.

With this survey information, the following specifics may be determined:

Module size and weight limits
Acceleration loads imposed by shipping
Foundation design parameters
Feasible module handling and transportation methods

Within the limits set, there are other factors to be considered to determine the ultimate module sizes and weights on a given project.

Field labor availability, cost, and capability
Transportation
Engineering and procurement constraints
Cost versus module volume, weight, and area
Plant operability and safety
Plant characteristics and inherent layout requirements

There is no one ideal module size; the size and weight will vary depending on the unique conditions of each project. The optimum individual module size generally will be the largest that can be economically justified in light of the following:

Program objectives; relative importance of overall costs, schedules and a reduction
    in field forces
Available transport route and systems
Plant characteristics and plot layouts; the natural division of plant equipment into
    modules
Work content in the module which translates into reduced labor costs versus the
    added costs of framing, bracing, transportation, and handling
The state of the art in engineering for module design

Most module programs will contain a range of module sizes, dictated mainly by the particular plant characteristics and circumstances. The size and weight limits must be established in concert with the marine and land transport methods. Once established, the dimensional and weight limits must be strictly observed during the design and fabrication stages. Formal dimensional and weight control programs are required to insure that later expensive surprises are avoided.

The site installation concept influences the detailed design. Early decisions in this regard must be made. A key point is the module base support level. Except for certain modules, which because of their inherent configuration must be elevated on supports above grade, the decision depends on whether those modules containing equipment normally mounted on grade-level foundations will have their base frames mounted above or below grade. An early and rigorous analysis of the factors affecting the decisions on the module support levels and the factors affecting pipeway module design is indicated. Attention must be given to special routing requirements of underground systems because of the differences between modular and conventional plants; one of the most important is the imposition of extremely heavy loads during the movement of the modules at the site.

Module Identification

Once the essential criteria have been established for the modules, conventional plot layouts and P&IDs for each plant facility must be examined creatively with the objective of identifying natural physical groups of equipment. Trial layouts in plan and elevation must be made to embody significant field work content within the established size and weight criteria. Due consideration must be given to assuring plant safety, operability, and maintainability. From these efforts a preliminary set of module candidates for each process unit should be developed and subjected to rigorous evaluation by the multi-disciplined module team. The evaluation should assess the cost, schedule, engineering, procurement, transportation, and construction suitability of each of the proposed modules.

The flow of information and module team interaction in this evaluation process is shown in Figure 4. The structural engineering participation in a modularization is much heavier than the normal involvement in a conventional project and a correspondingly greater demand on this discipline must be anticipated throughout the conceptual and detailed design phases of a modular project.

The module team must maintain a current awareness of the equipment procurement activities, the identity of other prefabricated components, and the potential for inclusion/exclusion of these elements in the module program.

In designing the module, it is advantageous to use vertically aligned equipment items wherever possible, and to stack equipment rather than spread it out as in the conventional plant layout. Provision must be made for operating and maintenance requirements. Equipment can be fabricated, erected, transported, and hooked up, but still have such a tight configuration that it is impossible to maintain. When all design criteria decisions have been made and the individual modules have been identified, the detailed design may proceed.

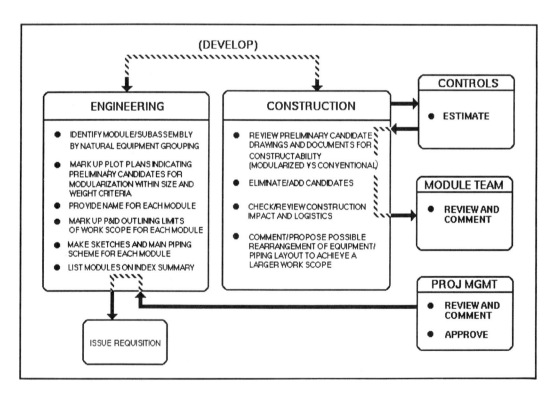

Figure 4 Flow chart of module team interactions.

Contracting Plan

All of the planning, engineering, and design work should be directed toward support
of the contracting plan which has been established for module fabrication. The impact
of the type of contract chosen will affect the timing and degree of engineering detail
required for the bid packages.

PROCUREMENT

On a modularized project three elements of procurement strategy are particularly significant: schedule, type of contract, and sourcing geography. Procurement strategy
for the modules must be carefully thought out and a specific plan of action established
at an early date.

The equipment content for each module must be set, and engineering for the modules should proceed as rapidly as possible to support early selection of a module fabricator. Almost invariably, the schedule constraints attending these activities dictate
an extensive overlap between engineering and procurement/fabrication so that lump-
sum engineering definition of modules is not practical. Module fabrication contracts
are preferably let on a unit price basis to satisfy these schedule considerations.

Concurrently with the engineering and module procurement, the purchase of the
long delivery equipment items contained on the modules must be expedited. A large
proportion of engineered items become part of the natural equipment groupings on the
modules. Specification, purchase, and vendor data for this equipment are all on the
critical path for module design. Innovative ways to shorten the procurement path are
necessary. Since transportation costs can be significant, major equipment and module
fabricator selection decisions should be made simultaneously to optimize the geographical
sourcing.

Similar schedule constraints are present in the procurement of bulk materials. If
the module fabricator is selected early on a unit price basis, the supply of module bulk
materials should be normally included in his scope of work. Exceptions would include
those critical long lead bulk materials and specialty items which must be identified and
placed on order prior to fabrication award.

The award of fabrication may be made on the basis of unit price competitive bids
or it may be on the basis of noncompetitive engineering judgment. Because piping
bulk materials comprise an important and voluminous class of bulk materials, the module
activities must be supported by an extremely comprehensive piping material control
program during the engineering, procurement, and fabrication phases. The program
must have the capability to integrate MTOs (material takeoffs), inventories, and delivery
tracking data by individual stock code/size and to sort on a demand basis by module,
by isometric, by source, by end user.

Wherever possible, the module fabrication contracts should be placed on a process
plant unit basis. To the extent practicable all modules for a given plant should be
fabricated by one contractor.

Work in the module contractor's yard is on an assembly line basis. Late delivery
of project-furnished equipment and materials can disrupt this assembly line, leading to
extra charges. Great emphasis should be placed on equipment suppliers' schedule performance. Expediting efforts should be maintained at a high level for these critical items.

Each module represents a significant element in the field construction program.
The proper sequencing and timely delivery of the modules is critical. The module fabricators capability and reputation for on-time delivery is extremely significant in selecting the firm to assemble the modules.

FABRICATION

Module fabrication is a combination of two separate operations normally present on a
conventional project: shop fabrication and field erection.

Project management is primarily concerned with these elements: shop fabrication, inspection, and expediting normally associated with vendor supplied equipment, and planning and surveillance requirements normally associated with field construction management.

Identifying firms qualified in this particular combination of skills with sufficient resources to provide 1, 2, or 3 million fabrication jobhours is fundamental to successful execution.

In recent years, shipyards have been directing their resources toward offshore oil platform and module construction work. Their organizations and facilities are well suited for this work; but, because of certain fundamental differences, there are areas of work procedures, quality control, and construction management that need to be modified for successful module fabrication projects. It is always best to anticipate that a strong resident owner's technical management team will be required to oversee this vital part of the project. Shipyards are not the only type facility plant suited to module fabrication, but they have most of the essential requirements for module fabrication and assembly. Regardless of the firm selected to do the work, the organization and facility must be able to deliver a quality product to meet strict schedule requirements.

Time should be allotted in the fabrication schedule to adequately test out the individual modules and to thoroughly check out the tolerances for field hookup prior to shipment. All piping systems should be pressure tested and all instrumentation and electrical control loops tested for system integrity and continuity before shipment. Repairs, corrections, and modifications are more easily and economically made in the shop when done by shop craft personnel familiar with the systems being supplied.

TRANSPORTATION

The transportation of the modules from the point of fabrication/assembly to the jobsite is a major and expensive activity not encountered in the conventional project.

Route Survey

A successful cost effective module transportation program starts with a thorough route survey which covers the movement of the completed modules from likely fabrication yards to their placement at the jobsite. The survey should be given early priority and will typically involve both land and marine transport. The transport of bulky heavy modules on land and sea requires the choice of specialized types of heavy haul vehicles and vessels. Choices must be made early to provide the basis for module design, to permit timely contracting/chartering of these services, and to resolve logistics-related questions. Landlocked sites represent a particular challenge to the project team.

Modes of Transportation

Depending upon the conditions, the land transport vehicle options would include: conventional trucks or tractor-trailer units, rail cars, and heavy haul transporters.

Most modules will exceed the size and weight limitations of conventional truck and rail systems. Land transport of most modules will probably use some combination of special purpose heavy haul transporters. These versatile but expensive vehicles are available in two basic types: crawler or rubber tired. These may be tractor-drawn or self-propelled. The rubber-tired or crawler, self-steerable bogies are designed to be assembled in combinations to suit load, size, weight, and route conditions. The bogies incorporate hydraulic jacking mechanisms to raise and lower their load-carrying platform. This is useful in loading and unloading modules and can be an important element in the module handling concept adopted for the project.

Sea transport of heavy, bulky items of assembled equipment has progressed significantly during the past decade. This trend was accelerated as the benefits of modularization became recognized. The state of the art in this field today has developed along the following lines:

The heavy lift vessel is capable of utilizing its own gear for the loading and discharge of modules. These self-propelled vessels are rated on the capacity of their derricks. At present vessels are in operation with capacities exceeding 1000 tons. This type of vessel is a valuable tool for a project that has a few large pieces to move over an extended period of time.

Roll-on/roll-off heavy lift vessels are powered vessels with a flat deck capable of carrying very heavy outsized pieces. These vessels vary in size and presently the largest units operating have a capacity of 2200 freight tons with 1100 square meters of unobstructed deck space.

Roll-on/roll-off barges are nonpowered ocean-going units which are towed from one location to another. The size used from Japan to the U.S. Gulf is 123 meters by 30.8 meters and has a usable clear deck space of 3000 square meters. These are capable of handling 15,800 freight tons.

The break bulk cargo vessel could be used for modules having a weight of 200 tons or less. Modules would be designed for lift-on and lift-off. The cargo can be stowed either in the hold or on the deck. Modern vessels, self-sustaining up to 100 tons are available for chartering. In the 100-200 ton range, shore or loading cranes would be used.

Shipping Protection

For modules shipped on deck, specifications for exposure protection must be developed for use by the various design disciplines working on the project. Each module should be reviewed on an individual basis to determine whether additional protection is necessary.

Shipping Stresses

Shipping stresses are dependent upon the shipping route, size, and characteristics of the carrier, module characteristics, and the season of shipment. Some of these parameters will be known at the time of design. It may be necessary to assume the others and this can be done in a conservative manner usually without too much penalty. If the route and carrier are established in sufficient time, it will be possible to run model basin tests or to utilize past tests to more precisely establish the proper design factors. Most qualified shipping companies have considerable experience and can be of help in setting these.

CONSTRUCTION

Meaningful construction plans are derived from four sources:

1. Schedule considerations
2. Impact of the direct jobhour transfer on all support activities, organization, and indirect costs
3. Development of handling methods and techniques to receive, transport, and set the identified modules, subassemblies, and vendor packages
4. Constructability of the entire plant recognizing the decreased flexibility brought about by the fact that modules comprise significant preconstructed sections of the plant

Schedule Considerations

The modular project activities must merge with the nonmodular activities in the construction phase. This fact will govern the planning steps required to integrate module fabrication, transportation, and placement into the main project plan. Certain degrees of planning freedom exist within each of the module activities, but early recognition of their interdependence and identification of critical constraints are essential for a successful overall plan.

A well thought-out field construction sequencing plan should encompass the following:

> The heavy haul and rigging concepts already adopted
> Preferred sequence of module deliveries to optimize construction planning objectives such as minimal rigging interferences, manpower resource leveling, overall completion milestones, and the like
> Earliest and latest individual module delivery need dates
> Identification of critical constraints

Once developed, essential requirements from the plan should be made available to the modules marine transport contractor and the module fabrication contractor to guide them in preparing their respective plans. These plans should include the following:

> Marine transportation
> > Stowage plans by voyage and vessel name
> > Schedule of arrival and departure dates for each voyage with estimated loading, unloading, and voyage durations
> > Identification of critical constraints and degrees of freedom with respect to dimensional/weight limitations, stowage, and ship alternatives
> Module fabrication
> > Preferred sequence of module fabrication
> > Manpower-loaded fabrication schedule
> > Identification of critical constraints such as materials and equipment deliveries, craft manpower limitations, and engineering schedules

During the planning stage conflicts of objectives and constraints will develop. Joint planning sessions led by the project manager and attended by construction marine transportation and module fabrication representatives will be necessary to optimize the project plan. Cost studies may be ordered to objectively select those tradeoffs required to produce the best plan.

Before the construction start date, all material requisitions and/or subcontracts covering piling fabrication, underground pipe fabrication, temporary facilities, construction equipment, tools, consumables, site preparation, haul roads, temporary power and water, fencing, dirt and spoils disposal and fill material will have been prepared, and some of these material contracts will be in progress. During this predominantly civil stage, construction of foundations, piling installation, installation of underground piping, electrical, and sewers will be essentially completed in the process and utility areas. When the first modules arrive at the jobsite, a concentrated mechanical effort will be initiated. The off-plot is typically built using conventional construction methods as it probably will have a low module content. This can be used to advantage to help with manpower leveling and to maintain field work flexibility. During the predominantly mechanical phase, the modules will be set, interconnections made, and systems checked out and tested. Precommissioning will start prior to total mechanical completion.

Mechanical completion of off-plot substations, electrical, cooling water, tankage, and steam systems will be accomplished as required for start-up of process and utility plants.

Typically, the construction of a utility plant will start with construction of foundations and installation of underground piping, electrical, and sewers and be practically complete when the first modules arrive. During this period, nonmodularized equipment will be set on foundations or stored, depending on access requirements. Module deliveries will be in a predetermined sequence, the modules will be set, all interconnections made, and as systems are completed, checkout and testing will begin. Precommissioning will begin and extend through mechanical completion. All process units will follow the same sequence.

Construction Nonmanual Organization

Organizational requirements during the early phases of a construction program involving large modules differ considerably from a conventional construction effort. This difference results from relocation of a large portion of the initial structural and mechanical work from the jobsite, allowing the underground civil effort to be carried to a further state of completion before the major emphasis shifts to the mechanical program.

A large reduction of jobsite infrastructure is generally possible because of the transfer of jobhours to the fabrication shop. This cost advantage must not be allowed to erode during the course of the field operation.

Contingency Plan

An inherent part of an implementation plan for module construction is the need to address the possibility that it may not be feasible to maintain the desired delivery schedule for one or more of the modules. These circumstances might involve:

Late equipment delivery
Labor problems
Major quality control problems on complex equipment
Material shortages

Part of the early work scope in the implementation phase will be to develop a contingency plan that can be implemented on short notice in the event that circumstances dictate. These items should be addressed in the contingency plan:

What type of adverse circumstances can and should be covered?
Which modules are on the critical path and what impact would these have on other areas of the project if they were delayed?
What options are open to alleviate the detrimental effects of any of these adverse circumstances on the project?
In what preference should options be adopted?
What monitoring systems should be implemented in order to pick up signals that the execution of the job is in trouble at the earliest possible moment?

THE CASE FOR MODULARIZATION

In the foregoing paragraphs we have seen some of the special requirements of the modular plant from the viewpoint of the project manager. Modularization is undertaken only when there are certain very specific construction constraints. In these instances, the advantages of modularization more than offset the disadvantage of additional cost elements. The more important of these conditions that lead to justification of a modular approach include:

A construction site that is located in an undeveloped and remote area which lacks the necessary skilled manpower resources

A construction site with hostile environmental conditions, climatic or other, that reduces labor productivity to an unacceptably low level

Quality requirements and/or limited availability of special fabrication tools, facilities, skills, or techniques that necessitate assembling hardware in a controlled environment

Some examples of projects in which modularization is warranted are:

Offshore petroleum drilling and production platforms
Arctic oil production facilities
Desert area processing facilities
Remote area power generation facilities
Prison facilities using prefabricated concrete elements

There is no doubt that the future will see expanded use of modular concepts in exploration of new frontiers including outer space and areas under the ocean surfaces.

The expansion of remote area resource development has accelerated the use of modularization. Some of the benefits of modularization in these cases are:

Fewer, less-skilled field construction personnel are required

Fabrication, assembly, testing, and checkout of major sections of sophisticated plant hardware are all accomplished by skilled labor in an environmentally controlled shop, usually resulting in a more reliable, higher quality plant

An earlier onstream completion date than would otherwise be possible with the resultant overall cost savings and/or a better rate of return on investment

Modularization may offer a solution to reducing the overall time span of a project where there is a shortage of skilled site labor or where the site conditions are extremely difficult by relocating or transferring much of this work to a fabrication yard. Although the costs are usually higher than they would be for a conventionally executed project, they are substantially lower than they would be for a conventionally executed project at the specific site under the specific conditions expected.

8
Climatic and Remote Conditions

JOHN H. CASSIDY   *J. H. Cassidy & Associates, Scottsdale, Arizona*
R. D. SORBO*   *Standard Alaska Production Company, Anchorage, Alaska*

Planning and execution of projects in remote areas, under severe climatic conditions, pose new and different problems, usually without established solutions. A general discussion of these problems is of great interest to the project manager, as is the application of these principles to a specific project. Hence this chapter will be devoted to Arctic project management, the experiences of a major oil company on the North Slope of Alaska.

Arctic conditions add a complex variable to the challenging task of project and construction management. Because of the severity and sensitivity of the environment and the remoteness of the work site, the simplest engineering and construction tasks are no longer routine.

Arctic winters can be brutal and prolonged. Summers are brief. Winter temperatures of -50°F are common, with wind chill factors down to -160°F. Access to and within the work site is limited much of the year. Because of the environment, construction productivity is low and wages are high. Not only is labor costly, but the remoteness of the sites dictates the provision of transportation, food, and lodging for workers, driving up project costs even more.

Fortunately, innovative methods have been developed that minimize the impact of the Arctic environment on projects. With very careful planning and a healthy respect for Mother Nature, projects can still be completed in a timely and cost-effective manner.

Large-scale Arctic projects in the United States are not uncommon, thanks to the development of the Alaskan oil fields beginning in the early 1970s. We will point out here what's unique to Arctic projects, and identify key areas the project manager must be aware of and control, such as:

General description of Arctic work	Procurement
Concept of modularization	Modular construction
Project controls	Arctic construction
Engineering	Logistics

GENERAL DESCRIPTION OF ARCTIC WORK

The effect of the cold environment cannot be overstated; it is the single most important item that makes Arctic work so unique from projects in more temperate areas. As one

---

Current affiliation: IT Corporation, Martinez, California

old timer so accurately noted, you still get the four seasons, but they are early winter, winter, late winter, and next year's winter!

Depending on exact location, winter and the first snows can set in by September and last until April or May. Extreme temperatures are prevalent from October through March, with February and March being the most severe. With temperatures hovering around -40°F to -50°F and howling winds, the weather's effect on man and machinery is devastating. Exposed flesh freezes rapidly, and special precautions are required for equipment to withstand the extreme cold. Darkness adds to the misery of winter, depending on how far north you are. In midwinter the sun doesn't rise above the horizon for several months.

During the hostile winter conditions, outside work is kept to a minimum, however, it is essential that all work requiring direct access to the tundra is accomplished during this period. This includes all pile support installations for pipelines together with total installation of cross-tundra electrical transmissions systems. Every effort is made to avoid outside work during the darkest winter period extending from mid-December to mid-February.

In the summer, the Arctic can enjoy almost 2-1/2 months of continual daylight, when the sun never sets. From mid-April to about mid-August, light is sufficient to carry on outside work 24 hours a day. In the summer, temperatures can occasionally top 70°F (Figures 1 and 2).

Site accessibility is also subject to the perversities of cold weather. True, freezing temperatures allow for ice roads and good road transportation, but many items are too big for truck or rail transport, and must be shipped by sea. Once again, depending on location, sea transportation may be severely limited by the ice pack surrounding the land. As the major oil companies developing the Prudhoe Bay oil field in Northern Alaska have learned, the ice pack recedes for only 5-6 weeks each year. When the ice does move offshore, barge convoys bringing bulk supplies and production equipment must unload their cargo quickly and leave before the ice returns. Failure to depart prior to the return of the ice pack can impose a serious burden on the module movement program for the following year, including the expense of replacing barges crushed by the encroaching ice pack (Figures 3 and 4).

Certain innovations in engineering and construction have been developed to cope with the Arctic environment and its impact on equipment, people, and project costs/schedules. "Modularization," "low temp materials," "sealift," "L-48 (lower 48 states) construction" suddenly become buzzwords with new meaning. Upfront planning becomes much more critical; a schedule slippage of one month in the delivery of an item may result in a slippage of a year because of Arctic logistics.

Arctic project management is difficult and demanding, but also extremely satisfying if executed properly. Let's take a closer look.

CONCEPT OF MODULARIZATION

Modularization is a clustering of production facilities into compact, transportable units to allow assembly in a cost-effective environment for subsequent transportation to the remote final location for installation. A good analogy would be to envision the facilities as a big puzzle. The modules represent pieces of the puzzle, which are ultimately joined together as an operating facility.

All modules are common in the sense they have a floor, known as a "skid base." The skid base is usually 7-8 feet above grade, leaving enough room for the module movement equipment to maneuver underneath. The skid base is not only required for transportation purposes, it also acts as the module foundation. Structural steel, equipment, and piping, are added to this foundation to complete the module. A completed module that is enclosed looks much like a giant house. Modules are enclosed to protect the components from the cold. Metal-insulated paneling is the enclosure material of choice. Only modules containing sensitive items are enclosed. If a module is made up

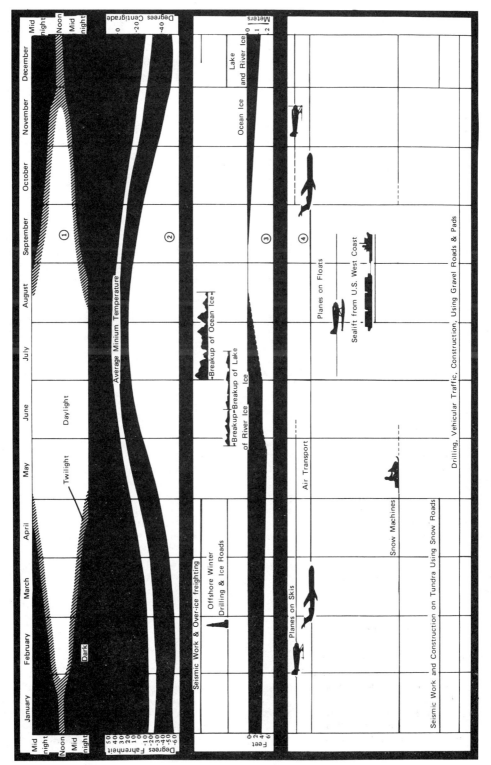

Figures 1-4 Time charts of Arctic weather conditions.

of piping components only, it need not be enclosed if sufficient piping insulation and heat tracing are provided.

Enclosed modules normally have their own heating, ventilating, and air-conditioning systems, as well as their own safety systems. Depending on their function, they may also have their own computer facilities and working/living quarters.

Cost is the overriding factor that drives modularization. Because Arctic construction is so expensive, modularization allows the great majority of the assembly work to be performed in an area of acceptable productivity and wage rates. Only a relatively small portion of the facility work must then be performed in the Arctic region, with its correspondingly higher costs.

Modules are typically "sealifted" via large barges from their assembly sites. The actual logistics considerations, movement equipment, and timing will be discussed later. At this point, let us say that the sealift involves the detailed planning and execution of very complex and large equipment moves.

Module Characteristics

Module design weight has historically been limited to 90% of the maximum capacity of the crawlers—normally used in tandem—utilized for carrying the modules. Past experience has shown that module weight tends to grow as the design progresses. A 900-ton module might grow to 1000 tons, and would require two 500-ton crawlers for module transport. Modules weighing 2600 tons have been successfully deployed, but only with special overload waivers from the crawler manufacturer. However, module movement technology is constantly improving, and in the mid-1980s is approaching the point of moving modules in the 4500-plus ton range. Maximum module size is typically 70 feet wide × 135 feet long × 100 feet high. Barge size is normally the limiting factor. Depending on barge size and vertical clearance on the route, some of these dimensions may be changed.

The minimum module width is a function of the clearance required between the trestles, the structure temporarily supporting the module prior to placement on the piles, and the transportation equipment. A typical minimal width of roughly 40 feet is based on the assumption that a crawler is used to transport the module. Also, a 1- to 6-foot eccentricity of the center of gravity is assumed. The module can be narrower than 40 feet if there is no offset of module weight or the module is light enough (200 tons or less) to be picked up by crane and transported by a single steer trailer/lowboy unit or dollies which do not have the same width requirements as the crawlers.

Although there are no overriding structural limitations, the module should not be too long to accommodate the turn radius of roads and structural rigidity. Due to deflection limitations, heavy girders are required for spanning the distance between crawlers.

Module height tends to be below 75 feet because of stability requirements during transportation. Elevations of bridges, high-voltage power lines crossing gravel roads at the jobsite, and other considerations may also limit module height.

PROJECT CONTROLS

Barge access to the Arctic is impossible during most of the year due to the ice pack. The ice recedes from the coast for only an average of 5-6 weeks during August and early September. Heavy modules and equipment and materials must be moved and landed during this short period. This window sets the schedule for all of the construction projects. Missing the window could mean delays in completing work of a full year.

Thus, the critical factor in setting the project schedule is to determine the annual sealifts to be used for transporting the module shipments. Once the last module shipment has been set, the completion date can be determined by the additional time required after arrival to complete the installation.

Project estimates and cost control are handled much the same as conventional projects. The only differences that the project manager need recognize are the higher wage rates and lower productivity factors in the Arctic, and the extra expense associated with modular design/transportation.

Scheduling for Sealift

Detailed design engineering must start early enough to ensure a continuous flow of the required materials to the module assembly site to support the construction schedule. Early predesign, planning, and constructability reviews are an absolute necessity to ensure minimal schedule/cost impact during the construction phase. At the 20-25% detailed design completion stage, the design basis is normally "frozen" to minimize change impact. The required design lead time varies with the type of work to be performed. Sealifted modules need, on the average, about 28 months from start of design definition to sealift in order to avoid cost impact. Design for nonmodular revamp work done in the Arctic, on the other hand, can begin from 10 to 20 minths prior to installation, depending on the size and nature of the project. Front-end engineering tends toward simultaneous and parallel efforts since it is usually on the critical path. A typical scenario would appear as outlined by Figure 5.

During this early engineering period, numerous plans/strategies must be developed to ensure optimal project execution. Examples are:

Project master schedule with milestones
Module assembly schedules
Module assembly site requirements
Plant site construction requirements
Module assembly contracting plan
Long delivery items list

Once these are established, more detailed planning may take place to consider the following:

Sealift operations plan
Engineering, procurement, and construction schedules
Module assembly detailed construction schedules
Module assembly progress schedule

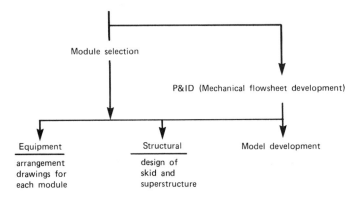

Figure 5 Front-end engineering.

Plant site installation schedule
Precommissioning schedules for systems
Other supporting controls and schedules

In setting the various strategies and schedules, it is important to consider the following items which are somewhat unique to Arctic modular work:

Given the extremely tight time frame that can be dictated by ice-free sea conditions, the critical path typically goes through front-end engineering, long-lead equipment supplies, skid fabrication/assembly, and through pipe spool isometric production/spool fabrication. This results in a need to stop feeding design changes to structural steel and spool fabricators. Subsequent design changes must be accommodated at the module assembly site.

Bid documents and procedures should be developed that permit taking bids on material and equipment for which design data is minimal but can progress sufficiently to be firm at time of award. Firm arrangement or outline drawings/loadings must be requested from bidders.

Any delay in the bidding, analysis, recommendation, and award periods for long lead equipment/subcontracts must be minimized. A commitment to this goal must be made at the start of the project.

The sealift weather window is not flexible and sealift will proceed regardless of the extent of module work that cannot be completed; the remaining work must be done in the Arctic at greatly increased costs. Barge shipments must usually depart the U.S. West Coast about the first to the second week in July in order to approach the Arctic during ice breakup. The barges make landfall about the second to third week in August.

In order to minimize work in the Arctic, design freeze dates must be identified early in the job and rigorously maintained. Design criteria changes must be avoided.

Module construction should not start until engineering is about 80 to 90% complete to minimize rework for reimbursable-type contracts. For lump-sum contracts, engineering should be between 90 and 95% complete prior to award.

If a marshalling yard at or near the module assembly site isn't available with the capacity to store equipment and materials whenever delivered, then supplies must be delivered in sequence with construction activities. This requires detailed construction planning. If equipment arrives late, storage space will already be occupied, thus causing delays.

Material control and tracking of bulk commodities should be performed per module. This facilitates expediting and simplifies identification and location of items that have become critical, but entails significant extra engineering effort.

Lead time based on past experience must be built into the pipe spool and critical equipment schedules.

Process modules containing long-lead equipment items such as separator vessels and compressors and drives are natural contenders for sealifting in the latter years of the project. It is also highly preferable that all possible work be completed on these more complex modules in the Lower 48.

It is highly preferable that service modules containing electrical generating and heating equipment are among the first to sealift. This allows temporary heating and lighting for construction completion activities, and equipment preservation.

Installation of pile supports and pile caps must be completed prior to the arrival of modules. Pile installation is normally accomplished during March when the tundra is frozen. Pile cap installation and necessary welding may be accomplished during the warmer period just prior to the arrival of modules on the summer sealift.

External pipe installation and testing operations are normally planned for the winter period unless permits for additional gravel roads, allowing year-round construction, have been applied for and received. Any necessary Arctic prefabrication work precedes this, under covered central fabrication facilities and in parallel with the pipe support installation activities.

It is preferable that certain strategic modules are in position to give continuity and focus to other outside Arctic construction works. Examples of this are pipeline systems where the presence of block valve houses, manifold buildings, and launcher/receiver buildings enable pipeline contractors to terminate their systems without having to remobilize operations at some later date.

Shop fabrication to support module yard assembly must follow a carefully prepared execution plan. Site and vendor selection must be done early and consideration given to who should buy the materials. The vendor's qualifications to meet the stringent Arctic specifications must also be evaluated. In addition:

Plan module assembly pipe spool and valve priorities exactly, and fabricate and deliver accordingly

Allow a minimum of 10 to 11 months after skid arrival for assembly of major modules (100,000+ craft hours)

Purchase a nominal surplus of ordinary bulk materials so that the assembly yards can sustain work without interruption

When consideration has been given to all of the above, the following represent "typical" schedules for a module project:

Figure 6—overall project schedule
Figure 7—typical process module schedule
Figure 8—module schedule-mobilization to loadout

Project Costs/Estimates

Arctic project costs/estimates are developed in essentially the same manner as for conventional projects, with adjustments made in those areas where costs are influenced by the uniqueness of the work. The most notable of these areas are summarized below:

Construction may be done at more than one location (e.g., module assembly yard and final site). This can lead to additional costs for materials handling and shipping plus multiple mobilization and demobilization. In addition, some owners elect to provide their own L-48 assembly sites with the associated cost. Regardless of who provides the assembly site, it needs to be recognized as a cost unique to modular work.

Fixed schedules due to sealift require cost premiums to meet material deliveries and module assembly deadlines. These premiums are often substantial, but must be paid in order to meet the fixed sealift date.

Exotic and costly construction materials are needed to combat the cold weather, and some fail rigid shop tests, necessitating refabrication and delays.

High transportation costs are not unusual for materials, particularly if sealifting or air freight is required. Sometimes large modules can be divided into smaller modules that can be shop fabricated and easily trucked to the Arctic rather than sealifted. Truckable modules reduce transportation costs, eliminate the large assembly yards, and remove the fixed schedules required by sealift.

Construction costs, due to Arctic weather and remote location, can be more than double the Gulf Coast norms. This is a result of reduced productivity and high wage rates. Labor productivity varies at the Arctic depending on whether the work is indoors or outdoors, and whether it is done during the summer or winter. Outdoor productivity in winter is about 1.3 times lower than summer

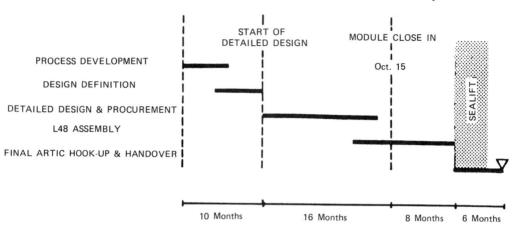

Figure 6 Overall project schedule.

productivity. Careful early planning is done to schedule the indoor work during the winter and the outdoor work during the summer to the maximum extent
possible.

If large module assembly is required, plans should include doing the maximum work
on the modules at the assembly yard, leaving little for Arctic completion. Most
precommissioning (e.g., loop testing and instrument calibration) can be done
before sealift if it is carefully documented. Hydrotesting and equipment cleaning also fall into this category. If items such as these are not completed in
the L-48, they can be transferred to the Arctic for execution at a cost of up to
four times as much when executed in the more hostile environment.

Specifications should be closely scrutinized to determine, on a case by case basis,
where low-temperature materials are really needed. Costly materials and shop
fabrication delays can also be avoided by an expanded shop inspection and
expediting program.

Cost data for Arctic projects can originate from multiple sources, in part because
more than one engineer and constructor are working on each project, and in
part because of the multiowner relationship caused by the extreme cost of development. A normal project has only one owner, one engineer, one constructor, and multiple materials' suppliers. Therefore, the task of cost-data coordination to produce consistent cost tracking and reporting is magnified.

Because of the remoteness of most Arctic locations, transportation and room/board
must be provided for all workers, a cost borne by the owner. Depending on
exact job location, duration, and size, this can amount to substantial sums.
Not only is there the fixed cost for the initial capital investment, there are
the high operating costs.

Because work is normally performed 6 to 7 days per week, overtime pay becomes
a major factor, not only for the craft but for the staff/supervisors who must
be compensated for their long hours as well.

The cost of sealift and loading/unloading operations can be staggering; one major
oil company spent roughly $50 million in one year's sealift involving 14 barges.
Sealift costs vary according to tonnage shipped, number of barges, and so on,
but will generally cost in excess of $1.5 million per barge and can go much
higher.

Because of the inordinate construction support required in the Arctic, indirect
construction costs can be extremely high; $30-40 per craft hour is the norm,
depending on the size of the allocation base.

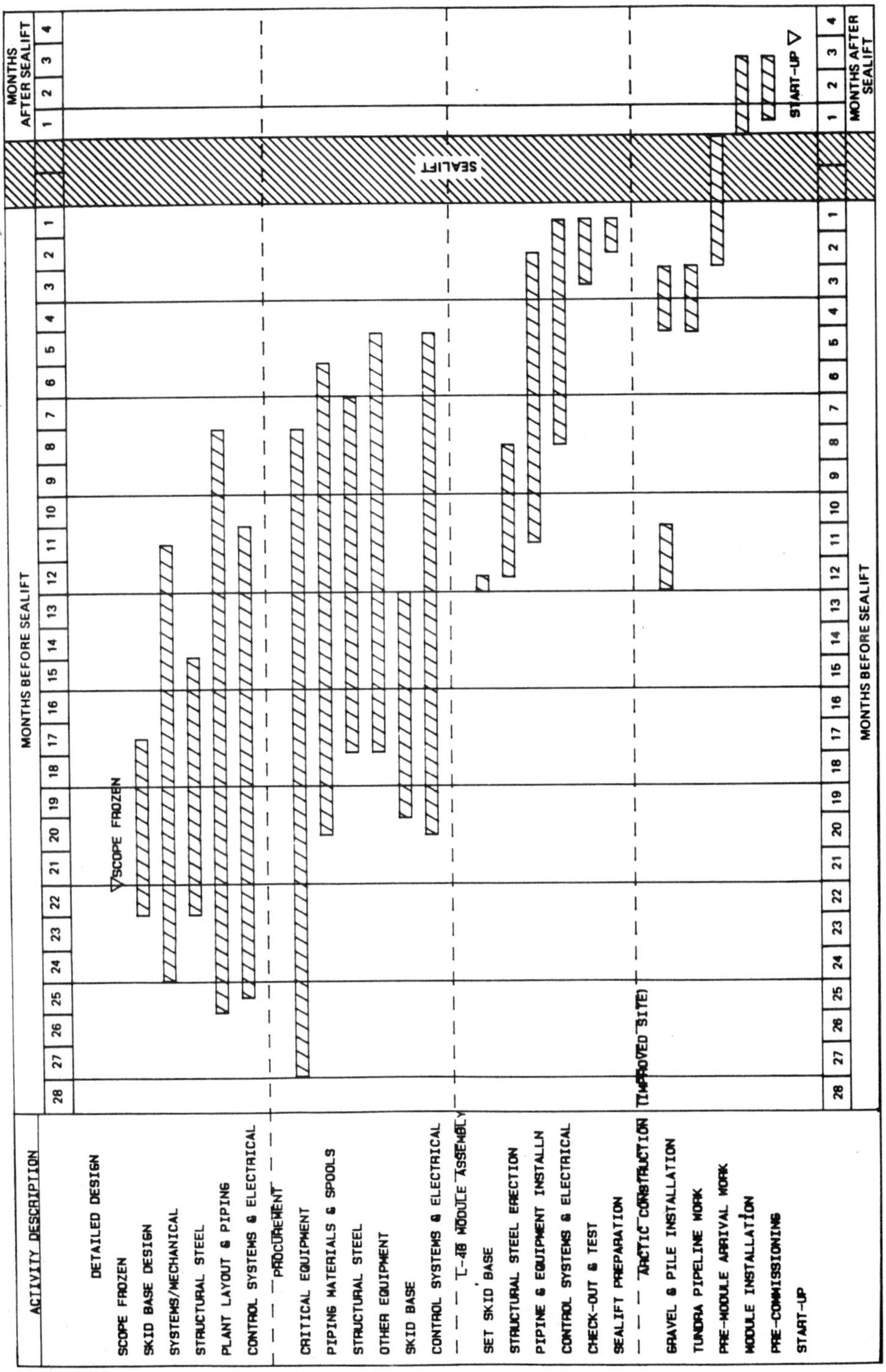

Figure 7 Typical process module schedule.

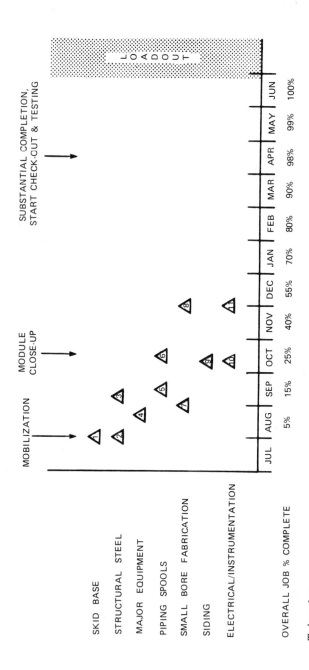

Figure 8 Module schedule—mobilization to loadout.

Triangles:

(1)   Skid base "walk away" date
(2)   All priority steel delivered (everything but miscellaneous steel, ladders, platforms, etc.)
(3)   Balance of structural steel
(4)   All major equipment
(5)   All priority spools (to be determined by construction, but generally all spools under 4")
(6)   Balance of spools

(7)   60% of pipe and fittings
(8)   Balance of small bore materials
(9)   All siding delivered
(10) All major electrical items; 60% of electrical/instrument bulks; 50% of instrumentation; all location drawings and conduit schedule
(11) Balance of electrical/instrument items; cable schedule, termination drawings

Tables 1 through 7 give some typical unit manhour rates for recent Arctic work. The following general notes apply to all of these tables.

1. Unless otherwise noted, all manhours given are for inside module work.
2. Unless otherwise noted, manhours do not include foremen or general foremen.
3. Foremen time runs 16.6% of journeymen time.
4. General foreman time runs 8.3% of journeyman time.
5. Hydrotest and air leak test runs 26% of total piping manhours.
6. Outside module tie-in and interconnecting piping work during the summer should be estimated at the same manhour units for inside work.
7. For outside winter work of unit manhours described in this chapter, the unit manhours should be increased 30%.
8. For inside winter module work (heated module), the unit manhours for handling should be increased 10%, and 6% for all other unit manhours.
9. Manhour units are for direct hours only. Support craft (laborers, teamsters, carpenters, and operators) run 25% to 35% of direct craft manhours. The 25% range should be used on large contracts (in excess of 40,000 manhours), and the 35% range should be used for all contracts being executed during the winter months (this period of time constitutes snow removal, etc.).
10. The direct craft normally includes pipefitters, electricians, ironworkers, painters, and insulators.
11. Direct and support craft mobilization and demobilization is eight (8) manhours per man total (4 manhours each way). Labor rates applied to these hours are straight time plus PT&I (no premium pay).
12. Direct and support craft pad travel manhours are calculated by dividing the total craft manhours by ten (10) and multiplying the result by the percent found on the schedule of normal average travel.
13. Off-slope travel time should be calculated at one round trip every nine weeks for craft labor. As a general rule, use $500/trip in 1983 dollars for budget estimates

ENGINEERING

Harsh Arctic weather conditions require unique engineering solutions, special metallurgies, and a healthy respect for Mother Nature. Permafrost, ice lenses, freeze/thaw cycles, and other soil conditions also affect the facility design. Even in remote Arctic locations, the impact of the facilities on the environment must be minimized by centralizing the facilities.

In certain Arctic regions, most of the ground surface is composed of tundra. This material is normally frozen from early November until late May. During the summer months, the tundra thaws to a depth of several feet, and forms a marshy and environmentally delicate surface. Little activity is permitted on the tundra at this time. Facilities requiring year-round access must be constructed on gravel pads interconnected by a gravel road system.

With modular design, facilities are configured around the method of transportation and installation of the modules. The design must inherently consider the method of transportation (barge, truck, rail, or various combinations), the method of L-48 loadout (crane, crawler, truck, rail, rubber-tire-vehicle), and the method of final placement (typically crane lift or crawler jacking). Often, the method of transportation restricts the locations of the L-48 assembly site and the timing of construction (i.e., sealift departure date).

Module designs also must address how the module is prepared for shipment to minimize field manhours and time. This includes such items as removal of exterior appurtenances, platforms, lights, ventilation hoods, and so on, sealing of openings to ensure

Table 1 Unit Manhours for Carbon Steel Butt Welds for Pipe

Size (inches)	STD pipe to 3/8" wall	XS pipe to 1/2" wall	Schedule no.					
			20	30	40	80	100	XXS & 160
1/2-1	1.58	1.80	—	—	1.58	1.80		2.25
1-1/4	1.80	1.80	—	—	1.80	1.80		2.48
1-1/2	1.80	2.02	—	—	1.80	2.02		2.93
2	2.25	2.25	—	—	2.25	2.25		3.60
2-1/2	2.70	2.93	—	—	2.70	3.93		4.05
3	3.15	3.15	—	—	2.93	3.15		4.73
4	3.38	4.05	—	—	3.38	3.38		6.75
6	4.50	5.63	—	—	4.50	5.63		11.03
8	5.85	7.43	5.85	5.85	5.85	7.43	12.0	18.95
10	6.98	9.00	6.98	6.98	6.98	11.48	18.2	29.48
12	8.10	10.58	8.10	8.10	9.23	14.83	24.5	40.28
14	9.68	12.83	9.68	9.68	11.25	21.60	33.9	51.08
16	11.25	14.85	11.25	11.25	14.85	25.20	40.6	62.33
18	13.28	17.33	13.28	15.30	19.35	29.70	47.7	75.83
20	14.18	18.90	14.18	18.90	21.15	37.58	59.1	91.80
24	15.53	22.73	15.53	—	29.93	46.80	81.1	33.43
30	17.40	—	—	—	—	—	—	—
36	19.49	—	—	—	—	—	—	—
42	22.50	—	—	—	—	—	—	—

Notes:
1. Above unit manhours include fit-up, tack weld, and all position welding.
2. For miter welds add 50% to butt weld labor unit.
3. Use 35% of labor unit for cutting and beveling of pipe or 20% for cutting/20% for beveling.
4. For slip on flanges add 25% to the labor rate for the schedule of pipe being used.
5. See applicable specification on 3/4" or greater wall thickness for stress relievings requirements.
6. Use 50% of labor rate for field shop welding.
7. For stainless steel pipe and fittings add the following to the above labor units for butt welds only: stick welding = 50%; heliarc welding = 100%.

Table 2 Unit Manhours for Flanged Bolt-ups (Raised Face and/or Flat Face)

Size (inches)	150#	300#	600#	900#	1500#	2500#
1/2-1	.98	1.10	1.22	—	1.58	2.07
1-1/4	1.10	1.22	1.34	—	1.80	2.19
1-1/2	1.10	1.22	1.34	—	1.80	2.19
2	1.50	1.58	1.70	—	1.94	2.43
2-1/2	1.70	1.80	1.94	2.03	2.07	2.66
3	1.83	1.94	2.07	2.19	2.43	2.80
4	2.43	2.80	3.30	3.53	3.78	4.26
6	3.04	3.77	4.50	4.62	4.86	5.72
8	3.90	4.37	5.35	5.47	6.08	7.29
10	4.86	5.35	6.32	6.93	7.90	9.36
12	5.71	6.56	8.02	8.40	9.72	10.94
14	6.56	7.53	10.08	10.58	10.94	—
16	7.29	8.40	12.15	13.14	14.22	—
18	8.75	10.21	14.58	15.66	—	—
20	9.10	10.94	15.75	—	—	—
24	10.94	12.15	18.27	—	—	—
30	14.21	15.80	—	—	—	—
36	18.48	20.54	—	—	—	—
42	24.03	26.70	—	—	—	—

Notes:
1. Unit manhours include all handling and bolt-up in place with gasket for one set of flanges.
2. Use 40% of above for unbolting of existing items.
3. For torque requirements add 50% to above manhours.
4. Orifice bolt-ups include two (2) bolt-ups and one (1) unbolt.

Table 3 Unit Manhours for Pneumatic Tubing at Instruments

Description	MHR/LF
1/4" Copper PVC-coated including fittings	.24
1/4" Stainless steel including fittings	.32
3/8" Copper PVC-coated including fittings	.36
3/8" Stainless steel including fittings	.40
1/2" Stainless steel including fittings	.50
3/4" Stainless steel including fittings	.96

Table 4 Unit Manhours for Rigid Galvanized Conduit

Conduit size (in)	"Conduit only"	MH/LF if GUA fittings are used
1/2	.125	.275
3/4	.150	.329
1	.174	.384
1-1/4	.200	.440
1-1/2	.224	.493
2	.250	.549
2-2-1/2	.374	.824
3	.449	.987
3-3-1/2	.549	1.207
4	.674	1.482
5	.872	1.918
6	1.120	2.464

Fittings and supports must be added to the above "conduit only" unit manhours per the following schedule; above unit manhours are 10 conduit clamps, the fittings and supports in Class I or Class II areas will be 85% of the total labor. In unclassified areas the fittings and supports will be 65% of the total labor. If type "GUA" fittings are specified fittings and supports will be 120% of the total labor.

Table 5 Unit Manhours for Terminations

Description	MHR/LF
Terminate single conductor @ T. B. tag and terminate	
Coax	.16
Shield	.10
#12 and smaller	.16
#8-#10	.24
#2-#6	.32
#1/0-#1	.40
#2/0 and larger	.60
Terminate type Mc cable outer jacket	
3/C #2 and smaller	.20
3/C #2/0-3/C #1	.32
3/C #500-3/C #3/0	.56
3/C #14	.40
50/C #18	.32

Table 6 Unit Manhours for Cable Trays

	MHR/LF			MHR/LF	
Width (inches)	Above grade	In[a] utiliway	Width (inches)	Above grade	In[a] utiliway
	Cable tray galvanized			Cable tray aluminum	
6	.31	.16	6	.25	.13
9	.34	.17	9	.28	.14
12	.38	.19	12	.31	.16
18	.45	.23	18	.39	.20
24	.50	.25	24	.44	.22
30	.60	.30	30	.50	.25
36	.75	.38	36	.62	.31
	Tray covers galvanized			Tray covers aluminum	
6	.06	.030	6	.05	.03
9	.07	.035	9	.06	.03
12	.09	.045	12	.07	.035
18	.10	.050	18	.09	.04
24	.13	.070	24	.10	.05
30	.14	.070	30	.13	.07
36	.15	.080	36	.15	.08
	During winter[b]				
To open utiliway	0.1/LF	0.3/LF			
To close utiliway	0.1/LF	0.15/LF			
Construct utiliway[c]	0.58/LF				

[a]Utiliway; timber duct for tray and cable, top of duct at grade.
[b]Snow removal: extra support crafts
[c]Does not include excavation, backfill or covering.

Table 7 Unit Manhours for Structural

Description	Manhours[a]
Fab and erect steel members	.042/lb
Erect prefab steel members	.0225/lb
Install handrail and miscellaneous steel	.10/lf
Install grating	.19/sf

[a]Above unit manhours include all handing, aligning, and to proper elevation.

dust and water tightness, addition of temporary supports and bracing, and removal of items sensitive to vibration during transportation, such as piping connected to rotating equipment, instruments, electronic devices and instrumentation.

The operating and maintenance (O&M) philosophy developed for each Arctic project has a significant bearing on the facility design. Decisions concerning unmanned versus manned, automatic versus manual, and local versus centralized control are required at the onset of any project. These decisions have a substantial influence on the project's design and configuration. For remote Arctic facilities, the high O&M costs must be included in any cost analysis to determine the optimum facility design. Even such items as operator shift rotation (i.e., operator continuity), emergency response times, and acceptable adverse weather conditions affect O&M costs and ultimately, the facility design.

A number of the technical problems that must be solved during engineering are not process-oriented, but construction-oriented. For this reason, sound construction planning is an essential element of facility design. Feedback from prior projects can simplify some aspects of the design and provide improved constructability. Some of the most simple design improvements yield tremendous cost savings for Arctic-installed projects.

Government permits and regulations affect even remotely situated Arctic projects. Environmental permits are required for excavation and placement of gravel, and hydrocarbon emissions. State and federal regulations govern spill containment, safety, fire protection methods, and fire-fighting equipment/access. Transportation of oversized and overweight loads requires specific logistics permits. During certain times of the year, movement over roads and tundra is severely restricted or virtually eliminated. All of the above permits and regulations have various degrees of impact on the project's design.

Conventional Versus Arctic Module Design

From an engineering standpoint, Arctic modular design differs from conventional plant design in the following areas:

The majority of the construction is usually performed at a non-Arctic location to minimize costs. Construction is completed at the final location. Engineering design and execution must recognize the distinction between non-Arctic work versus final installation work. Designs are required to enable the maximum quantity of materials to be installed in the warm weather construction sites and thus limit costly Arctic work.

Module transportation requires innovation and improvisation, until methods have become established and optimized.

Significant structural steel is needed for the module skid base and module framework to withstand the acceleration forces during transportation, particularly barge transportation. The steel framework is also required to support the insulated paneling which will enclose the module.

Temporary bracing or tie-down of equipment is required for transportation.

Arctic temperature storage and service conditions require appropriate material selection and operating procedures. Use of low-temperature materials for piping and steel, and heavy duty heating systems are significant cost elements.

Sealift puts a critical constraint on the construction schedule. It is a "drop dead" date. The barge must depart on a set date or risk not being able to deliver its cargo. Engineering progress must be achieved on schedule.

Heating and ventilating in enclosed modules require extensive use of space heaters and fan controls to maintain satisfactory temperatures.

Access to equipment for maintenance in enclosed modules is severely restricted, since space is minimized to keep costs low. Optimum layout planning is required.

Operating systems may be "split up" between modules, especially piping, electrical, and control systems. This requires additional pipe fittings and junction/terminal boxes, and careful attention to interface points.

Concrete foundations are not used for modules: modules are elevated above ground and process/equipment loadings are transferred into pipe piles.

Movement of crawlers and rubber-tired vehicles carrying modules has to be allowed for in plot plan layout and in establishing module dimensions.

Extensive loss prevention designs in the form of gas/fire detection/prevention equipment are required.

Higher home office engineering costs exist, particularly in structural design. Module dimensions, once established, cannot easily be changed.

A higher completion percentage in engineering is required before module assembly can begin because of the interaction of all the module components/systems.

Because module size is directly proportioned to module cost, module area is kept to a minimum. Modeling takes on an important role in ensuring that the optimum layout/design is selected. It also provides an excellent means to assure satisfactory detailed design from a dimensional and interference standpoint, because modules are inherently congested. Finally, models provide the operating, maintenance, and construction groups an opportunity to view the design and make appropriate changes. Models can also be used to simulate module placement.

Module Transportation Design

Module weight and size limitations must be established before engineering starts, to ensure that transportation from the module assembly site to the plant site is practical and economical. A rigorous weight control program is essential for design checking and transport requirements to ensure that maximum allowable weights are not exceeded.

The design must also account for the fact that modules must be transported in such a manner that asymmetrical loading on the module and on the transporter is minimized. Variables that occur during transportation are acceleration and deceleration caused by sea action, tilting due to road grade and camber, and windforce. The effect of these variables on the module must be recognized and addressed during module design.

A typical weight analysis for a module expressed in percentages is given below:

Skid base	20
Superstructure	30
Piping	15
Mechanical	30
Instruments/electrical	5
	100%

PROCUREMENT

Material and equipment procurement is yet another area within the project management realm that requires special attention and planning when dealing with Arctic projects. Material lead times are often lengthy because of two major factors:

1. Required delivery dates as a result of modularization and/or sealift constraints
2. Long lead times due to Arctic specifications

Consider the procurement requirements for a large compressor. On a conventional project, the compressor purchase order might be issued roughly 20 months before start-up. This would allow approximately a year for fabrication, and 8 months for installation. In the case of an Arctic modular project, the compressor would have to be ordered roughly 27 months before start-up because of the unique requirements for L-48 module assembly and sealift.

Consider the requirements for high-yield and/or low-temperature materials. These materials are required because of ambient temperature averaging 6°F with extremes to -85°F for outdoor service and also for indoor service because of process and design parameters which call for operation if module heat is lost. High pressure combined with the low-temperature conditions dictate API 5LX type pipe. Strictly low-pressure, low-temperature service dictates ASTM A333 piping materials and associated fittings.

Charpy tests are another material specification area affected by the uniqueness of Arctic work. The Charpy impact test is one method for determining material suitability to a specified cold temperature.

Charpy impact requirements determine the ability of the material to withstand fracture under certain conditions. As the temperature decreases, a material generally becomes more brittle and breaks easier. Charpy tests performed at specified design temperatures (i.e., -50°F) are an indication of material brittleness. Design standards have been developed to address the extremely low temperatures. Consequently, materials with properties to meet these standards have been developed, and therefore, the "somewhat specialty" nature of these low temperature materials adds to the leadtime.

Material Shipping Considerations

Because of remoteness and accessibility restraints associated with most Arctic sites, the project manager needs to be aware of the following:

Direct shipment to the Arctic site adds 4-plus weeks to the normal L-48 delivery.
Transportation is expensive, and consolidation of shipments is necessary to achieve cost effectiveness.
Barge transportation to a nearby warm weather port is often used, with subsequent truck transport to the final destination. Some restrictions on barge availability/frequency to the warm weather port must be anticipated.
If truck transport is used, it is possible that the haul road will have reduced load allowances during the spring thaw period. Typically lasting 6-8 weeks, road-loading limits may be reduced by 50% during the thaw. Also, different portions of the road may be subject to different thaw periods.
Air freight may be the only means of shipping temperature or mechanically sensitive items. In the event that air freight is not possible, shipping schedules may have to be adjusted in order to ship during acceptable periods in the case of temperature-sensitive items. Mechanically sensitive items may require special shipping precautions (special shipping bearings, etc.). In extreme cases, the manufacturer may claim the warranty has been invalidated as a result of less than desirable shipping modes.

Critical Materials

Generally speaking, the following items qualify as long-lead delivery items on Arctic projects:

Large-bore low-temperature/high-yield pipe, fittings, and flanges
Low-temperature structural steel
Large rotating equipment or complex process equipment
Module skid bases
Large-diameter valves
High- and medium-voltage cables
Insulated metal panels for module enclosure

These considerations require not only careful delivery date scheduling, but they also require careful material take-off strategies to avoid shortages and unacceptable amounts of surplus at job conclusion.

Other items of note are:

1. Long-lead material requires additional BEC (bid, evaluate, commit) time because it traditionally takes longer to take off and source.
2. The specialized nature of materials limits suppliers. In some cases, only foreign suppliers are available. Not only does this lengthen the procurement cycle, it also complicates delivery logistics. Also, one needs to consider the implications of foreign currency fluctuations if dealing with costly, long-lead items.
3. Not only are suppliers limited, but acceptable suppliers may have limited production capabilities, serving to further lengthen lead times.
4. Because of the specific qualities required for Arctic equipment and materials, additional quality verification should be anticipated. In addition, aggressive field expediting must be provided because of the criticality of schedule maintenance involving modules to be sealifted.
5. Once again, the criticality of material delivery relating to sealifted modules necessitates extraordinary material tracking systems in the home office and field office.
6. Not all materials and equipment will be delivered to the L-48 module assembly site; some will go directly to the final location. This requires extra effort on behalf of the procurement function to ensure the vendor, transporter contractor, and construction contractor understand the plan and their respective responsibilities.

MODULAR CONSTRUCTION

Construction of modular oil field facilities in the Arctic is a multiphase process which begins with Lower-48 fabrication/assembly, and is followed by sealift transportation and final installation in the Arctic. The concept behind this unusual construction technique is to complete as much fabrication in the Lower-48 states as possible, thereby reaping the benefit of lower labor rates and more available labor supply.

Modular design/construction is quite unique. Not only is L-48 work somewhat "disjointed," but total project construction work must be further separated to distinguish the L-48 work from that to be performed in the Arctic. Because of the extremely high labor rates associated with Arctic work, it is usually a "given" that as much work as possible be done in the L-48. This construction objective will, or should, drive the engineering design and construction planning philosophies to ensure that this can happen. With a wage rate difference between the L-48 and Arctic of $30-60 per manhour, failure to embrace this concept can be quite costly. Experience has proved to be the best teacher on how to maximize L-48 construction. The major factors are a supportive engineering/procurement schedule, an engineering design that recognizes the benefits of minimizing the Arctic work, and good construction planning. As an example of the evolution of the concept, some major oil companies have reduced Arctic modular hook-up times from approximately 1 year to under 6 months through sensitivity to the above factors. The resultant cost savings and production benefits realized from earlier start-up have been impressive.

Lower-48 Assembly

Site Improvement and Contractor Selection

Lower-48 assembly first requires the selection of an assembly site with a port via which the completed modules may be barged. Once a site is located, improvements are often necessary. These may include additions of docks, channel dredging to accommodate draft of barges, foundation installation, utility installation, and site grading and paving.

Once a site is established and engineering appropriately complete for the desired contract type, a bid package is issued and a contractor chosen. The basis for evaluating and choosing a subcontractor for Lower-48 assembly work is much the same as that used on a conventional project. If engineering is substantially complete prior to bid package issuance and sufficient time is allowed for an orderly construction sequence, a lump-sum contract strategy may be used. If time constraints dictate that construction must start prior to a comfortable level of engineering completion or that the construction time frame is unduly short, a cost-reimbursable contract may be more appropriate. The latter allows the owner the control needed to assure substantial completion in the Lower-48.

L-48 and Arctic construction work are normally handled by separate contracts and/or contractors, although that is not always the case. From an owner's standpoint, it is best to at least award the contracts at different times. Often the "plum" of being awarded the Arctic work will cause the L-48 contractor to try and perform better than he otherwise might. From a resource/experience standpoint, it is often better to have separate L-48 and Arctic contractors because the financial, staffing, facility, and equipment requirements of the often overlapping efforts can tax the resources of even some of the largest contractors.

Module Assembly

The L-48 total craft manhours associated with a large module can go as high as 200,000 per module, although the norm is closer to 100,000. A typical assembly scenario is shown in Figure 8.

Modular assembly is characterized by very detailed construction planning. Because module components are closely spaced to reduce size/costs, congestion of construction workers and corresponding low productivity is a major factor. Thus, manpower loading/leveling takes on new importance. In addition, careful planning is required to ensure components are installed in the proper sequence, so that access for yet-to-be installed items is maintained.

Laydown areas around the modules is an important consideration in establishing the layout of the site, as is how the completed modules are to be moved. Even though the yet-to-be completed modules may not be moved for almost a year, a loading pattern must be addressed during site layout to ensure adequate room for maneuverability, etc. during loading operations. Often, the 7-8 foot clear space underneath the module skid base is used for storage or workshops if layout room is constrained.

Module construction is initiated with the delivery of the skid base (usually fabricated by a specializing vendor and weighing 200-500 tons), which must normally have at least a minimal concrete foundation to support the completed module weight. Once the base has been set and leveled, structural steel erection begins. Depending on design and material availability, piping and equipment installation follow. Work proceeds until all items, including electrical and instrument items, have been installed. A critical item during assembly is the installation of the metal insulated paneling for the module sides and roof. Since the majority of module work is performed in the winter in order to meet a summer sealift schedule, protecting the work from inclement weather as early as possible is a major consideration. However, enclosure must not occur so soon as to interfere with component placement inside the module. Also, temporary lighting and ventilation systems must be provided once the module is essentially enclosed.

Survey control is extremely important since the modules will ultimately be joined together. Piping interface connections between modules should be checked regularly to ensure major misfits do not occur once the modules are joined together in the Arctic. Failure to exercise proper survey control will potentially result in increased setting time at the final location, and may even result in hasty torch cutting of interference points (piping, steel) so as not to delay setting operations. One approach to the fit-up problem is to cluster-build the modules in the L-48 in the exact configuration they will ultimately be placed. To do this, a spacious assembly yard is required.

Inherent with module design and its distinct parcelling of facilities is the fact that operating systems (piping, control loops) are split up. A complete system may be spread over numerous modules. While this does not necessarily cause a problem with the physical installation of the work, it does present problems during testing and check out. For example, testing one piping system may now involve 10 different tests if the system is in 10 different modules! Since systems cover all disciplines, module quality control activities can be more time consuming than similar activities for conventional plant design.

Final Completion and Documentation

Try though they might, it is not unusual for a company to fail to totally complete the L-48 work, giving birth to the term "transfer work." Transfer work is typically that work which optimally could have been completed in the L-48, but because of extenuating circumstances, must now be completed in the Arctic. Identification and cataloging of transfer items is extremely important and time consuming. Since it is highly possible that the L-48 contractor will not be the same as the Arctic contractor, the transfer work listing will identify possible credits from the former, and a possible change order to the latter. Depending on job conditions, the transfer work manhours can represent a substantial amount of the Arctic work and thus should be minimized.

Not only is documentation of transfer work necessary, documentation of completed work takes on a greater importance than with conventional plant design. Since typically two construction groups, L-48 and Arctic, are involved, the completed work quality control documentation must now serve the added purpose of identifying what has been done, and thus acts as a check and balance system with the transfer work system. Because of the added importance of this documentation as a communication tool, careful thought must go into the preparation and use of forms and into the delineation of operating systems for check-out purposes.

Because the L-48 assembly site is by definition remote from the final operating site, an effort should be made to have operating and maintenance representation at the site, at least temporarily. Without this representation, active operating/maintenance participation will not occur until after the modules have arrived at the Arctic. Some changes will be identified at that point, but they will be roughly twice as costly as in the L-48. While the construction staff may disdain the idea, the project manager will save substantial sums by ensuring this happens. Optimum walk-through times are at approximately 60% construction complete, and again at 90% construction complete.

Sealift Preparation

Hopefully, at the end of the L-48 construction cycle, the staff and craftsmen still have a little pizazz, because once the facility is complete, it really isn't. We move to an activity appropriately named "sealift preparation." Sealift preparation is a labor-intensive, 4-6-week preparation of the modules for barge shipment. Barge shipment means acceleration and rolling forces, and possible moisture migration into the module. Piping must be secured or removed from the nozzles of critical rotating equipment, instruments must be wrapped, exterior stairs and platforms may have to be removed, and general cargo—"bits and pieces"—must be crated or containerized. When final delivery is made, the process will be reversed. The thoroughness required for this effort should not be underestimated. Most companies have detailed specifications for dealing with the unexpected during barge shipment. Although bottled soft drinks have reportedly made the voyage upright, there are more tales about the ferocity of the open sea which typically must be crossed.

ARCTIC CONSTRUCTION

Contractor Selection

Prior to the arrival of the facilities in the Arctic, a bid package is issued to allow selection of a contractor who will complete the module interconnections, final construction, and commissioning. Depending on the level of construction completion achieved in the L-48, and the completeness of engineering on the project, either a lump-sum or a cost-reimbursable-type contract may be appropriate. Also, consideration in determining the contract strategy should be given to the impact on construction from the operations group for the existing facilities. This impact is often uncontrollable and may surface during tie-in work, commissioning, or even routine construction in and around operating areas.

Selection of the proper contractor is always a difficult task. Although bid price is certainly a factor, an exceptionally high amount of consideration should be given to the contractor's previous Arctic experience and technical expertise. The selection of a low-bid contractor with no Arctic background will often prove more costly than having chosen an experienced one with a higher initial bid.

Modules and Production Sites

Once a contractor is selected, the barges have arrived, and the modules transported and set, final construction and commissioning begins. Prior to the arrival of sealift, construction has hopefully been completed on those activities which can be done prior to module availability. Key activities include placing module pilings and installing power cables and temporary underground utilities. Upon arrival of sealift, the first objective is to set the modules in their final location and connect power leads. This minimizes the need for temporary heating and lighting equipment. The appropriate safety systems are also placed into service at this time.

Arctic construction sites are generally characterized as improved when production and support facilities already exist, or remote when no facilities are available. For improved construction sites, work crews are transported to their assigned work sites from central lodging facilities. Project size and crew numbers dictate the size of the fleet required to transport personnel to the work sites. Allowances are made for personnel plus their complement of bulky Arctic clothing, emergency hardware and, in some instances, personal tools.

Transportation to remote work locations may be accomplished by air, sea, or land. In addition to transportation, warm-up and/or emergency survival shelters may be warranted. The transportation equipment itself may be the warm-up and emergency survival shelter. Personnel going to remote sites are furnished with appropriate survival gear before departure and radio equipped transportation remains with the work crews at all times.

Construction methods and applications for interior module completion work are not significantly different from the methods employed in more temperate climates. However, outside work such as gravel placement, pipeline work, and powerline construction requires consideration of several notable differences:

1. Allowances for severe cold temperatures
2. Allowances for prolonged periods of minimal light
3. Production improvement techniques developed for the Arctic

Arctic temperatures require that surveying instruments be winterized to assure reliability. Arctic-grade lubricants are used on moving parts and as a practice, level bubbles are inspected to ensure they have been filled with alcohol or ether/alcohol. Electronic distance measuring equipment requires high quality batteries fully charged when not in use as a prevention against condensation and resultant freezing of moving parts and eyepieces.

Surveying requires that crews be prepared to remove snow or that the crews are supported with snow removal equipment when establishing surveying points. Installing survey monuments in the active freeze/thaw layer requires measures that negate the effects of soil heaving and thawing on established monuments. Monument areas are checked regularly to ensure they have not been affected by soil thaw or heave.

In most cases, pipeline construction requires the installation and maintenance of a gravel pad, snow pad, or ice road for access to the work. Portable shelters that completely enclose the welding operation are used for personnel and joint protection during the welding operation.

During periods of severe cold, engine-driven welding and support equipment runs continuously or is moved indoors if the work location is adjacent to heated shops. Welding leads and remote control leads are furnished with Arctic-grade insulation to minimize insulation cracking. Welding hood lenses are susceptible to freezing when the operators' breath condenses on the lens, and heavy winter dress, including insulated welding gloves, affects operator agility, reducing efficiency.

Material failure and personnel exposure are the primary considerations when hydrotesting and pneumatic testing are performed. Pipe materials are specified for cold temperature service. High nickel (1%) welding electrodes are used along with mandatory year round preheat and interpass temperature control to prevent thermal and mechanical cracking at the weld joints. Pressure testing is normally performed at temperatures above -20°F and all materials exposed to the test pressure are evaluated to ensure the test can be performed safely. The specified hydrotesting test medium used year around is a solution of 60% glycol and 40% water. Hydrotesting performed at the L-48 fabrication site utilizes this same mixture to avoid the problem of frozen liquids in the event of poor line draining. Total water solutions can be used for hydrotesting under controlled conditions where piping configurations allow total drainage of the tested system.

Electrical materials can also be adversely affected when installed during extremely cold weather. Outdoor cable is normally installed during warm weather periods; however, when cold weather installations must be made, heated shelters are constructed to maintain heat in the cable pulling area. Insulation breakdown and ground faults have occurred when cable was pulled without proper warming.

Extremely cold conditions often result in ice deposits forming on the bare metal ends of stripped cable, increasing the probability of loose connections due to loss of dexterity and hand sensitivity. Rigid galvanized conduit becomes brittle in cold weather resulting in cracking and peeling of the galvanized coating during forming or bending. Prevention measures include bending conduit in a field shop. Even usual routine electrical construction activities such as conduit seal pouring and installing adhesive-coated insulation require a moderately warm environment.

Installation of concrete in the Arctic is accomplished by essentially the same practices as those used wherever concrete is poured and cured at temperatures below 40°F. Cold weather protective equipment is common and noticeably more elaborate because cold weather installations are the rule rather than the exception.

A few concrete construction practices used in the Arctic are the use of Type II cements (high, early strength) and admixtures for concrete poured in the tundra active layer. Non-cement slurries are used for the tundra freeze layer and foamed-in-place backfill (Poleset) for pole lines and pipe support pilings.

Underground utilities are installed in the gravel pads either by direct burial (usually temporary) or more often in utiliways. Utiliways are wood channels with removable covers, constructed in the gravel mat, flush with the ground surface. During summer thaw groundwater must be dealt with. Groundwater should be removed from utiliways before it freezes and complicates construction or maintenance.

Major Gravel Programs

Gravel excavation sites are normally controlled by state authorities. A permit application must be submitted accompanied by project plans and proposals. Gravel handling practices used in the Arctic do not differ greatly from most sites where frozen soils with high water content are handled. Gravel borrow pit operations include activities such as dewatering, ripping, and blasting. Overburden is stockpiled where it can be reused and excavation site slope maintenance is continuous during the summer when the surface layer thaws.

Major gravel programs are normally scheduled in late summer because that is the optimum time to thaw and drain the gravel. Where thawed and drained soil is not critical, gravel programs are carried on the year round.

Equipment

The selection and preparation of construction equipment for use in cold regions has always posed major challenges to construction. Preparation standards for use on commonly inventoried construction equipment vary from vendor to vendor, although some equipment manufacturers have limited Arctic equipment line packages available. As a result, companies operating in the Arctic are developing their own methods for adapting construction equipment to cold regions and the amount of experimentation is substantial. Most adaptation is being done by equipment operators and mechanics working together to solve cold weather-related operational and maintenance problems.

To prevent freeze-up, it is often necessary to operate stationary heavy equipment 24 hours a day. This results in high fuel and maintenance costs. Where maintenance functions must be performed outdoors, repairs take from two to three times longer than in-shop repairs. Additionally, when roads are gravel surfaced, a high rate of glass damage and tire wear can be expected.

Human Resources

Due to the nature of construction activity in the Arctic and the inherent cost of ongoing construction overhead, work is scheduled 365 days a year. Regular professional employees of the owner companies typically work a rotation schedule of relatively frequent cycles. Eighteen days on followed by 10 days of rest and relaxation is an example of one commonly used rotation. Others would include: 3 weeks on/2 weeks off, 1 week on/1 week off. Typically, clerical/secretarial staff work a shorter rotation, usually one week on/one week off. These schedules are recommended to allow the employee R&R while providing adequate job coverage and continuity.

Contractor personnel traditionally work longer variations of this schedule such as 4 weeks on followed by 2 weeks R&R or 4 weeks on followed by 1 week R&R. These schedules are more desirable because contracts are relatively short term, thus allowing contractor employees job continuity without the need for replacements.

Normally each position is performed by two people alternating work schedules regularly. To ensure continuity, a detailed handover accompanied by written notes is essential to avoid duplication and to not hamper previously initiated action.

In recognition of the demand placed on personnel assigned to the Arctic, a compensation package should be developed to offset the negative factors. For the professional staff, several increments are normally added to base salary to compensate for the unique financial factors associated with working in the Arctic and the separation from the family.

Living Conditions

Travel to the work site is normally provided at company expense for regular employees. In addition to commercial air service, one major oil company provides two round-trip flights per day via company-leased aircraft.

Some major oil companies provide room and board accommodations for staff and contractors in dormitory-type arrangements. To maintain morale, entertainment and recreational facilities are provided. Primary lodging facilities are normally equipped with exercise areas, game rooms, movie theaters, cable television, and radio stations. When possible, special entertainment programs and guest speakers are provided during the year. Newspapers are flown in daily. One major oil company has engaged a consulting firm to work with employees on personal and family-related problems and to provide counseling for work burnout and loss of interest. These tend to be a problem when craft employees are required to work for prolonged periods without breaks, and thus should be considered when establishing rotation schedules.

Safety

Significant resources are expended on safety programs. Company safety programs are estimated to cost 30% to 100% more than similar programs in the L-48. As with most safety programs, the emphasis is on prevention through training, audits of working conditions, safety meetings/classes, and safety devices. Medical clinics staffed with professional medical personnel are normally located in the vicinity of the construction sites. However, full life-support equipment is usually not available and medical evacuation provisions are a necessary back-up. Safety training sessions concentrate on the hazards one would normally expect on a site. Particular emphasis is given to the following high exposure areas:

- Falls resulting from 9 months of winter conditions. Falls have a direct relation to reduced mobility from wearing heavy winter clothing and reduced visibility due to weather protection confinement.
- Fire hazards and fire protection are of paramount importance. Many temporary construction facilities are heated by nonpermanent devices. A higher than normal concentration of combustibles exists in the form of clothing, insulation, and lumber used for temporary shelter.
- Frostbite and prolonged exposure to the cold. Instructions are given to newly hired personnel on appropriate Arctic dress. More intensive training is given to personnel traveling to remote sites where exposure to high winds, whiteouts, fog conditions, and equipment breakdown demands self-discipline and the recognition of potential danger.

Offshore and Remote Site

Arctic contractors and construction managers have experimented with various types of conveyances to move personnel and material to remote work sites. The predominant method for moving heavy or bulk materials is by wheeled or tracked vehicles over ice roads or over the natural tundra. Ice roads and ice platforms are constructed by spraying water on the tundra to protect it, or in the case of offshore work, on the natural ice to reinforce it. Helicopters and fixed wing aircraft are used primarily for transporting personnel. On occasion, Hovercrafts or water craft have been employed when the pack ice recedes.

Remote site temporary facilities require particular attention to safety and emergency evacuation planning. It is not uncommon to have costly equipment staged specifically for emergency situations. Remote site planning also calls for above-normal fire watch personnel, fire protection and detection resources, and backup communications equipment.

LOGISTICS

The schedules for design, procurement, and installation of Arctic projects are more sensitive than other projects due to sealift/transportation constraints. If large modules are required, they automatically have a fixed shipment date due to the necessity of barging them for Arctic arrival during the summer period. If this time frame is not met or the ice does not break up sufficiently to allow passage of the sealift barges, all facilities will be delayed by one year until the next breakup. Smaller materials can be trucked, but there are cost penalties if they are delayed. These cost penalties arise from the inability to quickly demobilize and/or mobilize in the event of material short-ages. The most significant penalties arise from the loss of production which could re-sult from a missed sealift or delayed materials.

For Alaska work, trucking can be entirely overland or, preferably, by barge to the lower Alaskan coast, rail to Fairbanks, and over the Alyeska haul road to a north-ern location. The schedule should allow 4-6 weeks for either case, but many shipments can be delivered in 3 weeks under good conditions. It should be noted that the haul road thaws in May and early June, at which time permissible truck loading is reduced by half, and the road can be impassable for days. Logistics planning involving large modules which must be sealifted is the most complex and prevalent. If we consider northern Alaskan work, ice conditions in the Beaufort Sea create a "weather window" which determines when barges carrying modules and other major equipment can reach land, unload their cargo and depart for the L-48 in time to avoid the return of the ice pack.

Module movement logistics considerations are normally dictated by the following:

 - The Arctic ice pack across the northern coast of Alaska recedes from the coast for a mean of only 33 days each summer. This occurs during August and early September.
 - The nearly 4000 mile trip from the West Coast to Northern Alaska takes approxi-mately 5 to 6 weeks.
 - The loaded barges begin the trip in mid-June, pick up any additional cargo in the Seattle area, and depart from Puget Sound on or about July 15th. Gulf Coast location barges would leave in early May, and journey through the Panama Canal.
 - Arrival at the edge of the ice pack, near Wainwright, Alaska, occurs during the last week in July. Daily ice reconnaissance flights are used to determine when passage to the final destination is possible.
 - When the Arctic ice cap recedes, the barges are towed the remaining distance, normally a two-day trip, to unload.
 - The return of the barges is almost as crucial as the first leg of the journey. Barges which have not left by the time the ice cap returns will be unavailable for the following year's sealift. Moreover, barges trapped by the ice would be crushed during the winter months. Generally, these retrograde barges arrive on the West Coast the first week in October.

Description of Transport

Trucking

There are many different types of trucks to haul heavy equipment so each circumstance must be examined to determine the appropriate equipment.

Generally, moving large heavy loads overland is easier west of the Mississippi than east of the Mississippi. Careful engineering and logistics coordination is required for any load over 50,000 lbs. Typical limits for heavy haul overland west of the Mississippi are:

Dimensions: 14'H × 14'W × 60'L
Weight: 130,000 lbs (65 tons)

It should be noted that any move is constrained by the equipment available to move it and at this upper limit, only a few carriers can handle it. Typical limits for heavy haul overland moves east of the Mississippi are:

Dimensions: 14'H × 14'W × 60'L
Weight: Estimated 65,000-90,000 lbs.

All such moves are "permit moves," requiring specific state and local permits for travel over a specified route.

Barges

The standard barge used by many oil companies for sealift purposes measures 400 × 100 ft. The load limit for this size barge is 12,500 tons, which produces a draft of approximately 16 feet. For rough calculations, 100 tons equals 1 inch draft and 1000 tons equals 1 foot draft (starting with a 4-foot draft when empty). The water depth at some Northern Alaskan ports limits draft to 9 feet which allows about 5000 tons of cargo.

For barges having drafts exceeding the dockside water level, a portion of the cargo is transferred offshore to a separate barge. This cargo transfer can involve the transfer of general cargo only, or it may require the transfer of a module. Generally cargo lightering is done by cranes mounted on crane barges. Module lightering requires the ballasting of both the linehaul barge and lighter barge. The module transfer is done with crawlers.

Although barges 76 feet wide are also available, the 100 foot size is economically preferable because double the number of modules can be shipped. Also barge acceleration forces are less for the wider barge.

With respect to barge loading, the weight distribution of the modules must be such that the barge trim and list are satisfactory and that no undue stresses are imposed on the barge. In addition, the center of gravity, height, and windsail area of the modules must be within certain limits to ensure dynamic stability. Finally, the stow plans must conform to contingency criteria developed to prohibit certain critical modules and equipment from being stowed on the same barge to minimize production losses should a barge be delayed.

Universal Trestles

Trestles are needed to temporarily support modules during construction and transportation. They are also used to secure modules to the barge during sealift. They are composed of quadrapods and spreader beams, and are reusable for each year's sealift, after minor modifications. The quadrapod is a four-leg, self-standing unit which can be bolted onto the top of the spreader beams. A spreader beam is a plain frame built with two longitudinal, wide flange beams tied together with transverse beams. By combining different length spreader beams, either by bolting or welding, the required length can be obtained for a particular module.

Transportation Girders

For small modules and skids, generally weighing 200 tons or less, a transportation girder system has been developed to support these modules similar to the universal trestle system, except at only 54 inches off the ground. This allows these modules to be loaded, offloaded, and transported using platform (rubber-tired vehicles) trailers in lieu of expensive and logistically difficult crane lifting.

Crawlers and Rubber-Tired Vehicles (RTVs)

Crawlers are the major transportation equipment for loading and setting modules. Their relatively slow rate of travel (.35 MPH average) makes these vehicles ill suited for long distance module transport. RTVs are more attractive for longer distances, with a rate of travel of up to 5 mph. RTV capacity is limited to approximately 1400 tons. RTVs are usually not self-propelled, so normally a prime mover, the equivalent of a large truck with a towing/pushing mechanism, is used.

The widths of the transportation roads limit the width of the RTV system. Thus, although RTV systems would seem to have unlimited capacity by simply adding more tires and axles, the weights and dimensional constraints described above limit the capacity. Additionally, since the RTVs are limited in width, the transverse stability of the modules when on RTVs can become questionable. This is especially true for heavy, high center of gravity modules. Transverse stability is not as much of a problem when using crawlers.

There are three reasons that crawlers are not as susceptible to instability while transporting heavy, high center of gravity modules. First, the crawlers weigh more than similar capacity RTV systems, thus lowering the combined crawler and module center of gravity height and achieving a more stable condition. Second, the distance from the center of the load to the effective center of overturning resistance is greater for a crawler than for a similar capacity RTV system. Third, tire failure on the RTVs, no matter the cause, is dangerous due to the domino effect it has on the remaining tires.

Handling General Cargo

Certain preplanned standards are set for the handling of general cargo. Minimum uniform standards of export packing are required to alleviate handling problems of the cargo during offload. A uniform interproject general cargo identification system is recommended to ensure individual cargo traceability. Where possible, general cargo with the same designation facility is stowed on the same barge.

General cargo is stowed on the barges in a manner that minimizes barge deck space utilization. Stow optimizaiton requires the general cargo to be stowed around and under the modules on the barge deck. Consequently, the general cargo stowed under the aft of the modules is removed prior to module offloading. This is done at dockside if the barge is light enough to approach the dock directly. However, if the deadweight of the cargo causes a barge to draw more water than the depth of the dock approach allows, some of the cargo is transferred to lightering barges and brought to the dock by way of shallow draft barges. When only a portion of general cargo requires transfer to lighter barges, the cargo is transferred with both the barge and lightering barge in a "live" or floating condition.

General cargo is offloaded using a combination of cranes and forklifts. The cargo is stacked in rows and the description and staging location are recorded. The rows are arranged so that proper access is available for later retrieval of the cargo.

Records indicate that truck loads of general cargo have averaged 15 tons per truck. To maintain a scheduled offload rate of 150 tons per hour, approximately 10 trucks per hour should depart the docks on a regular schedule. The roundtrip is dependent upon the distance to the inland staging sites from the docks and the truck offloading equipment available at those sites.

Module Unloading

On arrival, the barges are secured in docks in a preplanned sequence, ballasted to the bottom of the bay, and offloaded. Modules are normally moved to a staging area by crawlers. The RTVs, module weight permitting, are used to move the modules to their ultimate locations. If possible, RTVs are not used to load or offload modules because the congestion of cargo on the barges does not allow room for prime movers and RTVs can overload the barge deck plate because of their concentrated loading. The tracked crawler vehicles are not subject to this problem since they bridge two or three of the trusses under the deck at any given time. In addition to being a crucial factor with respect to barge deck loadings, the ground contact pressure of the loaded module movement vehicles is a design factor for gravel roads, especially where culverts are embedded under the roadway.

XIII
INTERNATIONAL
PROJECTS

UNIT OVERVIEW

The marketing and execution of projects on a worldwide basis requires, for the company and the individual, a pioneer spirit, the ability to perform under adverse conditions, with, as a potential reward, a euphoriant atmosphere upon completion seldom experienced on the sheltered domestic project, for international work isn't a job; it's total immersion for the individual, the family, the team.

This unit will discuss marketing strategies, project execution, formation and maintenance of the project team, and social and behavioral considerations for the individual and spouse in the host country.

MARKETING

An oft-stated truism is that potential profits are commensurate with the degree of risk and exposure: high risks, high potential profits; controlled risks, modest potential profits. The international marketplace is an excellent example of this principle, a high-risk, fiercely competitive arena: one that demands the best business people, strategists, diplomats, as well as engineers and builders.

The foundation for entry into the international market is an absolute corporate commitment; this is not an area for casual sorties. The acceptable levels of investment and risk should be established early in the game. Then a realistic entry plan compatible with the levels of investment and exposure must be developed. Several basic assessments must be made: the capabilities, strengths, and weaknesses of your company in an international setting; the geographic areas to be penetrated, the targeted position in selected markets, the types of projects, the likely competition; financial goals; the action plan—what, when, where.

At some point, as a result of one or more strategies, a potential project is identified. An evaluation has to be made: to bid or not to bid, that is indeed the question, and, for those firms that eventually succeed, the answer isn't found in ad hoc meetings or executive pronouncement. Rather, the decision follows a definitive selectivity analysis established as part of the action plan.

Let's say that the analysis of a specific inquiry results in a decision to bid. We strategize again; this time a multifaceted pursual strategy. We ask many questions of ourselves, organization, competition, financing, special problems, evaluation criteria, and the like; and prepare ourselves for the proposal effort, concurrently initiating a full-scale intelligence-gathering program.

There is only one purpose for the proposal: get the job. Everything in the proposal must be oriented toward this rather simple objective, yet the field is littered with the muddled proposals of losers. A superior proposal, a clear understanding of the client's wants, a unique facet, such as a preliminary design not requested—this is the stuff of winning proposals. The proposal should send a clear message—select us!

PROJECT EXECUTION

The project management function for the international project is analogous to the role on the domestic project: the goal—to build a quality plant, on time, within budget, to the client's satisfaction, achieved through the application of well-known management principles—plan, organize, direct, control.

The specific needs of the international project will dictate the plan; the initial plan, and a host of intermediate plans, all geared to adjust to the unexpected, but all tough enough to restrain excursions and keep the project on course. International projects have diverse and ever-changing personalities. It is the volatile personality of these projects that has intrigued and captivated the international project manager.

The varied elements comprising the international project are detailed in this unit, including such considerations as the degree of client sophistication, plant location, local laws and regulations, ethos and mores, logistics, climatic conditions, contractual obligations, communications, quality control, personnel, infrastructure, material supply, modularization and preassembly, site working conditions.

One or more of these elements will control the project for a brief or an extended period. The manager has to direct his full attention to resultant upsets to the master plan, but must maintain peripheral vision to keep a rein on the project, drawing all project activities within the corridor pointed directly at the project goal.

Complex project organizations, including joint venture project directorates and other multicompany arrangements, are common, particularly for projects in the developing nations. These organizations must deal with all of the elements discussed, and with themselves, with special attention to the social and business environment of the host country, the needs of an expatriate staff, and frequently an extensive labor pool provided by a third country.

Each element and each principle are interrelated; the summation yields the unique personality characteristic of the international project. The impact of the interrelationships must be identified, evaluated, and addressed continuously, forcing all excursions back into the project mainstream.

Thus, while we see a basic management analogy—domestic and international—we see an intensity of element activity and interaction, a dynamic role for each part of the basic project plan that differentiates the international project from the domestic project to such a degree that we must conclude the project management roles are uniquely different.

PROJECT STAFF

The intangible personality of the project is determined by the synergistic mix of tangible and intangible factors, none of which is more elusive than the quality and commitment of the staff, and one of which can alter the seemingly intractable personality more dramatically.

An experienced international project manager can review a project staff and predict, with a reasonable degree of certainty, the ultimate fate of the project. For each individual on the staff there is a delicate balance: the negatives—actual or imagined inconvenience; the positives—responsibility, travel, money. The seesaw can go either way; the leadership of the project manager can help qualified people adjust, and his experience and judgment will direct him to other solutions when required.

Good staffs don't just happen. Planning and hard work produce good staffs, and the effort is expended before the airline tickets are purchased. The final step before assignment of an individual to the staff is the mutual acceptance of the Employee Assignment Agreement, a contractual commitment of the employer and employee, covering all terms and conditions relative to the assignment.

The traits of the staff members should be well known to the project manager, either directly or by discussions with individuals known to the manager and the employee. The most important trait is the ability to work well with others. Turnover on international projects is caused more by poor interpersonal relationships than by deficiencies in technical skills. Character defects are serious in the close confines of an international assignment.

The pressures on the expatriate employee and family are great: work pressures, family pressures, cultural shock.

The good project manager should participate in staffing activities on any project, but involvement is mandatory on international projects.

SOCIAL ASPECTS

The project manager on the international project cannot be aloof, an island unto himself. Nor can his family. The staff requires social attention. As does the client. Clients in developing countries, and to a degree in industrialized nations, expect the project manager, and frequently his family, to participate in a variety of social activities. The spouse is an important member of the team.

A very normal mistake made by the novice internationalist from the West on a tour of duty in a Third World country is the belief that deep down all people are the same. This belief is totally without foundation; the differences are multiple and profound. It is better to accept the differences as real, treat them as real, than to attempt with good intentions to seek a common psyche where none exists.

To think that what works at home must work everywhere is a naive trap. To push the thought that one's own customs are better—and it has been done and will be done in the future—is a tragedy. Americans admire the practice of frank and open discussion; tell it like it is. A highly respected trait; reserve it for the domestic project.

Another concept is that nationalities are monolithic—Burmese are Burmese, and so forth. Shall we say Americans are Americans? If you believe this, you've forgotten the differences in the principal geographical sections of the United States, and the differences between the inner city and the provincial rural areas. Overseas the differences are magnified. Geographical neighbors are as different from each other as they are from foreigners. It is important to appreciate that the needs and desires of foreigners shouldn't be categorized, that an understanding of many aspects of another society will remain incomprehensible.

SOURCES OF BACKGROUND INFORMATION ON INTERNATIONAL PROJECTS

African Development Bank, Abidjan, Ivory Coast.
Area Handbooks. Foreign Affairs Studies Institute, American University, Washington, D.C.
Asian Development Bank, Manila, Philippines.
Chase Manhattan Bank, New York.
Citibank, New York.
Embassy Post Reports. U.S. Department of State, Washington, D.C.
Export-Import Bank of the United States, Washington, D.C.
Foreign Corrupt Practices Act. U.S. Department of Justice, Washington, D.C.

Inter-American Development Bank, Washington, D.C.

International Construction Week. New York: McGraw Hill.

Lucas, C. L. *International Construction Business Management.* New York: McGraw-Hill, 1986.

Overseas Business Reports. Superintendent of Documents, U.S. Government Printing Office, Washington, D.C.

United States Agency for International Development, U.S. Department of State, Washington, D.C.

United States Chamber of Commerce, International Division, Washington, D.C.

United States Department of Commerce, International Trade Administration, Washington, D.C.

United States Department of Commerce, Office of Major Projects, Washington, D.C.

United States Department of State, *Countering Terrorism*, Washington, D.C.

World Bank, Washington, D.C.

Worldwide Projects, Westport, CT: Intercontinental Publications.

1

International Marketing

WILLIAM L. KELLEY *Morrison-Knudsen International Company, Inc., San Francisco, California*

The international marketplace for engineering and construction services is a challenging, exciting, risky, and fiercely competitive arena. For those who successfully penetrate it there are prospects of substantial financial and professional rewards.

With this perspective in mind, let us further recognize that the international marketplace is constantly changing. In decades past, reasonable success could be achieved simply by preparing and submitting proposals or bids. This minimal approach can no longer ensure survival.

The 1980s will be remembered as a period in which we were faced with fewer opportunities, more intense competition, prospective clients who were more sophisticated and demanding, narrowing of the technological gap between industrialized and developing countries, and the export difficulties promulgated by a strong U.S. dollar to 1986.

It is no longer enough to be good engineers, builders, or developers. We have to be good business people, strategists, and diplomats as well. Penetrating and surviving in the international marketplace demands that we undertake the most innovative and aggressive marketing and business development programs that our time and budget constraints can support.

There is no attempt here to paint a picture of gloom. On the contrary, the potential rewards can be fully motivating. However, to reap rewards on more than a hit and miss basis we must recognize, accept, and successfully deal with some important considerations in the international marketplace.

THE DECISION AND PLAN

The process should begin with a firm corporate decision to pursue operations on an international scale. This commitment can be to enter the market, or to expand existing operations geographically or technically, as circumstances may permit or demand. In either case, considerable homework needs to be done before the first overseas airline tickets are purchased.

The heart and soul of the process is a realistic and strategic plan, to include as a minimum:

Internal assessment of capabilities, strengths, weaknesses
External assessment of market opportunities, countries, types of projects, potential competition
Objectives, i.e., organizational, operational, financial
Action plans for allocation of resources and for scheduling and budgeting them

All four aspects of the plan are critically important for success. They should be examined and updated on a continuous basis so that the plan is dynamic and realistic and does not become static or stagnant. Constant market research of published information is helpful in this regard.

Country assessment is particularly important. We need to analyze countries from the standpoints of political and economic stability, country development programs, restrictive legal and monetary regulations, and import/export activities with other countries. This kind of information is available from many published sources including those of our own Department of Commerce.*

Data should be synthesized and translated into composite country ratings ranging from high to low priority as potential marketplaces. Despite this selective procedure, one may not be immune from local government upheavals and revolutions, civil wars, country economic collapses, and periods of runaway inflation. This emphasizes the need for current information. Conditions in developing countries do change, and changes frequently occur so rapidly as to nullify benefits of judgment which once was sound.

Another important assessment relates to what we have to sell, or more specifically, how we perceive the marketing of our service will compete in the international marketplace. Realistic internal appraisals of project capability and external analyses of potential competition are absolute prerequisites.

Whether we are pursuing solely, or any combination of, engineering, procurement, construction, or construction management, most marketing strategies are common to all. The only real difference is in price-based competitive bidding in which the low bidder usually, but not always, gets the job.

LAYING THE GROUNDWORK

Given a marketing plan for which we have identified our strengths and weaknesses, examined the external environment, established objectives, and formulated action plans, let's move on to some of the important aspects of implementing the plan through development of new business.

Once we have objectively determined where we want to work and what work we want to do, the identification of projects follows logically. One of the most effective means of project identification is through local country presence personified by local representatives, principals of local firms, our embassy commercial attaches, our project managers, and our own visits from home offices.

The Office of Major Projects of the Department of Commerce furnishes an effective service with direct links to our country embassies, in identifying and tracking projects. Foreign country embassies and consulates in the United States may be sources of information as well. Also, there are many publications which contain announcements of new projects, including those of the *Commerce Business Daily*, international lending institutions such as World Bank, African Development Bank, Interamerican Development Bank, Asian Development Bank, and a variety of trade journals. But reliance solely on these sources will limit opportunity because of the time factor. Much earlier identification and tracking of projects is necessary to ensure a competitive position.

For major programs or projects, this early identification and tracking may take the form of developing and nurturing personal relationships with top officials of pro-

---

*
 An excellent source of country information is the series of AREA Handbooks prepared by Foreign Area Studies (FAS) of The American University, Washington, D.C. The Handbooks are designed to be useful to anyone who needs a convenient compilation of basic facts about social, economic, political, and military institutions and practices. Some 108 country volumes currently comprise the series.

spective clients years before projects transcend through the aspiration stage to become reality. This kind of dedication is part of the success story behind many mega-size projects in the past.

Back to local presence. Better stated, it is the quality of local presence that is important. This does not mean that one must incur the expense of opening and supporting a local business development office. But it does suggest the engagement of a local representative, and/or a local engineering firm as a potential partner. Local intelligence gathered by the representative or local firm concerning upcoming projects is indispensable. Early information obtained before general release enhances the ability to identify and select projects of interest.

The local representative may be an engineer, lawyer, businessman, or other professional. He must be competent, enthusiastic, possess local know-how, and be a known and respected member of the local community. He is called upon to make critical judgments which can materially affect success or failure.

The use of one or more local engineering or construction firms for marketing partnership efforts and to provide local know-how and support services is also of prime importance. Selection of one or more local partners is critical to gaining a reputation for success or being relegated to "also-ran" status internationally. The local partner should be financially and technically sound, and enjoy a good professional reputation in the market of mutual interest.

PROJECT SELECTION

The next logical step in the marketing process is project selection. Each project under consideration should pass a selectivity test. Is the project real or only an aspiration? Is it within our capability? Our capacity? Is the prospective client well established? Is the project soundly financed or, are we to arrange financing? Are there overriding legal or monetary regulations? How can we overcome them? Are there any other risks? Who are the competitors? These and other factors can be assessed on a numerical scale to assist decision making. For example, such a selectivity analysis might include the following considerations:

1. Potential profitability
2. Competition
3. Type of contract
4. Contract risks and liabilities
5. Country political/economic stability
6. Monetary regulations
7. Experience in similar projects
8. Experience with client
9. Experience in locale
10. Desire for more backlog in this specialty
11. Client contacts
12. Client's credit
13. Project staff availability
14. Staff support in locale (local partner)
15. Staff availability for personal follow-up
16. Staff availability for proposal
17. Potential for work continuity
18. Number and caliber of competitors
19. Competitor inside track (is project "wired?")
20. Other criteria

PROJECT PURSUAL

Once a project has passed the selectivity process—and the severity may vary according to level of willingness to take risk, or just sheer hunger for new work—the real "homework" begins.

There are three general approaches to seeking new business:

1. Solicited, competitive proposals, usually preceded by submittal of qualifications, shortlisting or making the bidders list, and followed by selection to propose or bid.
2. Unsolicited, sole source proposals in which we can, in effect, create market opportunities by perception of project needs and assisting to arrange project financing. The U.S. Trade Development Program (TDP) is an example of such financing source for lead-in studies.
3. Repeat business, that is, continuity from one phase of project development to the next, without competition. Of course, the key strategy leading to these opportunities is sound project performance.

All of these are important means of garnering new business. Let's assume we have an RFP (request for proposal) or a bona fide invitation to propose or bid on a project. A primary order of business should be to devise a multifaceted pursual strategy. Answering the following questions will help to accomplish this:

1. What are the key objectives of the project?
2. What is the client really looking for in the proposal?
3. What special problems are to be addressed?
4. What are the client's proposal evaluation criteria?
5. Who are the evaluators and what are their individual interests in the project?
6. Has contact been made with the client's principals at the highest level? With what result?
7. Has a local partner been lined up?
8. Shall we joint venture with another international firm?
9. Can we JV with a firm already prequalified to reduce competition?
10. Is the project financed?
11. If not, what financing sources should we consider?
12. Who are the competitors?
13. What do we perceive as their strengths? Their weaknesses?
14. How do our strengths and weaknesses compare to those of the competitors?
15. What unique features should be included in the proposal?
16. What are the objectives of a site inspection?
17. Shall we plan an oral presentation to the client?
18. Is the proposal to be priced?
19. If so, are prices to be presented "up front" or in a second envelope? Will price be the only selection criterion?
20. What type of contract is expected?
21. What are the local country tax requirements?
22. What other local monetary or legal regulations or restrictions?
23. Where is work to be performed (e.g., can design be done in the home office)?
24. Is technology transfer a key objective of the client?
25. What level of local personnel input to the project is expected?

INTELLIGENCE GATHERING

Usually, good answers to all of the foregoing questions are essential. The client's RFP or bidding documents will provide some, but not nearly enough, information. The rest has to come from digging deeper.

Most important is our perception of what the client really wants. Despite what we read in the RFP or bidding documents and what the prospective client told us, our proposal strategy must recognize what he is really looking for. What are his wants? Highest quality? Lowest price? Shortest time schedule? A state-of-the-art technical approach?

It is unlikely that we can offer him all of the above. But if we are unable to identify his real wants, then our homework has been inadequate and our proposal time and cost may well be wasted. Notice that we say "wants," not "needs." Telling a prospective client what we think he needs, if radically different from his terms of reference, is risky. It's better to give him an alternative proposal. Even this may be regarded as an offensive infringement on his pride of authorship of his RFP or bidding documents.

How do we determine the client's "real wants"? The client isn't just the name of an organization. It is people. Decision makers, each one having his own motivations. Be they board members or proposal evaluation committee members, our job isn't fully accomplished unless we reach each one, talk to them, and find out what it is that each one individually regards as important. We'll never read all this in the RFP or the bidding documents.

Of course, some of these assessments aren't all that easy. We have to deal with distortion of information as it flows from one person to another. Consider the potential problem of a communication between two people. Here are at least five different interpretations of the same information:

What he meant to say
What he thought he said
What he said
What you thought he said
What you said he said

Thorough and effective intelligence gathering, its interpretation, and its use to best advantage are crucial to success in the international marketplace. This is more difficult to accomplish overseas. Ambiguities in local laws, remote locations, language difficulties, and other uncertainties are some of the reasons.

THE PROPOSAL

Much can be said about organizing for and preparation of a winning proposal or bid. If we are in a competitive bid situation, usually only price, schedule, financial stability, quality of experience and resources, and financing offer (if any) are relevant.

However many contract awards are made on a negotiated basis. While success may depend on some or all of the above features, two others come into strategic play: (1) interpersonal relationships with people of the prospective client, and (2) the written word in the proposal. Conveying the real proposal message with effective writing is essential.

Below is a list of 7 key ingredients of a winning proposal.

1. Message. That we understand the project, the owner's "real wants," and are prepared to satisfy them with our resources and company commitment.
2. Response. Complete and direct response to the RFP or bidding documents. The client wrote them, or at least approved them, and expects to see them addressed in their entirety.
3. Disclosure. Comprehensive documentation of all relevant company experience. Careful attention to personnel resumes, rewriting them to emphasize pertinent experience.
4. Creativity. Something unique or innovative to set us apart from the competition.

5. Price. Usually but not always a significant factor in competitive proposals or bids.
6. Financing. More than ever, an important consideration—even a requirement. Bids are usually adjusted by financing terms offered, so the product of price and financing determines the "bottom line."
7. Style. Well composed, concisely written, logically organized, properly referenced, and attractively presented.

In preparing the proposal strategy, all of the homework already accomplished needs to be woven into the plan. Some RFPs (most for engineering work) include an evaluation system to award proposals a number of points in selected categories. Typical evaluation criteria may include a point distribution as shown below.

Qualifications of proposed personnel, particularly the project manager: up to 50%
Experience on similar projects: range of 25-35%
Proposed work plan and approach: range of 25-35%

Cost, or level of estimated effort in terms of manhours or manmonths may well be the deciding factor. If so, in times of a strong U.S. dollar it very definitely places a U.S. firm at a disadvantage overseas.

Obviously, if evaluation criteria are specified, every effort needs to be made to achieve the maximum possible score.

Various techniques are employed in proposal writing, i.e., getting the message across. Aside from proposal outlines, schedules and tables of contents, one technique which has come into wide use is called the "story board."

It employs modules organized for each strategic message intended for the proposal. Each module is composed of:

A topical sentence describing the module theme
A theme expressing the strategic message in, say 400-800 words
Graphics or art work to illustrate the theme

Modules from their earlier skeleton form and further developed during the proposal preparation process are posted on the wall of a control room. When finished they tell the complete story.

This technique permits early organization of the proposal contents, allows continuous management overview, directs the tone of the proposal toward its strategic objectives, clearly establishes writing assignments, and produces a balance of content.

A carefully conceived financing package is often a proposal requirement. This subject is covered in a separate chapter.

Formal oral presentations, in addition to written proposals, sometimes are important steps in the proposal process. However, overseas clients generally are less interested in receiving them than in the United States.

What about postproposal strategies? Continuous contact with the prospective client, in an effort to answer his questions and to further demonstrate our commitment to his project, can be well worthwhile. If our proposal was not selected, a postmortem will be of value to determine how we went wrong or how the competition outdid us.

CONTRACT NEGOTIATIONS OR "CLOSING THE DEAL"

The next marketing phase is the contract negotiation. That is, provided our proposal, "fully responding to the client's real wants," has been successful. Or unless the owner has solicited price-competitive bids as the sole criterion for contract award.

This is a particularly critical phase. The outcome directly affects project financial results, performance efficiency, liability exposure, and client relations.

Negotiating is a human relationship, a psychological confrontation which involves some conflicts of interest. It is an activity in which, if successful, most of the needs of two or more parties are satisfied. Both (or all) parties gain something in a successful negotiation. It is not a win-lose conflict, but an optimization of interests. It is a melding of these interests, some common and some opposing, through communication and resolution to reach a mutually acceptable agreement. It is a win-win situation.

Since the primary purpose of all negotiating is to resolve human conflicts of interest, strategies are employed by each party in negotiations.

Some negotiators employ a hardline strategy in which the goal is victory, the participants are adversaries, application of pressure is relentless, and efforts are focused on winning a contest of will. While this approach may yield agreement, it may cause a breakdown of negotiations. It likely will result in a strained client relationship with continuation of adversary attitudes.

By contrast, other negotiators employ a softline strategy in which the goal is agreement, the participants are friends, yielding to pressure is continuous, concessions are significant and efforts are focused on maintaining amicable relations while trying for a rapid conclusion of the negotiations. This approach will also yield agreement, but probably not a good one. It is often referred to as "giving away the store."

Still other negotiators employ a principled strategy in which the goal is a mutually acceptable agreement, the participants are problem solvers, application of pressure is tactical and discriminate, and efforts are focused on problems, interests, options, and criteria. This strategy, while it may embody judiciously selected elements of either the hardline or softline approach, has much greater potential for achieving a good agreement with which all parties are satisfied.

Employment of effective negotiating strategy requires several attributes of the negotiator:

1. Clear and comprehensive knowledge of the services being offered
2. Detailed knowledge of all elements of cost
3. Good business judgment
4. Recognition of the difference between cost and the value of the services to the client
5. Mental agility in the choice of tactics and options
6. Good facility in human relations
7. Good physical condition

PROJECT EXECUTION

What has the running of projects to do with marketing? A great deal. The success or failure of project execution is a prime influence on future success in the marketplace. A satisfied client is a significant asset. They communicate with each other. Referrals can have a powerful effect. What is better than the opportunity for repeat business with a satisfied client, with no competition?

No single factor for continued success is as important as the performance of people assigned to overseas projects.

In selecting and preparing personnel for overseas assignments, a delicate balance is required among the factors of professional capability, personal character traits, language proficiency, costs, and past and potential working relationships with clients. The scenario is radically different from domestic operations where client contacts are usually with the home office. Here, problems in performance can be solved by adjustments from the home office staff, and relocation and travel are relatively simple.

Adherence to a rigid criteria in selection and preparation of personnel is unrealistic. However, identification of the project manager is critical, since he will be the principal emissary with significant influence on success.

The ideal candidate for overseas manager is not only technically proficient, but is also an independent decision-maker. He acts as a company spokesman, marketing executive, and understands scope-budget-action plans. He is the company psychiatrist, father confessor, and arbitrator; yet he remains highly production oriented. He is fully understanding and sensitive. If possible he should be a prolific writer and multilingual. He must be an accomplished speaker, plus a diplomat, and much more.

The selection, preparation, and dispatch of employees to the overseas project—and the successful line-up of a local firm—are of course simply the opening maneuvers of a campaign that requires continued management attention. Since no overseas project can be considered an "island," the spatial abyss can be bridged in several ways. Executive management and engineering supervisory visits to the project offices and construction sites should be a matter of course for personal contact with clients. In addition, nontechnical support and humanistic logistics should be afforded to overseas project personnel, such as company publications and correspondence of general interest, telephone contact with families for personnel on single status assignments, and special home leave trips.

Personal messages on the telex should receive priority attention, as personal details are a key to morale for individuals and families away from their home base. In addition, such items as airline tickets, travel schedules, documentation, and medical exams are necessary for support.

With project execution accomplished, the basic marketing cycle for a single project is complete. Continued success demands that marketing be a continuing program and not just be only project-specific.

SOME AXIOMS

In our quest for new work, several other characteristics of the international marketplace should be recognized to assist in seleciton of opportunities and determination of business development strategies.

1. In less developed countries there is opportunity for us in programs requiring basic, grass-roots technology; however, in the intermediate developed countries, opportunities, other than in state-of-the-art technology, are diminishing. The point is not to go after projects that are really reserved for local firms. The representatives can help in this regard, as the prospective client may not necessarily be fully candid with us directly.
2. Whether we deserve it or not, Americans are regarded by our friends overseas as being myopic to local differences in culture and customs, and inept in the use of foreign languages. Certainly all of us are well advised to do our homework in these areas in advance. Our receptivity will be immeasurably improved, and so also will be our level of understanding.
3. There is an ever-increasing incidence of opportunities for U.S. firms to furnish only high-level review and supervision of projects (i.e., "rubber stamping"). Thus, without adequate opportunity to really control quality, budget, and schedule, if things go badly we are vulnerable to catching the discredit.
4. For large projects, international joint ventures are increasingly common. Clients may favor such ventures for the introduction of complementary technology, or for political reasons. We may favor joint ventures to reduce overall cost. Thus, it behooves us to become acquainted and maintain current communication lines with other firms of our choice in the industrialized world.
5. There is an ever-increasing tendency of overseas clients to require all or the majority of project work to be done in their own country—even in their own

offices. This places more burden on us to identify and relocate specialists. And, the cost of the project increases. An alternative is to secure client concurrence to placing some of his people in our home office.

6. With regard to proposals and competitive bidding, there are some differences in professional practices in Europe compared to those in the United States. If our competitors are European, their proposals for studies, preliminary designs, or bidding documents are likely to include less effort, lower cost, and shorter time schedules than those we normally would produce. Their philosophy is to defer some engineering to subsequent phases of the project, and their priced proposals for earlier phases appear more attractive to uninitiated clients. In our view, the showdown of this philosophy and the real cost resulting from it surface during construction. In this kind of competitive arena, we have either to adapt to the competition, or better, to convince our prospective clients that the most economical project is one which has thorough engineering up front.

Likewise competitive bidding philosophy of some of our foreign competitors differs from ours in the United States. We tend to figure costs and cover the unknowns with contingencies, whereas some competitors forego contingencies with the expectation for recovery in claims. Granted, this kind of arena offers tougher competition.

THE FUTURE

With the mid-to-late 1980s as a reference, and the aid of a trusty crystal ball, one can climb out on a limb and predict a short-term scenario, of 5 to 10 years, in the international marketplace:

1. In general, there is reason for optimism that things will improve. The basis for this expectation is that the economic stability of most of those countries which were healthier financially in the 1970s will recover.
2. Companies at the cutting edge of high technology will find increasing opportunity in developing countries.
3. More grass-roots-level opportunities will emerge in traditional market sectors of less developed countries.
4. We will experience continued heavy competition from the industrialized world, but with some relief as their currencies become stronger and the U.S. dollar yields some of its relative strength.
5. Arranged project financing will continue to be a key to success, but the disparity in financing terms offered will be mitigated by changes in relative strengths of currencies.
6. Mega-size project opportunities will emerge again, with improvement of financial stability in some countries. Types of projects will depend on recovery of slackened prices of minerals and coal, and on oil prices and their effect on world production.
7. Geographically, we may expect Asia to continue to be a center of opportunity. Latin America will gradually recover form its economic doldrums and offer increased opportunity. Action in the Near and Middle East will be dependent not only on oil prices and production but also political factors. In the longer term (perhaps mid-to-late 1990s), Africa should emerge with new development programs to the extent that it too can be an important focus for U.S. marketing.

SUMMARY

International marketing is an art. Success depends on effective application of various aspects of the art, as dealt with briefly in this chapter. And, we cannot rule out "dumb luck" as an occasional assist.

It would appear appropriate as a summary to state the following strategic considerations, each of which can play a key role in our quest for success.

1. Market planning. Develop and continually adapt it to changing conditions
2. New technology. Strive to stay at the forefront
3. Local country presence. Establish and maintain it
4. Selectivity. Practice it carefully with regard to countries, clients, projects, capability, and competition
5. Action planning. Be proactive rather than reactive
6. Pursual strategies. Be creative, aggressive, flexible, and tenacious
7. Homework. Know that winners do it best
8. Local cultures, customs, and languages. Understand and respect them
9. Competition. Know and respect it.
10. Joint ventures. Form them when circumstances dictate their desirability
11. Clients' real wants. Discern them and respond accordingly
12. Human factor. Recognize that we sell to people, not organizations
13. Contract negotiating. Hone skills and apply proven techniques
14. Project performance. Recognize that it is crucial to continuity of service and development of new business

Clearly, international marketing is more demanding and entails significantly greater risks than we experience on our home front. But the potential rewards are commensurate for those of us who successfully meet the challenge.

2

Operational Differences on International Projects

JOSEPH F. STOY*   *Petrochemical Industries Company K.S.C., Safat, Kuwait*

Foreign projects in the early 1980s accounted for one third of the combined workload of American contractors. The number of foreign projects is expected to continue to grow for many years at a rate faster than domestic projects. This is due to the sudden rise in wealth of certain nations and to the liberalization of financing for under-developed and developing nations. These nations have a large potential demand for products which they plan to exploit by constructing their own manufacturing facilities. Several nations have embarked on super projects, not only to supply their own demand, but to supply part of the world market. They view this as an economic necessity—the improvement in trade balance—or, simply as a good investment opportunity, since they have favorable positions in one or more economically advantageous areas—raw materials, financing, inexpensive and abundant labor, low-cost energy, geographic location, and so forth. Most of this expansion is for products that have matured in the developed nations.

Some developing countries with a feedstock position are starting a second wave of expansion: the processing of intermediate bulk chemicals and goods into finished products. They are investing in or acquiring downstream companies to gain experience and know-how, and to develop direct consumer feedback, which hopefully will lead to product improvement or new product lines, supported by captive research facilities. Their goal is to compete equally or advantageously with developed countries in the world market place.

All of this means a continued growth of foreign projects with the likelihood that today's young engineer will spend much of his career working overseas.

PROJECT CLASSIFICATION

Projects can be classified, from the viewpoint of the engineering contractor, as domestic, overseas, or foreign. A domestic project is one executed for a native concern in its native land. An overseas project is one executed for a native concern in a foreign land. A foreign project is one executed for a foreign concern in a foreign land.

Overseas projects were initially handled in much the same manner as domestic projects. The know-how, codes and specifications, engineering services, procurement

---

*Retired

services, construction management services, and materials were based on American standards and supply. All that was left was the translation of operating manuals and the text on drawings and specifications, usually handled by the client. The majority of the foreign projects, certainly well into the 1960s, were handled in the same manner as the overseas projects.

Projects in the developing countries today are in transition; some clients have reached a high level of sophistication, others haven't. Severely fragmented plans of execution are common. A typical scenario is a host of separate contracts, know-how, basic engineering, detailed engineering, procurement services, construction subcontracts, normally with a project management contractor who may or may not have construction management responsibility.

OWNER CLASSIFICATION

The owner of the facility may be a novice, or an astute leader of the industry. A classification of owners might be as follows:

American-based multinational
Foreign-based multinational
Private organization
Government organization
Joint venture

The types of firms involved in the project will affect the amount of coordination required, how firms interface, how rapidly decisions are made, the number of alternatives to be studied, the amount of assistance required in start-up and plant operation. Experienced clients evaluate options prior to contract award, whereas novice organizations generally do not. Even the simplest project requires limited cost/benefit analyses. The evaluation of alternatives during the course of a project will detract significantly from the efficient execution of the work, leading to schedule delays and budget overruns—a common occurrence in Third World programs.

ENGINEERING CONSIDERATIONS

The degree of engineering completeness for overseas and foreign projects must be a magnitude greater than for comparable domestic projects. All systems should be dimensioned and provided with extensive and accurate bills of material to permit maximum shop fabrication and minimize material shortages or surpluses.

Foreign pipe fabrication shops tend to have smaller capacities than U.S. shops. The result is the use of several shops for a major international project. Managing contractors are often required to supply all of the materials to the shop and the field. The piping materials program should be sufficiently flexible to divide materials between the various fabricators and subcontractors. A recent major European project involved 13 pipe fabricating shops and 4 piping erection contractors. The division of materials was crucial: a surplus of material to one shop or subcontractor meant a shortage to another.

Most overseas engineering offices are not geared to handle super projects. If the work is to be done overseas, several offices will be required to support a large project to prevent an unacceptable stretchout. Some multinational firms have offices in three or four European countries and routinely program large projects into several offices. The work is normally divided by process units or principal process elements, or split up to suit individual office capabilities.

PROCUREMENT CONSIDERATIONS

Equipment and bulk materials for overseas work are generally purchased on a world-wide basis. The procurement organization has to have worldwide capabilities including the ability to survey and evaluate all phases of source support.

Codes, laws, nationalistic attitudes, political restraints on source, cumbersome customs procedures, and a myriad of other inconveniences will try the patience of the most experienced international buyer. Quotations will cover a wide range of pricing, exceptions, terms and conditions, currencies, and the like. The exercise may then be compounded by a new set of conditions, additions to the bid list, and a new bid evaluation team, all at the initiative of the novice or sophisticated client.

Financial or governmental requirements for the project may specify the types of currencies to be expended and the total expenditure of each, particularly if a surplus of some currency exists in the treasury. Shipping and air travel may be limited to national carriers. All procurement activities may be directed through ministerial agencies; precise paperwork is a must. Licensed agents, selected by the owner, are common—don't bypass them in an effort to expedite orders.

Countries may be excluded from supplying materials. Certificates of origin may be required as proof of compliance. And payment through specified financial clearing houses with limitations for clearance imprinted on checks is normal.

CONSTRUCTION CONSIDERATIONS

Construction of international projects is generally on a subcontracted basis. If local labor is insufficient or unqualified, recruitment from other countries through labor brokers or agents is necessary. Imported labor requires the establishment of housing, recreational facilities, and catering services. The alternative is to construct a modular plant to minimize the cost associated with imported labor.

Construction schedules are longer, sometimes much longer. This is partly due to longer lead-time requirements for the recruitment of staff, marshalling of subcontractors, shipping time, and the building of infrastructure, such as offices, shops, roads, and the like. This longer lead-time resultant may be beneficial; extended planning should produce a more orderly construction program.

COMMUNICATIONS

The various means used to transmit information in the execution of a domestic project are taken for granted. The cost is essentially negligible. This is not the case, however, on an international project, where courier service and other special handling are mandatory.

Mail service can suffer due to the insistence of the country of origin to use national carriers for air mail service. A carrier may not make daily flights or may not go to the country of destination. Customs may cause delays of bulk mail unless a prior project agreement has been reached. The practice of reducing mail bulk by microfilming or magnetic tape has not gained any appreciable acceptance due to rehandling of information to obtain a hard copy.

The telephone frequently has limited use on certain foreign projects when the work is executed in various countries due to differences in working hours, time zones, and the work week. Transmittal of information electronically using facsimile or computer links is still limited to the occasional emergency use. Routine use is cost-justified only on larger projects.

SUMMARY

Overseas and foreign projects are enjoyable and challenging, with the advantages of travel, meeting new friends, learning new customs. But, don't equate overseas work to domestic work—this isn't the sheltered domestic environment, not for the company, not for the employee, not for the family. Approach the assignment with an open mind and enthusiasm, and the experience will be rewarding for you and your company.

3

Executing the International Project

ARTHUR C. BURNS* *The Ralph M. Parsons Company, Pasadena, California*

International projects have distinct personalities. These projects, especially large or complex ones located in remote areas, involve many considerations that are not a part of comparable domestic projects. The management and execution of an international project requires the recognition and acceptance that all facets of project operations are modified to suit the specific needs of the project. From conception to completion, these project personality factors contribute to the challenges that are associated with international work.

The management and execution philosophy for an international project is the same as that for a domestic project: the accomplishment of established goals through leadership, direction, inspiration, and delegation utilizing effective methods and controls. Similarly, the principles of project operation for an international project are equivalent to those for a domestic project. Owing to the specific nature of the international project, application of the project principles must be flexible and directed toward the individualistic and complex personality that exists. Of the basic project management and execution principles, the following are most applicable to international projects.

1. Plan your work—work your plan
2. Document—achieve proper communications
3. Be knowledgeable—where you are—how you got there—and where you are going
4. Maintain effective controls—no surprises
5. Lead—do not follow; follow up—do not assume
6. Select and maintain a winning team
7. Keep foremost in mind: time—quality—money

The performance of an international project calls for the full range of project activities employed on domestic projects, with functions modified to suit any unique situations. Successful accomplishment is the goal of all projects.

THE DOMESTIC PROJECT

As a rule, the domestic project is executed by a single contractor. On large projects, a project management group may be established to delegate and supervise work assigned to supporting project offices. The engineering work is normally performed in a single office location. Client representation is ever present and computer aids

---

*Retired

for design and controls follow established corporate procedures. Procurement work is performed in the same locale as engineering. Primary sources of supply are domestic; however, there may be some international sources of supply for selected equipment and materials. The construction activity at the work site uses labor and subcontract personnel from within the site area and its immediate surroundings. Specialty contractors also are employed. Project characteristics determine the size and type of project organization and the work plan. The single contractor, managing contractor, or managing construction contractor approach may be utilized. Project activities follow established corporate guidelines. The lines of communication are short and direct.

THE INTERNATIONAL PROJECT

The international project follows the same basic guidelines with modifications made and special emphasis given to the specific international aspects. The same basic functions are performed.

A summary functional organization chart showing a joint venture arrangement for a project is shown in Figure 1. With the agreement of contractors A and B to joint venture, a management committee is established, made up of several senior management members from each company as well as the project director who has been assigned the responsibility for the work. The project directorate is the project management group serving under the project director. Key personnel, such as project managers, procurement, construction, planning, controls, cost, fiscal, etc., are assigned from the contractors to the joint venture project directorate. The project directorate reports directly to the client and also to the joint venture management committee.

The production work is divided between contractors A and B. The engineering, procurement, and construction planning report directly to the project directorate. The construction site work is performed under the site manager, who is the deputy project director. He reports to the project directorate.

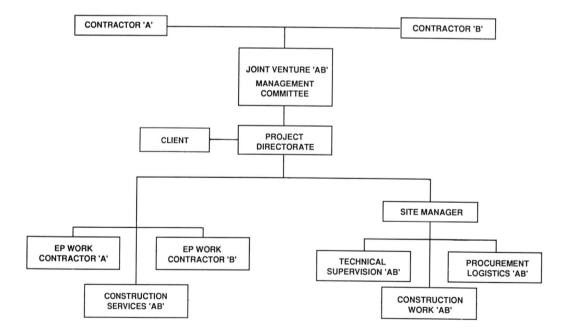

Figure 1 Joint venture functional organization.

Common project procedures, standards, and references are issued, with each office operating as a separate entity that is coordinated by the project directorate.

Numerous questions arise relating to the basis for organizing, planning, performing, and controlling the work. Decisions must be made during the initial planning stage that affect the entire program. Typical questions include:

Do we understand the work scope? Is it complete?
Should we go as a single contractor? Partnership? Joint venture?
Who is our competition? Strong and weak points?
What restraints are imposed? Regulations? Their cost?
What engineering can be performed in the country local to the work site?
Who has the best experience for selected engineering assignments?
What computer-aided designs are available?
How many participants should be involved in the work program?
What are the basic critical factors? Site access?
Are there restrictions on sources of supply? Local? Worldwide?
What degree of logistics is involved? Customs?
Should modularization be considered? To what degree? Prefabrication?
What sources of construction labor are available? Local? Expatriate?
What is performance qualification of labor? Is training required?
What is source of supervision? Equipment?
Should construction work be subcontracted?
What controls should be implemented?
What does the project schedule reveal? Critical path? Logistics?
What degree of materials management is required?
What are the financial arrangements? Funds? Payment? Taxes? Exchange rate?
What are contractual requirements? Guarantees? Reports?
What lines of communication should be used?
What organization best suits the project?

These basic questions are only part of the data that forms the initial conceptual planning for the project. The primary question is, "How do we form the best project organization and execute the work in the most optimum fashion, within the limits of any imposed restraints?"

PRIMARY CONSIDERATIONS

Having stated that international projects follow the basic fundamentals with modifications to accommodate the specific personality of each project, it is prudent to identify and discuss these special considerations. Each international project requires individual assessment. The primary considerations listed below may be incomplete or more than necessary. They are not ranked in order of importance; all are vital and interwoven. When taken together, they provide a synergistic impact upon the successful performance of work.

International projects: Primary considerations

Project philosophy	Contractual obligations
Nature of client	Financial aspects
Work site location	Engineering aspects
Applicable laws and regulations	Procurement aspects
Ethos and mores	Logistics
Hostile site conditions	Construction aspects
Project inquiry	Work-phase relationship
Project size and complexity	Project planning and controls
Work scope definition	Communications

Quality control/assurance   Contractor associations
Project personnel relations   Work assignments
Infrastructure   Project plan and work program

Each of these primary considerations is discussed below in detail and presents answers to various questions relating to the project managing and execution activities.

Project Philosophy

Project philosophy is a group of principles relating to the science of the industry and comprising logic, practical wisdom, ethics, and theory of applied industrial knowledge. It ranks as the primary consideration that makes up the specific personality of a project, and provides the basis for many project activities. International projects entertain many of the same principles as domestic projects; however, their impacts are more intensified and more variable.

The project philosophy as expressed by the owner/operator is contained in his prepared project database. Preliminary work studies, project goals and objectives, guidelines and regulations, all result in providing the bases for a work program that will suit the project philosophy.

The project evolution must be considered. It represents the answer to the questions "why is there a project?" The need for a project holds a top position in formulating project philosophy. Most projects grow into reality because of financial attractiveness. There are those projects that result from business necessities and political reasonings. The discovery of attractive feedstocks may serve to ignite the spark of project initiation.

Another chief component of project evolution stems from the changing and developing market picture. What products can be sold? Where is the best market location? What are the projected market trends? What are the costs and timing? What are the economics? How about financing? These questions all exist at the initial stage of project evolution. These initial market surveys and project economics are usually conducted by the owner/operator, although many international contractors have performed them also.

With the marketability (products defined with respect to quality and quantity) established, the next step calls for process design optimization studies. These process studies are generally carried out in conjunction with the marketing study. Evaluation of feedstocks (operating schemes vs. product refinements) is carried out. Ancillary facilities are identified, work programs planned, and economic studies performed. Suitable variables are introduced to provide for evaluations ranging from worst cases through normal to most attractive conditions.

The initial studies take into account all of the philosophy factors: the selection of the plant site requires extensive evaluation; environmental requirements temper the contemplated facilities; the process complexity will affect the operations and maintenance programs; the life-cycle economics stand out as an important principle. It reflects money through the application of facility utilization via planned and projected programs that are modified to meet the established economical ground rules.

Each philosophical principle has a direct impact upon the project. Also, each principle provides for the interrelations with other principles, that when combined, evaluated, and taken into consideration, comprise the project personality.

The owner/operator presents the philosophy of his project in his inquiry document and suggested contractual terms and conditions for the work to be performed. The principles and requirements presented reflect not only the evolution of the project, but also upon the work program and future operations. Project timing exerts its influences. An accelerated competition likely will get the work program off to an early start, thereby precluding a normal contract approach. This affects the type of contractual agreement and necessitates special ground rules for developing and executing the work program.

Project philosophy represents realism. It is reflected in all project activities. The impacts and interrelations of the philosophical principles must be identified, evaluated, and adhered to throughout the project work program.

Nature of Client (Owner/Operator)

The client (owner/operator) exerts appreciable influence over the planning and execution of a project. On international work, the greater the degree of sophistication of the client, the greater the basis for outlining the work requirements. Procedures, specifications, standards, regulations, and operating restraints are identified, providing a basis for evaluating work proposals. Where the client has little sophistication and/or is a part of a governmental agency, the outline of the work requirements does not always provide the necessary guidelines to plan and perform the work. Here it is necessary to refer to contractual obligations and develop and employ the criteria that are necessary to facilitate the work effort. Often, a project inquiry has been too general in nature, forcing the bidder to use his own criteria as the basis of his offer. As a result, evaluation is essentially impossible and rebidding is generally called for after a common set of basic criteria has been developed. Both time and money are wasted. The same analogy applies to project operation. A higher degree of client sophistication results in an efficient mode of project operation. When such client sophistication is absent, the contractor must develop suitable criteria.

Client philosophy must be sought, recognized, and thoroughly understood. Again, this philosophy is expressed in the various criteria that define the work scope and outline the guidelines for executing the work. Is the emphasis placed upon low investment costs or low maintenance costs? Is operation reliability the prime concern? What constitutes mechanical completion and final acceptance? Obviously, the less experienced client calls for a greater effort on the part of the contractor to ensure that contractual obligations are recognized, understood, and fulfilled. For example, on a major project for a foreign government, long after the plant had been operating satisfactorily, client exceptions were made because several units had fewer pumps than called for in the contract. The fact that other units had 10 to 20 percent more pumps than specified in the contract was of no consequence. An exception adjustment required negotiation.

Client philosophy is also revealed in the work performance route selected. If the work is adequately defined and there is time, the client may request lump-sum offers with bonus/penalty arrangements on completion. Where the work definition is not firm, the work will be performed under a reimbursable contract. Here the bonus/penalty arrangement on both time and moneys may be applied. Target costs, partial lump-sum offers, profit sharing, all are reflected in the philosophy of the client. The current trend for international projects calls for the selection of a managing contractor to prepare the preliminary designs and proposal engineering. The client then solicits worldwide bids from contractors whom he considers qualified to perform the production work. Lump-sum contracts are negotiated for engineering, procurement, and construction (EPC). The managing contractor is then called upon to manage and coordinate the project activities on behalf of the client.

A client may choose to serve as managing contractor. When this is deemed advisable, he may select personnel from major contractors to be part of his management team. It is likely that future project management teams will be comprised of representatives from the client and contractor organizations.

International projects call for close scrutiny of the financial picture. The payment of project moneys per agreement is vital to project operation. The money picture must remain in balance with all parties in agreement. Lack of moneys or excessive delays result in untenable situations where everyone loses.

The nature of the client has a marked impact upon international projects.

Work Site Location

The location of the site where the facility will be constructed has a marked influence upon project execution. When the work is to be carried out in a developed country, a project execution route would be established using local engineering, manufacturing, and construction talent. In this case, a project management group would be established within the country to oversee the work performed by experienced contractors. Procurement, too, would originate within the country, with materials and equipment imported from surrounding countries. Possibly, the prime contractor has an office or will make joint venture agreements with local contractors.

Reference is made here to two grass-roots refinery projects that were performed in the same country within a workspan of 5 years. One project involved an independent owner/operator; the other, a major owner/operator. Surprisingly, the mode of operation was very similar. The outline of project work programs is summarized below. There is very little difference between project operations. As would be expected, the major owner selected the process configuration, participated in project management, and took charge of start-up operations. The balance of project operations was essentially the same, allowing for the difference in the magnitude of the work scope.

Activity	Independent owner	Major owner
Process design	By contractor	By owner
Front-end engineering	By contractor	By contractor
Project directorate	By contractor	By owner-contractor
Engineering design		
Process units	Subcontractor X	Subcontractors A, B, and C
Utilities	Subcontractor Y	Subcontractors C and D
Offsite	Subcontractor Z	Subcontractor D
Procurement	By contractor	Bulks by contractor Equipment by subcontractors
Construction management	By contractor	By contractor
Construction work	Various subcontractors	Various subcontractors
Project controls	By contractor	Contractor and subcontractors
Operation startup	By contractor	By owner

In effect, the project operations of both projects were equivalent to that of domestic projects modified to comply with the practices of the country.

Obviously, there is a need to establish a working arrangement with in-country representatives who have specialized talents that can be brought into the project planning program.

The other extreme in project operation calls for the work to be performed in a country that is not developed industrially. Here the mode of operation cannot enjoy the execution benefits of a domestic project. The social aspects, along with established customs and conventions, play a greater role in performing the in-country work. The industrialization programs carried out in Saudi Arabia from 1975 are prime examples of this type of project execution. On the two industrial city projects at Jubail and Yanbu, the work programs were carried out under a joint team of the owners' representatives and the managing contractors. All work programs were carried out within the Kingdom. Worldwide services for plant components were obtained on a complete EPC basis. Needless to say, these two industrial undertakings are in the special class category: Both used extensive manpower to accomplish the objectives; but each had a separate personality. Other major work programs carried out in Saudi

Arabia, such as gas plant expansion facilities, grass-root refineries, industrial plants, petrochemical plants, energy facilities, pipelines, terminals, airports, and industrial buildings, all entailed specific modes of project execution that followed established guidelines.

Economics is a chief consideration when establishing a plan of execution for the project. Work site location has significant effects on project economics. Allowing for owner and local government restraints, the site factors may well be primary considerations for executing the work. Labor: Is it available locally or must it be imported? Labor rates: Is there economy in modularization? Supervision questions follow along the labor lines. Climatic conditions: Will they impact labor performance and material storage? Infrastructure: What facilities are required? Campsite? Residential? Offices? Preconstruction working facilities? Will they be temporary or will they become a part of the permanent facility? Access: How do we transport materials and manpower to the site?

Environmental consideration is associated with the site location. Stated restrictions must be met. If environmental restrictions have not been specified, good judgment and consideration of future obligations must prevail.

Communications are an important factor. Satellite communications is becoming a standard mode of operation; however, its use must comply with established regulations. Although the immediate exchange of information may appear costly at first, its contribution to successful job performance far outweighs its cost. It is the vital link of the project activity.

Applicable Laws and Regulations

Each country has its own laws governing business aspects, particularly those of foreign corporations who choose to perform work in its domain. It is natural for these laws and regulations to offer protection to local entrepreneurs. It is necessary for expatriate firms to be acquainted with the local laws and regulations and to comply with them. This matter should be resolved by the contractors' corporate legal experts.

The registration of a company and the selection of a local partner or agent representative are critical endeavors. Care must be exercised to obtain the most compatible and rewarding association from the many offers. By conducting its business activity, the contractor agrees to operate within the laws regarding employment of workers, including their benefits. It is important to note that the expatriate workers and supervisors brought in by the contractor are liable to conduct themselves within the confines of the applicable local laws and regulations. Here, close scrutiny and adherence must be given to the ethos and mores of the particular locale of the country.

It is the aim of the country involved to become more self-sustaining and achieve improved development of its people and resources. It is quite natural, then, to request that local talent be employed. This can create problems relating to the project operations. Local engineering firms may be limited to a single work discipline which necessitates the participation of additional firms as well as some on-the-job training. Updated surveys provide sufficient knowledge of the qualifications and potential of the local firms.

The local technical firms selected to participate on the project must receive project coordination and supervision. This calls for the temporary assignment of key expatriate personnel in the country. Since expatriate supervision is extremely costly, its size should be minimized, while maintaining its effectiveness. It may be more economical to perform the work back in the contractor's home office; however, this may not be what the project guidelines specified. Work assignments and development of national technical firms require proper considerations.

As in the case of technical talent, the regulations may call for maximum use of local procurement resources and local development of manufacturers and suppliers. Local materials are to be used where feasible. Designs must take this into account.

The technical procedures called for may not be recognized in the current fabrication modes of operation. Rejections may be high, and cost and deliveries adversely affected. Here, a procurement plan providing details of performance and supply and outlining compliance factors is mandatory. Since equipment and materials represent 50% of project costs, it is extremely vital that the execution plan be thorough and carried out effectively.

The project construction approach, too, may be guided by the requirement to use local forces. The contractor must consider the following questions: What labor forces exist—should subcontractors be utilized solely? What degree of supervision is available locally? What is the labor atmosphere—labor productivity—labor stability? Are there sufficient infrastructure facilities at or near the project work site? What are the construction practices? What must be provided externally? The economics of labor performance is a significant factor. The ratio of manpower to supervision and to equipment will affect the designs, time schedules, and cost of the work.

Project communications will be affected by the host country's laws and regulations. They may offer restrictions through customs, censorship, and regulations. Communication delays must be identified; the computer-satellite communications link may be unacceptable.

It is vital to learn the manner in which local business is conducted. Knowledge of general business decorum can be obtained from various commercial institutions. There are reasons why things are performed in a certain way. Perhaps various tax situations can be avoided by properly adhering to the established methods of doing the work.

Ethos and Mores of the Country

It is difficult to establish the impacts and effects that the social and living aspects of a country place upon the satisfactory performance of a work project. Much more importance is placed upon the technical and production efforts and their related cost impacts. Yet, the degree of contractor compliance with a country's way of living directly affects job performance and economics.

It is unlikely that the countries comprising the international community possess equivalent standards of living. The host country's government controls, work practices, religion, and social customs, may differ significantly from those of the contractor, but they are adequate for the way of life within the country. Accordingly, in addition to adhering to the laws and regulations, it is most important to carry out the in-country activities within the accepted confines of the social standards and customs. Typical areas for consideration include:

    Religion
    Equal opportunity
    Dominant home life
    Work periods/prayer time
    Holidays (national and religious)
    Social activities
    Dress codes
    Business arrangements
    Schooling
    Recreation
    Communications

The country's inhabitants accept the roles of the expatriate companies and their contribution toward the improved development of their resources and living standards. They are tolerant of the expatriate and his way of living. However, they do expect and are entitled to receive proper consideration for their way of living. The ability and desire of expatriate workers and their family members to accept these factors of ethos and mores promotes the stabilization of personnel and excellent relations within the country. Both of these are prime factors to be understood for successful project execution.

Hostile Site Conditions

Climatic conditions at the work site represent a prime consideration for design and execution of the international project. These climatic factors must be recognized from the start, evaluated, and allowances made for them in the design and execution phases of the work.

Work programs carried out in the Arctic, Middle East, and mountainous regions demonstrate the impact of the site climatic conditions. A brief discussion of these three work regions is presented:

Arctic Regions

The excessive winter weather and restricted access to work sites create major obstacles to the conventional design and execution program. There may be very short periods of time when there is suitable access to the site. Winter construction in a severe climate, along with its related infrastructure, is extremely costly. All facets of project operation must be evaluated to minimize expensive work factors. If site condition and logistics will allow, modularization of units or unit components should be employed. The use of an intermediate fabrication yard for modules and preassembly work will reduce manpower requirements at the site and also enhance working conditions, productivity, and costs. When site conditions preclude the use of large modules, the preassembly work will be limited to the applied logistical support restraints. Road, rail, and water shipments may have to be combined. Special shipping of heavy equipment may be restricted to times when the ground is frozen and can sustain the weights.

Many construction projects may be shut down during periods of severe cold. Because of the mobilization costs associated with international projects, winter shutdowns are generally too costly. Permanent building shells and temporary buildings (constructed during summer weather) can be employed for fabrication areas. Campsite facilities must accommodate the winter climates. Schedule consideration should be given to minimal winter work and high work activities during summer work periods.

Severe winter climate conditions result in extremely low labor utilization and performance factors, with an attendant increase in costs and schedule. All of the cold climate impacts must be considered and evaluated while developing the initial project work plan.

Desert Regions

In these areas the climatic impacts result from the excessively high temperatures and accompanying dust and sandstorms. Scorching temperatures impact on worker productivity. Certain functions such as concrete pours and curing must be carried out with weather as a major consideration. Large pours can be scheduled to allow curing during the cooler part of the day. Specifications will call for a halt to the concrete work operations above specified ambient temperatures. Ice machines are operating at capacity to keep the heat of reaction of concrete at acceptable limits. Some work programs may start in the early morning, shut down during the heat of the day, and resume work late in the afternoon when the heat effects are reduced.

Campsite living is geared to air conditioning. In addition to the heat (dry and humid), the dust and sandstorms must be dealt with. Severe storms call for work stoppage. Protection of material and equipment becomes a prime concern. For critical materials such as instrumentation, the use of pressurized air shelters is effective. The shelter is inflated with refrigerated filtered air. Storage protection against ex-

cessive solar heat must be provided. The material specifications should call for materials suitable to withstand these weather extremes.

Maintenance of construction equipment requires special attention. First, you cannot afford to have too much spare idle equipment; second, you cannot afford to experience excessive numbers of equipment failures. The heat and sand demand expanded
maintenance programs. Some of the experienced owners/operators have developed material storage requirements. Different classifications are used and various equipment
and materials are assigned to the classification. Each has its own degree of weather
storage protection requirements.

Mountainous Regions

Limited access is associated primarily with projects performed at high elevations. Logistics becomes the principal factor. Designs must be altered to conform. On some
projects, materials were hauled by burro pack, with strict size and load requirements.
Current projects planned in the inland regions of Africa and South America are prime
examples of this concern for logistics. There are no roads, and rail and waterways
are limited. Suggestions such as tractor-hauled hydrofoil skids along with air transport may appear to be farfetched, yet they may well be the answer.

At high elevations the atmosphere is a factor. Workers may be subjected to lack
of sufficient oxygen at the work site. Here an intermediate assembly area at lower
altitudes plus oxygen packs may prove to be the solution.

Other Factors

Extreme weather conditions have been recognized as the chief hostility factor. There
are other factors such as native acceptance. On a project in southeastern Turkey,
a construction crew encountered a village of devil worshipers. At night they conducted
a raid, damaging the installation made during the day. Obviously, the matter had to
be resolved. Fortunately, a direct confrontation by the construction chief resulted
in diplomatic settlement. Workers recruited from the area worked on the project during the day, but at night they were on opposing raiding parties. On other projects
there are reports that hostile native tribes have attacked workers and caravans.

These hostile factors contribute toward the personality of the individual project.
Their resolutions make the work extremely challenging.

Project Inquiry

Generally, prior to the issuance of a project inquiry document, the owner requests
potential contractors to submit their written qualifications for that project. This is
normally followed by a presentation in which the work program is thoroughly reviewed and a degree of familiarity is established between the owner and the potential contractor. The project inquiry document is then issued to selected qualified contractors.
This document sets the stage for the contractor's project planning and execution activities. The work scope is defined, ground rules are established, contractual obligations set forth, constraints and restraints identified. This document is of major
significance. It is becoming increasingly more common for the inquiry to state "no
exceptions allowed." This facilitates contractor selection and project execution. It
reflects that the owner has already studied alternatives and wishes to proceed with
a specified program. After complying with the inquiry requests, the bidder may identify and explain any exceptions and interpretation as an alternative or an exception
to his base proposal.

Let us examine some of the key considerations and their impacts. Obviously, the
contractor's qualifications have been examined and reexamined. Has he constructed
the same or similar units? How did he perform? Does he possess an adequate knowledge of international operations? Specifically, how do each of the project disciplines
perform their work? What is his financial position? Who are candidates for key pro-

ject positions and what personnel depth exists? What are the seleciton criteria? What cost factors must be considered? It behooves the owner to select a contractor that has the highest overall qualifications for the work. This becomes the primary step toward a successful operation of any project.

A summary of the principal factors of contractor selection is presented in Table 1. Key items are assigned a weighted value with the factors serving as a checkoff list. In some instances the numerical ratings are equated to an equivalent monetary amount combined with the potential contractor's bid price. It represents the expected total contractor cost of the work.

By examining the inquiry document thoroughly and evaluating his own capabilities, the contractor sets forth his plan to perform the work. A typical project plan sets forth the following:

Complete understanding of requirements
    Assess work scope requirements in manhours and costs
Work assignments
    Who does what work?
    Where will work be performed?
    Who has responsibility and authority?
Organization to manage and execute work
    What represents the best team?
    Joint venture—go it alone—selectively use subcontractors?
Project schedule
    Establish critical milestones
    Prepare detailed schedules for EPC
    Tie down acceptance criteria
Manpower loadings for EPC on unit component basis
Restraints and regulations plus their impacts
    Are there restrictions or advantages in utilizing technical and construction
    contractors from within the country?
Worldwide procurement
    Sources of supply
    Work quality and controls
    Logistics
    Costs
Work plans for EPC
Candidates for key project positions
    They should be involved from the start.
Project controls program
    Budgets
    Costs
    Materials
    Data collection/reporting
    Feedback
Computer utilization
    Designs
    Scheduling/WBS
    Budget/controls/reporting
    Material controls
    Progress
    Communications
Financial aspects
    Project funding
    Method of payment
    Degree of financing
    Tax liabilities

Table 1 Contractor Selection Criteria

Items	Factors
Key personnel	Ability-suitability-experience-knowledge-performance record-current assignment
Engineering	Manpower quality and availability-computer usage-design programs-facilities-procedures-technical reserves-flexibility-standards-performance record
Procurement	Worldwide experience/capability-task force-commodity buying-organization-procedures-personnel quality-availability-quality control-logistics-performance
Engineering/designs	Relationships with project director and corporate management-working relationships with project and corporate work disciplines-technical ability-design systems-computer model technology-document control-performance
Project controls	Cost systems-planning/scheduling reporting methods-computer usage-data bank-material controls-trending-forecasting-change control-departmental support
Construction	Resident manager and key staff-capability-experience-organization-construction plan-site familiarity-work control effectiveness-business relations-contractor associations-interproject relations
Corporate management	Participation level-project recognition-project support-initiative to act on project needs

      Internal exchange rates
      Bonus/penalty conditions
    Contract review
        Obtain clarification when necessary
        Recognize its importance
        Identify bases for changes and their impacts
        Tie down authorities and responsibilities
    Execution plan identifying who does what

The inquiry document and its response represent the index or summary for the management and execution of the project. It is stressed that international projects create international events that require international resolutions. The astuteness of international business operations requires the use of personnel who have international experience.

Project Size and Complexity

International projects may range from a small individual unit to a large multiple unit grass-roots complex. The facility may use a normal process design or incorporate a new process design development. Each style of facility calls for its own means of execution. The degree of contractor participation and the type of contractor to be considered is determined by preparatory work performed by the owner/operator. While contractor selection is generally based upon his degree of expertise, those having the greatest degree of experience should be able to apply their knowledge and construct a more attractive facility. The substitute for experience calls for innovative and creative approaches to the designs and work execution.

Worldwide sources for the performance of engineering, procurement, and construction are available for all types of projects. Competition is keen and excellent work is performed by all contractors. It is likely the owner/operator has categorized the worldwide contractors into various groups to be considered for different projects. The small and/or normal projects falling into the "typical" project class will be offered to a group of contractors who are smaller and production oriented. Multiple complexes (grassroots or existing facilities), new developments, and large mega projects call for special execution considerations. The owner/operator will very likely consider utilizing only major worldwide contractors to perform front-end work definition and proposal engineering and later serve as managing contractor when the production effort is contracted out to various contractors.

The contractor's performance is dictated by the size and complexity of the work, modified to suit the specific requirements of the owner/operator. Small and normal projects follow the routine EPC execution programs. Major projects are organized and executed to conform to owner/operator guidelines.

Work Scope Definition

The completeness of the work scope definition plays a major role in planning and executing the international project. The project planning and execution requires complete knowledge of project guidelines and restraints and what exactly is to be done.

It might be assumed that the responsibility for defining the work scope is that of the owner/operator, and its definition is provided for in the project inquiry. This assumption is correct; however, it is the degree of completeness of the work definition that must be considered. The work scope presented by the owner/operator generally spells out what facilities or what products are required. However, the work scope offered by the owner/operator may require considerable expansion in order to plan and execute the work program. There are occasions where major owner/operators offer a feedstock analysis and ask what can I produce? What should I produce? When can I sell it? What costs are involved? This represents an extreme case; however, it is not infrequent. This calls for assays of the feedstock, market surveys, process design and optimization, process selections, support facilities, operation and maintenance appraisals. Also entailed are project economics involving marketing and transporting costs with matrix evaluation of principal variables such as feed costs, operating costs, money return, investment costs and the like. The investigation may take into consideration site location and total infrastructure support. Such program evaluations represent extreme challenges and entail extensive considerations.

The bidder should make no assumptions and/or interpretations of the project inquiry. If there are questions, ask: have them clarified. With the end objectives defined, there are likely to be many questions relating to work performance. A site survey is generally necessary. All site conditions plus industrial and residential infrastructure should be assessed. Leave nothing to chance—evaluate and plan—general assumptions must be replaced with investigations. Who can do what work, having what quality, in what time period, for what price. The old adage that money is way ahead of what's in second place rings true. A well thought-out plan is the result of extensive investigations and thorough evaluations of their impacts and application. It can be called ingenuity, creativity, and innovativeness. It boils down to doing the job properly.

The investigation of work scope covers more than the site and its related conditions. Worldwide sources of material supply must be checked out and vendor performances evaluated. Quality control in performance and familiarity with and adherence to regulations and standard requirements should receive emphasis. Worldwide engineering and construction companies also should be evaluated to determine where their participation can be used.

The regulations (governmental and owner requirements), along with the terms and conditions of the contracts, are very much a part of the work scope definition.

Financial concerns may affect contractual arrangements which in turn may alter the basis for performing the work.

Contractual Obligations

The contract is the agreement between the owner/operator and the contractor to perform the work. As the project's legal document, it must be understood fully by all concerned. In addition to its typical terms and conditions, the contract for international projects will very likely call for employing local (in-country) talents.

A restriction may be placed upon the location for performing engineering and procurement.

It is common for the contract to reference local laws and regulations calling for selected engineering designs to be performed by national firms. In many instances, these technical firms, while capable, are not familiar with the specific nature of the work. It is necessary for the contractor to conduct surveys to become fully knowledgeable of the country's resources. This facilitates work assignments (sometimes on-the-job training), the degree of expatriate supervision required, and the schedule and development of the project execution plan.

The supply of equipment and materials also may be directed to facilitate the development of local suppliers and manufacturers. Import duties as well as stated regulations may dictate the use of local firms for supply. This may not represent the most economical approach; however, it is the contract restraint that is to be employed. Important factors here are the quality of goods and their timely delivery. Large orders may overtax the local producers' capabilities, reducing quality and impairing delivery. Also the materials may not comply fully with design standards. These factors must be recognized by continuous surveys and allowances made in the overall project plan.

There may be additional restrictions upon procurement. For example, worldwide procurement may be acceptable; however, all operations must originate within the country and outside materials and equipment must be obtained through local agents who are established for worldwide vendors.

The construction activity may also be called upon to utilize local labor and subcontractors to the fullest degree. By way of updated surveys and work activities, knowledge is available regarding the qualifications and performance of labor and subcontractors. Many firms may not have been exposed to the specific work atmosphere and there may be tendencies to overstate capabilities. Factors relating to labor performance must be analyzed thoroughly.

The contractual definition of "mechanical completion" must be understood and agreed upon. This also applies to financial matters relating to payment schedules, invoice supporting data, monetary rates of exchange, taxes, insurance, and warranties. These important facets must be reviewed thoroughly by personnel with the applicable expertise. A major owner/operator may deviate appreciably from his normal contractual terms and conditions; however, for a governmental owner/operator or its representative, the specific wording of the contract is of utmost importance. It may be written in the native language of the country and its translation must retain the specific meaning of the contract. The expression "a little is lost in the translation" is quite meaningful. Obviously, a changing contract resulting from misinterpretation plays havoc with the successful execution of a project—the contract can't be a "moving target."

Financial Aspects

The financial aspects of any project require top priority. Monetary transactions represent the prime purpose of the business world. The availability of financial resources has an immediate impact upon any work program.

Many international projects receive financial assistance to some degree. After arriving at the decision to proceed with a work program, it is necessary to consider the financial sources. What financing can be obtained and for what terms? The project work program and timing of events present the money outflow picture. Financing must be arranged to suit these conditions with some degree of flexibility. Project financing arrangements should be left to the financial experts. The impact of project financing represents a concern to the project management team.

With the advent of mega projects and with the high cost of moneys, it is necessary to reach an amicable agreement concerning the transfer of project funds. The international project introduces the currency exchange rate factor. The program of spending and invoicing is very time consuming and penalizes the spender. Late invoicing, with its substantiating data, could delay reimbursement for several months. The advance funds method of monthly or semimonthly advances that are reconciled with known expenses is an improvement. However, owing to invoicing delays, there is still an appreciable amount of estimating costs involved. The zero bank balance represents a very workable plan. Here it is vital that anticipated major expenditures are foreseen and their timing identified. These methods are applicable to a reimbursable-type of contracted work program. The establishment of agreed-to milestone payments reflects the general approach to major lump-sum work programs. It is based upon the payment of moneys at recognized and agreed-to accomplishments. The milestone payment method can be based upon the attained progress on the work program.

An international project entails worldwide procurement, and thereby places great emphasis upon the currency exchange rates. Allowances must be made for fluctuations, and the skills of the financial experts employed to avoid adverse money conditions. Obviously, it is most desirable to obtain moneys as early as possible and also to achieve attractive monetary exchange rates. With the high values of moneys, this activity, while monitored by project management, should be delegated and handled by skilled financial experts.

Taxes represent another key international project consideration. Some states in the United States still apply the unitary tax principle that calls for any corporation who conducts some business in the state to be subjected to income tax on its entire worldwide operation. As a result, many corporations are hesitant to become involved and do business elsewhere. A full understanding of the tax laws of the country where business is to be carried out is mandatory. There may or may not be reciprocal tax agreements with the United States. If not, without proper contractual arrangements, a corporation could be subject to double taxation: once by the project country and once by the United States. In-country and out-country contracts that call for specific and separate services to be performed have been used to resolve unnecessary tax liabilities.

In addition to corporate taxes, it is also necessary to consider personal taxes that may be levied upon employees that work in-country. Employee allowances and taxes must be accounted for in dealing with personnel who accept foreign project assignments.

International projects, especially those where the owner is a government agency of the host country, require that money matters be understood and explicitly tied down. Many times payments are delayed because the invoice documentation is unacceptable. The ensuing arbitrations cost time and money. Make sure the requirements are understood, then make sure they are adhered to by all parties. This consideration is applicable to the release of retention moneys. Obviously, the purpose of retention moneys is to ensure that the contractor will provide acceptable and timely constructed facilities. Generally the release of retention moneys is contingent upon the acceptance of the facility by the owner. The definition of mechanical completion and final acceptance must be suitably negotiated at the time of contract award. Many times the acceptance proceedings are carried into the operating phase of the work program, and work that is called out is intermixed with maintenance and warranties.

Another key part of the project financial program is a cost identification basis that is amenable to both owner and contractor. Such identification and trending provide the accurate source of where the money is spent. If the contract is lump sum, this cost basis is the proprietary tool of the contractor. Financial matters are conducted in accordance with the agreed-to contracted terms and conditions. A key part of this cost basis and its trending is the agreement as to what constitutes a contract change, its cost and impact, and its acceptance. This is an area of great controversy on international projects.

Engineering Aspects

The application of engineering expertise is presented in detail elsewhere in this text. Our purpose here is to review briefly the modifications to a normal engineering program incurred by the international project. It has already been mentioned that international projects entail international engineering. Also emphasis is placed upon the utilization of technical firms of the host country in which the work is performed.

It is recognized that the owner/operator (privately or government owned) wishes to contribute to the development of local talents for all facets of the work. The problem that faces the contractor is, that while the local firms have competent expertise in one or two disciplines, they are small and generally lack the process-oriented experience. Their methods and procedures do not match those of the managing contractor. Their willingness to apply their abilities to the project needs is a major attribute.

In efforts to obtain a balance between costs and performance, the managing contractor must evaluate the capabilities of local technical firms. He may even arrange or participate in joint venture agreements in an effort to combine talents for a specific project. Work parcels must be assigned selectively for compatibility with the expanding abilities of the local firms. Assignments involving civil works, roads, buildings, infrastructure, structural, and some electrical, equipment, and mechanical work represent typical work activities to be performed by local firms. The disciplines involving instrumentation, electrical, special equipment and mechanical design may exceed the production abilities of local firms and can be best performed by specialized firms or the managing contractor. But there is no hard and fast rule for the utilization of local talent.

Regardless of where the engineering design is carried out, it must result in design products that fully comply with the project requirements. The use of computer facilities for designs has arrived at the productive stage. Three-dimensional designs, along with electrical, equipment, and piping isometric designs by computer, are becoming normal operations. Computer design has also expanded into material takeoffs and prerequisite procurement functions. These factors, along with the development of working models, must be considered when making the engineering work assignments.

The developing trend calls for the prime contractor to perform the initial engineering work. The basic criteria, diagrams, flow plans, equipment designs, layouts, and models up to 30 to 40% completion are a part of the work definition and proposal work. The specifications, data sheets, drawings, and model become a part of the bid package for a selected component of the work. Qualified second-tier contractors and specialty contractors are then solicited to perform production engineering, procurement, and construction work. The second-tier contractor may arrange for joint venture and partnership agreements in an effort to better qualify to perform the work. The selection of the production firms requires evaluation to ensure that capabilities are not exceeded. A supervisory team will be placed in the production firm's offices to monitor the work.

Many foreign engineering firms do not possess a procurement or construction ability. Their project control features may be quite limited. Here again, ingenuity must be demonstrated in arranging for and performing the work with the single-source type concept of responsibility.

Bear in mind that the true cost of engineering is reflected through the cost of equipment, materials, designs, and operation. The cost of performing engineering is small when compared with the affected costs. The old adage "Do it once—Do it right" is quite applicable.

Procurement Aspects

In general, over 50% of the investment cost of a project represents moneys that are expended and controlled by procurement. Procurement is a vital part in the project cycle. With the technical data received from engineering, it is procurement's responsibility to seek out qualified suppliers, thereby obtaining the tools, equipment, and materials in harmony with established budgets and schedules so that the construction program at the site can be performed in an effective manner.

With the award of an international project to a contractor, a deluge of offers from suppliers worldwide follows. Each soliciting company desires to participate in the project and offers a range of services. Many firms have associations within the country of the work site as well as in major countries throughout the world. Maintaining an up-to-date list of suppliers and their qualifications will facilitate the preparation of an international source of supply for various materials. Since there is a tendency for some suppliers to overstate their production capabilities, it is most important to check vendor plant facilities on a regular basis.

When evaluating the offers of international suppliers, it is important to ensure that the vendors are knowledgeable and fully understand the commercial, technical, and time requirements of the order. Many suppliers assume that the project requirements are similar to their own standard supply. These assumptions are costly in terms of money and time. The fabrication shop procedures and housekeeping will affect the quality of the final product. If not in compliance, such items as mill and fabrication tolerances and specifications/standards and procedures all add up to a major project crisis. It is essential that the suppliers are knowledgeable and capable of performing to suit the project needs. The major fabricators turn out quality products; however, even they require evaluation, follow-up, and technical assistance.

As mentioned in the discussions of contract and government regulations, the international project owner wishes to use services that are local to the site location country. If work performance and product quality are acceptable, the local sources of supply should provide for economical supply.

Sometimes the actual purchasing operation is to be performed "in-country." Arrangements must be made to allow for the impacts of this mode of operation.

On major projects it may prove desirable to initiate "blanket order" or "umbrella"-type project commitments for selected equipment and material commodities. Items such as pressure vessels, heat exchangers, pumps and drivers, compressors, structural steel, piping, electrical, and instruments should be considered. This calls for developing a selection criteria and identifying the estimated quantities of goods for the various categories of materials. The production EPC contractors can issue no-cost purchase orders for the equipment or materials covered by the initial blanket orders. Multiple sources of supply offer economical advantages as the fabrication costs on an international basis can fluctuate rapidly. Another accepted route is to supply the production EPC contractor with sources-of-supply lists and let them strike their own negotiations. This allows for the control of vendor workloads and lump-sum pricing of total EPC contracts.

The economy of the project may call for maximum prefabrication, preassembly, and modularization work performed outside of the work site country. The economics and adherence to specification requirements must be considered. Sometimes this presite work is performed at a manufacturer's plant; other times a fabrication yard is used. The transportation costs plus labor costs must be reviewed. Project achievements regarding time, work quality, and money must be constantly monitored.

Expediting and inspection (vendor quality control) are key procurement activities. The expediting is essentially the same as for domestic projects. However, the communication gap may be severe. Many of the international suppliers do not comprehend the urgency requirements of a project. These facets must be reckoned with and suitable allowance made for anticipated slippages. The delay of shop drawings as well as final product can result in severe cost impact.

Products must comply with drawings and specifications. The increased complexity of fabrication requirements calls for the inspection by specialists having the proper certifications. These certified inspectors are not too abundant throughout the international scene. Currently, a high degree of international inspection is performed by certified U.S. inspection personnel. Both expediting and inspection services may be obtained via subcontracted services. This has not proved to be totally acceptable and should be supplemented with inspections made by contractor-qualified personnel. The need to make corrections or modifications in the field should be avoided on international projects, as associated costs are extremely high.

Material logistics is a prime factor in the procurement cycle. Preparatory to initiating the shipment of goods, it is necessary to package, crate, and protect the shipment from damage in transit. Formal crating specifications should be prepared and used. Invariably, when the crating is performed on a competitive basis it may not be satisfactory. Materials damaged in transit, whether resulting from failure of placement restrictions, shifting cargo, or improper crating, require costly and time-consuming repairs. Of course, there are insurance coverages, but usually it is impossible to wait for litigation settlements—the work must go on. Once repaired, the associated costs are never recouped. The best thing to do is to prevent in-transit damage by adequate crating and packaging. Protecting materials and equipment from salt water corrosion is a prime consideration. It is amazing what damage can result if equipment and/or material is shipped on deck with inadequate protective packaging.

Material arriving at the work site must be inspected for compliance with quantity and condition. Material receiving reports are issued with the condition of materials noted. With computerized records and control, the material receiving part of materials management can be carried out promptly and efficiently. When repairs are indicated, prompt action must be taken. It is unlikely that economics and time will permit the return of any damaged items to a manufacturer's plant. They must be repaired at the work site, preferably by the manufacturer or under his supervision.

Proper storage protection must be provided for equipment and materials stored and installed at the work site. Different classes of protection are involved. Moisture, freezing, sand and dirt, corrosion, and deterioration must be dealt with. Wearing parts of machinery along with instruments and electrical controls require special protection. The use of filtered air-conditioned storage balloon warehouses may be feasible for special items. Plastic seals, heavy greasing, thorough cleaning and servicing, are all a part of the various storage protection measures. Excessive heat and ice damage also must be considered. Theft must be taken into consideration.

Prior to the operation startup, it is necessary to have critical spare replacement parts on hand. The delivery time for a replacement part may exceed the ingenuity of maintaining continuity of operation. This start-up activity occurs at the time of transfer from construction to operations and there is a tendency to underevaluate its importance. Obviously start-up spares are quickly followed by normal spares and selected surplus materials. The operating supplies, especially those considered critical to maintain operations, must receive equal consideration with the start-up spares.

In their guarantees and warranties, manufacturers often wish to impose their standard conditions, limiting the time coverage, conditions that are not compatible with international projects. Negotiations may result in price increases in an effort to achieve warranties and guarantees favorable for the international project. It is understandable that longer periods of service guarantees represent additional moneys. Proper protection, installation, and servicing are vital; if they are not in accord with the manufacturer's procedures, the likelihood of collecting on warranties is remote. The terms of repair also require scrutiny; repairs at the manufacturer are too costly. A field-conditioning and accompanying backcharge must be negotiated.

Disposal of surplus materials is another task. It may not be possible to package and ship them to another site. Import restrictions may prevent their shipment out of the country. The owner/operator will obviously pick and choose from surplus materials to suit his needs, with the balance disposed of at a fraction of their cost. The moral here is to employ effective materials management controls to minimize the surplus material picture.

Logistics

While logistics of materials is a part of the procurement function, its role on an international project is important enough to require special mention. The movement of equipment and materials from the manufacturer or fabricator's work area to the work site involves logistics. The logistics program must be included as a part of the initial project execution plan. The sequencing and delivery of materials per schedules have far-ranging impacts upon the project work program. Allowances for shipping, consolidation, weather delays, import/custom clearances, and land shipment must form a part of the overall work plan and schedule. In the mid-1970s there were excessive delays encountered after cargo vessels had registered at the ports of Beruit, Lebanon, and Jedda and Dammam in Saudi Arabia. Fortunately, new facilities have corrected these delays; however, they could be encountered in other areas.

A site investigation at the outset will reveal many useful logistic features. A pioneer port, followed by a permanent facility, may be the most feasible facility for receiving materials at the site. The use of concrete barges and roll on-roll off (Ro-Ro) barges may also prove most feasible. The peculiarities and restrictions of the site conditions plus the local country regulations will become a part of the basic design criteria. They affect all phases of the project, including its cost.

Essentially, all international projects will require marshalling or loading and shipping facilities from various international ports. This allows for shipment consolidation. On mega projects, the logistics plan may call for using chartered ships for transporting the materials and equipment. On other major projects existing shipping lines will be used, and the project rates negotiated.

A simplified flow plan showing logistics and traffic operations is presented in Figure 2. The solid flow lines depict the movement of materials and the dashed flow lines indicate the paperwork route.

It is appropriate to utilize the services of a freight forwarding agent to handle the shipping paperwork routine and arrange for the marshalling and shipment operations. This applies at the port of embarkation and also at the receiving port area. These firms are thoroughly familiar with the laws and regulations. The in-country agent can facilitate customs inspections and arrange for storage and shipment to the work site. When using these services, it is most important for project representatives to monitor and inspect the loading and unloading operations. In this way in-transit damage is readily identifiable and assignments of responsibility are facilitated.

Extreme accuracy is required to ensure that the paperwork identifies quantities and materials that are actually shipped. When there are discrepancies between paperwork and shipments, the materials are held in customs until reconciliations are accepted. Obviously, this will have an impact on the work site work program.

Some countries may specify that the materials and equipment be shipped via ships of the country. Also, registered ships may be required. These requirements are contained in the contract and are recognized as restrictions that may have an impact on schedules and costs.

All facets of logistics affect project execution. For example, on a refinery project in southeastern Turkey, not only were the receiving port facilities somewhat limited, but there were over 50 tunnels on the railroad route to the site. There was no road access. The tunnels had been routed via soft mining so they were not straight,

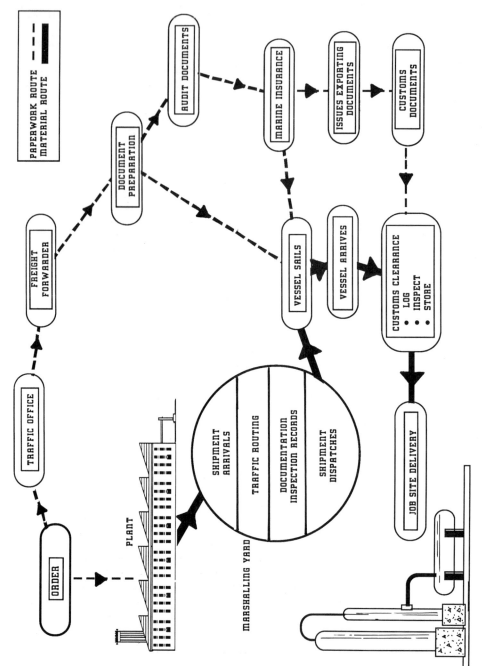

Figure 2 Flowchart of logistics and traffic operations.

and it was necessary to obtain special railway cars and construct mock-up sections to simulate the equipment that was to be shipped. Alterations to the tunnels and also to the designs and fabrication of some equipment were necessary.

The utilization of modular construction enhances the logistical activities. Projects carried out on the North Slope of Alaska have an open water access of several weeks during the late summer months. Accordingly, all fabrication and shipping activities are geared to meet these dates. With modular units becoming much larger, logistics become more vital. Movement of expensive ocean shipments requires complete evaluation. Table 2 identifies the primary modularization factors that should be evaluated when considering the use of modules. Each factor must be considered and resultant impacts identified. The impacts can be evaluated through a feasibility study.

Construction Aspects

The construction program is most affected by the local and governing conditions of the country in which the work is being performed. All activities must comply with the country's laws, regulations, and traditions. Since the project construction forces represent the total company entity to the host country, it is necessary to establish and maintain effective liaison with governmental and local businesses. There are many types of liaison involvement: work visas, work regulations, health, worker and social benefits, security, and assistance in complying with the manner in which business is normally performed in the country. The establishment and maintenance of good liaison contributes to the success of the operation. It recognizes that the construction force has the position of a visitor who is performing work that is beneficial to the country in a manner that demonstrates full cooperation and consideration.

Site conditions vary. Although the project may be part of an existing complex, it probably will be a grass-roots facility, with all of the plant facilities and associated infrastructure provided by the contractor. Previous discussions have set forth the fact that the site conditions plus in-country facilities will play a major role in determining the project work plan.

An outline of a typical construction plan is shown in Table 3. The principal factors are listed in chronological sequence. This plan forms a part of the project execution plan. It must be specific to provide for effective planning and execution of the work.

Local resources must be evaluated fully and applied selectively to the project work plan. Because many countries are in the development stage, the use of local resources

Table 2 Modularization Factors

Site conditions	Accessibility-labor picture
Economics	Increased engineering-lower field costs
Schedule	Evaluate-may be little impact
Feasibility	Evaluate each site and fabrication area
Fabrication	Work area vs. sources of material/labor
Module size	Site and logistic restraints
Work quality	Labor factor-controlled work area
Logistic restraints	Accessibility-time-size
Shipping risks	Concentrated shipments-ocean travel
Site work	Appreciable activity plus module installation

Table 3 Construction Plan Outline

Workscope definition

Site visit-regulations-government relations

Organization-management team

Planning and scheduling-procedures

Requirements and availability
    Manpower
    Supervision
    Construction equipment
    Contractors

Constructability reviews

Infrastructure-industrial-residential-civic

Materials management-prefab-logistics

Work restraints

Contract administration

Communications-completions-turnovers

Work performance-progress-productivity

Costs-trends-forecasts-changes

Security-safety-work quality

Training-start-up assistance

Closedown activities

---

may necessitate an extensive training program established and operated by the contractor. Responses to proposal inquiries may have to include a complete description of the craft training programs offered.

The size of the project impacts the labor requirements. Taking the rule-of-thumb, from 6000 to 10,000 manhours per million dollars (U.S.) in construction costs, an appraisal of total labor manhours can be established. Data from past projects will provide a basis for labor assignment to the various work crafts and nonproductive categories. Productivity estimates, gained from past experience and appraisals of current work activities, can be assigned and a relatively accurate labor/supervision and equipment support picture obtained. Once the requirements have been established, it is necessary to assess the available labor. Comparative evaluations with schedule considerations and local talent availability will indicate the degree of participation of expatriate labor.

On various international projects it may prove most feasible to utilize a total expatriate work force. Here, partnership or joint venture arrangements or contractor-subcontractor arrangements may be established. The international work forces such as those from European countries, Asia, Japan, South Korea, and the South Pacific are of outstanding quality and perform exceptionally well. The economics of the cost of a worker in the international area is quite high and generally prohibits the consideration of using labor from the major industrialized countries. Labor surveys of the international labor sources are proprietary in nature; however, references can be obtained from technical libraries and international labor organizations.

The effective utilization of field supervision is crucial for optimum project performance. Supervisors are expensive and there is a tendency to minimize the number to be utilized. However, this can be a false economy as supervisors do the immediate work planning and represent a key element of the overall work force productivity. On international projects constructed in non-industrialized countries in the late 1970s and early 1980s, the ratio of supervisor to workers varies from 1 to 8 to 1 to 10 for the heavy working crafts such as pipefitters, boilermakers, masons, steel workers, to ratios of 1 to 2 to 1 to 5 for electrical and instrumentation. At times the skills of the supervisors are called upon to perform selected special work.

For most international projects, a major construction firm serves as the managing contractor and the construction work is performed by various EPC contractors. The work coordination is the responsibility of the managing contractor. As of the mid-1980s the trend is toward lump-sum-type contracts. With high costs involved, it is imperative that the work definition, including site and in-country restraints, and work programs be of sufficient detail. Even so, mishaps will occur which will result in numerous negotiations relating to extra work and unanticipated delays.

The need to assess productivity is common for both domestic and international projects. The responsive corrective measures for international projects entail a much greater impact than for domestic work. The factors that enter into productivity assessment must be recognized and given respective evaluation weights. The ratio of progress achieved versus labor spent reflects merely the indicated type of productivity. The progress curve type of evaluation on a unit of work basis will give the true productivity of a specific craft relative to its progress picture. As indicated in Table 4 and Figure 3, some productivity factors cannot be controlled. The work week and weather factors are those that we accept; the balance of factors are subject to good construction management.

The assigned productivities reflect project costs. They become a part of the economic evaluations of "stick built" versus a modularization program. The evaluation of project progress vis-a-vis project productivities on a work breakdown structure can pinpoint areas of impact and concern. With the computer programs available, this evaluation and consideration of alternative work programs is performed readily.

Table 4 Typical Productivity Analysis

Factors	Weight %	Performance (assigned) %	Weighted average %	Remarks
Weather	10	60	6.00	All factors: heat, cold, rain
Work week	15	60	9.00	40-hr week vs. extended time
Craftsmen	15	75	11.25	Quality-availability-turnover
Supervision	10	70	7.00	Performance-experience
Work complexity	5	60	3.00	Size-equipment-specialties
Schedule	10	70	7.00	Adequacy of time
Congestion	10	70	7.00	Work areas-simultaneous work
Materials	15	60	9.00	Availability-storage
Local practices	5	70	3.50	Regulations-restraints-laws
Location	5	60	3.00	Site availability-infrastructure

65.75%

Labor factor - 1.52 (based upon contractors norm)

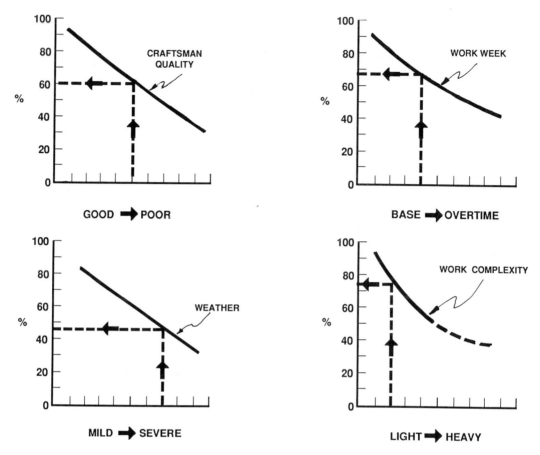

Figure 3 Productivity factors.

Materials management is a very important construction activity for international work. All material activities within the country are managed by the resident manager at the site. Local purchases, customs, in-country logistics, warehousing, and inspection certification form the nucleus of materials management. The tracking of materials in transit reflects on the long range planning programs. Traditionally, specific detailed work planning is done when the specific materials and equipment are on site and identified. Obviously, with such project impact, the materials management requires top consideration.

Work-Phase Relationships

A time relationship exists between engineering and construction on all projects. Each component (engineering and construction) has its own relationship factors and the entire project reflects the combined effects of the project components. This work-phase relationship between engineering and construction is most important for international work. The type of contract covering the work has a marked impact upon the work-phase relationship. There are always exceptions for individual projects with their specific activities, so be aware that the stated relationships are of a general nature.

It is desirable that a good filing program for work-phase relations be maintained for past projects, and the project size, complexity, type of contract, and work plan noted.

Figure 4 shows progress curves developed for engineering and construction of an international project. The purchasing commitment curve is superimposed. The basis for the data is a reimbursable-type contract when there has been little preproject activity. Where there has been appreciable preproject activity, the phase progress curves can be established by referencing the equivalent progress of engineering at the start of work. The production phases of work are projected to occur between the 20% and 85% progress points for both engineering and construction. Monthly progress rates of 5 to 7% per month for engineering and 4 to 6% for construction represent a good planning average for a major international project. A domestic project would have slightly higher progress rates. The buildup and closedown periods of work (i.e., from 0 to 20% and from 85% to 100% progress) will likely average out at a rate of progress of about 3% per month.

The work-phase relationship between engineering and construction is identified by the time span between the 50% progress points of the two curves, the 85% engineering progress, and the start of construction. The 50% progress points time span is quite critical. A domestic project would have a span of 10-12 months. An equivalent international project would span 16-22 months, depending upon the influence of project factors such as fabrication and logistic activities. The 85% engineering point represents the milestone that calls for the release of data and arrival of materials and equipment to start and sustain the mechanical construction activity. The start of the construction activity should occur about the time that the engineering progress is in the 25-30% range.

The phase relationship of the 50% progress points can be checked by noting the time (expressed as a percent) of the project. Noting the need to adjust the start of work (based upon preproject accomplishments), these 50% progress points should fall in the 25-35% of total project time for engineering and 65-75% of total project time for construction.

After developing these types of curves, constant trending, allowing for changes, etc., should be maintained. These data will develop into suitable check points for the scheduled activities.

Project Planning and Controls

The concept of project planning and controls is the same for international projects as it is for domestic projects. It is more complex, contains more variables, and the impacts can be far greater. The degree of involvement by other contractors on international projects necessitates that the master plans be prepared and that the flowdown information be disseminated to the proper work components.

The concept of time-quality-money must recognize that for international projects the stakes are high. Snowballing potentials are great; a small error or delay can result in a tremendous impact on the international project.

It is imperative that the definition of work be fully presented to and understood by those who will perform the work. Thoroughness and exactness are vital. The initial work plans should be well prepared, not just a general summary of what we would like to see accomplished. Since these initial work plans and accompanying procedures provide the basis for the future project operations, it is essential that they are complete, concise, and accurate. Their preparation requires using the work breakdown structure for various identifiable project components. It is necessary to tie down who does what and when, and to tie down budgets of performance and costs along with computer-generated schedules. A word of caution here. There are times when the computer-generated text may lead to its ineffectiveness because of the abundance of data that must be analyzed. In other words, develop the data, but print and report only salient information. Schedulers can go back to the computer to ask for alternative plans and reports if the occasion merits it.

In project managing, a key observation is the recognition of realism in reports and data as well as the validity of reporting. It is not intended to question the accuracy of the report. Instead, it recalls past projects that issued reports and compared them

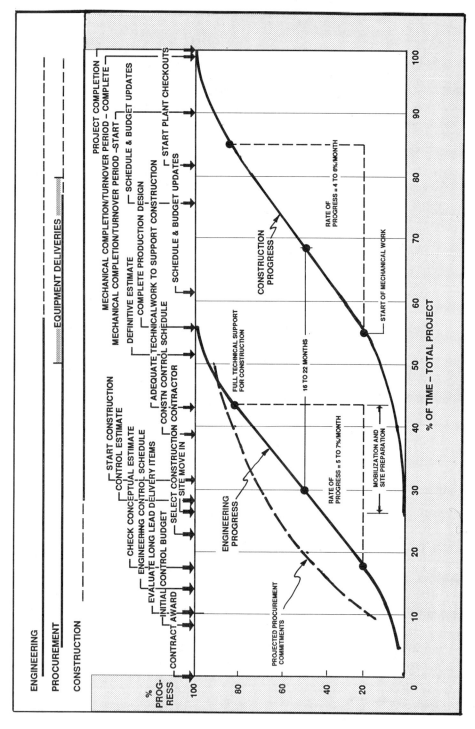

Figure 4 Work-phase relationship—engineering and construction.

to the final position. Based upon the information at hand, how accurate is it? This, along with computer projections, will give an accurate picture of where the project stands as well as where it is going. The work deviations caused by redo work, changes, or omitted items can be evaluated and their impacts recognized.

Risk analysis programs have been used in estimating to provide for an accuracy contingency. Various percentage factors are provided for the different items based upon an appraisal of firm data. The result is the contingency percentages. This same risk analysis can be applied to cost projections, work schedules, and work progress. The computer programs here reflect a significant tool in assisting in the management and control of project functions. Of course, true project control calls for data evaluation, the implementation of any remedial activities, and the follow-through to see that it was done.

In summary, international projects do not have the flexibility of domestic projects. Hence, work impacts are more severe and costly. This necessitates effective planning and controls.

A necessary part of the project planning activity is to establish detailed milestones and critical milestones of the project activities. These milestones can be tabulated via computer printouts with established dates showing the required timing of the milestone. The milestones can also be depicted in a schedule form tieing down scheduled accomplishments versus time and/or progress. Typical milestones for a scoping and proposal engineering effort are shown in Figure 5. Typical milestones for a released project are shown in Table 5.

The milestone accomplishments have been used as the basis of payment. The various milestones are weighted as to their value, and corresponding payments are made.

Schedulewise, the milestones reflect key markers of project activity enroute to successful completion. Their accomplishment per schedule serves as a reference relating to the status of the work and pinpoints where remedial action should be applied.

Another facet of project planning and control is manpower evaluation. Figure 6 shows the evaluation of the peak manpower to perform a project. The total manhours of one million and a schedule of 10 months have been established. The performance time to build up, peak, and reduce force is assumed. Arithmetically, the average number of men is calculated by dividing the manhours by the total number of hours. The illustration shows this as 625 men. By equating the area of the rectangle (representing average requirements) to the area of the trapezoid (representing the actual peak requirements) the peak manpower of 960 men is obtained. The manpower buildup, peak, and reduction can be programmed for each craft or unit component. The resultant manhour requirement is obtained by vectorial addition.

Communications

Communications is a key element for international projects. This refers to the spoken word as well as to written documentations, plans, and drawings. Most projects use the English language as the primary language for communicating. This is carried out at the senior supervisory level. Below that, the languages of communication become diversified. Contractual language may revert back to the country's native tongue. Many misunderstandings and costly activities can result from the communications gap.

Although the saying "It loses something in its translation" tells the story, it is necessary to use translators and other means to insure that proper communications are achieved. Many times, meetings can become quite tedious as translations and explanations are carried out. Also there are times when literal translations only confuse the issue. There is no immediate remedy; however, computer language translation programs can help to transcend the language barrier of communications.

Part of the communication concept is to ensure that communications are carried out properly and that information and data are issued to appropriate project personnel in a timely fashion. Oral discussions involving interpretations, criteria, decisions, and so on require documentation. The use of project notes identifies the discussion

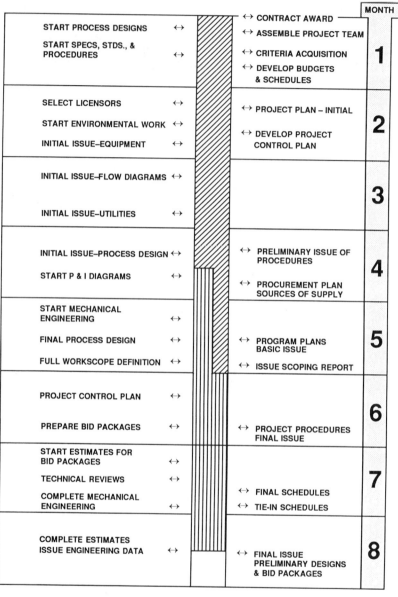

Figure 5 Milestone summary—scoping and proposal engineering.

Table 5 Milestone Summary—Released Project

Phase I work Preliminary	Phase II work Engineering	Phase III work Construction	Phase IV work Start-up
Project release	Long-lead equipment	Implement construction plan	Implement operations plan
Data acquisition	Implement organization	Contractor selection	Develop operative manuals
Product slate	Start engineering	Site move in	Start operator training
Process configuration	Implement budgets/schedules	Initial site activities	Order supplies/chemicals
Plans/schedules	Issue procedures	Initial infrastructure	Establish maintenance plan
Procedures	Initial infrastructure	Start site preparation	Start plant checkouts
Operation plans	Establish site team	Implement budgets/schedules	Start commissioning
Project plans	Finalize sources of supply	Site improvement work	Plant start-up
Complete process	Order equipment/materials	Definitive estimate	Performance tests
Final design criteria	Complete equipment engrg.	20% construction status	Operation acceptance
Initial designs	Drawing release schedule	Start equipment erection	Follow-up
Complete environmental study	Start design models	Cost/schedule trending	
Complete plans	25% engineering status	50% construction status	
Complete scoping	Set up logistics	Update budgets/schedules	
Work scope definition	Update budgets/schedules	Start plant checkouts	
Bid specifications	Final operating plans	Start punchlist work	
Estimate and review	50% engineering status	85% construction status	
Request bids	Update budgets/schedules	Start mechanical completion	
Environmental acceptance	Start spare parts program	Plant turnovers	
Update estimate	85% engineering status	Plant completions	
Review bids	Develop operation manuals	Plant acceptance	
Award recommendations	Complete designs	Closeout	
	Start support engineering	Move off	
		Project completion	

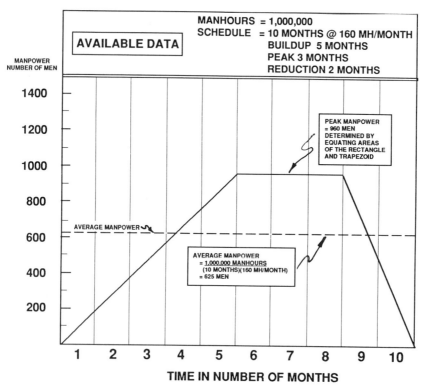

Figure 6 Peak manpower evaluation.

and also designates who is to take any necessary action. The distribution of data is important. It is necessary to advise the proper people of actions that may affect their work. A blanket issue is costly from the point of view of taking people's time to read and digest a message that is of no particular concern. Sometimes, even in cases of client involvement, the amount of information released can be too mcuh, resulting in tedious, time-consuming explanations.

An effective communication tool is the follow-up for requested information. Follow-ups should confirm that the communications have been received. So often we await information and after a follow-up check, find out that the request was never received. As a part of document control, all forms of written communication are identified by a code number and maintained in registered files that are periodically audited. When receipt of data is vital, an acknowledgment copy is included with the transmittal so that it can be returned to the sender. The use of electronic mail, via computers and satellite, facilitates communications between various engineering offices and with construction. While still quite costly, it is also possible to hold television conferences via satellite. These features allow for shorter lines of communications and immediate exchange of thoughts. The transmittal of reports and performance data is also instantaneous.

The periodic progress report is an important communication tool. In its preparation it causes the originator to thoroughly understand what is reported. It provides the client with a concise picture of the status of the work program and of recent accomplishments. These reports for international projects must be tempered to suit the specific client and country. For example, on a major project in Saudi Arabia, progress reports are published in both Arabic and English. Remember that progress reports are the principal means of informing the client's management of the work status. In effect, its presentation is indicative of the contractor's performance ability at this management level.

A typical communications interface diagram is shown in Figure 7. It covers a project having a managing contractor supervising two separate contractors performing engineering and procurement and a third contractor performing the construction work. There are five primary communication locations: the client, managing contractor, and the three contractors—representing ten communication channels. It is likely that the client and managing contractor will have representatives located in the offices of the contractor.

All client communication is between the client and managing contractor. As indicated, the managing contractor issues communications relating to direction, coordination, controls, and contractual matters to the three contractors. They, in turn, supply the managing contractor with reports and information relating to their work program. There is direct communication between the engineering contractors relating to technical and execution coordination. Also each engineering contractor maintains direct communication with the construction site relating to execution and reporting matters. A distribution list is established for each office to ensure that information is issued to the appropriate project personnel.

It should be noted that communications can be in the form of written communications, oral discussions, and personnel visitations.

The international project calls for communications to be direct and simple; and that extra effort be exerted to ensure that complete understandings are obtained.

Quality Control/Assurance

Discussions on procurement and logistics emphasize the need to obtain materials and equipment that comply with specifications and are in good condition. The primary means of accomplishing this is through quality control and assurance efforts. This applies to all phases of project operation, particularly fabrication of materials and equipment. The quality of work, if not maintained, can be reestablished only at the expense of time and money. International projects emphasize the impact of these control factors, and thereby call for extra effort in maintaining the quality of performance.

Quality control of engineering, construction, and general project operation is achieved by qualified personnel performing selective checking operations and audits. Naturally, construction work entails qualifications, inspections, and testing under the direct control of the contractor. Shop fabrication and material supply represent work performed by others and require inspection services to ensure that they comply with the established criteria.

International fabricators and suppliers may be licensors of well known U.S. firms, familiar with the applicable codes and regulations. Many have up-to-date fabrication facilities. Many client quality control criteria require that the work be inspected by licensed inspectors certified in applicable x-ray and nondestructive testing areas. As mentioned earlier, inspectors of this quality are in short supply and many worldwide inspections are performed by U.S. inspection personnel.

Although subcontract inspection is available worldwide, many clients decline to use this service because it lacks the proprietary atmosphere of contractor responsibility.

Performance of international vendors should be recertified by inspections on an annual basis or more frequently. An unknown vendor should be inspected prior to an award to ensure that his production and quality capabilities are acceptable.

On a special fabrication, a highly qualified manufacturer encountered embrittlement of weld metal on a thick wall (10 inches) high-pressure high-temperature vessel. Previous fabrication of similar vessels had been satisfactory. An exhaustive metallurgical-welding inspection audit was performed. In an effort to accelerate the work schedule, the number of weld passes was reduced by approximately 50% (from 140 to 75).

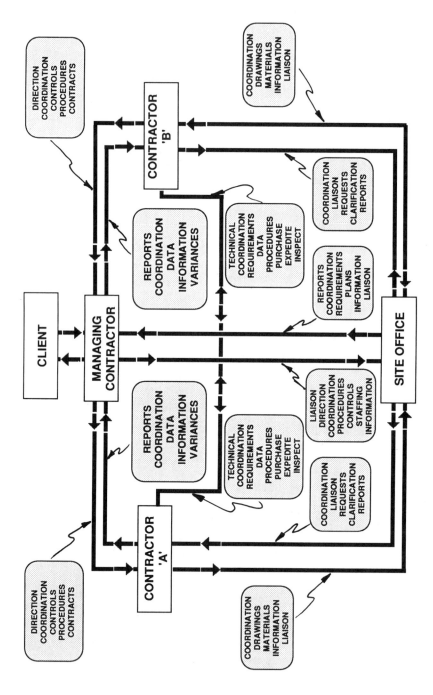

Figure 7 Project interface diagram.

The resultant weld pass deposit was too thick to be properly annealed by the next weld pass. By increasing the number of weld passes, thereby reducing the thickness of the weld pass deposit, a successful solution was achieved at no increase in cost. The harmonious working relationship between the fabricator and the inspection team of the contractor played a key role in this successful fabrication.

Another international fabricator overstated his capabilities and produced inferior quality products that required extensive repairs. The time delays and additional costs were excessive. Unfortunately, there was no preaward inspection and workmen certifications. Defective workmanship was not acknowledged, and ultimately the work was removed from the vendor shop and placed with a qualified and reliable firm.

It is important to know with whom you are dealing and make sure that performance is compatible with requirements.

Inspection of equipment upon arrival at destination represents a logistic milestone. This certifies the condition of materials and equipment which can be compared with the preshipping inspection. Lack of this arrival inspection when materials are received at the site leads to unnecessary activities of repair and assignment of costs.

Project Personnel Relations

International projects call for the assignment of selective key personnel to the site. These personnel fall into the following classifications:

> Management staff
> Supervisors
> Technical engineers
> Planning and scheduling engineers
> Cost engineers
> Procurement staff
> Subcontractor administrators
> Financial manager

These positions may be filled by personnel from around the world. As a result, it is necessary to establish definite standards outlining the working and living conditions for the site. This is handled by the personnel department of most companies. Since personnel activities have an impact on the project effort, it is necessary for project management to become involved with establishing policies on overseas benefits and with the selection of personnel to fill the available positions.

Prior to the selection of personnel, a complete knowledge of work site conditions and benefits must be known. All personnel assigned to the work site area should be treated fairly and in compliance with established policies. No exceptions. The decision as to whether a position is married (family) status or single status requires careful consideration. Once made, it must be adhered to at all times. It is expensive to relocate personnel to an overseas assignment. A complete brochure outlining the assignment terms and conditions should be issued to each prospective family. It is essential that these terms and conditions are fully understood by the employee and family and a work agreement executed. It is costly to have disgruntled employee families on an overseas project, and it is costly to effect replacements. Everyone must be aware of the site condition, especially employee families who have not lived overseas before.

Overseas projects require a longer work week and working conditions are associated with the unique characteristics of the work site. Generally, however, the expatriate worker recognizes that the work is similar to past international projects and accepts the new conditions. The major influence of the foreign assignment on the expatriate worker is his living environment. Family activities become of major importance as they relate to lifestyle. Complaints can be numerous and will show up in the working arena. Transportation status, living costs, taxes, schooling, recreation, close associations, and the exposure to the ethos and mores of the country can become in-surmountable for some people.

When these factors cannot be reconciled and adversely influence the performance of the employee, there are two choices to be considered: one is to live with the situation and attempt to resolve it; the other is to replace the employee and his family. Both choices are costly. Although there is a tendency to "live with the situation" and attempt resolution, it has been the experience of the author that replacement is the proper action. While it is expensive in tangible costs, it restores work harmony and provides for an overall more economical mode of performance.

As a part of the international work assignment, it is necessary to prepare a plan for emergencies and arrange for its implementation. Primarily this entails provisions for medical services, illnesses, and deaths. Existing medical facilities can be evaluated from site surveys and suitable arrangements must be made where greater capabilities are required. Also arrangements and procedures must be made to accommodate the death of any worker or their family members.

On one project in Saudi Arabia a young girl with a fractured arm went unattended for several days as she awaited medical aid. Also, the death of a worker in India created a hysterical situation when the body was cremated locally, because laws would not permit exporting the corpse.

Throughout the work site construction program, visits are made by various project team members from the engineering offices. While at the site, they too must comply with established procedures and protocol. They will remain on the home office payroll and generally have their salaries adjusted to correspond with the work schedules. The arrangement for temporary assignments of short duration should follow the corporate policies of the companies involved.

In summary, expatriate workers are expensive. The trend is to minimize their requirement to select key personnel and complete the roster from local workers or those from other international countries where working costs are lower. The selection of people to do the work is most critical. Their selection also includes the capability and ability of their families to conform to the appropriate lifestyle.

Infrastructure

What facilities are available and how can they be used? These are key questions to be answered and considered when preparing the project execution plan. Other questions that arise are: What other facilities are needed? Should they be temporary or permanent in nature?

If the work site is located in an existing community, it is likely that all of the infrastructure facilities (industrial, commercial, and residential) can be provided through existing facilities. Fabricating shops and support activities, along with housing and commercial facilities, are available. However, when the work site is located in a sparsely populated area, the availability of infrastructure facilities is another matter. Such facilities may be available from communities in the surrounding areas. It is not uncommon to have a work site location 50 miles or more away from some of the industrial, commercial, and residential infrastructure facilities.

The industrial facilities represent small fabricating shops, pipe fabrication, rebar bending and fabrication, concrete batch plant (normally located at the worksite), equipment servicing facilities, preassembly work areas, storage facilities, etc. These facilities are established for a single project and are of a temporary nature. If there is other construction going on in the area, it is common for much of the industrial infrastructure facilities to serve all projects. Cooperation and effective scheduling are necessary for each project to maintain its activities.

The residential infrastructure facilities may consist of a complete living complex with its own stores and community facilities such as medical, recreational, postal, religious, banking, fire, security, and limited schooling. The business offices relating to the project may also be included. These types of facilities can be provided, in total, by international firms who specialize in these services. A layout of the compound is prepared; residences established for families and living quarters provided for single workers. Sometimes living facilities for the single worker are located separately and nearer to the site area. In most cases, worker transportation is provided by buses. On major projects involving several prime managing contractors, the owner/operator, or the contractors involved may develop the project commercial and residential infrastructure as a joint activity.

Figure 8 identifies the various infrastructure support facilities. Six classifications are presented and specific infrastructure facilities are associated with each classification. Each contractor working on the international project must identify the infrastructure facilities that are applicable to serve his needs. There may be common facilities involving other contractors or segregated facilities to serve his specific needs. On major projects the administration of the work site infrastructure facilities requires the full attention of designated construction management.

Prior to initiating the plans for the infrastructure facilities, it is necessary to decide whether it will be temporary or become a part of the permanent community and industry. Invariably, temporary infrastructure is left to become a part of the permanent facility. By recognizing this situation in the development stages, it can be arranged so that the temporary and permanent facilities are in harmony.

If the work site and community are located in a remote area, it is necessary to provide suitable facilities for all personnel, including permanently assigned operators, to ensure their continuity of service.

Contractor Associations

Large domestic and international projects require several major contractors to work in concert. Such domestic projects employ project work agreements to define the working association and activities that will enable each contractor to execute his work program as planned. The international project is the same; however, there appears to be an even higher degree of cooperation offered. There is a fellowship that provides for the axiom "you help me and I'll help you."

When starting out on an assignment in Germany, a new contractor was entertained by representatives of five competing firms. Each representative offered advice as to how the business at hand was conducted. Visits to working sites followed. Obviously the new contractor was able to benefit greatly from the advice he received. The area of competitiveness remains, but the atmosphere of "let's help each other" prevails.

The international project entails living facilities as well as work plans. While each contractor provides his own facilities, there are common facilities that can be enjoyed. These follow primarily along the commercial infrastructure. It allows for a greater field of diversity among the families as well as the workers.

The principal association activities among contractors who are working in the same general area are the following:

Work agreements and regulations
Planning meetings
Coordination meetings
Training and safety programs
Common major construction equipment
Common infrastructure facilities
Common recreational facilities
Emergency assistance
Spirit of cooperativeness
Acceptance of contractors position

Each contractor must contribute toward these association activities. Their joint participation strengthens the effectiveness of the various work programs and also the international living conditions.

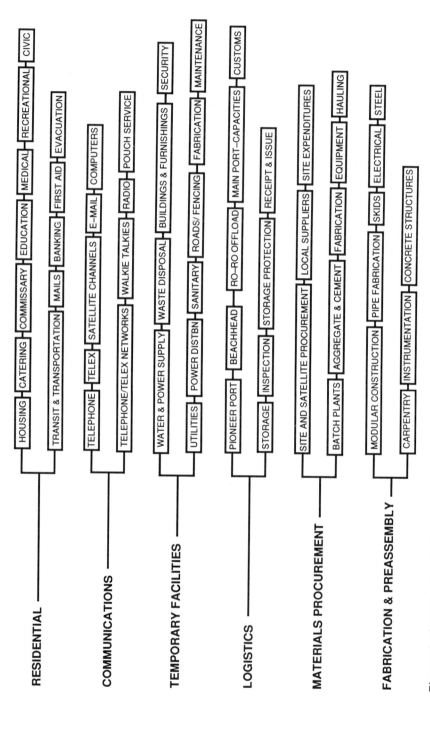

Figure 8   Construction infrastructure support.

The relationship of smaller contractor workers follows the same reasoning. They may be quartered in separate camps. Likely they will use their own messing facilities, but will use common industrial and recreational facilities.

The adage "To make a friend is to be one" holds true for the international project contractors. These relationships are beneficial to all concerned.

Work Assignments

Essentially all of the discussions presented in this chapter relate to the work tasks and the assignment of work. At the outset of a project, the owner/operator is charged with assigning the work and providing the bases for subsequent work assignments. Contractors are aware of the potential work assignments. In efforts to form the strongest team, several contractors may agree to joint venture to perform the work. This provides for more talented and experienced personnel to participate on the project.

With mega projects the work definition and preliminary engineering provide the basis of preparing inquiries for specific plant components, and selecting or assigning the production work to the most qualified teams. Competitive assessments are made as a part of the selection process to ensure that cost perspectives are considered. Along with the performance capabilities, there may be need to consider financial assistance.

The work assignment plan is an integral part of the project execution plan. The selected participants are called upon to develop their work plans for the components of work that have been placed under their control.

A typical work assignment of a mega project is shown in a functional organization form in Figure 9. A managing contractor is in charge of a project that entails offshore facilities and onshore facilities. The division of work is based upon using selected expertise for the various components of the work. Each selected contractor has full responsibility for his work from engineering through purchasing and construction to operations.

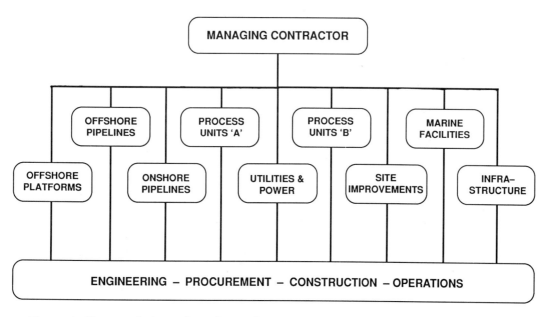

Figure 9 Mega project—work assignments.

Representatives of the managing contractor will be assigned to coordinate the work activities of the selected contractors to ensure that all of the project activities are proceeding according to the overall work plan.

From the managing contractor's point of view, the project organization serves to delineate the work assignments and provides the basis for coordinating the work program. Lines of communication are formed to allow the individual contractors the freedom to carry out their activities under the surveillance and guidance of the managing contractor. The work performed in project offices will utilize the full resources of the participating firms under optimum conditions. This is geared to time schedules, budgets, and work quality.

Project Plan and Work Program

All projects require the early preparation of a project execution plan. Obviously, the plan is based upon the available information including site observations, projected regulations, and previous experiences. The initial issue of the plan provides for the basic operating decisions. The execution plan is updated as additional information is obtained.

The purpose of the plan is to present the planned events and to tie down critical milestones and work accomplishments. Very likely the work plan will reveal areas of potential conflicts. Here alternative measures can be evaluated and selections made. The plan should present how various project disciplines propose to do their work. The primary components of the plan are as follows:

    Work scope definition
    Identification of regulations
    Summary of operations
    Project organizations
    Work assignments
    Contractor associations
    Project coordination procedures
    Basic design standards and specifications
    Schedules and work breakdown structures
    Work plans (by work phases)
        Summary
        Engineering
        Procurement
        Construction
        Operations
        Budgets and costs
        Key position descriptions
        Key personnel
        Reporting criteria
        Closeout procedures

The international aspect of the work will have an impact on all of the components of the work plan. There are many factors that influence the work program. Each must be recognized and considered fully in the development of the plan and also in the execution of the work. Assumptions and approximations must be replaced by investigations and identified references. The factual data should reflect a more streamlined work performance, thereby reducing costs. The analogy "an ounce of prevention is worth a pound of cure" holds true for having a proper work program.

SUMMARY

International projects essentially use the same basic principles that are employed for domestic projects; however, many new factors must be considered. Each project develops and retains its identity, which calls for the recognition of the various considerations presented herein. They are important and represent a vital part of the work program. Emphasis should be placed upon empathy. It is most important that an international project be viewed from an international position, especially that of the host country.

The actions and reactions of activities of international projects have great intensities. It is vital that experienced personnel be utilized and that work plans be developed and executed in the international atmosphere. The factors relating to time, quality, and moneys become highly visible.

The reward of a successfully executed international project comes from the recognition of the worldwide efforts performed in a harmonious fashion toward the accomplishment of established goals.

4

Staffing the International Project

DAVID G. TURNER, JR.* *Brown and Root Inc., Houston, Texas*

A project may be referred to as an international project when a large portion of the effort must be expended in a country other than the usual place of assignment for the project manager.

The calibre of the project staff is an early indicator of project success or failure for any project; for international projects the consideration is critical. The project manager must actively participate in selection of the staff and subsequent maintenance and personnel administration.

When an employee is relocated to a foreign country he generally suffers a degree of actual or imagined inconvenience. The negatives: absence from home, family, friends; personal hardships and personal risks; concern over loss of career opportunities while away from the home office. There are positives: increased job responsibilities; world travel; additional income.

The intent in staffing an international project is to provide equitable compensation to the employee to offset real personal and financial disparities during the assignment.

NOMENCLATURE

A definition of principal terms used throughout this text is appropriate.

Contracting Office. This is the home office where the work award was made, located in a country other than the one where a major portion of the work will be done. The project manager reports to the management of the contracting office.

Point of Origin. The city where an employee has his permanent home.

Jobsite. The location of the work in the other country. It may be a subsidiary project office doing design work or the field construction site.

Contracting Office Employee. An employee transferred to the job site from the contracting office.

Expatriate Employee. Any employee who is a national of a country other than the job site country.

Local Hire. An employee who is a national of the job site country or a resident of that country with proper working papers.

---

*
Present affiliation: Turner-Eatherton Incorporated, Houston, Texas

Third Country Nationals. Employees who are nationals of countries other than the contracting office country or the job site country, contracted to work at the job site.

BASIC DATA REQUIRED TO PREPARE THE STAFFING PLAN

The first step preparatory to staff planning is the comprehensive site survey for the total project. Data from this survey is used to develop the initial staffing plan. And, the plan is further refined during the proposal effort. Upon job release the first phase staff is mobilized, and, thereafter, there is a steady build-up to the project peak, followed by a long, gradual reduction to project completion.

Throughout the life cycle of an international project turnover is a constant and serious problem. There is no easy solution to this problem, which has devastated many a jobsite, but a good initial plan, sound employee relations practices, and a keen awareness of employee issues on the part of the project manager will contribute significantly to a healthy and productive job site atmosphere.

Let's look at the information that we expect to obtain from the site survey to assist us in the development of a staffing plan and site-specific personnel practices.

Restrictions on use of expatriate personnel.

Requirements for work permits.

Use of local employees: mandatory, encouraged, optional, forbidden; technical, administrative, skilled labor, unskilled labor.

Area contracting and subcontracting practices, capabilities, availability.

Immigration regulations, including family work restrictions.

Forecasts of local labor availability by crafts, current and anticipated based on projected area workload at time of project release.

Projected labor productivity, labor relations history, recent historical data, absenteeism rates.

Labor wage rates: union agreements, if applicable, with expiration dates by craft; otherwise, area practices.

Nonmanual salary scale. Complete salary survey to determine levels for expatriates and local hires; important to note that out-of-scale salary levels on one job can have serious areawide repercussions.

Historical and projected data on inflation and currency stability.

Availability of housing, schools, food, transportation, public services.

Tax provisions in the host country must be researched; use reputable local legal sources, and talk to qualified representatives of other companies in the area.

Local laws regarding movement, dress, and currency restrictions.

Criteria for single versus married status for staff.

Communication services available in the area: local and international facilities.

Climatic data including relevant individual and family needs: natives, expatriates.

Normal allowances for living costs, hardship allowances, any other considerations exercised by similar firms active in the area.

Legal and/or contractual benefits required to be paid to employees including but not limited to the following: provisions for (a) overtime premiums for work in excess of normal work week, (b) holiday work, (c) job shutdown on normal workday, (d) absent from work, and the like: travel time and travel allowances, bussing practices; height premiums for work above normal working elevations; paid sick leave, medical examinations, hospitalization, laboratory and pharmacy services, extended medical care for the family, prenatal and postnatal care, paid leaves for pregnancy; company subsidized lunches; housing or lodging allowances in lieu of housing; clothing allowances; leaves for marriage, death of relative, employee's wife giving birth.

Bonus and other incentive programs, severance and termination payments including conditions and notification, longevity payments.
Scholarships for employees and their children.

Many sources will normally be available in the host country to assist in data collection for the site survey. There are several organizations in the United States that can provide assistance for site survey planning (Organization of Resource Counselers, National Foreign Trade Council, Association of International Resources).

THE STAFFING PLAN

A first-pass analysis should be made by the project or appropriate discipline staff prior to the site survey to help orient the data collection effort. When the returns from the site survey are in, a good quality working draft can be prepared to serve as a basis for preliminary commercial planning (conceptual estimates, proposal initiation, and so forth).

An organization chart should be prepared showing all positions to be filled with start dates and assignment durations for each job title/classification. A determination is then made as to the most probable source for each principal personnel category. Normal sources include the temporary assignment of contracting office personnel, hiring of expatriate personnel, hiring of local employees, contracting for third country nationals.

We are then in a position to recommend a definitive compensation and benefits policy—a total personnel policy—for each type of employee.

PROJECT RELEASE

The staffing plan is further refined during the estimating and proposal period. The final plan, submitted with the proposal, should be totally responsive to the needs of the project and the RFP. The successful contractor is now at the point of project release; many diverse and parallel activities are initiated, including staffing.

The assignment of people to a project outside of their native country is most complex. It should not be attempted without a clearcut understanding of all terms and conditions between employer and employee. Experience has shown that the best vehicle to achieve a clearcut understanding is the Employee Assignment Agreement.

Recruitment will now start in earnest. Although project-specific needs cover a wide range of variables, principal categories are normally as follows: management, professional, technical, administrative (contracting office employees, third country nationals, and local hires, with the local content ranging from very low to moderate); skilled craftsmen (frequently a high ratio of third country nationals); laborers (local hires and major labor contracts with third country firms). The makeup of the skilled craftsmen and labor categories is determined by the level of industrial development in the host country.

The Employee Assignment Agreement is the contractual commitment between employer and employee most commonly used for the basic expatriate staff and expatriate craftsmen, and will be discussed in detail in this text. Agreements with local hires, both manual and nonmanual, have to be developed in compliance with the laws and regulations of the host country. Agreements with third country nationals, other than the basic staff, vary widely with the method of recruitment; the prime contractor might recruit a pipefitter team directly from Colombia, or contract with a firm from the Philippines for a totally self-supported labor pool.

Employee Assignment Agreement

Employee Assignment Agreements are normally required of all employees based at the job site for extended periods, referred to as extended assignments. For short-term assignments, normally up to 3 months or an agreed-to period, standard company travel policy governs. The treatment is the same as a business trip: expenses are reimbursed; the employee remains on his regular payroll at base salary.

The agreements will differ depending upon the origin of the employee, the level of the job, and individual considerations. Radically different conditions can be detrimental to morale: consistency should be stressed in the negotiation of expatriate assignment conditions. Portions of the agreement, as applicable, and all uniform job site practices, should be included in the inquiry documents for subcontracted labor.

The following is a check list of items to be included in the agreement.

Type of Assignment. Brief explanation of the scope of the project and a general description of the duties with the position title.

Job Description. Detailed specification: the work to be done, job classification, responsibilities, authority, reporting relationships.

Family/Single Status. A clear statement is required. If there is a possibility of a change from single to family status after an initial period, this should be stated to minimize any future misunderstanding.

Working Hours. Frequently working hours will be longer than the normal work week. A base salary adjustment may be granted to compensate for anticipated extended work weeks.

Duration of Contract. State the expected duration. Include terms and conditions for assignment extension.

Compensation. Rate and type of currency. Payment may be split between currency of the job site country and the country of residency or citizenship. Stipulate the pay period and the procedure for depositing nonlocal payments in the employee's bank account.

Overtime Provisions. If overtime is to be paid, all related policy should be stated.

Benefits. Be absolutely clear: what's in, what's out, examples, sample computations. Point out normal benefits that will be eliminated during the assignment. As an example, unemployment insurance and disability coverage may be eliminated. Typical items: legal requirements (host country, home country); status of company retirement and savings plans; status of medical, dental, hospitalization plans; social security; and so forth.

Home Maintenance Allowances. If the cost of maintaining an owned or leased house during the period of foreign residency is offered as part of the total package, the terms should be outlined.

Living Accommodations and Allowances. If a consideration, there are several approaches: company housing, private housing, cash in lieu of housing. The partial or full payment of utilities, furniture, household effects, supplies, etc., and the items to be provided by the employee have to be clarified.

Hardship Allowance. An allowance to compensate for inconvenience, risk, and the like, usually expressed as a percentage of salary.

Visa Requirements. Define the visa and work permit requirements. Assistance to the employee and the employee's family is normally provided by personnel and traffic departments. Costs are for the project account.

Travel Conditions. The project travel policy covering the type of air passage for the employee and accompanying family members should be stated.

Local Transportation. Specify mode of local transportation: company car, company car pool, employee responsibility. Cover arrangements, if any, for family members.

Shipment of Household and Personal Effects. Define the policy for transporting these items, and job-related personal files.

Temporary Quarters at Jobsite. When the employee first arrives at the job site, hotel or guest house accommodations may be supplied for a period of time during the settling-in period prior to the move to permanent quarters.

Schooling. Provisions for schooling, either at the job site or elsewhere are stipulated. Alternatively, cash allowances may be offered; if so, it is necessary to prepare itemized inclusion and exclusion lists.

Medical Attention. Several approaches, depending on project policy and job site location: company doctors and facilities; company direct payments; insurance policies, partially or totally funded by the company. Cover transportation policy when proper medical attention is deemed to be unavailable locally. If family care is different than employee care, state differentiation.

Emergency Leaves. Cover policy in the event of the death of a resident family member, serious illness or death of an immediate family member outside the job site country, or other emergencies. Wide latitude should be given to the project manager or his delegate to resolve issues of this type since there will always be events not covered by the agreement.

Vacation. A far more complex issue than for a domestic site. Define the method of accrual, timing, and transportation costs to be paid, if any. For a lengthy project, transportation is normally furnished back to the contracting office country or the point of origin. Equivalent fare may be paid to an alternative location, if stated in the agreement.

Communication Policy. Long distance telephone calls to home; define the amount to be absorbed by the project, with the remainder charged to the employee.

R&R Leaves. Evaluate the advantages of short interim vacations for highly stressful projects: extended long work weeks, heavy schedule pressure, civil unrest in the job site vicinity, etc. Cover the subject as appropriate in the agreement, but give the project manager freedom to implement in a judicious manner.

Taxes and Tax Equalization Programs. This is one of the most confusing and difficult areas of international work. General requirements, let alone detailed requirements, aren't usually understood by the employee. Clear displays with numerous examples should be prepared, with an open door to the qualified company tax people.

Completion. By virtue of acceptance of the assignment, the employee contracts to complete the period of the assignment. Historically, there has been a high incidence of turnover on international assignments. Contractual agreements should include penalties for failure to complete the assignment, including transportation of employee, family, and household goods to the point of origin. Funds, referred to as holdback, may be retained by the project, payable upon completion of the assignment. Bonus payments, if a consideration, are payable only under the conditions of the bonus program.

Things to Look for in the Expatriate Employee

More than any other single trait, the international project requires people who can work well with others. Turnover, voluntary and involuntary, is caused more by poor interpersonal relationships than by deficiencies in technical skills. On an international project, the employees not only have to work closely with one another at the workplace, they and their families will live in close proximity. Character defects, unimportant in a domestic assignment, may become intolerable in the close confines present on an international assignment.

The key people on the project should be picked from the permanent staff of the company. The cost of relocation is high, but the cost of replacement is higher. Select people with excellent credentials, known to perform well in an independent mode. Prior successful international experience is invaluable, especially when that experience has been in the same country.

Current employees should be given preference for principal staff assignments. If suitable candidates aren't available, the next source should be former employees whose capabilities, performance records, character, and experience are well known. Then seek outside people recommended by key staff personnel.

Normal recruiting procedures should be followed if the preceding efforts are unsuccessful. These would include: review of current resume files; advertisements in trade journals and newspapers; search firm referrals; word of mouth.

A thorough reference check should be made on anyone considered for an international project covering their work history, prior overseas experience, interpersonal relations, family situation, and an evaluation of their ability to adjust to the specific project conditions.

It is essential that the candidates for these assignments be contacted early, and that the scope of the proposed job, the duration, and all pertinent information be disclosed. It is imperative, when staffing an international project, to prepare a first-class orientation program, one that provides consistent information to the prospective team members. Some companies have successfully used video tapes to orient candidates to conditions at the job site. The candidates should have the opportunity to ask questions at the end of the presentation. Additionally, there are firms that specialize in providing orientation for international employees. These firms have a good track record in the indoctrination of people assigned to areas where special sensitivity is required.

The agreement should be discussed at length and all of its provisions explained in detail. There should be open dialogue about what the employee may expect upon completion of the assignment. This applies to all staff employees, permanent and project-hired.

The candidates should make a tentative commitment to accept the position, or reject the position, at the initial interview or shortly thereafter, and prior to a firm offer from the company. The project manager should interview all screened candidates and make all final selection decisions.

EMPLOYEE RELATIONS DURING EXECUTION

The requirements for personnel assistance to the expatriate employees will vary with the location and size of the project. No matter how small the project, someone must be designated to attend to the local needs of the employees; this may well fall upon the project manager.

There is a need for home-base coordination for employees who have accepted a transfer to the job site. Someone in the home office must be responsible for maintenance of continuing personnel activities: salary reviews, performance appraisals, insurance coverage, investment and retirement programs, service awards, mail, and other related functions. It's also important that temporarily assigned employees neither feel forgotten nor lose touch with the home base during their absence. This bond is an important morale booster for the relocated employee. The project manager plays an important role in reassuring the transferred employee of company interest and commitment to his career development.

Pressures From Many Directions

There are many pressures on the expatriate employee and his family.

Work Pressures. Frequently the employee will feel isolated and resentful. Judgments often have to be made with less than normal support. The work habits of expatriates and third-country nationals will be foreign to many members of the team, and will require team and individual attitude adjustments. Language barriers and communication problems are difficult. More than normal personnel administration is required to minimize disruptive and counterproductive influences.

Family Pressures. Married employees assigned on single status come under special pressures. Minor worries can grow into major concerns. The lack of frequent communication and mail delays create serious problems for many employees.

Also, there are problems for married employees whose wives and children accompany them. Educational systems are different. Where local schooling isn't available, children have to be sent away to school, sometimes considerable distances. The employee's wife may be unhappy because of restrictions, unfamiliar food, a total change in lifestyle. Shopping may be inconvenient or facilities may be limited. Accustomed recreational facilities may be absent. And, there is always the normal worry about family members and friends back home.

Cultural Shock. The culture, climate, and environment of the host country will be enormously different than home. Difficulties encountered in the new location will be magnified, as difficulties back home are minimized or forgotten. Conversely, the opportunities to broaden the family horizons tend to be overlooked, while brooding over the good things back home.

Personnel administration at the job site is necessary to counsel the staff that these pressures are always present and to put them into proper perspective when they occur.

The continuous communication of project plans to the staff is a beneficial counter to depression caused by the aforementioned pressures. A well-planned project newsletter, with family news as well as project news, is a positive antidote. Changes to personal plans for job-related reasons deeply involve not only the employee and the employee's family, but the entire expatriate community.

Staff Turnover

This is a situation exacerbated by low morale. On an international job, loss of a key employee can severely upset the project. It is difficult to plan adequately for staff turnover. The project manager should maintain an active and well-prepared succession plan to replace key employees who resign or otherwise become inoperative.

PROJECT COMPLETION

The staffing responsibilities for a project continue until mechanical and contractual acceptance, completion of punch lists, resolution of supplier and subcontractor claims, and termination or reassignment of all personnel. Personnel administration activities at the end of the project are simplified by advance planning and discussions of the plan with the staff. The project manager has an obligation to the staff to see that promises made are kept. The project manager also must protect his company against excessive or unwarranted interpretations made by the staff. There will be problems: anticipate them, keep communication channels open.

SUMMARY

The good project manager participates in the staffing activities on any project. This involvement is mandatory on international projects. Staffing and personnel administration are keys to project success, on the current project, and, through the establishment of his reputation with his superiors, peers, and subordinates, on all future endeavors.

5

Social Aspects of Project Management in Developing Countries

VIRGINIA QUINN   *Freelance Writer, Consultant, Washington, D.C.*

The social relationships between management, staff, and client are of great significance for an international company. In a domestic situation, when nationality is shared, the company manager may choose to limit involvement with a client to business. Apart from the annual Christmas party, the manager may also choose to remain socially aloof from the staff, and spouses and families are not necessarily introduced.

On the overseas job, and particularly in developing countries, the project manager heads a conspicuous and circumstantially interdependent group. The client and local partner are much more likely to exert themselves as hosts and to show they prefer closer contact. The project manager's spouse will almost certainly be acquainted with the expatriate staff, and probably will be required to entertain or counsel their families. Family members find friends, at least initially, within the company.

Wherever the pressures of beginning a project's first phase coincide with resettling in a foreign environment, the project manager's functions are magnified. The relationships rapidly forming among the staff and their families often affect performance and need attention. One of the most important responsibilities of the management role is to establish an early and mutually satisfactory personal alliance with the client, and sometimes with the client's family and associates.

CULTURAL DIFFERENCES

Many Westerners expect that deep down inside all human beings have the same emotional and physical responses to external stimulae. Time and again people say, when speaking of the common folk of another culture, "They get hungry just like me, they love their children and want the best for them just like me, and are afraid of dying just like me. Our only difference is in how we express these things."

This is not true. Differences are multiple and profound, and some will remain eternally incomprehensible to an outsider. For instance, an estimated 200,000 Iranians have perished in the battle with Iraq, many of them untrained farmers or children. Observers report that ecstatic parents push young boys forward in the belief that death in a Holy War will take them directly to Paradise. These common folk do not want the best for their children "just like me."

Even the requirement for food, the basic way we have learned to feel hunger, is not consistent. The ascetic, or indoctrinated, Vietnamese footsoldier's monthly food supply could be carried in a backpack; the American had to be resupplied every few days. Supplementary foraging and relative size did not account for the disproportionate rate of consumption.

We are prone to take the fundamental traditions and habits of our society so much for granted that our views seem inevitable. The commonplace in other lands sounds bizarre. The arranged marriage system retained in modern India, Japan, and Burma is too utterly strange to be discussed rationally with my neighbors. Foisting a mate I decide is best for her on my daughter would be considered intolerable abuse. We forget that the privileges and freedoms unquestioned in one society are controversial in others. Referring to a law written into China's 1978 Constitution, anthropologist Steven Mosher stated, "Beijing's birth control program will be exportably only to countries whose citizens have no inalienable rights vis-à-vis their government, (a precondition) rare elsewhere. . . ."

The professional who accepts an assignment abroad, without realizing that a culture in which he or she was not raised cannot be totally understood, will never be fully successful in the international arena. The project manager who feels secure in past experience, and comes armed with a list of strict business "do's and don'ts," cannot operate effectively in the Third World. Not only will these project managers be continually mystified by their partner's behavior and the client's rationale, neither client nor partner will be able to understand the reason for confusions.

FALLACIES

The main fallacy is in thinking that what works at home must eventually work anywhere. It is erroneous to promulgate the idea that the practices of one's own country are better, or morally superior, and should be imposed to improve the host country standards. A difficult concept for the American is the habit of frank and aggressive public debate—this just isn't done in the Third World.

Fortunately, the adage that "East is East and West is West and never the twain shall meet," is incomplete. Taken alone, as it generally is, the line indicates a dead end. Kipling's verse is more perceptive:

> And the end of the fight is a tombstone white
>   with the name of the late deceased,
> And the epitaph drear; A Fool lies here
>   who tried to hustle the East.

Both segments express Occidental frustration in dealing with the Orient yet apply universally. The project manager working within a different social system needs to add a phrase to the one-line quote, ". . . unless I am adaptable." On every continent, the expatriate company director should focus on the words "fight" and "fool" in the verse. Whether in Africa, South America, or Asia, a beginning is made by discarding the inflexible approach.

In picking Deng Xiaoping 1985 Man Of The Year, *Time Magazine* describes a leader "who is willing to bow and bend." According to the cover article, the concept of individualism has a negative connotation in Chinese society, but after collectivization lowered farm output to an alarming degree, Deng daringly led a reform movement to abolish communes. Leasing the land back to individuals has brought a phenomenal increase in productivity: "In a country . . . racked by periodic famines throughout four millenniums of recorded history, the average citizen has, finally, enough to eat." *Time* credits the turnaround to Deng's flexibility in his search for the solution to an ancient problem.

DIFFERENT CODES, UNFAMILIAR OR UNETHICAL

Differences in ASEAN* and U.S. business practices were discussed by Amaret Sila-on, Vice President of the Siam Cement Company, at a seminar in San Francisco in 1981. He stressed that while U.S. corporations are structured and divided into functional units to permit trained professionals to manage objectively, the extended family is still a powerful underpinning of companies in his region. Siam Cement, for example, has a dealer network for building materials which accounts for about $250 million of business a year. Half of the dealers are blood relatives and another quarter are related by marriage. The value of developing personal relationships in that area is inestimable, for businesses are not always consistently protected by law. A handshake, with the paternalistic owner, may be as binding as a letter of intent or a contract.

Mr. Amaret further pointed out that geographical neighbors are as different from each other as they are from far distant territories. No one is typical and it is a mistake to lump nations of the Third World by religion, ethnic group, per capita income, or general sensitivity to the West. At the same time, it is unwise to ignore such factors.

The key, again, is flexibility and the understanding that some aspects of every society will remain incomprehensible. That knowledge will prevent foolish or precipitous action in response to a partner or client who seems to be shady or tricky.

Misunderstandings frequently occur when the incorruptible foreigner refuses to negotiate with government officials who are following some acknowledged but unwritten financial procedure. U.S. companies have precise directives regarding irregular payments of any kind. The IRS would not consider unreceipted expenditures for services such as delivering the mail or getting a driving license to be deductible. The inability to understand foreign concepts of taxation has probably caused more social friction between Americans and their partners than any other single cultural difference.

A project manager for an engineering consultant imported a sizable amount of electronic equipment into a small African country. When he tried to clear the shipment from customs he was informed it was lost, but could probably be found if his local partner was given the task of clearing the goods. After conferring with his team of four other Westerners, he declared that he would not let this sort of thing get started, and continued to proceed through official channels.

The local partner soon complained he was suffering severe financial loss because he had 50 people standing by waiting for the equipment. The project manager told him the reason for the delay. The partner asked for a budget of about 10% of the value, and the responsibility for clearing the equipment through customs. The project manager refused.

The partner explained that this caused two difficulties. One, he had a lot of staff on the payroll who couldn't work without equipment. Two, the customs personnel would accuse him of cheating them out of their rightful income. The project manager was unmoved.

Since the partner was no more used to dealing with Westerners than the project manager was in working in a foreign culture, he attempted to apply pressure by stopping the cleaning of the office toilet rooms. He stopped supplying soap, towels, and toilet paper. The project manager and expatriate staff complained bitterly, and began keeping supplies in their desks.

The partner next installed a padlock on the outer door so that each employee wanting to use the facility would need to come to his office and ask for the key. The project manager and staff were outraged, and compelled to go home when nature called.

Following this softening-up process, the partner threw a dinner for the project manager and the staff. He invited his friends and colleagues and after an evening of eating and drinking again asked the project manager to be allowed to take over the clearing of the electronic goods. The project manager, in a spirit of cooperation, care-

---

fully explained to the group that this proposal was illegal. He said he would not endanger the reputation of the company he worked for by condoning an illegal act.

The local partner argued convincingly, "I have heard that it is necessary to tip service people in America. Isn't that the same as tipping the Customs to get your equipment?"

"Absolutely not. In America you tip after a service is provided and never—never—do we tip government officials."

"But I have heard," replied the partner, "that if you don't tip, you won't get any service next time. And in any case, tipping is not illegal here; we don't get arrested. It is our customary means for encouraging officials to do their jobs well."

The argument could not be resolved, the project collapsed, the Westerners departed, and the local partner went bankrupt. The project manager believed he had upheld the finest traditions of business and professional ethics. His company backed his decision and discontinued their involvement in overseas projects.

Although a larger company rarely reaches the point of withdrawing from the field over a single incident, the episode described above is essentially factual. Future project managers will doubless find themselves mired in equally contentious situations or, perhaps, in real danger of bodily harm. Today, the management position carries that possibility.

KIDNAPPING, TERRORISM, VIOLENCE

Location alone sometimes exposes the team to harm. If an apparently stable or strongly entrenched government falls, such as those in Iran or Haiti, the company may not have time or the means to bring isolated team members out. Irrigation experts supervising ongoing projects in the Jiroft Plain far south of Tehran were unable to communicate during the worst of the siege on the American Embassy. The very fact that they did not know what was happening in the capital or try to travel north protected them. For the moment, they were unwittingly safe where they were. Because of the project director's close relationship to previous government officials, now turned revolutionaries, the team was informed of the situation and managed to escape through Pakistan.

Unlike the nearly completed project which must terminate when hostilities start, an occasional new project fails because it has been prematurely conceived. An A.I.D.-funded technical assistance program for the National Planning Board of Lebanon was intended to give impetus to reconstruction, and got underway during the comparative calm of 1983. Personnel mobilized to Beirut by the consultant had to be evacuated twice in the first several months. The team financial specialist received a leg wound from shrapnel while departing but returned willingly with the group as soon as easing tensions allowed. After a final evacuation of family and team, the project director attempted to continue technical assistance from outside of Lebanon for a few months more. Explosive events then stopped the reconstructive planning entirely, but the surprising twist of this project was the psychological effect of location. The team seemed to be excited not only by the work but also by the dangerous situation in which they were working. They were not ready to leave the battle zone and it was difficult for the project director to remember his responsibility for their safety. A higher level of management recognized the problem and intervened.

Crisis management is a topic offered in university courses to executives and graduate students. Public relations firms contract to teach corporations how to cope with terrorist attacks. The U.S. Department of State emphasizes preparedness in a booklet, *Countering Terrorism*, which is quickly available to anyone requesting information. Though the State Department may unofficially advise, "Say a prayer," they do not take the matter lightly. Security suggestions to minimize the likelihood of terrorist strikes against the offices and homes of U.S. business representatives abroad are listed, as well as where to find aid in a foreign country.

The international community, including North American firms and employees, has been hard hit by kidnappings and extortion in South America. In Southeast Asia, a Danish highway engineer who had just discovered a serious breach in materials quality, was followed from the job site by the disgruntled contractor and shot in the face while driving back to town. However, the number of managers taken hostage or actually threatened physically does not compare with the countless controversies which deteriorate to petty squabbling in the multinational office and reduce staff efficiency. Beyond the office, a careless disregard for prevalent habits and mores may be construed as a deliberate slight.

CRITICAL DECISIONS: TABOO OR NOT TABOO

The business lunch is a worldwide institution, giving people of disparate backgrounds further opportunity to assess character and exchange ideas. In several Asian countries, the food is often followed by an invitation to join in an hour of relaxation at a massage parlor or communal steam bath with young ladies in attendance. An obvious problem arises for the foreigner who does not find participation morally comfortable, and has not had the foresight to indicate this view.

Few Americans would think of offering their Caterpillar client from Peoria a similar nonbusiness atmosphere to supplement business discussions. Fewer still are the Asian partners who would presume, without thought, that every foreigner will enjoy exotic postmeal activities. Extraordinary indeed are those who have not attempted to prevent confusion or offense. The Asian avoids loss of face and bad feelings by dropping hints before issuing the invitation; the unobservant recipient consents and becomes compromised. Once in the massage parlor, at the Geishing party, or hotel suite, retreat is a snub and the previous failure to listen has caused the partner or client to commit a social blunder.

An opposite dilemma, which could occur in the Middle East, results from a man seeking, however casually or innocently, the company of women. The manager working in an Arab nation must be very aware that errant social behavior is likely to have much more serious consequences than destroying client relations. Consciously or unconsciously breaking a social taboo, wherever the unacceptable has been defined according to Islamic law, can lead to legal prosecution or jail.

In parts of Latin America, the male counterpart is virtually forced to extend lunch or dinner with heavy drinking. Then, upon moving to an Arab country, he discovers that alcohol is banned and a disastrous quantity of tea substituted by the Moslem. Buddhist Thailand's staggering murder rate is largely due to crimes of passion, yet a state of superficial harmony is the achievement desired in the office. Face-to-face criticism is seen as the worst form of violence and "constructive" criticism, especially in public, is always destructive. As in Thailand, the outward show of respect is everywhere a rule. What seems like everyday good manners becomes a business imperative, and foreign companies are not immune. To resolve conflict, at the lowest level, the intelligent boss depends on the private chat and appeals with praise instead of embarrassing sarcasm.

THE FAMILY ROLE

When a project manager is accompanied abroad, family reactions to local conditions have a definite impact. To a lesser degree, because of lesser rank in the developing country office and thus in the community, the attitudes of the families of expatriate staff members can influence others in the multinational work force.

There is a saying among Westerners living and working abroad that a project manager is only as successful as his wife will allow him to be. Feminists do not bother to protest this expression because overseas management positions are nearly exclusively filled by men. The spouse, usually a woman, is either a positive element in his professional life or the chief undermining factor.

Most clients want to have some sort of social relationship with managers, and the client's wife is frequently eager to meet and entertain the incoming foreigner. The manager, in turn, enlists his wife to help him gain the client's confidence. Usually upon arriving, the manager's family will be welcomed and presented with gifts during their hotel stay, and will be included in the festive occasions of the local families before they are settled in a house of their own. Probably the manager's wife will enjoy the reception and the deference, be enormously interested in exploring with a guide, and reciprocate happily—especially at first.

But what if the wife cannot function in the strange or backward environment, is baffled by the sudden elevation of status, feels bored or besieged, hates the food, dislikes the client's wife, makes extravagant demands, or wants a return ticket home?

Everyone is bound to hear. Her servant will relate everything to the deputy manager's servant.

Foreign community enclaves are much like small towns. Even in a vast capital city, expatriate families are thrown together. Required to arrange their own entertainment, they mix interminably, and celebrate holidays as if they were ancestrally related. Warm friendships quickly cool and grow frigid. Horror stories are rife.

One wife needed a safe place to store a trunk of clothing while she spent several months out of the country. The local partner graciously agreed to have the trunk put in his office storeroom. Before leaving, the manager's wife decided she wanted a dress from the trunk. When she opened it and couldn't immediately pull out the dress, she angrily accused the partner of stealing. The scene took place in front of his staff. Later apologies, after the misplaced garment was found, were useless. Her strident behavior irretrievably damaged the manager's ability to work with the local partner, caused the partner great shame, and strained the working relationship between companies.

Such an event would not have been possible in the home country because the trunk would never have been stored in the office. In overseas locations, the company quite often takes the place of friends, neighbors, and family, and is expected to provide services that no employee or dependent would otherwise request.

On an agriculture extension project in another country, the staff shared a car which was to be used for business purposes. The project manager's wife had always had a company car at her disposal and felt cheated. To protest the unfair treatment, she commandeered the car early in the morning on the day the lending agency mission arrived in town to inspect the project, and kept it until late afternoon. Since the business car was the only vehicle available to them, the project manager, the lending agency mission, and the agriculture department officials were on foot.

They were not a sympathetic group. The company was obliged to replace the project manager, and was not invited by the government to propose on new projects. Years passed before the lending agency forgot and forgave.

Protective work laws generally keep the accompanying spouse from a rewarding job. Running the household can be a time-consuming and laborious task, but hardly compensates for the lack of contact, salary, and fulfillment to those accustomed to a career. Her husband travels to project sites, the home office, and other countries, but she may be unable to go with him because of the cost or immigration regulations. She may simply have to stay behind with the kids.

To the adventurous, such drawbacks do not matter, or are not allowed to overwhelm. The picture is not always drear. Women in remote mining camps study through correspondence courses. A wife isolated in Sulawesi, Indonesia, used the tour to earn her law degree. National universities and museums welcome foreigners willing to share talent or language. The perpetual student and the volunteer teacher are stimulated by the roving style of living. They, and the rare man who follows his wife to her overseas post, complement and support the project manager.

IT CAN BE DONE

Astrologically, aspect is the apparent position of one planet with respect to another. The social aspects of each country require similar examination in relation to the job. And throughout the developing world, these questions recur:

> Because the vocabulary of certain tropical countries does not include the word "No," should the visitor stop using it too?
>
> How does the project manager with no taste for certain kinds of consumption (alcohol, etc.) escape the client who insists that "real men" indulge together in such to excess?
>
> If we modify our behavior in an attempt to be courteous, or bend a principle to fit the surroundings, aren't we caving in?
>
> Do we really know what our responses mean to our clients and partners?

There are no simple answers. Reading a book about local customs helps, and can prevent breaking major taboos, but nothing written can cover the small individual crisis. Common sense and patience are easy enough to pronounce, but difficult to implement.

Paternalism, the compadre system, shifting ground rules, and cultural differences aside, the overall basic question is still, "Can I manage projects in foreign countries and maintain my own code of personal conduct?"

The answer is yes. Japanese businesses have operated with huge success in the United States, Europe, the Mideast and, against historical animosity, in other Asian nations. Though, as Gunnar Myrdal suggests in *Asian Drama*, Japanese companies may also have been the most willing to buy the competitive advantage, that surely is not the only reason. Every professional in the international arena respects two things: Quality of product or service, and hard work. A project manager will succeed if, in addition, he or she brings to the client and partners two traits: flexibility and sincerity. For then, "there is neither East nor West, border, nor breed, nor birth, . . . though they come from the ends of the earth."

XIV
COMMUNICATIONS

UNIT OVERVIEW

Communications—necessary or not? A simple question. We all say yes, then proceed, frequently, to do all in our power to abort communications, all the time feeling that we have communicated with precision, faultlessly. We don't consider with whom we're communicating: our objective—and we are dedicated to achievement by objectives—to "sell" that person; yet, we write to ourselves, the "objective" lost in a sea of prose. We think grammar is the essence of writing; it's not, the message is. Let's not be clumsy; we don't want the recipient to view us as a dolt. But the message is the thing, not the prose.

Then comes the stand-up presentation. First time, nervous, ill-prepared, the facts will speak, etc. Busto—sale lost. But was I selling? Never really crossed my mind. You are always selling! Selling yourself, your ideas, your group, your company. Why do you think there was a stand-up presentation in the first place? Someone, your supervisor, or others, had a purpose, and you were a principal. Next time I'll do better. Will you? Only if you devote the same amount of time and the same degree of enthusiasm to the presentation that you would devote to your daily technical and professional work, and consider the presentation to be just as important.

COMMUNICATING FOR DESIRED RESULTS

Effective communication is an essential element of a project: all good projects are blessed with good communications. People talk out problems, "for-the-record" letters aren't written, cost/benefit and tradeoff actions are initiated with a minimum, but appropriate, level of documentation, and so forth. If good communications don't advance a project, you can be absolutely certain that ineffective communications will retard it.

It is a pleasure to see the owner and contractor project teams work in harmony with a common purpose to solve problems until the project objectives are attained. How disagreeable it is to see hidden agendas, conflicting objectives, politics, witch hunts, and the like, destroy a project. Approximately 40% of your life each week, excluding sleep time, is spent at work. And when the job goes sour you fret the other 60% of the time. Why not make this major segment of your life enjoyable, rewarding. It won't always work, but no single factor will do more to turn things around than an improvement in communications within your environment.

There are many rules and much has been written about how to improve communications within the business world. Try this: With whom are you communicating; Why are you communicating; How will you communicate.

On the project level, straighten out a few things to give communication a chance to work. Settle, beyond a shadow of a doubt, or to the best of your ability within restraints imposed, the following on every project that you manage: scope, specifications, budget, schedule. Ascertain the nuances of politics, risk, and any other outside influence that can even remotely impinge on your commitment to do the best job for your company and the client.

WRITTEN COMMUNICATIONS

The project manager has to stop being too concerned with the traditional techniques of writing—what you learned in elementary school—and become more concerned with the instrument, the receiver, that will pick up the message—a very complex human mind.

It isn't the communication the writer thinks he's sending that counts. What will be acted upon is the message the reader thinks he received. Your meaning of words—the dictionary meaning of words—isn't important. The effects of the words are what the reader will be aware of.

Anyone who becomes a project manager doesn't need a course in writing to become an effective writer. He already knows more grammar than he should and gets preoccupied with more rules than exist. Be concerned about people and how to convey to them your needs so they will help you to do your job better.

A principal reason why we procrastinate and worry our way out of effective writing is our need to protect a delicate ego. We just can't make a mistake—this also, incidentally, is a fatal flaw in the field of project management, where a "good answer now" beats a "perfect answer later." Some learn to bear up under the humiliation of a mistake better than others. We call them "Top Project Managers."

THE STAND-UP PRESENTATION

When you stand up, face the client or the boss, and present a program, any impression left by a prior written document will be altered. One of four things will happen, two good, two bad: a good program will be enhanced; a poor program will be confirmed; a good program will be negated; a poor program will be salvaged. No status quo!

A presentation is a very special business animal. There is only one purpose: the selling of a concept or a program to a specific group. A presentation isn't a "speech" or a "talk"; it's a formal business vehicle—deadly serious.

Presentation goals can be many: you want a contract, or a change in scope, or a schedule extension, or an internal development budget, or, whatever you have determined to be the business result you want; but, one thing at a time: one subject, one presentation.

That's a presentation; no more, no less.

RECORDS: A NUISANCE—YES; A NECESSITY—YES

A mundane subject, true. But, over the past few decades we have progressively degenerated into a highly litigious society. There is one future communication that will explore past communications, and that is a lawsuit. Prepare for the future by protecting the past. Establish an economical and efficient record retention and retrieval program.

SELECTED REFERENCES

Corbett, E. P. J. *English Handbook: Choices and Conventions.* New York: John Wiley and Sons, Inc.

Bartlett, J. *Familiar Quotations.* Citadel Press, New York, 1983.

Gow. *Human Engineering.*

W. O. Meadke, et al. *Information and Records Management.* Glencoe Press, New York: 1981.

Hayakawa, S. I. *Language in Thought and Action,* 4th ed. New York: Harcourt Brace Jovanovich, 1978.

Carnegie, D. *Public Speaking and Influencing Men in Business.* Association Press.

Records Control and Storage Handbook with Retention Schedules. Itasca, NY: Bankers Box and Records Storage System.

Thomas, V. S., Schubert, D. R. et al. *Records Management: Systems and Administration.* New York: John Wiley and Sons, Inc., 1983.

Mitchell, W. E. *Records Retention.* New York: Ellsworth Publishing Company.

Perrin, P. G. *Reference Handbook of Grammar and Usage.* New York: William Morrow, & Co., Inc., 1972.

Baker, S. *The Complete Stylist and Handbook,* Third Edition. New York: Harper and Row, 1984.

Karrass, C. L. *Winning in Negotiations.* Los Angeles: Center for Effective Negotiating.

1

Communicating for Desired Results

LAWRENCE L. BISSETT *National Institute for Chemical Studies, Charleston, West Virginia*

H. GILBERT WEIL *General Project Manager, Consultant, Bridgewater, New Jersey*

Effective communication is an essential element of a project. All project managers bring some measure of planning, leading, organizing, and controlling to a project. Nevertheless, results frequently are limited by ineffective communications. In the truly superior project, communication is approached carefully and applied effectively. It imparts animation to the skeleton of a project organization. The owner and contractor project teams work in harmony with a common purpose, supporting and stimulating each other, and cooperating to resolve problems to achieve the project objectives. Alternatively, hidden agendas, conflicting objectives, politics, witch hunts, and the like can turn a project into a disaster. Let's analyze how better results can be attained for your project through more effective communications.

To facilitate the presentation, assume the project organization consists of the owner's project manager and project team, and the contractor's project manager and project team. The owner's project manager may be selected from a central engineering group servicing several operating divisions of a company, or from an operating division. In either case the owner's project manager is responsible to a senior executive of the operating division, referred to as the project sponsor, for the success or failure of the project. There are many variations of this basic project organization, depending on the structure of the principal organizations, but the ultimate performance and accountability rests with three key people: project sponsor, owner's project manager, contractor's project manager. We will focus here on communications as they apply to and are viewed by the owner's project manager.

FUNDAMENTAL CONSIDERATIONS

With whom are you communicating?

The project manager must extract clear objectives from the sponsor. The project team must understand where the project is headed, and anticipate and deal with problems. The contractor has his own way of doing things, and his methods must be understood and applied by team members in the most effective way for the benefit of the sponsor: the system should accommodate the project; the project should not accommodate the system. The project team must communicate effectively with the contractor to execute the work on schedule, within budget. The nature of communications in each case is different, and so is the manner in which one proceeds in order to be most effective.

Why are you communicating?

Are you conveying information? Are you outlining plans and objectives and getting understanding and acceptance? Are you leading, motivating others to do what you want them to do? Reporting? Problem solving? Your reason for communicating is the principal consideration in deciding how to communicate.

How will you communicate?

Time is a costly commodity. The wise manager learns to conserve time in his communications as well as in all other endeavors. Yet he must also judge when communication has effectively taken place; sometimes more time is required than he would like to invest. A logical pattern helps to make communications more effective with less expenditure of time. As we proceed, these considerations will be developed to illustrate principles with general application to project execution—logic relative to "the why" and "the how" in our dealings with different groups and individuals. Finally, additional considerations are presented for universal consideration.

COMMUNICATIONS WITH PROJECT SPONSORS

At the start of a project, the most important communication channel is between the project manager and the sponsor. The subject is the project objectives of the sponsor. Frequently the sponsor's initially stated objectives will be broad, and will be progressively defined over the course of the project. The project manager will find his plans, schedules, budgets, once firm, now in disarray. Therefore, as soon as possible learn what results the sponsor really wants. Be specific. Several basic objectives follow.

Performance Specifications

Production capacity. Product quality. Whatever, depending on the nature of the project. The sponsor expects the thing being built to do something under certain circumstances, and you must understand exactly what it is supposed to do, or more precisely, what the sponsor expects it to do.

Project Scope

The physical facility must be described in sufficient detail to permit the cost to be estimated, at a suitable level of accuracy. Quantify the major components, estimate the bulk materials, develop field labor requirements and productivity, etc. Prepare enough drawings to be sure that you and the sponsor envision the same final product. Would you have a contractor build a house for you based solely upon a set of performance specifications?

Budget

Before you set the project in motion, be sure that the sponsor is willing to fund the project scope as you understand it. Your judgment of the allowance required for contingencies will depend on agreement between you and the sponsor regarding change; how to control change, under what conditions to permit change, and so forth. Use these discussions to judge the quality of the information being provided to define the scope. At this point don't worry about saving time. A clear understanding between the sponsor and the project manager of the issues to be resolved in order to arrive at an adequate budget, including an allowance for contingencies, is necessary to avoid undesirable situations later.

Schedule

While the budget is being developed and agreed to, get agreement for the schedule as well. Is the project weather sensitive? Is the sponsor in a hurry—of course he is, but is he willing to pay the premium for a crash project? Discuss with the sponsor the schedule for preparing the facilities for operations, and starting them up. He should be planning for those activities as well, or perhaps he expects you to do this. Be sure that not only the completion date, but the intermediate milestones and the associated cash flow are acceptable to the sponsor.

Part of the art of communication is knowing what questions to ask. Some sponsor's objectives are not as obvious as those above, and the project manager must think about how to elicit those also, by asking questions.

Political Considerations

A myriad of questions arise. Is the project in a foreign country? What are the constraints on imports? Are indigenous materials available? Does the sponsor have favored suppliers or customers who must be on bid lists? What local politicians will be involved in evaluating the taxable assets? Are they reasonable? Is the project to be built in an agricultural area, or an urban area? What steps will the sponsor take to accommodate the political dynamics created by the execution of the project?

Safety/Environmental Considerations

The component of a project budget required for safety and environmental protection is steadily increasing. There are short- and long-term implications for the sponsor. In the short term, the project manager invests in safety during the execution of the project because the resulting improved productivity saves project funds, and he has to live within the terms of agreements with the proper authorities for disposal of refuse, noise reduction, and so forth, during construction. In the long-term, the design of the project will be based on criteria for long-term safety and environmental protection standards. The project manager must be sure that the owner understands all of those standards and is prepared to go before the regulatory bodies to secure approval for them.

Publicity/Image Aspirations

Does the sponsor want some favorable publicity from the project to enhance his sales program or his acceptance in the community? Will he be showcasing the project and perhaps interrupting construction? What funds should be budgeted for site tours, publications, entertainment, and the like?

Management of Risk

For reasons of economy or schedule compression, does the sponsor want to take risks? Will fallback plans and funds be provided? Who will decide what risks are acceptable?

These are only examples of the questions and answers—communications—which should take place between the project manager and the sponsor. The point is, clear objectives are vital to the success of the project. They should describe all of the business needs, be well thought out and documented, and be firm enough to provide the basic direction and tone for all project planning and execution activities.

After documenting the sponsor's objectives, the project manager develops his project plans: budget, schedule, and organization, including the continuing role of the sponsor; execution plans for engineering, procurement, and construction; controls, resource management, and reports—all will be described in detail. When the plan is complete, it must be presented to and understood by the sponsor, because it will be the basis for subsequent monitoring, controlling, and reporting of progress toward the required result.

Project managers usually want, but seldom find, sponsors who will be relatively uninvolved. Assuming that the sponsor has studied and agreed to the project plan, the project manager must next ascertain to what extent the sponsor wants to monitor progress, or keep in touch. First, agree upon the frequency and format for reporting progress. Typically, one should report actual cost and progress versus the plan, programs to correct deviations from the plan, and major problems and events on a monthly basis. The project manager might recommend a formal presentation to the sponsor on a quarterly basis to review progress and forecast results. Openness and candor are encouraged. If the project manager perceives that the sponsor's objectives might not be achieved, the sponsor must be informed as early as possible and an understanding reached. Most sponsors are reasonable, but they don't appreciate surprises when the opportunity to explore options and make decisions has passed.

Obviously, the sponsor is very important to the project manager. He controls the funds for the project. Communications with the sponsor following the rationale given will allow the project manager to direct the execution of the project with the assurance that a final result is being approached in a cost-effective manner, that he has proper backing, and that the project will be perceived to be a superior accomplishment by all parties.

COMMUNICATIONS WITH THE PROJECT TEAM

For the purpose of discussion, the project team is considered here to be that organization reporting to the owner's project manager—that person charged with the responsibility of guiding the selected contractor to achieve the objectives of the owner. In order for the project team to be a team, certain specific communications must take place when the team first comes into existence. This is part of team building.

Organization

The project manager can make assignments, but understanding and acceptance throughout the team comes only with discussion. Assigned personnel must understand accountability and authority, what roles are expected, and what latitude is allowed. Power influences must be properly distributed to assure a system of checks and balances, yet allow for appropriate decisiveness. The limits of responsibility should be clear, without overlap or gap.

Expectations

When lines of responsibility, accountability, and authority are clear, further discussion among team members is needed to bring out the expectations of the total team for each team member. These discussions can be surprisingly revealing because they are influenced by the usually diverse backgrounds of the team members. They are important for maintaining morale so that team members don't feel let down when a member fails to meet an expectation of which he was unaware. The door should be open to build trust and confidence.

Honesty and Candor

From the beginning, the project manager must work to establish honest, open communications. Develop healthy relationships between team members. Eliminate adversarial relationships, cultivate mutual support. Strive for an environment in which people can admit to their weaknesses. The effectiveness of the team will be directly proportional to the effectiveness of its communications. Some people cannot develop the necessary relationship to a team. The project manager may be faced with a choice between a reduced level of group dynamics and replacement of the individual. As team leader the project manager must be the role model for open and honest communications.

Objectives

Finally, the project manager is ready to discuss the objectives of the team and of the individual members as they relate to the objectives of the sponsor. If the team is congealing, personal objectives will be subordinate to team objectives. If honesty prevails, the project manager may be able to identify certain personal and political objectives detrimental to the thrust of the project, and deal with them constructively.

After the team relationships are established, and clear and explicit objectives are agreed to, the team can plan how to do its work. This communication is important to the project manager so that he can later monitor the performance of team members. The project manager presents the project plan, including budget and schedule. Each team member then presents an execution plan for his or her project component. Each plan is discussed by the team until interactions are understood and accepted. In the end, the project manager should feel confident that the combined individual plans support the project plan, and the individuals are personally committed to the project.

Communication is an important element of motivation; motivation is an important element of leading; leading is an important element of the project manager's work. In his day to day leadership, the project manager must keep in close touch with his team. Daily brief, informal meetings are recommended. Team members should be kept informed of progress and problems, and they should reciprocate. The progress expected for each day should be understood, and consistent with the individuals' plans. Changes to plans should be discussed and understood by the team. In a successful team, the quality of communications is such that members seldom surprise other members. Such a team environment doesn't just happen; the project manager builds it and nourishes it every day, and the nature and quality of his communications are the keys.

COMMUNICATIONS WITH CONTRACTOR COUNTERPARTS

The points discussed relating to communications for team building and planning within the project team apply to communications with the contractor counterparts as well. The project manager's task here is more difficult because he will probably be less familiar with personalities, politics, and power struggles within the contractor's organization.

Relationship to the Contractor's Project Manager

The two project managers must be able to develop mutual trust and confidence. They must be open and candid with each other, and mutually supportive. Assigning of blame can have no part in their relationship; if either fails, both fail. Each must feel that the other is available at any time for discussion, help, or constructive confrontation. Only if their communications are of this quality can the communications in the contractor's organization be of comparable quality.

Since the owner's project team represents the sponsor and understands the sponsor's objectives, it is in a position of leadership. Several principles are important to the exercise of this authority.

Lines of Communication

The project managers must agree on the appropriate lines of communication between their organizations. Open communications are good, but random, undisciplined communications aren't. Consideration must be given to approvals required for control, security, priority setting, and cost and schedule targets, at a minimum. Since the project manager is usually the one who is aware of all of the project considerations, he usually requires that he or his designate approve any significant nonroutine communications so that they are controlled, but not stifled.

Blurring of Organizational Boundaries

There is a danger if one does not quite succeed in establishing open, disciplined communications. Almost everyone feels good about open communication, but too often this is an idealistic concept. Therefore, when the project manager succeeds in opening most, but not all, communication lines, a funny thing happens. The open paths of communication become conduits for messages blocked from normal paths because of personality conflicts, internal politics, and so forth. Messages get through, crossing organizational boundaries, violating procedure. The project may benefit in isolated cases, but the breakdown in discipline is counterproductive in the long term.

Planning Routine Communications

Ideally the proper lines of communication between the owner's and the contractor's project teams will be open. Routine communications should be planned in detail for such activities as process design, procurement plans, engineering standards and specifications, material control, and field progress reporting. Some reflection on these examples will clarify why a plan is needed. The level of monitoring, review, and approval for each is a different activity. Project management must exercise judgment in developing the plan so that communications are not restricted unnecessarily, yet control is maintained for the various documents.

Task Force Direction

Assuming that a good team atmosphere has been developed between the project teams, the owner's team will have access to the individuals at work in the contractor's task force. Members of the owner's team must be careful not to communicate information that could be construed as giving direction to the task force. Such direction must come through the contractor organization. Failure to be sensitive to this issue will quickly lead to a breakdown of trust between teams.

Sharing Concerns

Weekly meetings between the project teams to discuss concerns can be very constructive. The participants must have the kind of relationship that lets them expose worries, hunches, and gut feelings without having to justify them. An informal atmosphere helps; a working lunch has merit. The object is to get issues out on the table, with bits of the puzzle being contributed by everyone in a position to know, so that a problem can be recognized early and its impact minimized.

Impediments

Be alert for political, organizational, or other impediments to communication in organizations. Look for the hidden organization. Once you've found it—it's there—see if it can be brought out in the open and put to constructive use.

A constructive, mutually supportive relationship between the project teams will help eliminate friction and wasted effort. Healthy communications will promote such a relationship and keep you informed about any breakdowns. The superior project manager will find it worthwhile to establish and maintain effective communications.

Communications with the Contractor's Task Force

The owner's project team should mix with, observe, and listen to the contractor's task force. Initially, the contractor may oppose this. A level of trust has to be developed for this to be acceptable. The benefits are many.

You will have your own data for quality, cost, and schedule control.

You will learn of problems and be able to get early resolution. Treat problem-related information with great sensitivity, lest your sources "dry up."

You will be able to reinforce the authority of the contractor's project management. Always bear this in mind when communicating anything to the task force.

You can help motivate. You represent the owner, the "boss"; your compliments are especially significant.

ADDITIONAL CONSIDERATIONS

Don't Waste Time. Clear, concise communications conserve time and avoid misdirection. "Yes" and "no" can be stated briefly. Early problem identification and resolution saves lots of time.

Meetings. Volumes have been written on running effective meetings; do it. This is another way to use time effectively.

Focus on Plans. Most communications relate to plans. Getting understanding and acceptance of plans and then using plans as a focal point for communications is very effective.

Foreign Environments. Projects in foreign countries raise problems of communications to another order of magnitude. Learn the language. Learn to "read" eyes. Get the listener to tell you what he thinks you said. And remember, "one picture is worth a thousand words."

Minimize Interfaces. If the nature of the project can justify it, a task force will provide better communications than other forms of project organization.

What's Really Going On? Some people can't see forests for trees, some people aren't objective, etc. Find out who your best observers are and use them.

Computer/Word Processors. Computers and/or word processors are becoming increasingly effective tools for the project manager to gather, organize, and evaluate information, and communicate within and between project teams and other participants.

CONCLUSION

Effective communications in a project environment bring many benefits.

Improved economy of time, effort, and money by keeping everyone focused on the sponsor's objectives

Improved leadership through motivation

Repeat business—superior project performance, followed by owner awareness

Effective communications make the difference between average and superior project performance—the key to a synergistic relationship between sponsor, contractor, and project manager.

In conclusion, a slightly humorous real-life anecdote may serve to underline the importance of these fundamentals.

One time, while on assignment in Puerto Rico, a project manager was explaining "Management by Objectives" to a gathering of Puerto Rican engineers. To illustrate objectives, he used winning a football game, scoring a touchdown, and achieving a first down as long-term, short-term, and immediate objectives. He was warming to the subject and going on to explain programs, strategies, and tactics (pass, set up running game, etc.) when he noticed a glaze settling over the eyes of his audience. He had ignored the first fundamental for optimizing communications. He had failed to consider with whom am I communicating! And consequently, was using an illustration that was totally foreign to them—American football.

2

Written Communications

HENRY E. FRANCIS*   *The Ralph M. Parsons Company, Pasadena, California*

The primary professional concern of a project manager is, of course, to complete the project on time and within the budget. But he can't do it alone. So he writes and he writes; mostly to help other people help him reach that goal. A project manager must be an expert in communications engineering. To be so, means putting aside concerns over the traditional techniques of writing and becoming more concerned with the instrument that will pick up his message; a very complex human mind. It isn't the communication the writer thinks he's sending that counts. What will be acted on is the message the reader thinks he received, modified by individual emotional reactions. The writer must be less concerned with his own "meaning" of the words and more concerned with the likely effects of the words. The mind he is trying to reach is fully as complex as his own. It belongs to a person who is overworked, underpaid, frustrated in business; misunderstood and unappreciated by family, friends, society. Perhaps not, but assume so. The message must cut through all of these impedances, and more, with the least possible distortion if it is to help get the job done.

What readers want first of all is recognition of their importance and needs. People don't do their best work if they are being put down. If the attitudes in the message reflect these needs, the rest of the communication has a chance of getting through. But remember, most workers already have more on their desks than they would like, and you're adding to the burden. If it is difficult for them to read, for any reason, they're likely to miss the message, get the wrong message, or not bother to read it at all. In which case you might better have spent your time doing something constructive.

Not many busy people would be likely to read beyond the following introductory paragraph to a letter (the paragraph following it was three times as long):

> This is an interim design review. This new tabulated logic diagram format representation presents a large number of circuits that materially saves on the production of a corresponding number of drawings which would normally be required. The trade-off price, however, that is being paid for these paper-savings is that it hampers, or denies in large measure to the reader the basic underlying reason for why there is a logic diagram in the first place—namely, to depict a sequence of events that guides the reader's mind's eye to grasp in factual and repeatable terms a conveyance of sophisticated and complex thoughts of the initiating engineers. The awkwardness of the new format is because of the disruption of thought of having to physically crank into the format a different insertion item each and every step of the process concurrent with trying to read and maintain rational thought of the complex circuit.

---

* Retired

Try to rewrite that paragraph into something easy to read (you can cut out about half the words) and you will begin to see at least one element of the unreadable.

Basic problems in writing often result from problems confronting the writer. Two of these are the feeling of inadequacy and self-doubt. Under these emotional handicaps a writer often falls back on two things: dignity and decorum. Writing becomes stiff, labored, and tedious. The writer gets lost in long involved sentences and communicates along with the content, coldness, lack of sympathy, and even arrogance. These problems usually resolve themselves when he starts concentrating on the complex mind he wants to influence at the other end of the chain. A writer cannot possibly understand all the possible nuances of all the possible reactions to the message. But some time spent trying to understand human behavior in general, will impart a better ability to understand a particular person's likely reaction.

There are many less dictatorial ways of saying this:

> I gave, to all persons who, at different levels, participate in the operations described in this program, strict instructions, for them to be impregnated of the importance and the necessity of taken measures. They are responsible for implementing it in their field.

A project manager doesn't need a course in writing to become an effective writer. He probably already knows more grammar than he needs and gets preoccupied with more rules and supposed rules than are required for clear expression. Instead of being concerned about writing as such, be concerned about people and with how to get across to them the attitude and information they need to get the job done.

GETTING STARTED WRITING

Some subjects are of such immediate and overwhelming importance that finding time to write what is necessary is no problem; everything else is dropped and the message begun. Other subjects, often those whose long range importance is much greater, lack the sense of urgency and can be put off, and put off, and put off. The solution is simple, if not easy: clear a spot on the desk, shut the door, and begin. Every manager eventually works out for himself a ranking of priorities of writing chores. How well he manages to communicate with his lieutenants and with the project record will be, to some extent, the measure of his success. Nothing gets written unless at some time he sits down and begins. Start writing at any point in the message. Start with things that will eventually be left unsaid. Start with thoughts that would be embarrassing if they actually saw the light of print. Start with the easiest part. But start! There is time later to review, to reorganize.

A common emotional reason for delaying the writing is the need to protect a delicate ego. Any decision-making is a risk-taking: you could be wrong. And while none of us is perfect, some bear up under the humiliation of error better than others. For those with an ego that bruises easily, it is even more devastating to have a lapse in judgment engraved forever, or practically forever, in the project files for all to see.

Another temptation project managers are prone to is to keep to themselves some essential knowledge so that everyone else doesn't know as much as they do. Hoarding information that a project couldn't go forward without can provide a comforting sense of security though it may be potentially disastrous in every other respect. The tender ego has many vulnerable faces that can be protected by not writing.

There isn't much outside help for these conditions. For those who must protect their ego by failing to record decisions or information that might later be second-guessed but need to be on the record, there are other ways to make a living. We have to apply some version of Harry Truman's, "If you can't stand the heat, get out of the kitchen."

Fortunately, tender egos are not a major problem in project management. Most managers suffer an occasional pang or two, but usually they are easily salved over, and they sit down and begin writing in spite of these and the pressure of time.

THE ACT OF WRITING

At the first, creative impulse, writing has little to do with spelling, punctuation, or grammatical rules. What possible difference can it make in a draft, to take an extreme example, if you say "Him and I received the vessels." These are mechanical matters best left to editing, that is, a second or later draft, so put them out of mind in the beginning. Of course, the writer must have some communication with himself for a later draft, or for an assisting editor, so it's best to spell words close enough to the accepted spelling that they can be remembered or communicated. The same goes for punctuation; a misplaced comma can sometimes result in a whole new meaning, but, again, these mechanics are only of minimum concern.

The first-line editor should be the writer himself, but often, when time is pressing, the secretary or typist who types the first draft is called upon to serve this function. To be effective, of course, such assistance requires a secretary who is capable of mechanical editing, and, even more importantly, a writer who is capable of delegating the responsibility. Here is an actual paragraph sent to a typist with instructions to type exactly as written because the writer didn't want the meaning changed:

> To avoid such changes, it is felt that we let the supplier identify the device wiring by his standard method. One of our suppliers identified the wiring between device terminal and terminal block terminal by identify terminal block terminal on device and device location with its terminal on terminal block terminal. This system proved to have minimum . . . .

Even a typist with little language ability could have, if he or she had been allowed to, asked the writer to explain and indirectly pointed out that it is mostly gibberish. After the secretary, if there is no formal editing available and you still lack time to perform this task yourself, get a friend or someone else who is "good" in English to read the first typed draft for mechanical and obvious meaning problems. Second-party editing, regardless of time considerations, should be reserved for routine communications only; important proposals or other documents demand the writer's own full attention through all composition stages, including editing. In any case, mechanics are a later editing problem, not a primary writing problem. So begin to write with your mind purged of all concern for "correctness." Save editing for a later time.

Next, spend a little time getting a clear image of the audience. You have already defined the reaction you want, but what kind of unwanted reactions might arise out of this particular audience? What are the sore spots? How can they be avoided? Keep them in mind. There seems to be some adjunct to Murphy's law that says if something written can be misinterpreted, it will be, in terms of some readers' particular bias. Any reader has more on his mind than your concerns. How will this audience react to your particular views?

So now to *organize* what you want to say, what you may have already drafted in a very rough form. You can't possibly tell anyone all you know on any subject. Don't try. More than that, most of what you know isn't important to the purpose of your message. Spend some time selecting the information you want to include. Decide what you need to say to help your reader understand what you want him to understand. Leave out the insignificant details. Don't bore or confuse him with facts that don't further your primary cause for writing.

Engineering writing is really fairly easy from the standpoint of overall organization. A logical route from beginning to end usually suggests itself. Management writing doesn't always fall into place quite as easily. It may take a little more time to determine the easiest, and hopefully, the shortest road to lead the reader to where you want him to go. So make an outline.

An outline has little to do with the kind of formal, balanced points and subpoints, with parallel construction of parts that some of us were taught in school. It is really just a list of the points we want to discuss and the order in which we want to discuss them. If some points are parts of larger points it doesn't hurt your understanding of what you're trying to do to show that by numbering and indenting. But if all you came up with is an unnumbered list of points in random order, you'll have all you need.

My first thinking about this chapter went something like this:

1. Attitudes
2. Starting
3. Writing
4. Presentation

At that point, my general approach was decided. The next step was to go back to each point and decide what elements I would take up under each item. With a couple of intermediate tries I ended up with this outline which I followed to write the chapter:

I. Introduction—Attitude and Success
   1. The reader as human
   2. Emotional responses
   3. The desire to communicate
II. Getting Started Writing
   1. Finding time
   2. Protecting the tender ego
      a. The risk of taking a position
      b. The risk of sharing knowledge
III. The Act of Writing
   1. Delegating the mechanics
   2. Organizing
      a. Defining the goal
      b. Limiting the content
      c. The shortest path
   3. Setting the Style
      a. The language level
      b. Tone—the human relationship
IV. The Art of Presentation
   1. Written
      a. Visual elements
      b. Length
   2. Oral
      a. The presenter

All of this is preparation for writing. If it seems like a lot of time spent without producing anything, just remember that a plant isn't built without site preparation.

Style

After writing is finished, any number of changes can be made. Information can be added or subtracted, positions of sentences or paragraphs can be changed, and all kinds of mechanical problems can be remedied—*this* is the stage for editing, again, best done by the writer himself. The one thing that cannot be changed, the element that is cast in concrete once you have set it down, is style. Style is in the structure of the language and the choice of words. It is the *attitude* with which a thought is expressed.

We are not machines, and unless we're programming computers, we're not communicating with machines. We're dealing with other humans whose reaction to our writing is not a simple ON-OFF. A major part of our communication is dependent on the kind of person we are, at that moment, on that piece of paper. We need to come across as someone the reader will respect, and therefore with whom he would like to deal on the subject we're writing about. This not only requires some feeling for the reader as another human; it also requires some self-knowledge and understanding of the kind of person we should be in the writing situation we're in.

What kind of person is this manager of a quality assurance program?

> The research of industrial products on which we can rely on and the demonstration of this attempt, leads the enterprises to reveal the means brought into play to reach this aim.

The kindest thing we can say about the opening sentence to a quality assurance program is that the writer has no clear idea about what he thinks he thinks.

Language

The best writing style is usually a middle level of language: not too formal, not too informal. This level of language aims at giving the reader an ease of understanding with the right kind of feeling about the subject and the author. The next example did not come, I am happy to say, from engineering writing. It came instead from a government bureau, but it illustrates well what happens when a writer tries to communicate on too high a level of language abstraction:

> There exists no single mechanism for the internalization or externalization which uniformly constitutes the socially most desirable internalization mechanism in all externalization situations.

Did you understand that—even fleetingly? Try this.

> If concise quantities and concepts are not deterministic at the outset, then a range of probabilistic values are postulated and used parametrically.

Sentence length and structure are also elements of style. There is no easy answer as to proper length. Just writing short sentences won't do. That breeds boredom. The easiest and most pleasant reading is of sentences of variable lengths of 1 to 40 words. The lengths must be varied to give emphasis (short sentences are more emphatic than long ones), rhythm, and variety.

Besides sentence length there is the matter of kind of sentence structure. Writing all simple sentences doesn't guarantee simplicity. Some thoughts are naturally more important than others in a reasoned discussion. The less important must be subordinated in the sentence, or the message isn't accurate. A sure way to generate interest with sentence structure is to see that it, too, is varied. Note how monotonous this collection of simple sentences gets:

> An 8-inch gas line extends from Pipeway Skid 313A for 360-feet to Module 4A. An 8-inch gas line connects the Intermediate Manifold Module to existing pipeway 870-feet away. At Gathering Center #2 there is a 2-inch diesel line hooking up the Emergency Generator 150-feet away. Nine lines 8-inches to 28-inches in size connect the intermediate manifolds to a pipe rack 20-feet away. An 8-inch gas line from this module travels 620-feet to its tie-in point. There is an 18-inch produced water line from the module to a flange connection 460-feet away. At Gathering Center #1 there are 2-2-inch diesel lines for the Emergency Generator 370-feet long. There is a 2-inch nitrogen line and an 8-inch gas line extending 50-feet from pipeway skid 329-feet to an exisitng pipe rack.

Writing all long sentences gets boring as well, besides becoming too involved for both the reader and the writer. We have to develop an eye for misshapen and over-complicated construction. If you find too many short simple sentences boring, consider that one overlong, complex sentence can sometimes be frightening:

> Compressor suction and side-load pressures are based on the assumption of a four percent line loss from the chillers and economizers to the compressor inlet nozzles for source pressures less than 25 psia, and a three percent loss when the source pressure exceed 25 psia, while the compressor discharge pressure allows for 12 psi differential from the compressor discharge nozzle flange to the condenser discharge flange.

The element of style that most affects the reaction of the reader is tone. Although tone is easy to identify, it isn't easy to define. All writing—business and technical as well as sales—is an attempt to convince somebody of something: to buy, to act, or to think in a certain way. But no one can be persuaded unless the writer first has the reader's good will. Here is a project manager who tried to lump all his scapegoats into one paragraph. Guess who will go the extra mile for him!

> The owner's decision to work toward the study team's original milestone mechanical completion date contributed to the not so successful execution of the various project elements and is responsible, at least in part, for a higher project cost and later-than-desired project completion. Review of each project segment reveals less than desired throughness in sound establishment of commitment. Smith's design engineering was conducted over the same time frame as Jones', and Brown's assembly essentially had the same construction time; however, decisions for a design basis and selection of an untried assembly contractor did not contribute to a project team dedicated to successful project completion.

With patience and practice anyone can learn the elements of writing. But, in the short term, it is difficult for some people to learn to think, or to be sensitive to the feelings and concerns of others. Tone is the reflection of the conscience and character of the writer and of his attitude toward the reader. A writer by word or by deed must show respect for the quality of his reader's mind. He must avoid hostility, and avoid any implication of personal superiority.

Tone is sometimes not in the language at all, but in the organization and detail of the subject matter. For instance, look to the degree of detail included in an instruction. It's easy to create a bad tone by including too much, while the easiest way to insure a good tone is simply to have respect for the intelligence of the reader. What excuse is there for this information: Lightning can cause damage by direct strike—a totally gratuitous definition, certainly for a professional audience.

A writer who has respect for his reader and who is sincere and interested in what he's trying to say won't get into problems with tone. He'll avoid the pomposity, the superiority, or the hostility that is prevalent in much of management prose. And he'll also avoid the uncertainty, the servility, and the antagonism that creeps into reports and letters going up the chain of command.

First we need to decide just what we are trying to persuade the reader to accept; then we can look more perceptively at our own attitude to see what tone our writing is setting. This following paragraph is easy to read, simple to follow, and the tone implies a message from one knowledgable engineer to another:

> 5. SDI Vent Stack Design: There will be a vent on the Satellite Drilling Island to relieve gasses from separators in the event of a major equipment overhaul. The release will be an infrequent event, occurring less than once every two years. The vent has been sited so that H_2S and hydrocarbon concentrations are dispersed to safe levels before workers come in contact with them.

PRESENTATION

There is more to winning confidence and support for a project, a report, or an instruction than merely presenting acceptable data. In the human side of communication we need also to be concerned with the outward nuances that contribute to a favorable impression—those elements of a presentation that have nothing to do with the data, its validity, or its value.

In a large corporation the mechanical elements of presentation do not usually present problems. Corporate practice and adequate secretarial help will usually ensure that elements offensive to the eye: uneven typing, crowded spacing, even misspellings, don't become issues. But the writer always should keep in mind his own reaction to messy communications and act accordingly. A handwritten memo may be faster, but if it is difficult to decipher it will be ineffective.

As to graphics, besides keeping the content simple enough to create the impression of capability, especially without arrogance, the supporting illustrations have to be artistically subdued and simple. Too elaborate graphics can be confusing; too small type often can't be read. Graphics for engineering need to reflect the popular image of the engineer: no frills, no artiness—completely objective.

CARRYOVER TO SPOKEN COMMUNICATION: SOME BASICS

Oral presentations are more difficult. All the elements relating to written communication apply. In addition to the presence of a human "presenter," the salesmanship that goes into an oral presentation is enhanced or degraded by the complex functions of language that go beyond communicating data. Those making the presentation must deal with a whole array of nonlanguage symbols that augment language in what has been called a "dancing of attitudes." There are certain images to create in the minds of the audience. These images represent what the presenter thinks he is and how he wants his company to be perceived.

The first image to create is that the group is trustworthy and can be relied upon. The second is that those who prepared the data are competent. The third is that everyone involved in the presentation is sincere and honest. If there is any one quality that needs to come through, it is sincerity. In addition, a respect for the administrative and technical knowledge of the audience must be demonstrated. In a subtle way, the presenter is a supplicant asking the audience for a favor—of understanding him in the way he wants to be understood. This places the presenter in an equivocal position. He must communicate competence in technical and administrative leadership while, at the same time, showing proper respect for his audience.

To inspire confidence, an engineer making a presentation must fit the popular image of a conservative, right-thinking person. Time and images change, but regardless of fashion, he or she should be conservatively dressed and well groomed. As a complement to appearance the speaker should speak simply and enunciate distinctly, with a minimum of mannerisms; and extend the same principles to demonstrations and presentation graphics when these are needed.

Creating the image that the speaker and the team behind him are competent and sincere, then, is the result of an accumulation of symbols that involve dress, mannerisms, attitudes, and technical knowledge. To produce all of these necessitates the feeling of what kind of person the audience would like to listen to and follow. And the audience isn't likely to be much different from those preparing the presentation. The kind of symbols that appeal to them are likely to be the same kind that will appeal to the audience.

SUMMARY

The first step toward becoming an effective communicator is to discard any notion that you are a master craftsperson, completely competent in the matters of technical or any other communication. Exact communication between humans using any set of language symbols is clearly impossible no matter how elementary the subject. The only tool we have for transmitting knowledge and experience is this haphazard system of symbols that has a little objective information and an abundance of subjective stimuli. What can be done to use it effectively?

The most desirable quality any communicator can have, in writing or speech, and which is remarkably lacking in most, is humility. Once you recognize the magnitude of the task and the inadequacy of the tools, it is hard to escape feeling humble. When you become fully aware that exact communication isn't possible, that ambiguity is always present, that more is always left out than is said, and that more is read into it than is intended, you'll work harder to write more precisely, more simply, and to sense elements that might cause an emotional short circuit in the audience.

Concentrate on the audience to help them understand the experience you are trying to communicate. While no one can possibly understand all the possible nuances of all the possible influences and reactions to your message, if you'll spend some time trying to understand human behavior in general, you'll be better able to anticipate a particular human audience's reaction to your symbols.

3

The Stand-Up Presentation

WILLIAM R. SEARS   *W. R. Sears & Co., Inc., San Francisco, California*

The project manager is, above all, a communicator. Let's develop here one phase, an important phase, of communication—the stand-up presentation.

A project manager cannot get very far without fine-tuning his general abilities in spoken and written expression. It's often the case that he became a project manager because he captained the effort from inception to award of a job, including numerous client contacts, management of the proposal effort, and effectiveness in the stand-up presentation.

It has been said that a good proposal or good presentation won't necessarily win the job for you; but, a poor one will virtually guarantee that you will lose it. The client looks at a proposal as a key presentation, a window through which he peeks to see how you are organized, how you think, how you are disciplined, and how you will conduct yourself throughout the project. When you stand up, face the client, and present your game plan and the credentials of your project team and your company, the impressions left by the written proposal will be altered. One of four things will happen: a good proposal will be enhanced; a poor proposal will be confirmed; a good proposal will be negated; a poor proposal will be salvaged. The client decision may just ride on your presentation!

There are several aspects of spoken expression that need attention: face-to-face conversations—sometimes called one-on-one selling, and participation in group meetings, are two common endeavors. While important, and with special dynamics of their own, they are quite different from a stand-up presentation.

Let's define what we mean by a presentation, and more particularly what we don't mean. We do not mean a "speech" or a "talk" or an "address" or any other terms associated with what in college are lumped under the heading of "public speaking." In all these cases an individual rises to his feet, broadcasts his ideas, and then sits down. Applause—that's it. Whether something happens or not is moot. That depends on the speaker, the subject, the audience. A presentation is a very special business animal with no uncertainty as to purpose. Yes, outwardly it is a form of public speaking. But the goal, the why, the how, the development distinguish it from other public utterances.

A presentation starts with what you want your audience to say "yes" to, either explicitly or implicitly. Thus, you set out with only one goal: the selling of a concept or program to that specific audience. The goal can be broad: you want a contract, a schedule extension, a basic specification change – whatever you have settled in advance in your own mind as the business result you want.

Accordingly, a presentation starts out with action desired. Then, it backs up to where you are currently and thus narrows down what you will say to this simple litmus test: Does it contribute to getting them to say yes in the time I have allotted? If it does, it goes in; if it doesn't, it stays out, however enamored you are with the point—this isn't the vehicle for self-serving argumentation.

That's a presentation—no more, no less.

We will devote a considerable amount of discussion to what happens before you ever set pencil to paper. The philosophy, the attitude, the management savvy, the sales awareness of the presenter are all ingredients vital to success in presentation. The most common deficiency is inadequate preparation. As to the visible outcroppings which the audience sees and hears, and which the world calls "the presentation," these we will deal with also. There will be sufficient detail so that a conscientious project manager will do quite well if rules and suggestions are followed, and caveats observed.

THE TECHNICAL PERSON AND THE TECHNICAL PRESENTATION THAT "SELLS" ONE'S IDEAS, PLANS, AND CONCEPTS INTERNALLY

The Technical Presentation

Let us restate: Whatever the desired result, a presentation is distinctive in that the presenter starts out with what he wants the audience to accept and agree on—the result he seeks—as the reason for making the presentation at all. Thus, all presentations start with an aim, a goal, an objective. Once we settle on that, we are well on our way to a presentation, as distinct from a speech.

In a technical company, a technical presentation is one with considerable technical content. That's what's so deceptive about the process. Because of that very technical content, and the need for considerable technical specificity, one can lose sight of the fact that a presentation must have an objective. Yet without one, it is purposeless and useless. The technical person upon whom this idea has dawned and to whom the need to "sell" ideas, plans, concepts, budgets, and projects has become acute, finds the presentation, when done properly, to be a most useful vehicle.

We are now ready to examine how the technical person can become proficient in the selling process, a procedure which provides the vital skeleton for this technical presentation.

The Problem

What's the problem?

Simply stated, with some notable exceptions, managers and engineers when called on to perform what must be classified as selling, often do it poorly. This is true whether what is being sold are concepts, ideas, services, products, budgets, requisitions.

How it this? Why is this? The three reasons, in reverse order of importance are:

1. They don't know how. They simply do not have the business savvy as a basis, nor the communications skills as a medium, to carry off these assignments with the proficiency required. They have been chronically bad writers of technical proposals—a frustration voiced loudly by many management executives.
2. They don't know it's part of their job. They believe that engineering as a business function is independent from other business functions. They believe there are divisions of labor and that they, the technical people, must conceive the solutions to the technical problems and then produce systems embodying these solutions. But the suggestion that a manager or an engineer should be called on to "sell" his ideas isn't generally understood.
3. They have no incentive. More money for performing communication tasks might work—probably not. Additional recognition for excellence could have some value. The one incentive that might appeal to the engineer is the knowledge, sincerely expressed by the top manager, that such effort is a key element in

an undertaking worth doing. Given this sense of need many otherwise recalcitrant managers and engineers might soften their views.

The Nature of the Technical Person: The Attitudes
Toward Selling in a Project Environment

To win the technical person's enthusiasm for selling ideas with proficiency calls for an examination of how his attitudes about selling were formed.

What sort of person is he? A statistical review of the technical community shows a high incidence of the following characteristics.

> As a child, he was a tinkerer. He had crystal sets, chemistry sets, mechanical interests. Excelled in arithmetic. As a rule, he was quiet, retiring, less verbal—more thing-oriented than people-oriented.
>
> By the time he got one or two college degrees, he was the product of an upbringing essentially in physical sciences and technical concerns—at the expense, vast data shows, of liberal arts and the gratifications derived from being accepted by other people.

Extroversion in others is abhorrent to the technical person. He finds his rewards in the achievement of things—experiments that succeed, formulas that work, equations that are solved. His whole rearing through engineering school is that the work should speak for itself. Along with it comes his early exposure to salesmen and selling. His judgments are based on his impressions of those he meets, and they are frequently negative.

The Psychological Barriers Confronting Managers and
Engineers in Selling in a Project Environment

It is no surprise to management that technical managers and engineers, the people who usually become project managers, have barriers to surmount before they can even neutralize their handicaps and capitalize on the strengths which make for effective selling of their ideas internally.

1. *Upbringing.* We have already seen how the technical person being thing-oriented, does not arrive at his desk with a career built on human satisfactions. Gratifications come when things, formulas, systems, equations, machines work.
2. *Attitude Toward Selling and Salespeople.* The very word "selling" conjures up an image he finds distasteful. Even though one rarely analyzes the salesperson's job or function in society, one does see, in the persons of people traditionally costumed in selling functions, certain attributes of selling.

   Selling is lonely: the field salesperson works alone a good deal of the time. It is fatiguing being "out" for long periods of time, the bulk of it little more than canvassing or peddling. The salesperson always has a subordinate status to that of the prospect—subject to rudeness or insolence which one must swallow without outward signs of pain. The earnings are uncertain, especially for those on commission. There is little security in it. Failure, resulting often from causes beyond the control of the salesperson, almost always redounds to one's discredit.
3. *Rejection.* If there is one major reason salespeople fail, and which explains why technical people are repulsed by selling, it's the fear of rejection. Yet for a salesperson to succeed, resolving this as a way of life is a key to survival. This is doubly true for the project manager.
4. *Structuring of the Job.* In all but the most complex selling job, the most successful companies with the most successful sales forces dictate a very high percentage of what sales personnel do and say.

Training involves pumping into them a carefully prepared body of knowledge, information, propositions, and responses—to accommodate every situation—and training them
for the kill.

This so-called "structuring" is a regimen which reasonably intelligent people can
conform to, still leaving room for individual peculiarities. But to the manager and engineer, enamored of "new approaches," "new state-of-the-art" behavior, the boredom
of repetition so common in much selling, constitutes an impossible way of life.

Specifics of Technical People's Attitudes

With all this churning in the minds of technical people, there is small wonder that their
attitudes toward selling range from doubt to rejection.

How are these attitudes manifested?

1. Overt attitudes
   a. Technical people believe other technical people resent being sold. They
      say so openly.
   b. Technical people believe it takes pressure to get someone to buy. They
      resent being pressured and they resent applying pressure. They so so
      openly.
   c. Technical people honestly doubt that "selling" is necessary, and believe
      the ringing truth of ideas will cause customers to buy. They frequently
      say things to this effect in open conversations.
   d. Technical people believe that if we must "sell" at all, the most important
      ingredient of selling is simply conveying information in a logical fashion.
2. Covert attitudes
   In addition, managers and engineers harbor feelings which they rarely express,
   but which, nevertheless, condition their attitudes and help explain why they
   can't generate enthusiasm for the selling assignment.
   a. Selling has no status in their valued circles of recognition. Engineers
      seek honors in the technical community from their peers. Achievement
      comes in the form of certain awards: a plaque, a testimonial. Nowhere
      in professional societies or among professional colleagues does one earn
      esteem for selling prowess.
   b. Selling has a poor reputation generally. Engineers often equate selling
      and salespeople with all the negative attributes associated with an image
      of pushiness, aggression, deceit.
   c. They believe that selling in technical industries is the last refuge for those
      individuals who could not make the grade technically.

Neutralizing Negative Attitudes by Managers and Engineers

Persuading technical people to adopt sound selling practices to gain their objectives
is far from an impossible task. Once management takes the proper steps, the con-
verts may become so enthusiastic that the pendulum will swing in the opposite direction.
They will begin neglecting their other duties, infected by the enthusiasm and enjoy-
ment of meaningful and successful interpersonal relations.

We must first realize that, of the numerous broad categories accounting for all salespeople, the technical industries can really effectively use only one. This is the person
of the highest calibre, the broadest talents, the greatest imagination and creativity.
Today's highly professionalized marketing executives, who inhabit the regions of ultimate decision are top-drawer functionaries of first magnitude. They are virtually,
without exception, college trained, with one or more advanced degrees in several re-
spectable disciplines: history, economics, sociology, psychology, business administration, philosophy, languages, as well as physics, chemistry, engineering. A technical person can feel quite comfortable in this league with colleagues who are, vocation-
ally speaking, equals.

The most critical aspect of this work, distinguishing one from others who bear the selling label, is the broad demands of the job:

One must be alert to changing conditions in industry. One must be able to consume vast amounts of relatively unrelated data and arrange them in such order as to focus on one's situation for results one seeks.

One must have personal charm and know-how, possess exceptional intelligence and an ability to read other people's wishes and needs, and an ability to respond nimbly and quickly.

One must be able to withstand withering fire and return volleys of one's own. One must recognize when one needs the specialized support of managers and engineers, and so organize a selling effort that makes the customer want to buy.

One must offer such impeccable credentials, in the technical side of business, that one wins immediate regard and respect from those one must influence.

One must be able to catalog the likes and dislikes of as many as 20 or 30 individuals, who each play a role in the process of decision—recognizing the influence of each, winning the approval or nonobjection of those who can say "no" but cannot say "yes."

One must understand the dynamics of customer team receptions in order to locate the true centers of decision power and pull from one's memory those appeals which will win them to one's way of thinking. One must ultimately win a consensus of approval that approaches unanimity before a contract materializes.

Such an individual is no ordinary person—and a far cry from the caricature many managers and engineers have of the salesperson and his function.

CONCRETE STEPS MANAGEMENT CAN TAKE TO SPUR MORE EFFECTIVE PRESENTATIONS BY PROJECT MANAGERS AND PROJECT ENGINEERS

How to Improve

With an appreciation of the real nature of the presentation challenge, the management of a company has two specific areas in which it can produce dramatic gains.

The first step is to deal with what it has. Management can take concrete steps to insure that the managers and engineers currently on board come around to a positive attitude toward management's need for presentation effectiveness, and to act to fill that need.

The second step is to deal with what it is going to have—with the next generation of managers, engineers, and technical personnel—the younger men and women on the threshold of opportunity.

With a careful eye on the role these young men and women will ultimately play in winning new business, and their qualifications to become the custodians of the company, management today can significantly influence the calibre of tomorrow's technical staff.

The Concrete Steps Management Can Take

Orientation

Management groups and technical departments must receive orientation on what marketing, selling, presentations, and communications are and why they are necessary business functions. They are activities of overriding importance bearing directly on the company's profit and growth.

Put Technical Information into Its Appropriate Perspective

It is fair to assume that reasonable people will respond to a review of how presentation professionalism fits into a company's life structure. It follows that technical information for the "customer"—the internal decisionmaker—is but one of the many kinds he receives before responding favorably. This puts into proper perspective the need for communication practices required to package ideas in a form suitable for the "customer."

Once these concepts are understood, a useful realization will unfold and the barriers to proficiency in presentations will crumble.

Explain the Singular Role of Technical People as the Only Believeable Carriers of Information from the Standpoint of Key Business Decision Making

Such an undertaking assails doubts even further on the true value of participation in the presentation effort—the unrelenting effort for greater business efficiency.

Realizing that only he will be believed by upper tiers of budget and project approvals because he is the steward of managerial and technical understanding is an important step. With it, can come appreciation that his soloist role, properly staged, can indeed move them—but not without staging.

Understand the Technical Person's Natural Impediments to Becoming Proficient in Selling

This calls for a noncritical accommodation to the simple fact that many technical people haven't been indoctrinated with the necessity to market their ideas either internally or externally. The steps described here will serve to meet these facts of life and to help management to lead managers and engineers into a new area of endeavor in which they will be professionally at ease.

Correct the Misconceptions of Technical People

A progressive management can catalog objections and meet them with a full respect for the feelings of technical personnel.

Technical People Resent Being Sold. Everybody resents being sold. But, everybody loves to buy. It falls on the managers and engineers representing the company to overcome their preconceived image of the stereotyped salesperson, and to develop their own image as alert and aware representatives—the "selling" of their technical strengths.

It Takes Pressure to Get Someone to Buy, and My Colleagues Resent Pressure and I Won't Apply Pressure on Them in My work. This is true only in certain forms of selling. We are talking about a very professional activity: the marketing of professional services to professional people, where we package our talents in a truly technical portfolio. Managers and engineers should strive to develop the sophistication and clarity required for the effective presentation of complex issues. Develop the powers of expression to create a favorable impression on the customer, and the selling of technical ideas will follow. Many people, not just engineers, fail to understand that impressions come first, the audience is tuned in or out by impressions, and content is blocked out.

All This is Nonsense Because the Only Thing That Really Counts Is a Good, Sound, Technical Approach. Our Management and Engineering Superiority Are Really All That's Needed. This is often true. Particularly when you are fortunate enough to own or have exclusive licensing rights to a demonstrably cost-effective process or product; but let's skip order taking. Let's agree that the best presentation isn't going to sell an inferior product or service. Move to the broad middle ground of commerce, where others are as good as you are. Or, enter a new field against entrenched opposition. Do you think your view that you have superior anything is enough to close a sale? Well, it isn't. Package it, work at it, sell it.

Being good technically, without a well-rounded communications approach and awareness, isn't enough. You know your product is good; your audience doesn't. You must communicate your beliefs to your audience, "selling" your company, your product, yourself.

The Customer Needs Information. Anybody Can Deliver it to Him. Communication is a complex business discipline. Anybody can take out tonsils—all it takes is 10 years of medical school. Anybody can draw up contracts, after 3 years of law school. Communication, like any other specialty, calls for expertise. The doctor trains. The lawyer trains. Why should one believe an interpersonal skill such as communication doesn't require training and expertise. A good bit of the trouble in the world, in society, can be traced to an inability to communicate. Don't fall for the trap that anybody can communicate—that communication is some sort of second-class discipline. Wise managers and engineers enlist all the support they can get so that their ideas are presented in the most compelling light.

My Colleague Managers and Engineers Will Look Down On Me for Excellence Here. Do you remember when the athlete was the Big Man On Campus and the student was the Nerd? Well, this didn't go out with high button shoes, but it did go out, starting with the no-frills military veterans and peaking in the 1970s and 1980s. Today, intelligence is respected and it's the athlete on the campus who is viewed with indifference. Your colleagues will respect you for having acquired another level of professional excellence in the ubiquitous and demanding field of human relations.

Selling Proficiency Has a Poor Reputation Generally. This is true in part. If you are talking about door-to-door canvassers, suedeshoe hucksters, door-to-door delivery persons, pad-in-hand-order-takers, okay. But if you want to hear management expressions of awe, admiration, and regard, listen to the references they make about the people proficient in getting ideas across succinctly, with conviction and punch. In particular, listen to management conversations in the corridors and the executive dining rooms. No higher tribute is paid to top-notch technical people than that which follows an effective, telling, organized effort. The complexities of selling ideas and concepts in industry call for such dexterity and finesse that only truly accomplished individuals can carry it off.

Selling is the Last Refuge of Managers and Engineers Who Don't Have It Technically. Anyone who spends full time in a marketing assignment generally gets out of touch with his engineering skills. One winds up, in time, using engineering know-how more for administrative than for creative reasons.

It is the lament of many engineering managers that they are not doing as much engineering as they would like to do. For that reason engineering proficiency cannot be equated with engineering management proficiency. This does not mean that a top technical person should forsake one's calling. It does mean that one must expand his horizons to see one's role in a marketing effort as vital for the company's overall success.

Define Selling Effort As Part of Every Manager's and Engineer's Job

Step one is simply to amend technical job descriptions with a clause calling for participation in customer-oriented efforts.

Once technical persons appreciate that they are supposed to perform well in presentation assignments and to be as proficient in skills of expression as in skills of technical creativity, they will respond to appeals for improvement more readily. They simply must know that management believes it's part of their job.

Install a Long-Term Training Program

Properly conditioned, informed, and motivated, a manager or engineer will respond to training in the specifics of marketing behavior. Such a program need not orient them to being full-time sales engineers. A long-term training program in marketing skills serves to qualify management and engineering personnel in the rudiments of selling skills. If they don't excel, they at least won't lose the battle.

Start Now to Upgrade Future Manpower

In the final analysis, the purest form of top-notch manager or engineer who excels
in attendant duties of proposal writing or technical presentation is the one who wants
and likes to do it. It's all well and good to improve those we have. Like any good
athletic coach, one plays the game with the material one has. But if a company is to
build for growth, it must systematically breed its own managers and engineers who
excel in communication arts, in addition to their technical excellence. The personnel
group should actively maintain a program to recruit promising young managers and
engineers with proclivities in this vital area.

There should never be any compromise on selecting first for technical superiority.
But where two candidates are equal in other respects, preference should be shown
to the one who will one day be on the podium, performing a marketing job with finesse
and skill.

Provide Meaningful Incentives for Marketing
Achievements by Managers and Engineers

While one should not make disparaging remarks about money, it is not certain that the
normal monetary inducements that attract most salespeople would produce an equivalent
response in the technical community. A manager or engineer responds to recognition
of his peers. Awards, testimonials, and personal notes from supervisors can have almost magical effects.

Finally, the really basic comfort that managers and engineers can have from asso-
ciating themselves with a marketing undertaking is a belief in its contribution to an
effort of value, and the opportunity to have their creative thoughts incorporated in
the total program.

The key to this is the company's top management. If management will proclaim
unabashedly that engineers who excel in selling their ideas are major contributors to
the company thrust, and if their efforts receive recognition from management, the up-
turn in interest and in sales volume will be striking.

This is a no-risk, win-win situation for management. Innumerable case histories
show that technical people, when encouraged in this effort by their superiors, reacted
favorably. Across a broad base of U.S. industry the results of programs such as the
preceding are noteworthy: 15 to 25% of the participants responded with enthusiasm,
and retained their enthusiasm; 5 to 10% rejected the concept; the remainder, the large
middle ground, worked at and improved their communication skills, converting a minus
to a plus.

STEPS TO A MORE EFFECTIVE STAND-UP PRESENTATION

The telephone rings. Your boss says he wants a "presentation" for a delegation of
visitors. You say okay.

(TIME PASSES)

The meeting breaks up. You're leaving the room. Your boss puts his arm around
your shoulder and whispers, "Terrific. Just what I wanted."

Between those two conversations, where do people who excel in presentations concentrate their energies?

The Objective

Able presenters get a clear understanding from the person giving the assignment on
the objective, the specific subject, the time available. They identify interest level
and technical competence of the audience, in what specific facility the presentation
will take place, with attendant questions about logistics, whether to have passouts,
souvenirs, or other gifts, the availability of existing graphic aids.

Strategizing the Objective

Able presenters speculate about how to determine what visitors really need to learn, how to win their interest, how to emphasize benefits—substantiated by features, proven by supporting data, experience or testimonials – how to anticipate and accomodate their possible objections, and finally on what to ask for.

Data Management

People who do this well assemble all the resources they can, human and material. They set a timetable of spendable time between "now" and the delivery time. They then "back upstream" to "now," allocating time for rehearsal, graphics rework, graphics creation, graphics and presentation design, conferences and strategies, to "now". Here's where they start going back downstream having allocated time periods for those vital efforts.

They process the material and informational resources, much as in a smelter or concentrator. They reduce the vast amount of available information to only that which they estimate best suits the assignment and the final audience. They make three cuts: a rough, a midway, and a final. They then proceed to "storyboard" their ideas.

Opening

Competent presenters concentrate a lot of time on having a truly effective, attention-getting opening that will raise the level of interest of the audience.

Summary

Professionals always summarize. A recap makes certain that vital points are brought home for the third time. Most presentations lend themselves to the classic formula of "tell'em what you're going to tell'em, tell'em, tell'em what you told them."

Graphic Aids

Truly competent presenters realize how effective charts, slides, overheads, blackboards, passouts, working material can be. They seek all sorts of ways to use them. They design aids simply, with one-idea-at-a-time concepts for all visuals.

Timing and Rehearsal

Professionals never "wing" it. The more they know a subject "cold," the more they review it. They "tailormake" for each audience a presentation although they may be using standard, long-familiar data.

Appearance and Delivery

A well-prepared, well-appearing presenter, remarkably, can, it almost seems, have only a fair delivery and, yet, come away being seen as impressive, informative, and competent. Physical appearance and grooming can make such a difference.

Naturally, the deliberate speaker with minimal talents is excelled by the well-practiced veteran who may come by good presentation naturally and easily. Even so, it is a learnable skill. As with all professionals, the best performers are not those who play the most, but those who practice the most.

All Audiences Want It Said Succinctly

The Advanced Manufacturing Engineering Council issued these suggestions to presenters at its annual conference. It's a cry by technical people for lucidity before their technical audiences.

1. Speak at a brisk pace but slow enough to be able to form your words without slurring them.
2. Have memory-jogging notes but do not read the presentation verbatim.
3. When displaying 35 mm slides, do not project them for too short a period. Over 30 seconds, however, is too long. Also, display as many detailed slides as considered necessary; do not have one slide do all the work.
4. Do not alternate from viewgraph to 35 mm from projection to projection. Show them in batches: one batch 35 mm, the other viewgraphs.
5. Keep your eyes on the audience, even when at the blackboard or pointing something out on the screen.
6. Let your voice project. Power is generated from the diaphragm, not the throat.
7. Do not keep your hands in your pockets. Use them for natural gestures.
8. Do not apologize for inadequate preparation or for any foul-up. Just do the best you can under the circumstances.
9. Have as your objective the fulfillment of the need for information on the part of the audience.
10. Do not underestimate the audience's intelligence, but at the same time do not overestimate their background knowledge.
11. Maintain enthusiasm for your subject; enthusiasm is contagious.
12. Do not fail to see the forest because of the trees. Always let your audience know the "big picture," but before you can do that, you yourself must know what it is.
13. Do not deluge the audience with too much information. Have a few points and drive them home with illustrations, case histories, hypothetical instances, and the like.
14. End your talk by reviewing the main points you want the audience to remember. Do not end with a whimper or with last minute new information.
15. One sure way to dispel stage fright is to become thoroughly immersed in your subject matter and in your desire to "spread the gospel."
16. Do not go over your allotted time. If it's a multispeaker seminar, you will be cutting into someone else's time. A seminar that has publicized its start and stop times should adhere to them since the attendees have scheduled their day around those times.

How Emotional Stimuli Affect Acceptance of Presenters

For the individual making a presentation to a group, many of the rules of interpersonal behavior routinely apply, and more are magnified. In the main, each of us is like a mirror. If a person smiles at us, we tend to smile back. If one frowns, we tend to frown back. Thus, the presenter learns from this phenomenon that as the originator of impressions one has numerous creative opportunities. He can precondition listeners and viewers to reduce or ignore barriers to communication, and conversely to erect and maintain them. The difference can be, among many other factors, the element of these "emotional" stimuli.

These emotional stimuli, whether audio or video, emerge from the presenter conforming to or conflicting with the recipients' pattern of values.

In a community of military officers, the unshined shoes of a visitor would arouse negative emotional responses. Why? Such oversight conflicts with the group's customs and understandings.

In the customer community, these kinds of ingredients have been, at times, considered negative emotional stimuli: chewing gum, shortsleeve shirts, using a toothpick, loud neckties, white socks, suede shoes.

How much of a price does the originator of such stimuli pay in emotional currency? This varies by group. The effective presenter assesses whether he wants to pay this cost and behaves accordingly.

How You Look Affects What They Accept

Look attractive, feel attractive, be attractive; after all, you can't expect men not to judge by appearances.

Ellen Glasgow

Keep up appearances; there lies the test. The world will give thee credit for the rest.

Charles Churchill

Eat to please thyself; dress to please others.

Benjamin Franklin

A peasant's dress befits a peasant's fortune.

Sir Walter Scott

Costly thy habit as thy purse can buy,
But not expressed in fancy; rich, not gaudy;
For the apparel oft proclaims the man.

Shakespeare

SUMMARY

There is no second chance to make a good first impression. Most presentations fail not merely because of the cosmetic shortcomings—graphic aids that are too busy, speakers who mumble, rambling discourses without logical start of finish—but because of surface irritants that the audience sees right away, resents right away, and thus turns away from the speaker right away. Good presentations start with a philosophic commitment to serve the audience's informational and psychological needs.

Everything begins with a management commitment, and ends with you—preparation, appearance, communication.

4
Records Management

THOMAS B. MITCHELL* *Davy McKee Constructors, Inc., Cleveland, Ohio*

ELIZABETH A. BASTA *Cleveland Electric Illuminating Company, Cleveland, Ohio*

What does records management have to do with project management? Why devote time and space to records management in a volume concerning project management? We will try to answer these questions.

Whether a given project experiences success or failure in attaining its objectives, there will be records created of what took place. Whatever the result, there will be inquiries, reviews, audits, and research into what happened.

We take it for granted that proper information accumulated in orderly, accessible modes is very helpful to successful project management. It will not overcome failure due to poor management or other causes, but it will at least provide the best compilation of information concerning what happened.

Conversely, we believe that a project with unplanned, uncontrolled documentation is like a rudderless ship. It may drift along and eventually reach its objective. But the course would be shorter with reliable guidance.

Generally, the records management environment is determined at the corporate level. If there is good records management within the entire organization, project record management will also be good. The project manager should at least understand the principles involved in records management. He can then lend support to compliance by the project.

If records management is not practiced by the parent organization, however, what better place to start than with a specific project?

REASONS FOR RECORDS MANAGEMENT

1. Successful project management depends upon information. Technological advances are changing the ways in which information is collected and transmitted. Recorded information is proliferating in both electronic and conventional forms, abetted by increasing complexity in all aspects of life.

2. Cost/benefit analyses apply to records management as well as to any other form of economic activity. There is a cost to create records and to store them thereafter. Failure to manage records has its cost too. Benefits obtained through records management include control of costs, faster access to needed information, and better security against physical loss or damage to vital records.

---

*Retired

3. Proper classification, storage, and protection of records, permits retrieval of information when needed at minimum cost. Information retrieval is important even after the project is completed. Questions arising then may be difficult to answer. Those familiar with the project may be unavailable. Proper selection, indexing, storage, and protection of records will facilitate preparation of answers.
4. There are operational, contractual, and legal requirements for retaining certain records. A properly executed records management program will assure compliance.
5. Other benefits obtainable through records management include improvements in information systems and procedures, better forms design, and elimination of redundancies.

DEFINITION OF RECORDS MANAGEMENT

Records management is the systematic control of the recorded information required in the operation of an organization. It includes the creation, maintenance, retrieval, and final disposition of records, all at the lowest possible cost.

BASIC PROGRAM FOR RECORDS MANAGEMENT

The first step for implementing a program for records management is to identify the records used by the organization. For an existing, functioning organization, inventory procedures are appropriate. For a fledgling organization, such as a project, determination of the records to be used must be part of administrative planning. In either case, the records identified are then evaluated as to importance and/or significance. Retention periods are determined. Appropriate storage facilities need to be arranged. Finally, procedures for the disposal of expired records are prepared.

A coordinator to develop and administer the program is needed. However, responsibility for executing the program belongs to the operating functions which create and maintain records. If the program is large, a records staff may be needed to operate inactive storage and record disposal facilities. Active management support is essential to attain the maximum benefit from a records management program.

Inventory

An inventory identifies and provides information as to the physical volume of records which must be evaluated.

Records must be classified into "Record Series" by categories according to the purpose for which created. A record series is defined as a group of identical or related records which meet these criteria:

1. Are used and filed as a unit
2. Can be stored as a unit
3. Can be disposed of as a unit

For example, cancelled checks are a record series consisting of a single, identical document. A purchase order file folder is also a record series, although it may contain several different forms and other documents related to the purchase transaction.

Information needed concerning each record category includes:

1. Title and description, purpose, source, frequency issued, storage media, size, retrieval need, and filing method
2. Inventory volume (a legal-size file drawer equals two cubic feet)

3. Alternative sources for the same information
4. Retention recommendations

After evaluation and comparison with possibly similar records series in the custody of other operating functions, the information obtained is used to prepare a Records Retention Schedule.

Evalutation of Records Series

Records series, like books, are not all of equal worth or created for identical purposes. Both worth and purpose may change with time. There are three primary classes into which records may be categorized. A particular record may, in time, belong to each class. An original, signed, construction contract is an example of such a record. In order of importance to the organization, these classes are:

1. Operational
2. Legal
3. Historic

All recorded information needed to fulfill the objectives of an organization form the operational records. Obviously this is the largest class of records with the greatest potential for benefits from records management.

Legal records are those which must be maintained beyond operational needs. Retention may be mandated by law, by contract, or by reason of potential liability. For example, inspection reports may need to be retained to comply with a government regulation. Purchasing files may be needed to fulfill a contract condition. Insurance policies for liability coverages should be retained indefinitely, even though expired.

Within each of the above classes, certain records may be considered vital for at least part of their retention period. Vital records are those deemed essential in the event of a disaster to enable the organization to:

1. Resume operations
2. Reconstruct its legal and financial status
3. Fulfill its financial obligations to outside interests, employees, and stockholders

Timecards and other documents used in preparing payrolls and customer billings for current accounting periods are typically vital documents. Note that after preparation of the payroll and billings, these documents support the computations, but are no longer vital.

Historic records and items may have significance, although of limited value in current operations. Items such as the original corporate charter, photographs, original manuscripts, and product samples are often worth saving. However, items in this classification are not the primary reason for records management.

Retention Periods

A retention period must be determined for each record series. This can be a major task requiring much study as there are operational, contractual, and legal aspects to this determination. It is advisable to obtain concurrence from operating, financial, administrative, and legal staff with the periods established.

For most records, operational needs will require the longest retention period. Perhaps not more than ten percent of all records need be kept for legal reasons after meeting operational needs. An even smaller percentage of records will qualify as historic.

Suggested sources to consult for the purpose of establishing records retention requirements include:

1. In-house policy directives
2. In-house systems and procedure manuals
3. Contracts, together with specifications and exhibits, or other directives which control the operation
4. Regulations promulgated under federal, state, or local laws which affect the operation. Some specific laws to consider are the Federal Income Tax Code, the Occupational Safety and Health Act, the Enmironmental Protection Act, and Workers' Compensation Acts.
5. Code of Federal Regulations, which is published annually and updated weekly by the *Federal Register.*

A file should be established on regulations that affect records for which the organization is responsible. Because of the tremendous volume of changing regulations, research for compliance is an ongoing effort which will often require the assistance of legal counsel.

Records must also be appraised for historic significance. Some records may have short operational value, but should be saved indefinitely because of potential historic value.

Storage Facilities

Record storage facilities can be located at the site of operations or in a disaster-resistant facility at a remote location. Storage containers may vary from cardboard boxes to racks for computer tapes requiring controlled environment. Selection of proper facilities depends upon cost, availability, record series classification, and the record media (paper, disc, tape, film).

Records series used in ongoing operations are filed in desks, cabinets, and similar equipment near work stations. Constraints encountered are space and the need to protect vital records series. These constraints are generally met by removing less active records to an accessible nearby location. Vital records may be duplicated, with one set sent offsite to a secure location. Automatic dispersal by electronic means is often feasible. Offsite, for this purpose, is defined as being sufficiently remote to avoid destruction of both record sets by a common disaster.

Inactive, infrequently referred-to records should be removed to storage at less expensive locations.

Prime office space in daily use is the least efficient and most costly place to store records that are not frequently used. It is better to select lower cost space which can be efficiently arranged to maximize storage capacity.

Assuming a rental value of $20/square foot per year, a four-drawer, legal-size file cabinet with provision for access costs $150 per year in floor space. However, at a $5 rental rate, with room to store 8 feet vertically, the cost is $10 per year in floor space.

Paper records can be placed in one cubic foot cardboard cartons to be stored on metal racks. The contents of a four-drawer legal size file cabinet can be stored in cartons on racks which cost about $30 to provide.

Consideration should also be given to alternative media for retaining information. Computer-generated data may be retained on magnetic tapes or discs. Paper records may be stored in micrograph form. Storage space for these media is minimal when compared to paper records. However, the cost of copying and retrieving records on these media, including equipment and supply purchases, should be measured against the savings in storage space.

Cost is only one factor to consider in selecting storage space. Other considerations include:

1. Accessibility. How often will records be delivered to, retrieved, and/or removed from storage?

2. Custodial supervision. Who is to look after stored material? Commercial facilities for storing retained records often provide this service. Otherwise, your organization may have to.
3. Retrieval. Does the storage facility have equipment for reproducing stored material, whether in paper, magnetic, or photographic form? Are there electronic means for transmitting information to you if speed is essential?
4. Capacity. Is there room to expand the storage area?

Records Disposal

A records management program is of no value without provision for disposal of records which are no longer needed.

Disposal must be in accordance with a defined program; and each disposal action must be documented to record when, how, and by whom the action was accomplished. This document is of value in the event of future inquiry.

Generally, disposal is most effective if the records are destroyed. Shredding or incineration are effective means. However, nonsensitive paper records may be sold to paper reprocessors or consigned to waste disposal facilities.

MANAGING THE RECORDS PROGRAM

Responsibility

Management must take full responsibility for the records program. Commitment to the program is essential; without it, matters will drift into a familiar pattern of duplication, redundancy, confusion, and waste.

A records coordinator should be appointed. Preferably, the coordinator should devote full time to records management. Certainly this is necessary until a program is fully underway.

Implementation of the records program is the responsibility of management at all levels in the organization. The coordinator will administer the program, advise, assist, and recommend solutions to problems when necessary. Responsibility for operating inactive storage facilities may be given to the coordinator or to an operating function, as appropriate.

Written Procedures

New work habits or ways of doing things are best explained in writing. A written procedure for records management need not be lengthy or complex. There are five items to cover:

State the objectives and define any new terms
Explain the procedure for identifying and classifying each record series
Describe the preparation of retention schedules for each function
Develop procedures for transferring records to storage and for retrieving documents when needed
Develop procedures for disposal or destruction of records no longer needed

Primary objectives of a records management program include efficient filing and retrieval of information in whatever form it is recorded, cost savings, protection against loss, and compliance with contractual and legal requirements.

To start a records inventory, first identify each record series found in the scope of the inventory. Classifying each record series as operational, legal, or historic is part of the inventory procedure.

Retention schedules are prepared from information obtained during the record series inventory. A typical retention schedule for an operating function will list each record series, indicating the time, usually in years, each is to be retained in active, inactive, or offsite storage. Record series not slated for ultimate disposal should be noted as "permanent." At this point, the records coordinator must become involved to analyze the assembled information for practicality, redundancy, and for compliance with retention requirements. Recommendations by the coordinator must be reviewed and discussed with the manager of the operating function. The retention schedule, amended if necessary, should then be submitted to the appropriate persons in the accounting, legal, and operating functions for approval. The completed schedule provides a blueprint for administering the records management program.

Procedures for transferring records to and withdrawing information from storage are then to be devised. Preferably, a form on which to identify the date, source, contents, and retention period for each storage container is used. Copies of this form are to be attached to the storage container and held by the functions responsible for the record series and for custody in storage. Generally, each storage container holds only material from one record series. Provisions for tracking retrievals and returns to storage can be made on the storage form.

Disposal of records that have outlived their retention period must be carefully documented. It is well to take the precaution of securing final approval for disposal from the function responsible for the records concerned. Choose a method of disposal consistent with the form and content of the records. Shredding or incineration achieve total destruction. Obtain a signed acknowledgment of disposal by the person who executed the disposal order. This acknowledgment becomes useful in the event of future inquiries.

Tracking Implementation

The records coordinator is responsible for tracking progress in implementing the records management program. Periodic progress reports should be given to all levels of management until the program has been completely installed. Thereafter, periodic status reports are desirable.

Progress reports for each operating function involved would provide useful information as to the status of the following steps:

1. Identify record series
2. Take inventory
3. Retention schedules
4. Inactive files to storage
5. Disposal of expired records

After installation of the program, periodic status reports should be prepared to inform management of the storage capacity for inactive records, the volume of records in storage, and the number of movements in and out of storage. These reports are prepared by the custodian of the inactive storage facility.

TECHNIQUES FOR RECORDS MANAGEMENT

Records management requires systematic control of all recorded information generated or used in the organization. Usually this information will be in the form of conventional paper documents. However, it is important to remember that provisions for the storage and retrieval of information recorded via other media must be included in the program.

When evaluating records to establish retention periods, only the information recorded should be considered. Many times destruction of records on microfilm, punch cards, or tape is delayed because they take up so little space and are inexpensive or no trouble to retain. The retention period should be determined without regard to the medium which contains the record. For example, accounts payable vouchers, whether on film or in hard copy form, should be destroyed solely on the basis of operational and/or legal need. Prompt destruction of records in accordance with established retention periods will prove the integrity of the program.

Advancing technologies are often viewed as making the records management task more difficult. Changes in the way information is created, and automated control of that information, can actually make the job easier. Most organizations have or can obtain the following resources for records management applications:

1. Word processing equipment can be used to prepare and maintain file indexes, records center inventories, destruction lists, etc.

2. Accessibility of reprographic equipment results in multiple copies of almost all business records so precaution must be taken to retain only "record copies." This simple duplication process, on the other hand, may be used to solve some vital records protection problems.

3. A wide array of micrographic equipment and systems is available to meet the most unique filing and records management needs. Consider security filming to protect your vital records and/or archival filming for permanent storage of historic records. Design a unitized microfilm system for large volume and/ or frequently referenced material. Combine that microfilming program with a computerized retrieval system. Film large engineering drawings or maps on 35-mm film and mount on space saving key punch aperture cards for easy retrieval.

4. Computer-generated records are excellent candidates for computer-output microfilm. COM is a method of converting machine-readable data directly from computer tape to microfiche at high speed. This microfiche requires only a fraction of the space to store, is easier to handle, and is less expensive to distribute and duplicate than paper records.

5. A relatively new and promising technique that will greatly simplify future records management is optical scanning, the success of which depends upon the quality of data base planning.

Rapid technological advances provide unlimited possibilities, but good, workable records management systems must be established before they can be automated. An index prepared with computer or word processing equipment will be only as good as the manual system it was generated from.

The complexity of the systems available will necessitate cooperation and a good working relationship with the computer analysts, micrographics experts, and other specialists in the organization.

XV
MANAGEMENT SKILLS

UNIT OVERVIEW

Each of us, prior to or during our first exposure to the business world, passed through a phase where we perhaps viewed the skills of those in management with a degree of awe. The effective management of people and events to achieve lofty goals does, indeed, create a mystique, felt by those within an organization, observed by others from without.

For many years management was treated as a pure art form, with the emphasis on the personalities and the idiosyncrasies of the manager. Personality is extremely important, but if we were to catalog the personalities of all the managers we have read about we would fill every square on the board. It was quite common at one time to see young executives assume the personality traits and habits of their leader or mentor, relating management success exclusively to style rather than content.

Recent decades have seen the emergence of management as a pseudoscience with an emphasis on technique—the programmed approach. A continuing and natural evolution has produced what we perceive today as a beneficial blend of style and methods; a blend of human relations and systems: the consummate manager.

What does all of this mean to the fledgling project manager? If we are to grow in the world of project management, or, eventually, into line management, we obviously must develop quality management skills, recognized and respected by our subordinates, peer group, and superiors. All too often however, we see people with high potential never achieve goals that are realizable and expected.

Certain attributes are prerequisites: some innate (intelligence, awareness, common sense); some developed (education, experience, prescience). We should appreciate that the successful managers of the past weren't in fact all style: they had well-developed techniques—perhaps understood by them, perhaps not—but, their techniques worked. It fell to later generations to analyze and evaluate these methods for the edification and enhancement of the modern manager.

Much has been written about managers and management. Let's keep it simple. There is no mystery. With the proper prerequisites, and an emphasis on common sense, you as a manager can go a long way if you will develop management skills—skills that can be "acquired." The benefits of these acquired management skills are many! Let's consider just a few.

Consistency. In all phases of life, with parental guidance as an excellent example, we seek consistency in treatment. No better place to apply this principle than in the management of a project team.

Problem solving. Use established techniques to solve routine problems. Leave your mind free to concentrate on complex issues.

Enhancement of style. If we are well-founded in the basics, we will find that the comprehension and implementation of a systems approach will help us to develop a mature style based on a solid foundation and convert future potential to present effectiveness.

Comfort zone. As we understand and introduce programs of management into our portfolio we will expand our management "comfort zone" and be better equipped to maintain our posture when project-threatening events occur.

Several basic project-oriented management skills will be discussed here that should be of value to the experienced manager as well as the novitiate.

TIME MANAGEMENT

To paraphrase Peter Drucker, Time is a unique resource, totally perishable, always in very scarce supply. We suggest you use it with great care, ration it, apply it in a systematic manner.

To get more done, you must manage time properly. The basic concepts of time management involve an understanding of your time habits, development of a systematic action plan for time utilization, elimination of time wasters and procrastination, and the ability to create and manage personal and group time.

A key project document is the schedule, whether manual or computer-based, short-term, long-term, or milestone. Plan your own time with the same degree of care that you plan project time, albeit on a mini scale. Prepare daily, weekly, long-term, and milestone personal calendars, using whatever format is comfortable for you. Keep them simple and current.

The ultimate test of personal and group time management has been, is, and will always be the meeting or conference. A meeting can either be a waste of an enormous amount of time: X people times Y hours equals an unrecoverable resource Z; or, initiate a highly productive course of action through the combined ingenuity of the team.

The mechanics of conference management are well covered in the literature. Excluding brief ad hoc meetings to sort out the facts on some current issue, there are two principles that must be adhered to in order to have a successful meeting. First, every meeting should have a purpose, a product. Second, every meeting may be classified by type: information sharing, problem solving, decision making, planning evaluation. Have a purpose for the meeting, organize by meeting type, understand meeting mechanics, keep the meeting on track, and, you will utilize the valuable resource of time in the most effective manner for the benefit of the project.

EFFECTIVE DELEGATION

Many project managers who were successful prior to the mid to late 1960s were ineffectual during the "Mega Period" from the late 1960s through the late 1970s. More than one company suffered through weak performances by their "Top Man." Why was this?

If a project is one that you can "see," or "put your arms around," certain basic management deficiencies don't exert undue influence. As projects grew in size and complexity, however, the need to use project management control programs and the need to work with and through the staff became mandatory. Many hands-on, personality-oriented managers adjusted. Many didn't.

Effective delegation was the key to the successful management of the mega project. Project management grew, almost overnight, from a highly technical exercise to a true management profession.

Delegation comes in two packages: one good, one bad.

Good Delegation: The leader prepares a well-defined scope of work; packages it; assigns it to a person qualified to handle the work; establishes realizable targets—time, money, quality, product; and sets up appropriate control programs to monitor progress.

Bad Delegation: The leader describes an element of work in vague terms; assembles a loose package of material some of which may be relevant; hands it to the most available staff member; sets targets of "now or later" (usually tomorrow); and, after looking over the designate's shoulder every day for a week, decides that he'll do it himself, and drops all his other activities. Exaggeration? Certainly! Close to the target? Close enough!

The process of delegation is a dynamic process of relationships, unique in that it involves all of the management and human skills: accountability, authority, responsibility; organizing, planning, controlling; leadership, motivation, communication; time management, performance management, problem solving, negotiation.

PROBLEM SOLVING AND PROBLEM PREVENTION

Complex problems, particularly client relations problems, frequently can be reduced by a separation of variable techniques to several single variable problems—reduced to the parts. Each single variable problem, often recognizable and well understood, can then be attacked independently and in parallel to minimize solution time.

Complex problems are multivariable, that is, composed of a mixture of single variable problems, and are intricate in structure, but may be relatively easy to resolve if analyzed in a methodical manner. Through analysis, we may also learn that an apparent complex problem is, in fact, a single variable problem masked by peripheral or nonrelevant issues. The young project manager can prevent years of ineffectual problem solving, with a resultant loss of subordinate and peer group leadership recognition, by developing a system for problem evaluation and resolution, and in so doing will further gain through the progressive development of a building-block file of standard solutions to basic and common problems.

An organized approach to problem solving requires that we collect information about the problem, find the cause of the problem, and take appropriate action. Since many possible causes might explain the problem, a technique called "is" and "is not" is most useful. Simply stated, the "is not" identifies conditions that appear to contribute to the problem but which are not affected by the deviation, helping to prevent hipshooting, that is, jumping on the first "logical" solution proposed, a common management ailment.

Good decisions take into account three key elements of choice: establishing objectives, the goals which we seek to achieve through a selected course of action; generating alternatives, the various routes available to reach the goal; examining adverse consequences, determining the risk inherent in the several available courses of action.

The game plan should consider limitations imposed by outside sources either beyound your control or restrictive to your control. There are always elements on a project that, overtly or covertly, will prevent you from meeting your objectives. Build preventative and contingency actions into the original plan, relying heavily on your experience and feel for the project. Then reassess the project frequently; you will find that you have a new project, that "The Project" is setting its own goals. A project, unfortunately, isn't an inanimate object, but very much has a life of its own. Much

of the effort put into initial planning isn't utilized because there's little certainty that
the program will be completed as planned.

All of us have benefited from the deterministic approach to computerized scheduling. It is often better, however, to plan contingency actions rather than arbitrarily
allow extra time to solve problems clearly identifiable in the original plan. Problem
avoidance through contingency planning, early problem identification, and periodic
reassessment of the total project is a key to a successful project. If a problem is identified in the original plan, attack the problem rather than blocking out time for a later
solution.

There are no black and white answers to most management problems. This is even
more so for project management problems, where time is of the essence. We hope,
working in the gray zones, to be able to neutralize the major damaging effects of these
excursions, forcing an acceptable level of tolerance so we can get on with the main
event, the project. Find a good solution under the circumstances. If we understand
value/cost/quality relationships we will appreciate that the optimum system doesn't
provide maximum quality or information. Perfection is a fault in a project manager,
a practice that encourages strategies by default in other critical areas. We have just
so much time—the irreplaceable resource.

PERFORMANCE MANAGEMENT

Performance management is a primary tool available to the project manager for the
improvement in results-oriented behavior of the project team. Performance management is the use of external events to change behavior. It reinforces the management
of people in an organization; it is used to manage the results. Three important terms
in performance management implementation should be understood: Antecedents, Behavior, Consequences.

Antecedents are the events before the action. We issue a variety of instructions,
set the scene, disseminate information. We provide the antecedents. The antecedents
can be tangible, such as written directives, schedules, budgets; or intangible, such
as pep talks, counseling sessions, personal example. A project environment is created.

Behavior is the observation and evaluation of actions of an individual and of the
group. Since behavior is what an individual or a group accomplishes, it can be measured and quantified: the number of drawings issued, the yards of concrete poured,
the number of people tardy.

Consequences are what happens after the action. The results can be either positive or negative, with recognition for the achiever, counseling for the laggard. Consequences should be balanced in degree and application against the impact of the corresponding behavior. And there should be personal impact, with a minimal delay in the
administration of the consequence.

The ABCs of performance management—antecedents, behavior, consequences—
are easy building blocks to increased project success. The keys to how we manage
performance are: be specific, choose obvious data, use good timing on follow-up.

THE ART OF NEGOTIATION

Negotiation is the art of applying influence to increase the probability of a particular
outcome. It differs from direct control where authority can be exercised to obtain
compliance. Successful project managers, lacking formal line authority, negotiate
daily to influence diverse interests to take actions necessary to meet the objectives
of the project.

There are two basic strategies to negotiation: one treats the other party as an
opponent; one regards the other party as a collaborator. Choose the strategy that
best fits the particular circumstances of the particular negotiation.

A win/lose strategy seeks to win at the expense of an opponent. This strategy is necessary when any concenssions would be very costly to one's own position. A win/win strategy seeks to collaborate on a mutually agreeable solution to seemingly conflicting interests. This strategy is essential when the other party's commitment is crucial to achieving the desired outcome.

THE PERSONNEL DEPARTMENT AND THE PROJECT

At first glance it may seem odd to include this topic in a unit dedicated to the skills of management. A common project management failing, however, particularly on complex or overseas projects, is the excessive involvement or lack of involvement of the manager in personnel activities.

Jobsite agreements. Will you apply uniform personnel practices, and, do you honestly believe you understand the complexities of relocation?

Day by day activities. Do you have the time to review, take action, and follow up on the myriad of personal problems incidental to the management of a project team?

Project completion. In addition to reassignment, we have to consider leave of absence, layoff, and termination. As the project winds down, other issues should command your attention.

You have just so much time. To spend an inordinate amount of your limited time with the details of personnel management that probably could be handled better by skilled personnel professionals, simply means that other issues where your skills are vital are being resolved by default. This doesn't mean you shouldn't be involved; what we have here is an excellent opportunity to practice "good delegation." Further, there are few more damaging practices than taking the initiative in highly personal issues—people issues—and failing to carry through because of the time-pressure of subsequent events.

The services provided by a modern personnel group are many and diversified: staffing, compensation, benefits, training and development, performance evaluation, new employee orientation; statutory assistance (Equal Employment Opportunity (EEO), Affirmative Action Programs (AAP), overtime legalities); evaluation of emerging legal considerations (employment-at-will, sexual harassment, age discrimination, medical discrimination, U.S. citizenship); jobsite assignments (short-term, long-term, assignment conditions); project completion (leave of absence, layoff, termination).

Personnel, working with the legal group, can establish uniform ground rules for standard problems, and give the manager sound advice on special problems. Delegate personnel management in a constructive manner for the benefit of the project team.

SELECTED BIBLIOGRAPHY

General Management

Batten, J. D. *Tough-Minded Management*. New York: American Management Association, 1963-1969.

Dowling, W. F., Jr., and L. R. Sayles. *How Managers Motivate: The Imperatives of Supervision*. New York: McGraw Hill, 1971.

Greenleaf, R. K. *Servant Leadership*. Paulist Press, 1977.

Harvard Business Review—On Management. New York: Harper & Row, 1955-1975.

Levinson, H. *Executive*. Cambridge, MA: Harvard University Press, 1981.

Decision Making

Cooper, J. D. *The Art of Decision Making*. New York: Doubleday & Company, 1961.

Emory, C. W. and P. Niland. *Making Management Decisions*. Boston: Houghton Mifflin, 1968.

Kepner, C. H. *Improving Plant Productivity*. Kepner-Tregoe, 1982.

Kepner, C. H., and Benjamin B. Tregoe. *The New Rational Manager*. Princeton, NJ: Princeton Research Press, 1981.

Kepner-Tregoe Journal XIII (1, 4); XIV (2, 4).

Kinsley, G. R. Potential Accident Analysis. *Professional Safety*. July 1983.

Nora, J., R. Rogers, and R. Stramy. *Transforming the Workplace*. Princeton, NJ: Princeton Research Press, 1986.

Tregoe, B. B. Decision Making Process. In *Handbook for Professional Managers*. L. R. Bittel and J. E. Ramsey (eds.). New York: McGraw Hill, 1985.

Negotiation

Albert Warschaw, T. *Winning by Negotiation*. Berkley Books, 1980.

Buskirk, R. *Handbook of Management Tactics*. Hawthorne Books, 1976.

Cohen, H. *You Can Negotiate Anything*. Lyle Stuart, 1980.

Fisher, R., and W. Ury. *Getting To Yes*. Boston: Houghton Mifflin, 1981.

Nierenberg, G. I. *The Art of Negotiating*. Cornerstone Library, 1968.

Schatzki, M. *Negotiation, The Art of Getting What You Want*. New York: New American Library, 1981.

Seltz, D. D., and A. J. Modica. *Negotiate Your Way To Success*. New York: New American Library, 1980.

Time Management

Drucker, P. F. How Effective Executives Use Their Time. Unpublished article.

Lakein, A. *Hydrocarbon Processing*, February 1977, pp. 145-162.

Prince, G. M. Training HRD, October 1977, pp. 39, 40.

Richards, G. W. and A. MacKenzie, *Hydrocarbon Processing*, July 1981, pp. 225-236.

Weber, R. A. *Time and Management*. New York: Van Nostrand Reinhold, 1972.

Personnel Practices

Burack, E. H., and N. J. Mathys. *Human Resource Planning: A Pragmatic Approach to Manpower Staffing and Development*. Brace-Park Press, 1980.

Lawler, E. E., III. *Pay and Organization Development*. Reading, MA: Addison-Wesley, 1981.

Milkovich, G. T., and J. M. Newman. *Compensation*. Business Publications, 1984.

Morgan, P. V. International Human Resource Management: Fact or Fiction. *Personnel Administrator*, September 1986.

Northrup, H. R., and M. E. Malin. *Personnel Policies for Engineers and Scientists, An Analysis of Major Corporate Practice*. Philadelphia: Industrial Research Unit, The Wharton School, 1985.

Rayman, J. and B. Twinn. *Expatriate Compensation and Benefits-An Employer's Handbook*. London: Kogin Page, 1983.

1

Time Management

HEBAB A. QUAZI[*] *Kinetics Technology International Corporation, Monrovia, California*

One thing we don't have enough of in our life is time. Peter Drucker says:

> Time is a unique resource: no matter how great the demand, there is no more
> to supply—it is totally inelastic. And time cannot be stored. It is going by the
> second, and you either get something out of it or you don't. However, you can-
> not regain it. Time is totally perishable, and so it is always in very scarce
> supply.

Yet, most people really do not have a systematic, objective approach to programming
their activities and to planning for the effective use of time.

Like anyone else, project managers have to use their time effectively. To get
more done, you must manage time properly. The basic concepts of time management
involve an analysis of your time habits, development of a systematic action plan with
proper goals and priorities, elimination of time wasters and procrastination, and the
ability to create and manage personal and group time.

In the overall concept of managing a project, a project manager's action plan
should include: a well thought out road map for managing time effectively, including
plans for long-term, short-term, and daily activities; setting priorities with estimates
of the degree of flexibility; delegation of activities with reporting requirements; conference planning and control. He also should plan how to utilize his discretionary
time effectively. The project manager must take time to evaluate the time management
habits of his subordinates and, if required, extend help to make them better time
managers. This will lead to an increased effectiveness of the project team.

BASIC CONCEPTS

Here are the basic elements of a systematic approach to time management.

Time Habits Analysis

The systematic approach to time management should begin with an analysis of your
present approach to time management. You need to ask yourself some provocative
questions to give you an outline of your goals, needs, and habits as they relate to
the use of time. Questions developed by Alan Lakein for self-appraisal of time
management are given below. Your answers to these questions will help you develop
a planning system for your activities—your own time-management system.

---

[*] *Present affiliation:* Martech International, Inc., San Dimas, California

Questions for time-management self-appraisal

1. What are your lifetime goals?
2. How would you like to spend the next five years?
3. What are the advantages to you of making better use of time?
4. What are the disadvantages you could avoid by making better use of time?
5. What are the long-term benefits of making better use of your time now?
6. What are the emotional, physical, and rational blocks to delegation?
7. What can you do when you have spare time on your hands?
8. How can you increase your ability to control you own time?
9. What will you do the next time you confront a time-choice conflict?
10. What does better time management mean to you?
11. What are you avoiding?
12. What can you eliminate?
13. Account for the 168 hours in the last seven days.
14. What have you been doing in the last six months which you should do less?
15. What should you do more of in the future?
16. What should you give up from the past?
17. What should you gain now for the future?
18. What are your goals in the personal area: physical, emotional, rational?
19. What are your goals in the areas of work and professional development?
20. What are your goals with regard to family and friends?
21. List instant tasks under each area of your life.
22. List instant tasks to bring you closer to your lifetime goals.
23. How can you improve your handling of paperwork?
24. How can you reduce your internal interruptions?
25. How can you reduce external interruptions?
26. What are the other questions you should ask yourself for better time use?

Action Plan

Developing an action plan is very important. The information derived from analyzing your past time management habits will help you develop your action plan for effective use of your time. The key milestones of your plan should be based on personal and corporate goals and priorities. It should take into consideration long-term as well as short-term goals and activities. The plan should include a list of tasks with the order of priority and time to be allocated to each. The plan should have flexibility to allow for periodic changes because of unanticipated demands, some of which may have very high priority.

In developing the plan take into consideration the limitations or restrictions imposed by outside sources beyond your control. These elements can prevent you from completing your task within the planned time limit. Materials or services which must be obtained from outside sources, or actions of others which might delay your progress, are restraints which must be reconciled. By identifying and recognizing the restraints in advance, you can develop alternative plans to avoid or eliminate them or moderate their adverse effects.

Goal Setting

You should know your goals. You may be working hard but, if you don't know where you are going, you may be spinning your wheels. It is very important to identify what you would like to do or like to have on a long-range as well as short-range basis. Start by listing all the things you want to achieve in your lifetime, and for the next five years, and for the next six months. The lists should include your personal, professional, and business goals. Next, you need to develop a list of activities that will help you reach each goal. Now is the time to assign priorities to your goals and devise a plan of activity for reaching each goal.

Prioriies

Setting priorities enables you to do what should be done instead of dealing with what comes along. For most of us, it is natural to do the easy and familiar things before tackling the more important and often more difficult ones. But from a benefits or importance point of view, it is best to begin with the top priority items first. Most of the important tasks require a fairly large amount of time to be spent in one stretch. We need to learn to identify the activities that demand blocks of undisturbed time.

In setting priorities, an ABC priority system is frequently used. Important items that must be done are rated as As, with Cs as the least important. You can make sure that the As get the attention they deserve, if they are identified and time is allocated. Sometimes it will be necessary to break a large activity down to small parts for ease of planning or getting a discrete part done in a reasonable time frame.

Now list all the A items that have to be done in a day, week, or a month. Then review the list for determining priorities among As and arrange in order of A1, A2, A3.

In assigning priorities, one thing to keep in mind is that what appears to be an "A" item today may not remain an "A" 6 months from now because of changes in criteria or the environment. It is important to review the list from time to time.

Time Wasters

A time waster is anything that prevents you from achieving your objectives effectively. Visitors dropping in, meetings that go on and on, unimportant phone calls, and the like are among the host of time wasters that will invade our daily work life if we are not careful. Managers who habitually procrastinate become interruption-prone and actually invite interruptions.

Time wasters can be grouped by the principal management functions in which the time wasting activity occurs. Richards and Mackenzie have listed 40 of the more common time wasters, grouped by management function. These are shown below. Scan them and identify the ones in your life.

Planning
Unable to set priorities
Lack of objectives/planning
Crisis management, shifting priorities
Attempting too much at once/unrealistic time estimates
Waiting for planes/appointments
Travel
Haste/impatience
Organizing
Personal disorganization/cluttered desk
Confused responsibility and authority
Duplication of effort
Multiple bosses
Paperwork/red tape/reading
Poor filing system
Inadequate equipment/facilities
Staffing
Untrained/inadequate staff
Under/overstaffed
Absenteeism/tardiness/turnover
Overdependent staff
Directing
Ineffective delegation/involved in routine details
Lack motivation/indifference
Lack coordination/teamwork

Controlling
    Telephone interruptions
    Drop-in visitors
    Inability to say "no"
    Incomplete/delayed information
    Lack self-discipline
    Leaving tasks unfinished
    Lack standards/controls/progress reports
    Visual distractions/noise
    Overcontrol
    Not being informed
    People not available for discussion
Communicating
    Meetings
    Lack/unclear communication, instructions
    Socializing/idle conversation
    "Memoitis"/overcommunication
    Failure to listen
Decision-making
    Procrastination/indecision
    Wanting all the facts
    Snap decisions

Conference Planning

As a project manager, you attend a lot of meetings. Some are initiated by you, some by members of your project team, some from outside your project organization. Despite all good intentions, most of the meetings do not deliver the desired results.

Having a good meeting involves good planning, concentration, and a genuine participation by the group's entire membership. We assume that we all know how to conduct ourselves in a meeting, but that is seldom true. George M. Prince reports that by study of videotapes of hundreds of meetings it was learned that very few people know how to avoid the sort of actions that result in wasting a lot more time and energy than they should in a meeting.

There are five basic types of meetings:

1. Information sharing. An organized exchange of data
2. Problem solving. Seeking options and alternatives
3. Decision making. Selecting a course of action from options and alternatives
4. Planning. Projecting future options and alternatives in terms of what, who, when, how, where, why, and with what
5. Evaluation. Reviewing results achieved, then focusing on the future

Each of these meetings has some specific product that the group attempts to produce. In real situations more than one type or, in an extreme case, all five types are wrapped up in one meeting.

For a successful meeting, advance notice about the meeting should be circulated or distributed to the participants to help them prepare for the meeting. The meeting notice should contain the following information, as a minimum.

(a) A one sentence headline that tells what the meeting is about
(b) Another sentence that tells what the meeting should accomplish
(c) The date and time of the meeting, including an estimate of how much time will be required
(d) The names of those who should attend the meeting
(e) The name of the person who is calling the meeting
(f) The location of the meeting

The advantage of stating the subject and purpose before a meeting is that the individual requesting the meeting will think through the purpose and focus on what he really wants from the meeting. Also, once the purpose of a meeting is made explicit, everyone knows when the meeting goes off track. The time estimate establishes a target that is usually absent from the meeting.

If you are the meeting caller, usually you chair the meeting. The chairperson has the responsibility to keep the discussions on track, help draw conclusions, and assign follow-up action. After the meeting it is a good practice to prepare meeting notes and distribute them to the participants. The notes should identify the action items, who should take them, and the timing.

PROJECT NEEDS

A project manager has full responsibility for the project. Based on the project scope and goals, he will need to list all the action items at the beginning of the project. Next, action items should be classified into long-term and short-term items with proper priorities assigned to each. The project manager must be well informed to be able to make decisions on the project quickly to meet its needs and to benefit the project as a whole. To do this, the project manager has to do a lot of advance planning, put the planning into action, check against the desired goals and, if necessary, redirect the activity. All these efforts take a lot of time, and even more if we add the time-wasters. As project manager, you will need to organize your activities, utilizing the best time management techniques.

PROJECT ACTION PLANS

At the very beginning of the project, the project manager is responsible for developing project execution plans, based on the specific project needs and goals. These plans are in the areas of engineering and design, cost, scheduling, procurement, quality assurance and control, manpower, construction, safety.

Based on these plans, you list the long-range, short-range, and daily activities separately. The long range may be on a half year or an annual basis, depending on project life. The short range schedule may be weekly or monthly. Now you assign priorities for the action items, based on project goals and objectives.

Once the priorities are assigned, develop the daily, short-range and long-range schedules. Schedules should be flexible enough to accommodate unscheduled emergency items. At certain time intervals, review the schedule and adjust, if necessary, for changed conditions, environment, or priorities.

DAILY CALENDAR

The daily calendar or schedule will generally vary, based on the management style or personal habits of each project manager. In general, the daily calendar should show the top priority items scheduled in the early part of the morning, when less outside disturbances are expected. Also, consider taking care of important calls in the early part of the morning.

Important letters, memos, or notes, should be written early in the day when your mind is clear, and you are less likely to be interrupted. Schedule about one-half hour to accommodate the unexpected or to schedule overruns from the morning activities. If nothing comes up, then that time can be used to do something that will improve the overall effectiveness of the project.

The midday is best used for luncheon meetings, such as a staff lunch, project management lunch, or business lunch. It is important to keep the lunch brief and within the scheduled lunch break.

The afternoon is a good time to get status reports from the project leaders on the problem areas. This may involve a one-on-one meeting or a group meeting. Keep meetings to a minimum.

A project manager is responsible for seeing that the project staff develops good time management habits. Afternoon activities may also include one-on-one meetings with individual staff members to review their time management habits, performance on the job, and their professional development.

For effective project control, a daily check of the status on critical items and on other sensitive schedule and cost elements may be helpful. These action items may be scheduled in the afternoon. A good practice is to end the work day by reviewing the next day's schedule and adjust it, if necessary. Quite often it will not be possible to finish all the action items planned for the day. If a full day of work is scheduled for the next day, consider staying late or coming in early the next day to work on those unfinished items.

A typical project manager's daily calendar is given below:

Daily Calendar

7:00	Write memo to Engineering V.P. on manpower
8:00	Initiate meeting notice on process compressor at 9:30 AM
8:15	Meet Project Management V.P. on project cost and schedule
8:30	Call customer Project Manager on compressor fabrication and delivery problem
9:00	Call Construction Manager at job site
9:30	Staff meeting on compressor fabrication and delivery problem
10:30	Review and comment on project engineering past performance and recovery plan
11:00	Reserved
12:00	Project Management Luncheon on productivity
1:00	
1:30	Meet with Project Engineer and Project Controls Manager on engineering recovery plan
2:00	
2:30	Meet Project Controls Manager and Cost Engineer on Cost Report
3:00	
3:30	Meet Project Electrical Engineer on improved performance
4:00	
4:30	Review today's achievement and update tomorrow's calendar
5:00	
6:00	

SHORT-RANGE ACTIVITIES

The short-range activities on a project include at least monthly work progress evaluation in the areas of engineering, procurement, and construction. A project manager is responsible each month for reporting the work progress, with explanations of deviations from the schedule and cost, and developing a recovery plan in the areas of shortfall. In addition, he is responsible for customer relations. At least once a month, review the status and revise future plans to improve or strengthen relationships with customers. Also, review interrelationships within the project team on a monthly basis. If required, the project manager should help facilitate cooperation and team-building spirit among team members.

Reports of project status are made, in fact, to both the customer's management as well as to the project manager's own management. Making this happen every month on a predetermined date requires a lot of planning and organization. Let's look at a typical project manager's short-range plan—one week.

Short-Range Plan

(First Week of the Month)

Monday	Project review (internal) of work progress, presented by discipline leaders
Tuesday	In-house issue of work progress and recovery plan
Wednesday	Draft Progress Report to client's management
Thursday	Issue Report to client
Friday	Issue Project Status Report to own management

LONG-RANGE ACTIVITIES

Based on the lifespan of the project, this may be a half year or an annual review and readjustment of the project execution plans, based on a reassessment of the project goals and priorities.

Reassessment of the whole project, and review of what the original project goals and priorities were may be necessary. If any of these have changed or altered because of an uncontrollable environment, the project manager should review every project execution plan and make necessary changes to meet new conditions. Finally, development of an orderly implementation plan should begin.

These activities will demand a significant time of both the project manager and the project team members in the sixth month, or twelfth month, as the case may be. Your work calendar for that month should be scheduled such that your regular project work is disturbed to a minimum.

A typical long-range activity calendar is shown below.

Long-Range Plan

(6th or 12th Month)

1st week	Review project goals and priorities (beginning with present)
2nd week	Review project execution plan and identify changes required
3rd week	Review changes with client
4th week	(1) Update project execution plan
	(2) Develop implementation plan

SUMMARY

A project manager has total responsibility for successful execution of the project. To achieve that end requires development of systematic plans to reach that goal. These demand effective and efficient utilization of time. In addition, project team members need guidance to learn to use their time most effectively. This will bring improved performance. In developing your good time management habits, remember the basic elements of a systematic approach to time management.

2

Effective Delegation

RONALD H. GERSTENBERGER   *Consultant, Amherst, New Hampshire*

ESTABLISHING THE OVERALL CONTEXT

Delegation is a complex subject. Deeply involved with human interrelations and management skills, delegation perhaps ranks second to the process of decision making in its complexity and may well be one of the least understood of all management techniques.

If we consider that two major classifications of skills are required in project management, it is usually conceded that technical skills are the prime requisite; perhaps to a significantly higher degree than in general management, and perhaps to the detriment of skills in human relations. If we assume that the educational background of most project managers is highly technical and specialized, it is also probably safe to assume that nontechnical, unspecialized human skills have been played down somewhat. However, the best project managers are well balanced and strong in both technical and human skills.

This discussion of delegation is surrounded by chapters relating to such skills as time management, negotiating, problem solving, and performance management. All are associated with human skills and all are interrelated. When you begin to recognize the importance and interrelationships of human skills in management, you begin to understand the importance of the skill of delegation.

ESTABLISHING THE SPECIFIC CONTEXT

The definition of words and terms has significance in establishing a specific and proper context. Even in highly theoretical areas, not only straightforward dictionary definitions but meaningful definitions by authors, lecturers, teachers, and others have placed things in a context which has led to the development of methods, systems, and techniques of much value. The same is true in regard to delegation. With this background, let's establish the specific context of this chapter on delegation by first defining the words in the unit title—Management Skills, and then in the chapter title—Effective Delegation.

A common definition of the word *management* is getting things done through and with other people. This is a simple yet thought-provoking definition. Or we could expand the definition in this way: accomplishing goals and objectives through the effective and efficient use of other people to the mutual benefit of both parties.

A simple dictionary definition of the word *skill* is competent excellence in performance; an ability that comes from knowledge and practice.

The purpose of this unit is to increase your knowledge and competence so that you may excel in getting things done through and with other people. Or better yet, to increase your knowledge and competence so that you might excell in accomplishing goals and objectives through the effective and efficient use of other people to the mutual benefit of both parties.

Defining the word *delegation* is not as straightforward. The American Management Association defines delegation as, essentially, giving other people things to do. In the dictionary definition of the verb *delegate*, we find words such as *appoint as representative, entrust or commit power, authorize*. And in the dictionary definition of the noun *delegation*, we find words with similar meanings such as *appointed to act for another, entrustment, invested with authority*. Strong words indeed.

A common misconception associated with delegation is that it is simply giving work to others, relieving the delegator of responsibility. After all, isn't that what management is all about—getting things done through others? And further, the thinking often is that it is the best way to avoid doing unpleasant things yourself. Or what about the opportunity to get something done that perhaps you don't feel you have the necessary background, experience, education, or skill to do yourself?

The American Management Association further states that managing is getting things done through other people, and delegation is giving other people things to do. They rightfully contend, then, that management and delegation are interwoven and that one who cannot delegate effectively cannot manage. Now that's a strong indictment which adds a degree of urgency to this chapter. The AMA also states that management is a dynamic process of relationships with other people, and that delegation is probably the most dynamic part of the process. There is nothing cut and dried or simplistic about it, then, is there?

Are you beginning to see the importance of delegation and why it is a management skill?

BACKGROUND OF DELEGATION

Is delegation something new in management? Hardly. In the Book of Exodus, Chapter 18, Jethro, Moses' mentor, and also his father-in-law, exhorts and instructs Moses to delegate much of his heavy, self-inflicted workload to able men. Jethro simply tells Moses that unless he does so, he, Moses, will become just another burnout statistic of little or no value to anyone.

Pay close attention to Jethro's instructions to Moses on the skills of delegation. They are similar to the skills any good mentor would pass on to his protege today; that any good delegator would pass on to his subordinate. Jethro's instructions were: select capable people; teach them; show them by example; give them responsibility and authority over segments of the work; keep control; maintain overall accountability. In addition, Jethro told Moses the people he selected should be trustworthy, God-fearing, available, and teachable. Take heed, there is much knowledge and wisdom to be gained from these passages.

THE PROCESS OF DELEGATION: A DYNAMIC PROCESS OF RELATIONSHIPS

It is almost impossible to think of delegation without the superior/subordinate relationship coming immediately to mind. Most managers and subordinates think of the process of delegation as the superior assigning work, responsibility, and commensurate authority to the subordinate while retaining overall accountability. Little thought, however, is generally given to other required management and human skills such as communication, leadership, negotiation, training, motivation, etc., which really are at the very heart of effective delegation.

Accountability, Authority, and Responsibility

Every manager must have a succinct understanding of three management relationships in the process of delegation: accountability, authority, and responsibility.

Accountability

Beginning at the top, here are some simple statements on accountability. I will leave it to you to think the statements through in relation to their management application and their delegation implication.

> Accountability is a unique project management function and obligation
> Accountability for meeting team goals and objectives always remains with the project manager
> Accountability always flows upward; from the subordinate to his superior
> Accountability is results oriented
> Accountability cannot be delegated

Authority

Let's now make some similar statements about authority.

> Authority is generally negative in its connotation
> Authority means authorization to do, to proceed—it does not necessarily mean power
> Authority authorizes the subordinate to carry out the plans of his superior, to achieve the results the subordinate has been asked to achieve
> Authority implies the right to make effective decisions within the limits of one's responsibility to accomplish measurable results for which one is held accountable
> Authority and responsibility go hand in hand and must coexist equally if a subordinate is to be held accountable
> Authority, within policy, procedural, and position description limits, can, should, and must be delegated
> Authority, when delegated, creates accountability

Responsibility

Lastly, some statements about responsibility.

> Responsibility, when delegated by the project manager, does not relieve the project manager of accountability to his superior for accomplishing team goals and objectives
> Responsibility is assigned downward
> Responsibility is accepted by the subordinate when a task is delegated or work is assigned
> Responsibility must be completely defined by the superior to the subordinate
> Responsibility for making decisions should be delegated as far down in the organization as the decision can effectively be made
> Responsibility is the subordinate's obligation to successfully accomplish to the best of his ability the specific assignment delegated by the superior to whom he is accountable
> Responsibility and authority go hand in hand
> Responsibility is both individualistic and commonistic
> Responsibility can and is delegated but not fully or totally

Can we now come up with meaningful statements about the management relationships of accountability, authority, and responsibility in the process of delegation? Let's give it a try.

Accountability cannot be delegated and is a unique function and obligation of the project manager upward to his superior to meet intermediate goals and the end objective of the project.

Authority, within defined limits, is always delegated by the project manager to a subordinate, authorizing the subordinate to make decisions within his limits of responsibility to achieve accountable, measurable results in carrying out the plans of the project manager in meeting intermediate goals and the end objective of the project.

Responsibility, within limits and with commensurate authority, is completely defined and delegated downward by the project manager to the subordinate who accepts the responsibility and obligation to make decisions and successfully complete, to the best of his ability, the specific assignment delegated by the project manager to whom he is accountable in meeting intermediate goals and the end objective.

We have already established that management and delegation are tightly interwoven and that one who cannot delegate effectively very probably cannot manage effectively.

Organizing, Planning, and Controlling

We know that delegation is assigning to a subordinate the responsibility and commensurate authority to accomplish a goal or objective or some other unique or specific result. We also know that to properly delegate, the superior must establish the standards and the objectives, review progress, guide the subordinate toward the results desired, and apply controls only as necessary to obtain the desired results.

Organizing

The management function of organizing has several activities associated with it. One of these activities is delegation. Organizing works this way: a manager analyzes the work, defines the work, and delegates the work in accordance with various methods and techniques. From the standpoint of organizing, perhaps the single most important consideration is pushing the responsibility for making effective decisions as far down in the organization as possible. This, of course, requires delegation. There is no other way to accomplish this important element of organizing.

Planning

Looking now at planning, the American Management Association points out that the last step in the planning process is to assign responsibility to the right people. What better lead-in to delegation is there? And does not the process of delegation itself require the application of the planning process? The answer is a resounding yes! For example, the establishing of intermediate goals and the end objective (goal setting) is an important part of planning. In fact it is the single most important part of the planning process. Without planned goals and objectives, desired results cannot be identified and you just may be delegating activity type work (busywork) without the ability to control the work to accomplish a specific or unique result.

Controlling

Controlling can be defined as a process used to maximize the probability that results will conform to the plan. It is a process permitting responsibility and commensurate authority to be delegated while overall accountability is retained. Delegation itself implies an overtone of control which originates from superior/subordinate, accountability/authority/responsibility relationships. What you as a project manager need is a good, effective, and timely early warning system in the form of feedback to inform you of any and all deviations from the plan, and assurance that the goals and objectives will be met. The best kind of control is not statistical in nature, but personal control. And personal control is only possible when responsibilities, standards of performance, goals, and objectives have been clearly, concisely, and completely communicated by the superior to the subordinate—the what, the why, the how, the when; coaching the subordinate in the desired results; checking on variances from desired results; and reviewing the intermediate and end results.

Human Skills, Management Skills, and People

There is little doubt that the biggest constraint in accomplishing goals and objectives is people. This being the case, we would be remiss if we fail to recognize and mention the importance of both human and management skills—communication, motivation, negotiating, training, leadership, performance management, problem solving, time management, and so on—in effective delegation: getting things done through and with people to the mutual benefit of all parties.

Volumes could be written about each relationship between delegation and the human and management skills. Just how significant this would be to you as an individual is questionable. The problem is that these relationships are personal and depend on the individual's development in the knowledge and application of human and management skills. Also, we are all unique individuals with free will; with a high degree of knowledge in some areas and less in others. We are, in fact, distinct and unique personalities. The solution, then, is to point out certain key elements of each skill as it relates to delegation to stimulate your thinking to determine your current slot or role in the relationship and to determine your strengths and weaknesses and need for improvement. We will take them one at a time beginning with the human skills.

Communication, Motivation, Training, and Delegation Relationships

Communication, in spite of serious attempts to improve the process, continues to be one of the foremost problems of management. It is the key skill in any person-to-person, one-on-one relationship; the only type of relationship occurring directly between the superior and subordinate in the delegation process. Communication is the key skill in the delegation process. And, do not ignore the importance of listening. It might just be the most important element of the communication process in its relationship to delegation in particular, and to management in general.

Motivation by definition means providing an inducement, an incentive, prompting a person to act in a certain way. Money is commonly thought to be the greatest motivator. However, surveys and studies have found that money is seldom number one and often is far down the list of motivational factors. The acceptance of responsibility and authority and the accomplishment of important team goals is gratifying, self-assuring, and confidence building to the subordinate. And helping the superior satisfy his accountability to his superior improves the position of the subordinate in the eyes of his superior. Remember, if the subordinate has trouble or fails to accomplish the desired result, it is in almost every case the fault of the superior rather than the subordinate; perhaps because of a failure in communication, confusion on what has been delegated, misunderstanding of relationships, etc. Do not, however, let one such incident of demotivation spoil the superior/subordinate relationship and don't back off. Adjust and repair and continue to delegate, learning from the experience.

Training is a strong motivating factor. In a situation where the subordinate is weak in certain management skills, it is the responsibility of management to train the subordinate in his area of need. Delegation of work to such an individual can be limited to his capabilities but not for an extended period of time. It would not be to the mutual benefit of both parties. You just cannot continue to motivate the subordinate by only delegating work he is totally capable of handling. To overcome this situation you must consider training to prepare the subordinate to take on greater responsibility. The best training is controlled on-the-job training. This means delegating work beyond the known capability of the subordinate. There is a risk involved, for the superior always retains accountability. It is, however, a worthwhile risk. On-the-job training means training the subordinate in the area between his known capa-

bility and the required capability to accomplish the desired results. This is not so
much continuing education as it is continual training. Extensive training, however,
is a senior management responsibility, but you can make a significant incremental contribution.

Delegation itself is a human skill. It is not secondary to any other human or management skill. Do not lose sight of this fact.

Leadership, Negotiation, and Time Management Relationships

There is no question that the superior is the key figure in the delegation process.
The best type of leader in the superior/subordinate delegation process is the "serv-
ant/leader" type. There are many articles and books on the servant/leader—read
one or more of them and you will surely incorporate some of the principles in your
management style.

Delegation requires person-to-person, one-on-one negotiating. Negotiating is
part of the communication process. Good delegation techniques will always lead to
a win-win situation to the mutual benefit of both parties. On the other hand, poor
delegation techniques only lead to a win-lose or lose-lose situation. Both are unacceptable to the delegation process.

Time management cannot be separated from delegation. No one person, including
project managers, can do everything. Significant amounts of work must be delegated
if a manager is properly managing his time. Perhaps this is a good time to also point
out that a manager can't go to the other extreme and delegate all or even nearly all
his work. Since management is the development of people, it requires the manager
to properly plan, organize, guide, and control the work—a responsibility that cannot
be totally delegated.

Problem Solving and Performance Management

We stated earlier that delegation perhaps ranks second to the process of decision-making
in its complexity. Then we stated that responsibility for making decisions should be
delegated as far down in the organization as the decision can effectively be made, and
that authority implies the right to make effective decisions within the limits of one's
responsibility to accomplish measurable results for which one is held accountable. It
should be sufficient to say that there is a direct relationship between decision making
and the delegation process.

In performance management, it is obvious that the superior/subordinate relationship comes into play as do many other relationships. It doesn't seem to matter from
what angle we approach the delegation process, it always seems to end up as a relationship. We have covered most of the more meaningful relationships. One yet remains: the relationship the project manager has with himself.

Keep in mind that as a project manager you are limited to what you can accomplish yourself but you are unlimited if you work effectively through others. Isn't that
the heart of management? So maybe you don't have the confidence in yourself to delegate. Or maybe you fear taking the rap for less than expected results. And maybe
there are many other reasons, better yet, excuses. Who's perfect? Let me ask you
a question. How much time do you spend on implementing less than perfect decisions?
Having established the fact that your superiors are not perfect, don't you feel better
already? All this leads to one point . . . if you are going to succeed in the very important human skill of delegation, you must be willing to delegate. It's that simple.

Let's look at a few reasons why many managers fail to delegate.

What about "the job will not be done the way I would do the job." That certainly
is true as no two people will ever do anything or everything exactly the same way.
Don't worry about it. The fact is that the subordinate may do a better job than you
would have done. Now there's something to worry about! Not really, the best possible job is always the desired result and to the mutual benefit of both parties.

Or what about "I love doing this particular kind of work and prefer not to delegate this job," or "I dislike doing this particular kind of work but I'm the only one capable of doing this job." It isn't easy, but don't hold back on delegating work you love doing yourself or work you dislike doing but are capable of doing. When you delegate such work, you will find the work easy to control. Why? Because when you delegate work you are capable of doing or love doing, you know exactly what you want and can communicate the desired results to the subordinate. Thus, feedback becomes informal and meaningful, primarily because of self-control on the part of the subordinate and, the desired results are controllable. On the other hand, if you delegate work you dislike or work that you feel incapable of doing, you will not only have difficulty in communicating the desired results but feedback becomes statistical in nature and therefore less meaningful, resulting in less control of the desired results.

Lastly, what about "the subordinate lacks training and experience to perform the job and accomplish the desired results." And whose fault is this? What an indictment against the manager himself! Delegated work is a perfect and unbeatable tool in training and the giving of opportunity for gaining experience.

To repeat, to be effective in delegation, you must be willing to delegate. However, even to become willing is more difficult than it sounds. But don't use the above excuses.

Good managers do not delegate work just to keep people busy. This accomplishes nothing and serves as a demotivator. It communicates to the subordinate that the superior is more interested in activity than productivity. It's the same activity trap we read about in time management. Activity or busywork seldom achieves desired results and seldom leads to goal or objective accomplishment.

Some managers get very touchy if they feel a subordinate is making even the slightest attempt to move in on their management territory. Although frequently the threat is more imagined than real, this sometimes surfaces if you delegate work to an aggressive, or even assertive, subordinate. If you are one of the touchy ones, here's one piece of scriptural advise—"work out your own salvation with fear and trembling" (Philippians 2:12). You do have a problem if things like this bother you.

Finally, one of the most essential parts of the dynamic process of delegation is trust. Successful delegation demands mutual trust on behalf of both parties and effective delegation depends on it. Trust is developed as relationships develop.

CONCLUSION

Delegation is a dynamic process of relationships concerned with results, and not cut-and-dried, simplistic methods, systems, or procedures. Sit down and draft your own thoughts: the steps to successful delegation; on what delegation is or isn't; on what delegation does; on the do's and don'ts of delegation. The field of project management is already oversaturated with methods, systems, and procedures—and, too little emphasis on human engineering.

My hope then is that your thinking will have been stimulated enough to begin to apply what you may have learned here. And that you might excel in accomplishing goals and objectives through the effective and efficient use of other people to the mutual benefit of both parties.

3

Problem Solving and Problem Prevention

BENJAMIN B. TREGOE   *Kepner-Tregoe Inc., Princeton, New Jersey*

The project manager plays a special role in today's organization. Pressured by dead-lines, responsible for workers inside and outside the organization, dependent on vendor's promises, subject to unexpected shifts from decisions made by others, he or she is still expected to accomplish major tasks on time and within budget.

Developed and used originally by design and construction engineering companies in the process plant industries, project management is now being used in a wider variety of settings, including software development, real estate, report production, and in providing many of the growing services in the U.S. economy. The growth of project management techniques is a reflection of growing competition in which success or failure often hangs on meeting a target date. To succeed in today's business environment, project managers must know how to allocate resources, estimate costs, and devise a critical path, but they also need practical tools for problem solving and problem prevention.

PREVENTING TROUBLE

A project manager at one of America's largest construction companies emphasizes the importance of problem prevention in a recent article in *The Kepner-Tregoe Journal*.

> Techniques of scheduling have become very sophisticated in recent years. Most project managers are aware of the dollar costs of missing a step in the plan. But few managers shore up these detailed plans with effective preventive and contingent actions. Much of the effort put into planning is wasted because there's little certainty these steps will be completed on time!

In well run projects, as much time is devoted to defining and planning the project as to implementing it. It is in these early stages that clear thinking about potential problems is so critical. An often overlooked resource is the project manager's own experience and the experiences of those managers and workers inside and outside the organization who have suffered through the imperfect process of moving from bubble to bubble on PERT charts toward completion of previous projects.

During project planning, as the sequence of activities and the timing of each part of the project are laid out, potential problems and opportunities begin to surface. Before a critical path or one of the standard sequencing techniques is completed, the experienced project manager knows where to expect trouble. By asking, "What hap-

Table 1 Construction of a Natural Gas Plant in Saudi Arabia

Potential Problems	Likely Causes	Preventive Action	Contingent Actions
If a technical problem cannot be resolved on site, then construction will be delayed	Equipment needed to repair the problem not available	Requisition all equipment needed for technical repairs on similar projects	Ask Saudi Arabian government to expedite shipment of "emergency repair" equipment through customs
	Technical expert not available	Train engineers to be sent to the site in technical repairs	Maintain a list of troubleshooters who could be sent to the site on short notice

pens if the preceding step is not completed on time?" a scenario can be envisioned: workers stalled, high inventory costs, line managers getting involved to "fix" the problem—a constructive "what if" program.

AN OUNCE OF PREVENTION

Once a project manager can identify future trouble, he or she can use valuable experience and skill in either preventing or minimizing the trouble. After specific potential problems are defined, likely causes are sought. Preventive actions are established to stop the likely causes. And, because all trouble cannot be prevented, contingent actions are set up to minimize the effect on the project. Both the preventive and contingent actions are built into the original plan. This process is called Potential Problem Analysis.

Let us assume a project manager is planning the construction of a natural gas plant in Saudi Arabia. Using Potential Problem Analysis, he thinks about what might go wrong and how to handle it (Table 1).

Potential problems can be brought to mind in a number of ways. Thinking in general about the new project or similar past projects helps visualize generic problems. More specific problems are generated by focusing on individual steps in the plan. The project manager can typically uncover even more future hazards by involving key players who will help complete the project.

By thinking about causes and preventive and contingent actions, project managers improve the quality of the plan and avoid the tendency to build in extra days "to allow for problems." It is far more effective to anticipate what will go wrong and take appropriate action to prevent its occurrence.

SHORING UP THE PLAN

The most effective problem prevention attacks critical problems. The project manager quoted earlier comments.

> Most project managers interpret "critical" to mean tight deadlines. A step in a construction plan is also critical if it involves new technology, the coordination of individuals unfamiliar with one another, a critical sequence of interrelated activities, completion by workers not under your control, or where failure would be disastrous.

Table 2 Action Plan for Utility Building

Action steps	Schedule	Responsibility
1. Order material	Day 1 to Day 2	Engineers
2. Excavate for foundations	Day 1 to Day 2	Laborers
3. Build form for footings and slab[a]	Day 2 to Day 3	Carpenters
4. Pour concrete	Day 3 to Day 4	Cement supplier and cement workers
5. Cure concrete	Day 4 to Day 6	—
6. Deliver materials[a]	Day 5 to Day 6	Materials supplier
7. Install framing	Day 7	Carpenters
8. Install siding	Day 7 to Day 11	Carpenters
9. Install windows, doors	Day 7 to Day 9	Carpenters
10. Install electrical	Day 11 to Day 13	Electricians
11. Construct roof framing	Day 11 to Day 13	Carpenters
12. Add roofing	Day 13 to Day 14	Roofers
13. Install vent in roof	Day 14 to Day 15	Carpenters
14. Paint building	Day 14 to Day 19	Painters

[a]Critical steps

Table 2 is a 14-step plan a project manager devised to construct a utility building. Two critical steps are identified—steps 3 and 6.

Step 3 is the more critical because its failure would stifle the entire project. Focusing on this step, the engineer considers specific potential problems. The probability and seriousness of each potential problem are then assessed. Here is his analysis of the most significant problem identified:

Potential Problem: Step 3	Probability	Seriousness
If the new forms are not completed on time, then the project will be delayed (H = High; M = Medium; L = Low)	High	High

As in the previous example, the engineer considers likely causes, preventive actions, and contingent actions as shown in Table 3. With these preventive actions in place, the project manager has considerably more confidence that the steps in the plan can be completed on time, and he is ready to handle the problems that do occur with clear contingent actions.

An added and often overlooked benefit in using this systematic approach to solving potential problems is the greater ease of communication permitted by clear identification of what might go wrong and how to handle it. Project managers report that this approach helps build a team spirit with outside vendors and with both peers and subordinates within the organization. Relations with top management are generally smoother as well.

Table 3 Potential Problem Causes with Matching Preventive and Contingent Actions

Likely Causes	Probability	Preventive Action	Contingent Actions
The foreman and workers are unfamiliar with the new forms	High	Hold training sessions beforehand Have a manufacturer's representative present during forming operation	Allow for overtime to pour concrete Change concrete mix to permit faster curing
The forms are untested	Low	—	Revert to old form

The same thinking process can be used to discover opportunities. Suppose the raw materials arrived early. Rather than preventing this, you might try to promote it and, in place of contingent actions designed to minimize the effects of a problem, you might exploit, or maximize, the effects. The cost and time savings achieved through opportunities can offset unexpected problems encountered elsewhere.

SAFETY FIRST

One of the widest uses of Potential Problem Analysis is accident prevention. George R. Kinsley of Rollins Burdick Hunter of Pennsylvania wrote an article for *Professional Safety*, the official publication of the American Society of Safety Engineers, in which he identifies the following Potential Accident Questions:

> What could go wrong?
> What has gone wrong in the past?
> What do our critics say will go wrong?
> What do the prognosticators of doom and gloom say?
> What is the worst thing that can happen? Lesser versions?

These questions help elicit specific potential problems which can be analyzed the same way other potential problems are: What could cause this problem? How can it be prevented? What contingent action will minimize the damage if the problem occurs?

PROBLEM SOLVING

Even the best planning does not anticipate every problem. "Many engineers feel that Murphy's Laws are principles of engineering," one project manager quipped. When unexpected problems arise, the project manager's goal is to return the project quickly to the carefully designed plan everyone expects to see completed. At the onset of these unforeseen problems, the project manager must:

> Collect information about the problem
> Find cause
> Take appropriate action

Collecting information is accomplished by involving everyone in the project who has relevant data. This information becomes the basis of the search for cause.

Finding the cause of a problem requires a separate thinking process called Problem Analysis, which defines the what, where, when, and extent of the problem—the complete picture. Since many possible causes might explain the problem, Problem Analysis relies on a technique called "is" and "is not." The "is not" identifies objects, places, and items similar to the problem, but which are not affected by the deviation. For example, if you are only having trouble with the car door on the driver's side (is), the car door on the passenger's side would be an (is not).

Testing for Carcinogens

Scientists working for the U.S. government, charged with protecting the public from dangers, test, evaluate, and either recommend or reject a wide variety of pharmaceuticals and food additives. In recent years, many government scientists have adopted project management techniques following criticism of several specific research projects. (Red dye number 2 was banned in the United States but not in Canada; while red dye number 40 was banned in Canada but not in the United States.)

Recently a group of these scientists reviewed the results from a comprehensive study of a substance suspected of causing cancer. The chemical additive had been introduced to test groups of mice and rats in varying amounts. The study showed a number of urinary bladder neoplasms, specifically, different cell types growing inside previously defined cell types in the treated rats. Several of the rats given the high dose and several given the intermediate dose developed the problem. While this appears to show a link to cancer, the percentages indicated marginal statistical significance.

These scientists could neither permit nor reject the additive until they clarified whether or not the substance caused cancer. They therefore assembled the data in a Problem Analysis format together with possible causes. They specified the facts about those rats that had the neoplasms (is) and also provided information about the corresponding (is nots). For instance, rats (is) had the problem but mice (is not) were in good health. After assembling (is) and (is not) data they asked what was different about the (is) compared to the (is not). That information is called distinctions and helps narrow the search for cause. Table 4 illustrates how these research scientists arrayed the data from 18 months of chemical testing.

The most probable cause best explains the (is) and (is not) data. Three of the possible causes were quickly eliminated, including the most obvious one: that exposure to the test chemical caused neoplasia. If that were true, the mice would have been affected. One would also expect the female rats to be affected, but they were not. There is no difference in susceptibility between males and females. In addition, substances that cause cancer in the urinary bladder tend to cause cancer in the kidney and ureter, which were not affected. Note that without the (is not) data the first possible cause would be plausible. It falls out only because it fails to explain the (is not).

A second possible cause was that the neoplasms are a secondary effect following inflammation or calculus formation. This does not explain why some male mice had calculi but no neoplasms.

The best fit of all the possible causes, the one which best explains the (is) and (is not) data, was spontaneous occurrence.

In addition to pinpointing the cause of the neoplasms, Problem Analysis improved communication among the scientists and with the public—a major concern for these project managers. "Contrary to popular opinion," a toxicologist explains, "scientific decisions are seldom a mere reflection of clear patterns and incontrovertible results." Like the manager of the Saudi Arabian gas plant project or the utility building, toxicologists need a way to spell out their assumptions to share with peers and superiors, and, sometimes, the general public.

Table 4 Problem Analysis in Regulatory Control Deviation: Excess of Urinary Bladder Neoplasms in Treated Male Rats

Is	Is not	Distinctions (difference of is compared to is not)
What		
Treated rats	Treated mice	Exposed in utero
Treated male rats	Treated female rats	Females—low spontaneous rate; no inflammation; no calculi
Excess of urinary bladder neoplasms	Neoplasm in muscles or connective tissues	
Where		
Urinary bladder	Kidneys, ureters	A common target of neoplasia
Epithelium	Connective tissue or muscle layers	Directly in contact with excretions
When		
At the end of the experiment	During the experiment	Exposed to longer duration of contact with the chemical
Extent		
5.2% in treated groups	Greater than 5.2%	The same percentage of rats in the control group of another study using the same strain of rats developed neoplasma
3 rats in the intermediate group, 3 in the high group, 1 in the low dose group	More or fewer	

Problem at the Construction Site

Let us return to the Saudi Arabian gas plant construction project, which has developed a problem: rust on the gears of a special $300,000 air compressor designed to run a series of pneumatic tools.

The project manager gathers those people who have information about the problem and who are familiar with the newly arrived equipment. Using Problem Analysis they search for the cause. The specification of the problem is shown in Table 5.

The ad hoc team, much like a Quality Circle or Quality Team in a manufacturing plant, suggests a number of possible causes from experience:

Gear not preserved by the manufacturer
Wrong preservative used
Gear left unprotected at the export packer's
Gear not boxed properly
Ocean spray hit it during shipment
Box left open at the jobsite before installation

Table 5 Deviation: Rust on the Gear

	Is	Is not
What	air compressor gear A	air pumps, pinion, casing, gears B and C
Where	Saudi Arabia gear box	U.S. outside
When	August after customs	before before
Extent	10% of teeth	other 90%

Each of these possible causes would allow air or water to make contact with the gear and cause rust.

Unfortunately, none of these possible causes explains the problem. The gear was preserved, packaged, and shipped with great care. Besides, none of these causes indicates why 10% of the teeth of one gear are rusted but not the other 90%. This again shows the value of the (is not) in isolating cause. Imagine for a moment what might happen without the (is not). The team would be much more likely to assume any one of the six causes is correct. In such a situation, legal action may be triggered by the mere suspicion that another party is at fault.

Using the technique described earlier called distinctions—distinctions narrow the search for cause—the team seeks the cause by asking, "Is there anything different about the gear with the rust as compared to the other gears?" But all the gears are alike; there are no obvious distinctions.

Unable to find the cause, but certain that the six suggested causes are incorrect, the team assigns two members who would be using the pneumatic tools to look more clearly at the rusted gear. Their commitment is very high and they are more familiar with the equipment than the project manager is. By direct examination, they note that the "rust" is actually dried red dye used to test the gears in the factory before shipping. This dye is completely harmless.

The gear is restored, the compressor works, and the project stays on schedule. There really is no "problem" in this case. But without a system for finding cause, which stimulates communication and that has the confidence of the entire team, a problem like this might delay the project. Imagine the project manager trying to "fix" each of the six possible causes listed above.

In our observation, managers are often quick to "jump to cause." A single explanation is proposed, or a person is blamed, and managers light on that explanation. In managing projects or in solving day-to-day problems, managers need the skill to find the causes of problems without jumping to the first solution someone proposes.

THINKING BEYOND THE FIX

Good troubleshooters—project manager, maintenance workers, managers—capitalize on successful problem solving by thinking beyond the fix. They ask where else this problem might occur and where else this solution might be implemented. In the red dye on the gears case, there was additional equipment being shipped by manufacturers. The project manager and the problem-solving team were on the lookout for red dye on other equipment.

At a large midwestern utility, a team of maintenance mechanics were called in to repair a faulty turbine during routine maintenance. They found that the ball bearings inside were crumbling. After they replaced the bearings, a senior operator asked if the twin turbine, currently running near capacity, might have the same problem.

They arranged to take a look on the night shift when demand for power is low. "The ball bearings fell into my hand like dust," the operator reports. The utility estimates a savings of $850,000 in fuel replacement costs from this operator's foresight by asking, "Where else might this fix apply?"

STATISTICAL PROCESS CONTROL

A growing number of companies and project managers are using Problem Analysis to bolster their overall efforts to improve quality. All of us are familiar with Statistical Process Control, a technique to help managers and operators identify quality deviations and control the manufacturing process. SPC is an intelligence gathering device that detects problems during the manufacturing process and corrects them before they reach quality control inspection. But Statistical Process Control does not identify all the factors that cause product quality to deviate from the norm. In those instances where SPC is unsuccessful at pinpointing the reason for a deviation, many organizations are using Problem Analysis.

In a dual casting and engine plant in Latin America, department managers laid out an optimistic three-year plan to reduce rejects and raise productivity.

Using a project management approach, they established clear measures for the end of each year. Reports were issued daily. Each time a problem was identified, a quality team used Problem Analysis to find cause.

The plant manager reports that they not only exceeded the goals of the three-year plan, but they went from last place in productivity worldwide among all plants operated by this company to sixth place among several hundred.

DECISION MAKING

While problem solving and problem prevention are vital to keeping a project on track, decision making is equally critical to overall success. The systematic process for decision making is called Decision Analysis.

Project managers who must design new equipment for clients outside their organization and who must oversee the building and testing of the equipment make decisions of far-reaching significance. In many instances, the failure of the new equipment to meet its stated purpose can be traced to poor decisions made at the front end of the project.

A group of engineers who design and build new equipment at geothermal power plants under construction by the U.S. government is expected to implement sound decisions that satisfy their client. "Sometimes we build what they ask for," an engineer with seven years experience comments, "but it does not achieve its goal." In this fairly typical scenario, the client presents these engineers with an alternative, never making clear what the objectives were for the decision.

Good decisions take into account the three key elements of choice: objectives, alternatives, and adverse consequences.

> Establish Objectives. Objectives are the goals which the selected course of action seeks to achieve. The degree to which these goals are missed, met, or surpassed will determine the success of the decision.
> Generating Alternatives. Alternatives represent the various routes available to reach the goal. Processes for generation and evaluation of alternatives identify the alternative that best meets the objectives.

> Examining Adverse Consequences. Almost every possible course of action is in-
> herent in each alternative. This part of decision making establishes peril,
> enabling the manager to determine whether the risk is prohibitive.

An engineer specializing in fusion and hazardous waste management, who has overseen
numerous large-scale projects in geothermal power, describes one experience with
clients who are fixed on a single alternative.

> We were asked to install a parallel well pump. Installing a parallel well pump rep-
> resents a decision, actually a single alternative, selected by the client. The ap-
> proach we find most helpful when a client presents a chosen alternative is to ask
> questions—pleasantly—about the decision. Pleasantness is critical. If a major
> client presents you with an alternative, you can only ask questions pleasantly.

What Were They Trying to Accomplish?

> Through questioning, we learned that the client wanted to double the water flow
> in the line going to the well. They also wanted this accomplished quickly and
> cheaply. We asked if they would be willing to consider other alternatives. They
> agreed.
>   A parallel pump appears at first to be a good alternative, but it would not
> double the flow of water in the line. In fact, a 10% increase is about all we could
> have accomplished. In addition, these pumps are very expensive and require a
> lead time of several months before delivery. We knew the chosen alternative
> would not work. With the client's objectives before us we were faced by a classic
> design Decision Analysis.
>   The question was, how could we best double the flow of water in the line?
> Finally, we recommended a new control valve, which could be installed several
> months earlier than a parallel pump at a saving of thousands of dollars. Most
> importantly, the new control valve met all critical objectives including doubling
> water flow in the line.

The Engineer's Role

> To meet complex technological challenges, engineers must be allowed to tap the
> full range of their expertise. Engineers who build exactly what their clients ask
> for without completely understanding the objectives are going into battle with
> duds in their ammunition box. Complete objectives allow designs to be completed
> in a "blaze of glory." With incomplete requirements, the "objective duds" will get
> you every time.

The point is simple: in good decision making, Objectives come before Alternatives.
Short of that, managers wind up "shooting from the hip."
    The final element of decision making is Adverse Consequences—those risks asso-
ciated with the alternatives. With the adverse consequences in mind, managers can
select that alternative which Balances Acceptable Risk with Maximum Benefit.
    Adverse Consequence thinking is the starting point of Potential Problem Analysis.
Potential Problem Analysis allows project managers to go beyond identifying potential
problems to planning how to eliminate or minimize them.

SETTING PRIORITIES

Another key management skill helpful to project managers in reaching their goals is
Effective Priority Setting. The process that helps set priorities is Situation Appraisal.

Table 6 The Rational Processes

Patterns of thinking	Time	Rational process
Organizing: Setting priorities among various concerns	Present	Situation Appraisal
Investigating: Finding out why something went wrong	Past	Problem Analysis
Making a choice: Setting criteria and evaluating alternatives	Present	Decision Analysis
Implementing: Anticipating what might go wrong and protecting the decision	Future	Potential Problem Analysis

In addition to setting priorities, Situation Appraisal helps managers decide which of the other rational processes (Potential Problem Analysis, Problem Analysis, Decision Analysis) should be used to resolve each concern:

> *Problem.* A step in the project was missed or something is not performing as expected
> *Decision.* A course of action must be selected from a range of alternatives
> *Potential problem.* Something might go wrong that will affect a project adversely

Situation Appraisal is the last of the four "rational processes" (Table 6).

Situation Appraisal begins by listing all the concerns: problems, decisions, and potential problems a manager faces. These concerns are then broken down into manageable pieces by asking questions that have stood the test of time:

> What evidence do you have that this is a concern?
> What do we mean by . . . ?
> What is actually happening?
> Do we think one action will resolve this concern?
> Can we improve on the way we have handled this situation?
> What could go wrong with this decision?

A project manager who is told "There's a foul up with the pipefitters," may gain a much clearer picture of what is happening by separating that "problem," which becomes:

> Wrong equipment was ordered
> Tools locked up; no one has the key
> Blueprints missing

The next step in Situation Appraisal is to set priorities. Priorities are determined by investigating three aspects of each concern:

> *Seriousness.* How much money or equipment and how many people are involved?
> *Urgency.* Is there a deadline?
> *Growth.* Will the situation deteriorate further if we do not act?

Using these criteria, the high-priority concerns will stand out from the others. Those concerns that are highest in seriousness, urgency, and growth must be addressed first.

The final step in Situation Appraisal is to plan the resolution of concerns. Using the criteria in the rational process chart, managers can determine which rational process will help them resolve the concern. Use Decision Analysis if a choice must be made. Use Potential Problem Analysis if a decision is to be implemented, or if something might go wrong. Use Problem Analysis if this concern requires finding out why something went wrong. Now the project manager is ready for resolution.

A project manager at a large utility comments:

> Situation Appraisal has been used at the highest level to list all concerns of all departments. This has helped top management keep on top of each concern of significance to the facility. Implementation of radiation protection activities has been one major concern. Following Situation Appraisal, we have assigned individual tasks to resolve this concern. Overall this has helped management organize complex start-up operations, and has helped other employees understand where we are going.

Situation Appraisal is the gateway to problem solving, problem prevention, and decision making. Together, the four "rational processes" equip managers to handle the threats and opportunities associated with project management. They are necessary enhancements to standard project management tools.

STATE OF THE ART

At this writing, project managers in construction and engineering companies, manufacturing sites, government, and service industries are currently strengthening their project management skills with these systematic processes for problem solving, problem prevention, and decision making.

Many organizations build systematic problem solving and decision making into their day-to-day operations. Here are a few examples:

- Project managers at one of the world's largest construction companies working together with project managers from a major utility for whom they are building a new plant share information about problems using the systematic Kepner-Tregoe approach called Problem Analysis
- Managers at a high-technology research and design company anticipate problems and search for causes of current problems in various stages of designing, testing, and producing communication equipment for a government agency
- Maintenance technicians at a computer manufacturer specify each problem they are not familiar with before attempting a fix
- Technicians in the U.S. Air Force and U.S. Navy collect specifying data (what, where, when, extent of the problem) to find out why computerized equipment fails in state-of-the-art military equipment
- Line workers at an automobile engine plant specify product defects using Statistical Process Control (SPC) then search for cause using Kepner-Tregoe Problem Analysis
- Medical researchers at the Center for Disease Control in Atlanta specify the incidence of newly reported diseases by using the what, where, when, extent format
- Operations managers in a major North American bank plan projects, anticipate problems, and modify plans using a computer-based job aid which incorporates systematic problem solving and problem prevention into project management

In every business environment and the government, workers and managers are using Problem Analysis and Potential Problem Analysis to manage projects and daily responsibilities more effectively. Project managers are using Problem Analysis and Potential Problem Analysis to find causes of problems and to prevent future trouble, to improve communication with peers, subordinates, line management and vendors, and to help get projects back on track.

Kepner-Tregoe has recently developed Pro Counsel, a computer-based aid to problem solving, decision making, and planning. Three parts of this software series, Trouble Shooter, Planning Pro, and Decision Aide, are currently in wide use by project managers. Trouble Shooter helps find causes of problems. Planning Pro synergizes key elements of project management with Potential Problem Analysis. Decision Aide helps organize the decision-making process.

A VIEW OF THE FUTURE

As projects become more complex technologically, as more and more specialists, many from outside the project manager's organization, are needed to complete projects, and as competitive pressures tighten time frames while demanding ever higher quality, project managers will have greater need of a systematic approach to problem solving and problem prevention.

The half-life of an engineer has been estimated at about 6 to 10 years. Add to this the geometrical increase in information commonly known as "the information explosion" and it is immediately clear that project managers cannot be content experts. They cannot master the minuscule details of the functions of every piece of equipment, or the properties of every raw material, or every complex new engineering process vital to each project. To monitor and control projects in the years ahead, project managers need some way to collect information, organize it, and make use of their own and their colleagues' experience and judgment. They need a process for managing information.

Nowhere is this more obvious than in high technology companies. For example, project managers at one of the world's largest computer manufacturers see their careful plans foiled by unexpected, if welcomed, technological breakthroughs. A new chip or a circuit board improvement means an engineering change order that invalidates the carefully designed project plan for building, testing, shipping, and installing a computer.

This improvement may upgrade the unit's capabilities but at a considerable price. A new chip may be incompatible with the software. Or it may not function with the maze of chips and circuits as previously designed. Since computer systems are a series of interrelated components, analagous to stereo systems, the change may pose difficulties for the overall interaction of the components of the system. Since the technological breakthrough that precedes the change has never been used in an actual computer system, the engineer can't know exactly what its effects will be.

Following an engineering change order, the manufacturing project manager at this computer company indicated that the new random access memory chips (RAMs) were to be standard. Shortly after installation, however, they began to fail, which in turn posed a threat to the plan to test, ship, and install these medium-sized computers.

The engineers compared the failing RAMs to the older RAMs that had not failed. A key distinction appeared: the specifications. After checking with the supplier of the new RAMs, they verified that the supplier had not met the company's specifications. A manufacturing engineer in this multibillion dollar company comments:

> Without a systematic process for finding the causes of problems, we might not have focused on the differences between the two types of RAMs. Instead, we might have returned to the old chip—allowing us to meet the orders for the product but reducing the sophistication of the unit.

As engineering change orders become a way of life in high technology industries, and as the sophistication of technicians increases, project managers need a practical system for communicating about actual and potential problems.

Problem Analysis, Decision Analysis, and Potential Problem Analysis are part of the core curriculum which this computer maker uses to develop the management skills of the engineers and technicians who in turn will develop "artificial intelligence," a computer discipline which seeks to imitate human reasoning.

SUMMARY

Our experience and our discussions with project managers indicate the need for a systematic approach for problem solving and problem prevention, growing out of sound questions devised to elicit critical data. In the future, these skills will be even more valuable to project implementation. And, while project management relies on a range of excellent planning techniques, problem solving and problem prevention have not yet become as closely associated with managing projects as PERT, WBS, or the other planning techniques engineers commonly use. The project managers using the systematic approach described here report smoother implementation of projects, quicker return to plan when mishaps occur, and heightened communication and confidence.

Project managers in the future can be expected to invest more time and effort in the planning phase of project management in which problems can be anticipated and in many instances prevented. This is particularly true in high technology environments where actions are more likely to have an adverse effect on some other part of the project and where clients, either internal or external, occasionally request products and services that are unfeasible, that do not accomplish their intended purpose, or that violate accepted guidelines.

4

Performance Management

PHILIP L. HELMER   *Helmer Pacific Inc., Kent, Washington*

Performance management is one of the primary tools available to the project manager for improving the results-oriented behavior of the project team. It provides a strong lever that can be applied to move the team to a higher plane of accomplishment. To see how and why it works, we have to understand the needs, motivation, and attitudes of individual team members, and their interaction within the group.

Projects are executed within a limited time frame. A team is gathered to perform the work and is dissolved when the project is finished. All but a few key members of the team are phased in and out of the project as it runs its course. A proposal or planning team gets the program underway. The baton is passed to programmers and front-end engineers. Information is developed by discipline engineers and flows to designers, the procurement group, and, finally, to the field forces.

In many cases, staff members have never worked together in the past and may not do so in the future. The project manager has to mold the staff as quickly as possible into a high yield team. Today, when fast track projects are the norm, it is imperative to form a close-knit team rapidly. Once the members acquire the feeling of a team, they can be managed as a team—not before.

But, how do we climb the steep learning curve? A project manager has little formal line authority over team members. The manager may know all or most of the team members, but not equally well, and has no hire-fire or visible reward status. Most prior relationships were casual. He must either directly, on a small project, or indirectly through the staff, on a large project, persuade the team to believe in, to commit, to a common goal. His or her personality and enthusiasm will have the greatest influence on the team. The project manager can, as the team leader, become the role model for the entire staff.

We climb the steep learning curve through personal persuasion, enthusiasm, role modeling: in short, leadership. We enhance our ability to lead through the application of time-tested management techniques. Both authoritarian and participative leaders use management skills—many similar, many different—to create a scenario for success. We need to create the challenge of success; people want to succeed, want to be winners, want to be on the winning team. Winning is, in large measure, its own reward.

We have to develop a team identity. A project team, formed from within a corporate matrix, or supplemented from without through hiring, has an overwhelming need for group identity, group recognition. As the team grows into a recognized entity each member will seek help from and provide reinforcement to the other team members. The "club" has been formed! Individuals will motivate others, and in turn will be motivated by others. Without comradery the cohesive internal forces necessary to produce successful projects will be lacking.

NEEDS, MOTIVATION, ATTITUDE

The motivation of an individual is a most complex subject. To be an effective manager within the confined environment of a project team, requires a basic awareness of the psychological needs of people. Several well-known and well-publicized theories have been proposed.

Maslow said there is a hierarchy of human needs which must be satisfied in a particular ascending order: survival, safety, social, respect, creative fulfillment. If the basic needs aren't satisfied the individual will not respond to the stimuli of higher needs. Simply stated, a hungry or threatened person cannot be concerned about the respect of others or their creative talents.

Herzberg said certain basic or "hygiene" factors were not motivators, contrary to accepted views at the time. Hygiene, or those things everyone needs to exist, such as good pay and good working conditions, are not motivators. He believed that motivation came only from a chance to grow and succeed.

Or, as Watson proposed, motivation can be external, stimulated by the prior experiences of the group members.

While there is no unanimity of acceptance for any theory, and all are oversimplifications, a recommended approach is to be cognizant of the several concepts and acquire an awareness so that as situations develop you may be able to relate to one or more parameters, thus guiding you toward a suitable course of action. An ability to handle interpersonal issues will help a project manager create a positive team attitude. It is important for a project manager to commit himself to the shaping of the attitudes of his team. The attitudes of people inevitably determine their behavior, what they think and do, and how they will respond to project direction and team participation.

To shape the attitudes of the team requires an understanding of the professional needs and motivational activators of each team member. Their individual perception of the project and their role on the project, and their perception of the manager, will determine their attitude. A designer wants to continue to improve his design to the ultimate perfect solution. Only when the drawing is physically torn from his board will he stop. Or, he may consider the goal to be time-oriented: shortest project schedule, fastest completion of his work.

Adversarial relationships, conflicting goals, and the like cannot easily coexist and must be resolved. It takes time and repeated personal contact to resolve these differences and work out the "people problems." Try to give as many team members as possible a chance to voice their views. And, while listening skillfully, and with genuine interest, we, as managers, have to keep our targets in view, those goals assigned to us by our management and our client. A project can never be considered to be a democratic environment. Among other things the team doesn't want democracy, although they will convey such a need repeatedly.

ANTECEDENT, BEHAVIOR, CONSEQUENCE

We have looked at the team and what makes it tick. As we inspect how to adjust its performance, it is worthwhile to define a couple of terms. Performance equals Behavior plus Accomplishment. Upon repetition, it also becomes a result of its prior Consequences. Performance Management is the use of external events to change behavior. It reinforces the management of people in an organization. It, therefore, is used to manage the results. Let's tackle step by step this concept of Performance Management.

First, the events before the action. We give commands and exhortations, write instructions, draw diagrams, explain and answer questions, and so forth. We set the scene, provide tools and information. We provide the Antecedents. The antecedents can be tangible: written instructions, a CPM schedule, a list of deliverables with deadlines, a detailed budget; or intangible: pep talks, discussions, counseling sessions, question and answer periods, or, body langugage, personal example, manner of dress. An environment will exist on every project, whether as a result of deliberate planning, or by happenstance.

Second, the observation and evaluation of Behavior. We measure, count, sample, and track an action or series of actions. To be useful, this data must be observable, preferably by the group. The doer should be able to observe the data frequently in order to gauge where he or she and the measurements stand. When the group is able to observe the data, reinforcement and understanding result. The data must be measurable both discretely and accurately.

Since behavior is what someone does or accomplishes, it can be observed: the number of letters written, the number of calculations performed, the individual specifications prepared, the number of drawings designed, the purchase orders placed, the yards of concrete poured, the tons of steel erected. We could also observe the number of people who came early or stayed late, or the number who ate lunch at their work station, or who went out and came back late. Or we could count the minutes spent on the phone, the sales calls made, the errors found and corrected, or the dollars spent. We count whatever leads us toward or away from the desired behavior. And, we must consciously feed back the data to each doer and the rest of the team. A word of caution: this is a constructive management tool; convey the impression of a witch hunt or yourself as a bean-counter and the program will fail.

Third, what happens after the action. The Consequence of the action may be either positive or negative. We give resounding applause for the achiever; counseling for the laggard. These are consequences we can get or give, and they can be shared with the team. Consequences should be balanced in degree and application against the impact of the corresponding behavior. There should be personal impact. Delays in administering consequences cause a loss of impact in a geometrical relationship. A kind word or a stinging rebuke given long after the action has been completed does little to reinforce the consequence. People fear the hot stove because the hurt is instantaneous. We try to make the consequence occur after every important behavior and randomly after lesser events. It is equally important to avoid bribery; consequences given in anticipation of expected action. If we receive candy without doing our chores, why do them.

The ABCs of Performance Management—Antecedent, Behavior, Consequence—are easy building blocks to increase project success. The keys to how we make this work are: be specific, choose obvious data, use good timing on follow-up.

Frequently we find it hard to establish a beginning for the ABCs. The initial steps come quickly and easily if the steps are small. After stating the Antecedents, look for a small positive accomplishment. And immediately give the Consequence. After several repetitions, the size or length of Behavior can be expanded and lengthened between Consequences. Careful early monitoring and attention lead quickly to the establishment of desirable routines.

PERFORMANCE MANAGEMENT IN ACTION

Let's look at some examples of Performance Management in Action.

> Our secretarial pool arrives late, leaves early. Few letters are produced, and many, even after revisions, contain numerous errors. The in-boxes are always full.

We start with the quality of work. We have a session explaining the problem and the need for quality. We demonstrate the improvement in performance resulting from a reduction in recycle. Perhaps a discussion of how the in-boxes could be periodically emptied, giving the staff a chance for relaxation and cleanup. Following this meeting

we start counting recycle or errors and discussing the results in daily or weekly briefings. We might prepare a chart showing the trend, with a reward for the individual
showing the best record. Plan to single out and praise the first series of documents
that are error-free. Then, evaluate the change in production and reward the best
producers. Give recognition to the clean in-box.

The next phase includes making the day interesting with a chance for professional
growth. Consider periodic brief early morning talks on the project programs described
by the letters and reports, the equipment covered by the specifications. Offer anno-
tating and proofreading help and seminars to improve skills. Offer growth positions
to the star performers. Quid pro quo! This exercise may be very dull to you but it's
not to the secretarial staff, whose support you need more than you know.

> Our project team misses deadlines consistently. Regardless of the task and the
> effort expended, everything seems to be late. Repeated rescheduling is required
> —still, milestones are missed.

Here is our chance to bring the staff together and explain the problem and its impact
on the program. We begin by finding the most minute milestones within several principal tasks—milestones which follow so closely that the sequence is immediately obvious. We then monitor the completion of each mini-milestone and report performance
at special staff meetings, until the problem is resolved. We emphasize the progress
the team is making and publish interim results. We ask for the team's help in identifying hold-ups. A few charts and graphs to show progress will be helpful. Initiate
planned personal contacts to discuss the problems, ideas, and attitudes of the staff
members. Incorporate worthwhile concepts and give appropriate credit. Once a team
starts to win a few small engagements, the synergism of winning prepares a team for
the major conflicts in any field of endeavor.

SUMMARY

Performance Management is an important management technique. We set the stage:
Antecedent. We measure achievement: Behavior. We have a result: Consequence.

Unless an antecedent is established, there is no basis for evaluation of behavior.
Ground rules must be set so each person will know what behavior is expected, and,
in turn, will be able to understand the result, or consequence.

A result, or consequence may be considered to be good or bad, but measured
against what? The profits from the project were good, or were they? Should they
have been significantly better?

Good performance is managed performance. Performance that is managed will produce good results against real targets.

Many project managers have little awareness of the terms used herein; the ABCs.
But they intuitively practice the principles of Performance Management. With a formal
awareness of the principles the good managers will apply them more often to the benefit of the project and the staff. The new project manager will have an excellent tool
to make his or her first-time project a success.

5

The Art of Negotiation

THOMAS A. HASKINS *The Haskins Organization, Littleton, Colorado*

The role of project management has expanded as projects have grown in size, technical complexity, schedule constraints, and budget limitations. Problems with communication, productivity, quality control, and client coordination have all become more critical. As a result, the effectiveness of management techniques has had an increased impact on the success of projects. The skill with which negotiations with team members, clients, and senior executives are conducted is, today, a critical element of project management.

NEGOTIATION APPLIED TO PROJECT MANAGEMENT

The topic of negotiation brings to mind tense bargaining sessions between a trade union and employer, or disarmament talks among international diplomats. Applications of negotiation techniques to project management are less dramatic, less calculated, and usually less adversarial. There are, however, several aspects of project management where negotiations may have a significant impact on the project.

Contract Terms and Compliance

The terms of every contract signed between two parties for a project are negotiated. As circumstances evolve, decisions often need to be made about how to comply with the contract. How well each party fulfills the contract will be the product of protracted negotiations after the original signing.

Construction and Procurement

Even in situations where prices are established by bidding, the delivery dates and interpretation of specifications are typically negotiated with each subcontractor and each supplier.

Design Input from Clients

Clients, directly or indirectly, provide a project team with budget, schedule, and design requirements, as well as reports of field conditions, operating data, and the like. When client negotiations are conducted successfully, clients will provide this information early in the project, thus permitting the orderly execution of the work.

Assignment of Personnel and Office Space

Project teams in an engineering firm negotiate for team members and workspace within the office. The selection of people and office location is the outcome of a series of negotiations.

Management of Multidisciplinary Teams

Conflicts between technical disciplines within a project team are inevitable. How these conflicts are resolved and what impact they have on each of the active projects is determined by how effectively the conflicting interests of the several parties are negotiated.

Senior Executive Involvement

The project manager and the senior executives of an engineering firm can compromise each of their bargaining positions with the client in their personal attempts to keep the client satisfied. How well they present a unified position to the client strengthens subsequent negotiations.

STATEMENT OF BASIC PRINCIPLES

Influence

Negotiation is the art of applying influence to increase the probability of a particular outcome. It differs from direct control where people can exercise their authority to obtain compliance. A project manager does not have direct authority over the clients, vendors, senior executives, and technical disciplines involved with the project. Successful project managers carefully apply their influence to manipulate these diverse interests in order to meet the objectives of the project.

Most factors which detract from successful technical projects result from a lack of initiative by the people involved. The client must provide information, approvals, and decisions on a timely basis. Designers must challenge assumptions about operating economies and construction costs and check out the implications of the designs they are developing. The production team must take the initiative to find errors and coordinate details with others in order to minimize field problems. People are influenced to take more or less initiative by the outcome of negotiations.

Initiative varies with the personalities of individuals. Some organizations encourage more initiative among their members than others. However, initiative also varies with the outcome of negotiations. Successful negotiations leave both parties more willing to look out for each other's interests. Quality is enhanced through individual initiative when negotiations are viewed by all parties as constructive.

Implicit Strategies

There are two basic strategies to negotiation: one treats the other party as an opponent; one regards the other party as a collaborator. The two strategies produce very different results. The actions of most people reflect an implicit strategy that they would not have consciously adopted. The challenge is to deliberately choose the strategy which best fits the particular circumstances of the particular negotiation.

Win/Lose Strategy

This strategy seeks to win at the expense of an opponent. Information about one's own constraints are kept from the opponent so it is not used to their advantage. This strategy includes dramatizing the desired outcome in order to weaken the resistance to one's real objectives. Comments by the opponent are regarded as overstatements of their position. Solutions are often presented as ultimatums, offering the opponent no choice but to give in. This strategy is effective where compliance can be tightly controlled. This strategy is necessary when any concessions would be very costly to one's own position.

Win/Win Strategy

This strategy seeks to collaborate on a mutually agreeable solution to seemingly conflicting interests. Information is openly shared with the other party in order to improve the collaboration. Efforts are made to learn the constraints faced by each other. Each party conveys their understanding of each other's position. Neither achieves their ideal solution. Together they find a new alternative which is more attractive than the opposing ideal solution. This strategy is effective where the outcome is dependent on follow through after the negotiation. This strategy is essential when the other party's commitment is crucial to achieving the desired outcome.

De-Escalation of Adversary Tactics

It is not enough to introduce a collaborative approach if one is confronted with an adversarial opponent. The tactics deployed by the opponent need to be neutralized first. Collaborative gestures will then influence the opponent to take a less adversarial stance.

Neutralizing Adversarial Tactics

Any tactic seeks to increase the chances of one's desired outcome. An adversarial tactic tries to weaken any opposition to the desired outcome. All of the actions which comprise an implicit "win/lose" strategy are adversarial tactics.

There are several responses which will neutralize adversarial tactics. The most difficult is to "see through" the tactic and to "withhold a reaction." The more one understands the opponent's position, the easier this becomes. Instead of responding directly to their actions or comments, ask for more information about their concerns; this tends to neutralize the tactic. Acknowledging one's awareness of the counter-objectives and circumstances has the same effect. Tactics are further neutralized by stating the limits of what one will consider and defining the additional problems created by the "other" solution.

Making Collaborative Gestures

Several followup moves will encourage an opponent to collaborate on an alternative solution. Withholding one's evaluation of their position eliminates their need to defend the problems they are trying to resolve. Acknowledging the circumstances they face reduces their inclination to dramatize their problems. Proposing alternatives which make concessions to one's own ideal solution encourages the opponent to do the same.

HISTORICAL CONTEXT

Project management is beginning to follow the history of industrial management. Frederick Taylor pioneered the fragmentation of work concept at the turn of the century. Industrial jobs were simplified and specialized into tasks which minimized the critical and creative thinking required by employees. Very little information was required by anyone in a specialized task to fulfill their responsibilities. Communication was kept on an "as-needed" basis. Employees reacted to the lack of dialogue with company leaders by taking increasingly adversarial stances against management. The rapid growth of trade unions soon followed.

Companies responded to the surge of "labor problems" by expanding the ranks of middle management. Overhead increased as nonproductive jobs were fragmented, according to the Taylor philosophy. Management became a profession which enabled people with little knowledge of a firm's production technology or markets to rise up within the organization. Comprehensive problems with communication, turnover, productivity, quality control, and coordination were given to managers to solve with isolated efforts. Middle managers were also informed on an "as-needed" basis, and found themselves frequently ineffective and underutilized.

Recently, we have begun to see a thinning out of middle management ranks. Quality circle spinoffs are expanding the dialogue with leaders and the involvement of the workforce in the decisions which affect their work. Top management is becoming more visible to the rank and file. Hands-on experience in production or sales is contributing more to career advancement. Union leaders are delivering more concessions and fewer ultimatums at the bargaining table. Industrial firms are shifting from adversarial to collaborative approaches to solving the same problems that they faced at the turn of the century.

Project management is faced with a similar transition. Project managers cannot be familiar with all the interactions of a major project. The size and complexity of projects necessitate very specialized roles for most team members. The volume of details results in only a few people having an overview of the project. Schedule and budget figures are withheld from team members who might compromise design decisions or impede progress if they were aware of either set of figures. Project managers within matrix organizations find department heads, and even team members, taking an adversarial stance to the successful accomplishment of their project. Project managers still remark on how they feel underutilized in spite of the vast number of details they are handling. Employees and project managers are in very similar positions to their counterparts in industrial firms.

Several factors will assist a transition in project management comparable to the trend in industrial firms. Increasing use of computer-aided design (CAD) systems for drafting and design work will make information from other disciplines more accessible. Team members can be relied on to do more critical and creative thinking with the manhours freed-up by automated document production. Large projects are being subdivided to facilitate improved control of budgets, schedules, design quality, and document accuracy. Increased skills among project managers to deal with people effectively will have the largest impact on the transition to a collaborative approach.

This transition will provide several benefits to the negotiations which occur within a project. Project managers will find team members less adversarial as the concept of the wide-angle view of the project is developed. The individual team members will take more initiative to coordinate details with other disciplines, to catch errors in documents, and to challenge solutions. Project managers will be in a better bargaining position to get cooperation to meet a deadline or follow through on a client-generated change if there has been a history of collaboration on prior staffing decisions. In each case an improvement will result from adopting a win/win strategy to achieve a desired outcome. Employees have frequently been regarded as potential opponents to the attainment of project objectives, many of which they were unaware of, or didn't understand. The attitude of the project workforce will make or break a job. The participative employee is a relatively new and highly beneficial concept.

THE ACTIVE PROJECT

Design Quality Control

Design quality is normally nonnegotiable. It is assumed the team will do the best job in the allotted time. The manhour budget is, more often than not, dictated, with a progressive stepwise relaxation as the project proceeds. Designers input to the first manhour estimate. However, after the project terms have been agreed upon with the client, the designers are issued their first ultimatum: to work with less hours than estimated.

There will surely be a design budget overrun. The management posture, in this instance, is quite variable. Anxious to protect the liability and reputation of the firm, the first management directive may be to do whatever has to be done to satisfy the needs and goals of the client. A second management directive, issued considerably later, may be less tolerant of a budget overrun than might have been reasonably assumed by the discipline engineers at project initiation. And, management directives may be inconsistent in the treatment of similar problems on different projects.

Events of this type communicate several messages to those in the trenches, none favorable. This is what they hear: initially, protect quality and schedule at the expense of budget; later, protect budget at the expense of quality. And in a complex project, with a few intermediate directives, a matrix of conflicting priorities can emerge. But, in the long run the designer knows he will only be rated on the quality of his work.

Quality isn't a negotiable commodity to the professional design engineer; in fact, it's a potential career-threatening excursion. An adversarial relationship immediately develops when it appears to the designer, regardless of what management may have intended, that the management solution to a tight commercial situation is a compromise in quality. The outcome is a standoff, where neither side gives credibility to the position of the other, with an inevitable result—both design quality and financial performance suffer.

Scope, Schedule, Budget

Successful project managers build a collaborative position from the start of a project and avoid ultimatums. The project manager conducts a kickoff meeting where he reviews the schedule and budget for each discipline. He acknowledges that the manhours may be less than each discipline had estimated for the proposal more than a year ago. Rather than a pep talk, the manager asks each discipline to make a realistic review of the work items and manhours required, and to look for engineering approaches that reduce manhours with acceptable tradeoffs, and without compromising the quality of the project.

The project manager isn't "giving away the store." Let's start with the premise that a quantity of work will take a fixed expenditure of resources—plus or minus. The best chance to bring in the optimum budget-schedule-quality combination is a frank discussion of the problem up front. Experience has shown that an arbitrary demand to meet an unrealistic program results in an excessive consumption of resources, frequently masked until the final deterioration of the project.

During the immediate period following the kickoff meeting, the project manager negotiates the scope with each discipline, and specifically what it will take to achieve the required design goals. The negotiation provides the project manager with the technical and communication background to pursue future progress evaluations in a nonadversarial atmosphere.

As the project evolves, the project manager meets with discipline leaders regularly to brief them in a broad manner, giving them more than they "need to know" to manage their own efforts. He reviews how they might respond if particular setbacks occur in the progress of the project; solicits their evaluations of design and document quality; keeps visibly well-informed about the circumstances facing each discipline leader; and all other actions related to a team effort. These actions maintain his collaborative stance with the discipline leaders in later negotiations for rework, tighter schedules, and different staffing. These actions also influence the discipline leaders to take preventative steps to minimize the effect of setbacks, and to plan the sequence and timing of remaining work.

When setbacks do occur, the project manager does not present an ultimatum for what has to happen to meet the deadline. He presents a problem in need of a solution. Knowing he needs the initiative and commitment of the discipline leaders to overcome the setback, he gives them the job of proposing alternative solutions.

The subsequent negotiation follows a collaborative, win/win strategy. The project manager can use his previously established position to acknowledge the design quality objectives that the discipline leaders will be protecting. He can rely on previous conversations to have the discipline leaders propose solutions which address the schedule and budget constraints of the project in addition to their own concerns. Neither the discipline leaders nor the project manager will feel like they have given in to a more powerful opponent's position. Their involvement in developing the solution will encourage them to take the initiative to keep the solution on track.

Management of Teamwork

Teamwork is more easily preached than practiced on projects within technical organizations. Conflicting schedules and limited availability of manpower put technical disciplines at odds with each other. An optimum design solution for one technical discipline may be suboptimal for another. Each discipline holds information that affects another's work. Each is in a position to create delays or rework for another. A lack of communication between disciplines will result in conflicts and errors within a set of documents. Teamwork is critical to the quality of a project.

Faced with an opposing discipline taking an adversarial stance, other members of the team typically abdicate responsibility for the outcome of the project. People become less inclined to coordinate details with the other discipline. Progress that is held up goes unchallenged. People act content to wait for needed information to be delivered. They become less willing to rethink their technical solutions or to accommodate the manpower constraints of another discipline. Meetings deteriorate into restatements of each discipline's position. Decisions are consequently imposed on the team, with very little commitment being generated. The limited authority of a project manager is no match for this level of opposition within a project team.

A successful project manager takes an active role in orchestrating the teamwork on his project. Early in a project, he establishes the climate for a mutual understanding of interdisciplinary needs. He stays current, learning what needs have been fulfilled, what items have been added, what items are outstanding. By being current on the needs of each discipline, he is in a better bargaining position to negotiate the fulfillment of those needs. The project manager offers to expedite decisions which involve the client or more than one other technical discipline. This role also makes the project manager more aware of how his own actions may be holding up progress or creating confusion.

The successful project manager is careful to not become overinvolved in technical details. The orchestration of teamwork is easily mistaken as a golden opportunity to enter into design decisions. The project manager makes a distinction between being aware and being involved. He uses the information about details to hold the technical discipline leaders accountable for meeting the needs of the other disciplines. To personally expedite the information would let them off the hook and discourage subsequent teamwork. The project manager conducts a protracted negotiation with each discipline to get each of the needs of the other disciplines met. The emphasis that the project manager places on the needs and progress of other disciplines influences the team members to collaborate on outcomes outside the scope of their individual efforts, a difficult problem in a matrix organization, an easier problem in a task force.

Management of Client Relationships

Clients usually can't accept the project team running over the budget or missing deadlines. Clients often know less about technical considerations than the project team and are suspicious of technical justifications for design decisions and schedule changes. And, those clients with technical training often become overinvolved in design decisions to protect their own interests. Client representatives may need to build coalitions among the executives within their own organization in order to get approval for submittals by the project team. They are held accountable for protecting the client's interests, at the expense of the project team, if necessary. Being conciliatory would appear to compromise the interests of the client organization.

The successful project manager continually works at shifting the naturally adversarial relationship with his client toward a collaborative one. Early in the project, he establishes a dialogue with the client representative. He concentrates on asking questions which demonstrate his interest in the client's situation. The project manager looks for opportunities to help the client get approvals within the client organization. He goes out of his way to keep the client informed of events, decisions, and progress. He solicits the client's evaluation on appropriate matters and openly discusses problems before the client would otherwise find out about them. He strives to make his counterpart look good.

These collaborative tactics can improve the working relationship with the client by encouraging the client to contribute to the outcome of the project without interfering with its progress. A client will be more willing to alter the tactics being used to keep the project team "on their toes" if the client is being dealt with collaboratively. This is often referred to as "building trust." Trust is a byproduct of negotiations.

Clients expect to find the project manager conciliatory at the beginning of a project. At this point, it is crucial to be very attentive to the client, but less than totally agreeable. A collaborative strategy does not depend on giving in to the client's wishes. Instead it makes their circumstances and objectives important and seeks other solutions to satisfy them. The client's willingness to consider alternative solutions depends on how they are dealt with from the start.

SUMMARY

The topic of negotiation differs from traditional advice about effective communication and management practices. Negotiation techniques make the distinction between adversarial and collaborative strategies. Much well-intended communication, spurred on by management textbooks, has an adversarial effect on the client or team members. Many of the problems which are identified as the result of personality differences are merely the outcome of a series of adversarial negotiations. Negotiation provides a framework for diagnosing why textbook management practices may not be working in a particular instance.

Much is preached about the importance of listening. Very little is put into practice. The fact that it constitutes "good management technique" is not enough to encourage consistent implementation. Within the context of negotiation, the payoff from effective listening is much more immediate. The process of asking questions and listening uncovers the other party's concerns. It enables one to anticipate responses to one's own proposals and to present solutions compatible with their point of view. We call this "an improved bargaining position."

Effective listening also demonstrates one's willingness to collaborate with the other party. Someone who is about to impose their own solution typically dominates a con-

versation. Asking questions and listening does far more to steer an adversarial negotiation to a collaborative one than any pronouncements of intentions to do the same.

Negotiation also contributes a long-range viewpoint to generic problems, frequently
permitting managers to solve future problems in brief meetings. One can look at the
effect of previous conversations and decisions on the other party. One can set objectives for the negotiation at hand and identify those which need more time. One can
look at slowly building a collaborative relationship and realizing that the source of
one's own frustration is merely the other party's deployment of several different adversarial tactics.

Negotiation is an art, not a science. It changes the probabilities of particular
outcomes. It does not prescribe specific actions to take in order to achieve specific
results. The awareness of how one's actions are influencing a negotiation will enable
project managers to control the diverse interests within a project more effectively.
The improvements in technical and commercial performance of the projects will follow.

6

The Personnel Department and the Project

DONALD A. SPIKER* *Davy McKee Corporation, San Ramon, California*

Call it personnel, employee relations, or the currently popular designation—human resources—the services provided by this essential staff department can be an important contributor to project success and can relieve the project manager of the often time-consuming details of employee-oriented activities. For our purposes here, we will use the older and, perhaps more widely used term, Personnel, in discussing this department's relationship to the project as a whole. It is not appropriate, nor is it the intent here to define in detail the total range of services which a modern and comprehensive personnel function should be able to provide the total organization. Rather, we will focus on those personnel functions directly related to an individual project and which have relevance to the successful implementation, conduct, and completion of that project.

PROJECT TEAM CONCEPT

A project team is assembled generally from a larger organizational unit, and is brought together with a unity of purpose, the project. Most organizations whose business activities require the project team concept face similar problems regardless of the nature of the business purpose. We find the project team concept in government, industry, education, and even in the political arena where investigating committees are a form of project team assembled to pursue a specific task. The project team is normally assembled from existing members of the organization who are assigned to the project for its duration and who then return to their previous "permanent" department or position in the organization at project completion. Frequently, the members of the project are relocated within the building facilities so that they can function in close physical proximity for the life of the project. It is also not unusual for employees to have a "permanent" or "payroll" job title and classification, for example, Senior Engineer, but when assigned to the project, may be given a project title for the duration of the project—for example, Supervising Engineer, Electrical. There may or may not be a change in base compensation consistent with the title change; generally, there is not. At the completion of the project, the employee returns to the Electrical Department as a Senior Engineer or may be assigned to a new project with an even different title. All of these factors impact on the conduct of the Personnel function in a project-oriented organization and require the personnel practitioner to have a high tolerance for ambiguity, or in a single word, *flexibility*. Many of the standard personnel policy solutions become inappropriate to administer the ever-changing problems in the project team concept.

Present affiliation: Management Consultant, Walnut Creek, California

PERSONNEL DEPARTMENT ROLE

Although a team is formed to devote its energies toward a specific project, team members remain employees of the total organization and the Personnel Department continues to provide its normal services to individual members of that team: benefits administration, training and development programs, maintenance of records, etc. Each project, however, seems to develop unique problems and circumstances brought on by contractual requirements, project location, client industry considerations, client preferences, and by the "style" of the project manager. These unique circumstances require flexibility and innovativeness on the part of Personnel to provide effective solutions for the project without creating inconsistencies which impact on the organization's normal policies. The Personnel Department, then, must provide staff assistance to the project manager in all employee-related functions, offering suggestions and recommendations for unique problem solutions consistent with the goals of the project as well as those of the organization. The most common areas of project-oriented problems are staffing, compensation, relocation allowances, and field assignment conditions. Of these, perhaps the most critical, and certainly the highest priority, is staffing.

Staffing

Staffing the project with competent and cooperative people is one of the first and most important functions of the project manager. In many cases, the project manager has been selected even before the contract has been awarded, and, the client has been advised and has approved the selection. In turn, the project manager may have begun his own deliberations over the selection of his project staff. Frequently the names of key staff members for the project will have been proposed to the client prior to the contract award. And, the client may request the assignment of certain key personnel based on their performance on earlier projects. While this may be desirable from a client relationships point of view, these employees may be currently engaged on other projects and unavailable. When all these initial considerations have been resolved and the contract is awarded, the balance of the staffing effort moves ahead.

The first source is the existing workforce. Project managers tend to prefer staff members they have previously worked with and who have proven abilities; further, this reinforces any team spirit that was previously developed on other projects. There are, of course, other highly qualified employees in the organization that the project manager has not worked with. The Personnel Department must be prepared and equipped to supply the project manager with resumes or other data on those employees for his consideration. Many companies maintain a computerized Skills Inventory system which contains data about each employee, the different projects he has worked on, as well as the varying positions he has held on those projects, and the type of project, his education, age, and other relevant information. This kind of system is also valuable in the proposal stage, particularly where specific employees are to be listed as available for that client's project. A Skills Inventory system can be maintained as part of the basic personnel database on a mainframe computer but also adapts easily to a PC which can be maintained and operated by the Personnel Department.

When the system is maintained on the mainframe, the project manager then has access to the records of employees at other locations of the company, thereby broadening his base for selection. It should be noted that initial selection by the project manager doesn't necessarily establish that the employee is available. He may be involved in another project where both that project manager and/or the client might object to his early release or, in the case of a branch office, they may be reluctant to lose a competent employee on a potentially permanent basis. One solution is to tap employees from another office of the company on an on-loan basis. This implies that the employee will be lent to the new project office on a temporary basis with a scheduled return date to the lending office and will remain on the payroll of his permanent office. The lending office feels more comfortable with this payroll arrangement and the more secure expectation of their employee's eventual return. When the employee is granted a transfer, he relocates permanently to the receiving office and becomes a continuing permanent employee at the new location. Whether on-loan or permanent transfer, the Personnel Department provides coordination by establishing effective dates, arranging for transfer of all personnel records, ensuring current enrollment in benefit programs, and either assisting in arranging temporary accommodations for the on-loan employee or providing orientation to the new area for the permanent transfer, including contact with a reliable realtor.

When the project manager is unable to fill his project needs from the existing workforce, it may become necessary to hire new employees for some selected positions. This can result from a heavy workload and the unavailability of excess manpower from the current staff or the need for some specialized talent or work experience which the company doesn't have on the payroll. In this circumstance, the Personnel Department plays a key role in creating a flow of qualified applicants for the open positions. Efforts may include newspaper advertising, soliciting employee referrals, the use of employment agencies or executive search firms, or the use of other community resources such as engineering societies, universities, personal contacts among others. The Personnel Department's responsibility is to attract the applicants, screen out the obviously unqualified, ensure that resumes/application forms are complete, maintain an applicant flow log of these applicants for legal purposes, and refer the qualified applicants to the project manager or his designate for interviews and final selection.

The applicant flow log is a necessary tool to comply with the Equal Employment Opportunity/Affirmative Action Programs discussed later. Basically, the log contains information on each applicant for employment including name, position applied for, date of application, sex, and race (by observation only) and whether the applicant was hired. The maintenance of these data isn't difficult except that the project manager and/or his staff may arrange employment interviews with friends and associates from other companies without the Personnel Department's knowledge. The project manager and his staff must be made aware of the need for the Personnel Department to be advised of all applicants, not only to meet legal requirements, but as a good business practice. The applicant rejected for that project may be highly qualified for another open position in the company.

Once an applicant is selected, the Personnel Department must check references to verify the information that the applicant has supplied: prior employment dates and employers, salaries, and educational achievements. It has become increasingly difficult to verify prior work performance, particularly if it has been unsatisfactory in any way. Employment verifications are subject to libel and slander laws and supervisors in most organizations have been instructed to refrain from unsatisfactory references. In addition, most prior supervisors are reluctant to prevent someone from obtaining another position, even though the work performance under their supervision was unsatisfactory.

A note about educational qualifications is warranted. It is becoming more common for applicants to falsify their educational achievements. A B.S. easily gets upgraded to an M.S. or a non-degreed applicant with 3-plus years of college level work conveniently grants himself a B.S. degree. It seems surprising that many employers do not attempt to check on the applicant's stated educational achievements. Verification is easy and simple and most colleges and universities are more than cooperative. The Personnel Department should verify all college/university level degrees for all applicants prior to hire. If this timing is impractical, then hiring should be made contingent on a satisfactory verification. This is particularly important in the engineering industry where the degree and/or professional registration may become critical.

Several additional approaches to staffing should be mentioned here: the use of temporary or project employees, contract or job shop employees, and consultants. These are all widely utilized, primarily for short-term assignments or, in the case of the consultant, for a specific task requiring special talent not available in the company. Temporary employees are hired by the project for a limited period of time and are usually paid on an hourly basis, that is, only for hours worked. They do not accrue vacation and are not paid for absence from illness, but most employers do pay for holidays which are observed by permanent employees. Since the employee benefit plans, medical, pension, and so on, are designed for permanent full-time salaried employees, temporary employees do not qualify, by definition. The employer must pay all statutory benefits, social security, unemployement insurance, and worker's compensation. Temporary employees typically receive a premium rate of pay in comparison to a permanent employee of the same salary grade and skill level. A common premium is 10-15%.

The advantage to the employer is a lower labor cost although, with the payment of statutory benefits and the salary premium, these savings are minimal, 10-15%, or less. Temporary employees can, of course, be converted to permanent when manpower needs require and would receive credit for the temporary period toward service-related benefits. The ability to employ on a temporary basis becomes restricted in a healthy labor market when permanent positions with full benefits are readily available.

A job shop is a separate company or agency which supplies manpower on a temporary, contractual basis. Job shoppers are employees of the job shop or agency, not the employer using their services. The agency is responsible for salary payments to the shoppers, withholding of taxes and other statutory benefits, and for providing worker's compensation and liability insurance coverage. The job shop bills the employer at the end of each pay-period for all hours worked by his people. The basic contract between the job shop and the employer is negotiated by the Personnel Department, including rates of pay for each classification and for the additive to base pay. This additive, normally in the 30-40% range, is intended to cover statutory benefits, administrative overhead and profit for the agency. In addition, the base rates charged are generally higher than the rate for permanent employees of the same grade and skill level, although this higher rate is not necessarily paid entirely to the employee.

After the contract is in place, the project is then able to contact the agency and request personnel as needed. The advantages here are the ready availability of personnel, frequently on a few hours notice, and the ease of terminating job shoppers who do not perform adequately. The advantage to the job shopper is a somewhat higher than normal pay rate and the possibility that one of the temporary assignments will be come a permanent position at the employer's request. The contract generally provides for this eventuality, either for a fee or after a period of job shop employment, usually 90 days.

Job shop is a term related to the engineering industry; temporary agency is probably more widely used. These agencies tend to limit their scope to a single job family, namely, engineers, draftsmen and designers, accountants, data processing personnel, nurses, or clerical groups. The skills in these jobs are highly transferable between companies and industries, the work is essentially similar, and little or no training or break-in time is required.

A consultant is a person with unique knowledge, talent, or abilities, generally in a professional discipline, and provides his knowledge to other persons or organizations on a fee basis. A bona fide consultant is an independent contractor and not an employee of the organization using his services. This becomes an important consideration under both state and federal laws. For an employee, the employer is responsible for the withholding of taxes and other statutory benefits; for an independent contractor, the employer has no responsibility in that regard. This determination is based on the degree of control exercised by the employer; the more control, the more an employee. The true consultant would have more than one client, an office [perhaps in his home, but a bona fide office], business cards and stationery, and a business telephone listing, all indicating that he is an independent business person. In addition, although the employer controls the end result of the consulting work, the means or method for accomplishing it would be the consultant's responsibility.

Consultants are widely used in engineering and technical areas because of the frequent need for thorough knowledge and expertise in very specific areas. Consulting rates vary and are subject to negotiation between the consultant and the user and the conditions are normally contained in a written agreement (Exhibit A, end of chapter). Some consultants may require a guaranteed minimum number of days or a retainer fee but most are open-ended and permit the use of the consultant only as required. The need for a consultant and the rate of compensation would be the province of the project manager or the general manager. The role of the Personnel Department is to ensure that a written agreement has been executed and to maintain such agreements on file.

A staffing schedule prepared by the project team will provide the necessary information to the Personnel Department as to effective dates of assignment for the various engineering disciplines and the field construction staff. These dates should be within a one month level of accuracy. As changes occur, the schedule should be updated so that Personnel can initiate necessary actions to hire or relocate employees. At the end of the project, a demobilization schedule is equally important, and should be developed in comparable detail.

Compensation

An effective compensation program is a key motivator in any organization and requires professional expertise in its design and administration. To be effective, a compensation program must be consistent and equitable as perceived by employees and should be designed to reward the better performers to a greater degree than the poorer performers—Pay for Performance is currently a popular term. The design, implementation, administration, and maintenance is a basic responsibility of the Personnel Department.

The key elements of a compensation program include accurate job descriptions, an effective classification system, a competitive salary structure, and a program for adjusting salaries that motivates employees to improved performance levels with the end result of maintaining the company in a reasonably competitive position. To borrow an old cliché, "It's easier said than done."

One pervading consideration of compensation is the company's concern with confidentiality. A major factor seems to be relativity; an employee becomes concerned or dissatisfied with his own compensation in relation to the compensation of his associates in the same job or grade level, if his own is lower. Thus, most organizations try to keep individual salaries confidential, which is virtually impossible in the project organization. Not only do employees compare notes themselves, but some one or more persons in the project team is responsible for preparing client billings of hours worked and labor rates. The salary information has to be available for that purpose and its confidentiality cannot be insured. Some years ago, the writer was employed by an organization that was very concerned that confidentiality, particularly with respect to executive salaries. Yet, each payroll period, a complete report of paid sick leave taken was published showing hours and hourly rates. Although names were not included, employee numbers were and it was a simple matter to speculate who employee number 00001 was, the President. And there was his hourly rate; a simple multiplication produced his annual base salary. Confidentiality is always sought but seldom achieved and this is a factor in the relation of compensation to the project team.

A brief description of the ingredients of a compensation program may assist in understanding the relationship to the project and in suggesting areas where the project manager may need assistance from the Personnel Department. The collection of tasks, duties, and responsibilities that an individual performs is a position, secretary to the project manager for example. All like positions are classified as a job; again, all secretaries regardless of their department. The process of job evaluation is concerned with relating one job to another to determine its relative worth to the organization for the purpose of assigning a grade or level to each job. The job of mail clerk is obviously worth less to the company than the position of Chief Engineer, but as we move away from the extremities, these differences in worth become more difficult to evaluate. A salary structure, then, is a series of levels or grades with a progressively higher salary range assigned to each succeeding grade. A salary range is expressed in dollars and encompasses a minimum and maximum rate. Thus, each job assigned to a salary range and grade would be paid within that minimum and maximum rate. The number of grades or levels is dependent upon factors that vary from industry to industry but a common number is 12 to 15 in the engineering industry.

The difficulty lies in evaluating in which grade a job belongs when the duties, responsibilities, and training and preparation for widely diverse jobs must be compared; truck driver versus registered nurse, for example. At this precise point in time, there is an increasingly intense debate in the United States on this subject, called comparable worth, involving a number of law suits. The debate has polarized around jobs which are typically filled by women versus those typically filled by men, but the problem is inherently more complex. A technical problem lies in the inability of the job classification systems available today to accurately weigh diverse job content and to produce consistent results upon repeated application. A fundamental problem lies in the free labor market concept, where individuals should have the opportunity to earn as high a level of compensation as they can attain, while at the same time, employers should pay no more than is required to employ the necessary skills.

Even with an effective internal compensation system, one element still missing is the salary levels of competitors for comparable grade levels and responsibilities. The Personnel Department should be able to develop sources for obtaining general salary data from competitor companies through salary survey groups, state and federal data, and through personal contacts. Most industries have some vehicle for sharing salary data on a confidential basis without identifying individual company participants. Marketplace benchmarks are essential ingredients to an effective compensation program.

The project-related compensation problems generally evolve around the assignment of a member to the project team in a position which is inconsistent with his current salary level or the hiring of a much-needed specialist whose salary requirements are substantially in excess of existing team members and/or the company grade level to which his position would normally be assigned. In the case of the assignment, the incumbent salary may be either too high or too low to fit the salary grade assigned to the project position. If too low, a salary increase in the same grade may be warranted or a promotion to a higher grade with an increase might be considered, but any action taken should be consistent with the company's compensation guidelines. When the salary is too high, it may result from the assignment of a senior person to a lower level position because no other assignment is available. While this may not raise serious problems internally, it may be of concern to a client who might object to a higher salary cost to fill that position.

The hiring of the specialist may be easier to resolve. He can be retained as a consultant, if appropriate, where rates of compensation are less restricted by company policy and contractual obligations or perhaps an alternative choice of specialist may be available at a more reasonable rate. If he must be employed at the higher rate, project team members are less concerned about an inconsistent salary for a short-term specialist than they might be for a permanent employee.

The essential concern with project-related salary administration is to avoid any salary action which may seem appropriate for the project but which may be inconsistent with overall company policy. If an employee is granted an excessive salary increase on assignment to the project, upon completion and return to his permanent department there are few alternatives other than salary reduction to maintain consistency and salary structure integrity. Even though such action may have been planned and the employee advised in advance, it would be wise to avoid this circumstance.

One additional compensation subject should be mentioned—the project bonus. Project contracts may provide for a total bonus based on specific factors: completion dates, costs, etc. If earned by the project performance as a whole, individual bonus amounts must be determined for members of the project team who contributed to the project's success. This is normally the prerogative of the project manager although the client may want to offer some input from his vantage point. Bonuses are paid after completion when project objectives have been met, and the role of the Personnel Department is to ensure that such bonus payments to individual employees are credited to compensation-related benefits as appropriate.

The Personnel Department should provide advice and recommendations to the project manager prior to any action involving compensation. It is easier to conceive innovative solutions before problems occur than to correct inappropriate decisions after the fact. In summary, professional compensation programs can contribute substantially to the effective management of a project. Nothing is more devastating to the successful interaction of project team members than an ineffective, mismanaged program that provides widely divergent compensation to employees performing essentially similar work at comparable performance levels.

The total compensation "package" includes base salary, possible overtime pay, project allowances, perhaps a project bonus, and an employee benefits program. Over the years, employees have come to expect a basic benefit program from all employers and tend to overlook this element as a major factor in total compensation.

Benefits

Employee benefit programs have a long history and have become an integral part of the monetary rewards of employment today. They were intended to afford protection to the covered employee or his dependents in the event of unpredictable events causing financial hardship whether it be illness, injury, disability, or death, and to assist in financial planning toward retirement, e.g., pensions and savings plans. A typical employee benefits program today would include medical coverage, life insurance, accident insurance, long-term disability coverage, a pension program or savings plan or both and, increasingly, dental coverage, legal coverage, and child day care for working parents. Generally, benefit programs are funded through private insurance carriers and the cost or monthly premium is usually shared between the employer and employee.

In recent years, the cost of benefits has been escalating into a major cost consideration ranging from 25 to over 40% of base salary. Escalating medical coverage costs along with federal social security contributions have played a major role in these increases. Social security contributions in 1987 were 7.15% of the first $43,500 earned. This is a dual contribution by both the employee and employer, with increases scheduled. Despite these increasing costs, benefits programs are not likely to be eliminated, although many companies have been reducing their benefits costs in recent years by increasing the employee contributions to these programs. As of this writing, some of the benefit programs remain as the only vehicle for tax-free or tax-deferred compensation from an employer—medical coverage, pensions, and savings plans, for example.

The role of the Personnel Department here may include the design of programs, depending upon the size of the organization, but certainly includes administration, including orientation of new employees, enrollment and cancelation of coverages, maintenance of adequate records, and frequently, claims for medical coverage and life insurance. One of the important functions that requires continuing emphasis is employee communication about the value of benefit programs. The cost to the employer of 25-40% of payroll is "silent." The employee never sees it in his paycheck and the employer gets little credit for providing this element of compensation. The Personnel Department should make use of all communication channels available—bulletin boards, employee publications, meetings—to ensure that employees have an understanding and awareness of the value of this factor of total compensation.

Other Personnel Functions

Many other services are normally provided by the Personnel Department which are directed toward the total organization as well as the project.

Training and Development

Many organizations maintain a full-time staff whose primary function is to assess training needs and to develop internal programs to accomplish those objectives. Frequently, the staff is involved in evaluating and recommending outside educational programs for attendance by staff employees. Some companies maintain a close liaison with a local college or university to provide courses on the company premises, either during or after normal work hours. There is usually no cost to the employee and he can receive credit toward a degree. A competent training and development staff can provide valuable assistance to the project manager as well as the total organization.

Performance Evaluation

An important function of Personnel is the coordination and administration of a performance evaluation system for all employees in the organization. Past reviews may be helpful to the project manager in his initial selection of the project team and to focus on some special talent or ability that might be needed during the life of the project. The types of performance review systems are many and varied and range from a simple numerical rating of traits such as quality of work, quantity of work, and initiative, to complex and sophisticated instruments requiring professional psychological services for their development. An important consideration is the reliability of the system or its ability to produce consistent results. A principal concern here is the raters themselves; there should be an effective training effort for the raters before they use the system. Evaluations should be conducted periodically, either annually or more frequently when an employee makes a significant change in job duties and responsibilities. Some organizations relate performance evaluations to salary increases on a direct basis while others intentionally avoid this relationship. Whatever approach is taken, its primary goal should be to improve employee job performance in the future. Too often it serves only as a report card of the past.

New Employee Orientation

This function is simply the process of indoctrinating a new employee to the organization. Benefits programs must be explained and new employees enrolled, a myriad of other forms signed, organization work rules and working hours discussed, and the new employee made to feel welcome to the organization. One of the common tools here is an Employee Handbook containing most of the information a new employee might need, but there is a potential legal problem with some wording in handbooks, as discussed later.

   Working closely with the project manager and the project team, Personnel should provide quality staff assistance in achieving project goals within the parameters established by overall company policy and practice. Although flexibility and consistency may seem somewhat incompatible, they can be achieved by an effective Personnel Department.

STATUTORY REQUIREMENTS

Certain elements of normal business activity have been regulated by state and federal legislation for many years. The most common of these are payments for work in excess of the standard work week (overtime) and nondiscrimination in employment and other personnel actions. Federal minimum wage legislation, although long standing, provides a base in 1987 of $3.35 per hour and has little impact on the type of organizations involved in project management activities. The legislation currently in effect for overtime and nondiscrimination provides for enforcement. Deliberate and willful noncompliance can result in either criminal or civil actions.

Overtime

Successfully meeting project schedules frequently requires the project team to work overtime, which may require additional compensation for some members of the team. In the United States, the standard work week is considered to be 40 hours, a result of long-standing federal legislation, the Fair Labor Standards Act (FLSA). The FLSA was originally enacted in 1938 and has been amended a number of times. This Act established the minimum wage concept, maximum straight time hours (40), overtime pay, child labor standards, and later, equal pay for equal work.

With respect to overtime payments, the Act provides that covered employees will receive premium pay at one and one-half times the straight time hourly rate for all hours worked in excess of 40 per week. Covered employees are defined as nonexempt, that is, they are not exempt from the FLSA. The Act further provides that certain executive, professional, and administrative positions do not have to be paid overtime payments for hours worked in excess of 40 per week if the duties and responsibilities of the position meet the criteria established in the Act. These positions are defined as exempt, that is, they are not covered by the overtime provisions. However, in conjunction with this "no-overtime" provision, the Act requires that exempt employees must receive full salary for any week in which any work is performed without regard to the number of days or hours worked. In essence, the exempt employee is guaranteed a fixed weekly rate of pay in exchange for no overtime payments.

In addition, each state may have its own legislation regulating hours of work and overtime payments. A few states, California included, are more restrictive than the federal legislation, requiring overtime payments for hours worked in excess of 8 per day as well as 40 per week for covered employees but also follow the federal definitions, in general, for exemptions. The importance of more restrictive state legislation is the added cost to employers and the impact on flexible work schedules. It has become increasingly popular to give employees some freedom in scheduling their own work hours where the type of business will permit. Thus an individual might choose to work 10 hours one day to make up for the 2 hours taken off for personal reasons another day. If the total weekly hours worked were 40, there would be no overtime payment under FLSA but there would be 2 hours premium pay for the 10-hour day under California provisions. California does permit four 10-hour days per week without overtime payments, but it requires a ballot with 2/3rds of the employees voting in favor both to implement or discontinue it—a cumbersome procedure.

At this writing, the California Industrial Welfare Commission is beginning a review of the 8-hour-day rule which has been in effect for many years. Any change will require public hearings and, as might be expected, support for making the change comes from employer associations, and opposition from employee groups. Change will not be easily accomplished, but if it should occur it would permit substantially increased flexibility in work schedules without requiring overtime payments and could benefit certain groups of employees such as working mothers and part-time students, as well as employers.

The definition of exempt versus nonexempt is made by the employer, subject to possible future review and challenge by the U.S. Department of Labor or state enforcement agenices. The Personnel Department should be the final arbiter in this area since this is a major element of their expertise. There are many guidelines available and the careful and accurate classification of positions can avoid unnecessary premium overtime payments. Despite this, some industries prefer to be conservative and classify positions as nonexempt which could probably be successfully defended as exempt.

It has also become increasingly common in some industries to pay overtime to selected exempt employees even though not required by law. These payments are normally made at straight time, as opposed to premium time, and it is not unusual for all members of the project team to receive compensation since many contracts provide reimbursability for such payments. This practice has evolved in part from competition, many employers are paying such overtime, and in part from the discrepancy

which may occur when the weekly compensation of nonexempt employees earning overtime pay exceeds the compensation of their immediate supervisor, who is exempt.

While overtime must be paid nonexempt employees for any hours worked in excess
of 40, overtime for exempt employees is generally paid on some pre-established schedule rather than on a casual basis. This scheduled overtime should be planned in advance for two or more weeks, and the days and hours should be announced. The
schedule might be 9 hours per day, Monday through Friday, for a 45-hour week or
six 8-hour days, Monday through Saturday, for a 48-hour week. If the exempt employee chose to work additional hours over 45 or 48, he would not be compensated.
Scheduled overtime should be authorized by the appropriate management member, using a simple form listing the names of the employees involved, the scheduled work
week, the inclusive dates, and the necessary signature approvals, including the client,
if necessary and appropriate.

In some areas, overtime payments do not generate any other additional salary-
related benefits. Additional vacation is not accrued because of the overtime or, if
the group life insurance coverage were expressed as one times annual salary, this
insurance amount would not be increased by the overtime payments. In these benefits
areas, salary means the normal base rate for a 40-hour week. Conversely, overtime
payments are normally credited to total compensation for purposes of pension plans
and savings plans.

Overtime payments are based on hours worked in the work week. The establishment of the work week is an employer's prerogative; the normal work week is a fixed
and regularly recurring period of 168 hours, seven consecutive 24-hour periods. It
may begin on any day of the week and at any hour of the day. An employer may change
the established work week, but only if the change is intended to be permanent and
is not made to evade the statutory overtime pay requirements. When the employer's
business is normally conducted on a Monday through Friday basis, the work week
will have little effect on overtime payments; however, where there is an uneven workload each week, the judicious establishment of the work week may assist in minimizing
such payments.

The Personnel Department should ensure that positions are classified correctly
and, in conjunction with the Payroll Department, that overtime is being paid in accordance with the law. In general, problems develop as a result of employee complaints,
although the Department of Labor has broad authority to review all payroll records
at any time, and to interview employees, if necessary. In addition, employee demographics should be considered in planning an overtime schedule of any length; a work
force with a long commuting time might prefer a 48-hour week split into four 10-hour
days and one 8-hour day rather than six 8-hour days when commuting time is considered. The cost of overtime would be identical. Finally it should be noted that
some studies have demonstrated a diminishing return in overtime hours worked, specifically 12-hour days on a continuing basis may result in minimal, if any, production
increases over a 10-hour day although the cost would be an additional 2-3 hours pay
per day.

Equal Employment Opportunity and Affirmative Action Programs (EEO/AAP)

The nation's concern with discrimination in employment began in 1941 through a series
of Presidential Executive Orders applicable to employers holding government contracts,
although the spirit of these Orders was seldom followed or enforced in the succeeding
20 years. The federal government's objective of ensuring equal employment opportunity was provided renewed emphasis by Executive Order 10925 in 1961 establishing
the President's Committee on Equal Employment Opportunity. Executive Order 11114
in 1963 extended coverage to contractors engaged on construction projects financed
or assisted with Federal funds. In 1964, broader legislation was enacted in the Civil
Rights Act, and the problem of coordinating the many different federal EEO programs
became intense. In a move designed to improve administration and enforcement, Execu-

tive Order 11246 was issued in September 1965 transferring responsibilities to the U.S. Department of Labor; and the Secretary of Labor immediately established the Office of Federal Contract Compliance (OFCC) as the enforcement agency. There have been subsequent amendments and revisions but E.O. 11246 and the OFCC remain today as the principal elements of this national program.

Generally, E.O. 11246 is applicable to all government contractors, subcontractors, first-tier subcontractors, vendors, and contractors on federally assisted projects and requires that:

They not discriminate against any employee or applicant because or race, color, religion, national origin, or sex

Help wanted advertising identify them as an Equal Opportunity Employer

They will furnish required information and reports and permit access to records to ascertain compliance

Their contracts may be cancelled for noncompliance

They will include the same provisions in every subcontract and purchase order and take action, as directed by the OFCC, to insure compliance of subcontractors and vendors

Obviously the coverage is broad and the number of companies affected substantial. Government contracts call up a vision of the defense industry but it is probably safe to assume that a vast majority of the Fortune 500 companies have government contracts of various sorts, not necessarily related to defense, and all their subcontractors and vendors are thus covered.

The enforcement powers of the OFCC are also broad; they may recommend that the Department of Justice bring suit in federal courts to enjoin noncompliance or to bring criminal action against a contractor for false information, cancel all or any part of a contract, and prevent contractors from receiving any future contracts until compliance is achieved. Clearly, these powers of enforcement have gained the attention of employers and Equal Employment Opportunity has become a way of life for companies of any size.

Among the several continuing requirements of this legislation are the annual work force report, EEO-1, and the preparation and maintenance of a written Affirmative Action Program (AAP). The EEO-1 is a numerical matrix of the work force by job levels: Officials and Managers, Professionals, Technicians, Clerical, etc., by race (White, Black, Asian, Hispanic, and American Indian) and by sex. These data are easily maintained in the personnel database and the preparation of the report is relatively simple. The AAP, however, is more complicated and the general requirements are contained in E.O. 11246.

The AAP specifies that the company representatives responsible for the program, usually the personnel manager and general manager, provide an analysis of the current workforce: race, sex, job title, and so on; the size of each minority group in the company compared to the size of the minority groups in the work force in the area; the employer deficiencies in each group; and plans to correct those deficiencies.

The AAP may be requested and reviewed at any time by the OFCC, and if not satisfactory, the employer may be declared in noncompliance and given a reasonable period to make necessary changes and correction. The prime contractor is responsible for compliance by subcontractors so that a current AAP may be a prerequisite to obtaining a subcontract.

A program of this import should, and usually does, have the attention of the top management but some of the day-to-day tasks fall to the Personnel Department. Applicant flow logs should be maintained which include data about each applicant for employment, including the position applied for, the date of application, sex and race of the applicant (by observation only), and the final successful candidate. The employment application and other employment forms must be free of any discriminatory questions or requests for information. Generally, prior to employment, requests for information may not ask for any protected data which would divulge race, religion, sex, age, or any other fact which could be used in a discriminatory fashion to deny employment. After employment, many of these data are required, and legally obtainable, in order to satisfy governmental reporting requirements.

The Personnel Department also has the primary responsibility to prepare the AAP and to insure that all supervisory actions are in compliance. Records must be maintained, supervisors must be trained and counseled, and on occasion, the general manager's influence must be solicited to persuade a recalcitrant project manager to take appropriate action so that compliance can be maintained and existing and future contracts protected. Project managers who are hiring must be aware of the announced goals in the AAP and, as in the rest of the organization, consistently seek to avoid discrimination in personnel-related actions. Although the EEO/AAP programs and requirements may seem onerous to employers at times, they should be viewed as an adjunct to the basic objective of hiring the best qualified person for the available position.

In addition to the long-standing legislation on overtime and discrimination, some new considerations affecting the employer/employee relationships are emerging, either by legislation or through precedent based on court decisions. The role of the Personnel Department is becoming increasingly complex requiring substantial effort to achieve compliance with the changing facets of governmental regulation.

EMERGING LEGAL CONSIDERATIONS

During the previous decade, the free-market aspects of employment have been subjected to an increasing scrutiny by attorneys and the courts. Whether this results from an enhanced awareness of a litigious society of the "spoils of war" or to employers' seeming disregard of social values, or both, the number of lawsuits contesting employers' personnel actions has increased dramatically and is causing a searching review of policies and practices that have been part of the employer/employee relationship for many years. One growing concern at this time is the concept of wrongful discharge versus employment at will.

Employment at Will

In the past, it has been a general rule that, unless hired for a specific period of time by contractual agreement, employment could be terminated by an employer at any time, without notice and with or without cause. Terminated employees are beginning to challenge this concept in the courts and are doing so successfully. Many employer documents (employee handbooks and personnel policies) refer to "discharge for cause" and by implication, at least, suggest that lacking cause the person is to be employed for life, or until retirement age. This is frequently supplemented by Personnel Departments who advise new employees about "career opportunities." The courts are increasingly recognizing that these employer-initiated documents and statements constitute an implied contract and are deciding in the employee's favor by awarding monetary damages, reemployment, or both.

The thread which seems to run through these court decisions is that an employer might become liable for a termination which is particularly unfair and carried out in an abusive way and/or one which is made because the employee has refused to go along with a violation of some public law or policy. The employers' liability for wrongful termination has been translated into monetary damages by the courts, in some cases substantial dollar amounts, and rehire of the terminated employee is often required.

The Personnel Department's role here is to insure that all company documents clearly avoid any reference or implication that employment is "forever." This would include employee handbooks, the company personnel policies, or any other written documents, and the personnel representative should be careful of any verbal commitments or implications as well. The employee handbook has special significance because it is written with the newly hired employee in mind. It is optimistic in tone and frequently refers to "careers" and "retirement," giving the impression of long-term employment. In many handbooks, the section on termination defines "termination for cause" as misconduct, insubordination, failure to follow orders, to name a few reasons, leaving the reader, and recently, the courts, with the impression that lacking any misconduct, employment will continue until retirement. In addition, it would seem wise to review all intended terminations with the personnel manager, who should be satisfied that the reasons for termination are valid in accordance with established company policies and not capricious or abusive.

Privacy

Another contemporary consideration is the degree of privacy that should be available to U.S. citizens, and therefore employees and/or employers. In the writer's earlier experience, a personnel record was the province of the employer, a private record; employees were not permitted to see their own folder. Consequently, all manner of documents, notes, performance evaluations, and derogatory memos, found their way into the personnel record and the employee had no knowledge that they were there. This is no longer the case in California and other states; employees may request and must be granted a reasonable opportunity to review their own records. When this legislation was first enacted in California, there was some apprehension on the part of personnel managers who predicted undesirable consequences; in fact, nothing much has happened. Some employees never ask to see their records; others ask frequently, but seemingly out of curiosity and not necessarily with any ulterior motive. Employers have become more responsive to employee rights and are insuring that an employee has seen, and maybe even signed, any controversial document that may be placed in the record, performance evaluations, for example. Employees may, of course, refuse to sign documents they feel are detrimental, but at least, having seen the document and been advised it would be placed in the record, they have little substantive complaint.

Another element relating to privacy was touched on earlier, employment references. It is good policy to limit employment verification information provided to other employers to name, position, title, and dates of employment of the ex-employee. Frequently the ex-employee will advise the potential new employer of his previous salary as part of the application process. If so, this may also be verified if requested. Supervisors and managers should decline all requests for employment references on prior employees and refer all such requests to the Personnel Department. Specifically, supervisors should not comment on prior unsatisfactory work performance or personal habits such as absence, tardiness, or use of drugs or alcohol.

Sexual Harassment

Another recent development is the concept of sexual harassment. In the classic example, the male supervisor harasses the female subordinate, asking for sexual favors in return for promotion or even continued employment, but there are cases where the roles are reversed and one must assume, there are, or will be, cases involving the same sex.

In some cases it has been held that the employer has a degree of responsibility for his supervisors' actions which may be impractical. Employers do have the clear responsibility to develop a policy statement and to advise their supervisory personnel that sexual harassment will not be tolerated and of the ensuing disciplinary results if it is encountered.

Age Discrimination

Age is yet another factor which has been used as a basis for discrimination in employment and other personnel actions and which is now prohibited by law. It warrants discussion here, separate from the EEO/AAP section because of its impact on the upper end of the age continuum, the termination of a career, or retirement. For a number of years, federal legislation has prohibited discrimination against those between the ages of 40 and 70, and recently, this upper limit has been removed entirely. Some states, California for example, had removed the upper limit prior to the federal action. The removal of this upper limit primarily affects retirements. Prior to this legislation, many companies had a mandatory retirement age of 65; now employees may continue working as long as their work performance warrants continued employment. In other words, they cannot be terminated or forced to retire for reasons of age alone.

Employees who feel they have been terminated because of age have resorted to the courts, filing civil suits against the ex-employer for damages, and have been successful. Juries have been particularly sympathetic to the plight of the older person whose termination appears to have been discriminatory and whose opportunity to acquire another position at a comparable salary rate seems limited. As a countermeasure, many companies have offered financial inducements for the older employee to voluntarily accept early retirement. These have included substantial cash severance payments, improved monthly retirement benefits or both.

The lower threshold of age discrimination, 40, applies primarily to the hiring function; applicants for employment may not be rejected for consideration on the basis of age alone; and to internal personnel action, promotions, transfers, work assignments, etc. In essence, people above the age of 40 are protected from age discrimination.

In practice, hiring discrimination based on age is difficult to establish because other factors are usually not equal: prior work experience, educational qualifications, etc. The Personnel Department, through the applicant flow log mentioned earlier, can determine whether a pattern of age discrimination is developing in a company and recommend countermeasures.

U.S. Citizenship

In 1986, Congress passed the Immigration Reform and Control Act intended to permit certain current illegal aliens to apply for permanent residency and to control the flow of future aliens. The rules for the implementation of this Act as formulated by the Immigration and Naturalization Service require for the first time that all U.S. citizens prove their legal status when applying for a job. Proof must be submitted to the new employer within 24 hours, verified by the Personnel Department, and records maintained for possible inspection by the Immigration Service. The law imposes fines ranging from $250 to $10,000 for employers who knowingly hire illegal aliens. While this legislation may not seem to be a problem in project-oriented organizations, there are a number of foreign-born engineers who have obtained legal entry to the United States with the assistance of a U.S. employer. If they should leave that employer and seek other employment in the United States, they may not be eligible for continued residence and may, in fact, be an alien not legally qualified to work. The Personnel Department must verify that all new hires are U.S. citizens or otherwise in an alien status permitting employment.

Medical Discrimination

Still another area of discrimination is emerging slowly, medical discrimination. Although still in its early stages, there are efforts by various gorups to implement legislation which would prohibit discrimination in employment for victims of cancer and AIDS. While it is premature to speculate on the eventual outcome of these efforts,

it seems likely that this question will receive increasing attention during the coming
years.

JOBSITE ASSIGNMENTS

Many projects require work to be performed in more than one physical location. This
is particularly true of engineering/construction projects where the engineering is typically done in the home or branch office, while the construction is, of course, done
at the jobsite location. The staff at the jobsite would include all construction personnel, usually a warehousing and procurement group, and frequently, selected engineers
from the home office. The movement of personnel to the jobsite raises a number of
questions about length of assignment, relocation, allowances, and other factors which
should be carefully analyzed and provided for in policy statements and/or assignment
letters.

Short-Term Assignments

Most projects require the assignment of specialized employees on a short-term basis,
typically one to three months, although some companies may consider a short term
to be 6 months or less. The employee does not relocate on a permanent basis, rather,
he goes on a single status basis, does not move any household goods, and lives in
temporary accommodations at the site. Since he is maintaining two residences, his
expenses for housing and other selected costs are reimbursed either through payment
of actual expenses or through a per diem. If the assignment is in excess of one month,
reimbursed trips home are provided on a predetermined basis, once per month, for
example. The housing may be provided through barracks at the site, employer-leased
apartments, or at a local hotel/motel. The short-term assignment is the most difficult
one for the employee and family, particularly if school-age children are involved. Some
companies provide a temporary salary increase as motivation to the employee to accept
the many inconveniences associated with a short-term assignment.

Long-Term Assignments

Long term is any assignment longer than the defined short term and frequently is
for the duration of the project. The employee and family are relocated to the jobsite
area, household goods are moved and/or stored, and the family establishes a new "residence" at the site location. The construction employee and his family are conditioned
to frequent relocation because mobility is a prerequisite of a construction career; their
lives are organized around this concept. Many find this to be an exciting and rewarding career with the opportunity to live in a variety of locations and to acquire many
friends throughout the world. Some construction families, however, prefer to establish a home base, normally not at the home office location, and the family remains there
while the employee accepts assignments on a single-status basis. Childrens' schooling
is uninterrupted and the employee visits home as time or cost permit.

   The home-office-based employee is in a somewhat different position. He has generally established a long-term residency in the home office vicinity and perhaps has
"deeper roots." His family has not acquired the mobility of the construction family
and may find relocation an undesirable hardship. Nevertheless, his services are required at the jobsite and he must be flexible in this regard. The home office employee
may also opt to leave his family at the permanent residence depending on the distance
and length of assignment. Longer distances and assignments generally lead to family
relocation. Given today's real estate considerations, many home office employees who
do relocate to the jobsite do not dispose of their permanent residences but choose to
lease their homes during the absence. When a family decides to let their permanent
residence remain empty until their eventual return, a whole new range of problems
arises such as gardening, maintenance, and security during the absence.

An essential difference between the career construction employee and the home office employee is the future expectation. The construction employee expects another assignment but doesn't know where; the home office employee expects to return to the location of the home office.

Assignment Conditions

Assignment to a field jobsite, whether long or short term, whether construction or engineering personnel, creates a need to establish the specific conditions of that assignment. In effect, a project policy must be developed to meet the exigencies of relocation to a new residence. Some elements of basic company policy will remain unchanged; vacation accrual, benefit programs, and paid sick leave are applicable at any location. Holidays observed may require some modification to be compatible with a client's policy or with the practices in a different location. Other factors will require a specific policy statement so that employees assigned to the jobsite will be aware of all conditions in advance.

Single/Family Status

Single status is intended for employees who are unmarried or whose assignment is on a short-term basis. Those who are eligible for family status, but who voluntarily elect single status, receive the single status allowances/accommodations only.

Travel

This includes the cost of transportation from the employee's location to the jobsite; family transportation is included for family status employees. Travel is normally by airline economy fare or by personal automobile at a cents per mile rate established by company policy. The current popular rate is 22 cents per mile. Upon satisfactory completion of the assignment, travel is provided to return to the point of origin or go on to the next project. Travel expenses include airfare or mileage, meals and lodging enroute if required, and/or transportation to and from airports. When a personal car is driven, the project or company policy may establish the number of days allowed in transit based on mileage; usually 350 to 400 miles per day are required.

Household Goods Shipments

For long-term assignments, the employee household goods are moved to the jobsite location with a weight limit usually established at 12,000-15,000 pounds. Packing is included and goods not shipped may be stored as long as the combined total weight does not exceed policy maximum. In addition, insurance is provided on both goods shipped and stored, and the monthly storage charges are paid by the company. Automobiles may be shipped or driven. Some items are normally excluded from shipment, pets and boats, for example. Some experienced construction personnel maintain a trailer or mobile home and move that from site to site, in lieu of the cost of shipping household goods. Many companies prefer to have moving arrangements made by an experienced traffic department so that they can obtain the best rates and otherwise monitor costs.

Settling-In Expense

For the long-term relocation, a settling-in allowance is frequently provided, intended to assit with the added costs of one-time problems such as new draperies, TV antenna, telephone installation and hook-up, and so on. This amount is frequently related to family size; $1000 for husband and wife plus $500 for each dependent child, for example. In some cases, this allowance is also provided at the completion of the project (settling-out allowance) to assist with the same costs upon return to the permanent residence.

Living Allowance

This should be an allowance that is intended to compensate for any excess living costs
at the job site and/or for the extra cost of maintaining two residences for the short-
term assignment. Theoretically, then, the cost of housing, food, and other goods
and services should be an element of the formula. In fact, company practices vary
widely and there seems to be no common agreement on this allowance. Some pay only
for short-term assignments; some pay for all assignments. Some pay on an actual
expense reimbursement, while others establish and pay a per diem amount. In some
cases, the housing portion is separate from other costs and the actual cost of housing
is paid, with a smaller per diem paid for other living expenses.

The determination of the amount to be paid is made in many ways. Some companies
use a standard policy of reasonable and actual expenses or a per diem regardless of
location; others may use company representatives to make a survey of local costs at
the site and use these data to establish an amount, which could vary from one location
to another. Third-party consultants are also available who specialize in providing cost
data for many locations or who will make a current survey of any location requested.
Some company criteria may include family size or income level to establish a different
allowance for each employee while others may pay the same per diem to each employee
regardless of family size or income level. The IRS has established per diem costs for
many U.S. cities which they consider equitable and this may serve as a guideline to
some company policies. A few companies have adopted assignment incentives, a percentage of base salary, in lieu of living allowances.

Local Transportation

This is always a problem for employees on short-term assignments whose initial travel
is by air. On a construction site, there are frequently pick-up trucks available for
transportation to and from work, but in many cases their use is restricted on weekends
or for other personal uses. One solution is to rent or lease passenger vehicles to
be shared by two or three single status short-term employees, or provide a monetary
allowance for this purpose.

Home Visits

During the short-term assignment on single status, most companies provide periodic
trips home. This would include the travel costs and ground transportation if travel
is by air. The most commonly used period is one trip each month. Alternatively,
the same costs could be reimbursed for the spouse to visit the job site, if appropriate.
Home visits are not normally provided to the employee on long-term assignment because
his family is usually with him. One exception might be the employee who elected single
status and left his family at the permanent residence, thereby eliminating the cost
of relocating his family. Some companies would provide this employee with periodic
trips home in lieu of the moving expense.

Other Allowances

Basically, allowances are intended to keep the employee whole; to protect him against
any excess costs as a result of the assignment. Less common than the ones already
discussed include federal and state tax differentials, pool and garden maintenance
costs for the permanent residence, an area or hardship allowance for assignments to
locations with difficult living conditions, and winter allowances to cover the additional
costs associated with extreme cold weather climates.

As with compensation, the various allowances and assignment conditions should
be competitive. Other employers are generally willing to share information on assignments, perhaps more readily than on compensation. The Personnel Department,
through employer associations and other contacts, should participate in surveys to
keep abreast of practices in the industry. The development of assignment conditions

should be a joint effort of the Personnel Department and the project manager. They should be issued to key project team members, the Accounting Department, and the traffic manager or other person responsible for making moving arrangements (Exhibit B, end of chapter). Some companies provide an assignment letter to each employee going to the job site so that ambiguity doesn't exist as to status and conditions of employment.

PROJECT COMPLETION

During the course of a construction project, many factors can combine to alter the original schedule: weather, change orders, slow delivery of materials, work stoppages. Nevertheless, the project team should be aware of all these, and as the project draws to a close, should develop a demobilization schedule showing the dates of release for each employee. The Personnel Department must be advised of these release dates in order to assist in whatever action will occur. Some employees will be reassigned to other projects at a field location, some will return to the home office, either to another project or to their "permanent" department, and still others will have no assignment. Regardless of the action to be taken, a performance evaluation of each employee's project performance should be made by the person(s) who has been directly responsible for his work. Over a period of time, these project performance evaluations will focus on the strong areas of each employee's performance and will assist in developing more effective and more homogeneous project teams in the future. The Personnel Department should maintain these written evaluations and they should be available for review by the project manager who is forming the next team.

Reassignment is relatively uncomplicated. Appropriate allowances are provided as previously discussed and the employee moves on, either to the home office or to the next field location. When new assignments aren't immediately available, there are several alternatives depending on the estimated period of time the employee may be idle.

Leave of Absence (LOA)

An LOA is a short-term absence without pay, usually from 30 to 90 days. It may be requested by the employee for personal reasons or may be initiated by the company. Both the employee and the company have high expectations of early return to active employment. All accrued vacation is paid in a lump sum and could amount to 4-6 weeks pay or more. Severance pay is not normally granted for an LOA, but frequently the employee is permitted to continue his employee benefits programs by payment of the normal employee premiums which are deducted from his vacation pay for the three-month period. If assignment conditions have not become firm at the conclusion of the three-month period, the leave might be extended for an additional three months. If the employee is recalled prior to the expiration of the leave, he simply returns to the active payroll and some adjustment is made for any benefits overpayment.

Layoff

When the possibility of the next assignment appears to be further in the future than three months, a layoff may be more appropriate than an LOA. A layoff generally implies that the employee's work performance has been acceptable, but there is simply no current assignment available. A severance payment is usually made either in a fixed amount or based on years of service. Again, all accrued vacation is paid, but the employee has not been permitted to continue his employee benefits programs. The continuation of medical coverage is the subject of current federal legislation, the Consolidated Omnibus Budget Reconciliation Act (COBRA), and beginning in 1986, all terminated employees are allowed to continue their medical coverage for 18 months through payment of the entire premium, both the employee's and employer's share, plus a 2% administrative surcharge. COBRA also allows spouses and dependents to continue coverage provided they are covered prior to termination. Since the monthly cost of quality family medical coverage is reaching the $200-300 level, this may be of minimal importance to the employee who has no current income.

The layoff status implies that the employee is subject to recall when work levels permit and he is not yet a terminated employee, however, he is eligible to apply for unemployment insurance benefits during this period. During this period of layoff, many pension plans offer the continuation of some or all of the period of absence as credited service under the plan so that it is to the employees advantage to return to work upon recall. There is generally a maximum time limit to the status of layoff, 1-2 years is common, and if no recall has occurred during that period, the layoff is converted to a termination.

Termination

This is the final severing of the employer/employee relationship. This may occur at the completion of the layoff period by policy statement, may be initiated by the employer for employee misconduct or other cause, or may be the result of an employee resignation. The various benefit plans contain termination provisions and these would be activated, normally allowing the employee one additional month's coverage. Eligibility for unemployment insurance would depend on the provisions of the state laws and the reasons for termination. In general, the employee is eligible for unemployment insurance benefits unless he has resigned or been terminated for cause. Again, if not previously paid at layoff, all accrued vacation would be paid at this time. Terminated employees, of course, may be rehired and frequently are, but the termination may have interrupted their continuous service with the employer as related to eligibility for service-related benefits, such as vacation and sick leave.

SUMMARY

The line responsibility for any project lies clearly with the project manager; he must make the difficult decisions and stand responsible for the results. This burden can be eased by the timely and effective use of all staff services in their areas of expertise. The role of the Personnel Department is to assist and guide the project manager in all employee-related functions so that the human resources of the project function together efficiently and effectively to achieve the project goals: timely completion, within budget, with quality work performance and safety, and a reasonable profit for the organization.

EXHIBIT A

CONSULTANT'S AGREEMENT

THIS AGREEMENT made and entered into on this ____ day of _____, ___, by and between _____ hereinafter referred to as "Principal", and _____, an independent consultant, hereinafter referred to as "Consultant";

WITNESSETH, THAT

WHEREAS, in consideration of the mutual promises and agreements herein contained, beginning on the above date, the Principal hires Consultant and Consultant agrees to work for Principal under the following terms and conditions:

1. Principal agrees to pay Consultant at the daily, hourly, monthly rate (one rate only) shown in Paragraph 9, Part A, for any professional services rendered by mutual agreement during the period of this Agreement. Principal agrees to provide Consultant with at least the number of days of work as shown in Paragraph 9, Part B, during a calendar year, Consultant will receive additional compensation for each additional day of work at the same daily rate shown in Paragraph 9, Part A.

2. Consultant agrees to hold himself available during the term of this Agreement and to provide consultancy services at such times and in such places as may be reasonably requested by Principal.

3. In the event that Consultant is called upon by Principal to render the services contemplated in the Agreement, Principal shall reimburse or prepay Consultant for reasonable travel and living expenses while on assignment away from his home and for required business communication.

4. Consultant agrees during the period in which he is engaged in performing services for Principal, or at any time thereafter, not to disclose to any person, firm or corporation any information concerning the business affairs of Principal which he may have acquired in the course of, or incident to his services hereunder, for his own benefit and to the detriment or intended or probable detriment of Principal.

5. All rights of Consultant under this Agreement are expressly declared to be non-assignable and nontransferrable and in the event that any attempted assignment or transfer is made, then and in that event Principal shall have no further liability hereunder. In the event Consultant becomes unable to perform the services contemplated by this Agreement, all rights and obligations hereunder of either party shall cease and terminate forthwith, except that any payments due for services rendered up to such occurrence will be paid.

6. It is understood and agreed that in the performance of such services as may be required under this Agreement, Consultant shall act as an independent contractor and not as an employee of Principal, and Principal shall have no obligations or liability as an employer on account of this Agreement. Principal's only obligation under this Agreement shall be compensation for services as provided for in Paragraph 1 and reimbursement for reasonable expenses as provided in Paragraph 3 hereof.

7. Upon execution of this Agreement, Consultant shall provide evidence to Principal that he maintains the following insurance coverage:

    (a) Workers Compensation - Statutory Compliance

    (b) Automobile Liability - at least $_____ Bodily Injury and $_____ Property Damage.

8. All business data developed in the course of this work shall be the property of Principal and shall be used by Consultant solely in his work for Principal. During the term of this Agreement, Consultant agrees that he will not represent or advise any party considered to be a competitor of Principal.

9. This Agreement shall terminate as shown in Part D below and may be renewed if mutually acceptable to both parties.

    A. Daily, Hourly, Monthly Rate:_____.

    B. Guaranteed number of days:_____.

    C. Agreement commencement date:_____.

    D. Agreement termination date:_____.

By:_____

ACCEPTED BY:_____

ADDRESS:_____

_____

SOCIAL SECURITY NO.:_____

DATE:_____

EXHIBIT B

ASSIGNMENT CONDITIONS

DOMESTIC ASSIGNMENTS

Construction Personnel to Field Projects

Long-Term Assignment (over 3 months)

1. Duration of Assignment

    Long-term assignments shall be defined as assignments in excess of 3 months.

2. Salary

    The base salary rate will not be changed at the beginning of a field assignment. Employees who are on a field assignment at the occurrence of an approved annual salary review will be reviewed for a possible salary adjustment at that time.

    Time sheets will be completed and approved at the field location in accordance with standard procedure or any special instruction at that location. Payroll checks will be handled by the Payroll Department based on the employee's instructions.

3. Single/Family Status

    All long-term assignments are intended to be on a family status basis. If the employee elects not to relocate his family to the field location, all allowances will be on a single status basis.

4. Travel and Relocation

    A. Travel to the field location will be by economy air transportation or by personal automobile with reimbursement at $.22 per mile for one car only. Reimbursement will also be made for reasonable and actual expenses enroute including transportation to and from airports, meals and, if appropriate, lodging when supported by receipts. Similar costs will be reimbursed for the return trip upon satisfactory completion of the assignment.

    B. Field construction personnel will receive travel time pay for travel to and from the assignment location. One day's travel pay will be allowed for travel by air or for 400 miles per day if by automobile. One day's pay will be 8 times the employee's regular straight time hourly rate. Travel pay will be paid for weekend travel.

    C. Reimbursement will be allowed for actual cost of moving and/or storage of household goods and effects when the employee travels from point of hire or permanent residence to area of assignment or from assignment to assignment. The combination of movement and storage shall not exceed a net weight of 15,000 pounds for a family or 7,500 pounds for a single status employee. While in movement or storage, goods will be insured for $3.50 per pound. Employees should make personal arrangements for additional insurance coverage if their goods contain items of unique value or unusual cost. In lieu of shipment of household goods, reimbursement will be allowed for the actual cost of moving a trailer not to exceed the cost of moving 15,000 pounds of household goods.

D. All arrangements for moving of household goods and effects or for transportation of trailer must be arranged by the Home Office Procurement Department and all requests for reimbursement must be supported by receipts. Charges for storage-in-transit will not be allowed unless approved in advance by the Project Manager.

E. A settling-in allowance of $500 per family or $325 per single employee (or married man on single status) will be paid to employees who are reimbursed for cost of moving household goods and effects. In addition to the settling-in allowance, the employee will be reimbursed for lodging for a maximum period of two weeks. Employees who are reimbursed for cost of moving a trailer are entitled to a settling-in allowance but no lodging reimbursement.

F. When an employee has satisfactorily completed an assignment and another assignment is not available, and the employee is placed on a leave of absence or layoff status, or is temporarily assigned to the Home Office, he will be allowed moving and travel expenses, including settling-out allowance, to his residence of record, point of hire, the Home Office, or another location of equal distance in accordance with Company policy. The project to which the employee was last assigned will be responsible for this expense.

G. If an employee is discharged for cause, quits, or requests a leave of absence before assignment is completed, he will not be entitled to additional reimbursement for moving and travel expenses for himself or his family.

5. Per Diem

During the term of the assignment, the employee will receive a per diem allowance of $40 beginning after the completion of the settling-in period (lodging reimbursement). Per diem will be paid while on vacation during the project, on sick leave, and on expense-reimbursed trips of short duration. Per diem will not be paid for any period of leave of absence. This per diem is subject to periodic management review for adequacy based on general cost of living considerations, specific cost conditions at the field location, and other factors.

6. Local Transportation

A. The senior company construction representative at the site will be furnished a vehilce for business-related travel. This will include travel from his place of residence to the job site, but in no event is this to be utilized by the employee or members of his family for personal transportation.

B. Other senior members of the site management staff may also be furnished a vehicle, under the same conditions as above, if so authorized by the Project Manager.

7. Overtime/Workweek

A. The standard workweek will be 40 hours. Workweeks in excess of the 40 shall be established by the Project Manager at the project. Such extended workseek shall be considered as scheduled, approved overtime.

B. Employees will receive compensation for approved overtime in accordance with their overtime code.

C. Casual overtime to complete concrete pours, hydrotesting, etc. will not be compensated.

D. Extended workweek payments to the Project Manager require prior approval of the General Manager.

8. Holidays/Vacation

Employees will continue to accrue paid vacation in accordance with the standard Company vacation policy. Taking of any vacation during the field assignment must be scheduled commensurate with the requirements of the project and approved by the Project Manager. All employees will observe the holidays established for the project rather than the Home Office holidays. Employees required to work on a project holiday may be given a compensatory day off prior to completing the field assignment. Employees will not be paid for any accrued but unused holidays.

9. Employee Benefits

Permanent salaried employees will be eligible for all the benefit programs in accordance with the provisions of those Plans.

10. Policy Changes/Deviations

Any changes to or deviations from this policy statement will require the prior approval of the General Manager.

XVI

THE YEARS AHEAD

UNIT OVERVIEW

As we look to the future we will attempt to portray a most likely environment for the
project manager. Time will undoubtedly erode the validity of some views, enhance
others, and, unforeseen events will further distort the picture presented today. If
the manager is trained by education and molded by experience to cope with the future
as depicted, he or she will be comfortable in any future environment, for the very essence of the forecast is a constantly changing and complex society. Successful individuals will have a sensitivity to emerging issues and be quick to respond to change.

The makeup of this unit, oriented toward the future, is the result of many revisions. The editors had only one objective: to better prepare the managers of today
for the most likely issues of tomorrow. The result is a unit that views the future, both
short term and long term, addresses the problem of declining productivity in the domestic sector, presents a need for a "project management information system," and
promotes the concept of the profession of project management.

FUTURE DECADES

Robert L. Kimmons, in the introductory chapter, New Directions, and James H. Loweree,
in the closing chapter, The Years Ahead, view the progressive transition of the project
management role from a technically oriented manager to an international business-ori-
ented manager: one who will have the ability to appreciate and use technology advantageously; one who will understand the needs of people in whatever social setting exists.

As Bob perceives the future, the project management profession will be central
to the resolution of a host of challenges attributable to conditions such as the following:

Increased world population	Production and distribution of food
Innovative financing	Waste treatment and disposal
World energy supplies	Infrastructure
Regional water shortages	Construction productivity

In Jim's view the needs of the developing and emerging nations for food, shelter, and
clothing will create a galaxy of projects, initiating industrial development and further
projects; the market place will be the world. The basic needs of the United States are

the modernization of wornout infrastructure, particularly in the field of transportation, and as time evolves a determination by the United States as to exactly what its position is in the family of industrialized nations.

The concept of the project-driven organization, a concept now in its infancy, will in future years be a fundamental business consideration in any environment where there are substantial time-related capital-intensive projects. We will also see the continual growth of the "involved client" concept, spawned during the mega project period when the major operating companies made a basic decision to manage their own money with their own senior people.

An appreciation and comprehension of the building block concepts of the involved client and the project-driven organization are imperative as we look to the future, for we will encounter them time and again, not only in the sophisticated arena of the established domestic corporations, but as capabilities are developed the concepts will be adopted by the ministeries and nationalized companies in the developing nations.

THE IMMEDIATE FUTURE

Manuel Peralta, for many years Manager, Exxon Project Management, and currently an executive with NASA, has taken a hard look at the immediate challenges for the project management profession in the domestic sector. Manny introduces the series of challenges with a critical evaluation of declining productivity in the United States, emphasizing that the prime function of any company is the management and control of capital expenditures, the foundation for productive capacity.

The key to the management and control of capital expenditures is a systems view of project management: project execution planning, contracting approach, estimating and scheduling, and the quality and depth of the project management resources of the company.

> *Project execution planning.* The execution plans for projects must be developed in a disciplined manner in order to optimize results.
> *Contracting approach.* The single most significant project execution decision affecting job performance is the selection of the contracting approach and the prime contractor.
> *Estimating and scheduling.* Realistic estimates and schedules and workable "early warning" indicators are necessary to give management flexibility in decision-making.
> *Project management.* Future managers will be technically qualified business people with strong interpersonal relationships.

PRODUCTIVITY: THE GREAT UNKNOWN

The limitation on the development of our natural resources for the betterment of all is the productivity of people, the human resource. Declining productivity is insidious, a creeping paralysis that isn't identified until a business fails, or a domestic industry withers in the face of foreign competition. In the past, identification hasn't always generated a broad-based root cause acceptance of the real issues.

The degree to which an improvement in productivity will be recognized as a beneficial influence on future events is, therefore, arguable, but it is hoped that the educational efforts of a few trailblazer organizations will enlighten all of us, for productivity is indeed a key to the future. The channeling of the energies of skilled workers in industrialized nations and the harnessing of the untapped energies of unskilled labor forces in underdeveloped nations will determine the success of companies and the growth of nations.

General Carroll H. Dunn, Project Director, Construction Industry Cost Effectiveness Project, The Business Roundtable, and Dr. Richard L. Tucker, Director of the
Construction Industry Institute at the University of Texas and Dr. Shirley S. Tucker,
Tucker and Tucker Associates, present the views of their fine organizations on the
critical issue of productivity in the United States.

Carroll reviews the role of The Business Roundtable, an association of business
Chief Executives who examine public issues that affect the economy and develop positions which seek to reflect sound economic and social principles. A principal thrust
of the group is to improve the efficiency and productivity of the construction industry.
The goal is greater productivity, with more construction for the money, not less money
for construction. A series of reports, available upon request, clearly demonstrate
that substantial savings in construction costs can be achieved through the cooperative
efforts of owners, contractors, and labor.

Richard and Shirley Tucker emphasize the dependency of productivity improvement
on the effectiveness of communications. A productive environment requires an organizational structure with an effective communication system. Management must have
useful and timely information reflecting current conditions at the work place in order
to initiate prompt corrective action.

THE LAST TWENTY YEARS: A SNAPSHOT

As Santayana said:

Those who cannot remember the past are doomed to repeat it.

Kenneth A. Fischer, for many years a Senior Project Manager with Davy McKee, and
currently serving in a similar capacity with John Zink, has developed a thought-provoking discussion: the comparison of a current project and a similar one of 20 years
ago.

Ken Fischer started with the fact that today's projects cost more than yesterday's,
but questioned the universal acceptance of the premise that the cost differential is
primarily due to a deterioration in productivity. In order to get a handle on what had
changed in the industry over a 20-year period, he elected to analyze home office hours,
reasoning that most of the changes in physical plants could be identified by changes
in home office engineering, controls, and staffing expenditures.

A study was initiated with two primary questions: "why" home office hours have
increased; "how much" has the increase been. The "why" factors determine what has
happened in the process plant industry; the "how much" factors determine the relative
weighting of the various contributors to escalating costs.

Project A, a hypothetical project completed 20 years ago, was compared to an assumed recently completed Project B of identical capacity, and identical product. There
is a tendency to conclude that the two plants are "identical," but in fact the plants
are "equivalent," and not "identical." To answer "why" home office hours increased,
the changes in plant, people, and tools were evaluated. The changes in these elements,
representing the difference between an "identical" project and an "equivalent" project,
were quantified to determine their relative contribution to home office job growth. The
conclusion of the study was that changes in plant accounted almost totally for jobhour
growth. Certain directional but less definitive conclusions were drawn for total plant
cost.

A general conclusion of this study, applicable to either a qualitative or quantitative
assessment of industry, is that we should have a thorough knowledge of the database
before comparing two "apparently identical" activities over a finite time frame. The
evidence of a general deterioration in productivity in the United States is irrefutable,
but the data to support such a conclusion in the engineering services industry just
doesn't exist.

The "arbitrary" identification of productivity deterioration as the overwhelming reason for the escalation in the cost of new plant construction, adjusted for constant dollars, can lead to erroneous conclusions and potentially ineffective corrective actions. Supportable results can only be obtained by a "separation of variables" technique familiar to the research community, or in plain talk, compare "apples and apples."

A PROJECT MANAGEMENT INFORMATION SYSTEM

Dr. C. William Ibbs, Professor of Civil Engineering, University of California, Berkeley, has reviewed the state of the art in project management information systems, and evaluated their suitability for the project management profession. Bill then proposes an approach to a PMIS.

Current management information systems are ineffective for two reasons:

They are designed and operated for intraorganizational and often nonproject purposes.

Their underlying basis assumes rationality of organizational and decision-making behavior. Information conducive to creative, anticipative, and predictive thought is, at best, subjugated by minutiae.

Why do things go wrong?

A decision isn't made—the default of no-choice is activated
A decision is wrong for reasons of:
  Not enough right information
  Not enough time to analyze the alternatives thoroughly
  An error in judgment
A decision is in conflict with other interests

A need is stated to provide project participants with the software tools necessary to develop an information system suited to their particular needs at a reasonable cost. A general purpose package called the Management Information System Generator (MIG) has been conceptualized capable of generating a project-specific PMIS.

THE PROFESSION

Dr. John R. Adams, Professor, School of Business, Western Carolina University, and an acknowledged leader of programs for the advancement of the profession of project management, reviews the development of the profession, past and present, and then outlines the Project Management Institute program for the enhancement of the status of the project manager in the future.

John states the need for project managers to regulate themselves, or society will provide regulations, therefore the drive to develop a recognized profession. Five attributes are generally identified as being common to all recognized professions.

A unique body of knowledge
Standards of entry
A code of ethics
Service orientation to the profession
A sanctioning organization

PMI has made significant progress in each of the five categories; much work, however, remains to be done.

1

New Directions

ROBERT L. KIMMONS *   *Ebasco-Humphreys & Glasgow, Inc., Houston, Texas*

Technological change continues to occur at an increasing rate. Tremendous challenges, some of which have overwhelmed mankind in the past, now, for the first time, will be overcome.

Project management will be at the forefront in implementing fundamental changes to improve the way we live. Collectively, as a profession, we must prepare for the challenges.

Some have conjectured that the day of the mega project is past. A quick look into the near future reveals that all of the past mega projects, those realized and those that have only been contemplated, are a mere speck compared to those on the horizon.

As project managers we will be judged on how well we are able to manage these projects; this will be determined by how well we prepare for the task of managing.

CHALLENGES

Future projects will be directed toward the resolution of challenges that we can identify today. The eight most significant are these:

1. Increased world population and changing distribution patterns
2. Innovation in financing new projects
3. A significant crisis in world energy resources
4. Regional water shortages
5. Adequate food production
6. Environmental priorities for waste treatment and disposal
7. Infrastructure extensions and renovation
8. Costs of construction

Concurrently, fundamental swings will occur in the social norms and behavior which will affect how these challenges will be met.

COMMENTARIES ON THE EIGHT CHALLENGES

1. Increased World Population and Changing Distribution Patterns

Overall, the world population is increasing, primarily in countries with a lesser share of the world's developed resources.

---

*
Current affiliation: Kimmons-Asaro Group Limited, Inc., Houston, Texas

In industrialized countries with better health and sanitation facilities, the rate of population growth is less rapid. The average age is increasing, and this is resulting in a largely nonproductive group who must rely on their own savings or government-funded social programs for survival.

In some areas of the world, large numbers of people relocate both from country to country and from region to region within the same country. These movements create intergroup friction which dissipates slowly over time as groups become integrated and homogenous.

The world is truly becoming smaller. Goods are distributed worldwide, creating tremendous market potential for some products. Increased opportunities of international travel expand product knowledge and consumer desire.

The long-term trend, although not without temporary setbacks, is toward free trade and a weakening of national trade barriers.

2. Innovation in Financing for New Projects

There can be no projects until someone has agreed to pay the bills. Progress is made by those individuals, firms, and governments who strive to do the impossible and are constantly straining for those things which are just out of reach. Financing the work can certainly be counted as a very difficult milestone in any of these endeavors.

To meet the need for every-increasing amounts of capital and the greater risks involved, complex multisource financial arrangements will be developed with very unique characteristics to conform to the money available, the tax implications, the risks and liabilities entailed, and the profit potential offered. The project manager of the future will need a comprehensive knowledge of the effect these financial arrangements will have on the execution of the project. The effect of accelerating or delaying the project schedule on the cost of money and the meshing of any changes in available cash flow to the project requirements are typical of those concerns that may be encountered by project management.

3. A Significant Crisis in World Energy Resources

The world's extreme dependence upon crude oil for energy is complicated by the concentration of the deposits in relatively few nations and the reliability of supply dependent upon political considerations. The crisis experienced in the 1970s has been alleviated by major conservation effort, and the price-driven search for additional proven reserves.

Oil is a nonrenewable resource. It will have to be replaced as an energy source at some time in the future. A period of low-cost crude oil will tend to accentuate the problem as the search for alternative energy sources will be deferred until a more favorable payout is possible. Any alternative will require a long developmental lead time. Some cogeneration projects have gone ahead, but other areas of energy conservation programs are lagging as the payouts have made investments less attractive. Worldwide energy policies are vital issues and may have to be mandated to avoid future disruption to world supply.

Currently, the most acceptable alternative, from both technical and commercial viewpoints, is nuclear power. A need will almost certainly be present for standard "off-the-shelf" designs for these plants, and some work has already been done in this direction. There are, however, extremely difficult social pressures to defuse before this source of power will gain proper public acceptance.

Consideration must also be given to producing energy from biomass, hydrogen from other than hydrocarbon sources, fuel cells, solar power, wind power, as well as from the more conventional hydropower route where geography makes this feasible.

4. Regional Water Shortages

Climatic changes, contamination of existing sources, and depletion of aquifers are leading to a shortage of water in many areas. Diversion of water by construction of canals and pipelines, utilization of salt water conversion, and even such ideas as towing of icebergs from the polar regions have been proposed to alleviate the ecologically threatened parched areas of the Earth.

Some solution for supplying water to the arid parts of the world will have to be found. Attention must be focused as well on the pressing problems of populated areas which will soon be faced with an increasing scarcity of water.

5. Adequate Food Production and Distribution

The disparity in the distribution of food throughout the world cannot be tolerated. Technological advances in food production, preservation, and packaging have lessened the chances of a catastrophic worldwide famine, which was feared until recently. Future efforts must be directed toward continued improvement of production and the resolution of distribution problems. Elimination of hunger is equally important as the eradication of disease.

Farm productivity has increased by moving from the small individual farm to concentrated crop raising, dairy, and meat production in the hands of a few large enterprises. The next step is obvious; however difficult for traditionalists to accept. We will move from the small individual kitchens to the large purveyors of mass-produced food, a step hastened by the increasing proportion of people employed outside the home; people who no longer have time to spend in preparing food.

6. Environmental Priorities for Waste Treatment and Disposal

Exploding populations and massive industrial development worldwide have created a severe overload on traditional waste disposal systems. Dumping presents very serious problems at the present scale.

Many of the disposal methods used in the past have led to contamination of natural resources, almost eliminating them for future use. High temperature incineration will find many applications in the future, as will substantially more use of recyclable products and resources. But, in the long term, the greenhouse effect must be analyzed and solved.

7. Infrastructure Extensions and Renovation

Technological development is continuously introducing new needs in the area of infrastructure support for our daily life. In developing nations these will require new construction. In those countries already industrialized, many of these facilities will need to be refurbished, updated, or replaced.

Our lifestyle in the future will change markedly. Technological advances will be reflected in how our homes are designed, as well as how our public and office buildings are used. There is a widespread consensus that we are on the brink of technology that will render a large portion of urban housing throughout the world obsolete. New materials, new lifestyles, and changing family groupings, radically changed appliances with sophisticated control circuits, together with escalating land costs, will work together to make substitution of existing structures economically and socially advantageous.

Projections of increased leisure time will change our views of how we spend our time off the job. People will work in or convenient to their home, networked to connect them with factories, laboratories, central processing facilities, libraries, and other information sources. There will be pressure to provide entertainment and educational opportunities to fill the spare time that many people will have.

8. Costs of Construction

Investors will resist the continuing upward spiral of building costs and will insist upon elimination of unproductive and unnecessary expenditures. This direction has already been set with the Business Round Table's Construction Industry Cost Effectiveness Task Force recommendations. The more progressive firms will take advantage of these studies and move aggressively to reduce construction costs.

Labor unions will experience an unsettled period, and will survive only if they can make a radical change in their approach. The line between worker and management is becoming less defined in the modern organization, and 20th century attitudes can no longer be applicable to life as it will have to be lived in the 21st century.

SUPPORTING DEVELOPMENTS

There are developments in motion which will have a great influence on the nature and management of future projects.

Increased Focus on Research

A substantial dedication of resources is being made to research. The research budgets of some companies now exceed the capital budgets. Research has been facilitated by the recent explosion of knowledge, and many investigations not previously possible are being undertaken today. Typical of the industrial segments where concentrated research development is being done are:

Computer hardware and software
Pharmaceuticals
Biotechnology
Genetic engineering
Fermentation chemistry
Ceramics
Refractories
Adhesives
Catalysts
Hypersonic aircraft
Medical equipment/supplies
Electric power storage

New concepts, themselves the subjects of intensive research, contribute to industrial development in general and include:

Fiberoptics
Lasers
Optical scanning
Automation
Robotics
Membrane separation
Supercritical extraction
Radiation
Artificial intelligence
Holography

New Methods and Tools

Within the time span of only one generation, the slide rule has faded into history, supplanted first by the electronic calculator and then by the computer. Project managers learned to hand construct logic diagrams, and since have seen more complex planning done faster and easier, first by mainframe computers and now by the personal computer.

All manner of manufacturing and process plant operations have been brought under computerized control, with a resultant continual optimization of operations.

Merchandising affects the future workload of project managers. New techniques in global marketing concepts will certainly create opportunities for products as yet undiscovered and for worldwide traffic in these items.

Development of Oceans, Seas, and Outer Space

The investment made in space exploration has paid dividends in acceleration of technical knowledge. Some of this has already found application in computer control, communications, and new materials for different fields.

Because of the investments required and the risks involved, development of space-related industries will probably not follow a steady upward curve. Inevitably, progress will continue to provide opportunities for mega project managers in the space programs.

The frontier of the Earth is the expanse of virgin territory under the oceans and seas. Underwater production of minerals, food, and energy will follow the leadership of the offshore deepwater oil production activities.

New Materials

Engineered plastics and polymer matrices will become the new commodity chemicals, replacing steel, aluminum, and metal alloys in some of their traditional applications. Our growing knowledge of chemistry will enable us to design specific materials to suit particular applications. There will have to be a shift in the source of some of the raw materials required for manufacture of these new products. Dependence upon hydrocarbons will diminish in favor of a renewable supply.

The fallout from space program innovation has benefited other industries. We can expect this synergism to continue and to provide new materials for our future projects.

THE CHANGING PROJECT ENVIRONMENT

The environment in which projects will be run in the future will differ from the traditional.

The Changing Profile of the Owner

A fundamental difference stems from the restructuring that has occurred in industry throughout the world. Restructuring is thought of as the elimination of nonproductive segments of the corporation.

Social changes and the advent of modern information systems mean that the relationship between management and labor in the future will be altered. Customs and values throughout the world are being transferred across national borders and integrated procedures will result. There are major trends toward vastly expanded international corporate cooperation.

Third world countries, particularly those with extensive petroleum production facilities and reserves, have not only built refineries but also large downstream plants to produce commodity petrochemicals. This has created some dislocation of production from existing plants and hastened the shutdowns of smaller, inefficient plants elsewhere.

Traditional ownership by multinational industrial firms will be replaced by ownership by government agencies and joint ventures between government-owned firms and local or international private capital.

Outmoded trade and antitrust policies hamper efficient movement on a worldwide scale. Some of these policies are obsolete in today's commerce; however, changes may come very slowly.

Changes in Engineering/Construction Firms

A significant change is taking place in the makeup of the contractor side of project execution. Earlier there was a very strong opinion on the part of the owner to support single responsibility. This started to change in the late 1970s toward a philosophy of getting the best firm to handle each particular segment of the project. This led to a contractual arrangement known as "construction management" where the owner selected a firm for its management capability. The firm, acting as an agent for the owner, "ran" the job. The large energy companies, in many instances, went further and seconded top management people to a "project directorate."

Engineering firms, formerly very labor-intensive businesses, now require a large investment in equipment and software. Even without the recession in worldwide construction in the early 1980s, there would probably have been a substantial reduction in the growth rate of the number of engineers and designers employed by engineering/construction firms. The recession forced contractors to concentrate on reducing their overheads by cutting staff size and by the aggressive elimination of middle management and extension of the span of control throughout. This latter was probably long overdue because of the tremendous influence of improved management information systems.

Even where the owner insists on single responsibility, most large projects will be executed by a joint venture company or a consortium of engineering and construction firms each bringing its own expertise. Management of these projects will require extensive managerial capability to mesh the differing corporate objectives, attitudes, and cultures.

An internationalization of the contracting industry has been underway over the past decade which has had an impact on the way business is conducted throughout the world. Where laws permit, existing companies have been acquired by firms from other countries. Local or branch offices have long been the norm among major international contractors, but these have gained a very pronounced local image. Partial ownership and long-term joint ventures have also been tried, achieving greater or lesser success depending largely upon the ability of the individuals to work together. This has led to a rapid diffusion of engineering/construction technology throughout the entire world with corresponding shifts in the distribution of the workload.

Some recent trends in the engineering/construction industry in the United States for example, will affect how these firms work in the future.

Reduction in staff has eliminated most of the marginal performers.
Early retirements have meant that many of the older, experienced engineers, designers, and construction superintendents and foremen are no longer employed.
Hiring has been eliminated or restricted so there are few younger people learning the business.
Computerization of engineering, design, drafting, project control, and information systems has developed so rapidly that the programs of some firms are in a shambles. They have written programs for obsolete mainframe computers; meanwhile commercial software programs comparable in capability are becoming available which use much smaller, faster computers.
There will be more and better supervision on future projects by senior management. This will be possible because of improved management information systems. Senior management will be better informed and will participate more directly in supporting the project objectives.

The success of the project management concept in achieving project objectives, particularly in cases where the project manager has been a strong authority figure, will result in a growing trend to reinforce the authority of the project manager. This has already been done on a small scale and involves giving almost complete authority to the project manager by eliminating the matrix organization aspects. In the future "project-driven" organization the project manager, because of experience, reputation, and general expertise, will have total project authority. This concept ensures a higher degree of harmony and less confusion on the project with a resultant productivity improvement.

PROJECT MANAGEMENT TECHNOLOGY

Project Management Tools

Planning, scheduling, estimating, and cost management have developed to a high degree of sophistication. These developments will continue and soon will give the project manager full on-line access to information that previously took days or even weeks to extract. The comprehensive database libraries and new software programs capable of seeking out bits of data, making comparisons, extracting performance exceptions, and condensing a high volume of information into a meaningful statement will be invaluable in focusing the project manager's attention on the critical areas which really require it.

Constructability

With the relatively new concept of constructability analysis, the process, plot plan, specifications, design, and planning for projects will be optimized, affording opportunities to eliminate unnecessary expenditures. Computer programs will impose a more structured discipline as well as eliminate the number-crunching tedium of estimating.

Productivity

Individual, group, and equipment performance will be improved due to a real emphasis on productivity throughout all phases of the project. Definitions of realistic performance expectations, continuous monitoring of performance against the plan, frequent feedback of performance results, and a reward system based upon results will assure that productivity improvements are achieved.

THE PROJECT MANAGER

What changes will the project manager need to weather in adapting to the new requirements of advances in project management?

- There will certainly be more interdisciplinary involvement required on the part of the project manager. For the project manager entrenched in engineering, this may be a difficult step to take. A much broader knowledge of finance, law, personnel administration, and business will be essential, along with a firm foundation in project management technology.
- The future for project managers calls for a high degree of flexibility and devotion to promoting good working relations among the project team members and with the client in the ever-changing environment of a project.
- Most importantly, the new breed of project manager will have to be a manager in all senses of the word. In the past, a project manager could be successful because of personality, track record, or merely expertise in his own discipline. Management skills are necessary today, and will be more so in the future for the successful management of projects.

CONCLUSIONS

In recognition of the powerful forces for success that are wrapped up in the project management concept, the forthcoming years will offer new opportunities and challenges to the project management profession.

Advances in our body of knowledge will continue into the future at a rapidly escalating rate. The project managers who run the most successful projects in the future will be those who are best able to assimilate and take advantage of the new developments.

2

Development of the Profession

JOHN R. ADAMS *Western Carolina University, Cullowhee, North Carolina*

A recent comment by Dr. Linn Stuckenbruck—Professor of Systems Management at the University of Southern California, past Secretary of the Project Management Institute, consultant, and project manager on a number of multibillion dollar utility and federal government projects—on how he became a project manager is highly revealing:

> Most of us never really plan to be project managers—it happens almost by acci-
> dent. Top management is having problems with some existing product, process,
> project, or project manager, and immediate action is indicated. The expedient solu-
> tion is to implement a new project or appoint a new project manager. In either
> case, volunteers are seldom requested. The new project manager is called in by
> the boss and told, "Congratulations, you're it—the new project manager. Now
> your first meeting on this problem . . ." Notice that the project is immediately a
> "problem." You are selected, of course, because you are either (1) the top tech-
> nical expert available to deal with the problem, (2) an experienced and well-trained
> line manager knowledgeable of this type of problem, or (3) a promising youngster
> to be "challenged." In any event, you just "happen" to be available, an individual
> in the right place at the right time.

Most of us who have been project managers have experienced something similar to this at one time or another. In this way we become members of what has been called "the accidental profession" (Davis, 1984), meaning that we had neither planned to be project managers nor had we prepared for such a position. It can even be argued that we had not become professionals at all, for a profession is an occupation people plan for, study for, prepare for, and build a career within. To the contrary, we entered the new job with no formal preparation and not much of an idea about what skills were needed, what knowledge was available, or how to go about dealing with this new chal- lenge. We probably had no conscious intention of building a lifetime career as a pro- ject manager. In most cases the thought never entered our head that this new job was different from the technical position in which we had been working. Most of us now would also agree that with better preparation we could have done a much better job on our first project. We would certainly have had an easier time of it, and would have made far fewer mistakes.

For the specialized management discipline known as project management, the situa- tion described above is the rule rather than the exception. Project management is an action-oriented field, and the individuals practicing in the field are so busy managing projects that few people stop to think about how to manage projects. When a project manager is named, seldom is time provided in which to study and learn about the new field, and there is precious little opportunity for learning about it anyway. As a result, the new project manager is left to learn this trade the hard way—through the "school of hard knocks," or by "trial and error." The time, money, and energy wasted as a result are incalculable.

Yet, project management is essential in today's complex world of rapidly expanding technology, increasing control by federal, state, and local governments, growing pressures from environmental protection and other special interest groups, and rapidly changing economic conditions. Project management is a management technique specifically designed to deal with a high rate of change, and I suspect that we can all agree that our organizations are facing a variety of demands for rapid change. We will review how project management developed, and then analyze how it came to be the "accidental profession." The conclusion is that this situation is unlikely to meet future needs for qualified project managers. An alternative approach, that of developing a recognized project management profession, is described. Current activities designed to develop project management as a profession are briefly reviewed. We will conclude with a projection of what project management might be like in the future if efforts to develop it as a profession prove successful.

DEVELOPMENT OF PROJECT MANAGEMENT

The concept of project management is not new. Even a cursory review of the concept demonstrates that construction of the Great Wall of China, the Egyptian Pyramids, the Eiffel Tower, and the Panama Canal are all projects in the classical sense of the term. Throughout history major construction efforts and military campaigns stand out as examples of project management at work. Until recently, however, the management of projects has not been singled out as a specialized skill needed by society. Rather, management of the project was left to those who conceived of the work, and was generally performed by those technical persons responsible for designing the product produced by the project. What has changed in more recent times is the technical complexity of the project, the diversity of skills needed to implement complex projects, and the managerial tools now available that make modern project management feasible.

Modern Project Management

As technology advanced during the twentieth century, the complexity of project efforts increased dramatically along with the diversity of skills which had to be integrated to yield the final project results. The problems of developing new products, particularly military weapons, became so great that for the first time project management techniques were "borrowed" from the construction field and applied to other product areas. For years major construction efforts had involved developing special purpose organizations which were devoted to completing the task and which were dissolved upon completion of the project. As other programs took on the size, complexity, and importance of such construction efforts, these organizational techniques were applied with some success. The Manhattan Project, which resulted in the development and production of the first atomic bomb, serves as a notable example of the early and effective use of project management for priority endeavors.

By the mid-1950s, however, advanced technology projects had reached a level of complexity that defied logical and detailed management with the planning and scheduling techniques then available. Almost simultaneously DuPont Corporation and the U.S. Navy Polaris Missile Program developed specialized techniques for planning, scheduling, and controlling the interaction of tasks needed to accomplish very large and complex modern projects. DuPont's critical path method (CPM) and the Navy's program evaluation and review technique (PERT) both used the now familiar arrow diagramming technique to divide a project into its component tasks and logically sequence them into a "map" of the project. Estimates of the duration of each task were then used to calculate the longest amount of time needed to accomplish all tasks. This is known as the "critical path" through the network. CPM went on to include a consideration of individual task costs, while PERT concentrated on the probabilities of accomplishing tasks within the estimated time durations. Many revisions have been made over the years to improve these basic techniques, and the two methods have grown together such that, in common usage, the terms CPM and PERT are now used almost interchangeably to refer to the techniques of arrow diagramming and "networking." The important point is that these two methods, particularly after the development of computer programs to handle the necessary analyses, provided radically new and revolutionary management techniques specifically designed as an aid in managing projects. The development of what we now call "project management" can be traced back to the introduction of these new management techniques. Thus the "field of project management" as we know it today has a relatively short history, dating back only to the late 1950s (Moder et al., 1983).

During the 1960s development of project management concentrated almost exclusively on these managerial tools. As the capabilities of computers grew and they became more available to project managers, elaborate computer programs were written allowing the application of PERT and CPM techniques to ever larger projects. For a time the U.S. Department of Defense mandated the use of PERT and its derivatives in the management of all major weapon system development programs. Perhaps more than any other single factor, this requirements was responsible for the rapid spread of these "project management tools." Willingly or not, essentially all major contractors to the U.S. military had to learn and use these tools, or cease doing business with the military. As a result, a large group of individuals became knowledgeable of and able to apply the new project management tools. Toward the end of the decade, the military directives were liberalized somewhat into the Cost/Schedule Control System Criteria (C/SCSC), a set of requirements that are still in effect today. While these criteria do not mandate a particular method or technique of networking, they do require that scheduling, budgeting, and control techniques originating in the early PERT and CPM models be used in the management of certain specified classes of military contracts, including those involved in major weapon system developments. Versions of these criteria have also been adopted by other federal government agencies (Moder et al., 1983). In general, the 1960s were characterized by the development of computerized models for implementing networking techniques, the elaboration of these techniques to allow a more thorough analysis of the progress being made on the project, and the application of these techniques to ever larger and more complex projects.

By the early 1970s, essentially all of the analytical tools available to the modern project manager had been developed and computerized. The computer support systems needed for these tools in projects of significant size, however, were large, expensive, centralized installations requiring special facilities and large support staffs. As a result, the expansion of project management tools was tied to the expansion of the computer systems themselves. Only the largest projects—integrated programs, major construction efforts, the development of a nation's natural resources—could justify the cost of using such computer systems and could gain access to them. It also became widely recognized that the largest projects could not be adequately managed without the use of project management tools. Thus project management came to be associated with large projects and computers. As the cost of computers dropped and they became more accessible throughout the ranks of management, project management tools were successfully applied to smaller projects.

Meanwhile, it had been recognized that project management involved much more than simply applying a set of computerized tools. Establishing temporary organizations to conduct projects displaced personnel and disrupted the normal functioning of more permanent organizations. The necessity for accurate and current data required project personnel to cut across established organizational lines, creating new organizational relationships and information flows. Authority relationships had to change. The difficulties became even more acute when an organization was involved in several projects at the same time. The literature of project management in the 1970s concentrated on dealing with these broader managerial issues and integrating these concerns with the use of project management techniques. Thus the concepts of the project and matrix organization were elaborated. Leadership theories, team-building, small group dynamics, and conflict management were all identified as necessary skills for an effective project manager. Procurement, contracting, and contract management were recognized as playing a major role in many projects. In general, during the 1970s the accepted view of project management evolved from a purely technical to a managerial perspective (Kerzner, 1984). Project management became accepted as much more than the application of specialized tools usually requiring computerized support. Rather, project management was recognized as a unique field of management, with its own specialized problems and its own set of skills needed to deal with these problems. At the close of the decade, however, there was little agreement on what these unique problems were or what skills were most necessary for the effective project manager. It was agreed that implementing project management involved much more than simply applying computerized or technical tools to resolve a problem; rather a philosophy of project management had to be developed and accepted.

Clearly, project managers have consistently made effective use of innovative technical advances in the management field. This is particularly true in the use of computers for managing planning, scheduling, and budgeting information. As we look to the future, it is clear that project managers will continue to use these technical improvements. Thus, more projects are being managed with the aid of computers. As the size and cost of computers have been reduced, the use of formalized planning, scheduling, and control techniques has been successfully extended into ever smaller projects. These techniques are now available to all project managers, and the effect of changed estimates or conditions can be evaluated quickly and easily on microcomputers even in remote field offices. This kind of development in the technical aspects of project management will continue and will help in spreading the recognition of project management as a specialized management field. The major changes to be expected as the field of project management continues to develop, however, involve the way in which individuals become responsible for managing major projects. These changes will result from a public recognition of the effect project managers as managers have on society as a whole.

An Accidental Profession?

Most project managers find it difficult to examine their occupation in perspective and philosophize over its contributions and its place in society. After all, most project managers are not philosophers. By education, training, experience, and inclination project managers are much more likely to be pragmatic, dynamic, objective-oriented "workaholics" than the quiet, reflective person we think of as a philosopher. Project managers are generally educated in a technology appropriate to the project they are managing, a project that is defined by a carefully worded and documented objective to be achieved. They are trained in the art of breaking that objective into its component tasks and in sequencing those tasks in the manner best calculated to achieve the objective on time, within budget, and meeting all performance requirements and specifications. Individuals usually accept the position of project manager in the belief that they will accomplish something that is useful and worthwhile beyond the basic need to provide themselves employment. Their experience with projects quickly demonstrates the pressure, stress, conflict, and time-critical nature of the job. Because of the very nature of their work, therefore, as well as by their education, training, and inclination, project managers almost invariably have an abiding preoccupation—almost an obsession—with "getting the job done." This obsession leaves very little time for philosophizing.

Nevertheless, project managers as a group have a unique and pervasive impact on the culture that surrounds them, for it is their skill and effort that implement change within our society. Project managers oversee the development of transportation systems to provide ever faster and more efficient movement of people and products to wherever they are needed. Project managers are responsible for the construction of the production facilities that provide the products needed by a technological society, and the buildings needed to house our working, recreation, and family activities. Project managers develop the drugs that improve our health and extend our lives. They provide the motion pictures, stage plays, operas, and athletic contests that entertain us. They even conduct the elections, social programs, and military efforts by which governments carry out their business. On a much smaller scale and within an individual organization, project managers select or develop new computer programs for use in any number of applications. They conduct market research efforts to predict potential sales of a new product, or they analyze alternatives to determine the best course of action in a specific situation. These efforts, narrower in scope, are as critical to the organization concerned as the much broader efforts are to society as a whole. What all projects have in common is that they create change. If a project manager leaves the organization or the society within which he or she works in the same condition it was in when the project started, it is a clear sign that either the project or the project manager, or both, has failed. Indeed, one measure of the magnitude and importance of a project is the amount of change it engenders within the relevant social structure. In effect, project managers create the changes that determine what the world will be like in the future.

It is a widely recognized and accepted fact that the individual, organization, or social structure that does not change as its environment changes will eventually cease to exist. Since project managers implement change, their importance to society is self-evident. In most cases where an identifiable group is important to the success of the social structure, that group is identified and singled out for varying levels of respect and attention. The group typically becomes known as a profession. We have only to look to doctors, lawyers, educators, and engineers for examples of this process. Not so the project manager—at least not yet—perhaps because project management has only recently been recognized as a specialized and unique field. We should be embarassed to admit that all it takes today for an individual to become known as a project manager is to claim the title. There is essentially no way today to challenge that claim.

By their nature, however, projects end. This means that the project manager must look for a new position. For most individuals selected to be project managers, the end of a project is the chance either to return to their technical occupation or to move into more permanent "line management" positions. This latter is true particularly if the project has gone well, for it has provided the opportunity to demonstrate an ability to manage. In fact, most successful project managers have managed only one or two projects prior to a career in line management. In such a case, project management has provided a valuable training ground for line management, and this is a valid and useful service to provide for an organization or for a manager. Unfortunately, it does not do much for developing the field of project management.

The real problem with this "accidental profession" approach to selecting project managers is that it provides no means for developing and identifying those individuals qualified to take responsibility for the really big and important projects: the space programs, the major transportation and regional development programs, the major drug, genetic, and medical treatment program — the projects that will shape the future dimensions of our society. For that we need a way by which project managers can develop and grow as project managers. We need a structured method by which individuals can (1) study what project management is all about, (2) enter the project management field at a relatively low level of responsibility to learn and to demonstrate the needed skills, (3) be promoted to positions and projects of ever-increasing responsibility and magnitude, and eventually (4) achieve a reputation that would warrant assignment of a major project responsibility. In other words, what is needed is a means by which an individual can choose to make project management a career. This cannot be accomplished if we remain "the accidental profession."

As we look to the future we must expect that the importance of effective project management will be more widely recognized by society as a whole. This recognition will inevitably generate social pressures to assure that those who practice project management, particularly on large and important projects which involve major expenditures of public funds or which may affect public safety, have the experience and competence to manage society's investment in the future. In general, there are only two basic responses to such pressures from society: either society will provide regulations by law to assure that only experienced and capable project managers hold critical project positions, or project managers will regulate and conduct themselves in a manner that convinces society that such laws are unnecessary. Most groups avoid control and regulation by law, with the accompanying loss of freedom to determine what knowledge and behavior is appropriate for gaining group membership. The generally accepted way for groups to do this, and to provide for developing a core of skilled, reputable practitioners, is by developing a recognized profession out of the field. If this can be accomplished in project management, an individual would still be able to make use of project management as an extremely useful step in a general management career. The career project managers, however, would form the core of experienced professionals qualified to assume the responsibilities of the major projects which are likely to have an impact on society.

DEVELOPING A PROFESSION: ITS ATTRIBUTES

Before project management can be proposed as a recognized profession, we must agree on just what would constitute that profession. There are five attributes that are generally identified as being common to all recognized professions (Meginson et al., 1986). These are listed below and described briefly. Please note that if these attributes are to be useful to project managers, they must be representative of all recognized professions, including law, medicine, engineering, accounting, and all other occupations generally considered to be representative of "the professions."

1. *A Unique Body of Knowledge.* This first attribute implies principles and concepts that are unique to the profession and are codified and documented so that they can be studied and learned through formal education. In most professions, the body of knowledge is taught in graduate or professional schools; for example, the specialized body of knowledge of the legal profession is taught in law schools. A degree does not necessarily qualify an individual to practice in the profession, but it does provide a means of assuring that the individual has at least been exposed to the basic principles on which the profession is based. Every profession has at least one degree that can be earned by those wishing to acquire a knowledge of the profession's principles. Several professions offer several levels of degrees, allowing specialization within the profession.

2. *Standards of Entry.* Defined minimum standards for entry into the profession imply progression in a career; entry standards define the place from which a career path begins. All professions must have an accepted route open to the public by which a person can become a recognized member of the profession. Law, engineering, accounting, and medicine all have entry standards, typically involving formal education leading to an academic degree; several years of experience, as in an apprenticeship program or as a beginner in the profession; test score requirements, which may or may not be legally enforceable; or some combination of the three.

3. *A Code of Ethics.* Ethical standards, or a code of ethics, are common to most professions. The purpose is to make appropriate behavior explicit and to provide a basis for self-policing of unethical behavior, thus avoiding or limiting the necessity of legal controls.

4. *Service Orientation to the Profession.* The service orientation is actually an attitude of the members of the profession, by which members are committed to better-

ing the profession itself. Professionals will commit their time, money, and energy to attending conventions, publishing their ideas and experiences, and generally contributing to the body of knowledge and the administration of the profession. A professional's commitment to the profession is frequently stronger than to the employer. In many cases professionals will leave their employing organization rather than violate the profession's standards of ethics or practice.

5. *A Sanctioning Organization.* The authenticating body or sanctioning organization has many purposes. It sets standards and acts as a self-policing agency. It promotes publications and the exchange of ideas, encourages research, develops and administers certification programs, and sponsors and accredits education programs. Through public information and recognition of professionals, such organizations provide a voice for their profession. In a word, the purpose of an authenticating body is to administer the profession.

It holds that if these attributes are common to all professions, then project management is a profession only to the extent that these characteristics are represented in its structure. To attain the status of a profession, we must develop and incorporate these attributes into some structure capable of sustaining and expanding the professional ties that bind qualified project managers to the profession. It will not be easy to develop project management as a profession without the career paths necessary to hold people in the field, and it will be difficult to forge career paths without a true profession in which to build them. Career paths and the profession of project management must be developed simultaneously. That is, as the field's professional attributes are strengthened, it becomes much more feasible for individuals to build their careers within project management. Table 1 shows the interaction of the professional attributes with the activities that lead to developing personal careers. Their mutual support is obvious. What remains is to determine how the field of project management currently measures up to each of the attributes of a profession.

PROJECT MANAGEMENT: THE POTENTIAL

First, we need to recognize that project management is not engineering. It is not architecture, medicine, accounting, or research. Project management is the management of certain aspects of all these fields, and more. The key term in project management is management, and it is generally recognized as being the management of specialized activities to achieve a fixed, predetermined objective or goal (Adams and Campbell, 1982). With that in mind, let's review the current status of project management with regard to the attributes of a profession to see just where we stand.

1. A Unique Body of Knowledge

A project management body of knowledge (PMBOK) exists and is reasonably well defined. This statement may seem obvious to many project managers who believe as the members of the PMI Standards Committee did in 1979 that all experienced project managers understood what should be in a PMBOK, and the task of defining and documenting it would be a simple matter of writing down what everyone understood to start with. Eight years and three committees later, and as the current Chairman of PMI's PMBOK Committee, we are heading into one more round of revising, documenting, gaining approval, and publishing a revised PMBOK. Agreement on the written details of "what we all understand" is terribly difficult to obtain, but it is slowly coming together. Our body of knowledge is broad in scope and encompasses many technologies, from accounting to contracting, from finance to organization behavior. It now exists in an outline (work breakdown structure) form and has recently been modified from six to eight major sections. The key to gaining acceptance has been the long-term commitment to provide for revisions, modifications, and elaborations to reflect changes in the field. This com-

Table 1 Individual Contributions in a Growing Profession

Attributes of profession	Personal Career Building Activities			
	Education	Experience	Certification	Contributions to professional organizations
Specialized body of knowledge	Education provides "academic" knowledge	Experience provides "practical" knowledge	Certification recognizes minimum level of knowledge	Contributions to professional organizations build a body of literature
Standards of entry	Standards of entry provide required knowledge standards for educational programs	Experienced personnel set standards for entry	Certification provides recognition of proficiency	Standards establish minimum qualifications for contributions
Code of ethics	Education contributes to philosophy	Experienced personnel demand enforcement	Certification requires acceptance of ethical standards	Contributions provide evidence of acceptance of ethics
Service motive	Education promotes attitude of service	Experience provides ability and incentive to serve	Certification implies recognition of service obligation	Contributions provide evidence of service motive
Sanctioning organization	Sanctioning organizations provide accreditation for education	Sanctioning organizations enforce ethics and standards that experienced personnel demand	Organization administers certification program	Contributions and membership support development of the profession

mitment is represented in a standing set of committees, one committee for each major section of the body of knowledge, which annually reviews concerns and recommends needed modifications. After many years of work, we are just reaching a level of stability sufficient to consider sponsoring the publication of formal texts to provide consolidated study materials for the PMBOK. The key to achieving any agreement at all has been an insistence on considering project management as the management of technically oriented projects, and not the technology itself.

2. Standards of Entry

The acceptance of defined minimum standards for entry into the profession of project management is still in the distant future, but a good start has been made. The Project Management Institute is using the engineering model, in which entry to the profession can be gaiaed by education—one can be hired into an engineering job directly out of college with an engineering degree; by examination—one can obtain engineering jobs by passing the professional engineers' exam; or preferably by a combination of the two—many practitioners earn a degree, gain experience, and then go on to take the professional engineers' exam, thus gaining status in their profession. The Project Management Professional certification exam has been offered for several years now, and there are several hundred certified project managers today. Western Carolina University's Master of Project Management degree, cosponsored by PMI, is currently the only such degree in a nationally accredited school of business or engineering within the United States, although several other universities are taking the first steps toward developing their own degree programs. Even more encouraging, the University of Quebec at Montreal has asked PMI to accredit their 10-year-old Master of Project Management Degree. Other degree programs exist in Australia, England, and perhaps elsewhere in the world. The existence of these programs simply demonstrates the demand for formal educational standards for project managers.

3. A Code of Ethics

We have lots of ethics in project management, but most of them are borrowed from the technologies in which project management is used. This approach has worked reasonably well in the past on a project by project basis, but the technically oriented ethics appropriate to an engineering construction project, for example, may be totally inadequate for a pharmaceutical project aimed at developing a new drug. As part of its certification program, PMI has developed and published a set of ethical standards which it believes to be appropriate to the project manager at large. These are quite global in nature; they are certainly not intended to supplant ethical standards appropriate to the particular technologies involved in specific projects, and they need to be developed and refined. They have been rather widely accepted by the PMI membership, however, and they provide a good start in this area. Along with the ethical standards, PMI has established a standing Ethics Committee to review and propose modifications to the standards, and to hear complaints of ethical violations. This committee can recommend corrective or punitive actions to the PMI Board of Directors in the event that alleged ethical violations are substantiated.

4. Service Orientation to the Profession

This is currently perhaps our strongest claim to professional standing. Drawing only from the PMI experience, there are now nearly 6,000 project managers in some 68 countries, representing more than 38 chapters, who are committed to developing project management as a profession. The willingness of these chapters and members to commit their own time and money to participate in PMBOK and certification reviews, advise universities in setting up degree programs, write articles and books for publication, and carry on the administration of a major international professional association is simply remarkable. Further, it appears that this service orientation is not unique to PMI. INTERNET in Europe, the Project Management Forum in Australia (PMF), and the Engineering Advancement Association of Japan (ENAA), to name only a few, all report high levels of interest and activity. The interest and support needed to create a new profession seem to exist and be waiting only for leadership and direction.

5. A Sanctioning Organization

The final requirement for generating a new profession is the authenticating body that provides leadership, establishes standards, and provides a means of communication and coordination among practitioners. The Project Management Institute is attempting to provide this service, mainly because no other project management organization has taken the lead in this area. PMI is the largest of the project management professional organizations, and is represented in the greatest number of countries. INTERNET is another possibility, but to date has shown little interest in such activities as developing and documenting a body of knowledge, sponsoring degree programs, or developing and administering a certification program. Most of PMI's activities are centered in the U.S. and Canada. The organization has demonstrated a remarkable willingness to make their work available to other project management organizations for adaptation and potential use within other countries.

There is clearly a tremendous amount of work to be done by countless numbers of people if project management is to become a recognized profession. Nevertheless, a start has been made, and the basis has been established within each of the five major attributes of a profession on which to build a new profession. It remains to be seen if project managers worldwide have the energy, the desire, the commitment, and the leadership to establish a new and recognized profession. I believe that they do, and that project management will be recognized in the not too distant future as the newest of the professions. In fact, it is necessary that this happen. There is simply too much to be gained by the individuals concerned, by the organizations they represent, and by the society they serve to allow this opportunity to slip by unfulfilled.

CONCLUSION: VISION OF A NEW PROFESSION

It remains only to point out what a profession of project management would mean to the project management professional. In the first place, entry to the profession would be attained through a program of formal education available at a wide selection of universities in several countries. The "typical" professional project manager would receive an undergraduate degree in a "technical" specialty, where the term technical could refer to engineering, architecture, finance, computer information systems, social welfare, theater arts, or in whatever field the individual will be managing future projects. Several years experience in that field, with highly favorable evaluations, would prepare the individual for advancement into project management. Project management education would be obtained at the graduate level, followed by entry into the profession as an assistant project manager, a project coordinator, a project specialist, or functional manager responsible for providing extensive support to projects. As performance warrants, the individual would be promoted to manager of a small project, then on to larger projects. At some point during this period, the individual would probably sit for exams and become a certified project manager. Contributions to the profession and personal recognition would be in the form of research, publications, and participation in the local, national, and/or international activities of a project management professional organization.

Again, as performance warrants, our project manager might next become an in-house project management consultant, or a general project manager of a very large, critical, society-affecting project activity. Finally, with this level of skill and experience, our project manager might become a private consultant to other organizations, or a senior-level project management executive, a manager of projects, or a vice president for projects.

This, of course, is only a general concept for a professional project manager's career, and it would necessarily vary due to the type and size of the organizations involved, as well as the performance and desires of the individual. The major gain for the individual, the organizations, and for society as a whole is that the project manager continually builds on demonstrated knowledge and abilities. At each step in a career the individual can be evaluated to determine qualifications for moving on to the next more demanding level of performance. Of course, line managers will still use project management as a stepping stone in a non-project management career, but the professional project managers will provide that core of highly qualified individuals needed to manage the critical projects of major significance to society.

A radical change from present practice? Yes, but a logical and necessary progression from the situation that exists today. If such a profession of project management can be developed, society will benefit from a greatly improved ability to determine who should be entrusted with the task of shaping the future.

REFERENCES

Adams, J. R. "From the Education Director's Desk," a column appearing in each quarterly issue of the *Project Management Journal* (formerly the *Project Management Quarterly*). December 1983-March 1986.

Adams, J. R. and B. W. Campbell. *Roles and Responsibilities of the Project Manager*. Drexel Hill, PA: Project Management Institute, 1982.

Davis, J. G. "The Accidental Profession." Reprinted in the Special Summer Issue of the *Project Management Journal*, August 1984, p. 6.

Kerzner, H. *Project Management: A Systems Approach to Planning, Scheduling, and Controlling*, 2nd ed. New York: Van Nostrand Reinhold Co., 1984.

Meginson, L. C., D. C. Mosley, and P. H. Pietrie, Jr. *Management: Concepts and Applications*, 2nd ed. New York: Harper & Row Publishers, 1986, pp. 16-17.

Moder, J. J., C. R. Phillips, and E. W. Davis. *Project Management with CPM, PERT, and Precedence Diagramming*, 3rd ed. New York: Van Nostrand Reinhold Co., 1983.

Stuckenbruck, L., in a personal interview with the author.

3

Productivity: A Key to the Future

RICHARD L. TUCKER *Construction Industry Institute, Austin, Texas*

SHIRLEY S. TUCKER *Tucker & Tucker Associates, Austin, Texas*

Many indicators imply significant downward trends in construction productivity during recent years. The Business Roundtable's Construction Industry Cost Effectiveness Project developed information showing that construction costs rose at a rate 50% greater than the rate of inflation during a 20-year period starting in the mid-1960s. Other data indicate similar trends.

A productive work force is critical to improving project efficiency, particularly in the more developed nations. As the standard of living improves in other countries, labor productivity will become a critical element of all projects. Since onsite labor represents 25-40% of total construction costs, major efforts to lower project costs must include significant programs oriented toward labor productivity.

LABOR PRODUCTIVITY

As a basis for examining labor productivity, it might be useful to examine a typical craftsman's time utilization. The percentages listed below are merely estimates, but are considered to be representative of many projects. Perhaps as little as 40% of a typical worker's day is utilized productively. Certainly the value will vary from project to project, and worker activities may consume much higher percentages. However, many industry experts consider the 40% value, if in error, on the optimistic side.

Productive	40%
Unproductive	
Administrative delays	20%
Inefficient methods	20%
Work restrictions/jurisdictions	15%
Personal	5%

If only a portion of a typical worker's time is spent productively, then one approach to productivity improvement is to focus on the unproductive portion of time. For example, if the values listed are assumed, then the 60% of unproductive time should be addressed. Any productivity improvements must represent a conversion of unproductive time into productive time. Moreover, attention should be concentrated on those elements that offer the greatest potential for improvement and impact on overall project efficiency.

The assumed values listed above provide guidance. Personal time, such as breaks and intentional idleness, is relatively low. Even if it is twice the assumed value of 5%, it does not offer, per se, a fertile opportunity for direct attention as a productivity focus. Craftsmen are typically self-motivated and accomplishment oriented. Jobsite surveys show high levels of frustration, absenteeism, and turnover among workers on sites that are poorly managed. Conversely, worker satisfaction is much higher, and personal time is less, on projects that are efficiently managed. Thus, the personal time element naturally will be reduced as a result of improvements in other project areas.

Jurisdictional restrictions and unreasonable work rules can be the source of significant labor inefficiencies. Although these are normally attributed to the union sector, opportunities also exist on many nonunion projects. Among the most prominent opportunities for improvement is a reduction in the number of crafts necessary to install a particular piece of work. For example, piping installation can involve crews of riggers, hangers, fitters, welders, scaffolders, insulators, operators, instrument specialists, and others. Even without jurisdictional problems, the logistics of efficient utilization of so many crafts makes high productivity difficult. Of course, any jurisdictional disputes will further compound productivity losses. Minimization of jurisdictions and work restrictions is an area for productivity improvement, but reflects a needed industry change. It is unlikely that major improvements can be made on specific projects. Even more, opportunities for improvement are relatively limited once a project has begun.

Inefficient tools and construction methods are major sources of labor inefficiency. Indeed, with the exception of improvements in heavy construction equipment, little progress has been made in construction methods during the past several decades. Major developments are needed in construction technology. Certainly automation, robotics, and computer utilization are appropriate areas. Again, the opportunities for development of new methods are more of an industrywide nature and are relatively limited for specific projects.

The most project-oriented and sizeable opportunity for labor productivity optimization lies in the area of administrative delays. Many studies have shown that sizeable portions of a worker's time are spent in waiting for materials, tools, equipment, instructions, and services furnished by project management. Reduction of administratively caused delays is project specific, within the realm of project management, and of sizeable potential for productivity improvement. It offers a prime area of focus for efficient labor utilization, and should be pursued initially as part of any productivity program.

REDUCTION OF ADMINISTRATIVE DELAYS

The basic philosophy for reduction of administrative delays is represented in Figure 1. For a program to be effective, it must be recognized that management actually installs nothing. Only the craftsmen put work in place. Thus, the principal role of management is to provide support to the work force in the form of directions, information, materials, tools, equipment, etc. Such a limited view of management does not mean that management can disregard its obligation to set standards and enforce discipline. Those functions are included in its supporting role.

Unfortunately, the support role of management appears simplistic. It is actually quite complex. The logistics of providing all of the necessary support material to every craftsman at all times are beyond the capabilities of any present-day computer or software.

A primary difficulty is in communications. Two persons have one potential channel of communication between them. For three persons, there are three potential channels of communication. For 5 persons, the number grows to 10 and it compounds with the number of persons. For 1,000 persons, for example, there are approximately 500,000 potential channels of communications whereas there are approximately 50 million potential channels for a project involving 10,000 persons. Considering all of the representa-

MANAGEMENT

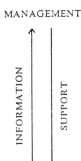

WORKERS

Figure 1 Management-worker relationship.

tives of owners, designers, site managers, craftsmen, vendors, inspectors, etc. on a large project, at least 10,000 persons are involved; thus, communications are difficult.

As shown in Figure 1, management cannot perform its support role without adequate information. The best information regarding necessary support services should come from those closest to the work, the craftsmen. However, continuous communications between every worker and manager are not possible, so an organizational structure with a communications system is necessary. Such a structure thus becomes the heart of any program to maximize productivity on modern day projects.

INFORMATION TOOLS

Most projects utilize line organization structures for information flow both to and from management. Communications through such structures are imperfect because of the numbers of steps involved. For optimum productivity, upper management must have useful and timely information reflecting conditions at the work place. In addition to normal cost reports, memos, and results of meetings, the following types of information sources are useful:

    Unit rate measurements
    Craft questionnaries/interviews
    Work sampling
    Craft and foreman delay surveys
    Equipment/tool room surveys
    Time lapse photography

These information sources are in addition to normal schedule and cost reports, and are for the purpose of productivity optimization. Thus, the accuracy of the information received is not nearly as important as the credibility and timeliness of the information received. Moreover, the level of effort involved in obtaining the information may be a factor in its usefulness. Each information source is described briefly below.

Unit rate measurements are obtained by dividing regular measurements of quantities of work completed by work-hours expended. The resulting ratios can then be compared to historical data or project estimates to obtain productivity factors. Although such information is needed for overall project evaluations, it is normally limited in its ability to provide insight into specific actions necessary for improvement.

Considerable information can be obtained from questionnaires and interviews with craftsmen and foremen. Although such information is a compilation of perceptions and

Observer's Name: _____ Badge #: _____ Date: _____ Day of Week: _____

Area Surveyed: _____ Area #: _____ (4) Time Survey Started: _____ (1) Stopped: _____ (2)

(3)   (5)   (6)

Activity / Craft	Labor	Carpnt	Concrt	Rebar	Paint	Electricl	Pipe	Instrmt	Insultn	M Wrt	BlrMkr	Rigging	HEOps	StlWkrs	ShtMtl	Totals
1. Late Start/ Early Quit																
2. Personal																
3. Obtaining Direction																
4. Gathering Tools/ Materials																
5. Moving Empty																
6. Idle																
7. Engaged in Fabrication																
8. Engaged in Installation																
TOTALS																

The number involved in direct activities #7 _____ + #8 _____ = _____ divided by the total number of observations, results in _____ percent involved in indirect work.

Figure 2 Work sampling data sheet. In full, the columns starting with "Labor" and proceeding to the right include Laborer, Carpenter, Concrete, Rebar iron worker, Painter, Electrical, Pipefitters, Insulators, Millwrights, Boilermakers, Riggers, Heavy equipment operators, Structural iron workers, and Sheetmetal workers.

is thus of questionable accuracy, it provides insight into problem areas and opportunities for improved efficiency. The biggest limitation of questionnaires and interviews is their time consumption. Thus, their use must be infrequent.

Work sampling offers apparent accuracy and statistical credibility. Data are obtained by trained observers traversing a site in a random fashion and recording workers' activities on a form such as that shown in Figure 2. Data are then compiled and presented in subcategories related to direct work, support work, or idle time. The process is viewed with suspicion by workers unless it is adequately explained in advance. The data are subject to interpretation and the method is relatively time consuming.

Efficient and nonadversarial methods for information development involve the use of craft and foremen delay surveys. Sample forms for such surveys are shown by Figures 3 and 4. A craft delay survey can be completed at a tool box session in a matter of a few minutes. Data can be quickly compiled for an entire site. The foreman delay survey is perhaps more feasible, since foremen are more comfortable with paper work

Craft Delay Survey

Date: _____ Craft: _____ Area: _____

I lost the following amounts of time yesterday due to:

Cause	Lost Time (Hours)					
1. Waiting on Materials	0	<1/2	1/2–1	1–2	2–4	>4
2. Waiting on Tools	0	<1/2	1/2–1	1–2	2–4	>4
3. Waiting on Equipment (or Breakdowns)	0	<1/2	1/2–1	1–2	2–4	>4
4. Rework	0	<1/2	1/2–1	1–2	2–4	>4
5. Waiting on Instructions/Information	0	<1/2	1/2–1	1–2	2–4	>4
6. Waiting on Permits	0	<1/2	1/2–1	1–2	2–4	>4
7. Waiting on Another Craft	0	<1/2	1/2–1	1–2	2–4	>4
8. Lack of Manpower	0	<1/2	1/2–1	1–2	2–4	>4
9. Overcrowding	0	<1/2	1/2–1	1–2	2–4	>4
10. Other (State) _____	0	<1/2	1/2–1	1–2	2–4	>4

Figure 3 Craft delay survey.

Date: _____   Name: _____

Number in Crew: _____   Gen. Foreman: _____

                                 Foreman Name: _____

PROBLEMS CAUSING DELAY

	Manhours Lost				
	Number of Hours	X	Number of Men	=	Manhours
Changes/Redoing Work (Design Error or Change)	_____	X	_____	=	_____
Changes/Redoing Work (Prefabrication Error)	_____	X	_____	=	_____
Changes/Redoing Work (Field Error or Damage)	_____	X	_____	=	_____
Waiting for Materials (Warehouse)	_____	X	_____	=	_____
Waiting for Materials (Vendor Furnished)	_____	X	_____	=	_____
Waiting for Tools	_____	X	_____	=	_____
Waiting for Construction Equipment	_____	X	_____	=	_____
Construction Equipment Breakdown	_____	X	_____	=	_____
Waiting for Information	_____	X	_____	=	_____
Waiting for Other Crews	_____	X	_____	=	_____
Waiting for Fellow Crew Members	_____	X	_____	=	_____
Unexplained or Unnecessary Move	_____	X	_____	=	_____
Other: _____	_____	X	_____	=	_____
_____	_____	X	_____	=	_____

Comments: _____

_____

_____

Figure 4 Foreman delay survey.

than are craftsmen. A survey form can be completed by each foreman as time cards are filled out near the end of each day. Since a foreman is in a position of familiarity with crew activities, the submitted data should be quite reliable. Information from craft and foreman delay surveys, although limited to administratively caused delays, is reasonably accurate and offers specific information for improvement.

Equipment surveys, tool room surveys, and similar studies are normally utilized when specific information from other sources implies their need. Typical forms are shown in Figures 5 and 6.

The most precise information can be obtained through time-lapse photography. Such information is particularly useful where significant numbers of craftsmen and

Tool Description	Order Filled	Order Not Filled	Expendable Description	Order Filled	Order Not Filled
Band Saw			Band Saw Blade (Regular)		
Battery			Band Saw Blade (SS)		
Bolt Cutters			Buffing Wheel		
Comalong			Buring Tip		
Comb, Wrench			Drill Bits		
Drill			Face Shield		
Extension Cord			File (Regular)		
Grinder (Right Angle)			File (SS)		
Grinder (Air Pencil)			Galvanizing Point		
Grinder (Elect. Pencil)			Grinding Wheel		
Grinder Wrenches			Impact Pin		
Hilti Drill			Pipe Dope		
Hilti Bits			Rock Cone		
Impact Head			Sandpaper		
Impactor			Tape (Duct)		
Pipe Taps			Tape (Masking)		
Pipe Wrench			Tape (Teflon)		
Rosebud			Tap Magic		
Safety Belt			WD-40		
Safety Glasses			Welding Lenses		
Torch			Wire Brush (Regular)		
Tripod			Wire Brush (SS)		
Other			Other		

Tool Room Number: _____ Location: _____
Date: _____ Time Survey Started: _____ Stopped: _____
Tool Room Personnel: _____

Figure 5 Tool room survey.

Observer's Name: _____   Badge #: _____   Date: _____   Day of Week: _____

Area Surveyed: _____   Area #: _____ (1)   Time Survey Started: _____ (3)   Stopped: _____ (5)   (2) (4) (6)

Activity \ Equipment	Cherry Pickers	Hydro-Cranes	Friction Cranes	Manlifts	Forklifts	Back-hoes	Loaders	Dumps	Dozers	Com-pactors	Delivery Trucks	Totals
1. Active (Engaged in Work)												
2. Passive (Holding a Load)												
3. Traveling (With a Load)												
4. Traveling (Empty)												
5. Down (Due to a Malfunction)												
6. Idle (In Area)												
7. Idle (In Yard)												
8. Moving Bulks/Clean-up												
TOTALS												

The number involved in direct activities #1 _____ + #2 _____ + #3 _____ =

Divided by the total number of observations results in _____ percent involved in Direct Work.

Figure 6 Equipment utilization survey.

activities can be captured in the field of view of the camera. The method is extremely useful for improvement of crew-controlled activities.

IMPROVEMENT ACTIVITIES

Productivity improvement can be most readily obtained through principles of participative involvement. Today's construction workers are better educated and their abilities can be utilized in determining solutions to problems as well as in problem identification. Construction workers are naturally creative and their creativity often can be captured in suggestions for productivity improvement. Participative involvement is normally utilized in the following three areas:

> Information gathering
> Feedback sessions
> Construction effectiveness teams

Information gathering is accomplished through the tools described previously. The process of information gathering from craftsmen and foremen is, in itself, a participative activity and often results in productivity improvement resulting from increased communications and awareness.

A natural follow-up to the information gathering activities is that of feedback sessions, where data gathered by way of the information tools is discussed. Such sessions can be held infrequently and need not involve all participants. Foreman feedback sessions, conducted on a biweekly or monthly basis, are particularly useful. Indeed, many problems are resolved during such sessions. Results from surveys and other information sources provide natural agenda items for discussion.

More specific and deliberate activities relate to construction effectiveness teams. Such teams can be similar to quality circles as are used in the more steady-state industries. Conversely, they can function as problem-solving teams which are established to address problems that have been identified by management. Although the two groups may differ in origination and tenure, their activities are similar. Construction effectiveness teams are ad hoc groups that meet regularly, operate in a methodical fashion, and make recommendations to management for productivity improvement. Their use can embody all of the principles of participative involvement in information gathering, problem identification, and implementation of productivity improvement suggestions. They inherently result in improved communications.

CLOSURE

Future improvements in construction productivity are quite realizable. Significant long-term improvements can result from realistic attention to jurisdictional and work restriction issues. Major improvements in productivity can be obtained from concerted research and development of new construction equipment and methods.

Immediate productivity gains can result from drawing upon the knowledge and creativity of craftsmen through improved communications. The improved communications result from participative involvement emphasis in gathering information and designing solutions to problems associated with administrative delays.

All such activities are complementary and supportive. Emphasis upon communications and productivity improvement will also result in improved quality, safety, and other desirable project features.

4

The Business Roundtable

CARROLL H. DUNN   *The Business Roundtable, New York, New York*

All who participate in the construction industry have a common interest and a common opportunity to make things better for ourselves, for each other, for the economy, and for the nation. The goal is greater productivity and more construction for the capital invested.

Roger Blough, a former Chief Executive Officer of United States Steel Corporation and a strong advocate of improved cost effectiveness in the construction industry, made the following points in 1983:

> Construction is important to the economy as a whole and, therefore, to everybody. It affects costs, prices, and our international competitiveness both in our own and foreign markets
>
> Construction dollars are not being used effectively
>
> Declining cost effectiveness is not the fault of any one group. Owners, managers, contractors, unions, workers, suppliers, and governments all share the responsibility
>
> Cost effectiveness in construction can be improved to the advantage of all without inequity to any group, if we recognize it as a national problem and seek cooperative instead of adversarial solutions

We will describe here how one organization, The Business Roundtable, normally not considered a part of the construction industry, has committed itself to continued improvement in that industry.

WHAT IS THE BUSINESS ROUNDTABLE

The Business Roundtable is an association of business chief executives who examine public issues that affect the economy and develop positions which seek to reflect sound economic and social principles. Membership includes a wide spectrum of enterprises: manufacturers, extractive industries, banks, retailers, insurance companies, transportation and communication companies, and utilities. Membership is by invitation, and a representation of category of business as well as geographical location is considered.

One public issue which has been and continues to be of great concern to The Business Roundtable is the efficiency and productivity of the construction industry. This is a natural interest since member companies spend billions of dollars annually for construction services; approximately one-third of the national total. There is also a broader rationale: Construction is the largest industry in the United States and, therefore, important to the economy as a whole, and to each of us, since it affects costs, prices, and competitiveness in both domestic and international markets.

HOW DID THE BUSINESS ROUNDTABLE COME ABOUT?

In 1969, a group of business executives, appalled at the rapid inflation in the cost of construction, formed an organization which they called the Construction User's Anti-Inflation Roundtable. Roger Blough served as the Chairman of the organization. They began efforts to find ways to promote quality, efficiency, and cost effectiveness in the construction industry. Their initial focus was broad-based but oriented toward labor-related cost factors.

In 1972, this Anti-Inflation Roundtable, along with two other organizations, merged to form The Business Roundtable. At that time the construction aspects of the new Roundtable's activities were assigned to a Construction Committee made up of executives from the member companies with responsibilities in the construction area. They fostered the development of autonomous "Local User Councils" in a number of metropolitan areas of the country. These councils provided a vehicle for owners to become better informed on local issues and activities impacting the cost of construction. A national forum for the exchange of ideas and concerns in the industry was then established, with two general conferences scheduled each year.

In 1977, the Construction Committee concluded that an in-depth study was needed to investigate construction industry practices, to identify and define the problems, and to develop long-range programs to solve or mitigate these problems. Their theme was "If there is a better way to do construction, let us find it." A task force of six construction executives was formed to scope the study effort. They identified five areas of study: Project Management, Construction Technology, Labor Effectiveness, Labor Supply and Training, and Codes and Regulations. They proposed, and The Business Roundtable Policy Committee approved, an 8 to 10 year study in four phases. The first phase was to develop a detailed plan; the second, a period of research and preparation of reports to include recommendations for action; the third, develop a strategy and plan to bring about needed action; and the final and continuing phase was the implementation of recommendations.

WHAT HAS BEEN ACHIEVED

The Construction Industry Cost Effectiveness Project was launched in late 1978. A task force which ultimately included over 250 construction experts, representing more than 125 companies and other organizations including contractor associations and academic institutions, spent four years gathering and analyzing data. Out of that effort came a series of detailed findings and, more importantly, a set of practical, workable recommendations with the potential of saving a minimum of ten billion dollars a year in industrial, commercial, and utility construction.

These findings and recommendations have been published in a series of 24 reports including a one-volume summary report. As a part of their commitment to construction industry improvement, The Business Roundtable has furnished these reports free for the asking. Over one and one half million copies were distributed by the end of 1985. The reports, listed in Table 1, are available on request to:

The Business Roundtable
200 Park Avenue
New York, NY 10166

There is nothing revolutionary about the reports. They offer neither easy answers nor startling new discoveries. And, no overnight remedies. They do, however, con-

Table 1 Construction Industry Cost Effectiveness Project

This Project is a long-range, four-phase effort to develop a comprehensive definition of the fundamental problems in the construction industry and an accompanying program for resolution of those problems leading to an improvement of cost effectiveness in the industry. The focus is on primary improvement in the industrial, utility, and commercial segments of the industry and it has been developed from the point of view of owners or users of construction. Efforts by all segments of the industry are vitally necessary if major improvement is to result.

The report series includes:

PROJECT MANAGEMENT—Study Area A
    A-1 Measuring Productivity in Construction
    A-2 Construction Labor Motivation
    A-3 Improving Construction Safety Performance
    A-4 First and Second Level Supervisory Training
    A-5 Management Education and Academic Relations
    A-6 Modern Management Systems
    A-7 Contractual Arrangements

CONSTRUCTION TECHNOLOGY—Study Area B
    B-1 Integrating Construction Resources and Technology into Engineering
    B-1 Technological Progress in the Construction Industry
    B-3 Construction Technology Needs and Priorities

LABOR EFFECTIVENESS—Study Area C
    C-1 Exclusive Jurisdiction in Construction
    C-2 Scheduled Overtime Effect on Construction Projects
    C-3 Contractor Supervision in Unionized Construction
    C-4 Constraints Imposed by Collective Bargaining Agreements
    C-5 Local Labor Practices
    C-6 Absenteeism and Turnover
    C-7 The Impact of Local Union Politics

LABOR SUPPLY AND TRAINING—Study Area D
    D-1 Subjourneymen in Union Construction
    D-2 Government Limitations on Training Innovations
    D-3 Construction Training Through Vocational Education
    D-4 Training Problems in Open Shop Construction
    D-5 Labor Supply Information

REGULATIONS AND CODES—Study Area E
    E-1 Administration and Enforcement of Building Codes and Regulations

---

solidate the knowledge and wisdom of the industry in one package, and they make clear in a unique way what is wrong and what needs to be done.

It is important to realize that the CICE recommendations operate on many different levels. Some are applicable to foremen in the field, some to the front office. Some apply to the owner, others to the contractor. They apply to large projects and to small projects, to new construction and to revamp and maintenance projects. Obviously, not every recommendation applies to every project, and certainly not all can be applied by anybody at any one time. The total effect is what counts and that, hopefully, will lead to better, less costly projects.

There are a total of 223 recommendations contained in the reports. All are reasonable and practical and, when implemented, have produced favorable results. Of the recommendations, 92 are addressed to owners, 56 to contractors, and 28 require joint actions by owners and contractors. The remaining 47 involve labor, government, academia, or are general in nature.

Since 1983, CICE implementation committees aimed at owners, contractors, organized labor, government as an owner and regulator, academia, and technical and professional societies have been at work.

There are definite indications that things are happening in the industry, and many companies—contractors and owners—as well as government agencies are realizing that change is the only route, not just to prosperity, but to economic survival.

Through the efforts of a Business Roundtable Task Force of Chief Executive Officers, word is getting to other CEOs about CICE and its recommendations. Attitudes are changing. And chief executives are getting involved in the construction process to a degree unknown in the past. Some are asking tough questions of themselves and their organizations:

> What are we doing to educate our people who manage contractor work about cost-improvement and CICE?
> How do we select contractors to bid for our business? Do we consider their track record in such areas as safety, cost control, and labor management? Do we consider how they respond to CICE recommendations?
> Do our contractor selection procedures and our contractual arrangements give our contractors incentives to improve cost-effectiveness?
> Do our managers monitor contractor safety performance? Do we pay the same attention to contractor absenteeism and turnover as to those factors among our own employees?

A FEW EXAMPLES

During the revamp of an oil refinery in Texas, one of the main elements was a worker motivation program that, together with excellent safety performance, saved the job a million and a half dollars at a cost of one-tenth of the savings.

At a consumer products plant, a $24-million project came in 11% under budget. Construction personnel worked with design engineers at an early stage to show how changes in layout and site arrangement could reduce field construction costs. Analysis showed this strategy was the principal reason for the underrun.

An engineering and construction company used value-engineering techniques to save $22 million on a major project.

A billion dollar defense project realized significant savings because right from the start the work was organized around CICE principles with the owners, the major contractors, and the subcontractors participatory to a commitment to create a success story—to prove that owners, contractors, and labor working together can achieve cost effectiveness.

In the academic area, a number of actions have taken place. Stanford University and Texas A&M have established short, intensive Construction Executive Courses. These are for upper-level managers in engineering and construction firms and owner organizations. These courses are analogous to the senior business management short courses which have long been offered by many universities. Owner and contractor personnel who have attended these programs are enthusiastic and report a direct application to their work. Similar programs in continuing education will be developed at other schools and will make important contributions to the upgrading of the construction management process.

CONSTRUCTION INDUSTRY INSTITUTE

A new and promising development in the academic area is the establishment of the Construction Industry Institute at the University of Texas at Austin. CII is the result of a realization growing out of the CICE project that there was a need for a national center to provide a coordinated effort for construction research and the dissemination of information.

The Institute is an innovative concept for research in construction. CII brings together owners, contractors, and academia in an effort to develop information to improve the U. S. construction industry. Its mission is to increase cost effectiveness in the industry and thereby strengthen the competitive position of U. S. business in the international market place.

Specific objectives of the Institute are:

To develop a national forum for issues related to the cost effectiveness of the construction industry
To bring together experienced management, technical personnel, and their companies who share a broad view of the construction industry, and are willing to participate and pool their expertise to improve it
To identify important issues which impact the cost effectiveness of the construction industry, support and direct research, prepare and offer recommendations, and define the measurable results expected from implementation
To disseminate both credible information of value and state-of-the-art knowledge to the construction industry through appropriate vehicles of communication and education
To establish and maintain appropriate liaison with other organizations active on construction industry issues of mutual interest.

Since CII serves as a continuing entity to keep the recommendations of the CICE project before the public, it closely parallels The Business Roundtable's efforts toward implementation of CICE recommendations. For this reason, the Roundtable has supported and continues to support and participate in CII, with the belief that CII will provide, from its research activities, results which complement and extend CICE. It also will be a continuing source of expertise and research capability for undertaking additional problem areas outside the CICE recommendations.

WHAT OF THE FUTURE?

It is abundantly clear that all involved in the construction industry should have a common interest and a common opportunity to make things better—better for ourselves, for each other, for the economy and for the nation. The goal—greater productivity and more construction for the money—not less money for construction.

While a great deal has happened in the past few years, there is much left to do. There are still many firms, important to this industry, that haven't been made aware that productivity can be improved and construction costs can be reduced through the cooperative efforts of owners, contractors, and labor.

CII has been, is, and will be a force for change and improvement in the industry. In its brief existence, it has grown in membership and achieved recognition in the industry as a viable research institute and a national forum for construction research. Through the participation of numerous universities in its research programs, not only are current problems being resolved, but, as the results of research are incorporated into academic programs, the education and training of future construction managers will be dramatically improved.

The significance of programs discussed here and their promise for the industry lies not only in the individual research projects, important as they are, but in the long-term commitment of owners and contractors to the idea of industrywide research and problem solving. In the future, it will be one of the most productive outgrowths of the CICE project.

The Business Roundtable will continue to maintain its interest in improvement of cost effectiveness in construction. This includes continued activities of its Construction Committee and support of Local User Councils and the efforts of the Construction Industry Institute.

5

The Effects of Changing
Project Requirements

KENNETH A. FISCHER *John Zink Company, Tulsa, Oklahoma*

The project manager faces constant challenges in the changing environment in which he operates. The changes in project methods and technology over the past several decades are staggering. Over the short term, these changes are not so discernible.

The impact of short-term change is highly visible in the project outcome; that is, in ever-escalating project costs. The sensitivity of top management to escalating costs has placed great emphasis on the area of project cost control. A significant dedication of resources has been made in the development of worker productivity measurement as a result of the continual outcry over its perceived decline.

Today's project costs are often compared with costs of similar past projects and the increases are attributed to poor productivity and/or lack of control. Cost control and productivity measurement are attempts to deal with the result of change. To effectively control costs the underlying change itself must be identified and controlled.

A large engineering organization made an attempt to identify the changes that have been attributed to project cost escalation. This study concentrated on the reasons for the escalation of home office jobhours and costs over the period from 1960 to 1980. The results were compared with escalation of total plant cost over a similar time frame.

By examining the results of this study, the project manager will become aware of the types of change that have occurred over this period of time and the magnitude of their impact on project costs. By understanding the effect of short-term change, the project manager will be better able to control the resulting impact on jobhours and on costs. The methods employed in the study are also of interest, as they can be employed by other organizations and industries to identify change and the corresponding effect on costs.

BASIC CONCEPTS

The most important objectives of the survey were to determine "why" the home office jobhours required to execute projects have increased and "how much" this increase has been. The "how much" was then compared with project total installed cost escalation over the 20-year period covered by the survey.

The survey methodology was not intended to be a rigorous analysis that might be expected to produce statistically reproducible results. Rather, it was an informed judgment survey based upon the experience and opinions of a large number of managers and senior company personnel whose careers spanned the 20-year period. The specific numerical results, therefore, may be questioned. The value of the survey, admittedly, lies not in the specific numerical results, but in the approach used to collect the data and the analysis and evaluation used to obtain the final results.

The survey was based on certain concepts, which are explained in the following paragraphs and are essential to an understanding of the survey approach and the conclusions reached.

The survey identified change by asking "why" project execution jobhours have increased. Project "A" was done 20 years ago. Project "B" is a recently completed project. The capacities and products are identical. The plant, people, and tools are equivalent.

There is a tendency to conclude that any increase in two "identical" plants is due solely to a decline in worker productivity. A more careful scrutiny though, reveals that the two plants are not "identical." There is a great difference in the elements listed as "equivalent," i.e., plant, people, and tools.

These components change constantly with time. The plants differ because of changes in materials and technology over the 20-year span. The people involved in design, construction, and operation of the plant have also changed. The tools used in engineering and construction are markedly different from those of two decades ago. Thus, the projects are "identical" only when viewed with respect to capacity and product.

To answer "why" jobhours have increased over the years, the survey looked closely at the changes that have occurred in the plant, people, and tools. These changes are the difference between an "identical" project and an "equivalent" project. When these are identified, they account for all of the project jobhour growth. Before identifying these changes specifically, the following generalization was developed using intuitive logic. The effects of changes in people and tools to project jobhours are addressed thus:

> If the project had been executed with the people of 20 years ago using today's tools a reduction in jobhours and cost would be expected. Modern tools unquestionably improve productivity and provide higher output from the people. This premise is illustrated by the lower dotted line in Figure 1.
>
> If the project had been executed with today's people using the tools of 20 years ago, we would expect an increase in jobhours and cost. Increased specialization and the generally accepted decline in output or in productivity would increase jobhours. This premise is illustrated by the upper dotted line in Figure 1.

Since historical project unit jobhours for individual engineering activities have not changed significantly over the past 20 years, we rationalize that the increase in project jobhours due to productivity decline are roughly being offset by a decrease in jobhours due to today's more sophisticated tools. Thus we expect a project executed today for a plant physically "identical" to one of 20 years ago would require approximately the same number of jobhours, shown by Figure 1 as a shaded band.

Why then are jobhours and costs increasing on today's projects? A leading cause must be the difference in the plants being built. We are building "equivalent" plants rather than "identical" ones.

The survey identified many changes in plant, people, and tools. The magnitude of the changes were quantified. The results were evaluated against the effect of inflation. The increase in project jobhours due to these changes was found to be 25% over the 20 years. When analyzed against inflation statistics for the past 15 years, total plant cost escalation was 16% above that resulting from inflation alone. This order of magnitude increase in jobhours and costs is due to the changes in the plant, people, and tools.

If the premises set forth in Figure 1 are accepted, and the tools and people components nearly cancel each other, the jobhour and cost growth result almost entirely from changes in the plant itself.

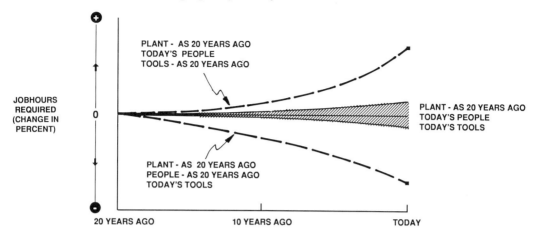

Figure 1 Productivity and jobhour comparison over 20 years.

SOURCES OF CHANGE

To this point we have talked about why project jobhours have increased in terms of change in the general project components of plant, people, and tools. The first object of the study was to identify the specific things that had changed in those components. We may reasonably assume that changes will continue on future projects and that the project manager must anticipate them and identify their possible effects to control pyramiding jobhours and costs.

A large number of experienced personnel were requested to list the reasons why the scope of their work had increased or decreased in their area of expertise. The individuals polled represented a complete cross section of engineering, procurement, construction, and project control backgrounds. They had an average of over 20 years in the engineering/construction industry and a history of employment across all sectors of the process plant industry.

The responses to this poll were tabulated, compared, and found to fall into nine separate categories of change. These were called the "why" factors and are listed below:

1. Technology
2. Schedule
3. Quality
4. Personnel
5. Owner
6. Computer
7. Motivation
8. Tradeoffs
9. Measurement

A brief description of each of these "why" factors was developed.

Technology

Technological improvements in our society have grown exponentially in recent years. This growth has impacted project jobhours as project complexity increased both in the nature of the plant itself and in the growing sophistication of the project execution and design methods. Specific elements of the technology "why" factors include:

> Proliferation of industry codes and standards
> Increased government regulation
> Sophistication of hardware
> The "paperwork" explosion
> Increases in plant scale
> Energy conservation considerations

Of these elements the most significant were judged to be:

Industry Standards and Government Regulations

Changes in engineering standards cover quantity, scope, and sophistication. For example, at the beginning of the survey period there was only one pressure piping code. Today there are more than half a dozen piping codes for refinery, chemical plant, pipeline, nuclear, etc.

In the 1960s, the ASME Section VIII Code had only 228 pages. Today there are two volumes and Division 1 & 2 total over 1200 pages.

OSHA and EPA were nonexistent. Owner specifications have also experienced similar growth, affecting both project jobhours and plant complexity.

Sophistication of Hardware

Today's projects utilize advanced hardware, complicated controls, and complex equipment. As an example, today's plant utilizes electronic instrumentation and computer controls. The earlier equivalent plant had analog pneumatic controls. Similar changes are evident in all engineering disciplines and have created an increasing need for specialization as opposed to yesterday's generalists.

The "Paperwork Explosion"

Advances in technology have added to plant complexity. More paperwork is required. This change is most evident in the nuclear industry where the paperwork borders upon the unmanageable. This in itself is a significant factor in the huge professional service and schedule overruns experienced on many of the nuclear plants.

There is more equipment in an equivalent plant requiring more piping, instrumentation, wire, and concrete resulting in more drawings, calculations, and records.

An identical project 20 years ago might require one or two filing cabinets. Today's project might require one or two rooms for recordkeeping.

Many more examples of technological growth can be cited within the diverse specialized industries. It is only because of offsetting improvements in method and procedure technology that associated project jobhour growth has not been more pronounced.

Schedule

For any endeavor, an optimum time frame can be determined to allow maximum efficiency. In project work, the engineering/construction schedule is often accelerated over the optimum because of the economic leverage exerted to get the facility into operation and optimize the life cycle financial return to the owner. Product value, product obsolescence, and operational profitability demand shorter schedules for project execution. Fast track schedules with phased startups increase project jobhours over historically based expectations.

Schedule overruns are usually identified as such. The associated jobhour overruns are generally not used to adjust the estimating data. Jobhour overruns resulting from unsuccessful attempts to shorten schedules unrealistically are not easily identified and can creep into historical records. This leads to significantly greater jobhour estimates and future work seems to expand to use up the hours available. In an effort to control this cycle of escalation, the project manager must plan and execute schedule optimization procedures and minimize inefficiencies due to false starts, incomplete information, and rework. He must avoid the pitfall of shortening activities beyond the physical limitations of reality. In spite of a desire to attain the goals which are set, the project manager must produce an attainable plan considering all of the constraints present. A poor schedule paying lip service to unreasonable goals will inevitably lead to escalating jobhours. Project completion will also frequently be delayed beyond that of a more realistically planned job.

Components of change in the schedule factor which contribute to jobhour growth include:

> False starts
> Incomplete information
> Inefficient procedures
> Superfluous controls
> Excessive management involvement
> "Fast track" schedule prerequisites

Of these, the following were judged to have the most impact on project execution changes over the period:

False Starts/Incomplete Information

On projects with tight schedules, the tendency is to start working everyone in every area on day one. This gives the impression of a team that "hits the deck running." The cost of this impression will never justify the shortlived optimism it generates initially. Work in some areas will be unsupported by the information required and will result in guesswork and assumptions. Work in other areas will be halted after a brief interval to await completion of work activities elsewhere.

Guesswork, starts, holds, and rework require additional coordination, meetings, correspondence, etc. as well as cause errors and mistakes in downstream work. More paper is generated, and the requirement for resources escalates.

Fast Track Prerequisites

To shorten an optimum schedule, the level of manpower must be increased, with a resultant need for exceptional care in planning. The project manager must have faith in the capability of his organization and formulate a plan to avoid excessive inefficiencies. He must be able to communicate the logic of his plan or he will be pressured to initiate counterproductive activities. The trend to shorter schedules has become a major obstacle to achieving project objectives. If not properly planned and administered, a fast track schedule program will result in significant jobhour growth, and frequently an extended schedule.

Our competitive environment has led to acceptance of a reduced schedule as a major factor in contractor and vendor selection, sometimes even surpassing that of cost differences. A project manager must be capable of developing and presenting a realistic plan, jobhour budget, and the attendant schedule fully thought-out and supportable.

Quality

The increase in expected quality of engineering over the past 20 years has parallelled the growth in technology. A greater degree of accuracy is implied as a result of today's more sophisticated methods. Yesterday's approximations and judgment decisions have been replaced by detailed computer analyses with a resulting stack of paper detailing every conceivable alternative; some significant, some not.

Project managers today are innundated with schedule and cost reports, manhour distribution accounts, material status reports, percent progress charts; all broken down in minute detail. Project management does not require accounting accuracy in anything but final cost reports. A project manager cannot wait until the figures are unquestionably accurate. Early trends are needed. Too much detail masks trends and impedes an analysis of the total picture. It is more important for the project manager to have significant information early to improve his decision-making ability than have an excess of facts obscuring details later.

The continuous search for better quality has driven project jobhours up disproportionately to the attained value of the improved quality. These are the identified elements of the quality factor:

> Zero-defect objective
> Specialization
> More than the required accuracy
> Need to "prove" everything
> Vendor quality requirements
> Unnecessary specification requirements
> Desire to reduce field jobhours
> Excessive standardization

The most significant of these as determined by the study were:

Reducing Field Manhours

As the cost of field labor increased and schedules shortened, efforts were made to reduce field work and rework due to engineering errors. These efforts have significantly increased engineering scope as well as jobhours. This shift of work from the field to the office is justified in many cases, but it must be carefully evaluated for each project.

The extended use of a design model for the detailing of small bore piping versus field routing is a good example of an engineering/field tradeoff that is often questionable.

Many projects maximize shop and offsite pipe fabrication, modular design, packaged equipment, shop painting and insulation, etc. Engineering documents are necessarily more extensive to support these practices, and the resultant jobhours far exceed those for an "equivalent" project of twenty years ago. Increasing engineering scope to optimize field operations has become accepted. The project manager should evaluate the cost effectiveness in each and every case.

Vendor Quality

Manufacturers have also experienced an escalation in jobhours and costs. Located at the bottom of the competitive ladder on a project, they are the first to feel the pressure of a buyer's market. To remain competitive, they reduce their services and scope of work. The burden is transferred to the engineer. Lack of timely and accurate vendor information is a major factor in lower productivity in an engineering office.

Electrical vendors previously had application engineers very familiar with the specific equipment to do relay and component selection based on receipt of minimum specifications. Cost of this service was included in their quoted price for the equipment. Now, even if such service is provided, it is an extra and invariably expensive. It may not meet the schedule requirements so the project is expected to provide the complete specifications/design.

Vendor drawing quality has deteriorated. More review and comments by the engineer increase the jobhours. Vendor drawings sometimes circulate through the approval chain of vendor/engineer/client five or six times. This adds to the work of the expeditors and inspectors and causes additional field rework and delays in plant startup.

Increased use of packaged equipment is misleading as a method to reduce home office jobhours. In order to tailor the package to the project specifications and still allow bidding by several vendors, the engineer will spend almost as many hours as it would take to design the system. The shift of work from the vendor to the engineer must be accounted for on projects executed during a "buyers" market.

Unnecessary Specification Requirements/Zero Defects

With the proliferation of client, industry, and government specifications, less judgment decisions are made by engineers. There is a rule for everything, but the costs of searching for and administering these rules have increased. Complex specifications may be misapplied, may be conflicting, and can be misunderstood or misinterpreted even by experienced specialists.

Custom design as opposed to manufacturer's standards has become the accepted practice. Additions are made to specifications to cover a theoretical or a one-in-a-million happenstance. Seldom is anything deleted from a specification. As we strive for the perfect specification which protects against all possible problems, we are striving for a "zero-defects" objective. Unless we are dealing with a special circumstance in which there really is a "zero-defects" objective understood by the one paying the bill, the costs will soon outweigh the benefit. The cost of fixing the error becomes far less than preventing it in the first place. Many of today's projects are probably operating past the breakeven point.

A periodic review of client and contractor specifications is required to prevent costly escalation of unjustified quality levels. Such reviews and continuing justification of specification requirements should be conducted on a regularly scheduled basis to control specification escalation. Though this is generally not an assigned project function, every project manager should realize the cost impact of excessive specification requirements and take steps to see that it is minimized on his projects.

To summarize the survey conclusions, there exists a breakeven point beyond which increased quality does not produce a justifiable return on the investment. Technical specialists should be conscious of the cost objectives of the project and review any restrictive portions of their specifications. The decline in vendor quality should not be quietly accepted, but the terms of the purchase order should be enforced. Engineering/field tradeoffs must be examined for cost effectiveness. The project manager should encourage his team not to pursue quality for its own sake, but to insist only on that required by the contract.

Opposition to technical excellence may be unpopular, but the project manager's goal should be to balance acceptable quality with budgeted cost.

Personnel

The people factor is the most controversial and difficult to define. The survey revealed a consensus that individual productivity had probably declined over the 20 years. This decline has been offset by an equal increase due to improved technological aids.

Because of the competitive nature of the contracting business, productivity and unit manhours per activity receive a high level of management attention and obvious problems are usually corrected quickly. Long-term productivity trends are usually not recognized when they do not result in jobhour escalation because of offsetting improvement in tools. An understanding of the long-term productivity decline could potentially reduce unit manhours when coupled with the technological advances. Such a reduction has not been achieved over the past 20 years due to a lack of attention to the changes as they have affected people. For the technically inclined, sociological factors are difficult to evaluate while systems are more readily understood. The project control systems have been developed to measure unit manhours and physical progress. They do nothing but measure changes against a constant target. It is the target itself that should be addressed for effective control. This requires an understanding of why and how people work.

The survey identified the following components of the people factor that have a direct impact on the decline of productivity of project personnel:

A declining experience level
Specialization
Organizational procedures
De-emphasis of individual initiative

The best tool the project manager can employ to minimize the deterioration of these
personnel factors is providing a team approach to project execution. This will lead
to positive motivation. Communication of the project objectives, projection of a positive
attitude, and an "all in the same boat" philosophy all tend to foster "team spirit." If
done intelligently, peer pressure and the inherent desire to be part of a winning team
will motivate project personnel to perform at their limit.

Owner

The list of elements for the owner factor is extensive. Increased sophistication of personnel, specialist involvement in project execution, demands for planning and justification of methods, increased numbers of resident engineers, reporting requirements,
changes as a result of complexity, and the extensive review/approval requirements
are just some of the elements of growth in this "why" factor. Yesterday's "minimum
acceptable" standard seems sometimes to have been replaced by a "maximum possible"
approach. Additional demands by the owner seem to have a tendency to become project
execution standards. Over a period of several projects with demanding owners, project personnel become brainwashed into thinking the "maximum possible" approach is
necessary for successful execution.

To remain competitive and prevent escalating owner requirements from becoming
standard operating procedure, the project manager should start each project from a
minimum requirements base. Owner requirements can be added as appropriate, making
sure that the owner fully understands the attendant cost and schedule impact. Returning to the base minimum at the start of each project will remind everyone of the basic
objectives of project execution and will help control escalation and change.

The owner must also exercise restraint in controlling changes and escalation. A
periodic review of requirements and their cost effectiveness should be a part of internal
procedures. The differing nature of projects is a consideration, and requirements
should be tailored to individual project needs.

Computer

Although the computer could be considered as an element of the technology factor,
its impact has been of such magnitude that it was considered as a separate factor.
Change elements of the computer factor include:

Computer-aided drafting
Design programs
Management information/control systems
Decreased flexibility
Increased level of detail
"Bean counting" mentality
Excessive paper generation

The computer is a large contributor to the technological improvements which offset project manhours increased by other factors. This improvement in jobhours, however,
has to be balanced against computer hardware and software charges. For an "identical" project, using the computer to support the engineering and project control systems
of 20 years ago, the result would be a net savings. The survey participants believed
that the net effect of the computer on today's "equivalent" project has been to increase
both jobhours and costs. This trend is a result of the increased level of detail offered

by the computer and its significant misapplication. We have become obsessed with a
reliance on the computer even for operations which are neither cost effective nor useful.

Intangibles

We should also consider three factors which we classify as "intangibles," which can
affect project jobhours and costs in both positive and negative ways. While the six
factors described above represent significant quantifiable change over the past 20 years,
the three intangible factors have not significantly changed in the potential impact they
can make on any individual project.

The first intangible factor is motivation. An efficient project team organization
and the assignment of qualified personnel are prerequisites. The type of organization,
task force or matrix, is of secondary importance although a task force environment
itself fosters a positive team attitude. Of prime importance is the project manager's
role in setting common objectives and realistic goals, in demonstrating a "can do" attitude, and in establishing open communications among those on the project. On projects
where the owner also assigns his own personnel to the contractor's office, the chances
of project success will not be materially improved unless the two groups have a joint
commitment to these principles.

An integrated team approach requires a project manager who is confident in his
organization, willing to admit mistakes, and skilled in negotiating differences of opinion.
Although initially more difficult, the integration of the project team will ultimately be
justified by an effective group of people having a common goal and accomplishing a
difficult but rewarding task.

The second intangible factor is the establishment of tradeoffs early in the project.
This involves an analysis of the required quality level and timing of the project against
overall costs. With the initial project objectives as a starting point, tradeoffs must
be made to specifically define the expectations for the project. The tradeoff to be evaluated is "how much is the additional insurance going to cost" against "how much will
be realized in the prevention of errors." Escalation of plant costs indicate that the
cost versus quality evaluation is sometimes not given the proper attention.

The following list includes major areas which should be evaluated against cost for
each project:

Contractor	Client
Material specifications	Material specifications
Field rework level	Reporting requirements
Computer usage	Operability
Administrative procedures	Ease of maintenance
	Start-up ease
	Energy efficiency
	Product quality
	Schedule requirements
	Time value of money

The third intangible factor is the basis and method for measuring project growth. Project jobhours and cost are often compared without a sufficient analysis of the project
and the work scope differences. Such elements as changes in execution requirements,
stage of project development, contracting and execution approach, market conditions,
check list basis for reimbursable versus nonreimbursable job classifications, and so
on. All must be taken into consideration along with the tangible factors when comparing similar projects executed at different times.

These three intangible factors have the potential to increase or decrease the project jobhours in relation to the 26% growth falling out of the survey data. They are
influenced greatly by the actions of the project manager and can have significant impact on a project.

In summary, each of the nine "why" factors and their subfactors have the potential to both increase or decrease project jobhours and costs. They contain a mix of the general plant, people, and tools components identified under basic concepts. The survey did not attempt to divide the "why" factors into either increase/decrease components or plant/people/tools components. This was considered to be too complex and unnecessary to obtain the desired results.

EFFECT ON JOBHOURS

The initial objective of the study was realized with the identification of the "why" factors as the sources of change. The next objective was to determine "how much" the "why" factors had affected the project jobhours over the period.

A work sheet was developed for each of the tangible "why" factors listing its subfactors. The worksheet for "Technology" is shown in Figure 2. The numbers from -5 to +10 across the top represent the percentage increase or decrease in jobhours during the past 20 years.

The worksheets were returned to the personnel who had participated in the "why" survey. They were requested to indicate the percentage change in jobhours attributable to each subfactor based on their own experience and judgment. Where the change exceeded the listed percentage increase or decrease, space was allowed to write in the desired percent change. More than 300 of these worksheets were completed and returned. The responses were separated by function, averaged, tabulated, and weighted by typical percentage of project contribution, yielding the results presented in Table 1.

For each function the percentage increase and decrease were combined to give a net growth or decline due to each "why" factor. It was not surprising that the greatest growth was in the controls area. Current practice places great emphasis on detailed reporting and forecasting. Twenty years ago controls were minimal.

The impact of the "why" factors on project team growth was the subject of much controversy among those surveyed, so a different approach was used. The participants

TECHNOLOGY	NEGATIVE						POSITIVE										
	5	4	3	2	1	0	1	2	3	4	5	6	7	8	9	10	
INDUSTRY STANDARDS																	
GOVERNMENT REGULATIONS																	
MORE HARDWARE ALTERNATIVES																	
HARDWARE COMPLEXITY																	
PAPER WORK																	
PLANT SIZE																	
ENERGY CONSERVATION																	

Figure 2 Example of survey worksheet.

Table 1 Percent Jobhour Growth (Decrease) Over 20 Years

	Engineering 73.5%			Procurement 17%			Controls 7.6%			Home Office Construction 1.9%			Net Weighted Subtotal 100%	Project Team	Net Weighted Total
Weighting	-	+	Net	-	+	Net	-	+	Net	-	+	Net			
Technology	0	6	6	2	7	5	0	5	5	0	8	8	6		
Schedule	0	6	6	0	4	4	2	11	9	0	4	4	6		
Quality	2	4	2	0	2	2	0	14	14	0	5	5	3		
Personnel	1	3	2	0	3	3	0	7	7	0	7	7	3		
Owner	1	7	6	1	5	4	1	24	23	0	6	6	7		
Computer	9	5	(4)	2	3	1	11	3	(8)	0	5	5	(3)		
Total	13	31	18	5	24	19	14	64	50	0	35	35	+22	+4	+26

were asked how many project team members were required on a medium-sized project 20 years ago and today. There was general agreement that where one project engineer ran such a project 20 years ago, four to five people are required today, including a project manager, project engineers, purchasing manager, control manager, scheduler, etc. A 200% growth was assessed for the project function.

In the opinion of the experienced personnel surveyed, home office jobhours required to execute a project have increased 26% over the past 20 years. This increase is due to change defined by the "why" factors and due to changes in plant, people, and tools over this time span. Not all change increased jobhours. The total weighted growth was 36%, but this was offset by a decrease or jobhour savings component of 10%.

Based on the premise that the people and tools components offset each other, much, if not all, of this 26% growth is attributable to the differences in the plant being built. Today's plant may be "equivalent" to one built 20 years ago, but it is certainly not "identical." The acceptance of this premise isn't necessary to benefit from the results of this survey. The true benefit is the identification of the causes of jobhour growth and their relative magnitude. Whether related to plant, people, or tools, the "why" factors will continue influencing jobhour growth and must be addressed in order to control project jobhours and costs.

Although the "why" factors were used as a basis to analyze home office jobhours, there is strong reason to believe that their application may be far more widespread than this in the service industries. They affect equipment, material, construction, and operation as well and could be used in studies of growth in these areas.

COST ANALYSIS

Once the magnitude of the jobhour growth had been quantified, the remaining questions addressed by the survey pertained to the effect of this growth on the project cost.

The cost analysis first determined the escalation of total plant cost due to all known factors, namely, inflation, productivity, and the "why" factors. For this analysis published historical cost data were utilized where available. The pure inflation rate was subtracted. The remaining growth can be attributed to the "why" factors identified in the study or the difference between an "identical" and an "equivalent" plant.

Accurate and pertinent historical cost data were not available in usable form for the entire 20-year period, so the analysis here was based on 15 years. The data for all of the cost elements (equipment, material, and construction) are based on the actual cost of purchased material and all components of construction. It includes both the effects of inflations and the change factors. Professional services are based only on salary escalation and thus exclude those change factors which must be added based on the results of the "how much" survey.

Figure 3 shows the historical salary escalation over the past 15 years. This escalation represents a 2.9 inflation multiplier (a 290% increase) in professional services salaries. The survey indicated an additional 26% growth which must be added to this escalation to include the effects of change factors consistent with the other components of total plant cost. To adjust for a 15-year time span a 20% growth was considered reasonable. When added to the 2.9 inflation multiplier the resulting and all-inclusive cost multiplier is 3.5.

With the professional services component now consistent, the dashed curve in Figure 4 was plotted based on the historical cost multipliers (MLTP) for each project component shown in the accompanying table. The total plant cost multiplier obtained from the weighted component multipliers was 3.3. Note that the percentage of each component to total plant cost has not significantly changed over the 15-year period.

The curve in Figure 4 was smoothed out by assuming an equal 7.7% growth in each year to account for the 3.3 multiplier. No attempt was made to determine actual yearly growth rates and the intermediate points on the curve don't represent the intermediate cost increases.

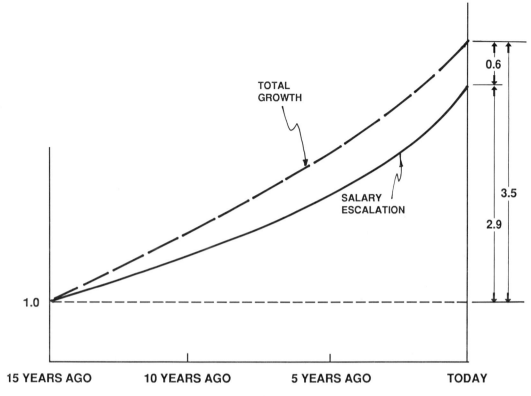

Figure 3 Professional services cost escalation.

To evaluate this total plant cost curve, a measure of pure inflation alone was required. The best measure was judged to be the Consumer Price Index (CPI). Although it can be argued that the CPI also reflects productivity changes, no better basis was found. When plotted with the total plant curve there is a 16% difference (3.3 divided by 2.85).

The total growth in plant cost over 15 years exceeds that which can be accounted for by inflation by 16%. How much of this 16% can be attributed to productivity deterioration depends on how well productivity is reflected by the CPI. The conclusion is that a large part if not all is due to the changes in the "why" factors.

Though certainly not completely rigorous, this analysis substantiates the contention that today's equivalent plants cost more due to factors other than inflation and productivity declines.

SUMMARY

The escalation in plant cost over the past 20 years has been due to changes in these three components:

    The physical facilities of the plant
    The design and construction personnel
    The tools used in design and construction

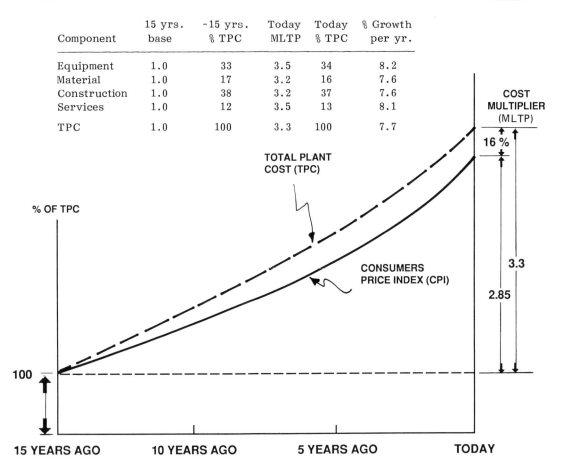

Component	15 yrs. base	-15 yrs. % TPC	Today MLTP	Today % TPC	% Growth per yr.
Equipment	1.0	33	3.5	34	8.2
Material	1.0	17	3.2	16	7.6
Construction	1.0	38	3.2	37	7.6
Services	1.0	12	3.5	13	8.1
TPC	1.0	100	3.3	100	7.7

Figure 4 Plant cost escalation.

The survey rationalized the offsetting effects of people and tools, concluding that a large part of the cost escalation must be attributed to changes in the plant design. We are not building "identical" plants even though they may be said to be "equivalent" to some built 20 years ago.

Based on this premise, the study identified six tangible "why" factors and three intangible factors which affect project home office manhours. Experienced personnel identified, in detail, areas of change for each of the "why" factors. Each gave a judgment as to the percent increase or decrease in jobhours attributable to each factor. The net result indicated a 26% growth in project home office jobhours over the 20 years. Most, if not all, of this growth is also attributable to changes in the plant as opposed to a decline in productivity.

A cost analysis was then made utilizing available historical data and the 26% growth in jobhours. This analysis indicated an increase in plant costs by a factor of 3.3 over a 15-year span. Approximately 16% of this growth cannot be accounted for by comparison to the general rate of inflation for the same period.

The 16% above inflation represents the growth due to changes in the physical plant component over the 15 years.

These conclusions were based on the judgment of experienced personnel whose careers spanned the time frame studies. There is room for difference with the specific statistical values. The value of the survey results is not the absolute value of the growth in jobhours or in total plant costs, but rather in the organized identification of the factors contributing to this growth.

These factors provide the project manager with a convenient checklist of things which can and will impact the cost of his project. Many of these factors are controllable. By targeting and controlling the factors applicable to his specific project the manager can minimize overall costs. Many organizations have recently followed similar procedures under the label of "productivity improvement." On a project basis this means identifying factors which affect cost and eliminating or reducing the scope of those not absolutely required. This process is true cost control and should be part of every project.

6

Relational Decision Making and Communications for Project Management

C. WILLIAM IBBS   *University of California-Berkeley, Berkeley, California*

Project management communications, as a delivery system, have gradually evolved to an unprecedented level of sophisticaiton. Yet the profession faces challenges as large as at any previous point in time. These challenges are the result of project and process "complexification," sources of which include project size and technology, scarce resources, international competition, and political regulatory concerns. Better, though not necessarily more formal, communication and information processing will have to be the principal control factors in the future project management world (1).

Current management information systems (MIS) are ineffective for two reasons:

They are designed and operated for intraorganizational and often nonproject purposes.

Their underlying basis assumes rationality of organizational and decision-making behavior. Information conducive to creative, anticipative, and predictive thought is, at best, subjugated by minutiae.

This chapter has two very important objectives, where the intent is to satisfy the needs of two different readerships. The first objective is to present a comprehensive overview of contemporary information, decision, and communication theory, as each relates to project management. For those readers interested only in these management concepts, the first few pages will be the key.

Since the world of project management is so dependent on computerized management information systems, this chapter also has another goal. That second objective is to outline a new MIS concept that would take advantage of the opportunities provided by these modern theories. This section by itself may interest another constituency. This schematic outline should be useful to system designers and project managers alike because it looks at the heart of the project management profession; essentially, the management of information and the people who possess or need that information.

A concept central to this entire discussion is that of relational communications. For the purposes of the present discussion, relational communications are considered to be the whole set of explicit, implicit or assumed information, and movement of information pertinent to a project. This information may be used solely by the individual, but more likely will be transmitted between individuals or institutions. It is necessarily dynamic, meaning reflective of the shifting, time-dependent relationships in an inter-organizational project team.

PREDECESSOR CONCEPTS

Control

The engineering construction community has historically dealt with complexity by varying degrees of control. Prime examples are multiple subcontracting and supervisory levels. Professional construction management evolved as a management tool when owners, as an example, could no longer efficiently regiment several prime contractors on the same site.

Both primers and weighty tomes exist on the subject of managerial control (2,3). At the risk of oversimplification, three points deserve special attention:

W. Ross Ashby's Cybernetic *Law of Requisite Variety* formalizes the hunch that the more the variety (complexity) that needs to be controlled in the environment, the greater the variety required in the resources to do the controlling (4,5).

Galbraith expressed a corollary: ". . . the greater the task uncertainty, the greater the amount of information that must be processed among decision makers during task execution in order to achieve a given level of performance" (6).

Organizational participants are not engaged in a *zero-sum* control game (Fig. 1). Tannenbaum found that by increasing the control exercised by the rank and file simultaneously with the control by other organizational members, the total *amount* of control in the organization is increased (7).

Management science theorists such as Boland have explored a concept called power-over versus power-with, or alternatively, control-over and control-with (8). Situations A and X in Figure 1 are schematically illustrative of control-over and control-with, while condition B represents true socialistic management. From his extensive work Boland has concluded that ". . . information requirements, as *currently framed*, are concerned exclusively with 'control-over'" (emphasis added).

There is a dawning realization though that much of project management is too complex for a control-over style (9). Instead, swinging control down and through the organization to the lowest practical level that still allows adequate information flow upward to top management, is gaining favor (10). Just as clearly, reporting flexibility and sortability (generally by exception) of information is and will continue to be the essential mechanism by which wading through the reams of typical project data is at all possible.

AMOUNT OF CONTROL EXERCISED

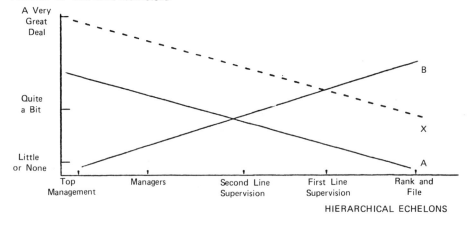

Figure 1 Control in organizations. From Ref. 7.

Planning and Scheduling

The literature is rife with complaints about current planning and scheduling practices. Prevalent criticisms seem to fall into three separate categories:

> Current techniques translate actions in an uncertain world into rigid, necessarily logical sequence, or else into probabilistic and stochastic variables that are arduous to quantify, even unrealistic.
>
> To derive control and operative benefits from scheduling, the schedule has to be updated very frequently. This effort is wasted if the communication channels are so slow that the new schedule is outdated by the time that it arrives on location, as frequently happens.
>
> It is difficult to make the transition from an alphanumeric presentation of a schedule to the mental perception of the brain where construction sequences are mostly modeled in images. Levitt argued strongly in favor of time-scaled bar charts, and other graphical representations (9). Note though that it still requires significant cognitive effort to translate activities represented by labeled bars into mental images and sequences.

The flurry of new planning and scheduling research is ample proof of dissatisfaction with the status quo; for example, the global method, diagonal network analysis, and fuzzy logic (11-13).

Thus, the following points emerge as necessary performance specifications for a Project Management Information System (PMIS):

> Since the future is unknown, all schedules will require reworking when the unexpected materializes. This fact should be explicitly recognized. Channels of communication should exist to handle this frequent occurrence effectively and efficiently. Schedule precision may have to be scaled back in trade-off with this timeliness concern, in accordance with the owner's priorities.
>
> Planning and scheduling techniques are in a state of flux. It is not clear if one superior technique will emerge or if implementers will use a variety of techniques based on circumstance or preference. This situation requires great flexibility in future management information systems.

Information, Communications, Decisions

Why do things go wrong?

Information

It is first useful to look at current information handling practice, particularly why things go astray.

Borrowing on the work of Mason and Mitroff (14), and Sanford and Adelman (15), three primary forms of decision-making error can be identified:

> A decision is not made; the default of no-choice is activated
> A decision is wrong for reasons of:
>> Not enough right information
>> Not enough time to analyze the alternatives thoroughly
>> A literal error in judgment
> A decision is in conflict with other interests

In the first case, the daily fire-fighting to which managers must attend is extremely distracting, even counterproductive. As Gresham's law of planning posits: Daily routine drives out planning. March and Simon have noted that when an individual is confronted with highly programmed and highly unprogrammed choices, the former will take precedence in the absence of overriding time pressures (16).

These unprogrammed or ill-defined decisions present difficulty to classically trained project managers. Poorly defined decisions may not be strictly necessary to the project, but they would still enhance it in some way. Value engineering is a good example. For all its theoretical merit, it is commonly paid only lip service for this reason.

To identify these opportunities, the entire project team must scan its task environment continuously. This requires time, and often an enormous variety of support information. Remedies to this dilemma may include a special project staff consultant whose charge is to seek such windows of opportunity. Naturally, a MIS with real-time, flexible inquiry capacity would be helpful. For the future, the rapidly burgeoning fields of artificial intelligence and knowledge-based expert systems offer promise of an escape from this mire (17-20).

The rational decision-making model accepts errors mainly on the basis of their being wrong. Time and information availability are accepted scarce resources in the accelerated world of project management, and consequently at the root of many mistakes. But decision quality can just as easily suffer from too much time and information. Schroder and Suedfeld's experiments on information overload and complexity are classic, and their findings can be graphically portrayed by Figure 2 (21).

Decision can also be wrong because of literal errors in judgment and analysis. This becomes apparent upon reviewing any traditional rational decision model, such as put forward by Thatcher (22). Highly simplified and summarized, the steps and intellectual input are:

1. Generate as many feasible choices as possible
   Information (hunches) and ingenuity (creativity)
2. Compare the consequences of the outcome
   Analytical skills and experience
3. Choose the best alternative based on identified objectives
   Analytical skills but mostly judgment and intuition

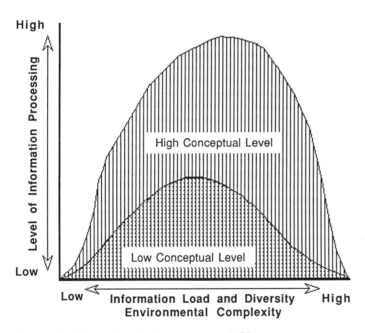

Figure 2 Information load vs. processibility.

It appears that with difficult, unstructured problems, the rational model of decision-making collapses. The decisionmaker has to rely on hunches, experience, creativity, intuition and judgment. To reduce errors of judgment then, an information system should attempt to enhance these faculties.

With fully structured decision problems, this type of error is only possible due to insufficient correct information. It may also be the result of improper training and education.

Communications

Galbraith's information processing model of organizations identified seven organizational strategies to coordinate activities (6). These strategies are depicted in Figure 3. Strategies 1-3 are the basics followed by most organizations, consciously or not. Strategies 4-7 were the options for improvement available to organizations at the time of his writing (1973).

Within this context, it seems fair to say that the construction industry has not accepted the concept of slack resources as a viable alternative. Rather, the creation of self-contained tasks has been most popular; viz., subcontracting.

The results are well known. This process has alleviated the overall coordination problem by decentralizing most decisions. But as projects and the environment grew in complexity, many communication deficiencies developed, mainly due to:

Interdependence
Organizational structure and technology
Differentiation
Dynamism in project teams

Increasing interdependence of participants is a staple on projects of even moderate complexity. *The higher the degree of interdependence, especially technical dependency, the more that organizational resources must be dedicated to coordination and away from the line aspects of the endeavor.* This, in turn, impacts indirect project costs disproportionately whether the interdependence is pooled, sequential, or reciprocal. Construction changes and design clarifications are two obvious examples of interdependence.

Recognition that temporary crisis networks are inefficient solutions to complex communication problems has driven interest in the recent emergence of a quasidiscipline: Interface management. Individuals who have been trained to blend knowledge of psychology, management organizations, and information theory, will soon be indispensable to large service corporations like construction.

The structural differences and changes between and within organizations during the lifetime of a project create significant communication barriers. The importance of a correct structural fit between the organization and its environment is evident in the light of contingency theory, the basic tenets of which hold that (23):

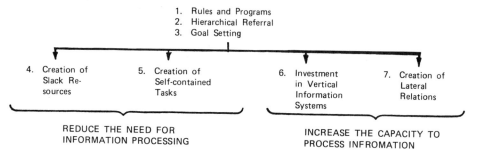

Figure 3 Organization design strategies.

1. There is no one best way to organize
2. Any way of organizing is not equally effective
3. The best ways to organize depend on the nature of the environment to which the organization must relate

This theory has had no known application to construction as of this time, but certainly holds promise.

Another important element to this topic is differentiation. Differentiation has been called the *difference in cognitive and emotional orientation among managers in different functional departments*. It occurs in the dimensions of organizational structure and interpersonal, time, and goal orientation, all of which is highly characteristic of project management (23).

To maintain and even nurture technological efficiency (as brought about by specialization), differentiation will have to be retained. In some extreme cases the technical core may have to be isolated from external influences. *For project management, the prescription is to respect and even promote culture differentiation, while balancing it with needed project integration*. This trade-off is an age-old "prisoner's dilemma" and is always likely to be project management's greatest challenge.

As guidance one must recognize that some individuals are more naturally qualified to fill marginal or interface positions at the boundary between different organizations. Most importantly, PMIS must accommodate the vocabulary, format, content, and other special needs peculiar to this crucial role.

As a last note in this section on communication, the dynamic relationships between project management organizations demand recognition. *Dynamism* is a theoretical construct for a tricky practical problem, namely the moving targets of interest level and information needs during an active project. To the extent that these relations can be predicted or associated (even loosely) with schedule milestones, a PMIS should be designed to oblige automatically such relational communications.

Decisions

The criticality of decision making in project management has been addressed by several researchers, including Kepner and Tregoe (24). Their main concepts are:

Problem analysis
Decision analysis
Potential problem analysis

They defined a problem as *a deviation from some standard or norm of desired performance*, implying that once the deviation has occurred and has been identified, then the right course of action can be decided (p. 231). This typical after-the-fact procedure requires improvement. Through systematic scheduling of programmable decisions, decisions of encounter can be effectively converted into programmed decisions. The sporadic use of this practice is not denied—it is the explicitness which needs to be encouraged.

Most attempts to schedule decision making intersperse decisions with physical activities in regular critical path method (CPM) logic. The associated problems will not be discussed here, but have been touched upon by Slavin (13). It has been said that one of the main benefits of CPM scheduling lies in the mental construction of the project in the activity domain. Analogously, decision scheduling would represent the construction of a project in the decision domain. Naturally these domains are highly interdependent, but due to different behaviors they should be separated.

Kepner and Tregoe's third concept, potential problem analyses, considers an extremely important aspect of project management—the ability to predict the future. Some of the steps are: list the specific potential problems, assess the risk of each potential problem, identify some of the possible causes.

It is clear that it is not within the bounded rationality of Simon's Administrative Man to list all potential problems, or to assess the risk, etc. Implicit in the usefulness of "potential problem analysis" are concepts such as the ability to see the picture in its entirety, creativity to generate potential problems, subconscious heuristic rules to reduce the mental search domain, and intuition to know what could happen.

Intuition, Creativity, and the Brain

It is now well established that the two hemispheres of the brain have different modes of information processing. This duality implies that the same information is processed in two different ways.

For most right-handed individuals, the analytic, logical, and verbal functions are housed in the left hemisphere of the brain. This is designated as the L-mode of thinking and knowing. Conversely, the right hemisphere's mode of information processing is characterized as simultaneous, holistic, spatial, and relational. Intuition and leaps of insight, those moments when everything seems to fall into place without logical deduction, are R-mode phenomena (25).

Most individuals have a dominant cognitive style, and according to Sanford and Adelman, engineers (and other professionals) manifest a preference for the L-mode due to professional training (15). The problem is that important aspects of project management, such as planning and potential problem analysis, depend in part on R-mode processes, while project professionals prefer, and their MIS exclusively handle, L-mode information.

It appears that R-mode cognition can be developed in individuals through training programs. Although it is too early to claim success, some seem to be highly productive. For example, Edwards improved the drawing and perception skills of artists by training the subjects to use the right hemisphere as the dominant mode of cognition.

It is not clear how these concepts can be implemented in project management, but it seems highly probable that future MIS will be required to transmit R-mode information. As computers take over more logical functions, the human intellectual domain will recede towards the unstructured decision problems, creativity, and R-mode processing.

Information System Requirements

The distinction between management information systems (MIS) and decision support systems (DSS) is that MIS answer what-is questions, and DSS answers what-if questions. Although many systems used in project management today include what-if features, such as interactive indications of the impact of a schedule change, they primarily function in the MIS mode.

The project management profession was quick to embrace computerized systems when they first appeared. The first generation of construction MIS features the automation of batched payroll and cost accounting systems. The second generation of MIS automated most other business functions of the firm and also included scheduling capabilities.

The third and present generation brought the *integrated* and *interactive* MIS. The interpretation of integrated varies widely depending upon the sophistication of the system under consideration. Commercially available MIS and those developed for proprietary use now have features such as advanced multicolor graphics capabilities, including time-scaled bar charts and cash flow diagrams, user-defined formats of reports, what-if scheduling answers, multiproject resource management, and more. Still, they suffer from a common shortcoming; namely, they reflect little information about which most project inquiries, correspondence, and conflicts are concerned. The majority of systems has yet to lose the appearance of computerized versions of former manual systems in favor of the liberation offered by computers. Too often deviations are reported as present but without explanation as to why they occurred. Criticism of current MIS does not imply that they should be abandoned. It suggests that they should be developed to include those aspects which would make existing information more useful and the project mosaic more coherent.

The recent schools of thought on organizational models are (26):

> Closed system models
>> Rational models: 1900-1930
>> Natural models: 1930-1950
> Open system models
>> Rational models: 1960-1970
>> Natural models: 1970-present

Close investigation will reveal that present construction MIS are predominantly based on closed system rational models, which appear outdated in this context. The present management science paradigm is based on the open system natural models.

Construction projects are inherently task specific and contractually rigid. For this reason, the rational models are more appropriate to construction project management. But due to the interdependencies and complexities in this environment, it seems imperative to use open system rational models in designing project information systems.

A fourth generation of MIS which follows this philosophy has recently been introduced by Tuman (27). The distinguishing feature of this generation is that it transmits information interorganizationally. Reports indicate there is a lively interest in such systems and that several firms are working toward that goal.

The importance of correct MIS design was reflected in March and Simon's statement that once a pattern of communication channels has become established, this pattern will have an important influence on decision-making processes and particularly on non-programmed activities (16). The very existence of an MIS establishes criteria for the adequacy of information used in decision making.

As early as 1967, Ackoff, in his essay titled "Management Misinformation Systems" refuted the belief that MIS design can be based on the user's perception of information needs. Other design methodologies and frameworks soon proliferated.

Among the best known work is Mason and Mitroff's (14). They constructed their framework around the proposition that an information system consists of at least one *person* of a certain *psychological type* who faces a *problem* with some *organizational context for which he or she needs evidence* to arrive at a *solution* (i.e., to select some course of action), and that the evidence is made available to him through some *mode of presentation.*

The originality of that framework was based upon the inclusion of the *psychological type*, for which they used a four-category taxonomy: thinking vs. feeling, and sensation vs. intuition; and the methods of generating and guaranteeing the *evidence.*

Differences in the characteristics of these methods for evidence generation have been responsible in part for the decision models which evolved for developing DSS (also applicable for MIS), as discussed by Huber (28):

> The rational model. Portrays an environment where organizational decisions are consequences of organizational units using information in an intentionally rational manner to make choices on behalf of the organization.
> The political/competitor model. Portrays an environment where organizational decisions are consequences of the application of strategy and tactics by units seeking to influence decision processes in directions that will result in choices favorable to themselves.
> The garbage can model. Organizational decisions are consequences of intersections of problems looking for solutions, solutions looking for problems, and opportunities for decisionmaking. Although it was not categorized as such, this model fits the criteria for the R-mode information processing well.

The program model. Organizational decisions are consequences of the programs and programming of the units involved.

Huber points out that no practical DSS should be based on only one decision model, and that it ideally should be based on a blend of these models depending on the unique situation of the organization that it would serve.

A major principle in MIS design is to base information requirements on the decision that managers should not make the decisions that they actually make. Without further refinement this causes a difficulty: an analysis of the decision process is used to design the MIS, but the decision process is highly influenced by the information system. By this reasoning the information system is both the cause and the effect of the decision process. Boland seems to address this problem when he argues for an extended framework as shown in Figure 4 (8).

An understanding of the organizational condition depends on a sense-making process. This, in turn, is predicated on a rationalizing framework consisting of the norm, myths, rituals, and goals of the symbolic organization.

The applicability of this reasoning model to the project environment is that the criteria used for decision making are in effect of those elements of the symbolic organization which are normally not transmitted through the formal information system, while the MIS design is based on the decisions it attempts to serve. Although a specific embodiment of the MIS may make unanticipated decisions possible, it does not cause the criteria for decision making to change, unless the criteria-changing elements are also transmitted.

March and Simon stated: "Humans, whether inside or outside administrative organizations, behave rationally, if at all, only relative to some set of given characteristics of the situation" (16). Huber added: "Organizaitons attempt to create and maintain within themselves decision environments describable with the rational model. In addition they attempt to convince their members and outside observers that they are successful in this regard. Of course they are only partially successful in either of these attempts" (28).

For example, a contractor whose decisions are guided by the practice to maximize short-term cash flow will develop an MIS based on those requirements. This MIS could provide input to new kinds of decisions, but unless the criteria are changed, the decision will still be based on short-term cash flow. On the same project the architect/engineer's decision process may be dominated by the ideal to win long-term design commissions.

Dissimilar orientations such as these are responsible for many project disagreements and may be one of the main factors contributing to the wrong project decisions which

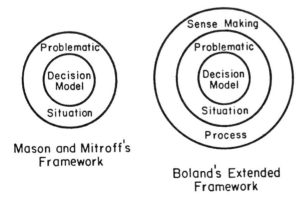

Mason and Mitroff's
Framework

Boland's Extended
Framework

Figure 4 MIS design framework.

are due to conflict in interest of the disciplines. If an MIS could be used to reduce the equivocality of the sense-making processes of the participants, the antagonistic atmosphere of construction projects could be reduced. To accomplish this, the MIS will have to be able to disseminate strategic information interorganizationally to the project participants.

Ad Hoc Project Organizations

The ability to transmit digital information interorganizationally will have far-reaching impacts on the project environment. Whereas project structures currently are comparatively loose, true relational communications will lead to greater unity in the ad hoc project hierarchy.

Research of project management still tends to focus on one participant and his or her intraorganizational presence. The wider field of management science is more complete in this fashion and provides a reasonable basis for useful extrapolation.

Depending on one's vantage point, definitions of formal organizations emphasize different areas of the social continuum of real world organizations. Since construction projects are short-term, purposeful arrangements, the following definitions from a rational systems perspective are expected to fit ad hoc project organizations well.

Chester Barnard defined formal organizations as: "a system of consciously coordinated activities of forces of two or more persons." Scott's more recent definition is: "an organization is collectively oriented to the pursuit of relatively specific goals, and exhibiting a relatively formalized social structure" (26).

To aid in boundary resolution, it is proposed that the ad hoc organization will include all those participants whose authorities and stakes in the project are based on contractual or statutory law. Outside the boundary will be those who only have a common law interest in the project.

For interorganizational MIS purposes, practical economies will predict that only those participants with high density of information exchange will be included in future generations of MIS.

For the ad hoc organization to function as a unit, individuals employed by participating organizations will have to develop lateral ties with people who are physically and organizationally separated. This will require unusual attention to the behavioral aspects of the design of an interconnecting MIS, and flexibility in the individuals who will have to function in a situation possibly as complex as a three-dimensional matrix organization. Since such project allegiance and loyalty is common on successful projects, it seems both possible and necessary to enhance it with adequate communication channels.

Control should be extended to the lowest practical level. In an ad hoc organization it is possible for some of the units to "disappear" through default. It will thus be necessary for the MIS to have holographic characteristics. When necessary, each participant should have access to the entire image of project information. This can only be achieved through a common database.

Experience with MIS indicates that new or different requirements are discovered as soon as a system is implemented. This will be especially true for ad hoc organizations due to the novelty of relational communications and the diverse organizational background. It will be necessary to consider every initial project MIS implementation not only as an instantly usable product, but also as a prototype that will evolve in a stepwise fashion.

Due to the dynamic nature of the relational communication network, the MIS will require a mechanism to make decisions on various attributes and functions of the network. Based on an organizational structure and anticipated changes in it, the program should be able to disseminate the right information to the right person at the right time.

Electronic Communication

Another compelling force in MIS system design is the phenomenally rapid changes taking place in the computer and telecommunication fields. In project management, desk-top personal computers with the power of 10-year-old mainframes are common. High-resolution graphic software and hardware facilities are affordable, and satellite transmission of data from remote projects is an everyday occurrence. Unfortunately, the hardware technology has undeniably outstripped the development of the information reporting systems.

Recent advances useful to the concept of relational communications include:

Commercial relational database managers.

Improved man-machine interfacing that requires less effort and computer skill from nonprogrammers.

Electronic mail, voice-grams, and videotex.

Broadband networking systems to integrate automated office devices, to provide distributed networking for industry standard computing hardware, and even several independent video channels for teleconferencing and security applications.

Several competitive common data carriers are established and deliver service virtually worldwide.

Progress by national and international standards organizations is converging into universal protocol standards for networking and data transmission.

Computer-aided design and drafting systems are commonly used in engineering offices. It would be feasible and convenient to disseminate design drawings in digital form.

Random-access memories with 512,000 bits of information on a single chip are commercially available and four million bits in an advanced state of experimentation. Among other advantages, this will make higher resolution color computer graphics more readily available.

Laser-scanned optical disks (12-inch diameter) which can store 5 gigabytes. (This information compares with a library of 17,000 average novels.) Presently these are read-only memory devices that would be employed for permanent records.

Hyperfast supercomputers, with processing speeds orders of magnitude above conventional mainframes and parallel processor arrays, will allow truer simultation and more detailed computational analysis.

It is a comparatively short step to the advent of audio and even video electronic mailboxes. Coordinated document transfer, essential for project management, is on this mailbox horizon as well. These trends will place even more demands on the information systems used by project managers.

A PROPOSED PMIS

Custom Software

Today's project managers view computerized information systems as a necessity, not a luxury. Yet, to get the type of special help and information which they seek from these systems, the trend among large firms has been to either customize existing packages or write a wholly proprietary code. Many valid reasons exist for this individuality in MIS development, but the fact remains that the industrywide cost of developing custom software is substantial.

A possible solution to the resulting hodgepodge may be an organized effort to develop a system so broad in scope and flexible in application that it would win general acceptance by satisfying most needs. This investigation has indicated that such standardization would be impractical if not impossible at this time.

Another approach is to provide project participants the software tools necessary to develop an information system suited to their particular needs at a low cost that is low relative to any in-house development effort. Following this approach a general purpose package has been conceptualized. It is called the Management Information System Generator (MIG), and is capable of generating a project-specific PMIS.

In the MIG system the user will, after a thorough investigation of project communication needs, specify the required features of PMIS in a problem-oriented language called Information Definition Language (IDL). With IDL as input, MIG will generate the computer code that will eventually form the source code for PMIS, including the specifications of various features such as the database characteristics. Figure 5 graphically illustrates this process.

Overview of PMIS

Based on the previous discussions, PMIS is envisioned as a project-oriented interactive computer communication network. The concept is further predicated on the assumption that most senior members of firms participating in the project will have regular access to an internal MIS through a computer terminal. PMIS will extract information for project use and disseminate related information through the same terminals that are used in daily company operations.

PMIS will be hosted by a central computer system which will be controlled by a *sponsor*. All the major project participants will have access to PMIS via their own in-house computers (called satellite computers), which will continue to execute the internal data processing requirements. This interconnected computer network is illustrated in Figure 6.

The form and medium of data communication between the host and satellite computers will depend on the density of information flow and the cost/benefit ratio, and would range from ordinary telephone lines to microwave satellite links, or any other future medium. The competitive interest of commercial common carriers will ensure economical means of digital data transmission.

The functions of the central computer will include:

Requesting information from and disseminating information to satellite computers
Processing the information in some prescribed manner
Recording information on a central data base as required

In order to execute these functions and act as messenger between satellite computers, possibly of different manufacturers, several nested interfaces will be necessary. The system layout is illustrated in Figure 7 in conceptual form.

System Sponsorship and Initiation

Questions always surround any proposal like this, especially the crucial issue of who could afford this development expense. Two options exist: first, private owners who have large capital construction budgets for many similar projects; second, a less likely option, service bureaus acting alone or in conjunction with professional construction management firms. The clear trend of increased owner participation in project planning and management is an impetus to such forecasts.

System initiation will not be a trivial undertaking. IDL will be a high-level English-like computer language that will allow the user to build a wide variety of features into the PMIS that is to be generated. Some aspects of the project team dynamism can be built into PMIS. For example, by integrating the schedule and information network, PMIS can determine from some prespecified triggering activity or decision when to commence distribution of progress reports to a specific subcontractor, and to what level of detail.

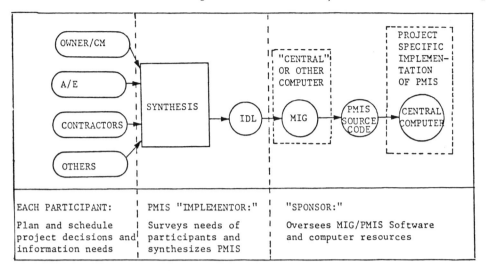

Figure 5 Implementation of PMIS.

MIG could provide some guidance in PMIS design through the availability of stand-ardized features and a menu of project plants. It would also reduce the tedium of code writing. The quality of the implemented version of PMIS will be highly dependent on the skill that goes into the implementation. Therefore the preparation for implementation will be a crucial aspect of the use of the system.

Present practice includes a preconstruction meeting, where the formats and distribution pattern of correspondence are discussed. In using MIG this procedure will assume a much greater importance, requiring methodical analysis and planning of all the communication requirements of the project.

In the event an unforeseen change is required in the communication network, MIG will be used to generate a new PMIS, without voiding the existing project database.

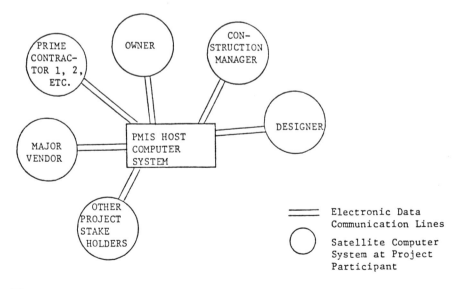

Figure 6 PMIS computer communication network.

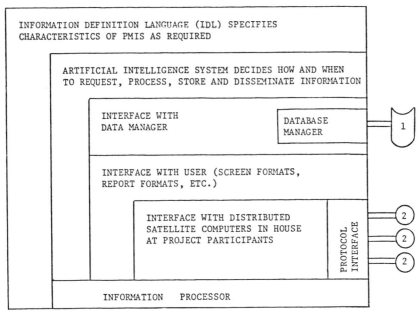

1) Database
2) Satellite Computers

Figure 7 Internal layout of PMIS.

Achieving this goal requires a great deal of data independence. It is expected that
a relational database will allow adequate flexibility in forming new relations of data.

PMIS in Operation

How a specific implementation of PMIS will function will depend on the implementor's
perception of the communication needs of the project. New uses will continuously evolve
as the system's capabilities are explored. In addition to the artificial intelligence features, PMIS will transmit information in all its generic forms; text, data (alphanumeric),
and images. The following are examples of modes of operation and features.

> It will function as a sophisticated electronic mail system. At sign-on, PMIS will
> make available all new messages directed to the user (with the option to read
> or respond later, in which case the user will be prompted at the next sign-on).
> The messages could have the specific participant as original addressee or it could
> be copied for messages to others by the system, based on the participant's
> sphere of interest.
> PMIS will keep records of messages, responses, dates, delays, etc. Appropriate
> performance criteria for project team members can be based on these statistics—
> for example, average response delays for A/E clarification requests.
> The filing system will allow message searches by a variety of categories: keywords,
> dates, etc.
> Batch mode of operation can be used with satellite computers acting as intelligent
> terminals to reduce connect time and cost.
> Any desirable statistics may be added to the system: weather, work force, labor
> hours, status of purchase orders or change orders, to name a few.

Anticipated changes in the organizational structure of the ad hoc project organization will be built into the PMIS. Unanticipated changes will require a regeneration of the PMIS.

Security of data will be defined by the PMIS implementor; access to information may be limited in any desirable way.

Due to the growing interest in computer-aided design among designers, it may become common to use digitalized three-dimensional models instead of design drawings. PMIS should be able to operate in high-resolution graphics mode to manipulate and rotate simulated three-dimensional images.

PMIS will use a project information flow model based on anticipated decisions and the information required for these decisions. This model can be used in a simulation before the project starts to derive expected information flow densities on individual communication channels; this could help in planning the managerial resources required for the project.

PMIS can accumulate actual information flow statistics on a project. This will further aid in forecasting the human resources required in information processing (i.e., managing) the future projects.

At close-out, the central computer can read back to any satellite computer those parts of the database that may be required for intraorganizational libraries.

Since the PMIS database will also contain, in relational form, sequences of problems, decisions and consequences together with data needed to define overall measures of project success, this information can be used in computerized training of future project managers, in a simulation module.

Developmental and Practical Matters

Due to the constraints of economy and practical implementation, PMIS will, especially initially, not have all the features of the ideal system described earlier. It will be necessary to limit its features to those that are most valuable in the control process.

It appears that the best way to increase understanding of the relational information needs of the ad hoc project organization is through the development and implementation of a prototype PMIS. A limited PMIS is technically feasible at this point by utilizing existing electronic mail systems and telephone lines or common data carriers for transmission of large data files.

Several firms now offer "black boxes" (protocol processors) that make communication between computers of different vendors possible. A more sophisticated PMIS could incorporate such processors until they are made obsolete by protocol standardization.

The star configuration proposed in Figure 6 is feasible for initial and low-volume implementations. In sophisticated high-volume systems it may be necessary to use a virtual host computer, distributed among the satellites, due to the roughly quadratic increase in processing cycles at a centralized host, compared to a linear increase in transactions.

SUMMARY

The first section of the chapter is a normative analysis of the requirements of management information systems (MIS) for construction project management. To establish a broad, general system, theoretic MIS design framework, the requirements are examined from viewpoints such as control, planning, scheduling, and decision making. A survey of current construction MIS reveals important weaknesses for use in project management, which relate to the coordination of the project participants from a diverse organizational background.

An approach to alleviate this problem is to consider the project participants as units of ad hoc project organization. The interorganizational communication necessary for the functioning of the ad hoc project organization is called relational communications to denote the dynamic nature of the interorganizational relationships.

The second part of the chapter reviews recent advances in computer and electronic communications which could be implemented in an automated project MIS. Finally, all these concepts are synthesized in a conceptualization of an advanced communication system.

The distinguishing feature of this system is that it offers project participants the computer software tools to generate a project management information system with characteristics as uniquely required by a specific project. Since the system manipulates generic forms of communication (text, alphanumeric data, voice, and images), it can be used not only in construction but also in any other project environment.

Undoubtedly the future project management world will be an exciting venture with challenges, frustrations, and even disappointments unimaginable. What is clear though is that tomorrow's managers will need better project information than today's management information systems provide. Even the decisionmaking and communication techniques of tomorrow will have to be different. That difference will be evolutionary, and from the base provided in this chapter, project managers should be well prepared.

REFERENCES

1. Grobler, F., C. W. Ibbs, Jr., and L. T. Boyer, "Relational Communications for Project Teams." *Proceedings of the 14th Annual Seminar/Symposium of the Project Management Institute*. October. Toronto: Project Management Institute, 1982, pp. V-L.1-V-L.14.
2. Peters, T. J. and R. H. Waterman, Jr. *In Search of Excellence*. New York: Warner Books, 1982.
3. Drucker, P. F. *Management: Tasks Responsibilities, Practices*. New York: Harper & Row, 1973.
4. Beer, S. *Brain of the Firm*. New York: Herder and Herder, 1972.
5. Churchman, C. W. *The Design of Inquiry Systems*. New York: Basic Books, 1971.
6. Galbraith, J. *Designing Complex Organizations*. Reading, MA: Addison Wesley, 1973.
7. Tannenbaum, S. *Control in Organizations*. New York: McGraw-Hill, 1968.
8. Boland, R. J., Jr. "Control, Causality and Information System Requirements." *Accounting, Organizations and Society*, Vol. 4, No. 4, New York: Pergamon Press Ltd., 1979, pp. 259-272.
9. Levitt, R. E. "Superprojects and Superheadaches." In *1981 Proceedings, PMI/INTERNET Symposium*. pp. 487-491.
10. Rockart, J. F. and M. E. Treacy. "The CEO Goes Online." *Harvard Business Review*, January-February 1982, pp. 82-88. *Organizational Communications*. New York: McGraw-Hill, 1977.
11. Martin, A. P. "The Global Method." In *1981 Proceedings, PMI/INTERNET Symposium*, pp. 619-630.
12. Winsor, R. "Diagonal Network Analysis, A Management Tool for the Future. In *1981 Proceedings, PMI/INTERNET Symposium*, pp. 299-308.
13. Slavin, M. W. "Fuzzy Logic and Refinery Outage Scheduling—An Artemis Case History." In *1981 PMI/INTERNET Symposium*, pp. 270-273.
14. Mason, R. O. and I. I. Mitroff, "A Program for Research on Management Information Systems." *Management Science 19*, 475-487 (January 1973).
15. Sanford, E. and H. Adelman. *Management Decisions: A Behavioral Approach*. Cambridge, MA: Winthrop Publishers, Inc., 1977.
16. March, J. G. and H. A. Simon. *Organizations*. New York: John Wiley and Sons, 1958.

17. Ibbs, C. W., Jr. *Proceedings of a Workshop for the Development of New Research Directions in Computerized Applications to Construction Engineering and Management Studies.* University of Illinois Construction Research Series Technical Report No. 19; July 1985; 127 pp.
18. Ibbs, C. W., Jr. "Future Directions for Computerized Construction Research." In *3rd National Conference on Microcomputers in Civil Engineering.* November 1985, Orlando, FL, pp. 239-246.
19. O'Connor, M. J., J. M. De La Garza, and C. W. Ibbs, Jr. "An Expert System for Construction Schedule Analysis." In *ASCE Proceedings on Expert Systems in Civil Engineering*, Seattle, April 1986, C. Kastem and M. C. Maher, editors; pp. 67-77.
20. De La Garza, J. M. and C. W. Ibbs, Jr. "An Improved Construction Scheduling Expert Systems." In *1986 Congress on International Building (CIB) Proceedings.* Washington, D.C., pp. 683-691.
21. Schroder, H. M. and P. Suedfeld. *Personality Theory and Information Processing.* New York: The Ronald Press Co., 1971.
22. Thatcher, J. R. "The Rational Project Manager." In *1981 PMI/INTERNET Symposium*, pp. 231-246.
23. Huse, E. F. *Organization Development and Change.* St. Paul: West Publishing, 1980.
24. Kepner, C. and B. Tregoe. *The Rational Manager.* Princeton: Kepner-Tregoe, Inc., 1976.
25. Edwards, B. *Drawing on the Right Side of the Brain.* Los Angeles: J. P. Tarcher, 1979.
26. Scott, R. W. *Organizations: Rational, Natural and Open Systems.* Englewood Cliffs, NJ: Prentice-Hall, Inc., 1981.
27. Tuman, J., Jr. "Building Information Management Systems for Major Advanced Energy Projects. In *1981 Proceedings, PMI/INTERNET Symposium*, pp. 525-535.
28. Huber, G. P. "The Nature of Organizational Decision Making and The Design of Decision Support Systems." *MIS Quarterly*, June 1981, pp. 1-10.

7

Project Management in the Future

M. PERALTA   *National Aeronautics and Space Administration, Washington, D.C.*

It has become increasingly clear that the United States is not keeping pace with foreign competition either at home or abroad. There has been an outpouring of disquieting statistics in recent years that underscores the seriousness of the issue and the implications for the future. The increased burden of government regulations and the decline in research and new capital investments are among the factors contributing to our nation's present lackluster economic performance.

A common judgment is that we have to tighten up our economy, increase our productivity, and pare off our excess. Being fit and lean is not only important for survival, but also to meet the challenges of tomorrow. Trimming the fat and regaining a sound footing will take time. The economy has been undergoing a realignment of priorities and a fundamental shakeout. Structural readjustments have caused severe short-term discomfort, but will provide a solid foundation for the future.

At the federal government level, President Reagan stressed the need to eliminate federal waste and inefficiency with the formation of the Private Sector Survey and Cost Control, stating "It is simply not right for us to squander money that our grandchildren will be held accountable for. We must reverse the process."

The Private Sector Survey on Cost Control authorized a team of private citizens to search out overlap, duplication, and nonessential administrative activities in the Executive branch of the federal government and to recommend ways to eliminate them. The private sector was asked to bring management expertise and skill to bear on finding the means to control expanding government spending.

At the industry level, the Business Roundtable has sponsored the Construction Industry Cost Effectiveness Project. This study includes an in-depth review of key problems facing the U.S. construction industry and proposals to alleviate the problems. It is one of the most comprehensive analyses ever undertaken of the cost effectiveness of the construction industry.

The Business Roundtable initiated the study because of its concern with the cost effectiveness of the construction industry and the importance that high productivity in this sector has on the overall well-being of our economy. More than 115 organizations volunteered to be active participants in the study and to look into such areas as project management, construction technology, government regulations and codes, and labor effectiveness, supply, and training. The study identified a number of problems that are currently hampering cost-effective construction. If the recommendations of the study are implemented, Roundtable sources indicate that there could be savings of at least ten billion dollars a year.

In addition to government and industry efforts, many companies are taking steps to ensure that their organizations will remain competitive by more careful scrutiny and selectivity in assigning priorities to individual business segments and capital projects.

Weaker segments are being eliminated and projects that are not sustainable in today's environment are being dropped or deferred.

FUTURE CHALLENGES

A prime function of any company is the management and control of capital expenditures, the foundation for productive capacity. Let's assume a company has selected an economically sound venture project. The key to success for the venture will be execution management to achieve the cost, schedule, and quality objectives of the company; by definition, project management.

Most sophisticated companies take a systems view of project management. Project management is the cornerstone for effective project controls, from project inception to facility startup. The major activities in a systems view of project management include project execution planning, contracting approach, estimating and scheduling, and the project management resources of the company.

Project Execution Planning

The first area of challenge is the execution planning for projects. The degree of influence and significance of decision making is inherently greatest during the early phases of a project and diminishes rapidly with time. Project execution should not simply be allowed to happen; it must be planned in an orderly, disciplined manner to assure optimum project results.

Execution planning should take place on all projects; formally on large complex ventures and less formally on smaller projects. The execution plan should be timely, appropriately comprehensive, and should encompass items such as project objectives, organizational roles and responsibilities, the bases for estimates and schedules, and contingency planning for identified potential constraints.

In the area of risk management there should be a close linkage between the execution plan and the estimate and schedule objectives. The execution plan should be a living document, updated continually to reflect the needs for specificity and the incorporation of significant changes.

In prior years a "seat of the pants" approach to execution planning served the industry reasonably well for most projects. The absence of a project execution plan, or a poorly conceived plan, however, was more often than not the chief culprit for those jobs that drifted far off course. The future can be expected to be less forgiving, and will demand greater emphasis on execution planning, particularly for complex or interactive projects.

Contracting Approach

The second area of challenge is contracting. A standard approach for the execution of major projects is to place the responsibility for engineering, procurement, and construction with a prime contractor. These activities normally represent about 90% of the cost of a project. Selection of the contracting approach and the prime contractor is the single most significant project execution decision affecting job performance. In the future it will be imperative to optimize the contracting approach for each project and to select the contractor who will provide the best performance and business terms.

Optimum contracting will produce substantial savings: up to 10% of the total project cost, and often more. For reimbursable cost projects, considerable value should be placed on the contractor's management, key project personnel, and control systems. Owners should not attempt to duplicate the efforts of contractors; rather, they should look to the contracting industry to provide the specific skills and detailed systems required for the efficient execution of projects. Success in the contracting industry in the future will be limited to those contractors responsive to the compelling need of owners for project optimization.

The future will see a broad array of project configurations as a result of the optimization of contracting execution. On large projects indirect costs tend to grow faster than job size. And engineering and labor productivity tend to decrease as projects grow in size. A well-supported directional conclusion is that a single prime contractor configuration may not be the best contracting strategy on large projects. Splitting large projects into separate components that can logically be handled as independent units frequently results in measurable gains in efficiency. Innovative incentive approaches have also led to enhanced contractor execution performance and control.

Estimating and Scheduling

The third area of challenge is estimating and scheduling. The specific nature of the challenge applies to larger and more complex projects: to establish realistic cost and schedule objectives and improve "early warning" indicators, thus giving management the maximum time to evaluate options and take corrective steps. Over the last decade or two the capital cost estimates used for the funding of major projects, and in particular large "first of a kind" projects and mega projects, have been significantly exceeded, sometimes by a factor. The result has been cancellations, deferrals, and other drastic actions. The principal contributors to inordinate cost and schedule growth have been new technology, remote locations, poor definition, resource limitations, and third-party effects. It has become evident that current planning, estimating, and scheduling techniques do not properly anticipate the effects of these factors on the cost and schedule objectives.

In the future it will be necessary to expand existing estimating and scheduling systems to recognize the impact of complexity factors in order to reduce the vulnerability of large projects to unacceptably high cost and schedule growth. One such approach entails the use of risk management techniques. Risk areas should be identified, the probability of occurrence evaluated, and the potential cost and schedule variances quantified. Comprehensive risk management programs will have to reinforce the development of essentially sound projects, provide clear early warnings of excessive risk levels for marginal ventures, and be sufficiently sophisticated to protect potentially viable projects from "risk compounding." A risk management evaluation should be included as part of the execution plan for all projects of intermediate complexity or higher to assist the project team in project execution.

Project Management

The fourth area of challenge, and the fundamental ingredient in the project management business, is the mobilization, integration, and management of human resources. A major challenge is the training, education, and development of the personnel who will staff the project teams of the future; people not only on the leading edge of technology for their profession, but people with strong interpersonal relations and broad management skills. The environment of the future will be a quantum extension of the large and complex projects we have seen in the past. The areas we have discussed will become basic to the successful companies of the future: execution planning, contracting approach, sophisticated control tools.

Project teams, and certainly the project manager, will have to be business oriented, with a high comfort factor in areas such as financial controls, personnel motivation, productivity, and general business management. The vitality and willingness to adjust to changing times, the ability to contribute to positive team attitudes, the skills to deal constructively with internal political issues, the handling of uncertainty, the nurturing of client and partner relationships, and the ease of movement in international circles. All of these will be the hallmark of the members of the future project staff.

SUMMARY

Today's environment is a highly competitive one, and it will be more so in the future. There will be many challenges to the project management profession. We have high-lighted several critical areas, and others will evolve with time.

> *Project execution planning.* The execution plans for projects must be developed in a disciplined manner in order to optimize project results.
> *Contracting approach.* The single most significant project execution decision affecting job performance is the selection of the contracting approach and the prime contractor.
> *Estimating and scheduling.* Realistic estimates and schedules and workable "early warning" indicators are necessary to give management flexibility in decision making.
> *Project management.* Future managers will be technically qualified business people with strong interpersonal relationships.

8

The Years Ahead

JAMES H. LOWEREE *Management Consultant, San Francisco, California*

Certain views of the business world of the future can be made with relative safety, others can't. Assuredly, there will be events in the future, unknown to us today, that will dramatically alter the marketplace as we know it and as we project it. We can say that the needs of the developing and emerging nations for food, shelter, and clothing will create a galaxy of projects, initiating industrial development and further projects. We can expect the continuous creation of new industries in the industrialized nations with each advance in high technology. When we glance back, however, we see gross errors in projections due to unpredictable world events: political, social, economic, ecological. So it will be with projections made here.

Qualifications in past projections have emphasized political, social, and economic factors. It might be stated today that a significant variable in the future will be ecological: the interaction of people and the environment. As the world becomes more industrialized the natural regenerative power of the atmosphere and the oceans and waterways will be inadequate. A major upset in the delicate ecological balance of this world of ours could drastically rearrange the order of priorities for the future. Ultraviolet radiation, acid rain, and contaminated aquifers are relatively new phenomena. The author [1] questioned in 1971 the possible susceptibility of plankton to future changes in the environment. Plankton, microscopic organisms in fresh and salt water, are a major source of oxygen in our atmosphere. NASA and NOAA [2] noted in a 1989 update on ozone depletion in the stratosphere that excessive ultraviolet radiation destroys plankton.

We will offer here, with caution, our views of the future: the marketplace, the organization of companies, the project manager, and project management tools.

A LOOK AT THE FUTURE

As we look to the future, it is reasonable to predict an acceleration in the transition from the technically oriented project manager to a manager who possesses a full range of business skills. The marketplace will be the world, with a host of projects directed toward satisfaction of the needs of the total population. We see a basic restructuring of management in manufacturing and contracting organizations to recognize the enormous sums of money that will be committed to new plant construction, perhaps altering forever the classic concept of line organizations. The managers of these complex projects of the future will not be drawn from top management; they will be top management, for in the capital-intensive industries the ascendant path will be project management. And, as we look to the future it is incumbent upon us to have an awareness of the embryonic present; further, we must glance back at the past frequently, for an understanding of the past will contribute to a better forecast of the future.

Remember the Past

In 1951 a well-known sanitary systems engineer delivered a paper on pollution abatement. He said:

> The right to discharge wastes must be defended as strongly as the rights for all other appropriate uses of public waters.

In the discussion that followed, the statement wasn't questioned. The statement wasn't a proclamation of new policy for a profession; rather, it was an affirmation of early law based on the principle of infinite dilution: that the assimilative capacity of streams is a natural and infinite asset available to all.

If we had projected the future for the manufacturing and service industries and for government in the 1950s, we probably wouldn't have mentioned the environment; we certainly would have been oblivious to the hypnotic buzz word introduced to the public in the mid-1960s—ecology. The annual expenditures of industry today for the maintenance and improvement of the environment are considerable. Many of the principal multinational energy contractors have established divisions dedicated solely to the marketing and engineering of systems for the prevention, treatment, and disposal of noxious effluents. The projections that we might have made in 1950 would have made interesting reading today—a quantum miss! We wouldn't have projected the removal of asbestos from public buildings and private residences as big business—it is! Projections are, unfortunately, conditioned and strangled by a fixation on the mainstream of the present, with a resultant polarized view of the future. We have today, however, a far more inquisitive professional; one who will assess the past objectively and see the full spectrum of the future. But we will still make mistakes, some serious, as we look ahead. The successful companies and individuals will retain a sensitivity to emerging issues and be quick to respond to change.

The Marketplace

A key market in the years to come will surely be the emerging and developing nations: those with untapped abundant natural resources; overpopulated regions on the brink of starvation; restless political settings with upward pressures for an improved standard of living; agrarian economies seeking to become industrialized; newly industrialized nations striving to compete in the open market. If we consider the wide range of consumer goods available to all but the poorest people in the industrialized nations, and compare the population of those few nations to the population of the "Third World," the full range of the ultimate consumer market comes into perspective—all preceded by massive infrastructure programs. It is not uncommon to see a developing nation install a basic chemical plant, with the unit cost of production considerably in excess of offshore pricing, in order to initiate a domestic industrial base.

The picture in the United States, arguably the most advanced industrialized nation, is completely different from the international outlook. We say arguably, open to doubt, since the steady decline in productivity and the shrinking position of industrial production compared to military expenditures poses the question of the real ranking of the United States today in the industrialized world. On the management front you can mortgage the future or invest in the future: U.S. industry has chosen the former, Asian industry the latter.

The most demanding need for capital projects in the United States is in the general field of infrastructure: an alarming number of bridges have been found to be unsafe; secondary roads in major East Coast cities are on the point of decay; local and regional flight paths are cluttered; passenger and commercial rail systems are antiquated; urban rapid transit systems, where they exist at all, are no longer rapid; and so forth.

A visionary might see the creation of a revitalized national railroad system with "Grand Central Stations" in major cities as the catalyst for a rejuvenation of the "inner cities" as well as the offloading of congested airlanes. Finally, modern urban/suburban rapid transit systems could offload our crowded freeways, an abysmal failure in transportation planning considering the magnificent Los Angeles complex is projected to have an average speed of 10 mph in the 1990s.

A pressing need in the industrial sector is the resurrection of the "Rust Belt" with a more selective heavy industrial mix, and the upgrading of outdated and inefficient petroleum refineries, chemical plants, and manufacturing facilities. It must be stressed, however, that a high degree of uncertainty is inherent in any forecast of the industrial sector due to the extreme pressures exerted in world trade by the surging industrialization of Asia, with low-cost labor, high technology capability, creative management, and an uncompromising work ethic. It is far from inconceivable that the United States is steadily drifting toward a "broker" role.

A transition "in toto" to a broker role is highly unlikely, however, since the defense budget, geared to a self-sufficient concept, should be adequate to maintain the "minimum critical" industrial base, although a lack of basic long-range planning reveals inconsistencies, such as the importation of raw steel with domestic finishing. Further, an important element of a basic defense policy has to be energy independence, but again we see inadequate forward planning. During an energy crunch we initiate research and pilot plant programs for the production of energy from alternative sources on a crash basis. When the crunch eases it's back to normal. The national policymakers seem to appreciate that fossil fuel energy resources are limited, and output is subject to international political manipulation, but fail to understand the need for constancy in planning, since many alternative means for energy production, such as shale oil, tar sands, and politically sensitive nuclear projects take five to ten years from conception to production, and span business cycles.

The Organization of Companies

The concept of the project-driven organization, now in its infancy, will in future years be a fundamental business consideration in any environment where there are substantial time-related capital-intensive projects. While the concept has only recently gained recognition and acceptance, the groundwork was laid, although not identified as such, from the mid-1960s through the mid-1970s, the era of the energy-related mega projects.

The major energy companies came to the conclusion that the historical delegation of total project management authority to multinational contractors was incompatible with the magnitude of the investments and the risks. The stakes were just too high. The first visible sign of the "involved client" was the formation of a project directorate, a blend of owner and contractor personnel on a common project team. In some cases the joint directorate concept evolved into an owner-dominated directorate, when the owner had the capability to provide total project management and had available staff, or an owner-controlled directorate with senior staff positions and discrete areas of responsibility assigned to one or more of the major international contractors.

The growth of the involved client concept was gradual throughout the hectic mega project period but no doubt was hastened by large cost and schedule overruns on cost-reimbursable projects. The energy companies made a basic decision: we will manage our money with our senior people. This decision not only initiated the era of the involved client, but an even more significant concept, the recognition that the management of major capital projects requires the talents of the best people in the organization, which in turn led to a progressive restructuring and realignment of executive responsibilities within organizations.

The building block concepts of the involved client and the project-driven organization were established. An acceptance and a comprehension of the total impact of these concepts are imperative as we look to the future, for we will see these principles in action not only in the sophisticated arena of the established domestic corporations, but as capabilities are developed the concepts will be adopted by the ministries and nationalized companies in the developing nations.

The impact of these fundamental changes has, in turn, resulted in a drastic restructuring of the multinational contracting industry, firms that cut their teeth in the
process plant, heavy construciton, and energy-related fields. Projects within these
companies were managed in a way that reflected the organizational structures of the
companies: functional in the early years, matrix and task in later years.

The matrix style has received its share of attention in the literature as a result
of the intensive focus on organizational structure and behavior, and perhaps due to
the classification of organizations by type with styles identified by name. In actual
practice the process plant engineering and construction firms located in New York City
in the 1940s (Foster Wheeler, Kellogg, Lummus) operated in a pure matrix style. The
task force style was implemented with exceptional results on the Manhattan Project during World War II, although the purists could cite any major task-oriented activity such
as the massive construction projects during the early Egyptian and Chinese civilizations.
The modern task force style was developed and enhanced principally through government space programs. If we look back before we look ahead, we will appreciate that
the matrix style sought to achieve compromise between the formal line organization and
the needs of projects, and the task force style addressed the symptoms rather than
the cause.

In the future companies will be formed and managed in a way that reflects the organizational needs of projects. The project itself is the principal motivating force that
will drive the company, thus it is aptly called the project-driven company. The best
organization will develop from an understanding of where the action is: the action is
the project, not the discipline organization. The successful organizations will practice
a new general management role: control with a light touch from the top, emphasizing
forward planning, decentralization of operations, with high accountability. Centralized
control. Decentralized operation. The project-driven organization!

The basic restructuring, which got underway following the dramatic drop in crude
oil prices in 1981, hopefully will be led in the future by modern management teams:
teams geared to innovation, flexibility, adaptability, responsive to change, capable of
change, without ties to traditional behavior. Why must this be? The project-driven
organization will demand the best to compete on a worldwide basis, stay abreast of technological improvements, react to market shifts, weather energy crises, interest rate
fluctuations, and all the other uncertainties of a turbulent world economy. One long-
awaited resultant will be the reversal of the "formal authority" and "implied authority"
roles of the line and project management, with project management emerging as the
"prestige profession."

The Project Manager

We've reviewed the marketplace and the organization of companies as we see the future.
The purpose of these projections is not to forecast the future in an absolute sense,
since that would be foolhardy; rather it is to paint a most likely and directionally correct picture of the probable environment for the project manager of the future, in order
to prepare managers for the challenges ahead. A manager, trained by education and
molded by experience to cope with the future as portrayed, will be able to handle anything that the future brings.

The future project manager will indeed be the CEO of a major enterprise. The
needs of the world, ranging from complex infrastructure programs through facilities
to provide food, clothing, and shelter, to consumer goods will be staggering.

You may spend most of your career in foreign countries. Indeed, you may work
for a foreign company. You will have to remain technolgoically up to date, for the world
will move fast. You will have to be comfortable in the executive suite, and in diplomatic
receptions. You will have to understand not only the native language at a jobsite,
but the cultures and mores of the people. Human relation skills in your own society
won't suffice; you will have to extend those skills to be interactive with the pulse of
other societies.

There was a period when the young project manager honed his or her business skills in MBA programs. This will be important in the future, but it is suggested that postgraduate training emphasizing international relations and languages may be more important, and those universities offering degrees in project management would do well to include a good selection of liberal arts electives in their programs. The future international project manager might be a person with a limited conversational command of several languages and the ability to move across borders easily, but a more effective approach will be fluency in the language and familiarity with the customs of one or two countries and the ability to settle down for an extended stay in a foreign culture.

A period of conversion will occur as companies move senior line personnel into project positions, but in time professional project managers will develop from within, assuring the company of long-term project capability. The move from line management to project management isn't easy; the line manager makes relatively few decisions, but these must be studied, deliberate, and correct, with long-term effects on employees and the company. The project manager makes many decisions, hopes most are right, and has little to do with long-term company policies and personnel practices. The line manager seeks the best possible result; the project manager seeks the best result possible—two worlds: different strategies, different tactics.

The project manager of the future will be a well-rounded business person, a thinking person. Future corporate executives will be trained within the ranks of project management.

Project Management Tools

We have working tools, such as scheduling methods, that need enhancement; developmental tools, such as estimating, that will remain developmental until management confidence levels permit action on the output without supplemental support; and tools that are in their infancy such as decision-making programs.

The software programs available to the project manager today, excluding proprietary in-house programs, were, with very few exceptions, developed by government, or by firms marketing software, or in the universities. There is a dearth of "user-specified" criteria. Complaints abound that project management systems have to be tailored to fit commercially available programs, yet if the developers of the present systems hadn't taken the initiative there wouldn't be anything to help us today.

Complaints aren't the answer. As the project management profession evolves in an orderly progression, one of the first milestones of an established profession will be a clear "user panel" directive. Firms specializing in appropriate software can then prepare user-oriented programs on a competitive basis to satisfy the needs of the project manager.

If there is a principle that should be followed by a user panel it would be "keep it simple." If, on the other hand, a "cradle to grave" concept is followed, the author can assure the profession that progress will be slow and expensive. It is beneficial to prepare an integrated flow sheet, in other words, a building block approach, to depict interactive considerations, but each element should be developed separately without regard to interaction, starting with the simplest. Test that element, put it into practice, modify it, and approve it for general use. Then move on to the next element. As each succeeding element is approved the basic flow plan and the elements will require revision, including interactive modifications as appropriate. Eventually an integrated flow plan will be completed that will be "proofed" and will have been progressively fed into the mainstream.

Several years ago the author witnessed a "cradle to grave" bulk materials control program, which after the expenditure of hundreds of thousands of dollars and years of effort, was never used and was finally abandoned. Two basic errors were made, among others: first, a simplistic view was taken that the problem was totally one of inventory control; second, progressive specification substitution, criticality, and delivery time for shortages were treated minimally.

The in-house development of project management programs should be scoped, budgeted, scheduled, and monitored by user groups. Better yet, a professional project management organization, such as the Project Management Institute, should take the lead and prepare user specifications for the competitive preparation of software programs by selected suppliers.

Most current systems are time savers and labor savers. They sort out lots of data, preserve valuable resources, save money. It is important that systems of this type be developed further so we have usable estimating programs, material control programs, and the like. It is expected that we will pass through this manual substitution phase quickly, and move on to the main act—the thinking programs.

Our profession, by default, permitted others to develop whatever programs we use today. As we approach the next generation of project management programs, the thinking programs, do we really want to be on the sidelines? It is unreasonable to expect those outside our profession to understand the issues faced by a project manager directing an international mega project. But, programs will be developed; some will be satisfactory, some will not; we would do well to lead the effort.

A productive first step might be an outline of a prioritized project management information system (PMIS). A program that should be high on any listing would be the general approach to resource allocation under a variety of preset and variable conditions. With a resource allocation database we would be ready to attack evaluative systems: problem anticipation, definition, solutions, options, risks; the "what if" and "why" programs. Finally we could venture into business systems and produce a universal PMIS database.

Lastly, all systems of the future must be communicative. Richard Tucker pointed out to the author that the basic formula for channels of communication, $(n)(n-1)$ divided by 2, is sobering when we deal with large numbers of people: 45 channels for 10 people, approximately 5000 channels for 100 people. As we march toward a highly systems-oriented future we must never forget that systems are tools, people are resources. People perform best when motivated. But people don't perform at all if they don't get the message.

SUMMARY

The projections offered are, at best, educated guesses, but if the future manager is comfortable in the environment created here, he or she will adapt well to most course corrections as we forge ahead. The future project manager will be a business person: one who will have the ability to appreciate and use technology advantageously; one who will understand the needs of people in whatever social setting exists. Worldwide projects will be directed toward infrastructure, industrialization, consumer goods, and basic needs. Domestic projects will stress infrastructure, high technology, environment, defense, and space programs. The project-driven organization will recognize the authority of the project manager, and from the ranks, select the executives of tomorrow.

REFERENCES

1. Environmental Design Manual, Foam Latex Facilities, C F Braun, Alhambra, California, December 1, 1971.
2. National Aeronautics and Space Administration (NASA) and National Oceanic and Atmospheric Administration (NOAA), News Conference, February 17, 1989. Reported by Philip Hilts, *The Washington Post*.

Index

Academia
  computer usage, 93
  materials management, 95
  organization, 92-93
  planning and controlling, 94
  quality management, 94-95
  research and development, 95
Aerospace projects
  F-15 program, 7
  government role, 700-701
  NASA, 7
  prime contractor role, 700
  product design and performance, 699-700
  project life-cycle, 698-699
  project management approach, 6
  scope, 697-698
Artic conditions (*see* Climatic and remote conditions)
Audit (*see* Finance)

Bid preparation and award (*see also* International, marketing; Proposal management)
  bid review, 213-219
    general, 213-216
    lump-sum, 216
    reimbursable, 216-219
  contracting, 207-210
    plan, 209-210
    principles, 207-208
    sequence of activities, 208-209
  contractor, 62, 207, 210-211
    objectives, 207
    responsibilities, 62
    screening, 210-211
  owner, 62, 207
    objectives, 207
    responsibilities, 62
  proposals, invitations for, 211-213
  scoping the project, 266-267

Business Roundtable (*see also* Productivity)
  Construction Industry Institute, 1040-1041
  how it was formed, 1038
  what has been achieved, 1038-1040
  what it is, 1037-1038
  view of the future, 1041-1042

Cash flow (*see* Finance)
Change control (*see* Project controls, change control)
Claims management (*see also* Contracts; Project controls, change control)
  case studies, 269-275
  phases of a project, 298-325
    phase 1—contract formation, 298-303
      contract types, 299-300
      key contractual clauses, 301-303
      rights and obligations, 301
    phase 2—contract administration, 303-311
      contractors and subcontractors, 304-305
      documentation, 307-310
      early warning signs, 310-311
      schedules, 305-307
    phase 3—claim/dispute resolution, 311-323
      asserting a claim, 322-323
      changes, 311-312
      claim posture, 316
      claim preparation, 316-317
      claim procedure, 317-318
      defending a claim, 322-323
      pricing the claim, 318-321
      rights and obligations, 313-316
    phase 4—preparation for litigation, 323-325
      legal theory, 325
      litigation management plan, 324-325

Claims management (cont.)
  phases of a project (cont.)
    phase 4–prep. for litigation (cont.)
      litigation team, 323-324
      privilege, 324
  system for claims management, 298
Climatic and remote conditions (*see also*
     Construction)
  Arctic construction, 808-812
  Arctic description, 787-789
  engineering, 797-803
  logistics, 812-815
  modularization, 788-790, 805-807
  procurement, 803-805
  project controls, 790-797
Communications (*see also* Management
     styles)
  considerations, 106, 833, 861-865, 895-
    896, 901
  counterparts, 899-901
  project team, 898-899
  sponsors, 896-898
  standup presentations, 912-921
    effective presentations, 918-921
    management support, 915-918
    technical presentations, 912-915
  written communications, 904-908
    act of writing, 905-908
    getting started writing, 904
Computer applications
  computer-aided design and drafting,
    433-441
    advanced techniques, 435-437
    advanced techniques, problems with,
      437-438
    CAD/CAM development, 438-439
    cost justification, 438-439
    CRT development, 435
    early applications, 433-434
    future developments, 440
  computer-aided project management,
    53-60, 93
    needs of, 53-58
      consultant, 54-55
      contractor, 54-55
      industry, 53
      owner and operator, 55
      project, 57
      project manager, 56
      project team, 58
    project manager, benefits to, 53
    responsibility, 59
    system design, 60, 93
    training, 58-59
Constructability (*see also* Construction)
  construction, 362

Constructability (cont.)
  engineering, 357-360
    electrical, 360
    equipment design, 358
    foundations, 358-359
    instrumentation, 360
    layout, 357-358
    piperack, 359
    piping, 359-360
    structures, 359
  procurement, 361
    specifications, 361
    vendor drawings, 361
Construction (*see* Climatic and remote
     conditions; Constructability; Con-
     struction management; Home office
     construction staff; Inspection; Labor
     relations; Modularization; Multipro-
     ject management; Offshore oil and
     gas projects; Productivity; Project
     controls, cost control, scheduling;
     Quality assurance and quality con-
     trol; Safety and security; Site mate-
     rials management)
Construction management (*see also* Con-
     struction)
  field cost control, 501-508
    contract changes, 507-508
    cost breakdown structure, 501-502
    direct costs, 503, 505
    indirect costs, 502-504
    labor costs, 502
    productivity, 505-506
    subcontract costs, 506-507
    types of costs, 501
    work breakdown structure, 501-502
  field organization, 495-499
    contractor's organization, 35, 41, 496,
      498-499
    direct hire, 496-497
    multiple subcontracts, 496, 498
    owner's organization, 495-496, 498-499
    quality assurance and quality control,
      498
    type of contract, 495
  field scheduling, 509-518
    field scheduling activities, 510-511
    field scheduling techniques, 511-513
      charting, 513
      logic networks, 511
      look-ahead scheduling, 511-512
      milestone reviews, 512-513
      sampling, 511
      schedule statusing, 512
    master schedule, 509-510, 514
    progress measurement, 513-518

Construction management (cont.)
  field scheduling (cont.)
    progress measurement (cont.)
      earned workhour concept, 515
      physical percent complete, 513-515
      resource utilization, 517-518
    reporting, 518
  methods of execution, 489-493
    construction offshore, 491-492
    construction in LDC's, 491
    continental European construction,
      491
    domestic construction, 489-493
      direct hire, 489-490
      multiple subcontracts, 490
    low cost labor, 492
Contingency reserves (*see also* Project
      controls, estimating)
  definition, 67
  initial cost estimate, 67-68, 388
  management of contingencies, 68, 77-78
  setting up a reserve, 69-70
  techniques, 70-74
    cost relevance, 72-74
    identification, 70-71
    influence diagramming, 71-72
    other techniques, 74
    successive estimating, 71
Contracts (*see also* Claims management;
      Joint ventures; Performance
      tests; Project completion)
  architect/engineer, 268
  basic considerations, 236-240
    clarity, 238-239
    get it in writing, 236-237
    legal advice, 240
    meaning of contracts, 240
    perfection, 239-240
    standard forms, 239
    terms and conditions, 237-238
    why have a contract, 236
    workable contracts, 236
  general discussion, 61-62, 235, 240-
      241, 495, 526-527, 532, 1078-
      1079
  guarantees and warranties, 64, 277-281
    elements, 64, 279-281
      liabilities, 64, 280-281
      scope, 279-280
      time frame, 280
    express guarantees, 277-280
    implied warranties, 278-279
  laws, compliance with, 282
  tort, 282
  types of contracts, 241-248
    cost-plus, 241-242, 245-248

Contracts (cont.)
  types of contracts (cont.)
    guaranteed maximum, 243-244
    lump-sum, 242-243, 245-248
    project management, 245
    unit price, 244-245
Cost control (*see* Project controls, cost
      control)

Delegation (*see also* Management styles)
  accountability, 947
  authority, 947
  communications, 949-950
  controlling, 948-949
  human skills, 949
  leadership, 950
  management skills, 949
  motivation, 949-950
  organizing, 948-949
  planning, 948
  responsibility, 947
  time management, 950
  training, 949-950
Document control (*see* Project controls,
      document control)

Engineering
  civil, structural, and architectural,
      417-423
    building authorities, 420-421
    code considerations, 421-422
    construction, 423
    design approach, 418-419
    procurement, 422-423
    retrofits, 422
    schedule, 418-419
    scope of work, 417-418
  design considerations, 395-400
    communications, 395-396
    delegation, 395
    preconstruction, 265-266
    product, 399-400
    reviews, 397-398
    standards, 396-397
  electrical, 429-432
    coordination with construction, 432
    coordination with other disciplines,
      431
    cost areas, principal, 430-431
    schedule, 430-431
  instrumentation and process control,
      407-415
    computer control, 413-414
    consultants and suppliers, 409-410
    coordination, 411-412
    documentation, 411

Engineering (cont.)
  instrumentation and process control
        (cont.)
     start-up, 413
     types of process control, 407-408
  mechanical, 401-406
     documentation, 401-403
     shop visits, 405
     specifications, 403
     technical bid evaluation, 404-405
     vendor data, 405
  piping design and plant layout, 425-428
     design approach, 426-247
     pipespool design and fabrication, 428
     piping materials, 427
     plant layout, 425-426
     vendor data, 427-428
Estimating (see Project controls,
        estimating)
Expediting (see also Procurement)
  area expediting, 457-459
  methodology, 456
  new concepts, 459-460
  organization, 455-456
  project expediting, 456-457
  reports, 459

Fast track projects, case study, 719-725
Finance
  cash flow forecasting, 191-206
     case study, 192-203
     general applicability, 203-206
     guidelines, 191
  financial audits, 581-584
     audit program, 582-584
        stage 1, 582-583
        stage 2, 583
        stage 3, 583-584
     what to audit, 581
     when to audit, 582
     who benefits, 584
     who conducts audit, 582
     why audit, 581
  project financing, 179-190, 848-850
     benefits, 179-180
     characteristics, 179, 848-850
     industry opportunities, 181
     marketing a financing, 187-190
     project opportunities, 181
     structuring a finance, 180-187

Home office construction staff (see also
        Construction)
  client contracts, 481
  construction procedures, 481
  equipment company, 480-481

Home office construction staff (cont.)
  expediting, 480
  field progress monitoring, 479-480
  field staff assignments, 479
  labor relations and safety, 482
  proposals, 480
  quality assurance and control, 481
  rigging calculations and standards, 481
  scheduling, 480

Inspection (see also Construction; Pro-
        curement)
  field inspection, 466
  field quality control, 466-467
  installation quality control, 467-468
  planning, 463-464
  quality assurance plan, 461-462
  shop inspection, 462-466
  strategy, 461-462
Insurance (see also Personnel management)
  analysis of risks, 286
  casualty insurance, 289
     aircraft, 291
     airport construction liability, 290
     comprehensive general liability, 289-
        290
     marine, 291
     professional liability, 291-292
  definition of risks, 285
  loss/accident record, benefits of, 294
  property insurance, 282-283, 286
     builders risk, 286-288
        all risk, 287-288
        fire, 286-287
        fire and extended coverage, 287
     contractors equipment, 288
     ocean marine cargo, 288
  special types of insurance, 293
  surety bonds, 294-295
  worker's compensation and employer's
        liability, 282-283, 292
     Canada, 293
     United States, 292-293
  wrap-up insurance programs, 293-294
International
  marketing (see also Bid preparation
        and award; Proposal management)
     decision, 821-822
     execution, 827-828
     future, 829-830
     groundwork, 822-823
     guidelines, 828-829
     intelligence gathering, 824-825
     negotiations, 826-827
     plan, 821-822
     project pursual, 824

International (cont.)
marketing (cont.)
project selection, 823
proposal, 825-826
project execution
client, nature of, 839
communications, 833, 861-865
construction, 833, 855-858
engineering, 832, 850-851
ethos and mores, 842-843
financial, 848-850
infrastructure, 868-869
laws and regulations, 841-842
location, 840-841
logistics, 853-855
philosophy, 838-839
planning and controlling, 858-861
procurement, 833, 851-853
project inquiry, 844-846
project pursual, 867-868
project size and complexity, 846-847
quality assurance and control, 865-867
scope of work, 847-848
social aspects
cultural differences, 883-884
ethos and mores, 885-886
fallacies, 884
family role, 887-888
taboo, or not taboo, 887
terrorism, 886-887
staffing the project (*see also* Personnel management)
project phases, 877-881
completion, 881
production, 880-881
release, 877-880
staffing plan, 875-877

Joint ventures (*see also* Contracts)
considerations, 254-255
corporations, comparison to, 252-254
definition, 249-250
liabilities, 251
participants, obligations of, 252
partnerships, comparison to, 250
purpose, 249
tax consequences, 251
terms of agreement, 256-263

Labor relations (*see also* Construction)
collective bargaining, 485-487
history of labor legislation, 483-485
local unions, 488
open shop, 488
prejob conference, 487-488

Management styles (*see also* Communications; Delegation; Performance management; Project manager; Superior project manager; Time management)
autocratic, 109
environment, 113
leader behavior, 110-111
managing the boss, 114
participative, 109
perceived, 109
preferred, 111-112
selecting a style, 111-112
Matrix organization (*see* Project organization)
Mega projects, case studies
Bechtel, 745-757
Fluor, 737-744
James Bay project, 102
mass transit projects, 102-103
Modularization (*see also* Construction)
construction, 783-785
definition, 771
engineering, 776-781
fabrication, 781-782
organization, 772-773
planning, 773-776
procurement, 781
transportation, 782-783
why and when, 785-786
Multiproject management (*see also* Construction; Project management)
classification, 760-770
grassroots complex, one owner, 761-765
multiprojects, one contractor, 760-761
multiprojects, one area, 765-770
definition, 759
Municipal projects
municipalities as clients, 653-657
engineering services, 654
municipal organizations, 653-654
politics, 653
types of projects, 654-656
performing the work, 657
public works, 98
selection of engineering firms, 656
competitive bids, 656
negotiated bids, 656
typical projects, 657-658

Negotiating
historical context, 973-974
principles, 972-973
project management, 971-972, 974-977

Offshore oil and gas projects (*see also* Construction)
  environmental considerations, 679-680
  execution, 676-681
   definition, 676
   identification, 676
   plan, 676, 680-681
  history, 671-672
  management team functions, 681-683
  management team organization, 683-689
  preproject planning, 676-678
  project development, pattern of, 672-673
  projects, nature of, 674
  risks, 674-675
  selection of engineering and contractor, 678-679
Organizational factors (*see also* Project organization)
  adverse effects of, 15-23
   counteractions for, 15-23
  factors, 15-23, 92-93
  helpful effects of, 15-23

Performance
  management (*see also* Management styles)
   antecedent, 968-969
   behavior, 968-969
   consequence, 968-969
   definition of, 967-968
  tests (*see also* Contracts)
   base performance levels, 619
   demonstration test run, 619-620
   equpiment testing, 620-622
   philosophy, 617-618
   process unit testing, 622-626
   single unit/multiunit testing, 620
   unit hydraulic limits, 619
Personnel management (*see also* International, staffing the project; Insurance)
  basic functions, 980-986
   benefits, 985
   compensation, 983-985
   performance evaluation, 986
   staffing, 980-983
   training, 986
  emerging legal considerations, 990-993
   age discrimination, 992
   employment-at-will, 990-991
   medical discrimination, 992-993
   privacy, 991
   sexual harassment, 991
   U.S. citizenship, 992
  jobsite assignments, 993-996

Personnel management (cont.)
  jobsite assignments (cont.)
   assignment conditions, 994-996
   long-term, 993-994
   short-term, 993
  project completion, 996
   layoff, 996-997
   leave of absence, 996
   termination, 997
  statutory requirements, 986-990
   EEO/AAP, 988-990
   overtime, 987-988
Petroleum production projects
  capital projects, 659-660
  design tradeoffs, 662
  environmental considerations, 662
  external influences, 661-662
  project coordination, 662-663
  technology, 660-661
Pharmaceutical projects
  design considerations, 667-668
  pharmaceutical processes, 666-667
  project management, 665-666, 668-669
Planning (*see* Project execution planning)
Problem solving (*see also* Project management)
  decision making, 960-961
  future, 964-965
  preventing trouble, 953-956
  problem solving, 956-959
  setting priorities, 961-963
  state of the art, 963-964
  thinking beyond the fix, 959-960
Procurement (*see also* Expediting; Inspection; Traffic)
  bidders list, 447
  bidding process, 451-452
  blanket orders, 449
  control, 450-451
  control forms, 451
  coordination plan, 451
  organization, 446-447
  planning, 445-446
  standardization, 447-449
Productivity (*see also* Business Roundtable; Construction)
  definition, 525-526
  execution strategies, 526-528
   constructability, 527
   contract compatibility, 526-527
   industrial relations, 527-528
   organization, 526
   work continuity, 527
  improvement, 528-529, 1027-1029
   administrative delays, 1028-1029
   analysis, 1027-1028

Productivity (cont.)
  improvement (cont.)
    communications, 529, 1028-1029
    information sources, 529, 1029-1035
    management commitment, 528-529,
      1028-1029
    participative involvement, 1035
  measurement, 528, 855-858
  national, declining, 1077-1078
Project completion (*see also* Contracts)
  closure work breakdown structure
    (CWBS), 594-609
    administrative issues, 607-609
      disposal of physical facilities, 607
      financial report, 608-609
      personnel issues, 607-608
    client-related issues, 601-603
      confirm remaining deliverables, 601
      invoice for final payment, 602
      negotiated settlement, 601-602
      obtain certifications, 602
    CWBS outline, 595
    field issues, 604-606
      as-built drawings, 605
      demobilization, 605-606
      final field report, 605
      fix-up, 604-605
      punch list, 604
    internally-initiated issues, 594-601
      communicate closures, 600
      control project charges, 599-600
      financial audit, 596
      identify certification needs, 596
      identify subcontractor commimtents,
        596, 598, 599
      identify vendor commitments, 596,
        597, 599
      identify remaining deliverables,
        594-595
      open work orders, 599
      screen incomplete tasks, 599
      warranty program, 600-601
    organizational issues, 606-607
      critique, 606-607
      technical data retention, 607
    subcontractor-vendor issues, 603-604
      confirm commitments, 603
      negotiate backcharges, 603-604
  completion issues, 587-594
    effective completion, 588-589
    emotional issues, 592-594
    intellectual issues, 592-593
    miniproject concept, 587, 590-591
    natural completion, 589-590
    unnatural completion, 590
  emotional issues, 609-615

Project completion (cont.)
  emotional issues (cont.)
    change in attitude, 611
    dissatisfaction with next assignment,
      610
    diversion of effort, 610-611
    fear of no future work, 610
    loss of interest, 609, 611
    loss of motivation, 610
    personnel changes, 611-612
    personnel unavailability, 612
    resolution, 612-615
Project controls
  change control (*see also* Claims manage-
      ment)
    administration of changes, 563-564
    effects of changes, 564
    inevitability of change, 561-562
    monitoring effects of changes, 564
    origin of changes, 562
    project management considerations,
      565-566
  cost control (*see also* Construction
      management)
    administrative reporting, 553-554
    construction costs, 558-559
    definition, 551
    front-end activities, 552-553
    home office costs, 554-555
    material costs, 555-556
    plan development, 551-552
    subcontract costs, 556-558
  document control (*see also* Records
      management)
    flow sheet, 575-576
    importance, 575
    monitoring functions, 577-578
      ledger sheet, 578
      visual map, 578
    recording functions, 576-577
      log books, 576
      logging blocks, 577
  estimating (*see also* Contingency re-
      serves)
    capital expenditure programs, 377-378
    contingency, 388
    estimate classification systems, 382-
      387
    estimating pitfalls, 381-382
    future considerations, 1079
    phased approvals, 380
    project changes, 378-379
    scope changes, 388
  scheduling (*see also* Construction)
    forecasts, 373-374
    future considerations, 1079

Project controls (cont.)
  scheduling (cont.)
    objectives, 365-366
    preparation, 368-372
      considerations, 368-369
      detailed schedules, 369-372
      master schedule, 369
      schedule integration, 372
    progress, definition of, 543
    progress, determination of, 543-548
      earned value, 546-548
      forecasting, 548
      identification, 544-545
      quantitative analysis, 545
    system development, 367
    system selection, 366-367
    utilization, 372-373
Project-driven organization (*see also*
      Project organization)
  administration, 50-51
  approach, 49-50
  company organization, 1083-1084
  definition, 49
  matrix, comparison to, 51
  training, 50
Project execution planning (*see also*
      Project controls; Project
      management)
  benefits of planning, 347-348
  components of a plan, 332, 337-346, 350
    client objectives, 337-341
    contracting strategy, 342, 1078-1079
    risk identification, 342-346
    roles and responsibilities, 341-342,
      1079
  definition of, 336
  need for, 336
  plan details, 332-333
  plan development, 94, 331, 349-350
  timing, 346-347
  using a plan, 347
  workshop, 305-355
    approach, 350
    benefits, 355
    conditions, 351
    design, 351-354
    objectives, 350
Project management (*see also* Interna-
      tional; Multiproject management;
      Problem solving; Regulatory
      requirements; other project
      entries)
  approach, 5-6
  changing project requirements
    change, sources of, 1045-1052
      computer, 1050-1051

Project management (cont.)
  changing project requirements (cont.)
    change, sources of (cont.)
      intangibles, 1051-1052
      owner, 1050
      personnel, 1049-1050
      quality, 1047-1049
      schedule, 1046-1047
      technology, 1045-1046
    concepts, 1043-1044
    cost analysis, 1054-1055
    home office hours, effect on, 1052-
      1054
    summation, 1055-1057
  definition, 1-2, 5, 97-98
  execution steps, 101
  future years
    challenges, 1007-1011
    contracting approach, 1078-1079
    estimating and scheduling, 1079
    execution planning, 1078
    management technology, 1013, 1079,
      1085-1086
    market place, 1011-1013, 1081-1083
  history, 7-9, 81-82
  management support, 64-65
  profession, 1015-1025
    attributes, 1020-1021
    development, 1015-1020
    potential, 1021-1024
    vision of a new, 1024-1025
  project management information system
    (PMIS)
    approach, 11
    predecessor concepts, 1060-1065
      communications, 1063-1064
      control, 1060
      decisions, 1064-1065
      information, 1061-1063
      intuition, 1065
      planning and scheduling, 1061
    proposed PMIS, 1069-1073
    system requirements, 1065-1068
  social responsibility, 82-84
  regulatory restraints, 84-88
Project manager (*see also* Management
      styles; Superior project manager;
      other project entries)
  authority, 105-107
    delegated, 105
    perceived, 106-107
    range, 106
  future roles, 1013, 1079, 1084-1085
  qualities, 98-101
  responsibilities, 101
  role, 97

Project organization (*see also* Organizational factors; Project-driven organization)
  ad hoc, 11-12, 1068
  matrix
    conflict, 28, 106
    definition, 25
  project organizations
    basic, 29-30, 92
    conceptual phase, 32
    construction, 35, 41
    contractor role, 27
    front-end, 33
    engineering, 31, 34, 37
    owner role, 26-27, 43
    process plants, 99
    selection of appropriate, 26
  project personnel
    key, 38-40, 42
    personalities, 62-63
    position descriptions, 38-40, 42
    work assignments, 43-44
  task force
    applicability, 46
    advantages, 48
    definition, 25, 45
    disadvantages, 48
    organization, 30, 36, 45
Project, small (*see* Small projects)
Project viability
  determination of, 139-144
  project conception, 133-135
    case study, 134-135
    evaluation of alternatives, 134
    stages, 133
  project scope, 145-149
    components, 145-146
    cost estimates, 147-148
    development, 148-149
    schedule, 147-148
    technical definition, 146-147
Proposal management (*see also* International, marketing; Bid preparation and award)
  data base, 222-223
  characteristics, 221-222
  preproposal effort, 223
  proposal contents, 225-228
  proposal effort, 224
Purchasing (*see* Procurement)

Quality assurance and quality control (*see also* Construction)
  quality assurance, 535, 567-573
    basic elements, 569-572
      audits, 572

Quality assurance and quality control (cont.)
  quality assurance (cont.)
    basic elements (cont.)
      corrective action, 571
      design control, 569
      document control, 569-570
      inspection, 570
      material control, 570
      records, 571-572
      services control, 570
      test control, 570-571
    definition, 535, 567-568
    levels of application, 572-573
    manual, 568-569
    organization, 568
    program, 568-569
  quality control, 531-535
    contract compatibility, 532
    definition, 531
    erection control, 534-535
    inspection, 533
    material control, 533-534
    program, 531-532
    specifications and codes, 533
Records management (*see also* Document control; Project controls)
  basic program, 924-927
  managing the program, 927-928
  techniques, 928-929
  why have records management, 923-924
Regulatory requirements
  case study, 169-178
  federal regulatory requirements, 168-169
  impact on project management, 167-168
Research projects
  managing a research program, 704-707
  project management, 9-11, 95, 703-704
  research program, definition of, 704
Risk management (*see* Insurance)

Safety and security (*see also* Construction)
  safety, 537-540
    fire, 539
    injury or illness, 538-539
    managing safety, 538
    permit-to-work systems, 539-540
    safety as good business, 537
  security, 540
Scheduling (*see* Project controls, scheduling)
Site
  materials management (*see also* Construction)

Site (cont.)
  materials management (cont.)
    consumables, 522-523
    control system basics, 471-473, 519-
      520
    definition, 519
    material preservation, 521
    productivity impact, 473-475, 519
    programs, current, 469-471
    purchasing, 520
    receiving, 522
    storage areas, 521-522
    surplus disposal, 523
    view of future, 475
    warehousing, 521
  selection
    environmental factors, 160-161
    evaluation factors, 156-157
    field investigations, 155-156
    foreign sites, 161-164
    keys to success, 154-155
    mathematical models, 157-159
    mistakes, 152-154
    principles, 151-152
Small projects
  current practice, 711-712
  definition, 712
  engineering shortcuts, 716-717
  organization, 714-715
  project controls, 715-716
  scope, 712-713
Superior project manager (*see also*
    Management styles; Project
    manager)
  authority of project manager, 126
  ethics, 120
  human relations, 117-120
    client, 117-119
    management, 120
    peer group, 119-120
    staff, 120
  Graduate-On-Line-Diagnosis, 128-129
  leadership, 126
  management styles, 115-116
    active dominant, 116
    active persuasive, 116
    basic, 115-116
    passive conforming, 116

Superior project manager (cont.)
  management styles (cont.)
    passive controlled, 116
    variable, 115-116
  project manager personality, 121-126
    achiever, 121
    communications, 125-126
    cost, value, quality understanding,
      123-124
    relevancy of perfection, 122-124
    take charge attitude, 121
    thinking person, 122
    time management, 124
  superior project, 27, 127-128
    definition, 127
    determinants of success, 27, 127-128
  superior project manager, 115

Task force organization (*see* Project
    organization)
Tennessee Valley Authority
  history, 647-648
  project management approach, 648-650,
    651-652
  unique management considerations, 650-
    651
Time management (*see also* Management
    styles)
  concepts, 937-941
  daily calendar, 941-942
  long-range activities, 943
  project action plans, 941
  project needs, 941
  short-range activities, 942-943
Traffic, 453-454 (*see also* Procurement)

Utility projects
  construction management, 639-641
  contracting with federal government,
    643-644
  definition and scope, 629-632
  design management, 632-639
  fossil-fueled plants, 641-642
  international projects, 644-645
  nuclear-fueled plants, 642-643

Zero-defect projects, case study, 727-
  735